1 MONTH OF
FREE
READING

at
www.ForgottenBooks.com

By purchasing this book you are
eligible for one month membership to
ForgottenBooks.com, giving you
unlimited access to our entire
collection of over 1,000,000 titles via
our web site and mobile apps.

To claim your free month visit:

ISBN 978-0-265-62560-6
PIBN 10435683

A TREATISE

ON THE

BANKRUPTCY LAW

of the United States

By

HAROLD REMINGTON

of the bar of New York City

formerly referee in Bankruptcy; author of "Bankruptcy Law for Students."

111 Broadway, New York City

SECOND EDITION

VOLUME I

THE MICHIE COMPANY, LAW PUBLISHERS

CHARLOTTESVILLE, VA.

1915

T
R 2844 b
1915

v, 1

Publisher's Preface

The author of this treatise, Harold Remington of the New York Bar, is already well known to the profession by reason of the first edition of his treatise, which was published in 1908.

Mr. Remington has brought to his work a valuable aggregate of qualifications. He was a practising attorney before the Bankruptcy Law was passed, being engaged largely in commercial law practice, so that in viewing the different provisions of the Bankruptcy Law he has been in a position to appreciate their respective uses and value as seen from the standpoint of history and comparative jurisprudence. Since the enactment of the Bankruptcy Act, his experience in bankruptcy matters has covered every field, placing him thus far in advance of most text-book writers. For eleven years he was sole Referee in Bankruptcy in one of the busiest commercial centres of the United States, having the administration of that law in a community of upwards of two-thirds of a million of inhabitants. While there, during the greater part of his administration of the law, there was given to him somewhat wider jurisdiction than most referees possess, in that for many years the appointment of receivers, the issuance of preliminary injunctions, etc.—elsewhere reserved to the judges themselves—were also in his hands. He had much to do, during the formative period of the practice under the Act, with the establishment of methods and procedure in bankruptcy, and was well known from his published decisions and otherwise, as one of those who did much to formulate bankruptcy practice. Naturally, too, referees in bankruptcy find his treatise replete with matters of invaluable and special interest to them.

It was during his refereeship that he brought out the first edition of REMINGTON ON BANKRUPTCY, then in two volumes, which very soon worked itself into the confidence and affection of the profession.

Upon Mr. Remington's resignation of the refereeship, he framed the Amendments of 1910 to the Bankruptcy Act, to Section 47a, giving trustees the rights of levying creditors; also to Section 60 (b), bringing the date of preferences down to the date of the recording of written instruments; and also to Section 48, regulating the compensation of receivers and trustees, which, up to that time, had been the cause of much scandal in bankruptcy administration. These amendments were both suggested and framed by him, and they have done much to strengthen the law in some of its weak points. Mr. Remington not only drafted these amendments, but also advocated their passage as well as the passage of the Amendments of 1910 before the Judiciary Committees of the House and Senate, and in recognition of the services he had rendered was presented by the President of the United

States with the pen with which those important amendments were approved. Mr. Remington is now engaged in the active practice of the law in New York City.

So there is probably no one in the United States who has had wider or more varied experience in bankruptcy matters than has the author of this treatise, not only in the field of bankruptcy legislation but also as a court in administering the law and as an attorney engaged in its active practice. It is from this storehouse of experience that the present treatise has been drawn; and in its preparation, covering many years of labor, the author has analyzed, criticized and classified all the published decisions in bankruptcy throughout the United States and its dependencies.

The present edition has been very painstakingly revised. During the last few years a great many important decisions, some of them making marked changes, have been made in bankruptcy, and points have been discussed and decided that are of the greatest importance to the practitioner.

To those not already acquainted with the plan of this treatise, it would be well to say that it is not arranged upon the method of treating bankruptcy law as a mere statute, to be annotated section by section, but rather as a jurisprudence, which it most assuredly is, being the result of centuries of growth in England and the United States. Thus the arrangement is philosophical and logical, taking up a bankruptcy case from its inception to its termination. The busy practitioner can, almost without an index, turn to the appropriate part of the treatise by pausing a moment to recollect what place in the ordinary course of a bankruptcy proceedings the particular question he wishes to investigate would be most likely to arise.

A feature which has been unique in this treatise is that the author has stated, fearlessly and clearly, the propositions of law as he considers them to have become established through the decisions, then, under each of these propositions thus worded in his own language, he has placed excerpts from the opinions of the leading cases in support or contra to the proposition enunciated. Thus, the practitioner is not only given the proposition of law, carefully stated with all its modifications, but also brief extracts from the opinions of courts in relation thereto. In this way the work is not only a treatise, but is also fairly a digest, saving the practitioner the necessity of resorting to the original reports, in many instances, in order to see whether or not the cases may be truly applicable.

With these few words concerning the qualification of the author and the construction of the treatise, the publishers present to the profession the second edition of REMINGTON ON BANKRUPTCY, hoping for it the same success that attended the first edition.

THE MICHIE COMPANY,
Law Publishers,
Charlottesville, Va.

TABLE OF CONTENTS.

INTRODUCTION.

Synopsis.

PART I.

CONSTITUTIONALITY, GENERAL NATURE AND CONSTRUCTION OF THE ACT OF 1898; AND JURISDICTION TO ADJUDGE BANKRUPT.

CHAPTER I.

CONSTITUTIONALITY OF THE ACT.

Synopsis of Chapter.

CHAPTER II.

In General, the Nature, Objects and Construction of Law and of the Procedure under It, and Forms and Orders.

Synopsis of Chapter.

CHAPTER III.

Jurisdiction to Adjudge Bankrupt.

Synopsis of Chapter.

DIVISION 3.

SUBDIVSION "A".

SUBDIVISION "B".

CHAPTER IV.

ACTS OF BANKRUPTCY.

Synopsis of Chapter.

PART II.

PROCEDURE IN PUTTING THE DEBTOR INTO BANKRUPTCY.

CHAPTER V.

PETITION IN VOLUNTARY BANKRUPTCY.

Synopsis of Chapter.

CHAPTER VI.

PARTIES AND PETITION IN INVOLUNTARY BANKRUPTCY.[1]

Synopsis of Chapter.

DIVISION 1.

DIVISION 2.

DIVISION 3.

DIVISION 4.

CHAPTER VII.

DIFFERENT PROCEEDINGS BY OR AGAINST SAME DEBTOR PENDING AT SAME TIME.

Synopsis of Chapter.

DIVISION 1.

DIVISION 2.

DIVISION 3.

CHAPTER VIII.

COMMENCEMENT OF PROCEEDINGS, SERVICE OF PROCESS AND RULE DAYS FOR PLEADINGS.

Synopsis of Chapter.

CHAPTER IX.

INTERVENING OF CREDITORS IN OPPOSITION TO PETITION.

Synopsis of Chapter.

CHAPTER X.

ANSWER, DEMURRER AND MOTION.

Synopsis of Chapter.

CHAPTER XI.

PROVISIONAL REMEDIES.

Synopsis of Chapter.

DIVISION 1.

DIVISION 5.

CHAPTER XII.

TRIAL.

Synopsis of Chapter.

CHAPTER XIII.

DISMISSAL.

Synopsis of Chapter.

CHAPTER XIV.

ADJUDICATION.

Synopsis of Chapter.

DIVISION 1.

DIVISION 2.

DIVISION 3.

CHAPTER XV.

THE BANKRUPT—HIS DUTIES AND RIGHTS OF PROTECTION FROM ARREST AND FOR STAY OF SUITS.

Synopsis of Chapter.

DIVISION 1.

DIVISION 2.

DIVISION 3.

CHAPTER XVI.

SCHEDULES.

Synopsis of Chapter.

PART III.

ADMINISTRATION OF THE ESTATE AFTER ADJUDICATION.

CHAPTER XVII.

Referees in Bankruptcy.

Synopsis of Chapter.

DIVISION 5.

SUBDIVISION "A".

CHAPTER XVIII.

NOTICES TO CREDITORS.

Synopsis of Chapter.

CHAPTER XIX.

MEETINGS OF CREDITORS.

Synopsis of Chapter.

CHAPTER XX.

Proofs of Claims.

Synopsis of Chapter.

CHAPTER XXI.

PROVABLE DEBTS.

Synopsis of Chapter.

DIVISION 1.

DIVISION 2.

DIVISION 3.

CHAPTER XXII.

YEAR'S LIMITATION FOR FILING CLAIMS.

Synopsis of Chapter.

CHAPTER XXIII.

ASSIGNMENT OF CLAIMS.

Synopsis of Chapter.

CHAPTER XXIV.

ALLOWABLE CLAIMS.

Synopsis of Chapter.

DIVISION 1.

SUBDIVISION "A".

·CHAPTER XXV.

ALLOWANCE, DISALLOWANCE AND RE-EXAMINATION OF CLAIMS.

Synopsis of Chapter.

DIVISION 1.

CHAPTER XXVI.

TRUSTEES.

Synopsis of Chapter.

DIVISION 1.

PART IV.

ASSETS AND TITLE TO ASSETS.

CHAPTER XXVII.

KINDS OF PROPERTY PASSING AND NOT PASSING TO THE TRUSTEE BY VIRTUE OF THE BANKRUPTCY.

Synopsis of Chapter.

CHAPTER XXVIII.

How Title Vests in Trustee.

Synopsis of Chapter.

CHAPTER XXIX.

When Title Vests; and Status of Property after Filing of Petition.

Synopsis of Chapter.

DIVISION 1.

DIVISION 2.

VOLUME II

CHAPTER XXX.

Trustee's Title and Right to Assets.

Synopsis of Chapter.

PART V.

DISCOVERING, COLLECTING AND SEPARATING ASSETS.

CHAPTER XXXI.

DISCOVERING ASSETS; GENERAL EXAMINATIONS OF BANKRUPTS AND WITNESSES.

Synopsis of Chapter.

CHAPTER XXXII.

JURISDICTION OF THE BANKRUPTCY COURT WHERE ANOTHER COURT AL-
READY HAS CUSTODY: CONFLICT OF JURISDICTION.

Synopsis of Chapter.

DIVISION 1.

DIVISION 2.

CHAPTER XXXIII.

JURISDICTION OVER ADVERSE CLAIMANTS.

Synopsis of Chapter.

DIVISION 1.

CHAPTER XXXIV.

RECEIVERS AND TRUSTEES AS DEFENDANTS IN PLENARY SUITS.

Synopsis of Chapter.

CHAPTER XXXV.

LIMITATIONS OF PLENARY ACTIONS BY AND AGAINST TRUSTEES.

Synopsis of Chapter.

CHAPTER XXXVI.

SUMMARY JURISDICTION OVER THE BANKRUPT, HIS AGENTS AND PERSONS
NOT ADVERSE CLAIMANTS; ALSO OVER PROPERTY IN CUSTODY.

Synopsis of Chapter.

PART VI.

CONVERTING THE ASSETS INTO MONEY.

CHAPTER XXXVII.

APPRAISAL.

Synopsis of Chapter.

CHAPTER XXXVIII.

SALE OF ASSETS.

Synopsis of Chapter.

CHAPTER XXXIX.

Synopsis of Chapter.

PART VII.

Costs of Administration, Distribution and Closing of Estates.

CHAPTER XL.

Costs and Expenses of Administration.

Synopsis of Chapter.

CHAPTER XLI.

DISTRIBUTION TO CREDITORS.

Synopsis of Chapter.

DIVISION 1.

DIVISION 4.

SUBDIVISION "A."

SUBDIVISION "B."

SUBDIVISION "C."

CHAPTER XLII.

CLOSING AND REOPENING OF ESTATES.

Synopsis of Chapter.

DIVISION 1.

DIVISION 2.

VOLUME III

PART VIII.

CRIMES AND CONTEMPTS.

CHAPTER XLIII.

CRIMES AGAINST THE BANKRUPTCY ACT.

Synopsis of Chapter.

CHAPTER XLIV.

CONTEMPTS.

Synopsis of Chapter.

PART IX.

COMPOSITION WITH CREDITORS.

CHAPTER XLV.

NATURE AND EFFECT OF COMPOSITION.

Synopsis of Chapter.

CHAPTER XLVI.

PROCEDURE ON COMPOSITION.

Synopsis of Chapter.

DIVISION 1.

CHAPTER XLVII.

Opposition to Comfirmation of a Composition.

Synopsis of Chapter.

DIVISION 1.

PART X.

DISCHARGE.

CHAPTER L.

NATURE AND HISTORY OF DISCHARGE.

Synopsis of Chapter.

CHAPTER LI.

PETITION FOR DISCHARGE.

Synopsis of Chapter.

DIVISION 3.

CHAPTER LII.

OPPOSITION TO DISCHARGE.

Synopsis of Chapter.

DIVISION 1.

DIVISION 2.

CHAPTER LIII.

EFFECT OF DISCHARGE ON THE RIGHTS OF THE PARTIES.

Synopsis of Chapter.

DIVISION 1.

SUBDIVISION "A."

CHAPTER LVI.

REVIEW OF THE REFEREE'S ORDER BY THE JUDGE.

Synopsis of Chapter.

CHAPTER LVII.

APPEALS, REVIEWS AND ERROR PROCEEDINGS FROM DISTRICT COURTS TO THE
. CIRCUIT COURTS OF APPEAL.

Synopsis of Chapter.

DIVISION 1.

SUBDIVISION "A."

CHAPTER LVIII.

APPEALS AND PETITIONS FOR REVIEW TO SUPREME COURT.

Synopsis of Chapter.

DIVISION 1.

DIVISION 2.

TABLE OF CASES

TABLE OF CASES

[ALL REFERENCES ARE TO SECTIONS]

[ALL REFERENCES ARE TO SECTIONS]

—k

—m

[ALL REFERENCES ARE TO SECTIONS]

REMINGTON ON BANKRUPTCY

INTRODUCTION.

Synopsis.

(a) Release from Debts Not Main Nor Essential Idea of Bankruptcy Law, but Merely Incidental.
(b) Jewish Sabbatical Year of Release.
(c) Modern Bankruptcy Law Not Criminal Statute.
(d) "Cessio Bonorum."
(e) English Bankruptcy Acts True Origin American Bankruptcy Law.
(f) Origin and History of Old English Bankruptcy Acts.
(g) First English Bankruptcy Act, 1542, 34 Henry VIII.
(h) Acts of 13 Eliz. 1570 and of 1 and 23 James I.
(i) Queen Anne's Act, 1705, and First Provisions for Discharge of Bankrupt.
(j) Bankruptcy Law at Time of American Revolution.
(k) First Bankruptcy Act of United States, 1800.
(l) Act of 1841.
(m) Act of 1867.
(n) Meaning and Idea of Bankruptcy Law To-Day.

(a) Release from Debts Not Main Nor Essential Idea of Bankruptcy Law, but Merely Incidental.—To gain a proper conception of bankruptcy law and of its place in jurisprudence, it is well first to exclude from the idea certain popular misconceptions of its origin, scope and function.

Bankruptcy law is popularly conceived to be a law devised mainly for releasing debtors from the bondage of hopeless indebtedness. This is undoubtedly the first idea that springs to mind when bankruptcy law is mentioned. But it is a wholly inadequate idea. Release from debts is not necessarily a part of bankruptcy law at all[1] and from the standpoint of history is a mere incident to its original object. To be sure, one of the most beneficent features of the bankruptcy laws of present times and one of the most potent arguments in their favor is the privilege granted in them to bankrupts who have given up all their property toward satisfying their debts and have truthfully revealed all information in relation to their affairs, of obtaining a release from the unpaid remainder of their debts. But

---

1. This proposition is strongly dissented from in Hardie v. Dry Goods Co., 21 A. B. R. 457, 165 Fed. 588 (C. C. A. Tex.), quoted post at § 17, the court, however, basing its opinion upon what it conceives to be the fact that "In nearly all and every voluntary bankruptcy brought under the present law the administration or distribution of the bankrupt's property has been practically concluded before filing the petition," which is certainly an incorrect statement if meant to be applicable generally.

this release from debts is, as above noted, merely an incident of the later development of bankruptcy law, not its original object.

(b) Jewish Sabbatical Year of Release.—Were the granting of release from debts, on the contrary, the distinguishing object of bankruptcy law, one might be justified in tracing the law to a remote origin—before the days, indeed, of David and Solomon, more than 3000 years ago, when the Israelites every seven years had their sabbatical year of release. The fifteenth chapter of Deuteronomy contains, quite explicitly stated, the first law known in history providing for the release of debtors from their debts, and, were the popular idea correct, the first bankruptcy law. It reads as follows:

"At the end of every seven years thou shalt make a release. And this is the manner of release: Every creditor that lendeth aught unto his neighbor shall release it. He shall not exact it of his neighbor or his brother; because it is called the Lord's release. Of a foreigner thou mayest exact it again; but that which is thine with thy brother thine hand shall release; save when there shall be no more poor among you."

This old Jewish law evidently was found to be, as it necessarily must have been, quite impracticable in its operation. As the stated seventh year approached, new business with poor people must have flagged and old creditors have become nervous and impatient. But in those days defects in laws did not require formal amendment for their correction, but were helped out in a way that is a lost art to modern legislators—the invocation of Divine wrath.

"Beware that there be not a thought in thy wicked heart saying, 'The seventh year, the year of release, is at hand' and thy eye be evil against thy poor brother and thou givest him naught, and he cry unto the Lord against thee and it be a sin unto thee. Thou shalt surely give him and thy heart shall not be grieved when thou givest unto him."

It may well be believed that nothing short of Divine command could have prevented grief, notwithstanding, from entering the heart of the unfortunate creditor of those days.

(c) Modern Bankruptcy Law Not Criminal Statute.—Nor is modern bankruptcy law to be looked upon as a criminal statute, although it must be conceded a quasi criminal origin in the statute of King Henry VIII. To be sure, it has created by its terms certain offenses punishable by imprisonment, as for instance, the concealment of assets and the perpetration of false oaths in relation to the bankrupt's affairs, but these criminal provisions will be found in present law to have become simply incidental to the real objects of the law, mere aids in carrying them out.

(d) "Cessio Bonorum."—The criminal idea—again digressing to antiquity—seems to have been prominent in the old Roman laws against insolvent debtors, the cruelty of which was monstrous until the time of

Julius Cæsar, when the law known as Cessio Bonorum, which might be translated freely "the law relating to assignments for the benefit of creditors," incorporated into Roman jurisprudence the humane principle that where an insolvent debtor had turned over honestly and fully all his property for the benefit of his creditors, he would not be liable either to capital punishment, imprisonment nor slavery, as theretofore might have been his fate. However, this provision of Cessio Bonorum was far removed from the releasing of an insolvent from his remaining debts, such as is to be found in modern bankruptcy law. The law, Cessio Bonorum, of Cæsar's time, might be thought to have been the prototype of bankruptcy law and in many features it did resemble such a law. It provided for the surrender of all assets by the insolvent and for his examination; and it granted him, in case of his full compliance with its provisions, immunity from personal punishment, although no release from debts. But the main feature distinguishing it from bankruptcy law was that its operation could not be invoked by creditors in the first instance, for it was purely a voluntary proceeding on the debtor's part, in this regard corresponding more to the laws of the present day providing for voluntary assignments for the benefit of creditors than to a true bankruptcy law.[2]

(e) English Bankruptcy Acts True Origin American Bankruptcy Law.—American Bankruptcy Law finds its true origin in the English Bankruptcy Acts, which were, originally at least, quasi criminal in their nature. In the first of the English acts the bankrupt was always referred to as "the offender," the odium of crime being thus cast upon the word "bankrupt" that has clung to it to this day. But the true conception of bankruptcy law, as will later more fully appear, is neither that it is simply a law for releasing debtors from debts nor a law for suppressing crime.

(f) Origin and History of Old English Bankruptcy Acts.—It is well briefly to trace the origin and history of the old English Bankruptcy Laws, that a better understanding of the growth of the law and a clearer conception of its place in American jurisprudence may be had.

As Europe began to emerge from the shadows of the Middle Ages, commerce sprang up. Perhaps, indeed, it was the springing up of commerce rather that caused the shadows to lift.

Particularly did England advance with rapidity in the development of commerce, owing, no doubt, to the greater security of her laws, for England was a vast sheep raising country in those days, and history and human nature combine to demonstrate that where every one has his property exposed to easy theft and despoiling, as is necessarily such property, the laws and property are likely to be more stringently enforced and more conscientiously obeyed; and thus naturally in England are found the first attempts at the better protection of commerce by way of bankruptcy laws.

2. See Justinian's Code, Dig. 2, 4, 25, 48, 19, 1 Nov. 4, 3.

Whatever the cause, the fact remains that the commerce of England was the best protected commerce in Europe and that such was the case even before the time England became mistress of the seas and when in fact she was of little power on the seas at all. Foreign merchants began to flock to her shores. Among them were many Lombards from Italy, the first bankers and brokers of Europe, who settled in London and gave their name to Lombard Street. They not only developed the system of exchange that has become the life of commerce, but also gave the name "bankrupts" to traders who failed, the table or "banque" of the broker who failed being broken or "rupt" as a symbol of his failure. As will later be noted the first English statute on the subject was entitled an "Act against those who do make bankrupt."

The needs of this growing commerce brought to light the inadequacy of English Common Law to the protection of trade. During the Dark Ages and Middle Ages, before the time of the Lombards, the Common Law had grown up and become more or less crystalized. Equity had also established its principles, and no doubt the remedies afforded by these two jurisprudences had been found to be entirely adequate to the needs of those early times. Commerce then was restricted. English sailors and merchants then were few and made but short ventures from home. England was mostly agricultural and pastoral, and had a quick market in the Low Countries and France close at hand. Its manufactures were small and the needs of the people little. The handicraftsman waited for an order before he did a stroke of work. Two or three times a year the farmer deserted his plow and resorted to the fair, and there met the seller of goods and enjoyed a week of boisterous holiday, his shopping being enlivened by carousing and drunken brawls. This was commerce before the discovery of gold in America made men restless and eager for venture, before the springing up of modern trade. In those days creditors undoubtedly had found the Common Law remedies of execution, distraint and the more lately developed "foreign attachment by the custom of London" amply sufficient to protect them from the frauds of debtors. Industrial Society had been in a fixed state. There had been little occasion for one to get largely in debt, and still less opportunity for him to get so without everybody knowing it. There had been little opportunity, for instance, for gathering together a mass of goods, purchased on credit, and then running away with them or their proceeds.

No one could likely have been found who would have been able to buy in bulk and the roads were bad and the tracing of strangers easy. There were no telegraphs to aid in overtaking absconders, to be sure; but, on the other hand, the absconder did not have the railway upon which to whirl out of sight. Troubles between debtor and creditor had been generally individual troubles—no retail merchant had had a multitude of creditors such as bankrupts have to-day; he could not have got into that condition. This being so, the Common Law remedy of execution, especially as supplemented in parts of England by the later developed law of foreign attachment, had fulfilled all needs. These remedies were adequate where the contest was simply between two or at most a few individuals, where it was a duel between the debtor and one creditor as a rule, or at most a contest between the debtor and two or three creditors, so to speak; but they became wholly inadequate where many creditors were involved. With the coming, however, of the opportunity and inclination to make commercial ventures and to obtain a stock of goods on hand in advance of demand and to do business on credit, came also the need for a better means of protecting the common interests of the creditors of the merchant.

The Common Law maxim, "The law favors the diligent creditor," upon which was founded the principle that the creditor making the first seizure by execution or attachment was entitled to precedence to the full amount of his claim over the creditor making the next levy, and so on, was found to work injustice in the new state of commerce where a great body of creditors owed by a single debtor was involved, each having contributed to the common fund and being equitably entitled to share in what was left in proportion to his unpaid for contributions, and a better principle was found in the maxim of equity "Equality is equity," which is the dominant principle of bankruptcy law.

It was, then, the growth of commerce and of trading on credit and the consequent springing up of a community of interest among all the creditors of the merchant that made the old remedies of execution and attachment, designed simply for litigation between a few individuals, insufficient and brought about the first English Bankruptcy Act in the reign of King Henry VIII in the year 1542.

(g) First English Bankruptcy Act, 1542, 34 Henry VIII.—The first English Bankruptcy Act is instructive to one desiring to acquire a true conception of bankruptcy law of the present time. The following points in it are to be particularly noticed: First, its quaint preamble, which, were all bankrupcies fraudulent, as they happily are not, would furnish a good preamble for a bankruptcy act to-day, so like was the human nature of the days of Henry VIII to that of the twentieth century; next, that the law is framed against debtors and in no way for them, no discharge or release from debts being provided for; next, that it is concerned wholly with fraudulent debtors, not at all with those who are simply unfortunate; and, in truth, as industrial society was then constituted, mere misfortune unconnected with fraud was hardly capable of producing sweeping results; finally that that community of interest amongst creditors which the old Common Law remedies did not contemplate nor provide for, finds expression in the seizure of the bankrupt's property by a common agent acting in behalf of all creditors and by the pro rata distribution amongst them of the proceeds of the bankrupt's goods seized, which are distinguishing features of all true bankruptcy laws.

The text of the law is given below: 34 and 35 Henry VIII, ch. 4 (1542-3):

"An Act against Such Persons as Do Make Bankrupts."

Where (as) divers and sundry persons craftily obtaining into their hands great substance of other men's goods, do suddenly flee to parts

Acts of Bankruptcy. unknown, or keep their houses, not minding to pay or restore to any (of) their creditors, their debts and duties, but at their own wills and pleasures consume the substance obtained, by credit, of other men, for their own pleasure and delicate living, against all reason, equity and good conscience: Be it enacted by authority of this present parlia-

Courts. ment, That the lord chancellor of England, or keeper of the great seal, the lord treasurer, the lord president, the lord privy seal, and other of the King's most honorable privy council, the chief justices of either bench for the time being, or three of them at the least, whereof the lord chancellor, or keeper of the great seal, lord treasurer, lord president or the lord privy seal, to be one, upon every complaint made to them in writing by any parties grieved concerning the premises shall have power and authority, by virtue

Jurisdiction. of this Act, to take by their wisdoms and discretions, such orders and directions, as well with the bodies of such offenders aforesaid, wheresoever they may be had, or otherwise, as also with their lands, tenements, fees, annuities and offices, which they have in fee

Seizure of Assets. simple, fee tail, term of life, term of years or in the right of their wives, as much as the interest right and title of the same offender shall extend or be and may then lawfully be departed with, by the said offender and also with their money, goods, chattels, wares, merchandises and debts wheresoever they may be found or

Appraisal and Sale. known. And to cause their said lands, tenements, fees, annuities, offices, goods, chattels, wares, merchandises and debts to be searched, viewed, rented and appraised; and to make sale of the said lands, tenements, fees, annuities and offices, as much as the same offender may then lawfully give, grant or depart with, or otherwise to order the same for true satisfaction and payment of the said cred-

Pro Rata Distribution of itors: that is to say to every of the said creditors
Dividends to Creditors. a portion, rate and rate alike, according to the quantity of their debts. And that every direction, order, bargain, sale and other things done by the said lords authorized, as is aforesaid, in writing signed with their hands, by authority of this act, shall be good and effectual in the law to all intents, constructions and purposes against the said offenders, their heirs and executors forever, as though the same order, direction, bargain and sale had been made by the said offender or offenders, as his or their own free will and liberty by writing, indented, enrolled in any the King's Courts of record.

II. And be it also further enacted by the authority aforesaid, That if after any such act or offense committed, and complaint

"General Examination." thereof made to the said lords as is aforesaid, any party grieved concerning the premises knowing, supposing or suspecting any of the goods, chattels, wares, merchandises, or debts, of such offender or offenders, to be in custody, use, occupying, keeping, or possession of any person or persons, or any person or persons to be indebted to any such offender or offenders, do make relation thereof to the said lords, to whom authority is given by this present act as is aforesaid, that then the said lords shall by virtue hereof have full power and authority to send for and convent afore them by such process, ways or means, as they shall think convenient by their discretions, all and every such person and persons so known, supposed or suspected, to have any such goods, chattels, wares, merchandises, or debts, in his or their custody, use, occupation, keeping or possession, or supposed or suspected, to be indebted to such offender or offenders; and upon their appearance to examine them and every of them as well by their oaths, as otherwise by such ways and means, as the said lords, by their discretions, shall think meet and convenient for and upon the specialty, certainty, true declaration and knowledge, of all and singular such goods, chattels, wares, merchandises, and debts, of any such offenders as be supposed or suspected to be in his or their custody, use, occupation, or possession, and of all such debts as by them or any of them, shall be supposed or suspected to be owing to any such offender, and if any such person or persons upon such examination do not disclose, plainly declare and show the whole truth of such things as he or they shall be examined of, concerning the premises: then every such person or persons so examined, and not declaring the plain and whole truth concerning the premises upon due proof thereof to be made, before the said lords therefor authorized, as is aforesaid, by witness, examination, or otherwise, as to the same lords shall seem sufficient in that behalf, shall lose and forfeit double the value of all such goods, chattels, wares, merchandises, and debts by them or any of them so concealed and not wholly and plainly declared and shown; which forfeiture shall be levied and recovered by the said lords having authority as is aforesaid, by such ways and means as to them shall seem requisite and convenient. And the same forfeiture to be distributed and employed to and for the satisfaction and payment of the debts of the said creditor or creditors, in such like manner, rate and form as above declared, concerning the ordering of the goods and chattels of the said offenders, keeping their houses, or flying to places unknown, as is aforesaid.

III. And be it also further enacted by the authority aforesaid, That if after any such person or persons' shall keep his or their houses, **Fraudulent Claims.** or flee to parts unknown, as is aforesaid, any person or persons do fraudulently by covin or collusion, claim or demand any debt, duty or other thing by writing or otherwise, of any such offender or offenders, other than such as he or they can and do prove to be due by right and conscience in form aforesaid, before the said lords having authority by this present act, as is aforesaid, and the same to proceed bona fide, without fraud or covin: that then every such person and persons, so craftily demanding or claiming any such debt, duty or other thing, as is aforesaid, shall forfeit and lose double as much as he or they shall so claim or demand. And the same forfeiture to be levied, recovered and employed, in manner and form as is afore rehearsed.

IV. And be it also further enacted by the authority aforesaid, That if any such person or persons, which shall keep his or their **Fraudulent Levies** houses, or flee to parts unknown, as is aforesaid, or in- **and Judgments.** tend to delay, or defraud their creditors deceitfully by covin or collusion, suffer or cause any other person or persons, to recover against him or them any debts, goods, chattels, wares or merchandises, without just cause and title so to do, proceeding bona fide, without fraud or covin, that then upon complaint thereof made to the said lords having authority by this present act, as is aforesaid, the same lords shall have power and authority by virtue hereof to convent and call before them the said recoverer or recoverers, and after such fraud, deceit, covin or collusion, shall plainly appear, or be duly proved before the said lords, authorized, as is aforesaid, all the said goods and chattels, of the said offender so recovered, shall be chargeable, employed, ordered and delivered toward the payment of the true and due debts of the said creditor, after the manner, form and rate, as is afore specified, by the discretion of the said lords, having authority by this present act, the aforesaid false and feigned recoveries notwithstanding, so that always such false and feigned recoveries shall not be in force, or any execution thereby had of or upon any goods, chattels, lands, or tenements of any such offender or offenders, until such time as all his or their true and due debts and duties, shall be fully satisfied, contented and paid to his or their creditors. And nevertheless after that the said true debts and duties, shall be fully satisfied and paid, as is aforesaid as well the body of the said offender, as his lands, tenements, goods and chattels, shall be charged and liable to the execution of the said recovery according to the tenor, force, and effect of the same.

V. And be it also enacted by the same authority, That if any such person or persons which shall be indebted, do withdraw himself **Absconding Bank-** out of this realm, and other the King's dominions, into **rupts Outlawed.** any foreign realm, or country, to the intent thereby to abide and remain, in defraud of his creditors: that then upon complaint in writing concerning the premises thereof made to the said lords having authority, as is aforesaid, the same lords shall by virtue and authority of this present act, have full power and authority to award proclamations to be made in such places as to them shall be thought meet and convenient, commanding by the same such offender in the King our sovereign lord's name, to return with all convenient speed into this realm, and to yield his body before the said lords, having authority as is aforesaid, or one of them. And if the said person within three months next after he shall have knowledge of such proclamation, or as soon after as he conveniently may, do not repair, and yield his body as is aforesaid, that then the body of all and every such offender and offenders shall be judged, taken and deemed to all intents and purposes out of the King's protection, and that also all goods, chattels, lands, tenements and debts of every such offender shall be by the order and discretion of the said lords employed and distributed amongst his creditors equally and indifferently rate for rate, in like manner and form as is afore declared: And that also every person or persons that shall willingly help to aid, embezzel or convey any such person or persons, their said goods, chattels, wares, or merchandises out of this realm, and **Punishment of Accom-** other the King's dominions, into any foreign realm **plice as Effecting Fraud-** or place, knowing the said person or persons to de- **ulent Removals, etc.** part or withdraw themselves, or convey their said goods, chattels, wares, and merchandises for the cause and intent aforesaid, shall suffer such pains by imprisonment of their bodies, or pay such fine to our sovereign lord the King, his heirs or successors, as to the said lords having authority by virtue of this present act, shall seem meet and convenient for their said offence or offences.

VI. Provided always, and be it enacted by the authority aforesaid, That if the creditors of any such offender or offenders, which **No Discharge from** shall keep his or their house or houses, or which shall **Unpaid Debts.** absent or withdraw themselves into places unknown, for the cause aforesaid, be not fully satisfied and paid or otherwise contented for their debts and duties by the ways and means afore specified and declared, that then the said creditor and creditors, and every of them, shall and may have their remedy for the recovery and levying of the residue of the same debts or duties, whereof they shall not be fully satisfied and paid, or otherwise contented in form aforesaid against the said offender or offenders, in like manner and form as they should or might have had, before the making of this act, and that the said creditor and creditors, and every of them, shall be only barred and excluded by virtue of this act, of and for all and every such part and portion of the said debts and duties, as shall be paid, satisfied, distributed, or delivered unto him or them by the said lords having authority as is aforesaid, and of no more portion or parcel thereof, anything herein specified that may be taken or construed to the contrary notwithstanding.

(h) Acts of 13 Eliz. 1570 and of 1 and 23 James I.—Twenty-eight years after the statute of Henry VIII was passed, Queen Elizabeth's parliament, in 1570, passed the second English bankruptcy law. Its preamble sets forth,

"Forasmuch as notwithstanding the statute made against bankrupts in the thirty-fourth year of the reign of our late sovereign lord King Henry the Eighth, those kind of persons have and do still increase into great excessive numbers and are like more to do if some better provision be not made for the repression of them and for a plain declaration to be made and set forth who is and ought to be taken and deemed for a bankrupt: Therefore, be it enacted, etc."

The statute goes on to limit its provisions as to who may be declared bankrupt to the classes of traders, merchants and dealers in money; and to declare what offenses should be sufficient to constitute the fraudulent debtor a bankrupt—for the law was still treating bankruptcy as a crime and the bankrupt as a criminal and none of the acts prohibited were sufficient to make one guilty of bankruptcy unless they were done with intent to hinder or defraud creditors. These "offenses" constituted what would now be denominated acts of bankruptcy and were five in number; thus, the body and property of the debtor were declared to be subject to seizure as a bankrupt's, if with intent to defraud or hinder creditors, first, the debtor should have departed the realm; or second, have kept to his house or absented himself; or third, have taken sanctuary; or fourth, have suffered himself collusively to be arrested for a fictitious debt; or fifth, have suffered himself to be outlawed, etc.

This law of Queen Elizabeth, then, in general simply amplified and made more definite the law of King Henry VIII, but in doing so it made a statute containing almost all the essential features of the bankruptcy law of the present day, excepting that it did not grant discharge to bankrupts and did not prohibit preferences amongst creditors and did not allow debtors voluntarily to go into bankruptcy. By the law of Elizabeth the operation of bankruptcy law was confined to merchants, brokers and traders, which limitation continued in all succeeding bankruptcy acts both in England and the United States until about the middle of the nineteenth century; the kinds of fraudulent acts that should be held sufficient to make one a bankrupt were defined; the recovery from third persons of property fraudulently conveyed to them by the debtor on the eve of his bankruptcy, was provided for; the provisions of the former law for bringing in an examining witnesses touching the bankrupt's property were amplified; the former rule for distributing the bankrupt's assets pro rata amongst his creditors was preserved.

In this law of Elizabeth, as in fact in all these laws until the reign of Queen Anne, nearly two hundred years after the first bankruptcy law to King Henry VIII, there was no provision whatsoever for discharging the bankrupt from his remaining debts. On the contrary, each law contained express provision that his remaining debts should not be construed to be released notwithstanding all his assets may have been divided up ratably amongst his creditors; and in addition, the law of Elizabeth expressly provided that if the bankrupt should afterwards acquire any new property, the right to it should immediately vest in all his creditors, both old and new, and that it should be administered by the bankruptcy commissioners as part of the bankrupt's estate, no matter how long a time meanwhile might have elapsed.

One could, with considerable interest and not a little profit, follow along the years after these first bankruptcy acts in the study of the development of bankruptcy law as it progressed in the successive enactments made from time to time in the reigns of the subsequent English sovereigns, but space will permit only the briefest reference to them. In the reign of Elizabeth's successor, James I, the law was twice changed, in the first James I, ch. 15, and 21st James I, ch. 19. Then there was a long period during the strenuous times of the English contest with the Stuart dynasty—Cromwell's time and until the Restoration—that the laws against those "who do make bankrupt" were left untouched.

(i) Queen Anne's Act, 1705, and First Provision for Discharge of Bankrupt.—In the eighteenth century bankruptcy law was again modified, the principal change to note being that, by the statute of Queen Anne, passed in 1705, known as 4th Anne, ch. 17, the prominence of the criminal idea was taken away and for the first time[3] a discharge was granted to the bankrupt from his remaining debts, if he had surrendered all his assets and made full disclosure to his creditors. The first provision in modern bankruptcy law for the discharge of the debtor is as follows:

"And be it further enacted that all and every person and persons so becoming bankrupt as aforesaid, who shall, within the time limited by this act, surrender him, her or themselves—and in all things conform as in and by this act is directed—shall be discharged from all debts by him, her or them due and owing at the time that he, she or they did become bankrupt."

Later on at various times were added further qualifications upon the right to a discharge from debts, amongst others that the bankrupt's assets

3. Hardie v. Dry Goods Co., 21 A. B. R. 457, 165 Fed. 588 (C. C. A. Tex.).

should equal a certain percentage of his debts, that a certain per cent. of his creditors should assent to his discharge, etc., etc., although it would seem to have been a sufficiently rigid requirement that the bankrupt should in all things have conformed to the many different provisions of the law in order to be entitled to discharge.

(j) **Bankruptcy Law at Time of American Revolution.**—With these preliminary discussions one is placed in a position to summarize impressions and to understand what was meant by bankruptcy law at the time our forefathers severed the colonies from the mother country and went on making laws of their own. Bankruptcy law at that time, it is evident, was a law directly towards furnishing a better protection to creditors against the devices of dishonest debtors than was afforded by the Common Law with its more limited remedies of execution and attachment, and only incidentally granted a discharge to such bankrupts as conformed fully to its requirements.

As it then was constituted, it might have been defined as a law devised for seizing the person and property of fraudulent and dishonest debtors, for punishing them for their frauds and for distributing their effects ratably amongst their creditors, and if their assets reached a certain percentage of their debts, of granting them a discharge from the remainder of their debts. It had quite as ample provisions for making searching examination of the bankrupt and of witnesses as there are in the bankruptcy laws of to-day. However, at least one of the distinguishing features of bankruptcy law as it is constituted at the present time, namely, voluntary bankruptcy, was wholly lacking and contrary to the theory of the early law, and this definition therefore will not suffice for bankruptcy law at the present time. At the time of our separation from England, English bankruptcy law did not allow a debtor to go voluntarily into bankruptcy as at present—voluntary bankruptcy, indeed, would have been quite foreign to the purpose and idea that the bankrupt was an escaping offender with creditors in hot pursuit. On the other hand, it exempted from its operation everybody except traders, brokers and merchants[4]—in general, those dealing in money and in buying and selling—they alone could be declared guilty of the offence of bankruptcy, whilst nowadays anybody (except under the law of 1898 a municipal, railroad, insurance or banking corporation) may go voluntarily into bankruptcy although there do remain still some restrictions as to those who may be forced into bankruptcy. Lastly, the provisions of the present law avoiding preferential payments to creditors received with notice did not then exist. A fraudulent conveyance, to be sure, even then could be set aside, but the mere paying by an insolvent debtor of one creditor, on an honest debt, without the paying of a like proportion to his other creditors, which is what is meant by a preference, was not the subject of

4. Friday *v.* Hall and Kaul Co., 216 U. S. 449, 23 A. B. R. 610.

any special provisions of bankruptcy law even if the creditor knew it
was a preference at the time he took it, the bankrupt's creditors being relegated to the Common Law for their only remedies for recovering property
from third persons. Such were the outlines and such the theory of English
bankruptcy law at the time the Colonies separated from their mother
country. It will be found, indeed, that these same ideas prevailed in the
first bankruptcy law enacted in the United States.

By the Constitution the right to regulate and control bankruptcies was
given over to the Federal Government, the framers of the Constitution
appreciating the wisdom of uniform rules in matters of bankruptcies precisely as in other matters relating to commerce. Indeed, the interstate
commerce clause and the clause authorizing uniform bankruptcy laws are
to be found side by side in the same section of the Constitution.

(k) First Bankruptcy Act of United States, 1800.—The first bankruptcy law of the United States was passed in 1800, during the administration of John Adams. It followed in its main features and even in its wording the English bankruptcy laws, and was essentially a law *against* debtors,
framed along the lines of suppressing fraudulent and criminal practices
rather than along the lines of providing a general system for the rational
and equitable administration of insolvent estates, no provision at all being
made for one voluntarily to become a bankrupt, the distinguishing feature
of the later bankruptcy laws, without which a bankruptcy law can not be
said to have arrived at the full statute of a general system of administering insolvent estates which it is at present. Indeed, like the laws that had
gone before it in England, its operation even adversarily was limited, only
traders, merchants, underwriters and brokers being within its purview.

This law was a tentative exercise of federal power over the subject of
bankruptcies, being limited by its own terms to five years, but it was even
shorter lived than that, being repealed in less than four years, in 1803. The
people of the United States had not awakened to the realization that they
had formed a nation, and in general they resented federal laws. Moreover, this law came at about the same time the hated Alien and Sedition Laws
were creating such an upheaval in American politics and it fell under the
same ban of popular opposition. It seemed to the people of those days that
the federal government was drawing around the necks of the people the
cord of a strongly centralized and domineering government. By the Alien
Act, the Federal Government, they thought, had been assuming arbitrary
and despotic power and by the Sedition Act, been attempting to muzzle
free speech, and now, by the Bankruptcy Act, it was still further drawing
to itself power, assuming the pursuit of debtors and obliging creditors to
resort to federal courts to litigate their rights. Instead of a court close at
hand, to which suitors had always been accustomed, now, by this new and
much distrusted law they must travel great distances to the federal courts
and bring themselves and witnesses there at a great loss of time and money;

and naturally they resented the law; and it went down in the general revolt that found expression in Jefferson's election; and for nearly forty years, that is to say until 1841, when the Whigs came into power, there was no national bankruptcy law in the United States and the permissive power of Congress over the "subject of bankruptcies" was not exercised, but was left in abeyance.

(1) Act of 1841.—In 1841 was passed the second national bankruptcy law of the United States. Although this law, like its remote predecessor of 1800 was short lived, being repealed within two or three years, for political reasons, this being the most heated period of the States' Rights controversy, yet the law itself was a most admirable one and was the first law on the subject of bankruptcies constructed on broad lines. It was the first American law that wholly abandoned the original idea that bankruptcy law was a law only to be invoked by creditors. In this law appeared all the essential elements of a true bankruptcy law. It provided a general system for administering all insolvent estates of living persons except those under guardianship, by its provisions for the first time debtors being allowed voluntarily to bring their estates into the bankruptcy courts for equitable distribution and its operation no longer being confined to merchants and those who dealt in money. To be sure it also provided, like all its predecessors, for the punishment of offenders, but it recognized on the other hand, the justice of granting to the honest debtor who had surrendered all his assets and truthfully revealed all facts in relation thereto and had aided his creditors in realizing as much as possible from the estate, a discharge and release from his remaining debts—the justice of lifting from his shoulders the burden of hopeless debt, that otherwise would have obliged him either to abandon all business enterprise or else to do business under cover of another's name. This law of 1841 contained ample provision for the seizure of property; for its sale and equitable distribution amongst creditors; for the recovery of property fraudulently conveyed and also for that conveyed by way of preference in the payment of one creditor over others; it also contained the usual provisions found in bankruptcy law for bringing witnesses into court and obliging them to submit themselves to examination on the general subjects of the bankrupt's business and behavior. However, it must be conceded that whilst the law was a great advance over all its predecessors in most particulars yet it had certain serious defects that undoubtedly hastened its fall. Among the faults that hindered it from being an ideal system for the United States, was that its courts were long distances apart, were not close to the people. It would be admittedly a great hardship to-day, in this period of quick and cheap travel, were creditors all over an entire district obliged to take train and come to the United States Judge every time they needed to appear in the Bankruptcy Court against, perhaps, a neighbor of their own town. How much more burdensome, then, must it have been, to have had to resort to the United States Judges in those days of stage coaches and bad roads!

It was nearly another quarter of a century after the repeal of the law of 1841 before the next national bankruptcy act of the United States was passed, the last before our present one.

(m) Act of 1867.—In 1867 was passed the third bankruptcy act of the United States. This law remained in force for eleven years, being repealed in 1878.

By a review of some of the causes that brought about this repeal light may be thrown upon certain parts of the present law wherein it was attempted to rectify the defects of the former law.

By the law of 1867, in the first place, it was too easy to throw a debtor into bankruptcy and too hard for him to obtain his discharge after he once became bankrupt, there were so many grounds named in the Act for declaring a debtor bankrupt, and so many for preventing his discharge. The present law sought to avoid these defects by limiting the number and nature of the acts of bankruptcy and grounds of opposition to discharge; and also in another way, by changing the definition of insolvency. The usual definition of insolvency is the inability of a debtor to meet his obligations as they mature in the due course of business. Now, according to that definition, in times of panic when money is scarce, everyone, almost, would be insolvent and the possible consequences of such holding would be that creditors would be enabled to throw many debtors into bankruptcy most unjustly; such, indeed, was found to be the result of the operation of the law of 1867, and the complaints were justifiable. In avoiding such consequences, the framers of the present law made a different definition of insolvency, and one corresponding more closely to its true meaning, namely, that a debtor should not be held to be insolvent, unless his assets, at a fair valuation, should be found to be less than his liabilities. Upon reflection it will be seen that this change in the meaning of insolvency obviates many of the faults of the law of 1867.

Other causes contributing to the downfall of the law of 1867 were the distance of the courts from the people, the same fault found in all the preceding laws in this country; and the excessive fees allowed to the officers of the court and attorneys practicing in bankruptcy.

In re Wells, 8 A. B. R. 75, 114 Fed. 222 (D. C. Mo.): "The Act of 1867 carried with it many evils, real or supposed. One of such evils was its oppressive and expensive features. The estates were eaten up by a most vicious fee system. The litigation was all, or practically all, in the Federal Courts, generally sitting at a great distance from the debtor, the claimant and the witnesses. It was the purpose of the present statute to correct this and limit the fees and expenses, and have the greater part of the litigation where the parties resided."

In re Oakland Lumber Co., 23 A. B. R. 181, 174 Fed. 634 (C. C. A. N. Y.): "Nothing contributed so much to bring about the repeal of the Act of 1867 as the large expense of administration, the small estates being entirely absorbed in fees. The more economical the administration of the present Act the longer will it continue as an important adjunct to trade and commerce."

The law of 1898 was framed with special view to the avoidance of these faults.

Thus, the fault of extravagance of administration has been guarded against by stringent provisions limiting the compensation of the officers of the court to exceedingly low rates of commission and prohibiting any extra or other compensation to them "under any form or guise whatsoever;" also by strict prohibition of unnecessary appointments of receivers, requiring that they be appointed only when it is "absolutely necessary" to do so for the preservation of the estate, the appointment of receivers being discouraged whenever resort to injunction will suffice. Indeed, the whole spirit of the Act of 1898 breathes economy in administration and makes of this law a peculiarly business law.

The fault of distance of the bankruptcy courts from the people which was so serious a defect in the administration of all former bankruptcy laws of the United States has been guarded against by providing that there shall be at least one referee (the judicial officer who constitutes practically the bankruptcy "court"), for each county, thus bringing the bankruptcy court home to the people and making of it quite as much a "people's court" as is their own county probate or insolvency court.[5]

(n) Meaning and Idea of Bankruptcy Law To-Day.—This somewhat extended review of the origin and history of the Bankruptcy Laws of the past from which the present system of bankruptcy law has sprung, places one in a position more intelligently to define the idea of bankruptcy law as it exists to-day in the United States, not meaning by this that the definition so arrived at would have been a proper one at all stages of history; for, as already noted, the idea and objects of bankruptcy law have undergone considerable development and change since the time the first harsh statutes of England were passed to repress and suppress the "offense," as it was then considered to be, of bankruptcy and to punish the offender.

Justice Miller, in Wilson v. City Bank, 17 Wall. (U. S.) 473, says: "The primary object of a bankruptcy law is to secure a just distribution of the bankrupt's property among his creditors: the secondary object is the release of the bankrupt from the obligation to pay his debts."

United States District Judge Ray, who was a member of the Judiciary Committee of the House of Representatives that passed the Act of 1898, and was chairman of the Judiciary Committee that secured the passage of the Amendment in 1903, and is one thoroughly familiar with the spirit

5. See post, § 24, note 24 (2).

of the Bankruptcy Law of 1898 says, in rendering his opinion in In re Leslie found in 9 Amer. B. R. on page 567.

"The main purpose of the bankruptcy law is to prevent preferences and secure a fair and equitable division of the bankrupt estate among the creditors, not to grant discharges. This end accomplished, the bankrupt is granted a discharge from all his debts."

As bankruptcy jurisprudence now stands in the United States, then, it may be said to be a system of laws for the taking possession of the assets of an insolvent, either upon his own initiative or in case he has done certain acts called acts of bankruptcy, considered to demonstrate his unworthiness or incapacity properly to continue his business, upon the initiative of his creditors; for recovering such of his assets as have been transferred fraudulently to third parties or unfairly to particular preferred creditors or have been seized by creditors while the debtor was insolvent; for selling the assets and distributing the proceeds equitably amongst his creditors; and finally for granting to him, in case he has surrendered all his assets and disclosed to his creditors in bankruptcy the truth about his business, a discharge from the unpaid deficit of his debts.

It will at once be seen that a law concerned with such broad objects must be far reaching in its administration.

When Congress passed the law of 1898 the people in general little comprehended the magnitude of the work done. Its passage was secured chiefly because of its one feature, the release of debts. A great multitude of victims of years of industrial depression were lying stranded on the rocks of hopeless debt. These debtors were skulking along the streets hardly daring to lift their eyes to passers by lest they might remind some creditor of an almost forgotten if not forgotten debt. Either so or the debtor was doing business under the name of his wife or other relative, or as "agent" or "trustee," as he would variously style himself; everybody understanding the real situation except perhaps the courts themselves, whose rules of evidence obliged them oftentimes to find that an experienced business man was merely agent or trustee for a wife who owned nothing originally and hardly knew where the place of business she was made to say she now owned was located, and generally knew nothing in particular about it. But this was the natural result of the barbarism of a country that had no bankruptcy system and these debtors, living their lives of falsehood and pretense, were the legitimate fruits of lack of civilization. These were probably the most potent arguments in securing the passage of the present bankruptcy act; but, after all, the scope of the work done was infinitely broader.

By this law Congress has superimposed upon the forty-eight widely varying systems of commercial law of the different states, one vast, uniform system of jurisprudence governing the dealings of men with one another in every part of the country, and in their most minute ramifications. Be it in Texas, Oregon, Missouri, Maine or Pennsylvania, almost every commercial transaction is conducted with an eye to the effect of the bankruptcy law upon it. If one or the other of those dealing becomes later a bankrupt, at once the provisions of this law must be searched to ascertain the rights of those involved. If neither party becomes bankrupt, yet if the property involved may have come from some bankrupt before his bankruptcy still the law may be operative. And when it is considered that the great bulk of commercial law practice is taken up with questions that only arise when one or the other of the parties has become insolvent it is then realized how vast the effect of bankruptcy law must be upon commercial transactions and the practice of commercial law. Attachments, executions, receiverships, assignments, fraudulent conveyances—these are the leading topics under commercial law practice and yet not one of them becomes of any importance unless the debtor be an insolvent or unless insolvency somewhere exist along the line.

By this law also the opportunity for one creditor to obtain a preference out of the insolvent estate over other creditors is prevented. The condition of affairs that existed when there was no bankruptcy law preventing preferences is well remembered. Those were days when the law of the survival of the fittest had unrestrained operation. No confidences were possible between a debtor and his creditors. The debtor who found his affairs getting into bad shape dared not breathe a word of his condition to any creditor, lest such a one would become alarmed and come down upon him with the sheriff. Nor did one creditor dare confer with another about their common debtor's affairs lest the other creditor take immediate action and get ahead of him.

There were no mutual confidences possible, for it was the reign of the old common law whose fundamental maxim, translated into popular language, is "first come, first served." The maxim "The law favors the diligent creditor" too often came to mean "the law favors the favorite creditor," the wife or other relatives or some powerful commercial house or bank which was carrying a cognovit note or chattel mortgage for ready levy or for the taking of quick possession.

The commercial world was given over to the unrestrained rule of the "survival of the fittest."

At the hint of coming insolvency began a frantic race for priority. More than likely the debtor himself would already have given a chattel mortgage to some favored creditor or relative and in addition have made an assignment to his own attorney. An attorney specially skilled in such manipulations, would send his clerk to file the mortgage or deed that was the usual incident to the debtor's failure, with instructions to apprise him the moment the filing was done so that immediately thereafter a deed of assignment might be filed. Whilst all this was going on, creditors on their part, would be hurrying out legal papers, one for the appointment of a receiver, another for an execution and so forth.

Those were strenuous times, indeed, when lawyers stayed up all night preparing papers and when sheriffs made levies at midnight—oftentimes to find a receiver or assignee already in charge.

By the passage of the bankruptcy act, preventing preferences amongst creditors, annulling seizures by legal process within four months of bankruptcy, and granting discharge to bankrupts, all this has been changed. Under the protection of the bankruptcy act, a debtor may now be candid with his creditors and may call them in and frankly relate to them his troubles. They, on their part, may deliberate among themselves and devise the best means for mutual benefit. No one can obtain an advantage over his neighbor, for preferences and seizures by legal process on the eve of insolvency are forbidden, and nullified, and the debtor, on his part, has nothing to fear from his own candor—at worst, having merely to surrender his assets for equal distribution, but, in doing so, running little risk of spending his remaining days under the yoke of debt; and these collateral benefits of the act are recognized among business men as affording great possibilities of future development most advantageous to the amicable adjustment of the affairs of failing debtors.

Such is the bankruptcy law of the present time, its object, history and place in jurisprudence, far reaching in its results, intimately bound up with the every day affairs of business life, humane and beneficent, just and efficient in its rules, one of the steps toward a higher civilization and better justice.

PART I.

CONSTITUTIONALITY, GENERAL NATURE AND CONSTRUCTION OF THE ACT OF 1898; AND JURISDICTION TO ADJUDGE BANKRUPT.

CHAPTER I.

Constitutionality of the Act.

Synopsis of Chapter.

§ 1. Power to Enact Bankruptcy Laws.—The only power Congress has to pass a national bankruptcy law must, of course, be found conferred in some clause of the constitution. This power is expressly granted in § 8 of Article 1 of the Constitution in the following words: "Congress shall have power to establish * * * uniform laws on the subject of bankruptcies throughout the United States."[1]

And it is interesting to observe that the clause giving to the Federal Congress control over interstate commerce was placed side by side with the clause giving to it the power to enact uniform laws for the protection of that commerce in the event of business failure.[2] Indeed, historically considered, the regulation of interstate commerce and its protection by uniform laws were among the chief causes of the formation of that "more perfect Union" which we now enjoy as the "United States of America."

§ 2. Constitutional Requirements—"Uniformity" and on "Subject of Bankruptcies."—The law so established must be uniform through-

---

1. Hurley v. Devlin, 18 A. B. R. 627, 151 Fed. 919 (D. C. Kans.), quoted at § 17.

2. **Bankruptcy Law a Commercial Regulation.**—See interesting article at end of 15 Am. B. R. by Mr. James M. Olmstead, Referee in Bankruptcy at Boston, "Bankruptcy Law a Commercial Regulation."

out the United States;[3] and be upon the "Subject" of bankruptcies.[4]

§ 3. "Uniformity" Geographical, Not Personal.—That is to say, the law must operate everywhere in the United States precisely alike, but it need not operate precisely alike upon all classes of people nor in all States upon the same kinds of property, provided in all States it operates alike on all persons of the same class and on all property seizable by creditors under their respective State laws.[5]

§ 4. Distinctions between Persons, Not Lack of "Uniformity."— The law is not unconstitutional because of its making distinctions between artificial and natural persons, nor between classes of artificial persons.[6]

§ 5. Recognition of Diverse Exemption Laws, Priority Laws, Dower Rights, etc., Not Lack of "Uniformity."—Nor is it unconstitutional because of its recognizing diverse exemption laws.

Thus, in one State the exemptions are different from those in another State and the trustee takes different classes of property, yet the law is uniform because in each State it gives to creditors at least all that in such State would belong to them without bankruptcy law.[7]

Hanover Nat'l Bank v. Moyses, 8 A. B. R. 1, 186 U. S. 181: "It was many times ruled (under the law of 1867) that this provision was not in derogation of the limitation of uniformity because all contracts were made with reference to existing laws, and no creditor could recover more from his debtor than the unexempted part of his assets. Mr. Justice Miller concurred in an opinion to that effect in the case of Beckerford, 1 Dill. 45.

"Mr. Chief Justice Waite expressed the same opinion in In re Deckert, 2 Hughes 183. The chief justice there said: 'The power to except, from the operation of the law, property liable to execution under the exemption laws of the several States, as they were actually enforced, was at one time questioned, upon the ground that it was a violation of the constitutional requirement of uniformity, but it has thus far been sustained, for the reason that it was made a rule of the law to subject to the payment of debts under its operation only such property as could by judicial process be made available for the same pur-

---

3. Hanover Nat'l Bk. v. Moyses, 8 A. B. R. 1, 186 U. S. 181; Leidigh Carriage Co. v. Stengel, 2 A. B. R. 383, 95 Fed. 637 (C. C. A. Ohio); Obiter, Singer v. Nat'l Bedstead Mfg. Co., 11 A. B. R. 276 (N. J. Ch.); Obiter, Hargardine-McKittrick Co. v. Hudson, 10 A. B. R. 225, 122 Fed. 232 (C. C. A. Mo.); Hills v. McKinniss Co., 26 A. B. R. 329, 188 Fed. 1012 (D. C. Ohio): "It seems to us that this act must be construed, if the language reasonably permits such construction, to secure uniformity in the fullest measure and to avoid an interpretation unless the same be compelled by the language of the statute, which permits a dishonest or tricky debtor to easily escape its provision."

4. Singer v. Nat'l Bedstead Co., 11 A. B. R. 276 (N. J. Ch.).

5. Hanover Nat'l Bk. v. Moyses, 8 A. B. R. 1, 186 U. S. 181, quoted at § 13; Leidigh Carriage Co. v. Stengel, 2 A. B. R. 383, 95 Fed. 637 (C. C. A. Ohio); Obiter, Singer v. Nat'l Bedstead Mfg. Co., 11 A. B. R. 276 (N. J. Ch.); Thomas v. Woods, 23 A. B. R. 132, 170 Fed. 764, (C. C. A. Kans.); Obiter, Darling v. Berry, 13 Fed. 659 (C..C.).

6. Leidigh Carriage Co. v. Stengel, 2 A. B. R. 383, 95 Fed. 637 (C. C. A. Ohio).

7. In re Rouse, Hazard & Co., 1 A. B. R. 240, 91 Fed. 96 (C. C. A. Wis.); In re Cohn, 22 A. B. R. 761, 163 Fed. 444 (D. C. N. Dak.).

pose. This is not unjust, as every debt is contracted with reference to the rights of the parties thereto under existing exemption laws, and no creditor can reasonably complain if he gets his full share of all that the law, for the time being, places at the disposal of creditors. One of the effects of a bankrupt law is that of a general execution issued· in favor of all the creditors of the bankrupt, reaching all his property subject to levy, and applying it to the payment of all his debts according to their respective priorities. It is quite proper, therefore, to confine its operation to such property as other legal process could reach. A rule which operates to this effect throughout the United States is uniform within the meaning of that term, as used in the constitution.'

"We concur in this view, and hold that the system is, in the constitutional sense, uniform throughout the United States, when the trustee takes in each State whatever would have been available to the creditors if the Bankrupt Law had not been passed. The general operation of the law is uniform although it may result in certain particulars differently in different States."

Nor is it lacking in "uniformity" because of its recognizing the various orders of priority of debts of the State law, under § 64 (b) (5).[8]

Nor because it recognizes the different dower rights of the various States.[9]

§ 6. State Law Governing Title, Not Lack of "Uniformity."—Nor because the title of the property is to be governed by the state law in cases where the peculiar provisions of the bankruptcy law itself do not confer title.

Property that will pass to the trustee in one State may not, because of diversity of laws, pass in another State; as, for instance, unrecorded conditional sales contracts are void as to creditors in some States and the property covered by them passes to the trustee; in other States they are not void and the same class of property does not pass; yet the law operates uniformly because the creditors still get all the property they would have had had there been no bankruptcy law.[10]

§ 7. "Subject of Bankruptcies" Not Necessarily Entire nor Confined to Original "Subject."—The "subject of bankruptcies" to which the constitution refers is confined to that general "subject" as recognized in the jurisprudence of England and America at the time of the adoption of the constitution.

Obiter, Singer v. Nat'l Bedstead Mfg. Co., 11 A. B. R. 276 (N. J. Ch.): "Of course, Congress can not extend its power to pass laws on the 'subject of bankruptcies,' by merely giving names to laws or by arbitrarily defining certain conduct of natural persons or corporations as acts of bankruptcy. Congress is confined to the 'subject of bankruptcies' as that subject was recognized in 1787."

Nevertheless the laws so established are not confined in their operation to the same class of persons not the same methods of procedure prevailing on the subject of bankruptcies "when the constitution was adopted."

---

8. In re Rouse, Hazard & Co., 1 A. B. R. 240, 91 Fed. 96 (C. C. A. Wis.).
9. Thomas v. Woods, 23 A. B. R. 132, 170 Fed. 764 (C. C. A. Kans.).

10. Hanover Nat'l Bk. v. Moyses, 8 A. B. R. 1, 186 U. S. 181, quoted, ante, § 5.

§ 8. Operating on Others than "Traders," Not Outside of "Subject."

—Thus the law is not unconstitutional because of its operating on others than traders, although bankruptcy law, at the time the Constitution was created, was confined exclusively to traders and was supposed to be peculiarly applicable to them.

Hanover Nat'l Bk. v. Moyses, 8 A. B. R. 1, 186 U. S. 181: "Mr. Chief Justice Fuller delivered the opinion of the court: By the fourth clause of section eight of article 1 of the Constitution the power is vested in Congress 'to establish * * * uniform laws on the subject of bankruptcies throughout the United States.' This power was first exercised in 1800. 2 Stat. 19, ch. 19. In 1803 that law was repealed. 2 Stat. 248, ch. 6. In 1841 it was again exercised by an act which was repealed in 1843. 5 Stat. 440, ch. 9; 5 Stat. 614, ch. 842. It was again exercised in 1867 by an act which, after being several times amended, was finally repealed in 1878. 14 Stat. 517, ch. 176; 20 Stat. 99, ch. 160. And on July 1, 1898, the present act was approved.

"The act of 1800 applied to 'any merchant, or other person, residing within the United States, actually using the trade of merchandise, by buying or selling in gross, or by retail, or dealing in exchange, or as a banker, broker, factor, underwriter, or marine insurer,' and to involuntary bankruptcy.

"In Adams v. Storey, 1 Paine 79, Mr. Justice Livingston said on circuit: 'So exclusively have bankrupt laws operated on traders that it may well be doubted whether an act of Congress subjecting to such a law every description of persons within the United States, would comport with the spirit of the powers vested in them in relation to this subject.' But this doubt was resolved otherwise, and the acts of 1841 and 1867 extended to persons other than merchants or traders, and provided for voluntary proceedings on the part of the debtor, as does the act of 1898.

"It is true that from the first bankrupt act passed in England, 34 & 35 Hen. VIII, ch. 4, to the days of Queen Victoria, the English bankrupt acts applied only to traders, but, as Mr. Justice Story, in his Commentaries on the Constitution, pointed out, 'this is a mere matter of policy, and by no means enters into the nature of such laws. There is nothing in the nature or reason of such laws to prevent them being applied to any other class of unfortunate and meritorious debtors.' Section 1113. * * *

"Sturges v. Crowninshield, 4 Wheat. 122, 195, was cited, where Chief Justice Marshall said: 'The Bankrupt Law is said to grow out of the exigencies of commerce, and to be applied solely to traders; but it is not easy to say who must be excluded from, or may be included within, this description. It is like every other part of the subject, one on which the legislature may exercise an extensive discretion. This difficulty of discriminating with any accuracy between insolvent and bankrupt laws, would lead to the opinion that a bankrupt law may contain those regulations which are generally found in insolvent laws; and that an insolvent law may contain those which are common to a bankrupt law.'

"In the case, In re Klien, decided in the Circuit Court for the District of Missouri, and reported in a note to Nelson v. Carland, 1 How. 265, 277, Mr. Justice Catron held the Bankrupt Act of 1841 to be constitutional, although it was not restricted to traders, and allowed the debtor to avail himself of the act on his own petition, differing in these particulars from the English acts. He said among other things: 'In considering the question before me, I have not pretended to give a definition; but purposely avoided any attempt to define the mere word "bankruptcy." It is employed in the Constitution in the plural, and as part of an expression; "the subject of bankruptcies." The ideas attached to the word in this connection, are numerous and complicated; they form a subject of extensive and complicated legislation; of this subject, Congress has general jurisdiction; and the true inquiry is—to what limits is that jurisdiction restricted? I hold, it extends to all cases where the law causes to be distributed the property of the debtor among his creditors; this is its least limit. Its greatest, is the discharge of a debtor from his contract. And all intermediate legislation, affecting substance and form, but tending to further the great end of the subject—distribution and discharge—are in the competency and discretion of Congress. With the policy of a law, letting in all classes, others as well as traders; and permitting the bankrupt to come in voluntarily, and be discharged without the consent of his creditors, the courts have no concern; it belongs to the lawmakers.'

"Similar views were expressed under the act of 1867, by Mr. Justice Blatchford, then district judge, in In re Reiman, 7 Ben. 455; by Deady, J., in In re Silverman, 1 Sawy. 410; by Hoffman, J., In re California Pacific Railroad Co., 3 Sawy. 240; and in Kunzler v. Kohaus, 5 Hill. 317, by Cowen, J., in respect of the act of 1841, in which Mr. Justice Nelson, then chief justice of New York, concurred. The conclusion that an act of Congress establishing a uniform system of bankruptcy throughout the United States, is constitutional, although providing that others than traders may be adjudged bankrupts, and that this may be done on voluntary petitions, is really not open to discussion.

"The framers of the Constitution were familiar with Blackstone's Commentaries, and with the bankrupt laws of England, yet they granted plenary power to Congress over the whole subject of 'bankruptcies,' and did not limit it by the language used. This is illustrated by Mr. Sherman's observation in the Convention, that 'bankruptcies were, in some cases, punishable with death by the laws of England, and he did not choose to grant a power by which that might be done here;' and the rejoinder of Gouverneur Morris, that 'this was an extensive and delicate subject. He would agree to it, because he saw no danger of abuse of the power by the legislature of the United States.' Madison Papers, 5 Elliot 504; 2 Bancroft 204. And also to some extent by the amendment proposed by New York, 'that the power of Congress to pass uniform laws concerning bankruptcy shall only extend to merchants and other traders; and the States, respectively, may pass laws for the relief of other insolvent debtors.' 1 Elliot 330. See, also, Mr. Pinkney's original proposition, 5 Elliot 488; the report of the committee thereon, 5 Elliot 503; and the Federalist, No. 42, Ford's Ed. 279."

Compare, Leidigh Carriage Co. v. Stengel, 2 A. B. R. 383, 95 Fed. 637 (C. C. A. Ohio): "The history of the bankrupt laws in England shows that a bankrupt law, when our constitution was adopted, which applied to all members of the community alike, would have been a great anomaly. The first Bankrupt Act passed in England was St. 34 & 35, Hen. VIII, ch. 4, 'against such as do make bankrupt.' The provisions of this act were extended and expanded by Act 13, Eliz., ch. 7; by Act 21, Jac. I, ch. 19; by Act 7, Geo. I, ch. 31; by Act 5, Geo. II, ch. 30; by Act 46, Geo. III, ch. 135; by Act 6, Geo. IV, ch. 16; and by Act 1 & 2, Wm. IV, ch. 56. From the days of Henry VIII to the days of Victoria, the English bankruptcy acts applied only to traders, and it was not until the Act of 1861 that the bankruptcy extended to nontraders. The United States Bankruptcy Law of 1800, the first bankrupt law passed after the constitution was adopted, was an involuntary law, and applied only to traders, bankers, brokers, and underwriters. 2 Stat. 19, § 1.

"The question of the classes of persons to be affected by the Bankrupt Law is one largely, if not wholly, within the discretion of Congress. Chief Justice Marshall said in Sturges v. Crowninshield, 4 Wheat. 122, 194: 'The Bankrupt Law is said to grow out of the exigencies of commerce, and to be applicable solely to traders; but it is not easy to say who must be excluded from, or may be included in, this description. It is, like every other part of the subject, one on which the Legislature may exercise an extensive discretion.' * * * Certainly it can not be said that, in enacting the present law, Congress has passed the limits of such discretion. The proper purposes of a bankruptcy act like the present are: First (and this was its original purpose), to enable creditors to protect themselves by summary process against the frauds of their debtors in evading the payment of debts; second, to distribute the assets of the debtor equally among his creditors; and, third, to relieve debtors from the burden of debts which, through business misfortunes and otherwise, they have incurred, and which they are unable to pay. * * * The reason why bankruptcy legislation was limited to traders for so many centuries was because it was considered that traders were the class having the greatest opportunity, and therefore most likely, to commit the frauds which bankruptcy acts were passed to prevent."

§ 9. "Voluntary Bankruptcies" Not Outside of "Subject."—It is not unconstitutional because of its permitting voluntary bankruptcies, although bankruptcy law as developed in the mother country, at the time the framers of the Constitution used the words "on the subject of bankruptcies" was wholly adversary in its character and did not permit one to petition voluntarily for his own adjudication. This is the holding of the Supreme Court in Hanover Nat'l Bk. v. Moyses, 8 A. B. R. 1, 186 U. S. 181, quoted in the preceding paragraph.

Compare, Leidigh Carriage Co. v. Stengel, 2 A. B. R. 383, 95 Fed. 637 (C. C. A. Ohio): "In England, until 1849, there was no provision by which petitions in voluntary bankruptcy could be filed, though there had previously been acts for the relief of insolvent debtors from an early period; and parliament had, as Mr. Justice Vaughan Williams points out in In re Painter [1895], 1 Q. B. 85, recognized that the State has an interest in the debtor being relieved from his liability, so that he shall not be weighed down by the burden of indebtedness from discharging the duties of a citizen and may employ himself in honest industry."

§ 10. Dealing with One Part Only of "Subject."—And thus, also, Congress may enact an entire system of bankruptcy laws, or simply may deal with one or more parts, or phases, of the "subject of bankruptcies."

Obiter, Singer v. Nat'l Bedstead Mfg. Co., 11 A. B. R. 276 (N. J. Ch.): "A more or less indefinite, and I think misleading, notion has sometimes been expressed that the Constitution has committed to Congress the whole subject of bankruptcy and insolvency for appropriate legislation, and that therefore whenever Congress passes a general bankrupt law, which it has done four times, each time naming it a 'uniform system of bankruptcy,' all power on the part of the States to legislate upon the subject of bankruptcy or insolvency is immediately suspended. The premise may be deemed to be correct, but it seems to me that the conclusion is entirely erroneous. Congress is not obliged to legislate on the whole subject of bankruptcy; it may deal with only one or several parts. It is the enactment by Congress of a law applicable to a particular case which suspends any State law which otherwise would be applicable to that case. If every case of bankruptcy or insolvency were within the operation of a National Bankrupt Act, then no possible State law on the subject of bankruptcy or insolvency would have any vigor, but every such law would ipso facto be suspended.

When the present Bankruptcy Act [Act, July 1, 1898, ch. 541, 30 Stat. 544 (U. S. Comp. St. 1901, p. 3418)], was under discussion in Congress, my recollection is that a large and influential body of our national legislators earnestly proposed to enact merely a voluntary law—a law under which debtors could come into a bankrupt court, lay down their assets and get a discharge. Would anybody seriously argue that if such a 'uniform system of bankruptcy' had been enacted by Congress it would have had the effect to suspend the operation of State bankruptcy and insolvent laws under which insolvent debtors or fraudulent insolvent debtors are brought involuntarily into court and stripped of their assets for the benefit of their creditors?

"The present 'system of bankruptcy,' which Congress saw fit to enact in 1898, does not pretend to cover the whole field of either voluntary or involuntary bankruptcy and insolvency. Corporations are not allowed to become voluntary bankrupts [changed by Amendment of 1910]. Large classes of natural persons and corporations are excluded absolutely from the operation of the involuntary system. All corporations as well as natural persons are excluded if their debts do not amount to $1,000. It would be a most extraordinary state of affairs if transportation companies, insurance companies and many other kinds of business corporations not within the classes enumerated in the present Bankrupt Act, and also manufacturing, mercantile and trading corporations, whose debts do not amount to $1,000, could not be subjected to the operation of our New Jersey statute, which provides a means for winding them up and distributing their assets. The result would be that such corporations, when insolvent, could not be wound up at all at the instance of their creditors. The Bankrupt Act [Act, July 1, 1898, ch. 541, § 4B], expressly provides that nominal banks and banks incorporated under State or Federal laws shall not be adjudged involuntary bankrupts, the intention plainly being to leave these respective banking corporations to be wound up under national or State statutes particularly applicable to them.

"It is perfectly plain that State systems of voluntary and involuntary bankruptcy may remain today in full operation upon large numbers of insolvent natural persons and corporations who can not be brought within the operations of the National Bankrupt Act under any possible state of facts.

"It is also, it seems to me, equally plain that a State system of involuntary insolvency also remains in full operation upon persons and corporations, who are as possible bankrupts within the operation of the National Bankruptcy Act, so far as the State system deals with cases of which the bankrupt courts under the Federal act can obtain no jurisdiction. To state the point otherwise, I may say that to my mind there is no distinction between an insolvent insurance company, railroad company or laundry company, which owes $1,000 of debts and has committed an act of bankruptcy, on the one hand, and an insolvent manufacturing, mercantile or trading company which has committed no act of bankruptcy, or does not owe debts amounting to $1,000, on the other hand, in respect of the operation of the national Bankrupt Act and the New Jersey Insolvent Corporation Act. In neither instance is a case presented of which the Federal bankrupt court can take cognizance. Each case, therefore, is within the full and complete operation of the New Jersey statute.

"As I read the present Bankrupt Act, the intention of Congress is that every case of bankruptcy or insolvency of which the bankrupt court has jurisdiction is to be dealt with exclusively by that court. The intention of the act is to supply the law of certain cases, and to supply a special court to enforce that law. All other cases of bankruptcy or insolvency are left to be dealt with as the State Legislature may see fit.

"It may be conceded that Congress can provide a law for only a limited number of cases of bankruptcy and insolvency, and expressly prohibit the enactment of any other bankrupt or insolvent laws by the States. For present purposes the concession may be that Congress might pass a voluntary system of bankruptcy, and enact that there should be no other law on the subject of bankruptcy or insolvency, voluntary or involuntary, throughout the United States. Even if this be a sound view, it need not be considered, because the present Bankrupt Act contains no words prohibiting States from passing insolvent or bankrupt laws which deal with cases which are not within the operation of the National Bankrupt Act—which are expressly excluded from it. It would be a singular result, indeed, if because Congress has not seen fit to provide a bankrupt law applicable to corporations engaged in operating railroads, steamboats, insurance companies, laundries, livery stables and large numbers of other business enterprises, the inference must be drawn that Congress did not intend that any bankrupt or insolvent laws should be applied to this class of corporations, but that State insolvency laws applicable to them should be suspended."

§ 11. Do Not Delegate Legislative Power.

—The laws so established do not, in contravention of constitutional law, attempt to delegate legislative power because of their recognition and enforcement of the diverse laws of the several states and of changes in such laws from time to time in the matters of exemptions, dower, priority of payment and the like.[11]

§ 12. Do Not Violate Constitutional Guaranty of "Due Process."

—Discharge in bankruptcy and adjudication of bankruptcy without notice to creditors interested, or without personal service of notice, do not violate the constitutional guaranty of due process of law.[12]

Hanover Nat'l Bk. v. Moyses, 8 A. B. R. 11, 186 U. S. 181: "Notwithstanding these provisions, it is insisted that the want of notice of filing the petition is fatal because the adjudication per se entitles the bankrupt to a discharge, and that the proceedings in respect of discharge are in personam, and require personal service of notice. The adjudication does not in itself have that effect, and the first of these objections really rests on the ground that the notice provided for is unreasonably short, and the right to oppose discharge unreasonably restricted. Considering the plenary power of Congress, the subject-matter of the suit, and the common rights and interests of the creditors, we regard the contention as untenable.

"Congress may prescribe any regulations concerning discharge in bankruptcy

11. Hanover Nat'l Bk. v. Moyses, 8 A. B. R. 1, 186 U. S. 181, quoted ante, § 8, and post, §§ 12, 13.

12. In re Billing, 17 A. B. R. 841, 45 Fed. 395 (D. C. Ala.); Compare obiter, In re Continental Corporation, 14 A. B. R. 538 (Ref. Ohio).

that are not so grossly unreasonable as to be incompatible with fundamental law, and we can not find anything in this act on that subject which would justify us in overthrowing its action.

"Nor is it possible to concede that personal service of notice of the application for a discharge is required.

"Proceedings in bankruptcy are, generally speaking, in the nature of proceedings in rem, as Mr. Justice Grier remarked in Shawham *v.* Wherrit, 7 How. 643. And in New Lamp Chimney Co. *v.* Brass and Copper Co., 91 U. S. 662, it was ruled that a decree adjudging a corporation bankrupt is in the nature of a decree in rem as respects the status of the corporation. Creditors are bound by the proceedings in distribution on notice by publication and mail, and when jurisdiction has attached and been exercised to that extent, the court has jurisdiction to decree discharge, if sufficient opportunity to show cause to the contrary is afforded, on notice given in the same way. The determination of the status of the honest and unfortunate debtor by his liberation from encumbrance on future exertion is matter of public concern, and Congress has power to accomplish it throughout the United States by proceedings at the debtor's domicil. If such notice to those who may be interested in opposing discharge, as the nature of the proceeding admits, is provided to be given, that is sufficient. Service of process or personal notice is not essential to the binding force of the decree."

§ 13. Do Not Impair Obligation of Contracts.

§ **13. Do Not Impair Obligation of Contracts.**—The laws so established do not contravene the constitutional prohibition against the impairment of the obligation of contracts by virtue of discharging debtors from the obligations of their contracts; for such prohibition is solely upon the states, not upon the United States.[13]

Hanover Nat'l Bk. *v.* Moyses, 8 A. B. R. 7, 186 U. S. 181: "As the States, in surrendering the power, did so only if Congress chose to exercise it, but in the absence of congressional legislation retained it, the limitation was imposed on the States that they should pass no 'law impairing the obligation of contracts.' In Brown *v.* Smart, 145 U. S. 454, 457, Mr. Justice Gray said: 'So long as there is no national bankrupt act, each State has full authority to pass insolvent laws binding persons and property within its jurisdiction, provided it does not impair the obligation of existing contracts, but a State can not by such a law discharge one of its own citizens from his contracts with citizens of other States, though made after the passage of the law, unless they voluntarily become parties to the proceedings in insolvency. Yet each State, so long as it does not impair the obligation of any contract, has the power by general laws to regulate the conveyance and disposition of all property, personal or real, within its limits and jurisdiction.' Many cases were cited, and, among others, Denny *v.* Bennett, 128 U. S. 498, where Mr. Justice Miller observed: 'The objection to the extraterritorial operation of a State insolvent law is, that it can not, like the Bankruptcy Law passed by Congress under its constitutional grant of power, release all debtors from the obligation of their debts. The authority to deal with the property of the debtor within the State, so far as it does not impair the obligation of contracts, is conceded.'

"Counsel justly says that 'the relation of debtor and creditor has a dual aspect and contains two separate elements. The one is the right of the creditor to resort to present property of the debtor through the courts to satisfy the

13. In re Milling Co., 16 A. B. R. 454, 457 (D. C. Tex.).

debt; the other is the personal obligation of the debtor to pay the debt, and that he will devote his energies and labor to discharge it,' 4 Wheat. 198; and 'in the absence of property the personal obligation to pay constitutes the only value of the debt.' Hence the importance of the distinction between the power of Congress and the power of the States. The subject of 'bankruptcies' includes the power to discharge the debtor from his contracts and legal liabilities as well as to distribute his property. The grant to Congress involves the power to impair the obligation of contracts, and this the States were forbidden to do.

"The laws passed on the subject must, however, be uniform throughout the United States, but that uniformity is geographical and not personal, and we do not think that the provision of the act of 1898 as to exemptions is incompatible with the rule."

§ 14. May Impose Enforcement on State Courts.—Congress constitutionally may impose the burden of enforcing the substantive rights conferred by the law upon the courts of the several states.

Obiter, Singer v. Nat'l Bedstead Mfg. Co., 11 A. B. R. 276 (N. J. Ch.): "It may be that Congress cannot impose upon the State courts the duty of administering any system of bankrupt laws, but if Congress sees fit to pass general laws on the subject of bankruptcy, without providing the judicial machinery for their administration, all State courts having jurisdiction of bankruptcy or insolvency cases would be obliged to enforce the laws on that subject enacted by Congress, and any conflicting State laws, or any State laws whatever applicable to the cases to which the Federal laws applied, would be superseded. A very complete 'system' of bankruptcy laws could, I think, be enacted by Congress without creating any special bankrupt Courts, at all. Such a code would be enforceable by all the Courts, State or Federal, having jurisdiction of any case to which the code applied, the code being the 'supreme law of the land.' * * *

"In the present instance, Congress has seen fit to provide a more or less elaborate code of bankruptcy laws applicable to certain specified cases, and to erect special tribunals who have exclusive cognizance of those cases, and who have to a large extent exclusive jurisdiction to administer this code of laws. The result is that the State courts lose jurisdiction of those cases, if they ever had any, because State laws which are applicable to them are suspended, and the State courts are not permitted to administer the Federal Bankrupt Law except to a very limited extent."

Hall v. Chicago, etc., R. Co. (Sup. Ct. Neb.), 25 A. B. R. 53: "The bankruptcy laws of Congress, enacted pursuant to the powers delegated to it by the Federal Constitution, are binding upon the State as well as the federal courts; the State courts are bound to respect the rights acquired under them, and it is not to be believed that any of our State courts will attempt to override or nullify any of such laws."

§ 14½. Uniformity of Court Procedure Essential.—But it is essential to its "uniformity" that the bankruptcy act be administered in accordance with uniform court process and procedure; and it would fall short of its purpose were its administration subjected to the forty-eight differing systems of court procedure of the different states.

Compare observation in Hills v. McKinniss Co., 26 A. B. R. 329, 188 Fed. 1012 (D. C. Ohio): "A system of bankruptcy, national in its character, to be uniform in its operation must of necessity be unique in its method of administration."

CHAPTER II.

In General, The Nature, Objects and Construction of The Law and of The Procedure under It, and Forms and Orders.

Synopsis of Chapter.

§ 15. In General.—The bankruptcy law of the United States is a system of jurisprudence originating in the English laws as the same were developed during the two or three centuries preceding our Revolution; and it has for its objects, first, the securing of possession of an insolvent's assets, the procuring of their equitable division among creditors, preventing and avoiding attempts of one creditor to obtain advantage over other creditors therein; and second, the liberation of worthy debtors from the burden of unpaid debts. Such proceedings are proceedings in rem; they proceed in accordance with equitable principles, and the law is to be fairly and reasonably construed with a view to effecting its objects.

§ 16. Definition and History of Bankruptcy Law.—For the history of bankruptcy law and a definition of the idea of the law, the reader is referred to the Introduction to this treatise, ante.

Grunsfeld Bros. *v.* Brownell, 11 A. B. R. 602 (New Mex. Sup. Ct.): "The best definition which we have been able to find of a bankrupt law is in 5 Cyc. 237, which is: 'A bankrupt law, in modern legal significance, means a statutory system under which an insolvent debtor may either on his own petition or that of his creditors be adjudged bankrupt by a court of competent jurisdiction, which thereupon takes possession of his property, distributes it equally among his creditors, and discharges the bankrupt and his after-acquired property from debts existing at the initiation of the bankruptcy proceedings.'"

§ 17. Objects and Purposes.—The objects and purposes of modern bankruptcy law are twofold: First, to secure possession of an insolvent's assets and procure their equitable division among creditors, preventing and avoiding attempts of one creditor to obtain advantage over other creditors therein; and second, to free the worthy debtor from the burden of unpaid debts. See the following expressions from the courts.[1]

MacDonald *v.* Tefft-Wellar Co., 11 A. B. R. 806, 128 Fed. 381 (C. C. A. Fla.): "The object of the Bankrupt Law is twofold—the benefit of the creditors and the relief of the bankrupt. Mr. Justice Story describes a bankrupt law as 'a law for the benefit and relief of creditors and their debtors in cases in which the latter are unable or unwilling to pay their debts.' 2 Story, Const., § 113, note 2. Mr. Stephen speaks of it as 'a system of law of a peculiar and anomalous character, intended to afford to the creditors of persons engaged in trade a greater security for the collection of their debts than they enjoyed at common law under the ordinary remedy by action.' 2 Steph. Com. 189. It cannot be necessary that both objects shall be attainable in order to warrant proceedings in bankruptcy. In many, perhaps a majority, of cases, the relief to the bankrupt is the only question, for there are no assets to distribute, and in many other cases the benefit and relief of creditors is the only object. A bankrupt may through fraud have lost his right to a discharge. An insolvent corporation whose property, including all franchises, has been distributed to creditors in involuntary proceedings in bankruptcy, takes little, if anything, by a discharge."

Continental Nat'l Bk. *v.* Katz, 1 A. B. R. 20 (Superior Ct. Ill.): "There are two principles which lie at the foundation of the Bankrupt Act: (1) that the debtor may be discharged from his provable debts; and (2) that his collectible assets may be divided equitably and ratably between his creditors."

Stevens *v.* Nave-McCord Co., 17 A. B. R. 615 (C. C. A. Colo.): "The discharge of the bankrupt from his debts and the equal distribution of his unexempt property among his creditors of the same class were the chief objects which Congress sought to attain by the enactment of this statute. The preference of one or more creditors over others of the same class was one of the principal evils at which the statute was leveled. Witness the prohibition of the allowance of the claim of a preferred creditor and of his participation in the meetings of creditors until he surrenders his preference and the right granted to the trustee to recover from him the property he has obtained thereby or its value."

Swarts *v.* Fourth Nat'l Bk., 8 A. B. R. 676, 117 Fed. 1 (C. C. A. Mo.): "No one can become familiar with the bankruptcy law of 1898, without a settled conviction that the two dominant purposes of the framers of that act were: (1) The protection and discharge of the bankrupt; and (2) the distribution of the unexempt property which the bankrupt owned four months before the filing of the petition in bankruptcy against him, share and share alike, among his creditors. All the earlier sections of the act are devoted to the security and relief of the bankrupt, and, when the distribution of his property is reached, the provisions relating to it are all drawn from the standpoint of the insolvent, and not from that of his creditors. The rights and privileges of the bankrupt, and the equal distribution of his property, dominate every provision, while the rights, wrongs, benefits, and injuries of his creditors are always incidental, and secondary to these controlling purposes."

[1867] Wiswall *v.* Campbell, 93 U. S. 347: "Congress, in enacting the Bankrupt Law (that of 1867) had apparently in view (1) the discharge under some

---

1 In re Swofford Bros. Dry Goods Co., 25 A. B. R. 282, 180 Fed. 549 (D. C. Mo.); In re Adams, 1 A. B. R. 99 (Ref. N. Y.). See, also, speech of Hon. Swager Sherley, Congressional Record of March 1, 1910.

circumstances, of an honest debtor under legal liability for debts he could not pay; and (2) an early pro rata distribution, according to equity, of his available assets among his several creditors."

U. S. ex rel Adler *v*. Hammond, 4 A. B. R. 738, 104 Fed. 862 (C. C. A. Tenn.): "The general purpose of the act so far as it relates to creditors, is that the assets of the debtor liable to the payment of their dues shall be speedily collected and distributed to them in accordance with the equitable rules thereby prescribed. As concerns the bankrupt the leading purpose is that having surrendered to his creditors all his property subject to their demands, he shall be released from all further liability from his debts and be given a clear field for future effort."

Ross *v*. Saunders, 5 A. B. R. 350, 105 Fed. 915 (C. C. A. Mass.): "The fundamental right of the bankrupt under the statute is to surrender all his assets and obtain his discharge. The fundamental right of the creditor is to have all the assets of the bankrupt applied to his debt, subject to his obligation to submit to a discharge when they have been thus applied."

Farmers Bank *v*. Carr, 11 A. B. R. 733 (C. C. A.): "The essential principle of the Bankruptcy Law is that all of the bankrupt's property be divided equally, without preference, to the payment of his debts. It abhors preferences."

In re Leslie, 9 A. B. R. 567, 119 Fed. 406 (D. C. N. Y.): "The main purpose of the bankruptcy law is to prevent preferences and secure a fair and equitable division of the bankrupt estate among the creditors, not to grant discharges. This end accomplished, the bankrupt is granted a discharge from all his debts."

In re Edes, 14 A. B. R. 383, 135 Fed. 595 (D. C. Me.): "The evident intention of Congress in passing the Bankrupt Law of 1898 was to provide an ample and complete method of administering and disposing of the assets of insolvents. The court created by this law was given jurisdiction which is in the broadest sense equitable. It is the evident intention of Congress to place the details of the administration of the estate within the jurisdiction of the court."

Brown *v*. Barker, 8 A. B. R. 453, 68 App. Div. 594, 74 N. Y. Supp. 43: "It is well for us to keep in mind that the three fundamental objects, which the Bankruptcy Act was intended to secure and accomplish were: (1) That a debtor who had been unfortunate, and become unable to pay his debts, might be released therefrom, and be enabled to commence his business life anew relieved of the burden, provided that he had not been guilty of fraudulent or other improper practices. (2) That, as the condition and price of being so released, he should turn over to his assignee, fully and unqualifiedly, all of his property which was subject to the demands of his creditors. (3) That this property should be applied equitably and ratably to the payment of his various debts, rather than that creditors should be allowed to pursue it for their own individual and diverse interests, with the result that one might secure payment in full of his claim and another get nothing. This object was emphasized in the act by those provisions which, within certain limits, took away, even from the vigilant creditor, any advantage which he might have secured prior to the filing of the petition in bankruptcy."

Blake *v*. Valentine, 1 A. B. R. 373, 89 Fed. 691 (D. C. Calif.): "The National Bankruptcy Act establishes a uniform system and regulates, in all their details, the relations, rights and duties of debtor and creditor."

Hicks *v*. Knost, 2 A. B. R. 155, 94 Fed. 627 (D. C. Ohio): "The object and purpose of the law is (1) to discharge honest bankrupts from their debts and (2) to secure to their creditors an equal distribution of their estate."

1 R Bky—3

In re Blount, 16 A. B. R. 101, 142 Fed. 263 (D. C. Ark.): "The main object of the Bankruptcy Act is to secure an equal distribution of the assets of an insolvent among all his creditors and prevent preferences. The duty of the courts is to carry this intention of Congress into effect to the extent which the language of the Act justifies. Mere schemes and artifices to avoid the letter and spirit of the law will not be tolerated."

In re Harr, 16 A. B. R. 217, 143 Fed. 421 (D. C. Mo.): "One of the main objects of the Bankruptcy Act is to protect unfortunate, but honest debtors. Fraudulent debtors are not intended to be protected, nor to escape payment of their just liabilities."

Leidigh Carriage Co. v. Stengel, 2 A. B. R. 383, 95 Fed. 637 (C. C. A. Ohio): "The proper purposes of a bankruptcy act like the present are: First (and this was its original purpose), to enable creditors to protect themselves by summary process against the frauds of their debtors in evading the payment of debts; second, to distribute the assets of the debtor equally among his creditors; and, third, to relieve debtors from the burden of debts which, through business misfortunes and otherwise, they have incurred, and which they are unable to pay."

In re Forbes, 11 A. B. R. 790, 128 Fed. 137 (D. C. Mass.): "The equal and equitable distribution of the estates of insolvents and their discharge from the obligation of their debts are the ends sought by proceedings in bankruptcy."

Barton Bros. v. Produce Co., 14 A. B. R. 504, 136 Fed. 355 (C. C. A. Ark.): "The spirit of the Bankrupt Act is commendable. Its purpose is to release the honest debtor from the burden of debts which he is unable to longer carry; to give freer play to his energies and enterprises, that he may thereafter be better able to support himself and those dependent upon his earnings, and thereby be in position to render a better service to the State and to society. The beneficent policy is conditioned always upon the bankrupt's full and complete surrender of all his unexempt property for the benefit of his creditors. He must be honest in this respect. He must neither conceal nor withhold knowingly anything from his creditors which they are entitled, under the law, to know or receive. Whenever the court is impressed with the belief, after due inquiry and examination, that in the main the bankrupt has intended and tried to comply with the law, he should be dealt with liberally on his petition for manumission from his debts. On the other hand, in order to obstruct gross abuses of the spirit of the Bankrupt Act, that it may not aid the dishonest debtor in being acquitted of his honest debts, while withholding aught that he should surrender for the benefit of his creditors, it is the duty of the court to look into the heart of his transactions."

Compare In re Hicks, 6 A. B. R. 183, 107 Fed. 910 (D. C. Vt.): "Involuntary proceedings in bankruptcy are not mere suits against the bankrupt for the collection of debts, but are broader, for the equal distribution of his property among his creditors."

Coal Land Co. v. Ruffner Bros., 21 A. B. R. 474, 165 Fed. 881 (C. C. A. W. Va.): "The prime purpose of the Bankruptcy Act is to secure an equal distribution of an insolvent's estate among the creditors."

Hurley v. Devlin, 18 A. B. R. 627, 151 Fed. 919 (D. C. Kans.): "Before passing to a consideration of the precise question involved in this controversy, it may be well to advert to a few general principles of the law, and to state some of the fundamental propositions underlying the rights of the respective parties to this litigation. First, it may be observed, as has been so often announced by the courts, that the federal Constitution and the acts of Congress passed in pursuance of the power it confers are the supreme law of this country, binding alike on all persons, all courts, and the Legislatures of the several states. By § 8 of the Constitution the people of this nation, in their individual, and the several states in their sovereign, capacities, conferred upon the Congress of the United States the express power to enact 'uniform laws on the subject of bankruptcies throughout the United States,' and in pursuance of the power thus conferred the national bankrupt law was enacted. The object and purpose of Congress as portrayed by this act was to take in charge the property of insolvent debtors who had committed acts of bankruptcy, through proceedings had in the bankruptcy courts, divide this property between the bankrupt, his wife and children, if any, on the one hand, and his creditors on the other, in proportion to their provable demands, and grant a discharge to the bankrupt debtor from further liability for his debts in so far as the Bankrupt Act grants a discharge. * * * In the exercise of this supreme power, Congress acts untrammeled by any State laws, whether organic or statutory, and it was within the power of Congress to preserve to the bankrupt debtor, his wife and children, just such rights in the bankrupt estate as are by the terms of the act provided, or, in the exercise of such power, to have cut off and destroyed all such claims and exemptions, and all others, leaving all the estate to the creditors and nothing to the bankrupt or his family, as Congress in its wisdom might deem proper."

In re Tindall, 18 A. B. R. 773, 155 Fed. 456 (D. C. S. Car.): "The main object of the Bankrupt Act and one of its most beneficial results, was an equal distribution among the creditors of the estate of the bankrupt."

Compare Hardie v. Dry Goods Co., 21 A. B. R. 457, 165 Fed. 588 (C. C. A. Tex.): "Originally, in bankrupt laws, the discharge of the bankrupt may have been incidental, and the main purpose the equal distribution of his goods among creditors; but to say it now, and of the present law, we must shut our eyes to the actual practice in our courts. In nearly all and every voluntary bankruptcy brought under the present law the administration or distribution of the bankrupt's property has been practically concluded before filing petition, and the sole object of the petitioner is to be relieved of his debts, and in number the voluntary cases are about four to one of the involuntary. See Report, Dept. of Justice, 1907. And the same may be said of the voluntary cases under the Act of March 2, 1867, c. 176, 14 Stat. 517, which was passed mainly to relieve the unfortunate debtors ruined by and through the vicissitudes of the great Civil War. For these considerations, we are disposed to deny that in the present bankruptcy law the discharge of the honest debtor is a mere incident which could have been omitted without impairing its symmetry and efficiency; and, on the contrary, to assert that the release of the honest, unfortunate, and insolvent debtor from the burden of his debts and his restoration to business activity, in the interest of his family and the general public, are the main, if not the most important, objects of the law."

In re Adams & Hoyt Co., 21 A. B. R. 161, 164 Fed. 489 (D. C. Ga.): "It is the paramount law for the administration of estates of insolvents. Its provisions * * * seek to bring about equality among creditors of the same class."

In re Frazin & Oppenheim, 24 A. B. R. 598, 183 Fed. 28 (C. C. A. N. Y.): "The object of Congress in enacting the bankruptcy law was to secure the efficient and fair administration of estates."

James v. Stone, 24 A. B. R. 288, 181 Fed. 1021 (C. C. A. N. Car.): "But, under the circumstances of this case, it cannot be reasonably insisted that a court of justice should, by its decree, proclaim to the public that one who concealed his goods, for the purpose of defrauding his creditors, had dealt fairly with his fellow man and that such an individual is entitled to the benefits of an act intended to promote honesty and fair dealing."

In re Levenstein, 24 A. B. R. 822, 180 Fed. 957 (D. C. Conn.): "Neither this law nor any of its predecessors was passed by Congress for the particular purpose of enabling the debtor to cancel his debts. The primary purpose of all such laws is to distribute the assets of the bankrupt equally and fairly amongst his creditors, and as an incident thereto the present law provides that he may, if his dealings have been fair and honest, be discharged from the balance of his indebtedness as an incentive to a further honest effort to obtain a livelihood."

Baylor v. Rawlings, 28 A. B. R. 773, 200 Fed. 131 (C. C. A. Neb.): "The purpose of a voluntary proceeding in bankruptcy is in consideration that the bankrupt promptly surrender all of his non-exempt property to the bankruptcy court, to the end that all of his creditors, without preference or priority, may take share and share alike in percentage of the property thus surrendered; then the bankrupt is given an acquittance of such percentage of his debts not thus paid, and may commence his business life anew."

Its purpose, also, is to protect interstate commerce by superimposing upon the forty-eight differing and confusing systems of State jurisprudence, the one vast uniform system of rights and remedies of the Bankruptcy Act, governing the relations of debtors and creditors in the event of business failure.

In re Beckhaus, 24 A. B. R. 380, 177 Fed. 141 (C. C. A. Ills.): "When the amended section [§ 60 (b) relative to preferences] is read against the background of the nature and purpose of the act, our interpretation we believe is confirmed. The act is a national act. It practically supplants the State insolvency laws. We think it clear that Congress recognized the vast sweep of interstate commerce and meant to free interstate traders from the confusion attendant upon a multiplicity of variant local laws. Therefore the act in all its parts ought to be interpreted in a national view, doing away as far as possible with the variances in the local laws."

Acme Harvester Co. v. Beekman Co., 27 A. B. R. 262, 222 U. S. 300: "It is the purpose of the bankruptcy law * * * to establish a uniform system of bankruptcy throughout the United States, to place the property of the bankrupt under the control of the court, wherever it is found, with a view to its equal distribution among the creditors."

§ 18. Bankruptcy Proceedings, Proceedings in Rem, Also in Personam.—Bankruptcy proceedings are proceedings in rem.[2]

2. In re Benedict, 15 A. B. R. 232, 238, 140 Fed. 55 (D. C. Wis.); In re Reynolds, 11 A. B. R. 760 (D. C. Mont.); In re Elmira Steel Co., 5 A. B. R. 486 (Ref. N. Y.); Southern Loan & Trust Co. v. Benbow, 3 A. B. R. 9, 96 Fed. 514 (D. C. N. Car., reversed, on other grounds, in 3 A. B. R. 710); In re Continental Corp'n, 14 A. B. R. 538 (Ref. Ohio); In re Reese, 8 A. B. R. 411, 115 Fed. 993 (D. C. Ala.); In re Beals, 8 A. B. R. 644, 116 Fed. 530 (D. C. Ind.); Acme Harvester Co. v. Beekman Co., 27 A. B. R. 262, 222 U. S. 300; Hills v. McKinniss Co., 26 A. B. R. 329, 188 Fed. 1012 (D. C. Ohio); Johnson v. United States, 20 A. B. R. 724, 163 Fed. 30 (C. C. A. Mass.), quoted at § 2323; In re Am. Brew. Co., 7 A. B. R. 463, 112 Fed. 752 (C. C. A. Ills.), quoted at § 444.

General View of Amendments of 1910.—For a general resumé of the different amendments passed in 1910, see parallel column statement, annexed to the speech of Hon. Swager Sherley, to be found in the Congressional Record of March 1st, 1910.

Hanover Nat'l Bk. *v.* Moyses, 8 A. B. R. 1, 186 U. S. 181: "Proceedings in bankruptcy are, generally speaking, in the nature of proceedings in rem, as Mr. Justice Grier remarked in Shawham *v.* Wherrit, 7 How. 643. And in New Lamp Chimney Co. *v.* Brass and Copper Co., 91 U. S. 662, it was ruled that a decree adjudging a corporation bankrupt is in the nature of a decree in rem as respects the status of the corporation. Creditors are bound by the proceedings in distribution on notice by publication and mail, and when jurisdiction has attached and been exercised to that extent, the court has jurisdiction to decree discharge, if sufficient opportunity to show cause to the contrary is afforded, on notice given in the same way. The determination of the status of the honest and unfortunate debtor by his liberation from encumbrance on future exertion is matter of public concern, and Congress has power to accomplish it throughout the United States by proceedings at the debtor's domicile. If such notice to those who may be interested in opposing discharge, as the nature of the proceeding admits, is provided to be given, that is sufficient. Service of process or personal notice is not essential to the binding force of the decree."

In re Beals, 8 A. B. R. 644, 116 Fed. 530 (D. C. Ind.): "The adjudication of bankruptcy proceeds in rem, and all persons interested in the res are regarded as parties to the bankruptcy proceedings."

Carter *v.* Hobbs, 1 A. B. R. 224, 92 Fed. 594 (D. C. Ind.): "The adjudication proceeds in rem, and all persons interested in the res are regarded as parties to the bankruptcy proceedings. These parties include not only the bankrupt and trustee, but also all the creditors of the bankrupt."

But compare trenchant remarks of Holt, J., in Whitney *v.* Wenman, 14 A. B. R. 592, 140 Fed. 960 (D. C. N. Y.): "It is claimed that the order passing the receivers' accounts was a judgment in rem. The counsel asserts that proceedings in bankruptcy are proceeding in rem, and that probate proceedings are proceedings in rem, and that a receiver's accounting is analogous to an executor's accounting. But in the first place the term 'a judgment in rem' is one which has various meanings. As Judge Holmes says, in Tyler *v.* Court of Registration (175 Mass. 76): 'No phrase has been more misused.' An adjudication of bankruptcy upon a petition in an involuntary proceeding is a judgment in rem, in the sense that it determines the status of the bankrupt; but the ordinary proceedings taken in a bankruptcy proceeding to decide questions arising in it are not, as I understand it, proceedings in rem. A proceeding, for instance, to determine a disputed claim, would not bind anybody except the parties to it. So a decree admitting or refusing to admit a will to probate is a proceeding in rem, so far as it determines the status of the will, but all the proceedings in the administration of an estate in the Surrogate's Court which result in orders are not proceedings in rem. A decree passing an executor's accounts, for instance, is of no effect against parties not cited. Butterfield *v.* Smith, 101 U. S. 570; Hood *v.* Hood, 19 Hun 300; Ib. on Appeal, 85 N. Y. 561; Black on Judgments, § 644. Many judgments which are sometimes called judgments in rem, but which are more properly described as being quasi in rem, bind only the parties, such as judgments on attachments or in foreclosure. Freeman *v.* Alderson, 119 U. S. 185; Black on Judgments, § 793; Freeman on Judgments, § 617. I think, therefore, that the proceeding to pass the receivers' accounts was not a proceeding in rem, and that the order entered upon it was not binding upon the defendants. If that is so, it was not binding upon the complainant, for estoppels by judgment must be mutual. Suppose the complainant, instead of objecting to the items in the receivers' accounts, had brought a separate action against the receivers to recover the value of the money and property which they delivered to the defendants."

The petition for adjudication, as also the petition for discharge, is a suit between the debtor and his creditors to determine his status, first as a bankrupt, and then as one released from his debts.

In re Levenstein, 24 A. B. R. 822, 180 Fed. 957 (D. C. Conn.): "Now just one moment's thought about the petitions for adjudication and discharge. They are in form and in fact proceedings in equity, in which the bankrupt is petitioner and his creditors are respondents. The bankrupt undertakes to show that he is an honest man, but has been unsuccessful; that he has committed no fraud, but has been the victim of misfortune. If he can establish these facts, he goes free; if he cannot, he has wasted his' time and bothered the court to no good purpose. Congress has pointed out to him the way to go about it, and he is bound to follow that path with precision and exactness."

It is better expressed to say that proceedings in bankruptcy are proceeding in rem first for the determination of the.status of the debtor as a bankrupt and then for the administration of his estate.

Indeed, they are both proceedings in rem and, in some phases, also proceedings in personam.[3]

§ 19. And All Persons Bound.

§ 19. **And All Persons Bound.**—Thus all persons are bound thereby (as to the proceedings that are strictly "bankruptcy proceedings," although not necessarily as to "controversies" arising out of the bankruptcy proceedings).[4]

In re Beals, 8 A. B. R. 644, 116 Fed. 530 (D. C. Ind.): "These parties include not only the bankrupt and trustee, but also all the creditors of the bankrupt."

In re Reynolds, 11 A. B. R. (D. C. Mont.): "An adjudication of bankruptcy operates in rem, and from the moment of the adjudication the bankrupt's estate is under the jurisdiction of the bankruptcy court, which will not permit any interference with its possession, even though it be by an officer of a state court acting under its process. Being a proceeding in rem, all parties interested in the res are regarded as parties thereto, including the bankrupt and trustee, as well as the creditors, secured and unsecured. The adjudication vests in the trustee or temporary receiver the title of the bankrupt's property, and stays all seizures made within four months."

Thus, all creditors are parties and bound thereby.[5]

3. Dressel v. North State Lumber Co., 5 A. B. R. 744, 107 Fed. 256 (D. C. N. C.); In re Tybo Min. & Reduc. Co., 13 A. B. R. 62, 132 Fed. 697 (D. C. Nev.); Hills v. McKinniss Co., 26 A. B. R. 329, 188 Fed. 1012 (D. C. Ohio). Compare, In re Magid-Hope Silk Mfg. Co., 6 A. B. R. 610, 110 Fed. 352 (D. C. Mass.).

4. Southern Loan & Trust Co. v. Benbow, 3 A. B. R. 9, 96 Fed. 514 (D. C. N. Car., reversed, on other grounds, in 3 A. B. R. 710); Carter v. Hobbs, 1 A. B. R. 215, 92 Fed. 594 (D. C. Ind.). Compare, In re Continental Corp'n, 14 A. B. R. 538 (Ref. Ohio).

5. Hackney v. Hargreaves Co., 13 A. B. R. 164, 68 Neb. 624; In re Pekin Plow Co., 7 A. B. R. 369, 112 Fed. 309 (C. C. A.); In re Frazier, 9 A. B. R. 21, 117 Fed. 746 (D. C. Mo.); In re Beerman, 7 A. B. R. 431, 112 Fed. 662 (D. C. Ga.).

Bear *v.* Chase, 3 A. B. R. 751, 99 Fed. 920 (C. C. A. S. C.): "Upon the adjudication of the bankrupt, all creditors become parties to the bankruptcy proceedings by operation of law, and particularly those creditors by whose act the bankruptcy was caused."

Of course all creditors "proving claims" become parties.[6]

But as to proceedings not "bankruptcy proceedings" proper but merely "controversies" arising out of or in the course of bankruptcy proceedings, persons not made parties thereto are not bound thereby. Thus, an order requiring a bankrupt to assign a life insurance policy to the trustee does not purport to pass upon the rights of a person to whom he had already assigned it.[7] And notice to creditors is not necessary to the binding force of the decree of adjudication;[8] nor of the subsequent proceedings in the administration of the estate.

And creditors are entitled to such notice only as the statute prescribes.[9]

In re Reese, 8 A. B. R. 413, 115 Fed. 993 (D. C. Ala.): "Proceedings in bankruptcy are in the nature of a proceeding in rem, and certainly a creditor who has received notice of the filing and that he has been scheduled as a creditor, is charged with notice of whatever transpires in the further administration of the bankrupt's estate."

Or as may be prescribed by a valid rule of court.[10]

Nor is personal notice of the application for discharge essential to the binding force of the discharge decree.[11]

Nor is personal service essential to the effectiveness of the adjudication in subsequent litigation for the recovery of assets in another district.[12]

§ 20. Bankruptcy Proceedings, Proceedings in Equity.—Bankruptcy proceedings are a branch of equity jurisprudence.[13]

6. In re Keller, 6 A. B. R. 334, 350 (D. C. Iowa).

7. In re Madden, 6 A. B. R. 614, 110 Fed. 348 (C. C. A. N. Y.).

8. In re Billings, 17 A. B. R. 80, 145 Fed. 395 (D. C. Ala.). Obiter, In re Mason, 3 A. B. R. 599, 99 Fed. 256 (D. C. N. Car.).

9. Hanover Nat'l Bk. *v.* Moyses, 8 A. B. R. 1, 186 U. S. 181. See ante, § 12.

10. In re Wollowitz, 27 A. B. R. 558, 192 Fed. 105 (C. C. A. N. Y.) decided under a rule of the Southern District.

11. Hanover National Bk. *v.* Moyses, 8 A. B. R. 1, 186 U. S. 181. See ante, § 12.

12. Hills *v.* McKinniss Co., 26 A. B. R. 329, 188 Fed. 1012 (D. C. Ohio).

13. In re Swofford Bros. Dry Goods Co., 25 A. B. R. 282, 180 Fed. 549 (D. C. Mo.); Missouri Elec. Co. *v.* Hamilton Brown Co., 21 A. B. R. 270, 165 Fed. 283 (C. C. A. Mo.), quoted post at § 552; Natl. Bank *v.* Abbott, 21 A. B. R. 436, 165 Fed. 852 (C. C. A. Mo.); In re Cooke, 5 A. B. R. 434, 109 Fed. 631 (D. C. N. Y.); Westall *v.* Avery, 22 A. B. R. 673, 171 Fed. 626 (C. C. A. N. Car.). Also, In re Faulkner, 20 A. B. R. 542, 161 Fed. 900 (C. C. A. Kan.); In re Broadway Sav. Trust Co., 18 A. B. R. 256 (C. C. A. Mo.); Swarts *v.* Siegel, 8 A. B. R. 689, 117 Fed. 16 (C. C. A. Mo.); In re Waugh, 13 A. B. R. 187, 133 Fed. 281 (C. C. A. Wash.); In re Lipke, 3 A. B. R. 569, 98 Fed. 970 (D. C. N. Y.); Lockman *v.* Lang, 11 A. B. R. 597, 12 A. B. R. 497, 132 Fed. 1 (C. C. A. Colo.); In re Herzikopf, 9 A. B. R. 746, 118 Fed. 101 (D. C. Calif.); In re Siegel-Hillman Dry Goods Co., 7 A. B. R. 351, 111 Fed. 983 (D. C. Mo.); In re Christensen, 4 A. B. R. 99, 101 Fed. 802 (D. C. Iowa); In re Rude, 4 A. B. R. 319, 101 Fed. 805 (D. C. Ky.); In re Edes, 14 A. B. R. 384, 135 Fed. 595 (D. C. Me.); Mason *v.* Wolkowich, 17 A. B. R. 714 (C. C. A. Mass.); In re Huddleston,

Bardes *v.* Bank, 4 A. B. R. 173, 178 U. S. 533: "Proceedings in bankruptcy generally are in the nature of proceedings in equity; and the words 'at law,' in the opening sentence conferring on the courts of bankruptcy 'such jurisdiction, at law and in equity, as will enable them to exercise original jurisdiction in bankruptcy proceedings,' may have been inserted to meet clause 4, authorizing the trial and punishment of offenses, the jurisdiction over which must necessarily be at law and not in equity."

Dodge *v.* Norlin, 13 A. B. R. 176, 133 Fed. 363 (C. C. A. Colo.): 'This is a proceeding in bankruptcy and a proceeding in bankruptcy is a proceeding in equity."

In re Rochford, 10 A. B. R. 609, 124 Fed. 187 (C. C. A. S. Dak.): "The administration and distribution of the property of bankrupts is a proceeding in equity, and when authorized by act of Congress it becomes a branch of equity jurisprudence."

In re Hoffman, 28 A. B. R. 680, 199 Fed. 448 (D. C. N. J.): "Courts of bankruptcy are courts of equity."

And the rules of equity control rather than those of law;[14] and this is so although certain issues may be triable to a jury by the statute, such jury being the jury to which the chancellor always has had the power to refer questions of fact for their advice.[15]

§ 21. Bankruptcy Act Covers Only Specified Cases of Insolvency.
—The bankruptcy act was not intended to cover all cases of insolvency, but only such cases as are within its provisions.[16]

§ 22. Bankruptcy Act Remedial and to Be Fairly Construed.—
The bankruptcy act is remedial and should be interpreted reasonably and according to the fair import of its terms with a view to effect its objects and to promote justice.[17]

---

1 A. B. R. 572 (Ref. Ala.); In re Pinkel, 1 A. B. R. 333 (Ref. N. Y.); Westall *v.* Avery, 22 A. B. R. 673, 171 Fed. 626 (C. C. A. N. Car.); Gillespie *v.* Piles & Co., 24 A. B. R. 502, 178 Fed. 886 (C. C. A. Iowa); In re Levenstein, 24 A. B. R. 822, 180 Fed. 957 (D. C. Conn.); In re Stewart, 24 A. B. R. 474, 178 Fed. 463 (D. C. N. Y.).

14. In re Stewart, 24 A. B. R. 474, 178 Fed. 463 (D. C. N. Y.); In re Cooper Bros., 20 A. B. R. 393, 159 Fed. 956 (D. C. Pa.); In re Irwin, 22 A. B. R. 165, 174 Fed. 642 (D. C. Pa.); Westall *v.* Avery, 22 A. B. R. 673, 171 Fed. 626 (C. C. A. N. Car.); In re N. Carolina Car Co., 11 A. B. R. 490, 127 Fed. 178 (D. C. N. Car.); In re Chambers, Calder & Co., 3 A. B. R. 537, 98 Fed. 865 (D. C. R. I.).

No notice to lienholder, no pleading of lien, order silent, yet purchaser protected free of liens and lienholder given lien on proceeds, because in a court of equity. McKay *v.* Hamill, 26 A. B. R. 164, 185 Fed. 11 (C. C. A. Pa.).

15. See post, § 405, et seq.

16. In re Wilmington Hosiery Co., 9 A. B. R. 581, 120 Fed. 180 (D. C. Del.); Singer *v.* Nat'l Bedstead Co., 11 A. B. R. 276 (N. J. Ch.). See ante, "Subject of Bankruptcy," § 7, et seq.; post, § 102.

Amendments to Bankruptcy Act Not Retroactive.—In re New Amsterdam Motor Co., 24 A. B. R. 757, 180 Fed. 943 (D. C. N. Y.).

17. Southern Loan & Trust Co. *v.* Benbow, 3 A. B. R. 9, 96 Fed. 514 (D. C. N. Car., reversed, on other grounds, in Frazier *v.* Southern Loan & Trust Co., 3 A. B. R. 710); In re Scott, 3 A. B. R. 628, 96 Fed. 607 (D. C. N. Car.); Blake *v.* Francis-Valentine Co., 1 A. B. R. 372, 89 Fed. 691 (D. C. Calif.); [1867] In re Muller, Fed. Cas. No. 9912; [1867] In re Silberman, Fed. Cases No. 1728; Atchison, etc., R. Co. *v.* Hurley, 18 A. B. R. 396, 153 Fed. 503 (C. C. A.).

Botts *v.* Hammond, 3 A. B. R. 775, 99 Fed. 916 (C. C. A. Md.): 'A's was well said in Blake *v.* Francis-Valentine Co., the National Bankruptcy Act is remedial, and should be interpreted reasonably and according to the fair import of its terms, with a view to effect its objects and to promote justice.'

Brown *v.* Barker, 8 A. B. R. 453 (Sup. Ct. N. Y. App. Div.): "We may take judicial notice that the present bankruptcy act is the result of a long continued agitation and discussion and that it is our duty, if possible, to so construe its provisions, liberally, if necessary, as to secure the objects for which it was created, rather than, by a narrow or technical construction, to defeat them."

In re Scott, 11 A. B. R. 331 (D. C. Del.): "Further, the Bankruptcy Act includes a large body of remedial legislation."

Impliedly, In re Edes, 14 A. B. R. 384, 135 Fed. 595 (D. C. Me.): "The Federal Courts have in fact liberally interpreted the whole statute as giving full equitable powers to the Court."

In re Beatty, 17 A. B. R. 743 (C. C. A. Mass.): "As the statutes of bankruptcy are to have an honest and practical interpretation, we are not to inject into what we have quoted therefrom, such phraseology as would require that the cause of the receivership need be solely insolvency."

In re Faulkner, 20 A. B. R. 542, 161 Fed. 900 (C. C. A. Kans.): "Bankruptcy proceedings are equitable in their nature, and should be as far as possible conducted on broad lines to accomplish the ultimate purpose of distributing the assets of a bankrupt pro rata among his creditors."

And the bankruptcy court has jurisdiction to make such orders, issue such process and enter such judgments, in addition to those specifically provided for as may be necessary to carry out the provisions of the Bankruptcy Act.[18]

Attempted judicial construction of the unequivocal language of a statute or of a contract serves only to create doubt and to confuse the judgment. There is no safer nor better settled canon of interpretation than that when language is clear and unambiguous it must be held to mean what it plainly expressed, and no room is left for construction.[19]

Where things are described particularly in a section of the statute the section is to be construed as meaning to cover nothing except the things described.[20]

The district court, save in exceptional cases, will defer to a decision of the Circuit Court of Appeals of another circuit where it is not in conflict with the decision of its own appellate tribunal.[21]

§ 23. Celerity of Procedure Intended.

—The bankrupt act contemplates that proceedings in bankruptcy shall progress with all reasonable

18. Bankr. Act, § 2 (15). In re Donnelly, 26 A. B. R. 304, 188 Fed. 1001 (D. C. Ohio).

19. Swarts *v.* Siegel, 8 A. B. R. 697, 117 Fed. 13 (C. C. A. Mo.). In one case, it is held, that in the construction of the Bankrupt Act, the maxim "expressio unius, exclusio alterius" has no application. In re Bay City Irrigation Co., 14 A. B. R. 370 (Ref.

Tex.); In re Toledo Portland Cement Co., 19 A. B. R. 117, 156 Fed. 83 (D. C. Mich.). Compare, rules laid down in Stevens *v.* Nave-McCord Co., 17 A. B. R. 615.

20. Stephens *v.* Merchants' Bank, 18 A. B. R. 560, 154 Fed. 341 (C. C. A. Ill.).

21. In re Baird, 18 A. B. R. 655, 154 Fed. 215 (D. C. Pa.).

despatch compatible with the due and orderly administration of justice and
a proper regard for the fundamental rights of the citizen.[22]

Boyd v. Glucklich, 8 A. B. R. 393, 116 Fed. 131 (C. C. A. Iowa): "The Bankrupt Act contemplates that proceedings in bankruptcy shall go forward with all
reasonable dispatch compatible with the due and orderly administration of
justice and a proper regard for the fundamental rights of the citizen."

Obiter, In re Paine, 11 A. B. R. 354, 127 Fed. 246 (D. C. Ky.): "The Bankruptcy Act furnishes much evidence of its purpose to require the winding up of
estates as speedily as possible."

[1867] Wiswall v. Campbell, 93 U. S. 347: "Prompt action is everywhere required by the law. In Bailey v. Glover, 21 Wall. 346, we said, speaking through
Mr. Justice Miller that 'It is obviously one of the purposes of the Bankrupt
Law that there should be a speedy distribution of the bankrupt's assets. This
is only second in importance to securing equality of distribution. The Act is
filled with provisions for the quick and summary disposal of questions arising
in the progress of the case, without regard to the usual modes of trial attended
with some necessary delay.'"

Obiter, West v. McLaughlin Co., 20 A. B. R. 654, 162 Fed. 124 (C. C. A.
Mich.): "One purpose which runs through the act is to require the prompt and
expeditious winding up of estates."

In re Lisk Mfg. Co., 21 A. B. R. 674, 167 Fed. 411 (D. C. N. Y.): "The Bankrupt Act was passed for the benefit of creditors, on the principle that when a
bankrupt's property is insufficient to pay its debts in full, there shall be an
equitable division thereof pro rata among them, and this fundamental rule requires the court, not only to preserve the estate and prevent its dissipation, but
that the property and assets of the bankrupt should be collected or marshaled
and the amount realized distributed without unnecessary delay."

But they are not to be so summary as to deprive parties of a reasonable
opportunity to defend. While proceedings in bankruptcy may be summary,
they should not be so summary as to deprive the bankrupt of those fundamental rights and privileges that belong to every citizen, among which are
the rights to be advised of the demand made upon him and the right, after
being so advised, to have a reasonable time to prepare his defense and produce his witnesses.[23]

Lockman v. Lange, 12 A. B. R. 497, 504, 132 Fed. 1 (C. C. A. Colo.): "A
proceeding in bankruptcy is a proceeding in equity. * * * If it is so sum-

22. Compare post, § 388½ and §
718. Blanchard v. Ammons, 25 A. B.
R. 590, 183 Fed. 556 (C. C. A. Ariz.);
Obiter, In re Koenig & VanHoo-
genhuyze, 11 A. B. R. 618, 127 Fed.
891 (D. C. Tex.); U. S. ex rel Adler
v. Hammond, 4 A. B. R. 738, 104 Fed.
862 (C. C. A. Tenn.). Obiter, In re
Nippon Trading Co., 25 A. B. R. 695,
182 Fed. 959 (D. C. Wash.); In re
Mexico Hardware Co., 28 A. B. R. 736,
197 Fed. 650 (D. C. N. Mex.), quoted
at § 824; In re Syracuse Paper & Pulp
Co., 21 A. B. R. 174, 164 Fed. 275 (D.
C. N. Y.). Obiter, In re Faulkner, 20

A. B. R. 542, 161 Fed. 900 (C. C. A.
Kans.), quoted at § 734. Also see to
the same general effect, Paxton v.
Scott, 10 A. B. R. 81; In re Crenshaw,
2 A. B. R. 623, 95 Fed. 633 (D. C. Ala.);
In re Cornell, 3 A. B. R. 172, 97 Fed.
29 (D. C.). Instance, In re Swofford
Bros. Dry Goods Co., 25 A. B. R. 282,
180 Fed. 549 (D. C. Mo.).

23. Boyd v. Glucklich, 8 A. B. R.
393, 116 Fed. 131 (C. C. A. Iowa). Inferentially, In re Faulkner, 20 A. B. R.
542, 161 Fed. 900 (C. C. A. Kans.),
quoted at § 734.

mary that it is not governed by the specific times fixed for pleadings and for the taking of evidence by the rules and practice in equity, it is not so summary that rights of person or of property may be taken from the parties to it without opportunity to frame or to try the issues that are tendered."

§ 24. Economy of Administration Intended.—The Bankrupt Act was framed in a manifest spirit of economy and is to be administered economically.[24]

24. Compare to same effect post, §§ 522½, 2011; In re Marks, 22 A. B. R. 54 (Ref. Ga.); In re Allert, 23 A. B. R. 101, 173 Fed. 691 (D. C. N. Y.); In re Kyte, 19 A. B. R. 768, 158 Fed. 121 (D. C. Pa.). Impliedly, In re Harper, 23 A. B. R. 918 (939), 175 Fed. 412 (D. C. N. Y.), quoted at § 899. Norcross v. Nathan, 3 A. B. R. 622 (D. C. Nevada).

(1) **Abuse of Power of Appointment of Special Masters.**—A practice has grown up in some districts of referring to special masters various matters that form part of the regular duties of referees, thus putting estates to additional and unnecessary expense. The practice is to be reprehended in view of the manifest spirit of economy in which the present law was framed. See post, §§ 522½, 2011.

For an instance of this practice see, In re Hoyt & Mitchell, 11 A. B. R. 784, 127 Fed. 968, the district judge there having referred to a special master the auditing of the trustee's reports, a duty clearly enjoined on the referee by the statute and General Orders in Bankruptcy as well.

For another apparent instance of such abuse, see Laffoon v. Ives, 20 A. B. R. 174, 159 Fed. 861 (C. C. A. Wash.), where, it appears, the re-examination of an allowed claim was referred to a special master—clearly an ordinary duty of the referee.

For other instances of such abuse, see In re Huntenberg, 18 A. B. R. 697, 153 Fed. 768 (D. C. N. Y.), and In re Wilcox, 19 A. B. R. 91, 156 Fed. 685 (D. C. N. Y.), wherein the judge referred to the referee as special master, or master commissioner, applications of claimants for orders on the trustee to surrender certain moneys.

Also, In re Photo Engraving Co., 19 A. B. R. 94, 155 Fed. 684 (D. C. N. Y.), wherein the judge referred to the referee "as special master" the question as to whether a city salesman's wages were entitled to priority where the adjudication of bankruptcy occurred before the amendment of 1906.

Also, In re Strobel, 19 A. B. R. 109, 160 Fed. 916 (D. C. N. Y.), wherein the judge referred to the referee "as special master" the motion of an adverse claimant to property.

Instance, In re Bevier Wood Pavement Co., 19 A. B. R. 462, 156 Fed. 583 (D. C. N. Y.), wherein the court appointed a special master to determine the validity of a claim for royalties against a bankrupt corporation.

Instance, In re Gregnard Lith. Co., 19 A. B. R. 743, 155 Fed. 699 (D. C. N. Y.), wherein a "special commissioner" was appointed to determine the priority of expenses of administration where the estate was too small to pay in full.

Instance, In re Schiebler, 20 A. B. R. 777, 165 Fed. 363 (D. C. N. Y.), wherein the referee was appointed as "special commissioner" to determine the reasonableness of attorney's fees prepaid under § 60 (d).

Instance, In re Huddleston, 21 A. B. R. 669, 167 Fed. 428 (D. C. Ga.): "The question of the propriety of the fee for Persons & Persons (attorneys for the bankrupt) was referred to the referee in bankruptcy as special master."

Instance, where referee was allowed extra compensation, In re Albert, 23 A. B. R. 101, 173 Fed. 691 (D. C. N. Y.).

Instance, In re Fenn, 22 A. B. R. 833, 172 Fed. 620 (D. C. Vt.) wherein the referee was appointed special master to determine the amount for which a claim should be allowed for dividends.

Instance, In re Watts-Woodward Press, Inc. (C. C. A.), 24 A. B. R. 684, wherein a special master was appointed to determine the validity of an unrecorded chattel mortgage on property in the possession of the receiver and sold by him, apparently after adjudication of bankruptcy.

(2) **Present Law Brings Courts Close to, Suitors.**—The present Bankrupt Act brings the bankruptcy courts close to suitors since it provides for a referee for each county. In re Steiner, 5 A. B. R. 214 (D. C. Mass.).

(3) **Malicious Prosecution of Bankruptcy Petition.**—A bankruptcy proceeding is not a mere civil suit. It is sui generis, and is far reaching and drastic in its effects. Whether accompanied by seizure of property or not,

In re Oppenheimer, 17 A. B. R. 60 (D. C. Pa.): "Economy is strictly enjoined, by the well-known policy of the Bankruptcy Act, in the administration of bankrupt estates."

In re Young, 16 A. B. R. 109 (D. C. N. Car.): "The principal object of the Bankrupt Law was to secure to creditors their portion of the bankrupt estate and at a minimum cost."

Fellows v. Freudenthal, 4 A. B. R. 495, 102 Fed. 731 (C. C. A. Ills.): "This provision is in harmony with the purpose manifested throughout the act, to so limit all allowances as to secure economical administration of proceedings and estates in bankruptcy; and [it is] the duty of the Courts to construe and administer the act in conformity with that purpose."

In re Curtis, 4 A. B. R. 27, 91 Fed. 737 (C. C. A. Ills.): "The policy of the present Bankrupt Act, in contrast with the provisions of the previous law, disclosed clearly the design of Congress that the administration of bankrupt estates should be had at the minimum of expense. Under the former law much scandal had arisen because of the large cost of administering estates. The present act, so far as it specifies the amount of fees of officers whose services may be required in execution of the law, fixes them at a low figure, possibly much lower than is compensation for the service; but it is not for us, for that reason, to disregard the law, or seek to thwart the design of Congress, however inadequate we may think the compensation allowed. This thought is well expressed by the court below in the opinion filed. It is there said:

"'The present bankrupt law was evidently intended to reduce to the lowest minimum the costs of administration, as regards fees of officers created by the act, as well as those of attorneys who may be called to assist the court in the preservation and distribution of the bankrupt estate.'"

In re Ketterer Mfg. Co., 19 A. B. R. 646, 155 Fed. 987 (D. C. Pa.): "Economy in the administration of estates is the policy of the present law, and is to be strictly enforced."

Faulk v. Steiner, 21 A. B. R. 623, 165 Fed. 861 (C. C. A. Ala.): "The Bankruptcy Act was framed with the purpose of securing to the creditors a distri-

it places an embargo on the bankrupt's right to dispose of his property and to do business generally. No prudent person will buy from him, and all those dealing with him are liable to have their transactions investigated and questioned by litigation. Hence, for maliciously instituting or maintaining a bankruptcy petition action will lie. Wilkinson v. Shoe Co., 15 A. B. R. 554, 141 Fed. 218 (U. S. C. C. Mo.).

(4) **Threats That Creditors "Will Get Nothing" in Case of Bankruptcy.—** It is common to hear threats that creditors "will get nothing" if bankruptcy is resorted to. The following is an observation of a court on the subject: In re Floyd, 19 A. B. R. 438, 154 Fed. 757 (D. C. N. Car.): "This proposition is seriously contended for in order, it seems, to carry out the promise originally made to the creditors when the assignment was made that bankruptcy would yield them practically nothing in the way of dividends, and the apparent purpose is to carry out

this promise by diminution of the assets, if possible, so as to deter other creditors who might have the temerity to resist the ex parte terms of a voluntary assignment. * * * Perhaps another reason for their objection to bankruptcy and to the jurisdiction of this court was that it offered an opportunity for looking into the transaction, which seems to have been suspicious of fraud, and their efforts to consume the assets left to the creditors will not be tolerated in a court of bankruptcy, governed, as it is, by the rules in equity."

(5) **Abuse of Prolonged Receiverships in Conducting Business.—**Compare post, § 388½.

(6) **Libel in Bankruptcy Petition.—** A material and pertinent allegation of a pending bankruptcy petition charging fraud and collusion was held absolutely privileged in Rosenberg & Dworstsky, 24 A. B. R. 583, N. Y. 139 App. Div. 517.

bution of the bankrupt's estate at a minimum cost. The policy of the act is one of economy, and to promote this policy, Congress sought to provide against the improvident and unnecessary appointment of receivers."

Hardware Co. *v.* Huddleston, 21 A. B. R. 731, 167 Fed. 433 (C. C. A. Ga.): "The proceedings of courts of bankruptcy should be so administered as to preserve the assets of the bankrupt estates for the benefit of the creditors."

In re Oakland Lumber Co., 23 A. B. R. 181, 174 Fed. 643 (C. C. A. N. Y.): "Nothing contributed so much to bring about the repeal of the Act of 1867 as the large expense of administration, the small estates being entirely absorbed in fees. The more economical the administration of the present act the longer will it continue as an important adjunct to trade and commerce."

§ 25. Official Forms and Orders in Bankruptcy.—Necessary rules, forms and orders as to procedure and for carrying the act into force and effect are to be prescribed and may be amended from time to time, by the supreme court of the United States.[25]

§ 26. Are Advance Interpretations as to Procedure, and to Be Followed, Though Not to Override Statute Itself.—These rules, forms and orders, are to be taken as interpretations, in advance, of the meaning of the act itself relative to procedure under it.

Impliedly, In re Jamieson, 9 A. B. R. 681, 120 Fed. 697 (D. C. Ills.): "For the purpose of making the proceedings under the act more specific, the Supreme Court adopted and established certain rules, orders, and forms to be followed in the execution and application of the statute. * * * These rules have the same weight in this case as though they were included in the express language of the statute."

Impliedly, Orcutt Co. *v.* Green, 17 A. B. R. 75 (C. C. A. N. Y.), "* * * the order being simply somewhat of an amplification of the law with respect to procedure, but nothing which can be construed as beyond the powers granted to the court by virtue of the law itself."

Contra, In re Edes, 14 A. B. R. 384, 135 Fed. 595 (D. C. Me.): "While this General Order has no force as legislation, and while it is not even a judicial interpretation of the Statute, it is an order of the Supreme Court of the United States based upon the bankruptcy statute. It cannot be held to be in derogation of such statute."

The rules and orders are obligatory and binding upon courts of bankruptcy and must be followed.[26] Indeed, one case has held they confer substantive rights as well as prescribe rules of practice.[27]

But the forms and rules prescribed as to pleading indicate only the form in general and are not exclusive.

In re Paige, 3 A. B. R. 679, 99 Fed. 538 (D. C. Ohio): "In answer to a petition for involuntary bankruptcy, the respondent is entitled not only to deny insolvency, but also to set up any defense and counterclaims which may show

---

25. Bankr. Act, § 30 (a); In re Johnson, 19 A. B. R. 814, 158 Fed. 342 (D. C. Ark.).

26. In re Scott, 3 A. B. R. 625 (D. C. N. Car.). Apparently, In re White, 14 A. B. R. 241, 135 Fed. 199 (D. C.

Penna.). To same effect, Gage *v.* Bell, 10 A. B. R. 696, 124 Fed. 371 (D. C. Tenn.).

27. In re Scott, 3 A. B. R. 625 (D. C. N. Car.).

him to have been solvent at the time when it is charged the act of bankruptcy was committed. The forms and orders prescribed by the Supreme Court indicate only the form in substance of the answer, but are not exclusive in their provisions."

In re Bellah, 8 A. B. R. 310, 116 Fed. 49 (D. C. Del.): "Rule 11 of the general orders in bankruptcy deals with amendments to a petition and schedules, but was not intended to abrogate or restrict the general power of amendment in other respects vested in the court."

And in general the forms and rules are merely directory as to procedure, and will not override the provisions of the statute themselves as to substantive rights.[28]

Burke v. Guarantee Title & Trust Co., 14 A. B. R. 31, 134 Fed. 562 (C. C. A. Pa.): "It is true that among the forms promulgated by the Supreme Court is 'Schedule B (5)' in which is contained the words: 'Property claimed to be exempted by the State laws, its valuation,' etc. But waiving the question whether in this instance the property claimed and its valuation were not stated in substantial accordance with this direction, it is enough to say that we do not understand it to be anything more than a direction. It could not have been intended to be mandatory. These forms were not designed to effect any change in the law. They are 'forms,' and nothing more. As was said by the Supreme Court (General) orders 38, 89, they are to be 'observed and used with such alterations as may be necessary to suit the circumstances of any particular case;' and, under the circumstance of this case, we decline to hold that the failure of the bankrupt to precisely observe one of them was fatal to his claim, because we could not do so without subordinating substance to form, and refusing a legal right, merely on account of a defect in procedure, which has caused no injury to any one, and which, if requisite, might be cured by amendment. General Order 11; In re Duffy (D. C.), 9 Am. B. R. 358, 118 Fed. 926; In re White (D. C.), 11 A. B. R. 556, 128 Fed. 513."

West Co. v. Lea, 2 A. B. R. 463 (C. C. A. Va.): "The fact that the official form for involuntary petitions contains an allegation of insolvency, does not make such an allegation material where the statute provides that other facts alone constitute a sufficient case for an adjudication."

In re Ingalls Bros., 13 A. B. R. 512, 137 Fed. 517 (C. C. A. N. Y.): "The authorities hereinbefore cited do or do not correctly declare the meaning of § 57 (n). If they do correctly declare it, the Supreme Court is powerless to vary it."

Nevertheless, the simple forms prescribed by the Supreme Court should be followed, and there should be no unnecessary departure by using the more prolix forms of chancery.

Gage v. Bell, 10 A. B. R. 696, 124 Fed. 371 (D. C. Tenn.): "It is to be observed that Form No. 6 does not contemplate any other pleading than that of a brief and simple denial (1) that the defendant debtor has committed the act

---

28. Inferentially, Lipman v. Stein, 14 A. B. R. 30, 134 Fed. 235 (C. C. A. Pa.).

All Pleadings of Fact in Bankruptcy to Be Verified.—All pleadings in bankruptcy containing matters of fact should be verified. Bankr. Act, § 18

(c). "All pleadings setting up matters of fact shall be verified under oath." Rogers v. Mining Co., 14 A. B. R. 253, 136 Fed. 407 (C. C. A. Alaska); In re Bellah, 8 A. B. R. 310 (D. C. Del.).

of bankruptcy, or (2) that he is insolvent, and (3) an averment 'that he should not be declared a bankrupt for any cause in said petition alleged.' At first I was inclined to hold that no other pleading whatever was permissible than this, and that under it any defense whatever, whether by demurrer or otherwise, could be made that would defeat the petition for any cause. But yielding to the license given by General Order No. 38, that the several forms shall be observed and used with such alterations as may be necessary to suit the circumstances of any particular case and conforming to the practice in other districts, reluctantly and with constantly increasing regret, I allowed other and special pleadings to be framed, and now, as in this case, in almost every case there are demurrers, formidable answers after the manner of pleadings in chancery, with exceptions, replications, etc., until the practice has departed from the simple forms prescribed and degenerated into those of a suit in equity. I doubt if this is proper practice."

CHAPTER III.

§ 27. In General.—The United States District Courts are, by the Act, erected into bankruptcy courts; their jurisdiction as such is limited, each

District Court being confined to the adjudication and administration of the estates of those debtors only who have resided or been domiciled or have had their principal place of business within the district the greater portion of the six months next preceding the filing of the petition; and of those debtors who are nonresidents of the United States or have been adjudged bankrupts outside of the United States, and have property within the district; in voluntary cases having jurisdiction over all natural persons and over all corporations except municipal, railroad, banking and insurance corporations, and in involuntary cases being confined to debtors who owe $1,000 or more and who, if natural persons, are not wage earners nor farmers, or, if corporations, are moneyed, business or commercial corporations and not municipal, railroad, banking nor insurance companies.

§ 28. U. S. District Courts Created into Bankruptcy Courts.—
The United States District Courts are, by the Act, created into bankruptcy courts.[1] They are still the United States District Courts, but are sitting "in bankruptcy." The machinery of the District Court is used, subject to such modifications as the Bankruptcy Act requires for its administration.

§ 29. Jurisdiction in Bankruptcy Limited, Though Bankruptcy Courts Not Inferior Courts.—Jurisdiction in bankruptcy is limited.[2]

Taft v. Century Savings Bk., 15 A. B. R. 597, 141 Fed. 369 (C. C. A. Iowa): "The District Court as a court of bankruptcy is undoubtedly a court of limited jurisdiction."

And the bankruptcy courts are expressly limited in the exercise of bankruptcy jurisdiction to their territorial limits.[3]

In re Steele, 20 A. B. R. 446, 161 Fed. 886 (D. C. Ala.): "The act of Congress creating courts of bankruptcy provides for one court only within the territory prescribed. Courts of bankruptcy have no jurisdiction outside of their territorial limits as prescribed by the act of Congress creating them. A United States district judge, even though a judge of the northern and middle districts of Alabama, has no jurisdiction, while holding court in the middle district thereof, to make an order appointing a referee in bankruptcy for the northern district of

---

1. Bankr. Act, § 1 (8): "Courts of bankruptcy shall include the district courts of the United States and of the Territories, the supreme court of the District of Columbia, and the United States court of the Indian Territory, and of Alaska." Blake v. Valentine, 1 A. B. R. 373, 89 Fed. 691 (D. C. Calif.).

2. In re Billing, 17 A. B. R. 86, 145 Fed. 395 (D. C. Ala.); Edelstein v. U. S., 17 A. B. R. 652, 149 Fed. 636 (C. C. A. Minn.); In re First Nat'l Bk. of Belle Fourche, 18 A. B. R. 273 (C. C. A.), quoted at § 30; In re Elmira Steel Co., 5 A. B. R. 485 (Ref. N. Y.). But compare evident misconception of meaning of expression "limited jurisdiction," In re Marion Contract & Const. Co., 22 A. B. R. 81, 166 Fed.

618 (D. C. Ky.): "The bankruptcy courts can hardly be called courts of limited jurisdiction inasmuch as they are vested exclusively with all jurisdiction in bankruptcy proceedings throughout the entire country."

Questions of Jurisdiction to Be First Heard.—Questions of jurisdiction are to be first heard. See post, § 413½. Also, see In re King, 24 A. B. R. 606, 179 Fed. 694 (C. C. A. Ills.), quoted at § 412.

3. Bankr. Act, § 2; In re Owings, 15 A. B. R. 475, 140 Fed. 739 (D. C. N. Car.); [1867] Lathrop v. Drake, 91 U. S. 516; In re Britannia Min. Co., 28 A. B. R. 651, 197 Fed. 459 (D. C. Wis.); In re Harris Co., 23 A. B. R. 237, 173 Fed. 735 (D. C. N. Y.).

Alabama. A United States district judge, even though a judge of the northern and middle districts of Alabama and residing in the middle district, has no jurisdiction or authority to go into the northern district, while the judge of the said northern district is holding court therein, and make an order appointing a referee in bankruptcy and prescribing a rule for the reference of proceedings in bankruptcy to said referee so appointed by him, without the concurrence of the judge of the said northern district." But compare opinion of conflicting judge, In re Steele, 20 A. B. R. 575, 161 Fed. 886 (D. C. Ala.).

And have no jurisdiction over persons not parties to the bankruptcy proceedings who are in another district, unless they are interested in the res in the custody of the bankruptcy court.[4]

But the bankruptcy courts are not inferior courts.

In re Billing, 17 A. B. R. 86, 145 Fed. 395 (D. C. Ala.): "The District Court of the United States is a court of limited but not inferior jurisdiction. Congress has conferred upon it original and exclusive jurisdiction to adjudge bankruptcies, and its judgments therein are supported by the same presumptions which are indulged in favor of the judgments of all superior courts of general jurisdiction. When jurisdiction is shown to have attached, the indisputable presumption, save when the question is raised by appeal or an attack upon the adjudication for fraud in its procurement, is that there was sufficient evidence to support the judgment."

Edelstein v. U. S., 17 A. B. R. 652, 149 Fed. 636 (C. C. A. Minn.): "It is true the District Court as a court of bankruptcy is one of limited jurisdiction—that is, limited in respect of the subjects over which it may exercise jurisdiction—but it is unlimited in respect of its power over proceedings in bankruptcy, specifically made subject to its jurisdiction by § 2 of the Act. When judgments are rendered by that court upon questions arising in such proceedings they possess all the incidents of finality and conclusiveness appertaining to judgments of courts of general jurisdiction. Its judgments, unless reversed on appeal or of error, import absolute verity."

In re First Nat'l Bk. of Belle Fourche, 18 A. B. R. 266 (C. C. A.): "While the jurisdiction of the national courts is limited, they are not inferior courts, and their judgments possess every attribute of finality and estoppel which pertains to those courts of general jurisdiction."

§ 30. Limitations as to Residence, Occupation, etc., Jurisdictional.

—The limitation of the operation of the bankruptcy act to those having their residence, domicile or principal place of business within the particular district for the requisite period of time, and also the exclusion from involuntary proceedings of wage earners and farmers, etc., and of municipal, banking, railroad or insurance corporations and of corporations which are not moneyed, business nor commercial corporations are jurisdictional matters: they concern the jurisdiction of the court over the subject matter and not merely over the person, the court's jurisdiction being confined to those classes of cases and not extending over the entire "subject of bankruptcies;" and the lack of the requisite conditions is not a personal privilege, waivable by the respondent; nor may jurisdiction be conferred by

4. In re Harris Co., 23 A. B. R. 237,   173 Fed. 735 (D. C. N. Y.).

consent to adjudge a person bankrupt who does not come within the limitations.[5]

Taft *v.* Century Sav. Bk., 15 A. B. R. 597, 141 Fed. 369 (C. C. A. Iowa): "From this section it appears that all persons are not subject to the provisions of the Bankruptcy Act. Wage earners, or persons engaged chiefly in farming or the tillage of the soil, or persons or corporations not owing debts to the amount of $1,000, are either expressly or by necessary implication, excluded.

"The District Court, as a court of bankruptcy, is undoubtedly a court of limited jurisdiction. Congress alone had power to determine the subjects over which it might exercise jurisdiction. As said by the Supreme Court in Johnson Company *v.* Wharton, 152 U. S. 252, 260.

" 'The distribution of the judicial power of the United States among the courts of the United States is a matter entirely within the control of the legislative branch of the government.'

"It is suggested that the bankruptcy court had jurisdiction over the alleged bankrupt in this case by due service of the subpœna upon him, and over the subject matter by virtue of the Bankruptcy Act, which confers upon it plenary jurisdiction in bankruptcy proceedings. But this does not solve the question. It was said by the Supreme Court in Windsor *v.* McVeigh, 93 U. S. 274, 282, that:

" ' 'All courts, even the highest, are more or less limited in their jurisdiction. They are limited to particular classes of actions. * * * Though the court may possess jurisdiction of a cause, of the subject matter and of the parties, it is still limited in its modes of procedure, and in the extent and character of its judgments. It must act judicially in all things, and cannot then transcend the power conferred by the law. * * * The judgments mentioned * * * [in the cases referred to for illustration] would not be merely erroneous. They would be absolutely void, because the court in rendering them would transcend the limits of its authority in those cases.'

"To the same effect are the following cases: Ex parte Lange, 18 Wall. 163, 176; Cornett *v.* Williams, 20 Wall. 226, 250. In the last-cited case, it is said:

" 'The settled rule of law is that, jurisdiction having attached in the original case, everything done within the power of that jurisdiction, when collaterally questioned, is to be held conclusive of the rights of the parties, unless impeached for fraud.'

"Applying the foregoing principles to the statute under consideration, it appears that Congress limited the jurisdiction of the District Court, as a court of bankruptcy to cases in which the debtor owes at least $1,000. Cases in which the debtor owes less than that sum are not brought 'within the power' of its jurisdiction, and debtors owing less than that sum are not subject to the provisions of the Bankruptcy Act. It has been held by the Circuit Court of Appeals for the Seventh Circuit that a petition in involuntary bankruptcy must show clearly that the debtor is not a wage earner or engaged chiefly in farming or the tillage of the soil. In re Taylor, 4 Am. B. R. 515, 102 Fed. 728. To the same

5. In re Plotke, 5 A. B. R. 176, 104 Fed. 964 (C. C. A. Ills.). Inferentially, In re Elmira Steel Co., 5 A. B. R. 486 (Ref. N. Y.). Inferentially, In re Clisdell, 2 A. B. R. 424 (Ref. N. Y.). Compare, also, In re Columbia Real Estate Co., 4 A. B. R. 411, 101 Fed. 965 (D. C. Ind., affirmed in 7 A. B. R. 441); In re Reisler Amusement Co., 22 A. B. R. 501, 171 Fed. 283 (D. C. N. Y.);

In re Lipphart, 28 A. B. R. 705, 201 Fed. 103 (D. C. N. Y.). And compare § 414, and "Adjudication," post, § 437, et seq.

Incidentally, it is to be noted that by the Amendment of 1910 the classification of corporations subject to bankruptcy has been changed. See post, § 80.

effect is the decision of this court in In re Plymouth Cordage Company, 13 Am. B. R. 665, 135 Fed. 1000, and the decision of the Circuit Court of Appeals of the Fifth Circuit in Beach *v.* Macon Grocery Company, 9 Am. B. R. 762, 120 Fed. 736. We observe no difference in principle between the omission of an averment bringing the debtor without the exception as to wage earners or persons engaged chiefly in farming or the tillage of the soil and the omission of an averment bringing the debtor within the class which owes debts to the amount of $1,000 or over. These provisions are both, in our opinion, jurisdictional, and either of the omissions just mentioned shows that the debtor proceeded against is not within the class of persons subject to the provisions of the Bankruptcy Act, or subject to the jurisdiction of the court in bankruptcy. The petition in this case was therefore defective in not disclosing that the debtor owed at least $1,000, and for that reason it conferred no jurisdiction upon the court to subject Cohen, the debtor, to the provisions of the Act."

In re Garneau, 11 A. B. R. 679, 127 Fed. 677 (C. C. A. Ills.): "He was a sojourner merely, and not a resident, of East St. Louis. We look upon this transaction as an imposition upon the jurisdiction of the court. The Congress did not intend that one may select any court of bankruptcy which he pleases in these broad United States, and be enabled, through a pretentious removal to the district of that court, to obtain his discharge from his debts. To allow that to be done would open the door to grave frauds upon creditors, which we are not disposed to countenance.

"It is objected that the petition to dismiss for want of jurisdiction comes too late; that the adjudication in bankruptcy is a judgment; that the only relief to the creditor was to appeal within 10 days from that adjudication. To so hold would be to deny in 99 cases out of 100 all relief whatever, and to make easy the perpetration of fraud. In voluntary cases the adjudication passes ex parte and forthwith. The time of appeal would have passed before creditors would in most cases receive notice of the adjudication, and the record made by the bankrupt would show nothing erroneous. Here there were no laches chargeable to the creditors, for promptly upon ascertaining the facts from the examination of the bankrupt the petition to dismiss was made. But, aside from that, it would be the duty of the court sua sponte, when it is led to suspect that its jurisdiction has been imposed upon, to inquire into the facts by some appropriate form of proceeding, and, for its own protection against fraud or imposition, to act as justice may require. Morris *v.* Gilmer, 129 U. S. 329." This case quoted further at § 33 note 11.

In re Taylor, 4 A. B. R. 515, 102 Fed. 728 (C. C. A. Ills.): "The defense to proceedings in involuntary bankruptcy that the person sought to be declared a bankrupt is within the exceptions of § 4, is not simply personal to the bankrupt —it goes to the jurisdiction of the Court and may be raised by any creditor."

Compare, obiter, Louisville Trust Co. *v.* Comingor, 7 A. B. R. 427, 184 U. S. 18: "Jurisdiction as to the subject matter may be limited in various ways, as to civil and criminal cases, cases at common law or equity, or in admiralty, probate cases, or cases under special statutes, to particular classes of persons, to proceedings in particular modes and so on."

In re Keystone Coal Co., 6 A. B. R. 378, 109 Fed. 872 (D. C. Penna.): "The question here involved is jurisdictional. Unless this court is vested with jurisdiction over this corporation by statutory grant, none exists."

Compare, inferentially, In re Brett, 12 A. B. R. 492, 130 Fed. 981 (D. C. N. J.): "The demurrant insists that the first two causes of demurrer deal with jurisdictional defects in the petition, and that it is beyond the power of the court to permit an amendment of the petition which shall relate back to the time when the

petition was filed. The purport of the argument is that the petition is so defective in form and substance that the court acquired by it no jurisdiction of the
subject matter of the proceedings, or of the person of the alleged bankrupt. But
it is not the petition that confers upon the court jurisdiction of the subject matter.
That is done by the law. Jurisdiction of the person is acquired by filing a petition, and serving a copy of it, with a subpœna, upon the alleged bankrupt. The
demurrant by its demurrer necessarily admits that the petition has been filed, and
the record of the case shows that a copy of the petition and the subpœna have
been served on the alleged bankrupt. The court therefore has jurisdiction both
of the subject matter and the person."

But compare, In re Mason, 3 A. B. R. 599, 99 Fed. 256 (D. C. N. Car.): "Entire want of jurisdiction over the res may be taken advantage of at any time
and attacked collaterally. But where objection goes only to the jurisdiction
over the person, it must be taken properly. A creditor cannot prove his debt,
participate in the election of trustee and distribution of assets, and then, upon
application for discharge, object to jurisdiction on account of bankrupt's nonresidence."

And also compare First Nat'l Bk. v. Klug, 8 A. B. R. 13, 186 U. S. 204: "The
conclusion was, it is true, that Klug could not be adjudged a bankrupt, but the
court had jurisdiction to so determine, and its jurisdiction over the subject
matter was not and could not be questioned."

Compare, also, In re Urban & Suburban, 12 A. B. R. 690 (D. C. N. J.): "The
Bankruptcy Act confers on the courts jurisdiction of the subject matter of bankruptcy proceedings, and jurisdiction of the company was in this case acquired
by due service of a subpœna and of a copy of the petition in bankruptcy. The
jurisdiction of subject matter and of the company was, therefore, complete at
the time of adjudication. In re Williams, Fed. Cas. No. 17,700; Roche v. Fox,
Fed. Cas. No. 11,974."

In re Frischberg, 8 A. B. R. 610 (Ref. N. Y.): "If the court had jurisdiction
of the subject matter and this it undoubtedly had by reason of the doing business, residence or domicile of the alleged bankrupt within the statutory period
of time, then it is immaterial whether jurisdiction of the person was thereafter
acquired by the service of process or by the voluntary appearance of the bankrupt; such jurisdiction could be acquired by either method."

It is analogous to the jurisdiction of the court in other proceedings for
the determination of the status of a person or the administration of estates.

Nevertheless, it was held (before the Amendment of 1910 enlarging the
classes of corporations subject to bankruptcy) by the Circuit Court of Appeals, in several cases, that neither the allegation nor the fact that a corporation is engaged principally in manufacturing, trading, etc., is jurisdictional.[6]

In re Broadway Savings & Trust Co., 18 A. B. R. 254 (C. C. A. Mo.): "The
contention of counsel for the petitioner that the omitted allegation, or the fact
that the desk company was engaged principally in one of the pursuits which
subjected it to the adjudication, was jurisdictional, has received deliberate and
studious consideration, and our conclusion, the reasons for it, and authorities

6. Compare, apparently to this same
effect, In re New England Breeders'
Club, 22 A. B. R. 124, 175 Fed. 501 (C.
C. A. N. H., reversing 21 A. B. R. 349, 165
Fed. 517), although the court is careful
to state that the record in the case did
not affirmatively disclose the lack of
jurisdiction, but on the contrary affirmatively alleged it.

in support of it may be found in our opinion in In re First National Bank of Belle Fourche, which is filed herewith. Our judgment is that neither the allegation nor the fact was jurisdictional, because neither conditioned the power of the court to hear the cause and decide every issue in it between the parties. It had the same jurisdiction of the cause and of the parties, and the same power to determine the issues between them, whether the desk company was or was not engaged in one of the pursuits mentioned in section 4b of the bankruptcy law. The only difference the decision of that issue made was that if it was so engaged the court should have given judgment for the petitioners, and if it was not so occupied it should have refused to adjudicate the desk company a bankrupt."

In re First National Bank of Belle Fourche, 18 A. B. R. 266 (C. C. A. Mo.): "The contention that the fact that the Widell Company was principally engaged in manufacturing conditioned the jurisdiction of the court and the validity of the adjudication, that the judgment is a nullity because this fact did not exist, and that its invalidity may be shown at any time by collateral attack, or otherwise by proof that the Widell Company was not engaged in any pursuit which subjected it to adjudication in bankruptcy, disregards the fundamental distinction between the facts essential to the jurisdiction of the court over the subject matter and the parties and those requisite to establish the cause of action. Jurisdiction of the subject matter and of the parties is the right to hear and determine the suit or proceeding in favor of or against the respective parties to it. The facts essential to invoke this jurisdiction differ materially from those essential to constitute a good cause of action for the relief sought. A defective petition in bankruptcy, or an insufficient complaint at law, accompanied by proper service of process upon the defendants, gives judication to the court to determine the questions involved in the suit, although it may not contain averments which entitle the complainant to any relief; and it may be the duty of the court to determine either the question of its jurisdiction or the merits of the controversy against the petitioner or plaintiff. Facts indispensable to a favorable adjudication or decree include all those requisite to state a good cause of action, and they comprehend many that are not essential to the jurisdiction of the suit or proceeding. The fact that Widell Company was engaged in a manufacturing pursuit was not of the former, but of the latter, class. It was not essential to invoke the jurisdiction of the court over the parties to the proceeding and the property involved, because the Act of Congress gave that court, upon the filing of the petition of the creditors, jurisdiction to hear and determine the questions it presented, upon proper service of the subpœna upon the defendant. The facts which conditioned the jurisdiction of the court were the filing of the petition and the service of the subpœna. In re Plymouth Cordage Co., 13 Am. B. R. 665, 135 Fed. 1000, 1004, 68 C. C. A. 434, 438.

"Concede, for we do not stop to consider or decide, that the nonexistence of either of these facts might be shown at any time, by collateral attack or otherwise, to destroy the validity of the adjudication, and this is the extent of the effect of many of the authorities cited by the counsel here. Williamson v. Berry, 8 How. 495, 540, 12 L. Ed. 1170; Adams v. Terrell (C. C.), 4 Fed. 796, 800. Nevertheless, the fact that the Widell Company was, or that it was not, principally engaged in manufacturing, was not of this class. It did not condition the jurisdiction of the court, but the judgment which it ought to render, only. The court had the same jurisdiction to decide the issues between the parties, whether the Widell Company was or was not principally engaged in a manufacturing pursuit. The only difference the determination of that issue made was that if it was so engaged the court should have given judgment for the petitioners, and if it was not thus occupied it should have rendered judgment against them."

The argument of these last two cases is that such facts pertain, not to the subject matter, but simply to the cause of action. However, it would seem that did they pertain simply to the cause of action their nonexistence would be waivable; but, assuredly, neither consent nor waiver can confer jurisdiction in the bankruptcy court of one district to adjudge bankrupt a debtor not resident, domiciled nor having his principal place of business therein, although the ascertainment of such jurisdictional fact must be left to the same court for determination and its determination may not be subject to collateral attack. Nor would any attempt to administer in bankruptcy a banking corporation or other corporation not included within the designated classes subject to bankruptcy be otherwise than null and void. Such ruling is familiar in probate jurisprudence upon the subject of attempts to administer upon the estate of a decedent who was not a resident at the time of his death or otherwise within the statutory classification.

The ruling that the *fact* of occupation is not jurisdictional is purely obiter in each of these cases; and the ruling that the *allegation* of occupation also is not jurisdictional, evidently has reference to the unimpeachability of the record by collateral attack where the record does not *affirmatively* show the debtor does *not* belong to the particular class but simply omits all allegations whatsoever as to the occupation. As is later noted (§§ 437, 450), the record of adjudication imports jurisdiction where jurisdictional findings are merely omitted and makes the adjudication impervious to collateral attack, but if the record of adjudication affirmatively shows the debtor did *not* belong to one of the classes subject to bankruptcy it would without question be absolutely void on its face.[7] Section

---

[7] United States *v.* Freed, 25 A. B. R. 89, 179 Fed. 236 (D. C. Mass.); In re New York Tunnel Co., 21 A. B. R. 531, 166 Fed. 284 (C. C. A. N. Y.), quoted supra. Compare, partially to same effect, In re Hudson River Electric Co., 21 A. B. R. 915, 173 Fed. 134 (D. C. N. Y.).

But Bankruptcy Court Has Jurisdiction to Determine Whether Debtor Belongs to Class Subject to Bankruptcy.—But the bankruptcy court has jurisdiction to determine whether the debtor actually belongs to a class subject to bankruptcy. Compare, In re Altonwood Park Co., 20 A. B. R. 31, 160 Fed. 448 (C. C. A. N. Y.); In re New England Breeders' Club, 22 A. B. R. 124, 175 Fed. 501 (C. C. A. N. Y., reversing 21 A. B. R. 349, 165 Fed. 517); or has had residence or domicile a sufficient length of time. In re Tully, 19 A. B. R. 604, 156 Fed. 634 (D. C. N. Y.).

But Existence of Jurisdictional Facts Need Not Appear on Face of Record.—But the existence of jurisdictional facts need not appear on the face of the record. Bryant *v.* Kinyon, 6 A. B. R. 242, 53 L. R. A. 871 (Mich.); In re First Nat'l Bank of Belle Fourche, 18 A. B. R. 271 (C. C. A.). See post, "Effect of Adjudication on Rights of Parties," §§ 437, 450.

But if Lack of Jurisdictional Facts Affirmatively Appears on Face of Record, Decree Void.—But if the lack of jurisdictional facts affirmatively appears on the face of the record, the decree is void, the distinction being between mere failure to show jurisdiction and the affirmative showing, of failure of jurisdiction.

Inferentially, In re First Nat'l Bk. of Belle Fourche, 18 A. B. R. 271 (C. C. A.): "The petition contained no statement that the Widell Corporation was not engaged principally in a manufacturing pursuit, and no showing that the court was without jurisdiction of the case; but it set forth the substance of a good cause of action, and it was impregnable to attack after the adjudication." See post, "Effect of Adjudication on Rights of Parties," §§ 437, 450.

2 of the Act grants "jurisdiction" to adjudge bankrupt debtors who have resided or had their domicile or place of business within the district a certain specified time. Such residence, domiciliation, etc., are, therefore, declared to be jurisdictional. Of the same nature are the limitations regarding occupation and amount of debts: they are limitations upon or extensions of the general subject matter of "bankruptcies." In other words, not all "bankrupts" (as the general term may be used) may be adjudged involuntary bankrupts under the present Act but only those owing debts of $1,000 or more. On the other hand, the general subject matter of bankruptcy was originally confined to "traders," "bankruptcy" being predicated, originally, only of "traders;" but under the present Act the subject matter in this regard has been extended so that "bankruptcy" now embraces other classes than those to which it originally applied. Likewise, the exception of merely wage earners, farmers, etc., is in reality an extension of the subject matter of bankruptcy beyond its original meaning, for now involuntary bankruptcy may be predicated of *all* natural persons "except" wage earners and farmers, whilst formerly it was predicable only of "traders." Thus it will be seen that these limitations are jurisdictional, pertaining to the "subject of bankruptcies," as the same may be limited or extended, under the present law.

In re New York Tunnel Co., 21 A. B. R. 531, 166 Fed. 284 (C. C. A. N. Y.): "Although we think these objections are good, still if the appellants and petitioners have called our attention to a jurisdictional defect which makes the adjudication a nullity, we feel bound to consider it. If a petition for adjudication were made by only two creditors, the law requiring three, there would be a jurisdictional defect on the face of the record, making any adjudication void. On the other hand, if the aggregate amount of claims were stated to be $500 as required by law, and because of set offs or other reasons was in point of fact less, an adjudication would be an error to be corrected by appeal. So if the petition were against a railroad company there would be on the face of the record such a jurisdictional defect as would make an adjudication void. Whereas, if the corporation might or might not be considered within the act an adjudication, even if erroneous, would have to be corrected by appeal. At the time the adjudication was made in this case, building companies had been held in two districts of this circuit to be within the act; In re Niagara Contracting Co., 11 Am. B. R. 643, 127 Fed. 782; In re Rutland Realty Co., 19 Am. B. R. 546, 157 Fed. 296. In re Church Construction Co., 19 Am. B. R. 549, 157 Fed. 298. We have since decided in, In the Matter of the Kingston Realty Co., 19 Am. B. R. 845, 160 Fed. 447, that they are not subject to adjudication. It is, moreover, argued in this case that a tunnel company differs from a building company and is within the act. Lack of jurisdiction cannot be said to have appeared on the face of the record and therefore the adjudication made by the District Court, even if erroneous, is not a nullity, as we have held In the Matter of Altonwood Park Co., 20 Am. B. R. 31, 160 Fed. 448. The petitioners and appellants have proceeded throughout under the Bankruptcy Act. But they are strangers to the bankruptcy proceedings, having no right to prove their claims, to defend or to appeal. The most they can do is to call the attention of the court as amici curiæ to a want of jurisdiction of the subject-matter appearing on the face of the record. In re Columbia Real Estate Co., 4 Am. B. R. 411, 101 Fed. 965." This case quoted further at §435½.

DIVISION 1.

JURISDICTION AS DEPENDENT ON RESIDENCE, DOMICILE OR PRINCIPAL
PLACE OF BUSINESS OR ON OWNERSHIP OF
PROPERTY IN DISTRICT.

**§ 31. Limitations as to Residence, Domicile or Principal Place
of Business.**—No one may be adjudged bankrupt, upon his own petition
or upon the petition of another, by his own consent or contrary thereto,
except by the bankruptcy court of the district where he has had either his
residence, domicile or principal place of business for the six months or for
the greater portion thereof, preceding the filing of the petition.[8]

In re R. H. Williams, 9 A. B. R. 736, 128 Fed. 38 (D. C. Ark.): "Has this court
jurisdiction in bankruptcy when the party has not had his principal place of business, residence or domicile within the district for more than three months preceding the filing of the petition in bankruptcy against him? Section 2 of the
Bankruptcy Act of 1898 confers jurisdiction on the District Court to (1) 'adjudge
persons bankrupt who have had their principal place of business, residence, or had
their domicile within their respective territorial jurisdictions for the preceding six
months, or the greater portion thereof. U. S. Comp. St., p. 3422. It will thus
be seen that in order to adjudicate a debtor a bankrupt, such person must have
his principal place of business, residence or domicile within that district for the
preceding six months, or the greater portion thereof. The greater portion of
what? There can be but one answer to this: the greater portion of the six
months preceding the filing of the petition. This is the conclusion reached by
the United States Circuit Court of Appeals for the Seventh Circuit. In re
Plotke, 5 Am. B. R. 171, 44 C. C. A. 282, 104 Fed. 964."

And an established domicile is presumed to continue down to the filing
of the petition, in the absence of proof to the contrary.[9]

**§ 32. Limitation Where Debtor Nonresident or Where Adjudged
Bankrupt Outside of United States, but Owns Property Here.**—Or,
if he has neither his residence, domicile nor principal place of business
within the United States, or has been adjudged bankrupt in a foreign
country and has property in the United States, then he may be adjudged
bankrupt by the bankruptcy court where the property is located.[10]

**§ 33. Not All Three Qualifications—Residence, Domicile and
Place of Business—Coincidently Requisite.**—If the person have either

---

8. Bankr. Act, § 2 (1); In re Elmira
Steel Co., 5 A. B. R. 485 (Ref. N. Y.);
In re Garneau, 11 A. B. R. 679, 127
Fed. 677 (C. C. A. Ills.); Tiffany v.
LaPlume Condensed Milk Co., 15 A.
B. R. 413 (D. C. Pa.); Hills v. McKin-
niss Co., 26 A. B. R. 329, 188 Fed. 1012
(D. C. Ohio); In re Lipphart, 28
A. B. R. 705, 201 Fed. 103 (D. C. N. Y.).
   Bankrupt under Guardianship in One
State, Moving to Another.—Where the
bankrupt is under guardianship in one
state, even where insolvency proceedings are there pending against him, if
he remove to another state with his
guardian's consent, a residence of [the
greater portion of] six months in the
latter state is sufficient. In re Kingsley, 20 A. B. R. 427, 160 Fed. 275 (D.
C. Vt.).
   9. In re Oldstein, 25 A. B. R. 138, 182
Fed. 409 (D. C. Ore.).
   10. Bankr. Act, § 2 (1).

his residence, domicile or principal place of business in the district for the requisite period, it is sufficient: he need not have all nor any two therein.[11]

11. In re Harris, 11 A. B. R. 650 (Ref. N. J.); In re Brice, 2 A. B. R. 197, 93 Fed. 943 (D. C. Iowa); In re Clisdell, 2 A. B. R. 424 (Ref. N. Y.); Obiter, In re Hurley, 29 A. B. R. 567, 185 Fed. 851 (D. C. Minn.).

Residence and Domicile Distinguished.—Residence and domicile are different terms. Both mean a home instead of a mere staying place. Residence may be a more or less temporary home; but domicile is the permanent home place to which one expects ultimately to return for permanent abode when away and has no intention of leaving permanently when there. Compare, In re O'Hara, 20 A. B. R. 714, 166 Fed. 384 (D. C. Pa.).

In re Garneau, 11 A. B. R. 679, 127 Fed. 677 (C. C. A. Ills.): "There is, of course, a legal distinction between 'domicile' and 'residence,' although the terms are generally used as synonymous, the distinction depending upon the connection in which and the purpose for which the terms are used. 'Domicile' is the place where one has his true, fixed, permanent home, and principal establishment, and to which, whenever he is absent, he has the intention of returning, and where he exercises his political rights. There must exist in combination the fact of residence and the animus manendi. 'Residence' indicates permanency of occupation as distinguished from temporary occupation, but does not include so much as 'domicile,' which requires an intention continued with residence. 2 Kent 576. Residence has been defined to be a place where a person's habitation is fixed without any present intention of removing therefrom. It is lost by leaving the place where one has acquired a permanent home and removing to another place animo non reverendi, and is gained by remaining in such new place animo manendi. Tracy v. Tracy, 62 N. J. Eq. 807, 48 Atl. 533. In Shaeffer v. Gilbert, 73 Md. 66, 20 Atl. 434, the word is thus defined: 'It does not mean one's permanent place of abode where he intends to live all his days, or for an indefinite or unlimited time; nor does it mean one's residence for a temporary purpose, with the intention of returning to his former residence when that purpose shall have been accomplished, but means, as we understand it, one's actual home, in the sense of having no

other home, whether he intends to reside there permanently or for a definite or indefinite length of time.'"

In re Dinglehoef Bros., 6 A. B. R. 242, 109 Fed. 866 (D. C. N. C.): "Residence is personal presence in a fixed and permanent abode as distinguished from a temporary occupation, but it does not include as much as domicile, which requires an intention continued with residence. In a case in which the claimant of an exemption under the laws of North Carolina had no residence in such State except during a sojourn in a boarding house soon after her marriage, nor any right to her exemption except such as she acquired through her deceased husband, who was not a resident of the State, she has never been a resident and her intention to return to the State cannot avail her."

In re Williams, 3 A. B. R. 677, 99 Fed. 544 (D. C. Wash.): "Domicile, meaning that residence from which there is no present intention to remove or to which there is a general intention to return, cannot be changed except facto et animo." In re Owings, 15 A. B. R. 473, 140 Fed. 30 (D. C. N. C.); In re Clisdell, 2 A. B. R. 424 (Ref. N. Y., reversed on other grounds in 4 A. B. R. 95).

In re Berner, 3 A. B. R. 325 (Ref. Ohio): "Domicile and residence are distinct terms in bankruptcy proceedings. Residence may involve the intent to leave when the purpose for which it has been taken ceases; domicile implies no such intent. The abiding is animo manendi. One is a resident of a place from which his departure is indefinite as to purpose; and for this purpose he has made the place his temporary home, while if his intent be to remain permanently, it becomes his domicile. Residence for voting purposes, or for the benefit of the poor laws is not necessarily the same as residence in cases involving jurisdiction for judicial purposes. Where it is sought to be proved that there has been an abandonment of the old domicile and an establishment of a new one, the burden of proof lies upon those asserting such change."

And the question of residence or domicile is principally a question of fact and of intent. In re Williams, 3 A. B. R. 677, 99 Fed. 544 (D. C. Wash.); In re Clisdell, 2 A. B. R. 424

Thus, foreign corporations having their principal places of business within the district, although resident and domiciled elsewhere, are subject to bankruptcy in the district.[12] Likewise, one who is clerking in one district but running a store in another district is also subject to bankruptcy.[13]

§ 34. "For Preceding Six Months or Greater Portion Thereof" Defined.—This residence, domicile or principal place of business must have existed during the preceding six months or the greater part thereof; which means a length of time, either continuous or interrupted, aggregating more than three months, occurring sometime within the preceding six months.[14] And the provision of § 2, 1, does not require residence or domicile, etc., either at the beginning or at the end of the six months period.[15] It does not mean, as is maintained in In re Ray, 2 A. B. R. 158 (Ref. Wash.), that the bankrupt may file his petition, nor that creditors may file their petition against him, in the district wherein he has longest resided or been domiciled during the preceding six months, if such longest period is less than three months.[16]

And this means six months preceding the filing of the petition, not preceding the adjudication, for adjudications of courts refer to the conditions of things as they existed at the date of the commencement of proceedings

(Ref. N. Y., reversed, on other grounds, in 4 A. B. R. 95). Instance, In re Scott, 7 A. B. R. 35 (Ref. Mass.).

And the burden of proof of change of residence or domicile rests on the one asserting the change. In re Berner, 3 A. B. R. 325 (Ref. Ohio); In re Waxelbaum, 3 A. B. R. 267, 97 Fed. 562 (D. C. N. Y.); In re Clisdell, 2 A. B. R. 424; In re Grimes, 2 A. B. R. 160, 96 Fed. 529.

The residence, domicile or principal place of business must be bona fide. In re Garneau, 11 A. B. R. 679, 127 Fed. 677 (C. C. A. Ills.). In this case the court holds, that the removal of a person from one district to another, for the purpose of pretending to acquire a residence solely for the purpose of filing a petition in bankruptcy in a district in which he did not reside with the intention of leaving the place as soon as his discharge, does not make him a resident of the district, and the facts being disclosed upon his examination his creditors are entitled to have the proceedings dismissed for want of jurisdiction, the adjudication in bankruptcy not being conclusive upon them. See quotations from this case in the text of § 30 and in the present section, note to § 33, ante.

But domicile is not lost by the absconding of the debtor to escape prosecution for a criminal offense. In re

Filer, 5 A. B. R. 332, 108 Fed. 209 (D. C. N. Y.).

Estoppel to Deny Residence.—Where a bankrupt secures dismissal of bankruptcy proceedings against him in one district by plea of nonresidence and allegation of residence in another State he, and later on his administrator will be estopped to deny residence in the latter district. Long v. Lockman, 14 A. B. R. 172 (D. C. Colo.).

12. In re Magid-Hope Silk Mfg. Co., 6 A. B. R. 610, 110 Fed. 352 (D. C. Mass.); In re Marine Machine & Conveyor Co., 1 A. B. R. 421, 91 Fed. 630 (D. C. N. Y.); Dressel v. Lumber Co., 5 A. B. R. 744, 107 Fed. 255 (D. C. N. C.). Obiter, In re Elmira Steel Co., 5 A. B. R. 485 (Ref. N. Y.).

13. In re Brice, 2 A. B. R. 197, 93 Fed. 942 (D. C. Iowa).

14. In re Berner, 3 A. B. R. 325 (Ref. Ohio); In re Plotke, 5 A. B. R. 171, 104 Fed. 964 (C. C. A. Ills.); In re R. H. Williams, 9 A. B. R. 736, 120 Fed. 38 (D. C. Ark.).

15. In re Berner, 3 A. B. R. (Ref. Ohio). Contra, In re Stokes, 1 A. B. R. 35 (Ref. Wash.).

16. In re R. H. Williams, 9 A. B. R. 736, 120 Fed. 38 (D. C. Ark.); In re Plotke, 5 A. B. R. 171, 104 Fed. 964 (C. C. A. Ills.); obiter, In re Berner, 3 A. B. R. 325 (Ref. Ohio).

or as subsequently may be brought into the record by subsequent pleadings.[17]

Where a voluntary petition has been filed too short a time after the debtor's acquisition of a residence or domicile, the adjudication is to be set aside; but, thereafter, where sufficient length of time has elapsed, it may be reverified and refiled, and a new adjudication be had.[18]

§ 35. Actual Principal Place of Business Governs.—In determining the principal place of business of a corporation, it is its actual principal place of doing business that will govern.

Compare, In re Guanacevi Tunnel Co., 29 A. B. R. 229, 201 Fed. 316 (C. C. A. N. Y.): "It is next contended that the District Court for the Southern District of New York was without jurisdiction, because the company had not maintained its principal place of business in New York for the greater part of six months before the filing of the petition. Sec. 2 (1). This objection being jurisdictional, may be made by a creditor. The majority of the court do not think this contention well founded. The charter of the company provides that its principal place of business shall be at Phœnix, Arizona, and that it may have such other offices, principal and branch, as may be established by the board of directors. The statement in the charter is not conclusive, the question being where, in point of fact, was the company's principal place of business during the period fixed by the Act. The petition asserts that it was at No. 55 Liberty Street, New York City. This formal statement of the board of directors, resulting in an adjudication, at least creates a prima facie case which leaves the burden of evidence to meet it upon the creditors who seek to vacate the adjudication. The affidavits show that the Tunnel Company has never done any mining; that its activities have been principally connected with the sale of its stock and the payment of its running expenses, and that the only place in which the business has been conducted has been at 55 Liberty Street, in this city. It is true that this had ceased to be the office of the company in the sense that the company paid the rent and was, in point of fact, the office of Meloy, June 6, 1911, when the board of directors met there and authorized him to file the petition, but while the company's business was being transacted there, it may be held to have been established by the board of directors within the meaning of the charter provision. The books were kept there, all meetings of the board were held there and all moneys of the company were disbursed from there. No meetings were ever held at Phœnix except the technical ones required by the law of the State of Arizona. It is not necessary that the company should have actually transacted much, or even any, business at 55 Liberty Street during the period fixed by the Act. The question is, where was the principal place of business? Its business was small and irregular and it may have transacted little or none, but if it had any principal place of business at all, it was there. The petitioning creditor has not satisfied us to the contrary."

Thus it is its actual place of doing business that will govern, rather than its home office as designated in its articles of incorporation.[19]

---

17. But compare, apparently contra, In re Tully, 19 A. B. R. 605, 156 Fed. 634 (D. C. N. Y.).

18. Compare, to this general effect, In re Tully, 19 A. B. R. 605, 156 Fed.

634 (D. C. N. Y.), although in this case no reverification nor refiling was had.

19. Home Powder Co. v. Geis (C. C. A. Mo.), 29 A. B. R. 580; Dressel v.

On the other hand, its home office may be its principal place of business, although it operates manufactories and mines elsewhere.

In re Slate Co., 16 A. B. R. 408, 144 Fed. 737 (C. C. A. Mass.): "We are of the opinion that when a corporation operating factories, mills, or mines in various states, has a principal office where business is transacted of the character of that conducted at the Boston office of the Matthews Consolidated Slate Company, such principal office, rather than a factory, mill, or mine, according to ordinary understanding and speech, as well as according to the intent of Congress, constitutes the 'principal place of business,' within the meaning of the Bankruptcy Act. Not only is this the natural interpretation, but it seems to us the only practical interpretation; for, since there can be but one principal place of business, if regard is paid to the amount of property owned or kept in a particular jurisdiction, or to the amount of product there turned out, or to the number of workmen employed, it might follow that the inquiry would be, which is the largest mine or factory? a question having little relation to the purpose of administering the assets."

Or its chief executive office and hence its "principal place of business" may be in one state and its plant in another.[20]

Nor will the failure of a foreign corporation to obtain a certificate of permission to do business, prevent its principal place of business being within the district.[21]

In re Duplex Radiator Co., 15 A. B. R. 324, 142 Fed. 906 (D. C. N. Y.): "At all events, in my opinion, if a foreign corporation has, in fact, had its principal place of business for six months in this district, this court has jurisdiction, and the fact that it has not obtained a certificate from the Secretary of State, permitting it to do business here, does not divest this court of jurisdiction. If it has not complied with the law of this State in obtaining such a certificate, it is liable to the consequences provided by that law. But, in my opinion, the fact that no certificate was obtained does not change the fact that the principal place of business is where the principal business is done."

Where a corporation has been placed in the hands of a receiver who is merely proceeding with the liquidation of its affairs, it can hardly be considered as being still "engaged in business" at all, within the meaning of the act. This was, in effect, the holding in a case where a corporation, organized in one state but merely holding its annual meetings there, had been placed in the hands of a receiver in such state, who had taken possession of its assets in another state where it had until that time actually had its principal place of business.[22]

North State Lumber Co., 5 A. B. R. 744, 107 Fed. 255 (D. C. N. C.); In re Marine Machine & Conveyor Co., 1 A. B. R. 421, 91 Fed. 630 (D. C. N. Y.); In re Duplex Radiator Co., 15 A. B. R. 324, 142 Fed. 906 (D. C. N. Y.).

20. In re Pennsylvania Consol. Coal Co., 20 A. B. R. 872, 163 Fed. 579 (D. C. Pa.).

21. And see In re (Perry) Aldrich Co., 21 A. B. R. 246, 165 Fed. 249 (D. C. Mass.). Compare, analogously, In re Dunlop, 19 A. B. R. 361, 156 Fed. 949 (C. C. A. Minn.), quoted at § 1753¾. As to facts constituting principal place of business, Obiter, In re Elmira Steel Co., 5 A. B. R. 486, 109 Fed. 471 (Ref. N. Y.).

22. Compare post, §§ 97, 97½.

In re (Perry) Aldrich Co., 21 A. B. R. 244, 165 Fed. 249 (D. C. Mass.): "The corporation was not continuing business it had been organized to do, nor was it liquidating its affairs of its own accord through officers of its own selection. It had been ordered by a court having the right to do so, to stop doing that business; and acts done thereafter, merely in order to collect its assets or turn them into money, by officers of that court cannot as it seems to me be what is intended by 'business' in the expression 'principal place of business' as used in the Bankruptcy Act. The petitioners might perhaps have obtained jurisdiction here by filing their petition within three months following December 18th. That period having expired, it seems to me no longer possible to bring the case within the language of § 2 (1)."

But it has been held that a clerk or employee of another can hardly be held to have a place of business within the meaning of the statute; and that it is his employer rather than he who has the place of business.

In re Lipphart, 28 A. B. R. 705, 201 Fed. 103 (D. C. N. Y.): "It is intended among other things, by the bankruptcy law, that these proceedings should, as far as practicable, be carried on in the jurisdiction most convenient to all concerned. The debts of a clerk on a small salary would, most likely, be owing to the tradesmen doing business in the place where he lived. I think that a clerk or, for that matter, the general run of employees cannot be said to be in business or to have a place of business. It seems to me that 'place of business' means a place where a man is conducting a business of his own in which he is a principal. I am inclined to think that the statute contemplated 'place of business' as applying only to those who have a business of their own, but in this case it is only necessary to decide that a clerk, such as this bankrupt, did not have a place of business anywhere, and therefore he should have filed his petition at the place where he resided or had his domicile."

However, such ruling probably is too narrow. A clerk, even, is a business man, and has a place where he does his business, quite as much as a small shopkeeper or cobbler.

§ 36. Residence, etc., of One Partner Sufficient.—A partnership petition may be filed in any district wherein any one of the partners has had his residence, domicile or principal place of business long enough to have supported the jurisdiction of the court had he individually petitioned.[23]

Division 2.

Who May Become Voluntary Bankrupts.

§ 37. Who May Be a "Voluntary" Bankrupt?—Any natural person

---

23. Sec. 5: "The court of bankruptcy which has jurisdiction of one of the partners may have jurisdiction of all the partners and of the administration of the partnership and individual property.

In re Blair, 3 A. B. R. 588, 99 Fed. 76 (D. C. N. Y.).

As to vacating of adjudication for want of jurisdiction for lack of proper residence, etc., in the particular district; also as to collateral attack on same, see post, "Adjudication, Vacating of;" also, "Adjudication—Collateral Attack upon," §§ 437, 450.

Possession of bankrupt's assets by State Court receiver, sheriff or other officer, does not affect the jurisdiction of the bankruptcy court to adjudge the debtor bankrupt. In re Moench, 12 A. B. R. 240, 130 Fed. 685 (C. C. A. N. Y., affirming 10 A. B. R. 656).

and any corporation, being indebted, except a municipal, railroad, insurance or banking corporation, may be adjudged bankrupt upon his or its own petition, such debtor being termed a "voluntary" bankrupt.[24]

Before the Amendment of 1910 no corporation could be a voluntary bankrupt; but by that Amendment this restriction has been removed. However, not all corporations may become voluntary bankrupts; municipal, railroad, insurance and banking corporations are not entitled to become voluntary bankrupts. According to the strict terms of the statute *any* corporation may become a voluntary bankrupt, except a municipal, railroad, insurance or banking corporation, even though such corporation might not be, strictly speaking, a "moneyed, business or commercial corporation;" so that any corporation (except a municipal, railroad, insurance or banking corporation) may, doubtless, become a voluntary bankrupt that would be entitled by state law to make an assignment for the benefit of creditors or otherwise affirmatively invoke the action of the courts therein in behalf of creditors.[25]

§ 38. "Voluntary" Bankruptcy a Later Development.—Bankruptcy law at the time we derived our Common Law from England, and even until 1826 in England and 1841 in the United States, could not be set in motion at all by the debtor himself, but only by his creditors; that is to say, until then, there was only one kind of bankruptcy, adversary bankruptcy; or, as the rather ambiguous term of the present Act has it, "involuntary" bankruptcy. Before those years a debtor could not voluntarily file a petition to be adjudged a bankrupt, no matter how insolvent he might be, nor how wise a step such might be for his creditors and for himself as well. Before then, the law was chiefly a creditors' law, a swift and sharp remedy placed in the hands of creditors for seizing and distributing the estates of dishonest insolvents and of punishing the offenders, only incidentally granting any favors to the debtors, much less giving them the right of initiative; and it was only by slow steps and gradual progress (see Introduction, ante) that bankruptcy law came to approach the full measure of a general system for the administration of insolvent estates that it is, speaking in general terms, at the present time.

But, although the debtor is now permitted voluntarily to seek his own adjudication as a bankrupt, and although the operation of the law is not confined to those known at common law as traders as it originally was

---

24. Bankr. Act, § 4 (a), as amended June 25, 1910: "Any person, except a municipal, railroad, insurance, or banking corporation, shall be entitled to the benefits of this act as a voluntary bankrupt."

Thus, a farmer, though immune from involuntary proceedings, obiter, Olive *v.* Armour Co., 21 A. B. R. 901, 167 Fed. 517 (C. C. A. Ga.).

25. Of course, a corporation cannot be adjudged bankrupt, if, under the law of the state, it is not permitted to contract debts. In such case those dealing with the corporation must take notice of the limitation of its powers and should they extend credit their claims would not be provable in bankruptcy. In re Wyoming Valley Assn., 28 A. B. R. 462, 198 Fed. 436 (D. C. Pa.) see post, § 80.

confined at the time we derived our Common Law from England, never-theless, even so, it is not every debtor, yet, that may voluntarily bring into operation the functions of the Bankruptcy Act, nor that may be thrown involuntarily into bankruptcy by creditors.

§ 38½. **Insane Persons.**—Insane persons may not be voluntary bank-rupts;[26] except in lucid intervals.[27]

§ 39. **Partnerships Included.**—Partnerships are included among those who may become voluntary bankrupts, for § 5 (a) provides that a partnership during the continuation of the partnership business or after its dissolution and before the final settlement thereof, may be adjudged a bankrupt.[28]

§ 40. **But Not Mere Joint Contractors or Joint Owners.**—Mere joint contractors or joint owners are not permitted to file a joint petition. Nothing short of a partnership will authorize the joining of two or more individuals in one petition. Thus, husband and wife may not join in a single petition where simply bound on the same obligations.

But compare contra rule in the State of Washington, evidently by virtue of statute.

Obiter, In re Herbold, 14 A. B. R. 118 (D. C. Wash.): "Early in the admin-istration of the Bankrupt Act the district judge of this district stated from the bench that he would, for the purpose of the Act, consider the family relation as a partnership. Under the community law, a family undoubtedly partakes of the nature of a quasi partnership, but the statutes of the State have provided that while a partnership for certain purposes, still, etc., etc."

The partnership must be an "actual" partnership as distinguished from a partnership by "holding out."[29]

§ 41. **No Specified Amount of Indebtedness Requisite, Though Debts Must Be "Provable."**—It is not necessary that the voluntary bankrupt owe any particular amount of debts.[30] But it is necessary that the debts be such as are termed "provable." What debts are provable and what are not provable will later be discussed.[31]

If he owe any provable debt, it is enough: he is entitled to go voluntarily into bankruptcy.[32]

26. See as to involuntary cases, post, § 54; (1867) In re Pratt, Fed. Cas. No. 11371; (1867) In re Weitzel, Fed. Cas. No. 17365; obiter, In re Kehler, 18 A. B. R. 596, 153 Fed. 235 (D. C. N. Y., affirmed in 20 A. B. R. 669, 152 Fed. 674, and 19 A. B. R. 513, 159 Fed. 55).

27. Obiter, In re Kehler, 18 A. B. R. 596, 153 Fed. 235 (D. C. N. Y., affirmed in 20 A. B. R. 669, 162 Fed. 674, 19 A. B. R. 513, 159 Fed. 55).

28. See as to involuntary cases, post, § 56, et seq.

29. See post, § 63, et seq.

30. In re Schwaninger, 16 A. B. R. 427, 144 Fed. 555 (D. C. Wis.).

31. See post, "What Debts Are Provable," chap. XXI, § 625, et seq.

32. This has been held to be so in partnership cases, even though all firm obligations be outlawed, if the right of contribution still exists un-settled among the partners. In re Levy & Richman, 2 A. B. R. 21 (Ref. N. Y.).

In one case it was held, that a vol-

In re Schwaninger, 16 A. B. R. 427, 144 Fed. 555 (D. C. Wis.): "It is my belief that Congress had not in mind any purpose to discriminate against an unfortunate debtor who is oppressed by a single obligation, and that the will of Congress will be effectuated by making the definition above recited applicable to § 4, and treating the term 'debts' where it occurs in such section as the equivalent of 'debt'."

And if there is no provable debt he is not so entitled.

In re Yates, 8 A. B. R. 69, 114 Fed. 365 (D. C. Calif.): "But a cause of action against him for unliquidated damages for a personal tort, such as is involved in the action of Risdon v. Yates, before referred to, is not within either of the classes named. * * * With much stronger reason should the decree adjudging Yates a bankrupt be vacated, and the proceeding instituted by him be dismissed, because at the date of the filing of his voluntary petition there was no existing provable debt against his estate under the Bankruptcy Act. It will be time enough for him to apply for relief under the Bankruptcy Act, and to ask the court to pass upon the many questions which may arise in such a proceeding, when it shall be ascertained that he is indebted to some person upon a claim provable under the Bankrupt Act."

By the Amendment of 1910 the restriction of bankruptcy to those "owing debts," has apparently been removed with regard to voluntary bankruptcy; but undoubtedly the courts will continue to construe the law as applicable only to those owing debts, since the only jurisdiction vested by the Constitution in Congress in this regard is "over the subject of bankruptcies" and, manifestly, there can be no "subject of bankruptcies" without debts. This elimination was doubtless by inadvertence. The subcommittee of the Judiciary Committee of the Senate, to whom had been entrusted the house bill, had recommended to the whole Judiciary Committee the following amendment: "Any person who owes debts provable under this act to the amount of $500 or over, except a municipal, railroad, insurance or banking corporation, shall be entitled to the benefits of this act as a voluntary bankrupt." The Judiciary Committee of the Senate as a whole (like the Judiciary Committee of the House) desired to reject and did reject the limitation of $500, but in doing so the Senate Judiciary Committee also struck out the words "who owes debts provable under this act," as well as the words "to the amount of $500 or over;" the House, subsequently, during the last hours of the session, concurring in the Senate amendment without change. However, as above noted, it is still necessary that the bankrupt be a person "who owes debts."[33]

§ 42. Insolvency Not Requisite to Voluntary Bankrupt.—Nor is it necessary that he be insolvent. The reason of this is probably that, if he be solvent, it is nobody's business but his own if he chooses to have his

untary petition should be dismissed where the only debt was a nondischargeable debt. In re Maples, 5 A. B. R. 426, 105 Fed. 919. But this case is not correct in such ruling, because bankruptcy may be proper in behalf of creditors even though unprofitable to the debtor.

33. Compare, In re Walrath, 24 A. B. R. 541 (D. C. N. Y.).

creditors paid through the machinery of the bankruptcy court; and if, on the other hand, he be actually insolvent, why then he *ought* to go into bankruptcy. So runs the argument at any rate.[34]

§ 43. Creditors May Not Intervene to Oppose Voluntary Petition.
—For the reason above stated, a debtor is adjudicated bankrupt at once on filing his voluntary petition, and no one is permitted to file a defense to it.[35]

In re Jehu, 2 A. B. R. 498, 94 Fed. 638 (D. C. Iowa): "I know of no provision of the Bankrupt Act which authorizes creditors to file answers to a voluntary petition in bankruptcy."

Nat'l Bk. *v.* Moyses, 8 A. B. R. 10, 186 U. S. 181: "These are not issuable facts and notice is unnecessary. * * * Adjudication follows as matter of course."

In re Carbone, 13 A. B. R. 55, (Ref. Wash.): "Adjudication of bankruptcy will be granted to a voluntary petitioner whose petition sets forth the jurisdictional requirements. A creditor may not object to such adjudication, but has his remedy if the averments are false."

Thus, a creditor may not intervene and oppose it, by setting up that the petitioner is not insolvent.[36] And this is so, even in partnership cases where one of the partners does not consent; the defense of solvency not being available to creditors in a partnership petition filed by one partner, but only to the nonjoining partner.[37]

§ 44. What Action by Corporation Necessary.
—The Amendment of 1910, removing the restriction against the voluntary bankruptcy of corporations, does not, however, prescribe what corporate action is requisite for the voluntary bankrupt. The old Bankruptcy Act of 1867, under which the voluntary bankruptcy of corporations was permitted, in its § 37 specifically authorized the voluntary bankruptcy of the corporation "upon the petition of any officer of any such corporation or company duly authorized by a vote of a majority of the corporators present, at any legal meeting called for the purpose." Doubtless, there being no express regulation in the present act itself, such corporate action will be requisite as would be requisite under the laws of the State for invoking the action of the court in the analogous cases of assignments or of the filing of insolvency petitions therein.[38]

---

34. In re Jehu, 2 A. B. R. 498, 94 Fed. 638 (D. C. Iowa). Compare, to same effect, obiter, In re Chappell, 7 A. B. R. 612, 113 Fed. 545 (Ref. Va., affirmed by D. C.).

35. In re Carleton, 8 A. B. R. 270, 115 Fed. 246 (D. C. Mass.). Also a partnership case. Obiter, In re Garneau, 11 A. B. R. 679, 127 Fed. 677 (C. C. A. Ills.), quoted at § 30.

In re Ives, 7 A. B. R. 692, 113 Fed. 911 (C. C. A. Mich.): This was the case of a partnership filing a voluntary petition and being adjudicated bankrupt, creditors afterwards seeking to intervene to have the adjudication vacated.

36. In re Carleton, 8 A. B. R. 270, 115 Fed. 246 (D. C. Mass.).

37. In re Carleton, 8 A. B. R. 270, 115 Fed. 246 (D. C. Mass.).

38. Under the Act of 1867, the term "corporator" as used in the Bankruptcy Act, was held to be in general synonymous with "stockholder." In re Lady Bryan Mining Co., 4 Nat. Bankr. Reg.

The board of directors has the same authority, under the Amendment of 1910, to make application for the benefits of the provisions of the bankruptcy law, as it had to admit the corporation's insolvency for the purpose of involuntary proceedings, prior to the amendment.[39]

Under the Act of 1867, it appears that a subsequent ratification of an unauthorized corporate petition was ineffective, even though all formalities were observed in the attempted ratification.[40]

Under the Act of 1867, it was requisite that the voluntary petition of a corporation contains, annexed thereto, a certified copy of the resolution passed by the "corporators" authorizing the filing of the voluntary petition, such resolution to follow substantially the following prescribed form, which has been adapted, however, to proceedings under the Act of 1898.[40a]

"At a meeting of the stockholders (or, the Board of Directors or Trustees, as the case may be) of the ....Company (or Association or Society, etc.,) a corporation created under the laws of the State of .... held at ....in the County of ....and State of ...., on this ....day of ....A. D., ... the condition of the affairs of said corporation having been inquired into, and it being ascertained to the satisfaction of said meeting that the said corporation was insolvent, and that its affairs ought to be wound up, it was voted (or resolved) by a majority of the corporators (or stockholders, or directors or trustees) present at such meeting (which was duly called and notified for the purpose of taking action upon the subject aforesaid) that ....be and .... thereby authorized, empowered and required to file a petition in the District Court of the United States for the ...... District of ...., within which said corporation has had its residence, domicile or principal place of business during the greater portion of the preceding six months, for the purpose of having the same adjudged Bankrupt; and that such proceedings be had thereon as are provided by the act of Congress entitled "An act to Establish a Uniform System of Bankruptcy throughout the United States," approved July 1st, 1898, and acts amendatory thereof.

In Witness Whereof, I have hereunto subscribed my name as .... of said Corporation and affixed the seal of the same this .... day of .... 19.......

[Seal]   ....
                                          of said Corporation.

At any rate, authority granted at a meeting of stockholders called and held in conformity with the express statutory requirements of the old

---

144, 394, 1 Sawyer 349; Ansonia Brass Co. *v.* Chimney Co., 13 Nat. Bankr. Reg. 385, 64 Barber. 435, 91 U. S. 656.

It was also held that the action of the Board of Trustees, though by State law they were in charge of the management of the ordinary business of the corporation, was not sufficient action of the corporators—that the stockholders themselves must have acted. In re Lady Bryan Mining Co., 4 Nat. Bankr. Reg. 394, 1 Sawyer 349; Ansonia Brass Co. *v.* Chimney Co., 13 Nat.

Bankr. Reg. 385, 64 Barber 435, 91 U. S. 656.

Compare, analogously, post, § 167, "Admissions by Boards of Directors of Corporations."

39. In re Kenwood Ice Co., 26 A. B. R. 499, 189 Fed. 525 (D. C. Minn.).

40. (1867) In re Lady Bryan Mining Co., 4 Nat. Bankr. Reg. 394 (D. C. Nev.).

40a. For suggested form of voluntary petition of a corporation, see post, § 190 note.

Act of 1867, and the forms of the Supreme Court provided thereunder, would doubtless be held equally valid authorization under the present law, in the absence of express statutory or Supreme Court rule.

The law of 1867, under which voluntary bankruptcy of corporations was permitted, prescribed what corporate action was requisite to that end. It required the "petition of any officer of any such corporation or company, duly authorized by a vote of a majority of the corporators, at any legal meeting called for the purpose." No such requisite appears in the Amendment of 1910. In the absence of any expression, it would seem that at least such corporate action would be requisite for authorizing the filing of a voluntary corporate petition, as would be requisite to commit the fifth act of bankruptcy. The decisions as to what is requisite to bind the corporation in the commission of the fifth act of bankruptcy will, perhaps, be the nearest, in analogy, for determining what authority and action is requisite on the part of a corporation to authorize a voluntary petition in bankruptcy.[41]

Division 3.

Who May Be Thrown Involuntarily into Bankruptcy.

§ 45. Who May Be Adjudged Involuntary Bankrupt.—Any natural person having sufficient legal capacity, except a wage earner, or a person engaged in farming or the tillage of the soil, any unincorporated company, and any moneyed, business or commercial corporation, except a municipal, railroad, insurance or banking corporation, owing debts to the amount of $1,000 or over, may be adjudged an involuntary bankrupt upon default or an impartial trial, and will be subject to the provisions and entitled to the benefits of the act.

The classes of corporations which may be adjudged bankrupts involuntarily has been changed by the Amendment of 1910, so that now not only may those corporations which are engaged principally in manufacturing, trading, printing, publishing, mining, or mercantile pursuits be adjudged involuntary bankrupts, but, in addition thereto, any moneyed, business, or commercial corporation may be so adjudged, except a municipal, railroad, insurance or banking corporation.[42]

§ 45½. Must Owe $1,000 or More.—A debtor may not be thrown into involuntary bankruptcy unless he owes at least $1,000.[43]

---

41. Compare post, §§ 167, 168.
42. See post, § 80. Also, see Bankr. Act, § 4b, as amended June 25, 1910: "Any natural person, except a wage earner or a person engaged chiefly in farming or the tillage of the soil, any unincorporated company, and any moneyed, business, or commercial corporation, except a municipal, railroad, insurance, or banking corporation, owing debts to the amount of one thousand dollars or over, may be adjudged an involuntary bankrupt upon default or an impartial trial, and shall be subject to the provisions and entitled to the benefits of this act."

Involuntary proceedings are in no sense optional with the alleged bankrupt. In re Wakefield, 25 A. B. R. 118, 182 Fed. 247 (D. C. N. Y.).

43. Bankr. Act, § 4 (b).

Thus, in partnership cases, debts created by "estoppel" or by "holding out," after actual dissolution, etc., are not sufficient: they must be debts of an actual partnership.[43a]

§ 46. "Wage Earners" and "Farmers," etc., Excluded.—

Wage earners and farmers and tillers of the soil are excepted and no one can be adjudged bankrupt in involuntary proceedings who is a wage earner or is chiefly engaged in farming or the tillage of the soil.[44]

In re Taylor, 4 A. B. R. 515, 102 Fed. 728 (C. C. A. Ills.): "We think the court erred in holding that the alleged bankrupt being a farmer and therefore not coming within the provisions of the law governing involuntary bankruptcy, was a personal privilege, which could only be set up by the bankrupt in person. The question was jurisdictional rather than personal. The law (Bankr. Act, 1898, § 4) provides that any natural person, except a wage earner or a person engaged chiefly in farming or the tillage of the soil, may be adjudged an involuntary bankrupt upon default or an impartial trial. The alleged bankrupt did not appear or answer, but the appellant who had obtained a lien upon his property, appeared and set up the fact in an answer. There was nothing in the petition to bring the alleged bankrupt within the terms of the statute. It did not allege what the defendant's business or occupation was, and there was no allegation to show that he did not come within the excepted classes, which, under the law, are too important to be wholly ignored. Farmers and wage earners constitute a large majority of the people. These are excepted from that portion of the clause relating to involuntary bankruptcy, and the petition should either have shown what the business of the defendant was, or that he did not come within the excepted classes."

These exceptions, of wage earners and farmers, exclude from the operation of involuntary bankruptcy the vast majority of those engaged in the industrial life of the country;[45] and indicate an adherence, more or less accurate, to the original restriction of bankruptcy proceedings to traders and merchants.

Compare Brown & Adams v. Button Co., 17 A. B. R. 566 (C. C. A. Del.): "Bankruptcy is supposedly concerned with commercial matters and was early

---

43a. See post, § 63.
44. In re Pilger, 9 A. B. R. 245, 118 Fed. 206 (D. C. Pa.). Impliedly, In re Bellah, 8 A. B. R. 310, 116 Fed. 69 (D. C. Del.); In re Mero, 12 A. B. R. 171, 128 Fed. 630 (D. C. Conn.); Brake v. Callison, 11 A. B. R. 797, 129 Fed. 201 (C. C. A. Fla.); In re Callison, 12 A. B. R. 344, 130 Fed. 987 (D. C. Fla.); In re Brett, 12 A. B. R. 492, 130 Fed. 981 (D. C. N. J.). Obiter, Moore v. Green (as to farmer), 16 A. B. R. 652 (C. C. A. W. Va.). Obiter and impliedly, Edelstein v. U. S., 17 A. B. R. 649 (C. C. A. Minn.); Beach v. Macon Grocery Co., 9 A. B. R. 762, 120 Fed. 736 (C. C. A. Ga.). Impliedly, In re Levingston, 13 A. B. R. 357 (D. C. Hawaii); In re White, 14 A. B. R. 241, 135 Fed. 199 (D. C. Penna.); Hoffschlaeger v. Young Nap, 12 A. B. R. 514 (D. C. Hawaii). Sutherland Medicine Co. v. Rich & Bailey, 22 A. B. R. 85 (Ref. Ga.); In re Duke & Son, 28 A. B. R. 195, 199 Fed. 199 (D. C. Ga.); In re Dwyer, 25 A. B. R. 913, 184 Fed. 880 (C. C. A. Ills.).

45. In re Taylor, 4 A. B. R. 515, 102 Fed. 728 (C. C. A. Ills.).

confined to traders. And while it has gradually been extended and enlarged, the original idea has not altogether been departed from."

First Nat. Bank of Wilkesbarre *v*. Barnum, 20 A. B. R. 439, 160 Fed. 245 (D. C. Pa.): "By this, it is evidently intended to relieve from adverse proceedings those who, not being engaged in business or trade, depend for a living upon the result of individual labor effort, without the aid of property or capital." Quoted further at § 47.

And the exclusion of the classes named goes to the jurisdiction of the court over the subject-matter itself.[46]

The fact that the debtor has made an assignment will not alter the case,[46a] any more than if he had committed any other act of bankruptcy: he does not divest himself of his privilege by divesting himself of the means of carrying on his occupation.

§ 47. "Wage Earner" Defined.

—A wage earner is defined to be an individual who works for wages, salary or hire, at a rate of compensation not exceeding fifteen hundred dollars a year.[47]

But the mere fact that the debtor is in receipt of a salary of less than $1,500 per annum is not conclusive that he is a "wage earner." Thus, where a sole owner of a mercantile business transferred the business to a corporation, bearing his own name, three-fourths of the stock of which he retained, being also interested in a real estate business and being worth $90,000 outside of his holdings of stock in the corporation, it was held that he was not a "wage earner," exempt from involuntary bankruptcy, though he received only $900 salary for his services as president of the corporation, the court saying that manifestly Congress did not intend to exempt persons such as this from the operation of the law.[48]

The mere incidental earning of wages is not sufficient to make one a "wage earner" within the meaning of the act.

---

46. See ante, § 30.

46a. Olive *v*. Armour & Co., 21 A. B. R. 901, 167 Fed. 517 (C. C. A. Ga.).

47. Bankr. Act, § 1 (27); compare post, § 2171; In re Hurley, 29 A. B. R. 567, 185 Fed. 851 (D. C. Mass.); In re Wakefield, 25 A. B. R. 118, 182 Fed. 247 (D. C. Cal.).

Instances: (1) An ordinary day laborer who does work with his hands, lifting logs, holding a plow, driving his team, and similar service for different people at irregular intervals, lasting from a day to a week at a time, is a "wage earner."

In re Yoder, 11 A. B. R. 445, 127 Fed. 894 (D. C. Penna.): "Upon these facts I think it is clear that the bankrupt was a wage earner and not an independent contractor. He was a servant hired by successive masters, and was always paid by the day, never by the job. The fact that he used his horses and wagons in performing the services for which he was paid by the day does not seem to me of any special importance. A carpenter, or any other skilled mechanic, employs tools—often his own tools—to assist him in earning his daily wages, and the bankrupt's horses and wagons stand, I think, in precisely the same category. * * * He was not an independent contractor looking for his income to the profits that he might make by carrying out a contract for a lump sum, but was an ordinary day laborer, who did work with his hands, lifting logs, holding a plow, driving his team and similar service, for which he was paid at a fixed rate by the day."

(2) A stockholder and officer of a corporation may nevertheless be a wage earner within the meaning of the statute. In re Pilger, 9 A. B. R. 244, 118 Fed. 206 (D. C. Wis.).

48. Carpenter *v*. Cudd, 23 A. B. R. 463, 174 Fed. 603 (C. C. A. S. C.).

In re Naroma Chocolate Co., 24 A. B. R. 154, 178 Fed. 383 (D. C. R. I.): "A person who is engaged in a manufacturing or trading business does not come within the ordinary usage of the term 'wage earner' merely because while engaged as a manufacturer or trader, he may earn wages by working for another in a different occupation."

A music teacher giving lessons at so much an hour is not a "wage earner."

First Nat. Bk. of Wilkesbarre v. Barnum, 20 A. B. R. 439, 160 Fed. 245 (D. C. Pa.): "By this it is evidently intended to relieve from adverse proceedings those who, not being engaged in business or trade, depend for a living upon the result of individual labor or effort, without the aid of property of capital. But not all of this class are exempt, as is shown by the limit of $1,500. And the work done must be such as is compensated by wages, salary, or hire, other earnings not being put in the same category. These terms mean much the same thing, and are no doubt collectively used in order to cover the different possible kinds of employment comprehended within the general idea. Wages, as distinguished from salary, are commonly understood to apply to the compensation for manual labor, skilled or unskilled, paid at stated times, and measured by the day, week, month, or season. Commonwealth v. Butler, 99 Pa. 535; Lang v. Simmons, 64 Wis. 525, 25 N. W. 650; Campfield v. Lang (C. C.), 25 Fed. 128; Henry v. Fisher, 2 Pa. Dist. R. 7; Louisville, etc., R. R. v. Barnes, 16 Ind. App. 312, 44 N. E. 1113; Fidelity Ins. Co. v. Shenandoah Valley R. R., 86 Va. 1, 9 S. E. 759, 19 Am. St. Rep. 858; State v. Haun, 7 Kan. App. 509, 54 Pac. 120. And also by the piece. Pennsylvania Coal Co. v. Costello, 33 Pa. 241; Swift Mfg. Co. v. Henderson, 99 Ga. 135, 25 S. E. 27; Ford v. St. Louis R. R., 54 Iowa 728, 7 N. W. 126; Seider's Appeal, 46 Pa. 57; Adcock v. Smith, 97 Tenn. 373, 37 S. W. 91, 56 Am. St. Rep. 810. But not by the job. Heebner v. Chave, 5 Pa. 115; Berkson v. Cox, 73 Miss. 339, 18 South. 934, 55 Am. St. Rep. 539; Morse v. Robertson, 9 Hawaii, 195; Henry v. Fisher, 2 Pa. Dist. R. 7. Nor including profits on the services of others. Smith v. Brooke, 49 Pa. 147; Sleeman v. Barrett, 2 H. & C. 934; Riley v. Warden, 2 Exch. 59. Neither is it so broad a term as 'earnings', which comprehend the returns from skill and labor in whatever way acquired. People v. Remington, 45 Hun, 338; Matter of Stryker, 73 Hun, 327, 26 N. Y Supp. 209; id., 158 N. Y. 526; Jenks v. Dyer, 102 Mass. 236; Nuding v. Urich, 169 Pa. 289, 32 Atl. 409; Goodhart v. Pennsylvania R. R., 177 Pa. 1, 35 Atl. 191; Hoyt v. White, 46 N. H. 45. Indeed the act itself in exempting wage earners recognizes that there are other kinds. Salary, on the other hand, has reference to a superior grade of services. Hardman v. Nitzel, 8 Pa. Super. Ct. 22. And implies a position or office. Belle v. Indian Live Stock Co. (Tex.), 11 S. W. 346. By contrast, therefore, 'wages' indicate inconsiderable pay for a lower and less responsible character of employment. South Alabama R. R. v. Falkner, 49 Ala. 115; Gordon v. Jennings, 9 Q. B. Div. 45. Where salary is suggestive of something higher, larger, and more permanent. Meyers v. N. Y., 69 Hun, 29, 23 N. Y. Supp. 484; White v. Koehler, 70 N. J. Law, 526, 57 Atl. 124; State v. Duncan, 1 Tenn. Ch. App. 334; Palmer v. Marquette Rolling Mill, 32 Mich. 274. The word 'hire' is rather associated with the act of employment than the reward for services done; and in the latter connection is more on the plane of wages than of salary, although in a sense it comprehends both; and is also applied to engaging the use of property. We hire a coachman, a gardener, or a cook; or a carriage to take a ride. And may also be said to hire a superintendent, a bookkeeper, or a clerk, although it would seem more correct, in the latter instances, to say engage or employ. * * *

From these considerations, as it seems to me, but one conclusion can be drawn. A person, like the respondent, giving music lessons at so much an hour, is not a wage earner within the meaning of the act. Teaching is a profession, denoting a nicer relation and involving a finer character or work, and entitled, like that of the lawyer, doctor, the engineer, the architect or the minister, to be regarded as upon a higher plane. His work is mental, not physical. He labors with his head, not his hands. And while they may not be distinctly conclusive, it has its weight. He is the tutor, or instructor, of his pupil, not his servant; his, of the two, being the master mind. This is not to say that one who works for a salary, like the teacher in our public schools, may not be wage earners, within the meaning of the bankruptcy law. The fact of being under a salary makes a difference, and brings the case squarely within the act, although it may be noticed in passing, that in the school laws of the State teachers are said to be appointed, not employed or hired. But the compensation received by the respondent, in the present instance, is certainly not a salary. Neither is it wages."

Similarly, a married woman, having a family, pursuing the usual and ordinary domestic duties of a married woman, will not be deemed a "wage earner" within the meaning of Bankr. Act, § 4b, because, at certain times of the year, in her spare time, she, though supported by her husband, performs services for others than the members of her own family.[49]

§ 48. Farmer Must Be Engaged "Chiefly" in Farming, etc.—
Only those engaged "chiefly" in farming or in tilling the soil are exempt; mere incidental farming or tilling does not exempt.[50]

Bank of Dearborn v. Matney, 12 A. B. R. 483, 132 Fed. 75 (D. C. Mo.): "It is not every person engaged in farming or the tillage of the soil who is exempt from the operation of the Bankrupt Act, but it is a person 'engaged chiefly in farming or the tillage of the soil.'"

And mere ownership of a farm is not sufficient to exempt. Thus, a farmer's wife in whose name the farm had been placed in order to escape creditors, the husband managing the same, is not exempt from bankruptcy.[51] And a mere owner of a farm leased to another is not exempt.[52]

And a cattle dealer, using lands simply as a mere feeding station, relying more upon purchased feed from the market for preparing the cattle for sale than on his own agricultural products, is not engaged chiefly in farming nor the tillage of the soil.[53]

In re Mackey, 6 A. B. R. 577, 110 Fed. 355 (D. C. Del.): "'A person engaged chiefly in farming' within the meaning of the Bankruptcy Act is one whose

---

49. In re Remaley, 23 A. B. R. 29 (D. C. Pa.).

50. Bankr. Act, § 4 (b). Instance, Matter of Charles L. Leland, 25 A. B. R. 209, 185 Fed. 830 (D. C. Mich.). "Retired farmer" not exempt.

51. In re Johnson, 18 A. B. R. 74 (D. C. N. Y.).

52. In re Matson, 10 A. B. R. 473, 123 Fed. 743 (D. C. Penna.); Hoffschlaeger v. Young Nap, 12 A. B. R. 521 (D. C. Hawaii). Compare, Wulbern v. Drake, 9 A. B. R. 695, 120 Fed. 493 (C. C. A. S. C.), where the bankrupt cultivated part of his land himself through hired laborers but leased out a great portion of it to tenant farmers, besides keeping a store himself.

53. Bank of Dearborn v. Matney, 12 A. B. R. 482, 132 Fed. 75 (D. C. Mo.). Also, In re Brown, 13 A. B. R. 140, 132 Fed. 706 (D. C. Iowa).

chief occupation or business is farming; and one's chief occupation or business so far as worldly pursuits are concerned, is that which is of principal concern to him, of .some permanency in its nature, which he deems of paramount importance to his welfare, and on which he chiefly relies for his livelihood, or as a means of acquiring wealth, great or small."

But a stock dealer has been held to be within the exemption.[54]

A reviewing court, where the evidence was conflicting, sustained a lower court in finding that a farmer was not "chiefly engaged," where he also derived income from picnic grounds, whereon he maintained buildings, etc., for letting out to pleasure parties.[55]

It is impracticable, if not impossible, to define with precision the facts which will in all cases determine whether one is engaged chiefly in farming and each case must be decided on its own circumstances.[56]

In passing upon the question, all the debtors' activities and pursuits must be taken into consideration.

American, etc., Co. v. Brinkley, 27 A. B. R. 438, 194 Fed. 411 (C. C. A. Va.): "The creditors say that the so-called entity theory requires that in determining whether the debtor was engaged chiefly in farming, we must exclude from consideration anything he did in connection with any of the partnerships. We cannot assent to this contention. Whether a debtor is or is not chiefly engaged in farming or tilling the soil is a question of fact to be determined in each case in which it is sought to have him individually adjudicated. In passing upon that question, all the debtor's activities and pursuits must be considered as a whole."

And that one may principally devote his physical exertion, or his time; or his capital, to a given pursuit, while a factor entitled to consideration, is not, in all cases, determinative of the question whether that pursuit is his chief occupation or business.[57]

§ 49. But Incidental Other Occupations Not Fatal to Jurisdiction.

—Conversely, one engaged chiefly in farming is exempt, although incidentally he also conducts a small business not belonging to the exempted classes; thus, where he is incidentally a private banker in a small way, yet he is exempt;[58] or where incidentally a storekeeper.[59]

Wulbern v. Drake, 9 A. B. R. 695, 120 Fed. 493 (C. C. A. S. C., affirming In re Drake, 8 A. B. R. 137, 114 Fed. 229, cited in Dearborn v. Matney, 12 A. B. R. 485): "The statute does not apply to such persons only as are engaged solely in farming or tillage of the soil, but exempts from the provisions relating to involuntary bankruptcy all persons who are chiefly so engaged. It does not

---

54. In re Thompson, 4 A. B. R. 340, 102 Fed. 287 (D. C. Iowa, Dist. in Bk. v. Matney, supra); In re Dwyer, 25 A. B. R. 913, 184 Fed. 880 (C. C. A. Ills.).

55. Stephens v. Merchants' Bank, 18 A. B. R. 560, 154 Fed. 341 (C. C. A. Ills.).

56. In re Mackey, 6 A. B. R. 577, 110 Fed. 355 (D. C. Del.).

57. In re Mackey, 6 A. B. R. 577, 110 Fed. 355 (D. C. Del.).

58. Couts v. Townsend, 11 A. B. R. 126, 126 Fed. 249 (D. C. Ky.).

59. In re Mackey, 6 A. B. R. 577, 110 Fed. 355 (D. C. Del.); American, etc., Co. v. Brinkley, 27 A. B. R. 438, 194 Fed. 411 (C. C. A. Va.).

matter, therefore, if the person may have other business or other interests, if his principal occupation is that of an agriculturist, if that is the business to which he devotes more largely his time and attention, which he relies upon as a source of income for the support of himself and family, or for the accumulation of wealth, although, as before suggested, he may have other interests."

Rise *v.* Bordner, 15 A. B. R. 298, 140 Fed. 566 (D. C. Pa.): "The respondent may be said to have had several occupations. He had a store, he was agent for the sale of fertilizers and ran a farm. The question is, in which business he was actually engaged. This is to be determined by which was of paramount importance to him, on which he depended for a living about which there can be no serious question. * * * That it was upon the farm that he depended for a livelihood is evident; what is called his store being the merest excuse for one and yielding him but a pittance."

Or where incidentally an attorney at law and collector,[60] or justice of the peace,[61] or where, incidentally, the keeper of a dairy,[62] or of a commissary;[63] or where he is agent for fertilizers and plows as well as being a farmer.[64]

§ 50. "Farming" and "Tillage of Soil" Distinguished.—"Farming" is not synonymous with "tillage of the soil."[65]

Bank of Dearborn *v.* Matney, 12 A. B. R. 482, 132 Fed. 75 (D. C. Mo.): "The courts are generally agreed that the term 'farming' is not synonymous with a tiller of the soil. To constitute one a farmer it is not essential that he in person should till the soil, or that his operations should be limited to agricultural planting, sowing and cultivation of the soil. Yet the context indicates that the terms 'farming' and 'tilling of the soil' are more or less closely allied. The word 'farming' was doubtless employed in the act as a generic term, in a comprehensive sense. The lawmakers, coming from the wide extent of the Republic, with its diversified agricultural adaptability, are to be presumed to have had in mind their knowledge of the methods in different localities of conducting the business of farming. It is therefore reasonable to conclude that the term was not limited merely to the production of grains and grasses and the like. The farmer may cultivate all or a part of his land. He may be general or special. He may devote his cultivation to the production of corn, or wheat, oats, or rye, or grasses, whichever, in his judgment, may be the more useful and profitable. He may include also with these breeding, feeding and rearing of live stock, embracing cattle, horses, mules, sheep, and hogs, for domestic use and for market. If he find it more profitable to feed his agricultural products or his grasses to live stock than to rely upon marketing the surplus, he may not be limited to the quantity of live stock for such purpose to what he may breed or rear on his farm. For this purpose he may rely entirely upon the purchase of such live stock from his neighbors or on the market, and utilize his farm products in feeding and fattening such 'feeders' for market."

60. In re Hoy, 14 A. B. R. 648, 137 Fed. 175 (D. C. Iowa); Olive *v.* Armour & Co., 21 A. B. R. 901, 167 Fed. 517 (C. C. A. Ga.).

61. Sutherland Medicine Co. *v.* Rich & Bailey, 22 A. B. R. 85 (Spec. M. Ga.).

62. Gregg *v.* Mitchell, 21 A. B. R. 659, 166 Fed. 725 (C. C. A. Ohio).

63. Sutherland Medicine Co. *v.* Rich & Bailey, 22 A. B. R. 85 (Spec. M. Ga.).

64. Sutherland Medicine Co. *v.* Rich & Bailey, 22 A. B. R. 85 (Spec. M. Ga.); Rice *v.* Bordner, 15 A. B. R. 298, 140 Fed. 566 (D. C. Pa.).

65. In re Thompson, 4 A. B. R. 340, 102 Fed. 287 (D. C. Iowa).

Hoffschlaeger Co. v. Young Nap, 12 A. B. R. 510 (D. C. Hawaii): "One whose principal occupation is raising live stock and producing fodder for feeding them by cultivation of the soil is 'chiefly engaged in farming' but not chiefly engaged in 'tillage of the soil.'"

Corporations engaged chiefly in tillage of the soil are not within the exemption and they may be proceeded against in involuntary bankruptcy.[66]

But it has been held that partnerships engaged in farming or in the tillage of the soil are exempted.[67]

Wage earners and men of small salaries and farmers, then, are exempt from any liability to being proceeded against in involuntary bankruptcy, no matter if they owe more than a thousand dollars, be insolvent and have committed one of the acts known as acts of bankruptcy.

§ 51. Infants.—An infant may be the subject of bankruptcy if he owes debts upon which he is absolutely bound and which he cannot disaffirm.[68] But if the debts of the petitioning creditors are such as can be repudiated by the infant, it has been held that involuntary proceedings will not lie.[69] A fortiori, if all the debts are such as can be repudiated, bankruptcy proceedings will not lie.[70]

In partnership bankruptcies, if one of the partners is an infant, the partnership and the remaining partners may be adjudged bankrupt.[71] And the partnership assets will pass into the hands of the trustee.[72] But the proceedings must be dismissed as to the infant.[73]

After all, there seems no valid reason for any distinction between cases where the infant's debts are repudiable and where not. The immunity is granted because of the infant's lack of capacity; because, in short, he is an infant—not because the debts are repudiable. The right to repudiate the debt is a personal one and the debts themselves are none the less *provable*. Yet the reason of the exemption of infants is probably that it would be an act of frivolity for courts to take up the administration, for the sake of repudiable debts.[74]

---

66. In re Lake Jackson Sugar Co., 11 A. B. R. 458 (Ref. Tex.).

67. Sutherland Medicine Co. v. Rich & Bailey, 22 A. B. R. 85 (Spec. M. Ga.). Compare, however, post, § 56.

68. In re Brice, 2 A. B. R. 197, 93 Fed. 942 (D. C. Iowa): Infant engaged in business; In re Penzansky, 8 A. B. R. 99 (D. C. Mass.), where the only creditor was a judgment creditor in an action for breach of contract to marry. Contra, In re Duguid, 3 A. B. R. 794, 100 Fed. 274 (D. C. N. C.).

Thus, where the debt is a judgment for negligence, In re Walrath, 24 A. B. R. 541 (D. C. N. Y.); [1841] In re Book, 3 McLean 317, Fed. Cas. No. 1637.

69. In re Eidemiller, 5 A. B. R. 570, 105 Fed. 595 (D. C. Ills.). Obiter, In re Walrath, 24 A. B. R. 541 (D. C. N. Y.).

70. Obiter, In re Brice, 2 A. B. R. 197, 93 Fed. 942 (D. C. Iowa); Rex v. Cole, 1 Lord Raymond 443. Obiter, In re Walrath, 24 A. B. R. 541 (D. C. N. Y.).

71. In re Dunnigan Bros., 2 A. B. R. 628, 95 Fed. 428 (D. C. Mass.); In re Duguid, 3 A. B. R. 794, 100 Fed. 274 (D. C. N. C.).

72. In re Duguid, 3 A. B. R. 794, 100 Fed. 274 (D. C. N. C.).

73. In re Dunnigan Bros., 2 A. B. R. 628, 95 Fed. 428 (D. C. Mass.).

74. See note to In re Dunnigan Bros., 2 A. B. R. 628.

§ 52. Married Women.—Married women are subject to bankruptcy proceedings even in States where judgments in personam cannot be taken against them and debts can only be enforced out of their separate estate by proceedings in equity.[75] But not where they cannot be bound.[76]

§ 53. Indians.—Ruling has been made as to Indians of the Chickasaw and Choctaw tribes, that they are subject to bankruptcy;[77] so, also, as to those of the Umatilla Reservation.[78]

§ 54. Insane Persons.—A person judicially declared insane or incapable of managing his affairs, cannot commit an act of bankruptcy, nor will a court entertain a petition against him.[79]

In re Eisenberg, 8 A. B. R. 551 (D. C. N. Y.): "It must be assumed that Congress was familiar with the difficulties that would be encountered by the courts in attempting to administer in bankruptcy the affairs of lunatics, and did not intend to include cases other than those mentioned in section 8, where provision is made for the continuance and settlement of estates of which the courts had acquired jurisdiction before the insanity occurred."

And even if he has not been judicially declared insane, yet his actual insanity at the time of the commission of the alleged act of bankruptcy is a sufficient defense; at any rate where the act alleged involves volition on the bankrupt's part.

In re Ward, 20 A. B. R. 482, 161 Fed. 755 (D. C. N. J.): "That is the act of bankruptcy charged against Ward. But if he has been a lunatic and so unsound of mind as to have been wholly incapable of managing himself or his estate ever since May 1, 1904, he could not have conveyed his lands in November and December, 1907, 'with intent to hinder, delay and defraud his creditors.' 'An intent to hinder or delay creditors,' says Judge Bradford, in the Wilmington Hosiery Company's case (D. C.), 9 Am. B. R. 579, 120 Fed. 185, 'involves a purpose wrongfully and unjustly to prevent, obstruct, embarrass, or postpone them (creditors) in the collection or enforcement of their claims.' Without undertaking to determine the exact boundaries of the jurisdiction of our

---

75. MacDonald v. Tefft-Weller Co., 11 A. B. R. 800, 128 Fed. 381 (C. C. A. Fla.).
76. See discussion, obiter, In re Brice, 2 A. B. R. 197, 93 Fed. 942 (D. C. Iowa).
Married Women's Rights, as Variously Considered in Bankruptcy Reports.—See various instances, post, wherever the subjects of allowance of claims, title of the trustee, marshaling of lien, etc., occur. Where a wife is in partnership with her husband, the proceeds of an insurance policy, after the death of her husband and the bankruptcy of the partnership, are not to be held by her free from the claims of partnership creditors, for the statute does not attempt to exempt such proceeds from the beneficiary's own debts.

In re Day, 23 A. B. R. 785, 174 Fed. 164 (D. C. Tenn.).
77. In re Rennie, 2 A. B. R. 182 (Ref. Ind. Ter.).
78. In re Russie, 3 A. B. R. 6, 96 Fed. 608 (D. C. Ore.).
79. In re Funk, 4 A. B. R. 96, 101 Fed. 244 (D. C. Iowa); In re Ward, 20 A. B. R. 482, 161 Fed. 755. In re Ward, 28 A. B. R. 29, 194 Fed. 174, 179 (D. C. N. J.), quoted at § 417. Quære, In re Stein & Co., 11 A. B. R. 536, 127 Fed. 547 (C. C. A. Ills.). Quære, In re Burka, 5 A. B. R. 844, 104 Fed. 331 (D. C. Tenn.).

This subject will be considered post, "Change of Debtor's Class," § 95, et seq. Compare, as to voluntary bankruptcy, ante, § 38½.

bankruptcy courts in cases against lunatic bankrupts, it is sufficient to say that, in the present case, the defense of insanity cannot be striken out of the answer."

In re Kehler, 19 A. B. R. 513, 159 Fed. 55, 20 A. B. R. 669, 162 Fed. 674 (C. C. A. N. Y.): "If he (Kehler) committed the acts of bankruptcy alleged in the petition while insane, the adjudication is a wrong which, irrespective of technical objections to the pleadings and proceedings of his committee, should be righted. If, on the other hand, these acts were committed while sane, there was no error in continuing the case even though the bankrupt subsequently became insane. Section 8 of the Bankrupt Act provides that the insanity of a 'bankrupt' shall not abate the proceedings, and § 1 provides that the word 'bankrupt' shall include a person against whom an involuntary petition has been filed. It is manifest, therefore, that if Kehler committed an act of bankruptcy while sane, and by reason of such act the court obtained jurisdiction, it can continue the proceedings notwithstanding the subsequent insanity of the bankrupt. * * * The district judge correctly states the proposition as follows: "True, an insane person cannot commit an act of bankruptcy, but if Kehler was compos mentis at the time the acts were committed, the petition by creditors being filed before he was adjudged insane, I think the court acquired jurisdiction of the proceedings.' "

Indeed, the subsequent adjudication of insanity is only prima facie proof of the debtor's insanity at the time of the commission of the act charged.

In re Ward, 20 A. B. R. 482, 161 Fed. 755 (D. C. N. Y.): "But is the adjudication in the Court of Chancery of New Jersey conclusive on this court in this proceeding? It would not be so in an action at law against the alleged bankrupt. In such a case, 'when an inquisition is admitted in evidence, the party against whom it is used may introduce proof that the alleged lunatic was of sound mind at the time covered by the inquisition.' Den v. Clark, 10 N. J. L. 217, 18 Am. Dec. 417. The same rule applies in equity. Hunt v. Hunt, 13 N. J. Eq. 161; Yauger v. Skinner, 14 N. J. Eq. 389; Hill's Ex'rs v. Day, 34 N. J. Eq. 150, 16 Am. & Eng. Ency. Law, 606. I think it is equally applicable to a bankruptcy case where the adjudication of lunacy is made upon proceedings instituted after the petition in bankruptcy has been filed. The Funk case (D. C.), 4 Am. B. R. 96, 101 Fed. 244, is distinguishable from this because there the adjudication of lunacy was made, and the property of the lunatic put into possession of his guardian, before the petition in bankruptcy was filed. In the Kehler case (D. C.), 19 Am. B. R. 513, 153 Fed. 235, where a petition in involuntary proceedings was filed before the alleged bankrupt had been adjudged a lunatic, Judge Hazel denied the motion to dismiss the petition because the jurisdiction of the bankruptcy court attached before the alleged bankrupt was adjudged insane, and because of the presumption of the alleged bankrupt's sanity at the time the acts of bankruptcy were committed. It is not necessary to decide, in the present case, what may be the effect of an adjudication of lunacy and the appointment of a guardian or committee for the lunatic under a writ of de lunatico inquirendo before a petition in bankruptcy is filed against the lunatic. It may be that in such a case the bankruptcy court acquires no jurisdiction."

It is questionable whether the petitioning creditors will have the right to a personal examination of the alleged lunatic before trial.[80]

It has been held that a person under guardianship in one state may

80. In re Ward, 20 A. B. R. 482, 161 Fed. 755 (D. C. N. J.).

remove to another state, his guardian consenting, and acquire a new residence in the latter state, sufficient for adjudication of bankruptcy, where the laws in the latter state hold that the ward's disability does not follow him into other jurisdictions than that of the guardian's appointment.[81]

§ 55. Decedents.—A deceased person may not be proceeded against.[82] Thus, where a partnership is dissolved by the death of a partner, it has been held that it is not subject to bankruptcy, and that the voluntary petition of the surviving partner affects only his individual estate;[83] but the contrary has been held, in the case of an involuntary petition filed after the death of one partner where the surviving partners continue the business under the old articles of partnership.[84]

SUBDIVISION "B."

PARTNERSHIPS AND UNINCORPORATED COMPANIES.

§ 56. Partnerships Included.—All kinds of partnerships and unincorporated companies may be adjudged involuntary bankrupts, except, perhaps, those "chiefly engaged in farming or the tillage of the soil." Likewise may be adjudged voluntary bankrupts.[85]

This is so, for the special section of the statute governing partnership bankruptcies contains no restriction, nor is there any restriction elsewhere as to the kinds of partnerships that may be adjudged bankrupt. It simply provides in clause (a) that "A partnership, during the continuation of the partnership business, or after its dissolution and before the final settlement thereof, may be adjudged a bankrupt." There being a special statute prescribing the requisites in this particular, such special provisions will govern, except where limitations elsewhere laid down may be applicable. Thus, a partnership, even if it be not engaged in manufacturing, trading, printing, publishing, mining or in a mercantile pursuit, may be adjudged an involuntary bankrupt; also, perhaps, even if it be engaged in farming, although upon this latter point there may be some doubt, owing to the dual capacity of a partnership, as being both an entity, in which capacity it would not be a "natural person" and therefore would not come within the exemption, and also an association of natural persons, in which capacity it would come within the exemption, since they would be "natural persons" "chiefly engaged in farming or the tillage of the soil."[86]

---

81. In re Kingsley, 20 A. B. R. 424, 160 Fed. 275 (D. C. Vt.).

82. Obiter, In re Hicks, 6 A. B. R. 183, 107 Fed. 910 (D. C. Vt.); Adams v. Terrell, 4 Fed. 796 (C. C.). This subject will be considered post, "Change of Debtor's Class," § 95, et seq.

83. In re Evans (Rudolph v. Evans), 20 A. B. R. 406, 161 Fed. 590 (D. C. Ga.).

84. In re Coe, 19 A. B. R. 618, 157 Fed. 308 (D. C. N. Y.), quoted at § 57.

85. Bankr. Act, § 5. See, also, ante, § 39.

86. Holding such partnerships exempt from adjudication. Sutherland Medicine Co. v. Rich & Bailey, 22 A. B. R. 85 (Special Master Ga.). Compare ante, § 50.

§ 57. Only "During Continuance of Partnership Business or."—
The statute says, in § 5, clause (a), that a partnership may be adjudged bankrupt during the continuation of the partnership business or after its dissolution and before the final settlement of its affairs. The question then arises as to what constitutes a "continuation of the partnership business." Such "continuation" must be continuation as an actual partnership and does not include the status arising by estoppel of a retiring partner who has permitted himself to be "held out" as still a member of the firm.

In re Pinson & Co., 24 A. B. R. 804, 180 Fed. 787 (D. C. Ala.): "The existence of the partnership within the meaning of this section is its actual status as distinguished from a status created by estoppel against the former partner. If it has been dissolved by the partners inter sese before the filing of the petition, it is not thereafter an existing partnership, and the proceedings in bankruptcy cannot be said to have been instituted 'during the continuation of the partnership debts.' The jurisdiction of the bankruptcy court to adjudicate and administer attaches only upon a showing of an actually existing partnership, constituting a legal entity at the time of the filing of the petition."

§ 58. Or before "Final Settlement."—The question also then arises as to when a partnership is "finally settled" within the meaning of the bankruptcy act. It certainly does not mean that it is settled when it simply has been dissolved, for the section expressly says "after its dissolution" and "before" its "final settlement." Nor is it "finally settled" when its assets are all distributed, for then creditors still may resort to the individual estates of the expartners. Therefore the rule cannot be that a partnership is to be considered as "finally settled" merely when it has been dissolved and all its assets gone.

The true rule is that as long as there are any undistributed assets, or any unpaid debts, a partnership is not "finally settled" and so may be adjudicated bankrupt as such.[86a]

Holmes v. Baker & Hamilton, 20 A. B. R. 252, 160 Fed. 922 (C. C. A. Wash.): "The rule is well settled that where assets or debts of a partnership remain after dissolution the partnership is considered as subsisting as to its creditors until its property is subjected to the satisfaction of their claims."

Mere existence of unpaid debts has been held sufficient;[87] even though the debts be outlawed, provided there remain rights of contribution among partners, etc., to be settled.

In re Hersch, 3 A. B. R. 348, 97 Fed. 571 (D. C. N. Y.): "And incontestably, it seems to me, there is no 'final settlement' of the business of the firm, until its debts are paid or in some way extinguished, by the statute of limitations, or otherwise."

86a. In re Levy & Richman, 2 A. B. R. 21, 95 Fed. 812 (Ref. N. Y.); [1867] In re Stowers, Fed. Cas. No. 13516; [1867] In re Foster, Fed. Cas. No. 4962; [1867] In re Crockett, Fed. Cas. No. 3402; [1867] In re Noonan, Fed. Cas. No. 10292.

87. Obiter, In re Pinson & Co., 24 A. B. R. 804, 180 Fed. 787 (D. C. Ala.).

For a still broader rule, see In re Levy & Richman, 2 A. B. R. 21 (Ref. N. Y.): "As long as there exists a right in any party to sue for a settlement of partnership affairs, or to enforce an executory agreement of settlement, or to obtain reimbursement for moneys paid upon a partnership debt, or as long as there remains an unadministered partnership asset, or as long as there remains a partnership debt enforceable anywhere within the territorial jurisdiction of the United States, it cannot be said there has been a final settlement of the partnership."

But it has been held the debts must be debts of an actual partnership, not those of a partnership by "estoppel" or by "holding out."[87a]

In re Pinson & Co., 24 A. B. R. 804, 180 Fed. 787 (D. C. Ala.): "The act also provides for the adjudication of a partnership, so long as its affairs are unsettled. If there are outstanding firm debts at the time of the filing of the petition in the requisite amount, a proper case is made for adjudication, the other elements being present, though the partnership has long ceased to do business; otherwise, not. The partnership affairs are unsettled within the meaning of this section so long as partnership debts are left unpaid. Debts which are binding on the partners only by estoppel as to creditors without notice of dissolution are not firm debts.

"As the proof fails to show that the petition was filed during the continuation of the partnership business, as herein defined, or that the outstanding indebtedness at that time, excluding such as was created subsequent to the dissolution and which became that of the partnership only by estoppel in favor of such creditors as had no notice of its dissolution amount to $1,000, the adjudication of the partnership is denied."

§ 59. Partnerships as Entities.

§ 59. Partnerships as Entities.—Partnerships (although in some respects treated as mere associations of individuals) are treated in the present Bankruptcy Act in general as distinct entities.[88]

Mills v. Fisher & Co., 20 A. B. R. 237, 159 Fed. 897 (C. C. A. Tenn.): "A partnership, under the Bankruptcy Act of 1898, is a distinct entity, a 'person.' Section 1, ch. 19. As an entity it may be adjudged to be a bankrupt irrespective of any adjudication against the individual members."

In re Sanderlin, 6 A. B. R. 384, 100 Fed. 859 (D. C. N. Car.): "A partnership

---

87a. Compare post, § 63.

88. In re McLaren, 11 A. B. R. 144, 125 Fed. 835 (D. C. N. Y.); In re Stein & Co., 11 A. B. R. 538, 127 Fed. 547 (C. C. A. Ills.); In re Mercur, 10 A. B. R. 505, 122 Fed. 384 (C. C. A. Penna., affirming 8 A. B. R. 275, 116 Fed. 655); In re Bardon, 4 A. B. R. 31, 101 Fed. 553 (D. C. N. C.); In re Meyer, 3 A. B. R. 559, 98 Fed. 976 (C. C. A. N. Y.); In re Hale, 6 A. B. R. 35, 107 Fed. 432 (D. C. N. C.); In re Corcoran, 12 A. B. R. 285 (Ref. Ohio); Vaccaro v. Security Bank, 4 A. B. R. 474, 103 Fed. 436 (C. C. A. Tenn.); McMurtrey v. Smith, 15 A. B. R. 430 (D. C. Tex.); In re Farley & Co., 8 A. B. R. 267, 115 Fed. 359 (D. C. Va.); Manson v. Williams, 18 A. B. R. 674, 153 Fed. 525 (C. C. A. Me.), quoted at § 63; In re Evans (Rudolph v. Evans), 20 A. B. R. 406, 161 Fed. 590 (D. C. Ga.); In re Ceballos, 20 A. B. R. 459, 161 Fed. 445 (D. C. N. J.); In re Solomon & Carvel, 20 A. B. R. 490, 163 Fed. 140 (D. C. N. Y.); In re Stovall Grocery Co., 20 A. B. R. 537, 161 Fed. 882 (D. C. Ga.); In re Bertenshaw, 19 A. B. R. 577, 157 Fed. 363 (C. C. A.). Instance, In re Ullman, 24 A. B. R. 755, 180 Fed. 944 (D. C. N. Y.); American Steel & Wire Co. v. Coover, 25 A. B. R. 58 (Sup. Ct. Okla.); In re Union Bank, etc., Co., 25 A. B. R. 148, 184 Fed. 224 (C. C. A. Mich.); Francis v. McNeal, 26 A. B. R. 555, 186 Fed. 481 (C. C. A. Pa.).

and the individuals composing it are distinct legal entities and proceedings in bankruptcy by or against one does not of necessity involve the other."

Strause v. Hooper, 5 A. B. R. 225, 105 Fed. 590 (D. C. N. C.): "It is clearly the policy of the Bankrupt Act of 1898, to treat partnerships as legal entities which may be adjudged bankrupts in voluntary or involuntary proceedings, irrespective of any adjudication of the bankruptcy of individuals who compose such partnerships or firms."

In re Pincus, 17 A. B. R. 331, 337 (D. C. N. Y.): "The right to proceed in bankruptcy against a partnership as a 'legal entity' is new, and before the Act of 1898 unheard of."

In re Perley & Hays, 15 A. B. R. 54, 138 Fed. 927 (D. C. Mo.): "It is, I think, well settled that a partnership under the existing bankrupt law, is a distinct legal entity, which may be adjudged a bankrupt by voluntary or involuntary proceedings, irrespective of any adjudication of the individual partners as bankrupts."

In re Bertenshaw, 19 A. B. R. 577, 157 Fed. 363 (C. C. A.): "The decisions under the Act of 1898 concerning the relations of partnership and individual estates have not been overlooked, but upon many phases of these relations they are confusing and inconsistent. The uniform current of authority is that under this act a partnership is a distinct entity separate from the individuals who compose it, that it owns its property, and owes its debts, which are respectively separate and distinct from the individual property and the individual debts of its partners, and that an adjudication of the partnership a bankrupt apart from, or in addition to, the adjudication of its partners bankrupts, is indispensable to the jurisdiction of a court of bankruptcy to administer the partnership property." However, the court In re Bertenshaw proceeds to draw extreme deductions from the rule, which, it would seem, are not approved by the weight of authority. See post, §§ 65, 477½, 2232.

In re Junck & Balthazard, 22 A. B. R. 298, 169 Fed. 481 (D. C. Wis.): "The authorities all seem to concur in the view that for some purposes at least the partnership is to be considered a person and a separate entity that owns property and owes debts. The marked difference in the phraseology of the Act of 1898 from all other acts can lead to no other conclusion."

But see In re Carleton, 8 A. B. R. 274, 115 Fed. 246 (D. C. Mass.): "A partnership can be treated neither as an entity altogether separate from the partners, nor as merely the sum of them."

And also see In re Forbes, 11 A. B. R. 787, 128 Fed. 137 (D. C. Mass.): "To decide the present case, the general nature of partnership proceedings in bankruptcy must be considered, since there lies the origin of the confusion. For some purposes a partnership has been treated as an entity apart from the partners; for other purposes it has been treated as a congeries of partners. Some courts have suggested that the Act of 1898 has adopted for bankruptcy the theory of an entity separate from the partners. Sections 1 (19), 5a; In re Meyer, 3 Am. B. R. 559, 98 Fed. 976; In re Mercur, 11 A. B. R. 505, 122 Fed. 384. Yet this treatment of a partnership is irreconcilable with other provisions of the statute. Section 5h of the act provides that the partnership property (except in case of consent) shall not be administered in bankruptcy unless all the partners are adjudged bankrupt. This is, in effect, a provision that the partnership shall not be made bankrupt except by an adjudication of all its partners. Adjudication without accompanying distribution of the bankrupt estate would be worse than a vain form, for it would confuse inextricably questions of preference, lien, attachment, and the like. The remedy given by clause 'h' to the trustee is, in substance, the equitable remedy found so unsatisfactory in the days of Lord Eldon. See In re Wilcox (D. C.), 2 Am. B. R. 117, 94 Fed. 84, 95. The negative provision of clause 'h' is more definite than the affirmative provision in clause 'a' which does not declare under what circumstances the adjudication of a partnership shall be made, or what shall be its form or effect. Section 5b contemplates that the adjudication under a joint petition shall be both joint and several. If the adjudication were joint only, there would be no object in providing that the joint creditors alone shall elect the trustee. Still again, § 5c gives to the court which has jurisdiction of one partner 'jurisdiction of all the partners,' and says nothing about jurisdiction of the partnership as an entity. Read as a whole, Form No. 2 agrees with § 5h, and not with the theory of entity. It is in terms the petition of individuals. It sets out that 'they' owe debts which they 'cannot pay and that they' desire the benefits of the Bankrupt Act. The joint debts are styled 'the debts of said partners,' not the debts of the firm, and the joint assets 'the property, real and personal, of the said partners.' It is true that the last paragraph of the petition contains a prayer that 'the firm may be adjudged by a decree of the court to be bankrupts,' but the use of the plural shows that the word 'firm' is there a collective noun as further appears from the fact that the prayer is obviously intended to cover a separate as well as a joint adjudication."

Even the wording of the first clause of § 5 shows the tendency towards the treatment of partnerships as entities. It speaks of adjudging "a partnership," not merely "partners;" and of adjudging a partnership to be "a" bankrupt, not of adjudging partners to be bankrupts. As a consequence, it would seem that none of the restrictions as to what natural persons and as to what corporations may be thrown into bankruptcy, would apply to partnerships—all partnerships are subject to being proceeded against in involuntary bankruptcy.[89]

§ 60. **When Is a Partnership Insolvent?**—However, a partnership is not held to be insolvent unless the total of its assets and the total of the assets of all its individual members (in excess of their respective individual indebtedness), together, are insufficient to pay its debts.[90]

---

89. [1867] In re Winkens, 2 N. B. Reg. 349, Fed. Cas. 17,875; [1867] In re Shepard, 3 Ben. 347, Fed. Cas. 12,754; [1867] Crompton v. Conkling, 9 Ben. 225, Fed. Cas. 3,407; Nutting v. Ashcroft, 101 Mass. 300.

90. Worrell v. Whitney, 24 A. B. R. 749, 185 Fed. 1002 (D. C. Pa.), quoted at § 1348; In re Perhefter & Shatz, 25 A. B. R. 576, 177 Fed. 299 (D. C. N. Y.). Francis v. McNeal, 26 A. B. R. 555, 186 Fed. 481 (C. C. A. Pa.); Washington Cotton Co. v. Morgan & Williams, 27 A. B. R. 638, 192 Fed. 310 (C. C. A. Ga.); In re Duke & Son, 28 A. B. R. 195, 199 Fed. 199 (D. C. Ga.); In re Forbes, 11 A. B. R. 787, 128 Fed. 137 (D. C. Mass.). Compare In re Ullman, 24 A. B. R. 755, 180 Fed. 944 (D. C. N. Y.). Obiter, In re Wing Yick Co., 13 A. B. R. 757 (D. C. Hawaii); Vaccaro v. Security Bank, 4 A. B. R. 474, 103 Fed. 436 (C. C. A. Tenn.). Obiter, In re Blair, 3 A. B. R. 588, 99 Fed. 76 (D. C. N. Y.); Davis v. Stevens, 4 A. B. R. 763, 104 Fed. 242 (D. C. S. Dak.). Apparently contra, obiter, In re Sanderlin, 6 A. B. R. 386 (D. C. N. C.). Apparently contra, McMurtrey v. Smith, 15 A. B. R. 427 (Spec. Master affirmed by D. C.). But in this case it does not appear that the individual debts of the partner were first deducted, and only the excess of assets over and above his debts and exemptions added to the firm's assets. Compare post, § 1348. Also, see § 247. In addition, see Boyd v. Boyd et al., 20 A. B. R. 330 (Ref. Ga.). Contra, In re Everybody's Market, 21 A. B. R. 925, 173 Fed. 492 (D. C. Okla.).

In re Perley & Hays, 15 A. B. R. 54, 138 Fed. 927 (D. C. Mo.): "The question arises as to whether or not the properties of individual members of a firm are to be taken into consideration when the issue of insolvency is raised of the partnership of which they are members. * * * The real question is whether or not the bankrupts were insolvent within the meaning of the present Bankrupt Law, or, to state it in another way, whether or not the individual properties of the partners are to be considered in determining the question of insolvency. It has been held, in a number of cases that the individual properties must be considered, and I find no case to the contrary."

Compare, Tumlin v. Bryan, 21 A. B. R. 319, 165 Fed. 166 (C. C. A. Ga.): "It is true that a partnership may be treated as an entity, separate from its individual members, for the purpose of its adjudication as a bankrupt * * * but, in a suit to recover a preference, it is not only the insolvency of an intangible entity, but the insolvency of its responsible component parts, that lies at the foundation of the right to relief. If the component parts of the firm may be made to pay the firm's debts, the suit lacks reason and substance, and it cannot be held that the defendant has obtained a greater percentage of his debt than other creditors of the same class. If the members of the firm are solvent, all creditors may be paid in full. If the individual members of the partnership are not shown to be insolvent at the date of the payments, the preference is not voidable."

Contra, In re Bertenshaw, 19 A. B. R. 577, 157 Fed. 363 (C. C. A.): "The only logical conclusion, therefore, from the settled proposition that the partnership is an entity distinct from its members under this act, is that it is insolvent under this act when the partnership property, the only property this person has, is insufficient to pay the partnership debts, the only debts this person owes. Possibly the opposite conclusion has crept into the opinions of the courts, under this act from the decisions under the insolvency law of Massachusetts and the bankruptcy law of 1867, where that theory necessarily obtains, because under those laws the insolvency or bankruptcy of the partnership was conditioned by the express terms of the statutes by the insolvency or bankruptcy of the partners, and the partnership was not in the conception of those laws a distinct entity, but a mere aggregation of partners. When, however, the Act of 1898 made the partnership a person, required its consideration, adjudication and the administration of its property as a distinct entity, and declared it insolvent when its property was insufficient to pay its debts, the tests of insolvency under the insolvency law of Massachusetts and the Bankruptcy Act of 1867 were inapplicable to cases under it, and the only test was that declared by the act itself, the insufficiency of the property of the person, the partnership, to pay the person's, the partnership's, debts." But this case, it seems, pushes the doctrine of "entity" to an extreme. The dissenting opinion expresses the truer rule.

And this has been held to be the rule notwithstanding a private agreement among the partners limiting the liability of one or more members.[91]

§ 61. Adjudication in Firm Name.—Adjudication may be had in the firm name alone, without mention of the individual names of the members

---

91. In re Boyd, 20 A. B. R. 331 (Ref. Ga.). Contra, and that the assets of the individual partners are not to be considered, In re Bertenshaw, 19 A. B. R. 577, 157 Fed. 363 (C. C. A.); also contra, In re Everybody's Market, 21 A. B. R. 925, 173 Fed. 492 (D. C. Okla.).

of the partnership.[92]

Likewise, the partnership may be adjudicated bankrupt without adjudication of its individual members.[93]

In re Meyers, 3 A. B. R. 559, 98 Fed. 977 (C. C. A. N. Y.): "We are of the opinion that it is the scheme of these provisions to treat the partnership as an entity which may be adjudged a bankrupt by voluntary or involuntary proceedings irrespective of any adjudication of the individual partners as bankrupt, and upon an adjudication to draw to the administration the individual estates of the partners as well as the partnership estate, and marshal and distribute them according to equity."

Mills v. Fisher & Co., 20 A. B. R. 237, 159 Fed. 897 (C. C. A. Tenn.): "A partnership, under the Bankrupt Act of 1898, is a distinct entity, a 'person.' Section 1, cl. 19. As an entity it may be adjudged to be a bankrupt irrespective of any adjudication against the individual members."

Contra, obiter, In re Forbes, 11 A. B. R. 790, 128 Fed. 137 (D. C. Mass.): "But the rule that there can be no bankruptcy of a partnership without bankruptcy of all the partners (save exceptional cases, such as In re Dunnigan (D. C.), 2 A. B. R. 628, 95 Fed. 428 and the like) is based, not so much upon a nice examination of the words of the particular statute, as upon general principles of law. The equal and equitable distribution of the estates of insolvents and their discharge from the obligation of their debts are the ends sought by proceedings in bankruptcy. Bankruptcy, without insolvency, actual or presumed, is almost inconceivable. Bankruptcy without discharge for the honest debtor is a contradiction in terms. It is impossible to declare a partnership insolvent so long as the partners are able to pay its debts and theirs, whether out of joint or separate estate, and so the courts have generally held that a partnership is not insolvent unless by the insolvency of all its partners. See Vaccaro v. Bank of Memphis, 4 Am. B. R. 474, 103 Fed. 436, 43 C. C. A. 279; In re Blair (D. C.), 3 Am. B. R. 568, 99 Fed. 76; Davis v. Stevens (D. C.), 4 Am. Br. R. 763, 104 Fed. 235. Not the insolvency of any imaginary entity, as in the case of a corporation, but the insolvency of its human component parts, lies at the foundation of the bankruptcy of a partnership. Those who bring an involuntary joint petition must certainly prove this, and by the principles of sound pleading and the analogy of Form No. 2 they must allege it. As the bankruptcy of a partnership begins with an inquiry into the condition of its individual partners, the end of the proceedings is normally their discharge. So far as I know, the discharge of a partnership as an entity has never been suggested, and what would be the effect of such a discharge can hardly be imagined. Herein appears the difference between a partnership and a corporation. Under an adjudication merely joint, it is impossible to discharge the partners as individuals, even from their joint debts, for every joint debt of the partnership is also a separate debt of each partner, and separate debts can be discharged only after an individual adjudication operating upon the separate estate. For these reasons, this court of bankruptcy has consistently refused to make the adjudication of a partnership, unless all the partners be adjudged bankrupts at the same time. The confusion which inevitably results from any

---

92. Fidelity Trust Co. v. Gaskell, 28 A. B. R. 4, 195 Fed. 865 (C. C. A. Mo.). See analogously, In re Levingston, 13 A. B. R. 357 (D. C. Hawaii). Impliedly, contra, In re Forbes, 11 A. B. R. 787, 128 Fed. 137 (D. C. Mass.).

But, undoubtedly, the rule of In re Forbes would be modified where the names of the individuals were not known.

93. In re Solomon & Carvel, 20 A. B. R. 490, 163 Fed. 140 (D. C. N. Y.).

other rule is abundantly illustrated by the reports. Whether an adjudication of all the partners upon separate petitions carries an administration of the partnership estate need not be decided here. This may be implied from section 5h, but the implication is not strong. See In re Mercur, 11 A. B. R. 505, 122 Fed. 384, 58 C. C. A. 472."

So, the firm and some of the partners may be adjudged bankrupt even though one of the partners is not amenable to adjudication.[94]

§ 62. Adjudication in Name of Ostensible Partner.—A partnership may be adjudged bankrupt in the name of an ostensible partner where such name is the name under which the firm did business.[95]

§ 63. Only "Actual" Partnership Subject to Adjudication.—Only an actual partnership may be adjudicated bankrupt as a partnership, not one "by holding out." The creditor must be left to assert by action any rights he may have by virtue of the "holding out."[96]

In re Beckwith & Co., 12 A. B. R. 453, 130 Fed. 475 (D. C. Penna., reversed on the facts, but not on the law, in Jones v. Burnham, Williams & Co., 15 A. B. R. 85, 138 Fed. 986, C. C. A. Pa.): "To maintain the proceedings as to Jones a partnership in fact must be shown, and not a mere holding out, by which he may have become liable to creditors. * * * Otherwise the proceedings might be good as to some creditors, with respect to whom this was true, and not as to others, as to whom it was not. And we should also have instances where there was no joint estate to administer, nor any assets other than the personal liability of the individuals who had made themselves answerable, a condition which plainly is not contemplated by the Bankrupt Act. But the existence of a partnership may be deduced from facts and circumstances and does not have to be established by proof of an express agreement, either oral or written."

Buffalo Mill Co. v. Lewisburg Dairy Co., 20 A. B. R. 279, 159 Fed. 319 (D. C. Pa.): "A partnership in fact must of course be shown."

In re Evans (Rudolph v. Evans), 20 A. B. R. 406, 161 Fed. 590 (D. C. Ga.): "The purpose of the petition filed by creditors now is to bring the ladies named into the bankruptcy proceeding as partners in the firm of Evans & Co., upon

---

94. In re Duke & Son, 28 A. B. R. 195, 199 Fed. 199 (D. C. Ga.).

95. In re Harris, 4 A. B. R. 132, 108 Fed. 517 (Ref. Ohio, affirmed by D. C.). Compare, however, In re Kaufman, 23 A. B. R. 429, 176 Fed. 93 (C. C. A. N. Y.); In re Rushmore, 24 A. B. R. 55 (Ref. Okla.).

96. Compare, Jones v. Burnham, Williams & Co., 15 A. B. R. 85, 138 Fed. 986 (C. C. A. Pa., reversing In re Beckwith, 12 A. B. R. 453, 130 Fed. 475, but on the facts and not on the law): However, this was rather an attempt to prove an actual partnership by means of admissions than to prove an estoppel to deny partnership, which latter is the true partnership "by holding out." See In re Kenney, 3 A. B. R. 353, 97 Fed. 554 (D. C. N. Y., affirmed by C. C. A., 5 A. B. R. 355). Compare, In re Clark, 7 A. B. R. 96, 111 Fed. 893 (D. C. Pa., reversed on facts, but not on law, sub. nom. Rush v. Lake, 10 A. B. R. 455, 122 Fed. 561). Compare, Lott v. Young, 6 A. B. R. 436, 109 Fed. 798 (C. C. A. Mont.). Compare, analogously, In re Stoddard Bros. Lumber Co., 22 A. B. R. 435, 169 Fed. 190 (D. C. Idaho). Compare, ante, §§ 39, 57, 58.

Compare, analogously and suggestively, though not in relation to adjudication of bankruptcy. Mock v. Stoddard, 24 A. B. R. 403, 177 Fed. 611 (C. C. A. Idaho, affirming In re Stoddard Bros. Lumber Co., 22 A. B. R. 435, 169 Fed. 190).

the ground that they made certain statements to creditors and to mercantile agencies, after the death of their father, to the effect that they are still connected with the firm and liable for its debts. Statements of this sort could not re-establish the firm of Evans & Co. which had been dissolved by operation of law. The statements might render the ladies liable for credits given to Evans & Co. on the faith of such statements, but could not make them members of the firm. The old firm was dead, and I do not see how the statements of these ladies could make a new firm composed of themselves and Evans. While, as I have stated, they might be estopped by their statements from denying liability for credit given on the faith of their representations, they would not in this way establish a new partnership firm."

In re Pinson & Co., 24 A. B. R. 804, 180 Fed. 789 (D. C. Ala.): "Debts which are binding on the partners only by estoppel as to creditors without notice of dissolution of the partnership are not firm debts, upon the non-payment of which an adjudication against the firm may be based. * * * As the proof fails to show that the petition was filed during the continuation of the partnership business, as herein defined, or that the outstanding indebtedness at that time, excluding such as was created subsequent to the dissolution and which became that of the partnership only by estoppel in favor of such creditors as had no notice of its dissolution amounted to $1,000, the adjudication of the partnership is denied."

Such was the holding, indeed, in a case where two persons intending to form a corporation, which was, however, never organized, associated themselves in a mercantile business, one contributing a stock of goods and cash, which was deposited in bank and used in the business, the other contributing merely his personal services, the court holding that a partnership in fact existed, and affirming the rule.

Manson v. Williams, 18 A. B. R. 674, 153 Fed. 525 (C. C. A. Me., affirming In re Hudson Clothing Co., 17 A. B. R. 826, 148 Fed. 305): "We will observe, however, that the learned judge of the District Court found that there was a copartnership in fact between the two brothers under the style of the Hudson Clothing Company. He did not rest his conclusion in any way on the hypothesis of a copartnership by estoppel in the strict sense of the expression. This is important, because we regard the law as settled that, in bankruptcy proceedings involving a copartnership, the copartnership is, ordinarily, to be regarded as a true entity, precisely as the individual partners are. Various incidental reasons are given for this, the principal one of which is that otherwise there would be two classes of creditors whose equities otherwise are equal, one of which classes would share in the proceeds of certain property on the ground that two or more persons were estopped as to them from denying a copartnership, while other creditors who had contributed to the same enterprise would be left to what might remain of the property involved in the enterprise after the first class were paid, or to one or more individual estates. The fundamental reason, however, is that all through the various statutes of bankruptcy, whether in the United States or in England, which deal with copartnerships, the individuality and the entity of the copartnership are recognized to the same extent as the individuality and the entity of the several persons involved therein. The entire rule on this topic, so far as we have occasion to refer to it, is well deduced from Ex parte Sheen, 6 Chan. Div. (1877) 235, 22 Moak's Eng. Rep. 781."

And it must be proved to be a copartnership.[97]

> Compare, In re McLaren, 11 A. B. R. 141, 125 Fed. 835 (D. C. N. Y.): "Ordinarily an infant cannot be a copartner, and especially is this true in the absence of an agreement. It should seem improper to adjudicate a copartnership bankrupt because two of the alleged members admit its existence, and that they are members, all the other members denying any connection with it and denying the acts of bankruptcy."

And the burden of proof of the partnership rests on the petitioning creditors.[98]

§ 64. Individual Members Joinable with Partnership, in either Voluntary or Involuntary Proceedings.

—The individual members of the partnership may be joined with the partnership itself in either voluntary or involuntary bankruptcy proceedings, and may be adjudged bankrupts as individuals along with the partnership.[99]

In cases of voluntary bankruptcies, of course, no difficulty can be experienced, for no act of bankruptcy is necessary in voluntary bankruptcies, and so the partnership and its individual members can come into the same proceedings without difficulty.

In cases of involuntary bankruptcies, however, some theoretical difficul-

---

97. Evidence sufficient to prove partnership. Rush v. Lake, 10 A. B. R. 455, 122 Fed. 561 (C. C. A., reversing In re Clark, 7 A. B. R. 96, 111 Fed. 893); In re Beckwith & Co., 12 A. B. R. 453, 130 Fed. 475 (D. C. Penn., reversed, sub. nom. Jones v. Burnham, Williams & Co., 15 A. B. R. 85, 138 Fed. 986, C. C. A. Pa.); Buckingham Trustee v. First Nat. Bk., 12 A. B. R. 465, 131 Fed. 192 (C. C. A. Tenn.); Lott v. Young, 6 A. B. R. 436, 109 Fed. 798 (C. C. A. Mont.); In re Hudson Clothing Co., 17 A. B. R. 826, 148 Fed. 305 (D. C. Me.); Manson v. Williams, 18 A. B. R. 674, 153 Fed. 525 (C. C. A. Me., affirming In re Hudson Clothing Co., 17 A. B. R. 826, 148 Fed. 305).

Wife of Bankrupt as Partner.—A wife may not be a partner in a mercantile partnership with her husband in Arkansas, although a married woman may form such a partnership with another person. In re Suckle, 23 A. B. R. 861, 176 Fed. 828 (D. C. Ark.).

98. Jones v. Burnham, Williams & Co., 15 A. B. R. 85, 138 Fed. 986 (C. C. A. Pa., reversing In re Beckwith, 12 A. B. R. 453).

99. See post, §§ 70, 71, et seq.; In re Grant Bros., 5 A. B. R. 838, 106 Fed. 497 (D. C. N. Y.); Bank v. Craig Bros., 6 A. B. R. 381 (D. C. Ky.). In re Meyer, 3 A. B. R. 559, 98 Fed. 976 (C. C. A. N. Y., affirming Bank v. Meyer, 1 A. B. R. 565, 92 Fed. 896); In re Forbes, 11 A. B. R. 787, 128 Fed. 137 (D. C. Mass.). But compare, query, In re Stokes, 6 A. B. R. 262, 106 Fed. 312 (D. C. Pa.).

Also compare In re Farley & Co., 8 A. B. R. 266, 115 Fed. 359 (D. C. Va.): "The conclusion that I reach is, that when the members of a firm, which files a voluntary petition, desire to be adjudicated bankrupts individually, i. e., as against their individual creditors as well as against the firm creditors, they should each file an individual petition. And that in a case, such as the present, where there are two partners each desiring an individual discharge, there should be three orders of adjudication, and of reference, and that in all other proceedings the idea of three separate 'cases' should be carried out, certainly three separate estates are to be administered, and in strictness three discharges are sought."

"Consent" requisite only for administration of assets, not for adjudication. In re Everybody's Market, 21 A. B. R. 925, 173 Fed. 492 (D. C. Okla.).

ties arise, from the fact that in order to have the individual members adjudicated bankrupt as individuals there must have been some act of bankruptcy committed by them in their individual capacity.[1]

In re Meyer, 3 A. B. R. 559, 98 Fed. 976 (C. C. A. N. Y., affirming Chem. Nat. Bk. *v.* Meyer, 1 A. B. R. 565): "But, as the commission of an act of bankruptcy is indispensable to jurisdiction in an involuntary proceeding, the individual members cannot be adjudged bankrupts in such a proceeding who have not committed, or been participants in committing, one of the enumerated acts." This was the case of the assignment of a firm, the court holding that the partner who was the author of the assignment participated individually in the act.

Holmes *v.* Baker & Hamilton, 20 A. B. R. 252, 160 Fed. 922 (C. C. A. Wash.): "It is true that an individual member of a firm cannot be adjudged a bankrupt for an act of bankruptcy not committed by him or in which he did not participate; but that is not the case here presented. The act of bankruptcy in this case was committed by all the members of the firm. It was an act of omission, the failure to discharge the levy of an execution, a duty which vested as much upon the appellant as upon any member of the firm. Notwithstanding the dissolution of the partnership, it remained as it was before, the appellant's duty to see that the property of the copartnership was devoted to the payment of the partnership debts, as to which he had not been released."

Impliedly, In re Sanderlin, 6 A. B. R. 384, 109 Fed. 857 (D. C. N. Car.): "A partnership and the individuals composing it are distinct legal entities, and proceedings in bankruptcy by or against one does not of necessity involve the other." This case was reversed, but upon other grounds, in McNair *v.* McIntyre, 7 A. B. R. 638, 113 Fed. 113 (C. C. A.).

Bank *v.* Craig Bros., 6 A. B. R. 381 (D. C. Ky.): "At the hearing, the evidence showed that on the 23d day of July, 1901, A. J. Craig and John Craig, individually and as the persons composing the firm of Craig Bros., both joined in making a general assignment to James D. Canfield of all their property, individual and partnership alike, for the benefit of all their creditors, and it inevitably results from these admitted facts, whatever may be the truth upon the other issues involved, that there must, upon that ground, be an adjudication both against the firm and the individual members composing it. The proper rule seems to be that where both the partnership and each of the individuals who compose it make the assignment, the act of bankruptcy is committed by all of them. The adjudication should, therefore, embrace both the firm and the individual members."

But compare, In re Forbes, 11 A. B. R. 791, 128 Fed. 137 (D. C. Mass.): "If A & B, two partners, are insolvent, and A, by his voluntary petition or otherwise, commits an act of bankruptcy in connection with the firm, there is no reason, in the nature of things, that the joint adjudication should not be accompanied by an individual adjudication against him, and his individual assets and debts may thus properly be brought under the administration of the court of bankruptcy. Furthermore, if A has committed an act of bankruptcy

---

1. Compare post, § 171. Chem. Nat. Bk. *v.* Meyer, 1 A. B. R. 565, 92 Fed. 896 (D. C. N. Y., affirmed by In re Meyer, 3 A. B. R. 559, 98 Fed. 976). Obiter, In re Hale, 6 A. B. R. 35, 107 Fed. 432 (D. C. N. Car.). Also compare, inferentially and analogously, In re Lehigh Lumber Co., 4 A. B. R. 221, 101 Fed. 216 (D. C. Penn.). In re Ceballos & Co., 20 A. B. R. 459, 161 Fed. 445 (D. C. N. J.). To same effect in principle, Mills *v.* Fisher & Co., 20 A. B. R. 237, 159 Fed. 897 (C. C. A. Tenn.).

which involves the firm, there is no substantial reason of justice that B, the nonassenting partner, insolvent by the terms of the supposition (a partnership not being insolvent unless all its members are insolvent), and bound as to the joint debts and assets by A's act of bankruptcy, should not also be adjudged bankrupt individually as well as jointly. The joint adjudication is thus made to draw after it the separate adjudication of both partners. This is the rule required by convenience, and it is not contrary to justice. On the other hand, justice requires, and convenience does not forbid, that the nonassenting partner have the right to contest the issue of insolvency, substantially tendered by the petition."

Also compare Yungbluth v. Slipper, 26 A. B. R. 265, 185 Fed. 773 (C. C. A. Wash.): "In some of the decisions it has been said broadly that one partner may. not be adjudged bankrupt for the act of his copartner, and undoubtedly the statement is true as to certain acts of individual partners. * * * But we think the true doctrine is that, if the act of the individual partner is one for which the partnership itself may be adjudged bankrupt, the other members of the firm may also be adjudged bankrupt unless they can show in defense that the property of the firm, together with that of all the partners applicable to the payment of partnership debts, is sufficient to pay the same."

§ 65. Where Firm, Alone, Adjudicated, Whether Individual Estates Brought in for Administration.

—Where only the firm is adjudicated bankrupt and not the individual members also, the better opinion is that, nevertheless, the estates of the individual members are involved and should be administered in bankruptcy.[2]

In re Meyer, 3 A. B. R. 561, 562, 98 Fed. 975 (C. C. A. N. Y.): "We are of the opinion that it is the scheme of these provisions to treat the partnership as an entity which may be adjudged a bankrupt by voluntary or involuntary proceeding, irrespective of any adjudication of the individual partners as bankrupt, and upon an adjudication to draw to the administration the individual estates of the partners as well as the partnership estates, and marshal and distribute them according to equity. The assets of the individual estates and the debts provable against them can be ascertained without adjudicating the in-

---

2. Obiter, In re Farley, 8 A. B. R. 268, 115 Fed. 359 (D. C. Va.).

In re R. F. Duke & Son, 29 A. B. R. 93, 199 Fed. 199 (D. C. Ga.), following Francis v. McNeal, 26 A. B. R. 555, 186 Fed. 481, 108 C. C. A. 459. Obiter, In re Junck & Balthazard, 22 A. B. R. 208, 169 Fed. 481 (D. C. Wis.); In re Latimer, 23 A. B. R. 388, 141 Fed. 665 (D. C. Pa.); obiter, In re Ceballos, 20 A. B. R. •459, 161 Fed. 445 (D. C. N. J.); contra, In re Bertenshaw, 19 A. B. R. 577, 157 Fed. 363 (C. C. A.), wherein the dissenting opinion expresses, however, the truer rule. Also, compare § 477½, and post, § 2231.

Summary Orders on Nonbankrupt Partner and on Assignee of Partner. —In partnership bankruptcies it has been held that a summary order would lie upon the assignee of one of the members, to turn over individual assets, although the member was not himself a bankrupt. In re Stokes, 6 A. B. R. 262, 106 Fed. 312 (D. C. Penna.). But this decision seems to carry the rule beyond proper limits. While it might properly be conceded that a summary order would lie on the nonadjudicated partner to turn over assets, it would hardly seem that such an order would lie upon his assignee since the avoidance of assignments only follows by virtue of the bankruptcy of the identical person making the assignment. In an individual bankruptcy of a member of a partnership not itself bankrupt, a summary order on the assignee of the partnership will be refused. In re Mercur, 10 A. B. R. 505, 116 Fed. 655 (C. C. A.).

dividual partners bankrupt. The language does not require such an adjudication. The section is silent respecting a discharge of the partners individually. It does not, by terms or by implication, preclude an adjudication of the individual partners as bankrupt in the partnership proceeding; and, if there is such an adjudication, there is nothing to prevent the partners from receiving a discharge individually, if they are otherwise entitled to it under the act."

Dickas v. Barnes, Tr., 15 A. B. R. 569, 140 Fed. 849 (C. C. A. Ohio): "For the appellants, it is contended that the court, having refused to declare them bankrupts, had no authority to treat them and their property as if they were bankrupts. Although there are several assignments of error on each appeal, they all rest on this contention. The argument is that not being bankrupts they are not subject to the jurisdiction of the bankruptcy court; that the refusal to declare them bankrupts put an end to the authority of the court to retain control of their property for the purpose of the bankruptcy proceedings; and it is complained that the court by its order in effect denied to them the immunity to which they were entitled by reason of the provisions of the Bankruptcy Act. By § 4b wage earners and tillers of the soil are excepted from those who may be adjudged involuntary bankrupts. And for our present purpose we think the other appellants, who committed no act of bankruptcy, might be regarded as standing on the same footing as those who by reason of their occupation were exempt from an adjudication of bankruptcy. It may be conceded that but for the relation of these parties to the partnership, the contention they make would be supported by perfectly adequate reasons. But on account of that relation other conditions exist. One who combines with others in a partnership enterprise becomes bound for the payment of the partnership debts. As partner, he shares the fortunes of the partnership. In certain circumstances it may become subject to the exercise of the powers of a court of bankruptcy where its resources will be gathered in to satisfy the claims of creditors. One of those resources is the liability of the partner, for which his individual property stands charged. It is true that by virtue of the rule in equity, as well as in bankruptcy, for the marshaling and distribution of assets, his individual property is first applicable to the payment of his private debts, if there be any; the surplus then becomes assets for the payment of the partnership creditors. These consequences of partnership are not derived from the Bankrupt Act, but from the general law; and a partner is not relieved from them by his exemption from an adjudication of bankruptcy. If bankruptcy does not supervene, they would be worked out by a court of general jurisdiction, and the partner would be a party, a necessary party, to the record so that his liability for the firm debts could be enforced. In the bankruptcy court the partner may be brought before the court for the same purposes. In order to reach his property for the payment of the firm debts, it must be ascertained what surplus there will be after paying his private debts. It is said, however, that this must be done in a state court. But however this might be if he were a stranger, the partner is not to be regarded as a stranger, but as a party to the bankruptcy proceedings (Loveland on Bankruptcy, 2d Ed. 251, and cases in n. 42); and the court had authority to take such proceedings as were necessary to ascertain what assets were available and to subject them to the requirements of the case before it."

In re Wing Yick Co., 13 A. B. R. 757 (D. C. Hawaii): "Although a partnership may be adjudged bankrupt without adjudging the partners bankrupt, yet in the case of the bankruptcy of partnership, both the partnership property and the individual property of the partners are administered by the trustee, each partner being liable for all of the debts of the firm, and the assets of the partnership and of the individual partners are marshaled so as to prevent preferences, and secure the equitable distribution of the property of the several estates."

Even though as individuals they would not be amenable to bankruptcy.[3]

And this is so notwithstanding one of the partners is a wage earner, or farmer, and belongs to a class exempted from the operation of the bankruptcy act. Such was the holding of the Circuit Court of Appeals in Dickas v. Barnes, quoted supra.

And it is especially true where the act of bankruptcy, upon which the adjudication was made, involves the solvency of the firm.[4]

But a receiver or trustee of a partnership adjudged a bankrupt is not the receiver or trustee of the property of another unadjudicated partnership in which the members of the bankrupt partnership were also members, and he has no more right to seize or to administer such property without the consent of the nonadjudicated partners that he has to take and distribute the property of any other stranger.[5]

§ 65¾. Where Solvent Partner Exists and Does Not Consent.—

But it has been held that the partnership assets will not be so administered where there is a solvent partner who does not consent.[6] But it is very doubtful whether § 5 (h) refers to any other than cases of individual bankruptcy wherein it is sought also to administer partnership assets;[7] or where, in one partnership bankruptcy it is sought to administer the assets of another partnership not itself adjudicated bankrupt.[7a]

§ 65½. Act Must Be That of the Partnership.—The act alleged as

the ground for adjudication must be the act of the partnership.[7b]

In re Stovall Grocery Co., 20 A. B. R. 537, 161 Fed. 882 (D. C. Ga.): "It will be perceived that the act of bankruptcy alleged here is the transfer by an individual member of a firm of property with the intent to defraud individual creditors and firm creditors. This is not an act of bankruptcy on the part of the firm. The partnership entity must act, and what is relied on must be its act."

§ 66. Act Need Not Be Actually Committed by All Partners.—The

3. In re Duke & Son, 28 A. B. R. 195, 199 Fed. 199 (D. C. Ga.).

4. Francis v. McNeal, 26 A. B. R. 555, 186 Fed. 481 (C. C. A. Pa.).

5. Fidelity Trust Co., v. Gaskell, 28 A. B. R. 4, 195 Fed. 865 (C. C. A. Mo.).

6. In re Solomon & Carvel, 20 A. B. R. 488, 163 Fed. 140 (D. C. N. Y.); In re Blair, 3 A. B. R. 580 (D. C. N. Y.); obiter, In re Junck & Balthazard, 22 A. B. R. 298, 169 Fed. 481 (D. C. Wis.).

7. See post, § 2232. See dissenting opinion, In re Bertenshaw, 19 A. B. R. 577, 157 Fed. 577 (C. C. A.).

7a. Instance, Fidelity Trust Co. v. Gaskell, 28 A. B. R. 4, 195 Fed. 865 (C. C. A. Mo.).

7b. This subject is further considered in detail under the subject of "Imputed Acts of Bankruptcy—Agents of Corporations and Partnerships," post, § 171; also under the germane subject of "Transfers by Individual Partners Not Voidable as Preferences in Firm Bankruptcies," etc., post, § 2268½.

act of bankruptcy alleged in an involuntary petition need not be actually committed by all the partners.[8]

In re Forbes, 11 A. B. R. 791, 128 Fed. 137 (D. C. Mass.): "Even their privity is not essential. An act by one member of a firm, within the scope of his authority, in relation to joint property or joint debts, such as giving a preference, making a fraudulent transfer, should be imputed to all the members in this as in all other civil cases."

But the individual members may not also be adjudicated bankrupt unless they have each committed an act of bankruptcy.[9]

§ 67. But All Partners to Be Made Parties.

—But all the partners must be made parties: a petition will not lie for less than all.[10] Where one of them is dead, it is questionable whether partnership adjudication may be had.[11]

§ 68. Nonconsenting Partner Not Made Party, No Adjudication on Voluntary Partnership Petition.

—And a voluntary petition by less than all, where the nonconsenting partners are not made parties in any way, is irregular and will not warrant adjudication of the partnership,[12] and cannot be cured by subsequent consent of the nonconsenting partners through their attorneys.[13]

§ 69. Individual Petitions Not Amendable to Include Partnership.

—Individual bankruptcy proceedings against persons who are also members of a partnership cannot be amended so as to include the partnership. There is nothing in the record by which to amend, the right to amend going no further than to bring forward and make effective that which in some shape is already there.[14]

In re Mercur, 10 A. B. R. 505, 122 Fed. 384 (C. C. A. Penna., affirming 8 A. B. R. 275, 116 Fed. 655, distinguished in In re Kaufman, 14 A. B. R. 397, 136 Fed. 262): "The general right to amend, regardless of the time which has elapsed, is abundantly sustained by the authorities. * * * But to do so it is plain there must be in the record as it stands the substance of that which is asked for; the

---

8. In re Perlhefter & Shatz, 25 A. B. R. 576, 177 Fed. 299 (D. C. N. Y.). Compare Yungbluth v. Slipper, 26 A. B. R. 265, 185 Fed. 773 (C. C. A. Wash.), quoted at § 171. Impliedly, Holmes v. Baker & Hamilton, 20 A. B. R. 252, 160 Fed. 922 (C. C. A. Wash.), quoted at §§ 64 and 171.

9. In re Ceballos, 20 A. B. R. 459, 161 Fed. 445 (D. C. N. J.).

10. In re Winters, 3 A. B. R. 90 (D. C. Iowa); In re Altman, 2 A. B. R. 407, 95 Fed. 263 (D. C. N. Y., affirming 1 A. B. R. 680).

11. In re Evans (Rudolph v. Evans), 20 A. B. R. 406, 161 Fed. 590 (D. C. Ga.).

12. In re City Contracting & Building Co., 20 A. B. R. 171, — Fed. — (D. C. Hawaii).

13. In re Altman, 2 A. B. R. 407, 95 Fed. 263 (D. C. N. Y., affirming 1 A. B. R. 690); In re Winters, 3 A. B. R. 90 (D. C. Iowa); In re Russell, 3 A. B. R. 91, 97 Fed. 32 (D. C. Iowa). Notice to the nonconsenting partner may be given by publication, where personal service cannot be given. Obiter, In re Winters, 3 A. B. R. 90 (D. C. Iowa).

14. Compare, to same general effect, Royston v. Weis, 7 A. B. R. 584, 112 Fed. 962 (C. C. A. Tex.). Compare, In re Kaufman, 23 A. B. R. 429, 176 Fed. 96 (C. C. A. N. Y.), quoted at § 70.

right to amend can go no further than to bring forward and make effective that which is in some shape already there. * * * It is plain from this review of the proceedings that, while begun at the same time and carried on together side by side, they have from the outstart been individual in character, directed against the two parties who were the subject of them severally, and not because or by virtue of the partnership relations. The fact that it existed could not be obscured, but it has not been made the basis of any action taken, the references to it being incidental only and usually with the suggestion that it was not in any way involved. It is now proposed, however, to change this, and by a so-called amendment to recant and transform all that has been so far done. Instead of two distinct cases against each of the parties severally, we are to have practically one, which shall be effective against the partnership to which they happen to belong, the same as though it had been directed against it from the beginning. It is contended as a justification that both the partners having been brought into court, of necessity the partnership has been also. If this be true, the amendment is proper, but otherwise not. All the authorities agree that in contemplation of the statute a partnership is a distinct entity, which requires a petition specifically directed against it, alleging an act of bankruptcy in which it is expressly involved, and resulting in an adjudication of the partnership itself, irrespective of and in addition to any that may be made against the individual members. This is carried so far that without it, as it is held, there can be no effective discharge from the firm obligations, and, by some courts, that the proceedings against the partnership and the individual members are distinct cases, in which separate fees must be paid. * * *

"If this be so, whatever proceedings are instituted should disclose from the outstart the character which is proposed for them, and should maintain it to the close. It a partnership is intended to be reached, the petition and the proceedings under it should be appropriate to that end; if only the individual members, they should be governed by that circumstance. This is something more than a mere matter of form. It goes to the substance of the proceedings, involving, as it does, the question of notice and the rights of the parties to be affected."

Mahoney *v.* Ward, 3 A. B. R. 773, 100 Fed. 278 (D. C. N. Car.): "The fact that he happened to be a partner with Jones in one firm and with Cawthorn in another would not necessarily draw into the proceeding the two commercial firms, or justify each member of such firms to come into court, save themselves from complying with the law by paying costs; and being adjudged bankrupts even by a consent order."

Nor may *a nunc pro tunc* entry of adjudication of the partnership be made therein to revert to the time of the adjudication of the several individuals composing it as members.[15] But a joint voluntary petition of two persons who also compose a partnership, if it fairly appears that they were seeking to have the firm adjudged bankrupt, may be amended to specifically pray therefor.[16] And it has been held that a petition filed against an alleged partnership and its individual members, should it appear that no partner-

15. In re Mercur, 10 A. B. R. 505, 122 Fed. 384 (C. C. A. Penn., affirming 8 A. B. R. 275, 116 Fed. 655). Compare, Ludowici Roofing Tile Co. *v.* Penn. Inst., 8 A. B. R. 739, 116 Fed. 661, involving the Mercur bankruptcy.

Compare, analogously, In re Altman, 1 A. B. R. 689 (Ref. N. Y., affirmed in 2 A. B. R. 407).

16. In re Meyers, 3 A. B. R. 260, 97 Fed. 753 (D. C. N. Y.).

ship exists, may be amended so as to proceed solely against one of such members.[17]

§ 70. Secret or Silent Partners, on Discovery, Brought in.—But secret or silent partners may, on discovery, be brought in.[18]

However, where an adjudication is in form that of an individual, the subsequent discovery of a secret partner, the partnership doing business under the individual name, will not authorize the converting of the individual adjudication into a partnership adjudication by mere order; there must be allegations made by formal petition of the existence of a partnership and opportunity be given to the alleged partners to make the controversies authorized in partnership bankruptcy cases.

In re Kaufman, 23 A. B. R. 429, 176 Fed. 96 (C. C. A. N. Y.): "Counsel for Lena Kaufman contends that the record does not sustain the finding that she was a partner with her husband, but it is not necessary to go into that branch of the case. For the purposes of this appeal it may be assumed that for some time prior to the filing of the petition in bankruptcy there was a firm in the district doing business under the name of 'Isaac Kaufman,' the partners in which were Isaac Kaufman and Lena Kaufman. The existence of the firm, however, was not known or even suspected and in consequence the proceeding was instituted not against any partnership but against Isaac Kaufman individually. The difficulty with the order is that, after proceedings against the individual have progressed for a considerable time, much testimony having been taken, it undertakes to establish the pendency pari passi of another proceeding against the firm, which was never begun by filing any petition against it, and to put that second proceeding in the same condition as the first. In our opinion this cannot be done by a mere order; such a procedure would deprive the firm and the partner now sought to be brought in of the opportunity which the statute gives them to controvert the facts alleged in the petition and to have, if they so desire, a trial by jury on the question of insolvency and any act of bankruptcy alleged to have been committed. Sections 18d, 19a. This case is to be distinguished from those cited on the brief where the original proceeding was against a firm and, upon the discovery of a partner not originally named or known, he was brought in as one of the members of the firm."

§ 71. Petition by One Partner or Several Partners, Where Remaining Partners Do Not Join.—A petition may be filed by one partner or several of the partners, for adjudication of the partnership, where some of the remaining partners do not join.[19]

§ 72. Remaining Partners Not Joining, Petition Treated as Involuntary as to Nonconsenting Partner but Voluntary as to Creditors.—Where one or more partners less than all file a voluntary partner-

---

17. In re Richardson, 27 A. B. R. 590, 192 Fed. 50 (D. C. Mass.). See also, § 272.

18. Compare, In re Harris, 4 A. B. R. 132, 108 Fed. 517 (Ref. Ohio, affirmed by D. C.). Evidence as to whether one is a secret partner or not.

Rush v. Lake, 10 A. B. R. 455, 122 Fed. 561 (C. C. A., reversing 7 A. B. R. 96). Evidence as to whether one is a silent partner. In re Clark, 7 A. B. R. 96, 111 Fed. 893 (D. C. Wash.).

19. See cases cited in succeeding paragraphs.

ship petition to have the partnership, as such, adjudged bankrupt and the other partner, or some of the other partners, after notification, do not join with him therein, the petition is treated as an involuntary petition as to the nonconsenting partner, but as a voluntary petition so far as creditors are concerned.

In re Carleton, 8 A. B. R. 270, 115 Fed. 246 (D. C. Mass.): "The history in the United States of voluntary petitions filed by one partner with intent to put the firm into bankruptcy appear to be this: Section 14 of the act of 1841, provided:

"'That where two or more persons, who are partners in trade, become insolvent, an order may be made in the manner provided in this act either on the petition of such partners, or any one of them or on the petition of any creditor of the partners; upon which order all the joint stock and property of the company, and also all the separate estate of each of the partners, shall be taken, excepting such parts thereof as are herein exempted.' 5 Stat. 448.

"This enabled one partner to put all the members of his firm into bankruptcy, provided all were insolvent. No specific provision was made for proceedings in which one partner asserted and the other denied insolvency; but, so far as outsiders were concerned, the petition was treated as a voluntary one. See Chandler, Bankr. Law, pp. 9, 64; Ex parte Hall, Fed. Cas. No. 5,919; Ex parte Hull, Fed. Cas. No. 6,856; Bank v. Johnson, Fed. Cas. No. 133; Ex parte Galbraith, Fed. Cas. No. 5,187.

"Section 36 of the act of 1867, provided: 'That where two or more persons who are partners in trade shall be adjudged bankrupt, either on the petition of such partners, or any one of them, or on the petition of any creditor of the partners, a warrant shall issue in the manner provided by this act, upon which all the joint stock and property of the copartnership, and also all the separate estate of each of the partners, shall be taken, excepting such parts thereof as are hereinbefore excepted.'

"This section, though much resembling section 14 of the act of 1841, yet differed from it in this: Instead of authorizing one partner to put all the members of the firm into bankruptcy by a voluntary petition, it provided what should happen after all had been adjudged bankrupt upon the petition of one partner or of a creditor.

"General order 18 dealt with the matter further, and provided, substantially, as in the existing general order 8, that:

"'In case one or more members of a copartnership refuse to join in a petition to have the firm declared bankrupt, the parties refusing shall be entitled to resist the prayer of the petition in the same manner as if the petition had been filed by a creditor of the partnership, and notice of the filing of the petition shall be given to him in the same manner as provided by law and by these rules in the case of a debtor petitioned against; and he shall have the right to appear at the time fixed by the court for the hearing of the petition, and to make proof, if he can, that the copartnership is not insolvent, or has not committed an act of bankruptcy, and to take all other defenses which any debtor proceeded against is entitled to take by the provisions of the Act.'

"Under this act and general order it was held by many courts that a petition by one partner to put the firm into bankruptcy need not allege an act of bankruptcy; an allegation of insolvency, as in the case of a voluntary petition, was sufficient. In re Stowers, Fed. Cas. No. 13,516; In re Noonan, Fed. Cas. No. 10,292; In re Hathorn, Fed. Cas. No. 6,214; In re Penn, Fed. Cas. No. 10,927.

This was said in In re Gorham, Fed. Cas. No. 5,624; and in In re Grady, Fed. Cas. No. 5,654. It was assumed, more or less distinctly, in In re Bennett, Fed. Cas. No. 1,314; Id. 1,315; Re Prankard, Fed. Cas. No. 11,366; Re Moore, Fed. Cas. No. 9,750; Re Little, Fed. Cas. No. 8,390; Re Smith (D. C.); 6 Fed. 465. An examination of the files shows that this was the firmly-settled practice in this court under the act of 1867, and that to this extent the petition of one partner was deemed a voluntary proceeding, even as against a nonjoining partner. In some other respects the proceedings were treated as voluntary. In re Wilson, 2 Low. 453, Fed. Cas. No. 17,784. Yet in Metsker v. Bonebrake, 108 U. S. 66, 2 Sup. Ct. 351, 27 L. Ed. 654, the Supreme Court held that a case in which one partner petitioned and the other partner came in and confessed himself bankrupt was a case of 'compulsory or involuntary bankruptcy,' within the provisions of St. 1874, ch. 390, § 10 (18 Stat. 180), and Rev. St., § 5128, dealing with preferences. Mr. Justice Miller said:

"'We do not doubt that Metsker's was a case of involuntary or compulsory bankruptcy within the meaning of this amendment. The distinction intended by this language is clearly between the cases in which the bankrupt himself and of his own volition initiates proceedings in bankruptcy and those in which they are commenced by some one else against him. In the one case it is voluntary, and in the other compulsory. It is not a voluntary bankruptcy if the man is forced into it against his will by his partner, any more than by any one else; and it is compulsory and involuntary if he refuses to join in such case, and is forced into it, as much as in any other enforced bankruptcy.' Pages 70, 71, 108 U. S., page 353, 2 Sup. Ct., 27 L. Ed. 654.

"Section 5 of the act of 1898 provides that 'a partnership, during the continuation of the partnership business, or after its dissolution and before the final settlement thereof, may be adjudged a bankrupt.' Nothing is said in the act concerning the method or methods by which a partnership may be adjudged either by voluntary or involuntary petition. For direction in this matter, we must turn to general order 8, which is, in substance, general order 18 of the act of 1867. Taking the act and the general order and form No. 2 together, it appears to me safest to assume that the law regarding partnership petitions is substantially the same as it was under the act of 1867. Notwithstanding the decision of the Supreme Court in Metsker v. Bonebrake, it appears to me that this court is not compelled to hold, either under the act of 1867, and general order 18, or under the act of 1898 and general order 8, that this petition is so far involuntary as to permit a creditor of the firm to intervene in order to resist adjudication. See In re Murray (D. C.), 3 Am. B. R. 601, 96 Fed. 600. As to the petitioner, these proceedings are purely voluntary. As to him a creditor has no more right to intervene than in the case of any other voluntary petition. As to the nonjoining partner, the proceedings are in some sense involuntary. As to intervention by a creditor, it is most convenient, and most consistent with justice and the general scheme of the act, to hold that the right 'to make all defenses which any debtor proceeded against has a right to make' is confined to the nonjoining partner. If he makes no objection, then, so far as adjudication is concerned, the petition is to be treated generally as if it were altogether voluntary. Had this been an ordinary voluntary petition by both partners, the creditor could not have intervened to contest the adjudication. If partners are willing to be adjudged bankrupt, whether on the petition of one or on that of all of them, they are to have their way.

"Difficulties may arise in construing either act. For example, the court may have to consider what defenses are now open to the nonjoining partner. Under the act of 1867, as has just been stated, the petition needed to allege no more than insolvency, and the nonjoining partner might take issue on the alleged insolvency. Under § 11 of the act of 1867, insolvency was necessary to support a voluntary petition. There is no such requirement in the act of 1898, though forms Nos. 1 and 2 both require the voluntary bankrupt to set out his inability to pay his debts. This inability may, perhaps, be taken to represent insolvency, though inability to pay debts is not the precise equivalent of insolvency as defined in § 1 of the act of 1898. Under the act of 1867 it was suggested in some cases that one partner might put the firm into bankruptcy by a petition alleging either insolvency without an act of bankruptcy or an act of bankruptcy without insolvency. It would be somewhat difficult to apply this theory to the act of 1898, and the matter is stated here only to show that the difficulties involved in the conclusion here reached have not been overlooked."

Again, In re Carleton, 12 A. B. R. 475, 131 Fed. 146 (D. C. Mass.): "But so far as the present bankrupt (the partner filing the petition) is concerned, the partnership proceedings must be deemed voluntary."

In re Murray, 3 A. B. R. 601, 96 Fed. 600 (D. C. Iowa): "When a petition on behalf of part of the members of the firm is filed in the clerk's office, it must then be classed as a voluntary proceeding, and in the absence of the judge from the district or division, the clerk must refer the case to the proper referee. If, however, the nonjoining partner or partners, upon notification, should make defense to the petition, then the proceeding would become as to him an involuntary one."

In re Ceballos & Co., 20 A. B. R. 459, 161 Fed. 445 (D. C. N. J.): "But this proceeding is voluntary as to the petitioner, and involuntary as to his two co-partners."

In re Junck & Balthazard, 22 A. B. R. 298, 169 Fed. 481 (D. C. Wis.): "It thus appears that for certain purposes at least the petition, so far as Balthazard is concerned, is to be regarded as involuntary. * * * In the case of a non-assenting partner, the procedure as to him is the same as in an involuntary case; but as to creditors the petition is voluntary, and there is no room for the issue which the creditor Saveland attempts to raise by his intervention, and his answer may be stricken from the files."

And, if the other partner or partners upon notification, do come in and join, then the petition remains as a voluntary petition and adjudication can at once be made, either by the judge, or, in the judge's absence, by the referee, upon reference.[20]

§ 73. No Act of Bankruptcy Requisite, Even Where Not All Join.
—But no act of bankruptcy need be alleged where the petition is filed by one or more, less than all, and all do not join.[21]

In re Junck & Balthazard, 22 A. B. R. 298, 169 Fed. 481 (D. C. Wis.): "This disposes of the objection * * * that the petition was so far involuntary that it was defective without an averment showing that the firm had committed an act of bankruptcy. The better rule seems to be that in such case the ordinary averment that the firm has not sufficient assets to pay its obligations, and is willing to submit its property for distribution, is sufficient, and the filing of such

---

20. In re Murray, 3 A. B. R. 601, 96 Fed. 600 (D. C. Iowa).
21. Obiter, In re Carleton, 8 A. B.
R. 270, 115 Fed. 246 (D. C. Mass.); In re Forbes, 11 A. B. R. 787, 128 Fed. 137 (D. C. Mass.).

a petition by one of the partners is of itself considered the equivalent of an act of bankruptcy."

Or perhaps the act of bankruptcy is to be considered to be the filing of the bankruptcy petition on the part of the firm itself or the written admission contained therein that the partnership is unable to pay its debts and is therefore willing to be adjudged bankrupt.[22]

Compare, National Bank *v.* Moyses, 8 A. B. R. 10, 186 U. S. 181: "And he has committed an act of bankruptcy in filing the petition."

One case, however, has specifically held the filing of a petition in bankruptcy by one partner against his copartners cannot be deemed an act of bankruptcy on the part of the partnership.[23] But this ruling is probably based upon a rejection of the doctrine that the filing of a voluntary petition is itself the commission of the fifth Act of Bankruptcy,[23a] and that it lies within the implied authority of a partner to make such a written admission as will bind the firm.[23b] However, even the case mentioned was rightly decided, for the firm and the petitioning partner were both adjudged bankrupt, though the nonconsenting partners were not adjudged bankrupt for lack of any individual acts of bankruptcy committed by them.

§ 74. Not All Defenses Available, but Only Insolvency; Though Entitled to Jury on That Issue.

—The nonjoining partners may not make all defenses which would have been available against a petitioning creditor, but are confined to the single issue of insolvency notwithstanding the Supreme Court's General Order, No. VIII.[24]

In re Forbes, 11 A. B. R. 787, 128 Fed. 137 (D. C. Mass.): "A nonassenting partner cannot set up the want of an act of bankruptcy as a defense to a petition brought by his partner against the firm and partners, but (that) he may set up the defense of solvency. * *. * The nonassenting partner is entitled to trial by jury upon the issue of insolvency and upon that issue only. Upon the issue of partnership he is entitled to a trial by the court."

22. Blake *v.* Valentine, 1 A. B. R. 375, 89 Fed. 691 (D. C. Calif.); In re Forbes, 11 A. B. R. 787, on page 791, 128 Fed. 137 (D. C. Mass.).
23. Obiter, In re Ceballos & Co., 20 A. B. R. 459, 161 Fed. 445 (D. C. N. J.).
23a. See post, §§ 102, 164.
23b. See post, § 169.
24. Gen. Ord., No. VIII: "Any member of a partnership, who refuses to join in a petition to have the partnership declared bankrupt, shall be entitled to resist the prayer of the petition in the same manner as if the petition had been filed by a creditor of the partnership, and notice of the filing of the petition shall be given to him in the same manner as provided by law and by these rules in the case of a debtor petitioned against; and he shall have the right to appear at the time fixed by the court for the hearing of the petition, and to make proof, if he can, that the partnership is not insolvent or has not committed an act of bankruptcy, and to make all defenses which any debtor proceeded against is entitled to take by the provisions of the act; and in case an adjudication of bankruptcy is made upon the petition, such partner shall be required to file a schedule of his debts and an inventory of his property in the same manner as is required by the act in cases of debtors against whom adjudication of bankruptcy shall be made."
In re Junck & Balthazard, 22 A. B. R. 298, 169 Fed. 481 (D. C. Wis.), quoted at §§ 72, 73; In re Perlhefter & Shatz, 25 A. B. R. 576, 177 Fed. 299 (D. C. N. Y.).

But nonjoining partners are entitled to a jury to try the issue of insolvency.[25]

§ 75. Whether Partner May File Ordinary Involuntary Petition.
—It seems that a partner may not file a regular involuntary petition against the partnership of which he is a member, but that his only method of bringing his firm into bankruptcy is as above indicated.[26]

§ 76. Creditors May Not Intervene.
—Creditors may not intervene to resist the adjudication upon a petition filed by one partner.[27]

§ 77. Unincorporated Companies.
—Unincorporated companies may be adjudged bankrupt.[28]

§ 78. Definition of Unincorporated Company.
—It is generally understood to be a body or association occupying middle ground between partnerships and stock corporations, possessing some of the powers and privileges of both.[29]

§ 79. Private Bankers.
—Private bankers may be adjudged bankrupt.[30]

And a partnership may be a private banker. But a corporation cannot be a "private banker" within the meaning of the Act.[31]

Burkhart v. Germ. Am. Bk., 14 A. B. R. 222, 137 Fed. 958 (D. C. Ohio): "And it is urged that this bank, having some of the powers and privileges of a private corporation not possessed by individuals or partnerships, is a corporation, and not a partnership, and that therefore the petition must be dismissed. *. * * This bank is an unincorporated company, and under the laws of Ohio and for general purposes is a partnership, and for the purpose of banking is a private

25. In re Forbes, 11 A. B. R. 787, 128 Fed. 137 (D. C. Mass.); In re Murray, 3 A. B. R. 601, 96 Fed. 600 (D. C. Iowa).
26. Compare, obiter, In re Schenkein & Coney, 7 A. B. R. 162, 113 Fed. 421 (Ref. N. Y.).
27. See ante, § 43. In re Junck & Balthazard, 22 A. B. R. 298, 169 Fed, 481 (D. C. Wis.), quoted at § 72. Obiter, In re Carleton, 8 A. B. R. 270, 115 Fed. 246 (D. C. Mass.). The petition of one partner for adjudication of the firm should show clearly that it is the petition of one partner against the firm and that the other partners have not joined. In re Russell, 3 A. B. R. 91, 97 Fed. 32 (D. C. Iowa). And that he seeks discharge from firm as well as individual debts. In re Russell, 3 A. B. R. 91, 97 Fed. 32 (D. C. Iowa). Insanity of one partner, even if it began before the commission of the act of bankruptcy, will not defeat the subsequent adjudication of the partnership as bankrupt, as we have heretofore seen. In re Stein & Co., 11 A. B. R.

536, 127 Fed. 547 (C. C. A. Ills.). A partnership may be adjudged bankrupt after the death of a partner upon an act of bankruptcy committed by the surviving partner. Obiter, In re Stein & Co., 11 A. B. R. 536, 127 Fed. 547 (C. C. A. Ills.). As to deposit of costs in partnership cases, see post, § 289. As to service of process upon nonjoining partner, see post, § 310.
28. Bankr. Act, § 4; Burkhardt v. Germ. Am. Bk., 14 A. B. R. 222, 137 Fed. 958 (D. C. Ohio); In re Seaboard Fire Underwriters, 13 A. B. R. 722, 137 Fed. 987 (D. C. N. Y.).
29. Burkhardt v. Germ. Am. Bk., 14 A. B. R. 222, 137 Fed. 958 (D. C. Ohio).
30. Bankr. Act, § 4 (b). Obiter, Couts v. Townsend, 11 A. B. R. 128, 126 Fed. 249 (D. C. Ky.). Instance, Kersten v. Kersten, 6 A. B. R. 516, 110 Fed. 929 (D. C. Wis.).
31. In re Surety & Guarantee Trust Co., 9 A. B. R. 129, 121 Fed. 73 (C. C. A. Ills.); In re Oregon Trust and Sav. Bk., 19 A. B. R. 484, 156 Fed. 319 (D. C. Ore.).

banker, but the contention is that it must be deemed to be a corporation for the purpose of administering its assets in bankruptcy, and it is urged, that to hold otherwise would nullify the provisions of clause 6, § 1. The broad terms of clause 6, § 1, are, however, limited by §§ 4 and 5 in relation to who may become bankrupts. In this respect §§ 4 and 5 distinguish unincorporated companies and private bankers and ordinary partnerships from corporations. It is difficult to conceive of an unincorporated company (as distinguished from a corporation and an ordinary partnership) without any of the powers and privileges of a private corporation, for without any of these powers and privileges it would be an ordinary partnership. It is generally understood to be a body or association occupying middle ground between partnerships and stock corporations, possessing some of the powers and privileges of both, and is generally so recognized by the courts; and § 4 may have contemplated such an unincorporated company, thereby limiting the definition of 'corporations', at least for the purpose of adjudications in bankruptcy, to bodies organized under the laws making the capital subscribed alone responsible for their debts. Clause 6, as construed by counsel for the respondents, would conflict with § 5, and deprive creditors of the right to have the individual property of the partners administered for their·benefit by the bankrupt courts. It would be reasonable to treat as corporations bodies whose subscribed capital stock is alone responsible for their debts, but it would be contrary to the spirit and purpose of the Bankrupt Act to deprive creditors of the right to have the individual property of partners administered for their benefit by the Bankrupt Courts simply because the partnership contract invested the partnership with authority to exercise some of the powers and privileges of a corporation. * * * This bank is a partnership, formed for the purpose of carrying on its business of banking as a private banker, such as is contemplated by Laning's Rev. Laws, § 4891 (Bates' Ann. St., §§ 3170-1), et seq., and as such, may be adjudged a bankrupt."

SUBDIVISION "C."

CORPORATIONS.

§ 80. Classes of Corporations Included and Excluded.—The original restrictions of the Act of 1898 as to the corporations subject to bankruptcy, to those engaged in "manufacturing, trading, printing, publishing, mining, or mercantile pursuits" have been removed by the Amendment of 1910 which has restored, with exceptions, the limitations of the old law of 1867; so that now, "any moneyed, business or commercial corporation," may be subjected to involuntary bankruptcy, except that no "municipal, railroad, insurance, or banking corporation" may be so adjudged.[32]

---

32. Bankr. Act, § 4b, as amended June 25, 1910: "Any natural person, except a wage earner or a person engaged chiefly in farming or the tillage of the soil, any unincorporated company, and any moneyed, business, or commercial corporation, except a municipal, railroad, insurance or banking corporation, owing debts to the amount of one thousand dollars or over, may be adjudged an involuntary bankrupt upon default or an impartial trial, and shall be subject to the provisions and entitled to the benefits of the act."

Definition of Corporation.—Bankr. Act, § 1 (a) (6): "'Corporations' shall mean all bodies having any of the powers and privileges of private corporations not possessed by individuals or partnerships, and shall include limited or other partnership associations organized under laws making the capital subscribed alone responsible for the debts of the association."

Compare (1867) Winter *v.* Iowa, M. & N. P. Ry. Co., 7 Nat. Bankr. Reg. 289, 2 Dill. 487, Fed. Cas. No. 17,890: "The first ground of demurrer is that the defendant is not a 'moneyed, business, or commercial corporation,' within the meaning of the Bankrupt Act, and hence that the provisions of that act do not apply to it. 'The provisions of this act shall apply to all moneyed, business, or commercial corporations, and joint stock companies.' Section 37. Except as otherwise provided, corporations are within the Bankrupt Act (§ 48) and in my judgment the purpose of Congress in the use of the language above quoted from § 37 was to include all corporations of a private nature, organized for pecuniary profit. Instead of undertaking to enumerate by name or description the various kinds of such corporations, language broad enough to include them, and which would exclude corporations of a public, civil or municipal character, as well as those organized purely and strictly for religious, charitable, educational, and like purposes, was employed."

Compare (1867) Adams *v.* Boston, H. & E. Ry. Co., 4 Nat. Bankr. Reg. 314, Fed. Cas. No. 47. "Public corporations, created for municipal or political purposes, and such private corporations as are ecclesiastical, or eleemosynary, or established for the advancement of learning, are clearly not made subject to the provisions of the act. Private corporations are divided into ecclesiastical and lay. Lay corporations are divided into civil and eleemosynary. Civil corporations are created for an infinite variety of purposes; such as affording facilities for obtaining loans of money, the making of canals, turnpike roads and the like. The words of the thirty-seventh section, 'moneyed, business or commercial corporations,' would seem to have been intended to embrace all those classes of corporations that deal in or with money or property in the transaction of money, business or commercial for pecuniary gain, and not for religious, charitable or educational purposes. Accordingly, district courts of the United States in various districts have treated manufacturing, mining and similar corporations, and in one circuit at least, railway corporations, as subject to be dealt with under the provisions of the Bankrupt Act. But it is contended that the public purposes for which railways are created, and the public duties they are bound to perform, make them public corporations; and therefore such a construction should be given to the words of the statute as would exclude them from its operation. In the popular meaning of the term, nearly every corporation is public, inasmuch as they are created for the public benefit. But if the whole interest does not belong to the government, or if the corporation is not created for the administration of political or municipal power, the corporation is private."

Compare (1867) Rankin *v.* Florida, A. & G. C. Ry. Co., 1 Nat. Bankr. Reg. 647, Fed. Cas. No. 11,567: "A corporation created for the purpose of carrying on or pursuing any lawful business, defined by its charter and clothed with power so to do for the sake of gain, is clearly such a corporation. Now, this corporation is a common carrier, takes tolls, purchases, sells and mortgages property, contracts debts and other obligations, may sue and be sued. What more is necessary to fix upon it the character of a business corporation?"

It will be noted that the classification of the law of 1867 has not been readopted in its entirety, for the needed exceptions which were felt to be lacking in the law of 1867 have been engrafted in the Amendment of 1910. Thus, municipal, railroad, insurance, and banking corporations are not eligible nor subject to adjudication of bankruptcy. Thus, were it not for the exception in the statute, railroad corporations might be subject to bankruptcy as they were held to be under the law of 1867.[33]

Compare (1867) Winter v. Iowa, M. &. N. Ry. Co., 7 Nat. Bankr. Reg. 289, 2 Dill. 487, Fed. Cas. No. 17,890: "Railways fall within the designation of business or commercial corporations. * * * The question whether railroad companies are within the operation of the Bankrupt Act [Act of 1867] has several times been before the courts, and so far as the researches of counsel have extended, it has been uniformly decided that they were. * * * Under the laws of the state, railroads may mortgage their property, or it may be subjected to the payment of their debts by proper judicial order, and in this manner sold and transferred, and really the only question is whether insolvent railway companies shall be made to pay their debts under the collection laws of the state, or under the mode provided by the Bankrupt Act."

"There may be practical difficulties or embarrassments in the administration in bankruptcy of a railway company, owing to the nature of the property, and this might suggest reasons for excepting such corporations from the act, or for providing a special mode of proceeding; but it affords no sufficient grounds for a forced construction of the present statute so as to exclude such corporations from the scope of its operation."

Thus, insurance corporations, excepted by the Amendment of 1910, were held subject to bankruptcy under the law of 1867.[34]

Thus, banking corporations, excepted by the Amendment of 1910, would but for that exception, otherwise be subject to bankruptcy.[35]

Doubtless, steamship and steamboat companies, canal corporations and express companies are subject to voluntary and involuntary bankruptcy under the Amendment of 1910.

Compare obiter (1867) Sweatt v. Boston, H. & E. R. Co., 5 Bankr. Reg. 234, Fed. Cas. No. 13,684: "Steamship and steamboat companies, when incorporated and engaged in accomplishing the purpose for which they are created, and canal corporations not of a public character, are undoubtedly commercial corporations within the meaning of that phrase as employed in the Bankrupt Act, and as such are clearly subject to the provisions contained in § 39 of the same act. Created as railways are for the same general purpose as the other corporations named, they are legally known by the same denomination and are properly included in the same classification. All such corporations transact immense amounts of business, and may, perhaps, in view of that fact, be well enough called business corporations, but their true legal and constitutional denomination, in the opinion of the court, is that of commercial corporations, as they are erected for the purpose of transporting passengers and freight, which is a commercial business, as it involves intercourse and an interchange of commodities. Commerce among the states, as well as foreign commerce, is subject to the

33. Adams v. Boston, H. & E. Ry. Co., 4 Nat. Bankr. Reg. 314, 5 Am. Law Rev. 375, Fed. Cas. No. 47, quoted supra; In re California Pacific Ry. Co., 11 Nat. Bankr. Reg. 93, Fed. Cas. No. 2315; Sweatt v. Boston, H. & E. Ry. Co., 5 Nat. Bankr. Reg. 234, Fed. Cas. No. 13,684 quoted post, this section.

34. Compare, In re Independent Ins. Co., 6 Nat. Bankr. Reg. 200, Fed. Cas. No. 7017; In re Hercules Mut. Life Assur. Soc., 6 Nat. Bankr. Reg. 338, Fed. Cas. No. 6,402; In re Merchants' Ins. Co., 6 Nat. Bankr. Reg. 43; S. C., Biss. 162; Hill v. Reed (N. Y.), 16 Barb. 287.

35. Compare Gillett v. Moody, 3 N. Y. 479; Robinson v. Bank of Ithaca, 21 N. Y. 406; Mut. Ins. Co. v. Erie County Supervisors, 4 N. Y. 442; Talmadge v. Peel, 7 N. Y. 347; Hobbs v. National Bank of Commerce, 101 Fed. Rep. 75.

regulation of congress, and it is well settled law that the word 'commerce' includes navigation as well as traffic, and that the power to regulate extends to the vehicles of intercourse as well as to the commodities to be exchanged."

It will be observed with regard to the voluntary bankruptcy of corporations, that the Amendment of 1910 is broader than the old law of 1867, inasmuch as *any* corporation, "except a municipal, railroad, insurance or banking corporation," may, under the Amendment of 1910, petition for its own adjudication as bankrupt, whether or not it be a "moneyed, business or commercial corporation," whilst, under the old law of 1867, only "moneyed, business or commercial corporations" could do so; and yet, on the other hand, the Amendment of 1910, so far as relates to the involuntary bankruptcy of corporations, is not so broad as the old law of 1867 because it excepts "municipal, railroad, insurance and banking corporations."

Thus, it is possible that an educational institution, although neither a "moneyed, business or commercial corporation," may voluntarily petition for its own adjudication as bankrupt, under the Amendment of 1910, though not subject to involuntary bankruptcy.[36]

"Municipal corporations" are towns, cities, counties, parishes and the like, which are created and continued for public purposes.[37]

A corporation created for the purpose of carrying on any lawful business defined by its charter and clothed with power so to do, for the sake of gain, is a "business corporation," and amenable to the provisions of the Bankruptcy Act.[38]

But, of course, a corporation cannot be adjudged bankrupt if, under the law of the state, it is not permitted to incur indebtedness. In such case those dealing with the corporation must take notice of this limitation on its powers, and should they extend credit their claims would not be provable in bankruptcy.[39]

§§ 81 to 94 Inclusive. Jurisdiction over Corporations before Amendment of 1910.—The rules and decisions taken up with the definitions and distinctions originally imposed by the law of 1898 upon bankruptcy jurisdiction over corporations are no longer of importance.[40]

SUBDIVISION "D."

CHANGE OF DEBTOR'S CLASS; DEATH OR INSANITY; DISSOLUTION OF CORPORATION.

§ 95. Change of Debtor's Class after Commission of Act but before Filing of Petition.—Of course where a person belongs to one of the

36. Compare McLeod *v.* Lincoln Med. Col. of Cotner University (Nebr.), 96 N. W. Rep. 266.

37. Compare, impliedly (1867), Sweatt *v.* Boston, H. & E. R. Co., 5 Nat. Bankr. Reg. 234, Fed. Cas. No. 13,684.

38. In re Radke Co., 27 A. B. R. 950,

193 Fed. 735 (D. .C. Cal.).

39. In re Wyoming Valley Assn., 28 A. B. R. 462, 198 Fed. 436 (D. C. Pa.).

40. Volumes I and III of the first edition of "Remington on Bankruptcy," §§ 81 to 94 inclusive, may be referred to on this subject.

exempted classes both at the time he commits the act of bankruptcy and also at the time the petition is filed against him, no question can arise; no jurisdiction exists to declare him bankrupt.[41] Likewise no question exists where he belongs to a class not exempted from bankruptcy at both times; he is undoubtedly subject thereto.[42] Interesting questions arise, however, where a farmer or wage earner commits an act of bankruptcy and thereafter ceases to belong to one of the exempted classes, and also where one, subject to being proceeded against in bankruptcy, commits an act of bankruptcy, but, before the petition is actually filed against him, becomes a farmer or wage earner or dies or becomes insane. The law says a wage earner or farmer shall not be proceeded against. Shall the debtor thus escape and the creditors be thus frustrated? Will the court refuse to take jurisdiction because he is now a farmer or wage earner, so long as he was not a member of one of the exempted classes when he committed the act of bankruptcy? Likewise, shall his subsequent death or insanity frustrate creditors? And, on the other hand, if exempted from bankruptcy when he committed the act, will his later transfer to one of the nonexempt classes subject him thereto?

The general rule undoubtedly is that jurisdiction depends upon the state of things at the time the action is commenced.[43]

If at the time the debtor committed the act of bankruptcy he was a farmer or wage earner or otherwise not subjected to bankruptcy, but subsequently ceases to belong to an exempted class, the bankruptcy court will not, on that account, refuse jurisdiction.[44]

In re Matson, 10 A. B. R. 473, 123 Fed. 743 (D. C. Pa.): "No doubt the respondent, as the owner of a farm and lately engaged in its cultivation, would in common parlance, be classed as a 'farmer.' But while he still owns his farm and resides upon it, he has leased it for the current year on a money rent to his son, and had at the time the petition in bankruptcy was filed against him."

Obiter, Tiffany v. Condensed Milk Co., 15 A. B. R. 418 (D. C. Pa.): "This is not to deny the force of those cases which hold that where a person ceases to belong to one of the excepted classes, he becomes liable according to the class in which he is found at the time proceedings are instituted."

But if at the time the debtor committed the act of bankruptcy he belonged to one of the classes of those subject to bankruptcy, the court will not refuse to take jurisdiction, although at the time the petition was filed he had come to belong to one of the privileged or exempted classes.[45]

41. In re Pilger, 9 A. B. R. 244, 118 Fed. 206 (D. C. Wis.).

42. Instance, In re Charles L. Leland, 25 A. B. R. 209, 185 Fed. 830 (D. C. Mich.).

43. Mollan v. Torrance, 9 Wheat 537; In re Pilger, 9 A. B. R. 244, 118 Fed. 206 (D. C. Wis.).

44. Hoffschlæger Co. v. Young Nap, 12 A. B. R. 523 (D. C. Hawaii). Compare, In re Pilger, 9 A. B. R. 244, 118 Fed. 206 (D. C. Wis.).

45. Obiter, In re Pilger, 9 A. B. R. 246, 118 Fed. 206 (D. C. Wis., citing Everett v. Derby, Fed. Cas. No. 4,576); In re Naroma Chocolate Co., 24 A. B. R. 154, 178 Fed. 382 (D. C. R. I.).

Flickinger v. Nat'l. Bk., 16 A. B. R. 680, 145 Fed. 162 (C. C. A. Ohio): "A majority of the court is inclined to think that the statute should be regarded as having reference to the conditions existing at the time when the act of bankruptcy is committed."

Obiter, In re Mackey, 6 A. B. R. 577, 110 Fed. 355 (D. C. Del.): "No construction of the Bankruptcy Act is admissible which would permit an insolvent person, who had committed an act of bankruptcy within four months next preceding the filing of the petition, to evade the provisions of the statute, by engaging in farming after the commission of the act and before the filing of the petition."

Such also were the holdings in two cases where merchants, and in one case where a manufacturer, committed an act of bankruptcy, but each became a farmer before the petition was filed against him.[46]

In re Luckhardt, 4 A. B. R. 307, 101 Fed. 807 (D. C. Kas.): "The right of the creditor to proceed against his debtor within the four months limited after the commission of an act of bankruptcy, cannot be defeated by the debtor within that period changing his occupation to one of those exempted from involuntary proceedings by § 4 (b)."

In re Burgin, 22 A. B. R. 574, 173 Fed. 726 (D. C. Ala.): "The act itself does not otherwise specify the time when the status of the bankrupt is to be determined. Some of the district courts have construed it to refer to the time of the commission of the act of bankruptcy rather than of the filing of the petition, going upon the idea that the law should not be so construed as to permit the bankrupt, by a change of occupation between the commission of the act of bankruptcy and the filing of the petition, to defeat the operation of the law. The same reasoning would seem to demand a construction of the law that would prevent the bankrupt from incurring debts and acquiring assets in a non-exempt occupation, and then by ceasing to do business in such occupation, and engaging in an exempt occupation, and thereafter committing an act of bankruptcy, to defeat the operation of the law. This construction would require that the status of the bankrupt in this respect be determined as of the period during which he was engaged in the business in which he contracted the debts, and acquired or owned the assets subject to administration."

Compare, even broader rule, obiter, Tiffany v. Condensed Milk Co., 15 A. B. R. 417 (D. C. Pa.): "The principle to be deduced from them is clear. The liability of a person, whether natural or artificial, to bankruptcy is to be judged by the character of the pursuit in which such person was engaged at the time the debts due the petitioning creditors were incurred; with respect to which it may be conceded, that, as to a corporation, its actual business is to be considered, and not that which it might possibly have undertaken by virtue of authorized but unexercised powers."

And in other cases where merchants became wage earners.[47] On the other hand, in general, it is the actual occupation at the time of the filing

---

46. Flickinger v. Nat'l Bk., 16 A. B. R. 680, 145 Fed. 162 (C. C. A. Ohio). **Burden of Proof of Bankrupt's Status on Petitioning Creditors.**—The burden of proof of the bankrupt's status, whether he belong to a class of debtors subject to bankruptcy, is upon the petitioning creditors. In re Burgin, 22 A. B. R. 574, 173 Fed. 726 (D. C. Ala.).

47. In re Crenshaw, 19 A. B. R. 502, 156 Fed. 638 (D. C. Ala.); In re Naroma Choc. Co., 24 A. B. R. 154, 17 Fed. 382 (D. C. R. I.).

of the bankruptcy petition and for a reasonable period prior thereto that is to govern, not the occupation at a remote period.[48]

And one who continues in the exempt occupation cannot be adjudged bankrupt because of any act committed by him while so occupied even though the indebtedness charged in the petition in bankruptcy was incurred while he was in a non-exempt occupation.

In re Folkstad, 29 A. B. R. 77, 199 Fed. 363 (D. C. Mont.): "The law of bankruptcy is what Congress has made it, and not what expediency and convenience might desire it. The statute is clear and unambiguous. It declares that certain persons, having committed an 'act of bankruptcy', may on petition filed within four months thereafter be adjudged involuntary bankrupts. It expressly excepts persons engaged chiefly in farming or tillage. The effect is that these excepted persons cannot commit an 'act of bankruptcy'. An act is an 'act of bankruptcy' for the reason that he who commits it can because thereof be adjudicated an involuntary bankrupt.

"It is an 'act of bankruptcy' when the act is committed, or not at all. If the act is committed by one who then is not of the class that the law says may be adjudicated an involuntary bankrupt, it is not an 'act of bankruptcy,' and furnishes no foundation for involuntary proceedings.

"No former occupation can make the act of an exempt person an 'act of bankruptcy'. No subsequent change of occupation can deprive the act of a non-exempt person of its quality as an 'act of bankruptcy.' The act takes color only from the bona fide occupation of the actor at the time it is committed, and not from his occupation prior or subsequent thereto. Otherwise, a farmer of ten years' standing might be adjudicated an involuntary bankrupt because of debts incurred prior thereto in the vocation of merchant. By analogy, in reference to the time when insolvency is material, see West Co. v. Lea, 174 U. S. 598, 2 Am. B. R. 463.

"One who incurs debts in a non-exempt occupation, changes to an exempt occupation, and thereafter commits an act that in a non-exempt occupation would be an 'act of bankruptcy' is not subject to adjudication of involuntary bankruptcy because thereof, and of such debts still existing, or at all."

Likewise, where a debtor has both exempt and non-exempt occupations and contracts debts in one non-exempt occupation and acquires property in another he cannot escape bankruptcy on the ground of being at the same time a member of an exempt class, such as a wage earner.

In re Wakefield, 25 A. B. R. 118, 182 Fed. 247 (D. C. Cal.): "The reasoning which justifies a construction of the statute which will not permit an individual who has acquired property and incurred debts as a merchant to avoid bankruptcy by becoming a wage earner, either before or after an act of bankruptcy, applies with equal force to one who contracts debts in one non-exempt occupation, acquires property in another, and seeks to avoid an application of the statute to such debts and property by claiming that the act of bankruptcy was committed while he was a wage earner."

§ 96. **Death or Insanity after Commission of Act but before Filing of Petition.**—On the other hand, if a debtor belonging to one of the

48. In re Interstate Paving Co., 22 A. B. R. 572, 171 Fed. 604 (D. C. N. Y.).

enumerated classes subject to being proceeded against commits an act of bankruptcy but dies before the petition is filed against him, the court will refuse jurisdiction.[49]

Obiter, In re Hicks, 6 A. B. R. 183, 107 Fed. 910 (D. C. Vt.): "Valid proceedings cannot be begun against the estate of a deceased person, but only against the person and property of the living."

The ruling would be the same, it would seem on principle, if he become insane.[50] It must not be thought, however, that these rulings would be inconsistent, for the court would refuse jurisdiction in cases where the debtor dies or becomes insane before the petition is filed, simply because the court is not given jurisdiction over the estates of decedents or persons non compos mentis.[51] Were the bankruptcy courts given such jurisdiction, then doubtless the intervening death or insanity of the debtor would not affect the jurisdiction. Moreover, a contrary ruling would open the door to great frauds by permitting the most flagrant acts of bankruptcy to be committed by a debtor without remedy if he thereupon becomes a wage earner or farmer. The distinction seems also to be based somewhat on the fact that death and insanity are not within the debtor's control, whilst the other changes of class are more or less voluntary.

But, on the other hand, there is apparent authority in support of the contention that, unless there be an adjudication of insanity at the date of the commission of the act, jurisdiction will not be defeated by insanity intervening before the filing of the petition.

Obiter, In re Kehler, 19 A. B. R. 513, 159 Fed. 55, 20 A. B. R. 669, 162 Fed. 674 (C. C. A. N. Y.): "The district judge correctly states the proposition as follows: 'True, an insane person cannot commit an act of bankruptcy, but if Kehler was compos mentis at the time the acts were committed, the petition of the creditors being filed before he was adjudged insane, I think the court acquired jurisdiction of the proceedings.' "

In re Kehler, 18 A. B. R. 596, 153 Fed. 235 (D. C. N. Y., affirmed in 19 A. B. R. 513, 159 Fed. 55, 20 A. B. R. 669, 162 Fed. 674): "Counsel for the general guardian of the lunatic place stress upon In re Funk (D. C.), 4 Am. B. R. 96, 101 Fed. 244, where it was broadly held that a court of bankruptcy will not entertain jurisdiction of a petition by creditors to have a person adjudged a bankrupt who prior to the filing of such petition had been regularly and duly adjudged insane. In that case, however, the court expressed the opinion that in cases where the insanity had not been adjudged, and creditors sought the adjudication of the bankrupt, a court of bankruptcy might properly exercise jurisdiction and could hold the party responsible for acts committed prior to

49 See In re Pierce, 4 A. B. R. 489, 102 Fed. 977 (D. C. Wash.); [1867] Adams v. Terrell (C. C.), 4 Fed. 796.
50. Compare ante, § 54. See In re Funk, 4 A. B. R. 96, 101 Fed. 244 (D. C. Iowa). Compare, In re Stein & Co., 11 A. B. R. 536, 127 Fed. 547 (C. C. A. Ills.). See authorities cited in In re Burka, 5 A. B. R. 844, 104 Fed.

326 (D. C. Tenn.). But compare, In re Kingsley, 20 A. B. R. 427, 760 Fed. 275 (D. C. Vt.), where the court even held, that with the guardian's consent, he could acquire a new residence in another state, such guardianship disability not being recognized there.
51. In re Eisenberg, 8 A. B. R. 551, 117 Fed. 786 (D. C. N. Y.).

the ascertainment of his mental incapacity. This principle, in which I concur, would seem to justify a continuance of this proceeding. In re Eisenberg (D. C.), 8 Am. B. R. 551, 117 Fed. 786, the court declined to entertain jurisdiction in proceedings in bankruptcy instituted by the committee of a lunatic on the ground that he was not a qualified person to perform the duties required of him by the provisions of the Bankruptcy Act."

But if one of the partners of a bankrupt partnership is insane or dead at the time of the filing of the petition, the jurisdiction of the bankruptcy court over the partnership would not be defeated.[52]

§ 97. Dissolution of Corporation, or Its Ceasing Business, before Petition Filed.—A corporation's ceasing to do business after the commission of an act of bankruptcy does not defeat bankruptcy proceedings, as not being "principally engaged" in any business.[53]

Logically the dissolution of a corporation after its commission of an act of bankruptcy and before the filing of the petition would defeat the jurisdiction of the bankruptcy court. Being no longer a corporation it could not be a bankrupt corporation.

However, where such dissolution is a mere incident to a winding up of the corporate affairs, and the collection and distribution of its assets, such dissolution will not defeat the jurisdiction, the fiction of corporate entity giving way to the reality of business needs.[54]

In re Storck Lumber Co., 8 A. B. R. 86, 114 Fed. 860 (D. C. Md.): "The question raised by this motion to quash is not clear of difficulty, but it seems that it must be solved by applying the broad principle that the National Bankrupt

---

52. In re Stein & Co., 11 A. B. R. 536, 127 Fed. 547 (C. C. A. Ills.). Compare, In re Ives, 7 A. B. R. 692, 113 Fed. 911 (C. C. A. Mich.).

53. In re Moench & Sons Co., 12 A. B. R. 240, 123 Fed. 965 (C. C. A. N. Y.). Obiter, Tiffany v. Condensed Milk Co., 15 A. B. R. 417 (D. C. Pa.). But compare ante, § 35. See, as to possible effect of change of classification of corporations subject to bankruptcy introduced by Amendment of 1910, ante, § 80, it being no longer necessary to show the corporation to be "principally engaged." Obiter, Ballinger v. Nat'l Bank, 24 A. B. R. 44, — Fed. — (C. C. A. Calif.).

54. Compare, Scheuer v. Book Co., 7 A. B. R. 384, 112 Fed. 407, where the intervening dissolution of a corporation was held analogous to the intervening death of a natural person, after the filing of the petition. Obiter, Tiffany v. Condensed Milk Co., 15 A. B. R. 417 (D. C. Pa.). Compare, where, subsequent to the state insolvency proceedings an additional act of bankruptcy, by way of "written admission,

etc.," was committed, Coal & Coke Co. v. Stauffer, 17 A. B. R. 573 (C. C. A. Pa., affirming In re International Coal Min. Co., 16 A. B. R. 312, 143 Fed. 665, D. C. Pa.); White Mountain Paper Co. v. Morse, 11 A. B. R. 633, 127 Fed. 643 (C. C. A., affirming In re White Mountain Paper Co., 11 A. B. R. 491).

Dissolution by Governor's Proclamation for Nonpayment of Taxes— Entity Still Exists for Purpose of Winding Up.—Where a corporation has been dissolved by proclamation of the governor for nonpayment of taxes, its entity is still in existence for the purpose of winding up and it may by resolution declare its inability to pay its debts and willingness to be judged bankrupt. In re Munger Vehicle Tire Co., 19 A. B. R. 785, 159 Fed. 901 (C. C. A. N. Y., affirming 19 A. B. R. 914, 159 Fed. 901).

Obiter, Ballinger v. Nat'l Bank, 24 A. B. R. 44, — Fed. — (C. C. A. Calif.). Compare analogous proposition in In re Electric Supply Co., 23 A. B. R. 649, 175 Fed. 612 (D. C. Ga.).

Law is to govern the administration of the estates of all insolvent debtors who are within its provisions, and supersedes all the State laws having the like object, when its provisions are invoked by the requisite creditors, and acts of bankruptcy are proven. The Maryland statute for winding up insolvent corporations is in the nature of a proceeding in insolvency. * * * The National Bankrupt Act of 1898 superseded the State insolvent laws, and now, when commercial and manufacturing corporations are so numerous, and are sometimes used, as in this case, more as a cover from individual liability than for more legitimate uses, it can scarcely be supposed, as the Bankrupt Act especially provides for proceedings against commercial corporations, that it was intended that such a corporation could commit acts of bankruptcy, and escape the provisions of the Bankrupt Act by applying to be wound up under the State statute, and thus defeat the operation of the Bankrupt Law."

In re International Coal Min. Co., 16 A. B. R. 312, 143 Fed. 665 (D. C. Pa.): "To concede the contention of the respondent here, that the sale of the property of the alleged bankrupt by the sheriff of Philadelphia county on this peculiar writ worked a dissolution of the corporation so that proceedings in bankruptcy could not be instituted against it, would 'result in the anomalous situation that the commission of an act of bankruptcy would prevent the bankrupt act from taking effect'. But even under the act of 1870 the corporate existence does not entirely disappear upon the sale of the property and franchises upon an execution under that act, because the act 'excepts lands held in fee' from sale on the special fi. fa., 'which must be proceeded against and sold in the manner provided for in cases for the sale of real estate.' The title to this excepted real estate must remain in the corporation until sold, and a dissolution cannot take place so long as this asset exist, even under that act. But even if this were not so, the Bankrupt Act would so far control the matter of dissolution of the insolvent corporation as to prevent its legal extinction by superseding all State laws in conflict with its provisions to an extent necessary to enable creditors of insolvent corporations to have the assets of their insolvent debtor administered in accordance with its terms."

Inferentially, In re Storm, 4 A. B. R. 601, 102 Fed. 618 (D. C. N. Y.): "It is contended on the part of the alleged bankrupt that the voluntary proceedings for the dissolution of the corporation vacated the preference, while it is urged on the part of the petitioner that the proceedings confirmed the preference inasmuch as the lien created by the levy upon personal property would be confirmed. The levy of the execution created a lien, and the attention of the court is called to no statute providing that the voluntary proceedings should discharge the lien. The alleged bankrupt contends that voluntary proceedings taken by a corporation for dissolution extinguish the liens of all levies on executions. But it is not thought that a corporation may in such manner escape a levy upon its property. Hence it is concluded that the alleged bankrupt suffered numerous judgments to be entered against it, executions to be issued thereon, levy to be made, and property to be advertised for sale, and before the sale took proceedings calculated to continue the benefit of the levy. The act of bankruptcy was committed, and this court has jurisdiction to proceed with the administration of the estate."

In re Adams & Hoyt Co., 21 A. B. R. 161, 164 Fed. 489 (D. C. Ga.): "Assuming that the Adams & Hoyt Company, while insolvent, within four months prior to the filing of the petition in bankruptcy, committed certain acts of bankruptcy, I do not believe that it could escape and avoid the jurisdiction of the bankruptcy court by instituting a proceeding such as was instituted by this company in the superior court. The jurisdiction of the bankruptcy court attached, or its right to act arose, when the company, being insolvent, committed the acts of bankruptcy. Any other view of the matter would destroy the effect of the Bankruptcy Act entirely. It is the paramount law for the administration of estates of insolvents. Its provisions, which seek to bring about equality among creditors of the same class, cannot be avoided in this way. The effect of proceedings such as were instituted by this corporation in the superior court, if sustained, would be that an insolvent corporation could, in clear and gross violation of the Bankruptcy Act, transfer all of its property to one or more of its creditors, to the exclusion of all of its other creditors, and the corporation would thereby create a preference or preferences which would undoubtedly be set aside under the Bankruptcy Act, but the corporation would avoid the operation and effect of the Bankruptcy Act by this new method of procedure. The right of the bankruptcy court to take charge of the corporation's effects and to administer the same in accordance with the Bankruptcy Act, thereby bringing about equality of payment among creditors of the class, arose and was in existence at the time the petition in the superior court was filed. It still exists unaffected, in my judgment, by what was done in the superior court."

And it has even been held that the ceasing to do business before the commission of the act of bankruptcy will not defeat the jurisdiction.[55]

§ 97½. Assets in Hands of Receiver or Assignee No Defense.—

It is no defense to an act of bankruptcy that the assets are already sequestered by the state court nor that the state court's custody of the assets cannot be superseded by that of the bankruptcy court: the question is one of the commission of an act of bankruptcy, not one of the custody of the property in the event of adjudication.[56] However, such facts may have bearing upon the jurisdictional question, in cases of corporations, of their being principally "engaged in" one or the other of the jurisdictional occupations.[57]

§ 98. Death or Insanity after Filing of Petition, No Abatement.—

If, however, after the petition is filed, the debtor dies or becomes insane, the Bankruptcy Court does not lose jurisdiction, but proceeds as if he were still alive and clothed with full reason.[58]

Such would probably be the ruling in the absence of statute, but § 8 expressly provides that:

"The death or insanity of a bankrupt shall not abate the proceedings, but the same shall be conducted and concluded in the same manner, so far as possible, as though he had not died or become insane."

55. Robertson v. Union Potteries Co., 22 A. B. R. 121, 177 Fed. 279 (D. C. Ga.).

56. In re Sterlingworth Ry. Supply Co., 21 A. B. R. 341, 164 Fed. 591 (D. C. Pa.).

57. See ante, §§ 35, 97.

58. See ante, §§ 54, 96. In re Spalding, 14 A. B. R. 129, 134, 139 Fed. 243 (C. C. A. N. Y., reversing, on other grounds, 13 A. B. R. 223, D. C. N. Y.); In re Hicks, 6 A. B. R. 182, 107 Fed. 910 (D. C. Vt.). No abatement of involuntary proceedings by death of bankrupt after petition filed and before adjudication. Shulte v. Patterson, 17 A. B. R. 99 (C. C. A. Iowa). Obiter, In re Benedict, 15 A. B. R. 238, 140 Fed. 55 (D. C. Wis.). In re Risteen, 10 A. B. R. 494, 122 Fed. 732 (D. C. Mass.). Compare, under law of 1867, Frazier v. McDonald, 8 N. B. R. 237, Fed. Cas. No. 5,073. In re Larkin, 21 A. B. R. 711, 168 Fed. 100 (D. C. N. Y.); Partridge v. Andrews, 27 A. B. R. 388, 191 Fed. 325 (C. C. A. N. Y.).

And this is so, even though the subpœna has not been served.[59]

Shulte *v.* Patterson, 17 A. B. R. 99 (C. C. A. Iowa): "It is not denied that the provision of the Bankruptcy Act in respect of the death of the bankrupt prevents the abatement of a proceeding which has once been commenced and is pending, but it is said that it does not apply in a case which, although the petition has been filed, process has not been served upon the bankrupt. But here again we are met with the express provision of the Act that, when the petition is filed, that is the commencement of the proceedings; and when proceedings have been commenced they must be said to be pending. In actions that do not abate by the death of the defendant, and the one before us is of that character, it is not always necessary to their continuance that service of process shall have been previously made upon the defendant."

Thus, his right to a discharge will not be affected by his death;[60] nor by his becoming insane;[61] but, in the latter instance, a guardian ad litem should be appointed for him.[62]

§ 99. Rights of Widow and Children on Bankrupt's Death after Filing of Petition and before Adjudication.

—If the bankrupt die, after the filing of the petition but before adjudication, his widow and children will be entitled to the usual allowances:[63]

Proviso of § 8: "Provided, that in case of death, the widow and children shall be entitled to all rights of dower and allowance fixed by the laws of the state of the bankrupt's residence."

Section 8 of the act has been wrongfully construed to mean that, even after adjudication of bankruptcy and after the election of a trustee and when the estate is fully launched in the process of administration, if the bankrupt die, at once the further administration is to be changed so as to allow the widow and children their year's support, etc.;[64] provided the assets have not already been distributed.[65]

As to dower the situation is clear, for dower is an inchoate estate or interest likely to ripen into consummation at any time, and the assets come into the bankruptcy court already burdened therewith.[66] Dower rights are not lost by virtue of bankruptcy proceedings;[67] except as to personalty allowed by stat-

---

59. Compare, "Commencement of Proceedings," post, § 306, et seq.

60. Obiter, In re Miller, 13 A. B. R. 345 (D. C. Pa.).

61. In re Miller, 13 A. B. R. 345 (D. C. Pa.).

62. In re Burka, 5 A. B. R. 843, 107 Fed. 674 (D. C. Tenn.).

63. Compare, In re Dobert & Son, 21 A. B. R. 634, 165 Fed. 749 (D. C. Tex.), where, in accordance with State law, the court refused the widow's and children's allowances out of partnership assets.

64. In re Parschen, 9 A. B. R. 389, 119 Fed. 976 (D. C. Ohio); In re Newton, 10 A. B. R. 345, 122 Fed. 103 (D. C. Conn.); In re Dicks, 28 A. B. R. 845, 198 Fed. 293 (D. C. Ga.).

65. Inferentially, In re Slack, 7 A. B. R. 121, 111 Fed. 523 (D. C. Vt.). But. contra, see In re Seabolt, 8 A. B. R. 57, 113 Fed. 766 (D. C. N. C.).

66. See post, § 1166½. In re McKenzie, 15 A. B. R. 683, 142 Fed. 383 (C. C. A. Ark.); Thomas *v.* Woods, 23 A. B. R. 132, 178 Fed. 1005 (C. C. A. Kans.), quoted at § 1166½.

67. See § 1166½. In re Slack, 7 A. B. R. 121, 111 Fed. 523 (D. C. Vt.). Obiter, Hurley *v.* Devilin, 18 A. B. R. 627, 151 Fed. 919 (D. C. Kans.); Thomas *v.* Woods, 23 A. B. R. 132, 178 Fed. 1005 (C. C. A. Kans.), quoted at § 1166½.

ute "as part of dower," which will not be allowed if the bankrupt does not die until after adjudication.[68]

But as to the newly arising right to the widow's allowance, as held by these decisions, much confusion results.

A logical consequence of these rulings—In re Parschen, In re Newton, In re Dicks and In re Slack—would seem to be that both the bankrupt could have his exemptions and then, dying, his widow would have her widow's allowance, in addition to dower. Certainly, the title to exempt property never passes, so the exempt property may not be retained by the trustee even though not formally set apart until after the bankrupt's death, but must be delivered to the deceased bankrupt's representatives, for the trustee has title only *as of the date of the adjudication* and at that date the bankrupt was alive and entitled to the exemptions claimed. How these rulings can be harmonized with the usual procedure in cases of assigned estates is hard to discover. Title passes to the trustee as of the date of the adjudication. On that date the wife had inchoate dower right but no right to allowances. Now, according to the disapproved cases, owing to the happening of this subsequent contingency of death, the title thus already conveyed to the trustees is pro tanto defeated.

Pratt *v.* Bothe, 12 A. B. R. 533, 130 Fed. 670 (C. C. A. Ky.): "The Bankruptcy Act makes a final and sharply defined line in respect of the power of the bankrupt over his estate and the distribution of it as of the date of the filing of the petition against him. From that time his assets are in gremio legis, and he cannot, unless he compounds with his creditors, bind his assets. He may, of course, make new contracts and incur new obligations, but they are not chargeable to the funds which have become vested in the trustee until they have subserved the purpose of the bankruptcy proceedings, when, if anything remains, he acquires it."

Subsequent death of the assignor does not accomplish so much in cases of general assignments for the benefit of creditors. Moreover, the rule would not work uniformly. In estates where the trustee had been quick in distributing the assets or the bankrupt slow in dying, the widow would not get her allowance;[69] unless the trustee should sue the creditors, each for his pro rata share of the amount distributed. Furthermore, who is to fix the amount of the widow's allowance? Certainly not the bankruptcy court, for it has not the machinery. If it is to be fixed by the probate or surrogate court, then suppose it is fixed at so high a figure that the bankruptcy trustee would not have funds enough to pay it, as actually occurred in the Parschen case?

All these difficulties indicate that the decisions In re Parschen, In re Newton and In re Dicks do not state the true rule, even as inferentially modified by the decision in In re Slack, denying the right where all the assets have been distributed. The phrase, "the proceedings shall not abate," has refer-

68. In re McKenzie, 13 A. B. R. 227, 132 Fed. 986 (D. C. Ark.).

69. Inferentially, In re Slack, 7 A. B. R. 121, 111 Fed. 523 (D. C. Vt.).

ence exclusively to the pendency of a petition before adjudication, not to
the administration of an estate the title to which has already irrevocably
passed to creditors by virtue of the adjudication.

§ 100. Their Rights Where Death Occurs after Adjudication.—

The true rule is that, if the death of the bankrupt occur after the adjudication, the widow and children may not claim allowances out of the bankrupt
estate; their only right is to go into the State Court and get their allowance
there out of whatever estate the bankrupt had at the time of his death, including any unused exempt property.[70]

In re Seabolt, 8 A. B. R. 57, 113 Fed. 766 (D. C. N. C.): "The question then
remaining in this regard is whether Seabolt, having died after the proceedings
in bankruptcy were commenced, and after the consent of the partners was had
for exemptions from the partnership effects, the allotment which he would have
taken had he lived vests in his administrator. It is my opinion that it does. A
creditor pursuing a debtor by execution or other legal proceeding, for the purpose of subjecting his property to the payment of his debt, does not acquire a
lien upon that part of the debtor's personalty which is exempted by the law.
The exemption in North Carolina is in favor of a debtor against execution for
debt.

"The purpose of the law undoubtedly is to save the exempted property from
sale at the hands of creditors, for the benefit of the debtor and his family. This
is no doubt the humane object which the framers of our constitution and the
makers of our exemption laws had in view. A statute of exemption is properly
a remedial statute, evidently intended to prevent families from being stripped
of their last means of support, and left to suffer, or cast as a burden upon the public, and to rescue them from the hands of unfeeling creditors. Leavitt v. Metcalf,
19 Am. Dec. 718. It would be a strange construction of the law, therefore, to
hold that, whilst the exemption would obtain against what is known as an
execution, or other final process issued for the collection of a debt, it could still
be swept away by another proceeding on the part of creditors, and the debtor
and his family thus be deprived of its benefits. The right to the exemption
accrued to the debtor when the creditors instituted proceedings in bankruptcy
to subject his property to the payment of his debts, and upon the appointment
of a trustee in bankruptcy the title of the property reserved by the law as the
debtor's exemption did not vest in such trustee, but remained in the debtor,
awaiting the mere legal formality of having it appraised and set apart to him.
This being the case, the exempted property which would have been set apart and
allotted to Seabolt had he lived remained a part of his estate at his death, and
belongs to his administrator, and not to the trustee in bankruptcy; * * *
Therefore, when the administrator of Seabolt has in hand the money paid to
him by the trustee for the personal exemption, so much of it as is necessary
can be set apart as a year's support to the widow by a proceeding in the State
court under the statute providing for such cases."

In re McKenzie, 15 A. B. R. 684, 142 Fed. 383 (C. C. A. Ark., affirming 13 A. B.

---

70. Contra, In re Newton, 10 A. B.
R. 345, 122 Fed. 103 (D. C. Conn.); also
contra, In re Parschen, 9 A. B. R. 389,
117 Fed. 976 (D. C. Ohio). In re Dicks,
28 A. B. R. 845, 198 Fed. 293 (D. C.
Ga.). Compare, In re Slack, 7 A. B.
R. 121, 111 Fed. 523 (D. C. Vt.), where
the decision denying the allowance is
based on the fact that all assets had
already been distributed, and on the
law of Vermont that all debts are first
to be paid and the allowance to be
granted only out of the surplus.

R. 227): "Clause 5 of § 70 (a) defines the property to which the trustee in bank-ruptcy took title in this case and hence it is the only one that it is necessary for us to consider. * * * While she has an inchoate right of dower in the real estate of her husband while living, she has no right whatever in his personal property until his death. Her interest in the latter does not accrue until he dies, and then it attaches to the personal property of which he was seized or possessed at his death, only."   * *

"The adjudication in bankruptcy and the appointment and qualification of the trustee, disseised and dispossessed the bankrupt of all his personal estate not exempt from execution long before his death. Since at the time of his death he was neither seised nor possessed of any of it, the logical and unavoidable conclusion is that his widow had no right of dower or other interest in it under this statute, and her claim to it cannot be sustained. So are the decisions of the highest judicial tribunal of Arkansas whose construction of these statutes of that State is, upon familiar principles, controlling in this case. In cases wherein the debtor died while he was the owner and in possession of personal estate, the claim of the widow to one-third of it has been sustained by the court and declared to be superior to that of his creditors. * * *

"But in cases where the husband died after he had parted with the title or possession of his personal property the claim of the widow to a right of dower or other interest therein under the statutes of Arkansas, superior to that of his creditors, was denied on the ground that ownership and possession at the time of the death of the husband were indispensable conditions of the maintenance of such a claim."

In re McKenzie, 13 A. B. R. 227 (D. C. Ark., affirmed in 15 A. B. R. 679): "But it is claimed by counsel for the widow that the Bankruptcy Act extends the right of a widow to dower to the time the personalty of the estate is actually distributed, and that in contemplation of law the bankrupt is seised and pos-sessed of the bankrupt estate, for the purpose of the widow's dower, until the proceeds are actually distributed among the creditors.

"If this proviso were to be considered regardless of any of the other provi-sions of the Bankruptcy Act or the provisions of the former bankruptcy acts, there might be some reason for this contention; but it is a well settled rule of law that in construing any section of a statute the intention of the legislature must be gathered from the entire Act, and every part of it must be taken into consideration, and comparison may also be made with statutes in pari materia. Kohlsaat v. Murphy, 96 U. S. 153, 24 L. Ed. 844.

"The Bankruptcy Act of 1841 contained a similar provision as to the rights of wives in relation to dower. Section 2 of the Act, ch. 9, 5 Stat. 442.

"In Worcester v. Clark, 2 Grant Cas. (Pa.) 84, the Court had held in con-struing that Act, that this proviso alone saved the right of dower, but this was expressly overruled by the Supreme Court in Porter v. Lazear, 109 U. S. 84, 89, where the court say:

"Upon this question of construction we are not bound by the opinion of the State court, and have no hesitation in disapproving the dictum, and in holding that the proviso ruled on was not in the nature of an exception to, or restric-tion upon, the operative words of the act, but was a mere declaration, inserted for greater caution, of the construction which the act must have received with-out any such proviso, and that the omission of the proviso in the recent Bank-rupt Act (referring to the Act of 1867), does not enlarge the effect of the as-signment or of the sale in bankruptcy, so as to include lawful rights which be-long, not to the bankrupt, but to his wife.'

"Section 70 of the present Act vests the title of the bankrupt's estate in the trustee as of the date he was adjudged a bankrupt. Under the Act of 1867 (Rev. St., § 5044), the title of the bankrupt's estate, which vested in the assignee, related back to the filing of the petition. Section 8 of the present Act, provides that: 'The death or insanity of a bankrupt shall not abate the proceedings, but the same shall be conducted and concluded in the same manner, so far as possible, as though he had not died or become insané.'

"Under the Bankruptcy Act of 1867 (Rev. St., § 5090), the proceedings in bankruptcy would abate upon the death of the insolvent if it occurred prior to the issuing of the warrant. As the bankrupt may die after the filing of the petition before there is an adjudication, and consequently before the title to the estate becomes vested in the trustee, under the provisions of § 70, and the proceedings would not abate by reason of the death, there might have been some question as to whether the widow would be entitled to dower in the personalty of her husband under a statute such as is in force in the State of Arkansas. To remove all doubts on this subject this provision was undoubtedly enacted."

§ **101. Dissolution of Corporation after Filing of Petition.**—Section 8 has been held applicable, by analogy, to corporations. The dissolution of a corporation decreed by the State Court, after the filing of the petition in bankruptcy, will not abate the proceedings in bankruptcy, this being ruled in analogy to the principle of § 8.[71]

§ **101½. Burden of Proof of Debtor's Class.**—The burden of proof that a debtor is not a farmer or wage earner is upon the petitioning creditors;[72] or that it belongs to a class of corporations subject to bankruptcy.[73]

Walker Roofing Co. v. Mer. & Evans Co., 23 A. B. R. 185, 173 Fed. 771 (C. C. A. Va.): "The burden is on the petitioner in a proceeding of this character to show by a preponderance of the evidence that the company conducted a business which could be properly termed 'manufacturing', 'trading' or 'mercantile.'"

And it is to be established by a fair preponderance of the evidence.[74]

---

71. White Mountain Paper Co. v. Morse, 11 A. B. R. 633, 127 Fed. 643 (C. C. A. N. H., affirming In re White Mountain Paper Co., 11 A. B. R. 491); In re Burgin, 22 A. B. R. 574, 173 Fed. 726 (D. C. Ala.), quoted on analogous proposition at § 95.

72. In re Burgin, 22 A. B. R. 574,

173 Fed. 176 (D. C. Ala.).

73. In re H. R. Elec. Power Co., 23 A. B. R. 191, 173 Fed. 934 (D. C. N. Y.).

74. In re H. R. Elec. Power Co., 23 A. B. R. 191, 173 Fed. 934 (D. C. N. Y.); Walker Roofing Co. v. Mer. & Evans Co., 23 A. B. R. 185, 173 Fed. 771 (C. C. A. Va.), quoted at § 94.

CHAPTER IV.

ACTS OF BANKRUPTCY.

Synopsis of Chapter.

DIVISION 4.

SUBDIVISION "A".

SUBDIVISION "B."

DIVISION 5.

§ 102. No Act Requisite in Voluntary Bankruptcy—Petition Itself Act of Bankruptcy.

—Voluntary bankruptcy need not be based on the commission of an act of bankruptcy, or, rather, the act of bankruptcy upon which it is based is the written admission contained in the voluntary petition itself of the bankrupt's inability to pay his debts and his desire to be adjudged bankrupt for that cause, such written admission itself constituting the fifth class of acts of bankruptcy enumerated in the statute.[1]

National Bk. v. Moyses, 8 A. B. R. 10, 186 U. S. 181: "The petition must state that 'petitioner owes debts which he is unable to pay in full' and that 'he is willing to surrender all his property for the benefit of his creditors, except such as is exempt by law.' This establishes those facts so far as a decree of

---

1. See post, § 164. In re Fowler,   tine Co., 1 A. B. R. 372, 89 Fed. 691
Fed. Cas. No. 4,998; Blake v. Valen-   (D. C. Calif.).

bankruptcy is concerned, and he has committed an act of bankruptcy in filing the petition."

In re Forbes, 11 A. B. R. 791, 128 Fed. 137 (D. C. Mass.): "A voluntary petition is itself treated as an act of bankruptcy."

Contra (that it is not in itself an act of bankruptcy), obiter, In re Ceballos & Co., 20 A. B. R. 459, 161 Fed. 445 (D. C. N. J.): "It is important, in considering the cases decided under the Act of 1867, to bear in mind the provisions of that act. Section 11 expressly provided that the filing of a voluntary petition should be an act of bankruptcy. The present Bankruptcy Act contains no such provision. The filing of the voluntary petition in bankruptcy, under the present law, is not an act of bankruptcy. It simply institutes a proceeding in which the court acquires jurisdiction to adjudge bankruptcy if the facts warrant adjudication. It follows that the filing of a petition by one partner against his copartners cannot be deemed an act of bankruptcy on the part of the partnership." But this case totally ignores the fact that the insertion of the Fifth Act of Bankruptcy under the present statute, an act of bankruptcy not appearing in the Act of 1876, renders unnecessary any specific mention of the filing of the voluntary petition as an act of bankruptcy. And the decision is obiter, because the partnership was actually adjudged bankrupt without finding any other act of bankruptcy to have been committed by it.

§ 103. But Requisite in Involuntary Bankruptcy.—But involuntary bankruptcy must be based on the commission of an act of bankruptcy, and what constitutes such act is prescribed by statute.

Not even every person nor corporation nor partnership included in the various classes heretofore considered as being subject to involuntary bankruptcy, may be forced into bankruptcy. Other conditions must also, at the same time, exist. Such person or corporation or partnership must have committed what is termed an act of bankruptcy.

The Bankruptcy Act was not intended to cover all cases of insolvency, but only such cases as are within its provisions.[2]

Singer v. Nat'l Bedstead Co., 11 A. B. R. 279 (N. J. Ch.): "The present 'system of bankruptcy,' which Congress saw fit to enact in 1898, does not pretend to cover the whole field of either voluntary or involuntary bankruptcy and insolvency."

Thus, the mere fact that an individual or copartnership refuses or is unable to pay his or its debts is not an act of bankruptcy, although it may be evidence of insolvency. .

Davis v. Stevens, 4 A. B. R. 763, 104 Fed. 235 (D. C. S. Dak.): "It might be evidence of insolvency, but the mere fact that an individual or copartnership refuses to pay his or its debts is not an act of bankruptcy."

And the statute specifies what acts constitute acts of bankruptcy.

Bankr. Act, § 3 (a): "Acts of bankruptcy by a person shall consist of his having (1) conveyed, transferred, concealed or removed or permitted to be con-

---

2. In re Wilmington Hosiery Co., 9 A. B. R. 581, 120 Fed. 179 (D. C. Del.). Also, see ante, §§ 10, 21.

cealed or removed, any part of his property with intent to hinder, delay or defraud his creditors or any of them; or,

"(2) transferred, while insolvent, any portion of his property to one or more of his creditors with intent to prefer such creditors over his other creditors; or,

"(3) suffered or permitted, while insolvent, any creditor to obtain a preference through legal proceedings, and not having at least five days before a sale or final disposition of any property affected by such preference, vacated or discharged such preference; or,

"(4) made a general assignment for the benefit of his creditors, or being insolvent, applied for a receiver or trustee for his property, or because of insolvency a receiver or trustee has been put in charge of his property under the laws of a State, of a Territory or of the United States, or,

"(5) admitted in writing his inability to pay his debts and his willingness to be adjudged a bankrupt on that ground."

DIVISION 1.

FIRST ACT OF BANKRUPTCY; TRANSFERS, CONCEALMENTS AND REMOVALS WITH INTENT TO HINDER, DELAY AND DEFRAUD.

§ 104. First Act of Bankruptcy—Fraudulent Transfers, Removals and Concealments.—A debtor has committed an act of bankruptcy if within four months preceding the filing of the petition against him he has conveyed, transferred, concealed or removed or permitted to be concealed or removed any part of his property with intent to hinder, delay or defraud his creditors or any of them, such four months not expiring until four months from the date of recording or registering, where recording or registering is required or permitted, or where not so required or permitted, then from the date of taking notorious, exclusive and continuous possession.[3]

3. Bankr. Acts, §§ 3 (a) (1); 3 (b). See post, § 185. In re Larkin, 21 A. B. R. 711, 168 Fed. 100 (D. C. N. Y.); In re Duke & Son, 28 A. B. R. 195, 199 Fed. 199 (D. C. Ga.). Distinction between "concealment" and "transfer." Bank v. DePauw Co., 5 A. B. R. 345 (C. C. A. Ills.).

Instances of transactions held to hinder, delay and defraud creditors under the first class of acts of bankruptcy:

Discounted notes paid before maturity and the greater part of the debtor's property transferred to certain preferred creditors. In re T. & J. Farrell, 9 A. B. R. 341 (Ref. N. Y.).

Violation of sales of merchandise stock in bulk law. In re T. & J. Farrell, 9 A. B. R. 341 (Ref. N. Y.).

Payment of individual debt out of partnership funds. In re Gillette, 5 A. B. R. 119, 104 Fed. 769 (D. C. N. Y.).

Absconding debtor running away to avoid criminal prosecution and carrying with him assets not exempt from execution. In re Filer, 5 A. B. R. 332, 108 Fed. 209 (D. C. N. Y.).

Chattel mortgage made within the four months for a present loan to prefer certain creditors, of which purpose mortgagee had notice or reasonable grounds of inference, is in bad faith and constitutes an effort to hinder and delay creditors under § 3 (1). Obiter, In re Pease, 12 A. B. R. 66, 129 Fed. 446 (D. C. Mich.).

Assignment of individual assets of partners in bank partnership to receiver of the firm already in charge of the firm assets. In re Salmon & Salmon, 16 A. B. R. 126, 143 Fed. 395 (D. C. Mo.).

Instances of transactions held not to hinder, delay or defraud under the first class:

Mortgage covering all debtor's property, but sufficient equity left to

§ 105. Is Historically Original Act.—The first of these classes, namely, the class consisting of transfers, concealments and removals of property, with intent to hinder, delay or defraud creditors, is the only one that is not of comparatively modern origin. This class might, indeed, be denominated the original class, for it will be remembered that the first bankruptcy act of England, the Statute of King Henry VIII (see Introd., § (g), p. 5), only mentioned as its object those "divers and sundry persons who craftily obtaining in their hands great substance of other men's goods, do suddenly flee to parts unknown to keep their houses, not minding to pay or restore to any of their creditors their debts or duties."

§ 106. Same as Reprobated at Common Law or by Stat. Eliz.— Class 1 of Acts of Bankruptcy (save and except as to the four months' limitation) is also the same class reprobated at Common Law and by the Statute of Elizabeth, as being transfers, concealments or removals of property made with intent to hinder, delay or defraud creditors.[4]

Lansing Boiler Works *v.* Ryerson, 11 A. B. R. 558, 128 Fed. 701 (C. C. A. Mich.): "It is to be observed that subsection 1 of § 3 of the Bankrupt Act makes those conveyances, which, by the common law and the statute of Elizabeth, were held void, because fraudulent, a ground for adjudicating the grantor a bankrupt. * * * The language of subsection 1 of § 3 is the familiar language of statutes against conveyances fraudulent as against creditors, and we think there can be no doubt that Congress intended the words employed should have the same construction and effect as have for a long period of time been attributed to those words."

Some decisions erroneously speak of "frauds on the Bankruptcy Act" as being acts of bankruptcy although falling short of the ordinary definitions of what constitutes a hindering, delaying or defrauding of creditors.[5] But the courts may not create an act of bankruptcy not specified in the statute.

The rules of law relative to what acts are comprehended within this class 1 of acts of bankruptcy, namely, as to what amount to conveyances, transfers, concealments and removals of property made with intent to hinder, delay or defraud creditors, are to be ascertained from the decisions of each state upon the subject of transfers, concealments and removals of property made with intent to hinder, delay or defraud creditors, at any rate where not modified by statute from what constituted such fraud at common law. And so

take care of remaining creditors. Lansing Boiler & Eng. Wks. *v.* Ryerson, 11 A. B. R. 558 (C. C. A. Mich.).

Evidence too vague. In re Foster 11 A. B. R. 131, 126 Fed. 1014 (D. C. Pa.).

As to form and sufficiency of allegations under class 1 of Acts of Bankruptcy, see post, "Parties and Petition in Involuntary Bankruptcy," Chap. VI.

4. Githens *v.* Shiffler, 7 A. B. R. 453,

112 Fed. 505 (D. C. Pa.). Obiter, In re Bloch, 15 A. B. R. 751, 142 Fed. 674 (C. C. A. N. Y.); Rumsey *v.* Machine Co., 3 A. B. R. 704, 99 Fed. 699 (D. C. Mo.); Coder *v.* Arts, 22 A. B. R. 5, 213 U. S. 223, quoted at § 1498. Contra, In re Salmon & Salmon, 16 A. B. R. 127, 143 Fed. 395 (D. C. Mo.).

5. Rumsey *v.* Novelty Co., 3 A. B. R. 704, 99 Fed. 699 (D. C. Mo.).

this class will need no further explanation here. It must not be understood from this, however, that the class is of comparative unimportance; on the contrary, this class has always been reckoned one of the gravest and most frequently occurring acts of bankruptcy, and is therefore properly placed first in the list of them.

§ 107. Meaning of "Removed."—Thus, the word "removed" signifies here an actual or physical change in the position or locality of the property.[6]

§ 108. Meaning of "Permit."—Thus, also, one does not "permit" a removal who has neither power nor right to prevent it;[7] nor where the removal was done without the debtor's knowledge or collusion.[8]

§ 108½. Meaning of "Conceal."—To conceal is to hide or withdraw from observation; to cover or keep from sight; to prevent discovery or to withhold knowledge. Thus, a bankrupt conceals assets where he evinces an indisposition to disclose his real financial condition, as well as where he keeps his assets beyond the reach of his creditors.[9]

§ 109. Actual Intent to Defraud Necessary.—An actual intent to hinder, delay or defraud creditors, etc., must be proved.[10] But the statute being in the disjunctive, it is not necessary that the intent be an intent to defraud; it will be sufficient if there be an actual intent to hinder or delay.[11]

Such intent involves a purpose wrongfully or unjustifiably to prevent, obstruct, embarrass or postpone them in the collection or enforcement of their claims.[12]

Lansing Boiler Works v. Ryerson, 11 A. B. R. 561, 128 Fed. 701 (C. C. A. Mich.): "For it is the well settled law that a conveyance made in good faith whether for an antecedent or present consideration is not forbidden by such statute, notwithstanding the effect may be that it hinders or delays creditors by removing from their reach assets of the debtor."

Thus, an intent to avoid distribution in the bankruptcy court and to bring about a distribution in the state court is not an intent to hinder, delay or defraud.[13]

In re Wilmington Hosiery Co., 9 A. B. R. 581, 120 Fed. 179 (D. C. Del.): "Where an insolvent corporation, against which a bill was filed alleging its

6. In re Wilmington Hosiery Co., 9 A. B. R. 581, 120 Fed. 179 (D. C. Del.).
7. In re Wilmington Hosiery Co., 9 A. B. R. 581, 120 Fed. 179 (D. C. Del.).
8. Obiter, In re Belknap, 12 A. B. R. 326, 129 Fed. 646 (D. C. Pa.).
9. In re Glazier, 28 A. B. R. 391, 195 Fed. 1020 (D. C. Pa.).
10. In re Wilmington Hosiery Co., 9 A. B. R. 581, 120 Fed. 179 (D. C. Del.). Impliedly, In re Belknap, 2 A. B. R. 326, 129 Fed. 646 (D. C. Pa.); In re

McLoon, 20 A. B. R. 719, 162 Fed. 575 (D. C. Me.); Coder v. Arts, 22 A. B. R. 1, 213 U. S. 223, quoted at § 1498.
11. In re Hughes, 25 A. B. R. 556, 183 Fed. 872 (D. C. N. Y.).
12. In re Wilmington Hosiery Co., 9 A. B. R. 581, 120 Fed. 179 (D. C. Del.). Instance, In re Minard, 19 A. B. R. 485, 158 Fed. 377 (D. C. Ore.).
13. Contra, Rumsey v. Machine Co., 3 A. B. R. 704, 99 Fed. 699 (D. C. Mo.).

insolvency and praying the appointment of a receiver made answer admitting its insolvency, and a receiver was thereupon appointed who took possession of its property, the corporation did not thereby permit its property to be removed, with intent to hinder or delay its creditors, or any of them within the meaning of section 3a (1) of the Bankruptcy Act."

Contra, In re Salmon & Salmon, 16 A. B. R. 127, 143 Fed. 395 (D. C. Mo.): "Again, although the conveyances in question were undoubtedly made in good faith for the purpose of paying pro rata the debts of the makers, without preference other than the laws of the State provided, and although they might not be avoided at common law for any fraud inhering therein, yet as the making of these conveyances, taken in connection with the transfer of all the property of the bank theretofore made, must inevitably result in hindering and delaying the creditors of the grantors in the collection of their debts, and as the grantors in the making of these conveyances must be presumed to have intended the natural and probable effect of their act, it must be held, as a matter of law, the makers intended thereby to hinder and delay their creditors, and the making thereof constitutes an act of bankruptcy."

Nor is an intent to use the proceeds of a cash sale of all one's property to pay certain creditors in preference to others, a fraudulent intent, although it may be a preferential intent;[14] nor is a sale made by an insolvent to raise money to pay off a creditor who is threatening criminal proceedings and who eventually does reject payment and institute criminal proceedings show such intent;[15] nor does the removal of goods by a creditor in the bankrupt's absence without legal proceedings and without the bankrupt's collusion, constitute removal by the bankrupt with intent to defraud.[16] Much less is a fraudulent intent proved where a mortgage was given to raise money to pay to all creditors.[17]

But such intent may exist and the transfer be voidable as to creditors even though full consideration was paid.[18]

Obiter, In re Pease, 12 A. B. R. 66, 129 Fed. 446 (D. C. Mich.): "Even though a present, fair consideration be paid for property transferred to the hindrance, delay of or in fraud upon creditors, it will not save the conveyance. 'A sale may be void for bad faith, though the buyer pays the full value of the property bought.' This is the consequence where his purpose is to aid the seller in perpetrating a fraud upon his creditors, and where he buys recklessly or with guilty knowledge."

Obiter, In re Smith, 23 A. B. R. 864, 176 Fed. 426 (D. C. N. Y.): "So a person may transfer his property for a full and fair consideration, and receive that consideration, but if it is done with intent on his part to hinder, delay or defraud his creditors, the one making the transfer has committed an act of bankruptcy."

And such intent must be proved as to the particular transaction impeached.[19]

14. Githens v. Shiffler, 7 A. B. R. 453, 112 Fed. 505 (D. C. Pa.); In re Belknap, 12 A. B. R. 326, 129 Fed. 646 (D. C. Pa.).

15. In re Belknap, 12 A. B. R. 326, 129 Fed. 646 (D. C. Pa.).

16. In re Belknap, 12 A. B. R. 326, 129 Fed. 646 (D. C. Pa.).

17. In re McLoon, 20 A. B. R. 719, 162 Fed. 575 (D. C. Me.).

18. Coder v. Arts, 22 A. B. R. 1, 213 U. S. 223, quoted at § 1498.

19. Hoffschlæger Co. v. Young Nap, 12 A. B. R. 524 (D. C. Hawaii).

The badges of fraud must be considered all together, not separately; for frequently, if separately considered, they are inconclusive, whilst, if considered together, they may, by their number and joint operation, forge an invulnerable chain of proof of fraudulent intent.[20]

Failure to file a mortgage may be a badge of a fraudulent intent participated in by the mortgagee; but it is rebuttable and may be explained away.[21]

§ 110. Proof of Intent Aided by Presumptions.—The existence or absence of intent to hinder, delay or defraud may be aided by presumptions.

§ 111. Thus, Presumption against Fraud.—Thus, the presumption is against fraud.[22]

Davis *v*. Stevens, 4 A. B. R. 763, 104 Fed. 235 (D. C. S. Dak.): "In the absence of proof as to when and how assets were lost, the presumption is against fraud."

§ 112. Thus, Natural and Probable Consequences of Act Raise Presumption.—But an actual intent to defraud will be presumed when one does an act which he knows will produce that result, or the natural and necessary effect of which is to produce it.[23]

Bean-Chamberlain Mfg. Co., *v*. Standard Spoke & Nipple Co., 12 A. B. R. 610 (C. C. A. Mich.): "For the court to have complied with the request of the appellant, and instructed the jury that, ignoring the natural and necessary result of the transfers made, they should direct their attention solely to the good faith of the transaction, and, whatever the result of its conduct, acquit the appellant if they found it had acted in good faith, would have been misleading. It was the right of the jury to determine the intent, but in doing so it was the duty of the jury to consider the testimony and the natural presumptions which flow from acts done by design. If a company in failing circumstances wilfully places all its property beyond the reach of its creditors, that circumstance is a fact to be considered in determining whether it did so in good faith, without any intent to hinder, delay, or defraud its creditors."

Obiter, In re Pease, 12 A. B. R. 67, 129 Fed. 446 (D. C. Mich.): "The act of the debtor being a preference, his intent is inferable from his act."

But it must be proved that the debtor had knowledge of the essential facts which tended to produce the resulting consequences, else the presumption does not arise.[24]

Where proof is first made that the debtor was insolvent and was remov-

---

20. See post, §§ 1216½, 1496½; Houck *v*. Christy, 18 A. B. R. 330, 152 Fed. 612 (C. C. A. Kans.).

21. In re McLoon, 20 A. B. R. 719, 162 Fed. 575 (D. C. Me.).

22. Instance, In re Hallin, 28 A. B. R. 708, 199 Fed. 806 (D. C. Mich.).

23. In re Wilmington Hosiery Co., 9 A. B. R. 581, 120 Fed. 179 (D. C. Del.); Hoffschlaeger Co. *v*. Young Nap, 12 A. B. R. 521 (D. C. Hawaii); In re Salmon & Salmon, 16 A. B. R. 127, 143 Fed. 395 (D. C. Mo.); (1867) In re Black-Secor, 1 Nat. Bank Reg. 361. See citations under corresponding proposition relative to second act of bankruptcy, post, §§ 117 and 132. Also, rule applied in opposition to discharge. In re Nelson, 23 A. B. R. 37, 179 Fed. 320 (D. C. N. Y.).

24. Compare, to this effect, In re McLoon, 20 A. B. R. 719, 162 Fed. 575 (D. C. Me.).

ing his property out of the jurisdiction, it then rests upon the respondent to disprove the intent by satisfactory explanation.[25]

But the mortgaging of all one's property to a few creditors does not alone afford conclusive and irrebuttable presumption of intent to hinder and delay creditors within the meaning of the law.

Landsing Boiler Works v. Ryerson, 11 A. B. R. 560 (C. C. A. Mich.): "The court erred in assuming that because the mortgage covered the whole property of the debtor it necessarily followed that a case was made out under subsection 1 and that no proof of good faith could prevail against that assumption. Upon the vital question of the bona fides of the mortgage it was of importance to consider among other things, what was the value of the property mortgaged when compared with the indebtedness of the company."

Nor does a sale out of the usual course of business, alone raise a presumption of fraudulent intent.[26]

§ 113. Fraudulent Intent Distinguished from Preferential Intent.
—A fraudulent intent is to be distinguished from a preferential intent.[27]

Obiter, In re Belknap, 12 A. B. R. 329, 129 Fed. 646 (D. C. Pa.): "The intent to defraud is essential under this clause, and differs from the intent to prefer, which is essential to the act of bankruptcy described in § 3 (a) (2)."

Thus, a cash sale for full consideration by an insolvent debtor of all his property, where his intent was not to get the property away from all creditors but simply to use the proceeds in paying certain creditors in preference to all others, is not a fraudulent transfer, although the effect is to leave nothing for the remaining creditors.[28]

§ 114. Participation of Transferee in Fraudulent Intent Requisite.
—Participation of the transferee in the fraudulent design must be shown, in accordance with the usual rules as to fraudulent transfers.[29]

25. Hoffschlaeger Co. v. Young Nap, 12 A. B. R. 517, 521 (D. C. Hawaii).

26. Obiter, Houck v. Christy, 18 A. B. R. 330, 152 Fed. 612 (C. C. A. Kans.).

27. See post, §§ 1221, 1498. See citations in corresponding propositions under second act of bankruptcy, post, § 117. Baden v. Bertenshaw, 11 A. B. R. 308, 68 Kas. 32; In re Mingo Valley Creamery Ass'n, 4 A. B. R. 67, 100 Fed. 282 (D. C. Pa.). Obiter, In re Duffey, 9 A. B. R. 360, 118 Fed. 926 (D. C. Pa.). Impliedly, Manning v. Evans, 19 A. B. R. 217, 156 Fed. 106 (D. C. N. J.); Coder v. Arts, 22 A. B. R. 1, 213 U. S. 223; (Van Iderstine) Trustee v. Nat'l Discount Co., 23 A. B. R. 345, 174 Fed. 518 (C. C. A. N. Y.).

28. Githens v. Shiffler, 7 A. B. R. 453, 112 Fed. 505 (D. C. Penn.): But no showing appears to have been made in Githens v. Shiffler that the purchaser participated in the intent, yet this fact would hardly be sufficient to distinguish the case from In re Pease, 12 A. B. R. 66 (D. C. Mich.). It might have been a preferential transfer, if not a fraudulent transfer.

29. Declarations of Alleged Fraudulent Vendor—Whether Competent to Impeach Transfer.—As to whether declarations of the alleged fraudulent vendor made after the transfer are competent to impeach the transfer, compare, In re Foster, 11 A. B. R. 133, 126 Fed. 1014 (D. C. Pa.): "It may, perhaps, be true that declarations concerning the financial relation between Frank and himself, although made after the deed was delivered, are evidence in this issue between the bankrupt and the petitioning creditors. Upon this point the referee cited Johnson v. Wald, 2 Am. B. R. 84; but an examination of the report will show that it has no value as an authority. Evidence of

Thus, notice to the president of a creditor bank has been held to be notice to the bank.[30]

§ 114½. Great Latitude in Evidence Proper.—Great latitude in the admission of evidence is proper.

In re Luber, 18 A. B. R. 476, 152 Fed. 492 (D. C. Pa.): "In the investigation of questions of fraud, as a rule, great latitude is allowed in the admission of evidence, in order that the jury may be able to determine from all the circumstances whether the transaction was fraudulent or not. Questions of fraud can scarcely ever be proven by direct evidence, hence the necessity for the admission of all the circumstances fairly connected with the transaction."

Impliedly, In re Larkin, 21 A. B. R. 711, 168 Fed. 100 (D. C. N. Y.): "Where a person in debt transfers or conveys his property, all the surrounding circumstances and conditions under which it is done are to be considered in determining whether or not it was done with intent to hinder, delay or defraud his other creditors. The intent may be inferred from the acts done and the circumstances surrounding the transactions."

§ 115. Act to Be within Preceding Four Months.—The act of fraud must have occurred within the preceding four months.[31]

§ 116. Insolvency of Debtor Not Requisite, Prima Facie.—Insolvency of the debtor need not be shown by creditors under the first act of bankruptcy in order to make a prima facie case;[32] but if the debtor prove solvency, it is a complete defense, by statutory provision.[33]

DIVISION 2.

SECOND CLASS OF ACTS OF BANKRUPTCY—PREFERENTIAL TRANSFERS AND JUDGMENTS.

§ 117. Second Act of Bankruptcy—Preferences.—The second, and all the other four classes of acts of bankruptcy enumerated in the statute, are outgrowths of the wants of the business world of the present time, and are of comparatively recent development, answering to the demands of

similar declarations was no doubt received at the trial of that case, but there was no dispute concerning the fact that the vendee was a creditor, and the declarations were received without objection. In the Circuit Court of Appeals only one question was raised, and that concerned a different matter. But even if such declarations are evidence in an issue like this, the value of the testimony is evidently not great, and it certainly should be scanned with much care, especially since it stands alone without corroborating testimony. A peculiar result of sustaining the referee's finding might be, that in a suit by the trustee in bankruptcy against Frank, the bankrupt's declarations made after the transfer could not be heard to affect his vendee's title, unless, perhaps, collusion were first shown (Grimes Co. v. Malcolm, 164 U. S. 490; Padgett v. Lawrence, 40 Am. Dec. 232, note, and Horton v. Smith, 42 Am. Dec. 632), and we should have the anomaly of a cloud upon the vendee's title that depended solely upon evidence that could not be heard."

30. In re Gillette, 5 A. B. R. 119, 104 Fed. 769 (D. C. N. Y.).

31. See post, § 182, et seq.

32. In re Larkin, 21 A. B. R. 711, 168 Fed. 100 (D. C. N. Y.). See Bankr. Act, § 3 (c), (2). Also, see post, §§ 174, 177, et seq.

33. Obiter, Spencer v. Nekemoto, 24 A. B. R. 517. (D. C. Hawaii), quoted at § 1499½; In re Larkin, 21 A. B. R. 711, 168 Fed. 100 (D. C. N. Y.).

modern commercial life, whose complex and sensitive organization makes it quite as necessary to guard against the more delicate and subtle, but more common forms, of unfair dealings, as against the grosser forms condemned in the first named and original act of bankruptcy. And so, as might be expected, there is not found in them the implication of fraud and moral turpitude that is carried by the first and ruder class, although, of course, fraud and moral turpitude may in fact accompany any of them.

A debtor has committed an act of bankruptcy if (within the four months preceding the filing of the bankruptcy petition) he has transferred, while insolvent, any portion of his property to one or more of his creditors, with intent to prefer such creditor over his other creditors, such four months not expiring until four months from the date of recording or registering, where recording or registering is required or permitted, or where not so required or permitted, then from the date of taking notorious, exclusive and continuous possession.[34]

To be sure, this act does imply, something of unjust dealings; yet, in many if not in most States, until the passage of the National Bankruptcy Act, any insolvent debtor, except perhaps a corporation, was at liberty to pay in full whatsoever creditor he liked, although in so doing nothing might be left for any of the remainder of his creditors.

§ 118. Intent to Prefer and Intent to Defraud Different.—Intent to prefer is to be distinguished from intent to defraud; and a preferential transfer is different from a fraudulent transfer.[35]

§ 119. Definition of Preference.—The question involved in a study of this second and exceedingly important class of acts of bankruptcy, voluntary preferences as they might be termed, will come up again in a more interesting and complete form later on, when the treatment accorded by the bankruptcy law to those creditors who have received preferences is under consideration, in connection with §§ 57 and 60 of the Bankruptcy Act. In order, however, to present the salient features of preferences so that we may carry an idea of what is meant by this second class of acts of bankruptcy, it is proper to note the following definition and propositions:

A preference is a transfer made or seizure by legal proceedings procured or suffered by an insolvent debtor of some part of his property, the effect of which is to enable a creditor to obtain a greater proportion of his debt than some other creditor of the same class of priority.

---

34. Bankr. Act, § 3 (a) (2). In re Duke & Son, 28 A. B. R. 195, 199 Fed. 199 (D. C. Ga.).

35. See post, §§ 1221, 1498. See post, "Ninth Element of Voidable Preference," § 1397. Also, see ante, § 113. Baden v. Bertenshaw, 11 A. B. R. 308 (Sup. Ct. Kan.); In re Mingo Valley Creamery Ass'n, 4 A. B. R. 67, 100 Fed. 282 (D. C. Pa.). Obiter, In re Duffey, 9 A. B. R. 360, 118 Fed. 926 (D. C. Pa.); Githens v. Shiffler, 7 A. B. R. 453, 112 Fed. 505 (D. C. Pa.); In re Belknap, 12 A. B. R. 326, 129 Fed. 646 (D. C. Pa.). Impliedly, Manning v. Evans, 19 A. B. R. 217, 156 Fed. 106 (D. C. N. J.); Coder v. Arts, 213 U. S. 223, 22 A. B. R. 1; (Van Iderstine) Trustee v. Nat'l Discount Co., 23 A. B. R. 345, 174 Fed. 518 (C. C. A. N. Y.).

§ 120. All Elements of Preference Must Exist.—All the elements of a preference must exist and in addition thereto the transfer must have been made with the debtor's intent to prefer.[36] The literal reading of the statute might leave in doubt whether a preference in fact must be proved to have resulted so long as it is proved that the insolvent has transferred "any portion of his property" "with intent to prefer;" but the intent to prefer may not be inferred from a transfer which does not in fact create an actual preference, and if no actual preference exists, the intent to prefer becomes immaterial.[37]

§ 121. Thus, Depletion of Insolvent Estate Implied.—Thus, first, some portion of the debtor's property must have been appropriated by the transaction to the payment of a claim, and the insolvent estate thereby correspondingly diminished, preference implying the depletion of the insolvent fund.[38]

Naylou & Co. v. Christiansen Co., 19 A. B. R. 789, 158 Fed. 290 (C. C. A. Mich.): "Clause (2) of the third section of the Bankrupt Act * * * declares it to be an act of bankruptcy when the person has 'transferred, while insolvent, any portion of his property to one or more of his creditors with intent to prefer such creditors over his other creditors.' To fulfill these conditions three things must concur: The bankrupt must have transferred some part of his property to his creditors; he must have been insolvent at the time; and he must have intended, in doing it, to prefer those creditors over others. The record shows beyond doubt that the alleged bankrupt transferred some of its property to some of its creditors and that it had other creditors."

And appropriation without depletion is not sufficient.[39] But the depletion may be accomplished by indirect means as well as by direct means, as, for instance, by a transfer to a third party for the benefit of the creditor.[40]

§ 122. Thus, Fraudulent or Fictitious Debt Not Implied.—Thus, second, the claim upon which the preferential transfer is made, may be, and

---

36. Instance, In re Pure Milk Co. of Mobile, 18 A. B. R. 735, 154 Fed. 459 (D. C. Ala.).

37. Elements to be proved according to the summary, more or less complete, laid down in the case, In re Rome Planing Mills, 3 A. B. R. 123 (D. C. N. Y.): "In order to make out a case in an involuntary bankruptcy proceeding based on subd. 2, § 3, the petitioners must prove first, a transfer of the debtor's property to a creditor; second, the debtor's intent to prefer such creditor; third, the insolvency of the debtor at the date of the transfer."

38. In re McGee, 5 A. B. R. 262, 105 Fed. 895 (D. C. N. Y.), a transfer of accounts to third party to sell and raise money to retire an outstanding obligation. Troy Wagon Works v.

Vastbinder, 12 A. B. R. 352 (D. C. Pa.), a transfer of notes taken for goods sold to creditor originally selling the same goods although original sale claimed to be a case of consignment and not of sale.

39. Martin v. Hulen, 17 A. B. R. 510 (C. C. A. Mo.). Instance, In re Perlhefter & Shartz, 25 A. B. R. 576, 177 Fed. 299 (D. C. N. Y.).

40. In re McGee, 5 A. B. R. 262, 105 Fed. 895 (D. C. N. Y.); Goldman v. Smith, 1 A. B. R. 266, 93 Fed. 182 (D. C. Ky.), which was a case of transfer to pay one who guaranteed overdrafts that were used to prefer. See, further, the corresponding proposition under the subject of voidable preferences, post, § 1278, et seq.

usually is, the genuine claim of a bona fide creditor, a preference implying a debt and not a fraudulent or fictitious transaction.[41]

§ 123. Thus, Creditor's Claim Must Be Pre-Existing Debt.—Thus,

third, the creditor's claim must have a debt, a pre-existing debt, and the transfer will not amount to a preference if made contemporaneously with the rising of the claim, preference implying a preceding credit.[42]

Thus, agreements for liens, made at the time of the passing of the original consideration, if valid as equitable assignments as against creditors under State law, and not requiring record or registry, will be held to be equitable assignments in bankruptcy.[43]

Thus, where the bankrupt, in purchasing a stock of goods, gave a chattel mortgage thereon, covering all additions, and immediately consolidated therewith his old stock, it was held to be contemporaneous, or, at any rate, no depleting of the assets.[44]

§ 124. Thus, Transfer by Debtor Requisite.—Thus, fourth, the

debtor must have made a "transfer" of property (or, perhaps, have "permitted" or "suffered" the creditor to obtain the judgment whose enforcement would have operated to appropriate property of the debtor), preference implying a change of title in the form known as a transfer, namely, by the voluntary action of the debtor, or, perhaps, a seizure by legal proceedings assented to by the debtor.[45]

The word "transfer" is used in its most comprehensive sense and is intended to include every means and manner in which property can pass from the possession and ownership of another, and includes sales and every other and different mode of disposing of or parting with property, or the possession of property, absolutely or conditionally, as a payment of money, pledge, mortgage, gift or security.[46]

Thus, the voluntary confession of judgment in favor of certain creditors

41. Compare, In re O'Donnell, 12 A. B. R. 621, 131 Fed. 150 (D. C. Mass.). In this case, the court held the assignment of money due under building contract made to secure an accommodation indorser was a preference. See, further, the corresponding proposition under the subject of voidable preferences, post, § 1279, et seq.

42. Bankr. Act § 60 (a); In re Flint Hill Stone & Const'n Co., 18 A. B. R. 83 (D. C. N. Y.). See citations and propositions under the subject of voidable preferences, post, §§ 1314, et seq.

43. Wilder v. Watts, 15 A. B. R. 57, 138 Fed. 426 (D. C. S. C.). See post, § 1370, et seq.

Definition of "Pre-Existing Debt—Antecedent Debt," see post, § 1314.

44. Martin v. Hulen, 17 A. B. R. 510 (C. C. A. Mo.). See citations and

propositions under the subject of voidable preferences, post, § 1276, et seq.

45. Bankr. Act, § 60 (a); In re Riggs Restaurant Co., 11 A. B. R. 508, 130 Fed. 691 (C. C. A. N. Y.). Chattel mortgage. But in New York an attachment is neither a "transfer nor a judgment." In re Schenkein & Coney, 7 A. B. R. 162 (Ref. N. Y.). See citations and propositions under the subject of voidable preferences, post, § 1328, et seq.

46. Bankr. Act, § 1 (a) 25 of the Statute of 1898; Carson, Pirie & Co. v. Trust Co., 182 U. S. 438; Boyd v. Lemon & Gale Co., 8 A. B. R. 81, 114 Fed. 647; In re Riggs Restaurant Co., 11 A. B. R. 508, 130 Fed. 691 (C. C. A. N. Y.), involving a chattel mortgage. In re Edelman, 12 A. B. R. 238, 130 Fed. 700 (C. C. A. N. Y.).

and the permitting of levy and sale thereon, may be a "transfer" under § 3 (a) (2) as well as a "permitting" or "suffering" under § 3 (a) (3).

In re Nusbaum, 18 A. B. R. 598, 152 Fed. 835 (D. C. N. Y.): "When the alleged bankrupt, Philip Nusbaum, being insolvent, voluntarily confessed judgment in favor of certain of his creditors with intent to hinder, delay, and defraud his other creditors, and also with the intent to prefer such creditors over his other creditors, and permitted them, as he knew they would and as they did, to issue executions thereon and levy upon and sell all his property by virtue thereof, and put the proceeds of such sale of such property in their pockets in payment and satisfaction of their respective debts, as he knew they would and intended they should, he transferred same while insolvent, with intent to hinder, delay, and defraud his other creditors, and with intent to prefer the creditors in whose favor he confessed such judgments. It was not a sale by him in form, but it was 'a different mode of disposing of or parting with property, or the possession of property absolutely,' and 'as a security' first, and then, second, 'as a payment' to such preferred creditors. It was an act of bankruptcy under both clause 1 and clause 2 of subdivision 'a' of § 3 of the act, irrespective of clause 3 thereof. It was a 'transfer' within the plain definition of the term found in clause 25 of § 1 of the act. The act of bankruptcy was consummated, the transfer made, when the executions were issued and the sale by virtue thereof actually made, and the petitioning creditors were in time if they filed their petition within four months after such sale, as it is alleged they did. It was a transfer made by the alleged bankrupt who confessed the judgments that executions might be issued, levies made, sales made, and his property or its proceeds conveyed or transferred to his preferred creditors in payment of their debts. It was done to hinder, delay and defraud his other creditors."

And in another case, on demurrer, the court has intimated that the mere suffering of a judgment to be taken may be a "transfer" under § 3 (a) (2).

Obiter, In re Tupper, 20 A. B. R. 824, 163 Fed. 766 (D. C. N. Y.): "She has by such non-action assented to the judgment and preference. The fair inference is that she assents to the lien and desires to aid and take part in preferring these creditors over her other creditors. It may be a fair inference that she has 'transferred' while insolvent by way of security, in one of the modes referred to in subdivision 25 of § 1, this real property to these judgment creditors with intent to prefer such creditors over her other creditors. May not her intent to prefer this mode of transfer and the intent of Pardo & Hogan to obtain and receive and retain a preference be fairly inferred?"

§ 125. Thus, Transfer Must Have Been to Apply on Debt.—Thus, fifth, the transfer must have been made in satisfaction of a debt in whole or in part, and the property must have been sought to be applied on a debt, a preference implying a transfer to satisfy a provable claim.[47]

§ 126. Thus, Debtor Must Have Been Insolvent.—Thus, sixth, the debtor must have been insolvent at the time of the appropriation of the property.[48]

---

47. See citations and propositions under the subject of Voidable preferences, post, § 1339, et seq.

48. Bankr. Act, § 60 (a). See citations and propositions under the subject of voidable preferences, post, §

Troy Wagon Works *v.* Vastbinder, 12 A. B. R. 353, 130 Fed. 232 (D. C. Pa.): "But it is essential to a preference that the debtor should have been insolvent at the time, and unless this appears there is no act of bankruptcy."

§ 127. Must Be within Preceding Four Months or Notorious Possession Be Taken.

—Thus, seventh, the transfer or other appropriation must have been made within the four months preceding the filing of the bankruptcy petition, else it will not constitute an act of bankruptcy.[49] And if the transfer is of a kind requiring recording or registration in order to be valid against third parties, then the four months, it is provided, shall not begin to run until the date of such recording or registration or until the date the transferee shall take continuous, notorious and exclusive possession.[50] What constitutes "notorious, exclusive and continuous possession" depends on the character of the property.[51] Advertisement is not necessary. All the statute requires is that there be no concealment nor effort to prevent its being known.[52] But if the transfer is not of a kind requiring recording or registration, it is valid without record or registry.[53]

So, the fact that the instrument of transfer was executed and delivered within the four months in execution of a prior oral agreement to execute it, does not change the result or prevent the transfer being held a preference.[53a]

§ 128. Must Give Recipient Greater Percentage than Other Creditors.

—Thus, eighth, the effect of the transfer or other appropriation of property must have been to give the creditor receiving it a greater percentage of his claim than some other creditor of the same class in the order of priority, preference implying advantage of one creditor over another.[54]

Thus, where the actual effect was rather to prefer all the other creditors over the one receiving the transfer it will not be a preference, as for instance, where the transfer was by an insolvent debtor to one creditor (a responsible concern), on consideration of the latter's assumption of the former's debts.

1342, et seq. Also see Naylon & Co. *v.* Christiansen Co., 19 A. B. R. 789, 158 Fed. 290 (C. C. A. Mich.); In re Rome Planing Mills, 3 A. B. R. 123 (D. C. N. Y.); In re Morgan & Williams, 25 A. B. R. 861, 184 Fed. 938 (D. C. Ga.); In re Kassel, 28 A. B. R. 233, 195 Fed. 492 (C. C. A. N. Y.).

49. Bankr. Act, § .60 (a). Also, see post, § 1367. See Jones *v.* Coates, 28 A. B. R. 249, 196 Fed. 860 (C. C. A. Mo.).

50. See Bankr. Act, § 3 B; In re Woodward, 2 A. B. R. 233, 95 Fed. 260 (Ref. Tex.).

51. Jones *v.* Coates, 28 A. B. R. 249, 196 Fed. 860 (C. C. A. Mo.).

52. In re Woodward, 2 A. B. R. 233, 95 Fed. 260 (Ref. Tex.).

53. Jones *v.* Coates, 28 A. B. R. 249, 196 Fed. 860 (C. C. A. Mo.), decided under the law of Kansas.

53a. In re Smith, 23 A. B. R. 864, 176 Fed. 426 (D. C. N. Y.), quoted at § 1370, also, on other point at § 130.

54. Bankr. Act, 60 (a); In re Douglass Coal & Coke Co., 12 A. B. R. 539, 131 Fed. 769 (D. C. Tenn.). Compare analogously (but not placed on this ground), Spike & Iron Co. *v.* Allen, 17 A. B. R. 583 (C. C. A. Va.). Also, see post, § 1385, et seq.

Proof of transfer of all assets which are not exempt, leaving some creditors unpaid, is, of course, proof of this element. Gering *v.* Leyda, 26 A. B. R. 137, 186 Fed. 110 (C. C. A. Neb.).

Missouri Elec. Co. *v.* Hamilton Brown Co., 21 A. B. R. 270, 165 Fed. 283 (C. C. A. Mo.): "In this condition of its affairs the Missouri Company on October 17, 1906, in consideration of the release and satisfaction of its debt to the American Company, its largest creditor, and of the agreement of that creditor to pay its other debts out of the proceeds of the property which it assigned, conveyed to the American Company its bills and accounts receivable, its choses in action, and the proceeds of sales made or to be made of its real estate, plant, machinery, stock, chattels, rights, and franchises; and the American Company, in consideration of that conveyance, executed and delivered to the Missouri Company a written satisfaction and discharge of the latter's debt to it. If these writings had the legal effect which they purported to have, they reduced the indebtedness of the Missouri Company $139,018.36, transformed it from an insolvent to a solvent corporation, and left all its property and all the proceeds of its property still available for the discharge of its debts to other creditors. * * * The transaction evidenced by the assignment and the release, therefore, did not have the effect to prefer, nor did it evidence any intention of the debtor to prefer the American Company to its other creditors, but it had the opposite effect. It preferred the other creditors to the American Company."

§ 129. Debtor's Intent to Prefer Requisite.

—There is a final and ninth element requisite to make a preference an act of bankruptcy—the debtor's intent to prefer.[55]

The preference must have been made with the intent on the debtor's part to prefer one creditor over another. If no such extent exists, it is not an act of bankruptcy, although it may be in fact a preference.

In re Gilbert, 8 A. B. R. 101, 112 Fed. 951 (D. C. Ore.): "To authorize an adjudication of bankruptcy it must appear that the transfers of the securities by a debtor within four months of the filing of the petition were made with intent to prefer the creditors to whom they were made."

In re Douglass Coal & Coke Co., 12 A. B. R. 539, 131 Fed. 769 (Ref. Tenn., affirmed by D. C.): "I, nevertheless, do not think that a presumption of intent to prefer should be indulged in against an insolvent debtor by his mere act of paying certain creditors small sums in the usual course of business, and apparently in the effort to keep the business going, unless there is other and further evidence showing specific intent thereby to give such creditors an undue preference over others, although such might be the effect of the payment."

§ 130. Creditor's Intent Immaterial.

—The intent with which the creditor receives the preference is immaterial when it comes to the consideration of the preference as an act of bankruptcy, that is to say, when we come to regard the act as an act of the debtor, although as we shall see later on when we come to consider its effect upon the creditor's rights, the creditor's intent does become material. This distinction must not be lost sight of. But a voluntary preference will amount to an act of bank-

---

55. In re Rome Planing Mills, 3 A. B. R. 123, 96 Fed. 812 (D. C. N. Y.); In re Flint Hill Stone & Construction Co., 18 A. B. R. 81, 84 (D. C. N. Y.). Compare, post, discussion in §§ 1393, 1394. Impliedly, In re Nusbaum, 18 A. B. R. 598, 152 Fed. 835 (D. C. N. Y.), quoted on other points at § 124; In re McLoon, 20 A. B. R. 776, 162 Fed. 575 (D. C. Me.); In re Hammond, 20 A. B. R. 776, 163 Fed. 148 (D. C. N. Y.); In re Hallin, 28 A. B. R. 708, 199 Fed. 806 (D. C. Mich.); In re Truitt, 29 A. B. R. 570, 203 Fed. 550 (D. C. Md.).

ruptcy even though the creditor receiving it may not have known the transfer resulted in a preference at all, and even though he may have been wholly innocent. If the insolvent debtor in making the preferential transfer had the intent to prefer the creditor receiving it over his other creditors, then he has committed an act of bankruptcy. It is the debtor's intent that is material, not the creditor's, in determining whether the preference amounts to an act of bankruptcy.[56]

In re Rome Planing Mills, 3 A. B. R. 123, 99 Fed. 937 (D. C. N. Y.): "The intent which must be shown is that of the debtor. Reasonable cause on the part of the preferred creditor to believe that a preference was intended, is immaterial." In re Wright Lumber Co., 8 A. B. R. 345, 114 Fed. 1011 (D. C. Ark.): "It is not necessary, therefore, in order that the execution of this mortgage be an act of bankruptcy that the claimant, Alphin, knew, or had reasonable grounds to believe, when he accepted the mortgage that the bankrupt intended to prefer him over other creditors." In re Smith, 23 A. B. R. 864, 176 Fed. 426 (D. C. N. Y.): "The intent of the one receiving the deed or mortgage [transfer of property, subdivision 25, § 1, of the act] is entirely immaterial on the question whether or not an act of bankruptcy has been committed." Quoted further at §§ 132, 1370.

§ 131. Proof of Intent to Prefer.—Proof of intent to prefer involves proof of the debtor's knowledge of his own insolvent condition; for unless he knew he was insolvent he could not be presumed to have intended a preference.

Intent to prefer may be shown by circumstantial evidence. "Actions speak louder than words" in proof of intent.[56a] But intent to prefer will not be inferred from the mere making of the transfer or giving of the security, without more.[57] Proof of other preferential transfers at about the same time is evidence of intent to prefer in the case in hand.[58] The fact that there were no other debts then due and payable does not conclusively negative an intent to prefer.[59] Testimony of the debtor himself that he had no such intent is entitled to very little weight.[60] "Intent" is different from "motive."[61] The question of the intent to prefer is for the jury to determine, where a jury has been demanded.[62] "Intent" to prefer may exist although the transfer was made under pressure of coercion, or

56. But see In re Edelman, 12 A. B. R. 238, 130 Fed. 700 (C. C. A. N. Y.), where the act pointed out as indicating the intent was not the act of the debtor at all, but merely that of the creditor —the failure to record a preferential mortgage.

56a. (1867) Traders' Bk. v. Campbell, 14 Wall. 87, 6 B. Reg. 353.

57. (1867) Sparhawk v. Richards, 12 Bank Reg. 74; (1867) Gottman v. Honea, 12 Bank Reg. 493; (1867) In re McKay, 7 Bank Reg. 230; (1867) In re Connor, Lowell 532; (1867) In re Perrin, 7 Bank Reg. 283.

58. Atkins v. Bank, Crabbe 529.

59. (1867) Warren v. Bank, 10 Blatchf. 493, 7 Nat. Bank. Reg. 481.

60. (1867) Oxford Iron Co. v. Slafter, 13 Blatchf. 455, 14 Bank Reg. 380.

61. See note to Johnson v. Wald, 93 Fed. 640, 2 A. B. R. 84 (C. C. A. Ga.).

62. In re Bloch, 6 A. B. R. 300, 109 Fed. 790 (C. C. A. N. Y.). See note to Johnson v. Wald, 93 Fed. 640, 2 A. B. R. 84 (C. C. A. Ga.). Analogously, as to fraudulent removals, etc., Mfg. Co. v. Spoke & Nipple Co., 12 A. B. R. 614, 131 Fed. 215 (C. C. A. Mich.).

under threat of criminal prosecution.[63]

On the other hand, the fact that payment was made in order to avoid a threatened suit is not proof, in and of itself without more, of intent to prefer.[64]

§ 132. Proof of Intent to Prefer Aided by Presumptions.—Proof of intent to prefer is aided by various presumptions.[65]

The debtor is presumed to know the natural and probable results of his own acts.[66]

In re Smith, 23 A. B. R. 864, 176 Fed. 426 (D. C. N. Y.): "Intelligent and sane men are presumed to intend the well-known and obvious consequences of their own voluntary acts, and it cannot be rationally concluded that in sending for Gridley and executing that mortgage the day after the verdict referred to was rendered and which verdict was to be followed by a judgment and a lien on the real estate, Smith, well knowing he was insolvent, did not intend to prefer Gridley." Quoted further at §§ 130, 1370.

In re Wright Lumber Co., 8 A. B. R. 345, 114 Fed. 1011 (D. C. Ark.): "If it be said that the testimony shows that the bankrupt did not intend to prefer a claimant, the answer is that he was insolvent and he knew it, and he must be held to have intended that which was the necessary consequence of his act. He cannot be heard to say that he did not intend to do a thing when the necessary and logical consequence of his act was to do that very thing."

Thus, the transfer of all one's property affords a violent if not conclusive presumption of an intent to prefer, where there are other creditors unprovided for;[67] or, under certain circumstances, the transfer of a large part of one's property.[68]

See Boyd v. Lemmon, Gale & Co., 8 A. B. R. 81, 114 Fed. 647 (C. C. A. Miss.): Where "debtor firm, while insolvent took the money proceeds of the cash sale

---

63. (1867) Clarion Bank v. Jones, 21 Wall. 325; (1867) Sawyer v. Turpin, 91 U. S. 114; (1867) Giddings v. Dodd, 1 Dill 115; (1841) Strain v. Gourdin, 2 Woods 380; (1841) Arnold v. Maynard, 2 Story 349.

64. Lumber Co. v. Atwood, 18 A. B. R. 510, 152 Fed. 978 (C. C. A. Va.).

65. In re Douglass Coal & Coke Co., 12 A. B. R. 547, 131 Fed. 769 (Ref. Tenn.).

66. In re McGee, 5 A. B. R. 262, 105 Fed. 895 (D. C. N. Y.); In re Rome Planing Mills, 3 A. B. R. 123, 96 Fed. 812 (D. C. N. Y.); Bloch v. Farjicon, 6 A. B. R. 300, 109 Fed. 790 (C. C. A.). Impliedly, In re Grant, 5 A. B. R. 837, 106 Fed. 496 (D. C. N. Y.); In re Gilbert, 8 A. B. R. 101, 112 Fed. 951 (D. C. Oregon); Rex Buggy Co. v. Hearick, 12 A. B. R. 726, 132 Fed. 310 (C. C. A. Kas.); Johnson v. Wald, 2 A. B. R. 84, 93 Fed. 640 (C. C. A. Ga.). Analogously and impliedly, Plate Glass Co. v. Edwards, 17 A. B. R. 448 (C. C.

A. Iowa); (1867) Toof v. Martin, 13 Wall. 40; (1867) Wager v. Hall, 16 Wall. 584; (1867) Farrin v. Crawford, Fed. Cas. 4,686; (1867) In re Merchants' Ins. Co., Fed. Cas. 9,441. See citations under corresponding proposition relative to proof of intent to defraud under first act of bankruptcy, ante, § 123. Instance, In re Nusbaum, 18 A. B. R. 598, 152 Fed. 835 (D. C. N. Y.), quoted at § 124; instance where rule applied in concealment as bar to discharge, In re Nelson, 23 A. B. R. 37, 179 Fed. 320 (D. C. N. Y.). Compare post, § 2637½.

67. Compare, as to similar rule in reference to proving "greater percentage," Gering v. Leyda, 26 A. B. R. 137, 186 Fed. 110 (C. C. A. Neb.).

68. (1867) Wager v. Hall, 16 Wall. 584. See citations in In re Gilbert, 8 A. B. R. 106, 112 Fed. 951 (D. C. Oregon). Compare, In re Bloch, 6 A. B. R. 300, 109 Fed. 790 (C. C. A. N. Y.). Compare, Parsons v. Topliff, 119 Mass. 243, 249. Compare, Toof v. Martin, 13 Wall. 40.

of all their property to one not a creditor and applied the same to the full payment of the debts due by them to several of the creditors, leaving others unpaid, it is sufficiently proved that they thereby made a transfer of their property while insolvent to one or more of their creditors with intent to prefer such creditors over other creditors within the meaning of § 3 (a) (2)."

Thus, payment of some creditors in full, and refusal or failure to pay others, the debtor knowing his condition of insolvency, is conclusive proof of intent to prefer.[69]

Rex Buggy Co. v. Hearick, 12 A. B. R. 726, 132 Fed. 310 (C. C. A. Kan.): "If a merchant is hopelessly insolvent during the four months preceding the filing of a petition in involuntary bankruptcy against him and with knowledge of such condition of insolvency pays to certain of his creditors substantial sums of money in full satisfaction of their claims, and denies payment to others whose claims are due and equally entitled to payments, he has committed an act of bankruptcy within the meaning of § 3, subd. 'a,' ch. 2 * * *. His payment under such circumstances inevitably results in giving the creditors so favored a preference over the others. The debtor is presumed to intend the necessary result of his own intelligent acts. This doctrine is abundantly supported by authority."

But where all one's property is mortgaged to secure a few creditors, but the equity left is sufficient to provide for the rest, it is not a preference.[70]

Where, also, the creditor receiving the transfer assumes payment of the debtor's other debts, and is itself a responsible party, intent to prefer cannot be presumed, but rather, is rebutted.[71]

Thus, also, when a debtor, with knowledge of his insolvent condition, transfers property to some of his creditors without leaving enough to pay others a like proportion on their respective debts, an intent to prefer them will be conclusively presumed.[72]

In re McGee, 5 A. B. R. 262, 105 Fed. 895 (D. C. N. Y.): "Every one is presumed to intend the legal consequences of his act, and where an insolvent debtor transfers a large portion of his property to one creditor to the exclusion of others, such transaction must be taken as conclusive of an intent to give a preference."

So, also, the debtor's intent to prefer may be presumed from a transfer, while insolvent, of a large portion of his property to a single creditor.[73]

But, of course, the presumption of an intent to prefer creditors arising from the transfer of property by an insolvent debtor, is affected by the amount of such transfer and where the transfer is of a comparatively small

---

69. Johnson v. Wald, 2 A. B. R. 84, 93 Fed. 640 (C. C. A. Ga.); Naylon v. Christiansen, 19 A. B. R. 789, 158 Fed. 290 (C. C. A. Mich.), quoted ante, also, on other points at § 121.

70. Lansing Boiler & Eng. Works v. Ryerson, 11 A. B. R. 558, 128 Fed. 701 (C. C. A. Mich.).

71. Missouri Elec. Co. v. Hamilton Brown Co., 21 A. B. R. 270, 165 Fed. 283 (C. C. A. Mo.), quoted at § 128.

72. In re Gilbert, 8 A. B. R. 102, 112 Fed. 951 (D. C. Ore.); Obiter, In re Wright Lumber Co., 8 A. B. R. 345, 114 Fed. 1011 (D. C. Ark.).

73. In re Rome Planing Mills, 3 A. B. R. 123, 96 Fed. 812 (D. C. N. Y.). Compare, analogously, post, §§ 1401, 1406.

part of the debtor's property, the presumption does not arise.[74] And the mere paying of certain creditors small sums in the usual course of business,[75] and apparently in the effort to keep the business going, will not raise the presumption of an intent to prefer.[76]

Macon Grocery Co. v. Beach, 19 A. B. R. 558, 156 Fed. 1009 (D. C. Ga.): "It will be found, however, that in each of these cases a substantial preference had been made, that the preferential intent was always inferable, and that the consequent injury of other creditors was significant and distinct. The basic reason upon which all of these determinations are founded is substantially that every person of a sound mind is presumed to intend the necessary, natural and legal consequence of his deliberate acts. In each case the insolvency of the bankrupt was conceded or proven. Then, when he has made a payment to a particular creditor, he is presumed to have the intent to prefer him, as it will enable that creditor to obtain a greater percentage of his debt than will inure to others. But if the payment on the debt is of that infinitesimal sort that it can have no perceptible consequence, is an intent to prefer a necessary, natural and legal consequence of such payment? It would seem that the substantial or important character of payment or transfer must ex necessitate possess large evidential effect to show the intent to prefer. This may be gathered from the statement of Mr. Justice Field, in Toof v. Martin, 13 Wall. 40, 20 L. Ed. 481. Speaking for the court in that case, that great jurist declares: 'It is a general principle that every one must be presumed to intend the necessary consequences of his act. The transfer in any case by the debtor of a large part or all his property while he is insolvent to one creditor, without making provision for an equal distribution of its proceeds to all his creditors, necessarily operates as a preference to him.' If this is true, the converse would seem also true. If the alleged bankrupt, although aware of his insolvency, should make a payment of an amount not a large part of his means, but utterly trivial—a payment to which no creditor, in the absence of litigation, would possibly object—it is at least debatable whether such payment must necessarily demonstrate the unlawful intent to give a preference to one creditor to the injury of others. The doctrine which we are discussing, and which the courts have so strongly stated, presupposes that the payment is injurious to the other creditors. But where the facts show that no injury, of which the law would or could take an account, would result, the reason of the rule ceasing, it seems that the rule itself would cease. * * * We conclude, therefore, that the payment of 60 cents for soda water, coca cola and one bar of soap, and $2.15 for a dressed doll, in the absence of all other evidence to that end, does not raise the presumption of an intent to give the creditors paid a preference over his other creditors."

The debtor's knowledge of his insolvent condition may be presumed, for the presumption is that a debtor does know his own financial condition.[77]

---

74. In re Gilbert, 8 A. B. R. 102, 112 Fed. 951 (D. C. Ore.); In re Douglass Coal & Coke Co., 12 A. B. R. 539, 131 Fed. 769 (D. C. Tenn.).

75. Thus, the payment of $3.00 to a creditor a week before the filing of the petition. In re Stovall Grocery Co., 20 A. B. R. 537, 161 Fed. 882 (D. C. Ga.).

76. In re Douglass Coal & Coke Co., 12 A. B. R. 539, 131 Fed. 769 (D. C.

Tenn.). But compare, on demurrer, In re Ball, 19 A. B. R. 609, 156 Fed. 682 (D. C. N. Y.).

77. In re Gilbert, 8 A. B. R. 104, 112 Fed. 951 (D. C. Ore.); In re Jacobs, 1 A. B. R. 518 (D. C. La.); In re Silverman, 4 Bank Reg. 523; Wager v. Hall, 16 Wall. 584; Naylon v. Christiansen, 19 A. B. R. 789, 158 Fed. 290 (C. C. A. Mich.).

But it is a rebuttable presumption.[78]

In re Bloch, 6 A. B. R. 300, 109 Fed. 790 (C. C. A. N. Y.): "In such a case (not a case of a transfer of all the debtor's property) evidence by the alleged bankrupt to rebut the presumption that a preference was intended should be submitted to the jury, and an instruction that an intent to prefer is conclusively presumed, is erroneous."

And if the debtor establishes his want of knowledge and his honest belief that he was solvent, he rebuts the presumption of an intent to prefer.[79]

In re Gilbert, 8 A. B. R. 104, 112 Fed. 951 (D. C. Ore.): "There is a further presumption that the debtor knows his financial condition as to solvency, but this is a disputable presumption, and if the debtor honestly believes himself to be. solvent, or if he establishes his want of knowledge as to his insolvency, he then rebuts the presumption of an intent to prefer which arises from the fact of actual insolvency.

In re Rome Planing Mills, 3 A. B. R. 123, 96 Fed. 812 (D. C. N. Y.): "When this (the transfer while insolvent of a considerable portion of his property to one creditor) is proved, the burden is upon him to show that he was ignorant of his insolvency and had reason to believe he could pay his debts in full."

Thus, where the liability, other than that to the preferred creditor, was upon an old, forgotten guaranty still contingent at the time of the transfer, or upon some other indefinite or forgotten claim, the presumption is rebutted,[80] but exactness in knowledge of insolvency is not requisite.

Naylon & Co. v. Christiansen, 19 A. B. R. 789, 158 Fed. 290 (C. C. A. Mich.): "And no one connected with the company would profess any knowledge of its condition. But we are loath to believe that those who had charge of and were so much interested in the affairs of the company could be and continue so utterly ignorant of the financial condition of their company as the general terms in which their testimony was given would seem to indicate. It might well be that they did not know it exactly or even with any close approximation to the facts, and perhaps that was the test assumed when they gave their testimony. But that they should have no understanding of its condition while it was running down, its trade small, the disparity of its debts and its assets growing more and more apparent, and its inability to pay its debts becoming so acute that it could only pay them in driblets and when pressed by creditors, we are not prepared to believe. As against the literalness of such statements, we think it safer to rely upon the strong presumption that they had a general knowledge of its condition. However, the knowledge of its insolvency by the respondent is not of itself a material fact. It is only important as it bears upon the question of its intent in making these payments."

The taking of unusual steps in the transaction, or the failure to take the usual steps, may indicate intent. Thus, failure to record a real estate mort-

---

78. In re Gilbert, 8 A. B. R. 104, 112 Fed. 951 (D. C. Ore.). Inferentially, Merchants' Nat'l Bk. v. Cole, 18 A. B. R. 48 (C. C. A. Ohio).

79. In re Bloch, 6 A. B. R. 300, 109 Fed. 790 (C. C. A. N. Y.); [1867] Toof v. Martin, 13 Wall. 10.

80. Impliedly, Merchants' Nat'l Bk. v. Cole, 18 A. B. R. 48 (C. C. A. Ohio); In re Morgan & Williams, 25 A. B. R. 861, 184 Fed. 938 (D. C. Ga.), wherein the obligation was a forgotten claim for cotton "franchise."

gage, given within the four months' period for an antecedent debt, until several months after its execution, warrants a finding of an intent to prefer when taken in connection with facts denoting knowledge of insolvency.[81]

And the presumption that one intends the natural and probable effects of his own acts is predicated upon proof of his knowledge of the essential facts which tend to produce the resulting consequences.[82]

Thus, mere knowledge of insolvent condition, without more, may not be sufficient to raise the presumption of intent to prefer; as, for example, where one knowing himself to be insolvent gives a mortgage to raise money to pay—not one creditor, nor some creditors, but all creditors.[83]

There is also a presumption that a debtor knows of the existence of a debt,[84] although, of course, it is a rebuttable presumption, resting upon the debtor to rebut.[85]

DIVISION 3.

THIRD ACT OF BANKRUPTCY—PREFERENCES BY LEGAL PROCEEDINGS NOT VACATED NOR DISCHARGED.

§ 133. Third Act of Bankruptcy—Preferences by Legal Proceedings Not Vacated.—The third class of acts of bankruptcy is the suffering or permitting whilst insolvent any creditor to obtain a preference through legal proceedings and not having, at least five days before a sale or final disposition of the property affected by such preference, vacated or discharged the same.[86]

In re Rome Planing Mills, 3 A. B. R. 123, 96 Fed. 812 (D. C. N. Y.): "The following are the essential elements. * * * First, That a preference was obtained by a creditor through legal proceedings. Second, That the debtor suffered or permitted the preference and did not vacate or discharge the prefer-

---

81. In re Edelman, 12 A. B. R. 238, 13 Fed. 700 (C. C. A. N. Y.). But in this case the failure to record the mortgage, it will be observed, was not traced home to the bankrupt, yet it must be remembered that it is the bankrupt's intent and not that of the creditor that is involved in the giving and accepting of a transfer that results in a preference.

82. In re McLoon, 20 A. B. R. 719, 162 Fed. 575 (D. C. Me.).

83. In re McLoon, 20 A. B. R. 719, 162 Fed. 575 (D. C. Me.).

84. In re Pangborn, 26 A. B. R. 40, 185 Fed. 673 (D. C. Mich.).

85. In re Pangborn, 26 A. B. R. 40, 185 Fed. 673 (D. C. Mich.).

86. Bankr. Act, § 3 (a) (3). For other decisions construing this act of bankruptcy, see citations under the propositions hereinafter following.

In re McCartney, 26 A. B. R. 548, 188 Fed. 815 (D. C. Pa.); In re Putnam, 27 A. B. R. 927 (D. C. Cal.).

Instance, failure of partner who long since sold out to remaining partner, to discharge levy by firm creditor on former firm assets, a firm act of bankruptcy. Holmes v. Baker & Hamilton, 20 A. B. R. 252, 160 Fed. 922 (C. C. A. Wash.).

Instance [surety levying on judgment note given for money the same day loaned] United Surety Co. v. Iowa Mfg. Co., 24 A. B. R. 726, 179 Fed. 55 (C. C. A. Mo.), but this seems not to have been a case of true preference, since the advancing of the money for the payroll was apparently substantially contemporaneous with the levy of execution therefor.

Instance held not preference. In re Crafts-Riordan Shoe Co., 26 A. B. R. 449, 185 Fed. 931 (D. C. Mass.).

ence at least five days before a sale, or final disposition of-the property affected. Third, That the debtor was insolvent at the time the preference was obtained. The burden of proof is upon the petitioner. The debtor's intent is not an essential element. It is sufficient that the debtor obtained a preference and that the debtor has permitted it to remain undischarged."

The proceeding through which the preference is alleged to have been obtained must, of course, be a valid one, that is to say, if it were by levy of execution the levy must have been not a mere nullity; otherwise this act of bankruptcy has not been committed.[87]

§ 134. No Fraudulent Intent Implied.—In this act of bankruptcy no fraudulent intent is implied. On the contrary, the act rather implies helplessness on the part of the debtor; for the insolvent debtor finds it difficult to extricate himself from his dilemma where a creditor has levied an execution or attachment or otherwise obtained a hold on his property by legal proceedings. Of course, if, in fact the debtor be not insolvent, or if the levy be not upon a just debt or be not authorized, the debtor may extricate himself; but if the claim be just and the levy proper, and the debtor have no valid defense and is insolvent, he can scarcely avoid committing this act of bankruptcy, unless he can get some one to give bail for him. If he cannot procure bail and if he has no defense, then he is surely helpless and is helpless without necessarily any fraud, connivance, intent or action existing on his part at all. If he pay the claim in full and thus discharge or vacate the legal proceedings, he might avoid this third act of bankruptcy; but the payment itself would likely be held to be a preference, since he is insolvent and knows he is insolvent; and it would be thus an act of bankruptcy of the second class.[88]

§ 135. Intent to Prefer Not Requisite, So Long as Actual Preference Exists.—It is the result obtained by the levying creditor and not the intent of the debtor to prefer, that is the test.[89]

87. In re Samuel Bodek, 26 A. B. R. 476, 188 Fed. 817.

88. See post, §§ 136 and 141. 'See In re Miller, 5 A. B. R. 140, 104 Fed. 764 (D. C. N. Y.); In re Meyers, 1 A. B. R. 1 (Ref. N. Y.). Scheuer v. Book, 7 A. B. R. 384 (C. C. A. Ala.); In re Truitt. 29 A. B. R. 570. 203 Fed. 550 (D. C. Md.).

89. In re Rung Furn. Co., 14 A. B. R. 12, 139 Fed. 526 (C. C. A. Mass.). To the same effect, see Bradley Timber Co. v. White, 10 A. B. R. 329, 336, 121 Fed. 779 (C. C. A. Ala.), affirming White v. Bradley Timber Co., 9 A. B. R. 441, 119 Fed. 989); In re Ferguson, 2 A. B. R. 586, 95 Fed. 429 (D. C. N. Y.); In re Meyer, 1 A. B. R. 1 (Ref. N. Y.); In re Reichman, 1 A. B. R. 17, 91 Fed. 624 (D. C. Mo.); In re Moyer, 1 A. B. R. 577, 93 Fed. 188 (D. C. Pa.), a judgment entered within four months on warrants to confess given before four months. In re Rome Planing Mills, 3 A. B. R. 123, 96 Fed. 812 (D. C. N. Y.); In re Thomas, 4 A. B. R. 571, 103 Fed. 272 (D. C. Pa.); Parmenter Mfg. Co. v. Stoever, 3 A. B. R. 220, 97 Fed. 330 (C. C. A. Mass.). Contra, Duncan v. Landis, 5 A. B. R. 649, 106 Fed. 839 (C. C. A. Pa.). Nevertheless see, In re Kersten, 6 A. B. R. 516 (D. C. Wis.), where it seems to have been thought necessary to show some affirmative act, as, here, the debtor's appearance in State Court on creditors' application for the appointment of a receiver there and debtor's presentation of a list of names for the receivership. In re Tupper, 20 A. B. R. 824, 163 Fed. 766 (D. C. N. Y.); In re Truitt. 29 A. B. R. 570. 203 Fed. 550 (D. C. Md.).

The leading case upon this point is Wilson Bros. *v.* Nelson, 7 A. B. R. 142, 183 U. S. 191, (reversing In re Nelson, 1 A. B. R. 63, 98 Fed. 76, D. C. Wis.).

In this case of Wilson Bros. *v.* Nelson, the Supreme Court of the United States held, that in determining what constitutes the suffering or permitting of a preference by legal proceedings the statute makes the result obtained by the creditor and not the specific intent of the debtor, the essential fact, and that no intent on the part of a debtor either to hinder, delay, or defraud his creditors or to prefer one of them over another is required by the third act of bankruptcy. This was held in a case where a cognovit judgment was taken and levy made thereunder on a note given nearly fourteen years before that time, the debtor all the time being wholly innocent of any connivance, collusion or suggestion that the creditor take judgment, and being in total ignorance that any such judgment was going to be taken. The Supreme Court held, that, nevertheless, because, after levy made, the debtor had not procured its discharge or its vacating before five days before the time set for execution sale, he had committed this act of bankruptcy, for he had suffered and permitted a preference to be obtained and retained by his nonresistance to legal proceedings.

§ 136. "Continuing Consent."—In cases where the lien was obtained by levies under judgments obtained upon warrants to confess judgment, there may be said to exist, theoretically, a continuing "consent." Such was the fact in the case of Wilson *v.* Nelson, discussed in the preceding paragraph; also, in In re Thomas, 4 A. B. R. 571, 103 Fed. 272 (D. C. Pa.). Nevertheless, "continuing" or constructive consent, as in cases of warrants to confess judgment, is not necessary.[90]

Mere passivity on the debtor's part is sufficient to constitute "suffering" or "permitting." Active participation, co-operation or collusion in the legal proceedings, is not a requisite element.[91]

In re Rome Planing Mills, 3 A. B. R. 123, 96 Fed. 812 (D. C. N. Y.): "It is not necessary that the debtor should have done any affirmative act. If he remains passive and supine and permits his property to be taken by one creditor at the expense of others, he has 'suffered' or 'permitted' a preference to be obtained."

Bogen & Trummell *v.* Protter, 12 A. B. R. 288, 129 Fed. 533 (C. C. A. Ohio): "A debtor who does not pay a lawful debt when due and stands by while his creditor secures a judgment against him and levies upon his property certainly 'suffers and permits' such judgment to be taken, levy made, and preference thereby obtained."

Bradley Timber Co. *v.* White, 10 A. B. R. 326, 121 Fed. 779 (C. C. A. Ala.):

90. In re Rung Furn. Co., 14 A. B. R. 12, 139 Fed. 526 (C. C. A. N. Y.).

91. Impliedly, Wilson *v.* Nelson, 7 A. B. R. 142, 183 U. S. 191, reversing In re Nelson, 1 A. B. R. 63, 93 Fed. 76 (D. C. Wis.); In re Rung Furn. Co., 14 A. B. R. 12, 139 Fed. 526 (C. C. A. N. Y.). Compare, contra query before decision of Supreme Court in Wilson Bros. *v.* Nelson; In re Ogles, 1 A. B. R. 671, 93 Fed. 426 (D. C. Tenn.). See post, "Fourth Element of a Voidable Preference," §§ 1328, 1339.

"We doubt if any of the evidence of witness Roach was relevant to the issue involved. Whether or not an insolvent makes resistance to legal proceedings of a creditor to obtain preference is not very material. It may show good faith on his part, but the act of bankruptcy declared in the law is 'suffering or permitting' a judgment which will result in a preference, and a failure to vacate the same within at least five days before a sale or disposition of the property affected by such preference. The Bankrupt Law seeks to prevent, and, if obtained by any means, to set aside, preferences obtained against an insolvent within four months; and, in order to effect an equal distribution of an insolvent's property among creditors, it contemplates a resort to the bankruptcy court in all cases of such preferences, no matter whether the bankrupt has consented thereto or opposed the same."

Although of course, if active participation by the debtor actually occur, and the sale be completed, then there may exist a preferential "transfer" cognizable under the Second Act of Bankruptcy.[92]

Upon reflection, it will become clearly evident that, by the operation of this third act of bankruptcy, almost any insolvent debtor, except the absolutely exempted ones, can ultimately be brought into the bankruptcy court and adjudged bankrupt, without any bad faith or intent on his part. He can in other words, be compelled to commit this act of bankruptcy.[93]

§ 137. Debtor's Resistance to Suit without Release of Property Ineffectual.

—It will make no difference that the debtor resists the suit in good faith, files answer, contends at the trial and appeals the judgment before the sale, if the execution of the judgment upon the property is not stayed or the property otherwise released.[94]

Bradley Timber Co. v. White, 10 A. B. R. 326, 121 Fed. 779 (C. C. A. Ala.): "Whether or not an insolvent makes resistance to legal proceedings of a creditor to obtain preference is not very material."

But where a levy, which is alleged to constitute this act of bankruptcy, appears to be fatally defective, the act of bankruptcy is not committed; and the debtor has an undoubted right to contest the validity of the alleged levy in the proper tribunal.[95]

§ 138. Preference Must Have Been Obtained Thereby.

—A preference must have been obtained thereby.[96]

In re Chapman, 3 A. B. R. 607, 99 Fed. 395 (D. C. Ga.): "The difficulty

---

92. In re Nusbaum, 18 A. B. R. 598, 152 Fed. 835 (D. C. N. Y.), quoted at § 124.

93. (1867) See Warren v. Bank, 7 Nat. Bank Reg. 481; (1867) Coxe v. Hale, 8 Nat. Bank Reg. 562.

94. In re Rung Furn. Co., 14 A. B. R. 12, 139 Fed. 526 (C. C. A. N. Y.): In this case the court held, that the failure of an insolvent corporation to vacate a preference resulting from a judgment, levy and sale, is an act of bankruptcy within § 3a (3), even though the judgment debtor answers the suit, goes to trial in good faith and later and before the sale duly appeals from the judgment.

95. In re Samuel Bodek, 26 A. B. R. 476, 188 Fed. 817 (D. C. Pa.).

96. In re Kersten, 6 A. B. R. 516, 110 Fed. 929 (D. C. Wis.); Spike & Iron Co. v. Allen, 17 A. B. R. 588, 148 Fed. 657 (C. C. A. Va.); In re Rome Planing Mills, 96 Fed. 812, 3 A. B. R. 123 (D. C. N. Y.).

arises from the fact that in the suit the plaintiff obtained a general judgment. The reply is this, however, is that, while the plaintiff has a general judgment,. she is only proceeding to enforce it against the particular property on which she had the contract lien, and for that reason the proceeding to sell, whatever may have been the character of the judgment, is not a preferential proceeding. The plaintiff is only seeking for the time being to enforce the judgment against the property on which she had the contract lien, and the Bankruptcy Act could never have contemplated that a person should be adjudged a bankrupt for permitting the enforcement of a lien against particular property, when the lien as to the property was in no sense a preference under any of the provisions of the act. I see no practical difference between this execution proceeding, as it now is, against the property conveyed to the plaintiff to secure the debt, and an ordinary proceeding to enforce a mortgage against the particular property on which the mortgage was given. If a levy was made on property other than that as to which the plaintiff in the judgment had a special lien, and an attempt was being made to sell the same, and the defendant failed within five days of the time of sale to vacate or discharge the judgment, then, undoubtedly, it seems, an act of bankruptcy would be committed. To constitute an act of bankruptcy, under the clause in question, it would be necessary that the debtor should suffer or permit, while insolvent, a judgment to go against him, which judgment would of itself be a preference under the act; that he would then allow execution to be issued and levied, and proceedings to sell to be instituted by the necessary advertisement, and fail, within five days of the time of sale, to vacate or discharge the judgment. The sale which the defendant, by the act, must prevent, would consummate and make effective the preference given by the judgment. This is very different from the case at bar, in which an antecedent lien, not obnoxious in any way to the act, is being enforced by legal proceedings. In the first instance practical results beneficial to the creditors would be obtained by the institution of the bankruptcy proceedings, inasmuch as the preference created by the judgment lien would be annulled and vacated, and, as a consequence, the property of the defendant equally divided. Such is evidently the intent of this act of bankruptcy—that a preference might be avoided, and an equal distribution of the debtor's property result. In the case now before the court, the institution of the bankruptcy proceedings will not affect the lien of the judgment on the land which was about to be sold. Should the bankruptcy proceedings go on, the court must either allow the plaintiff to proceed to enforce her judgment as a special lien on this property, by execution of the City Court, as she is now doing, or must allow the trustee to sell the property subject to the lien, should it be thought probable that anything could be realized for the general creditors over and above the amount of the judgment. The court would declare it to be an act of bankruptcy in Chapman not to have prevented the sale, and would then, by its own order, allow the sale to go on. This is not, in my opinion, such a case as Congress had in view in enacting the clause in question."

Thus, the debtor must have been insolvent.[97] And insolvency at the time of the levying of the execution is sufficiently proved where insolvency is proved as of the subsequent date of the sale coupled with proof of no sub-

---

97. See ante, § 126. In re Rome Planing Mills, 96 Fed. 812, 3 A. B. R. 123 (D. C. N. Y.). Inferentially, In re Rung Furn. Co., 14 A. B. R. 12 (C. C. A. N. Y.). In re Crafts-Riordan Shoe Co., 26 A. B. R. 449, 185 Fed. 931 (D. C. Mass.).

stantial change of intervening financial condition.[98]

Thus, the preference must have given the creditor an advantage over other creditors of the "same class." A landlord's distraint, even were it a "legal proceedings" would not be obtaining a "preference" unless there were other creditors entitled to like priority with landlords under the laws of the United States or States, under class 5 of priorities, who did not receive like proportion; for, otherwise, the landlord is not in the "same class."[99]

Spike & Iron Co. v. Allen, 17 A. B. R. 588, 148 Fed. 657 (C. C. A. Va.): "The law in regard to preference by legal proceeding is that the existence of the lien obtained by the proceeding shall work a preference; that is, shall enable some one of the creditors of the insolvent debtor to obtain a greater percentage of his debt than other creditors."

Likewise, suffering judgment on a priority claim of a workman would not be sufficient if there is enough to pay all labor claims in full; although if the judgment be for more than $300 it will be a preference as to the excess.[1] Thus, again, property of the bankrupt must have been sequestrated in some form thereby.[2]

Presumably, all the remaining elements of a preference are likewise requisite.[3] Thus the claim must be that of a creditor[4] and proof thereof must be shown.

§ 139. Legal Proceedings Must Have Created the Preference.—

The preference must have been obtained through legal proceedings.[5]

In re Rome Planing Mills, 3 A. B. R. 123, 96 Fed. 812 (D. C. N. Y.): "The

---

98. Obiter, In re Crafts-Riordan Shoe Co., 26 A. B. R. 449, 185 Fed. 931 (D. C. Mass.).

99. In re Belknap, 12 A. B. R. 326, 129 Fed. 646 (D. C. Penna.).

1. Inferentially, In re Cement Co., 17 A. B. R. 375 (Sp. M. Mich., reversed on other grounds In re Toledo Portland Cement Co., 19 A. B. R. 117, 156 Fed. 83, D. C. Mich.).

2. Instance, In re Miller, 5 A. B. R. 140, 104 Fed. 764 (N. C. N. Y.), where a judgment debtor directed a levying officer to go to one owing the debtor, who thereupon paid the officer the amount owing. Instance, In re Harper, 5 A. B. R. 567, 105 Fed. 900 (D. C. Ills.), a case of garnishment in aid of execution where garnishee has the right to pay at once or at any time to the judgment creditor, held, clause as to "five days" not applicable.

3. See ante, § 119 to § 129, inclusive.

4. In re Crafts-Riordan Shoe Co., 26 A. B. R. 449, 185 Fed. 931 (D. C. Mass.).

5. Spike & Iron Co. v. Allen, 17 A. B. R. 588, 148 Fed. 657 (C. C. A. Va.). Instance, In re Mather v. Coe, 1 A. B. R. 504, 92 Fed. 333 (D. C. Ohio), receivership in State court whereby priority given to workmen that could not have been given them under the Bankruptcy Act. Instance, In re Kersten, 6 A. B. R. 516, 110 Fed. 929 (D. C. Wis.), receivership in State court whereby payments that would have been held preferences under the bankruptcy act and requiring surrender before further participation in dividends, would not be affected. Instance, In re Miller, 5 A. B. R. 140, 104 Fed. 764 (D. C. N. Y.), supplementary proceedings—payment by debtor's debtor to sheriff. Instance held not legal proceedings, In re Mero, 12 A. B. R. 171, 128 Fed. 630 (D. C. Conn.), liveryman's lien. Thus, likewise, a seizure under landlord's distress warrant has been held not to be a seizure by legal proceedings in Spike & Iron Co. v. Allen, 17 A. B. R. 588, 148 Fed. 657 (C. C. A. Va.), also in obiter, referred to, but not decided, In re Belknap, 12 A. B. R. 326, 129 Fed. 646 (D. C. Pa.).

words 'legal proceedings' as used in subd. 3 of § 3 have reference to any proceedings in a court of justice, interlocutory or final, by which the property of the debtor is seized and diverted from his general creditors."

§ 140. Vacating of Preference, Ineffectual unless Accomplished at Least Five Days before Sale.

—The preference must be discharged or vacated to avoid the charge of the act;[6] and it must have been discharged or vacated at least five days before a sale or final disposition of the property affected.[7]

In re Vastbinder, 11 A. B. R. 121, 126 Fed. 417 (D. C. Pa.): "It is not the mere obtaining of a judgment and levying execution on the property of the debtor while insolvent that makes him liable as a bankrupt, but the failure on his part, within five days before a sale or final disposition of the property levied on, to have the same vacated or discharged."

§ 141. "At Least Five Days before a Sale, etc."—Meaning of Term.

—The term "at least five days before a sale or final disposition of the property affected" means at least five days before the time fixed for the sale and it is not necessary for creditors to wait until the sale actually has taken place and thereby possibly have their whole proceedings rendered fruitless.[8]

In re Rome Planing Mills, 3 A. B. R. 123, 96 Fed. 812 (D. C. N. Y., cited in In re Miller. 5 A. B. R. 140, 104 Fed. 764, D. C. N. Y.): "It is not necessary that the creditor should wait until a sale has actually taken place. It would be a strange construction of an act designed to save and protect the debtor's estate, to hold that it can only be set in operation after the estate has been plundered and dissipated. The debtor has until five days before the day the sale is legally noticed in which to vacate or discharge the preference. If he has not done so at that time the creditor may proceed and file a petition and, upon a proper showing, may enjoin the sale. The act of bankruptcy is not consummated until the expiration of the time in which the debtor may vacate or discharge the lien, and the last day for doing this is five days before the day a sale of the property is advertised. In the case of a judgment, therefore, the petitioners must prove the entry of the judgment, the issue of an execution, the levy thereunder and the debtor's insolvency at the time of the judgment and levy. They must also prove that the property was actually sold at execution sale or that the sale was advertised for a day certain, and that the debtor had permitted the levy to stand until the sale was but five days distant."

Bogen & Trummell v. Protter, 12 A. B. R. 288, 129 Fed. 533 (C. C. A. Ohio): "The debtor still has the privilege of avoiding the act of bankruptcy, by discharging the preference at least five days before the time set for sale."

---

6. Wilson Bros. v. Nelson, 7 A. B. R. 142, 183 U. S. 191; obiter, In re Rome Planing Mills, 3 A. B. R. 123, 96 Fed. 812 (D. C. N. Y.); In re Vastbinder. 11 A. B. R.. 121, 126 Fed. 417 (D. C. Pa.); In re Rung Furn. Co., 14 A. B. R. 12, 139 Fed. 526 (C. C. A. N. Y.).

7. Wilson Bros. v. Nelson, 7 A. B. R. 142, 183 U. S. 191; In re Rome Planing Mills, 3 A. B. R. 123, 96 Fed. 812

(D. C. N. Y.); Impliedly, In re Hammond, 20 A. B. R. 776, 163 Fed. 548 (D. C. N. Y.).

8. In re Meyers, 1 A. B. R. 1 (Ref. N. Y.); In re Elmira Steel Co., 5 A. B. R. 488, 109 Fed. 456 (Spec. Master, N. Y.). Compare, In re Tupper; 20 A. B. R. 824, 163 Fed. 766 (D. C. N. Y.); In re Truitt. 29 A. B. R. 570, 203 Fed. 550 (D. C. Md.).

1 R B—10

Obiter, In re Hotel & Cafe Co., 15 A. B. R. 69, 138 Fed. 947 (D. C. Pa.): "It seems clear to me that it was the intention of Congress in framing this clause to fix the consummation of the act of bankruptcy at a period of five days before a sale. If this were not so and the act of bankruptcy is held not to have been consummated until a sale had taken place, creditors could not file involuntary petitions in bankruptcy until after the property of the alleged bankrupt had been swept away by an execution. In other words, it seems to me that it was the intention to fix the consummation of the act of bankruptcy upon an alleged bankrupt five days before the day of sale if at that time he had failed to lift the levy on his property. A petition can then be filed before the sale and the property administered in bankruptcy for the benefit of all the creditors."

Thus, it is incumbent upon an insolvent to discharge or vacate a lien secured by an attachment at least five days before the expiration of a period of four months following the date of the levy; otherwise he commits the third act of bankruptcy.[9]

Nevertheless, it would seem that the court must have fixed some time for the sale or other disposition of the property. Until such time is fixed it is impossible for this act of bankruptcy to be committed.[10]

In re Vetterman, 14 A. B. R. 245, 135 Fed. 443 (D. C. N. H.): "The concluding part of the clause, with reference to the sale or final disposition, is connected with what precedes, in respect to preference through legal proceedings, by the word 'and', thus making it one act of bankruptcy, culminating five days before sale or final disposition. If it were otherwise, and the inception and the culmination of the legal proceedings were separated by the word 'or,' it might be different. In such cases there might be two acts of bankruptcy.

"I find no authority for holding that a creditor's petition in an involuntary bankruptcy proceeding, which merely alleges that an attachment has been made in a legal proceeding, sets forth an act of bankruptcy, within the meaning of the statute of 1898. * * *

"This decision in no way touches the question whether an attachment creditor acquires a valid lien, whose attachment is more than four months old, when that part of clause 3 relating to the sale and the 'five days before' operates upon the situation."

However, in one case on demurrer, the court expresses the opinion that in states where a judgment operates, ipso facto, as a lien on real estate, the Third Act of Bankruptcy has been committed if the judgment debtor allows

---

9. Folger v. Putnam, 28 A. B. R. 173, 194 Fed. 793 (C. C. A. Cal.).

10. Seaboard Steel Casting Co. v. Trigg, 10 A. B. R. 594, 124 Fed. 75, 76 (D. C. Va.), where the allegation that the attachment has not "to this time been discharged" was held insufficient. But it has been held, though upon doubtful ground, that mere garnishment in proceedings in aid of execution in States where the debtor of the judgment debtor is at liberty to discharge his own debt by payment thereof at any time to the judgment creditor of his creditor, is sufficient without the fixing of any date, the law fixing the "final disposition" at any date chosen by such debtor of the judgment debtor. In re Harper, 5 A. B. R. 567, 105 Fed. 900 (D. C. Ills.); analogously, In re Miller, 5 A. B. R. 140 (D. C. N. Y.). But such holding would seem to make the issuance of any execution on a judgment equally an act of bankruptcy, in States where the debtor of the judgment debtor is at liberty likewise to apply his debt on the execution, without the institution of proceedings in aid of execution.

the four months to elapse without voluntarily going into bankruptcy or otherwise vacating the lien, even though no time for sale has been set, the court regarding the lapse of the four months period as the equivalent of the "final disposition" prescribed in the statute, a conclusion in which there is much force. Since the obvious purpose of bankruptcy law is to prevent one creditor gaining a preference over other creditors out of the insolvent fund, whether through the debtor's voluntary act or the creditor's own seizure by legal proceedings, it would follow in a well-rounded statute that the permitting of such a preference to become fixed beyond opportunity of nullification should be an act of bankruptcy.

In re Tupper, 20 A. B. R. 824, 163 Fed. 766 (D. C. N. Y.): "It has been held that this act of bankruptcy is not committed until a sale is at least advertised or the property affected by the preference is to be finally disposed of and the fifth day prior to the proposed sale or proposed final disposition of the property affected has arrived. In the case of personal property, a sale or proposed sale on execution issued on a judgment is, of course, the sale or final disposition intended, as there is no right of redemption. In the case of real estate, an advertised sale on execution or an actual sale would, in my judgment, be a final disposition, notwithstanding there is a right of redemption. In the case of real property, under the law of the state of New York the docketed judgment becomes an absolute lien so soon as docketed in the county where the real property is situated and is 'a disposition of the property', in a sense, for it has been by operation of law pledged as a security for the debt or amount of the judgment; but under the terms of the Bankruptcy Act such a lien, such a disposition of the real property, does not become final until the expiration of four months from its docketing in the county where the real property is situated. * * * An execution and levy and an advertised sale thereunder were wholly unnecessary to a final disposition of this property. On the 8th day of March, 1908, but for the filing of the petition in bankruptcy, the real property would have passed irrevocably and absolutely under the lien, and, as Tupper had become and was insolvent, it was not in her power to pay or discharge it. * * * Not so with personal property, for there there is no lien until execution is issued and generally levy made, and, even then, the lien ceases if within definite periods a sale is not advertised, and hence there is no final disposition of such property proposed until the same is advertised for sale. It seems to me that effect is to be given to the words 'or final disposition of any property affected by such preference.' 'Final disposition' is not a gift of the property to some third person or a voluntary transfer to the creditor in satisfaction of the preferential judgment, as that would be merely a sale in payment. Congress had in mind, when it enacted this law, the fact that there are different ways or modes of disposing of property, of enforcing executions, judgments, and liens, and it referred to the ordinary method of disposition by way of sale, and then used the words 'or final disposition' to cover every other method of passing the control and dominion of the property from the debtor, insolvent person, to another or to others either absolutely or as security to the preferred creditor to the exclusion of his other creditors. The purpose of the law is that no one creditor shall be preferred over the others by an insolvent person, but that all creditors shall share equally except as to honest liens created more than four months prior to the filing of a petition in bankruptcy. It was not intended that a creditor should obtain a lien on all the real estate of an insolvent person by a judgment filed and docketed, and then lie still, without issuing execution or making a

levy and advertising the property for sale for four months and until such judgment had become unimpeachable under the Bankruptcy Act or otherwise, thereby gaining a preference, an absolute security for the debt, and it might be
to the extent of the entire property of the insolvent person, and thus excluding
other creditors from any share in the estate. It has been held that an advertised or even a proposed sale is not in all cases necessary under subdivision 3
of § 3."

But if the lien were obtained more than four months and five days before
the time set for the sale, the petition could hardly be filed in time at all.

Nevertheless, if, before any sale actually has taken place and before the
bankruptcy petition is filed, the execution is stayed and the lien vacated, although not until within the five days before the time fixed for the sale, the
bankruptcy petition will be dismissed, at any rate where, before it was filed,
the petitioning creditors had actual notice of the vacating of the lien.[11]

Where the debtor has discharged an attachment lien by giving a redelivery
bond (turning over some property to the surety for security) but no judgment has yet been rendered in the attachment case, it has been held that
there has not yet been any "final disposition," such that the surety himself
could petition the debtor into bankruptcy.[12]

In one case,[13] however, although a suit and attachment were both begun
within the four months period, and the sale under the attachment had been
made, the proceeds being held by the sheriff pending trial, the court held
no act of bankruptcy had been committed because a sale under an attachment did not accomplish a "final disposition of the property," no judgment
having been rendered at the time of the filing of the bankruptcy petition.
But such construction is too finely spun: it is open to the same objection
as above noted that it is not necessary for creditors to wait until there has
been an actual "final disposition" of the property attached, so long as the
vacating is not accomplished within five days of either a sale or a final
disposition.

In computing the five days time the first day must be excluded and the
last day included; thus, where the execution sale was set for the twenty-
second day of the month, a petition filed on the seventeenth day is too
early.[14]

§ 142. How Vacating Accomplished and How Not.—Vacating must
not be accomplished by payment of the debt by the bankrupt out of the bankrupt estate, else an act of bankruptcy, although not one of the third class
of acts of bankruptcy, will have been committed.[15]

11. In re Doddy, Jordan & Co., 11
A. B. R. 344, 127 Fed. 771 (D. C. Penn.).
12. In re Windt, 24 A. B. R. 536, 177
Fed. 584 (D. C. Conn.); compare, suggestively, In re Crafts-Riordan Shoe
Co., 26 A. B. R. 449 (D. C. Conn.).
13. In re Crafts-Riordan Shoe Company, 26 A. B. R. 449, 185 Fed. 931 (D.
C. Mass.).

14. Bankr. Act, § 31; also Pittsburgh
Laundry v. Imperial Laundry, 18 A. B.
R. 756, 154 Fed. 662 (C. C. A. Pa.).
15. But compare obiter, in syllabus,
White v. Bradley Timber Co., 9 A. B.
R. 441, 121 Fed. 779, affirming 119 Fed.
989 (D. C. Ala.). In re Tupper, 20 A.
B. R. 824, 163 Fed. 766 (D. C. N. Y.).

Scheuer *v.* Book Co., 7 A. B. R. 384, 112 Fed. 407 (C. C. A. Ala.): "Such payment ought not to be considered in any just sense as the vacating or discharging of a preference within the intent and meaning of the third subdivision, § 3 (a), of the Bankruptcy Act."

That there was no defense to the justness of the claim, upon which the levy was made is no excuse.[16] But there is no legal obligation upon an insolvent debtor to have himself adjudged a bankrupt.[17]

A corporation cannot avoid the effect of having committed this act of bankruptcy, by subsequently going into liquidation, by proceedings for dissolution.[18]

Vacating is accomplished successfully by the giving of a bond releasing the property, where a third party is surety on the bond and no property of the bankrupt is transferred as indemnity.[19]

§ 143. Lien Must Have Been Obtained within Four Months— Mere Enforcement of Lien Obtained before, Insufficient.

—The lien must have been obtained within the four months preceding the filing of the bankruptcy petition.[20]

Owen *v.* Brown, 9 A. B. R. 717, 120 Fed. 812 (C. C. A. Colo.): "The contention of the appellants is that the judgment creditor obtained a preference and the act of bankruptcy was committed when the defendant's real estate was sold on execution, without regard to the date of the judgment on which the execution was issued, and regardless of the fact that the judgment was a lien on the real estate of the defendant sold on the execution from the date of its rendition. * * * This contention finds no support in the Bankrupt Act or on principle * * *.

16. Scheuer *v.* Book Co., etc., 7 A. B. R. 384, 112 Fed. 407 (C. C. A. Ala.).

17. Spike & Iron Co. *v.* Allen, 17 A. B. R. 583, 148 Fed. 657 (C. C. A. Va.); Summers *v.* Abbott, 10 A. B. R. 254, 122 Fed. 36 (C. C. A. Mo.); (1867) Wilson *v.* City Bk., 17 Wall. 473.

18. In re Storm, 4 A. B. R. 601, 103 Fed. 618 (D. C. N. Y.). Compare, White Mountain Paper Co. *v.* Morse, 11 A. B. R. 632, 127 Fed. 180 (C. C. A. N. Y.). The lien must have been obtained after the passage of the Bankruptcy Act; the statute is not retroactive. Owen *v.* Brown, 9 A. B. R. 717, 120 Fed. 812 (C. C. A. Colo.). Perhaps in point, In re Chapman, 3 A. B. R. 607, 99 Fed. 395 (D. C. Ga.).

19. Contra, In re Crafts-Riordan Shoe Co., 26 A. B. R. 449, 185 Fed. 931 (D. C. Mass.), wherein the court seems to think that simply because the creditor has security through a third party's becoming surety a "preference" was created, apparently overlooking the fact that a preference can only be predicated upon the transfer of the debtor's own property.

20. Inferentially, In re Chapman, 3 A. B. R. 607, 99 Fed. 395 (D. C. Ga.), quoted ante, § 138. Inferentially, In re Meyers, 1 A. B. R. (Ref. N. Y.). Inferentially, Metcalf *v.* Barker, 9 A. B. R. 36, 187 U. S. 165. Contra, and that the four months' time dates from the five days before the sale or proposed sale. Parmenter Mfg. Co. *v.* Stoever, 3 A. B. R. 220, 97 Fed. 330 (C. C. A. Mass.). This case it was sought to distinguish in In re Chapman, 3 A. B. R. 611. Also, In re Hotel & Cafe Co., 15 A. B. R. 288, 129 Fed. 533 (C. C. A. Ohio). But, if the date set for the sale is more than four months and five days from the obtaining of the lien, the question arises, whether a bankruptcy petition would lie? It would seem the levy must have occurred within the four months and the proposed sale must have occurred within the four months and five days of the filing of the petition; consequently, it might be easy to avoid this act of bankruptcy by having the date for the sale set later.

In re Deer Creek, etc., Co., 29 A. B. R. 356, — Fed. — (D. C. Pa.).

"The 'preference through legal proceedings' mentioned in subd. 3 is a preference obtained by such means within four months next preceding the filing of the petition in bankruptcy.

"Neither the third subdivision of § 3a, nor any other provision of the Bankrupt Act, contemplates that valid judgment liens on real property acquired before the passage of the act, or more than four months before the filing of the petition in bankruptcy, shall be vacated; or that the due enforcement of such liens by execution shall constitute an illegal preference, which would be exactly tantamount to vacating or annulling the lien itself."

In re Ferguson, 2 A. B. R. 586, 95 Fed. 429 (D. C. N. Y. a case of an execution levied within four months, approved in In re Chapman, 3 A. B. R. 607, 99 Fed. 395, D. C. Ga.): "The act of bankruptcy referred to in subd. 3, cl. a, § 3, must, I think, be limited to such acts as by construction of law and in the view of the Bankruptcy Act, work an injury to other creditors by securing to them a preference which the Bankruptcy Law is designed to prevent. The language of this subdivision shows this intent. This cannot apply, therefore, to· such levies and liens as are acquired long prior to the passage of the act, and more than four months prior to the petition, which the Bankrupt Act does not vacate or disallow. Such a lien the debtor cannot be required to satisfy or vacate."

Compare, In re Vetterman, 14 A. B. R. 245, 246, 135 Fed. 443 (D. C. N. H.): "This decision in no way touches the question whether an attaching creditor acquires a valid lien, whose attachment is more than four months old when that part of clause 3 relating to the sale and the 'five days before' operates upon the situation."

Apparently, contra, Parmenter Mfg. Co. v. Stoever, 3 A. B. R. 220, 97 Fed. 330 (C. C. A. Mass.): "The act of bankruptcy dating from the sale or from the five days anterior to the sale and not from the date of the attachment."

But the mere enforcement, within the four months period, of a lien obtained before the four months period, is valid and unaffected.[21]

And this is so even where a general judgment also was obtained, and the creditor is seeking to enforce the general judgment against the particular property on which he has the contract lien.[22]

DIVISION 4.

FOURTH CLASS OF ACTS OF BANKRUPTCY—ASSIGNMENTS AND RECEIVERSHIPS.

§ 144. No Implication of Fraud in Fourth Act.—As to acts of bankruptcy embraced within the fourth class, namely, the debtor's making of a general assignment for the benefit of his creditors, or being insolvent, his applying for a receiver or trustee for his property, or because of his insolvency, the putting of a receiver or trustee in charge of his property under the laws of a State, Territory or of the United States, it may also

---

21. Owen v. Brown, 9 A. B. R. 717, 120 Fed. 812 (C. C. A. Colo.). Compare, In re Vetterman, 14 A. B. R. 245, 135 Fed. 443 (D. C. N. H.). Also, see post, § 184. Also, see correlative subject, post, § 1444, et seq. Colston v. Austin, etc., Co., 28 A. B. R. 92, 194 Fed. 929 (C. C. A. Del.).

22. In re Chapman, 3 A. B. R. 607, 99 Fed. 395 (D. C. Ga.), quoted ante, § 138.

be said that there can be no implication of fraud on the debtor's part from these acts alone and unaccompanied with any artifice or design, for these acts at worst are merely constructively fraudulent.

Randolps *v.* Scruggs, 190 U. S. 533, 10 A. B. R. 1: "The assignment was not illegal. It was permitted by the law of the State, and cannot be taken to have been prohibited by the bankruptcy law absolutely, in every event, whether proceedings were instituted or not. * * * It had no general fraudulent intent."

Summers *v.* Abbott, 10 A. B. R. 254, 122 Fed. 36 (C. C. A. Mo.): "The deed of assignment covered all the property of the bankrupts. It was honestly made for the laudable purpose of applying all the property of the debtors to the payment, ratably, of all their debts. This is conceded. No claim is made that there was a secret trust reserved for the grantors' benefit, or that there was otherwise any fraud in fact in the execution and delivery of the deed. It was not made to hinder, delay, or defraud creditors, but to pay creditors. Fraud cannot be predicated of such a deed. It constituted an act of bankruptcy, which entitled the debtors' creditors, if they saw proper to do so, to have the administration of the trust transferred from the assignee to the bankrupt court, but this is no impeachment of the honesty of the transaction; and the debtors, when adjudged bankrupts, would be entitled to their discharge, precisely as though they had made no such assignment. It is also admitted that the appellant, who was named in the deed as assignee, accepted the trust in good faith, and for the purpose of executing it according to law and the terms of the deed; and that he did execute it intelligently, successfully, and honestly, is conceded. Neither fraud in fact nor in law can be imputed to such an assignee. The contention of the trustee in bankruptcy is that all assignments for the benefit of creditors since the passage of the Bankruptcy Act are fraudulent, and that every assignee under such a deed is a fraudulent vendee or assignee, and hence entitled to no compensation for his services. This contention is probably grounded on the assumption that it is the legal duty of an insolvent debtor who wants to apply his property to the payment of his debts to apply to the bankrupt court to be adjudged a bankrupt, and then turn his property over to the trustee of his estate in bankruptcy. But neither in the present nor any previous Bankrupt Law this country has ever had will there be found any provision making it obligatory upon a debtor to go into court and have himself adjudged a bankrupt. The Bankrupt Act declares the making of 'a general assignment for the benefit of his creditors' shall constitute an act of bankruptcy, but it nowhere declares that when the debtor has committed an act of bankruptcy he shall go into the bankrupt court and have himself adjudged a bankrupt. Many debtors who commit acts of bankruptcy struggle on and finally pay all the debts they owe, which is much more than would have been done had they gone into the bankrupt court and had themselves adjudged bankrupts. It is open to the creditors of one who has committed an act of bankruptcy to proceed to have him adjudged a bankrupt, but it is optional and not obligatory upon this creditors to do this. As a matter of fact, thousands of debtors commit acts of bankruptcy who are never adjudged bankrupts; their creditors preferring to let their debtor administer his estate, rather than turn it over to a bankrupt court."

It will have been observed that there are three distinct acts embraced within this class. Their consideration will now be taken up in their order.

GENERAL ASSIGNMENTS.

§ 145. General Assignment, Act of Bankruptcy.—A general assignment for the benefit of creditors is an act of bankruptcy.[23]

§ 146. Assignment Must Be General.—The assignment must be a general assignment. Thus, a direct transfer to creditors without the intervention of an assignee or trustee is not a general assignment for the benefit of creditors within the meaning of the Act.[24]

Missouri Elec. Co. v. Hamilton Brown Co., 21 A. B. R. 270, 165 Fed. 283 (C. C. A. Mo.): "A general assignment conveys all or substantially all the property of the debtor, while an assignment which conveys but a portion of it is a partial assignment, and not a general assignment. * * * This assignment did not convey the real estate of the assignor, which was about one-fourth of its property in value after the amount of the incumbrance upon the real estate had been deducted from its total value. * * * An absolute transfer by a debt or of both the legal and the equitable title to the assignee in trust for his creditors, so that the grantor retains no control of its use and no power to dispose of it, is indispensable to a valid assignment of such property for the benefit of creditors. Sandmeyer v. Dakota Fire & Marine Ins. Co., 2 S. D. 346, 352, 50 N. W. 353, and cases there cited; Smith & Keating Imp. Co. v. Thurman, 29 Mo. App. 186, 191. The conveyance here in question made no such transfer of the real estate of the debtor. A general assignment for the benefit of creditors is ordinarily a conveyance by a debtor without consideration from the grantee of substantially all his property to a party in trust to collect the amounts owing to him, to sell and convey the property, to distribute the proceeds of all the property among his creditors, and to return the surplus, if any, to the debtor. A conveyance of his property by a debtor directly to his creditor, or to his creditors, for their benefit, is not a general assignment for the benefit of creditors because it raises no trust."

Again, the mere appointment of a committee to sell the assets of a corporation is not "a general assignment;"[25] provided, however, no "transfer" of title to the committee be made; for, if title be transferred, assuredly it would be precisely a "general assignment for the benefit of creditors."

But it need not be by a formal deed of assignment.[26]

---

23. Bankr. Act, § 3 (a) (4); Clark v. Mfg. & Enamel Co., 4 A. B. R. 351, 101 Fed. 962 (C. C. A. W. Va.); West Co. v. Lea Bros., 2 A. B. R. 463, 174 U. S. 590, affirming Lea Bros. v. West, 1 A. B. R. 261, 91 Fed. 237; In re Romanow, 1 A. B. R. 461, 92 Fed. 510 (D. C. Mass.); In re Hirose, 12 A. B. R. 154 (D. C. Hawaii); Whittlesey v. Beeker & Co., 25 A. B. R. 672 (Sup. Ct. N. Y.). For other instances and various applications, see citations under succeeding propositions. That such assignments are voidable by the trustee, see post, §§ 1440 and 1604.

24. Obiter, Iron and Supply Co. v. Rolling Mill Co., 11 A. B. R. 200, 125 Fed. 974 (D. C. Ala., citing May v. Tenney, 148 U. S. 66, and Davis v. Schwartz, 155 U. S. 631).

25. In re Hartwell Oil Mills, 21 A. B. R. 586, 165 Fed. 555 (D. C. Ga.).

26. In re Salmon & Salmon, 16 A. B. R. 122, 143 Fed. 395 (D. C. Mo.). Obiter [held under facts of case not an act of bankruptcy], In re Federal Lumber Co., 26 A. B. R. 438, 185 Fed. 926 (D. C. Mass.).

In re Tomlinson Co., 18 A. B. R. 691, 154 Fed. 834 (C. C. A. Okla.): "Mc-Connell took possession of the property conveyed, and proceeded to execute the trust imposed upon him. In our opinion the instrument in question was a general assignment for the benefit of creditors within the true meaning of the Bankruptcy Act, and was an act of bankruptcy warranting the adjudication. The 'general assignment' there contemplated is to be taken in its generic sense, and embraces any conveyance at common law or by statute by which the parties intend to make an absolute and unconditional appropriation of the property conveyed to raise funds to pay the debts of the vendor, share and share alike. * * * The instrument in question does not contain any of the elements of a mortgage, as insisted upon by bankrupts' counsel. The idea that it was intended as a security for the ultimate payment of the debts of the vendor, or that a reservation of a right to redeem whenever the vendor should pay its debts was intended, is not remotely suggested by any of the terms of the instrument; in other words, there is no right of redemption reserved. The provision at the end of the instrument, requiring a surplus, if any, to be paid to the vendor, cannot be regarded as such reservation. It is nothing more than an expression of what the law implies."

Thus, a trust instrument for effecting a composition with creditors, wherein the debtor turns over all his property to an agent to sell and to distribute among creditors after reimbursing himself for expenses, is, in effect, a general assignment.[27] Thus, the confessing of judgment to one as trustee for all creditors is, in effect, an assignment for the general benefit of all creditors and is an act of bankruptcy.[28]

Thus, also, it has been held where the original deed of assignment has been lost, but the facts are proved that the debtor had intended to make an assignment in usual form and that the assignee had sent out notices as such, etc., the making of a general assignment was sufficiently proved and its specific terms were unnecessary.[29]

And if the transaction be such as, by the law of the State, would be held to be a general assignment, it will be an act of bankruptcy.[30]

And it is an act of bankruptcy, though it be not a valid assignment for all purposes.[31]

Griffin v. Dutton, 21 A. B. R. 449, 165 Fed. 626 (C. C. A. Mass.): "Such an assignment is sufficient in form, and constitutes an act of bankruptcy, if it purports to be a general assignment for the benefit of creditors, signed by the bankrupt and duly ratified by the trustee named therein. Nor is it necessary that the assignment should be valid for all purposes, as for instance, that the creditors should assent thereto. The language of the Bankruptcy Act is general. It

---

27. Impliedly (controversy not over its being declared an act of bankruptcy) In re Hersey, 22 A. B. R. 856, 171 Fed. 998 (D. C. Iowa).
28. In re Green & Rogers, 5 A. B. R. 848 (D. C. Penna.); Courtenay v. Finch, 27 A. B. R. 688, 194 Fed. 368 (C. C. A., N. D.).
29. Griffin v. Dutton, 21 A. B. R. 449, 165 Fed. 626 (C. C. A. Mass.), quoted post, this section.

30. In re Salmon & Salmon, 16 A. B. R. 122, 143 Fed. 395 (D. C. Mo.).
31. Canner v. Tapper Co., 21 A. B. R. 872, 168 Fed. 519 (C. C. A. Mass.). And probably if not a general assignment by state law it will not be such in bankruptcy. Impliedly, Missouri, Elec. Co. v. Hamilton Brown Co., 21 A. B. R. 270, 165 Fed. 283 (C. C. A. Mo.), quoted supra.

makes no distinction between strictly valid instruments and those which may be invalid for certain purposes. To limit its operation to those assignments which are in all respect valid would be contrary to the intent and purpose of the act."

Nevertheless, the act of assignment must be consummated by an acceptance by the assignee; so that an instrument of assignment never delivered, or one which is merely accepted conditionally, the condition not being fulfilled, will not suffice; as, for example, where the proposed assignee refuses to accept the trust because not all creditors have assented to the arrangement.[32]

It is still a "general assignment" though expressly limited to be for the benefit only of those who become parties by signing the agreement.

In re Courtenay Mercantile Co., 26 A. B. R. 365, 186 Fed. 352 (D. C. N. Dak.): "Counsel for the Mercantile Company contends that the restriction above quoted, limiting the creditors who shall receive the benefits of the deed to those who shall become parties to it and release their claims in full, destroys the character of the instrument as a general assignment, and converts it into a mere security for those creditors who shall decide to accept its benefits. I cannot adopt that interpretation. As to the effect of such a restrictive clause upon a deed of assignment for the benefit of creditors, there is great conflict in the authorities. In some jurisdictions, it is held to render the instrument void; in others, it is considered valid. 'As against the assignor it is uniformly treated as a general assignment.' * * *

"On the face of the instrument here involved, it was a disposition of all the property of the assignor for the benefit of his creditors. All the creditors had a right to accept its benefits. The assignor could in no way control this discretion. Their right to do this would continue until the estate had been distributed. The character of the instrument should be judged as of the time of its execution and delivery. * * *

"When a debtor assigns all his property in trust for the benefit of his creditors, provided they elect to accept the terms of the deed, he makes a general assignment for the benefit of creditors, within the meaning of section 3 of the bankruptcy Act."

But receiverships, etc., are not to be considered as coming under this head, although they may operate, in effect, like general assignments.[33]

§ 147. **Insolvency Not Requisite in Chief, Nor Competent as Defense.**—It is not necessary to prove the debtor was insolvent; the assignment itself is enough.[34]

---

32. In re Federal Lumber Co., 26 A. B. R. 438, 185 Fed. 926 (D. C. Mass.).

33. See post, subd. B, § 150. Compare, Rumsey v. Novelty Mfg. Co., 3 A. B. R. 704 (D. C. Mo.), wherein the court held the transaction not to be the equivalent of an assignment, but to be "in fraud of the Bankruptcy Act." But "Fraud on the Bankruptcy Act" is not an act of bankruptcy unless it amounts to a common law hindering, delaying or defrauding of creditors or to one of the other acts mentioned.

But compare [apparently holding the transfer to the receiver to be an assignment, although probably there was in reality an actual assignment made to him, in addition] Yungbluth v. Slipper, 26 A. B. R. 265, 185 Fed. 773 (C. C. A. Wash.),

34. Leidigh Carriage Co. v. Stengel, 2 A. B. R. 383, 95 Fed. 645 (C. C. A. Ohio); Clark v. Am. Mfg. & Enamel

West Co. *v.* Lea, 2 A. B. R. 463, 174 U. S. 590, affirming Lea Bros. *v.* West, 1 A. B. R. 261, 91 Fed. 237: "The mere statement in the statute, by way of recital, that a petition may be filed 'against a person who is insolvent and who has committed an act of bankruptcy', was not designed to superadd a further requirement to those contained in paragraph (a), § 3, as to what should constitute acts of bankruptcy. This reasoning also answers the argument based on the fact that the rules in bankruptcy promulgated by this court provide in general terms for an allegation of insolvency in the petition and a denial of such allegation in the answer. These rules were but intended to execute the act, and not to add to its provisions by making that which the statute treats in some cases as immaterial a material fact in every case. Therefore, though the rules and forms in bankruptcy provide for an issue as to solvency in cases of involuntary bankruptcy, where by the statute such issue becomes irrelevant, because the particular act relied on, in a given case, conclusively imports a right to the adjudication in bankruptcy if the act be established, the allegation of insolvency in the petition becomes superfluous, or if made need not be traversed.

"Our conclusion, then, is that, as a deed of general assignment for the benefit of creditors is made by the Bankruptcy Act alone sufficient to justify an adjudication in involuntary bankruptcy against the debtor making such deed, without reference to his solvency at the time of the filing of the petition, that the denial of insolvency by way of defense to a petition based upon the making of a deed of general assignment is not warranted by the Bankruptcy Law; and, therefore, that the question certified must be answered in the negative." Quoted further, § 149.

Day *v.* Hardware Co., 8 A. B. R. 175, 114 Fed. 834 (C. C. A. Ala.): "It is not necessary to allege or prove that the defendant is insolvent."

And the debtor will not even be permitted to defend on the ground that he is willing and able to prove affirmatively that he is solvent.[35]

§ **148. Intent to Defraud Not Requisite.**—It is not necessary to prove intent to defraud creditors.[36]

§ **149. Assignment Need Not Work Preference.**—Nor is it necessary to prove that the operation of the assignment would be to prefer some creditors over others, contrary to the distribution prescribed by the bankruptcy statute.

Here it is to be noted that, although under the old law of 1867 assignments for the benefit of creditors were not expressly made acts of bankruptcy, yet they were held to be acts of bankruptcy under another provision of the law, namely, as being intended to interfere with the operation of the

---

Co., 4 A. B. R. 351, 101 Fed. 962 (C. C. A. W. Va.); Salmon & Salmon, 16 A. B. R. 122, 143 Fed. 395 (D. C. Mo.); In re Richardson, 27 A. B. R. 590, 192 Fed. 50 (D. C. Mass.).

35. West Co. *v.* Lea Bros., 2 A. B. R. 463, 174 U. S. 590, affirming Lea Bros. *v.* West, 1 A. B. R. 261, 91 Fed. 237; Bank *v.* Craig Bros., 6 A. B. R. 381, 110 Fed. 137 (D. C. Ky.); Day *v.* Beck & Gregg Hdw. Co., 8 A. B. R.

175, 114 Fed. 834 (C. C. A. Ala.); Bray *v.* Cobb, 1 A. B. R. 153 (D. C. N. C.).

36. But for cases holding that such assignments in and of themselves do operate to hinder, delay and defraud, see In re Salmon & Salmon, 16 A. B. R. 122, 143 Fed. 395 (D. C. Mo.); Rumsey *v.* Machine Co., 3 A. B. R. 704, 99 Fed. 699 (D. C. Mo.); Whittlesey *v.* Becker & Co., 25 A. B. R. 672 (Sup. Ct. N. Y.).

bankruptcy law.[37]

West Co. v. Lea, 2 A. B. R. 463, 174 U. S. 590, affirming Lea Bros. v. West, 1 A. B. R. 261, 91 Fed. 237: "Under the English bankruptcy statutes (as well that of 1869 as those upon which our earlier acts were modeled), and our own bankruptcy statutes down to and including the Act of 1867, the making of a deed of general assignment was deemed to be repugnant to the policy of the bankruptcy laws, and, as a necessary consequence, constituted an act of bankruptcy per se. This is shown by an examination of the decisions bearing upon the point, both English and American. * * * Neither, however, the Act of 1867, nor the amendments to it, contained an express provision that a deed of general assignment should be a conclusive act of bankruptcy. Such consequence was held to arise, from a deed of that description, as a legal result of the clause, in the Act of 1867, forbidding assignments with 'intent to delay, defraud, or hinder' creditors, and from the provision avoiding certain acts done to delay, defeat, or hinder the execution of the act. Rev. Stat. 5021, pars. 4, 7. Now, when it is considered that the present law, although it only retained some of the provisions of the Act of 1867, contains an express declaration that a deed of general assignment shall authorize the involuntary bankruptcy of the debtor making such a deed, all doubt as to the scope and intent of the law is removed." Quoted further, supra, at § 147.

Likewise in England.[38]

SUBDIVISION "B."

RECEIVERSHIPS AND TRUSTEESHIPS.

§ 150. Receivership Not Considered "Equivalent" of General Assignment.—In the present statute there was originally only this one act, the making of a general assignment for the benefit of creditors, enumerated under class 4; and there was no provision whatsoever in the law making receivership acts of bankruptcy. Accordingly, litigants who did not wish to conduct the administration of an insolvent estate in the bankruptcy court soon learned to have receivers appointed and thus to evade the bankruptcy court. Attempt was then made to have these receiverships declared to be acts of bankruptcy as being the "equivalent" of general assignments, as being in reality disguised assignments. This construction was frowned upon and declared improper and a torturing of plain words.[39]

---

37. (1867) In re Kasson, 18 Nat. Bank. Reg. 379; (1867) Globe Ins. Co. v. Cleveland Ins. Co., 14 Nat. Bank. Reg. 311, 10 Fed. Cas. 488; (1867) In re Beisenthal, 14 Blatchf. 146; (1867) Reed v. McIntyre, 98 U. S. 513; (1867) Boese v. King, 108 U. S. 385.

38. Globe Ins. Co. v. Cleveland Ins. Co., 14 Nat. Bank. Reg. 311; West Co. v. Lea, 2 A. B. R. 463, 174 U. S. 590, affirming Lea Bros. v. West, 1 A. B. R. 261, 91 Fed. 237.

39. In re Empire Metallic Bedstead Co., 3 A. B. R. 575, 98 Fed. 981 (C. C. A. N. Y., affirming 2 A. B. R. 329, reversing 1 A. B. R. 136); In re Spalding, 14 A. B. R. 131, 137 Fed. 1020 (C. C. A. N. Y.).

See also, In re Gilbert, 8 A. B. R. 101 (D. C. Ore.), in which case the facts were briefly these: an unfriendly suit pending against a bankrupt partnership; a stipulation therein made by one partner that a receiver might be appointed to wind up the partnership and pay creditors, and a subsequent

Vaccaro *v.* Security Bk., 4 A. B. R. 474, 103 Fed. 436 (C. C. A. Tenn.): "A general assignment is the voluntary act of the debtor, whereby he transfers his property to a trustee for the benefit of creditors. Its nature and characteristics were well understood. It is not enough to say that if the same consequences ensue from the appointment of a receiver that the one act is the equivalent of the other in law. Under § 3 of the Bankrupt Act very serious consequences attach to the making of a 'general assignment.' The debtor may be ever so solvent and the act highly advantageous to his creditors, still it is technically an act of bankruptcy, and some creditors are quite likely to imagine that some advantage will accrue by an adjudication in bankruptcy.

"We are not disposed to construe the provisions of the fourth subdivision of § 3 as including anything as a general assignment unless it is clearly one of those assignments known to the common law as a general assignment.

"The mere fact that the consequences which attach to the appointment of a receiver for the purpose of winding up a partnership or a corporation are similar to those which result to creditors from a general assignment is not enough.

"If the procurement of the appointment of a receiver to wind up the affairs of an insolvent partnership be an act of bankruptcy at all, it must come under some other of the subdivisions of § 3. What we here decide is, that it is not a 'general assignment,' under that section."

But it was intimated in some of the decisions that had the claim been placed on the ground that the receivership amounted to a transfer of property with intent to hinder creditors, a different conclusion might have been arrived at.[40] Yet, even on this ground it was held not to be an act of bankruptcy.[41]

Nevertheless, even before the Amendment of 1903, receiverships were held to operate as acts of bankruptcy in certain instances, where their effect was to create liens by legal proceedings or preferences in favor of workmen or operatives under State law.[42] But this ground could not be urged where no showing was made that such priorities would be created in

transfer to the receiver; held, not an act of bankruptcy and not the equivalent of a general assignment.

Davis *v.* Stevens, 4 A. B. R. 763, 104 Fed. 235 (D. C. S. Dak.). Compare, analogously, to same effect, Merry *v.* Jones, 11 A. B. R. 625 (Sup. Ct. Ga.). Compare, analogously, to same effect, Ex rel Strohl *v.* Sup. Ct. Kings Co., 2 A. B. R. 92 (Sup. Ct. Wash.). Compare, to same effect, In re Baker-Ricketson Co., 4 A. B. R. 605, 97 Fed. 489 (D. C. Mass.).

But compare [though here there appears to have been an actual assignment expressly made to the receiver, subsequently] Yungbluth *v.* Slipper, 26 A. B. R. 265, 185 Fed. 773 (C. C. A. Wash.).

40. In re Empire Metallic Bedstead Co., 3 A. B. R. 575, 98 Fed. 981 (C. C. A. N. Y., affirming 2 A. B. R. 329, reversing 1 A. B. R. 136).

41. In re Burrell & Corr, 9 A. B. R. 178, 123 Fed. 414 (D. C. N. Y., affirmed by Circuit Court of Appeals, 9 A. B. R. 625); In re Wilmington Hosiery Co., 9 A. B. R. 581, 120 Fed. 179 (D. C. Del.); In re Baker-Ricketson Co., 4 A. B. R. 605, 97 Fed. 489 (D. C. Mass.); In re Zeitner Brew. Co., 9 A. B. R. 63, 117 Fed. 799 (D. C. N. Y.).

42. See Mather *v.* Coe, 92 Fed. 333, 1 A. B. R. 504 (D. C. Ohio). This was doubtful law in view of the fact that such priorities would be recognized in the bankruptcy distribution itself under Bankr. Act, § 64 (b) (5) as priorities given by State law, under the doctrine of the case in In re Laird, 6 A.

the particular case in hand.[43] And where the receivership was one for the dissolution of a corporation, but was procured in order to cover preferences suffered by legal proceedings in favor of certain creditors, it was held to be an act of bankruptcy;[44] but not where it was for dissolution of a corporation and was not a mere subterfuge.[45]

However that may be, the difficulty was obviated by the Amendment of 1903, by which the ground of receivership or trusteeship was added.

§ 151. Receivership and Trusteeships as Acts of Bankruptcy.—

So now, secondly, for a debtor, being insolvent, to apply for a receiver or trustee of his property, or, because of insolvency, to have a receiver or trustee put in charge of it, is an act of bankruptcy.[46]

Obiter, Lowenstein v. Henry McShane Mfg. Co., 12 A. B. R. 604, 130 Fed. 1007 (D. C. Md.): "I have not considered that question, as I am of opinion that in the creditors' bill in the State court praying the appointment of receivers upon the allegation that the corporation was unable to pay its debts, and was in fact insolvent, and the answer of the corporation admitting the facts alleged in the bill, and consenting to the relief prayed, and the action of the court in granting the relief prayed and appointing receivers, who have been ever since in charge, constitutes the condition of affairs intended to be covered by the Amendment of 1903, the words of which are 'or because of insolvency a receiver or trustee has been put in charge of his property under the laws of a State,' etc."

B. R. 1, 109 Fed. 550 (C. C. A. Ohio).

43. In re Baker-Ricketson Co., 4 A. B. R. 605, 97 Fed. 489 (D. C. Mass.).

44. Scheuer v. Book Co., 7 A. B. R. 384, 112 Fed. 407 (C. C. A. Ala.). Compare, analogously, In re Storm, 4 A. B. R. 601, 103 Fed. 618 (D. C. N. Y.).

45. In re Empire Metallic Bedstead Co., 3 A. B. R. 575, 98 Fed. 981 (C. C. A. N. Y., affirming 2 A. B. R. 329, and reversing 1 A. B. R. 136). Receiverships, before the Amendment of 1903 made them acts of bankruptcy, were held to be such acts in Scheuer v. Book Co., 7 A. B. R. 384, 112 Fed. 407 (C. C. A. Ala.), in which case, however, the receivership was not squarely held to be the act of bankruptcy, but the act of bankruptcy was the suffering of certain preferential levies and payments, and the subsequent receivership was held to be a mere cover or subterfuge. Held, not to be acts of bankruptcy: In re Empire Metallic Bedstead Co., 2 A. B. R. 329, 98 Fed. 981 (D. C. N. Y., affirmed in 3 A. B. R. 575); In re Harper & Bros., 3 A. B. R. 804, 100 Fed. 266 (D. C. N. Y.). Collusive receivership with nothing done by the receiver, Blue Mtn., etc. v. Portner, 12 A. B. R. 559, 131 Fed. 57 (C. C. A. Md.). Receivership

amounting to insolvency proceedings, but apparently merely incidental to foreclosure of liens, Singer v. Nat'l Bedstead Mfg. Co., 11 A. B. R. 276 (N. J. Ct. Ch.), wherein also appears an interesting discussion, obiter, couched in a somewhat hostile tone, towards the entire law, however.

Receivership Amendment Not Retroactive.—This amendment is not retroactive so as to make an act of bankruptcy out of a receivership created before the amendment, even if the petition in bankruptcy was not filed until afterwards. Seaboard Steel Casting Co. v. Trigg, 10 A. B. R. 594, 124 Fed. 75 (D. C. Va.). But if the receivership were applied for after the amendment, although the suit in which the receiver was appointed was started before the amendment, nevertheless it is an act of bankruptcy. In re Edw. G. Milbury Co., 11 A. B. R. 523 (D. C. N. Y.).

46. Bankr. Act, § 3 (a) (4): In re Bennett Shoe Co., 15 A. B. R. 497, 140 Fed. 687 (D. C. Conn.); In re Hercules Atkin Co., 13 A. B. R. 369, 133 Fed. 813 (D. C. Pa.); In re Spalding, 14 A. B. R. 129, 139 Fed. 244 (C. C. A. N. Y.). In re Pickens Mfg. Co., 20 A. B. R. —, 158 Fed. 894 (D. C. Ga.);

§ 152. As to Receiverships Applied for by Debtor—Debtor Must Have Applied Therefor.

—When the act alleged is the debtor's application for a receiver, it will be necessary for the petitioning creditors to prove that the debtor himself made the application.[47]

In cases of corporations, it is not always requisite that there be a formal stockholders' meeting, or a meeting of the board of directors: the application for the receiver may still be substantially the act of the corporation, especially where there is fraud or an attempt to evade the provisions of the bankruptcy law.

Mercantile Co. v. Hardware & Steel Co., 24 A. B. R. 216 (238), 177 Fed. 825 (C. C. A. Nev.): "We are not here dealing with the lawful act of the plaintiff in error acting in a lawful corporate capacity, but with the acts of certain individuals holding all the stock of the corporation and constituting its officers and directors, who, it is alleged, have 'conspired and agreed together to take such measures and do such acts as would hinder, delay and defraud the creditors of said corporation * * * and would evade the provisions of the laws of the United States in reference to bankruptcy, and prevent such creditors from obtaining a knowledge of the true condition of said corporation's affairs, and from having or participating in the choice of a person or persons to act as trustee of said corporation or its property.' With respect to the acts of these parties it is alleged: 'That in pursuance of said conspiracy and agreement said directors and officers acting for and on behalf and as the act and deed of said corporation, which was then and there insolvent as aforesaid, on the 6th day of August, 1908, caused to be filed in the District Court of the First Judicial District of the State of Nevada, in and for the county of Esmeralda, an application praying for the appointment of a receiver with a view to the dissolution of said corporation.' The application for a receiver in the name of the stockholder as set forth in the petition is charged to be the act and deed of the corporation; and it is further charged that the directors and officers of the corporation acting for and on behalf and as the act and deed of the corporation accepted the service issued in the case, and thereupon caused to be filed with the court an appearance and application for the appointment of a receiver. We think these allegations are sufficient and charge the corporation with having committed an act of bankruptcy in applying for a receiver of its property. The corporate entity cannot be so disguised that it can successfully masquerade in the name of a stockholder, and, evading the searching eyes of a court of equity, hinder, delay and defraud its creditors and defeat the provisions of the Bankruptcy Act. A court of equity looks through forms to the substance of things, thus preserving the rights of innocent parties against all forms of deception and fraud."

And it is not a defense that the law of the State does not permit the corporation itself to apply for a receiver.

In re Electric Supply Co., 23 A. B. R. 647, 175 Fed. 612 (D. C. Ga.), quoted at § 153; In re Kennedy Tailoring Co., 23 A. B. R. 656, 175 Fed. 871 (D. C. Tenn.), quoted at § 157. See Master's Report, In re Douglass Coal & Coke Co., 12 A. B. R. 543, 131 Fed. 244 (Tenn.). See Master's Report, In re International Mercantile Agency, 13 A. B. R. 725 (D. C. N. J.);

In re Beatty, 17 A. B. R. 739 (C. C. A. Mass.). Instance. In re Edw. G. Milbury Co., L't'd, 11 A. B. R. 523 (D. C. N. Y.), where the receiver was appointed in an action under the State statute to dissolve the corporation.

47. Obiter. In re Spalding, 14 A. B. R. 129, 139 Fed. 244 (C. C. A. N. Y.), quoted, post, § 159.

Mercantile Co. *v.* Hardware & Steel Co., 24 A. B. R. 216 (238), 177 Fed. 825 (C. C. A. Nev.): "It is further objected that the laws of the State of Nevada do not permit or authorize a corporation to apply for the appointment of a receiver; that the State court did not have jurisdiction over such an application, and that the application for a receiver for a corporation to be an act of bankruptcy under the Bankruptcy Act must be an application made under the laws of the State, that is to say, it must in every respect be a lawful application conforming to the laws of the State. This is not the language of the Bankruptcy Act; nor do we think it was the purpose of Congress to make the act of bankruptcy dependent upon the pretended regularity of the proceedings of the State court. That court may be imposed upon and its jurisdiction invoked to defeat the jurisdiction of the bankruptcy court as charged in this case. It is sufficient that the corporation is insolvent, and, being insolvent, has applied for a receiver whereby the property of the corporation is to be taken possession of and administered and distributed by the State court."

It has been held that mere consent, being passive, is not tantamount to an application;[48] but "consent" in form, may amount in fact to an "application."

§ 153. Debtor to Be Insolvent at Time of Application and Insolvent According to Bankruptcy Definition.

—And it must be proved that the debtor was insolvent at the time he made the application.[49] This insolvency must be insolvency according to the bankruptcy definition; namely, that the debtor's property is not sufficient even at a fair valuation to equal his liabilities; and it will not do simply to prove that he is insolvent within the usual meaning of the term, namely, unable to pay his debts as they mature in the usual course of business.[50]

In re Ellsworth, 23 A. B. R. 284, 173 Fed. 699 (D. C. N. Y.): "If the company, while insolvent, had voluntarily brought an action to wind up its affairs for the benefit of its creditors, and had applied for the appointment of receivers to take charge of its property, the superior right of the bankruptcy court could not safely be questioned; but the interposition of an answer in an action brought by a contract creditor, admitting therein the truth of the allegations of the bill and joining in the prayer for relief, is not believed to be the equivalent of the term 'being insolvent, applied for a receiver or trustee for its property.' In the equity action, the complainants applied for receivers on the ground that the Edward Ellsworth Company was unable to pay its debts as they matured, and that it would be to the advantage of creditors and stockholders to have its affairs wound up. Nowhere in the bill is it asserted that the corporation is

---

48. In re Gold Run, etc., Co., 29 A. B. R. 563, 200 Fed. 162 (D. C. Colo.).

49. Obiter, In re Spalding, 14 A. B. R. 129, 139 Fed. 244 (C. C. A. N. Y., reversing 13 A. B. R. 223), quoted post, § 159. Compare, In re Douglass Coal & Coke Co., 12 A. B. R. 545, 546, 131 Fed. 769 (Tenn.).

50. In re Douglass Coal & Coke Co., 12 A. B. R. 545, 546, 131 Fed. 769 (Tenn.); In re Pickens Mfg. Co., 20 A. B. R. 202, 158 Fed. 894 (D. C. Ga.).

Insolvency—A question for jury.—The question of insolvency is one for the jury. Blue Mtn., etc., *v.* Portner, 12 A. B. R. 559, 131 Fed. 57 (C. C. A. Md.). But where the facts are definitely established the question of solvency becomes one of law, on which the court may give binding instructions. In re Iron Clad Mfg. Co., 28 A. B. R. 628, 197 Fed. 280 (C. C. A. N. Y.).

insolvent, as that term is defined by § 1, subd. 15, of the Bankruptcy Act. In fact, the bill contains an affirmative allegation that the defendant is solvent. Such averments, together with the admission by the corporation of their truth and its consent to the appointment of receivers of its property, undoubtedly vested the circuit court, in view of the diversity of citizenship of the parties, with power and authority to act in the premises."

But admissions of the debtor, in his application for the appointment of a receiver, that his financial condition is such that he cannot hope to continue his business, that his credit is seriously impaired if not wholly destroyed, that it is impossible to raise the necessary capital with which to meet his maturing obligations, and that he is being threatened with suits which must result in levies, may amount to proof of insufficiency of assets to meet obligations, within the meaning of the Bankruptcy Act, notwithstanding that insolvency may have been formally denied.

In re Electric Supply Co., 23 A. B. R. 647, 175 Fed. 612 (D. C. Ga.): "When, therefore, the defendant alleges that, owing to the gross mismanagement of its affairs, 'its condition is such that it cannot hope to continue its business, that it is impossible to raise the necessary capital to meet its matured and maturing obligations, that its promissory notes, accounts, and other obligations are past due, that it is threatened with suits, which must result in levies and in the depletion of the assets,' it is but an elaborate declaration that it has nothing sufficient to pay its debts. This condition is not amended by its prayer to the State court for leave to surrender its charter and to go out of business, to sell its properties as quickly as possible and turn them into cash, and to stand off through the injunctive power of the State court all persons having claims against it while this process of disintegration is going on. It is true that the alleged bankrupt, with some astucity, is careful to say that it is not insolvent. It is careful also to adopt resolutions expressly denying insolvency. But the denial is unimportant in view of the recitals showing its utter incapacity to pay its debts. * * * It is true that in that case insolvency was distinctly alleged. Here, as we have seen, there is an attempt to deny it; but the averments of the Electric Supply Company, made in its petition to the Superior Court, sworn to by its president, and presented as a part of its answer here, so conclusively show insolvency that there can be no doubt that it was the true and substantial basis of the petition, and the court will not shut its eyes to the truth, * * * notwithstanding the pleader's art may have been utilized to defeat the operation of the bankruptcy law. * * * The court is constrained to make this determination because of consideration of law and the sworn admission of record made by the bankrupt above set forth."

But if the receiver was appointed on the application of the bankrupt, it is not material that insolvency be a ground of receivership under the State law; much less that such insolvency be established by the record of the State court.

Mercantile Co. v. Hardware & Steel Co., 24 A. B. R. 216 (238), 177 Fed. 825 (C. C. A. Nev.): "But our attention has not been called to any case that holds that under the first provision of the statute where the creditors' petition charges a single act of bankruptcy, viz, 'being insolvent applied for a receiver or trustee

1 R B—11

for his property,' the act of bankruptcy is dependent upon the record in the
court to which the application for a receiver is made; that is to say, we do not
find any case holding that unless the petition to the court for a receiver states
that the application is based upon the insolvency no act of bankruptcy has been
committed."

**§ 154. And Burden of Proof of Insolvency Not Shifted by Debt-
or's Failure to Produce Books and Appear for Examination at Trial.**
—Moreover, this proof of insolvency probably must be made affirmatively
by the creditors without the aid of the provisions of the later clause of this
section prescribing that the burden of proof of solvency shall rest on the
debtor in certain cases and in other cases that he must attend court with all
his books and papers, on failure to do which the petitioning creditors will be
relieved of proof of insolvency and the burden of proving solvency will shift
to the debtor. This later clause was not amended to include the amended
part of acts of bankruptcy and probably, therefore, the burden of proof of
the insolvency will rest on the creditor without aid therefrom.

**§ 155. As to Receiverships "Because of Insolvency"—Actual In-
solvency Not Requisite.**—On the other hand it would seem that where the
act complained of as ground of bankruptcy is the putting of a receiver in
charge because of insolvency, all that would be necessary would be to prove
that a receiver was put in charge of the property on the ground of insolvency, no matter whether the debtor actually be insolvent or not.[51]

Inferentially, but obiter, In re Pickens Mfg. Co., 2 A. B. R. 202, 158 Fed. 894
(D. C. Ga.): "Counsel for the petitioning creditors claim that insolvency stands
adjudicated against the company by the action of the State court and by the
company's action in connection with those proceedings, and that it is precluded
thereby from a further hearing here. The language of this Amendment of 1903
is peculiar in that it provides that 'being insolvent, applied for a receiver,' etc.,
and then in the disjunctive 'or because of insolvency a receiver or trustee has
been put in charge,' etc. This lends some point to the argument that where
insolvency is found as a fact by the state court, and a receiver appointed on that
ground, insolvency is adjudicated and will be assumed here. The practice, however, in the courts, so far as there has been a practice established, seems to
allow a hearing here on the question of insolvency, notwithstanding the fact of
the commission of an act of bankruptcy, under this amendment."

**§ 156. Whether "Insolvency" Alleged Need Be Insolvency Ac-
cording to Bankruptcy Definition.**—And it would also seem to be immaterial what definition may have been given to the word "insolvency" by
the court appointing the receiver.[52] Nevertheless, it has been held that the
insolvency must have been insolvency according to the Bankruptcy Act's
definition.[53]

51. In re Spalding, 14 A. B. R. 129,
139 Fed. 244 (C. C. A. N. Y.). Also,
see Master's Report, In re Douglass
Coal & Coke Co., 12 A. B. R. 545, 546,
131 Fed. 769 (Tenn.).

52. See Master's Report, In re
Douglass Coal & Coke Co., 12 A. B.
R. 545, 546, 131 Fed. 769.
53. Compare, In re Ellsworth Co.,
23 A. B. R. 284, 173 Fed. 699 (D. C. N.

In re Golden Malt Cream Co., 21 A. B. R. 36, 164 Fed. 326 (C. C. A. Ind.):
"Section 3, par. 'a,' subdiv. 4, of the Bankruptcy Act provides that it shall be an
act of bankruptcy, when because of insolvency, a receiver or trustee has been put
in charge of his property under the laws of a state; from which it is argued by
petitioners that the act of bankruptcy does not depend upon the actual status
of insolvency, as that status is fixed by the Bankruptcy Act, but upon the fact
that a finding of insolvency is disclosed in the record of the state court upon
the basis of which a receiver was appointed; and that such finding cannot, after
bankruptcy proceedings are begun, be recalled. We cannot concur in this
view of the law. The word 'insolvency,' as used in the Bankruptcy Act, means
insolvency within the meaning of the definition of that act. And though the
same words be employed in the finding of the state court to define a set of
facts different from the facts intended to be defined by the word in the Bankruptcy Act, the state court is not without power, by appropriate amendment to
so change its order that such order will set forth the real facts on which the
order was intended to act; for certainty a mere divergence of the definition ought
not to have the effect of making that an act of bankruptcy which in fact was not
intended by the bankruptcy law to be an act of bankruptcy."

§ 157. Whether "Insolvency" Must Be Ground for Receivership by State Law, and Appointment Based on That Ground.

—But if the re-
ceiver is put in charge "because of insolvency" under a statutory provision,
such statutory provision, it would seem, must provide insolvency as one of
the grounds for receivership. Merely that the application alleges insolvency
and the court finds insolvency will not suffice, it would seem, if "insolvency"
be not a ground for receivership under the law of the State whose court
appoints the receiver.[54]

In re Spalding, 14 A. B. R. 129, 139 Fed. 245 (C. C. A. N. Y., reversing 13
A. B. R. 223): "Inasmuch as in the present case the receiver was not appointed
upon the application of Spalding, it is immaterial whether Spalding was at the
time insolvent. It is also immaterial that the plaintiff in the action may have
alleged as one of the evidential facts of fraud that Spalding was insolvent. It
suffices that the court in exercising its authority did not purport to do so upon
that ground, and that the order appointing the receiver and reciting the grounds
for the action of the court is conclusive to the contrary. The receiver was
appointed because the court found that Spalding had disposed and was threatened
to dispose of his property with intent to defraud the plaintiff in the action
and other creditors, and assigned this as the only ground for its action in putting a receiver in charge of his property."

But compare, In re Underwear Co., 18 A. B. R. 620, 153 Fed. 224 (D. C. Conn.):
"The only decision in this circuit which offers aid in reaching a conclusion upon
the matter under consideration is In re Spalding, 14 Am. B. R. 129, 139 Fed. 245.
The law of New York under which, in that case, a receiver was appointed to
take charge of Spalding's property, did not cover insolvency as a jurisdictional
fact. The creditor's petition therein was granted upon other distinct grounds,
and insolvency was only brought in incidentally, and could not influence, much
less control, the judgment. In New York a corporation could have been pro-

Y.), quoted at §§ 153, 158, 159, 305.
54. Schumert & Warfield, Ltd., v.
Security Brew. Co., 28 A. B. R. 676,
199 Fed. 358 (D. C. La.).

ceeded against because of insolvency, but an individual could not. Under the laws of Connecticut there is no provision for alleging insolvency eo nomine as the cause for obtaining a receivership over the property and affairs of a corporation. * * * It seems to me that upon this record alone it must be apparent to any reasonable mind that the facts found by that court show that it was 'because of insolvency' that the receiver was appointed. The record certainly does not show conclusively that insolvency was not the cause, or one of the causes, which led to the appointment. It may be said to exhibit a prima facie showing of insolvency of sufficient force to put the respondent corporation in this court upon its proofs. If such a rule be adopted, no harm can come to any one hereafter. If applications shall be made to the State courts for receivers in cases where beyond question the corporation is solvent, the record in the state court will undoubtedly proclaim the fact in a convincing way. The situation is so serious that I cannot bring myself to believe that the spirit of the bankruptcy law will permit such a technical construction of section 3 subd. 4, of the Bankruptcy Act * * * as the respondents ask for; nor can I believe that the spirit of In re Spalding commands such action, although I am bound to admit that its letter might not unreasonably be so interpreted."

Likewise, mere temporary receivers appointed to preserve the property until the statutory inquiry to determine insolvency can be made, will not suffice.

Zugalla v. Mercantile Agency, 16 A. B. R. 75 (C. C. A. N. J.): "It will be observed that the New Jersey statute, under which this proceeding was begun, authorizes the issue of an injunction only after the court has, upon due notice, instituted an inquiry and heard proofs and allegations to satisfy itself 'that the corporation has become insolvent and is not about to resume its business in a short time,' etc. It is also to be observed that under this statute, receivers can be appointed only at the time of the issuing of the injunction, or at some time thereafter. It follows, therefore, that the receivers, with the drastic powers and authority conferred by the statute, can only be appointed after a judicial determination of the insolvency of the corporation. * * *

"It is manifest that the restraining order and the appointment of a receiver, covered by this order, are not the injunction and appointment of a receiver contemplated by the statute, after a judicial inquiry as to the alleged statutory insolvency of the corporation. The order was evidently made under the general equity powers of the Court of Chancery, and not under statutory authority. It was made, both as a restraining order and as an appointment of a receiver, to preserve in statu quo the property and assets of the corporation, in the custody of an officer of the court, until action could be taken under the statute, and the judicial inquiry contemplated by the statute and provided for in the preliminary order itself, with due notice to all parties in interest, had been completed."

However, the statute makes no distinction between "temporary" receivers and any other kind of receivers.

Blue Mountain Iron & Steel Co. v. Portner, 12 A. B. R. 559, 131 Fed. 57 (C. C. A. Md.): "That the Bankruptcy Act requires permanent receivers to be appointed would be to read into the statute something the lawmaking department —Congress—did not see proper to put there."

In re Kennedy Tailoring Co., 23 A. B. R. 656, 175 Fed. 871 (D. C. Tenn.):

"The Bankruptcy Act furthermore draws no distinction between temporary and permanent receivers, but makes the simple fact of a receiver having been placed in charge of the defendant's property on the ground of insolvency an act of bankruptcy."

And an allegation that the corporation merely was "in imminent danger of insolvency" has been held insufficient, on what appears, however, to be finely drawn distinctions.

In re (Perry) Aldrich Co., 21 A. B. R. 246, 165 Fed. 249 (D. C. Mass.): "It seems to me clear that the papers in the case wholly fail to show that the receivers appointed were put in charge of the defendant's property 'because of insolvency.' It is impossible to say, on what appears from them, that insolvency as defined in the Bankruptcy Act was one of the grounds upon which the court acted in making its decree. The allegations of the bill do not imply in-solvency, they go no further than to say that there is danger of insolvency,—in which sense is left uncertain. Whatever the kind of insolvency meant, the inference is that it does not yet exist. Whether the corporation was actually insolvent or not when the bill was filed or the receivers appointed under it, seems to me wholly immaterial unless it can also be made to appear that the court so found, either upon the evidence before it or the agreements of the parties, and made the fact at least one of the grounds of its action. In this case, the deposition of the learned justice of the Maine Supreme Court who heard the case and made the decree appointing the receivers has been taken by the parties opposing adjudication, and is before me. It leaves no doubt whatever in my mind not only that he understood both parties to say that the corporation was then solvent, but that he told counsel at the hearing that if a receivership was desired on the ground of insolvency it probably could not be granted, in view of the decision, then recent, in Moody v. Port Clyde Development Co., 102 Maine 365—and that, as he expressly states, he did not appoint the receivers by reason of the corporation's insolvency. It seems to me clear that such insolvency entered in no way into the result arrived at by the court. In view of this deposition it seems to me idle to discuss or consider any evidence as to what was or was not said by counsel, witnesses or parties at the hearing. If any one of them stated or argued that the corporation was insolvent, they must have done so without affecting in any way the action of the court."

But insolvency need not be a statutory ground for a receiver; it is sufficient if the State law other than that which is statutory makes it such.

In re Kennedy Tailoring Co., 23 A. B. R. 656, 175 Fed. 871 (D. C. Tenn.): "I find no authority holding that in order to constitute an act of bankruptcy under this section of the act, the appointment of a receiver must be made by the state court under a state statute. On the contrary, the fact that a receiver has been put in charge by a state court, although acting under its general equity power, seems to be recognized, implicitly at least, as constituting an appointment under the laws of the state. * * * In Lowenstein v. Mfg. Co. (D. C.), 12 Am. B. R. 601, 130 Fed. 1007; Hooks v. Aldridge (C. C. A., Fifth Circuit), 16 Am. B. R. 658, 145 Fed. 865, and Beatty v. Coal Mining Co. (C. C. A., First Circuit), 17 Am. B. R. 738, 150 Fed. 293. See, also, 1 Remington on Bankruptcy, § 151, p. 132. The case of Zugalla v. Mercantile Agency (C. C. A., Third Circuit), 16 Am. B. R. 67, 142 Fed. 927, does not, as I view it, hold to the contrary; the reference in that opinion to the fact that the receiver had not been appointed under the state statute, but under the general equity power of the court, not being made with reference to the question now under consideration, but to show that the appointment of the receiver was made merely for the purpose of taking custody of the property, and not as an appointment of a receiver on the ground of insolvency under the state statute."

Where the receiver is one "applied for" by the bankrupt, insolvency need not be a ground for the appointment of a receiver either under statute or general law. [55]

§ 158. Ground of Receivership, as Being "Insolvency" Provable Only by Record, unless Record Silent.—The fact that the receiver was put in charge on the ground of insolvency must be proved by the record of the Court that put him in charge, unless the record is silent.

In re Spalding, 14 A. B. R. 129, 139 Fed. 245 (C. C. A. N. Y.): "If the court had merely appointed a receiver without reciting the ground of its judgment, the record could have been referred to, or the grounds shown by evidence aliunde. Russell v. Place, 94 U. S. 608; Davis v. Brown, 94 U. S. 428, 429. But having recited the grounds, the recitals cannot be contradicted without impeaching the record, and this is inadmissible. In re Watts, 190 U. S. 35, 10 A. B. R. 113."

Blue Mountain Iron & Steel Co. v. Portner, 12 A. B. R. 559, 131 Fed. 57 (C. C. A. Md.): "It does not require argument to sustain the position that the order appointing the receivers being in writing must speak for itself, and no declaration of the judge who signed it can be given grounds on which to enter the order. Public records can neither be explained nor varied by parol testimony. They are conclusive, speak for themselves, and imply absolute verity. * * *

"The best evidence of the appointment of the receiver was the record of the proceedings in equity in the court which made the appointment. It was the basis of the issue, and could have been proved in no other way. The record was competent for this purpose, and no authority is cited holding that the best evidence of a proceeding in a court of equity is not the record of the proceeding."

In re Ellsworth Co., 23 A. B. R. 284, 173 Fed. 699 (D. C. N. Y.): "Inasmuch as the record in the Circuit Court action does not assert or claim that the Edward Ellsworth Company was insolvent, within the meaning of the Bankruptcy Act, this court is precluded from considering evidence aliunde to contradict the judgment or decree appointing receivers and setting forth the basis of such appointment." Quoted further at §§ 153, 159, 1305, 1909.

The papers in the case may not be used to contradict the recitals of the decree.[56] But where the decree is silent as to the grounds, the papers in the case may be consulted or evidence aliunde be produced.[57]

---

55. Mercantile Co. v. Hardware & Steel Co., 24 A. B. R. 216, 177 Fed. 825 (C. C. A. Nev.), quoted ante, §§ 152, 153.

56. In re Spalding, 14 A. B. R. 129, 139 Fed. 245 (C. C. A. N. Y.), 13 A. B. R. 223 (D. C. N. Y.).

57. Obiter. In re Spalding, 14 A. B.

In re Kennedy Tailoring Co., 23 A. B. R. 656, 175 Fed. 871 (D. C. Tenn.): "It is, however, settled by the weight of authority that, where the order of the state court appointing a receiver does not show the ground upon which it is made, extrinsic evidence may be introduced to establish that fact."

The testimony of the judge as to the real grounds of the receivership is not competent,[58] excepting, perhaps, where the reason for the appointment is not shown by the record.[59] The allegation in the pleadings of the ground of the receivership need not allege insolvency in hæc verbis: equivalent words are doubtless sufficient.[60] The suit itself need not be brought on the ground of insolvency; it is the appointment of a receiver on that ground that is the act to be alleged.[61] Insolvency must be one of the grounds urged and it must be a good ground in the law; but insolvency need not be the sole ground of the appointment;[62] and the statute is to be honestly, practically and fairly construed to effect its object, and not to be strictly construed to defeat it if possible.[63]

In re Beatty, 17 A. B. R. 743; 150 Fed. 293 (C. C. A. Mass.): "As the statutes of bankruptcy, are to have an honest and practical interpretation, we are not to inject into what we have quoted therefrom, such phraselogy as would require that the cause of the receivership need be solely insolvency. If insolvency, either as a distinct ground of proceeding or as coupled with others, was one of the substantial reasons for the appointment of the receiver, the case would come within the reasonable construction of the statute. The same line of reasoning disposes of a proposition which has been strongly urged on us, to the effect that the Superior Court, under the local rules administered in Massachusetts, had no jurisdiction to appoint a receiver on account of insolvency. The Superior Court is a court of general equity jurisdiction; and, if it exceeded its jurisdiction in the particular mentioned, the excess would be of the kind remediable only by appeal, and would not render its proceeding void. Such being the fact, and the statutes of bankruptcy being practical statutes, we have no doubt they are satisfied if the Superior Court did in fact appoint a receiver on the ground of insolvency, either as the sole ground of its proceeding or in a mixed case under the circumstances which we have explained."

R. 129, 139 Fed. 245 (C. C. A. N. Y.); Russell v. Place, 94 U. S. 608; Davis v. Brown, 94 U. S. 429. Apparently, Hooks v. Aldridge, 16 A. B. R. 662, 145 Fed. 865 (C. C. A. Tex.).

58. Blue Mtn., etc., v. Portner, 12 A. B. R. 559, 131 Fed. 57 (C. C. A. Md.).

59. Schumert & Warfield, Ltd. v. Security Brew. Co., 28 A. B. R. 676, 199 Fed. 358 (D. C. La.).

60. Impliedly, Hooks v. Aldridge, 16 A. B. R. 662, 145 Fed. 865 (C. C. A. Tex.). Analogously, as admission of actual insolvency, where receivership applied for by debtor. In re Electric Supply Co., 23 A. B. R. 647, 175 Fed. 612 (D. C. Ga.), quoted at § 153; In re Kennedy Tailoring Co., 23 A. B. R. 656, 175 Fed. 871 (D. C. Tenn.). In-

stance, contra, In re Ellsworth Co., 23 A. B. R. 284, 173 Fed. 699 (D. C. N. Y.).

61. In re Spalding, 13 A. B. R. 223 (D. C. N. Y.).

62. In re Beatty, 17 A. B. R. 743, 150 Fed. 293 (C. C. A. Mass.); In re Electric Supply Co., 23 A. B. R. 647, 175 Fed. 612 (D. C. Ga.); In re Kennedy Tailoring Co., 23 A. B. R. 656, 175 Fed. 871 (D. C. Tenn.); Hooks v. Aldridge, 16 A. B. R. 662, 145 Fed. 865 (C. C. A. Tex.).

63. In re Spalding, 13 A. B. R. 223 (D. C. N. Y.). Instance, apparently, Hooks v. Aldridge, 16 A. B. R. 662, 145 Fed. 865 (C. C. A. Tex.). In re Electric Supply Co., 23 A. B. R. 647, 175 Fed. 612 (D. C. Ga.), quoted at § 153. But compare, that it is to be strictly

The questions whether such receiver was appointed on the ground of insolvency and took charge of the property are for the jury.[64]

§ 159. Receiver Appointed but Not on Ground of Insolvency, Not This Act of Bankruptcy.

—If the receivership is applied for by others than the debtor himself and the application therefor is not made on the ground of insolvency, it is not an act of bankruptcy, although the debtor may, in fact, be insolvent.[65]

In re Douglass Coal & Coke Co., 12 A. B. R. 539, 131 Fed. 769 (D. C. Tenn.): "There is no doubt in this case about insolvency being established, in the legal sense; but Congress has used such language as makes it necessary that a receivership in a State court, in order to constitute an act of bankruptcy, must have been established, or the receiver appointed, on the ground of the corporation's insolvency. It is very much open to doubt whether Congress has not here used language which makes necessary a result which Congress itself intended to avoid. Looking to the practical bearing of the question, there is much reason to believe that Congress intended to make the appointment of a receiver in a State court conclusive as a ground of bankruptcy, without requiring this court to inquire into the grounds on which the receivership was created; but the language of the amendatory act is perfectly plain, in requiring that the existence of a receivership in a State Court, in order to be a ground of bankruptcy, must have been on account of the insolvency of the corporation, and this leaves open in any case to inquiry by this court the grounds on which the appointment of a receiver was made, and, if the appointment was made on any other ground than that of insolvency, it does not constitute an act of bankruptcy. Now, in the case here considered, the appointment was on account of breaches of covenants— covenants like the covenant to keep down taxes, and the like—and, although these particular acts or defaults strongly tend to show insolvency, they justify the appointment of a receiver, regardless of insolvency; and it seems that, in form, at least, the receivership was established on the ground of breaches of these covenants."

Thus, the appointment of a receiver over an individual judgment debtor's property, on the creditor's application in a creditor's action to set aside an alleged fraudulent conveyance, the statute of the State, not giving "insolvency" as a ground for the appointment of a receiver over the property of an individual, is not an act of bankruptcy.

In re Spalding, 14 A. B. R. 129, 139 Fed. 245 (C. C. A. N. Y.): "Giving subd. a (4) the construction which its language demands, we are of the opinion that it does not make a receivership an act of bankruptcy unless it was procured

---

construed, In re Ellsworth Co., 23 A. B. R. 284, 173 Fed. 699 (D. C. N. Y.), quoted at §§ 153, 159, 305.

64. Blue Mtn., etc., v. Portner, 12 A. B. R. 559, 131 Fed. 57 (C. C. A. Md.).
Doctrine Not Applicable to Cases of Receivership Applied for by Bankrupt. —The doctrine of § 158 is not applicable to cases of receivership applied for by the debtor. Mercantile Co. v. Hard-

ware & Steel Co., 24 A. B. R. 216 (238), 177 Fed. 825 (C. C. N. Y.), quoted at §§ 152, 153.

65. Compare, although perhaps rightly to be considered application by corporation itself, being by complaining stockholders, In re (Perry) Aldrich Co., 21 A. B. R. 246, 165 Fed. 249 (D. C. Mass.), quoted at § 157.

upon the application of the insolvent himself and while insolvent, and does not make the putting a receiver in charge of the property of an insolvent an act of bankruptcy unless this was done because of insolvency; and if the latter provision applies to any case where the trustee has not been put in charge pursuant to some statute of the State, or a receiver put in charge by a court acting under statutory authority, it certainly applies only when this has been done because of insolvency. In most of the States statutory provisions exist conferring jurisdiction upon designated courts for the appointment of receivers. The statutes of New York authorize the appointments of receivers of corporations in cases of insolvency, but there is no statute authorizing the appointment by any court of a receiver of the property of an individual merely upon the ground of his insolvency. The appointment in the present case was doubtless made pursuant to section 713 of the Code of Civil Procedure, which authorizes the appointment of a receiver of 'the property which is the subject of the action' upon the application of a party who establishes an 'apparent right to or interest in the property, where it is in the possession of an adverse party,' and when its custody by a receiver becomes expedient.

"Inasmuch as in the present case the receiver was not appointed upon the application of Spalding, it is immaterial whether Spalding was at the time insolvent. It is also immaterial that the plaintiff in the action may have alleged as one of the evidential facts of fraud that Spalding was insolvent. It suffices that the court in exercising its authority did not purport to do so under that ground, and that the order appointing the receiver and reciting the ground for the action of the court is conclusive to the contrary. The receiver was appointed because the court found that Spalding had disposed and was threatening to dispose of his property with intent to defraud the plaintiff in the action and other creditors, and assigned this as the only ground for its action in putting a receiver in charge of his property."

And where the surviving partner of an insolvent partnership joins with the administrator of the deceased partner in statutory proceedings for the appointment of a receiver in the probate court to wind up insolvent partnerships on the death of a partner, an act of bankruptcy has not been committed.

National Bank v. Arend, 16 A. B. R. 867, 146 Fed. 351 (C. C. A. Ohio): "It is conceded that this was not a case where 'because of insolvency a receiver has been put in charge of property,' because clearly the receiver was not appointed because of insolvency, but because of the death of a partner and to wind up the partnership. * * * But it is submitted that, since the firm and the surviving partner were insolvent and the latter joined in the application, he 'being insolvent applied for a receiver or trustee for his property,' and therefore committed an act of bankruptcy."

"But, as held by the court below, the surviving partner never really applied for a receiver. He had no power under the Ohio statute to apply for a receiver. He had the option of taking the interest of the deceased partner at the appraisement. He had thirty days in which to exercise this option. He did not want the interest at the appraisement, so he waived the thirty days and immediately declared his intention of not exercising the option. When he had done this, he had exhausted the power conferred upon him by the statute. It then became the positive duty of the administrator to apply for the appointment of a receiver to wind up the business."

And equity proceedings for the winding up of insolvent corporations and their reorganization have sometimes been upheld, by giving strict and literal interpretation to the terms.[66]

In re Ellsworth Co., 23 A. B. R. 284, 173 Fed. 699 (D. C. N. Y.): "True, it is claimed that there was collusion between the parties to the equity suit to defeat the operation of the Bankruptcy Act; but it is not contended that there was fraud or wrongful act by either of the parties to confer jurisdiction upon the circuit court. Such being the fact, the particular object sought to be accomplished in the equity action, the winding up of the business of the corporation or perhaps its reorganization, or readjustment of its affairs or any wrongs to dissatisfied creditors, that are supposed to ensue therefrom, are not thought material on this application." Quoted further at §§ 153, 158, 305.

§ 160. Appointment of Trustee as Act of Bankruptcy Not Necessarily Appointment by Court.

—The trustee need not have been put in charge by any court proceedings.[67]

Thus, this act of bankruptcy may be committed by the dissolution and winding up of corporations and other companies under statutes without court proceedings.[68]

And it has been intimated, that a statutory proceeding to wind up an insolvent corporation on petition of creditors, where no receiver nor trustee is expressly designated, but merely the sheriff sells the property and distributes the proceeds among creditors, is this act of bankruptcy.

In re International Coal Min. Co., 16 A. B. R. 311, 143 Fed. 665 (D. C. Pa.): "It is made an act of bankruptcy to put a receiver or trustee in charge of the property of a corporation under State laws by § 3, subd. 4, and the substitution of the sheriff to effect the same result will not defeat the provisions of the act." "In this proceeding, the property of the insolvent corporation is not placed in the hands of a receiver or trustee by that name, but it is so in effect, because the sheriff, after a sale of the property on execution, is required to distribute the net proceeds among the creditors of the corporation according to the rules established in cases of insolvency of individuals, and the same as a receiver or trustee would have been required to do under the law relating to insolvent debtors in the state." Subsequently, in this case, the corporation committed an additional act of bankruptcy, by admitting, in writing, its insolvency and its willingness to be adjudged bankrupt. See Coal & Coke Co. v. Stauffer, 17 A. B. R. 573, 148 Fed. 981 (C. C. A. Pa.).

---

66. See post, § 305.
67. In re Hercules Atkin Co., 13 A. B. R. 369, 133 Fed. 813 (D. C. Pa.).
68. In re Hercules Atkin Co., 13 A.

B. R. 369, 133 Fed. 813 (D. C. Pa.); In re Bennett Shoe Co., 15 A. B. R. 497, 140 Fed. 687 (D. C. Conn.).

DIVISION 5.

FIFTH CLASS OF ACTS OF BANKRUPTCY—WRITTEN ADMISSION OF INABILITY TO PAY DEBTS AND WILLINGNESS TO BE ADJUDGED BANKRUPT THEREFOR.

§ 161. Fifth Class of Acts of Bankruptcy.—The debtor commits an act of bankruptcy if he admits in writing his inability to pay his debts and his willingness to be adjudged bankrupt on that ground.[69]

§ 162. No Fraud Implied.—As to the fifth and last class of acts of bankruptcy, it is also to be said no fraud is implied; the act is wholly innocent. Indeed, nothing shows more clearly than do the last four statutory classes of acts for throwing a debtor into bankruptcy, how different the theory of bankruptcy law is nowadays from what it was in the time of King Henry VIII, when bankruptcy was felony, or from what it was even as late as King James' times, when it was still a felony and the bankrupt was specifically declared to be a felon by the statute itself, with all that the word felon implied in those days.

§ 163. Purpose of Act.—The purpose of creating this act of bankruptcy is at first hard to discover. It would seem that a debtor who had gone thus far would probably be willing to go further and file a petition in bankruptcy voluntarily and at much less cost and ceremony, too. But experience has shown that many an insolvent who ought to place his affairs in the hands of the court is unwilling or unable to take the step, though willing to admit in writing his inability to pay his debts and his willingness to be adjudged bankrupt on that ground.

It is also to be remembered that the Bankruptcy Act of 1867, though not mentioning the filing of a voluntary petition among the acts of bankruptcy formally set forth in § 39 of that Act, nevertheless in Section II provided that if the debtor should file a petition "setting forth * * * his inability to pay all his debts in full, his willingness to surrender all his estate and effects for the benefit of his creditors and his desire to obtain the benefit of this Act * * * the filing of such petition shall be an act of bankruptcy."

The framers of the present law gathered up this act of bankruptcy from the old law of 1867 and placed it in its proper order as one of the acts of bankruptcy specifically classified as such.[70]

---

69. Bankr. Act, § 3 (a) (5).
70. Before the Amendment of 1910 a corporation was forbidden voluntarily to go into bankruptcy, but this 5th act of bankruptcy afforded an easy and perhaps justifiable method of evading such restriction, so that in practice the prohibition upon a corporation going voluntarily into bankruptcy amounted merely to this: that it had to have the co-operation or consent of some of its creditors. See In re Moench, 12 A. B. R. 243, 130 Fed. 685 (C. C. N. Y.): "It is no doubt true that by committing either the fourth or fifth acts of bankruptcy, when three creditors stand ready at once to take advantage of it by filing a petition, the corporation achieves the object which the act forbids it to secure by

§ 164. Voluntary Petition Itself a Commission of Fifth Act of Bankruptcy.

—In theory, at least, it is this act of bankruptcy which is committed by every voluntary bankrupt in filing his petition for adjudication, for the petition expressly admits in writing the debtor's inability to pay his debts and his willingness and desire to be adjudged bankrupt because of it.[71]

National Bk. *v.* Moyses, 8 A. B. R. 10, 186 U. S. 181: "The petition must state that 'petitioner owes debts which he is unable to pay in full' and that 'he is willing to surrender all his property for the benefit of his creditors, except such as is exempt by law'. This establishes those facts so far as a decree of bankruptcy is concerned, and he has committed an act of bankruptcy in filing the petition."

In re Forbes, 11 A. B. R. 791, 128 Fed. 137 (D. C. Mass.): "A voluntary petition is itself treated as an act of bankruptcy."

§ 165. Admission to Be Unqualified.

—The admission must be unqualified, and must be made before the involuntary petition is filed.

In re Baker-Ricketson Co., 4 A. B. R. 606, 97 Fed. 489 (D. C. Mass.): "The vote of the corporation was not an act of bankruptcy, within the meaning of the statute, because it was not in itself a written admission, but merely authorized one of its officers to make that admission if a petition in bankruptcy was filed. This is not such an unqualified admission as is required by the statute. The paper signed by Mr. Ricketson does not support the allegations of the petition. Even if the petition be again amended so as to include this paper, it is hard to see how an admission, made after the petition has been filed, constitutes an act of bankruptcy of which the petitioner can avail himself."

Thus, an answer admitting insolvency, accompanied with a consent to the appointment of a receiver, is not equivalent to a written admission and willingness under this fifth act of bankruptcy.[72]

Likewise, a mere resolution of a board of directors authorizing an attorney to represent the corporation in any bankruptcy proceedings that might be brought thereafter and to consent to the appointment of a receiver is not sufficient.[73]

its own voluntary petition, but its doing so is not such a 'fraud upon the act' as to prevent the application of the plain language of the act to the facts presented."

Also, In re New Amsterdam Motor Co., 24 A. B. R. 757, 80 Fed. 943 (D. C. N. Y.): "If the corporation was within the scope of the Amendments of 1903, it could have become bankrupt by passing a resolution that it was willing to be so adjudged. In short, although the form was involuntary, the substance of such proceedings was voluntary."

71. Blake *v.* Valentine Co., 1 A. B. R. 372, 89 Fed. 691 (D. C. Calif.); In re Fowler, Fed. Cas. No. 4,998.

Contra, In re Ceballos & Co., 20 A. B. R. 459, 161 Fed. 445 (D. C. N. J.).

But this case seems to consider it conclusive that such a filing is not specifically mentioned as an act of bankruptcy under the present law whilst it was so mentioned under the law of 1867, failing altogether to observe that the Fifth Act of Bankruptcy under the present law renders such special mention now unnecessary.

72. In re Wilmington Hosiery Co., 9 A. B. R. 579, 120 Fed. 179 (D. C. Del.). But that the willingness to be adjudged a bankrupt on the ground of insolvency may be inferred from the admission of insolvency contained in the answer, see Brinkley *v.* Smithwick, 11 A. B. R. 500, 126 Fed. 686 (D. C. N. C.).

73. In re Southern Steel Co., 22 A. B. R. 476, 169 Fed. 702 (D. C. Ala.).

§ 166. Mere Admission of Insolvency Insufficient.

—Mere admission of insolvency, although made in writing, is insufficient. There must be also a written admission of willingness to be adjudged bankrupt on that ground.[74]

In re Wilmington Hosiery Co., 9 A. B. R. 579, 120 Fed. 179 (D. C. Del.): "A written admission of insolvency and consent to have a receiver appointed by the Chancellor cannot be regarded as a written admission of inability to pay debts and willingness to be adjudged bankrupt. No doctrine of equivalency is applicable in this connection." But there was an additional reason in this case, it would seem, namely, that the act was not alleged in the petition nor did it occur before the petition was filed, there being, moreover, no amendment to cover it.

Or perhaps willingness to be adjudged insolvent under the insolvency laws of the state, if they are in effect bankrupt laws.[75]

§ 167. Admissions by Boards of Directors of Corporations.

—The decisions seem to be somewhat in conflict as to whether or not it is within the proper function of the board of directors of a corporation to pass a resolution and have the same spread upon its records, admitting the inability of the corporation to pay its debts and its willingness to be adjudged a bankrupt upon that ground. But the true rule seems to be that it is within their power, where it is not forbidden to them by statute, either expressly or by necessary implication, nor by a by-law of the corporation itself.

Thus, it is held, that it is within their power, where not forbidden by statute or by-law.[76]

In re Moench, 12 A. B. R. 240, 130 Fed. 685 (C. C. A. N. Y.): "There is nothing in the Bankruptcy Act to indicate that the making of a general assignment for the benefit of creditors—which is the fourth of the specified acts of bankruptcy—may not be taken to be an act of bankruptcy when it is made by a corporation, and, if the corporation can commit the one act, there seems no sound reason for holding that it could not commit the other. Where, by statute, the making of such a general assignment is forbidden to a corporation, some question might be raised as to whether the corporation could commit the fifth act; but we need not now pass upon any such question, because since the passage of the Stock Corporation Law of 1890, and the amendments of chapter 688, p. 1824, Laws, 1892, the old prohibition in this State against the making by a corporation of a general assignment for the benefit of creditors has been done away with. * * * It would also seem to be reasonable to hold that the power to make the admission in writing could be exercised by the same

---

74. Inferentially, obiter, In re Empire Metallic Bedstead Co., 1 A. B. R. 136, 98 Fed. 981 (Ref. N. Y.). This case was reversed, on other grounds, in 2 A. B. R. 329 and 11 A. B. R. 674; Conway v. German, 21 A. B. R. 577, 166 Fed. 67 (C. C. A. Md.), quoted on other points at §§ 257, 268, 271.

75. Compare, inferentially, In re Storck Lumber Co., 8 A. B. R. 86, 114 Fed. 860 (D. C. Md.).

76. Obiter, In re Rollins Gold & Silver Min. Co., 4 A. B. R. 327, 102 Fed. 982 (Ref. N. Y.); In re Moench, 10 A. B. R. 656, 123 Fed. 965 (D. C. N. Y., affirmed in 12 A. B. R. 240, 130 Fed. 685). Inferentially, In re Imperial Corp., 13 A. B. R. 199, 133 Fed. 73 (D. C. N. Y.); Home Powder Co. v. Geis, 29 A. B. R. 580, 204 Fed. 568 (C. C. A. Mo.), decided under the laws of Arizona. See, as to authority suffi-

officers who have the power to make a general assignment, and, in the absence of the statute or by-law regulating the subject, such power resides in the directors."

In re Lisk Mfg. Co., 21 A. B. R. 674, 167 Fed. 44 (D. C. N. Y.): "Neither the state statute nor the by-laws of the corporation prohibited the directors from making a general assignment for the benefit of creditors; and hence the written admission, signed by the secretary of the corporation by order of the majority of the board of directors, was sufficient to authorize the creditors to institute the bankruptcy proceeding in question."

And that it is within their power, even where the directors are holding over and are merely de facto directors.

In re Riley, Talbott & Hunt, 15 A. B. R. 159 (Ref. Mich. affirmed by D. C.): "Where there has been a failure to hold a meeting of stockholders for the purpose of electing directors of a corporation, the previously elected directors hold over and become de facto directors whose actions cannot be attacked in a collateral proceeding, and such de facto officers have the power at a legally convened meeting to admit in writing the inability of their corporation to pay its debts and its willingness to be adjudged bankrupt under § 3a (5) of the Bankruptcy Act, 1898."

And it has been held that, in general, officers of a corporation who have power to make a general assignment have power to make the admission.[77] And that the assent of the stockholders is not required.[78] Also, that it is within their power though three nominal directors were not notified, they being out of the jurisdiction and hostile, being engaged in prosecuting attachment suits against the corporation.[79] And even where some of the directors, living or sojourning in another state, were not notified of the director's meeting at which the resolution was passed.

In re Lisk Mfg. Co., 21 A. B. R. 674, 167 Fed. 411 (D. C. N. Y.): "It is claimed in behalf of the bankrupt that the statute of the state (§ 29 of the general corporation law [Laws N. Y. 1901, p. 507, c. 214]) substantially provides that the business of the corporation shall be conducted by a majority of the directors at a meeting duly assembled, etc., and it is pointed out that the requirement of the by-laws of the Lisk Manufacturing Company indicates that such meeting of the board of directors was not regularly assembled or convened. Under § 5 of the by-laws of such corporation, special meetings of the directors were held at any time by oral notice or by notice in writing duly signed by each director. The by-laws do not provide that such meetings of

cient to file voluntary petition in behalf of a corporation under the Amendment of 1910, ante, § 44.

77. In re Lisk Mfg. Co., 21 A. B. R. 674, 167 Fed. 411 (D. C. N. Y.): "Officers who have power to make a general assignment under the laws of the state have power to make the specified admission."

78. In re Mutual Mercantile Agency, 6 A. B. R. 607, 111 Fed. 152, and cases cited therein; In re Machine & Conveyor Co., 91 Fed. 630, 1 A. B. R. 421 (D. C. N. Y.); In re Kelly Dry Goods Co., 4 A. B. R. 528, 102 Fed. 748 (D. C. Wis.). Obiter, In re Rollins Gold & Silver Min. Co., 4 A. B. R. 327, 102 Fed. 979, 985. Obiter, In re Peter Paul Book Co., 5 A. B. R. 105, 104 Fed. 788 (D. C. N. Y.).

79. In re Marine Machine & Conveyor Co., 91 Fed. 630, 1 A. B. R. 421 (D. C. N. Y.).

the directors shall be held in Canandaigua, the place of business of the bankrupt. In view of the manner in which previous business meetings were held by the directors, it was not absolutely necessary that oral notice should have been given, in the absence of bad faith, to directors living or sojourning in a distant state. For this reason, in my opinion, it was not necessary that C. D. McLaughlin, the director residing in Omaha, should have notice of the meeting. The situation was thought by a majority of the directors, after consultation with their counsel and thorough examination of the financial affairs of the corporation, to require immediate action by the board of directors, and under all the circumstances to secure the consent of the absent director was obviously unnecessary. * * * J. L. McLaughlin, another director, knew of the proposed meeting and its object. He must be deemed to have acquiesced in the action of the other directors or waived notice of the meeting."

Also that it is within their power though for several years the corporation had ceased to do business and though its charter had been declared void by the governor's proclamation for failure to pay taxes.[81] But it is also held, that it is not within their power where, by the laws of the State, the powers of the directors are so defined and limited as necessarily to exclude this power.[82] And, of course, it is not within the power of the board of directors to make the admission, and their act in so doing cannot be subsequently ratified by stockholders, where the statute permits only stockholders to do such act.[83]

And of course an officer cannot by writing a letter in the name of a corporation bind the corporation to this act, unless expressly authorized to do so.[84] But an unauthorized admission may perhaps be ratified.

In re Lisk Mfg. Co., 21 A. B. R. 674, 167 Fed. 411 (D. C. N. Y.): "Moreover, the Lisk Mfg. Co. in view of the facts must be held to have acquiesced in or ratified the action of its secretary in signing the resolution setting forth an admission of its inability to pay its debts, and its willingness to be adjudged a bankrupt. * * * The business of the bankrupt has been conducted by the receivers for more than six months with the evident assent of the new directors, the stockholders, and parties in interest; and under the circumstances the latter are equitably estopped to claim at this time that the resolution which is the foundation of this proceeding was unauthorized or was improvidently passed at a meeting of which all the directors were not notified and did not attend."

But not, of course, where the board of directors themselves would not have had the power to make the admission originally.[85]

---

81. In re Munger Vehicle Tire Co., 19 A. B. R. 785, 159 Fed. 901 (C. C. A. N. Y.).

82. In re Bates Machine Co., 1 A. B. R. 129, 91 Fed. 625 (D. C. Mass., distinguished in In re Moench, 12 A. B. R. 242; also, In re Riley, 15 A. B. R. 163); In re Quartz Gold Mining Co., 19 A. B. R. 667, 157 Fed. 243 (D. C. Ore.). Obiter, In re Gold Run, etc., Co., 29 A. B. R. 563, 200 Fed. 162 (D. C. Colo.).

83. In re Bates Machine Co., 1 A. B. R. 129, 91 Fed. 625 (D. C. Mass., distinguished in In re Moench, 12 A. B. R. 242; also, in In re Riley, 15 A. B. R. 163). To same effect, analogously, In re Independent Thread Co., 7 A. B. R. 704, 113 Fed. 938 (D. C. N. J.).

84. In re Southern Steel Co., 22 A. B. R. 476, 169 Fed. 702 (D. C. Ala.).

85. In re Burbank Company, 21 A. B. R. 838, 168 Fed. 719 (D. C. N. H.).

It is not forbidden even where the directors solicit the creditors to take the action, the creditors being bona fide creditors.[86] Nor is the bankrupt's solicitation of such action by creditors, such collusion as will defeat adjudication.[87]

In re Duplex Radiator Co., 15 A. B. R. 324 (D. C. N. Y.): "The mere fact that a corporation admits in writing its inability to pay its debts and its willingness to be adjudged a bankrupt on that ground, and thereupon requests certain creditors to file an involuntary petition, constitutes no ground of defense to the proceedings by a creditor who opposes the adjudication."

§ 168. Written Admission Notwithstanding Assets Already Sequestrated in Another Court.

—Nor does the fact that the property of the corporation has already been sequestrated under state insolvency proceedings, incapacitate the corporation to make such admission subsequently.[87a]

Coal & Coke Co. v. Stauffer, 17 A. B. R. 573, 148 Fed. 981 (C. C. A. Pa., affirming In re International Coal Min. Co., 16 A. B. R. 309, 143 Fed. 665): "It is true, that the law already referred to provides that the property and franchises of the corporation, sold under this special fi. fa., shall pass to the purchaser, thus, in effect, terminating the existence of the old corporation. If, however, the proceeding by which this property and franchises were sold, was an act of bankruptcy, it was void and of no effect. If it were not, still the existence of the corporation is not terminated in every respect by this requirement of the State law. It has often been held that, even where a charter expires by time, its existence will be considered as being extended for the purpose of winding up its affairs, securing creditors and satisfying the ends of justice, even without special statutory authority for that purpose, and we think that the paramount authority of the Federal Bankrupt Law is sufficient to keep alive the corporation in this case for the purposes of the bankrupt jurisdiction created by the said act, and to give efficacy to the admission made by the directors of the insolvent corporation as an act of bankruptcy."

It has been held, in a case the reasoning of which in this particular cannot be upheld, that where the United States Circuit Court has already taken possession of the assets through a receiver in an equity suit appointed on the ground of insolvency, the board of directors may not make such a written admission, and that they may be punished for contempt if they do so.[88]

Such holding manifestly confuses the jurisdiction to determine the status of the debtor as a bankrupt with the jurisdiction to prevent interference with property of the debtor already in the custody of a court.

---

86. In re Moench, 10 A. B. R. 656, 130 Fed. 685 (D. C. N. Y., affirmed in 12 A. B. R. 240, 130 Fed. 685). Impliedly, In re Duplex Radiator Co., 15 A. B. R. 324, 142 Fed. 906 (D. C. N. Y.). Contra, obiter, In re Bates Machine Co., 1 A. B. R. 129, 91 Fed. 625 (D. C. Mass.).

87. In re Moench, 10 A. B. R. 656,

130 Fed. 685 (D. C. N. Y., affirmed in 12 A. B. R. 240, 130 Fed. 685).

87a. See, analogous proposition, "Assets in Hands of Receiver or Assignee No Defense," ante, § 97½; also see, In re Sterlingworth Ry. Supply Co., 21 A. B. R. 341, 164 Fed. 591 (D. C. La.).

88. In re H. R. Electric Power Co.,

§ 169. Admissions by Partners.—Again, this fifth class of acts of bankruptcy affords a means for one partner to put the partnership into bankruptcy without the other partner joining; for the written admissions in the petition itself and prayer for adjudication are an act of bankruptcy themselves under the fifth class, and being presumptively made with the consent of the other partners, are binding on the partnership unless expressly repudiated.[90] And where the other partner afterwards stands by without protest, authority in one partner to make such a written admission will be presumed.[91] Adjudication may be made against the partners on such admission, both individually and collectively.[92]

In re Northampton Portland Cement Co., 24 A. B. R. 61, 185 Fed. 542 (D. C. Pa.): "The reasoning of the court in support of this ruling [West Co. v. Lea, 174 U S. 590, 2 A. B. R. 463] applies with equal force when the petition is based upon the bankrupt's admission that he cannot pay his debts and is willing to be adjudicated upon that ground."

§ 170. Insolvency Not Requisite, nor Is Solvency Competent as Defense.—It is not necessary to prove the debtor to be in fact insolvent.[93] All that is necessary is to prove that he admitted his inability to pay his debts; that he declared his willingness to be adjudged a bankrupt, the willingness of course being for adjudication on the ground of his inability to pay his debts; and that these admissions and declarations were in writing.

In re Duplex Radiator Co., 15 A. B. R. 324 (D. C. N. Y.): "When the act of bankruptcy alleged is an admission in writing of inability to pay debts and willingness to be adjudged a bankrupt on that ground, the question of insolvency is immaterial."

And evidence of solvency is inadmissible in defense.[94]

---

23 A. B. R. 191, 173 Fed. 934 (D. C. N. Y.).
Such Written Admission not Same Thing as Voluntary Bankruptcy.—The contention that the passing of such a resolution by the board of directors amounts to the same thing as a voluntary petition and therefore was within the former rule forbidding the voluntary bankruptcies of corporations [changed by Amendment of 1910] was held not well taken. In re Kelly Dry Goods Co., 4 A. B. R. 528, 102 Fed. 748 (D. C. Wis.). Obiter, contra, In re Bates Machine Co., 1 A. B. R. 129, 91 Fed. 625 (D. C. Mass.); In re Moench, 12 A. B. R. 242, 130 Fed. 685 (C. C. A. N. Y.), quoted, ante, § 163.

1 R B—12

90. In re Kersten, 6 A. B. R. 516, 110 Fed. 929 (D. C. Wis.). Compare ante, §§ 73, 102, 164. But compare, In re Ceballos, 20 A. B. R. 459, 161 Fed. 445 (D. C. N. J.), quoted at §§ 102, 164.
91. In re Kersten, 6 A. B. R. 516, 110 Fed. 929 (D. C. Wis.).
92. In re Kersten, 6 A. B. R. 516, 110 Fed. 929 (D. C. Wis.).
93. But compare erroneous doctrine of In re Ceballos & Co., 20 A. B. R. 459, 161 Fed. 445 (D. C. N. J.), criticised at §§ 73, 102, 164.
94. In re Moench, 12 A. B. R. 240 (C. C. A. N. Y., affirming 10 A. B. R. 656); In re Duplex Radiator Co, 15 A. B. R. 324 (D. C. N. Y.); In re Riley,

DIVISION 6.

GENERAL OBSERVATIONS APPLICABLE TO THE VARIOUS ACTS OF BANK-
RUPTCY—ACTS COMMITTED IN DIFFERENT CAPACITY—BURDEN OF PROOF
OF COMMISSION OF ACT—PROOF OF INSOLVENCY—PROOF OF INTENT—
TIME OF COMMISSION OF ACT.

**§ 171. Imputed Acts of Bankruptcy—Agents of Corporations and
Partners.**—The act of bankruptcy may be imputed, but when imputed must
be shown to have been committed by the person in a capacity binding the
debtor sought to be thrown into bankruptcy.

Thus, corporate and firm acts of bankruptcy must have been committed in
the capacity of agent of the corporation or of the firm. In case it is a
partnership or corporation that is the defendant, it must be proved that the
act was an act of the partnership or of the corporation itself and not
merely the individual act of some one connected therewith. The individual
must have been acting for the corporation or partnership, in order to bind
the corporation or partnership.[95]

Davis *v.* Stevens, 4 A. B. R. 763, 104 Fed. 235, 242 (D. C. S. Dak.): "The
fact that one partner of a copartnership embezzles the funds thereof and absconds and conceals himself constitutes no act of bankruptcy of that copartnership."

Hartman *v.* Peters, 17 A. B. R. 62, 146 Fed. 82 (D. C. Pa.): "This cannot be sustained. The act relied on was individual and single, being simply the conveyance by
John Peters of his farm to secure certain of the firm debts. The circumstances attending the transaction, and the parties benefited thereby may justify
the conclusion that it was fraudulently intended; or if not that, that it at least
effected a preference of the firm creditors secured. But with this the firm
itself, so far as appears, had nothing whatever to do; nor had Earl Peters, the
other member of it, who could not be affected, nor could his partnership interest, by the separate and distinct act of his copartner, dealing, not with the
firm property, but with his own. The petition should have been directed against
John Peters, and not, as it is, against the firm; and must therefore be dismissed.

Talbott, etc., 15 A. B. R. 164 (D. C.
Mich.). In re Lisk Mfg. Co., 21 A. B.
R. 674, 167 Fed. 411 (D. C. N. Y.).

95. Instance, Strellow *v.* Schloss, 17
A. B. R. 881, 149 Fed. 907 (D. C. Pa.),
department store conducted in manager's name, but manager not real
owner. Also, inferentially, In re Sanderlin, 6 A. B. R. 384, 109 Fed. 857 (D.
C. N. C.). This case was reversed, but
upon other grounds, in McNair *v.* Mc-
Intyre, 7 A. B. R. 638, 113 Fed. 113 (C.
C. A. N. C.). Compare, In re Wing
Yick Co., 13 A. B. R. 755 (D. C. Hawaii), in which case the judgment, the
failure to vacate which was the act of
bankruptcy complained of, did not run
against the firm expressly but merely
jointly against the individuals, yet
shown to be on a firm obligation. Inferentially, Bank *v.* Craig Bros., 6 A.
B. R. 381, 110 Fed. 137 (D. C. Ky.).
Compare, inferentially and analogously,
In re Lehigh Lumber Co., 4 A. B. R.
221, 101 Fed. 216 (D. C. Pa.). Compare, analogously, In re Schultz, 6 A.
B. R. 91, 109 Fed. 264 (D. C. N. Y.),
where the frauds of one partner towards his copartner as well as towards
creditors were held not to be imputa-
ble to the partnerships. See similar
proposition relative to opposition to
discharge, post, §§ 2484, 2485, 2486.
Also, see ante, §§ 64, 65½.

There are other questions in the record; but this is decisive, and they will not be considered."

In re Stovall Grocery Co., 20 A. B. R. 537, 161 Fed. 882 (D. C. Ga.): "It will be perceived that the act of bankruptcy alleged here is the transfer by an individual member of a firm of property with intent to defraud individual creditors and firm creditors. That is not an act of bankruptcy on the part of the firm. The partnership entity must act, and what is relied on must be its act."

Obiter, Spike & Iron Co. v. Allen, 17 A. B. R. 590, 148 Fed. 657 (C. C. A. Va.): "If the property sold was, as is contended, covered by the deed in trust. Warwick, the president, had no right to sell it, and his act was wrongful. There is no evidence that he sold it by authority of the company, or that the company ratified his action; nor are we advised that it was within the scope of the president's power to sell the property which composed the plant and operating machinery of ·the company. * * * If it be true that Warwick, without authority, disposed of property which was subject to the lien of the bondholders, this would be his act, for which he would be individually liable, but .the company cannot be held responsible."

Inferentially, but obiter, In re Perley & Hays, 15 A. B. R. 56, 138 Fed. 927 (D. C. Mo.): "That case (In re Meyers, 3 A. B. R. 559, 98 Fed. 976) seems to indicate that, in order to put a firm into bankruptcy, the act of bankruptcy complained of must have been committed by the firm."

Obiter, Mills v. Fisher & Co., 20 A. B. R. 237, 159 Fed. 897 (C. C. A. Tenn.): "But it is not an act of bankruptcy for which a firm may be adjudged a bankrupt, that one of its members, out of his individual estate, prefers one of his own or one of a firm's creditors. In bankruptcy the assets of a bankrupt partnership must be first applied to the payment of partnership debts and the individual assets to the payment of the individual debts. The joint creditors are only entitled to share in the surplus of the individual assets and the individual creditors only in the surplus of joint or firm assets. Bank. Act 1898, § 5. The application by one partner of his individual property to the payment of one firm creditor would be an individual act, and not the joint act of the firm, and, therefore, not an act for which the firm could be adjudged bankrupt. * * * Although the intent be to prefer a firm creditor it is not enough to sustain a proceeding against the firm." But in this case adjudication of the individual eventually was had on the ground that the transfer by the individual partner from his own estate diminished pro tanto the residuary funds to which firm creditors might be entitled to resort, and against which they might prove their claims.[96]

(1867) In re Redmond, Fed. Cas. 11,632, 9 N. B. Reg. 408: "It seems too clear to admit of argument, that in order to maintain proceedings in bankruptcy against partners as such, it must be alleged and proven, that the firm has committed an act of bankruptcy; and that when the act charged is the fraudulent conveyance of property, it must be of partnership property." "A conveyance by one partner of his individual property, although an act of bankruptcy as against him, will not sustain a proceeding in bankruptcy as against the firm, even though such conveyance was made with intent to hinder, delay or defraud firm creditors, or with a view of giving preference to a firm creditor. In such case the proceeding must be against such partner alone."

---

96. Hartman v. Peters, 17 A. B. R. 61, 146 Fed. 82 (D. C. Pa.); (1867) In re Redmond, Fed. Cas. 11, 632, 9 A. B. R. 408; (1867) In re Lloyd, Fed. Cas. 8429; (1867) In re Melick, Fed. Cas. No. 9399; (1867) In re McLean, Fed. Cas. 8879; (1867) In re Jewett, Fed. Cas. 7306. Also, see post, § 1291.

But a written admission by one partner that the partnership is unable to pay its debts and is willing to be adjudged bankrupt on that ground, has been held to warrant an adjudication both against the firm and its members individually.[97]

Likewise, the failure of a member of a partnership, long since dissolved, to vacate a preferential execution levy on former partnership property, he having sold out to his co-partner, has been held sufficiently an act of the partnership and of each member to warrant adjudication both of the firm and all members.

Holmes v. Baker & Hamilton, 20 A. B. R. 252, 160 Fed. 922 (C. C. A. Wash.): "It is true that an individual member of a firm cannot be adjudged a bankrupt for an act of bankruptcy not committed by him or in which he did not participate * * *; but that is not the case here presented. The act of bankruptcy in this case was committed by all the members of the firm. It was an act of omission, the failure to discharge the levy of the execution, a duty which rested as much upon the appellant as upon any member of the firm. Notwithstanding the dissolution of the co-partnership, it remained, as it was before, the appellant's duty to see that the property of the co-partnership was devoted to the payment of the partnership debts, as to which he had not been released."

Of course the act of a partner whilst engaged in the partnership business, or of an officer of a corporation whilst engaged in the corporate business, would be the act of the partnership and of the corporation respectively; indeed, only thus could a partnership or corporation commit an act of bankruptcy. Section 1 of the Statute, which, as we have seen, is taken up with definitions, sets forth in clause 19 that:

"'Persons' shall include corporations, except where otherwise specified, and officers, partnerships, and women, and when used with reference to the commission of acts which are herein forbidden shall include persons who are participants in the forbidden acts, and the agents, officers, and members of the board of directors or trustees, or other similar controlling bodies of corporations."[98]

Thus, a partner may make an assignment of the firm's assets for the benefit of creditors that will bind the firm.[99] He has, in general, sufficient authority to bind the partnership thereby even without the other partner's consent.

Yungbluth v. Slipper, 26 A. B. R. 265, 185 Fed. 773 (C. C. A. Wash.): "The only question which requires any extended discussion is presented by the contention that the appellant could not be adjudged a bankrupt on account of the individual act of bankruptcy of his copartner. Schafer made the assignment for creditors, and there is no proof that the appellant assented to it. There can

97. In re Kersten, 6 A. B. R. 516, 110 Fed. 929 (D. C. Wis.). Inferentially, In re Forbes, 11 A. B. R. 787, 128 Fed. 137 (D. C. Mass.). See ante, §§ 73, 169.

98. Compare, U. S. v. Lake, 12 A. B. R. 270, 129 Fed. 499 (D. C. Ark.).

Compare, In re Meyer, 3 A. B. R. 559, 98 Fed. 976 (C. C. A.).

99. Yungbluth v. Slipper, 26 A. B. R. 265, 185 Fed. 773 (C. C. A. Wash.), quoted § 171, post.

be no doubt that Schafer's act was an act of bankruptcy for which the partnership was properly adjudged bankrupt, for it was an act which affected the partnership business and disposed of the partnership assets."

So the act of a partner may be imputed to his partnership where the partner has participated in the partnership act of bankruptcy, but where he was acting solely as an individual, it would be questionable whether the partnership should be charged with the particular act of bankruptcy even though the partner may have been using partnership funds. Thus, where, without the knowledge or connivance of the other partner, one partner converts some of the partnership funds to his own use and absconds, it is not the act of the partnership and the partnership should not be adjudged bankrupt on the allegation that it has removed part of its property with intent to hinder, delay and defraud creditors. Even if it would not be difficult to put such a partnership into bankruptcy on other grounds, this particular act could not be charged against the partnership, because it was not the act of the partnership but of an individual member, acting solely for himself. But if the act be connived at by the other members of the partnership, it would be a partnership act of bankruptcy.[1]

Likewise, individual members of a partnership may not be adjudicated individually bankrupt along with the partnership unless proof be made of their commission of individual acts of bankruptcy or of their participation as individuals in a firm act.[2]

A transfer by one partner of all his individual property to pay a firm debt may constitute a preference, since the estate of each partner is—in its due order of priority after payment of individual debts—a fund to which partnership creditors may resort; and its depletion to satisfy one firm creditor over others is, pro tanto, a depletion of partnership assets.

Mills v. Fisher & Co., 20 A. B. R. 237, 159 Fed. 897 (C. C. Tenn.): "Nevertheless the right of a partnership creditor to share in the separate estate of the members of the copartnership gives him such an interest in the separate property of its members as to entitle him to prove his claim against the separate estate and to make such a claim the basis for an adjudication of bankruptcy against a member of a firm who has given a preference out of his estate. This was well settled under the former act and in this respect the present law has not changed the rule." Quoted supra, also, at § 1281.

Yet it has been held that if the act of the one partner is sufficiently the act of the partnership to bind the firm, it will be sufficient also for the adjudication of the other partners as individuals unless they can show in defense that the property of the firm, together with that of all the partners applicable to the payment of partnership debts, is sufficient to pay those debts.

---

1. In re Gillette, 5 A. B. R. 119, 104 Fed. 769 (D. C. N. Y.).

2. See ante, § 64. Also, In re Ceballos, 20 A. B. R. 459, 161 Fed. 445 (D. C. N. J.).

Yungbluth *v.* Slipper, 26 A. B. R. 265, 185 Fed. 773 (C. C. A. Wash.): "But the proceeding in this case was not only against the partnership, but was also against each individual member. In some of the decisions it has been said broadly that one partner may not be adjudged bankrupt for the act of his co-partner, and undoubtedly the statement is true as to certain acts of individual partners. Thus it has been held that neither a firm nor the other partners may be adjudged bankrupt for the act of a partner in preferring out of his individual estate one of his own or the firm's creditors. Mills *v.* J. H. Fisher & Co. (C. C. A., 6th Cir.), 20 Am. B. R. 237, 159 Fed. 897, 87 C. C. A. 77, 18 L. R. A. (N. S.) 656. But we think the true doctrine is that, if the act of the individual partner is one for which the partnership itself may be adjudged bankrupt, the other members of the firm may also be adjudged bankrupt unless they can show in defense that the property of the firm, together with that of all the partners applicable to the payment of the partnership debts, is sufficient to pay the same. The true construction of this feature of the bankruptcy law is, we think, best expressed by Judge Lowell, In re Forbes (D. C., Mass.), 11 Am. B. R. 787, 128 Fed. 137, a case in which, in view of section 5 of the Act, which provides that the partnership property (except in case of consent) shall not be administered in bankruptcy unless all the partners are adjudged bankrupt, he held that the partnership may not be made bankrupt except by an adjudication of all its partners, and that the only defense a nonconsenting partner can make to the petition is that the partners are able to pay the partnership debts and their own debts, out of the joint or separate estates."

But such holding is not to be approved. The true rule is that an individual act is essential to an individual adjudication, although the individual property of a nonadjudicated member may be drawn in for administration in the partnership bankruptcy as being property in which partnership creditors have an interest to the extent of any surplus left after satisfaction of the individual debts. Any other rule would lead to intolerable confusion and inconsistency.

§ 172. Burden of Proof in Prosecuting Bankruptcy Petition on Creditors.

The burden of proof is on the creditors, except for the contingency provided for in paragraph d, § 3 of the Act.[4]

The petitioning creditors must prove the allegations of their petition, and the burden rests upon them to do so. However, since the meaning of "insolvency" under the Act of 1898 requires proof of the existence and value of the assets and of the amount of liabilities, it would be almost a prohibitory requirement to place upon the petitioning creditors the burden of proof of insolvency, were it not for the right of discovery furnished by § 3 (d), requiring the bankrupt, in cases where the act of bankruptcy involves proof of insolvency, to produce books, documents and papers to explain his business and himself to appear and submit to examination at the time of trial. In thus requiring such production of evidence and testimony

---

4. In re Rome Planing Mills, 3 A. B. R. 123, 96 Fed. 812 (D. C. N. Y.); In re McLoon, 20 A. B. R. 719, 162 Fed. 575 (D. C. Me.). Also burden of proof that debtor belongs to class of corporations subject to bankruptcy is on creditors. Walker Roofing Co. *v.* Mer. & Evans Co., 23 A. B. R. 185, 173 Fed. 771 (C. C. A. Va.).

at the time of trial, the statute enables the petitioning creditors to maintain the burden of proof of insolvency; so even as to insolvency, the burden of proof rests on the petitioning creditors, subject to excuse in case the bankrupt fails to comply with the requirements as to discovery.

§ 173. **Intent Necessary Only in First Two Acts.**—Intent is not a necessary element and need not be proved except in the first two classes of acts of bankruptcy, namely, transfers, concealments and removals of property with intent to hinder, delay or defraud creditors and transfers of property with intent to prefer one creditor over another, as to which acts of bankruptcy proof of the debtor's intent is necessary.[5]

In the proof of any of the other acts of bankruptcy no regard need be given to the debtor's intent in doing or failing to do the act alleged. And the burden of proof of the intent (where intent must be proved) is on the creditors.[6]

§ 174. **Insolvency Requisite in All Instances, Except "Fraudulent Transfers," "Assignments," Receiverships "Because of" Insolvency, and "Written Admissions."**—Insolvency must be proved in all instances except, first, where the act complained of is a transfer, removal, etc., with intent to hinder, delay or defraud creditors; or, second, is a general assignment by the debtor; or, third, is the putting of a receiver in charge on the ground of insolvency; or, fourth, is the admission in writing of one's inability to pay his debts and his willingness to be adjudged a bankrupt on that ground.[7]

---

5. In re Rome Planing Mills, 3 A. B. R. 123, 96 Fed. 812 (D. C. N. Y.). See ante, §§ 109 and 129.

6. In re Bloch, 6 A. B. R. 300, 109 Fed. 790 (C. C. A. N. Y.); Merchants' Nat'l Bk. v. Cole, 18 A. B. R. 49, 149 Fed. 708 (C. C. A. Ohio).

7. As to proof of insolvency, see post, §§ 1343, 1344, et seq.

Insolvency is a question of fact for the jury. In re Blue Mtn., etc., v. Portner, 12 A. B. R. 559 (C. C. A. Mo.). Admissions of insolvency by the bankrupt are competent to prove insolvency; but they must amount to admissions of insolvency as defined by the Bankrupt Act, namely, inadequacy of assets to meet liabilities, and not as meant at Common Law, else they will be insufficient to make complete proof of insolvency. In re Doscher, 9 A. B. R. 555, 120 Fed. 408 (D. C. N. Y.); In re Perlhefter & Shatz, 25 A. B. R. 576, 177 Fed. 299 (D. C. N. Y.).

Instances of Proof of Insolvency under Petitions for Adjudication.— Offer of thirty cents on dollar as a composition to creditors is sufficient prima facie evidence of insolvency not to be overcome by mere estimates as to the value of his lease, good will and fixtures. In re Lange, 3 A. B. R. 231, 97 Fed. 197 (D. C. N. Y.); McGowan v. Knittel, 15 A. B. R. 1, 134 Fed. 498 (C. C. A. Pa.).

Judgment records not admissible if reopened generally and not specially to let bankrupt make whatever defense he desired. McGowan v. Knittel, 15 A. B. R. 1, 134 Fed. 498 (C. C. A., reversing Knittel v. McGowan, 14 A. B. R. 209, 134 Fed. 498, D. C. Penn.).

Record of judgment entered more than four months' preceding commission of alleged act of bankruptcy admissible. Knittel v. McGowan, 14 A. B. R. 209 (D. C. Penn., reversed in McGowan v. Knittel, 15 A. B. R. 1, 134 Fed. 498, C. C. A.).

Memorandum from books subsequently produced; witnesses testifying from memoranda taken from books not then, but subsequently produced; the alleged bankrupt is not prejudiced.

That is not quite the same as saying that insolvency need not be proved in the first class nor in any of the cases of the fourth class nor in the fifth; for it will be observed that in one instance, in class four, namely, where the debtor himself applies for a receiver, it must be proved that he was in fact insolvent.

Insolvency need not be proved in classes one, four and five; except that, as to class four, in case of receivership and trusteeship applied for by the debtor while insolvent, insolvency must be proved.

Whilst insolvency is not a necessary element of the first act of bankruptcy, solvency of the debtor is made by statute a defense to such charge.[8]

§ 175. When Creditors to Prove Insolvency in Chief It Must Be Insolvency at Time Act Committed.

—The insolvency to be proved, wherever its proof is required to be made by creditors, as part of their case in chief, is insolvency at the time the act was committed.

Acme Food Co. v. Meier, 18 A. B. R. 550, 153 Fed. 74 (C. C. A. Mich.): "If the act of bankruptcy be the giving of a preference under subdivision 2, or the permitting of a preference through a legal proceeding under subdivision 3 of the same section, there must be a state of insolvency at the time of the preference and solvency or insolvency at the time of the filing of the petition can only have a reflex importance, if any."

In re Rome Planing Mills, 3 A. B. R. 123, 96 Fed. 812 (D. C. N. Y.): "In

Knittel v. McGowan, 14 A. B. R. 209 (D. C. Penn., reversed, on other grounds, in McGowan v. Knittel, 15 A. B. R. 1, 134 Fed. 498, C. C. A.).

Claims on unmatured notes are admissible. Knittel v. McGowan, 14 A. B. R. 209 (D. C. Penn., reversed, on other grounds, in McGowan v. Knittel, 15 A. B. R. 1, 134 Fed. 498, C. C. A.).

Oral evidence, to prove bankrupt's reversionary interest in land conveyed, offered by bankrupt, rejected. Knittel v. McGowan, 14 A. B. R. 209 (D. C. Penn., reversed, on other grounds, in McGowan v. Knittel, 15 A. B. R. 1, 134 Fed. 498, C. C. A.).

Expense of preserving the estate pending adjudication of bankruptcy may be proper item of liability. Thus, the amount paid by a receiver to renew a hotel license has been held to be a proper item of liability. Knittel v. McGowan, 14 A. B. R. 209 (D. C. Penn., reversed, on other grounds, in McGowan v. Knittel, 15 A. B. R. 1, 134 Fed. 498, C. C. A.).

An instruction that the bankrupt's liquor license is an asset is not improper. Knittel v. McGowan, 14 A. B. R. 209 (D. C. Penn., reversed, on other grounds, in McGowan v. Knittel, 15 A. B. R. 1, 134 Fed. 498, C. C. A.).

Complaint that findings based on "wrecker's" values, or on "serap values." Motor Vehicle Co. v. Oak Leather Co., 15 A. B. R. 808, 141 Fed. 518 (C. C. A. Ills.).

"Fair valuation" is the valuation which the bankrupt itself could have gotten—the market value. In re Marine Iron Works, 20 A. B. R. 390, 159 Fed. 753 (D. C. N. Y.).

Bankrupt's guaranties to be counted among liabilities, even his oral guaranties, since the fact that the obligations are not in writing goes simply to the proof, not to the validity of the obligation itself. Hutting Mfg. Co. v. Edwards, 20 A. B. R. 349, 160 Fed. 619 (C. C. A. Iowa).

Fraudulently conveyed property not to be counted in, but preferentially conveyed property to be counted in. Acme Food Co. v. Meier, 18 A. B. R. 550, 153 Fed. 74 (C. C. A. Mich.).

But property which might be, but is not, claimed by third parties to be recoverable, as transferred to the bankrupt in fraud of such third parties' rights, is not to be excluded. In re Aschenbach Co., 23 A. B. R. 95, 174 Fed. 396 (C. C. A. N. Y.).

8. See post, § 177.

order to succeed under this subdivision [subd. 2, § 3a] the petitioners must prove * * * Third, the insolvency of the debtor at the date of the transfer."

But compare, evidently careless statement in syllabus to Knittel *v.* McGowan, 14 A. B. R. 209, 134 Fed. 498 (D. C. Pa.): "The evidence produced to show the indebtedness of an alleged bankrupt must be such as to satisfy the jury of its existence and that it is more than the value of his assets at the time the petition is filed."

§ 176. When Insolvency Not Part of Creditor's Case but Solvency Available as Affirmative Defense, Date of Solvency, Date of Petition.

—But in the case of the first class of acts of bankruptcy, namely, transfers and concealments made with intent to hinder, delay or defraud creditors, while insolvency is not an element for the petitioners to prove, yet the statute makes it a complete defense for the debtor or for creditors opposing the petition to allege and prove that the party proceeded against was not insolvent as defined in the Bankruptcy Act, at the time of the filing of the petition against him.[9]

And the burden of proving solvency in such cases rests, of course, upon the bankrupt.[10]

§ 177. Insolvency Not Necessary Element of Creditors' Case under First Act, but Solvency Complete Bar, in Defense.

—Insolvency need not be shown by the petitioning creditors under Act One of acts of bankruptcy unless so far as it may be involved as an evidential fact in the proof of "fraudulent intent" or "good faith."[11]

In re Pease, 12 A. B. R. 66, 129 Fed. 446 (D. C. Mich.): "The giving of the mortgage, therefore, was an act of bankruptcy under subd. 1 of § 3 without regard to Pease's financial condition at the time. Insolvency of the debtor is not an element of that subdivision."

Inferentially, Lansing Boiler Works *v.* Ryerson, 11 A. B. R. 558, 128 Fed. 701 (C. C. A. Mich.): "No question of solvency or insolvency or preference arises under this subsection except as they bear upon the issue of good faith in making the conveyance, saying nothing now of the provisions of Clause 2 of subsection 5 of section 3 which relieves the consequences of subsection 1 if the respondent can prove that at the date of filing the petition he was solvent." This case is distinguished by the same court in Mfg. Co. *v.* Spoke & Nipple Co., 12 A. B. R. 613.

In re Larkin, 21 A. B. R. 711, 168 Fed. 100 (D. C. N. Y.): "Some acts of bankruptcy must be committed while the person is insolvent. The first act of bankruptcy defined may be committed by the person charged when perfectly solvent. If a solvent person conveys or transfers, conceals or removes, or permits to be concealed or removed, any part of his property with the intent to hinder, delay, or defraud his creditors, or any of them, he commits an act of bankruptcy; and if within the ensuing four months he becomes insolvent, and

---

9. Bankr. Act, § 3 (1) (c). Also, see Elliott *v.* Toeppner, 9 A. B. R. 50, 187 U. S. 327; Acme Food Co. *v.* Meier, 18 A. B. R. 550, 153 Fed. 74 (C. C. A. Mich.), quoted at § 177.

10. Louisiana, etc., Soc. *v.* Segen, 28 A. B. R. 407, 196 Fed. 903 (D. C. La.).

11. Analogously, compare, In re Steininger, 6 A. B. R. 68, 108 Fed. 591 (C. C. A. Ga.).

a petition is thereupon filed against him, such petition may allege such acts as the act of bankruptcy, and the person may be adjudicated a bankrupt accordingly. Subdivision 'b' of § 3 provides: 'A petition may be filed against a person who is insolvent and who has committed an act of bankruptcy within four months after the commission of such act.' The wisdom of this provision is perfectly apparent. The first Act of Bankruptcy, so far as it relates to the conveyance or transfer of property, differs from the Second Act of Bankruptcy in this: That in the first there is a conveyance or transfer with intent to hinder, delay, or defraud creditors, while in the second the transfer is made with the intent simply to prefer one creditor or more over the other creditors. In the second case the transfer must have been made while the person making it was insolvent. The very tendency of the acts mentioned in the First Act of Bankruptcy is to create insolvency so far as creditors are concerned. The person is not to be permitted to convey, transfer, conceal or remove any part of his property with intent to hinder, delay, or defraud his creditors, and on becoming insolvent within four months thereafter to escape the bankruptcy law by showing that he was solvent when he so conveyed, transferred, concealed, or removed his property."

Since, as noted (ante, § 106), this first class of acts of bankruptcy comprehends precisely those acts which, by the established decisions, have been held to constitute acts done with intent to hinder, delay or defraud creditors, proof of insolvency is not necessary so long as the actual intent to defraud is otherwise proved.

But the special provisions of the Bankruptcy Act of 1898, § 3 (c), permit proof of solvency as a defense, and proof of solvency is a complete rebuttal.[12]

Obiter, In re West, 5 A. B. R. 734, 108 Fed. 940 (C. C. A. N. Y.): "It is not necessary for the petitioning creditors to prove the insolvency of the bankrupt when the alleged act of bankruptcy is that contained in subdivision 1 of § 3, which is in substance the conveyance of property with intent to delay or hinder his creditors, for by paragraph 'c' of the same section, solvency at the time of filing the petition is made a defense to proceedings in bankruptcy instituted under subdivision 1, and the burden of proving solvency is on the bankrupt. This burden devolved upon the opposing creditor."

The burden of proof of solvency is, of course, on the bankrupt.[13]

Acme Food Co. v. Meier, 18 A. B. R. 550, 153 Fed. 74 (C. C. A. Mich.):

---

12. Sec. 3 (c) (2): "It shall be a complete defense to any proceeding in bankruptcy instituted under the first subdivision of this section to allege and prove that the party proceeded against was not insolvent as defined in this Act at the time of the filing of the petition against him, and if solvency at such date is proved by the alleged bankrupt the proceedings shall be dismissed, and under said subdivision one the burden of proving solvency shall be on the alleged bankrupt."

Lansing Boiler Works v. Ryerson, 11 A. B. R. 558, 128 Fed. 701 (C. C. A. Mich.). Obiter, Lea Bros. v. West, 1 A. B. R. 261, 91 Fed. 237; In re Schenkein v. Coney, 7 A. B. R. 162 (Ref. N. Y.). See Master's Report, In re Douglass Coal & Coke Co., 12 A. B. R. 542, 131 Fed. 769 (Tenn.). Obiter and inferentially, West Co. v. Lea, 2 A. B. R. 463, 174 U. S. 590.

13. In re Crenshaw, 19 A. B. R. 502, 156 Fed. 638 (D. C. Ala.).

"Solvency when the petition was filed is important only as a defense to an act of bankruptcy under subdivision one of § 3, and the burden of showing this is on the defendant."

And creditors opposing the debtor's adjudication have the same burden of proving solvency thrust upon them that the debtor himself would have had.[14]

§ 178. Burden of Proof of Insolvency under Second and Third Acts in Petitioning Creditors.

—As to classes two and three of acts of bankruptcy, namely, transfers with intent to prefer one creditor over another, and permitting a creditor to obtain a preference by legal proceedings, the burden of proof rests, to be sure, on the creditors.[15]

§ 179. But Debtor to Appear and Also Produce Books at Trial, to Afford Discovery.

—But as to classes two and three of acts of bankruptcy, the debtor must appear at the trial with all his papers and books and make a complete exposure of all facts regarding his solvency, and if he does not attend with them and submit to examination, the burden of proving his solvency shifts over on to him.[16]

Bogen & Trummell v. Protter, 12 A. B. R. 288, 129 Fed. 533 (C. C. A. Ohio): "If he submits to examination and produces his books, and his insolvency does not appear, the burden is upon the petitioner to make the proof, but if he fails to appear for examination, or fails to produce his books, the burden is upon him to prove his solvency."

McGowan v. Knittel, 15 A. B. R. 2, 137 Fed. 453 (C. C. A. Pa.): "As the alleged bankrupt appeared in courts with his books, etc. (§ 3), the burden of proving that his property would not suffice to pay his debts rested upon the plaintiffs."

It is one thing to make a debtor prove his own solvency and quite a different thing to make the creditor prove the debtor's insolvency. From their very nature, the facts as to his solvency lie more within the debtor's knowledge than within that of his creditors; and it is only fair that the debtor produce the data and furnish explanation to aid the petitioning creditors to make proof of insolvency, and that in case he fail to do so the petition-

---

14. In re West, 5 A. B. R. 734, 108 Fed. 940 (C. C. A. N. Y.).

15. Knittel v. McGowan, 14 A. B. R. 209, 134 Fed. 498 (D. C. Penna., reversed, on other grounds, in McGowan v. Knittel, 15 A. B. R. 1, C. C. A. Pa.).

16. Sec. 3 (d): "Whenever a person against whom a petition has been filed as hereinbefore provided under the second and third subdivisions of this section takes issue with and denies the allegation of his insolvency, it shall be his duty to appear in court on the hearing, with his books, papers, and accounts, and submit to an examina-

tion, and give testimony as to all matters tending to establish solvency or insolvency, and in case of his failure to so attend and submit to examination the burden of proving his solvency shall rest upon him."

In re Bloch, 6 A. B. R. 300, 109 Fed. 790 (C. C. A. N. Y.). Obiter, Bray v. Cobb, 1 A. B. R. 153, 91 Fed. 102 (D. C. N. C., reversed, on other grounds, in Cobb v. Overman, 6 A. B. R. 324, 109 Fed. 65). See In re Edelman, 12 A. B. R. 238, 130 Fed. 700 (C. C. A. N. Y.). Also, see In re Coddington, 9 A. B. R. 243, 118 Fed. 281 (D. C. Penn.).

ing creditors be excused from the proof, and the burden of proving solvency be cast upon the debtor and upon creditors intervening to oppose the petition.

§ 180. **Destruction or Loss of Adequate Books, or Failure to Keep Them, No Excuse.**—That the requisite books or records have been lost or destroyed, is no excuse; if the debtor fails to appear with books and records sufficient to determine the question of his solvency or insolvency, the burden of proof is upon him to prove his solvency.

Bogan & Trummell v. Protter, 12 A. B. R. 288, 129 Fed. 533 (C. C. A. Ohio): "With these books missing, it was impossible to ascertain Protter's financial condition. The law expects a merchant charged with bankruptcy, to support his statements by his books, which speak for themselves. * * * In this case, the testimony showed the salesbook for 1902 was on hand just before the fire. It disappeared after the fire, although it was not burned up. So with the other books. No satisfactory explanation of their disappearance was furnished. It is not sufficient for an alleged bankrupt, when called upon to produce his books, to say, 'I don't know where they are.' It is his business to know where they are. They are the only proper proof of his financial condition. He must not only keep proper books of account, but preserve them, and produce them when called upon. He fails to do so at his peril. The court should have held that, under the circumstances, the burden of proving his solvency rested upon Protter."

That the debtor did not keep the requisite books or records is also no defense.[17]

§ 181. **Query, Whether Requirement of Production of Account Books at Time of Trial, etc., Applies to Receiverships as Acts of Bankruptcy.**—Owing to the failure to make any corresponding amendment to § 3 (d), when class four of acts of bankruptcy was amended in 1903 to include receiverships, it is a question whether in cases of receiverships as acts of bankruptcy the burden of proving the debtor's insolvency, which rests on the creditors, is aided by the right to require production of account books, etc., at the time of trial, as in cases of preference; and whether the failure

In re Perlhefter & Shatz, 25 A. B. R. 576, 177 Fed. 299 (D. C. N. Y.); Cummins Grocer Co. v. Talley, 26 A. B. R. 484, 187 Fed. 507 (C. C. A. Tenn.); In re Donnelly, 27 A. B. R. 504, 188 Fed. 1001 (D. C. Ohio).

It has been held, indeed, that outstanding accounts in favor of the bankrupt must be such as could be realized upon under an execution, in order to warrant consideration as assets. Louisiana, etc., Soc. v. Segen, 28 A. B. R. 19; S. C., 28 A. B. R. 407, 196 Fed. 903 (D. C. La.). But see post, § 1353, note 357.

Interlocutory Order Requiring Alleged Bankrupt, Who Denies Insol- **vency, to File List of Creditors and Schedule of Assets.**—It appears to have been the practice, without question, as reported in one case, to require an alleged bankrupt, who was denying insolvency, to amend his answer by attaching a list of creditors and assets. Young & Holland Co., 20 A. B. R. 512, 162 Fed. 663 (C. C. A. R. I.). Also, see post, § 334½.

What Constitutes Insolvency.—As to what constitutes insolvency, see post, §§ 1343, 1353, et seq.

17. Obiter, inferentially, Bogen & Trummell v. Protter, 12 A. B. R. 288, 129 Fed. 533 (C. C. A. Ohio).

of the debtor to bring in his books and to submit to examination shifts the burden of proving solvency over to the debtor. Of course, if the debtor defaults and files no pleading against the petition, the creditor may have adjudication, for § 4b says the debtor may be adjudged bankrupt "upon default or an impartial trial." If he does not default and yet absents himself from the court room and does not produce his books, his insolvency would be difficult to prove and creditors would likely not be aided by § 3 (d).[18]

§ 181½. **Interrogatories.**—There is no statutory provision for annexing interrogatories to an involuntary petition,[19] and such practice has been held unauthorized, in a case, however, where it was being sought thereby to obtain indirectly a "general" examination into the "acts, conduct and property of the bankrupt" before adjudication.[20] Yet the ordinary remedies by way of discovery pertinent to the issues framed on the petition ought not to be denied to petitioners in bankruptcy.

DIVISION 7.

FOUR MONTHS TIME FOR FILING OF PETITION.

§ 182. **Four Months Time for Filing of Petition.**—None of these acts are available as grounds for adjudging a debtor an involuntary bankrupt, unless the petition against him is filed within four months after the commission of the act.[21]

---

18. Of course creditors may call him and cross-examine him as to his solvency, at any rate, where the act of bankruptcy alleged is one of those where the bankrupt is required to attend with all his books and submit to examination. In re Coddington, 9 A. B. R. 243, 118 Fed. 281 (D. C. Penn.).

It is held, in one case, that the evidence produced to show the indebtedness of an alleged bankrupt must be such as to satisfy the jury of its existence. Knittel v. McGowan, 14 A. B. R. 209 (D. C. Pa.), but it is to be feared that this case lays down too exacting a rule: "satisfying" evidence is a high degree of proof and its requirement is next to the requirement of proof beyond reasonable doubt, and would hardly seem proper in bankruptcy cases, at least in this branch of bankruptcy law.

Bankrupt can not complain of error in court instructing jury that something was an asset which was not such. Knittel v. McGowan, 14 A. B. R. 209, 134 Fed. 498 (D. C. Penn., reversed,

on other grounds, in McGowan v. Knittel, 15 A. B. R. 1, C. C. A. Pa.).

19. In re Thompson, 24 A. B. R. 655, 179 Fed. 874 (D. C. Pa.).

20. Compare post, §§ 282½, 412½, 1543. Also, see In re Thompson, 24 A. B. R. 655, 179 Fed. 874 (D. C. Pa.).

21. Bankr. Act, § 3 (b): "A petition may be filed against a person who is insolvent and who has committed an act of bankruptcy within four months after the commission of such act. Such time shall not expire until four months after (1) the date of the recording or registering of the transfer or assignment when the act consists in having made a transfer of any of his property with intent to hinder, delay, or defraud his creditors or for the purpose of giving a preference as hereinbefore provided, or a general assignment for the benefit of his creditors, if by law such recording or registering is required or permitted, or, if it is not, from the date when the beneficiary takes notorious, exclusive, or continuous possession of the property un-

Thus, under the first act of bankruptcy, the act of fraud must be alleged and proved to have occurred within the four months.[22]

§ 183. Continuing Concealments.

—Where fraudulent concealment of property is the act alleged, in order to be a continuing concealment such as to bring the transaction within the four months period, there must be something more than the merely incidental concealment accompanying the ordinary fraudulent transfer.[23]

§ 184. Date of Levy Controls Where Preference by Legal Proceedings.

—Where the act of bankruptcy complained of is the suffering a creditor to obtain a preference by legal proceedings, as in case of an attachment, the four months does not begin to run until the levy of attachment, no matter how long the main case itself in which the attachment was issued, has been pending. It is the seizure of the property that creates the preference.[24]

But the due enforcement by execution within the four months period of judgment liens, obtained before the four months period, is not within the statute.[25]

§ 185. "Four Months," to Date from Recording, etc., Where Such Requisite; or from Notorious Possession, Where Not.

—In order to remove all incentive from the dishonest debtor of secretly committing an act of bankruptcy and keeping it quiet in the hopes that the four months period for beginning proceedings that will result in setting it aside shall elapse without action being taken, the statute provides in clause B, § 3, as above noted, that the four months period:

"Shall not expire until four months after the date of the recording or registering of the transfer or assignment (when the act consists in having made a transfer of any of his property with intent to hinder, delay or defraud creditors, or for the purpose of giving a preference as hereinbefore provided, or a general assignment for the benefit of creditors) if by law such recording or registering is required or permitted, or, if it is not, then from the date the beneficiary takes notorious, exclusive or continuous possession of the property, unless the petitioning creditors have received actual notice of such transfer or assignment."

Thus, where the act complained of is a preferential transfer, such transfer will date only from the date of recording or registry, if recording or registry is required by law; and if not so required, then only from the date of actual notice to the petitioning creditors or of the taking of actual, no-

---

less the petitioning creditors have received actual notice of such transfer or assignment."

22. Davis v. Stevens, 4 A. B. R. 763, 104 Fed. 435 (D. C. S. Dak.).

23. Bank v. DePauw Co., 5 A. B. R. 345, 105 Fed. 926 (C. C. A. Ind.).

24. In re Higgins, 3 A. B. R. 364, 97 Fed. 775 (D. C. Ky.).

25. See ante, § 143.

torious, exclusive and continuous possession by the beneficiary.[26] Acts which took place more than four months before the filing of the bankruptcy petition cannot form the basis upon which to make adjudication of bankruptcy, except in cases where record or registry is requisite and the petitioning creditors were without notice and neither public record was made nor notorious possession taken.[27]

A case well illustrating this point is In re Mingo Valley Creamery Association, 4 A. B. R. 67, 100 Fed. 282 (D. C. Pa.), where an insolvent corporation sold all its real estate and used the proceeds to pay up some creditors in full, to the exclusion of all the rest. The petition was not filed until after four months from the payment, but within four months from the time the deed was filed for record. This was held to be too late, for the act of bankruptcy was not the sale, nor deeding of the real estate, but the payments to the few creditors to the exclusion of the rest; and these payments had been made more than four months before.

§ 186. Either Record, etc., or Notice, or Notorious Possession, Suffices.

—If (where recording or registering is requisite) either public record is made, or actual and notorious, exclusive and continuous possession taken, it will suffice;[28] or if the petitioning creditors have had actual notice.

§ 187. Only Such Notorious Possession Requisite as Property Susceptible of.

—But only such notorious possession is required as the property from its nature is susceptible of.[29]

§ 188. Date of Filing Petition, Not Issuance nor Service of Subpœna, Controls.

—Delay in issuing the subpœna upon the respondent beyond the four months period will not make the proceeding too late, for it is the filing of the petition, not the issuance of the subpœna that determines the four months limit.[30]

§ 188½. Date of Joining of Sufficient Creditors, When Controls.

—It has been held that where two of the three petitioning creditors in an involuntary petition containing no averment that the creditors were less than twelve, were not shown thereby to be creditors, rendering the petition insufficient to authorize an adjudication, and after the lapse of more than three months other creditors join in the petition, the four months period within which preferential transfers under § 60b, or fraudulent transfers

---

26. Bankr. Act, § 3 (b). Compare, Little v. Hardware Co., 13 A. B. R. 422, 133 Fed. 874 (C. C. A. Tex.).

27. In re Girard Glazed Kid Co., 12 A. B. R. 295, 129 Fed. 841 (D. C. Penn.).

28. In re Bogen, 13 A. B. R. 529, 134 Fed. 1019 (D. C. Ohio); In re Woodward, 2 A. B. R. 233, 95 Fed. 260 (Ref. Tex.).

29. In re Bogen, 13 A. B. R. 529, 134 Fed. 1019 (D. C. Ohio); In re Woodward, 2 A. B. R. 233, 95 Fed. 260 (Ref. Tex.).

30. In re Lewis. 91 Fed. 632, 1 A. B. R. 458 (D. C. N. Y.).

under § 67e, as amended, commences to run is from the time the petition was made sufficient by the joinder of other creditors, and conveyances made more than five months previous to such time cannot be set aside under either of said sections.[31]

§ 189. Computation of Time of Four Months Period.—The four months period is computed by excluding the day the act was committed and including the day the petition was filed.[32]

Fractions of a day are not to be considered.[33] Where the last day falls on Sunday, the petition is in time if filed on Monday.[34]

---

31. Manning v. Evans, 19 A. B. R. 217, 156 Fed. 106 (D. C. N. J.).

32. Bankr. Act, § 31 (a): "When-. ever time is enumerated by days in this act, or in any proceeding in bankruptcy, the number of days shall be computed by excluding the first and including the last, unless the last fall on a Sunday or holiday, in which event the day last included shall be the next day thereafter which is not a Sunday or a legal holiday."
In re Stevenson, 2 A. B. R. 66, 94 Fed. 110 (D. C. Del.); In re Dupree, 97 Fed. 28; Dutcher v. Wright, 94 U. S. 553; In re Tonawanda Street Planing Mill Co., 6 A. B. R. 38 (Ref. N. Y.). Instance, In re Hill, 15 A. B. R. 499, 140 Fed. 984 (D. C. Calif.); In re Warner, 16 A. B. R. 519. 144 Fed. 987 (D. C. Conn.).

Compare, analogously, In re Holmes. 21 A. B. R. 339. 165 Fed. 225 (D. C. Vt.); Pittsburgh Laundry v. Imperial Laundry, 18 A. B. R. 756, 154 Fed. 662 (C. C. A. Pa.).

33. In re Tonawanda Street Planing Mill Co., 6 A. B. R. 38 (Ref. N. Y.). Analogously, Jones v. Stevens, 5 A. B. R. 571 (Sup. Jud. Ct. Me.). Apparently, In re Hill, 15 A. B. R. 499, 140 Fed. 984 (D. C. Calif.). Analogously, In re Warner, 16 A. B. R. 519, 144 Fed. 987 (D. C. Conn.).

Similarly, in determining availability of bank deposit as offset. Moore v. Third Natl. Bank of Phila. (Pa. Superior Ct.), 24 A. B. R. 568. See also, post, § 1180.

34. In re Stevenson, 2 A. B. R. 66, 94 Fed. 110 (D. C. Del.).

PART II:

PROCEDURE IN PUTTING THE DEBTOR INTO BANKRUPTCY.

CHAPTER V.

PETITION IN VOLUNTARY BANKRUPTCY.

Synopsis of Chapter.

§ 190. Points of Difference between Voluntary and Involuntary Petition—Duplicate Petitions—Schedules.
§ 191. Voluntary Petition to Show Residence, etc., and Existence of Debt.
§ 192. Need Show No Act of Bankruptcy Other than Debts Unable to Pay and Prayer for Adjudication.
§ 193. Need Not Show Insolvency.
§ 194. Signature and Verification.
§ 195. Adjudication Immediate, Creditors May Not Oppose.
§ 196. Petition May Be Dismissed by Court of Its Own Motion.

§ 190. Points of Difference between Voluntary and Involuntary Petition—Duplicate Petitions—Schedules.—The first step towards calling into action the machinery of the bankruptcy law is to prepare and file the petition.

In voluntary cases there need be but one petition prepared and filed, the requirement of triplicate filing applying only to the schedules, not to the petition itself. But in involuntary cases the petition must be prepared and filed in duplicate, one copy for the court's records, the other for service on the respondent.[1]

The voluntary petition must be accompanied with schedules of all the debtor's liabilities and assets, but there is no requirement that schedules shall accompany the involuntary petition; for, naturally, creditors are not in a position to know the facts, and since the schedules would become of use only in case the petition were granted and the debtor adjudged bankrupt, it might never become necessary to use them at all; for this reason ten days' time is given the bankrupt after he has been adjudged bankrupt within which to file his schedules when the proceedings are in involuntary bankruptcy.[2]

§ 191. Voluntary Petition to Show Residence, etc., and Existence of Debt.—The voluntary petition in bankruptcy must show jurisdiction.

1. Bankr. Act, § 59 (c): "Petitions shall be filed in duplicate, one for the clerk, the other for service on the bankrupt."
2. **Form of Voluntary Petition.**—See Appendix, Official Forms Nos. 1 and 2. For form of voluntary petition of corporation, suggested in the absence of a special form prescribed by the Supreme Court of the United States, see Appendix, Unofficial Form No. 54.
   Form of Involuntary Petition.—See Appendix, Official Form 3. The form of the involuntary petition of creditors is, in the nature of things, somewhat different in each case, since the indebtedness and names of the petitioning creditors vary and also the acts of the debtor complained of as grounds of action.

It must show a sufficient residence, domicile or principal place of business of the debtor within the district (or ownership of property therein in cases of nonresidents of the United States) to give the court jurisdiction;[3] and these allegations of residence, domicile, etc., must not be made disjunctively.[4] It must show that the petitioner owes debts which he is unable to pay;[5] and that they are "provable" debts.[6]

§ 192. Need Show No Act of Bankruptcy Other than Debts Unable to Pay and Prayer for Adjudication.

—The petition need show no act of bankruptcy other than the admission of inability to pay debts and desire to be adjudged bankrupt as prescribed in the official form.[7]

§ 193. Need Not Show Insolvency.

—It need not allege the debtor is insolvent.[8]

§ 194. Signature and Verification.

—The voluntary petition must be signed and verified by the petitioner. The requirements are essential.[9] The verification may be made before a notary public who thereafter becomes the attorney of record for the bankrupt.[10]

Voluntary Petition of Corporation.—The Amendment of 1910, authorizing the voluntary bankruptcy of corporations, does not prescribe what action is necessary on the part of the corporation to that end, nor what officer shall verify the petition.

Going into bankruptcy is a special act which requires special action on the part of the corporation; it is a cessation of business and a surrender of property, and, as such, is a power which usually resides with the directors, and is not a general duty of the president.[11]

In the absence of any rule of the Supreme Court the signature to, as well as the verification of, the petition should be made by whomsoever may have been expressly authorized by corporate action for that purpose. In the absence of any express authorization, it would seem that such signature and verification should be made by whatever officer or agent would be competent for a similar purpose under the assignment or insolvency laws of the State.[12]

In the absence of any restriction by statute, or by the corporation's charter

3. See ante, §§ 27, 31, et seq.
4. In re Laskaris, 1 A. B. R. 480 (Ref. N. Y.). See also, Official Form No. 1.
5. See ante, § 41.
6. See ante, § 41; post, § 625, et seq.; post, § 440.
7. See ante, § 102.
8. See ante, § 42.
9. In re McConnell, 11 A. B. R. 418 (Ref. N. Y.).
10. In re Kindt, 3 A. B. R. 443, 98

Fed. 403 (D. C. Iowa). Compare, analogously, In re Kimball, 4 A. B. R. 144 (D. C. Mass.).
11. In re Jefferson Casket Co., 25 A. B. R. 663, 182 Fed. 689 (D. C. N. Y.). Compare ante, § 167.
12. Compare ante, § 44. Dodge v. Kenwood Ice Co., 29 A. B. R. 586, 189 Fed. 525 (D. C. A. Minn.); In re Jefferson Casket Co., 25 A. B. R. 663, 182 Fed. 689 (D. C. N. Y.).

and by-laws, it is within the power of the board of directors to file a voluntary petition in bankruptcy.[13]

§ 195. Adjudication Immediate, Creditors May Not Oppose.

—If jurisdictional averments are sufficient, adjudication is at once entered. Creditors will not be heard in opposition. If the jurisdictional averments are sufficient, as soon as the voluntary petition is filed an order of adjudication is entered, either by the judge, or in case of the judge's absence by the referee, an officer whose duties will be later explained. The clerk usually inspects the petition to see if it is in proper form and enters the adjudication on the records of the court without delay;[13a] for, as heretofore seen (ante, § 43), a creditor cannot intervene to oppose a voluntary adjudication, for no one is supposed to have any object in opposing the debtor if he desires to have himself adjudged bankrupt; and, furthermore, as also before noted (ante, §§ 102, 192) the averments of the petition themselves constitute an act of bankruptcy.

Probably the rule prohibiting creditors from intervening to oppose the adjudication in voluntary cases would not, however, prevent creditors or any one else, for that matter, bringing to the attention of the court the lack of jurisdiction for want of the debtor's actual residence, etc. Such would seem to be a corollary of Bankruptcy Act, § 18 (g).

§ 196. Petition May Be Dismissed by Court of Its Own Motion.

—Either the adjudication is entered or the petition, if fatally defective, or if jurisdiction is wholly wanting, may be dismissed.[14]

In re Waxelbaum, 3 A. B. R. 395, 98 Fed. 589 (D. C. N. Y.): "No express provision is made in the act or in the rules as to when or how an inquiry into the truth of the jurisdictional facts alleged in a voluntary petition is to be made; but, considering the complication which would often arise, it seems evident that the jurisdiction, when challenged, should be inquired into as early as possible, so that the proceedings, if invalid, may be arrested in limine: and the alternative of adjudication or dismissal given by (Bankr. Act) § 18 (g) implies that the court should make such inquiry into the facts as may be necessary to determine whether to adjudicate, or to dismiss."

---

13. In re Guanacevi Tunnel Co., 29 A. B. R. 229, 201 Fed. 316 (C. C. A. N. Y.). Compare, analogously, as to power of directors to make "written admission" as act of bankruptcy, ante, § 167.

13a. In some districts, it is the duty of the attorney for the petitioning creditor to fill in a blank form of order of adjudication.

14. Bankr. Act, § 18 (g); In re Garneau, 11 A. B. R. 679, 127 Fed. 677 (C. C. A. Ills.). As to vacating of adjudication and dismissal of petition, see post, § 429, et seq. As to requisite deposit for costs, see post, § 285, et seq.

CHAPTER VI.

PARTIES AND PETITION IN INVOLUNTARY BANKRUPTCY.[1]

Synopsis of Chapter.

DIVISION 1.

1. See interesting article "Creditors' Petitions in Involuntary Bankruptcy," I. National Bankruptcy News 62.

§ 197. How Many Creditors and to What Amount Must Join as Petitioners.—Three or more creditors must join as petitioners, if the total number of creditors is twelve or more; but one creditor will suffice if all the creditors are less than twelve; and such creditor or creditors must hold claims aggregating not less than $500 over and above any securities, and the claims must be provable claims.[2]

§ 198. Whether Requirements Jurisdictional.—These provisions of the Bankruptcy Act, § 59 (b), are said to be jurisdictional.[3] This juris-

---

2. Bankr. Act, § 59 (b): "Three or more creditors who have provable claims against any person which amount in the aggregate, in excess of the value of securities held by them, if any, to five hundred dollars or over; or if all of the creditors of such person are less than twelve in number, then one of such creditors whose claim equals such amount may file a petition to have him adjudged a bankrupt." In re Blount, 16 A. B. R. 101, 142 Fed. 263 (D. C. Ark.).

3. In re Gillette, 5 A. B. R. 125, 104 Fed. 769 (D. C. N. Y.); In re Rogers Milling Co., 4 A. B. R. 540, 102 Fed. 687 (D. C. Ark.).

dictional defect is probably waivable.[4] And the petition must show on its face the requisite number of creditors and amount of claims held by them, although in fact there may be a deficiency.[5] But the defect is not fatal and may be supplied by amendment.[6] And it is not meant by "jurisdictional" that the requirements affect jurisdiction over the subject matter, such as limit the operation of involuntary bankruptcy to certain corporations and require certain residence, domicile, etc.

§ 199. Employees and Relatives Excluded.

—In computing the number of creditors of a bankrupt for the purpose of determining how many creditors must join in the petition, his employees (who were such at the time of the filing of the petition) and his relatives are not to be counted, unless they themselves have joined in the petition.[7]

§ 200. Directors and Officers Excluded.

—Directors and officers of corporations need not be counted in determining whether the total number of creditors is less than twelve, unless they themselves voluntarily join in the petition.[8]

§ 201. Date of Adjudication Determines Whether Requisite Number Have Joined.

—The date of the adjudication and not the date of the filing of the petition is the date to test whether sufficient creditors in num-

---

4. In re Gillette, 5 A. B. R. 125, 104 Fed. 769 (D. C. N. Y.); In re Mason, 3 A. B. R. 599, 99 Fed. 256 (D. C. N. C.).

5. In re Bedingfield, 2 A. B. R. 355, 96 Fed. 190 (D. C. Ga.); In re Stein, 12 A. B. R. 364, 130 Fed. 377 (D. C. Penna., disapproved in In re Plymouth Cordage Co., 13 A. B. R. 665, 135 Fed. 1000, C. C. A.).

6. See post, § 269.

7. Bankr. Act, § 59 (e).

8. In re Barrett Pub. Co., 2 N. B. N. & R. 80 (Ref. Ills.).

Fraudulently Preferred Creditors under Law of 1867.—And it was held under the law of 1867 that creditors who had been fraudulently preferred were not to be counted in in determining whether a sufficient number had joined in the petition. In re Gillette, 5 A. B. R. 124, 104 Fed. 769 (D. C. N. Y.). [1867] Compare, to same effect, In re Israel, 12 N. B. Reg. 204, Fed. Cas. 7,111; [1867] In re Hunt, 5 N. B. Reg. 493, Fed. Cas. 6,883; [1867] Clinton v. Mayo, 12 N. B. Reg. 39, Fed. Cas. 2,899; [1867] In re Rosenfields, 11 N. B. Reg. 86, Fed. Cas. 12,061.

Creditors Assenting to General Assignment.—And it has been held, under the present law, that creditors who have assented to the general assignment which is urged as the act of bankruptcy are not to be counted in. In re Miner, 4 A. B. R. 710, 104 Fed. 520 (D. C. Mass.): "For these reasons, because such is the letter of the act, because such was the construction of analogous provision in the Act of 1867, and because such seems to me the fair intent of the act as a whole, I hold that the creditors who have assented to the assignment are not to be reckoned in the computation required by § 59b."

Small Claims on Current Accounts of Grocers, etc.—In one case it has been held, that small claims of a few dollars or cents on current accounts of grocers, etc., purposely allowed to run in order to bring the number of creditors up to twelve and to defeat a single creditor who had been left out of a settlement arrangement should not be counted in, on the doctrine de minimis lex non curat.

In re Blount, 16 A. B. R. 97, 142 Fed. 263 (D. C. Ark.): "To treat the holders of such claims as creditors to be considered in determining the number existing for the purpose of preventing a bona fide creditor to institute proceedings of this nature, when an insol-

ber and amount of claims have joined.[9]

§ 202. But Date of Filing Petition Determines How Many Must Join and Total Indebtedness and Subsequent Payment or Assignment of Claims, or Offset Ineffectual.

—The date of the filing of the petition determines whether the number of creditors owed by the bankrupt is in fact less than twelve and consequently whether three must join or one alone is sufficient.[10] And this is so, for only those who were creditors at the time of the filing of the petition have provable claims and are interested in the bankruptcy. Thus, the payment of the debt of one of the petitioning creditors after the petition is filed will not cause the dismissal of the proceedings;[11] nor its assignment to one of the other creditors;[12] nor the payment of enough to reduce the aggregate below $500.00, where other creditors intervene bringing the amount back to $500.00.[13] Also creditors induced by the bankrupt's assignee under a general assignment not to join in the petition should, nevertheless, be reckoned as among the whole number of creditors;[14] or when so induced by the bankrupt himself.[15]

Creditors whose claims arose after the filing of the petition may not be counted in in ascertaining the number of creditors owed by the bankrupt, nor may such creditors join as petitioning creditors.

Moulton v. Coburn, 12 A. B. R. 557, 131 Fed. 201 (C. C. A. Mass.): "While we find in the statute an express privilege to creditors to join in a petition, we find nothing to contravene the ordinary rule of law that the allegations of a declaration, bill, or petition, are to be disposed of as of the time of filing or of beginning the suit. Thus, we find in the statute nothing to indicate that creditors whose debts are created after the filing of a petition are entitled to join, or that a bankrupt may defeat a petition by increasing the number of his creditors between the filing of the petition and the time of answer. That the statute permits a creditor to become a party to a proceeding already begun affords no indication that the substantial rights of the parties are to be determined as of any other date than that fixed by the filing of the original petition."

The purchase in by an assignee for the benefit of creditors, out of the funds of the estate, of claims of several creditors and then his reassignment

vent conveys all of his property, with the avowed intention of preferring all of his creditors except one, would be a violation, if not of the letter, certainly of the spirit of the bankruptcy law, and cannot be tolerated."

9. In re Plymouth Cordage Co., 13 A. B. R. 665, 135 Fed. 1000 (C. C. A. Okla.); Moulton v. Coburn, 12 A. B. R. 557, 131 Fed. 201 (C. C. A. Mass.).

10. In re Coburn, 11 A. B. R. 212, 126 Fed. 218 (D. C. Mass., referred to in In re Adams, 12 A. B. R. 369, 130 Fed. 788, D. C. Mass.; affirmed sub nom. Moulton v. Coburn, 12 A. B. R. 553, 131 Fed. 201, C. C. A.); Stroheim v. Perry & Whitney Co., 23 A. B. R. 695, 175 Fed. 52 (C. C. A. Mass., af-

firming Perry v. Whitney Co., 22 A. B. R. 772).

11. Quære, in Gage v. Bell, 10 A. B. R. 696, 124 Fed. 371 (D. C. Tenn.); obiter, In re Coburn, 11 A. B. R. 212, 126 Fed. 218 (D. C. Mass.).

12. Inferentially, In re Brown, 7 A. B. R. 102, 111 Fed. 979 (D. C. Mo.).

13. In re Ryan, 7 A. B. R. 562, 114 Fed. 373 (D. C. Penn., dist. in In re Stein, 12 A. B. R. 366); In re Beddingfield, 2 A. B. R. 355, 96 Fed. 190 (D. C. Ga.). Compare, Gage v. Bell, 10 A. B. R. 696, 124 Fed. 371 (D. C. Tenn.).

14. In re Coburn, 11 A. B. R. 212, 126 Fed. 218 (D. C. Mass.).

15. In re Brown, 7 A. B. R. 102, 111 Fed. 979 (D. C. Mo.).

of the same claims to several new persons in order to increase the number of creditors to more than twelve, so that three creditors must join in an involuntary bankruptcy petition against the debtor, will not defeat an involuntary petition filed by a single creditor, where, by the assignee's original purchase the original number of creditors was reduced below twelve, the effect of the assignee's purchase with funds of the estate being to extinguish them; and his subsequent attempted reassignment of them being ineffectual to restore their vitality as debts.[16]

An offset accruing after the filing of the petition is unavailable to reduce a claim.[17]

Indeed, in one case it has been held that the date of the occurrence of the act of bankruptcy—an assignment—was the date for ascertaining whether the total amount of indebtedness was less than $1,000, in that case the assignee and debtor having settled with sufficient creditors before the filing of the petition to reduce the total indebtedness below the requisite $1,000.[18] However, in that case the settlement having been made through the assignee under the avoided assignment, the case should not be taken as modifying the rule of the main proposition herein.

But the fact that the claim of one of the petitioning creditors was a claim acquired by assignment after the debtor had committed the act of bankruptcy—even though such act of bankruptcy be an assignment for the benefit of creditors—is no disqualification [19]

In one case it has apparently been held that a creditor purchasing a claim after the filing of the bankruptcy petition is not qualified to be a petitioning creditor.[20] But such a rule would be too broadly stated, preventing bona fide transfers of interest in pending choses in action; and the case of Stroheim v. Perry & Whitney Co., in which the apparent rule is made is better brought within the rule of § 203¼, as being a claim where the petitioning creditor was only colorably the assignee, the real party in interest being the sister of the bankrupt and the real holder of the note therein involved.

§ 203. **Different Claims Purchased in by One Creditor Lose Separate Identity.**—Claims purchased by one creditor for the purpose of securing the statutory amount requisite for bringing involuntary proceedings do not retain their identity as separate claims in the sense of the law relating to the question.[21]

---

16. Leighton v. Kennedy, 12 A. B. R. 229, 129 Fed. 737 (C. C. A. Mass.).
17. Obiter, inferentially, In re Bevins, 21 A. B. R. 344, 165 Fed. 434 (C. C. A. N. Y.).
18. In re Jacobson, 21 A. B. R. 921 (Ref. Mass.).
19. In re Perry & Whitney Co., 22 A. B. R. 772, 172 Fed. 744 (D. C. Mass.).
20. Stroheim v. Perry & Whitney Co., 23 A. B. R. 695, 175 Fed. 52 (C. C. A. Mass., affirming Perry v. Whitney Co., 22 A. B. R. 772, 172 Fed. 744).
21. Lowenstein v. McShane Mfg. Co., 12 A. B. R. 601, 130 Fed. 1007 (D. C. Md.); (Obiter) In re Worcester Co., 4 A. B. R. 505, 102 Fed. 808 (C. C. A. Mass.). Instance, held not bought in by one creditor, In re Bevins, 21 A. B. R. 344, 165 Fed. 434 (C. C. A. N. Y.).

In re Burlington Malting Co., 6 A. B. R. 369, 109 Fed. 777 (D. C. Wis.):
"Issue being taken upon the truth and bona fides of such claims, it now appears
by the undisputed proof that the claims so bought in were purchased by the
original petitioner and paid by him or his counsel in full, and that the purported
intervenors have no actual claim or interest. The procedure is an obvious subterfuge and the intervening petitions are summarily dismissed. In any view
the claims so appearing are provable only by the original petitioner, as purchaser and actual owner (In re Worcester County, 4 Am. B. R. 496, 505), and
furnish no aid for the purposes of jurisdiction."

They are simply several claims by one creditor.

Nor do claims thus bought in or assumed retain their separate identity
so as to prevent one certain creditor, whose claim is the only one not taken
care of, instituting or maintaining an involuntary petition; nor so as to
require him to obtain sufficient other creditors to join with him to institute involuntary proceedings.[22] Nor do claims contracted for on condition that
the creditor will join, retain their identity as separate claims.[23]

§ 203¾. **Actuality of Purchase of Claim.**—The court will inquire
into the actuality of the purchase of claims by petitioning creditors.[24] Thus,
where one of the petitioning creditors was a corporation, whose business it
was to purchase insolvents' assets and which had contracted for claims in
order to qualify for involuntary proceedings, all doubts as to the actuality of
the purchase will be resolved against the petitioning creditor.

Lowenstein v. McShane, 12 A. B. R. 601, 130 Fed. 1007 (D. C. Md.): "In
dealing with this case the court cannot shut its eyes to the evident character of
this proceeding in bankruptcy. A large enterprise, with much property and
many creditors, was being administered by a court of competent jurisdiction
through its receivers, and had been so administered for four months, lacking
one day. Two creditors who were dissatisfied with the results of their intervention in the receivership case turned to the bankrupt court. They were but
two out of a great number of creditors. But joining with them comes the Assets Realization Company, a corporation whose business it is to deal in the
property of insolvent estates. It is not a creditor of the corporation desiring
to protect itself by availing of the provisions of the bankrupt act to secure an
equal distribution of its debtor's property, but it bought up the claims—one at
100 per cent., and other at less—for the express purpose of qualifying itself to
join in the petition in bankruptcy, and take the administration out of a court
where the great bulk of the creditors have shown that they are willing it should
remain, and subject it to the added expense of the bankrupt court. It is evident that the Assets Realization Company has not laid out its money in buying

---

22. Lowenstein v. McShane Mfg.
Co., 12 A. B. R. 601, 130 Fed. 1007 (D.
C. Md.). See post, §§ 739, 574.

23. In re Blount, 16 A. B. R. 97 (D.
C. Ark.).

24. In re Perry & Whitney Co., 22
A. B. R. 772, 172 Fed. 744 (D. C. Mass.
aff'd sub. nom. Stroheim v. Perry &
Whitney Co., 23 A. B. R. 695, 175

Fed. 52). Also compare In re Perry &
Whitney Co., 22 A. B. R. 780, 172 Fed.
752 (D. C. Mass.), although, in the latter case, the lack of actuality purchase
does not stand out clearly. But compare, In re Halsey Elec. Generator Co.,
20 A. B. R. 738, 163 Fed. 118 (D. C. N.
J.), quoted at § 203½.

claims—one at least at as much as 100 per cent.—without the expectation of deriving some pecuniary advantage greater than that of a mere creditor seeking to bring about a ratable distribution of an insolvent debtor's assets. In such a case the court should be slow to lend its aid, and, I think, should resolve every doubtful question of fact or law against a petitioning creditor who assumes such an attitude toward a valuable estate."

Thus, where the sister of a debtor assigns notes held by her against him to different parties, in order to enable the assignees thereof to be petitioning creditors, but without consideration, the court will disregard the assignment as being merely colorable and not actual, and as creating an artificial condition.

Stroheim v. Perry & Whitney Co., 23 A. B. R. 695, 175 Fed. 52 (C. C. A. Mass., affirming In re Perry & Whitney Co., 22 A. B. R. 772): "The petition was filed on September 23, 1908. On September 10, 1908, a sister of Stroheim held several notes of the debtor. At that time she transferred to Skelly one note without any substantial consideration, for the sole purpose of enabling her brother's copartnership to secure a sufficient number of creditors to proceed with the bankruptcy petition. Beaumont came into possession of another note under the same circumstances and for the same reason. Evidently they were not creditors when they joined the petition, because evidently the whole transaction was purely colorable, and the notes still belonged to Stroheim's sister. Therefore they could not lawfully make the required oath to the involuntary petition. We concur fully with the conclusion of the learned judge of the District Court so far as these two signatures are concerned."

§ 203½. Assignee of Valid Claim Competent.

—But if claims actually are purchased by a creditor, or by one who later becomes a petitioning creditor, there is no good reason nor law why such purchase, if it be actually made, should change the debt. It is still a "provable" debt, and the motive of the purchaser will not detract from the legal rights of the parties, nor render him incompetent to act as a petitioning creditor.[26]

In re Halsey Elec. Generator Co., 20 A. B. R. 738, 163 Fed. 118 (D. C. N. J.): "It also appears that Murray and Van Slyck each hold an assigned claim, that neither of them has any financial interest in the claim held by him, and that each of them holds his claim solely for the benefit of his assignor. This fact, however, does not disqualify either of them as a petitioning creditor. The assignments were made by persons who originally claimed to be separate creditors of the alleged bankrupt for the respective amounts of the claims assigned. Murray and Van Slyck are trustees for their respective assignors, and, as they hold the legal title to the claims assigned, they are the owners of those claims, and, if they be valid claims, are creditors. There is no dispute as to the validity of any of the claims, except that of Murray." Quoted further at § 204.

In re Hanyan, 24 A. B. R. 72, 181 Fed. 102 (C. C. A. N. Y.): "There is nothing

26. (1867) In re Woodford & Chamberlain, 13 N. B. Reg. 575, Fed. Cas. No. 17,972, cited and distinguished in Leighton v. Kennedy, 12 A. B. R. 235, 129 Fed. 737 (C. C. A. Mass.). But compare, In re Beddingfield, 2 A. B. R. 355, 96 Fed. 190 (D. C. Ga.).

in this section, or in any other provision of the Bankruptcy Act, requiring that a petitioning creditor should have been one at the time of the act of bankruptcy. All that the act requires is that he have a provable claim against the alleged bankrupt when the petition is filed. With entire respect for those who have intimated a different opinion, I am not able to see upon what ground courts have the right to impose additional conditions, not stated in the Bankruptcy Act, upon the right of any creditor having a provable claim to join in an involuntary petition."

But it would seem from some rulings that where the purchase does not occur after the filing of the bankruptcy petition, the purchaser may not then join as one of the petitioning creditors, for the petitioning creditors must have been creditors at the time of the commission of the act or at the latest at the time of the filing of the bankruptcy petition.

In re Perry & Whitney Co., 22 A. B. R. 780, 172 Fed. 752 (D. C. Mass. aff'd sub nom. Stroheim v. Perry & Whitney Co., 23 A. R. R. 695, 175 Fed. 52): "The adjudication in involuntary proceedings, for which the bankruptcy act provides, seems to me intended to be the result of the respective rights and obligations of the debtor, and his creditors as they exist at the time of the act of bankruptcy, or of the filing of the petition. Whether there shall be adjudication or not concerns them, and does not properly concern anyone between whom and the debtor no relations existed at either of those times. I do not believe it to have been intended that adjudication should result from or depend upon an altered situation arising later, still less a situation artificially created in order to affect the proceedings, by one with whom the debtor has never dealt in any way. If the petitioner, Leahy, is recognized as a creditor entitled to maintain this petition, and adjudication is ordered, the respondent will have been adjudged bankrupt, not because there are three creditors having a right to complain of its assignment made September 10, who desired this result, but because Charles Jacobs, to whom the debtor owed nothing when the assignment was made, and who never had any claim of any sort upon the debtor, until more than four months had passed since the assignment was made, has now undertaken to interfere in proceedings with which he had until now no concern at all, for the purpose, openly declared by him, to have been his sole purpose, of enabling his sons, the attorneys for the original petitioners, to prevail in the controversy regarding adjudication."

But it is doubtful that such a rule is to be adopted as a general proposition, and the cases under it are better brought under different propositions. Of course, however, even under this rule, a creditor who acquires his rights from one who is already a petitioning creditor, would be himself competent as such.[27]

§ 204. Creditor's Claim Not to Be Split Up to Obtain Jurisdictional Number.

—A creditor's claim may not be split up into several demands in order to create the requisite number of petitioning creditors.[28]

27. See post, § 238.

28. Compare, where two notes held by one creditor, were, by an agent of the creditor, without authority transferred to two different parties, to make them competent as petitioning creditors. In re Perry & Whitney Co., 22 A. B. R. 722, 172 Fed. 744 (D. C. Mass.

In re Tribelhorn, 14 A. B. R. 493, 137 Fed. 3 (C. C. A. N. Y.): "He was the attorney for the petitioning creditors, and manifestly acquired a part of the demand of Schmidt for the purpose of being joined with Schmidt as a petitioning creditor. The Bankrupt Act does not sanction the splitting up by a single creditor of his demand into several demands in order to create the requisite number of petitioning creditors, and, if such a practice were tolerated, the provisions of § 59d would become practically nullified."

In re Halsey Elec. Generator Co., 20 A. B. R. 738, 163 Fed. 118 (D. C. N. J.): "It is contrary to the policy of the Bankruptcy Act to permit a creditor to split up his claim against the debtor and assign some of the parts to other persons for the purpose of qualifying them as joint petitioners in a bankruptcy proceeding." Quoted further at § 203½.

§ 205. Preferred Creditors to Be Counted in, if Necessary.—The claims of creditors who have received preferences (even if they no longer claim to be creditors), are, perhaps nevertheless to be counted in, if necessary to sustain jurisdiction.[29]

McMurtrey v. Smith, 15 A. B. R. 431, 142 Fed. 853 (Master's Report approved and adopted by D. C.): "An equal distribution of the assets of an insolvent among the creditors of the same class is the aim and policy of the Bankruptcy Law; it denounces the unequal treatment of creditors, makes it a ground for involuntary proceedings against the insolvent and authorizes recovery from the creditor who is chargeable with notice of preference when accepting payment beyond his pro rata. Will the law countenance an action whereby the very act of evading the law is interposed as a defense against its application? Can a debtor be heard to say: 'If I make a preference while insolvent, the Bankruptcy Law will be invoked and will administer my affairs for the benefit of all my creditors; but if I prefer for an amount large enough to leave less than $1000 in debts outstanding, the Bankruptcy Law will take its protecting hands away from the creditors whom I left unpaid?' Evidently the answer to this question is in the negative, unless the law expressly answers it in the affirmative, or, being silent, the conclusion from other provisions of the law is irresistible that the question must be answered in the affirmative."

In re Tirre, 2 A. B. R. 493 (D. C. N. Y.): "To exclude a debt upon the ground of a void preference would enable the parties to evade the Bankruptcy Act altogether and thus take advantage of their own wrong."

But are to be excluded, if they defeat jurisdiction, as, for instance, where all creditors but one or two are preferred.[30]

Stevens v. Nave-McCord Co., 17 A. B. R. 610 (C. C. A. Colo.): "A creditor, who has a voidable preference, may not be counted against the petitioner in computing the number of creditors that must join in a petition for an adjudi-

aff'd sub nom. Stroheim v. Perry & Whitney Co., 23 A. B. R. 695, 175 Fed. 52).

29. In re Cain, 2 A. B. R. 378 (Master's Report approved by D. C. Ills., citing In re Scrafford, 15 N. B. Reg. 104, 21 Fed. Cas. 866); In re Norcross, 1 A. B. R. 644 (Ref. Mo.). It is to be noted, however, that the preferred creditors in this case were opposing the adjudication. Obiter, compare, Leighton v. Kennedy, 12 A. B. R. 229, 129 Fed. 739 (C. C. A. Mass.).

30. In re Miner, 4 A. B. R. 710, 104 Fed. 520 (D. C. Mass.); (1867) In re Israel, Fed. Cas. 7,111; (1867) In re Currier, Fed. Cas. 3,492; (1867) Clinton v. Mayo, Fed. Cas. 2,899.

cation in bankruptcy, until he surrenders his preference. If he surrenders before adjudication, he may be counted.

"The argument, in support of the contention that creditors who have secured a voidable preference must be counted in computing the number of creditors that must join in the petition, is that such parties have provable claims, and that every one who has a provable claim, and who is not excluded by § 59e * * * is a countable creditor under the bankruptcy law of 1898. * * * Counsel reason with much force and cogency that these provisions of the bankruptcy law clearly show that a preferred creditor has a claim which may always be proved and filed, and which may thereafter be allowed upon his surrender of his preference, and that the express specification in 59e of the creditors who may not be counted in determining how many creditors must join in the petition excludes preferred creditors who are not thus mentioned from the latter category under the familiar rule 'Expressio unius est exclusio alterius', and thus unavoidably includes them in those that must be counted. The argument is very persuasive, but it is met by other considerations which must not be disregarded. A creditor who has a voidable preference may make and file his formal proof of claim without surrendering his preference, and in that sense his claim is provable. In other words, it is susceptible of a formal statement in writing under oath which may be filed in court, under §§ 57a and 57c. But the claimant may not secure an allowance of his claim, he may not vote upon it at a meeting of creditors, he may not obtain any advantage by means of it in the bankruptcy proceedings, until he first surrenders his preference. Sections 57g, 56a (30 Stat., 560 [U. S. Comp. St. 1901, pp. 3442, 3443]); Keppel v. Tiffin Savings Bank, 197 U. S. 357, 361, 367, 13 Am. B. R. 552. Cardinal rules for the construction of a statute are that the intention of the legislative body which enacted it should be ascertained and given effect, if possible, regardless of technical rules of construction and the dry words of the enactment; that that intention must be deduced not from a part but from the entire law; that the object which the enacting body sought to attain and the evil which it was endeavoring to remedy may always be considered for the purpose of ascertaining its intention; that the statute must be given a rational, sensible construction; and that, if this be consonant with its terms, it must have an interpretation which will advance the remedy and repress the wrong. U. S. v. Ninety-Nine Diamonds (C. C. A. 8th Cir.), 139 Fed. 961, 965, 2 L. R. A. (N. S.), 185.

"The discharge of the bankrupt from his debts and the equal distribution of his unexempt property among his creditors of the same class were the chief objects which Congress sought to attain by the enactment of this statute. The preference of one or more creditors over others of the same class was one of the principal evils at which the statute was leveled. Witness the prohibition of the allowance of the claim of a preferred creditor and of his participation in the meetings of creditors until he surrenders his preference and the right granted to the trustee to recover from him the property he has obtained thereby or its value. Section 56a, 57g, 60a, 60b (30 Stat. 560, 562 [U. S. Comp. St. 1901, pp. 3442, 3443, 3445]); Pirie v. Chicago Title & Trust Co., 182 U. S. 438, 449, 5 A. B. R. 814; Kippel v. Sav. Bank, 197 U. S. 356, 361, 13 Am. B. R. 552, 25 Sup. Ct. 443, 49 L. Ed. 790. The bankruptcy law contains no express provision that a creditor who holds a voidable preference may so use his claim as to obtain any advantage from it before he surrenders his preference. Should a provision be ingrafted upon this statute by construction by means of which he may avail himself of the Act itself to defeat one of its main purposes, a construction by means of which he may use the statute to retain a preference which it was one of the chief objects of the Act to avoid? For, if this statute be interpreted to mean that a debtor may confer voidable preferences upon all his creditors but two, and may thereby enable them to hold their preferences and be counted against an adjudication, the evil which Congress sought to remove is promoted, and the remedy it provided is impaired. Such an interpretation does not accord with the spirit of the law. It would not be a reasonable, sensible construction of it, and it seems to be contrary to the intention evidenced by the body of the statute. - The most persuasive argument against this conclusion is that creditors holding voidable preferences are not mentioned in § 59e in the list of those who may not be counted, and the rule that the specification of some is the exclusion of others. But, after a thoughtful consideration of this and the other contentions of counsel, the evil of preferences which the bankrupt law was enacted to remove, the remedy of an equal distribution of the property of the bankrupt which it was passed to provide, the prohibition of the use of their claims by preferred creditors until they surrender them which the Act contains, the general scope of the law and all its provisions read and considered together, and the duty to give to it a rational and sensible interpretation, have forced our minds to the conclusion that it was the intention of Congress that creditors who hold voidable preferences should not be counted either for or against the petition for an adjudication in bankruptcy until they surrender their preferences. This intention, thus deduced, must therefore prevail over the technical rules of construction which counsel for the appellees invoke."

In re Blount, 16 A. B. R. 97, 142 Fed. 266 (D. C. Ark.): "The main subject of the Bankruptcy Act is to secure an equal distribution of the assets of an insolvent among all his creditors and prevent preferences. * * * The duty of the courts is to carry this intention of Congress into effect to the extent which the language of the act justifies. Mere schemes and artifices to avoid the letter and spirit of the law will not be tolerated. * * *

"If the contention of counsel for the bankrupt is to be sustained, an insolvent debtor owing debts to 12 or more creditors can assign or convey his property for the benefit of some of his creditors, leaving some unprovided, provided the creditors thus discriminated against do not exceed two; and the bankruptcy courts are powerless to prevent this wrong, because they say that until the preferred creditors are actually paid out of the proceeds of the insolvent's estate, they are still his creditors. The reasoning of the referee, as well as the authorities cited by him, fully meet that contention and are approved by the court. When Mr. Ford, in consideration of the transfer to him of all the assets of the bankrupt, assumed the payment of all of the bankrupt's debts except that of the petitioning creditor Johnston, he not only became a trustee for the benefit of those preferred creditors, but under the laws of the State of Arkansas, as construed by its highest court, he became absolutely liable to them for their claims."

Leighton v. Kennedy, 12 A. B. R. 232, 129 Fed. 739 (C. C. Mass.): "* * * while, if preferred creditors should be counted against an involuntary petition, they could, by merely sitting still, give effect to preferences illegally received and defeat the purposes of the bankruptcy statute."

§ 206. Only Creditors Who Might Have Been Petitioners to Be Counted.

—Only such creditors as might have joined as petitioning creditors should be counted in ascertaining whether the number of creditors is

1 R B—14

less than twelve.[31]

§ 207. Erroneous Averment of Less than Twelve.

—If the petitioner erroneously avers that there are less than twelve creditors altogether and if less than three have joined as petitioners the case is not thereupon to be dismissed, but the bankrupt[32] or answering creditor must point out the remaining creditors and notice must be given them and also opportunity for sufficient of them to join.[33]

§ 208. Bankrupt to Supply List of Creditors, if He Claims Averment Erroneous.

—The bankrupt[34] or the answering creditor,[35] as the case may be, must file with his answer a sworn list of all the creditors, where he claims the petitioning creditor erroneously has averred the total number of creditors to be less than twelve.

In re Haff, 13 A. B. R. 367 (C. C. A. N. Y.): "Here, although the bankrupt averred the existence of a larger number of creditors in his answer to the earlier petition, he annexed only a partial list, and not a list under oath of all his creditors, with their addresses as provided for in said section."

The debtor must do more than state simply the names and addresses of his other creditors. He must also give the amounts of the respective debts; the consideration; the date due and in general a complete description so as to enable the petitioning creditor to negotiate with the others to join him

---

31. In re Miner, 4 A. B. R. 710, 104 Fed. 520 (D. C. Mass.). As to counting attachment creditors, see In re Schenkein & Coney, 7 A. B. R. 162 (Ref. N. Y.). Under the law of 1867 they could not be counted, In re Scrafford, Fed. Cases, No. 12,556.

32. Bankr. Act, § 59 (d): "If it be averred in the petition that the creditors of the bankrupt are less than twelve in number, and less than three creditors have joined as petitioners therein, and the answer avers the existence of a large number of creditors, there shall be filed with the answer a list under oath of all the creditors, with their addresses, and thereupon the court shall cause all such creditors to be notified of the pendency of such petition and shall delay the hearing upon such petition for a reasonable time, to the end that parties in interest shall have an opportunity to be heard; if upon such hearing it shall appear that a sufficient number have joined such petition, or if prior to or during such hearing a sufficient number shall join therein, the case may be proceeded with, but otherwise it shall be dismissed."

In re Plymouth Cordage Co., 13 A.

B. R. 665, 135 Fed. 1000 (C. C. A. Okla.); (1867) In re Williams, Fed. Cas., No. 17,700; (1867) Roche v. Fox, Fed. Cas., No. 11,974; In re Brown, 7 A. B. R. 102, 111 Fed. 979 (D. C. Mo., explained in In re Haff, 13 A. B. R. 362, 136 Fed. 78, C. C. A. N. Y.); In re Mammoth Pine Lumber Co., 6 A. B. R. 84 (D. C. Ark., distinguished in In re Stein, 12 A. B. R. 364, 130 Fed. 377, D. C. Pa. But In re Stein is itself disapproved in In re Plymouth Cordage Co., supra). Compare, In re Brett, 12 A. B. R. 492, 130 Fed. 981 (D. C. N. J.); In re Romanow, 1 A. B. R. 461, 92 Fed. 512 (D. C. Mass.); In re Mercur, 2 A. B. R. 626, 95 Fed. 634 (D. C. Penna.); In re Mackay, 6 A. B. R. 577, 110 Fed. 363 (D. C. Del.); Hoffschlaeger Co. v. Young Nap, 12 A. B. R. 515 (D. C. Hawaii). Compare, also, to same effect, inferentially, In re Haff, 13 A. B. R. 362, 135 Fed. 742 (C. C. A. N. Y.). Gage v. Bell, 10 A. B. R. 696, 124 Fed. 371 (D. C. Tenn.).

33. State B'k v. Haswell, 23 A. B. R. 330, 174 Fed. 209 (C. C. A. Iowa).

34. Gage v. Bell, 10 A. B. R. 696, 124 Fed. 371 (D. C. Tenn.). Also see cases cited under last two preceding notes.

35. As to answering creditor, State

in his petition.[36] And the same duty rests upon an answering creditor, where the bankrupt himself does not answer.[36a]

§ 209. Mode of Service of Notice.—The mode of service of such notice is left to the discretion of the court.

In re Tribelhorn, 14 A. B. R. 492, 137 Fed. 3 (C. C. A. N. Y.): "The mode of service is left to the discretion of the court. It not being contended that any of the creditors named were not actually served in due time to intervene if they had desired to do so, the mode of service upon them was immaterial."

Compare, In re Barrett Pub. Co., 2 N. B. N. & R. 80 (Ref. Ills.): "I am of the opinion that it is the duty in the first instance of the bankrupt to send out such notice, and that on the omission of the bankrupt so to do, that the duty then falls upon the petitioner."

Probably the usual ten days' notice would suffice. And one case holds that the court need not withhold entry of adjudication to give time for such notification, if the creditors—not shown in the answer—have already been informed of the pendency of the bankruptcy proceedings.[37]

§ 210. Joining of Additional Creditors.—And creditors may join with the petitioning creditors in contending for the adjudication of the bankrupt, after the filing of the petition.[38]

A creditor who files a petition in bankruptcy, has the right to request others to intervene, when such intervention becomes necessary to preserve the proceedings.[39]

§ 211. Creditors May Join though Sufficient Already Petitioning and May Plead Separately.—Creditors may join with the petitioning creditors as well as intervene to contest the adjudication, even though there are three petitioning creditors already. It would be strange, indeed, if other

---

B'k v. Haswell, 23 A. B. R. 330, 174 Fed. 209 (C. C. A. Iowa).

36. Gage v. Bell, 10 A. B. R. 696, 124 Fed. 371 (D. C. Tenn.). And the court may refer the answer and list to a special master to ascertain the full particulars. But where all creditors not set forth in the answer had been informed of the pendency of the proceeding but had not entered any appearance, nor asked to intervene, and there was nothing to indicate that they could have been induced to join in the proceedings, the court may refuse to withhold its adjudication to give the clerk time to notify such creditors. In re Tribelhorn, 14 A. B. R. 492, 137 Fed. 3 (C. C. A. N. Y.).

36a. State Bank v. Haswell, 23 A. B. R. 330, 174 Fed. 209 (C. C. A. Iowa);

Gage v. Bell, 10 A. B. R. 696, 124 Fed. 371 (D. C. Tenn.).

37. In re Tribelhorn, 14 A. B. R. 492, 137 Fed. 3 (C. C. A. N. Y.).

38. Bankr. Act, § 59 (f); In re Haff, 13 A. B. R. 362, 135 Fed. 742 (C. C. A. N. Y.); Ayres v. Cone, 14 A. B. R. 739, 138 Fed. 783 (C. C. A. S. Dak.); In re Plymouth Cordage Co., 13 A. B. R. 665, 135 Fed. 1000 (C. C. A. Okla.); In re Beddingfield, 2 A. B. R. 355, 96 Fed. 190 (D. C. Ga.); In re Bellah, 8 A. B. R. 310 (D. C. Del.); In re Stein, 5 A. B. R. 288, 105 Fed. 749 (D. C. Pa., disapproved, on other grounds, in In re Plymouth Cordage Co., 13 A. B. R. 665, 135 Fed. 1000, C. C. A. Okla.); State Bank v. Haswell, 23 A. B. R. 330, 174 Fed. 209 (C. C. A. Iowa).

39. Compare post, § 216; also see In re Smith, 23 A. B. R. 864, 176 Fed. 426 (D. C. N. Y.).

creditors should be cut off by the filing of the petition from doing more than merely to join therein and thus be denied any part in the management of the prosecution of the common right. Such creditors may file intervening petitions setting up acts of bankruptcy in their own way and may even add other acts, provided they have occurred within the four months preceding the filing of the intervening petition.[40] But they may not add acts of bankruptcy occurring more than four months before the filing of such intervening petitions.[41] The intervening petition may be amended. Thus, it may be amended to supply a defect in its allegations as to the number of creditors of the bankrupt.[42] The intervening petition may be withdrawn.[43]

§ 212. Involuntary Proceedings Not to Be Dismissed Except on Merits, etc., if Any Creditor Willing to Take Up Contest.

—The proceedings may not be dismissed for want of prosecution or otherwise than on the merits, or by the court on its own motion for failure to comply with court rules, if any creditor objects to the dismissal and will himself take up the contest and comply with the rules.[44]

§ 213. Time of Joining and Whether Counted in.

—They may join at any time before the decision of the court upon the issue of bankruptcy, and be counted to make up the requisite number of creditors and amount of claims.[45]

And they may so join even though the original creditors had not provable claims or were insufficient in number, or were otherwise disqualified.

In re Vastbinder, 11 A. B. R. 121, 126 Fed. 417 (D. C. Pa.): "It is urged, however, that as the original petition was insufficient, by reason of one of the petitioners being disqualified, it cannot be cured by the intervention of others; but that does not seem to be the law. The proceedings, as originally instituted, were formally sufficient, and even though some of the petitioning creditors were not as argued, entitled to prosecute them, they, nevertheless, inured to the benefit of all, and others may unquestionably come in for the purpose of supplying any deficiency."

40. In re Haff, 13 A. B. R. 362, 135 Fed. 742 (C. C. A. N. Y.). Also, In re Stein, 5 A. B. R. 288, 105 Fed. 749 (D. C. Pa.); In re Beddingfield, 2 A. B. R. 355, 96 Fed. 190 (D. C. Ga.). But other creditors cannot be compelled to come in and join. In re Gillette, 5 A. B. R. 119, 104 Fed. 769 (D. C. N. Y.).

41. In re Haff, 13 A. B. R. 362, 135 Fed. 742 (C. C. A. N. Y.).

42. In re Haff, 13 A. B. R. 362, 135 Fed. 742 (C. C. A. N. Y.).

43. Moulton v. Coburn, 12 A. B. R. 554, 131 Fed. 201 (C. C. A. Mass., affirming In re Coburn, 11 A. B. R. 212, 126 Fed. 218).

44. Impliedly, In re Cronin, 3 A. B. R. 552, 98 Fed. 584 (D. C. Mass.). Although this was a case where one of the petitioning creditors was objecting, yet the principle involved is the same and would apply to the case of any creditor. This case was distinguished in Moulton v. Coburn, 12 A. B. R. 555, 131 Fed. 121 (C. C. A. Mass.).

45. In re Plymouth Cordage Co., 13 A. B. R. 665, 135 Fed. 1000 (C. C. A. Okla.); In re Romanow, 1 A. B. R. 461, 92 Fed. 510 (D. C. Mass.); In re Beddingfield, 2 A. B. R. 355, 96 Fed. 190 (D. C. Ga.); obiter, In re Tribelhorn, 14 A. B. R. 491, 137 Fed. 3 (C. C. A. N. Y.); In re Crenshaw, 19 A. B. R. 502, 156 Fed. 638 (D. C. Ala.); In re Perry & Whitney Co., 22 A. B. R. 770, 172 Fed. 745 (D. C. Mass.); In re Charles Town Lt. & Power Co., 29 A. B. R. 721, 199 Fed. 846 (D. C. W. Va.).

Obiter, In re Crenshaw, 19 A. B. R. 502, 156 Fed. 638 (D. C. Ala.): "The first contention on the part of the respondent is that some of the original petitioners could not institute this proceeding on the ground or suggestion that said petitioners connived at a 'fraud on the law,' or attempted a fraud on the other creditors. * * * But, assuming that the rule invoked applied to this case as originally instituted, it would have no effect now because a sufficient number of creditors other than the original petitioners have entered their appearance and joined in the petition. Creditors other than the original petitioners may, at any time, enter their appearance and join in the petition, and creditors so joining in a petition subsequent to its filing may be reckoned in making up the number of creditors and amount of claims required by the act to support the petition."

But they may not join after the decision of the court upon the issues.[46]

In re Tribelhorn, 14 A. B. R. 491, 137 Fed. 3 (C. C. A. N. Y.): "After a hearing and dismissal of an involuntary petition (for deficiency of parties plaintiff) it is too late for any new creditor to intervene as a matter of right, and a denial of the application is proper."

And the words "at any time" are obviously not to be taken in an absolutely unlimited sense; there must at least be a petition pending before the court.[47] Creditors may join after the expiration of the four months period in order to make up the requisite number, even though the original creditors had no provable claims or were insufficient in number.[48]

§ 214. Whether Only Creditors Competent Whose Claims against Debtor Existed at Time of Commission of Act.

—It has been held that only creditors who were such at the time of the commission of the alleged act of bankruptcy or who held their rights against the bankrupt at that time, may petition the debtor into bankruptcy;[49] but such ruling is doubtful.[50]

---

46. Neustadter v. Chicago Dry Goods Co., 3 A. B. R. 96, 96 Fed. 830 (D. C. Wash.):

47. Obiter, In re Perry & Whitney Co., 22 A. B. R. 770, 172 Fed. 745 (D. C. Mass.).

48. In re Romanow, 1 A. B. R. 461, 92 Fed. 510 (D. C. Mass.); In re Mammoth Pine Lumber Co., 6 A. B. R. 84 (D. C. Ark.); In re Mackey, 6 A. B. R. 577, 110 Fed. 355 (D. C. Del.), approved by In re Haff, 13 A. B. R. 367, 135 Fed. 742 (C. C. A. N. Y.); inferentially, In re Plymouth Cordage Co., 13 A. B. R. 665, 135 Fed. 1000 (C. C. A. Okla.).

Whether Doctrine of Laches Applicable.—It has been held that though no time has been fixed by statute yet, as proceedings in bankruptcy are of an equitable nature, the court might perhaps apply the ordinary rules of laches. Stroheim v. Perry & Whitney Co., 23 A. B. R. 695, 175 Fed. 52 (C. C. A. Mass.).

Yet, it is not precisely true to say that the Bankruptcy Act specifies no time, since § 59f says: "Creditors, other than original petitioners may at any time enter their appearance and join in the petition or file an answer and be heard in opposition to the prayer of the petition," which would seem to indicate that the broadest liberality should be allowed as to the time of such joining.

49. In re Callison, 12 A. B. R. 344, 130 Fed. 987 (D. C. Fla., affirmed sub nom. Brake v. Callison, 11 A. B. R. 797, 129 Fed. 196). But compare, as to frauds against subsequent creditors, Beasley v. Coggins, 12 A. B. R. 355, 57 So. Rep. 213; Beers v. Hanlin, 3 A. B. R. 745, 99 Fed. 695 (D. C. Ore.); In re Brinckmann, 4 A. B. R. 551, 103 Fed. 65 (D. C. Ind.); (1867) In re Muller, Fed. Cas. No. 9,912; (1867) In re Burk, Fed Cas. No. 2,156.

50. In re Perry & Whitney Co., 22 A. B. R. 772, 172 Fed. 745 (D. C. Mass.).

At any rate the claims need not have been owned by the present creditor at the time of the commission of the act.[51]

Thus the assignee of a provable claim may intervene as a petitioner, although the assignment to him was subsequent to the filing of the petition.[52]

And the claims need not have been "provable" at the time of the commission of the act if "provable" at the time of the filing of the petition.[53] Two cases, however, hold that if the claim was an unliquidated tort claim for personal injury at the time of the commission of the alleged act of bankruptcy although reduced to judgment at the time of the filing of the petition, it may not be one of the petitioning creditors' claims.[54]

The better rule, in short, is that it is only necessary that the debt have existed at the time of the commission of the act of bankruptcy, not that the particular petitioning creditor have been at the time a creditor of the bankrupt.

In re Hanyan, 24 A. B. R. 72, 180 Fed. 498 (D. C. N. Y.): "There is nothing in this section, or in any other provision of the Bankruptcy Act, requiring that a petitioning creditor should have been one at the time of the Act of Bankruptcy. All that the act requires is that he have a provable claim against the alleged bankrupt when the petition is filed. With entire respect for those who have intimated a different opinion, I am not able to see upon what ground courts have the right to impose additional conditions, not stated in the Bankruptcy Act, upon the right of any creditor having a provable claim to join in an involuntary petition."

§ 215. Relatives, Officers, Directors, etc., Competent Petitioners.
—Members of the debtor's family may be petitioning creditors, as a wife and sons.[55]

And directors, officers and stockholders who are creditors may be petitioning creditors.[56]

First Nat. Bank v. Ice Co., 14 A. B. R. 448, 136 Fed. 466 (D. C. Pa.): "Having carried the company along as they had, by advancing money and lending their credit, they were not obliged to sit by and do nothing, simply because of their official relation to it."

§ 216. Solicitation by Bankrupt to File Involuntary Petition, or by Creditors Not to Resist Adjudication, Not Improper.
—It is not improper for the directors of a corporation to solicit creditors to file a petition

---

51. In re Perry & Whitney Co., 22 A. B. R. 772, 172 Fed. 745 (D. C. Mass.).

52. In re Fitzgerald, 26 A. B. R. 773, 191 Fed. 95 (D. C. N. Y.).

53. Compare post, § 228.

54. Beers v. Hanlin, 3 A. B. R. 745, 99 Fed. 695 (D. C. Ore.); In re Brinckmann, 4 A. B. R. 551, 103 Fed. 65 (D. C. Ind.). But these cases are clearly erroneous. The claim in each case was undeniably a "provable" debt at the time the petition was filed and that was enough.

55. Impliedly, Bankr. Act, § 59 (e); In re Novak, 4 A. B. R. 311, 101 Fed. 800 (D. C. Iowa).

56. Compare post, § 888. Home Powder Co. v. Geis, 29 A. B. R. 580, 204 Fed. 568 (C. C. A. Mo.). Obiter, In re Rollins Gold & Silver Mining Co., 4 A. B. R. 327 (Ref. N. Y.).

against the corporation, based on the fifth act of bankruptcy.[57] It is not such collusion as will defeat adjudication for a corporation to admit in writing its inability to pay its debts and its willingness to be adjudged a bankrupt on that ground, and to accompany the same with solicitation of certain creditors to file a bankruptcy petition against it.[58]

Nor is it improper for the creditors to solicit the bankrupt not to resist the petition for adjudication.

In re Billing, 17 A. B. R. 90 (D. C. Ala.): "It is neither immoral nor illegal nor contrary to public policy for petitioning creditors to urge upon their debtor, who is in fact insolvent, and has committed an act of bankruptcy, not to resist the adjudication in an involuntary proceeding, or for such debtor to heed the importunity of creditors at any stage in the proceeding against him. When such a debtor does no more than abandon resistance once begun to an effort to adjudicate him a bankrupt, and consents to be adjudged, because he deems it for the best interests of all his creditors, his conduct, whether induced solely by his own volition and judgment, or inspired by the solicitation of creditors, and whether or not there be any formal agreement between the debtor and the petitioning creditors as to his consent to an adjudication, does not work any fraud or wrong upon creditors. The law gives the creditors the right to force such a debtor into bankruptcy. Having the right under the law and facts of this case to force the debtor into bankruptcy, his creditors had a perfect moral and legal right to seek to end the prolonged litigation, by agreement to that end between themselves and the bankrupt. The bankrupt could lawfully consent in advance to a decree, which the law, on the evidence, would surely pronounce against him, if the litigation continued. In such a case the law seeks to bring about the equitable pro rata distribution of his estate among his creditors, according to the provisions of the bankruptcy statute. His consent only aids in carrying out the policy of the statute, and in bringing about a status, which the law, under the circumstances, declares ought to exist."

Nor, for that matter, is the bankrupt's solicitation of creditors not to file a petition in bankruptcy against him, improper.[59]

A creditor who files a petition in bankruptcy has the right to request others to intervene, especially when such intervention becomes necessary to preserve the proceeds.[60]

57. In re Moench, 12 A. B. R. 240, 123 Fed. 965 (C. C. A. N. Y., affirming 10 A. B. R. 656).

Nor is it improper for a debtor to request creditors to file an involuntary petition. (1867) In re Ordway Bros., 19 Nat. Bankr. Reg. 171.

58. In re Duplex Radiator Co., 15 A. B. R. 324, 142 Fed. 906 (D. C. N. Y.). But where a corporation itself desiring to go through bankruptcy is unable to get three creditors to file a petition but succeeds in getting two and induces a third creditor to assign its claim; and thereupon the two and the assignee of the third file the petition, it has been held, that the court should dismiss the petition as a collu-

sion to avoid the statute. In re Independent Thread Co., 7 A. B. R. 704, 113 Fed. 998 (D. C. N. J.). This is a doubtful rule. Contrast, inferentially, In re Moench, 12 A. B. R. 240, 123 Fed. 465 (C. C. A. N. Y., affirming 10 A. B. R. 656).

Creditor's attorney's promise to pay another creditor's claim himself, for joining in involuntary petition, is valid and enforceable against attorney. Bernard v. Fromme, 22 A. B. R. 585, 132 App. Div. (N. Y.) 922, 116 N. Y. Supp. 807.

59. In re Brown, 7 A. B. R. 102, 111 Fed. 979 (D. C. Mo.).

60. In re Smith, 23 A. B. R. 864, 176 Fed. 426 (D. C. N. Y.).

§ 217. Partnership Creditors Competent to Petition against Individual Partner.—Partnership creditors are creditors also of each partner and may be petitioning creditors against the individual partner.[61]

§ 218. Partnership as Petitioning Creditor in Firm Name.— Whether a partnership who is a creditor may be one of the petitioning creditors in its firm name, quære.[62]

§ 219. Authority of Corporate Officer to File Petition.—As to what is sufficient authority in àn officer of a creditor corporation to authorize him to file an involuntary petition, there has been one holding under the present law.[63]

§ 220. Secured Creditors Competent to Extent of Deficit.—Creditors holding securities are competent to join as petitioners. But their claims are to be counted in estimating the $500 only for the deficit left after the deduction of the value of their securities.[64]

In re Smith, 23 A. B. R. 864, 176 Fed. 426 (D. C. N. Y.): "I find nothing in the Bankruptcy Act which, even by implication, denies the right to a secured creditor or a judgment creditor to file a petition in bankruptcy against the one owing the debt. * * * All claims may be proved, unless of a class or classes of which this is not one, and, if there be a partial security by way of lien or otherwise, same may be allowed for the balance over the security, and in certain cases the lien or incumbrance or preference must be surrendered before the claim can be allowed."

§ 220½. Priority Creditors.—Likewise, creditors who would be entitled to priority of payment on distribution of the bankrupt estate would nevertheless be competent petitioning creditors, although their claims are to be counted in estimating the $500 only for the deficit left after deduction of the probable value of their priority.[65]

§ 221. Estoppel of Creditors by Connivance.—Creditors who have connived at the alleged act of bankruptcy, whether it be either actually or constructively fraudulent, or not fraudulent at all, are of course estopped from proceeding against the debtor in involuntary bankruptcy on that ground.[66]

---

61. §§ 1291, 1387½, 2268½; see also In re Hee, 13 A. B. R. 8 (D. C. Hawaii); In re Mercur, 2 A. B. R. 626, 95 Fed. 634 (D. C. Pa.); Mills v. Fisher & Co., 20 A. B. R. 237, 159 Fed. 897 (C. C. A. Tenn.), quoted at §§ 1291, 2263½.

62. In re Levingston, 13 A. B. R. 357 (D. C. Hawaii).

63. In re Winston, 10 A. B. R. 171, 122 Fed. 187 (D. C. Tenn.).

64. Bankr. Act, § 59 (B). Compare post, § 751. In re Blount, 16 A. B. R. 697, 142 Fed. 263 (D. C. Ark.); In re Fitzgerald, 26 A. B. R. 773, 191 Fed. 95 (D. C. N. Y.).

65. But Tax Collector under Statute Giving Right to Sue in Own Name after Three Months, Not Competent When.—In re Corwin Mfg. Co., 26 A. B. R. 269 (D. C. Mass.).

66. Obiter, Woolford v. Steel Co., 15

Obiter, Moulton v. Coburn, 12 A. B. R. 553, 131 Fed. 201 (C. C. A. Mass.): "A creditor who has assented in writing to the terms of a common law assignment for the benefit of creditors is not entitled, ordinarily, to join in an involuntary petition alleging as the sole act of bankruptcy the making of the general assignment to which he has expressly assented. This is not because he has ceased to be a creditor, but because, having voluntarily elected that the bankrupt's estate shall be administered under the assignment, and having accepted the provisions of the deed of trust, he is thereby estopped from action inconsistent with the agreement."

In re Marks Bros., 15 A. B. R. 459, 142 Fed. 279 (D. C. Pa.): "* * * it has been well settled that it is a just ground for refusing to allow a petitioner to complain of an act of bankruptcy which has been induced or brought about by himself. 'To hold otherwise would enable the unscrupulous to entrap a person into bankruptcy.' A party cannot thus take advantage of his own wrong."

Lowenstein v. McShane Mfg. Co., 12 A. B. R. 601, 130 Fed. 1007 (D. C. Md.): "As to Lowenstein and N. Frank & Sons, it is objected that, by their participation in the receivership proceedings in the State court, they have elected to proceed in that forum, and are estopped from petitioning bankruptcy. It appears that Lowenstein and N. Frank & Sons on November 28th, 1903, intervened in that case on the day after the receiver was appointed, and filed petitions in the Circuit Court No. 2 praying that court to appoint a coreceiver. These petitions came on for hearing on March 24, 1904, and a coreceiver was appointed by the court, although not the one urged by the petitioner.

"This action, it seems to me, was an election by those two creditors to avail of the proceedings in the State court, and it appears that, during the period between their intervention in that case and their filing the petition in bankruptcy, much was done by the receivers in the State court. The large business of the corporation was carried on, money was, by the orders of court, expended in the repairs of buildings, and leases to quite a number of tenants were effected at very remunerative rents, and sales of property have been negotiated. It seems to me that equitably, after four months' participation, these creditors should be held to be estopped from taking this proceeding, which would be destructive of the acts of the receivers."

§ 222. Mere Proving of Claims under General Assignment or Receivership No Estoppel.

—But the mere proving of claims under a general assignment for the benefit of creditors in the state insolvency courts will not operate to estop the creditors so proving them from filing an involuntary petition against the bankrupt.[67]

A. B. R. 40, 138 Fed. 582 (D. C. Del.); (1867) In re Williams, Fed. Cas., No. 17,706; Cummins Grocery Co. v. Talley, 26 A. B. R. 484, 187 Fed. 507 (C. C. A. Tenn.); In re Gold Run, etc., Co., 29 A. B. R. 563, 200 Fed. 162 (D. C. Colo.). Clark v. Henne & Meyer, 11 A. B. R. 583, 127 Fed. 288 (C. C. A. Tex.): This was a case where a proposal was made and acted on at a meeting of all creditors but one that the bankrupt should execute a transfer in the form of a deed of trust or chattel mortgage, in the usual form with power of sale and condition of defeasance, of his stock of goods and all evidences of indebtedness to a trustee to apply the proceeds of sale as therein stated in which event the court held the creditors were estopped from setting up such conveyance as a ground for the debtor's adjudication as bankrupt.

67. In re Hirose, 12 A. B. R. 154 (D. C. Hawaii); In re Curtis, 2 A. B. R. 226, 94 Fed. 630 (C. C. A. Ills., distinguished in Moulton v. Coburn, 12 A. B. R. 553, 131 Fed. 201, and also in

Perhaps obiter, Hays v. Wagner, 18 A. B. R. 167, 150 Fed. 533 (C. C. A. Ohio): "The claim of the Hayden-Clinton National Bank is assailed, not on the ground of its insufficiency but because the bank itself had filed a claim as a creditor under the Ohio assignment of April 29, 1904, relied upon as the act of bankruptcy. The petition below was filed July 16, 1904, and there is nothing in the record, as it now stands, to show that any claim was ever filed with the Ohio assignee by this bank, but the statement of evidence which was stricken from the record by the nunc pro tunc order does contain the information that on August 5, 1904, the bank presented to the assignee a claim amounting to $10,000, being a note for that amount, of which Hays was one of the makers. But, if this information were properly before us, it would not lead us to eliminate this claim. We think that, after joining in the petition below, the bank had a right, if it deemed it advisable, to present the note referred to in the Ohio assignment. It is not the same note, and, besides, it was presented after, and not before, the bank joined in the petition below. Having joined in the petition, the bank could not in that way withdraw from the litigation."

Nor will the proving of claims under a receivership estop them.[68]

§ 223. Actual Connivance at Act Essential to Estoppel.—Actual connivance at the act of bankruptcy or laches in objecting to it would seem to be the test.[69]

Obiter, Leidigh Carriage Co. v. Stengel, 2 A. B. R. 383, 95 Fed. 637 (C. C. A. Ohio): "It seems that the decisions in which it has been held that a creditor was estopped from instituting bankruptcy proceedings against one who has made a general assignment have been cases in which the petitioning creditor had induced and abetted the committing of the act of bankruptcy which he afterward relied upon in his petition, or where, after he learned of the act he acquiesced in it and did not at once, when he might have done so, file a petition in bankruptcy and avoid the act."

Impliedly, Sinsheimer v. Simonson, 3 A. B. R. 824, 95 Fed. 954 (C. C. A. Ky.): "The assignee wrote and asked from them statements of account, which they gave. It was not filed with the assignee for the purpose of becoming a party to the assignment, but was a mere answer to the inquiry * * *.

"Further, we are satisfied, from an examination of the evidence, that the reason why the petition in bankruptcy was not filed until February, 1899, though prepared shortly after the deed of assignment, was the promise of a speedy settlement and composition of the claims by the defendants, which might make unnecessary all the proceedings in bankruptcy. As the delay was due to the

---

Durham Paper Co. v. Seaboard Knitting Mills, 10 A. B. R. 29, 121 Fed. 179); Leidigh Carriage Co. v. Stengel, 2 A. B. R. 383, 95 Fed. 643 (C. C. A. Ohio); In re Canner, 21 A. B. R. 199 (Ref. Mass.). Apparently, but perhaps not really, contra, Durham Paper Co. v. Seaboard Knitting Mills, 10 A. B. R., 29, 121 Fed. 179 (D. C. N. Car.). Apparently contra, except in cases where the debtor has induced the proof by misrepresentation, obiter, Canner v. Tapper Co., 21 A. B. R.

872, 168 Fed. 519 (C. C. A. Mass.), quoted at § 224.

68. In re Salmon & Salmon, 16 A. B. R. 136, 143 Fed. 395 (D. C. Mo.).

69. In re Curtis, 2 A. B. R. 226, 94 Fed. 630 (C. C. A., affirming 1 A. B. R. 440, distinguished in Moulton v. Coburn, 12 A. B. R. 556, 131 Fed. 201, C. C. A. Mass.). Compare, to similar effect, as to proving claims, In re Folb, 1 A. B. R. 22, 91 Fed. 107 (D. C. N. Car.).

solicitation of the defendants, it could not have misled them into a change of any position. * * *

"The sale by the petitioners of two small bills of goods to the assignee, and the receipt of the money for the same, was not an act which was calculated to mislead any one into the belief that petitioners affirmed the validity of the assignment, and did not intend to impeach it. Haydock *v.* Coope, 53 N. Y. 68, is closely analogous upon this point, and supports our view. Under these circumstances, we do not think that the petitioning creditors, by their delay, misled the defendants or others to believe that they were not intending to file a petition in bankruptcy within the required four months."

§ 224. And Actual Connivance at or Express Assent to General Assignment May Suffice to Effect Estoppel.

—But where the very act of bankruptcy urged is the making of a general assignment, creditors who have assented thereto are estopped and may not be petitioning creditors nor be reckoned in ascertaining the number of creditors.[70]

Moulton *v.* Coburn, 12 A. B. R. 553, 131 Fed. 201 (C. C. A. Mass., affirming In re Coburn, 11 A. B. R. 212): "It must be assumed that the assenting creditor had knowledge of his rights under the Bankruptcy Act, and voluntarily chose to assent to the terms of the assignment in preference to exercising his rights under the act. Here was a complete election between rights under the assignment and rights under the Bankruptcy Act. That one small creditor alone cannot file a petition in bankruptcy, that he may have doubts of his ability to induce other creditors to join him, and that his remedy by a petition in bankruptcy is dependent upon the co-operation of other creditors, does not justify him in assenting to an assignment, and afterwards repudiating it if he can find a sufficient number of creditors to join him in a petition. The election results from his choice of rights which are inconsistent with the enforcement of rights under the Bankruptcy Act. That he may not have an individual right to prefer a petition in bankruptcy does not render impossible an election between such rights as the act confers and rights under an assignment. He has chosen between two rights, one of which is derived from an instrument in which a clear intention appears that he should not enjoy both."

Likewise, where the act of bankruptcy complained of is a receivership.[71] Likewise, where the petitioning creditor procured a judgment creditor to issue the execution complained of.[72]

A stricter rule is laid down in Durham Paper Co. *v.* Seaboard Knitting Mills, 10 A. B. R. 29, 121 Fed. 179 (D. C. N. C.), as follows:

70. In re Miner, 4 A. B. R. 710, 104 Fed. 520 (D. C. Mass.); In re Perry & Whitney Co., 22 A. B. R. 772, 172 Fed. 745 (D. C. Mass.). But compare Hays *v.* Wagner, 18 A. B. R. 167, 150 Fed. 533 (C. C. A. Ohio), quoted on other points, ante, § 222. **Express Assent by Mere Agent of Creditor.**—Previous assent by agent to other assignments, acquiesced in by creditor, may bind the creditor as to a present assent, where not repudiated. Stroheim *v.* Perry & Whitney Co., 23 A. B. R. 695, 175 Fed. 52 (C. C. A. Mass.).

71. Woolford *v.* Steel Co., 15 A. B. R. 40, 138 Fed. 582 (D. C. Del.); Lowenstein *v.* McShane Co., 12 A. B. R. 60, 130 Fed. 1007 (D. C. Md.).

72. In re Marks Bros., 15 A. B. R. 459, 142 Fed. 279 (D. C. Pa.).

"A petitioner who participates in, receives benefit under or assents to a general assignment, valid under the laws of the State, is estopped from afterwards filing or becoming a party to a petition in bankruptcy to avoid such assignment."[73]

But, in any event, where the express assent has been induced by the misrepresentations of the bankrupt, it will not operate as an estoppel.

Canner v. Tapper Co., 21 A. B. R. 872, 168 Fed. 519 (C. C. A. Mass.): "That a creditor who has become a party to a general assignment may not ordinarily join as a petitioning creditor in bankruptcy proceedings is settled. * * * Where the petitioning creditor has become a party to the assignment, relying upon the false representations of his debtor, the general rule stated in Moulton v. Coburn and in In re Romanow does not apply, and the exception to the rule suggested in the former case has its proper application. The false representations thus relied on need not be sufficient to form the basis of an action of deceit. The debtor who offers a general assignment to his creditors is bound to a fair disclosure of his circumstances without concealment or falsehood."

Similarly, a creditor who merely has presented a claim against the debtor in insolvency proceedings in a state court, under a law which is subsequently declared to be superseded by the bankruptcy act, is not precluded from joining in a petition seeking the debtor's adjudication as a bankrupt.[74]

§ 225. Corporation Creditor Not Estopped by Officer Acting as Assignee.

—A corporation creditor of an alleged bankrupt, which was not preferred, under the bankrupt's prior general assignment for creditors, is not estopped to join in the petition for involuntary bankruptcy by the fact that one of its officers in his individual capacity, acted as the assignee.[75]

§ 226. No Election of Remedies because of Previous Attack upon Preferences in State Court.

—It is not to be construed as an election of the remedies of the State court to first attack there, preferences under a general assignment. Attacking preferences under a general assignment by action in the State court does not estop the same creditors from attacking the same preferences by instituting bankruptcy proceedings against the assignor. The bankruptcy proceedings and the assignment proceedings are not similar suits on the same cause of action.[76]

§ 227. Creditors Holding Provable Claims, and Only Such, Competent.

—Creditors holding provable claims, and only such, are competent.[77]

73. To same effect, see In re Romanow, 1 A. B. R. 461, 92 Fed. 510 (D. C. Mass.), criticised in In re Canner, 21 A. B. R. 199 (Ref. Mass.).

74. In re Weedman Stave Co., 29 A. B. R. 460, 199 Fed. 948 (D. C. Ark.).

75. In re Winston, 10 A. B. R. 171, 122 Fed. 187 (D. C. Tenn.).

76. Leidigh Carriage Co. v. Stengel, 2 A. B. R. 383, 95 Fed. 637 (C. C. A. Ohio).

77. Bankr. Act, § 59 (b); In re Yates, 8 A. B. R. 69, 114 Fed. 365 (D. C. Calif.). As to what are "provable" claims and what are not, see post, "Provable Debts," ch. XXI, § 625, et seq., where the various propositions are taken up and discussed in full and authority cited.

Even the wife of the debtor has been held competent to be a petitioning creditor, in States where she may be his creditor.[78]

§ 228. Must Be Provable at Time of Filing Petition.—The provability must be at the time of the filing of the petition.[79] The claim need not be provable at the time of the commission of the alleged act of bankruptcy, although perhaps the original obligation must have existed in some form at that time.[80]

§ 229. Claims Arising after Filing of Petition Insufficient.—And a creditor whose claim arose since the filing of the petition has not a provable debt.[81]

§. 230. Contingent Claims Insufficient.—Contingent claims are not provable and are not sufficient for petitioning creditors' claims.[82]

But the fact that the damages cannot be fully ascertained and are not fully suffered until after the filing of the petition will not make the claim contingent in the sense of the bankruptcy law.[83]

And the bankrupt's liability as endorser before maturity of the obligation is a provable debt and the holder may be a petitioning creditor.[84]

The claim of a surety on a redelivery bond given to effect release from an attachment, where the attachment itself would be dissolved by the adjudication of bankruptcy, has been held not sufficient for a petitioning creditor's claim.[85]

§ 231. Surety's Claims.—A surety on a defaulting contractor's bond completing work at an expense greater than the balance of the contract

---

Partner's Claim for Contribution for Paying Firm Debts.—In re Pangborn, 26 A. B. R. 40, 185 Fed. 673 (D. C. Mich.).

78. In re Novak, 4 A. B. R. 312, 101 Fed. 800 (D. C. Iowa); In re Bevins, 21 A. B. R. 344, 165 Fed. 434 (C. C. A. N. Y.).

79. In re Bevins, 21 A. B. R. 344, 165 Fed. 434 (C. C. A. N. Y.).

80. See ante, § 214.

81. Obiter, In re Coburn, 11 A. B. R. 212, 126 Fed. 218 (D. C. Mass., affirmed in Moulton v. Coburn, 12 A. B. R. 553); obiter, In re Adams, 12 A. B. R. 368, 130 Fed. 788 (D. C. Mass.). See post, ch. XXI, div. 5, § 668, et seq.

But the mere purchase, after the filing of the petition, of a claim already existing at the time of the filing of the petition, is not prohibited, although compare, apparently though not really contra, Stroheim v. Perry & Whitney Co., 23 A. B. R. 695, this decision being better analyzed as coming under the rule of § 203¼, ante. See further, § 203¼.

82. See post, "Contingent Claims," §§ 611, 640, et seq.

83. See post, § 685, et seq. Also see In re Stern, 8 A. B. R. 569, 116 Fed. 604 (C. C. A. N. Y., affirming Manhattan Ice Co., 7 A. B. R. 408, 114 Fed. 400); In re Grant Shoe Co., 12 A. B. R. 349, 130 Fed. 881 (C. C. A. N. Y.), affirmed sub nom. Grant Shoe Co. v. Laird Co., 21 A. B. R. 484, 212 U. S. 445.

84. In re Rothenberg, 15 A. B. R. 485, 140 Fed. 798 (D. C. N. Y.). See post, § 643, et seq.

85. In re Windt, 24 A. B. R. 536, 177 Fed. 584 (D. C. Conn.), quoted at § 231.

price is a creditor of the contractor to the extent of its loss, and may file a petition against him.[86]

It has been held, that a surety before payment of any part of the principal's obligation is not a creditor, and cannot file a petition against him; but this is not correct law, by the great weight of authority.[87]

However, a surety on a redelivery bond on attachment has been held not to be competent because the adjudication of bankruptcy would itself defeat the creditor's claim.

> In re Windt, 24 A. B. R. 536, 177 Fed. 584 (D. C. Conn.): "* * * * The adjudication upon the petition would dissolve the Childs attachment lien. With such dissolution would disappear also the obligation of the administrator's decedent to respond to the officer on the receipt, and the mortgage note given to secure him from loss thereby would fail for lack of consideration. I do not think one can force another into bankruptcy by the use of alleged debts, which, by operation of law will be extinguished and therefore not provable, the instant the adjudication exists."

Such would not be the rule, however, where under the doctrine of § 1524, et seq., post, the creditor is permitted to proceed with his suit to judgment; and it is manifestly improper to adjudicate in advance that such action will not be permitted. Indeed, such action is most appropriate, since the very object of requiring a bond is to guard against the insolvency of the principal.

§ 232. **Unliquidated Claims Sufficient if Provable.**—Creditors holding unliquidated claims may be petitioning creditors provided their claims belong to some one or more of the classes mentioned in the Bankruptcy Act, § 63 (b) as provable, to-wit:[88] Contracts, express or implied; judgments; costs; or taxes; or are capable of being presented as such, as in cases where a tort may be waived and suit brought on implied·contract. Thus, for instance, unliquidated claims arising ex contractu are provable and sufficient for petitioning creditors' claims. Damages for breach of warranty upon a sale of personal property are claims arising on contract, and are provable although the amount thereof is undetermined and although an independent claim purely in tort, for deceit, might also lie.[89]

Likewise, damages for breach of contract of sale covering a period of time where the time for performance has not expired, is a provable debt if

---

86. Boyce v. Guaranty Co., 7 A. B. R. 6, 111 Fed. 138 (C. C. A. Ohio).

87. Phillips v. Dreher Shoe Co., 7 A. B. R. 326, 112 Fed. 404 (D. C. Pa.). But compare Swarts v. Siegel, 8 A. B. R. 689, 117 Fed. 13 (G. C. A. Mo.). Also, see post, "Claims of Sureties," § 642, et seq.

88. See post, §§ 704, 709.

89. Grant Shoe Co. v. Laird, 21 A. B. R. 484, 212 U. S. 445 (affirming In re Grant Shoe Co., 12 A. B. R. 349, 130 Fed. 881), quoted on other points at § 639½. Contra, In re Morales, 5 A. B. R. 425, 105 Fed. 761 (D. C. Fla.): In this case the court held, that a claim for breach of warranty upon a contract for the sale of cigars, not liquidated, could not be used as a basis for adjudication in bankruptcy, because it sounded in tort.

new contracts have been made so that the extent of the damages is ascertainable.

In re Stern, 8 A. B. R. 569, 116 Fed. 604 (C. C. A. N. Y., affirming In re Manhattan Ice Co., 7 A. B. R. 408, 114 Fed. 400): "The question as to what constitutes a provable claim in involuntary petitions in bankruptcy has been much discussed. It has been held that one having an unliquidated claim for damages for a tort was not such a creditor as to be entitled to institute involuntary proceedings. In re Brinckmann (D. C.), 4 Am. B. R. 551, 103 Fed. 65. So it has been held, that such claims and claims for rent to accrue under a lease or for breach of warranty are not provable as debts until they have been liquidated. * * *
"But in the case at bar, the question is not necessarily whether the claims are liquidated or unliquidated, but whether they are 'provable.' The statute provides that the petitioning creditors shall have 'provable claims.' Counsel for defendant corporation contends that damages to accrue in the future are not provable because they are uncertain in amount, and because not having yet accrued they are not yet in existence. But in actions for personal injuries, or for breaches of warranty in the sale of seeds, or for failure to deliver goods which have no recognized market value, the injured party is entitled to recover compensation for such elements of damage as are shown to be reasonably certain or probable, or such as naturally result in such cases and may be supposed likely to occur in the given case. * * *
"The petitioners herein proved that the amount of ice used by them in their business was about 1,000 tons a year; that under the new contracts which they were obliged to make they were paying an excess over the contract price with the petitioners of from 60 cents to $1.50 a ton; that the price of ice fluctuated from year to year; that they had made unsuccessful attempts to get their ice cheaper. Upon this evidence the court was justified in finding, and it found, that this evidence tended to show that the petitioners could not replace the contract without suffering a direct loss much in excess of $500, and that they were creditors for the requisite amount, and were not obliged to await the expiration of the time for which the contracts were to continue."

It is true that the Bankruptcy Act, § 63 (b) seems to imply that an unliquidated claim, even though arising on contract, is not "provable" until liquidated; from which it would follow, that it could not be used as a basis for involuntary proceedings, since the creditors must hold "provable" claims; and this is the holding in one case.

In re Big Meadows Gas Co., 7 A. B. R. 697, 113 Fed. 974 (D. C. Pa.): "It will thus be seen the demand is proved after liquidation and that prior thereto an application is to be made to the court for direction as to the manner of such liquidation. After careful and deliberate consideration of the question here involved, we have reached the conclusion that the unliquidated demand herein made only becomes a provable debt after it has been judicially ascertained and liquidated in the statutory method set forth. Such construction is in accord with other provisions of the act. The provisions requiring petitioning creditors should have claims aggregating five hundred dollars in excess of all securities evidences that Congress felt there should be definite, ascertained claims, and that too in excess of all securities, as a foundation on which to base a petition to adjudicate one a bankrupt. Where a claim against another has not been judicially ascertained and where its validity and certainty are evidenced by no paper, acknowledgment or other admission of the debtor, it would offend our sense of right to allow such self asserted claim to constitute sufficient ground for harrassing another with a petition in bankruptcy. It will readily be seen that an averred but unfounded claim might be made an effective weapon to enforce an unjust demand or even to bankrupt a struggling but solvent debtor."

But the wording of the Bankruptcy Act, § 63 (b) to the effect that unliquidated claims may be unliquidated and "thereafter proved" is not conclusive that such claims are not previously "provable;" and certainly, an unliquidated claim, if capable of being presented as a claim ex contractu, is discharged by the bankrupt's discharge although never, in fact, so presented, all which implies that the claim is all the time "provable," since only "provable" debts are discharged.

But unliquidated claims for torts which cannot be presented in form ex contractu as on implied contract, are not provable and are not sufficient claims for petitioning creditors; as for instance, damages for personal injury.[90]

§ 233. Preferred Creditors Competent.

§ 233. **Preferred Creditors Competent.**—Creditors who have received preferences within four months of the filing of the petition nevertheless have provable claims, and may join as petitioning creditors.[91]

Stevens v. Nave-McCord Co., 17 A. B. R. 610, 150 Fed. 71 (C. C. A. Colo.): "A creditor who holds a voidable preference has a provable claim in the sense that he may make and file the formal proof thereof specified by the bankruptcy law; but he may not procure an allowance of his claim, he may not vote at a creditors' meeting, and he may not obtain any advantage from his claim in the bankruptcy proceeding before he surrenders his preference."

"Such a preferred creditor may present or may join in a petition for an ad-

90. In re Yates, 8 A. B. R. 69, 114 Fed. 365 (D. C. Calif.); Beers v. Hanlin, 3 A. B. R. 745, 99 Fed. 695 (D. C. Ore.); In re Brinckmann, 4 A. B. R. 551, 103 Fed. 65 (D. C. Ind.). Both the cases, Beers v. Hanlin and In re Brinckmann, go too far, for the claims in those two cases were reduced to judgment at the time of the filing of the petition, although not at the time of the commission of the act of bankruptcy charged.

91. In re Wise, 2 N. B. N. & R. 151 (Ref. N. Y.); In re Thompson, 2 N. B. N. R. 1016 (Ref. Minn.); In re Herzikopf, 9 A. B. R. 90, 118 Fed. 101 (D. C. Calif.); In re Miller, 5 A. B. R. 140, 104 Fed. 764 (D. C. N. Y.), which was a case of "innocent" preference, however. In re Hornstein, 10 A. B. R. 308, 122 Fed. 273, 277 (D. C. N. Y.); In re Douglass Coal & Coke Co., 12 A. B. R. 551, 131 Fed. 769,

(Master's Report D. C. Tenn.). Compare, to same effect, In re Norcross, 1 A. B. R. 644 (D. C. Mo.); In re Cain, 2 A. B. R. 378 (D. C. Ill.). Compare Keppel v. Tiffin Sav. Bank, 13 A. B. R. 552, 197 U. S. 356. In re Fishblate Clothing Co., 11 A. B. R. 204, 125 Fed. 926 (D. C. N. Car.); In re Gillette & Prentice, 5 A. B. R. 119, 104 Fed. 769 (D. C. N. Y.), which was a case of fraudulent preference, however. Contra, In re Wing Yick Co., 13 A. B. R. 757 (D. C. Hawaii). Contra, In re Rogers Milling Co., 4 A. B. R. 540, 102 Fed. 687 (D. C. Ark.).

Under the law of 1867, compare, In re Bloss, Fed. Cas. 1,562; In re Calif. Pac. Ry. Co., Fed. Cas. 2,315; In re Stansell, Fed. Cas. 13,293; Rankin v. Railway Co., Fed. Cas. 11,567. Compare resume in Keppel v. Tiffin Sav. Bank, 13 A. B. R. 552, 197 U. S. 356.

judication of bankruptcy. But he may not be counted for the petition unless he surrenders his preference before the adjudication."

The fact that they will not be allowed to participate in the dividends unless the preferences are surrendered, is like any other objection to the substance of the claim. The claim is nevertheless provable; but it simply is not allowable unless the preference is surrendered, and it stands as any other unallowable though provable claim of a petitioning creditor would stand.

However, since the passage of the Amendment of 1903 making recoverable only such preferences as were received under circumstances indicating the creditor's collusion, the rule is that creditors who have received such preferences will not be counted for the petition without surrender, or at least offer of surrender, of the preference, before adjudication.[92]

The petition should show an offer to surrender; or should be amended to show it.[93]

If the creditor, however, offer in the petition to surrender his preference, then at any rate any disqualification is removed.[94]

Obiter, In re Vastbinder, 11 A. B. R. 118, 126 Fed. 417 (D. C. Pa.): "But, however this may be, it is conceded by all the authorities that a preferred creditor may surrender his preference and thus qualify, and since, as pointed out by Brandenburg, there is no one, prior to the selection of a trustee, to whom he can surrender, it is sufficient if he offers to do so in the petition or course of the proceedings; and that, in effect, is what has been done here."

But if the act of bankruptcy charged is precisely the giving of the preference to such creditor, such creditor may not, without surrender (or offer of surrender) of his preference, file the involuntary petition.[95]

§ 234. Attaching Creditors and Other Creditors Obtaining Liens by Legal Proceedings.—An attaching creditor whose lien was acquired within the four months may be a petitioning creditor, for he has a provable claim—merely his lien is null and void.[96]

92. Stevens v. Nave-McCord Co., 17 A. B. R. 610, 150 Fed. 71 (C. C. A. Colo.). One court has several times given such preferred creditors the option either of having the petition dismissed or of depositing the preference with the clerk of the court—a proceeding without express sanction in the statute, at any rate. In re Gillette, 5 A. B. R. 119, 104 Fed. 769 (D. C. N. Y.); In re Miller, 5 A. B. R. 140, 104 Fed. 764 (D. C. N. Y.).

93. In re Miller, 5 A. B. R. 140, 104 Fed. 764 (D. C. N. Y.). (1867) Compare, In re Rodo, 20 Fed. Cas. 153.

94. In re Wing Yick Co., 13 A. B. R.

757 (D. C. Hawaii); Stevens v. Nave-McCord Co., 17 A. B. R. 610, 150 Fed. 71 (C. C. A. Colo.). Obiter, In re Girard Glazed Kid Co., 12 A. B. R. 295, 129 Fed. 841 (D. C. Penn.).

95. Obiter, Leighton v. Kennedy, 12 A. B. R. 229, 129 Fed. 731 (C. C. A. Mass.).

96. See post, § 777; also see In re Hornstein, 10 A. B. R. 308 (D. C. N. Y.); In re Schenkein & Coney, 7 A. B. R. 162, 113 Fed. 421 (Ref. N. Y.); impliedly, In re Richard, 2 A. B. R. 506, 94 Fed. 633 (D. C. N. C.); contra, In re Burlington Malting Co., 6 A. B. R. 369, 109 Fed. 777 (D. C. Wis.); com-

In re Smith, 23 A. B. R. 864, 176 Fed. 426 (D. C. N. Y.): "I am not disposed to hold that judgment creditors who have obtained judgments within four months, on discovering that their debtors in fraud of the Bankruptcy Act have disposed of their property, may not abandon remedies by execution and supplementary proceedings in aid thereof and themselves institute bankruptcy proceedings, inasmuch as their liens, if any, fall the moment an adjudication in bankruptcy is pronounced. In view of the fact that all liens created within four months of the filing of the petition fall of their own weight under the provisions of the section quoted, reason and justice dictate that creditors having such liens, on discovering the true condition of the alleged bankrupt, and that the pursuit of remedies under their liens and to enforce same would be unavailing, may institute proceedings in bankruptcy and enforce the provisions of the Bankruptcy Act. If they have reduced their claims to judgment duly docketed, and have thereby created a lien on the real estate of their creditor, are they compelled to proceed to issue execution, levy and advertise a sale, with full knowledge that other creditors may institute bankruptcy proceedings, and make their efforts and expense fruitless? I think not. Having such a lien, they may file a petition in bankruptcy, and proceed under the law. They know their lien as such is made void by the very act they invoke in case adjudication is made. It is not an experiment with the law, or an attempt to evade it, or to enforce their lien and the Bankruptcy Act at one and the same time. From the necessities of the case, in view of the Bankruptcy Act, it is the honest method to pursue."

Nevertheless, before adjudication he should be required formally to surrender his attachment lien.[97]   And the filing of the petition itself does not amount to such a release.[98]

§ 235. Validity of Petitioning Creditor's Claim May Be Disputed.
—Whether a petitioning creditor's debt is a valid debt is a proper issue.[99]

But compare Gage v. Bell, 10 A. B. R. 701, 124 Fed. 371 (D. C. Tenn.): "The court is not now prepared to say that such proceedings are not admissible, but it very well may be said that a petitioning creditor, having a debt provable on the face of it, ought not to be compelled by the defendant debtor to enter into

pare, obiter, First Nat'l Bank v. Ice Co., 14 A. B. R. 448, 136 Fed. 466 (D. C. Pa.). Instance, In re Putnam, 27 A. B. R. 923, 193 Fed. 464 (D. C. Cal.).
Surety for Redelivery on Attachment, Whether Competent.—Though a surety in general is to be considered a creditor from the moment of signing, and therefore competent to be a petitioning creditor, and though an attaching creditor likewise is competent as such, yet a surety on the bankrupt's bond for redelivery on attachment has been held not to be competent, because the adjudication itself will defeat the claim, In re Windt, 24 A. B. R. 536, 177 Fed. 584 (D. C. Conn.). But such holding is to be criticised for failing to take into account the possibility that the court will permit the creditor to proceed to judgment in order to fix the liability of the surety, under the doctrine of § 1524, post.

97. In re Hornstein, 10 A. B. R. 308 (D. C. N. Y.); impliedly, In re Richard, 2 A. B. R. 506, 94 Fed. 633 (D. C. N. C.); contra, In re Schenkein & Coney, 7 A. B. R. 162, 113 Fed. 421 (Ref. N. Y.).

98. In re Burlington Malting Co., 6 A. B. R. 369, 109 Fed. 777 (D. C. Wis.).

99. In re Ferguson, 11 A. B. R. 371 (D. C. Pa.).
Assigned Taxes Sufficient.—A claim for taxes acquired by assignment is a sufficient claim for involuntary proceedings. Obiter, In re Cleanfast Ho-

litigation about it, legal and equitable, and antecedently to establish it by over-throwing all the defenses, real or fabricated, that the debtor may choose to set up by pleadings specially framed to present such issues. It is in effect tantamount to holding that a creditor with a disputed debt cannot be a petitioning creditor in bankruptcy; or, at least, not until he has cleared away all dispute and controversy, and established his debt by a judgment at law; for it would be, in effect, a requirement to do this, even if he must get such a judgment or its equivalent in the bankruptcy proceedings. And the result is that before we can inquire whether a debtor is insolvent, and has committed an act of bankruptcy, we must engage in a preliminary work of litigation in law and equity, and, possibly, even in admiralty as well, with each petitioning creditor, in order that we may know beforehand whether the debtor has any defense he may possibly make to the creditor's claim of debt. This is converting the language of the statute, 'three or more creditors having provable claims,' into a requirement that there shall be 'three or more creditors having proved and established debts,' before they may file the petition. Section 59b. If a debt is wholly wanting in existence, if it has been paid, for example, or if it has been fabricated for the purpose, of course the defendant should be allowed to show that fact in some form. But if it be a reasonably fair and honest claim of debt, which is provable in the sense that it is a claim that the court of bankruptcy after adjudication will hear and establish, if proved, the creditor should not be bound before the adjudication to so prove and establish it, but should be allowed to rely upon its provable quality, prima facie, to support an involuntary petition in bankruptcy."

§ 236. Withdrawal of Petitioning Creditors.—A creditor may withdraw from an involuntary petition on leave of court.

In re Coburn, 11 A. B. R. 212, 126 Fed. 218 (D. C. Mass., affirmed sub nom.

siery Co., 4 A. B. R. 702 (Ref. N. Y.). But compare, query, In re Bedding-field, 2 A. B. R. 355, 96 Fed. 190 (D. C. Ga.).

Tax Collector under Statute Giving Him Right to Sue in Own Name after Three Months.—In re Corwin Mfg. Co., 26 A. B. R. 269, 185 Fed. 976 (D. C. Mass.).

Corporation Which by Law Is Unable to Contract Indebtedness.—A corporation which, under state law, can not incur an indebtedness, may not be adjudged bankrupt even though it is shown that it would be insolvent. In re Wyoming Valley Assn., 28 A. B. R. 462, 198 Fed. 436 (D. C. Pa.).

Other Instances as to Provability of Claims Sought to Be Used in Involuntary Petitions.—Account originating with partnership, later continued with its successor, a corporation; payments thereon credited to partnership claim; balance due to corporation. Hoffschlaeger Co. v. Young Nap, 12 A. B. R. 517 (D. C. Hawaii).

Subcontractor's claim against head contractor, conditioned by contract on the owner's paying, is not sufficient.

In re Ellis, 16 A. B. R. 225, 143 Fed. 103 (C. C. A. Ohio).

Trust agreement not bill of sale. In re Halsey Elec. Generator Co., 20 A. B. R. 738, 163 Fed. 118 (D. C. N. J.).

Partner's claim for share of profits is not provable claim against the partnership. Obiter, In re Schenkein & Coney, 7 A. B. R. 162, 113 Fed. 421 (Ref. N. Y.).

A corporation that is a de facto partner can not prove its claim for its contributory share as a debt simply because it was ultra vires to be a partner. Wallerstein v. Ervin, 7 A. B. R. 256, 112 Fed. 124 (C. C. A. Penn.).

Unpaid stock subscription held, valid. Hays v. Wagner, 18 A. B. R. 163, 150 Fed. 533 (C. C. A. Ohio).

A debt owing but not yet due is nevertheless provable and permitted to share in dividends, so a creditor holding it as a claim is competent to be one of the petitioning creditors. (1867) Linn v. Smith, 4 N. B. Reg. 12.

Instance held valid, Cleage v. Laidley, 17 A. B. R. 598, 149 Fed. 346 (C. C. A. Mo.), charge of illegality; "gambling in futures" debt.

Moulton v. Coburn, 12 A. B. R. 553, C. C. A.): "A creditor misled may be permitted to withdraw." Citing In re Heffron, Fed. Cas. No. 6,321, and In re Sargent, Fed. Cas. No. 12,361.

Leave of court to petitioning creditors to withdraw an involuntary petition will be refused where the creditor's claim was settled by the bankrupt in order to induce withdrawal.[2]

Obiter, In re Stovall Grocery Co., 20 A. B. R. 537, 161 Fed. 882 (D. C. Ga.): "Two creditors have withdrawn their claims, leaving the total amount of indebtedness contained in the petition less than $500. I doubt if this can be done, especially in view of what seems to be the fact that these two claims that were withdrawn were purchased by a son of the members of the bankrupt firm. While the amount paid for the claims is not shown, such conduct, if tolerated, allows an alleged bankrupt, after bankruptcy proceedings have been instituted, to buy up the claims of creditors filing a petition against him, and thereby give the creditors whose claims are so purchased a preference; doing in this way the very thing which it is the purpose of the Bankruptcy Act to prevent."

Or, perhaps, where any of the other petitioning creditors objects.[3]

§ 237. Disqualification of Part of Petitioning Creditors.—Where one of the three original petitioning creditors turns out to be disqualified, yet the case will not be dismissed if there remain any intervening creditors who are qualified.[4] But the court need not hold the case where no creditors have yet intervened, and need not require notice to be given to other creditors, so they may come in and fill the vacancies in the complement.[5]

In re Tribelhorn, 14 A. B. R. 491, 137 Fed. 3 (C. C. A. N. Y.): "After a hearing and dismissal of an involuntary petition (for lack of sufficient number of petitioning creditors) it is too late for any new creditor to intervene as a matter of right and a denial of the application is proper."

§ 238. Change of Ownership of Petitioning Creditor's Claim— New Owner Substituted.—Where a transfer of ownership occurs in a petitioning creditor's claim, pending the suit, the transferee may be sub-

2. In re Beddingfield, 2 A. B. R. 355, 96 Fed. 190 (D. C. Ga.). And a petitioning creditor can not be allowed subsequently to disqualify himself by conniving at a perpetuation of the assignment which is charged as the act of bankruptcy. Hays v. Wagner, 18 A. B. R. 167, 150 Fed. 533 (C. C. A. Ohio).

3. In re Granite Quarries Co., 16 A. B. R. 823 (D. C. Mass.), in which case all wished to withdraw except one and that one held a disputed claim then being litigated; yet the court held the case to await the outcome of the litigation. In re Cronin, 3 A. B. R. 552, 98 Fed. 584 (D. C. Mass.); [1867] In re Heffron, 10 N. B. Reg. 213, Fed. Cas. 6,231; (1867) In re Sargent, 13 N. B. Reg. 144, Fed. Cas. 12,361. (1867) Compare, In re Indianapolls, etc., 5 Biss. 287, Fed. Cas. 7,023.

4. In re Vastbinder, 11 A. B. R. 118, 126 Fed. 417 (D. C. Pa.); In re Crenshaw, 19 A. B. R. 502, 156 Fed. 638 (D. C. Ala.), quoted at § 213.

5. In re Gillette, 5 A. B. R. 119, 104 Fed. 769 (D. C. N. Y.). To same effect, compare, In re Neustadter v. Dry Goods Co., 3 A. B. R. 98, 96 Fed. 830 (D. C. Wash.).

stituted in the place of the original creditor; thus, the trustee in bankruptcy of a petitioning creditor may be substituted.[6]

DIVISION 2.

ALLEGATIONS AND FORM OF PETITION.

§ 239. All Essential Facts of Capacity, Jurisdiction and Cause to Be Pleaded, According to Usual Rules.—All the essential facts giving capacity to the parties and jurisdiction to the court and forming the elements of the cause of action must be alleged, and their allegation must conform to the usual rules of pleading.[7]

In re Plotke, 5 A. B. R. 175 (C. C. A. Ills.): "The essential facts must appear affirmatively and distinctly, and it is not sufficient that jurisdiction may be inferred argumentatively. Wolfe v. Ins. Co., 148 U. S. 389; Parker v. Ormsby, 141 U. S. 81, 83."

Thus, the petition should give the details of alleged preferences, the amounts thereof, the names of those preferred; the amounts of alleged fraudulent transfers, the dates thereof, the persons to whom made, the values of the property transferred, and a sufficient description thereof; and like details, if available, should be given as to property alleged to be concealed.[8]

§ 240. Nature and Amount of Petitioners' Claims and Number Joining, to Be Shown.—The petition must show the nature of the petitioning creditors' claims.

In re White, 14 A. B. R. 241, 135 Fed. 199 (D. C. Pa.): "An involuntary petition which fails to state the nature of the claims of the petitioning creditors is defective, but amendable."

But the statement of the nature of the petitioners' claims need not be made with the particularity requisite in the proof of debt under § 57, Bankr. Act.[9]

In re Brett, 12 A. B. R. 496, 130 Fed. 981 (D. C. N. J.): "There is nothing in the Bankruptcy Act, or in the General Orders or forms prescribed by the

---

6. Hays v. Wagner, 18 A. B. R. 163, 150 Fed. 533 (C. C. A. Ohio).

7. Clark v. Henne, 11 A. B. R. 593, 127 Fed. 288 (C. C. A. Tex.); In re Pressed Steel Goods Co., 27 A. B. R. 44, 193 Fed. 811 (D. C. Mich.).

Caption.—The caption of a petition in bankruptcy is no part of the petition and is not jurisdictional.

In re Garman, 15 A. B. R. 587 (D. C. Hawaii): "If the body of the petition is sufficient and the petition is properly served the court has juris-

diction even though the caption be defective."

8. In re Sig. H. Rosenblatt & Co., 28 A. B. R. 401, 193 Fed. 638 (C. C. A. N. Y.).

9. Instance, In re Brett, 12 A. B. R. 492, 130 Fed. 981 (D. C. N. J.): "Owner and holder of promissory note for $100 dated January 15, 1904, and made by the alleged bankrupt, and payable to the creditor's order three months after date," is a sufficient al-

Supreme Court under the authority of the Act, requiring greater particularity. The provision of § 57 of the Act, which requires the consideration of the claim to be set forth and sworn to relates to the proof of the claim, and not to the averments of the petition."

They must be shown to be provable claims. It must also appear that the petitioning creditors' claims aggregate at least $500;[10] and that there are three creditors joining in the petition, unless the total number of creditors owed by the bankrupt is less than twelve.[11]

§ 241. Indebtedness, Residence, Domicile, etc., to Be Shown.—
It must be alleged that the debtor owes $1,000 or more.[12]

It must be alleged that the debtor has resided, had his domicile or principal place of business within the district for the greater portion of the six months next preceding the filing of the petition, or that he resides outside the United States, etc., and has property within the district, etc.[13] Where more than one of the facts of territorial jurisdiction are alleged, the allegation of the residence, domicile and principal place of business must not be made disjunctively.[14]

§ 242. Corporation to Be Brought within Class Subject to Bankruptcy.—
If the defendant is a corporation, it must be brought by allegation within one or the other of the classes of corporations subject to bankruptcy.[15]

Amendment of 1910.—Since the Amendment of 1910 it must be shown that such corporation is either a "moneyed," "business," or "commercial" corporation, and that it is not a "municipal, railroad, insurance or banking corporation."[15a]

§ 243. Bankrupt to Be Shown Not within Excepted Classes.—
The

legation without statement of consideration.

10. In re Hughes, 25 A. B. R. 556, 183 Fed. 872 (D. C. N. Y.); The exact amounts need not be determined. See post, citations under the subject of amendments to supply defective allegations, § 261, et seq. See also, post, § 268, et seq.

11. See post, citations under the subject of amendments to supply defective allegations in this particular, § 268.

12. See ante, § 45½.

13. In re Plotke, 5 A. B. R. 175, 104 Fed. 964 (C. C. A. Ills.). See ante, § 31, et seq. In re Blair, 3 A. B. R. 588, 99 Fed. 76 (D. C. N. Y.).

14. In re Laskaris, 1 A. B. R. 480 (Ref. N. Y.). Obiter, In re Clisdell, 2 A. B. R. 424 (D. C. N. Y.).

15. In re Imperial Film Exchange, 28 A. B. R. 815, 198 Fed. 80 (C. C. A. N. Y.). Obiter, Woolford v. Steel Co., 15 A. B. R. 33, 138 Fed. 582 (D. C. Del.), wherein it is held that filing demurrer with answer and going to trial waives insufficiency of allegations. For instance of an apparently wrong decision, see In re Stern, 8 A. B. R. 569, 116 Fed. 604 (C. C. A. N. Y.). But this case may perhaps be explained by the fact that the demurrer was put in with the answer, and that the parties went to trial without objection, thus suffering the actual facts pertaining to the business of the corporation to get before the court.

15a. Bankr. Act, § 4b, as amended in 1910: "* * * and any moneyed, business, or commercial corporation, except a municipal, railroad, insurance or banking corporation."

exceptions as to wage earners, farmers, etc., should be negatived in the petition where it is sought to put a natural person into involuntary bankruptcy.[16]

In re Mero, 12 A. B. R. 121, 128 Fed. 630 (D. C. Conn.): "There was nothing in the petition to bring the alleged bankrupt within the terms of the statute. It did not allege what the defendant's business was and there was no allegation to show that he did not come within the excepted classes, which, under the law, are too important to be wholly ignored. Farmers and wage earners constitute a large majority of the people. These are excepted from that portion of the clause relating to involuntary bankruptcy, and the petition should either have shown what the business of the defendant was, or that he did not come within the excepted classes." In this case, however, it is to be noted that the direct issue of fact was made by answer, after demurrer overruled. This case is further quoted post, § 245.

In re Bellah, 8 A. B. R. 310, 116 Fed. 69 (D. C. Del.): "In accordance with the elementary rule that in proceeding on a statute, the pleader must negative an exception in the enacting clause, a petition in involuntary bankruptcy against an individual is defective if it omits to aver that the defendant was not a wage earner nor a person engaged chiefly in farming or the tillage of the soil."

In re Brett, 12 A. B. R. 492, 130 Fed. 981 (D. C. N. J.): "In pleading upon statutes, where there is an exception in the enacting clause, the plaintiff should negative the exception. In accordance with this rule, the petition must contain allegations which fairly negative the exception of the Bankruptcy Act concerning wage earners and farmers." This case is further quoted post, § 245.

Contra, quære, obiter, Bank v. Craig, 6 A. B. R. 383, 110 Fed. 137 (D. C. Ky.): "It might, I suppose, be quite fairly inferred that the judges of that court, in framing the rules and forms, considered the question whether the allegation that the debtor was not a wage earner and was not chiefly engaged in farming or the tillage of the soil was essential, and concluded that it was not. Otherwise doubtless the form prescribed would have included it. They probably thought that the exceptions named in § 4, could not be specially and affirmatively pleaded if the facts justified it, and that they need not be anticipated or negatived in the petition. Settling Form 3 is strong evidence of this."

It would seem on principle that the same rule should prevail as to corporations; that is to say, it should be expressly alleged that the corporation is not a municipal, banking, railroad nor insurance corporation; yet it might very properly be held that all the corporations excepted from the operation of bankruptcy give undoubted evidence of their character by their names.

---

16. Ledbetter v. U. S., 170 U. S. 606; Conway v. German, 21 A. B. R. 577, 166 Fed. 67 (C. C. A. Md.); In re Callison, 12 A. B. R. 344, 130 Fed. 987 (D. C. Fla., affirmed sub nom., Brake v. Callison, 11 A. B. R. 797, 129 Fed. 196). Obiter, Edelstein v. U. S., 17 A. B. R. 649, 149 Fed. 636 (C. C. A. Minn.). Obiter and impliedly, Beach v. Macon Grocery Co., 9 A. B. R. 762, 120 Fed. 736 (C. C. A. Ga.); In re Levingston, 13 A. B. R. 357 (D. C. Hawaii); In re White, 14 A. B. R. 241, 135 Fed. 199 (D. C. Penna.). Impliedly, Armstrong v. Fernandez, 19 A. B. R. 746, 208 U. S. 324; Impliedly, Rise Admr. v. Bordner, 15 A. B. R. 297, 140 Fed. 566 (D. C. Pa.). Impliedly, In re Crenshaw, 19 A. B. R. 502, 156 Fed. 638 (D. C. Ala.).

§ 244. Exceptions Not Mere Matter of Defense.—The exceptions are not merely matters of defense to be pleaded by the debtor and not to be considered by the court unless pleaded. This is so, for there is no presumption that a natural person is or is not a wage earner or a person engaged chiefly in the tillage of the soil, or in farming. And it is not a mere personal privilege for the respondent to raise himself or to waive at pleasure. It is a jurisdictional matter.[17]

And the petition is demurrable for want of the allegation.[18]

And the same rule would seem to be applicable to corporations, as to not being "municipal," "railroad," "insurance" nor "banking" corporations.

§ 245. Negativing of Exceptions Not Necessarily by Direct Denial but Statement of Actual Occupation Sufficient.—The negativing need not be by direct denial but may be simply by way of affirmative allegation as to the character of the alleged bankrupt's chief occupation, showing inconsistency with his being chiefly a farmer or tiller of the soil, etc.[19]

In re Mero, 12 A. B. R. 121, 128 Fed. 630 (D. C. Conn.): "It is certainly necessary either to set forth the kind of business the defendant was engaged in so that one may be able to see that it is not of the excluded classes or to state specifically that it was not of the excluded classes." Quoted further ante, § 243.

In re Brett, 12 A. B. R. 492, 130 Fed. 981 (D. C. N. J.): "The petition must contain allegations which fairly negative the exception of the Bankruptcy Act concerning wage earners and farmers. The form in which the exception should be negatived· is immaterial. It may be done in the express language of negation or in affirmative language which clearly shows that the alleged bankrupt

17. See ante, § 30; also see In re Taylor, 4 A. B. R. 515, 102 Fed. 728 (C. C. A. Ill.). In re Duke & Son, 28 A. B. R. 195, 199 Fed. 199 (D. C. Ga.). Compare also, Conway v. German, 21 A. B. R. 577, 166 Fed. 67 (C. C. A. Md.), quoted at §§ 268, 271.

18. Obiter, Edelstein v. U. S., 17 A. B. R. 649, 149 Fed. 636 (C. C. A. Minn.). Also, see remaining cases cited, § 243.

19. In re Levingston, 13 A. B. R. 357 (D. C. Hawaii); In re Lackow, 15 A. B. R. 826 (Special Master, Pa.). Obiter, inferentially, In re Pilger, 9 A. B. R. 245, 118 Fed. 206 (D. C. Wis.). Instance, In re Charles L. Leland, 25 A. B. R. 209, 185 Fed. 830 (D. C. Mich.).

Failure of respondent to deny the negative allegation of the petition is an admission that the respondent does not come within any of the excepted classes. Hoffschlaeger Co. v. Young Nap, 12 A. B. R. 517 (D. C. Hawaii).

Answer affirming that the respondent comes within the excepted classes, the petition failing to negative the ex- ception, is conclusive where the case is set down for hearing on petition and answer and the petition should be dismissed. Obiter, Rise Amr. v. Bordner, 15 A. B. R. 297, 140 Fed. 566 (D. C. Pa.).

After the petitioners have introduced testimony tending to prove the negative of the exceptions, it then devolves upon the respondent to prove he comes within the exceptions, he being, in the nature of things, in full possession of evidence to disprove such averments if they are not true. Hoffschlaeger Co. v. Young Nap, 12 A. B. R. 517 (D. C. Hawaii).

Answering over waives a demurrer for failure to negative the exceptions, even though the answer expressly asserts an intention not to waive it. Bank v. Craig Bros., 6 A. B. R. 381, 110 Fed. 137 (D. C. Ky.).

And the defect may not be taken advantage of collaterally. Thus, not on discharge. Edelstein v. U. S., 17 A. B. R. 649, 149 Fed. 636 (C. C. A. Minn.).

is neither wage earner, nor a person chiefly engaged in farming or the tillage of the soil. * * * Although the exception of the statute is not negatived in the petition now under consideration in express words of negation, which is the form usually employed in common-law pleading, the averments concerning the debtor's residence and domicile, his principal place of business, and his owning and conducting a store and saloon, all in the city of Paterson, exclude the idea of his being a 'wage earner' or 'a person engaged chiefly in farming,' and do sufficiently negative the exception."

In re Taylor, 4 A. B. R. 515, 102 Fed. 728 (C. C. A. Ills.): "The petition should either have shown what the business of the defendant was or that he did not come within the excepted classes."

In re White, 14 A. B. R. 241, 135 Fed. 199 (D. C. Pa.): "Must show either by a negative averment that the alleged bankrupt is not one of the excepted classes, or there must be a specific statement as to his principal business."

In re Crenshaw, 19 A. B. R. 502, 156 Fed. 638 (D. C. Ala.): "A further contention is that the petition does not allege that the respondent was not a wage earner or farmer, and therefore it is insufficient. The original petition alleges that the respondent was engaged in trade under the firm name and style of Crenshaw & Co., which clearly implies that he was engaged in some mercantile pursuit, if it does not affirmatively show that he was not a wage earner or farmer."

This permission does not violate the rule against argumentative pleading, for it affirmatively shows the debtor's class.[20]

But the defect of failure to negative the exceptions is amendable.[21]

Beach v. Macon Grocery Co., 9 A. B. R. 762, 120 Fed. 736 (C. C. A. Ga.): "Where the petition to adjudicate a natural person an involuntary bankrupt is in the form prescribed in the General orders of the Supreme Court, and contains averments consistent with the alleged bankrupt being a merchant and not chiefly engaged in the tillage of the soil, if not sufficient for want of a specific charge that the alleged bankrupt is not a wage earner nor a person engaged chiefly in farming or the tillage of the soil, the defect may be cured by amendment."

However, it is at least preferable to deny in the words of the statute.[22]

It would seem that, as a general thing, so far as the rule requiring the negativing of exceptions is applicable to corporations, the name of the bankrupt corporation would itself be sufficiently indicative of its not being within the excepted classes; that is to say, as to its not being a municipal, railroad, banking nor insurance corporation.

§ 246. Act to Be Shown to Be within Four Months.—The act of bankruptcy must be alleged to have occurred within the preceding four months.[23]

---

20. But compare, analogously, In re Plotke, 5 A. B. R. 175, 104 Fed. 964 (C. C. A. Ills.): "The essential fact must appear affirmatively and distinctly: it is not sufficient that jurisdiction may be inferred argumentatively."

21. That the failure to negative the exceptions is remediable by amendment, see post, "Amendments," § 261, et seq.

22. Hoffschlaeger Co. v. Young Nap, 12 A. B. R. 514 (D. C. Hawaii).

23. Davis v. Stevens, 4 A. B. R. 763,

§ 247. Insolvency of Individual Partners, Whether to Be Alleged in Partnership Cases.—In partnership cases, where insolvency is an essential element of the act of bankruptcy, it has been held that the petition must show not only that the partnership assets are insufficient to pay firm debts, but that the excess of the individual assets of its members over their respective individual indebtedness would not add sufficient assets to make up for the deficiency.[24] But the contrary has also been held;[25] and it would seem, on principle, that the allegation that the debtor proceeded against, namely, the partnership, is insolvent should be all that would be requisite, and that the further question of the insolvency of the individual members would relate merely to the proof as to whether or not the debtor, the partnership, was in fact insolvent.

§ 248. Creditors to Be Shown to Have Existed at Time of Commission of Act.—It must affirmatively appear that another creditor or other creditors existed at the time of the act complained of than the creditors to whom the transfer was made. A subsequent creditor may complain only where a design existed to defraud future creditors.[26]

§ 249. Distinct Acts Alleged in Same Petition.—Distinct acts of bankruptcy may be alleged in the same petition, but they must all be shown to have occurred within the preceding four months.[27]

§ 250. Multifariousness.—The petition must not be multifarious; that is to say, it must not include several matters perfectly distinct and independent.

It is a temptation to the practitioner who is accustomed to joining any number of defendants in a fraudulent conveyance suit or a creditor's bill, asking for an injunction against this one and relief against that one and so forth, to join some fraudulent transferee as a party defendant to the petition in bankruptcy and to pray for an injunction to issue upon him forbidding him to dispose of the property in controversy; but such joinder is improper in bankruptcy. The reason of it becomes evident on reflection. A bankruptcy petition is a proceeding in rem to determine the status of a person;

104 Fed. 235 (D. C. S. Dak.); under first act of bankruptcy. Bradley Timber Co. *v.* White, 10 A. B. R. 329, 121 Fed. 779 (C. C. A. Ala., affirming 9 A. B. R. 441).

24. Vaccaro *v.* Security Bank, 4 A. B. R. 482, 103 Fed. 436 (C. C. A. Tenn.); In re Duke, 28 A. B. R. 195, 199 Fed. 199 (D. C. Ga.); In re Perlhefter & Shatz, 25 A. B. R. 576, 177 Fed. 299 (D. C. N. Y.).

25. In re Everybody's Market, 21 A. B. R. 925, 173 Fed. 492 (D. C. Okla.).

26. Brake *v.* Callison, 11 A. B. R.

797, 129 Fed. 196 (C. C. A. Fla.); In re Flint Hill Stone & Construction Co., 18 A. B. R. 83, 149 Fed. 1007 (D. C. N. Y.).

Recording of conveyance does not impart constructive notice of its fraudulent character to subsequent creditors so as to prevent the attacking of it on the ground that it was made in furtherance of a scheme to defraud subsequent creditors. Beasley *v.* Coggins, 12 A. B. R. 355, 57 So. Rep. 213.

27. Bradley Timber Co. *v.* White, 10 A. B. R. 329, 121 Fed. 779 (C. C. A. Ala.).

the adjudication settles the status of the defendant as a bankrupt, and all the world must take notice of it. Now, in other proceedings in rem to determine status, as, for instance, proceedings for determining one insane or otherwise non compos mentis, it would not for a moment be thought right practice to join some dishonest person who had been getting the ward's property away from him by fraud, even if the proceedings for the determination of the ward's unfitness longer to control his property were instituted precisely for the purpose of enabling the defrauding party to be reached. So in bankruptcy, a petition is multifarious that unites with the allegations and prayer for the adjudication of the debtor, allegations and prayer for the provisional seizure of the property by the marshal;[28] or for an injunction against attaching creditors;[29] or for an injunction against a receiver appointed by the State court, forbidding him to dispose of certain property in his hands.[30] Separate proceedings must be brought.[31]

Thus, whether the bankruptcy court will or will not have jurisdiction over assets of the estate in the possession of a state court receiver, or other court officer, is not an issue that can be raised on the hearing of the petition for adjudication of bankruptcy.[32]

In re Kingsley, 20 A. B. R. 424, 160 Fed. 275 (D. C. Vt.): "It is claimed by the guardian that he holds the property of the bankrupt under the insolvency laws of New Hampshire, which are not suspended by the bankruptcy enactments of Congress and, therefore, this court of bankruptcy cannot administer upon the estate of his ward. It is unnecessary to discuss that question now. The real question is that of jurisdiction of the court in adjudging Austin N. Kingsley a bankrupt. Having been a resident of Vermont for a period of more than six months gives him a right to apply to the court of bankruptcy for relief from all of his creditors, whether they are within or without the jurisdiction of Vermont or New Hampshire. The fact that he is under guardianship in New Hampshire and proceedings are pending there in the Probate Court,—a court that has no power to relieve an insolvent debtor except as to creditors residing in that State, or voluntarily coming within its jurisdiction,—does not deprive the bankrupt of seeking the benefits of the national acts of bankruptcy in the Federal court having jurisdiction of the district where the bankrupt has been domiciled for six months previous to the filing of his petition."

And, whether or not the preference which is alleged as the act of bankruptcy upon which adjudication of bankruptcy is asked, is voidable as against

28. In re Kelly, 1 A. B. R. 306, 92 Fed. 333 (D. C. Tenn.); In re Ogles, 1 A. B. R. 671, 93 Fed. 426 (D. C. Tenn.); Mather v. Coe, 1 A. B. R. 504, 92 Fed. 333 (D. C. Ohio). See, for proper practice, Philips v. Turner, 8 A. B. R. 171, 114 Fed. 726 (C. C. A. Miss.).

29. Mather v. Coe, 1 A. B. R. 504, 92 Fed. 333 (D. C. Ohio); In re Ogles, 1 A. B. R. 671, 93 Fed. 426 (D. C. Tenn.).

30. Mather v. Coe, 1 A. B. R. 504, 92 Fed. 333 (D. C. Ohio); In re Ogles, 1 A. B. R. 671, 93 Fed. 426 (D. C. Tenn.).

31. Mather v. Coe, 1 A. B. R. 504, 92 Fed. 333 (D. C. Ohio).

32. In re Kersten, 6 A. B. R. 516, 110 Fed. 929 (D. C. Wis.).

the preferred creditors, is not one to be decided at the adjudication on the petition.[33]

And it would be multifarious and without jurisdiction to join an assignee or receiver of the bankrupt, even when no relief were sought against him.[34]

§ 251. Petition a Pleading and to Conform to Usual Rules.—The petition is a pleading, and should conform to the usual rules of pleading in the manner of statement.[35]

§ 252. Thus, Petition to Set Up Facts, Not Legal Conclusions.—Thus, the petition should set up facts, not legal conclusions.[36] Thus, it will not do to allege that the petitioner has a provable claim, but the facts showing it to be one should be alleged.[37]

In re Nelson, 1 A. B. R. 63 (D. C. Wis.): "Issuable facts not conclusions should be alleged." Reversed, on other grounds, in 7 A. B. R. 142.

Nor will it do merely to say that the debtor within the preceding four months had transferred property with intent to prefer, or with intent to hinder, delay or defraud. The facts showing these various elements of the cause of action must be alleged.

§ 253. Facts Not to Be Alleged Argumentatively.—Nor should the facts be alleged argumentatively.

In re Plotke, 5 A. B. R. 175, 104 Fed. 964 (C. C. A. Ills.): "The essential facts must appear affirmatively and distinctly and it is not sufficient that jurisdiction may be inferred argumentatively."

§ 254. Facts Should Be Ultimate Facts, Not Evidence.—The facts stated should be the ultimate facts and not mere evidentiary facts.

In re Bellah, 8 A. B. R. 310, 116 Fed. 69 (D. C. Del.): "* * * the manner and details of the concealment being matters of evidence and not of averment."

§ 255. Allegations in Mere Words of Statute Insufficient; Ex-

---

33. Leidigh Carriage Co. v. Stengel, 2 A. B. R. 383, 95 Fed. 637 (C. C. A. Ohio).

34. In re Bay City Irrigating Co., 14 A. B. R. 370, 135 Fed. 850 (D. C. Tex.). But compare, Louisville Trust Co. v. Comingor, 7 A. B. R. 421, 184 U. S. 18, where an assignee for creditors was joined.

35. Clark v. Henne & Meyer, 11 A. B. R. 583, 127 Fed. 288 (C. C. A. Tex.).

36. In re Cliffe, 2 A. B. R. 317, 94 Fed. 354 (D. C. Penna.). In re Sig. H. Rosenblatt & Co., 28 A. B. R. 401,

193 Fed. 638 (C. C. A. N. Y.); In re Truitt, 29 A. B. R. 570, 203 Fed. 550 (D. C. Md.). Inferentially, In re White, 14 A. B. R. 241, 135 Fed. 199 (D. C. Penna.).

37. Hoffschlaeger Co. v. Young Nap, 12 A. B. R. 514 (D. C. Hawaii), which was a case under the second act of bankruptcy. Impliedly, In re White, 14 A. B. R. 241, 135 Fed. 199 (D. C. Penn.). But compare, inferentially, In re Hark Bros., 14 A. B. R. 400, 135 Fed. 603 (D. C. Penn.).

cept as to Fourth and Fifth Acts.—Allegations in the mere words of the statute are insufficient.[38]

> In re Hark Bros., 14 A. B. R. 400, 135 Fed. 603 (D. C. Pa.): "There is one rule, however, followed by all the courts, that allegations of acts of bankruptcy in a petition in the language of the Act without setting forth any other facts or circumstances are insufficient."
> In re Bellah, 8 A. B. R. 310, 116 Fed. 69 (D. C. Del.): quoting U. S. *v.* Carll, 105 U. S. 611: "'It is not sufficient to set forth the offense in the words of the statute, unless those words of themselves fully, directly and expressly, without any uncertainty or ambiguity, set forth all the elements necessary to constitute the offense intended to be punished.'"

Except undoubtedly, as to classes 4 and 5 of acts of bankruptcy, as to which the statutory words could not well be amplified without pleading merely evidentiary facts.

§ 256. Allegations of Residence, Domicile, etc., Not to Be Made Disjunctively.

—Allegations as to residence, domicile, etc., should not be made disjunctively.[39]

§ 257. Petition to Set Forth Essential Facts of Act Charged, Definitely and Certainly.

—The petition must allege, as fully, definitely and certainly as the petitioners' information permits, the acts charged and the essential elements of the cause of action and of the capacity of the parties and of the jurisdiction; and where it is incomplete it must contain explanation of its lack of completeness.

Thus, as to allegations of the first act of bankruptcy, fraudulent concealments, removals, etc., the allegations must be definite and certain.[40]

> Inferentially, In re White, 14 A. B. R. 241, 135 Fed. 199 (D. C. Penna.): "This is a demurrer to the petition, the second reason of which alleges that it does not set forth when the money which is alleged is owing to the several creditors became due, nor the amount of the securities held by the petitioners, nor the manner in which the value of the securities is fixed, nor does it set forth when the goods were sold. The petition in this respect conforms to the language prescribed by the Supreme Court under General Order 37. It is stated that the claims are for 'goods sold and delivered,' and that 'Hark Brothers purchased the same within one year from this date,' to-wit, the 21st day of October, 1904, the date of the execution of the petition. It is not necessary to state when the several amounts became due as it is alleged they have 'provable claims' nor is there anything to require them to state the amount of the securities held, nor the manner in which the value of the securities are fixed. This objection is overruled."

---

38. In re Cliffe, 2 A. B. R. 317, 94 Fed. 354 (D. C. Pa.); In re Pressed Steel Goods Co., 27 A. B. R. 44, 193 Fed. 811 (D. C. Mich.); In re Deer Creek Co., 29 A. B. R. 356, — Fed. — (D. C. Pa.).

39. In re Laskaris, 1 A. B. R. 480 (Ref. N. Y.).

40. In re Bellah, 8 A. B. R. 310, 116 Fed. 69 (D. C. Del.); In re Mero, 12 A. B. R. 171, 128 Fed. 630 (D. C. Conn.); In re Hark Bros., 14 A. B. R.

Likewise as to allegations of the second act of bankruptcy, preferential transfers.[41]

In re Ewing, 8 A. B. R. 269, 115 Fed. 707 (C. C. A. N. Y.): "The demurrer to the petition for the adjudication of Ewing as a bankrupt should have been sustained because the petition omits to aver that any of the payments alleged to have been made by Ewing, the alleged bankrupt, to Bouvier, were made with intent to prefer Bouvier over his other creditors."

In re Nelson, 1 A. B. R. 63, 98 Fed. 76 (D. C. Wis.): "The specific fact must be alleged with time, place and circumstances." Reversed, on other grounds, sub nom. Wilson v. Nelson, 7 A. B. R. 142, 183 U. S. 191.

In re Blumberg, 13 A. B. R. 343, 133 Fed. 845 (D. C. Pa.): The allegation here was that the transfer was made for "improper considerations." No specification of names nor amounts was made. The court says: "The difficulty of obtaining accurate information concerning fraudulent transfers of property or preferential payments has been suggested as an excuse for the vagueness of such averments as are found in this petition, and I am not insensible that such difficulty may often exist. Due allowance should be made for it, but the petitioning creditors are nevertheless bound to as full a disclosure as their information may enable them to make, supplemented by an explanation of its lack of completeness, so far as it may thus be lacking. Impossibilities are not expected of petitioning creditors, more than of other suitors; but they must found their case on something more than rumor, or vague hearsay, or mere suspicion."

In re Flint Hill Stone & Construction Co., 18 A. B. R. 83, 149 Fed. 1007 (D. C. N. Y.): "But here we have no allegation that the endorsements were not made at the time, or even that the mortgages were given to secure indorsements past or present, or that they were given not in due course of business for a present full and adequate consideration. The petition is silent as to the consideration. True, it says the mortgagees were indorsers, but it does not say the mortgages were given to secure such indorsements. Nor is there any allegation that the officers of the corporation knew of its insolvency when the mortgages were given. Neither does it affirmatively appear that, when the mortgages were given, the alleged bankrupt had other creditors. The petitioners were creditors when the petition was verified, but it is not alleged that they were such when the mortgages were given. For anything that appears, the chattel mortgages were for money borrowed to pay off and satisfy all the debts owing by such corporation, if any, existing at the time such mortgages were given. If such was the case, there was neither intent to hinder, delay or defraud, or to prefer one creditor over another. There must be an allegation either that the mortgages were given with intent to hinder, delay and defraud the other creditors of the alleged bankrupt, or that they were given with intent to prefer the mortgagees over the other creditors of the corporation. The petition should also allege that there were other creditors, and that the debts or indorsements secured by the mortgages were pre-existing or if then incurred

400 (D. C. Penn.); In re Flint Hill Stone & Construction Co., 18 A. B. R. 83, 149 Fed. 1007 (D. C. N. Y.); In re Sig. H. Rosenblatt & Co., 28 A. B. R. 401, 193 Fed. 638 (C. C. A. N. Y.); In re Hallin, 28 A. B. R. 708, 199 Fed. 806 (D. C. Mich.).

41· In re Vastbinder, 11 A. B. R. 121, 126 Fed. 417 (D. C. Pa.); Clark v. Henne & Meyer, 11 A. B. R. 593, 127 Fed. 288 (C. C. A. Tex.); In re Hallin, 28 A. B. R. 708, 199 Fed. 806 (D. C. Mich.).

It has been held essential to allege insolvency at the date of the transfer. In re Hammond, 20 A. B. R. 776, 163 Fed. 548 (D. C. N. Y.), quoted at § 262½.

or made that the mortgages were given for an inadequate consideration, etc.; as the case may be."

Mills *v.* Fisher & Co., 20 A. B. R. 237, 159 Fed. 897 (C. C. A. Tenn.): "The general averment that the firm of J. H. Fisher and Company have, within four months, 'paid out large sums of money in the settlement of the debts of the firm and thereby making preferences among creditors,' etc., is a vague drag net, specifying no act of preference which under any rule of pleading would justify an adjudication. * * * The dismissal of the petition, so far as an adjudication against the firm is sought, was not error."

In re Pure Milk Co., 18 A. B. R. 735, 154 Fed. 682 (D. C. Ala.): "The averment in the petition that the alleged bankrupt had within four months paid money to one or more creditors, with intent to prefer such creditors over its other creditors, is insufficient as an averment of an act of bankruptcy".

Conway *v.* German, 21 A. B. R. 577, 166 Fed. 67 (C. C. A. Md.): "The second and third paragraphs of section 4 of the petition were clearly insufficient, the first because too general, in that it did not state of what, or to whom the alleged transfer was made, with intent to give preference to one creditor over another."

And similarly as to allegations of the third act of bankruptcy—failure to vacate preferential legal proceedings.[42]

In re Rome Planing Mills, 3 A. B. R. 124, 96 Fed. 812 (D. C. N. Y.): "The petition must prove the entry of the judgment, the issue of an execution; the levy thereunder, the debtor's insolvency at the time of the judgment and levy, and also either that the property was actually sold at execution sale, or that the sale was advertised for a day certain and that the debtor had permitted the levy to stand until the sale was only five days distant."

In re Vastbinder, 11 A. B. R. 118, 126 Fed. 417 (D. C. Pa.): "* * * held insufficient where its only allegations as to the five days is merely that the attachment 'has not to this time been vacated.'"

In re Hammond, 20 A. B. R. 776, 163 Fed. 548 (D. C. N. Y.): "The next ground of objection is that the petition states that judgments were suffered to be entered against the bankrupts, but does not state that they were not vacated within five days before a sale or final disposition. * * * The demurrer will be sustained on all three grounds."

Thus, likewise, as to allegations of the fifth act of bankruptcy,—written admission of inability to pay debts and willingness to be adjudged bankrupt on that ground.

Conway *v.* German, 21 A. B. R. 577, 166 Fed. 67 (C. C. A. Md.): "* * * and the second, that they had admitted their inability to pay their debts, if intended to show the defendants admission of such facts, and the willingness to be adjudicated bankrupts, should have averred that such acknowledgement, as well of inability to pay, as the willingness to be adjudicated bankrupts, was made in writing. (Bankruptcy Act 1898, § 3, sub-section 5.)"

---

42. In re Cliffe, 2 A. B. R. 317, 94 Fed. 354 (D. C. Pa.); In re Vetterman, 14 A. B. R. 245, 135 Fed. 443 (D. C. N. H.); In re Pressed Steel Goods Co., 27 A. B. R. 44, 193 Fed. 811 (D. C. Mich.); In re Radke Co., 27 A. B. R. 950, 193 Fed. 735 (D. C. Cal.). See Seaboard Steel Casting Co. *v.* Trigg, 10 A. B. R. 594 (D. C. Va.).

Thus, the allegations as to the claims of the petitioners, and as to the domicile, residence or place of business of the debtor, must be made definite and certain.

In re Plotke, 5 A. B. R. 175 (C. C. A. Ills.): "The essential facts must appear affirmatively and distinctly, and it is not sufficient that jurisdiction be inferred argumentatively. Wolfe v. Ins. Co., 148 U. S. 389, 141 U. S. 81, 83."

Hoffschlaeger v. Young Nap, 12 A. B. R. 510 (D. C. Hawaii): "Allegation of debt as 'balance due upon goods, wares and merchandise sold and delivered to respondent by petitioner at respondents' request' is sufficient as to the nature of petitioners' claims."

§ 258. But No Greater Nicety nor Fullness Requisite than Nature of Facts Permits.—But no greater nicety nor fullness is required than the nature of the facts will permit.[43] Thus, as to the first act of bankruptcy.

In re Mero, 12 A. B. R. 171, 128 Fed. 630 (D. C. Conn.): "It is important that the allegations in this respect shall be as specific as possible but it would be unfair and contrary to the spirit and purpose of the Bankrupt Law to require greater detail than it is probable that creditors can furnish. I do not think it necessary to allege 'in what manner the said bankrupt indicated his intent.'"

In re Bellah, 8 A. B. R. 310, 116 Fed. 69 (D. C. Del.): "An averment in a petition in involuntary bankruptcy that the defendant at a certain time received a specified sum of money from a specified source, which sum 'he has ever since concealed and secreted with intent to hinder, delay or defraud his creditors,' is not defective for want of particularity; the manner and details of the concealment being matters of evidence and not of averment."

Thus, as to the second act of bankruptcy.

In re Lackow, 14 A. B. R. 514 (D. C. Pa.): "The time of making the preferential payment and its amount are both specified and the failure to state the names of the creditors is sufficiently accounted for. If their names had been known, it would have been necessary to set them forth, but I do not think that the Bankrupt Law intended to require from petitioning creditors the attempt to perform impossibilities. If they do not know the names of preferred creditors, and cannot learn them by proper inquiry and investigation, the petition is good, in my opinion, although it may only aver in general terms that the payment has been made, adding the reason why a more specific allegation is not possible."

§ 259. Prescribed Bankruptcy Forms to Be Adhered to as Closely as Facts Permit.—The regular forms prescribed by the Supreme Court should be adhered to as closely as the facts will permit.[44]

Gage v. Bell, 10 A. B. R. 696, 124 Fed. 371 (D. C. Tenn.): "It is to be observed

---

43. Inferentially, but obiter, In re Hark Bros., 14 A. B. R. 400, 135 Fed. 603 (D. C. Penna.); In re Vastbinder, 11 A. B. R. 121, 126 Fed. 417 (D. C. Pa.).

44. Impliedly, In re White, 14 A. B. R. 241, 135 Fed. 199 (D. C. Penna.). See also, Bradley Timber Co. v. White, 10 A. B. R. 329, 121 Fed. 779 (C. C. A. Ala.).

that Form No. 6 (89 Fed. xxx, 32 C. C. A. liv) does not comtemplate any other pleading than that of a brief and simple denial (1) that the defendant debtor has committed the act of bankruptcy, or (2) that he is insolvent, and (3) an averment 'that he should not be declared a bankrupt for any cause in said petition alleged.' At first I was inclined to hold that no other pleading whatever was permissible than this, and that under it any defense whatever, whether by demurrer or otherwise, could be made that would defeat the petition for any cause. But yielding to the license given by General Order No. 38, that the several forms shall be observed and used with such alterations as may be necessary to suit the circumstances of any particular case, and conforming to the practice in other districts, reluctantly and with constantly increasing regret, I allowed other and special pleadings to be framed, and now, as in this case, in almost every case there are demurrers, formidable answers after the manner of pleadings in chancery, with exceptions, replications, etc., until the practice has departed from the simple forms prescribed and degenerated into those of a suit in equity. I doubt if this is proper practice."

And the courts discourage the use of the complicated forms used in the federal chancery practice.[45] But the official forms are intended to execute the Act and not to add to its provisions by making that which the statute treats as immaterial in some cases, a material fact in every case.[46] And the provisions of § 57 as to the allegations required in order to make due "proof" of claims for participation in the dividends, need not be complied with in alleging the provable claims of the petitioning creditors in the petition itself.[47]

Where the prescribed forms are followed, or substantially followed, the allegation would, generally, be considered sufficient.[48]

§ 260. Answering Over Waives Defects.

Defective or insufficient statements of facts are waived by answering over without objection.[49] Likewise, all formal or modal defects, not reaching to the jurisdiction, are waived by answering over.[50]

§ 261. Amendments.

Amendments may be allowed to bankruptcy petitions, as to other pleadings.[51]

---

45. Gage v. Bell, 10 A. B. R. 696, 124 Fed. 371 (D. C. Tenn.); Bradley Timber Co. v. White, 10 A. B. R. 329, 121 Fed. 779 (C. C. A. Ala.).

46. West v. Lea Bros., 2 A. B. R. 463, 175 U. S. 590.

47. In re Brett, 12 A. B. R. 492, 130 Fed. 981 (D. C. N. J.); Hoffschlaeger Co. v. Young Nap, 12 A. B. R. 510 (D. C. Hawaii).

48. Impliedly, Conway v. German, 21 A. B. R. 577, 166 Fed. 67 (C. C. A. Md.), quoted at § 268.

49. In re Cliffe, 2 A. B. R. 317, 94 Fed. 354 (D. C. Pa.); Motor Vehicle Co. v. Oak Leather Co., 15 A. B. R. 804, 141 Fed. 518 (C. C. A. Ills.).

50. Leidigh Carriage Co. v. Stengel, 2 A. B. R. 383, 95 Fed. 637 (C. C. A. Ohio.).

51. Gleason v. Smith Perkins Co., 16 A. B. R. 605, 145 Fed. 895 (C. C. A. Pa.). In re Vastbinder, 11 A. B. R. 119, 126 Fed. 417 (D. C. Pa.), although this was not really an amendment of the pleading, but simply of the verification. Obiter, Woolford v. Steel Co., 15 A. B. R. 31, 138 Fed. 582 (D. C. Del.); In re Blumberg, 13 A. B. R. 343, 133 Fed. 845 (D. C. Pa.); Beach v. Macon Grocery Co., 9 A. B. R. 762, 122 Fed. 736 (C. C. A. Ga.); In re Weinman, 2 N. B. N. & R. 51 (Ref. Pa.); In re Mercur, 10 A. B. R. 505,

Armstrong *v.* Fernandez, 19 A. B. R. 746, 208 U. S. 324: "The errors assigned in reference to the action of the referee and of the court in permitting the amendments of the verification and other amendments we regard as without merit. The power of a court of bankruptcy over amendments is undoubted and rests in the sound discretion of the court. We think there is no abuse of discretion here and that the court was fully justified in its orders in reference to amendments."

In re Bellah, 8 A. B. R. 310, 116 Fed. 69 (D. C. Del.): "Rule 11 of the general orders in bankruptcy deals with amendments to a petition and schedules, but was not intended to abrogate or restrict the general power of amendment in other respects vested in the court."

In re Brett, 12 A. B. R. 492, 130 Fed. 981 (D. C. N. J.): "If the demurrer * * * should be sustained, the petition should not be dismissed without first giving the petitioners an opportunity to apply for leave to amend."

Obiter, Wilder *v.* Watts, 15 A. B. R. 67, 138 Fed. 426 (D. C. S. C.): "Amendments are usually allowed if the ends of justice will be promoted, but, as they are not matters of right, the court must exercise its discretion in permitting them. The amendment proposed states a new and independent cause of bankruptcy, not related to the original petition. The petitioners have given no reason why this alleged act of bankruptcy was not stated in their first petition."

Gleason *v.* Smith, 16 A. B. R. 605, 145 Fed. 895 (C. C. A. Pa.): "The power of the court to grant the amendment is undoubted. In the Bellah case * * * it was held that General Order No. XI, which relates to amendment of petitions, was not intended to abrogate or restrict the general power of amendment in the court."

Such amendments rest in the sound discretion of the court, which is not to be reviewed unless abused.[52]

And, in a proper case, it is error for the court to refuse to permit amendment.[53]

Amendment should be allowed to show insolvency at the date of the commission of the act of bankruptcy where the petitioner has alleged it only as of the date of the filing of the petition.[54] But a formal application should be made for leave to amend.[55]

§ 262. Must Be "Something to Amend by."—There must be some-

122 Fed. 384 (C. C. A. Pa.), also 2 A. B. R. 626 (D. C. Pa.); In re Shoesmith, 13 A. B. R. 645, 135 Fed. 684 (C. C. A. Ills.); In re Cliffe, 2 A. B. R. 317, 94 Fed. 354 (D. C. Pa.); In re White, 14 A. B. R. 241, 135 Fed. 200 (D. C. Pa.); In re Plymouth Cordage Co., 12 A. B. R. 665, 135 Fed. 1000 (C. C. A. Okla.). Impliedly, In re First Nat'l Bank of Belle Fourche, 18 A. B. R. 270, 128 Fed. 630 (C. C. A.). Instance, In re Mero, 12 A. B. R. 171, 128 Fed. 630 (D. C. Conn.). In re Nusbaum, 18 A. B. R. 598, 152 Fed. 835 (D. C. N. Y.); instance, In re Hammond, 20 A. B. R. 776, 163 Fed. 548 (D. C. N. Y.); inferentially, Ryan *v.* Hendricks, 21 A. B. R. 570, 166 Fed.

94 (C. C. A. Wis.); Conway *v.* German, 21 A. B. R. 577, 166 Fed. 67 (C. C. A. Md.), quoted at § 271; instance, In re Marion Contr. & Const. Co., 22 A. B. R. 81, 166 Fed. 618 (D. C. Ky.); In re R. L. Radke Co., 27 A. B. R. 950, 193 Fed. 735 (D. C. Cal.).

52. In re Sig. H. Rosenblatt & Co., 28 A. B. R. 401, 193 Fed. 638 (C. C. A. N. Y.).

53. Conway *v.* German, 21 A. B. R. 577, 166 Fed. 67 (C. C. A. Md.), quoted at § 271.

54. In re Pangborn, 26 A. B. R. 40, 185 Fed. 673 (D. C. Mich.).

55. In re Pressed Steel Goods Co., 27 A. B. R. 44, 193 Fed. 811 (D. C. Mich.).

thing already in the record by which to amend. The right to amend can go no further than to bring forward and make effective that which in some form is already there.[56]

In re Mercur, 10 A. B. R. 505, 122 Fed. 384 (C. C. A. Pa.): "The general right to amend, regardless of the time which has elapsed, is abundantly sustained by the authorities. * * * But to do so it is plain there must be in the record as it stands the substance of that which is asked for; the right to amend can go no further than to bring forth and make effective that which is in some shape already there."

But the mere general allegation (not objected to at the trial) of "other preferences" is sufficient to support an amendment, where the facts actually admitted in evidence tend to establish other preferences.[57]

§ 262½. Whether Other Acts May Be Added.—The addition of other acts of bankruptcy ordinarily is not permitted;[58] but may be permitted;[59] and it is a matter within the sound judicial discretion of the court whether to permit amendment by the inserting of additional acts of bankruptcy.[60]

It has been held, that where an alleged bankrupt fails to answer or plead to an involuntary petition, it may not thereafter be amended so as to allege acts of bankruptcy prior to the acts of bankruptcy set forth in a second petition.[61]

Indeed, the general allegation of "other preferences" or the general allegation merely that preferential payments have been made, is sufficient to amend by.

Impliedly, In re Hammond, 20 A. B. R. 776, 163 Fed. 548 (D. C. N. Y.): "The third ground of objection is that preferential payments are alleged to have been made, but no particular payments are recited, and no allegation is made that any transfer of property referred to was with intent to prefer the creditors to whom the property was transferred. Each of these grounds of demurrer is good in the sense that the objection is as to a jurisdictional fact which must be established in order to keep the estate in bankruptcy, but, inasmuch as other creditors' rights have accrued, and inasmuch as the petition was dated upon the 9th day of April, whereas the transfer in question was made upon the 4th

---

56. Compare, Ludowici Roofing Tile Co. v. Penn. Inst., 8 A. B. R. 739 (D. C. Pa.), involving the Mercur bankruptcy. Also In re Crenshaw, 19 A. B. R. 502, 156 Fed. 638 (D. C. Ala.). Obiter, In re Hamrick, 23 A. B. R. 721, 175 Fed. 279 (D. C. Ga.), quoted on other points at § 264.

But see In re Shoesmith, 13 A. B. R. 645, 135 Fed. 684 (C. C. A. Ills.), that "The jurisdiction comes from the Bankrupt Act and is not conferred by the accuracy and precision of the averments made in the petition."

Schedules filed simultaneously with involuntary petition apparently held enough in record to amend by, al-

though perhaps hearing also had been had. In re Pangborn, 26 A. B. R. 40, 185 Fed. 673 (D. C. Mich.).

57. Motor Vehicle Co. v. Oak Leather Co., 15 A. B. R. 804, 141 Fed. 518 (C. C. A. Ills.). Compare, In re Hammond, 20 A. B. R. 776, 163 Fed. 548 (D. C. N. Y.), quoted at § 262½.

58. In re Pure Milk Co., 18 A. B. R. 735, 154 Fed. 682 (D. C. Ala.).

59. In re Nusbam, 18 A. B. R. 598, 152 Fed. 835 (D. C. N. Y.).

60. Pittsburg Laundry v. Imperial Laundry, 18 A. B. R. 756, 154 Fed. 662 (C. C. A. Pa.).

61. In re Harris, 19 A. B. R. 204, 156 Fed. 875 (D. C. Ala.).

day of April, in order to secure a past indebtedness, and as the petition contains the general statement that preferential payments have been made to creditors while the alleged bankrupts were insolvent, this would seem to be a proper case for amendment of the petition rather than for absolute dismissal."

Of course, this rule does not prohibit the joinder of additional creditors, permitted expressly by the statute; nor does it prevent the insertion of jurisdictional "allegations," as to the nature of the claims, occupation of the debtor, etc., even where totally omitted from the original petition.[62]

In one case where the bankrupt had admitted in his answer the preference charged, whereupon the preferred creditor had intervened and answered, the court permitted an amendment by the addition of another preference which the bankrupt likewise admitted but which no creditor controverted; and adjudication was entered on the latter act.[63]

§ 263. Similar Acts of Series Added by Amendment.—Similar acts of bankruptcy in a series of like acts may be added by amendment.

Obiter, White *v.* Bradley Timber Co., 8 A. B. R. 672, 116 Fed. 768 (D. C. Ala.): "There is some authority for the proposition that, where the amendment offered shows acts of bankruptcy of a like character as the one attempted to be shown in the original petition the amendment will be allowed or authorized before or at the hearing of the cause."

§ 264. Acts Occurring within Four Months of Application to Amend, Added.—And acts of bankruptcy, occurring within the four months before the filing of the application for leave to amend, may be added,[64] even though occurring after the filing of the original petition.

In re Hamrick, 23 A. B. R. 721, 175 Fed. 279 (D. C. Ga.): "The additional grounds of bankruptcy set out by amendment in this case are later than the ground stated in the original petition, and counsel have urged that only acts of bankruptcy committed earlier than that originally alleged can be attached by amendment. As I have stated, I think the general order and the decisions on that have no application whatever to a case like this, where only one petition is filed, and the question here as to the allowance of the amendment is controlled by the general rule on the subject of amendments. I think the special master correctly held that the amendment should be allowed, and also correctly held that the facts did not sustain the original ground of bankruptcy, but did sustain the additional grounds, and that an adjudication should be entered in the case."

§ 265. But Occurring before and Not Originally Referred to, Not to Be Added.—But an act of bankruptcy not referred to in the original

---

62. State Bank *v.* Haswell, 23 A. B. R. 330, 174 Fed. 290 (C. C. A. Iowa), quoted at § 269.
63. In re Cleary, 24 A. B. R. 742, 179 Fed. 990 (D. C. Pa.).
64. In re Mercur, 2 A. B. R. 626, 95 Fed. 634 (D. C. Pa.); obiter, In re Haff, 13 A. B. R. 365, 136 Fed. 78 (C. C. A. N. Y.). Instance, In re Nus-

baum, 18 A. B. R. 598, 152 Fed. 835 (D. C. N. Y.). But compare, obiter, White *v.* Bradley Timber Co., 8 A. B. R. 671, 116 Fed. 768 (D. C. Ala.). Contra, where the petitioners were not ignorant of the act and especially where they participated in it, Wilder *v.* Watts, 15 A. B. R. 67, 138 Fed. 426 (D. C. S. C.).

petition, and occurring more than four months before the amendment is asked for, may not be added.[65]

In re Haff, 13 A. B. R. 362, 135 Fed. 742 (C. C. A. N. Y.): "The general rule seems to be that an original petition cannot be amended by setting out therein acts of bankruptcy not referred to in the original petition and occurring more than four months before the application for an order allowing the amendment."

In re Pure Milk Co., 18 A. B. R. 735, 154 Fed. 682 (D. C. Ala.): "If the petition originally filed was insufficient in averring an act of bankruptcy, then it in effect averred no act of bankruptcy. Leave to amend·may be granted, but will not generally be granted when the proposed amendment would introduce into the petition entirely new acts of bankruptcy. New acts of bankruptcy will not be permitted to be introduced into the petition after the four months' period has expired. A fortiori, where no act of bankruptcy is averred in the original petition, should an act of bankruptcy be permitted to be introduced after the four months' period has expired? * * * Here the petition avers no specific act of bankruptcy and the amendment is founded upon an act which it appears was committed more·than four months before the amendment is proposed to be made, which, it seems to me, is a much stronger case against the·petitioner's claim than when a new act of bankruptcy is sought to be introduced."

And the same rule applies to intervening petitions.[66]

§ 266. Except, Where Two Petitions Consolidated or Pending at Same Time, Earlier Acts in One May Be Adopted into Other.

—Where, however, two petitions against the same debtor have been consolidated, or are pending at the same time in different districts, earlier acts in one may be adopted into the other by amendment, under General Order No. 6.[67]

---

65. In re Walker, 21 A. B. R. 132, 164 Fed. 680. (C. C. A. Calif.); In re Perlhefter & Shatz, 25 A. B. R. 576, 177 Fed. 299 (D. C. N. Y.); Obiter, In re Riggs Restaurant Co., 11 A. B. R. 508, 130 Fed. 691 (C. C. A. N. Y.). [1867] In re Cole & Hoblitzer, 1 N. B. R. 516; [1867] In re Craft, 2 N. B. R. 111, Fed. Cas. 3,317; [1867] In re Leonard, 4 N. B. R. 562, Fed. Cas. 8,255; White v. Bradley Timber Co., 8 A. B. R. 671, 116 Fed. 768 (C. C. A. Ala.); (1867) Stern v. Schonfield, Fed. Cas. 13,377; analogously, In re Stephenson, 2 A. B. R. 66, 94 Fed. 110 (D. C. Del.); In re Maund, 1 L. R. O. B. Div. 194 (1895). Compare, In re Harris, 19 A. B. R. 204, 156 Fed. 875 (D. C. Ala.). But compare, In re Shoesmith, 13 A. B. R. 645, 135 Fed. 684 (C. C. A. Ills.). Contra, In re Strait, 2 A. B. R. 308 (Ref. N. Y.).

66. In re Walker, 21 A. B. R. 132, 164 Fed. 680 .(C. C. A. Calif.).

67. Wilder v. Watts, 15 A. B. R. 57, 138 Fed. 426 (D. C. S. C.). Compare,

obiter, Gleason v. Smith, 16 A. B. R. 605, 145 Fed. 895 (C. C. A. Pa.).

Gen. Order No. 6: "In case two or more petitions .shall be filed against the same individual in different districts, the first hearing shall be had in the district in which the debtor has his domicile, and the petition may be amended by inserting an allegation of an act of bankruptcy committed at an earlier date than that first alleged, if such earlier act is charged in either of the other petitions; and in case of two or more petitions against the same partnership in different courts, each having jurisdiction over the case, the petition first filed shall be first heard, and may be amended by an insertion of an allegation of an earlier act of bankruptcy than the first alleged, if such earlier act is charged in either of the other petitions."

But, for limitations of rule, see In re Harris. 19 A. B. R. 204, 156 Fed. 815 (D. C. Ala.).

And compare, In re Sears, 8 A. B. R. 713, 117 Fed. 294 (C. C. A. N. Y.): "The order allowing an amendment of the petition by the insertion of a special act of bankruptcy was erroneous, because it clearly appeared that such act of bankruptcy was not an earlier act than that first alleged, but was later. The case is controlled by the terms of General Order, No. 6 and as that makes explicit provision for it an amendment not within its terms is unwarranted."

§ 267. Amendment to Make Pleadings Conform to Facts Proved.

—Amendment may be allowed to make pleadings conform to the facts proved, or will be "deemed made."[68]

In re Lange, 3 A. B. R. 231, 97 Fed. 197 (D. C. N. Y.): "Though these were not set out in the petition, yet being of like general character as the one debt stated, though not for rent, they would have been allowed to be inserted in the petition by amendment, if applied for before the trial; and as the defendant cannot claim surprise, all the evidence being derived from his own testimony to his own book entries the amendment should be deemed made."

And where the evidence admitted actually proves another act of bankruptcy than the one alleged, the petition may be amended to conform to the facts proved.[69] Similarly, where a new trial is granted the original petition may be amended to conform to the facts developed at the first trial.[70]

§ 268. Failure to Show Requisite Number, and Amount or Nature of Claims Amendable.

—The failure of the petition to show on its face the requisite number of creditors and amount of claims held by them is not fatal but may be supplied by amendment.[71]

In re Plymouth Cordage Co., 13 A. B. R. 665, 135 Fed. 1000 (C. C. A. Okla.): "The fact that there is no averment that the creditors are less than twelve cannot be more fatal to the right of the petitioner to an adjudication in bankruptcy than the fact that he has made such an averment, which, upon the trial, proved to be without foundation in fact. The truth is that the contention of counsel for the respondent fails to distinguish between the averments essential to jurisdiction over the subject matter and the parties and those requisite to invoke a favorable adjudication upon the petition. Jurisdiction of the subject

68. In re Miller, 5 A. B. R. 145, 104 Fed. 764 (D. C. N. Y.); Motor Vehicle Co. v. Oak Leather Co., 15 A. B. R. 804, 141 Fed. 518 (C. C. A. Ills.); Hark v. Allen Co., 17 A. B. R. 3 (C. C. A. Pa., affirming In re Hark Bros., 15 A. B. R. 460). But compare, analogously, In re Pierce, 4 A. B. R. 554, 103 Fed. 64 (D. C. N. Y.). Apparently, In re Pangborn, 26 A. B. R. 40, 185 Fed. 673 (D. C. Mich.). In re Richardson, 27 A. B. R. 590, 192 Fed. 50 (D. C. Mass.).

69. In re Miller, 5 A. B. R. 145, 104 Fed. 764 (D. C. N. Y.); Motor Vehicle Co. v. Oak Leather Co., 15 A. B. R. 804, 141 Fed. 518 (C. C. A. Ills.).

70. In re Hark Bros., 15 A. B. R. 460, 142 Fed. 279 (D. C. Pa., affirmed in Hark v. Allen Co., 17 A. B. R. 3); Hark v. Allen Co., 17 A. B. R. 3 (C. C. A. Pa., affirming In re Hark Bros., 15 A. B. R. 460, 142 Fed. 279, D. C. Pa.), changing from fraudulent removal, etc., to preferential transfer.

71. In re Beddingfield, 2 A. B. R. 355, 96 Fed. 190 (D. C. Ga.). Compare, to same effect, In re Broadway Sav. Trust Co., 18 A. B. R. 255 (C. C. A. Mo.); In re First Nat'l Bank of Belle Fourche, 18 A. B. R. 265 (C. C. A. Mo.); State Bank v. Haswell, 23 A. B. R. 330, 174 Fed. 290 (C. C. A. Iowa); In re Pangborn, 26 A. B. R. 40, 185 Fed. 673 (D. C. Mich.). Contra, In re Stein, 12 A. B. R. 364, 130 Fed. 377 (D. C. Penn.).

matter and of the parties is the right to hear and determine the suit or proceeding in favor of or against the parties to it. The facts essential to invoke this jurisdiction differ materially from those essential to constitute a good cause of action for the relief sought. A defective petition in bankruptcy or an insufficient complaint at law, accompanied by proper service upon the defendants, gives jurisdiction to the court to determine the questions it presents, although it may not contain averments which entitle the complainant to any relief; and it may be the duty of the court to determine either the question of its jurisdiction or the merits of the controversy against the petitioner or plaintiff. Allegations indispensable to a favorable adjudication or decree include all those requisite to state a complete cause of action, and they comprehend many that are not requisite to the jurisdiction of the suit or proceeding. The averment that all the creditors of Smith were less than twelve was not of the former, but of the latter, class. It was not essential to invoke the jurisdiction of the court over the parties to the proceeding and the property it involved, because the act of Congress gave that court, upon the filing of the petition of the creditor, jurisdiction to hear and determine the questions it presented, whether they were questions of jurisdiction or upon the merits. Not only this, but the averment that the creditors were less than twelve was not even essential to a favorable adjudication upon the petition, because the Bankruptcy Law provided that if two other creditors, whose claims were sufficient in amount, joined in the petition of the cordage company, the court might proceed to adjudicate the issue of bankruptcy upon the merits, although the creditors exceeded twelve in number."

Ryan v. Hendricks, 21 A. B. R. 570, 166 Fed. 94 (C. C. A. Wis.): "The amendments related to the number of the petitioning creditors and the amount and nature of their claims, and to the occupation of the debtor. There is no doubt that at the time the original petition was filed Logerman was a bankrupt and all the conditions existed which made it proper for his estate to be administered under the Bankruptcy Law. If the original petition failed to set forth these conditions fully and clearly, the court did right in allowing the amendments; and the amendments, when made, related back to the time of the filing of the original petition and had the same effect as if originally incorporated therein."

Conway v. German, 21 A. B. R. 577, 166 Fed. 67 (C. C. A. Md.): "If, by this language of the lower court, it was meant to say that the statement of the amount and nature of the petitioner's claims as set forth in the petition was insufficient, we are inclined to disagree with the court, as the claims seem to be so stated as to give the defendants a full and clear understanding of what the debts are, and are in substantial conformity with the form prescribed by the supreme court of the United States for use of creditors filing involuntary bankruptcy petitions (Forms No. 3). If insufficient, however, the defect could have been remedied by filing an itemized or fuller statement of the petitioner's claim, which is in effect what was asked in the second paragraph of the application to amend, which we think also should have been allowed."

Thus, amendment may be allowed to supply the averment that there are less than twelve creditors.[72] Likewise, failure to state the nature of the pe-

---

72. Inferentially, In re Bellah, 8 A. B. R. 310, 116 Fed. 69 (D. C. Del.); In re Haff, 13 A. B. R. 362, 136 Fed. 78 (C. C. A. N. Y.); In re Plymouth Cordage Co., 13 A. B. R. 665, 135 Fed. 1000 (C. C. A. Okla.); In re Pangborn, 26 A. B. R. 40, 185 Fed. 673 (D. C. Mich.).

titioning creditors' claims is remediable by amendment.[73]

And in an intervening petition, amendment may be allowed to supply such deficiencies, if the original petition was defective in these particulars.[74]

And it makes no difference that attaching creditors' rights are affected by the amendment.[75]

§ 269. Omission or Defects in So-Called "Jurisdictional" Averments Amendable.

—Jurisdictional as well as other averments may be amended or inserted.[76]

In re Weinmann, 2 N. B. N. & R. 51 (Ref. Pa.): "A petition in bankruptcy may be amended with respect to jurisdictional averments as to the residence or place of business of the bankrupt."

State Bank v. Haswell, 23 A. B. R. 330, 174 Fed. 290 (C. C. A. Iowa): "This rule is also applicable to cases where jurisdictional facts which existed at the time the original petition was filed are subsequently made to appear for the first time by an amendment."

Thus, by inserting the averment that the bankrupt's creditors are less than twelve in number;[77] or, by inserting the residence or domicile of one partner, jurisdiction over one partner giving jurisdiction over all.[78]

Or, by inserting the averment that the bankrupt is not a wage earner nor a farmer.[79]

Obiter, Beach v. Macon Grocery Co., 9 A. B. R. 762, 120 Fed. 736 (C. C. A. Ga.): "The petition in the case is in the form prescribed in general orders of the Supreme Court, and besides contains averments consistent with the alleged bankrupt being a merchant, and not chiefly engaged in tilling the soil, and for that reason it is probably sufficient, or, if not sufficient because of the omission to specifically charge that the alleged bankrupt is not within the excepted class, the defect is one that may be cured by amendment."

Or, by inserting an averment of requisite residence;[80] or an averment that

---

73. In re White, 14 A. B. R. 241, 135 Fed. 199 (D. C. Pa.); Conway v. German, 21 A. B. R. 577, 166 Fed. 67 (C. C. A. Md.), quoted supra; Ryan v. Hendricks, 21 A. B. R. 570, 166 Fed. 94 (C. C. A. Wis.), quoted supra.

74. In re Haff, 13 A. B. R. 362, 136 Fed. 78 (C. C. A. N. Y.); State Bank v. Haswell, 23 A. B. R. 330, 174 Fed. 290 (C. C. A. Iowa), quoted at § 269.

75. Ryan v. Hendricks, 21 A. B. R. 570, 166 Fed. 94 (C. C. A. Wis.), quoted on other point, supra.

76. In re Plymouth Cordage Co., 13 A. B. R. 665, 135 Fed. 1000 (C. C. A. Okla.). Obiter, Woolford v. Steel Co., 15 A. B. R. 31, 138 Fed. 582 (D. C. Del.).

77. In re Plymouth Cordage Co., 13 A. B. R. 665, 135 Fed. 1000 (C. C. A. Okla.); In re Pangborn, 26 A. B. R. 40, 185 Fed. 673 (D. C. Mich.).

78. In re Blair, 3 A. B. R. 588, 99 Fed. 76 (D. C. N. Y.).

79. Armstrong v. Fernandez, 19 A. B. R. 746, 208 U. S. 324; In re Plymouth Cordage Co., 13 A. B. R. 665, 135 Fed. 1000 (C. C. A. Okla.), quoted at § 268; In re White, 14 A. B. R. 241 (D. C. Pa.); In re Bellah, 8 A. B. R. 310, 116 Fed. 69 (D. C. Del.); In re Brett, 12 A. B. R. 496, 130 Fed. 983 (D. C. N. J.); In re Pilger, 9 A. B. R. 245, 118 Fed. 206 (D. C. Wis.); In re Mero, 12 A. B. R. 171, 128 Fed. 633 (D. C. Conn.); In re Crenshaw, 19 A. B. R. 502, 156 Fed. 175 (D. C. Ala.); Ryan v. Hendricks, 21 A. B. R. 570, 166 Fed. 94 (C. C. A. Wis.), quoted at § 268; Conway v. German, 21 A. B. R. 577, 166 Fed. 67 (C. C. A. Md.), quoted at § 271.

80. In re Weinmann, 2 N. B. N. & R. 51 (Ref. Pa.).

the debtor is a corporation principally engaged in manufacturing, etc.[81]

But it has been held that a petition showing on its face less than $500 of debts belonging to the petitioning creditors, cannot be amended to include enough more to make up the jurisdictional amount;[82] and that this is so, although the ones sought to be added were omitted from the original petition through a clerical mistake. But this seems an improper ruling, if in fact there were sufficient in number originally.

And an intervening, joining, petition may be amended to supply jurisdictional facts omitted from the original petition, as well as to supply sufficient joining creditors.

State Bank v. Haswell, 23 A. B. R. 330, 174 Fed. 290 (C. C. A. Iowa): "The amendment as made in this case did not constitute the petition, within the meaning of § 60. It did not by its terms purport to be a petition. It alleged no new act of bankruptcy. It consisted merely in striking out such allegations of the original petition and substituting such other allegations as were requisite to show the joinder of the necessary parties, authorized by § 59d, and their status as creditors. The original petition then remained as if all the averments of the amendment had been bodily incorporated in it. Congress, by the provisions of § 59, which seems to have been enacted to meet just such condition of things as is disclosed by this record, very manifestly intended, not that the original petition should be supplanted by the amendment there provided for, but that it might be supplemented by the joinder of other necessary creditors. This is made clear, not only by the provisions of subdivision 'd,' but by the provisions of subdivisions 'e' and 'f' of the same section. They all contemplate the retention of the original petition as the pleadings upon which subsequent proceedings should be had. The general rule as repeatedly recognized by this court is: 'That the amendment to a petition which sets up no new cause of action, but merely amplifies and gives greater precision to the allegations in support of the cause of action originally presented, relates back to the commencement of the action.' Crotty v. Chicago Great Western Ry. Co. (C. C. A.), 169 Fed. 593, and cases cited. This rule is also applicable to cases where jurisdictional facts which existed at the time the original petition was filed are subsequently made to appear for the first time by an amendment."

§ 270. Misnomer—Amendment Allowable.—Where a misnomer of a party has occurred, the error may be corrected by amendment.[83]

§ 271. Amendment May Be Refused.—Amendment may be refused, where refusal would not be an abuse of discretion.

Woolford v. Steel Co., 15 A. B. R. 31, 138 Fed. 582 (D. C. Del.): "Where two petitions in involuntary bankruptcy were filed in the District Court of the United States for the District of Delaware against a corporation April 12, 1905, each alleging only one and the same act of bankruptcy, namely, the appointment because of its insolvency of receivers and putting them in charge of the prop-

---

81. Obiter, In re First Nat. Bank of Belle Fourche, 18 A. B. R. 270, 152 Fed. 64 (C. C. A.); In re Marion Contr. & Const. Co., 22 A. B. R. 81, 166 Fed. 618 (D. C. Ky.).

82. In re Stein, 12 A. B. R. 364, 130 Fed. 377 (D. C. Penn.).

83. Gleason v. Smith, 16 A. B. R. 606, 145 Fed. 895 (C. C. A. Pa.).

erty of the corporation December 12, 1904, by the Circuit Court of the United States for the same district, and each of the petitions was substantially defective, although curable by amendment; and where it further appeared that all of the petitioning creditors in each petition before the appointment of receivers by the Circuit Court took part in procuring or consented to and approved the appointment of receivers and, thus, aided and assisted in the commission of the act on which their petitions in bankruptcy were founded; and where it further appeared that there was no evidence that the corporation was insolvent within the meaning of that term as used in the Bankruptcy Act; and where it further appeared that the estate of the corporation was in course of administration by the Circuit Court through its receivers, and that the receivers had faithfully, diligently and efficiently discharged their duty, and that whatever delay may have occurred was the result of causes over which they had no control; and where it further appeared that the throwing of the corporation into bankruptcy would cause unnecessary expense, delay and confusion in the proper administration of its property: Held, that applications to amend the petitions should be denied and motions for the dismissal of the petitions should be granted."

"If the petitions had not been defective, the petitioners would have had a right under the Bankruptcy Act to proceed to support them by evidence and, if successful, to have the corporation adjudged bankrupt, regardless of any delay, confusion or expense attending such a course. But the petitions being fatally defective, leave to amend should not be granted, thereby withdrawing the administration of the property from the Circuit Court, unless for cogent reasons, not appearing in this case."

Wilder *v.* Watts, 15 A. B. R. 57, 138 Fed. 426 (D. C. S. C.): "In aid of the referee's conclusion that Watts committed an act of bankruptcy in the preferential payments, the attorneys for the petitioner, pending the hearing before me, asked leave to amend their petition, so as to charge these alleged preferential payments as acts of bankruptcy. Amendments are usually allowed if the ends of justice will be promoted, but, as they are not matters of right, the court must exercise its discretion in permitting them. As an adjudication in involuntary proceedings puts a stigma upon the person so adjudicated, he ought, in fairness, to have opportunity of answering; and the proposed amendment, duly verified, should have been served upon him. This was not done. The amendment proposed states a new and independent cause of bankruptcy, not related to the original petition. The petitioners have given no reason why this alleged act of bankruptcy was not stated in their first petition. They cannot claim ignorance, because one of the alleged preferential payments now, stated as an act of bankruptcy was made to parties who filed the original petition. There are respectable authorities holding that acts of bankruptcy occurring subsequent to those stated in the original petition cannot be allowed to be brought in by amendment. * * *

"It does not appear to me that the proposed amendment is 'clearly in furtherance of justice.' The petitioners have not shown any good reason, or any reason at all, why the acts of bankruptcy set up were omitted from the original petition, and have made no excuse for such omission; and, as it appears from the whole case that the alleged bankrupt has no assets to be administered, I fail to see how the interest of creditors can be served by harassing him with further proceedings."

It may be refused where the proposed amended pleading fails to state a cause of action.[84]

Impliedly, Pittsburg Laundry v. Imperial Laundry, 18 A. B. R. 756, 154 Fed. 662 (C. C. A.ʼ Penn.): "No reasons for the refusal are stated by the court, but they are readily apparent from an inspection of the amendments proposed, as they all lack the specific particularity requisite to the statement of an act of bankruptcy, or to sufficiently distinguish them from acts not in violation of the bankrupt law. * * * The other assignments of error refer to the refusal of the court below to allow the amendments to the petition above referred to. The whole matter of permitting or refusing amendments, is entirely within the judicial discretion of the court, and, in accordance with the general rule, will not be interfered with by a reviewing court, unless abuse of such discretion has been shown. As the record discloses no ground for such interference in this case, the decree of the court below is affirmed."

But, in a proper case, it may be error to refuse to permit amendment.

Conway v. German, 21 A. B. R. 577, 166 Fed. 67 (C. C. A. Md.): "In our judgment, the lower court erred in not allowing the amendment prayed for by appellants, with respect to the points now under consideration. Clearly petitioners should have been allowed to strike out the two sections of their petition referred to, if such action was deemed proper after the demurrer thereto was sustained; and it would not affect the petition if it otherwise contained proper averments, giving to the court jurisdiction, to adjudicate the defendants bankrupts. Sustaining the demurrer as to these two sections of paragraph 4, would not have caused the petition to be dismissed if otherwise sufficient, nor would the appellants have failed in their case, either because they did· not sustain the particular averments by proof,ʼ or had been allowed to strike them out. The amendment showing that the defendants did not belong to the class subject to be adjudged involuntary bankrupts, in that they were neither wage earners, nor persons engaged chiefly in farming, or the tillage of the soil, should have been allowed. Such an averment so far as this case is concerned, is a mere negative one, and not of a jurisdictional character. There is no contention made here by the defendants that they belong to the inhibited class, and hence cannot be adjudicated bankrupts, and as a matter of fact they do not belong to that class. Were they seeking to come within the inhibited class, it would be essential for them to make proof of their averment, but they are not, and while technically speaking it should have been stated in the petition, that they were not persons coming within that class, still it was not essential so to do, and in no sense affected the merits of the case, and the amendments desired should have been permitted."

§ 272. Amendment to Make Partnership Petition Out of Individual Petitions Refused.

—A petition to have a partnership adjudged bankrupt nunc pro tunc as of the date of the original adjudication of its several members in individual bankruptcy may be refused.[85]

---

84. Compare, analogously (petition to recover preferences), Johnson v. Anderson, 11 A. B. R. 294, 70 Nebr. 233.

85. In re Mercur, 10 A. B. R. 505, 122 Fed. 384 (C. C. A. Pa., affirming 8 A. B. R. 275, 739).

Amendment of Partnership Petition to Proceed against Individual Member. —A petition filed against a partnership and its members may be amended so as to proceed against one of such members individually. In re Richardson, 27 A. B. R. 590, 192 Fed. 50 (D. C. Mass.). See also, § 69.

But where the individual members have joined in one petition with the obvious intent to have themselves adjudicated bankrupt as partners but fail specifically to pray for the adjudication of the firm, the adjudication may be amended nunc pro tunc into a partnership adjudication.

In re Meyers, 3 A. B. R. 260, 2 N. B. N. & R. 111 (D. C. N. Y.): "I have no doubt that the petition in the present case was designed to procure a firm adjudication and the discharge of both bankrupts from the firm debts. The petition for adjudication is in the form prescribed by the Supreme Court for partnership cases, except that in the final prayer it does not ask that said 'firm' may be adjudged bankrupt, but only that the petitioners may be adjudged bankrupt. In the petition, however, they are described as the members, and the only members, of the firm of Meyers Bros.; and the schedules show that all their debts were debts as copartners in that firm. The order of adjudication follows the petition, and does not adjudicate the firm bankrupt, but only the two petitioners. In the notice for the first meeting of creditors, the two petitioners are described as 'formerly trading as Meyers Brothers.' A trustee was appointed of the bankrupt's estate and effects, which under the petition must include their joint and several estate."

§ 273. Amendment Relates Back to Date of Filing of Original.—
The amendment relates to and takes effect as of the date of the filing of the original petition.[87]

§ 274. Cause of Error to Be Stated in Application to Amend.—
The cause of the error in the original petition must be stated in the application for leave to amend.[88]

White v. Bradley Timber Co., 8 A. B. R. 671, 116 Fed. 768 (D. C. Ala.): In this case the petition had been dismissed for lack of stating any act of bankruptcy, and the motion to vacate the dismissal and for leave to amend failed to state reason for original omission. The court says: "The authorities are to the effect that, in the application for leave to amend, the petitioners shall state the cause of the error in the paper originally filed. It must be shown that the petitioners or their attorney had no knowledge of, and could not have ascertained with reasonable diligence, the facts sought to be added by the amendment, at the time the original petition was filed, or that the facts were omitted by inadvertence, mistake, or other reason which would excuse such omission."

In re Pure Milk Co., 18 A. B. R. 735, 154 Fed. 682 (D. C. Ala.): "Moreover the application to be allowed to amend does not comply with Rule XI. No showing is made why the act of bankruptcy now proposed to be averred was not set out in the original petition."

§ 275. Alleged Bankrupt to Have Reasonable Time to Answer Amended Petition.—An alleged bankrupt has a right to a reasonable time to answer an amended petition.[89]

---

87. In re Shoesmith, 13 A. B. R. 645, 135 Fed. 684 (C. C. A. Ills.); Bank v. Sherman, 101 U. S. 403; Ryan v. Hendricks, 21 A. B. R. 570, 166 Fed. 94 (C. C. A. Wis.); State Bank v. Haswell, 23 A. B. R. 330, 174 Fed. 290 (C. C. A. Iowa).

88. Gen. Ord. No. XI; In re Portner, 18 A. B. R. 89, 149 Fed. 799 (D. C. Pa.).

89. Lockman v. Lang, 12 A. B. R. 497, 132 Fed. 1 (C. C. A. Colo.); Wilder v. Watts, 15 A. B. R. 57, 138 Fed. 426 (D. C. S. C.).

§ 276. Prayer, Signature and Verification.—The petition must contain a prayer for adjudication,[90] and must be subscribed and verified.

§ 277. Verification by Attorney.—An attorney may verify a petition for his client under the same circumstances that would authorize him to do so in any other equity case in the United States Courts. And he may do so if he has knowledge of the facts and his client has authorized him to verify, or ratify his verification.[91]

Obiter, In re Herzikopf, 9 A. .B R. 90, 118 Fed. Rep. 101 (D. C. Calif.): "And no other evidence of his authority than the fact of his admission to practice in the District Court is required."

Rogers v. Mining Co., 14 A. B. R. 252, 136 Fed. 407 (C. C. A. Alaska): "May be made by the attorney in fact of the petitioning creditors."

In re Hunt, 9 A. B. R. 251, 118 Fed. 282 (D. C. Iowa): "In clause 9 of section 1 of the Bankrupt Act it is provided that the word 'creditor' shall include any one who owns a demand or claim provable in bankruptcy and may include his duly authorized agent, attorney or proxy. * * * As it is not declared that the petition shall be verified by the creditor in person, the verification will be sufficient if made by the agent or attorney representing the creditor, it being made to appear that the affiant has knowledge of the facts verified."

In re Chequasset Lumber Co., 7 A. B. R. 87, 112 Fed. 56 (D. C. N. Y.): "It fully appears that the persons who made the verifications were the ones most fully acquainted with the facts and apparently the only agents of the corporations who had the necessary knowledge to enable them to verify the petition. The verifications are deemed sufficient."

Obiter, In re Vastbinder, 11 A. B. R. 118, 126 Fed. 418 (D. C. Pa.): "There can be no doubt as to the right of an attorney in fact to make the necessary oath, where the facts are within his own knowledge and this will be assumed where the oath is in positive terms."

In re Levingston, 13 A. B. R. 357 (D. C. Hawaii): "An authorized agent is qualified to verify an involuntary bankruptcy petition when his principles are at a distance and he is acquainted with the facts."

But the attorney's oath must be positive and not qualified.

In re Vastbinder, 11 A. B. R. 119, 126 Fed. 417 (D. C. Pa.: "But in the present instance the oath is not positive, but qualified, to the best of the affiants' knowledge, information and belief; rather loose terms, which may be made to mean anything or nothing. The difficulty is, that the facts which are affirmed of knowledge are not distinguished from those which are based on information, thus in effect dissipating the force of the affidavit. The first ground of demurrer is, therefore, well taken, but as this is an amendable defect opportunity will be given to remedy it."

90. In partnership bankruptcies, a prayer that "said copartners may be adjudged bankrupt" is a prayer solely for adjudication of the partnership and does not include adjudication of its members as individuals. In re Wing Yick Co., 13 A. B. R. 757 (D. C. Hawaii).

91. Compare, analogously, In re Roukous, 12 A. B. R. 170, 128 Fed. 648 (D. C. R. I.). But see, contra quære, In re Nelson, 1 A. B. R. 63, 98 Fed. 76 (D. C. Wis.). This case was reversed, on other grounds, by the Supreme Court in Wilson v. Nelson, 7 A. B. R. 142, 183 U. S. 191. Also, contra (obiter), In re Simonson, Whiteson & Co., 1 A. B. R. 197, 92 Fed. 904 (D. C. Ky.).

§ 277½. Who to Verify for Partnership; for Corporation.—A member of the firm may verify for a partnership, and the president for a corporation.

In re Walker, 21 A. B. R. 132, 164 Fed. 680 (C. C. A..Calif.): "It cannot be doubted that, since a corporation must act through some agent, a verification in its behalf may be made by its president. Nor can it be doubted that a member of a partnership may properly verify a claim made on behalf of the firm of which he is a member."

But, doubtless, they are not the sole persons qualified for such purpose.

It is not necessary that the treasurer of a corporation verify an involuntary petition, where the corporation is a petitioning creditor. Such requirement concerns only proofs of debt after adjudication.

§ 278. Form of Oath.—No particular form of oath is requisite.

In re Bellah, 8 A. B. R. 310, 116 Fed. 69 (D. C. Del.): "While a petition in involuntary bankruptcy must be signed and verified in duplicate by the petitioning creditors, or those authorized to represent them, the Bankruptcy Act does not provide or require that such petition shall be verified by a formal affidavit or an affidavit of any sort, the only provision applicable to the verification of such petition being that 'all pleadings setting up matters of facts shall be verified under oath.' "

But the verification should be positive, not on information and belief.[92]

In re Ball, 19 A. B. R. 609, 156 Fed. 682 (D. C. N. Y.): "The Petition is to be followed by a verification. 'United States of America, District of ...., ss.: ...., ..., ..., being three of the petitioners above named, do hereby make solemn oath that the statements contained in the foregoing petition subscribed by them are true.' It would seem from the language of the prescribed form that a petition in involuntary bankruptcy is looked upon in the same light as a complaining affidavit in the matter of a criminal charge. The language 'your petitioners further represent that' is the statement of a conclusion and of an allegation which it is apparent must in all cases be made upon hearsay, information and knowledge derived from sources other than the actual personal knowledge of the party making the petition. The language of the verification is to the effect that the petitioners swear that the statement made by them is true. This statement is that they 'represent' or allege to the court the doing of certain things by the alleged bankrupt. The affiant swears that he charges certain acts against the bankrupt, and he implies that he has verified them so as to be willing to stand by the consequences of his charge. He is not testifying as to what he has seen or done. The verification is not equivalent to an oath that the person making the verification has actual knowledge that certain acts were done, because they occurred in the presence of the petitioner. The oath is not subject to the rules of competency with respect to hearsay testimony. On this account the insertion of the words in a petition, that it is made upon information and belief, neither add to nor detract from the strength of the allegation, and like-

92. See Supreme Court Form No. 3. "............ do hereby make solemn oath that the statements contained in the foregoing petition subscribed by them are true."

wise in the verification the additional statement, that the petitioners believe the matters which are stated to be alleged upon information and belief to be true, is mere surplusage, and while the language should not be used, it is no ground for dismissing the petition. The cases cited are not, in the opinion of the court, in contradiction of this view."

§ 279. Agent to Allege Capacity and Authority.—The person verifying for a corporation or as agent for another must state his capacity and that he is authorized.[93]

In re Bellah, 8 A. B. R. 310, 116 Fed. 69 (D. C. Del.): "A corporation can act only through its officers, or agents, and where its name is subscribed by an individual to a petition in involuntary bankruptcy, and the petition purports to be verified by the same person, it is necessary that such person should set forth under oath or affirmation that he was authorized to sign and verify the petition on behalf of the corporation. The omission of such an averment, unless remedied, is fatal; but is not an incurable defect, jurisdictional or otherwise."

In re Levingston, 13 A. B. R. 357 (D. C. Hawaii): "The authority of an agent to act for his principal in petitioning for adjudication in involuntary bankruptcy, is material and should be set forth in the affidavit or otherwise established."

§ 280. Amendment of Verification Permitted.—Even if the verification be irregular the petition will not, as a rule, be stricken from the files; for the court will usually give an opportunity for correct verification to be made.[94]

§ 281. Each Petitioner to Verify.—The petition must be verified by each petitioner.[95]

§ 282. Waiver of Objections to Verification.—Objections to the verification may be waived.[96] They may be waived by the bankrupt answering over, where the bankrupt is the objecting party;[97] or by the bankrupt appear-

---

93. (1867) In re Sargent, Fed. Cas. No. 12,361. Authority of president of corporation to institute or join in filing bankruptcy proceedings against a debtor, held to be conclusive under the terms of a certain by-law, until revoked by board of directors. In re Winston, 10 A. B. R. 171, 122 Fed. 187 (D. C. Tenn.).

94. In re Vastbinder, 11 A. B. R. 119, 126 Fed. 417 (D. C. Pa.); In re Bellah, 8 A. B. R. 310, 116 Fed. 69 (D. C. Del.). Inferentially, Bank v. Craig Bros., 6 A. B. R. 381, 110 Fed. 137 (D. C. Ky.). Inferentially, In re Nelson, 1 A. B. R. 63, 98 Fed. 76 (D. C. Wis., reversed, on other grounds, by Sup. Ct., 7 A. B. R. 142); Armstrong v. Fernandez, 19 A. B. R. 746, 208 U. S. 324, quoted at § 261.

95. Inferentially, Bank v. Craig Bros., 6 A. B. R. 381, 110 Fed. 137 (D. C. Ky.). But that all have not veri-

fied, is not jurisdictional; and the proper remedy is to move for a rule to require a proper verification, and if the rule is not complied with, to move to dismiss the petition for that reason.

96. Failure to File Petition and Schedules at Time of Verification.— Failure to file the petition and schedules at the time of their verification is not a jurisdictional defect to be taken advantage of after adjudication. In re Berner, 3 A. B. R. 325 (Ref. Ohio).

97. In re Plymouth Cordage Co., 13 A. B. R. 668, 135 Fed. 1000 (C. C. A. Okla.); Leidigh Carriage Co. v. Stengel, 2 A. B. R. 383, 95 Fed. 637 (C. C. A. Ohio); In re Herzikopf, 9 A. B. R. 90, 118 Fed. 101 (D. C. Calif.); In re Vastbinder, 11 A. B. R. 118, 126 Fed. 418 (D. C. Pa.); (1867) Roche v. Fox, Fed. Cas. No. 11,974.

ing and going into the merits notwithstanding his motion is solely to the jurisdiction;[98] or by the bankrupt's failure to raise the objection within the time limited for pleading.[99] Doubtless there are other things that would operate as waivers.

§ 282½. Annexing Interrogatories.—There is no statutory provision for the annexing of interrogatories,[1] and such interrogatories have been held improper in a case where it was sought thereby to obtain indirectly a "general" examination into the "acts, conduct and property of the bankrupt" before adjudication.[2] But, as previously remarked,[3] the ordinary remedies by way of discovery pertinent to the issues framed on the petition ought not to be denied to the petitioning creditors.

DIVISION 3.

FILING IN DUPLICATE.

§ 283. Involuntary Petition to Be Filed in Duplicate.—The petition in involuntary bankruptcy must be filed in duplicate, one copy for the clerk to keep for the files, the other for service on the bankrupt with the writ of subpœna. They are duplicate originals.[4]

§ 284. Waiver by Appearance.—The objection that it was not filed in duplicate is waived by answering over or general appearance within four months of the commission of the alleged act of bankruptcy.

In re Plymouth Cordage Co., 13 A. B. R. 668, 135 Fed. 1000 (C. C. A. Okla.): "The objection that a petitioner in bankruptcy failed to file a duplicate of his petition is waived by an answer by the bankrupt within four months of the alleged acts of bankruptcy without presenting the objection."

But it has been held that, where an involuntary petition is filed within the four months period, but the duplicate is not filed within such period, the proceedings are invalidated and the debtor cannot be adjudged bankrupt;[5] even though thereafter the respondent appears, generally, and without objection.[6] But this is not good law. The object of requiring the duplicate is to supply the respondent with a copy, and he may waive the privilege.

In re Plymouth Cordage Co., 13 A. B. R. 668, 135 Fed. Rep. 1000 (C. C. A. Okla.): "The copy for service on the bankrupt is for his benefit. The only object of requiring its filing is to give him a copy of the petition, in order to

---

98. In re Smith, 9 A. B. R. 98, 117 Fed. 961 (D. C. Conn.).

99. In re Simonson, 1 A. B. R. 197, 92 Fed. 904 (D. C. Ky.).

1. In re Thompson, 24 A. B. R. 655, 179 Fed. 874 (D. C. Pa.).

2. Compare post, §§ 412½, 1543; ante, § 181½. In re Thompson, 24 A. B. R. 655, 179 Fed. 874 (D. C. Pa.).

3. Compare ante, § 181½.

4. Bankr. Act, § 59 (c); In re Stev-enson, 2 A. B. R. 66, 94 Fed. 110 (D. C. Del.); In re Bellah, 8 A. B. R. 321, 116 Fed. 69 (D. C. Del.); In re Plymouth Cordage Co., 13 A. B. R. 667, 135 Fed. 1000 (C. C. A.).

5. In re Stevenson, 2 A. B. R. 66, 94 Fed. 110 (D. C. Del.).

6. In re Stevenson, 2 A. B. R. 66, 94 Fed. 110 (D. C. Del.); In re Dupree, 8 A. B. R. 321, note, 97 Fed. 28 (D. C.).

enable him to answer it. The right to it is a personal privilege, which he may demand and secure or may renounce and waive. As the only benefit of the privilege is to enable him more speedily and conveniently to answer the petition, an answer without a demand of the privilege is a waiver of it. It stops the bankrupt from thereafter insisting upon it, because it leads the petitioner to proceed and to incur expenses in reliance upon the renunciation of the privilege which has become functus officio by the answer."

Division 4.

Deposit for Cost and Poverty Affidavits.

§ 285. Deposit for Costs.—The party filing the bankruptcy petition, whether it be a voluntary or involuntary petition, must accompany it with a deposit of $30.00; $15.00 of which is for the referee, $10.00 for the clerk, and $5.00 for the trustee.[7] The deposit is the same in both voluntary and involuntary bankruptcies.

§ 286. Indemnity for Expenses.—In addition, indemnity for the expenses of the referee also may be—and usually is by rule of court—demanded in advance.[8]

§ 287. Poverty Affidavit.—In cases of voluntary bankruptcy the peti-

---

7. See Bankr. Act, § 40 (a), as to the deposit for the referee; § 48 (a) as to that for the trustee; and § 52 as to the clerk's fee.

Clerk Entitled to $5 per Diem Compensation for Days When Voluntary Petitions Referred during Absence of Judge.—The clerk is entitled to his statutory compensation of $5.00 per diem for days on which voluntary petitions in bankruptcy filed during the absence of the judge from the district are referred. United States v. Marvin, 212 U. S. 275, 22 A. B. R. 717.

8. The clerk is also entitled to reimbursement for his expenses necessarily incurred in publishing or mailing notices or other papers, and may charge a certain rate for each notice he sends, not as a fee but as a means of covering his estimated expenses in publishing or mailing notices. In re Hardware & Furniture Co., 14 A. B. R. 186, 134 Fed. 997 (D. C. N. Car.).

Gen. Order No. XXXV: "1. The fees allowed by the act to clerks shall be in full compensation for all services performed by them in regard to filing petitions or other papers required by the act to be filed with them, or in certifying or delivering papers or copies of records to referees or other officers, or in receiving or paying out money; but shall not include copies furnished to other persons, or expenses

necessarily incurred in publishing or mailing notices or other papers.

"2. The compensation of referees, prescribed by the act, shall be in full compensation for all services, performed by them under the act or under these general orders; but shall not include expenses necessarily incurred by them in publishing or mailing notices, in traveling, or in perpetuating testimony, or other expenses necessarily incurred in the performance of their duties under the act and allowed by special order of the judge.

"3. The compensation allowed to trustees by the act shall be in full compensation for the services, performed by them; but shall not include expenses necessarily incurred in the performance of their duties and allowed upon the settlement of their accounts.

"4. In any case in which the fees of the clerk, referee, and trustee are not required by the act to be paid by a debtor before filing his petition to be adjudged a bankrupt, the judge, at any time during the pendency of the proceedings in bankruptcy, may order those fees to be paid out of the estate; or may, after notice to the bankrupt, and satisfactory proof that he then has or can obtain the money with which to pay those fees, order him to pay them within a time specified, and, if he fails to do so, may order his petition to be dismissed."

1 R B—17

tioner may be excused from making these deposits—except the indemnity for expenses—upon filing what is called a poverty affidavit and proving to the satisfaction of the court an absolute inability to make the deposit.[9]

§ 288. Showing May Be Demanded in Addition to Poverty Affidavit.

—The mere filing of the poverty affidavit is not conclusive, although it is undoubtedly prima facie, proof. The court may demand other proof; and, in practice, the prospective bankrupt may be cross-examined as to his inability to make the deposit. Merely that he has no money, or no property except such as is exempt from levy of execution, or that it is inconvenient for him to get the money, will not suffice. There must exist absolute *inability* to raise money.

In re Levy, 4 A. B. R. 109, 101 Fed. 247 (D. C. Wis.): "Without adopting the extreme view there expressed (Sellers *v.* Bell, 2 A. B. R. 554, 94 Fed. 801), I am clearly of opinion that the statute intends to exempt a petitioner who has no means, from making the preliminary deposit of $25, and must be fairly interpreted to that end; that the affidavit in connection with the schedules establishes prima facie right to such exemption, subject, however, to investigation; and, if the inquiry is fairly answered respecting available means, and none appear held by the petitioner when the proceedings were instituted, nor obtainable through his individual earnings or efforts, the exemption must be allowed."

In re Bean, 4 A. B. R. 54, 100 Fed. 262 (D. C. Vt.): The court held that money subject to exemption "may be subject to an order for payment of statutory fees which are primarily for the benefit of the bankrupt and do not depend upon property not exempt but upon absolute inability."

In re Hines, 9 A. B. R. 27, 117 Fed. Rep. 790 (D. C. W. Va.): "A fair construction of the above language indicates that it was the intention of the act to allow voluntary bankrupts to file their petition without the payment in advance of the fees therefor, only in case they did not have, and could not obtain, the money with which to pay such fees. In other words, if the bankrupt was absolutely without money or effects of any kind, but was able to borrow from his friends money with which to pay the court costs, he could not properly make the affidavit required in this case, and it would be his duty to pay the fees. * * * The petitioner is not a pauper in the sense of the Bankruptcy Act. Exemptions allowed by the statute were not intended to cover exonerations from the payment of the fees provided for the court officers by that act. Having held that the statute does not confer upon a voluntary petitioner in bankruptcy the unqualified right to proceed upon his own affidavit as to his poverty, it follows that if, from the schedule filed by such petitioner, facts appear which are at variance with such affidavit, an order should be made requiring the bankrupt to deposit such fees before proceeding further with the case."

In re Collier, 1 A. B. R. 182, 93 Fed. 191 (D. C. Tenn.): "It cannot be * * * the intention of the statute to confer upon the petitioner the unqualified right to proceed in bankruptcy upon his own affidavit as to his poverty, nor that such affidavit should be taken as conclusive of the fact. * * * And the court will not be satisfied in doubtful cases until an inquiry has been made into the circumstances."

9. Bankr. Act, § 51 (a) (2); In re Mason, 25 A. B. R. 73, 181 Fed. 899 (D. C. Ala.).

Obiter, contra, Sellers v. Bell, 2 A. B. R. 554, 94 Fed. 801 (C. C. A. Ala.): "If these ideas are to find permanent lodgment in the minds of the judges of the courts of bankruptcy and become active, the carefully expressed provisions of the Bankruptcy Act granting the right to insolvent debtors to present their petition for relief in some cases in forma pauperis will not only be denied, but this humane and benevolent bounty from the government will be tortured into a most malignant snare. It is manifest that paragraph 4 of General Order 35 relates only to cases in voluntary bankruptcy, and the language shows that there may be such cases in which the petitioning debtor is not required to pay the fees of the clerk, referee, and trustee before or at the time of filing his petition, although he presents a schedule of property in excess of the exemptions allowed by the law of the State of his domicile and surrenders an estate in bankruptcy. Otherwise, it would be futile to provide that 'the judge at any time during the pendency of the proceedings in bankruptcy may order those fees to be paid out of the estate.' The terms of the affidavit, as prescribed by sec. 52, are 'that he is without, and cannot obtain, the money with which to pay such fees.' This affidavit may well be made in cases in which there is an estate to be surrendered, consisting not in money or in property that has a market value or can be converted into money by the petitioning debtor without substantial sacrifice of its value, and from which, therefore, he could not obtain the money in the exercise of perfect good faith towards the court and his creditors. Upon the presentation of his petition and schedules, accompanied by the affidavit in the terms of the statute, the clerk has no option as to filing the petition and taking the action thereon prescribed by the law. The judge of the Court of Bankruptcy, on the motion of parties interested, or on his own motion, after notice to the bankrupt, may have satisfactory proof that the bankruptcy has not made a full surrender of his assets, and that he then has, or can obtain, the money with which to pay those fees." But this case is obiter since it was concerned with an opposition to discharge on the ground of having committed a false oath in swearing to a poverty affidavit.

If afterward the court is satisfied that the bankrupt has obtained or can obtain the money for these fees, the judge, upon notice to the bankrupt, may order him to pay them, on penalty of a dismissal of the proceedings.[10]

In re Mason, 25 A. B. R. 73, 181 Fed. 899 (D. C. Ala.): "Money belonging to the petitioner, either in his hands or otherwise held subject to his order, is * * * subject to an order for the payment of the statutory fees."

§ 289. One Deposit for Partnership and One for Each Partner Adjudicated.

—It has been held that in partnership cases one deposit will not be enough: that there must be one deposit for each estate administered.[11]

---

10. Gen. Ord. No. XXXV (4); Anonymous, 2 A. B. R. 527 (D. C. Wash.). Apparently contra, Sellers v. Bell, 2 A. B. R. 529, 94 Fed. 801 (C. C. A. Ala.). But this was a case of opposition to discharge for swearing falsely that he could not obtain filing fees.

In re Herbold, 14 A. B. R. 119 (D. C. Wash.): In this case the court, obiter, says the bankrupt may be cited for contempt for not paying; but there is no authority for this assertion. Gen. Order No. XXV prescribes the remedy for noncompliance.

But the judge, not the referee (unless perhaps under local rule of court), must be the one to make the order, In re Plimpton, 4 A. B. R. 614, 103 Fed. 775 (D. C. Vt.).

11. Obiter, In re Mercur, 10 A. B. R. 510 (C. C. A. Pa.). Contra (in a voluntary case), In re Langslow, 1 A. B. R. 258, 98 Fed. 869 (D. C. N. Y.). Contra, In re Gay, 3 A. B. R. 529, 98 Fed. 870 (D. C. N. Y.).

In re Barden, 4 A. B. R. 31, 101 Fed. 555 (D. C. N. Car.): "Other sections might be quoted to illustrate the provisions peculiar to partnerships, but the foregoing are sufficient to show a recognition of the partnership as a distinct entity and the legislative intent to recognize different estates when a partnership and the individual partners are adjudged bankrupt—the sense in which the words 'each estate' is used in the section providing for the payment of the clerk's fees: * * * In short the proceedings are separate, the estates different. The only logical conclusion from the act itself—keeping in view the legislative intent deducible therefrom, 'estate' having no restricted technical meaning but meaning the ownings, real and personal property, choses in action, whatever may belong to the person as defined in the statute—is that Congress meant exactly what the statute provides. Clerks shall receive for their services to each estate a filing fee of ten dollars, that is ten dollars for filing the petition and schedules of the partnership and ten dollars for filing the petition and schedules of each individual member thereof—ten dollars for each estate to be administered. And if Congress thus used the words 'each estate' it is not probable the phrase 'in each case' was used in a more restricted sense. * * * As the estates must be kept separate, the petition and schedules being different, many questions may arise as to the estates of the firm or individual members, thus making several cases. Because the papers are or may be filed in the same file case, jacket or envelope does not of necessity make them one and the same case. * * * My conclusion is that the proper construction of the statute in proceedings where a petition is filed by a partnership to have a firm adjudged bankrupt, and petitions by the individual members of the firm, each petition and the accompanying schedules, constitute separate and distinct cases, hence the referee and trustee are entitled to a fee of ten dollars and five dollars respectively in each case—one on the partnership petition, and one on the petition of each individual member. The general idea of the bankrupt law is economy in its administration, but above this the law is just—just to bankrupts, just to creditors, and was intended to be just to the officers of the court. Any other construction would not be in keeping with the spirit of the law, but flagrantly unjust to the officers."

In re Farley & Co., 8 A. B. R. 266, 115 Fed. 359 (D. C. Va.): "The language of the act in respect to the fees of the referee and trustee is not so plain. Sections 40a and 48a. In each, the language is a fee 'in each case' to be deposited with the clerk at the time the petition is filed. If I am right in thinking that three petitions should have been filed in the matter in hand, it seems clear that the word 'case' as used in the act is intended to apply to the duties of these officers as to each estate. And even if separate petitions are not necessary, it still does not follow that the proceedings as to the three separate estates constitute only one 'case.' * * * If only a firm petition is filed and a discharge of the members of the firm quoad the firm liabilities only is wanted, then only one fee should be allowed to each officer. In such a case it is true that the several estates of the firm and the partners will be involved, but only the firm estate will be administered. If, however, the partners seek discharges, both as against the firm creditors and as against their respective individual creditors, it is evident that the several estates must be administered. In such cases several fees are allowable."

§ 290. Return of Deposit in Involuntary Cases, but Not in Voluntary.

—The deposit will be returned to the petitioners in involuntary cases out of the funds of the estates, but in purely voluntary bankruptcies it will

not be returned, because the money deposited by the bankrupt on the filing
of his petition would belong to his trustee in any event.

In re Matthews, 3 A. B. R. 265, 97 Fed. 772 (D. C. Iowa): "The provisions
of General Order No. 10 do not apply to the deposit of $25, which the clerk,
under section 51 of the Bankrupt Act, is required to collect from the bankrupt
when he files his petition. The money thus collected by the clerk is intended
to cover the statutory fees to be paid to the clerk, referee, and trustee as compensation for their services; and being paid to the clerk when the petition is
filed, the amount of the estate passing to the trustee is lessened by that sum, and,
if this amount should be now returned to the bankrupt, he would be receiving
part of his estate as it belonged to him before he filed his petition, which estate
by the adjudication became in fact the property of the creditors. The provisions of General Order No. 10 are intended to cover money which the bankrupt
or some third party may be called upon to furnish after the initiation of the
proceedings in order to meet expenses incurred by the officer for the purposes
specially recited in the order, which purposes do not include the money deposited with the clerk to meet the fees (not expenses) of the clerk, referee and
trustee. Money thus advanced, if the bankrupt has met the requirements of
the law with respect to turning over his estate to his creditors, is deemed to
have been obtained from sources other than the estate belonging to the creditors, and therefore provision is made for its repayment out of the estate. The
purpose of the order is to protect the officers from personal loss in the performance of their duties under the Bankrupt Act, but it is not the intent of the order
that the bankrupt shall be repaid the money which presumably he took out of
his estate to pay the fees of officers before he filed his petition in bankruptcy."

§ 291. Return Where Voluntary and Involuntary Petitions Both Pending and Adjudication on Voluntary.

—If a voluntary petition is
filed and adjudication had thereon during the pendency of an involuntary
petition against the same debtor, it has been held that the petitioning creditors may have their deposit and expenses repaid out of the estate in
the voluntary proceedings.

In re Stegar, 7 A. B. R. 665, 113 Fed. 978 (D. C. Ala.): "Creditors by commencing the involuntary proceedings, incur liability for costs and attorneys'
fees, and, if the petition be wrongfully filed, for damages. They also get in
position to avoid preferences and transfers which might not be assailable on the
adjudication under the later voluntary petition. The court cannot deprive petitioning creditors of these rights, or enlarge their liabilities, by dismissing
the prior involuntary proceeding in order to administer the estate under the
voluntary petition. How, then, are the rights of petitioning creditors to be
saved, if they are not allowed to proceed, and the administration of the insolvent estate is had under the insolvent's voluntary petition, subsequently
filed?

"A debtor who, without appearing in an involuntary proceeding, subsequently
files a voluntary petition, upon which he is adjudged a bankrupt, cannot complain of the filing of the involuntary petition. The court would never dismiss the
creditor's petition under such circumstances; and unless the petition were dismissed, or petitioners withdrew it, there could not, under the plain terms of the
Bankrupt Act, be any liability to the defendant. This liability out of the way,
it would remain to save the creditors harmless as to costs and attorney's fees.

This is easily effected by directing an adjudication on the voluntary proceeding, staying the involuntary proceeding in the meanwhile, reserving to petitioning creditors the right to prove their costs and expenditures under the adjudication on the voluntary petition with leave to bring forward the involuntary petition if subsequently it be found necessary to protect rights which could not be saved by adjudication under the voluntary petition."

This case (In re Stegar) lays down doubtful law, however, where no adjudication nor finding is actually made upon the involuntary petition. If creditors have not established their right upon the facts alleged by them, why should they be entitled to a return of their deposit for costs which otherwise would not be recoverable? Moreover, there is no rule of priority therefor laid down in the statute nor in the Supreme Court's orders.

There is a tendency in the courts continually to enlarge the number of allowances to be made out of insolvent estates beyond those limited in the statute. So many different claimants stand ready to dip into the estate for reimbursement that creditors always are in danger of being further and further postponed each year in bankruptcy administration. Besides the priorities specifically granted by the bankruptcy act itself, the list of those entitled to reimbursement out of the estate has been continually extended by judicial construction. The tendency of the courts to pay every litigant's expense bill out of the estate is contrary to the clear intent of the act. Certainly, if no showing is made by the petitioning creditors that they actually had the right of action alleged by them, they ought not to be reimbursed their costs and expenses out of the estate, simply because the bankrupt thereafter voluntarily petitions himself into bankruptcy.

CHAPTER VII.

Different Proceedings by or against Same Debtor Pending at Same Time.

Synopsis of Chapter.

§ 292. Statement of Situation.—Sometimes different proceedings are instituted contemporaneously against the same debtor in the same or in different jurisdictions; and likewise it frequently occurs that during the pendency of involuntary proceedings against a debtor he files a voluntary petition himself.

Complications thus are likely to arise requiring rules for the guidance of the court.

Division 1.

Practice Where Two or More Involuntary Bankruptcy Petitions Are Filed against the Same Debtor.

§ 293. Petition in District of Domicile First to Be Heard.—Where two or more involuntary petitions are pending at the same time against the same debtor, hearing shall be first had upon the petition filed in the district where the debtor had his domicile.[1]

This is so in the case of a corporation as well as in that of a natural person, the word "individual" as used in Gen. Order VI being the same as "person" and including a corporation.

In re United Button Co., 12 A. B. R. 766 (D. C. N. Y.): "While the use of the word cannot be regarded as fortunate for the purpose of clear expression, if the intent was to include corporations, yet it is concluded with some reluctance that such was the intent. It is of the greatest importance that the Bankruptcy Act should be administered with the utmost harmony as regards the several district courts, and that each of such courts should concede freely what is due to a particular court which has acquired jurisdiction and first undertaken the administration of a bankrupt's estate. Priority of jurisdiction should carry the right of administration, at least where it is followed by priority or adjudication, and, aside from the compulsion of General Order VI, such rule would prevail."

And the "district of his domicile" is the district wherein he has had his domicile for the preceding six months or the greater portion thereof.[2]

§ 294. In Partnership and Corporation Cases Petition First Filed, First Heard.

—In the case of a partnership, the petition first filed will be first heard;[3] and this is so whether all the different petitions were filed by creditors, or all by partners, and whether filed in different districts, or in the same district. In case one of the petitions be filed by creditors and the other by one of the partners, the general orders prescribe no express rule, but the petition first filed would properly be the one first heard. In the case of a corporation the same rule prevails.[4]

§ 295. Other Hearing Stayed.

—Hearing upon the other petitions may be stayed until adjudication is made upon the petition first heard.[5]

§ 296. Court Making First Adjudication Retains Jurisdiction.

—The court making the first adjudication of bankruptcy retains jurisdiction over all proceedings therein until the same are closed;[6] and may stay the

---

1. Gen. Ord. VI; In re United Button Co., 13 A. B. R. 454, 137 Fed. 668 (D. C. Del.); In re United Button Co., 12 A. B. R. 763, 132 Fed. 378 (D. C. N. Y.); obiter, In re Waxelbaum, 3 A. B. R. 395, 98 Fed. 589 (D. C. N. Y.); In re Isaacson, 20 A. B. R. 430, 161 Fed. 779 (D. C. N. Y.); In re Isaacson, 20 A. B. R. 437, 161 Fed. 777 (D. C. N. Y.).

2. In re Isaacson, 20 A. B. R. 430, 161 Fed. 779 (D. C. N. Y.); In re Isaacson, 20 A. B. R. 437, 161 Fed. 777 (D. C. N. Y.).

3. Gen. Ord. No. VI; In re Sears,

7 A. B. R. 279, 112 Fed. 58 (D. C. N. Y.).

4. In re Tybo Mining & Reduc. Co., 13 A. B. R. 62, 132 Fed. 697 (D. C. Nev.); In re Elmira Steel Co., 5 A. B. R. 484, 517, 528, 109 Fed. 456, 474, 480 (D. C. N. Y.).

5. Gen. Ord. No. VI; In re Tybo Mining & Reduc. Co., 13 A. B. R. 62, 132 Fed. 697 (D. C. Nev.).

6. Gen. Ord. No. VI. Two corporations with property and business so commingled as to be incapable of separation, both being bankrupt were in one case treated as a single corpo-

other proceedings.[7]

§ 297. But Court Having Right to Retain, May Relinquish.

—But the court having such right of retaining jurisdiction shall, if satisfied that it is for the greatest convenience of parties in interest, order the case to be transferred to one of the other courts where petitions have thus been filed.[8]

In re Isaacson, 20 A. B. R. 433, 161 Fed. 779 (D. C. N. Y.): "It may be assumed that General Order No. 6 is subject to the provisions of § 32 of the bankruptcy law, and that the case may be transferred and consolidated for the convenience of the parties, if brought within the provisions of § 32, in spite of the direction in the General Order that the court first adjudicating shall retain jurisdiction until the proceedings are closed."

But there must be clear warrant before the court abandons its duty to another court.

In re United Button Co., 13 A. B. R. 454, 137 Fed. 668 (D. C. Del.): "Unquestionable jurisdiction of the case, owing to the domicile of the bankrupt, existing here, the burden of satisfying this court that the greatest convenience of the parties in interest requires a removal of the case to New York, rests upon those seeking such removal. It is not going far to say that on general principles of policy a court having taken cognizance of a case within its undoubted jurisdiction should not abandon to other tribunals the performance of the duty it has assumed unless it has clear warrant for so doing. The Bankruptcy Act does not define or describe 'greatest convenience' or 'parties in interest,' as those phrases are used in § 32 and General Order VI. Both expressions are elastic and largely indefinite. It is manifestly too narrow a construction of the phrase 'parties in interest' to restrict it merely to unsecured creditors in bankruptcy. The bankrupt is not only literally but substantially a party in interest. A creditor holding a security which is sought to be set aside by the trustee in bankruptcy is also a party in interest. And it probably may be stated with accuracy that all persons whose pecuniary interests are directly affected by proceedings in bankruptcy are, within the true meaning of § 32 and General Order VI, parties in interest. What may be for the greatest convenience of parties in interest does not necessarily depend upon only one factor or circumstance entering into the situation. Proximity of the place of business of the bankrupt to the court entertaining proceedings in bankruptcy, though a circumstance sometimes entitled to weight is by no means conclusive, and the same may be said with respect to proximity to the place of manufacture. Proximity of a majority of the creditors of the bankrupt in number or in the amount of their claims is a circumstance which should also be duly weighed. And the

---

ration. In re Bridge & Iron Co., 13 A. B. R. 304, 133 Fed. 568 (D. C. Kans.).

Two corporations with property and business so commingled as to be incapable of separation, both being bankrupt, etc., compare post, §§ 304½, 305½.

7. In re United Button Co., 12 A. B. R. 761, 132 Fed. 378 (D. C. N. Y.).

Compensation of Receivers (before

Amendment of 1910) on Transfer.—In re Isaacson, 23 A. B. R. 98, 174 Fed. 406 (C. C. A. N. Y.).

8. Gen. Ord. No. VI; In re Waxelbaum, 3 A. B. R. 392, 98 Fed. 589 (D. C. N. Y.); In re General Metal Co., 12 A. B. R. 770, 133 Fed. 84 (D. C. N. Y.); In re Tybo Mining & Reduc. Co., 13 A. B. R. 62, 132 Fed. 697 (D. C. Nev.); In re Sears, 7 A. B. R. 278, 112 Fed. 58 (D. C. N. Y.). Instance where relinquishment refused, In re Pennsyl-

same may be said with at least equal force of a majority of the debtors of the bankrupt in number or in amount. Nor is the element of expedition or of economy in the administration of the estate in bankruptcy to be lost sight of. Taking into consideration all the circumstances disclosed by the petition, affidavits and exhibits, this court is not satisfied that the transfer of the case in hand to the District Court for the Southern District of New York would be for the greatest convenience of the parties in interest. I do not think that the petitioners have adduced the preponderance of evidence required of them as those on whom the onus of proof rests, to justify a removal."

Contra, In re General Metals Co., 12 A. B. R. 770, 133 Fed. 84 (D. C. N. Y.): "Under these circumstances, although neither district affords any very conspicuously superior advantages over the other as a place for the administration of the estate, I think upon the whole that the greatest convenience of the parties in interest will be subserved by having this estate administered in Colorado."

"Parties in interest" are not to be confined to unsecured creditors: all persons, including the bankrupt himself, are comprehended.[9] The burden of proof is on the parties desiring the transfer.[10]

The wish of the majority of the creditors is strong evidence, although not conclusive, as to the "greatest convenience."[11] Creditors who have received preferences which they do not offer to surrender will not be heard to urge their own convenience.[12]

§ 298. Amendment by Adopting Earlier Act from Other Petitions.
—The petition in the case first heard may be amended by adding any earlier act of bankruptcy alleged in any of the other petitions;[13] but, apparently, not by the addition of a later act.[14]

In re Sears, 8 A. B. R. 713, 117 Fed. 294 (C. C. A. N. Y.): "The order allowing an amendment of the petition by the insertion of a further act of bankruptcy was erroneous, because it clearly appeared that such act of bankruptcy was not an earlier act than that first alleged, but was later. The case is controlled by the terms of General Order No. 6, and, as that makes explicit provision for it, an amendment not within its terms is unwarranted. Except for that provision, such an amendment would have been permissible, and its allowance a reasonable exercise of judicial discretion; but the provision, by implication, limits the power of amendment to the single case in which an earlier act of bankruptcy is sought to be incorporated into the petition."

It seems, however, quite a misapplication of the rule, "inclusio unius, exclusio alterius," to hold that the mere permission granted in General

---

vania Consol. Coal Co., 20 A. B. R. 872, 163 Fed. 579 (D. C. Penn.).

9. In re United Button Co., 13 A. B. R. 454, 137 Fed. 668 (D. C. Del.).

10. In re United Button Co., 13 A. B. R. 454, 137 Fed. 668 (D. C. Del.).

11. In re United Button Co., 13 A. B. R. 454, 137 Fed. 668 (D. C. Del.).

An erroneous transfer is not to be corrected by motion to vacate or annul but by usual petitions for review or appeal. Kyle Lumber Co. v. Bush, 13 A. B. R. 535, 133 Fed. 688 (C. C. A. Ala.).

12. In re Sears, 7 A. B. R. 278, 112 Fed. 58 (D. C. N. Y.).

13. Gen. Order No. VI.

14. Wilder v. Watts, 15 A. B. R. 57, 138 Fed. 426 (D. C. S. C.).

Order No. 6 to adopt an earlier act of bankruptcy alleged in the superseded petition, excludes the adoption of a later act. Such holding misses the very object of the general order, which, doubtless, is merely to prevent creditors losing the benefit of any earlier act alleged in the superseded petition, right to plead which might.not exist in the petitioning creditors of the superseding petition, because of the expiration of the four months period.

§ 298½. **Which Petition to Be First Heard.**—General Order No. 7 provides:

"Whenever two or more petitions shall be filed by creditors against a common debtor, alleging separate acts of bankruptcy committed by said debtor on different days within four months prior to the filing of said petitions, and the debtor shall appear and show cause against an adjudication of bankruptcy against him on the petitions, that petition shall be first heard and tried which alleges the commission of the earliest act of bankruptcy; and in case the several acts of bankruptcy are alleged in the different petitions to have been committed on the same day, the court before which the same are pending may order them to be consolidated, and proceed to a hearing upon one petition; and if an adjudication of bankruptcy be made upon either petition, or for the commission of a single act of bankruptcy, it shall not be necessary to proceed to a hearing upon the remaining petitions, unless proceedings be taken by the debtor for the purpose of causing such adjudication to be annulled or vacated."

But this general order No. 7 has no applicability where only one of the petitions is answered at all, for the unanswered petition is then the first to be heard.[15]

DIVISION 2.

PRACTICE WHERE VOLUNTARY AND INVOLUNTARY BANKRUPTCY PROCEEDINGS ARE PENDING AT THE SAME TIME AGAINST SAME DEBTOR.

§ 299. **Subsequent Voluntary Petition Allowable though Involuntary Pending.**—The pendency of an involuntary petition before adjudication will not of necessity invalidate a subsequent voluntary petition filed in the same or another district.[16]

In re Waxelbaum, 3 A. B. R. 392, 98 Fed. 589 (D. C. N. Y.): "The first petition may be invalid for lack of jurisdiction * * * or other considerations may justify a subsequent voluntary petition and the question of jurisdiction must be determined on each petition and neither is necessarily conclusive of the other."

In re Ralph Carpenter, 25 A. B. R. 161 (Ref. N. Y.): "The debtor has the right to avail himself of the benefits of the bankruptcy law on his own application, and this right cannot be forfeited or rendered ineffectual merely because

---

15. In re Harris, 19 A. B. R. 204, 156 Fed. 875 (D. C. Ala.).

16. In re Lachenmaier, 29 A. B. R. 325, 203 Fed. 32 (C. C. A. Wis.); In re New Chattanooga Hardware Co., 27 A. B. R. 77, 190 Fed. 240 (D. C. Tenn.).

Compare, In re Sterne & Levi, 26 A. B. R. 259, 190 Fed. 70 (D. C. Tex.). Compare, to same effect, under law of 1867. In re Canfield, Fed. Cas. No. 2,380.

the creditors' petition is first filed and pending undetermined when the debtor files his petition."

§ 300. But Notice to Petitioning Creditors First, before Adjudication on Voluntary Petition.

—Where a voluntary petition is filed whilst involuntary proceedings are pending, notice should be given to creditors before entry of adjudication is made on the voluntary petition, and thereupon the court should give priority to whichever petition seems proper.[17] The adjudication should be made in that proceeding which, under all the circumstances, appears to be for the best interest of the entire estate.[17a] But if adjudication has already been made on the voluntary petition notwithstanding the prior filing and pendency of an involuntary petition which it is for the best interests of creditors to maintain, it is proper practice for creditors to have an order served in the voluntary case upon the bankrupt to show cause why the voluntary adjudication should not be vacated and the petition be dismissed.[18]

§ 301. Precedence to Involuntary Petition Where Creditors' Rights Require.

—Precedence should be given to the involuntary petition and no adjudication be entered on the voluntary petition until the involuntary petition shall have been heard and decided, whenever it appears that if the estate is administered under the voluntary petition preferences or other voidable transfers will be rendered unassailable by reason of the expiration of the four months limitation.[19] And an adjudication entered on the voluntary petition before the hearing on the involuntary petition will be set aside.[20]

§ 302. But Adjudication on Voluntary Petition an Absolute Right Where Creditors' Rights Not Imperiled.

—But the right of a debtor to file a voluntary petition and to be adjudicated bankrupt thereon can not be denied and precedence be given to the involuntary proceedings, where it does not appear that thereby voidable transfers will be rendered unassailable by reason of the expiration of the four months limitation.[21]

17. In re Dwyer, 7 A. B. R. 532, 112 Fed. 777 (D. C. N. Dak.).

17a. In re New Chattanooga Hardware Co., 27 A. B. R. 77, 190 Fed. 240 (D. C. Tenn.).

18. Inferentially, In re Waxelbaum, 3 A. B. R. 395, 98 Fed. 589 (D. C. N. Y.).

19. In re Dwyer, 7 A. B. R. 532, 112 Fed. 777 (D. C. N. Dak.). Inferentially, In re Stegar, 7 A. B. R. 665, 113 Fed. 978 (D. C. Ala.).

Compare, on facts, voluntary and involuntary petitions filed in different districts, involuntary first filed but voluntary first to be adjudicated. In re Sterne & Levi, 26 A. B. R. 259, 190 Fed. 70 (D. C. Tex.).

Precedence to Involuntary Petition, First Filed, Even Though Adjudication on Voluntary Petition First Made and Creditors' Rights Not Imperiled.— In re Sterne & Levi, 26 A. B. R. 259, 190 Fed. 70 (D. C. Tex.).

20. In re Dwyer, 7 A. B. R. 532, 112 Fed. 777 (D. C. N. Dak.). See post, § 442.

21. Compare, however, to the effect that such rule only applies to proceedings pending in the same district, In re Sterne & Levi, 26 A. B. R. 259, 190 Fed. 70 (D. C. Tex.).

In re Stegar, 7 A. B. R. 665, 113 Fed. 978 (D. C. Ala.): "Ordinarily, how-ever, it is true that the debtor has the right to avail himself of the benefits of the Bankrupt Law on his own petition, and that this right cannot be forfeited or rendered ineffectual merely because the creditors' petition is first filed and pending undetermined when the debtor files his petition. A debtor has the un-doubted legal right to contest the involuntary proceeding, which must neces-sarily be based upon some violation of the act, of which the debtor may not be guilty, and is therefore unwilling to be adjudged guilty, although desirous to have his estate distributed among creditors on his own petition. The debtor is not bound to postpone this right because of the involuntary proceeding, and may, unless he has waived the right, push his own proceeding, and at the same time contest the creditors' proceeding. A voluntary and involuntary petition are filed in different rights, and based on different grounds, though the effects of the adjudication may be the same in each proceeding. The two petitions not being filed in the same right, nor based on the same cause, and an adverse judgment to the petitioning creditors being no bar to an adjudication on the voluntary proceeding, the mere pendency of a prior involuntary petition, upon which there has been neither hearing nor adjudication, is not ground for abate-ment of the subsequent voluntary petition."

In re Lachemaier, 29 A. B. R. 325, 203 Fed. 32 (C. C. A. Wis.): "Ordinarily it is in the interest of creditors to have the adjudication entered at once upon the voluntary petition. They thereby obviate the expense, difficulty and delay incident to establishing issues which the defendant may vigorously oppose. It is only where, by reason of the time elapsed between the filing of the invol-untary petition and of the voluntary, creditors through the trustee might not be able to recover property and avoid preferences, that the court will suspend the voluntary petition or set aside proceedings based thereon, in order that the involuntary proceeding may be pushed."

But the adjudication on the subsequently filed voluntary petition will not invalidate the involuntary proceedings.[22]

§ 303. Stay of Involuntary Petition to Ascertain Propriety of Ad-judication on Voluntary.

—The involuntary proceedings need not be dis-missed but may be stayed until, in the course of the administration of the voluntary proceedings, it is ascertained that creditors' rights would be preju-diced, whereupon trial may be had upon the involuntary petition.[23]

---

22. Gleason v. Smith, 16 A. B. R. 606, 145 Fed. 895 (C. C. A. Pa.).

23. In re Stegar, 7 A. B. R. 665, 113 Fed. 978 (D. C. Ala.).

Deposit for Costs.—As to the right of the petitioning creditors in the in-voluntary case to reimbursement of their deposit for costs and their ex-penses out of the voluntary case, see ante, ch. VI, § 285, et seq.

Proof of claims or acceptance of div-idends in the voluntary proceedings will not be a bar or waiver of the right to prove the claims under the involun-tary proceedings, In re Stegar, 7 A. B. R. 665, 113 Fed. 978 (D. C. Ala.).

Consolidation of voluntary and in-voluntary proceedings "without prej-udice" does not mean that adverse claimants who have obtained posses-sion by replevin after the filing of the petition shall be permitted to retain possession. In re Briskman, 13 A. B. R. 57, 132 Fed. 201 (D. C. N. Y.).

As to voluntary and involuntary pe-titions in the same court under the law of 1867; In re Stewart, 3 N. B. Reg. 109, Fed. Cas., No. 13,419; In re Wie-larski, 4 N. B. Reg. 390, Fed. Cases, No. 17,619; In re Flanagan, 5 Sawy. 312, 18 N. B. Reg. 439, Fed. Cases, No. 4,850; In re Canfield, Fed. Cases, No. 2,380.

§ 304. Voluntary and Involuntary Petitions in Different Districts —Bankrupt's Domicile Preferred.—Where the involuntary and the voluntary petitions have been filed in different districts, the case should be heard in the district of the bankrupt's domicile, or else transferred to the district where it would be for the greater convenience of the parties in interest.[24]

§ 304¼. "Greatest Convenience of Parties in Interest."—Neither the Bankruptcy Act nor the General Orders define "greatest convenience" nor "parties in interest."[25] But "greatest convenience" depends on all the circumstances—proximity of a majority of the creditors, proximity of the place of business of the bankrupt, proximity of witnesses and other circumstances;[26] whilst the term "parties in interest" covers every party who has any interest in or connection with the case, among others secured, priority and unsecured creditors, also the bankrupt himself.[27]

§ 304½. Consolidation of Partnership, Corporation and Individual Petitions.—Where not only a partnership and its members have been adjudicated bankrupts, but also a corporation, the principal part of whose stock is owned by one of the partners (the corporate entity being, furthermore a mere fiction), even such apparently distinct proceedings have been ordered consolidated.[28]

DIVISION 3.

PRACTICE WHERE FEDERAL EQUITY PROCEEDINGS IN THE UNITED STATES CIRCUIT COURT IN WHICH A RECEIVER IS IN CHARGE OF THE ASSETS ARE PENDING IN THE SAME DISTRICT WHEREIN THE INVOLUNTARY BANKRUPTCY PETITION IS FILED.

§ 305. Whether Bankruptcy Proceedings Have Precedence over Federal Equity Proceedings in Same District.—Where federal equity proceedings, not in bankruptcy, are pending in the same district where the involuntary bankrupt petition is filed, the creditors have the absolute right to proceed with the bankruptcy proceedings regardless of expenses, delay or inconvenience or the fact that it would be to the best interests of the great majority of the creditors to have the assets administered in the United States Circuit Court.[29]

24. In re Waxelbaum, 3 A. B. R. 392, 98 Fed. 589 (D. C. N. Y.).
   But compare, In re Sterne & Levi, 26 A. B. R. 259, 190 Fed. 70 (D. C. Tex.), wherein the rule is laid down that, under such circumstances the involuntary petition—if first filed—should be given precedence, unless for convenience of parties.
25. In re Sterne & Levi, 26 A. B. R. 259, 190 Fed. 70 (D. C. Tex.).
26. In re United Button Co., 13 A. B. R. 454, 137 Fed. 668 (D. C. Del.); In re Sterne & Levi, 26 A. B. R. 259, 190 Fed. 70 (D. C. Tex.).
27. In re United Button Co., 13 A. B. R. 454, 137 Fed. 668 (D. C. Del.); In re Sterne & Levi, 26 A. B. R. 259, 190 Fed. 70 (D. C. Tex.).
28. Salt Lake Valley Canning Co. v. Collins, 23 A. B. R. 716, 176 Fed. 91 (C. C. A. Mont.). Compare ante, § 296; note and post, § 305½.
29. Compare ante, § 159.

Obiter, Woolford *v.* Steel Co., 15 A. B. R. 36, 138 Fed. 582 (D. C. Del.): "If the petitions were not defective, the petitioners would have a right under the Bankruptcy Act to proceed to support them by evidence, and, if successful, to have the Diamond State Steel Company adjudged bankrupt, regardless of any delay, confusion or expense attending such a course."

But if the petition in bankruptcy is defective the court may take into account the unwisdom of the bankruptcy proceedings in passing upon an application for leave to amend and may refuse amendment where ordinarily it would have allowed amendment.[30]

But, unless the equity proceedings come within the rules of supersedence laid down post, § 1582, et seq., the custody of the res will not be superseded.

Compare, In re Ellsworth Co., 23 A. B. R. 284, 173 Fed. 699 (D. C. N. Y.): "The Bankruptcy Act has not superseded the right and power of a court of equity to take charge of the property of an insolvent corporation for the protection of stockholders and creditors, marshal the same, recognize and enforce valid liens and priorities, and equitably distribute the surplus proceeds among its creditors. It is only where a receiver has been appointed in another court because of insolvency, as that term is defined in the bankruptcy law, or where the corporation on its own initiative has applied for the appointment of a receiver or custodian of its property, that an act of bankruptcy under § 3a, subd. 4, has been committed. This provision of the bankruptcy law must be strictly construed. * * * If the company, while insolvent had voluntarily brought an action to wind up its affairs for the benefit of its creditors and had applied for the appointment of receivers, the superior right of the bankruptcy court could not be questioned." Quoted further, ante, §§ 153, 158, 159.

DIVISION 4.
JOINDER OF DEBTORS WHO ARE NOT PARTNERS.

§ 305¼. Nothing Less than Actual Partnership Sufficient for Joinder of Parties.—Nothing less than an actual partnership will permit of a joinder of parties defendant.[31]

§ 305½. Inextricable Commingling of Corporate Affairs.—It has been held that where a corporation was organized in one state to take over the business of another corporation in another state and their affairs had become so commingled that they could not be extricated, the two might be joined, and that the court of the district first obtaining jurisdiction over both might retain it.[32]

And partnership, corporation and individual bankruptcies have been consolidated in cases where the fiction of corporate entity was to be ignored.[33]

---

30. Woolford *v.* Steel Co., 15 A. B. R. 36, 138 Fed. 582 (D. C. Del.).
31. Compare, § 40; also, § 63.
32. In re Alaska American Fish Co., 20 A. B. R. 712, 162 Fed. 498 (D. C. Wash.). Similarly, In re Bridge & Iron Co., 133 Fed. 568, 13 A. B. R. 304; compare, "Remington on Bankruptcy," § 296.
33. See ante, § 304½.

CHAPTER VIII.

COMMENCEMENT OF PROCEEDINGS, SERVICE OF PROCESS AND RULE DAYS FOR PLEADINGS.

Synopsis of Chapter.

§ 306. Filing of Petition Commencement of Proceedings.—The filing of the petition is the commencement of proceedings.[1] It is the time of the filing of the petition, not that of the issuance nor service of the subpœna thereon that controls.[2] The petition is "filed" when delivered to the clerk and marked "filed" even though not delivered at the office nor during office hours.[3] As previously noted (§ 190) in voluntary cases only one petition is to be filed, although it is to be accompanied by triplicate copies of the schedules; but in involuntary cases, on the other hand, the petition must be prepared and filed in duplicate—one for the court, the other for service on the alleged bankrupt.

§ 307. Service of Process, According to Federal Equity Practice.—Service of process shall be by service of the duplicate petition and subpœna according to federal equity practice, except that it is returnable within fifteen days; unless longer time be fixed by the judge.[4]

1. In re Hicks, 6 A. B. R. 182, 107 Fed. 910 (D. C. Vt.). As to effect of delay in filing petition after same sworn to, see ante, footnote to, § 282.
2. In re Appel, 4 A. B. R. 722, 103 Fed. 931 (D. C. Neb.); In re Lewis, 1 A. B. R. 458, 91 Fed. 632 (D. C. N. Y.); Shulte v. Patterson, 17 A. B. R. 99 (C. C. A. Iowa); In re Stein, 5 A. B. R. 288, 105 Fed. 749 (C. C. A.).
3. In re Wolf, 2 A. B. R. 322 (D. C. N. J.).
4. See Bankr. Act, § 18 (a): "Upon the filing of a petition for involuntary bankruptcy, service thereof, with a writ of subpœna, shall be made upon the person therein named as defendant in the same manner that service of such process is now had upon the commencement of a suit in equity in the courts of the United States, except that it shall be returnable within fifteen days, unless the judge shall for cause fix a longer time." Hills v. McKinniss Co., 26 A. B. R. 329, 188 Fed. 1012 (D. C. Ohio).

But an order that "process issue as prayed for" is not sufficient to warrant an extension of the return-day thereof; nor can an unwarranted extension of the time be cured by the elimination of Sundays and holidays. In re Francis,

§ 308. Service by Publication.—If personal service is not available, then service is to be had by publication; and such publication is to be in accordance with the federal equity practice relative to enforcing liens, except that the order shall, unless otherwise directed by the judge, be published not more than once a week for two consecutive weeks, the return day to be ten days after the last publication, unless the judge fixes a longer time.[5]

The day on which the defendant is to appear and answer, demur or plead must be designated in the order of publication, else the order is defective.[6]

Adjudication upon service by publication is as effective for all purposes as upon personal service; thus, for example, the trustee subsequently elected has precisely the same right to proceed to recover property in another district as if the adjudication had been based on personal service.[7]

Service by publication is constructive notice to the defendant, as well as to a state receiver in possession of his property.[8]

§ 309. Provisions as to Service Directory, Not Mandatory.—The provisions of Bankruptcy Act, § 18 (a), as to service of process, are directory and not mandatory, and failure to proceed in accordance therewith will not render the adjudication void, although it may be irregular and subject to correction on error.[9]

§ 310. Apply to Partnership Petitions Filed by One Partner.—The provisions of Bankrupt Act, § 18 (a), as to service of process, etc., apply to partnership cases filed by one or more, but less than all, the partners. Where the nonjoining partner or partners can be found personal service must be had, but if personal service cannot be had, upon filing an affidavit to that effect, an order of publication will be made.[10]

§ 311. Delay in Serving Subpœna.—Long delay in serving the subpœna or in the bankrupt's entering of appearance does not necessarily affect jurisdiction.[11]

---

etc., Co., Lt., 29 A. B. R. 13, — Fed. — (D. C. Hawaii).

5. See remainder of § 18 (a) of Bankruptcy Act: "But in case personal service can not be made, then notice shall be given by publication in the same manner and for the same time as provided by law for publication in suits to enforce a legal or equitable lien in the Courts of the United States except that, unless the judge shall otherwise direct, the order shall be published not more than once a week for two consecutive weeks and the return day shall be ten days after the last publication unless the judge shall for cause fix a longer time." Hills v. McKinniss Co., 26 A. B. R. 329, 188 Fed. 1012 (D. C. Ohio).

1 R B—18

6. Bauman Diamond Co. v. Hart, 27 A. B. R. 632, 192 Fed. 498 (C. C. A. Tex.).

7. Hills v. McKinniss Co, 26 A B. R. 329, 188 Fed. 1012 (D. C. Ohio).

8. Bauman Diamond Co v. Hart, 27 A. B. R. 632, 192 Fed. 498 (C. C. A. Tex.).

9. In re Stein, 5 A. B. R. 288, 105 Fed. 749 (C. C. A.).

10. In re Murray, 3 A. B. R. 601, 96 Fed. 600 (D. C. Iowa).

11. In re Frischberg, 8 A. B. R. 607 (D. C. N. Y.); In re Stein, 5 A. B. R. 288, 105 Fed. 749 (C. C. A.); In re Lewis & Bro., 1 A. B. R. 458 (D. C. N. Y.); Gleason v. Smith, 16 A. B. R. 606, 145 Fed. 895 (C. C. A. Pa.).

§ **312. Manner of Service.**—Service shall be made in the same manner as in federal equity practice.[12] Thus, in the absence of the respondent from his usual place of abode, service of the petition and subpœna, by delivering to and leaving a copy with some adult person who is a "member of or resident in his family" at such place, is good service.[13] And publication in such case is unnecessary.[14]

Thus, leaving the subpœna with the clerk of the hotel of which the alleged bankrupt is proprietor and where he usually resides, is valid service.[15] A foreign corporation having its principal place of business within the district may be served by service upon the commissioner of corporations of the State where he is the duly appointed attorney of the corporation to receive service.[16] But the writ of subpœna need not contain the special memorandum mentioned in Equity Rule 12.[17] It is improper to serve a receiver in charge of the assets of the alleged bankrupt.[19] Service on a director chosen at an adjourned session of the annual meeting is proper rather than upon one chosen at a special meeting, the former not being ousted from office.[20]

§ **313. Bankrupt's Waiver of Improper Service, etc.**—The bankrupt waives objections to the jurisdiction for failure to make proper service, and for improper verification of the petition, and that it was not filed in duplicate, by appearing and going on the stand to prove facts that would only be material on the merits.[21]

§ **314. Voluntary Appearance.**—The bankrupt may, of course, voluntarily appear and consent to the adjudication.[22] And this, although after long delay and when no subpœna has been served. But of course he may not consent thereto where he has not had his residence, domicile or principal place of business in the district the requisite period of time.

§ **315. Answer Day.**—The bankrupt or any creditor may appear and plead to the petition within five days after the return day, or within such further time as the court may allow.[23] The day on which the defendant is to appear, etc., should be designated in the order for publication.[24]

---

12. As to the manner of service of process on a lunatic, see In re Burke, 5 A. B. R. 843 (D. C. Tenn.). As to the fees of marshal, see post, "Costs of Administration."

13. In re Norton, 17 A. B. R. 504, 148 Fed. 301 (D. C. N. Y.).

14. In re Norton, 17 A. B. R. 504, 148 Fed. 301 (D. C. N. Y.).

15. In re Risteen, 10 A. B. R. 494, 122 Fed. 732 (D. C. Mass.).

16. In re Magid Hope Silk Co., 6 A. B. R. 610, 110 Fed. 352 (D. C. N. Y.).

17. In re Wing Yick Co., 13 A. B. R. 360 (D. C. Hawaii).

19. In re Bay City Irrigation Co., 14 A. B. R. 370, 135 Fed. 850 (D. C. Tex.).

20. In re Plasmon Co., 14 A. B. R. 487 (D. C. N. Y.).

21. In re Smith, 9 A. B. R. 98, 117 Fed. 961 (D. C. Conn.).

22. In re Frichsberg, 8 A. B. R. 607 (Special Master, N. Y., affirmed by D. C.). Bankruptcy proceedings may be instituted and process may issue though there may be a vacancy in the district judgeship at the time, In re Urban and Suburban, 12 A. B. R. 687 (D. C. N. J.).

23. Bankr. Act, § 18 (b); In re Cooper Bros., 20 A. B. R. 392, 159 Fed. 956 (D. C. Pa.).

24. Bauman Diamond Co. v. Hart, 27 A. B. R. 632, 192 Fed. 498 (C. C. A. Tex.).

§ 316. May Be Extended.—The time to answer may be extended by order of the court.[25] But the court must make the order and a mere extension of time by agreement is not operative unless all creditors consent, or unless, on notice to all, none object.[26]

25. Bankr. Act. § 18 (b); In re Cooper Bros., 20 A. B. R. 392, 159 Fed. 956 (D. C. Pa.).

26. In re Simonson, et al., 1 A. B. R. 197, 92 Fed. 904 (D. C. Ky.).

CHAPTER IX.

Intervening of Creditors in Opposition to Petition.

Synopsis of Chapter.

§ 317. Intervening of Creditors to Resist Petition.—Creditors, and persons claiming to be creditors, may intervene to resist the adjudicating of the debtor to be a bankrupt, as well as to contend for it.[1]

In re Billing, 17 A. B. R. 89 (D. C. Ala.): "It is often vital to the interests of creditors that the debtor's business, though in a critical condition, be not taken out of his control. The owner, left to the conduct of the business, may mend his fortune, and save loss to the creditors, when a trustee or receiver could not take the business and do as well. In recognition of this interest of the creditor in his debtor's remaining in control of his own affairs, the statute authorizes the creditor to intervene in involuntary proceedings, to prevent his debtor from being put in bankruptcy, unless he be insolvent and has committed an act of bankruptcy."

But the right of intervention should not be abused where the debtor is clearly insolvent and has undoubtedly committed the act of bankruptcy urged.

Obiter, In re Billing, 17 A. B. R. 89 (D. C. Ala.): "This provision was intended to arm the creditor with effective means, placed directly in his own keeping, of assisting the debtor to resist an improper effort to force him into bankruptcy, and also to give the creditor like effectual means of preventing his debtor and petitioning creditors from colluding to bring about the adjudication, when the debtor is not insolvent and has not committed an act of bankruptcy, and is unwilling to institute voluntary proceedings. It was not within the contemplation of the statute, when the debtor is, in fact, insolvent, and has

---

1. Bankr. Act, § 18 (b): "The bankrupt or any creditor may appear and plead to the petition within five days after the return day, or within such further time as the court may allow."

Also, § 59 (f): "Creditors other than original petitioners may at any time enter their appearance and join in the petition, or file an answer and be heard in opposition to the prayer of the petition."

Goldman v. Smith, 1 A. B. R. 266, 93 Fed. 182 (D. C. Ky.); Ayres v. Cone, 14 A. R. B. 739, 138 Fed. 783 (C. C. A. S. D.); In re Moench & Sons, 10 A. B. R. 590, 123 Fed. 965 (D. C. N. Y.). Instance, In re Taylor, 4 A. B. R. 515, 102 Fed. 728 (C. C. A. Ills.).

committed an act of bankruptcy, to give to the creditor the right to contest the adjudication, merely to keep alive a lien or levy, which would be destroyed if the petition be not defeated; for that is contrary to the spirit and purpose of the bankruptcy law. The contest of the petition for the latter purpose is an abuse of the statute."

§ 318. No Intervention to Contest Voluntary Petition.—Creditors may not so intervene in purely voluntary bankruptcies;[3] even if the voluntary petition be that of a partnership.[4]

§ 319. "At Any Time."—"At any time" in Bankrupt Act, § 59 (f), does not give creditors a right to appear and plead after the expiration of the five days or of the further time allowed by the court.[5] The term "at any time" must of necessity have some limitation and clause 59 (f) should be construed in the light of clause 18 (b). And at any rate, after the trial and submission of the case, even though before the rendering of a verdict or decision, a creditor may not be allowed to appear and plead and to raise new issues.[6]

§ 320. Attaching Creditor, etc., May Intervene without Surrendering Property Attached.—An attaching or execution creditor may intervene and resist the petition without surrendering the property attached.[7] It would be different were the attaching or execution creditor urging the adjudication for his attachment would be inconsistent with the adjudication—the facts he would rely on to establish the adjudication would show himself to be obtaining a lien by legal proceedings contrary to the very bankruptcy law he invokes: he might be a petitioning creditor but he would be obliged to abandon his attachment lien.[8]

§ 321. Mere Lienholder, unless Also Creditor, May Not Intervene.—But a mere lienholder or other party in interest who is not at the same time a creditor may not intervene.[9]

3. In re Carbone, 13 A. B. R. 55 (Ref. Wash.); In re Carleton, 8 A. B. R. 270, 115 Fed. 246 (D. C. Mass.).

4. In re Ives, 7 A. B. R. 692, 113 Fed. 911 (C. C. A. Mich.); In re Carleton, 8 A. B. R. 270, 115 Fed. 246 (D. C. Mass.).

5. In re Mutual Mercantile Agency, 6 A. B. R. 607, 111 Fed. 152 (D. C. N. Y.).

6. In re Mutual Mercantile Agency, 6 A. B. R. 607, 111 Fed. 152 (D. C. N. Y.).

7. In re Moench & Sons, 10 A. B. R. 590, 123 Fed. 965 (D. C. N. Y.). Inferentially, In re Taylor, 4 A. B. R. 415, 102 Fed. 728 (C. C. A. Ills.); [1867] In re Bergeron, Fed. Cas. No. 1,342; [1867] In re Hatje, Fed. Cas. No. 6,215;

[1867] In re Mendelson, Fed. Cas. No. 9,420.

8. See ante, § 234, et seq.

9. But where one of the original three petitioning creditors turns out to be disqualified the court will not retain the case in order that other creditors may be brought in. In re Gillette, 5 A. B. R. 119, 104 Fed. 769 (D. C. N. Y.).

Bankrupt Entitled to Answer Intervening Petitions.—Bankrupt can not be debarred of right to answer the intervening petitions. Obiter, In re Gillette, 5 A. B. R. 119, 127 Fed. 769 (D. C. N. Y.).

Where erroneous averment of less than twelve creditors, intervening creditor to give list if bankrupt fails to do so, see ante, §§ 207, 208.

In re Columbia Real Estate Co., 7 A. B. R. 441, 112 Fed. 643 (C. C. A. Ind.): "We are of the opinion from these provisions and their consistency with the general tenor of the act that the intention clearly appears that the only claimants who are entitled to hearing on the issue of involuntary bankruptcy, aside from the bankrupt, are the creditors of the bankrupt; that creditors having security or priority are excluded therefrom to the extent of their security or priority, and can be recognized only in that issue for unsecured or unpreferred amounts; that even as a creditor one who is secured and stands alone on his security can neither invoke nor oppose an adjudication of involuntary bankruptcy; and surely that this claimant of the mere rights of a mortgagee, through transactions with third parties, who is not a creditor of the bankrupt, can have no standing therein as a party."

If, however, the lienholder is a creditor and a fortiori if he is a creditor to an extent not covered by his security,[10] he may, of course, intervene.

§ 321¼. **Whether Receivers May Intervene.**—Nor may the receiver of the bankrupt corporation, who has been appointed in proceedings for dissolution of the corporation, intervene and defend that the corporation no longer exists but has been dissolved.[11] But it has been held that a receiver of a corporation appointed in an equity suit before the bankruptcy on the ground of insolvency, is a competent party to intervene to oppose adjudication;[12] but this ruling is not to be approved, because the receiver is merely a custodian of assets, not a rightful party in determining the debtor's status as a bankrupt.

§ 321½. **Whether Stockholders May Intervene.**—Stockholders considered merely as such, are not creditors of the corporation in which they hold stock and therefore cannot as creditors intervene to answer a petition in bankruptcy against the company. However, in a proper case the court of bankruptcy may permit them to intervene in the right of the corporation.[13]

§ 322. **Objections to Improper Intervention, by Motion to Strike from Files.**—Objections to the improper intervention of creditors should be by motion to strike their petition from the files—not by demurrer.[14]

10. Johansen, etc., Co. v. Alles, 28 A. B. R. 299, 197 Fed. 274 (C. C. A. Mo.).
11. In re Storck Lumber Co., 8 A. B. R. 86 (D. C. Md.).
12. In re H. R. Elec. Power Co., 23 A. B. R. 191, 173 Fed. 934 (D. C. N. Y.);
In re Gold Run Co., 29 A. B. R. 563, 200 Fed. 162 (D. C. Colo.).
13. See post, § 326.
14. Neustadter v. Chic. Dry Goods Co., 3 A. B. R. 96, 96 Fed. 830 (D. C. Wash.).

CHAPTER X.

ANSWER, DEMURRER AND MOTION.

Synopsis of Chapter.

§ 323. Answer.—Either the bankrupt or any creditor may within five days after the return day or within such further time as the court may allow appear and plead to the petition.[1] He may file an answer, demurrer or a motion, as in other cases.

§ 324. Demurrer to Petition.—Demurrer may be filed to the petition, in accordance with the usual rules.[2] The respondent may demur to one cause of action and answer to another. If he demur and answer to the same cause, the demurrer will be considered waived.[3] But if they be filed to separate causes, but overlap, they may both stand, under the aid of Equity Rule 37.[4]

§ 325. Amendment after Demurrer Sustained.—Where a demurrer

---

1. Bankr. Act, § 18 (b); § 59 (f); see citations ante, § 317. In re Cooper Bros., 20 A. B. R. 392, 159 Fed. 956 (D. C. Pa.).

2. Instance, In re Vastbinder, 11 A. B. R. 118, 126 Fed. 417 (D. C. Pa.); Bradley Timber Co. v. White, 10 A. B. R. 329, 121 Fed. 779 (C. C. A. Ala.); In re Hark Bros., 14 A. B. R. 400, 135 Fed. 603 (D. C. N. Y.); In re Brett, 12 A. B. R. 492, 130 Fed. 981 (D. C. N. J.). Obiter, In re First Nat. Bank of Belle Fourche, 18 A. B. R. 270 (C.

C. A.); Instance, In re Hammond, 20 A. B. R. 776, 163 Fed. 548 (D. C. N. Y.); instance, In re Putnam, 27 A. B. R. 923, 193 Fed. 464 (D. C. Cal.); In re Radke, 27 A. B. R. 950, 193 Fed. 735 (D. C. Cal.).

3. In re Koolin, 24 A. B. R. 534, 179 Fed. 1013 (D. C. Pa.); In re Cooper Bros., 20 A. B. R. 392, 159 Fed. 956 (D. C. Pa.).

4. In re Cooper Bros., 20 A. B. R. 392, 159 Fed. 956 (D. C. Pa.).

to a petition is sustained, the petition will not be dismissed without first giving the petitioners an opportunity to apply for leave to amend.[5]

§ 326. Who May Answer.

—The bankrupt or any creditor may answer.[6] Stockholders considered merely as such, are not, however, creditors of the corporation in which they hold stock and, therefore, cannot, as creditors, answer a petition seeking the adjudication of the company. - It is not doubted, however, that in a proper case the court of bankruptcy, in the exercise of its equitable functions, may permit stockholders to so intervene in the right of the corporation, as, for instance, where they would be allowed to prosecute or defend generally, in the name of the corporation, in any other court of equity.[7]

§ 327. Form of Answer.

—The rules with regard to answers follow the usual principles of pleading. The forms and orders of the Supreme Court indicate only the general form of the answer, and are not exclusive.[8]

The answer must be verified;[9] but verification may be supplied by amendment.[10]

§ 328. Time to Answer Amended Petition.

—An alleged bankrupt has the right to a reasonable time to answer an amended petition.[11]

Lockman v. Lang, 12 A. B. R. 497, 132 Fed. 1 (C. C. A. Colo.): "A single day is not a reasonable time for an alleged bankrupt who is not within the district, to answer an amended petition, which for the first time charges him with certain acts of fraud and bankruptcy."

§ 329. Defective Denial Cured by Going to Proof.

—Defective denial is cured where the parties proceed to the taking of the proof.[12] Thus, argumentative denials and denials of legal conclusions may be cured.[13]

5. In re Brett, 12 A. B. R. 492, 130 Fed. 981 (D. C. N. J.). Impliedly, In re First Nat. Bank of Belle Fourche, 18 A. B. R. 270 (C. C. A.). Instance, In re Hammond, 20 A. B. R. 776, 163 Fed. 548 (D. C. N. Y.).

6. Bankr. Act, §§ 18 (d), 18 (e), 59 (f); compare ante, § 317, et seq.; also, § 323.

7. In re Eureka, etc., Co., 28 A. B. R. 758, 197 Fed. 216 (D. C. Ark.).

8. In re Paige, 3 A. B. R. 679, 99 Fed. 538 (D. C. Ohio). See ante, § 26.

9. In re Harris, 19 A. B. R. 204, 156 Fed. 875 (D. C. Ala.).

10. In re Harris, 19 A. B. R. 204, 156 Fed. 875 (D. C. Ala.).

Form of Joining Creditor's Pleading. —See instance, State Bank v. Haswell, 23 A. B. R. 330, 174 Fed. 290 (C. C. A. Iowa): "The requisite number of creditors joined with the original petitioner, as authorized by that section, in an amendment which was filed. This amendment, after averring that the new parties had provable claims against the debtor, stated that they adopted all the averments of the original petition, which remained unchanged by the amendment, the same as though they had originally signed and joined in said 'petition.'"

11. Wilder v. Watts, 15 A. B. R. 57, 138 Fed. 426 (D. C. S. C.).

12. Troy Wagon Works v. Vastbinder, 12 A. B. R. 352, 130 Fed. 232 (D. C. Pa.).

13. Troy Wagon Works v. Vastbinder, 12 A. B. R. 352, 130 Fed. 232 (D. C. Pa.). In this case the court held, that a denial in general terms, that he did not "at any time commit any act of bankruptcy alleged" is sufficient as a denial of insolvency where the petitioners so regard it and proceed to the taking of the proof. Cummins Grocery Co. v. Talley, 26 A. B. R. 484 (C. C. A. Tenn.).

§ 330. Allegations Not Denied Need Not Be Proved.—Allegations in the petition not denied by answer need not be proved.[14]

§ 331. Answer Denying Act Pleaded but Showing Facts Sufficient to Constitute Another Act.—If the answer denies the specific act of bankruptcy alleged, but sets up by way of new matter facts sufficient to constitute a different act, for instance, an intentional preference, no reply being filed, adjudication will follow.[15]

§ 332. No Demurrer to Answer.—No demurrer to an answer will lie; the sufficiency of the answer can only be tested by setting the case for hearing upon the petition and answer.[16] If the parties proceed on the demurrer without objection it will be taken as a setting of the case down for hearing on the petition and answer, and a waiver of right to replicate.[17]

§ 333. All Defenses Available to Bankrupt.—The bankrupt may make all defenses that would have been available to him without bankruptcy, as well as those specially available to him by the particular provisions of the Bankruptcy Act.[18]

---

14. In re Elmira Steel Co., 5 A. B. R. 488, 109 Fed. 456 (Special Master N. Y.); In re Taylor, 4 A. B. R. 515, 102 Fed. 728 (C. C. A. Ills.).

15. Brinkley v. Smithwick, 11 A. B. R. 500, 126 Fed. 686 (D. C. N. Car.). Act charged in petition was transfer to hinder, etc.; answer denied the intent and act and stated it was a sale for cash and that the cash was all used to pay some creditors, leaving the rest unpaid, although insolvent. Held. to state a good ground for adjudication, as being a preference.

16. Goldman v. Smith, 1 A. B. R. 266, 93 Fed. 182 (D. C. Ky.); Vitzthum v. Large. 20 A. B. R. 666, 162 Fed. 685 (D. C. Iowa), quoted at § 1759½.

17. Goldman v. Smith, 1 A. B. R. 266, 93 Fed. 182 (D. C. Ky.); Vitzthum v. Large, 20 A. B. R. 666, 162 Fed. 685 (D. C. Iowa), quoted at § 1759½.

18. Instances of Defenses Raised.—Denial of ownership of property claimed to have been preferentially transferred and allegation that it was on consignment. Troy Wagon Wks. v. Vastbinder, 12 A. B. R. 352, 130 Fed. 232 (D. C. Pa.).

Jurisdiction of bankruptcy court over assets of the debtor's estate in the hands of a state receiver is not a question for consideration upon the petition for adjudication of bankruptcy. In re Kersten, 6 A. B. R. 516, 110 Fed. 929 (D. C. Wis.). Compare ante, § 97½.

Creditors may not be deprived of their rights to an adjudication on the ground that it will not benefit them, In re Hee, 13 A. B. R. 8 (D. C. Hawaii); nor on the ground that it will be against the best interests of the great majority of the creditors, Woolford v. Steel Co., 15 A. B. R. 36, 138 Fed. 582 (D. C. Del.): "If the petitions were not defective, the petitioners would have a right under the Bankruptcy Act to proceed to support them by evidence, and, if successful, to have the Diamond State Steel Co. adjudged bankrupt, regardless of any delay, confusion or expense attending such a course."

General denial puts in issue the existence of $500 of debts to petitioning creditors.

And if stipulation of counsel does not admit such indebtedness proof must be made. In re West, 5 A. B. R. 734 (C. C. A.).

Dissolution of the corporation does not defeat the operation of the bankrupt act. In re Storck Lumber Co., 8 A. B. R. 86, 114 Fed. 860 (D. C. Md.).

Validity of petitioning creditor's debt is a valid issue, In re Ferguson, 11 A. B. R. 371, 127 Fed. 407 (D. C. Pa.).

The alleged bankrupt may defend that, under the state law, it can not incur indebtedness. and, consequently that the claims of the petitioning creditors are not provable in bankruptcy. In re Wyoming Valley Assoc., 28 A. B. R. 462, 198 Fed. 436 (D. C. Pa.).

But compare, Gage & Co. v. Bell,

In re Paige, 3 A. B. R. 679, 99 Fed. 538 (D. C. Ohio): "The forms and orders in bankruptcy prescribed by the Supreme Court of the United States indicate the form, in substance, of the answer to be filed by the alleged bankrupt. The law does not contemplate that the respondent shall be confined to that particular form, and set out in his answer only such facts as are suggested by the order. * * * The respondent denies insolvency, but sets up, with great particularity, defenses and counterclaims which he alleges show him to have been solvent at the times charged, and when the act of bankruptcy was committed."

§ 333¼. Bad Faith of Petitioning Creditors No Ground for Dismissal of Petition.

—Bad faith on the part of the petitioning creditors in instituting the proceedings affords no ground for dismissing the petition. The motives of the parties are immaterial. Their rights are absolute.[19]

10 A. B. R. 701, 124 Fed. 371 (D. C. Tenn.): "The court is not now prepared to say that such proceedings are not admissible, but it very well may be said that a petitioning creditor, having a debt provable on the face of it, ought not to be compelled by the defendant debtor to enter into litigation about it, legal and equitable, and antecedently to establish it by overthrowing all defenses, real or fabricated, that the debtor may choose to set up by pleadings specially framed to present such issues. It is in effect tantamount to holding that a creditor with a disputed debt can not be a petitioning creditor in bankruptcy; or, at least, not until he has cleared away all dispute and controversy, and established his debt by a judgment at law; for it would be, in effect, a requirement to do this, even if he must get such a judgment or its equivalent in the bankruptcy proceedings. And the result is that before we can inquire whether a debtor is insolvent, and has committed an act of bankruptcy, we must engage in a preliminary work of litigation in law and equity, and, possibly, even in admiralty as well, with each petitioning creditor, in order that we may know beforehand whether the debtor has any defense he may possibly make to the creditor's claim of debt. This is converting the language of the statute, 'three or more creditors having provable claims,' into a requirement that there shall be 'three or more creditors having proved and established debts,' before they may file the petition. Section 59b. If a debt is wholly wanting in existence, if it has been paid, for example, or if it has been fabricated for the purpose, of course the defendant should be allowed to show that

fact in some form. But if it be a reasonably fair and honest claim of debt, which is provable in the sense that it is a claim that the court of bankruptcy after adjudication will hear and establish, if proved, the creditor should not be bound before the adjudication to so prove and establish it, but should be allowed to rely upon its provable quality, prima facie, to support an involuntary petition in bankruptcy."

Denial of Authority of Person Acting for the Petitioning Creditors.—Authority of attorney to appear for the petitioning creditors cannot be denied by answer, but only by rule upon the attorney himself.

Gage v. Bell, 10 A. B. R. 696, 124 Fed. 371 (D. C. Tenn.): "The defendant cannot, by answer or plea, set up want of authority in the plaintiff's attorney, but he must make a rule upon him to show his authority supported by affidavit as to the facts. * * * The reasons for this rule are well illustrated by this case. The courts could not conveniently do the business of litigation if either litigant could capriciously embody in his pleadings the collateral matter of the authority of the attorneys, respectively, to appear and file their pleadings. Every litigation would degenerate into a preliminary inquiry about the attorney's dealings with his client."

Authority of president of corporation to institute bankruptcy proceedings against debtor or to join in one, In re Winston, 10 A. B. R. 171, 122 Fed. 187 (D. C. Tenn.).

Claim of Petitioning Creditor Illegal as Based on Gaming Consideration.—Hill v. Levy, 3 A. B. R. 374, 98 Fed. 94 (D. C. Va.).

19. Not contra, Lowenstein v. McShane Mfg. Co., 12 A. B. R. 601, 130

§ 333½. Nor Is Collusion between Them and the Bankrupt Good Ground.—Nor is the fact that a receiver has been appointed by the bankruptcy court, through collusion between the petitioning creditors and the bankrupt, and in the bankrupt's interest, a ground for dismissing the bankruptcy petition itself.[20]

§ 333¾. Nor That No Assets Available.—Nor is it a valid defense that no assets are in sight or that adjudication will not benefit creditors;[21] for creditors have the right to have the debtor's status determined to be that of a bankrupt, besides which they are entitled to an opportunity to discover assets and to place themselves in position to take advantage of any future discovery of assets.

In re Pangborn, 26 A. B. R. 40, 185 Fed. 673 (D. C. Mich.): "It seems doubtful whether there may be enough of a surplus to go into the trustee's hands to make these proceedings of any great practical value; but whatever extent and force that consideration may have is not for the court."

§ 334. Motions.—Motions, as in other cases, may be filed.

§ 334¼. Requiring Bankrupt to Attach List of Debts and Assets, Where Insolvency Denied.—Whether the alleged bankrupt who denies insolvency may be required to attach to his answer a list of debts and assets has not been decided in any reported case, but seems to have been the practice in one case at least.[22]

There seems, however, to be no valid objection to the practice, as a means of affording discovery to the petitioning creditors, it being a proper exercise of the discretion of the court, in regulating the pleadings before it, to make the requirement.[23]

Fed. 1007 (D. C. Md.). Compare, § 203½.

20. Coal and Iron Co. *v.* Steel Co., 20 A. B. R. 151, 160 Fed. 212 (D. C. Ala.).

21. In re Hee, 13 A. B. R. 8 (D. C. Hawaii); impliedly, In re Kersten, 6 A. B. R. 516, 110 Fed. 929 (D. C. Wis.).

22. Young & Holland Co. *v.* Brande Bros., 20 A. B. R. 612, 162 Fed. 663 (C. C. A. R. I.).

23. See ante, § 179.

CHAPTER XI.

Provisional Remedies.

Synopsis of Chapter.

§ 335. Provisional Seizure of Property and Remedies of Creditors during Pendency of Petition.

—During the period intervening between the

filing of the petition and the adjudication, opportunity occurs for the bankrupt to dispose of the assets, selling them or removing them or hiding them or wasting them. Likewise abundant opportunity exists for third persons, with or without the connivance of the bankrupt, to make way with property belonging to the estate, and otherwise to defeat creditors.

Creditors, however, are not helpless in this contingency. They have several remedies available to them upon proper showing being made. They may seize property in the hands of the bankrupt by process issued in the same case, resembling the ordinary process of attachment before judgment; they may have restraining orders issued in the same case; they may arrest and detain the bankrupt for examination; they may have a receiver appointed in the same case to act in their behalf; or they may start independent suits themselves, as if bankruptcy had not intervened, and later may be reimbursed out of the estate for their proper expenses in so doing.

DIVISION I.

PROVISIONAL SEIZURE OF PROPERTY.

§ 336. Provisional Seizure on Affidavit and Bond.—To cover the period of the pendency of the petition §§ 69 and 3 (e) of the statute provide for a species of attachment to issue for the seizure of the property, the warrant for seizure issuing upon the filing of an affidavit which alleges the commission of an act of bankruptcy and neglect of the property of the debtor and the giving of a bond, similarly to the procedure in ordinary attachment cases where property of the defendant is seized before judgment and held to await the outcome of suit.[1]

In re Williams, 9 A. B. R. 736, 120 Fed. 34 (D. C. Ark.): "It confers on the creditors the right to institute proceedings against insolvent or fraudulent debtors, in order that the estate may be administered by the bankruptcy court and an equal distribution of the assets had. But in order to prevent a fraudulent disposition of the property pending the proceedings, it permits a seizure of the assets before the hearing, upon certain allegations and the execution of a

1. Application to Be by Creditors, Not Receiver.—The application should be made by creditors rather than by a receiver, In re Sunseri, 18 A. B. R. 234 (D. C. Pa.).

Section 69 reads as follows: "A judge may, upon satisfactory proof, by affidavit, that a bankrupt against whom an involuntary petition has been filed and is pending has committed an act of bankruptcy, or has neglected or is neglecting, or is about to so neglect his property that it has thereby deteriorated, or is thereby deteriorating, or is about thereby to deteriorate in value, issue a warrant to the marshal to seize and hold it subject to further orders. Before such warrant is issued and petitioners applying therefor shall enter into a bond in such

an amount as the judge shall fix, with such sureties as he shall approve, conditioned to indemnify such bankrupt for such damages as he shall sustain in the event such seizure shall prove to have been wrongly obtained. Such property shall be released, if such bankrupt shall give bond in a sum which shall be fixed by the judge, with such sureties as he shall approve, conditioned to turn over such property, or pay the value thereof in money to the trustee, in the event he is adjudged a bankrupt, pursuant to such petition."

Clause E of § 3 covers substantially the same ground and reads as follows: "Whenever a petition is filed by any person for the purpose of having another adjudged bankrupt, and an ap-

bond to pay the damages which the debtor may sustain by reason of the seizure if upon a final hearing it is adjudged that the same was wrongful, in the
same manner as in ordinary cases when the same object is sought by resort to
proceedings by attachment."

§ 337. Referee, in Absence of Judge, to Issue Warrant.—The referee may, on receipt of the certificate of the district clerk that the judge is
absent, exercise the powers of the judge for the taking of possession and
releasing of the bankrupt's property pending adjudication.[2]

§ 338. Allegation for Provisional Seizure Not to Be Made in Petition Itself.—The application for the warrant is a separate proceeding from
that for the adjudication of bankruptcy, and should not form part of the petition.[3]

§ 339. Affidavit Must Be Made.—Although §§ 3 (e) and 69, Bankr.
Act, are not identical, yet, in substance, they are so; and, although an affidavit
is not mentioned in § 3 (e), yet the "application" there mentioned presumably must be supported by affidavit. More than likely the two sections
should be read together and not as if they related to distinct proceedings.
Nevertheless it is possible that, where receivers are appointed under § 3 (e)
to make the seizure, the affidavit need not contain the recitals prescribed in
§ 69.

§ 340. Affidavit to Be Specific as to Facts Constituting Act of
Bankruptcy and Neglect of Property.—The affidavit for the warrant
should be specific and contain allegations of fact sufficient to prove the act
of bankruptcy alleged and the neglect of property complained of.

In re Kelly, 1 A. B. R. 308, 91 Fed. 504 (D. C. Tenn.): "Affidavits under this
§ 69 of the Bankrupt Act should be as specific as possible in their statements
of all the essential facts—indeed, should be quite as fully satisfactory in the
exhibition of the proof of the act of bankruptcy as the testimony to be produced
at the hearing of the petition for adjudication in a contested case—so that the
court may see precisely, from those facts, whether or not an act of bankruptcy
has been committed, or whether the alleged bankrupt has been neglecting his
property, so that it is deteriorating in value, etc. It is a formidable thing to
seize a man's property so summarily before he is heard, and should never be

plication is made to take charge of and
hold the property of the alleged bankrupt, or any part of the same, prior
to the adjudication and pending a
hearing on the petition, the petitioner
or applicant shall file in the same
court a bond with at least two good
and sufficient sureties who shall reside within the jurisdiction of said
court to be approved by the court, or
a judge thereof, in such sum as the
court shall direct, conditioned for the
payment, in case such a petition is
dismissed, to the respondent, his or
her personal representatives, all costs,
expenses, and damages occasioned by
such seizure, taking and retention of
the property of the alleged bankrupt.
"If such a petition be dismissed by
the court or withdrawn by the petitioner, the respondent or respondents
shall be allowed all costs, counsel
fees, expenses, and damages occasioned
by such seizure, taking or detention
of such property. Counsel fees, costs,
expenses and damages shall be fixed
and allowed by the court, and paid by
the obligors in such bond."
2. See Bankr. Act, § 38 (3); In re
Knopf, 16 A. B. R. 439, 144 Fed. 245
(D. C. S. C.).
3. In re Kelly, 1 A. B. R. 306, 91
Fed. 504 (D. C. Tenn.).

done upon the mere opinions of witnesses as to whether an act of bankruptcy has been committed, but only on a full showing of the facts of the case."

In re Sunseri, 18 A. B. R. 231 (D. C. Pa.): "I do not think the court should authorize such seizure in any case except upon a petition very clearly and definitely setting forth all the facts, not merely suspicions, and after exacting proper security."

But it is not necessary to allege that the property to be seized is not exempt from seizure.[4]

§ 341. Bond to Be Given.—A bond must be given to protect the bankrupt and creditors interested in the event the seizure was wrongly obtained.[5] And where seizure is by a receiver and a bond is not given the receivership should be vacated.[6]

§ 342. Neither Affidavit nor Bond Can Be Waived by Bankrupt.—The bankrupt cannot waive the filing of the affidavit nor the giving of the bond. Although the bond is in terms given to respond to the bankrupt for his damages in case the seizure is wrongful, yet it may inure to others for whom the bankrupt cannot waive.

In re Sarsar, 9 A. B. R. 577, 120 Fed. 40 (D. C. Tenn.): "This application must be refused, as the court cannot permit it to issue except upon compliance with the conditions of the statute. It is sufficient to say that the statute does not expressly authorize any waiver of the requirements of this section by the bankrupt, nor does it seem to contemplate that they may be waived. It is true that the statute, in terms, states that the condition of the bond shall be to indemnify the bankrupt for such damages as he shall sustain in the event the seizure shall prove to have been wrongfully obtained, but non constat that this bond may not inure to the benefit of any one interested in the property of the bankrupt which should be wrongfully seized, and that, at least in a court of equity, one so injured might be subrogated to the rights of the bankrupt in that behalf."

§ 343. Need Not Be Signed by Petitioners.—The bond need not be signed by the petitioners.[7]

§ 344. Surety Company Bond Sufficient.—A surety company bond is sufficient (under the United States Act of 1894) although only one surety is on it and that surety does not reside in the district.[8]

§ 345. Premium.—The premium for such bond has been held not to be a proper item of taxable costs;[9] but undoubtedly it is a proper charge where allowed or prescribed by rule of court.

4. Hoffschlaeger Co. v. Young Nap, 12 A. B. R. 510 (D. C. Hawaii).

5. Beach v. Macon Grocery Co., 8 A. B. R. 751, 116 Fed. 143 (C. C. A. Ga.); In re Haff, 13 A. B. R. 354, 135 Fed. 742 (C. C. A. N. Y.); In re Sunseri, 18 A. B. R. 234 (D. C. Pa.); impliedly, In re Sears, Humbert & Co., 10 A. B. R. 389 (Ref. N. Y.); impliedly, In re Sarsar, 9 A. B. R. 576, 120 Fed. 40 (D. C. Tenn.); In re Knopf, 16 A. B. R. 446, 144 Fed. 245 (D. C. S. C.).

6. In re Haff, 13 A. B. R. 354, 135 Fed. 742 (C. C. A. N. Y.).

7. In re Sears, Humbert & Co., 10 A. B. R. 389 (Ref. N. Y.).

8. In re Sears, Humbert & Co., 10 A. B. R. 389 (Ref. N. Y.).

9. In re Hoyt, 9 A. B. R. 574, 119 Fed. 987 (D. C. N. Car.). But compare note, In re Sears, Humbert & Co., 10 A. B. R. 393 (Ref. N. Y.).

§ 346. Receiver May Be Appointed to Make Seizure.—A receiver may be appointed instead of the marshal to make this seizure.[10]

The order should in terms provide that he should not take possession until the filing and approval of the bond required of the petitioning creditor by Bankr. Act, § 3 (e).[11] And the order should fix the time within which the petitioning creditors' bond should be given.[12] The receiver before adjudication of bankruptcy should not be appointed, without notice to the bankrupt; unless it is alleged and appears that to give notice of the application would in all probability defeat the very object of the appointment, in which event notice may be dispensed with.[13]

In re Francis, 14 A. B. R. 676, 136 Fed. 912 (D. C. Penna., affirmed sub nom. Latimer v. McNeal, 16 A. B. R. 43, 142 Fed. 451, C. C. A. Pa.): "The act does not expressly require that notice shall be given the alleged bankrupt before the appointment shall be made, but, as a rule, from the institution of proceedings in a suit until final judgment, every step is preceded with notice, and it is laid down as a general proposition that notice must be served upon the party before a receiver can be appointed, except (1) where the defendants or parties in interest have absconded, or are beyond the jurisdiction of the court, or cannot be found; (2) where there is imminent danger of loss or great damage, or irreparable injury, or the gravest emergency, or when by notice the very purpose of a receiver may be rendered wholly nugatory—as where the property may be removed without the jurisdiction of the court, or it is being collected, and the proceeds wrongfully appropriated. In such cases the court will lay its hand upon the property, through the appointment of a receiver, for the purpose of maintaining the status quo until the issues may be determined as to the right of ownership."

§ 347. On Dismissal, Property to Be Returned without Deduction for Care.—In case the petition is dismissed it has been held in some cases that the receiver must return the property to the defendant intact and that no costs nor expenses can be charged against the defendant for the custody and care;[14] whilst, in other cases, it has been held that not only the expenses of such care and preservation may be charged against the property but even that the expense of selling the perishable property may be so charged, such being the case notwithstanding the fact that the dismissal was on account of lack of jurisdiction, the lack of jurisdiction not appearing on the face of the petition.[15]

10. See post, division 4 of this chapter, § 390. Beach v. Macon Grocery Co., 8 A. B. R. 751 (C. C. A. Ga.). See inferentially, In re Sears, Humbert & Co., 10 A. B. R. 389 (Ref. N. Y.); inferentially, In re Haff, 13 A. B. R. 354 (C. C. A. N. Y.); In re Francis, 14 A. B. R. 676 (D. C. Pa.).

11. In re Haff, 13 A. B. R. 354, 135 Fed. 742 (C. C. A. N. Y.).

12. In re Haff, 13 A. B. R. 354, 135 Fed. 742 (C. C. A. N. Y.).

13. See post, § 381. See also, Latimer v. McNeal, 16 A. B. R. 45, 142 Fed. 451 (C. C. A.), quoted post, § 381; Faulk v. Steiner, 21 A. B. R. 623, 165 Fed. 861 (C. C. A. Ala.), quoted post, § 381.

14. In re Sears, Humbert & Co., 10 A. B. R. 389 (Ref. N. Y.).

15. In re De Lancey Stables Co., 22 A. B. R. 406, 170 Fed. 860 (D. C. Pa.).

§ 348. Respondent Allowed Expenses, Counsel Fees and Damages on Dismissal.

—In case the petition is dismissed by the court or withdrawn by the petitioners, the respondent shall be allowed all costs, counsel fees, expenses and damages occasioned by such seizure, taking or detention of property.[16]

In re Ghiglione, 1 A. B. R. 581, 93 Fed. 186 (D. C. N. Y.): "* * * the last paragraph of subd. e above quoted applies only to cases arising under the first paragraph of that subdivision, and where the application 'to take charge of and hold the property of the alleged bankrupt' prior to adjudication has been granted and the bond given. The allowance of 'counsel fees' in addition to costs can rest only on express statutory provision. It is contrary to the ordinary Federal practice, and seems to have been designed to afford a fuller measure of indemnity to the defendant than is ordinarily afforded in legal proceedings in the federal courts, for an unjustifiable interference with his property. Such interference may at times be ruinous, and by breaking up a man's business make him insolvent when he was not insolvent before. It is an available weapon which may be misused, and is therefore justly guarded by special provisions for the most complete indemnity to the accused. Ordinary cases of involuntary proceedings, not accompanied by such injurious interference, fall as respects costs under the provisions of Rule XXXIV, which does not allow counsel fees in addition to costs."

Hoffschlaeger Co. v. Young Nap, 12 A. B. R. 526 (D. C. Hawaii): "The counsel fee allowed in proceedings for seizing and holding the property of the presumed bankrupt is for special services and is a distinct matter."

Under § 983, U. S. Rev. Stat., allowing amounts paid witnesses to be taxed as costs, the affidavit must show that they have been actually paid.

The allowance of counsel fees is by special provision of the statute in cases of seizures.[17]

§ 349. Costs, Expenses, Counsel Fees and Damages Confined to Those Incident to Seizure.

—The costs, counsel fees, expenses and damages, taxable under the bonds are to be strictly confined to those incident to the seizure.[18]

Selkregg v. Hamilton Bros., 16 A. B. R. 476, 144 Fed. 557 (D. C. Pa.): "The bond as it is to be remembered, is given solely for the purpose of indemnifying the alleged bankrupts for taking their property out of their hands, before there

---

16. Bankr. Act, § 3 (e); In re Hines, 16 A. B. R. 541, 144 Fed. 147 (D. C. Ore.); In re Williams, 9 A. B. R. 739, 120 Fed. 34 (D. C. Ark.); Nixon v. Fidelity & Deposit Co., 18 A. B. R. 174 (C. C. A. Mont.); In re Nixon, 6 A. B. R. 693 (D. C. Mont.). This case of In re Nixon was a case of the dismissal of a petition as to two of five persons alleged to be partners. Selkregg v. Hamilton Bros., 16 A. B. R. 474, 144 Fed. 557 (D. C. Pa.); In re Smith, 16 A. B. R. 480 (D. C. Okla.); Hill Co. v. Supply & Equipment Co., 24 A. B. R. 84 (App. Ct. of Ill.).

17. Hoffschlaeger Co. v. Young Nap, 12 A. B. R. 526 (D. C. Hawaii); In re Hines, 16 A. B. R. 541, 144 Fed. 147 (D. C. Ore.); In re Williams, 9 A. B. R. 736, 120 Fed. 34 (D. C. Ark.); In re Ghiglione, 1 A. B. R. 580, 93 Fed. 186 (D. C. N. Y.). Compare, In re Phila., etc., Co., 11 A. B. R. 444 (D. C. Pa.). Compare, In re Morris, 7 A. B. R. 709, 115 Fed. 591 (D. C. Pa.).

18. In re Smith, 16 A. B. R. 478 (D. C. Okla.).

has been an adjudication against them; and it is only by failing to keep this in view, that any confusion arises. The master has lost sight of it slightly, in holding, that, as noted above, the respondents are entitled to such costs as would be allowed to a party in equity, in case of a dismissal. These costs, no doubt, are to be taxed in their favor, against the petitioning creditors, by the clerk, in the main proceedings. But they do not come in here, where we are fixing the responsibility of the bondsmen, both principals and sureties, which is another matter. The costs to be covered in the latter case are those which are strictly incident to the seizure proceedings, and ordinarily in any event would not amount to much. Where, as is often the case, application for a warrant to the marshal, like that for the appointment of a receiver, is heard ex parte, there would be nothing more than those for the filing of the moving papers, taken care of at the time by the parties."

Thus, the counsel fees taxable are simply those incident to the seizure. And none may be allowed for resisting the petition.[19]

In re Smith, 8 A. B. R. 56, 113 Fed. 993 (D. C. Ga.): "* * * the only counsel fees the court is authorized to fix and allow in this case is for services of counsel to the respondent performed in proper efforts to secure the discharge of the property from the writ of seizure; and for services rendered in opposing the petition and securing its dismissal no counsel fees can be allowed in this proceeding."

§ 350. Allowance Only to Respondents at Time Bond Given—Subsequent Respondents May Move for New Bond.

—The only liability for costs upon a bond given under Bankr. Act, § 3 (e), is to those who were respondents when the bond was given. Those who subsequently become respondents and wish to be protected may move for a new bond.[20]

§ 351. After One Recovery under § 3 (e), No Second Recovery under § 69 (a) Even though "Damages" Not Included in First Suit.

—After one recovery has been had under Bankr. Act, § 3 (e) on the bond, a second suit under § 69 (a) is not maintainable for the "damages" for the seizure, even though "damages" were not included in the first action. The cause of action is single—"for costs, counsel fees, expenses and damages" —and may not be split.[21]

§ 352. No "Seizure," No Counsel Fees, Expenses nor Damages.

—Where there is no seizure of property, no counsel fees, expenses nor damages may be allowed the defendant.[22] But, of course, costs are to be allowed defendant, if the petition is dismissed.[23]

19. In re Selkregg, 16 A. B. R. 474, 144 Fed. 557 (D. C. Pa.).
20. In re Spalding, 17 A. B. R. 667 (C. C. A. N. Y.).
21. Nixon v. Fidelity & Deposit Co., 18 A. B. R. 174 (C. C. A. Mont.).
22. In re Williams, 9 A. B. R. 736, 120 Fed. 34 (D. C. Ark.); In re Morris, 7 A. B. R. 709, 115 Fed. 591 (D.

C. Penn.); In re Ghiglione, 1 A. B. R. 580, 93 Fed. 186 (D. C. N. Y.); impliedly, Selkregg v. Hamilton, 16 A. B. R. 476 (D. C. Pa.); impliedly, In re Smith, 16 A. B. R. 478 (D. C. Okla.); impliedly, In re Spalding, 17 A. B. R. 667 (C. C. A. N. Y.).
23. In re Morris, 7 A. B. R. 709 (D. C. Penna.). Compare, In re Williams,

An injunction restraining certain persons from paying money to the bankrupt does not amount to a "seizure" within the meaning of this section.[24] Nor does an injunction restraining the sheriff or alleged bankrupt from disposing of the alleged bankrupt's stock of goods pending the hearing upon the petition for adjudication amount to such a "seizure;" nor is the injunction bond liable for counsel fees, damages, etc., assessable upon a bond given under Bankr. Act, § 3 (e).[25]

§ 353. Only Damages for "Seizure," Not for Instituting Bankruptcy Proceedings.—Thus, also, only damages for the seizure of the property are allowable, not damages for instituting the bankruptcy proceedings themselves.[26]

Selkregg v. Hamilton Bros., 16 A. B. R. 476, 144 Fed. 557 (D. C. Pa.): "But here again, the result of the institution of the proceedings in bankruptcy is not to be confounded with the seizure under the warrant to the marshal. The one was no doubt calculated to affect the credit, and so may have worked the financial injury of the firm, in a way that may make the petitioning creditors liable to action. But these consequential damages are quite different from those due to the taking possession of their canning factory, by which their business was directly interfered with, if that was in fact the case. Both steps may have combined to work their injury, but each, in its own way, and only that which is directly attributable to the one which we are considering is recoverable for here."

In re Moehs & Rechnitzer, 22 A. B. R. 286, 174 Fed. 165 (D. C. N. Y.): "The liability on the petitioning creditors bond is for damages caused by the appointment of the receiver. There is no liability for filing a petition in bankruptcy except for the usual costs, unless the petitioners acted without probable cause and maliciously, and in that case the remedy is a suit in the nature of a suit for malicious prosecution."

In re Ward, 29 A. B. R. 547, 194 Fed. 174, 179 (D. C. N. J.): "Such section [Bankr. Act, § 3] cannot be invoked to recover costs and expenses occasioned in making a successful defense to the charge of bankruptcy."

And even damages for loss of credit by the seizure may be mitigated by the debtor's own conduct.

§ 354. "Malicious Prosecution" for Wrongful Seizure.—The bond is not the only recourse of the debtor in case he is not adjudged bankrupt. In proper cases he may institute suit for malicious prosecution.[27]

9 A. B. R. 736, 120 Fed. 34 (D. C. Ark.). Inferentially, In re Spalding, 17 A. B. R. 667 (C. C. A. N. Y.).

24. In re Williams, 9 A. B. R. 736, 120 Fed. 34 (D. C. Ark.).

25. In re Hines, 16 A. B. R. 541 (D. C. Ore.).

26. In re Smith, 16 A. B. R. 478 (D. C. Okla.).

27. Wilkinson v. Goodfellow-Brooks Shoe Co., 141 Fed. 218 (D. C. Mo.); obiter, Selkregg v. Hamilton Bros., 16 A. B. R. 476, 144 Fed. 557 (D. C. Pa.); obiter, In re Haff, 13 A. B. R. 354 (C. C. A. N. Y.); [1867] Sonneborn v. Stewart, Fed. Cas. 13,176, reversed in 98 U. S. 187 because facts showed probable cause; King v. Sullivan, 92 S. W. (Tex.) 51; [Eng.] Brown v. Chapman, 3 Barr. 1418. Obiter, In re Moehs & Rechnitzer, 22 A. B. R. 286, 174 Fed. 165 (D. C. N. Y.).

Libel in Bankruptcy Petition.—A material and pertinent allegation of

§ 355. Property Claimed Adversely Not to Be Seized.—Property

claimed adversely and in the actual possession of the adverse claimant must not be summarily ordered seized.[28] The warrant of seizure must not be taken as giving any greater authority to seize property in the hands of adverse holders than would have existed without such warrant.

Obiter, Bardes v. Bank, 4 A. B. R. 163, at page 176, 178 U. S. 538: "The powers conferred on the courts of bankruptcy by clause 3 of § 2, and by § 69, after the filing of a petition in bankruptcy, and in case it is necessary for the preservation of property of the bankrupt, to authorize receivers or the marshals to take charge of it until a trustee is appointed, can hardly be considered as authorizing the forcible seizure of such property in the possession of an adverse claimant, and have no bearing upon the question in what courts the trustee may sue him." But as to this obiter, see Bryan v. Bernheimer, 5 A. B. R. 631, 181 U. S. 188, where the court says: "But the remark 'can hardly be considered as authorizing the forcible seizure of such property in the possession of an adverse claimant' was an inadvertence, and upon a question not arising in the case then before the court, which related exclusively to jurisdiction of a suit by the trustee after his appointment."

In re Kolin, 13 A. B. R. 533 (C. C. A. Ills.): "The court and the parties seem to have overlooked the ruling of this court in Boonville Nat. Bk. v. Blakey, 6 A. B. R. 13, 43, 107 Fed. 891, that a receiver is a mere custodian of property taken from the possession of the bankrupt until a trustee is appointed; that he does not exercise the powers of a trustee, and while he may take appropriate measures incident to the protection of the property in his custody, and, in case of perishable property may, under the direction of the court, sell the same when necessary, yet he is not authorized, nor can the bankruptcy court properly direct him, to take possession of property held and claimed adversely by third parties, or to institute actions for the recovery of property claimed to belong to the bankrupt's estate."

In re Sunseri, 18 A. B. R. 235 (D. C. Pa.): "When property alleged to have been disposed of by the bankrupt in fraud of his creditors is in the hands of third parties and a seizure thereof properly made under authority of the court, if such third parties set up an adverse claim to said property, which is more than merely colorable, and said parties are not merely the agent or representative of the bankrupt, the court can proceed no further than the ascertainment of these facts, but must relegate the parties to some proper plenary action."

In re Ward, 5 A. B. R. 215, 217, 104 Fed. 985 (D. C. Mass.): "* * * the jurisdiction of this court over plenary suits, and its jurisdiction by summary

a pending bankruptcy petition charging fraud and collusion was held absolutely privileged in Rosenberg v. Dworetsky, 24 A. B. R. 583, N. Y. App. Div.: "This allegation was certainly pertinent and material to the claim that the bankrupt had removed and concealed the goods. The alleged libel complained of, therefore, is a statement in a pleading or petition filed in a court in pending judicial proceedings, pertinent and relevant to the issue there presented. As such

it was absolutely privileged, and all this appearing upon the face of the complaint, said complaint was open to attack by demurrer."

28. See post, § 1652, et seq. and § 1796, et seq. Also, see post, § 391. In Rockwood, 1 A. B. R. 272, 91 Fed. 363 (D. C. Iowa); Beach v. Macon Grocery Co., 8 A. B. R. 751, 116 Fed. 143 (C. C. A.). See also, 11 A. B. R. 104. But see erroneous decision contra, In re Knopf, 16 A. B. R. 432 (D. C. S. C.); also erroneous decision

process and pending adjudication, to seize property in the hands of a third party and alleged to belong to the bankrupt, stand and fall together. In re Hammand they were said to ·stand together. In Bardes v. Bank the opinion was expressed that they fall together. For these reasons, I think the District Court is without jurisdiction to take property alleged to belong to the bankrupt out of the possession of a third party, as well temporarily and by summary process, as permanently and by plenary suits. * * *

"Counsel for the petitioners urged that the Supreme Court passed only upon the jurisdiction of this court over plenary suits, and that the jurisdiction by summary process was left undisturbed. It would be strange, however, if a court be without jurisdiction to determine the title or to affect the control of property by a plenary suit, where all parties must be fully heard, and yet has jurisdiction on summary process, and without hearing, to take possession of the same property or to restrain its use. I do not understand that the Supreme Court has held that the District Court may do by summary process that which it is forbidden to do in a plenary suit."

Compare, obiter, McNulty v. Feingold, 12 A. B. R. 338, 129 Fed. 1001 (D. C. Penna.): "This applies to the powers of receivers or the marshal to take charge of property of bankrupts in the possession of third persons after the filing of the petition, and until it is dismissed or the trustee is qualified, when that is absolutely necessary for the preservation of the estate (Bryan v. Bernheimer, 181 U. S. 188, 5 Am. B. R. 623), and would be a proceeding in bankruptcy, as distinguished from a controversy at law or in equity, within the true interpretation of § 23 (In re Rochford, 10 A. B. R. 608, 124 Fed. 182)."

In re Kelley, 1 A. B. R. 306, 91 Fed. 504 (D. C. Tenn.): "Warrant cannot be issued directing the marshal to seize property in the possession of third persons under claim of title."

And such property may not be summarily ordered seized, even though such adverse claimant in possession is being proceeded against as one of the

contra, In re Haupt Bros., 18 A. B. R. 585, 239 Fed. 153 (D. C. N. Y.); also erroneous decision contra, but obiter, In re Berkowitz, 23 A. B.. R. 227, 173 Fed. 1012 (D. C. N. J.).

Better practice to notify holder, unless great exigency exists. In re Sunseri, 18 A. B. R. 234 (D. C. Pa.): "It may be added that in all such proceedings, unless the property is of an exceedingly perishable nature or the circumstances of the case particularly urgent, it would be better before any order for seizure were granted to give the party in whose hands the property is alleged to be prior notice, and an opportunity to be heard on a rule to show cause."

Compare, In re Young, 7 A. B. R. 14, 111 Fed. 158 (C. C. A. Ark.), a case rightly decided but wrongly reasoned. The property seized was actually in the possession of the bankrupt and the right to seize it summarily was therefore unquestioned. See post, § 1794. The court also seems to consider that the Supreme Court in its case of Bryan v. Bernheimer, 181 U. S. 188, 5 A. B. R. 623, had acknowledged an error in its previous case of Bardes v. Bank, 178 U. S. 524, 4 A. B. R. 163. There was no such error and the two cases are clearly and necessarily distinguishable. Bryan v. Bernheimer related to seizures of property in the constructive custody of the bankruptcy court—a proceedings not tolerated in any jurisdiction; whilst Bardes v. Bank denied the right of the bankruptcy court to proceed summarily to seize property held all the time by adverse claimants.

Compare, Mather v. Coe, 1 A. B. R. 504 (D. C. Ohio). But compare, obiter, contra, In re Rochford, 10 A. B. R. 608, 124 Fed. 182 (C. C. A. S. Dak.). Stipulation between receiver and adverse claimant as to sale of property in adverse claimant's possession. See Ommen, trustee, v. Talcott, 23 A. B. R. 572, 175 Fed. 261 (D. C. N. Y.).

members of the partnership sought to be adjudicated bankrupt, if, in fact, such person is not a partner.[29]

Though property adversely held may not be summarily ordered seized, yet, if, under a general warrant of seizure, not specifically directed to such property, the receiver or marshal does actually seize the property, the real owner probably may not regain possession simply on proof of a taking from an adverse colorable possession, but must, on the merits, prove actual right of property or right of possession.

§ 356. Property in Actual Possession of Bankrupt, Though Claimed by Another, Seizable.

—But property claimed adversely and yet in the actual custody of the bankrupt, although as "agent" or "custodian" of the adverse claimant, may be summarily seized.[30]

Thus, where an officer of a bankrupt corporation was arrested on a criminal charge and, at the request of the jail authorities, handed over to them certain property claimed to belong to his wife, it was held that the United States marshal, acting under proper warrant had the right, and it was his duty, to seize such property.[31]

Before adjudication in bankruptcy has taken place though after petition filed, officers of court in possession under legal process are adverse claimants representing their several creditors, under and by virtue of a legal lien that has not yet been nullified, and such officers are not subject at such time to summary process from the bankruptcy court.[32]

Property summarily taken by the receiver or marshal from the possession of an adverse claimant must not be sold without the claimant's consent;[33] and where property is taken from the possession of an adverse claimant, without his consent, by a receiver in bankruptcy under an erroneous order which the claimant successfully resists on appeal, he is entitled to a return of the property without charge of any kind against either it or him.[34]

§ 357. Officer Making Seizure, to Determine Ownership at Own Risk.

—Responsibility of determining ownership of the property seized rests upon the marshal who may be liable for wrongful seizure.[35]

§ 358. Compensation and Expenses of Marshal or Receiver on "Seizure."

—Before the Amendment of 1910 fixed the compensation of marshals and receivers it was held, that the marshal was entitled to reasonable compensation where he made the seizure under Bankr. Act, § 2 (3) ;[36]

29. In re Nixon, 6 A. B. R. 693, 110 Fed. 633 (D. C. Mont.).

30. In re Moody, 12 A. B. R. 718, 131 Fed. 525 (D. C. Iowa); In re Bender, 5 A. B. R. 632, 106 Fed. 873 (D. C. Ark.).

31. LeMaster v. Spencer, 29 A. B. R. 264, 203 Fed. 210 (C. C. A. Colo.).

32. In re Andre, 13 A. B. R. 132 (C. C. A. N. Y.). Inferentially, Mather v. Coe, 1 A. B. R. 504, 92 Fed. 333 (D. C. Ohio).

33. Beach v. Macon Grocery Co., 8 A. B. R. 751, 116 Fed. 143 (C. C. A. Ga.).

34. Beach v. Macon Grocery Co., 8 A. B. R. 751, 116 Fed. 143 (C. C. A. Ga.).

35. See note to In re Rockwood, 1 A. B. R. 272.

36. In re Adams Sartorial Co., 4 A. B. R. 107, 101 Fed. 215 (D. C. Colo.).

and also to reimbursement of his expenses.[37]   And it was likewise held that
the receiver was entitled to reasonable compensation when he made the
seizure, and that the amount thereof was within the discretion of the court
and was not limited by § 2 (5) which prescribed merely the compensation for
continuing the business.[38]

Amendment of 1910.—The Amendment of 1910 to § 72, which was
inserted by the senate, includes the receiver and marshal among those who
"shall not in any form or guise receive, nor the court allow" them "any
further or other compensation than that prescribed by the act;" so that,
apparently, in cases where property is returned to the bankrupt on the dismissal of the petition any allowance to the receiver or marshal is cut off,
except commissions on monies disbursed, in accordance with § 48, and the
marshal's fees for service of papers and process, etc., in accordance with §
52.   However, § 48 is to be construed in the light of its object, which has
reference only to allowances out of the assets administered—not to compensation of receivers and marshals taxed as part of the costs against unsuccessful petitioning creditors and others, where the assets are not administered but returned intact to the respondent without adjudication of
bankruptcy; therefore, in cases where assets are returned to the respondent
on dismissal of the petition without adjudication and without administration, the compensation to be fixed as part of the costs against the unsuccessful petitioner or petitioners, would, it would seem, remain in the discretion
of the court.

DIVISION 2.

RESTRAINING ORDERS AND INJUNCTIONS BEFORE ADJUDICATION.

**§ 359. Jurisdiction to Enjoin after Filing of Petition and before
Adjudication.**—The bankruptcy court has power between the time of the
filing of the petition and the adjudication of bankruptcy (as well as afterwards), to enjoin all persons within its jurisdiction from doing any act
that will interfere with the due administration of the bankruptcy act.[39]

---

37. In re Smith, 16 A. B. R. 480,
146 Fed. 923 (D. C. Okla.). Recent
legislation having put the marshal
upon a salary basis, such compensation, probably, if allowed at all, would
go to the United States.

38. In re Kirkpatrick, Receiver, etc.,
17 A. B. R. 594, 148 Fed. 684 (C. C.
A. Mich.).

39. See post, "Restraining Orders
after Bankruptcy Court Has Assumed
Jurisdiction," § 1903, et seq.
As to enjoining legal proceedings
where the state court has acquired
jurisdiction, see post, § 1904, et seq.
Instance, In re Oxley & White, 25
A. B. R. 656, 182 Fed. 1019 (D. C.

Wash.); impliedly, In re Donnelly, 26
A. B. R. 304, 188 Fed. 1001 (D. C.
Ohio).
Perhaps, New River Coal Land v.
Ruffner, 20 A. B. R. 100, 165 Fed. 881
(C. C. A. W. Va.), quoted at § 1901.
But in this case it is not certain
whether adjudication had already oc-
curred or not.
Apparently, In re Jersey Island
Packing Co., 14 A. B. R. 690, 138 Fed.
625 (C. C. A. Calif.); In re Globe
Cycle Works, 2 A. B. R. 447 (Ref. N.
Y.). Obiter, Beach v. Macon Grocery
Co., 8 A. B. R. 751, 116 Fed. 143 (C.
C. A. Ga.).
In re Eastern Commission & Im-

In re Hornstein, 10 A. B. R. 308, 122 Fed. 266 (D. C. N. Y.): "It is plain that the judge of a court of bankruptcy may lawfully grant such restraining order, operative on and binding litigants in the State court, although strangers to the bankruptcy proceedings, as may be necessary for the enforcement of the provisions of the Bankrupt Act. This court has no hesitation in holding that express power is given by the Act of Congress to courts of bankruptcy to enjoin all persons within its jurisdiction, whether litigants in a State court or elsewhere, from doing any act that will interfere with or prevent the due administration of the Bankruptcy Act. If this is not true, how frail and worthless is the law. In the face of a statute conferring the power, comity does not require the courts of the United States to compel persons whose rights are seriously jeopardized by proceedings in a State court to resort thereto for protection. This restraining order was properly granted, and must be upheld, if the petitioners had the right to institute this proceeding in involuntary bankruptcy."

In re Krinsky Bros., 7 A. B. R. 535, 112 Fed. 972 (D. C. N. Y.): "Those who deal with a bankrupt's property in the interval between the filing of the petition and the final adjudication, do so at their peril. * * * and the moment it was suggested that proceedings had been instituted in this court, it was his duty to have paused and ascertained the status of the matter."

In re Weinger, Bergman & Co., 11 A. B. R. 424, 126 Fed. 875 (D. C. N. Y.), wherein an order restraining replevin proceedings was granted, after the filing of the petition and before adjudication, the court saying, "The fact that the bankruptcy court may not have yet made an adjudication and that no receiver nor trustee has yet been appointed, in my opinion, is immaterial."

In re Goldberg, 9 A. B. R. 156, 117 Fed. 692 (D. C. N. Y.): "Until the question of bankruptcy is determined, further proceedings in the action should be stayed, and until 12 months thereafter in case Goldberg is adjudged a bankrupt. Clearly the alleged purchaser at the sale should not be permitted to take or remove the property, if lawfully he may be prevented, nor should the sheriff be permitted to sell.

"It is claimed that such action should proceed to judgment, and a sale of the property attached be permitted; the distribution of the proceeds only being enjoined. There is no reason or necessity for such a course. If Goldberg is adjudged a bankrupt, the trustee will take and dispose of the property. If not so adjudged, these attaching creditors will proceed with their action. The right to the injunction sought in this case is plain. In re Lesser, 3 A. B. R. 758, 99 Fed. 913; Bear v. Chase, 3 A. B. R. 748, 99 Fed. 920. Indeed, the act itself suggests this as the proper remedy in such a case. Bankruptcy Act, § 11a; § 67f; § 2 (15)."

---

porting Co., 12 A. B. R. 305, 129 Fed. 847 (D. C. Mass.): In this case the bankruptcy court granted an injunction pending adjudication in bankruptcy, restraining an attaching creditor from proceeding to judgment against the bankrupt—the bankrupt having pledged some of its own property with the surety upon the redelivery bond that had been given to secure a release of the property attached. Indirectly therefore the bankrupt estate would be depleted by the attachment, so that it was proper to issue the restraining order.

Instance of restraining order, subsequently dissolved on the facts, In re Latimer, 15 A. B. R. 461, 141 Fed. 665 (D. C. Pa.). Apparently (but not clear whether before adjudication), In re Currier, 5 A. B. R. 639 (Ref. N. Y.).

Instance, In re Kleinhans, 7 A. B. R. 604, 113 Fed. 107 (D. C. N. Y.), restraining landlord from prosecuting summary proceedings in the state court to oust the receiver from occupancy of the premises of the bankrupt.

In re Hines, 16 A. B. R. 541, 144 Fed. 147 (D. C. Ore.): "The only purpose of the injunction was to restrain the debtor, and the sheriff, who had custody of the stock of goods, from disposing of them during the pendency of the proceedings under the petition to have the debtor adjudged a bankrupt; the purpose being to have the matter remain in statu quo until it could be ascertained whether or not the defendant was in reality a bankrupt, and whether his property should be taken charge of by the bankruptcy court."

Obiter, Beach v. Macon Grocery Co., 8 A. B. R. 751, 116 Fed. 143 (C. C. A. Ga.): "The sixty-ninth section of the Bankrupt Law provides a mode of protecting the alleged bankrupt's estate pending the adjudication of an involuntary bankrupt, and * * * the bankruptcy court can deal with the property of said Asa N. Beach through seizure by the marshal; or, under the court's general equity powers, the court can otherwise protect the property by the appointment of a receiver, or through an injunction, * * * an order on motion and notice may be made by the bankruptcy court restraining and enjoining Julia M. Dixon from disposing of or removing or incumbering any of the property described in the ancillary bill until the trial of the issue * * * in involuntary bankruptcy."

Apparently (but not clear whether before adjudication) In re Smith, 8 A. B. R. 56, 113 Fed. 993 (D. C. Ga.): "There can be no question of the power of the court between the time an involuntary petition in bankruptcy is filed and the selection of a trustee to make proper orders to protect and guard the bankrupt's estate for the benefit of creditors, as may be proper and right under the facts presented. Of course, the court will not unduly interfere with property claimed by third persons, and will not interfere at all with bona fide sales for fair consideration, and which are not obnoxious to the provisions of the bankruptcy act."

Apparently (but not clear whether before adjudication) In re Ball, 9 A. B. R. 276, 118 Fed. 672 (D. C. Vt.): "This stock of goods is a part of the estate to be administered by the trustees, upon which the petitioner has only a lien, which, to its lawful extent, is to be respected and adjusted in the proceedings. A sale by her upon the mortgages, as threatened, would defeat this right, and confessedly waste the estate and wrong the general creditors, while in administration by the trustee her claims will be saved to her, by being left to rest upon the proceeds. The injunction should therefore be continued pending the administration, which will leave the goods for the trustee, as a part of the estate, to be proceeded with under direction of the referee."

§ 360. No Injunction before Bankruptcy Petition Filed, to Preserve Status Quo.

—In one case it has been held that the bankruptcy court has jurisdiction before the filing of any bankruptcy petition to issue injunctions to preserve the status quo until a bankruptcy petition can be filed.[40] But in other cases in which the state court's authority was invoked, such jurisdiction before the filing of the bankruptcy petition has been denied.[41]

Ellis v. Hays Saddlery & Leather Co., 8 A. B. R. 109 (Kans. Sup. Ct.): "The National Bankruptcy Act of 1898 went into effect on July 1st of that year, but

---

40. Blake v. Valentine, 1 A. B. R. 372, 89 Fed. 691 (D. C. Calif., distinguished in In re Ogles, 1 A. B. R. 683, 93 Fed. 426).

41. Vietor v. Lewis, 1 A. B. R. 667, 53 N. Y. Supp. 944, 38 App. Div. 316. See also, post, § 402.

its operation was suspended so that involuntary proceedings against a debtor could not be commenced until November 1st. In August, 1898, a failing merchant gave a chattel mortgage on his stock of goods to secure a debt owing to the mortgagee, and the latter took possession. A general unsecured creditor (the plaintiff) then brought suit to enjoin a removal of the goods or their sale, alleging that the mortgage was executed in fraud of the Bankrupt Law, and praying that the property be held in statu quo, until November 1st, when proceedings in bankruptcy, which plaintiff alleged it intended to file against its debtor, could be made available. Held, that no cause of action for equitable relief was stated in the petition, and that a decree granting an injunction must be reversed."

Clothing Co. *v.* Hazle, 6 A. B. R. 265 (Mich.): "It is apparent that the object of this bill was merely to preserve an estate until a time should come when it could be administered under the new law, which at the time the bill was filed did not authorize the Federal courts to interfere. It is claimed that as these courts were powerless to protect creditors under the Bankruptcy Act, the State courts must have the power. This does not impress us as being a sound theory. The rights and remedies in such cases, under the State law, were settled. They existed and were open at this time. But counsel say that they might be superseded or supplemented for the four months following July 1st by another remedy so that they might, if they chose, avail themselves of a protective remedy afforded by the Bankrupt Act. We see no better reason why this should be than that an injunction should heretofore have been issued, in any case of fraud and danger, to impound the estate until creditors' claims should mature, judgment be obtained, execution issued and returned, to the end that a creditors' bill might be effectively filed. The exigency is as great in such a case as this, yet no one has heard of such a proceeding being permitted."

And such jurisdiction, on principle, does not exist.

§ 361. Injunction Issues in Case Itself, but No Part of Bankruptcy Petition.

—The petition for the injunction should be filed and the injunction be issued in the bankruptcy proceedings themselves.[42] But the allegations and prayer for an injunction should not be a part of the petition in bankruptcy itself, for fear of multifariousness.[43]

§ 362. Comity Requires Resort First to State Court, Except in Exigency.

—Where the property involved is already in the custody of the state court, comity usually requires resort to the state court first; but summary proceedings, may, in the court's discretion, be taken directly, and in the first instance, in the bankruptcy court.[44]

Resort to the state court first is not such an election as will prevent the subsequent issuance of the injunction by the bankruptcy court.[45]

42. In re Globe Cycle Works, 2 A. B. R. 447 (Ref. N. Y.); impliedly, In re Jersey Island Packing Co., 14 A. B. R. 689, 138 Fed. 625 (C. C. A. Calif.).

43. Mather *v.* Coe, 1 A. B. R. 504, 92 Fed. 333 (D. C. Ohio). As to proper practice, see course pursued in Philips *v.* Turner, 8 A. B. R. 172, 114 Fed. 726 (C. C. A. Miss.).

44. Inferentially, In re Hornstein, 10 A. B. R. 308, 122 Fed. 266 (D. C. N. Y.). Compare, on subject of comity, post, §§ 1637, 1860, 1904, 2699. Also compare Bear *v.* Chase, 3 A. B. R. 746, 99 Fed. 920 (C. C. A. S. Car.).

45. Bear *v.* Chase, 3 A. B. R. 746, 99 Fed. 920 (C. C. A. S. Car.); In re Hecox, 21 A. B. R. 314, 164 Fed. 823

§ **363. Notice of Hearing for Injunction.**—Notice of the filing of the petition for the injunction should be given;[46] unless for good cause shown dispensed with. But verbal notice of the order of injunction will subject the person restrained thereby to punishment for contempt for disobedience thereof.[47]

§ **364. Bankrupt May Be Restrained.**—The bankrupt may be restrained from disposing of the property.[48]

Indeed, it is preferable, on account of the saving of expense, to resort to an injunction rather than a receivership, wherever an injunction is available.

§ **365. Likewise Adverse Claimants.**—Adverse claimants in possession of property, may, before adjudication, on proper showing, be restrained by the bankruptcy court from disposing of property claimed to belong to creditors, notwithstanding proceedings to actually recover it may not be instituted by the receiver.[49] And adverse claimants in possession who come into such injunction proceedings and litigate the merits of the original transaction have thereby consented to the jurisdiction, such that upon an adverse adjudication thereon they may be ordered to surrender the property.[50]

And secured creditors may be enjoined from selling out their securities, even though by the terms of the agreement of pledge they might have such remedy;[51] although, where sale by the pledgee is authorized by the terms of the agreement of pledge, injunction would be granted only in cases of oppression or fraud.[52]

Adverse claimants may be restrained from taking legal action relative to the bankrupt's property in the meantime; thus, real estate mortgagees may be restrained from proceeding with a foreclosure suit started after the filing of the bankruptcy petition;[53] whether they were in possession or not[54] at the time of the filing of the bankruptcy petition.

§ **366. Also Court Officers in Possession.**—Receivers, assignees,

(C. C. A. Colo.). Compare Hooks *v.* Aldridge, 16 A. B. R. 664, 145 Fed. 865 (C. C. A. Tex.).

46. Beach *v.* Macon Grocery Co., 8 A. B. R. 751, 116 Fed. 143 (C. C. A. Ga.). Compare, inferentially, similar rule as to the appointment of receivers to make seizures, ante, § 346; post, § 381.

47. In re Krinsky Bros., 7 A. B. R. 535, 112 Fed. 875 (D. C. N. Y.). As to fees of marshal, see post, "Costs of Administration," § 2129, et seq.

48. Impliedly, In re Hines, 16 A. B. R. 541, 144 Fed. 147 (D. C. Ore.).

49. In re Currier, 5 A. B. R. 639 (Ref. N. Y.). Instance, In re Clifford D. Mills, 25 A. B. R. 278, 179 Fed. 409 (D. C. N. Y.). See, also similar proposition *after* adjudication, post, § 1905.

50. Philips *v.* Turner, 8 A. B. R. 171, 114 Fed. 726 (C. C. A. Miss.).

51. Impliedly, obiter, In re Mertens, 14 A. B. R. 226, 231, 134 Fed. 104 (D. C. N. Y.), quoted post, § 760 or rather § 761.

52. See post, § 761.

53. In re Donnelly, 26 A. B. R. 304, 188 Fed. 1001 (D. C. Ohio).

54. In re Donnelly, 26 A. B. R. 304, 188 Fed. 1001 (D. C. Ohio).

sheriffs and other court officers may meantime be restrained from disposing of assets of the estate in their possession.[55]

Impliedly, Coal Land Co. v. Ruffner Bros., 21 A. B. R. 474, 165 Fed. 881 (C. C. A. W. Va.): "In the act forbidding courts of the United States to stay proceedings in a state court, the courts of bankruptcy are specifically excepted and the bankruptcy law of 1898 expressly confers upon these courts the power to issue injunctions to stay proceedings within this exception."

§ 367. Restraining Order Ineffectual Out of District of Issuance.
—Undoubtedly the restraining order would be ineffectual to restrain parties outside the district.

In re Acme Harvester Co. v. Beekman Co., 27 A. B. R. 262, 228 U. S. 478: "As to the injunction, we are of the opinion that there was no power in the District Court to issue an ex parte injunction, without notice or service of process, attempting to restrain the Beekman Lumber Company from suing in a State outside the jurisdiction of the District Court. Such proceeding could only have binding force upon the Lumber Company if jurisdiction were obtained over it by proceedings in a court having jurisdiction, and upon service of process upon such creditor."

It would seem that the proper practice, where it becomes necessary to protect property located in another state, prior to adjudication of bankruptcy, would be for the creditors themselves to bring suit,[56] or for the receiver to institute ancillary proceedings in the other district.[57]

§ 368. Who May Petition for Injunction—Receiver—Creditors—Bankrupt.
—The petition may be filed by the receiver;[58] or by creditors.[59]

The petition also may be filed by the bankrupt in the interest of the estate.

Obiter, Blake v. Valentine, 1 A. B. R. 378, 89 Fed. 691 (D. C. Calif.): "But all the authorities which discuss this question are to the effect, as stated in Bump. Bankr. (10th Ed.) 229, that before the appointment of an assignee (or trustee)

---

55. In re Lengert Wagon Co., 6 A. B. R. 535, 110 Fed. 927 (D. C. N. Y.); In re Globe Cycle Works, 2 A. B. R. 447 (Ref. N. Y.); In re Goldberg, 9 A. B. R. 158, 117 Fed. 692 (D. C. N. Y.). Apparently, In re Hornstein, 10 A. B. R. 308, 122 Fed. 266 (D. C. N. Y.). Perhaps, New River Coal Land Co. v. Ruffner, 20 A. B. R. 100, 165 Fed. 881 (C. C. A. W. Va.). Instance, restraining sheriff, In re Oxley & White, 25 A. B. R. 656, 182 Fed. 1019 (D. C. Wash.).
Under what circumstances court proceedings will not be enjoined, see subject of "Conflict of Jurisdiction," post, § 1580, et seq; also, § 1636.

56. In re Schrom, 3 A. B. R. 352, 97 Fed. 760 (D. C. Iowa, distinguished in 9 A. B. R. 744).

57. See Bankr. Act as amended 1910 § 2 (20); also see post, Rem. on Bankr., §§ 1707, 1708, et seq.

58. In re Barrett, 12 A. B. R. 626, 132 Fed. 362 (D. C. Tenn.); impliedly, In re Hornstein, 10 A. B. R. 311, 122 Fed. 266 (D. C. N. Y.).

59. Impliedly, In re Currier, 5 A. B. R. 639 (Ref. N. Y.).
Impliedly, In re Jersey Island Packing Co., 14 A. B. R. 689, 690, 138 Fed. 625 (C. C. A. Calif.). In this case the court upheld a petition by unsecured creditors filed simultaneously with an involuntary petition in bankruptcy, to restrain the proposed sale of all the assets of the bankrupt under a trust deed. Instance, In re Latimer, 15 A. B. R. 461, 141 Fed. 665 (D. C. Pa.).

proceedings for an injunction to protect the property of the bankrupt may be instituted by the bankrupt or the petitioning creditor." This authority is incorrect, however, in holding that suits may be instituted before the filing of the bankruptcy petition, to hold matters in statu quo.

§ 369. **Verification.**—The petition for the injunction may be verified by attorney.[60]

§ 370. **Injunction Bond and Damages on Bond.**—Undoubtedly, the court has authority to dispense with the giving of the customary injunction bond. Certainly so, if it may do so in independent plenary suits instituted by the receiver or trustee, as held in some cases.[61]

Impliedly, In re Williams, 9 A. B. R. 736, 740, 120 Fed. 34 (D. C. Ark.): "* * * as the restraining order was granted without any bond, under the general equity powers conferred on the courts by § 2 of the Bankrupt Act. In equity cases, when an injunction is granted without a bond, only taxable costs can be allowed."

The same damages are not allowed on the injunction bond that are allowed on the bond for warrant to marshal to seize property, discussed in the preceding division.

In re Hines, 16 A. B. R. 541, 144 Fed. 147 (D. C. Ore.): "The injunction bond which was given in the present case cannot, under any process of reasoning, take the place of the bond intended to be executed under § 3e. Indeed, in the present instance, the property of the debtor was not taken into custody. * * * The conditions of the injunction bond are widely different from those prescribed for the bond to be given under § 3e, and if I were to look at the bond alone I could not adjudge, under its conditions, the relief demanded by way of costs; but, it not having been intended for that purpose, the defendant could in no way be entitled to the relief which he seeks under § 3e, because the relief there provided for can only be had upon the bond contemplated by the section. I must hold, therefore, that the plaintiff is not entitled under his cost bill to the attorney's fees prayed for, nor to the keeper's fees, damages, or expenses claimed by Hines for attending court."

DIVISION 3.

ARREST, DETENTION AND EXTRADITION OF THE BANKRUPT.

§ 371. **Arrest and Detention of Bankrupt, for Examination.**—The Judge may, at any time after the filing of a petition by or against a person, and before the expiration of one month after the qualification of the trustee, upon satisfactory proof by the affidavits of at least two persons that such bankrupt is about to leave the district in which he resides or has his principal place of business to avoid examination, and that his departure will defeat the proceedings in bankruptcy, issue a warrant to the marshal, di-

60. In re Goldberg, 9 A. B. R. 156, 117 Fed. 692 (D. C. N. Y.).

61. In re Barrett, 12 A. B. R. 626, 132 Fed. 362 (D. C. Pa.).

recting him to bring such bankrupt forthwith before the court for examination.

If upon hearing the evidence of the parties it shall appear to the court or a judge thereof that the allegations are true and that it is necessary, he shall order such marshal to keep such bankrupt in custody not exceeding ten days, but not imprison him, until he shall be examined and released or give bail conditioned for his appearance for examination, from time to time, not exceeding in all ten days, as required by the court, and for his obedience to all lawful orders made in reference thereto.[62]

§ 372. Warrant Not Proper Where Bankrupt Already Departed.
—The warrant cannot be issued for the purpose of procuring the return or as the basis for the extradition of a bankrupt who has already departed.[63]

§ 373. Writ of Ne Exeat Also Available.
—Arrest and detention under § 9 (b) are not the exclusive method of detaining the bankrupt. A writ of "ne exeat republica" may be issued in aid of the bankruptcy proceedings.[64]

Hoffschlaeger Co. *v.* Young Nap, 12 A. B. R. 510 (D. C. Hawaii): "The counsel for the plaintiff, however, said that they had moved for the writ, not under § 9 (b) but under § 2, subd. 15."

Although the writ of ne exeat cannot be issued unless a suit in equity is commenced, yet bankruptcy proceedings are held to be such a suit.[65]

And it may be issued where the specific bankruptcy provisions of § 9 (b)

---

62. Bankr. Act, § 9 (b).

Contempt for Squandering Assets after Filing of Petition.—In one case the bankrupt was punished for contempt for recklessly squandering assets which he knew his creditors had a right to have preserved after the filing of the bankruptcy petition against him. In re Smith, 26 A. B. R. 399, 185 Fed. 983 (D. C. N. Y.).

63. In re Ketchum, 5 A. B. R. 532, 108 Fed. 35 (C. C. A. Tenn.). See post, § 375.

64. In re Lipke, 3 A. B. R. 569, 98 Fed. 970 (D. C. N. Y.); Lewis *v.* Shainwald, 48 Fed. 500. Inferentially, In re Ketchum, 5 A. B. R. 532, 537, 108 Fed. 35 (C. C. A. Tenn.); In re Cohen, 14 A. B. R. 355, 36 Fed. 999 (D. C. Ills.); impliedly, In re Appel, 20 A. B. R. 890, 163 Fed. 1002 (C. C. A. Mass.); In re Berkowitz, 22 A. B. R. 231, 173 Fed. 1012 (D. C. N. J.).

Sufficiency of affidavit and process where the writ ne exeat regno is employed. Hoffschlaeger Co. *v.* Young Nap, 12 A. B. R. 510 (D. C. Hawaii): "Petition for a writ of ne exeat is

sufficiently supported by a sworn affidavit by one holding the positions of secretary, treasurer and manager of the plaintiff corporation, containing the allegations of respondent's indebtedness in a fixed amount for goods sold and delivered, or respondent's action in securing passage for himself and family on a steamer about to depart for a foreign land and that such departure would prejudice plaintiff's interest in such indebtedness.

"The order for process to issue was made on a separate piece of paper; it recited 'In the above case let the writ issue, etc.' This was sufficient, it being filed with the papers in the case and there being no uncertainty about its connection with the case.

"Plaintiff was allowed 24 hours to file the bond required by the order for process and it was filed in that time. This was sufficient."

Irregularities cured by nunc pro tunc order. In re Berkowitz, 22 A. B. R. 231, 173 Fed. 1012 (D. C. N. J.).

65. In re Lipke, 3 A. B. R. 569, 98 Fed. 970 (D. C. N. Y.).

for the detention of the bankrupt are inadequate, or the remedy under such provisions has already expired or is about to expire.[66]

In re Cohen, 14 A. B. R. 355, 136 Fed. 999 (D. C. Ills.): "No power can be exercised which does not clearly reside in the Act. But Congress intended to give, and, in my judgment, the above quoted language does give, every judicial power known to the law which the court may find necessary for the proper enforcement of the Bankrupt Act. * * * Certainly the writ of ne exeat is a judicial power known to the law. * * * It gives the power to issue any necessary writ 'agreeable to the usages and principles of law.' The writ provided for in § 717 is of time-honored usage. Originally it was based upon the principle that the law might require a party to be restrained within the king's realm. Surely it is equally in accordance with the principles of law that the court may for proper cause restrain a party within such territory that the hand of the court may without embarrassment be laid upon him when he is wanted. I think this power is clearly given by § 716, Rev. St., as one of the equity powers of a bankruptcy court, and, if there could be any doubt on that subject, it is removed by the enactment of § 2, subd. 15, of the Bankrupt Law. * * *
"The respondent had been previously arrested and examined before the court as provided for in § 9 (b) * * * and the ten days time limit fixed in § 9 (b) being about to expire this application is urged under the authority of § 2 (15) of the Bankrupt Act and §§ 716, 717, U. S. Rev. Stat."

And the bond given under ne exeat republica providing that the bankrupt shall not depart from the jurisdiction except upon leave of the bankruptcy court, is not satisfied by mere attendance when wanted, but requires leave to be obtained before any departure.

In re Appel, 20 A. B. R. 890, 163 Fed. 1002 (C. C. A. Mass.): "Was the learned judge of the District Court right in ruling that the bond given for the bankrupt's release was in effect a bail bond, binding him only to abide the decrees and orders of the District Court when rendered, and in other respects leaving him free to absent himself from the court's jurisdiction? The trustee contended in accordance with the wording of the bond, that it was conditioned upon his remaining constantly within the jurisdiction. An examination of the practice of the English Court in chancery, as set out in the decided cases and in accepted text books, leads us to the conclusion that the bond should receive its grammatical construction, and that it binds the bankrupt not to go into parts beyond the jurisdiction without leave of the court of bankruptcy, Musgrave v. Medex, 1 Mer. 49; Utten v. Utten, 1 Mer. 51; 2 Dan. Ch. Pr. (6th Am. Ed.), p. 1712. This rule has peculiar application to the case of a bankrupt who is required by the general scheme of the Bankruptcy Act to be constantly on hand in order that he may assist the trustee in his administration of the estate. We hold the decree of the District Court erroneous, and reverse it, because it sets out that the bankrupt's absence from Massachusetts was not a breach of the bond."

§ 374. Extradition.—The bankruptcy court has jurisdiction to extradite bankrupts from their respective districts to other districts.[67]

66. Thus, a year after the adjudication, In re Appel, 20 A. B. R. 890,   163 Fed. 1002 (C. C. A. Mass.).
67. Bankr. Act, § 2 (14).

And whenever a warrant for the apprehension of a bankrupt shall have been issued, and he shall have been found within the jurisdiction of a court other than the one issuing the warrant, he may be extradited in the same manner in which persons under indictment are extradited from one district within which a district court has jurisdiction, to another.[68]

Section 2 (14) refers to the same power that is stated more explicitly in § 10 (a).[69]

This remedy of extradition is available not only immediately upon the filing of the bankruptcy petition, but also later at any time during the pendency of the bankruptcy proceedings.

§ 375. Not to Be Based on Warrant under § 9 (b) Issued after Bankrupt's Departure.

—There is no jurisdiction to issue a warrant of arrest under § 9 (b) after the bankrupt has departed from his district and settled in another, as a basis for extradition proceedings to bring the bankrupt before the court for examination.[70]

§ 376. Not Available Merely to Procure Return for Examination.

—And extradition will be refused where its object and ground is the examination of the bankrupt.[71] Such examination may be obtained through ancillary proceedings instituted in the district of the bankrupt's present residence.[71a]

DIVISION 4.

RECEIVERS.

§ 377. Receivers.—After the filing of the petition and before adjudication and, for that matter, at any time before the appointment of the trustee, the bankruptcy court may appoint a receiver to act in behalf of creditors.

Under the old law of 1867 there was an officer called the messenger whose duty it was upon the filing of a bankruptcy petition to go out and take into his custody the bankrupt's property; but there is no such officer provided under the present law. The present law, however, in § 2, clause 3, provides even more wisely for this contingency, by authorizing the court, by which is meant either the judge or the referee, to

"appoint receivers or the marshals, upon application of parties in interest, in case the courts shall find it absolutely necessary for the preservation of estates, to take charge of the property of bankrupts after the filing of the petition and until it is dismissed or the trustee is qualified."[72]

68. Bankr. Act, § 10 (a).

69. In re Ketchum, 5 A. B. R. 532, 108 Fed. 35 (C. C. A. Tenn.).

70. In re Ketchum, 5 A. B. R. 532, 108 Fed. 35 (C. C. A. Tenn.). Ante, § 372.

71. In re Hassenbusch (unreported), 1 R B—20

affirmed in 108 Fed. 35, 47 C. C. A. 177.

71a. See post, §§ 1570, 1705.

72. In re Florcken, 5 A. B. R. 802, 107 Fed. 241 (D. C. Calif.); In re Kolin, 13 A. B. R. 533, 134 Fed. 557 (C. C. A. Ills.).

Bond to Pay Expenses, Where No

In re Kleinhans, 7 A. B. R. 604, 113 Feb. 107 (D. C. N. Y.): "The question presented here is not whether the receiver obtained title to the property of the alleged bankrupts by virtue of his appointment, but rather whether the bankruptcy court obtained such jurisdiction over the res at the time of filing the involuntary petition to have H. Kleinhans & Co. adjudged bankrupt as to justify this court's intervention in an attempt on the part of the lessors to oust the receivers and officers of this court to the detriment of the bankrupt estate, from the possession of the leased premises. Counsel for lessors contend that by § 70 of the Bankrupt Act, a trustee of a bankrupt's estate is vested by operation of law with the title of the bankrupt as of the date of the adjudication, and that in the absence of an express provision of the Bankrupt Act vesting title in the receiver as of the date when a petition is filed, it must be held, that the title continues in the alleged bankrupts until a trustee is appointed; and therefore the process of the State court to remove for non-payment of rent ought not to have been enjoined. This contention is unsound. Coincident with the filing of a petition in bankruptcy, either voluntary or involuntary, a court of bankruptcy acquires control over the estate of a bankrupt or person charged with acts of bankruptcy. It may immediately seize and lay claim to all property either in the actual possession of the bankrupt or such as may be reduced to possession. Power is conferred on the court to appoint marshals or receivers to take charge of the property of bankrupts. Section 2, subd. 3, Bankrupt Act. It is the immediate duty of the receiver of the property to preserve the estate intact, and to conserve the assets and estate of the bankrupt, pursuing the course pointed out by the act which will best promote and further the interests of the creditors. True, the receiver here is not vested with a title to the property of which he becomes custodian, nor does any provision of the Bankrupt Act vest him with powers similar to that of a trustee appointed by the creditors. The property, however, corporeal and incorporeal, either comes into his possession as an officer of the court, or such right to possession is obtained as will tend to retain intact the actual and visible assets of the bankrupt, to the end that, when an adjudication is made, the trustee may be vested not merely with the bankrupt's title to the property, but that he may have and receive the actual possession of all assets in the control of the bankrupt at the instant that the protection of the court was invoked."

Boonville Nat'l Bk. v. Blakey, 6 A. B. R. 13, 107 Fed. 891 (C. C. A. Ind.): "The authority for the appointment of a receiver in bankruptcy proceedings comes from the act and is limited by the act. The order of the court appointing him cannot be broader than the statute. The receiver is a statutory receiver, and not a general receiver. The latter is appointed by a court of chancery by virtue of its inherent power, independent of any statute. His authority is derived from, and his duty prescribed by, the order of appointment, and he is called a common-law receiver. Herring v. Railroad Co., 105 N. Y. 340, 12 N. E. 763. A statutory receiver is one appointed in pursuance of special statutory provisions. He derives his power from the statute, and to it must look for the duty imposed upon him. He possesses such power only as the statute confers, or such as may be fairly inferred from the general scope of the law of his appointment. We are therefore referred to the Bankrupt Act (30 Stat., Ch. 541) to ascertain the powers of the bankruptcy court to appoint a receiver, and the

Assets Shown.—Where the applicants for the appointment of the receiver show no assets, they may be required to give bond to pay the expenses of the receivership if sufficient assets applicable to that purpose be not discovered. In re McKane, 18 A. B. R. 594, 158 Fed. 647 (D. C. N. Y.).

extent of the power which the act confers upon him. By § 2, cl. 3, the courts of bankruptcy are invested with authority to 'appoint receivers or the marshals upon application of parties in interest, in case the court shall find it absolutely necessary for the preservation of estates, to take charge of the property of the bankrupts after the filing of the petition and until it is dismissed or the trustee is qualified,' and to (§ 2, cl. 5) authorize the business of the bankrupts to be conducted for limited periods by receivers and marshals or trustees, if necessary, in the best interests of the estates. These are the sole provisions of the act which authorize a receiver and define his duties. There is, however, another provision which may properly be considered in this connection. In § 69 it is provided that before adjudication upon an involuntary petition, when it shall appear to the judge that the property of the alleged bankrupt is being neglected, so that it will deteriorate in value, a warrant may be issued to the marshal to seize and hold the property subject to further order, upon the petitioning creditors giving bond to indemnify the alleged bankrupt for the damages he shall sustain if such seizure shall be proved to have been wrongfully obtained, and the property, when seized, shall be released upon bond filed by the alleged bankrupt conditioned to turn over the property or its value in money to the trustee in the event of adjudication of bankruptcy. * * * We can now discover, as we think, the general purpose of this law. It was that the property of the bankrupt should be vested in a trustee, to be selected by creditors; that such officer should have the general control and management of the estate, and the right to recover for the benefit of creditors all property transferred in fraud of the act. It contemplated that between the filing of the petition and the adjudication of bankruptcy an emergency might arise with respect to the care of bankrupt's property; and in involuntary cases for the protection of the property in the interval between the filing of the petition and the adjudication, the bankruptcy court was authorized to direct the marshal to seize and hold the property pending adjudication. So, also, in voluntary or involuntary cases, when it was found absolutely necessary for the preservation of an estate, the court should appoint a receiver or the marshal to take charge of the property of the bankrupt until the petition is dismissed or the trustee is qualified. It plainly was not contemplated that the receiver or the marshal so designated should supersede the trustee or exercise the general powers conferred upon a trustee. There is no such power specifically conferred or any provision in the act from which such power can reasonably be implied. Such temporary receiver, whether he be the marshal or another, is not a trustee for the creditors, but is a caretaker and custodian of the visible property pending adjudication and until a selection of a trustee. If in any sense a trustee, he is trustee for the bankrupt, in whom is the title to the property until it passes by operation of law as of the date of adjudication to the trustee selected by the creditors. The duty required and the power conferred clearly are that the receiver or the marshal should take possession of property that would otherwise go to waste, and hold it and preserve it, so that it might come to the trustee, when selected, without needless injury. There might also be an occasion when the business of the bankrupt ought not, in the interest of the creditors, to be temporarily suspended, as for example in the case of a hotel or other business, where the value of the good will required that it should be kept a going concern until the trustee should be appointed, and for a limited time after the trustee was appointed, that he might dispose of it profitably for the creditors."

In re Benedict, 15 A. B. R. 232, 140 Fed. 55 (D. C. Wis.): "The primary purpose of the bankruptcy court, and its first duty in point of time, is to collect and bring into custody the assets of the estate, and preserve the same until a trustee is qualified to take title thereto. To this end the Act of 1898 provides in case of necessity for the appointment of a receiver, who is practically a custodian. (Sec. 2, subd. 3.) The conditions now obtaining in every department of industry, and the wide scope of modern enterprise, render the prompt assembling of assets at once important and difficult. Business is largely conducted by great corporations, whose investments and operations are not confined to a single State or district, but often involve transactions and holdings in many States. When an involuntary petition is filed against such corporation, it is not uncommon that the assets are widely scattered. In the instant case the alleged bankrupt has stocks of goods in four different cities in this district. The several steps provided by the Bankrupt Act to secure an adjudication and the selection of a trustee involve considerable delay, although no opposition develops. This delay may be indefinitely prolonged by a demand for a jury trial and a final review by writ of error. Time must be allowed to assemble the creditors who are to select a trustee. From twenty days to four months may be designated as the usual period for these primary proceedings, although one case has been brought to my attention where two years were consumed in litigation before a trustee was chosen. In the meantime, what will become of these widely scattered assets situate beyond the territorial limits of the court of original jurisdiction? There seems to be no one whose duty it is to give any attention to such property. A dishonest bankrupt, having access, may dissipate or dispose of it, or entangle the title with liens and complications. It will be subjected to peril from theft as well as from fire, there being no custodian to protect or insure it. Unless some way can be devised under the Bankrupt Act to husband these scattered assets, the law discloses a structural weakness which seriously impairs its efficiency. * * * Naturally, the first question for consideration is whether such receiver has extraterritorial authority. The difficulty encountered at the threshhold lies in the limitation placed by the Bankrupt Act upon the jurisdiction of the courts by the language, 'within their respective territorial limits,' etc. It is difficult to see how such jurisdiction, so qualified, can be enlarged by an order. Any act by such receiver in Wisconsin pursuant to such order would amount to an attempted exercise of jurisdiction outside the territorial limits. The process and authority * * * are entirely inoperative in this district, and do not warrant the Illinois receiver to discharge any official function whatever in this district."

§ 378. Receivership Available Any Time before Appointment of Trustee.

—The provisional remedy of receivership is not limited, it is to be borne in mind, to the period before the adjudication; but is available at any time before the appointment of a trustee.

§ 379. Appointment by Referee before Adjudication.

—Before adjudication, upon receipt of the certificate of the District Clerk of the Judge's absence or inability to act and of the reference of the matter on that account, the referee may appoint the receiver.[73]

§ 380. Appointment by Referee after Reference.

—After reference of the case to the referee in charge of the particular case, the application for

---

73. Bankr. Act, § 38 (4) (3). In re Kelly Dry Goods Co., 4 A. B. R. 528, 102 Fed. 747 (D. C. Wis.).

the appointment of the receiver, like all other proceedings, should be made to the referee and not to the judge.[74] But, of course, the referee must wait until the certificate of reference has been actually received before proceeding to act in the matter.[75]

§ **381. Notice of Application.**—Notice to the creditors is not necessary;[76] nor is notice to the bankrupt necessary after adjudication of bankruptcy;[77] but notice to the bankrupt is necessary before adjudication, except in cases where it is alleged and shown that to give notice would likely defeat the very objects of the appointment.[78]

Obiter, Latimer *v.* McNeal, 16 A. B. R. 45, 142 Fed. 451 (C. C. Pa.), affirming In re Francis, 14 A. B. R. 675: "We are, indeed, clearly of opinion that except in rare cases a receiver ought never to be appointed without notice to the alleged bankrupt. Furthermore there occur well-recognized instances of such urgency as to dispense with notice; as where irreparable loss or injury is impending; or where notice might defeat the very purpose of the receivership."

And notice to the bankrupt may be excused where he has absconded.[79]

Faulk *v.* Steiner, 21 A. B. R. 623, 165 Fed. 861 (C. C. A. Ala.): "When the involuntary petition was filed, the petition to appoint a receiver was also filed, and the receiver was appointed immediately, without notice to the alleged bankrupt. No fact is alleged or shown by the record to authorize the appointment without notice. The Bankruptcy Act does not expressly provide that notice shall be given before the appointment shall be made, but it is a general rule that, from the institution of a suit until final judgment, every step that immediately affects the rights of a defendant should be preceded by notice, and with few and well-defined exceptions, no court is justified in appointing a receiver and seizing the property of a defendant without giving him notice and an opportunity to be heard. It is necessary to fairness and justice in all legal procedure that judicial action should be taken in open court on issue between the parties, or after an opportunity for such issue; and a regard for this rule 'will not only insure the rights of litigants, but will also protect from the unjust criticism so often made, and, what is of more importance, will secure the courts themselves against hasty and ill-considered action.' * * * The 23rd Gen. Ord. in bankruptcy provides that: 'In all orders made by a referee, it shall be recited, according as the fact may be, that notice was given and the manner thereof; or that the order was made by consent; or that no adverse interest was represented at the hearing; or that the order was made after hearing adverse interests.' The referee, in the appointment, disregarded

74. Gen. Order No. XII. In re Florcken, 5 A. B. R. 802, 107 Fed. 241 (D. C. Calif.); impliedly, In re Moody, 12 A. B. R. 718, 131 Fed. 525 (D. C. Iowa).

75. In re Florcken, 5 A. B. R. 802, 107 Fed. 241 (D. C. Calif.).

76. In re Abrahamson & Bretstein, 1 A. B. R. 44 (Ref. N. Y.):

77. In re Abrahamson & Bretstein, 1 A. B. R. 44 (Ref. N. Y.).

78. In re Francis, et al., 14 A. B. R. 676, 136 Fed. 912 (D. C. Pa., affirmed sub nom. Latimer *v.* McNeal, quoted ante, § 346).

79. Bauman Diamond Co. *v.* Hart, 27 A. B. R. 632, 192 Fed. 498 (C. C. A. Tex.).

the order. * * * It has been doubted if a referee is ever justified in appointing a receiver without notice before adjudication. Ross-Meeham Foundry Co. v. Southern Car Foundry Co., 10 A. B. R. 624, 124 Fed. 403. No principle is more essential to the administration of justice, whether, by a referee or a judge, than that no man should be deprived of his property without notice and opportunity to make his defense. A mistaken notion seems to have grown up in reference to bankruptcy proceedings that they are in some way an exception to this principle. * * * If it be conceded that a case may occur where a referee could lawfully appoint a receiver without notice—a question that it is not necessary now to decide—he is certainly not authorized to disregard the rule of equity procedure as to notice which controls a chancellor when appointing receivers. Under the well-established rule a chancellor will not appoint a receiver without notice except in a case of imperious necessity, when the rights of the petitioner can be secured and protected in no other way. It sometimes becomes necessary for the court to act without notice to the defendant, when he has absconded, or is beyond the jurisdiction of the court, or cannot be found, or when there is imminent danger of irreparable injury, or when, by giving notice, the very purpose of the appointment may be rendered nugatory."

It has been held that a state receiver should have notice of an application for the appointment of a receiver in bankruptcy proceedings.[80]

The appointment of a receiver without notice, however, is held not to be the depriving of the bankrupt of his property without due process of law.[81]

Latimer v. McNeal, 16 A. B. R. 45, 142 Fed. 451 (C. C. A. Pa.): "Now, as respects the matter of notice, it will be observed that the bankrupt act does not expressly require notice to be given the bankrupt before the appointment of a receiver, under the provision quoted. Such appointment, moreover, does not deprive the bankrupt of his property without due process of law, for the appointment is essentially for the temporary custody of his property with a view to its preservation."

§ 382. Bond of Receiver.—The receiver should give bond.[82]

Obiter, In re Erie Lumber Co., 17 A. B. R. 708, 150 Fed. 817. (D. C. Ga.): "These merchants, however, are not wholly without remedy. The bonds of the receivers, each in the amount of $7,500, are on file. They are conditioned for the faithful performance by the receivers of their duty; and those who have losses because these officers of the court have disregarded its orders and contracted debts in excess of the authority granted them may bring actions on these bonds to redress the wrongs."

§ 382½. Ancillary Receivers.—Ancillary receivers may be appointed.[83]

80. Bauman Diamond Co. v. Hart, 27 A. B. R. 632, 192 Fed. 498 (C. C. A. Tex.).

81. See ante, § 346. But compare, inferentially, Faulk v. Steiner, 21 A. B. R. 623, 165 Fed. 861 (C. C. A. Ala.), quoted supra.

82. Suit on Bond.—The receiver may be sued on his bond for failure to perform his duties, as, for instance, by persons selling him goods on credit when he has exceeded his authority in buying on credit. Obiter, In re Erie Lumber Co., 17 A. B. R. 708, 150 Fed. 817 (D. C. Ga.).

83. Bankr. Act, § 2 as amended in 1910 Babbitt, Trustee v. Dutcher, 216 U. S. 102, 23 A. B. R. 519, quoted post at § 1705.

For the entire subject of Ancillary Receiverships see also post, § 1705 et seq. For forms, see Appendix.

In granting an ancillary receivership, the court ordinarily looks at nothing except the pendency of the proceedings in the parent district, the appointment there of a receiver, and the presence of assets in the district where the application is made.[84]

An ancillary receiver must account to the court wherein he was appointed.[85]

As a general rule applications for the removal of an ancillary receiver, or for the increase of his bond, will be referred to the court wherein the bankruptcy proceedings proper are pending. This, however, is a matter of comity, and these questions may be disposed of without such reference.[86]

§ 383. Bankrupt, Whether Quasi Trustee for Creditors.

§ 383. Bankrupt, Whether Quasi Trustee for Creditors.—It has been held, sometimes expressly and at other times by necessary implication, that pending the appointment of a receiver or trustee the bankrupt himself is quasi trustee of the estate.[87] He certainly is such after adjudication of bankruptcy,[88] but not before adjudication,[89] and creditors before adjudication must protect themselves by resort to some one or more of the provisional remedies available—that is precisely what such remedies are for.

In bankruptcy the creation of a receivership affects the parties somewhat differently from what it does in other branches of practice. In bankruptcy, a receiver is a mere custodian appointed to care for property of a destructible or removable nature and the receivership does not to any great extent fix priorities of rights or of liens as is usually the case in other branches of jurisprudence.[90] Consequently the great strife that usually occurs over the validity and precise time of the appointment of a receiver is generally lacking in bankruptcy, for all preferences and legal liens, etc., within the entire four months of the adjudication are in the same situation, in general, and little is to be gained by setting the receivership aside unless it has been improvidently granted. Under the bankruptcy law a great many of the quick moves, by way of assignments, preferred mortgages, etc., made on the eve of a receivership are avoided by the mere filing of the petition itself and subsequent adjudication, and therefore the receivership does not figure in that regard.

---

84. In re Hayes, 27 A. B. R. 713, 192 Fed. 1018 (D. C. N. Y.).
85. Loeser v. Dallas, 27 A. B. R. 733, 192 Fed. 909 (C. C. A. Pa.).
86. In re Hayes, 27 A. B. R. 713, 192 Fed. 1018 (D. C. N. Y.).
87. In re Wilson, 6 A. B. R. 287, 289, 108 Fed. 197 (D. C. Va.); inferentially, In re Allen, 3 A. B. R. 38, 96 Fed. 512 (D. C. Calif.). Obiter and inferentially, Blake v. Valentine, 1 A. B. R. 378 (D. C. Calif.). Marsh v. Heaton, 1 Low. 278. Impliedly, In re Pot-

teiger, 24 A. B. R. 648, 181 Fed. 640 (D. C. P.), quoted post at § 1121. Compare post, § 1807. But compare, "Bankrupt Selling Goods In Usual Course of Business after Filing of Petition," § 1093, note.
88. Compare post, § 1121.
89. Compare post, §§ 1121, 1133 and 1807.
90. Compare, however, post, §§ 1137½, 1138, et seq., and 1207½.

§ **384. But One Ground, "Absolute Necessity for Preservation of Estate."**—There is but one ground for the appointment of a receiver in bankruptcy—such appointment must be "absolutely necessary for the preservation of the estate."[91] Inasmuch as the right to appoint a receiver is based upon the authority conferred by the statute, the application should state as ground for the appointment that it is "absolutely necessary for the preservation of the estate that a receiver be appointed," and the affidavit in support of the application should state facts that will make it evident that a receiver is absolutely necessary.

Faulk & Co. v. Steiner, 21 A. B. R. 623, 165 Fed. 861 (C. C. A. Ala.): "We are also required to consider the question whether there is anything in the record, as matter of law, to justify the appointment of a receiver. Aside from the Bankruptcy Act, the appointment of a receiver is an extraordinary remedy, and is granted with great caution and only in cases of necessity. The court acts with extreme caution, and requires a clear case of right and pressing necessity to induce it to make an appointment. Is the rule less strict as to the appointment of receivers in bankruptcy? The Bankruptcy Act was framed with the purpose of securing to the creditors a distribution of the bankrupt's estate at a minimum cost. The policy of the act is one of economy, and to promote this policy, Congress sought to provide against the improvident and unnecessary appointment of receivers. The authority to make the appointment is conferred and limited by the act. There is but one ground stated for the appointment. The act authorizes the appointment of receivers 'upon the application of parties in interest, in case the courts shall find it absolutely necessary, for the preservation of estates, to take charge of the property of bankrupts after the filing of the petition and until it is dismissed or the trustee is qualified.' * * * The petition to appoint the receiver should allege that the appointment is absolutely necessary for the preservation of the estate, and the facts should be stated either in the sworn petition, or in accompanying affidavits showing the necessity. The record falls far short of this rule, both as to averment and proof. Neither the petition, the affidavit accompanying it, the order of appointment, nor other parts of the record show that the appointment was absolutely necessary for the preservation of the estate. In a replication filed in a subsequent proceeding, it is alleged that Faulk & Co. agreed with Steiner and others that the involuntary petition should be filed and a receiver appointed. This feature of the case will be referred to later. It is sufficient at this point to say that the order appointing the receiver does not purport to have been made by consent, and the record nowhere shows such agreement to have been made. We think it appears from the record that the appointment was improvident, and in opposition not only to the form but to the substance of the law. We are of opinion that the District Court erred in refusing to discharge the receiver."

In re Oakland Lumber Co., 23 A. B. R. 181, 174 Fed. 634 (C. C. A. N. Y.):

91. Bankr. Act, § 2 (3); Bryan v. Bernheimer, 5 A. B. R. 623, 181 U. S. 188; In re Rosenthal, 16 A. B. R. 448, 144 Fed. 548 (D. C. N. J.). Obiter, In re Becker, 3 A. B. R. 412, 98 Fed. 407 (D. C. Pa.), quoted post, § 385. Obiter, In re Cornice & Roofing Co., 13 A. B. R. 586, 133 Fed. 958 (D. C. Ky.); obiter, Skubinsky v. Bodek, 22 A. B. R. 689, 172 Fed. 332 (C. C. A. Pa.), quoted post, § 1544. In re Desrochers, 25 A. B. R. 703, 183 Fed. 990 (D. C. N. Y.); In re Wentworth, 27 A. B. R. 515, 191 Fed. 820 (C. C. A. N. Y.).

"The power to take from a man his property, without giving him an opportunity to be heard, is both arbitrary and drastic and should not be exercised except in the clearest cases. Congress recognized the necessity for caution by limiting the appointment of receivers to cases where it is 'absolutely necessary' for the preservation of the estate. In other words, the reason for such an interference with the rights of property must be clear, positive and certain. Of course cases frequently arise where this remedy may be necessary—cases where there is reason to believe that the property may be stolen or secreted or turned over to favored creditors. But fraud cannot be presumed, neither can danger to the property be predicated, of acts which are honest and lawful. It cannot be presumed that an assignee under a State law intends to plunder the fund he is appointed to administer. Unless something be shown to the contrary the presumption is persuasive that during the interval between the filing of the petition and the appointment of a trustee, the property will be entirely safe in the hands of the assignee, especially if he be enjoined from disposing of it pendente lite. We are informed that it has grown into a well-established custom for the attorney for the petitioning creditors, when he files his petition, to apply at the same time for the appointment of a receiver, and that the application is usually granted. If such a practice exists we see nothing in the law to warrant it. It seems to us that the rule which obtains in all other jurisdictions where receivers are appointed is equally applicable to courts of bankruptcy, and that in no case should a remedy so far reaching in its effects be resorted to except upon clear and convincing proof. Cases have not infrequently come within the observation of the court where, after a receiver was appointed, the petitioning creditors were unable to establish their own status or to prove an act of bankruptcy, and the petition was dismissed, leaving the court with a receiver on its hands, with no proceeding in esse and no funds with which to pay him and the expenses incurred by him. Again, the appointment of a receiver creates an additional official to be paid from the estate. Nothing contributed so much to bring about the repeal of the Act of 1867 as the large expense of administration, the small estates being entirely absorbed in fees. The more economical the administration of the present act the longer will it continue as an important adjunct to trade and commerce. All these reasons combine in requiring that the power to appoint receivers should be exercised not as a matter of course, but cautiously, circumspectly, and always upon proof that the appointment is 'absolutely necessary.'"

And the affidavit should be positively sworn to else its averments will not, alone, support the appointment of a receiver.

In re Rosenthal, 16 A. B. R. 448, 144 Fed. 548 (D. C. N. J.): "The only facts presented to the referee in the present case were those contained in Abraham Rosenthal's petition, and they were merely that he and Michael Rosenthal were partners in the silk manufacturing business; that on November 1, 1905, the firm made an assignment to William Schmidt for the benefit of their creditors; that Schmidt thereupon took possession of their property, the estimated value of which was about $8,000; that he and Michael Rosenthal were about to file their petition in voluntary bankruptcy; that he 'verily believes that it will be to the benefit of all persons in interest that a receiver of this court do forthwith, seize and take possession of all property belonging to said partnership and now in the hands of said assignee.' There is no intimation in the petition that the assignee is doing anything prejudicial to the interests of creditors or in conflict with the provisions of the Bankruptcy Act. Nor, in the order made, is there any finding that it is absolutely necessary for the preservation of the bankrupts' estate that a receiver be appointed. It follows that the referee's order must be set aside and the petition on which it was made be dismissed."

Improvident and unnecessary appointments of receivers Congress sought earnestly to guard against. The appointment must not only be "necessary" but "absolutely" necessary. The law was framed in a manifest spirit of economy (see ante, § 24) and the expense of a receivership should be avoided, if at all possible.[92] Resort to injunction should rather be had wherever such remedy will be adequate.[93]

An assignment for creditors or a receivership is not a good ground in and of itself before adjudication; for the assignment or receivership is not nullified until adjudication and the custody of the state court, without its own consent, may not be disturbed until then.

In re Spalding, quoted in In re Oakland Lumber Co., 23 A. B. R. 181: "The question here presented was, upon facts substantially identical, decided by this court in In re Spalding, in May, 1905. As the opinion was delivered orally and has not been reported, we quote it at length: 'The fundamental error in the argument for the receiver and of the learned court below seems to be that both regard it as proper that a receiver should be appointed, practically as a matter of course, in every case where a petition in bankruptcy is filed. That is not the law and it is not good sense. The court has jurisdiction under the statute to appoint receivers only when it shall find it absolutely necessary for the preservation of estates. The petition upon which this receivership was granted not only fails to show that it was absolutely necessary, but shows affirmatively that it was absolutely unnecessary, as it shows the property to have been in the custody of a receiver appointed by the Supreme Court of the State of New York, and there is nothing in the record to show that the State court receiver is not an entirely proper and competent person to preserve the assets. What could the Federal receiver do under such circumstances? He has not title to any property. He is a mere custodian. He could not take the assets from the State court receiver. The bankruptcy court could not make any such order and the assets could only be taken from the State court receiver by an application in the State court itself. Furthermore, this appointment of receivers, as of course, is a great injustice to the bankrupt in the event that the petition is not followed by adjudication. And it is wasteful and an unnecessary expense to the estate in the event that there is an adjudication. The papers on this application are wholly inadequate. The order is reversed with instructions to vacate the receivership.'"

Contra, obiter, In re Ethridge Furn. Co., 1 A. B. R. 112, 92 Fed. 329 (D. C. Ky.): "* * * if after an involuntary petition in bankruptcy is filed against the assignor based upon the assignment, the Court of Bankruptcy may and ought to appoint a receiver to take charge of the assigned property."

Consent of the bankrupt to the appointment of the receiver will not obviate

92. In re Oakland Lumber Co., 23 A. B. R. 181, 174 Fed. 634 (C. C. A. N. Y.), quoted supra, § 384.

93. Impliedly, In re Oakland Lumber Co., 23 A. B. R. 181, 174 Fed. 634 (C. C. A. N. Y.), quoted supra. But compare, In re Huddleston, 21 A. B. R. 669, 167 Fed. 428 (D. C. Ga.).

the requirement that such receivership must be "absolutely necessary for the preservation of the estate."

Faulk v. Steiner, 21 A. B. R. 623, 165 Fed. 861 (C. C. A. Ala.): "The Bankruptcy Act makes no provision for the appointment of a receiver in bankruptcy by the consent of the alleged bankrupt. The appointment, by the terms of the act, is only authorized when it is absolutely necessary for the preservation of the estate. * * * The creditors, therefore, are the parties chiefly · interested in avoiding the expenses of an unnecessary receivership. It was not intended, we think, that the bankrupt, by his consent, could remove the limitation of the statute, and authorize the appointment of a receiver where it was not necessary for the preservation of the estate. Provisions of the act for the protection of the bankrupt cannot be waived by him if such provisions also serve to protect the bankrupt's creditors. In re Sarsar (D. C.), 9 Am. B. R. 576, 120 Fed. 40. In Whelpley v. Erie Ry. Co., 6 Blatchf. 271, Fed. Cas. No. 17,504, it was claimed that a party was estopped by consenting to the appointment of a receiver. Nelson, Circuit Justice, held: 'I do not assent to this view. The company waived the notice which is required by the rules and practice of this court before an injunction can be issued; but the order for the injunction, and for the appointment of a receiver, depended upon the judgment of the judge who granted them. Indeed, I am not prepared to admit that an order for an injunction, or a receiver, can be made in an improper case, even with the consent of both parties, more especially where the rights of third persons may be concerned.' The agreement of the alleged bankrupt that a receiver should be appointed—if such agreement has been made—should not, under the circumstances, be permitted to affect the rights of opposing creditors."

But, compare, loose statement, In re Huddleston, 21 A. B. R. 669, 167 Fed. 428 (D. C. Ga.): "After adjudication of voluntary bankruptcy, an application by creditors, in which the bankrupt unites, to appoint a receiver or custodian to preserve the assets of the estate, otherwise wholly unprotected, will usually be granted, especially in the absence of any charge of fraud or collusion, and where the creditors and other persons interested make no objection whatever. When a receiver is designated by the court, the subsequent election by the creditors of the same person as trustee is evidence of the fitness and competency of such person."

§ 384¾. **Who Eligible?**—The same rule should apply, in general, to the selection of a receiver, as to that of a trustee.[94] Thus, it has been held that where the appointment of a receiver has been brought about by the active interference and procurement of the bankrupt, the appointment will be set aside, no matter how high be the character or capacity of the person thus appointed; and this rule states sound doctrine and is a safe rule for guidance in the delicate and responsible matter of such appointments.

Coal and Iron Co. v. Steel Co., 20 A. B. R. 151, 160 Fed. 212 (D. C. Ala.): "There can be no question that in such cases as this, where it is shown that the appointment of a receiver or trustee in bankruptcy is brought about by active interference and procurement of the bankrupt, the appointment of the

94. See post, § 887, et seq.

same will be set aside on proper petition and showing to the court, it matters not how high the character or capacity of the receiver or trustee may be who is so attempted to be procured by the bankrupt. As is said by Lochren, District Judge, in the case of In re Hansen (D. C.), 19 Am. B. R. 237, 156 Fed. 717: 'It is well settled by all the authorities that the trustee represents the creditors, and not the bankrupt, in the administration of the estate; and that it is improper that the bankrupt shall actively interfere with the matter of his selection and appointment; and that if he does interfere, and the person aided by him is appointed by votes procured by such interference, the appointment should for that reason be disapproved. * * *' What is said here as to the application of this principle to trustees must of course apply with much more force to receivers, for whom the court alone is responsible. Many cases to the same effect might be cited, and I have found none contrary to the principle announced in the Hanson case, supra. The rule is based on sound reason, and is a salutary one. It often becomes the duty of the receiver directly to antagonize the bankrupt by efforts to discover secreted assets. Surely then, there should be no color of basis for any suspicion of partiality or sense of obligation on the part of the receiver toward the bankrupt."

However, in some instances, it may be almost imperative to appoint a partisan of the bankrupt as receiver; as, for example, in cases of assignments or receiverships before bankruptcy; for, in such cases, the assignment or receivership not being void until adjudication, the assignee or receiver of the state court must be left in charge until adjudication. Frequently it is of advantage to appoint such assignee or receiver, as receiver in bankruptcy, that he may be under the direct control of the bankruptcy court.[95]

§ 384½. Vacating of Appointment.

—The court may, of course, vacate the appointment of a receiver for proper cause; thus, such an appointment has been vacated where the receiver entered into an improper agreement with attorneys for the payment and distribution of their fees.[96]

§ 384¾. Receiver's Attorneys.

—The bankrupt's attorney should not be selected as counsel by the receiver.[97] It has also been held that the petitioning creditor's attorney should not be so selected.

In re Strobel, 20 A. B. R. 21, 160 Fed. 916 (C. C. A. N. Y.): "Such selection affords a ready opportunity for chicanery, fraud and perjury."

In re Hill Co., 20 A. B. R. 73, 159 Fed. 73 (C. C. A. Ills.): "The record discloses the further fact that the attorneys for whom the claim is made were actively engaged throughout the protracted contest in bankruptcy, as attorneys for the petitioning creditors, and were not independent counsel employed by the receiver within the spirit of the order referred to. It is the general rule that

---

95. See post, § 889. Also see instance where prior receiver in State court was elected trustee in bankruptcy and yet trouble arose. Loveless v. Southern Grocery Co., 20 A. B. R. 180, 159 Fed. 415 (C. C. A. La.).

96. Matter of Oshwitz & Feldstein,

25 A. B. R. 594, 183 Fed. 990 (D. C. N. Y.).

97. Compare, In re Strobel, 20 A. B. R. 21, 160 Fed. 916 (C. C. A. N. Y.) quoted above; also compare, In re Hill Co., 20 A. B. R. 73, 159 Fed. 73 (C. C. A. Ills.), quoted supra.

receivers are to select counsel not identified with the interests of one or the other party to the litigation, and for departure from the wholesome rule special circumstances and authorization are needful."

It is undoubtedly good law and good morals that the bankrupt's attorney should not be selected by the receiver for his counsel; but it is of questionable propriety to lay down any hard and fast rule that the petitioning creditors' attorney should not be so selected. On the contrary, the petitioning creditors' attorney is precisely the attorney who is presumably the best informed as to the real state of affairs. As a rule he has investigated the situation at a time when the parties, if guilty, have been more unguarded than they will ever afterwards be. He represents creditors who have taken the initiative. Now, simply because collusive petitions *may* be filed and have frequently been known to be filed is no ground for depriving creditors, where the petition has not been collusively filed, of the aid of the attorney who has been first to investigate and to act and is thus in the best position to be the most efficient. Some less clumsy method of meeting the evil of collusive bankruptcies ought to be devised. There ought to be no rule that he should be so selected but there certainly ought to be no rule either of court or of discretion, forbidding his selection. The vast majority of receiverships in bankruptcy occur where there is little if any litigation over the question of the debtor being adjudged bankrupt and there is little need of the receiver taking any attitude of judicial equipoise between contending parties. It is of more importance, as a rule, that he be active and alert, prompt and efficient in collecting and guarding the assets.

The court may, should the circumstances warrant such action, direct the receiver to dismiss an attorney employed by him, and to retain another; and this course will be followed whenever it appears that the attorney retained is either incompetent, or is not conducting the business entrusted to him in the interest of the creditors, or any of them, or where he attempts to serve some purpose of his own which is antagonistic or detrimental to the creditors. But where no such reason is shown, an order of this character will not be made.[98]

SUBDIVISION "A."

FUNCTIONS OF RECEIVERS.

§ 385. Powers, Functions and Relation to Court and Creditors.— Receivers in bankruptcy derive their powers from the bankruptcy act and are limited thereby. The object of their appointment is the preservation of the property so as to prevent its deterioration, waste, or loss.[99]

---

98. In re Champion Wagon Co., 28 A. B. R. 51, 193 Fed. 1004 (D. C. N. Y.).

99. Bankr. Act, § 2 (3) (5); Boonville Nat'l Bk. v. Blakey, 6 A. B. R. 13, 107 Fed. 891 (C. C. A. Ind.); In re

Harris, 19 A. B. R. 635, 156 Fed. 875 (D. C. Ala.); In re Rubel, 21 A. B. R. 566, 166 Fed. 131 (D. C. Wis.).

Bankruptcy Court Authorizing Receiver to Stipulate with Adverse Claimant for Sale of Property.—The

In re Kelly Dry Goods Co., 4 A. B. R. 530, 102 Fed. 747 (D. C. Wis.): "The purpose of the appointment of a receiver in bankruptcy is one of mere temporary custody, and the duties are of the utmost simplicity."

In re Benedict, 15 A. B. R. 232, 140 Fed. 55 (D. C. Wis.): "The Act provides in case of necessity for the appointment of a receiver, who is practically a custodian."

Obiter, In re J. C. Winship Co., 9 A. B. R. 641, 120 Fed. 93 (C. C. A. Ills.): "The receiver had no interest. He was a mere caretaker. He had no title."

In re Kolin, 13 A. B. R. 533, 134 Fed. 557 (C. C. A. Ills.): "The court and the parties seem to have overlooked the ruling of this court in Booneville National Bank v. Blakey, 6 A. B. R. 13, 43, 107 Fed. 891, that a receiver is a mere custodian of property taken from the possession of the bankrupt until a trustee is appointed; that he does not exercise the powers of a trustee, and while he may take appropriate measures incident to the protection of the property in his custody, and, in case of perishable property may, under the direction of the court, sell the same when necessary, yet he is not authorized, nor can the bankruptcy court properly direct him, to take possession of property held and claimed adversely by third parties, or to institute actions for the recovery of property claimed to belong to the bankrupt's estate."

But compare, broader rule, In re Fixen & Co., 2 A. B. R. 821, 96 Fed. 748 (D. C. Calif.): "Courts of Bankruptcy have authority not only under the special provisions of § 2 of the Bankruptcy Act, but also by virtue of their general equity powers, to appoint receivers."

Their duties are preservative rather than administrative.

Skubinsky v. Bodek, 22 A. B. R. 689, 172 Fed. 332 (C. C. A. Pa.): "Until after an adjudication the function of a receivership is not administrative of the estate in bankruptcy, but is solely preservative. And this is equally true whether receivers in bankruptcy are or are not authorized by the court to conduct the business of alleged bankrupts for limited periods * * * the granting of such authority and action thereunder prior to an adjudication of bankruptcy can in no legitimate sense be deemed 'process of administration of the estate under the act.'"

Thus, receivers have no power to voluntarily surrender property in their custody.[1]

Thus, perhaps, receivers may not sell assets other than perishable assets, except when authorized to conduct the business.[2]

Compare, In re Becker, 3 A. B. R. 412, 98 Fed. 407 (D. C. Penna.): "Objection is raised to a receiver's power to sell the property of the bankrupt.' The objection is based upon the language of clause 3 of § 2, which authorizes courts

---

bankruptcy court may authorize the receiver to make a stipulation for sale by an adverse claimant of property in the latter's possession. Ommen, Trustee v. Talcott, 23 A. B. R. 572, 175 Fed. 261 (D. C. N. Y.).

1. Inferentially, Whitney v. Wenman, 14 A. B. R. 45, 198 U. S. 552, quoted at § 1801; In re Rose Shoe Mfg. Co., 21 A. B. R. 725, 168 Fed. 39 (C. C. A. N. Y.). See post, § 1801.

2. Inferentially, In re Kelly Dry Goods Co., 4 A. B. R. 528, 102 Fed. 747 (D. C. Wis.); inferentially, obiter, In re Kolin, 13 A. B. R. 533, 134 Fed. 557 (C. C. A. Ills.); inferentially, In re Harris, 19 A. B. R. 635, 156 Fed. 875 (D. C. Ala.). But compare obiter, as to curing sale, after trustee elected, by order of confirmation. In re Fulton, 18 A. B. R. 591, 153 Fed. 664 (D. C. N. Y.).

of bankruptcy to appoint receivers, 'for the preservation of estates, to take charge of the property of bankrupts after the filing of the petition, and until it is dismissed or the trustee qualified.' It is argued that this limits the power of receivers and forbids them to do more than hold possession of the bankrupt's property during a certain interval. I do not think the argument is sound. The clause restricts the power of the court to appoint, confining it to cases of absolute necessity, and then goes on to state the purpose for which the appointment may be originally made. But, after a receiver has once gone into possession, it may become necessary to sell the property for the very purpose of preserving it, or its value—which is, of course, the essential matter—either in whole or in part. In such event, I think the court has ample power to order or confirm a sale, either under the power to preserve, implied by clause 3 itself, or under clause 7 of the same section, which empowers the court to 'cause the assets of the bankrupt to be collected, reduced to money and distributed.' "

In re Harris, 19 A. B. R. 635, 156 Fed. 875 (D. C. Ala.): "But I further stated in that case that this was confined only to such cases in which it was clear to the court that the property was, in fact, perishable in part or in its entirety, or would greatly deteriorate if held without a sale, and that only that portion which was of such nature could be ordered sold. Now, under these circumstances the receiver is not a general receiver, as designated by the courts in chancery under the common law, but he is a statutory receiver, clothed with the limited powers of the statute under which his receivership was created, and he cannot by the very terms of the statute go beyond the respective powers conferred upon him by the statute itself."

And, in general, no order of sale, other than that implied in the leave to conduct the business, should be entered until after adjudication, except in cases of perishable property.[3]

The receiver, properly, should have no interest to serve except the preservation of the estate.[4]

Obiter, In re Frazin & Oppenheim, 24 A. B. R. 598, 183 Fed. 28 (C. C. A. N. Y.): "The one thing, more than all others, which creditors and bankrupt alike have the right to expect from those having official duties to perform relating to the property of the estate is disinterestedness in its disposition and liquidation."

A receiver should not deal personally with the assets and he should have no "entangling alliances." However, in some rare instances it has been im-

---

3. Inferentially, In re Kelly Dry Goods Co., 4 A. B. R. 528, 102 Fed. 575 (C. C. A. Ills.). In this case, however, the court did not set aside the sale ordered by the referee, because a fair sum was realized and no damage done.

All Persons Dealing with Receiver Chargeable with Notice of Limitations of Authority.—All persons dealing with the receiver are chargeable with notice of the limitations of the receiver's authority. Thus, that he may borrow money but may not buy goods on credit. In re Erie Lumber Co., 17 A. B. R. 687 (D. C. Ga.).

Receiver Subject to Subpœna, as Any Other Witness.—Compare, to this general effect, Graphophone Co. v. Leeds & Catlin, 23 A. B. R. 337, 174 Fed. 158 (U. S. C. C.).

All Persons Dealing with Receiver Chargeable with Notice of Limitations of Authority.—Also, see In re Burkhalter [Rogers v. People's Bank] 24 A. B. R. 553, 182 Fed. 353 (D. C. Ala.), quoted at § 1780½.

4. Compare other sections of this Division 4, particularly §§ 384½, 384¾, 385.

plied that a receiver in carrying on the administration of the estate may buy from a corporation or firm with which he is connected. The question probably is largely dependent on circumstances.[5]

In re Frazin & Oppenheim, 24 A. B. R. 598, 183 Fed. 28 (C. C. A. N. Y.): "The purchases in question were made in good faith, with the approval of Mr. Merrill, the co-receiver, and we know of no principle upon which a receiver, under such circumstances, is obliged to account for profits made by a corporation in which he is a stockholder."

§ 386. Receivers May Sell Perishable Assets.

—Receivers may be ordered by the referee to sell perishable assets;[6] and may be ordered so to do by the referee[7] upon receipt of a certificate from the district clerk of the judge's absence.[8]

But the court will first satisfy itself that the assets are really perishable,[9] as either perishability, depreciation, or some other good reason must exist to warrant a sale by the receiver;[10] but he may not sell without notice to creditors, unless the goods be perishable.[11]

An ancillary receiver will not be granted permission to sell assets in the absence of an order of the court wherein the parent proceedings is pending.[12]

§ 386½. Whether May Sell Otherwise.

—It is clear the receiver may sell assets when ordered to conduct the business or when the assets are perishable, as appears from the preceding and succeeding paragraphs. But whether he may sell under other circumstances is doubtful, at any rate before adjudication.[13]

Certainly he may not do so without the consent of the bankrupt. And even the bankrupt's consent may not be sufficient; for creditors have the right to intervene and become parties. Furthermore, it is a requirement under the present act that there shall be ten days notice by mail given to all creditors of all proposed sales (§ 58), to which the only possible exceptions are those of perishable property, under the Supreme Court's General Order 18, and sales while conducting the business. In case of non-perishable property, especially real estate, an order of court not based upon such notice would be irregular, though possibly the defect could be cured by subsequent proceedings for confirmation of the sale, upon notice to creditors, after ad-

5. Compare post, § 2036.
6. Gen. Ord. No. XVIII. As to meaning of "perishability," see post, § 1944.
7. In re Kelly Dry Goods Co., 4 A. B. R. 528, 102 Fed. 747 (D. C. Wis.); In re Garner Co., 18 A. B. R. 728, 153 Fed. 914 (D. C. Ala.).
8. In re Kelly Dry Goods Co., 4 A. B. R. 528, 102 Fed. 747 (D. C. Wis.).
9. In re Harris, 19 A. B. R. 635, 156 Fed. 875 (D. C. Ala.).

10. In re Desrochers, 25 A. B. R. 703, 183 Fed. 990 (D. C. N. Y.).
11. See post, § 386½.
12. In re Brockton, 27 A. B. R. 577, 194 Fed. 233 (D. C. N. Y.).
13. But contra, In re Becker, 3 A. B. R. 412, 98 Fed. 407 (D. C. Pa.), quoted at § 385. Compare, In re Kelly Dry Goods Co., 4 A. B. R. 528, 102 Fed. 747 (D. C. Wis.). Compare, In re Kolin, 13 A. B. R. 533, 134 Fed. 557 (C. C. A. Ill.). Also, see § 1943.

judication and election of the trustee. Nevertheless, such attempted sales before adjudication are generally found to carry in their train complicated questions that render them exceedingly unsatisfactory in actual practice. And, in practice, it is usually found that, after all, the comparatively little delay occurring before the election of a trustee does not seriously impair the non-perishable assets, although litigants frequently are unduly anxious on that account.

At any rate a sale by a receiver without order of the court conveys no title.

In re Fulton, 18 A. B. R. 591, 153 Fed. 664 (D. C. N. Y.): "Further, although the point has not been urged, it does not seem that the receiver should have attempted to make a sale of the lease in question. Matters relating to rent or the possession of the property should be attended to by the receiver, and the appointment of a trustee should be facilitated in every way, in order that the title to the chattel real may devolve upon the trustee as soon as possible. It might be argued that a sale could be had by order of the court before the election of a trustee, and confirmatory deeds given thereafter. The title of the trustee relates back to the adjudication in bankruptcy, and he could be directed to execute a conveyance in order to carry out the terms of a sale. But nevertheless it is apparently certain that a sale of a chattel real by a receiver without the express direction of the court conveys no title. The defect in the sale cannot be cured by a motion to confirm the sale and to quiet adverse claims to the property sold."

A sale by a receiver after adjudication but before the appointment of a trustee has been attacked on the ground that the trustee was the only one who could convey title, since, on his qualification, his title reverts to the date of adjudication; but this position has been held untenable, on the ground that it is the court in either event that makes the sale.[14]

And a sale by the receiver is a judicial sale;[15] and the bankruptcy court has summary power to compel the purchaser to carry out his offer.[16]

§ 387. May Continue Business, but Only for "Limited Period."—
Receivers (and later on, trustees also) may be authorized to continue the business of the bankrupt;[17] but the business may not be conducted for more than a "limited" period. The term "limited period" is ambiguous. It may mean either a short period or a definite period. Probably it means both a short and also a definite period; or successive short and definite periods, to

14. In re Maloney, 21 A. B. R. 502 (Sup. Ct. D. of C.), quoted at § 1950.
15. In re Jungman, 26 A. B. R. 401, 186 Fed. 302 (C. C. A. N. Y.); compare post, § 1950.
16. In re Jungman, 26 A. B. R. 401, 186 Fed. 302 (C. C. A. N. Y.), quoted at §§ 1804, 1962.
17. Bankr. Act, § 2 (5): "Courts of bankruptcy shall have power to authorize the business of bankrupts to be conducted for limited periods by re-

ceivers, the marshals or trustees, if necessary in the best interests of the estate, and allow such officers additional compensation for such services but not at a greater rate than in this Act allowed trustees for similar services." Instance, In re Richards, 11 A. B. R. 581, 127 Fed. 772 (D. C. Mass.); instance, In re Restein, 20 A. B. R. 832, 162 Fed. 986 (D. C. Pa.); obiter, Skubinsky v. Bodek, 22 A. B. R. 689, 172 Fed. 332 (C. C. A. Pa.).

prevent the long drawn out continuance of business involving creditors and risking their moneys for years.

Compare, to this general effect, In re Lisk, 21 A. B. R. 674, 167 Fed. 411 (D. C. N. Y.): "To allow the receivers to conduct the business of the bankrupt for a prolonged period to the exclusion of rights of creditors demanding the right given them by the Bankruptcy Act to elect a trustee and administer the estate, is unwarranted."

But the conducting of the business may only be done when it is for the best interest of the estate, and the application and the order must show that it is for the best interest of the estate that the business be conducted.

Yet an order for the conducting of the business may not be collaterally attacked,[18] and it rests in the discretion of the court.[19]

Amendment of 1910.—One of the abuses to which the administration of insolvent estates is peculiarly susceptible is that of the prolonged conducting of business by the officers of the court. This evil the framers of the Bankruptcy Act attempted to avoid, by requiring that such conducting of the business should be only for a "limited period." However, this limitation did not fully effect its object, and the abuse of long continued receiverships in the conducting of business continued, with the result that the administration of bankrupt estates in some sections of the country came to be almost wholly carried on by receivers appointed by the court, rather than by trustees elected by creditors, at great additional expense to the estate, creditors at the same time being debarred from investigation into the affairs of their debtor. Frequently, also, such prolonged continuing of business under receiverships was connived at by the bankrupt, especially in cases of corporations, for the purpose of delaying and tiring out creditors and reorganizing the corporate affairs at their expense. One of the objects of the Amendment of 1910, limiting the compensation of receivers for the conducting of the business was precisely to prevent this abuse of prolonged court custody and to hasten the turning over of insolvent estates to the trustees elected by creditors, for administration.[19a]

§ 388. Expense of Continuing Business.—The expense of continuing the business may not be charged against the fund to the detriment of a prior lienholder thereon, without his consent, acquiescence or participation;[20] but may be so charged if the lienholder consents to the continuance of the business.[21]

---

18. In re Isaacson, 23 A. B. R. 98, 175 Fed. 292 (C. C. A. N. Y.).
19 In re Isaacson, 23 A. B. R. 98, 175 Fed. 292 (C. C. A. N. Y.).
19a. See Senate Judiciary Report No. 691. of the 61st Congress, 2nd Session. quoted at § 2116.
20. In re Bourlier Cornice & Roofing Co., 13 A. B. R. 585, 133 Fed. 958 (D. C. Ky.). See post, subject of "Costs of Administration," §§ 1996, 2036. In re Erie Lumber Co., 17 A. B. R. 687 (D. C. Ga.); In re Clark Coal & Coke Co., 23 A. B. R. 273. 173 Fed. 658 (D. C. Pa.), quoted at § 1966.
21. See post, subject of "Selling Free from Liens," § 1996. In re Erie Lumber Co., 17 A. B. R. 687 (D. C.

It has been held, in one case, that where a receiver persisted in carrying on the business of the bankrupt, that of a restaurant keeper, for nearly a year at a weekly loss of $100, without keeping proper account books, with an officer of the bankrupt in control of the moneys and without a proper bank account or separation of his private funds from the funds of the receivership, his account would be surcharged with a part of the loss.[22]

But, in general, a receiver in bankruptcy should not be surcharged for losses on sales during his continuance of the business.[23]

§ 388½. Additional Compensation for Continuing Business.

The receiver may be allowed additional compensation for conducting the business of the bankrupt.[23a]

Amendment of 1910.—But by the Amendment of 1910 this compensation is limited to commissions on moneys disbursed by him or realized from property turned over in kind by him—at any rate, so far as any allowance out of the assets is concerned.[24]

However, such limitation of compensation has reference to allowance out of the estate, so that, in the event of dismissal of the petition without adjudication, it is possible that other compensation than that by way of commissions or moneys disbursed may be charged against the petitioning creditors by way of costs, the obvious intent of Congress in limiting the compensation being to protect helpless insolvent estates from depletion through extravagant allowances therefrom.

§ 389. Power to Borrow Money, and Issue Receiver's Certificates.

—And when authorized by order of the court, receivers may borrow money and issue receiver's certificates.[25]

In re Erie Lumber Co., 17 A. B. R. 689, 150 Fed. 817 (D. C. Ga.): "Now, § 2 (5) * * * expressly vests courts of bankruptcy with the power to 'author-

Ga.); In re Clark Coal & Coke Co., 23 A. B. R. 273, 173 Fed. 658 (D. C. Pa.), quoted at § 1996.

Damages for Receiver's Breach of Contract.—Receivers are personally responsible for breach of their own contracts in the conducting of the business, and may be sued therefor. In re Erie Lumber Co., 17 A. B. R. 707 (D. C. Ga.): "If the receivers were guilty of any breach of contract with him, none of the creditors having interest in the fund are responsible for it. The receivers are each sui juris and personally responsible for any wrong ex contractu or ex delicto which they may have committed. The claim is unliquidated, and, even if liquidated, would as against antecedent liens have little or no superior dignity to a claim of a general creditor."

Receivers' certificates, whether receivers personally liable thereon, and whether may be sued in plenary action outside of bankruptcy court, see post, §§ 1780½, 1804½.

22. In re Consumers Coffee Co., 20 A. B. R. 835, 151 Fed. 933 (D. C. Pa.).

23. In re Isaacson, 23 A. B. R. 98, 175 Fed. 293 (C. C. A. N. Y.).

23a. Bankr. Act, § 2 (5): "Authorize the business of bankrupts to be conducted for limited periods by receivers, the marshals, or trustees, if necessary in the best interests of the estate, and allow such officer additional compensation for such services, as provided in section forty-eight of this act."

24. Bankr. Act as amended 1910, § 2 (5), § 48 (e), § 72; see post, § 2118, et seq.

25. Impliedly, In re Alaska Fishing, etc., Co., 21 A. B. R. 685, 162 Fed. 498 (D. C. Wash.). Obiter, compare, In re Clark Coal & Coke Co., 23 A. B. R. 273, 173 Fed. 658 (D. C. Pa.). Also

ize the business of bankrupts to be conducted for limited periods by receivers, the marshals, or trustees, if necessary in the best interest of the estates.' There was, therefore, no doubt of the power of the court to take the action it did. Authorized to operate the property through its receivers, it was equally competent for the court to raise on the credit of the values in hand the funds immediately necessary for its operation. Here was a large saw mill plant, with planing mill, veneering mill, large orders for its products, all belonging to a class of business which at the time and since then has been most notably prosperous. * * *

"It is, however, urged that the court may provide for the priority of receivers' certificates only in case of a railway or quasi public corporation. In view of the act of bankruptcy authorizing the continuance of a private corporation through a receiver, we do not think that this is true. The power to continue business implies the power to make debts, and to provide for their payment, which must include the power to borrow money for urgent necessities and for direct operating expenditures."

In re Restein, 20 A. B. R. 832, 162 Fed. 986 (D. C. Pa.): "All the authorities sustain the proposition that the court in bankruptcy has power to authorize a receiver to borrow money and issue certificates therefor and conduct the business for the purpose of preserving the assets of the bankrupt's estate. In this case the order was made because it was urged upon the court that it was necessary to do so to realize on the prospective assets, which all parties concerned agreed could be made out of the contracts which the bankrupt had with the United States government, so that the certificates were properly issued."

The court may, of course, limit the amount which the receiver may borrow; and loans made to him in excess of such limited amount, can only be binding on the estate upon a showing that the proceeds were used in conducting its business, and then only ratably with the claims of other creditors of the receiver.

In re C. M. Burkehalter & Co., 25 A. B. R. 378, 182 Fed. 353 (D. C. Ala.): "When the bank undertook to charge against funds of the estate, deposited with it by the receiver, notes on which it had advanced money to the receiver, without authority of court, it did so wrongfully for two reasons: in the first place, it had no right to appropriate the trust funds to unauthorized loans, until it had been determined by the court that the proceeds of the loans had been used by the receiver for the benefit of the trust estate. In the second place, it thereby preferred a claim that was entitled to no preference. It was for the court to determine whether the trust funds were sufficient to pay in full all claims against the receiver. The bank, by its action in appropriating the trust funds without order of court, deprived the court of the opportunity of ratably distributing the fund, if insufficient to pay all amongst those having equal claims to it. The payment was not in the usual course and was in violation of the

compare, In re Clark Coal & Coke Co., 22 A. B. R. 843, 57 Pittsb. Law J. 205.

Holders of Receivers' Certificates May Sue in What Forum.—See post, §§ 1780½, 1804½.

Priorities between Holders of Receiver's Certificates and Others Who Have Sold Supplies, etc., to Receiver.

—In re Restein, 20 A. B. R. 832, 162 Fed. 986 (D. C. Pa.). Compare, In re Erie Lumber Co., 17 A. B. R. 687 (D. C. Ga.).

Also between Holders of Receiver's Certificates and Lienholders.—In re Alaska Fishing, etc., Co., 21 A. B. R. 685, 162 Fed. 498 (D. C. Wash.). Compare post, § 1996.

court's order. Nor could the consent of the receiver to the bank's action improve the situation. The receiver was merely the agent of the court in handling the funds of the estate and was without authority to direct or consent to a misappropriation of them. The bank was charged with notice of the limitations upon the receiver's power to borrow money and of his want of authority to use the trust funds to pay unauthorized loans made to him. If the law were different, it would always be in the power of a receiver, with the bank's co-operation, to create a preferred indebtedness of double that authorized by the court, by borrowing twice the amount so authorized and applying the trust funds to the payment of the unauthorized portion of the loan to the exclusion of that authorized, the latter portion remaining a first lien on the assets of the estate."

§ 390. May Make Seizure, under Statute, Instead of Marshal.—

A receiver, instead of the marshal, may be appointed to make the seizure under § (3) of § (69).[26]

§ 390½. Compensation for Making Seizure.—The receivers are entitled to compensation for making seizure.[27]

Amendment of 1910.—Such compensation, where adjudication follows, is to be confined to commissions upon moneys disbursed or realized from property turned over to the trustee, in accordance with the rates prescribed in § 48 (d), with this additional proviso, that where the receiver is a "mere custodian" he receives a lesser rate of commissions.[27a] What constitutes being a "mere custodian" is not clear, although the apparent wording of the proviso to the amendment, § 48 (d), would seem to indicate that the receiver or marshal is to be considered a "mere custodian" whenever he "does not carry on the business of the bankrupt." However, the question as to when the receiver is or is not a "mere custodian" is open. Doubtless there may be instances arising where a receiver or marshal who does not "carry on the business of the bankrupt," may yet be more than a "mere custodian." The proviso limiting compensation of the custodian was meant to cover cases where the services performed were merely those of a "keeper."

See Report of Hearings before the Sub-Committee of the Senate Judiciary Committee on House Bill 20575 to Amend the Bankruptcy Act, Sixty-First Congress, Second Session.

§ 391. May Not Seize Property Held Adversely.—The receiver may

not seize property held and claimed adversely by third parties.[28]

---

26. See ante, § 346, et seq.
27. See Bankr. Act as amended in 1910, § 48 (d); quoted post, § 2132½.
27a. See post. § 2132½.
28. Booneville Nat'l Bk. *v.* Blakey, 6 A. B. R. 13, 107 Fed. 891 (C. C. A. Ind.). But it is to be noted that this was not an action to recover specific property but for a money judgment. Beach *v.* Macon Grocery Co., 8 A. B. R. 751, 116 Fed. 143 (C. C. A. Ga.).

Obiter, In re Kolin, 13 A. B. R. 533, 134 Fed. 557 (C. C. A. Ills.). Contra, In re Barrett, 12 A. B. R. 626, 132 Fed. 362 (D. C. Tenn.).

See similar proposition, ante, § 355; also, compare post, § 1652, et seq., and § 1796, et seq. Contra, In re Haupt Bros., 18 A. B. R. 585, 153 Fed. 239 (D. C. N. Y.); contra, In re Garner & Co., 18 A. B. R. 733, 153 Fed. 914 (D. C. Ala.), wherein the court even

§ 392. May Compel Surrender of Property Not Held Adversely.—
Jurisdiction exists in the bankruptcy court to order surrender, by summary
process, to the receiver of property in the hands of the bankrupt, or in the
hands of the bankrupt's agent, or in the hands of any one not adversely interested therein;[29] likewise, if in the hands of a levying officer, where the
levy has been nullified by the adjudication. And, in one case, it has been
held likewise, so, of the proceeds of sale in the hands of the judgment creditor under a lien levied within the four months, where the sale was made
after adjudication.[30]

In general, whatever property the bankruptcy court would have summary
jurisdiction to order surrendered later to the trustee it will have jurisdiction
to order surrendered in the meantime to the receiver.[31]

Thus, documents, title to which later would pass to the trustee, may
be ordered surrendered to the receiver in the interim, even though they
contain incriminating matter.

In re Harris, 221 U. S. 274, 26 A. B. R. 302: "If a trustee had been appointed,
the title to the books would have vested in him by the express terms of § 70,
and the bankrupt could not have withheld possession of what he no longer
owned, on the ground that otherwise he might be punished. That is one of
the misfortunes of bankruptcy if it follows crime. The right not to be compelled to be a witness against oneself is not a right to appropriate property
that may tell one's story. As the bankruptcy court could have enforced title in favor
of the trustee, it could enforce possession *ad interim* in favor of the receiver."

A petition presented by the receiver seeking an order of surrender
should clearly set forth the facts upon which his claim is based.[32]

**§ 393. Whether May Maintain Independent Plenary Suits to Re-
cover Property.**—Whether receivers may institute and maintain independent plenary suits to recover specific property has been variously decided, the contention arising over the apparent conflict between the principle

ordered the property sold! Contra,
but obiter, In re Berkowitz, 22 A. B.
R. 227, 173 Fed. 1012 (D. C. N. J.).
Stipulation between receiver and adverse claimant as to sale of property
in adverse claimant's possession. See
Ommen, Trustee *v.* Talcott, 23 A. B.
R. 572, 175 Fed. 261 (D. C. N. Y.).
29. In re Muncie Pulp Co., 14 A. B.
R. 70, 139 Fed. 546 (C. C. A. N. Y.);
impliedly, In re Lebrecht, 14 A. B. R.
445, 135 Fed. 877 (D. C. Tex.); In re
Michaels, 27 A. B. R. 299, 194 Fed. 552
(D. C. N. Y.); In re Franklin, etc., Co.,
28 A. B. R. 278, 187 Fed. 281 (D. C.
Pa.); obiter, In re Zotti, 26 A. B. R.
234, 186 Fed. 84 (C. C. A. N. Y. affirming
23 A. B. R. 304, 178 Fed. 304), quoted
at § 1807.
30. In re Breslauer, 10 A. B. R. 33,
121 Fed. 910 (D. C. N. Y.).

**When Contempt for Disobedience
of General Order to Turn Over Books,
etc., Made in Order of Appointment
of Receiver.**—It has been held that a
mere general order for the bankrupt
to turn over all books, assets, etc., to
the receiver, contained in the order of
appointment of the receiver, is not
sufficient to predicate contempt for
disobedience, where the agent representing the receiver on the demand had
no written credentials other than the
order itself. Skubinsky *v.* Bodek, 22
A. B. R. 699, 172 Fed. 332 (C. C. A.
Pa.).

31. In re Harris, 221 U. S. 274, 26 A.
B. R. 302.
32. In re Brockton, 27 A. B. R. 576,
194 Fed. 233 (D. C. N. Y.).

that a receiver in bankruptcy has no title except that of a custodian and that his functions are limited by the statute on the one hand, and the manifest necessity, on the other hand, for some one to act in behalf of all creditors in the period elapsing between the filing of the petition and the election of the trustee.[33]

Some cases hold that receivers may institute plenary suits to recover, as well as to defend possession of, property belonging to the estate.[34]

In re Fixen & Co., 2 A. B. R. 822, 96 Fed. 745 (D. C. Calif.): "A receiver in bankruptcy has power not only to take charge of property which is voluntarily turned over to him, but to institute legal proceedings to recover property belonging to the bankrupt."

Other cases hold that receivers have not such power and can not take possession of property held and claimed adversely by third parties nor institute actions for the recovery of property claimed to belong to the bankrupt's estate.[35]

The true rule doubtless is that, before adjudication at any rate, the receiver would not have the right to pursue third parties by plenary action, unless under the exceptional circumstances of their having gotten property away from him that was once in his custody; this being so because the bankruptcy case itself, before adjudication, is concerned not with property but with the status of a person; and a receiver therein would therefore not be in the position of a court officer seeking possession of assets in controversy, for the title to the assets does not pass until the adjudication. It is also possible that a distinction might exist between suits involving the assertion of those rights which are peculiarly conferred by the Bankruptcy Act and which depend upon the adjudication, such as suits to recover preferential transfers void under § 60 (b); and those suits common to all creditors.

But where the bankruptcy court authorizes a receiver to bring suit, his right to do so is so far res judicata that it can not be collaterally attacked in another court, even though such authority was erroneously granted.[36]

§ 394. May Not Sue for Money Judgment for Debt.—But the rule is settled that receivers may not institute suits in personam to recover money

---

33. See § 1717.
34. In re Barrett, 12 A. B. R. 626, 132 Fed. 362 (D. C. Tenn.). Obiter, In re Kelly, 1 A. B. R. 306, 91 Fed. 504 (D. C. Tenn.).
And will not when suing in the Federal Court in the same district, be required to give security for costs nor to become personally liable therefor unless it is shown the receiver is acting in bad faith, or unreasonably or oppressively; certainly not where there are assets in the bankrupt estate; nor even where there are no assets except when it is due to indemnify ad-

versary. In re Barrett, 12 A. B. R. 626, 132 Fed. 362 (D. C. Tenn.).
35. Title & Trust Co. v. Pearlman, 16 A. B. R. 463, 144 Fed. 550 (D. C. Pa.); obiter, In re Kolin, 13 A. B. R. 533, 134 Fed. 557 (C. C. A. Ills.); In re Schrom, 3 A. B. R. 352, 97 Fed. 760 (D. C. Iowa); Beach v. Macon Grocery Co., 8 A. B. R. 751 (C. C. A. Ga.); Booneville Nat'l Bk. v. Blakey, 6 A. B. R. 13, 107 Fed. 891 (C. C. A. Ind.); Frost v. Lathan & Co., 25 A. B. R. 313, 181 Fed. 866 (D. C. Ala.).
36. Slaughter v. Louisville, etc., Co., 27 A. B. R. 570 (Sup. Ct. Tenn.).

judgments upon mere debts.[37]

§ 394½. Whether May Compromise Controversy.

—It has been held that a receiver has no power to compromise a controversy, except in so far as such power may be incidental to the continuation of business, or otherwise incidental to the preservation of the estate.

[Southern] Steel & Iron Co. v. Hickman, 27 A. B. R. 203, 190 Fed. 888 (C. C. A. Ala.): "The receivers were interested primarily in getting iron for use in their operation of the plant and incidentally in releasing the bankrupt estate *pro tanto* from the defendants' claim. The jurisdiction of the receivers to treat with defendants arose solely from their need of this iron. As receivers, they had no authority to compromise claims against the bankrupt estate. Their action in so doing independently of their need for the iron would not have been binding upon the trustee. In trading for this iron, it was competent for them to incidentally protect the estate by making the amount received apply on the original order. This being the extent of their jurisdiction and authority in the premises, the parties will be held to have negotiated within these limitations, of which knowledge is imputed to them."

§ 395. Receiver Going into Other District than That of Appointment.

—It was held before the Amendment of 1910 and before the Supreme Court's decision in Babbitt v. Dutcher,[37a] that receivers could not go out of the jurisdiction of their appointment and institute actions, nor do any other official act.[38]

But the reverse is the law, especially since the Amendment of 1910 authorizing ancillary proceedings in aid of receivers and trustees, namely, that ancillary jurisdiction exists, and that receivers may be authorized to go into other jurisdictions to protect assets.[39]

But even so, they may only do so when specially authorized by the court appointing them.

---

37. Booneville Nat'l Bk. v. Blakey, 6 A. B. R. 13, 107 Fed. 891 (C. C. A. Ind.), evidently reversing Blakey v. Booneville Bk., 2 A. B. R. 459; inferentially, obiter, In re Kolin, 13 A. B. R. 533, 134 Fed. 557 (C. C. A. Ills.).

37a. See post, § 1705, et seq.

38. In re Schrom, 3 A. B. R. 352, 97 Fed. 760 (D. C. Iowa). Compare post, § 1705, et seq.

In re Benedict, 15 A. B. R. 232, 140 Fed. 55 (D. C. Wis., citing Booth v. Clark, 17 How. 327, and Hale v. Allinson, 188 U. S. 56): "In Great Western Mineral & Manufacturing Co. v. Harris, 198 U. S. 561, Mr. Justice Day, delivering the opinion, fully sustains the authority and reasoning of this early case, and commits the court again to the doctrine that the receiver in whom the title to assets has not been vested, but who relies upon his authority as an officer of the court, has no authority to do any official act outside the jurisdiction of the court appointing him."

In re Dunseath & Son Co., 22 A. B. R. 75, 168 Fed. 973 (D. C. Pa.): "The weight of authority is that the receiver appointed by the District Court of one district can not maintain an action in the District Court of another district to recover the assets in the hands of strangers. The extra-territorial power of a receiver was carefully considered in the case of Clark v. Booth, 17 How. 327, * * *, and it was there decided that the receiver possessed no such power. This case was referred to in the case of Hale v. Allinson, 188 U. S. 56, * * *, where Mr. Justice Peckam, in commenting on the case of Clark v. Booth, said: 'We do not think anything has been said or decided in this court which destroys or limits the controlling authority of that case.'"

39. See post, § 1705, et seq.

In re National Mercantile Agency, 12 A. B. R. 189, 128 Fed. 639 (D. C. Pa.): "As is well known a receiver has such power only as the court that appoints him chooses to give and unless he is authorized to leave the court of original jurisdiction and sue elsewhere, he is not competent to bring such a suit."

And authority so to do before adjudication was refused a receiver in one case.[40]

§ 396. Security for Costs and Bond for Injunction by Receiver.—

Security for costs will not be required where action is brought in the federal court of the same jurisdiction, nor will the receiver be required to become personally liable therefor, in the absence of bad faith or unreasonableness in bringing the suit; certainly not where there are assets in the bankrupt estate, nor even where there are no assets unless it is due to the adversary to indemnify against costs.[41]

Injunction bond need not be given, unless the court in its discretion deems it necessary.[42]

§ 397. Effect of Dismissal of Petition on Receivership.—

The dismissal of the petition before adjudication would probably have the same effect upon a receivership as in other equity cases; unless, perhaps, the receiver were appointed under § 69, or § 3 (e), as to which, see ante, § 344, et seq.

Thus the court has jurisdiction, notwithstanding the proposed dismissal, to determine the ownership of property in its custody.[43]

The effect of such dismissal, at any rate, is a subject of judicial action and may not be determined by mandamus.[44]

Where the decree of dismissal has been appealed from, a receiver will not be discharged when his retention is necessary for the preservation of the property.[45]

§ 397½. Duty to Turn Over Assets to Trustee.—

It is the duty of the receiver to turn over to the trustee, on his appointment, the assets remaining in his hands, without waiting for the court to pass upon his account and discharge him.

It has been held that he may retain a sufficient sum to cover the probable expenses of the receivership, but no more.[46]　But the better practice is

---

40. In re Schrom, 3 A. B. R. 352, 97 Fed. 760 (D. C. Iowa.).

41. In re Barrett, 12 A. B. R. 626, 132 Fed. 362 (D. C. Tenn.).

42. In re Barrett, 12 A. B. R. 626, 132 Fed. 362 (D. C. Tenn.).

43. In re J. C. Winship Co., 9 A. B. R. 641, 120 Fed. 93 (C. C. A. Ills.): obiter, In re Ward, 28 A. B. R. 36, 194 Fed. 174, 179 (D. C. N. J.); Instance, In re Eagle Laundry Co., 25 A. B. R. 868, 184 Fed. 948 (D. C. N. Y.).

44. Edinburg Coal Co. v. Humphreys, 13 A. B. R. 593, 134 Fed. 839 (C. C. A. Ills.).

Court Vacating Receivership.—In re Church Construction Co., 19 A. B. R. 549, 157 Fed. 298 (D. C. N. Y.).

45. In re Ward, 28 A. B. R. 36, 194 Fed. 174, 179 (D. C. N. J.).

46. In re College Clothes Shop, 27 A. B. R. 10, 192 Fed. 80 (D. C. N. Y.).

for the receiver to turn over all assets and obtain orders upon the trustee for the payment of such of his expenses as he himself has not paid.

§ 398. Costs and Expenses of Receiver Taxable against Petitioning Creditors.

—Where a receiver has been appointed, the costs and expenses of the receivership are taxable against the petitioning creditors.[47]

In re Lavoc, 15 A. B. R. 290 (C. C. A. N. Y.): "The question presented for review is whether petitioning creditors are liable for the expenses of a receivership in a case where, upon commencing a proceeding against a debtor to have him adjudicated a bankrupt, they have applied to the court and obtained the appointment of a receiver of his property, and the proceeding is subsequently dismissed as unfounded, the receiver meanwhile having entered upon his duties, taken charge of the property, and incurred expenses.

"There is no express provision in the Bankruptcy Act which authorizes the court of bankruptcy to compel petitioning creditors to pay the costs of a receivership under such circumstances, and the power of the court must, therefore, rest upon its implied authority to require those to bear the expenses of a proceeding which they have instituted without sufficient cause, and in the course of which they have invoked its assistance and asked it to put its machinery in motion for their benefit in such a way that expenses will accrue which must be borne either by them or the adverse party. Courts of equity frequently exercise this power in advance of taking action and in the absence of any statutory authority. Thus, in granting an injunction, it is common practice to require the plaintiff to give a bond or make a deposit in the registry to secure the adverse party against loss if the process be subsequently vacated. The precise question, however, has been considered frequently and determined by the courts. * * *

"Upon authority and because the principle is so just and reasonable, we adopt it and apply it to the case in hand."

Beach v. Macon Grocery Co., 11 A. B. R. 110, 125 Fed. 513 (C. C. A. Ga.): "The petitioners who instituted the proceedings and secured the appointment of a receiver are properly and equitably chargeable with the costs and expenses incurred by their wrongful application. In the event of their insolvency, any expenses incurred by the receiver should fall on him, and not on the defendants. He need not become receiver unless he chooses, or he may require a bond of indemnity before accepting the position. In a case, therefore, where the receiver has been wrongfully appointed, and the order subsequently vacated, it would be more equitable that the receiver himself should sustain the loss or expenses of the receivership paid by him than that they should be taxed to the successful defendants."

And it has been held, that the court may order the defeated party to pay the costs and punish him for contempt for failure to do so.

In re Lavoc, 15 A. B. R. 293, 142 Fed. 960 (C. C. A. N. Y.): "As the court below had competent power to make the order directing the payment of the receiver's expenses, it also had power to enforce its lawful order by a proceeding for contempt (Bankrupt Act, § 2, subd. 13). It is doubtful whether the enforcement

---

47. To same effect. obiter, In re Church Construction Co., 19 A. B. R. 549, 157 Fed. 298 (D. C. N. Y.). Compare, In re Hill Co., 20 A. B. R. 73, 159 Fed. 73 (C. C. A. Ill.), quoted at § 398½.

of the contempt proceeding is equivalent to the imprisonment for debt within the meaning of § 990 of the United States Revised Statutes (Mueller v. Nugent, 184 U. S. 1, 13, 7 A. B. R. 224), and whether that section is not by implication repealed, so far as it conflicts with the express provision to the contrary, in the Bankrupt Act. However this may be, § 990 has no application to a case in which imprisonment for failure to obey the lawful order of the court is permitted by the laws of the State. By the law of this State, § 1241, Code of Civil Procedure, disobedience of an order is punishable as for a contempt of the court where it requires the payment of money to the court or to an officer of the court. The order under review being one requiring the payment to the receiver of the expenses incurred by him, can, therefore, be enforced by the usual punishment for contempt. O'Gara v. Kearney, 77 N. Y. 423-426; Devlin v. Hinman, 161 N. Y. 115."

It seems, however, a severe and unusual, rather than "usual," remedy to enforce the payment of costs by imprisonment for contempt.

And it has been held that the moving party can only be held liable for the costs of a receivership, in excess of the assets thereof, where the proceedings which resulted in the receivership were instituted improvidently or without reasonable cause.[48]

But where the seizure resulted in preserving the value of the estate at a time of financial crisis rather than in inflicting a loss, the court refused in one case to assess the costs and expenses of the receivership against the petitioning creditors who had moved for the receivership.[49]

In re Ward, 29 A. B. R. 547, 194 Fed. 174, 179 (D. C. N. J.): "This section [Bankr. Act, § 3] created a new right in the debtor. He is to be reimbursed in case such seizure and detention occasioned him pecuniary loss. It has no application where the seizure and detention occasions no loss * * * as the taking over by the court of the bankrupt's property in this case had the effect of avoiding impending loss, and the restraints resulted in actual gain, none should be charged against the applicant for such receiver."

Amendment of 1910.—Since the Amendment of 1910, limiting the compensation of the receiver to commissions upon actual amounts disbursed by him or upon moneys realized from property turned over in specie to the trustee, the question arises as to what compensation may be allowed a receiver where no disbursements are made by him and where no adjudication takes place, and consequently no trustee is appointed. Doubtless, the proper construction of § 48 would be that that section is only applicable to cases where administration of assets is had, the obvious intent of the amendment being to avoid the abuse of extravagant allowances out of helpless insolvent estates, which was the immediate cause of the passing of this amendment.

The administration of insolvent estates differs from other forms of litigation. In other litigations there are two adversary parties, sitting on opposite sides of the trial table, each watching the other's every movement.

48. In re Metals, etc., Co., 27 A. B. R. 11, 195 Fed. 226 (C. C. A. Ill.).

49. Instance, In re Aschenbach Co., 25 A. B. R. 502, 183 Fed. 305 (C. C. A. N. Y.).

But insolvency administration is peculiar in this, that there is ordinarily a large number of parties interested, sometime scores and hundreds of them, scattered far apart and in distant parts of the country, each one of whom is interested in the estate, to be sure, but each one of whom has but a comparatively small share therein. "What is everybody's business is nobody's care;" so it has come to be true that there is nothing more helpless than an insolvent estate: it is the easy prey of the rapacity of unscrupulous attorneys, of misinformation on the part of the court, and of over-estimation of the worth of services rendered on the part of officers in charge of the administration.

The reason of the law fails where there is an alert and adversary party, such as the petitioning creditor, against whom the allowance of compensation is to be fixed. Where there are no assets for administration, obviously there can be no allowance, for lack of a subject out of which to grant allowance.

In the case supposed, however, the receiver would only be a "mere custodian," in any event, since the assets would not be administered nor the business conducted, and he would, therefore, even if § 48 were applicable and the assets be wholly converted into money, be restricted to the very meagre compensation of 2 per cent on the first $1,000 and one-half of one per cent on amounts above that sum, to which the "mere custodian" is limited by the Amendment of 1910.

§ 398¼. Whether Receivership Expenses Payable Out of Assets on Dismissal of Petition.

—It has been held that the expenses and compensation of the receiver may be paid out of the assets on dismissal of the petition, and that this is so, notwithstanding the dismissal was on the ground that the debtor was a corporation of a class not subject to bankruptcy.[50]

In re T. E. Hill Co., 20 A. B. R. 73, 159 Fed. 73 (C. C. A. Ill.): "On behalf of this assignee it is contended that he is entitled to the corporate assets 'without any deduction for the expenses of the receivership'—in effect, that it was not within the power of the court, after dismissal of the petition for adjudication of bankruptcy, to award payment for expenses or compensation of the receiver out of the funds in the custody of the court. The only reviewable question under his petition rests on this broad proposition, and it cannot be upheld, as we believe, when the jurisdiction of the District Court over the subject-matter is ascertained and recognized. Upon the filing of the petition for an adjudication of bankruptcy against the corporation and service of process, jurisdiction over parties and subject-matter was established (First National Bank of Denver v. Klug, 180 U. S. 202, 204, 8 Am. B. R. 12, and cases cited), and was

---

50. **Receiver's Attorney Fees—When Not Allowed as Part of Such Costs.**— See In re T. E. Hill Co., 20 A. B. R. 73, 159 Fed. 73 (C. C. A. Ill.), quoted post, § 2054. Compare ante, §§ 347, 397; post, § 418. Compare, Olive v. Armour & Co., 21 A. B. R. 901, 167 Fed. 517 (C. C. A. Ga.).

Motion That Funds in Receiver's Hands Be Paid Over to Trustee.—In re Vogt. 20 A. B. R. 243, 163 Fed. 551 (D. C. N. Y.).

Compensation of Receivers.—See post, § 2118, for the subject of compensation of the receiver.

complete for the hearing and determination of all the issues involved, whatever the ultimate conclusions of the court upon such issues. In re First National Bank of Belle Fourche, 18 Am. B. R. 265, 152 Fed. 64, 68, * * *; Columbia Ironworks v. National Lead Co., 11 Am. B. R. 340, 127 Fed. 99, 101. So, under § 2 (3) of the Bankruptcy Act, * * *, the power and duty of the court, in such case, is unquestionable, to appoint a receiver, when found necessary for preserving the estate in controversy, 'to take charge of the property * * * after the filing of a petition and until it is dismissed, or the trustee is qualified.' This preservation of res and statu quo is an elementary requirement in bankruptcy, when ground appears for the exercise of such power, and until the issues are decided the jurisdiction is exclusive. The receiver, upon appointment and acceptance, becomes the officer and hand of the court in performance of his duties, neither subject to the wishes or directions of the parties, nor dependent upon the result of the controversy for payment of expenses or services; and he is clearly entitled to protection by the court, in the exercise of such jurisdiction, for all expenses rightly incurred and services rendered under its orders, either in allowances out of the funds committed to his charge, or through provision otherwise made by the court to that end. The rule thus settled in reference to receivers in equity (High on Receivers, § 796, and Smith on Receiverships, § 350), applies with special force for protection of these statutory receivers. While it is the undoubted purpose of the statute to limit the functions of the receiver in bankruptcy (Boonville Nat. Bank v. Blakey, 6 Am. B. R. 1, 107 Fed. 891, 894), and his performance must be confined to the statutory requirements and directions of the court thereunder, the authority vested in the court is ample, as we believe, to provide for payment of needful expenses and compensation (within the prescribed limits) out of the property thus taken custodia legis. Assuming that the court may ultimately charge such expenses, in whole or in part, against the petitioning creditors, on dismissal of the proceedings, and further assuming for the argument, that they should be so charged in the case at bar, as contended, it is not the place of the receiver to move for relief of one or the other party, nor are his rights dependent upon the equities of the parties therein. So, the authorities cited in support of the contention that the receivership expenses were rightfully chargeable to the petitioning creditors (In re Lavoc, 15 Am. B. R. 290, 142 Fed. 960, * * * and cases reviewed; Link Belt Mach. Co. v. Hughes, 195 Ill. 413, 417, * * * 59 L. R. A. 673, and citations) are inapplicable upon the present inquiry. We are of opinion, therefore, that allowance out of the assets for expenses of the receivership was authorized, as within the statutory purposes of the appointment; and no other question of law is raised by the petition to review such allowance."

In re De Lancey Stables Co., 22 A. B. R. 406, 170 Fed. 860 (D. C. Pa.): "It was not the case where upon the face of a petition it is clear that the bankrupt belongs to an excepted class; for example, a transportation company or a railroad company. In such a proceeding any action attempted by the court would be wholly void, for no jurisdiction ever attaches; the petition is coram non judice. But, where there is an apparent right to file the petition, jurisdiction undoubtedly exists—that is, the right to hear, inquire, and determine—although the inquiry may result in a finding that the averments of the petition are not true, and that for this reason the proceeding can go no further. Therefore, as jurisdiction against the stables company existed—prima facie a trading or mercantile company—it follows that the court had a right to preserve the property, and as means to that end to appoint a receiver, and also to turn the goods and chattels into cash. This last step was necessary, for the cost of keeping and feeding the horses would soon have exhausted their value. Having, therefore, exercised the undoubted power of caring for the property and of transforming it into money, the expenses of so doing are properly chargeable against the fund; and, as there is no attack upon the reasonableness of the credits asked for in the receiver's account, these credits will be allowed."

§ 398½. Compensation of Receiver on Dismissal by Settlement with All Creditors—Amendment of 1910.—Of course, where settlement is made with all creditors but not by way of composition before adjudication, the compensation of the receiver may likewise be fixed by agreement, the prohibition of § 72 of the act manifestly referring only to allowances out of assets administered under the bankruptcy law.

DIVISION 5.

CREDITORS' INDEPENDENT PLENARY ACTIONS PENDING ADJUDICATION.

§ 399. Creditors' Independent Plenary Actions Pending Adjudication.—After the filing of the petition and before adjudication, creditors may institute suits for the recovery of property fraudulently transferred or concealed by the bankrupt either before or after the filing of the petition; and will thereafter, in case bankruptcy supervenes and their proceedings thereby be annulled or the lien of the proceedings be preserved for the benefit of all creditors, be reimbursed for all their expenses if such suits shall have resulted in the recovery of the property for the creditors.[51]

The clause, added to (2) of Bankruptcy Act, § 64 (b), authorizing such reimbursement, was added by the Amendment of 1903 chiefly to protect creditors during the time intervening between the filing of the petition and the adjudication against fraudulent transfers and concealments which could not be reached under warrant to the marshal or receiver to seize property, such warrants not operating to authorize the seizure of property held adversely by third parties but only of property in the posses-

---

51. Bankr. Act, § 64 (b) (2): "And, where property of the bankrupt, transferred or concealed by him either before or after the filing of the petition, shall have been recovered for the benefit of the estate of the bankrupt by the efforts and at the expense of one or more creditors, the reasonable expenses of such recovery" shall be entitled to priority of payment from the bankrupt estate.

But compare, Cruchet v. Red Rover Mining Co., 18 A. B. R. 814, 155 Fed. 486 (U. S. C. C. Mass.): "The bill did not allege the pendency of the bankruptcy proceedings in Colorado, nor was that fact brought to the attention of the court in any way. If it had been,

the court would have refused to take jurisdiction of the bill, since it would be manifestly destructive of the fundamental purpose of the Bankrupt Act and lead to endless confusion, for the Circuit Courts to entertain creditors' bills like the present one after the commencement of proceedings in bankruptcy against the insolvent. Nor are we aware that any Circuit Court has ever entertained such a bill and appointed a receiver where it had notice that bankruptcy proceedings had already been commenced against the defendant."

Frost v. Latham & Co., 25 A. B. R. 313, 181 Fed. 866 (C. C. Ala.).

sion of the bankrupt, or his agent; some cases as before noted having also denied to receivers, before adjudication, the power to institute proceedings or plenary actions to such end.

Until adjudication, creditors of course are entitled (and also were entitled before the Amendment of 1903) to make use of all the usual and ordinary remedies of creditors in the State or Federal Courts to recover property, for in case there be ultimately no adjudication, their right to sue in the ordinary tribunals would be undoubted.[52] Justly, creditors should not be deterred from making use of these ordinary remedies for their protection by the fear that subsequent bankruptcy will not only rob them of all special advantages but also throw the costs of suit upon them; consequently, this amendment to § 64 (b) (2) allowing them reimbursement was wise and opportune.

Even without the special provision of the Amendment of 1903 to § 64 (b) (2), creditors would be entitled, pending the hearing on an involuntary petition, to maintain independent plenary actions for the recovery of property.[53]

Obiter, Title & Trust Co. v. Pearlman, 16 A. B. R. 464, 144 Fed. 550 (D. C. Pa.): "It is further urged, that, unless power to sue is possessed by the receiver in a case of this kind, there will be a miscarriage of justice, the Pennsylvania statute requiring that proceedings to invalidate a sale in bulk, such as the one that is here complained of, shall be brought within ninety days from its consummation. But assuming this to be the case, it affords no argument for the existence of the power unless it is otherwise deducible. Even if there be this lapse in the law, we are not authorized, out of mere necessity, to raise up something to cover it. The truth is, however, that there is no such difficulty as is assumed. A sale of the character of that in question is made fraudulent and voidable by the local law as against creditors, and creditors therefore have the right themselves to take steps to avoid it. Ordinarily this would be by judgment and execution against the property alleged to have been fraudulently disposed of upon a sale of which the purchaser would be in shape to test the title of the alleged fraudulent vendee. But in requiring proceedings to be begun within ninety days after the consummation of the sale, of necessity something more direct and speedy is contemplated, it being practically impossible within that time to bring action and obtain judgment in order to do so. Neither would an attachment lie, under the Act of 1869 (Pa.), the fraud which justifies it having to be actual, and not merely constructive. Stewers Pork Packing Co. v. Sheener, 15 District 141. Under the circumstances the only relief available to general creditors is by bill, and this must therefore be regarded as intended to be given. Houseman v. Crossman, 177 Pa. 453. And if this be so any creditor would be entitled to sue on behalf of himself and others, either before or

---

52. Reading Trust Co. v. Boyer, 15 Pa. Dist. Rep. 45.

53. Obiter, Horner-Gaylord Co. v. Miller & Bennett, 17 A. B. R. 257, 147 Fed. 295 (D. C. W. Va.). This decision is in error, however, in holding that the bankruptcy court may maintain such plenary action. Compare, In re Schrom, 3 A. B. R. 352, 97 Fed. 760 (D. C. Iowa, distinguished in In re Williams, 9 A. B. R. 744). It is not clear but what the court in this case, however, was advocating ancillary bankruptcy proceedings rather than a resort by creditors to their ordinary remedies pending the hearing upon petition for adjudication. Compare, to same effect, In re Adams, 1 A. B. R. 104 (Ref. N. Y.).

after the institution of proceedings in bankruptcy, such suit, if after, being ancillary thereto, no trustee having yet been chosen. In re Schrom, 3 Am. B. R. 352. This remedy being open, the argument drawn from the necessity for authority on the part of a receiver to sue is effectually disposed of."

In re Ward, 5 A. B. R. 215, 219, 104 Fed. 985 (D. C. Mass.): "It is further urged that, if this court be without jurisdiction to keep from concealment or dissipation the property of the bankrupt in the hands of a third party pending adjudication, there will seldom be left much for the trustee to distribute among the creditors. This may be true, but the situation is created by Congress, not by the Court."

§ 400. Must Be for Benefit of All.—Probably, only those proceedings taken for the benefit of all creditors are strictly entitled to the benefits of § 64 (b) (2).

Yet the benefits of that section have been extended to cases operating to the advantage of all creditors although not so intended.[54] Thus, where an attachment lien, dissolved as to the attaching creditor by the debtor's bankruptcy, is preserved for the benefit of all creditors under § 67 (f) the lien for the costs also is preserved.[55]

§ 401. Independent Plenary Suits by Creditors Not Maintainable in U. S. District Courts.—Independent plenary suits by creditors may not be brought in the bankruptcy courts at all, either before or after adjudication. The jurisdiction conferred by the Amendment of 1903 upon the bankruptcy courts to entertain plenary actions against adverse claimants is limited to cases where the status of the debtor as a bankrupt has become established, so for that reason, alone, such suits would not be maintainable before adjudication. But, further than that, the Amendment of 1903 confers jurisdiction only in suits by "trustees," so that neither before nor after adjudication have creditors themselves the right to resort to the bankruptcy courts in independent plenary suits.[56]

Viquesnay v. Allen, 12 A. B. R. 406, 131 Fed. 21 (C. C. A. W. Va.): "* * * and the amendment if applicable here, likewise applies only to suits by trustees in bankruptcy."

§ 402. No Suit to Maintain Status Quo for Filing Bankruptcy Petition.—Before the filing of a bankruptcy petition creditors may not obtain restraining orders either in the State or Bankruptcy Courts to preserve

54. Compare, In re Francis-Valentine Co., 2 A. B. R. 522, 94 Fed. 793 (D. C. A. Calif.).

55. Receivers v. Staake, 13 A. B. R. 281, 138 Fed. 717 (C. C. A. Va.. affirmed sub nom. First Nat'l Bk. v. Staake, 15 A. B. R. 639, 202 U. S. 141); First National Bk. v. Staake, 15 A. B. R. 639, 202 U. S. 141 (affirming 13 A. B. R. 281).

56. Contra, Horner-Gaylord Co. v.

Miller & Bennett, 17 A. B. R. 257, 147 Fed. 295 (D. C. W. Va.). See post, § 715. Also compare, inferentially, contra, In re Haupt Bros., 18 A. B. R. 585, 153 Fed. 239 (D. C. N. Y.). Nevertheless, the bankruptcy court has jurisdiction to enjoin, pending the petition: In re Jersey Island Packing Co., 14 A. B. R. 690, 138 Fed. 625 (C. C. A. Calif.); Frost v. Latham & Co., 25 A. B. R. 313, 181 Fed. 866 (C. C. Ala.).

the status quo upon the ground that they are about to institute bankruptcy proceedings or will institute them as soon as possible.[57]

However, of course, such object may be the real object, but the application for the restraining order must be upon other grounds. Creditors under § 64 (b) may be allowed their costs and expenses where the effect of such prior action is to aid in the recovery of assets.

57. See ante, § 360.

CHAPTER XII.

TRIAL.

Synopsis of Chapter.

§ 403. Trial, in General, by Court.—After the issues are made up the case is set down for hearing. Bankruptcy proceedings, as already noted (ante, § 20), are a branch of equity jurisprudence; and the hearings in general are to be before the court, even as to the issue of bankruptcy.[1]

Thus, hearings are to be before the court as to whether the debtor belongs to a class exempt from bankruptcy.[2]

Adjournments of bankruptcy hearings and trials, may be had, in accordance with the ordinary rules, bearing in mind, always, however, that celerity of procedure is intended by the Bankruptcy Act.[3]

Amendment of 1910—Adjournment of Petition, in Composition Cases.—In the case of a composition before adjudication, under the Amendment of 1910, it is expressly provided that the hearing upon the petition for adjudication shall be delayed until it shall be determined whether the composition shall be confirmed.[3a] The right to such delay must, however, be exercised in a reasonable manner, and if the bankrupt is guilty of bad faith or laches or if there be no reasonable prospect of a consummation of the composition, it would seem that the adjudication need not be delayed

---

1. Bankr. Act, § 18 (d): "If the bankrupt or any of his creditors shall appear within the time limited and controvert the facts alleged in the petition the judge shall determine as soon as may be, the issues presented by the pleadings without the intervention of a jury, except in cases where a jury trial is given by this act, and make the adjudication or dismiss the petition."

2. Carpenter v. Cudd, 23 A. B. R. 463, 174 Fed. 603 (C. C. A. S. C.), quoted at § 408.

3. See ante, § 23.

3a. Bankr. Act, § 12a: "* * * and action upon the petition for adjudication shall be delayed until it shall be determined whether such composition shall be confirmed." See also, post, § 2358, et seq.

beyond a reasonable time for determining those facts; otherwise estates would be wasted and a convenient instrument would be furnished unworthy bankrupts for coercing creditors into unfair or improper settlements.[3b]

§ 404. **But Court May Submit Issue of Fact to Jury.**—Any specified issue of fact may, of course, be submitted by the bankruptcy court, acting as the chancellor, to the jury, for determination.[4]

In re Rude, 4 A. B. R. 319, 101 Fed. 845 (D. C. Ky.): "Bankruptcy proceedings are equitable in character, and while the court, or, possibly, the referee, might have had a jury to pass upon the amount of the attorney's fee, that was a matter of discretion, and not of right. The court does not understand that in equitable proceedings parties have a right to have an issue tried out of chancery by a jury. Section 19 of the Bankrupt Act, and section 648 of the Revised Statutes in relation to trials in Circuit Courts, do not, in my judgment, affect this result."

But certain holdings are to the effect that the right in bankruptcy practice is confined to those issues mentioned in the statute.[5]

§ 405. **Jury's Verdict, in General, Advisory.**—In case the court thus submits an issue to the jury, the determination of the jury, except in the one statutory instance hereafter mentioned, is merely advisory and not binding on the court;[6] and this exception is in cases where the Bankruptcy Act gives the respondent an absolute right to a jury trial.

Even after the bankrupt has waived the right of trial by jury the court may, of its own motion, direct the issues or any of them he may select to be tried by a jury. In this event the jury trial is not to be taken as being held under the provisions of the bankruptcy act, but as advisory merely, under the general powers of the court as a chancellor.

Oil Well Supply Co. v. Hall, 11 A. B. R. 738 (C. C. A. W. Va.): "It is very clear that the case below was not submitted to the jury under the provisions of the nineteenth section of the Bankruptcy Act (Act July 1, 1898, ch. 541, 30 Stat. 551 [U. S. Comp. Stat. 1901, p. 3429]). The respondents did not demand a jury. Indeed, the record states that a jury was waived. But the district judge, of his own motion, and for his own satisfaction, desired the aid of a jury in

---

3b. It has been the holding, in some unreported cases, however, that the right is absolute and the court without discretion.

4. Oil Well Supply Co. v. Hall, 11 A. B. R. 738, 128 Fed. 875 (C. C. A. W. Va.); Morss v. Franklin Coal Co., 11 A. B. R. 423, 125 Fed. 998 (D. C. Pa.); In re Neasmith, 17 A. B. R. 131, 147 Fed. 160 (C. C. A. Mich.); (1867) Barton v. Barbour, 104 U. S. 137; Carpenter v. Cudd, 23 A. B. R. 463, 174 Fed. 603 (C. C. A. S. C.).

5. In re Herzikopf, 9 A. B. R. 745, 118 Fed. 101 (C. C. A. Calif.). And In

re Neasmith, 17 A. B. R. 131, 147 Fed. 160 (C. C. A. Mich.).

6. Oil Well Supply Co. v. Hall, 11 A. B. R. 738, 128 Fed. 875 (C. C. A. W. Va.); In re Neasmith, 17 A. B. R. 131, 147 Fed. 160 (C. C. A. Mich.). The court is not restricted to the district court jury in such cases, so it appears, but may submit the issue to the Circuit Court jury, the two juries being interchangeable. Oil Well Supply Co. v. Hall, 11 A. B. R. 738, 128 Fed. 875 (C. C. A. W. Va.); Carpenter v. Cudd, 23 A. B. R. 463, 174 Fed. 603 (C. C. A. S. C.), quoted at § 408.

passing upon the question whether an act of bankruptcy had been committed, as charged in the petition. It is always within the discretion of a judge to seek the aid of a jury in solving a question of fact. In the court of chancery the chancellor can do this, either by ordering an issue out of chancery to be tried in the law court, or by impaneling a jury in his own court, and submitting the question to them himself. Wilson v. Riddle, 123 U. S. 615, 8 Sup. Ct. 255, 31 L. Ed. 280; Idaho, etc., Co. v. Bradley, 132 U. S. 509, 10 Sup. Ct. 177, 33 L. Ed. 433. In all such cases the verdict of the jury is advisory—not binding on the court, which must for itself determine the issues. This was the course pursued here. The judge presented the issue to the jury, but he afterwards adopted their conclusion, and gave effect to it by his own decree. This he need not have done if the jury trial had been had under the nineteenth section of the Bankruptcy Act. In carrying out his purpose to seek the aid of a jury, he used a jury in the court over which he was about to preside, and which best suited his convenience—the jury in the Circuit Court of Parkersburg. As the verdict of the jury was sought by himself to aid his conclusion, he could select any jury, especially as the jurors in the District and Circuit Courts of the United States can be used in every court."

§ 406. Except That on Issues of Insolvency and Commission of Act, Right Absolute.

—There is one mandatory exception to the rule that the issues are all to be tried by the court: The debtor himself, resisting his adjudication as bankrupt, may, as a matter of absolute right, have the issues as to his insolvency and as to his having committed the act of bankruptcy charged, determined by a jury.[7]

Elliott v. Toeppner, 9 A. B. R. 50, 187 U. S. 327: "The proceedings in the administration of the bankrupt estate are equitable in their nature but the bankruptcy courts act under specific statutory authority and when on an issue of fact as to the existence of ground for adjudication a jury trial is demanded, it is demanded as of right, and the trial is a trial according to the course of common law."

It is demandable as of right even on the question as to whether the debtor has made a general assignment, although the issue of insolvency in that in-

---

7. Bankr. Act, § 19 (a): "A person against whom an involuntary petition has been filed shall be entitled to have a trial by jury, in respect to the question of his insolvency, except as herein otherwise provided, and any act of bankruptcy alleged in such petition to have been committed, upon filing a written application therefor at or before the time within which an answer may be filed. If such application is not filed within such time, a trial by jury shall be deemed to have been waived." Blue Mtn., etc., v. Portner, 12 A. B. R. 559, 131 Fed. 57 (C. C. A. Mo.).

Carpenter v. Cudd, 23 A. B. R. 463, 174 Fed. 603 (C. C. A. S. C.), quoted at § 408. Impliedly, Buffalo Mill Co. v. Lewisburg Dairy Co., 20 A. B. R. 279, 159 Fed. 319 (D. C. Pa.), quoted

at § 408; In re Ward, 20 A. B. R. 482, 161 Fed. 755 (D. C. N. J.), quoted at § 408; impliedly, Schloss v. Strellow, 19 A. B. R. 359, 156 Fed. 662 (C. C. A. Pa.).

Disobedience of Interlocutory Order Requiring Alleged Bankrupt, Who Denies Insolvency, to Attach List of Debts and Assets Not Ground for Refusing Him Right of Trial.—Where the court has made an interlocutory order upon an alleged bankrupt who is denying that he is insolvent, requiring him to file a list of debts and assets by way of amendment of his answer, the bankrupt's disobedience of the order will not deprive him of the right to appear at the trial and oppose the petition. Young & Holland v. Brande Bros., 20 A. B. R. 612, 162 Fed. 663 (C. C. A. R. I.).

stance would be immaterial,[8] and it is demandable upon the question of the existence of a receivership as an act of bankruptcy.[9]

§ 407. But Jury Demandable by Virtue of Statute, Not Constitution.

—But it is demandable as of right solely by virtue of the Bankruptcy Act and not by virtue of any constitutional provisions.

In re Christensen, 4 A. B. R. 99, 101 Fed. 243 (D. C. Ia.): "It is equally well settled that proceedings in bankruptcy are of equitable cognizance, and therefore the provisions of the Seventh Amendment are not applicable thereto."

§ 408. Jury Confined, Where Demandable, to Two Issues.

—The jury so demanded by the bankrupt may only consider the two issues: Whether the act of bankruptcy was committed and whether the bankrupt was insolvent—the other issues are to be determined by the court alone.[10]

Carpenter v. Cudd, 23 A. B. R. 463, 174 Fed. 603 (C. C. A. S. C.): "Under these provisions it is clear that it is the province of the judge to hear and determine without the intervention of a jury all issues in cases of contested bankruptcy, unless the alleged bankrupt shall make seasonable application for a jury trial, in which case he is entitled as of right to a jury trial in respect to his insolvency, and any act of bankruptcy alleged to have been committed by him. Any other issue of fact involved in the question of bankruptcy, such, for instance, as that in this case, may in the discretion of the court be also submitted to the jury; but the finding of the jury upon such an issue, as in cases submitted to a jury by the chancellor in a court of chancery, is merely advisory, and not binding upon the court."

Thus, where the answer admits insolvency and the act of bankruptcy charged, but alleges that the debtor is not amenable to involuntary proceedings because chiefly engaged in farming, there is no issue warranting a jury trial.[11] Nevertheless, other issues may, from the nature of things, be involved in the question of insolvency and thus have to be left to the jury; as, for example, whether the debtor is a member of a partnership or whether the alleged partnership includes a certain respondent.[12]

---

8. See Day v. Beck & Gregg Hdw. Co., 8 A. B. R. 175, 114 Fed. 834 (C. C. A. Ala.). Apparently, contra, Simonson v. Sinsheimer, 3 A. B. R. 824, 95 Fed. 948 (C. C. A. Ky.).

9. Blue Mtn., etc. v. Portner, 12 A. B. R. 559, 131 Fed. 57 (C. C. A. Mo.).

10. Morss v. Franklin Coal Co., 11 A. B. R. 423, 125 Fed. 998 (D. C. Penna.). In this case the Court refused to permit the jury to pass on the issue as to whether the petitioners held provable claims.

Simonson v. Sinsheimer, 3 A. B. R. 824 (C. C. A. Ky.). But in this case the Court, obiter, limits the right to the mere question of insolvency; perhaps because in that case it was a mere question of law whether the act of bankruptcy (an assignment for the benefit of creditors) had been committed.

Obiter, In re Neasmith, 17 A. B. R. 131, 147 Fed. 160 (C. C. A. Mich.). Compare, same rule where one partner petitions for adjudication of the firm. In re Forbes, 11 A. B. R. 787, 128 Fed. 137 (D. C. Mass.).

Compare, where the question of membership of one of the respondents in a partnership was held to be involved in the question of insolvency, In re Neasmith, 17 A. B. R. 131, 147 Fed. 160 (C. C. A. Mich.).

11. Stephens v. Merchants Bank, 18 A. B. R. 560, 154 Fed. 341 (C. C. A. Ill.).

12. Compare, where the question of

Buffalo Mill Co. *v.* Lewisburg Dairy Co., 20 A. B. R. 279, 159 Fed. 319 (D. C. Pa.): "But if the respondent was a partner, it is admittedly decisive of the question of his solvency, and as he is entitled to go to the jury upon everything which affects or enters into that, the question of partnership must be kept open for their consideration."

Or may be involved in the question of the commission of the act of bankruptcy charged; as, for example, whether the debtor were insane at the time the alleged act was committed and therefore whether it was possible for him to have committed it.

In re Ward, 20 A. B. R. 482, 161 Fed. 755 (D. C. N. J.): "It will be observed from what has been said that in such a case as the present one the defense that the alleged bankrupt did not commit the act of bankruptcy charged against him involves the question of his insanity. * * * Evil intent is an essential element of the act charged. Section 19 of the act gives to an alleged bankrupt the right of a trial by jury of the question of his insolvency and of the question concerning his commission of an act of bankruptcy. * * * The question of the alleged bankrupt's sanity will therefore be submitted to the jury as an essential part of the defense that he did not commit the act of bankruptcy charged."

On the other hand, the bankrupt is not entitled to a trial of the mere question of intent to commit a preference, after having in the pleadings, substantially admitted the insolvency and the act of bankruptcy charged.[13]

And the issue of insolvency involves of course, the existence, validity and amount of debts; and the court may not predetermine such facts.

Schloss *v.* Strellow, 19 A. B. R. 359, 156 Fed. 662 (C. C. A. Pa.): "On February 28, 1907, there was a jury trial as to both insolvency and the act of bankruptcy; but the assignment of errors concerns only the issue as to insolvency, and the single point presented by the several specifications is whether, for the trial of that issue, the orders of September 29, 1906, and of January 30, 1907, had conclusively determined the validity and amount of the claims and of the petitioners, original and intervening. The case was tried and decided upon the theory that they had, and in this we think there was error. The precise question, as defined by the Bankruptcy Act * * *, was whether the property of Schloss would, 'at a fair valuation, be sufficient in amount to pay his debts,' and for the solution of that question it was quite as needful to ascertain the amount of his debts as the value of his property. These elements were both inherent in 'the question of his insolvency.' There was no separate issue as to his indebtedness. That was matter of evidential fact, and the plaintiff in error was entitled to a finding of the jury upon it, notwithstanding its supposed predetermination by the court."

§ 409. Jury Trial Not Available to Intervening Creditors.—None

membership of one of the respondents in a partnership was held to be involved in the question of insolvency, In re Neasmith, 17 A. B. R. 131, 147 Fed. 160 (C. C. A. Mich.). Also, Schloss *v.* Strellow, 19 A. B. R. 359, 156 Fed. 662 (C. C. A. Pa.). Compare, inferentially merely, Lennox *v.* Allen Lane Co., 21 A. B. R. 648, 167 Fed. 114 (C. C. A. Mass.).

13. In re Harris, 19 A. B. R. 204, 156 Fed. 875 (D. C. Ala.).

of the intervening creditors, however, have the right to demand a jury. It is a right personal to the bankrupt.

In re Herzikopf, 9 A. B. R. 745, 121 Fed. 544 (C. C. A. Calif.): "The argument for the appellants is that any defense which would be open to the bankrupt is open to all of his creditors, including the method of making it. The difficulty in the way of the appellants is that, except in certain specified particulars, within which the present case does not come, proceedings in bankruptcy are of an equitable nature (Bardes v. Hawarden Bank, 178 U. S. 524, 535, 4 A. B. R. 163, 20 Sup. Ct. 1000, 44 L. Ed. 1175), in respect to which, it must be conceded, the right to a jury trial does not exist. Of course, in the exercise of the jurisdiction at law conferred on the bankruptcy courts, as, for instance, the power to 'arraign, try, and punish bankrupts, officers and other persons, and the agents, officers, members of the board of directors or trustees, or other similar controlling bodies, or corporations for violations of this act, in accordance with the laws of procedure of the United States now in force, or such as may be hereafter enacted regulating trials for the alleged violation of laws of the United States,' there goes the concomitant right to trial by jury. But in proceedings not at law, but relating, as does the case at bar, to the question of the insolvency of the alleged bankrupt, and to acts of bankruptcy alleged to have been committed by him, it is quite clear, we think, that no right to a jury trial exists unless the Bankruptcy Act expressly or by necessary implication gives it. It is not claimed that it is expressly given to any creditor. It is given, with certain limitations, to the 'person against whom an involuntary petition has been filed' by the clause above quoted. But even the bankrupt is by the statute restricted in his right to a jury trial to the issues specifically mentioned, to-wit, his insolvency and any act of bankruptcy committed by him. These express limitations of the right to a jury trial clearly manifest, under the familiar maxims, 'Expressio unius est exclusio alterius,' and 'Expressum facit cessare tacitum,' the intention of Congress to withhold it from all others, and in all cases, in such of the proceedings in bankruptcy as are of an equitable nature."

§ 410. To Be Conducted According to Common Law.—If a jury trial be had on demand of the bankrupt it is to be conducted precisely as a jury trial is conducted according to the course of the common law.[14] Thus, for instance, a general exception to a refusal to charge several requests cannot avail if any one of the requests was properly refused.[15] But equitable defenses are not on that account to be excluded.

Acme Food Co. v. Meier, 18 A. B. R. 550, 153 Fed. 74 (C. C. A. Mich.): "Neither is there any sound reason for saying that the effect of calling for a jury to try the issues in respect to the alleged acts of bankruptcy operates

---

14. Elliott v. Toeppner, 9 A. B. R. 50, 187 U. S. 327; Duncan v. Landis, 5 A. B. R. 649, 106 Fed. 839 (D. C. Pa.). Where each party asks the court to direct a verdict it is equivalent to a request for a finding of facts and if the court directs the verdict both parties are concluded on the findings of fact, see Bradley Timber Co. v. White, 10 A. B. R. 329, 121 Fed. 779 (C. C. A.);

Acme Food Co. v. Meier, 18 A. B. R. 550, 153 Fed. 74 (C. C. A. Mich.).

15. Bean-Chamberlain v. Standard Spoke & Nipple Co., 12 A. B. R. 610 (C. C. A. Mich.).

Estoppel as to Residence by Pleadings Filed in Another Case.—Long v. Lockman, 14 A. B. R. 172, 135 Fed. 197 (D. C. Colo.).

to circumscribe the powers of the court to those technically belonging to a court of law. It is true that error upon such a trial by jury can be reviewed only by a writ of error. But that is because the act confers as a privilege the right of jury trial and such a trial can only be reviewed according to the course of the common law. Elliott v. Toeppner, 187 U. S. 327, 9 Am. B. R. 50. But in the case under consideration the only defense against the charge of an act of bankruptcy by making a deed which at common law was mala fide, is that the deed was made in good faith and intended as a mere security. Against the charge that these same conveyances were intended as illegal preferences the only defense is, that, in fact, they were mere securities and that defendant was solvent when they were made if his equity of redemption be valued as part of his property. In such a case to give the defendant the right of trial by jury and then deny the right to show the actual character of the conveyances would be to give and deny the right of jury trial by the same provision of law."

§ 411. Demand for Jury.—But the jury must be demanded;[16] and if the bankrupt does not demand the jury before or on the answer day, and demand it in writing, filed with the District Clerk, he will be deemed to have waived a jury trial.[17]

§ 412. Reference to Master Where Jury Not Demanded.—Where a jury is not demanded, the judge may refer the issues to a master commissioner to take and hear the evidence and report his findings.[18]

Clark v. Am. Mfg. & Enamel Co., 4 A. B. R. 351, 101 Fed. 962 (C. C. A. W. Va.): "There was no error in the action of the lower court in referring the case, as it did, to a referee. * * * Upon the filing of an answer to an involuntary petition in bankruptcy, it is quite usual, and in many instances the only way that the court can proceed, to have one of its referees take the evidence, and report upon the various questions presented, returning to the court the evidence taken for its consideration."

And the findings of fact of the Special Master will not be disturbed unless clearly against the weight of the evidence.[19]

But some real necessity for such reference must exist, to warrant burdening an insolvent estate with the additional expense of a special mastership.[20] And where a preliminary question of jurisdiction is raised, easily determinable, such necessity cannot be said to exist; and it has been held under such circumstances improper to refer all the issues at one time to a special master.

16. In re Ward, 20 A. B. R. 482, 161 Fed. 755 (D. C. N. J.).

17. Bankr. Act, § 19 (a): "* * * upon filing a written application therefor at or before the time within which an answer may be filed. If such application be not filed within such time, a trial by jury shall be deemed to have been waived."

Bray v. Cobb, 1 A. B. R. 153, 91 Fed. 102 (D. C. N. Car.); In re Neasmith, 17 A. B. R. 131, 147 Fed. 160 (C. C. A. Mich.).

18. In re Lavoc, 13 A. B. R. 400, 134 Fed. 237 (C. C. A. N. Y.). Impliedly, In re Rome Planing Mills, 3 A. B. R. 766, 99 Fed. 137 (D. C. N. Y.).

Obiter [reference held improper under facts of case], In re King, 24 A. B. R. 606, 179 Fed. 694 (C. C. A. Ills.), quoted at § 412.

19. In re Rome Planing Mills, 3 A. B. R. 766, 99 Fed. 137 (D. C. N. Y.). Also, see post, § 2840, subject of "Review of Referee's Orders."

20. In re King, 24 A. B. R. 606, 179 Fed. 694 (C. C. A. Ills.), quoted at § 412.

In re King, 24 A. B. R. 606, 179 Fed. 694 (C. C. A. Ills.): "While it is undoubted * * * that reference to a special master or like ministerial officer may be ordered, to hear and report the testimony (with or without advisory findings thereupon), when an issue triable by the judge alone involves extended testimony and its hearing in open court appears to be impracticable, we believe the act neither intends nor authorizes such general reference of issues as ordered in the instant case. The jurisdictional averments of residence and principal place of business were distinctly controverted, and it appears that the facts were readily ascertainable for solution of that primary issue. Orderly procedure required, as we believe, its determination by the district judge as a condition precedent to inquiry upon the other issues of fact raised by the pleadings. Direct hearing of the testimony upon an issue of such nature would seem desirable; but, if that course is impracticable, reference to a ministerial officer to take and report such testimony cannot rightly extend the hearing as well to the subordinate issues, not open to inquiry until jurisdiction to proceed therein is ascertained and found by the district judge. The court can confer no authority upon the referee (as master or otherwise) to decide these issues, nor to rule thereon either finally or temporarily."

§ 412½. Discovery, Depositions, Interrogatories, etc.

—There is no statutory permission for the filing of interrogatories with the petition,[21] and such interrogatories have been held improper, at any rate where a general examination into the "acts, conduct and property" of the bankrupt is thus sought to be obtained before adjudication.[22]

But there is no good reason for denying to suitors the ordinary remedies for discovery as to the issues raised on the petition allowable in other proceedings in equity. Bankruptcy is a proceedings in equity and equity rules prevail. The Supreme Court, moreover, in its general orders, has directed that where the Act of Rules of Bankruptcy are silent the practice should conform as nearly as possible to that prevailing in the federal equity courts.

§ 413. Trial to Be "Impartial."

—The trial must be an "impartial" trial.

Bankr. Act, § 4 (b): "* * * be adjudged an involuntary bankrupt upon default or an impartial trial."

Why congress qualified the word trial by the adjective "impartial" and prescribed that the trial must be "impartial" is hard to understand. The trial would be presumed to be impartial. Perhaps partiality is thus made a specific ground for reversal, although it is difficult to precisely define its limitations.

The bankrupt then, at the hearing or trial, is either adjudged bankrupt or adjudged not bankrupt.

21. In re Thompson, 24 A. B. R. 655, 179 Fed. 874 (D. C. Pa.).

22. In re Thompson, 24 A. B. R. 655, 179 Fed. 874 (D. C. Pa.); also compare post, § 1543 and ante, §§ 181½, 282½.

CHAPTER XIII.

DISMISSAL.

Synopsis of Chapter.

§ 414. Dismissal for Want of Jurisdiction.—The petition should be dismissed where jurisdiction is lacking. And the court should of its own motion dismiss the petition if it discovers it has been acting without jurisdiction.[1]

In re Columbia Real Estate Co., 4 A. B. R. 417, 101 Fed. 965 (D. C. Ind., affirmed by C. C. A., 7 A. B. R. 441): "Want of jurisdiction is a question that the court should consider whenever or however raised, even if the parties forbear to make it or consent that the case may be heard on its merits." Citing Metcalf v. Watertown, 128 U. S. 586.

This rule applies also to voluntary petitions.[2]

When jurisdiction is challenged, it should be inquired into as soon as possible.[3] The essential facts conferring jurisdiction must appear affirmatively and distinctly in the pleadings before the court will make adjudication; it is not sufficient that jurisdiction may be inferred argumentatively.[4]

---

1. In re Garneau, 11 A. B. R. 679, 127 Fed. 677 (C. C. A. Ills.): In re Waxelbaum, 3 A. B. R. 395, 98 Fed. 589 (D. C. N. Y.). Instance, In re San Miguel, etc., Co., 27 A. B. R. 901, 197 Fed. 126 (D. C. Pa.). Compare ante, § 30; post, § 441½.

2. In re Waxelbaum, 3 A. B. R. 395, 98 Fed. 589 (D. C. N. Y.); In re Garneau, 11 A. B. R. 679, 127 Fed. 677 (C. C. A. Ills.); post, § 431.

Compare, In re Tully, 19 A. B. R. 604, 156 Fed. 634 (D. C. N. Y.), where the court vacated the order of adjudication because of lack of sufficient residence at the time of the adjudication; but immediately readjudicated the debtor bankrupt as having meantime acquired sufficient residence, without requiring even the formalities of reverification or refiling, clearly an erroneous ruling. See post, §§ 431, 441½; also ante, § 30.

3. In re Waxelbaum. 3 A. B. R. 395, 98 Fed. 589 (D. C. N. Y.); In re King, 24 A. B. R. 606, 179 Fed. 874 (C. C. A. Ills.), quoted at § 412.

4. In re Plotke, 5 A. B. R. 175, 104 Fed. 964 (C. C. A. Ills.).

§ 415. Dismissal after Hearing Merits.—If the debtor after hearing is adjudged not bankrupt the petition is dismissed; and the proceedings of course end there, except as the litigation may be prolonged in the higher courts by appeal or writ of error.[5]

Thus, of course, after dismissal the court has no authority to hear controversies in regard to alleged claims against the estate.[6]

But the fact that after adjudication the estate may be able to pay all of its debts in full will not, of itself, prevent its administration in the bankruptcy court.[7]

§ 416. Dismissal as to Part.—The petition may be dismissed as to some and not all the alleged parties defendant.[8]

§ 416½. Dismissal on Composition.—Amendment of 1910.—It is contemplated by § 12 of the Bankruptcy Act as amended in 1910, that the petition for adjudication shall be dismissed upon distribution of the consideration after confirmation of a composition. This dismissal, however, is not to be made until the composition has been distributed;[8a] and during the meantime the case is to be considered as still pending.[9]

§ 417. Costs on Dismissal after Hearing Merits.—The court will allow costs against the petitioning creditors on dismissal after a hearing on the merits.[10] And where a receiver has been appointed, the costs and expenses of the receivership are taxable against the petitioning creditors.[11]

But in one case the court refused to tax against the petitioners the receiver's costs and expenses where the receivership had resulted in preserving the property during a financial crisis.

In re Ward, 29 A. B. R. 547, 194 Fed. 174, 179 (D. C. N. J.) quoted further at §§ 353, 398: "After the creditors' petition praying that William R. Ward be adjudged a bankrupt, was dismissed upon the ground that he was insane at the time of the commission of the alleged act of bankruptcy, the guardian

---

5. As to malicious prosecution of bankruptcy petition, see ante, § 354.
6. In re Sig. H. Rosenblatt & Co., 28 A. B. R. 401, 193 Fed. 638 (C. C. A. N. Y.).
7. In re Jamaica, etc., Co., 28 A. B. R. 763, 197 Fed. 240 (D. C. N. Y.).
8. Instance, In re Nixon, 6 A. B. R. 693, 110 Fed. 633 (D. C. Mont.).
8a. See post, § 237½.
9. [1867] In re Mickel, 19 N. B. Reg. 374, quoted post, § 237½.
10. Gen. Ord. XXXIV: "In cases of voluntary bankruptcy, when the debtor resists an adjudication, and the court, after hearing adjudges the debtor a bankrupt, the petitioning creditor shall recover, and be paid out of the estate, the same costs that are allowed to a party recovering in a suit in equity; and if the petition is dismissed the

debtor shall recover like costs against the petitioner."
In re Haesler-Kohloff Carbon Co., 14 A. B. R. 381, 135 Fed. 867 (D. C. Pa.); In re Ghiglione, 1 A. B. R. 580, 93 Fed. 186 (D. C. N. Y.); In re Morris, 7 A. B. R. 709, 115 Fed. 591 (D. C. Pa.).
11. See ante, "Receivers," ch. XI, div. 4.
It has apparently been held, that the court may order the defeated party to pay the costs and punish him for contempt for failure to do so. In re Lavoc, 15 A. B. R. 293 (C. C. A. N. Y.).
But there can be no counsel fees awarded on dismissal where there has been no seizure of property. See ante, § 398. Matter of the Aschenbach Co., 25 A. B. R. 502, 183 Fed. 305 (C. C. A. N. Y.).

ad litem appointed to defend on behalf of said bankrupt, and the general guardians of the said bankrupt, who were subsequently permitted to intervene to make a like defense, presented their petitions; the former praying for an allowance of $5,000 as compensation for services rendered as such guardian *ad litem*, to be paid by the petitioning and intervening creditors; and the latter praying the court to fix the costs, counsel fees, expenses and damages occasioned by the seizure, taking and detention of the bankrupt's property by the receiver of this court, at $11,063.20, to be paid by the same creditors."

"The present case is one where the seizure and detention was more constructive than actual. The estate that stood in the name of the bankrupt at the time of the appointment of the receiver, consisted almost entirely of marketable securities pledged as collateral for loans. The appointment was made in the midst of a financial crisis attended with a falling market, and the restraining orders that were issued coincident with said receivership prevented a sacrifice of said collateral, with the result that they were intact at the close of such receivership, with a market value considerably more than when such receivership began. Such results are not those aimed at in section 3e. This section created a new right in the debtor. He is to be reimbursed in case such seizure and detention occasioned him pecuniary loss. It has no application where the seizure and detention occasions no loss; and such section cannot be invoked to recover costs and expenses occasioned in making a successful defense to the charge of bankruptcy. As the taking over by the court of the bankrupt's property in this case had the effect of avoiding impending loss, and the restraints resulted in actual gain, none of the costs and expenses incident to such receivership should be charged against the applicant for such receiver. However, the costs and expenses that, in a sense, may be said to have been occasioned by the seizing and detaining of the property, are but a small part of the whole expense incident to this protracted litigation. Outside of the receiver's fees and his petty disbursements, all the expenses incurred and almost all of the services rendered by counsel, were in consequence of the contest over the question of adjudication; and as counsel of all the parties, in their arguments and briefs, have dealt with the recoverability of such expenses and fees generally, I will so treat them, regardless of the fact that the general guardians' prayer is limited to such as are recoverable under section 3e, and permit them to amend their petition in that particular. Under General Order 34, the guardians can recover only such costs as 'are allowed to a party recovering in a suit in equity.' And by section 2, cl. 18, of the Bankruptcy Act, the court has a discretionary power to impose the costs 'allowed by law' upon one or the other of the parties, or part against each and part against the estate."

§ 418. Costs on Dismissal for Want of Jurisdiction.—On dismissal for want of jurisdiction over the class of persons proceeded against, the court is without power to award costs; and may not tax costs against the petitioning creditors.[12]

12. Compare ante, §§ 347, 397, 398½. In re Ghiglione, 1 A. B. R. 581, 93 Fed. 186 (D. C. N. Y.); In re R. H. Williams, 9 A. B. R. 736, 120 Fed. 34 (D. C. Ark.). But compare, Olive *v.* Armour Co., 21 A. B. R. 901, 167 Fed. 514 (C. C. A. Ga.); also compare, In re De-Lancey Stables, 22 A. B. R. 406, 170 Fed. 860 (D. C. Pa.).

Compare, In re Ward, 29 A. B. R. 547, 194 Fed. 174, 179 (D. C. N. J.), quoted at § 417, where dismissal was because of debtor's insanity at time of commission of alleged act and where the receivership had resulted in preserving the estate at a time of financial crisis.

In re Phila. & Lewes Transp. Co., 11 A. B. R. 444 (D. C. Pa.): "I see no reason why the rule which denies to a court the power to award costs, when a case is dismissed for want of jurisdiction (Citizens Bk. *v.* Cannon, 164 U. S. 319) should not prevail in a court of bankruptcy as well as in other jurisdictions."

However, it has been held that where a bond for the seizure of property has been given in such case, damages and attorney's fees may be recovered, the giving of the bond creating a new right under the special provisions of the Bankruptcy Act.[13]

Moreover, it has been held that the court has not "lack of jurisdiction" when it decides that a debtor is not of a class subject to bankruptcy, for, all the time, the court had complete jurisdiction to determine precisely that question.[14]

Where a bankruptcy proceedings was dismissed for want of jurisdiction, after the estate had been partly administered, it was held that the court would allow only such costs as were actual disbursements, or were for services rendered, in the necessary preservation of the estate.[15]

§ 418½. Costs on Dismissal in Compositions before Adjudication. —Amendment of 1910.

—The Amendment of 1910, permitting compositions with creditors before adjudication of bankruptcy, contemplates the dismissal of the bankruptcy petition on distribution being made to creditors on confirmation of the composition. In such cases the compensation of the receiver or marshal is regulated by § 48, being limited to commissions not exceeding one-half of one per cent upon the amount distributed to creditors, and an additional one-half of one per cent thereon in the event that the business has been conducted.

Such compensation is additional to that payable to the distributing agent out of the composition fund deposited by the bankrupt.

§ 418¾. On Dismissal by Settlement Other than "Composition." —Amendment of 1910.

—The compensation of the receiver or marshal on dismissal of an involuntary petition by consent of parties, as, for example, in cases of settlement with all creditors other than by way of a statutory "composition," is not within the contemplation of § 48, nor within the prohibitions of § 72, as amended in 1910, such sections having reference only to allowances out of the assets in process of administration, or where compositions under § 12 are involved; and having no relation to cases where all parties, the debtor and all creditors, agree upon the compensation.

§ 419. On Dismissal, Ten Days Notice to Creditors to Be Given.

—If no adjudication takes place at all, either that the debtor is bankrupt or not bankrupt, but the petition is dismissed by the petitioning creditors, or by

---

13. Hill Co. *v.* Supply & Equipment Co., 24 A. B. R. 84 (App. Ct. of Ill.).

14. Hill Co. *v.* Supply & Equipment Co., 24 A. B. R. 84 (App. Ct. of Ill.), quoted ante, § 30. See also, discussions of § 30, ante.

15. In re Eagle Laundry Co., 25 A. B. R. 868, 178 Fed. 308 (D. C. N. Y.).

consent of parties, or for want of prosecution, ten days notice must be sent
by mail to all creditors, of the application or intention to dismiss.[16]

In re Plymouth Cordage Co., 13 A. B. R. 665, 135 Fed. 1000 (C. C. A. Okla.):
"Notice is indispensable and an order of dismissal without notice is erroneous."

The notices required by Bankruptcy Act, §§ 18 (g) and 59 (g), before dismissal are indispensable safeguards against the abuse of bankruptcy petitions
by unscrupulous and designing creditors to force preferential settlements
from debtors or to protect preferences or other improper transfers until the
four months' limitation for instituting another proceeding for their avoidance shall have elapsed, when by sudden dismissal without notice the rest
of the creditors would be left remediless, bankruptcy petitions becoming
thus instruments for acquiring preferences rather than for preventing them.
Congress was so much in earnest on the subject that it inserted the requirement in two different sections, one of which it amended in 1910 to make
even more explicit and mandatory; and by these repetitions it emphasizes
the importance which it attaches to the giving of notices to creditors of
applications for dismissal.[17]

---

16. See Bankr. Act, § 59 (g): "A
voluntary or involuntary petition shall
not be dismissed by the petitioner or
petitioners or for want of prosecution
or by consent of parties until after
notice to the creditors, and to that
end the court shall, before entertaining an application for dismissal, require the bankrupt to file a list, under
oath, of all his creditors, with their
addresses, and shall cause notice to
be sent to all such creditors of the
pendency of such application and shall
delay the hearing thereon for a reasonable time to allow all creditors and
parties in interest opportunity to be
heard."

And Bankr. Act, § 58 (a): "Creditors shall have at least ten days notice
by mail * * * of * * * (8) the proposed dismissal of the proceedings."

In re Lederer. 10 A. B. R. 492, 125
Fed. 96 (D. C. N. Y.); In re Lewis. 11
A. B. R. 683, 129 Fed. 147 (D. C. Del.);
In re Frischberg, 8 A. B. R. 610 (Ref.
N. Y.); In re Jamaica, etc., Co., 28 A.
B. R. 763, 197 Fed. 240 (D. C. N. Y.).

Contra, In re Levi & Klauber, 15 A.
B. R. 295 (C. C. A. N. Y.). This case
was decided before the Amendment of
1910 but it did not quote the statute
correctly even as it was before the
amendment, and the adoption of its
ruling would in effect have abrogated
the two clear, unequivocal sections of
the statute relative to dismissal of petitions. Section 59 did not, even before
the Amendment. provide that "an invol-

untary petition shall not be dismissed
for want of prosecution by the petitioner or petitioners therein, or by consent of parties, until after notice to
creditors." Such is not a correct quotation of the statute. The statute even before the Amendment of 1910 was so
worded as to be free from the possibility of such construction. It read
as follows: "A voluntary or involuntary petition shall not be dismissed by the petitioner or petitioners
or for want of prosecution or by consent of parties until after notice to the
creditors." Again, § 58 (a) always has
provided that "Creditors shall have at
least ten days notice by mail * * * of
* * * (8) the proposed dismissal of the
proceedings." It would be well to bear
in mind the admonition of the court
in Swarts v. Siegel, 8 A. B. R. 697, 117
Fed. 13 (C. C. A. Mo.): "Attempted
judicial construction of the unequivocal
language of a statute serves only to
create doubt and to confuse the judgment. There is no safer nor better
settled canon of interpretation than
that when language is clear and unambiguous it must be held to mean
what it plainly expresses, and no room
is left for construction."

The motion for dismissal should give
a good reason. In re Lewis, 11 A. B.
R. 683. 129 Fed. 147 (D. C. Del.).

17. Obiter, In re Frichsberg, 8 A. B.
R. 607, 610 (Ref. N. Y.). Obiter, In re
Ryan, 7 A. B. R. 562, 114 Fed. 373 (D.
C. Pa.).

In re Lewis, 11 A. B. R. 693, 129 Fed. 147 (D. C. Del.): "In the language employed in another connection by Judge Blodgett in the case of In re Heffron, Fed. Cases, No. 6,321, decided under the Bankruptcy Act of 1867. 'It would lead to underhand and secret negotiations between the debtor and a portion of the creditors and be a strong incentive for showing favors to a few creditors at the expense of the many.'"

But an order dismissing the proceedings without notice to other creditors than merely to the petitioning creditors is not wholly void, and at best is a mere irregularity.[18] The court would have had jurisdiction to enter a dismissal on other grounds without notice, as upon failure of the petitioning creditors to prove their case, and the mere ground upon which the dismissal is made would not warrant a fatal disregard of it, as if void on its face.

Amendment of 1910.—Owing to the particular difficulty in giving notices to creditors before the filing of schedules, some of the courts, before the Amendment of 1910, had come to rule that §§ 58 (a) (8) and 59 (g) were unenforceable, since no method was provided whereby the names and the addresses of the creditors could be ascertained. This defect has been cured by the Amendment of 1910, by which it is provided in § 59 (g), that courts shall, before entertaining an application for dismissal, require the bankrupt to file a list, under oath, of all the creditors with their addresses and shall cause notice to be sent to all creditors of the pendency of such application and shall delay the hearing thereon for a reasonable time to allow all creditors and parties in interest to be heard. As to the length of time of such notice and the manner of giving it, § 58 (a) already furnishes the guide, such section providing that there should be ten days notice by mail, etc., "of (8) the proposed dismissal of the proceedings."

§ 420. On Dismissal after Hearing Merits, No Notice Requisite.—

On dismissal, after hearing the merits, no notice to creditors is requisite.[19]

Neustadter v. Chic. Dry Goods Co., 3 A. B. R. 96, 96 Fed. 830 (D. C. Wash.): "It is my opinion that these provisions of the law relate to dismissals which in effect withdraw the cases without submission to the court for its decision upon the merits."

§ 421. Reinstatement on Dismissal without Notice.—

Where dismissal is made without notice to creditors, creditors not notified may have the proceedings reinstated; but creditors not notified must not be guilty of laches, else their application for reinstatement of the proceedings will be refused.[20]

---

18. Obiter, In re Jemison Mercantile Co., 7 A. B. R. 588, 112 Fed. 966 (C. C. A. Ala.); obiter, In re Plymouth Cordage Co., 13 A. B. R. 665, 135 Fed. 1000 (C. C. A. Okla.). Compare, obiter, Neustadter v. Chic. Dry Goods Co., 3 A. B. R. 96, 96 Fed. 830 (D. C. Wash.).

19. Cummins Grocer Co. v. Talley, 26 A. B. R. 484, 187 Fed. 507 (C. C. A. Tenn.).

20. In re Jemison Mercantile Co., 7 A. B. R. 588, 112 Fed. 966 (C. C. A. Ala.), distinguished in In re Plymouth Cordage Co., 13 A. B. R. 625, 135 Fed. 1000 (C. C. A. Okla.).

§ **422. No Dismissal if Any Petitioning Creditor Objects.**—It is not discretionary with the court to dismiss the petition if any of the petitioning creditors objects, no matter if satisfied it would be for the best interests of the creditors to do so and that the parties are acting in good faith. The right of a creditor to proceed is an absolute right.

In re Cronin, 3 A. B. R. 552, 98 Fed. 584 (D. C. Mass.): "Is the condition altered by the fact that the majority of the petitioners have come to desire a dismissal of the petition, which dismissal is resisted by the minority? Will the assent of the majority of the petitioners enable the court to act for the interest of the creditors by dismissing the petition, or has the minority the right to in-sist upon an adjudication, if an act of bankruptcy has been committed? I think that in this case the right of the minority is absolute."

In re Perry & Whitney Co., 22 A. B. R. 772, 172 Fed. 745 (D. C. Mass.): "It sufficiently appears from the record that this case is one in which only a comparatively inconsiderable minority of the creditors desire the administration of the estate in bankruptcy, and that by far the greater proportion of them in number and amount regard the common law assignment as more for their interest. * * * If there are three bona fide creditors whose claims amount in all to $500, Congress has given them the right to insist on bankruptcy, however great the majority of creditors who disagree with them."

And no dismissal will be granted on the application of two of the petition-ing creditors against the protest of the third;[21] not even where the court is satisfied it would be for the best interests of creditors.[22]

It has been held that where all the creditors except one and he with a dis-puted claim, consents to a dismissal either affirmatively or by failure to op-

---

21. In re Lewis, 11 A. B. R. 683, 129 Fed. 147 (D. C. Del.); In re Cronin, 3 A. B. R. 552, 98 Fed. 584 (D. C. Mass.).

22. In re Cronin, 3 A. B. R. 552, 98 Fed. 584 (D. C. Mass.).

No Dismissal of Petition for Adjudi-cation Simply Because of Collusive Receivership.—Birmingham Coal & Iron Co. v. Steel Co., 20 A. B. R. 157, 160 Fed. 212 (D. C. Ala.).

Nunc Pro Tunc Correction of Order of Dismissal.—Bernard v. Abel. 19 A. B. R. 383, 156 Fed. 649 (C. C. A. Wash.).

Motion to Dismiss Petition.—Ber-nard v. Abel. 19 A. B. R. 383, 156 Fed. 649 (C. C. A. Wash.).

Notice of Motion to Dismiss.—Ber-nard v. Abel. 19 A. B. R. 383, 156 Fed. 649 (C. C. A. Wash.).

Power to Amend Court Records.—Bernard v. Abel. 19 A. B. R. 383, 156 Fed. 649 (C. C. A. Wash.): "The prin-cipal question involved is whether the court had authority to vacate the judg-ment of dismissal, and to make a judg-ment nunc pro tunc at the time and under the circumstances stated. Courts have the power to amend their judg-ments, upon proper showing, within a

reasonable time, when no such change of circumstances has occurred as would make an amendment unjust to third persons or to the parties themselves. It happens sometimes, for instance, that applications to amend verdicts are granted even after error has been brought. Such amendments have often been allowed upon the Judge's notes of the evidence at the trial, or upon other evidence clearly establishing the jus-tice of the proposed amendments. This principle is distinctly stated in Matheson's Adm'r v. Grant's Adm'r, 2 How. 263, 11 L. Ed. 261. 'It is a fa-miliar doctrine,' said the Supreme Court in Insurance Co. v. Boon, 95 U. S. 117, 24 L. Ed. 395, 'that courts always have jurisdiction over their records to make them conform to what was ac-tually done at the time; and, whatever may have been the rule announced in some of the old cases, the modern doc-trine is that some orders and amend-ments may be made at a subsequent term, and directed to be entered, and become of record, as of a former term.' This power is one to make the record speak the truth."

pose, and therefore there are not the required three creditors remaining to insist on the continuance of the proceedings and no fraud or other deception appears, the court should dismiss the petition.[23]

§ 422¼. Court's Authority to Hear Controversies after Dismissal.

—After dismissal the court has no authority to hear controversies in regard to alleged claims against the estate.[24]

---

23. In re Sig. H. Rosenblatt & Co., 28 A. B. R. 401, 193 Fed. 638 (C. C. A. N. Y.).

24. In re Sig. H. Rosenblatt & Co., 28 A. B. R. 401, 193 Fed. 638 (C. C. A. N. Y.).

1 R B—23

CHAPTER XIV.

ADJUDICATION.

Synopsis of Chapter.

DIVISION 1.

ADJUDICATION IN GENERAL—DEFAULT ADJUDICATION—PREMATURE ADJUDICATION AND ADJUDICATION ON PLEADINGS.

§ 423. Adjudication on Voluntary Petition, "Forthwith;" on Involuntary, "Soon as May Be."—Voluntary petitions, as previously noted (§ 195), are heard without delay and if in due form and jurisdiction be not lacking, adjudication is made forthwith, without right in any one to contest the issue, save and except the limited right of a nonjoining partner to contest the issue of insolvency on a petition filed by a copartner.

The involuntary petition, on the other hand, has to be set down for hearing. It is heard by the judge, as we have seen, with or without the intervention of a jury, as the case may be. It is to be heard "as soon as may be;"[1] although delay will not affect the court's jurisdiction to adjudicate.[2] The adjudication is then made, or the petition is dismissed.

§ 424. Jurisdiction to Make Adjudication on Default.—Jurisdiction is given specifically by Bankr. Act, § 4 (b) to make adjudications upon involuntary petitions on default; although undoubtedly such jurisdiction would exist by virtue of the general jurisdiction to adjudicate bankrupt, elsewhere conferred by the law.[3]

§ 425. Default Adjudication by Referee in Judge's Absence or Inability.—If the judge is absent from the district, or the division of the district in which the petition is filed, at the time of the filing of a voluntary petition; or, in the case of an involuntary petition, on the next day after the last day on which pleadings may be filed, and none have been filed, the clerk forthwith refers the case to the referee having jurisdiction, for adjudication;[4] and the referee thereupon makes the adjudication.[5]

Of necessity the same rule would prevail if the judge were otherwise unable to act.

The "pleadings" of course refer to pleadings that raise an issue or are in opposition, not to pleadings that admit the allegations of the petition. Like-

---

1 Bankr. Act, § 18 (d).

2. In re Frichsberg, 8 A. B. R. 607 (Ref. N. Y.).

3. Bankr. Act, § 18 (e).

4. Bankr. Act, § 18 (f); In re Humbert Co., 4 A. B. R. 76, 100 Fed. 439 (D. C. Iowa).

5. Bankr. Act, § 38: "Referees respectively are hereby invested, subject always to a review by the judge; within the limits of their districts as established from time to time, with jurisdiction to (1) consider all petitions referred to them by the clerks and make the adjudications or dismiss the petitions."

wise, the filing of an answer admitting the allegations of the petition does not convert an involuntary case into a voluntary one nor permit an earlier reference to the referee.

In re Humbert Co., 4 A. B. R. 76, 100 Fed. 439 (D. C. Iowa): "Under the provisions of § 18 of the act, the clerk cannot send a case of involuntary bankruptcy to the referee for adjudication, except in cases wherein no issue is made by the bankrupt or any creditor upon the facts averred in the petition, and the judge is absent from the district or division thereof wherein the case is pending on the next day after the last day on which pleadings may be filed; and these necessary conditions cannot be ascertained except by fixing a proper return day in the mode already pointed out, and then awaiting the lapse of the ten-day period allowed for filing pleadings in opposition to the petition for adjudication."

Of course, the referee does not make the adjudication if the petition is defective in showing jurisdiction. Under such circumstances the referee doubtless has jurisdiction, under Bank. Act, § 38 (4), to require amendment of the petition, or even to enter a dismissal thereof, upon notice to creditors.

The referee may not, even in the absence of the judge, hear contested petitions.

In re Humbert Co., 4 A. B. R. 77, 100 Fed. 439 (D. C. Iowa): "If a contest is made on behalf of the bankrupt or any of the creditors, then the issues presented thereby must be tried by or before the judge."

Jurisdiction to adjudge bankrupt on contested petitions may be exercised under § 18, Bankr. Act, only by the "judge" as contradistinguished from the "court," which latter term may include the referee.

§ 426. Adjudication by Default a Judgment on Merits, Binding on All.—A default adjudication of bankruptcy is a judgment on the merits, and is conclusive upon all who, in the exercise of proper diligence, might have defended.[6]

In re Billing, 17 A. B. R. 86 (D. C. Ala.): "When, as here, the petition is filed by the proper parties, in the proper district, and makes all the jurisdictional allegations, and is uncontested, the failure to contest the petition by any person having the right, so to do, establishes the truth of the allegations of the petition. The law, thereupon, demands an adjudication of bankruptcy, which when thus rendered, is binding on all the world. Every creditor was conclusively charged with notice of the pendency of the proceeding and what was being done to bring about adjudication, and no creditor can be heard to set up want of knowledge or notice of the proceeding as an excuse for not controverting the petition before adjudication, or as a reason why it shall not bind him."

§ 427. Premature Adjudication on Bankrupt's Consent.—If the bankrupt enters appearance and files answer before the answer day and consents to an earlier hearing or consents to his own adjudication before

6. In re Gorman, 15 A. B. R. 587 (D. C. Hawaii).

answer day, and adjudication is thus had, such premature adjudication is voidable if any creditor appears on or before answer day; but if the time elapses for creditors to appear and none appear, the premature adjudication by the bankrupt's consent may not be attacked.[7]

In re Columbia Real Estate Co., 4 A. B. R. 419, 101 Fed. 965 (D. C. Ind., affirmed 7 A. B. R. 441): "Nor can there be want of jurisdiction over the subject-matter because the adjudication was had on the same day that the petition and answer were filed. There is nothing in § 18 of the Bankruptcy Act which precludes a waiver of process, a voluntary appearance of the bankrupt, and an answer admitting bankruptcy on the day the petition is filed. An adjudication on a voluntary appearance and an answer admitting the averments of the petition would certainly conclude the bankrupt who entered the appearance and filed the answer. It may be when an adjudication has been made without service of process, and before the expiration of 15 days, that the creditors might, upon seasonable application, procure an order vacating the adjudication so far as to allow them to plead and be heard in opposition to the petition. But such right must be exercised with reasonable promptness after actual or constructive notice of the adjudication. In the present case neither the bankrupt nor any creditor is objecting to the adjudication. Their acquiescence shows that they are content."

But compare, In re Humbert Co., 4 A. B. R. 76, 100 Fed. 439 (D. C. Iowa): "The return day having been thus fixed, then the case must remain in the clerk's office until the expiration of the ten days allowed to the bankrupt or any creditor to appear and contest the facts averred in the petition. A waiver on the part of the bankrupt of this period of time cannot deprive creditors of the right to appear in opposition to the petition, and until that time has elapsed it cannot be known whether a contest will or will not be made on behalf of creditors.".

And, of course, this is true, additionally, where such creditors had actual knowledge of the pendency of the proceedings before the adjudication.

In re Marion Contract & Construction Co., 22 A. B. R. 81, 166 Fed. 618 (D. C. Ky.): "They by no means attempt to say that they could not have intervened before the adjudication, and have been made parties under clause 'b' of § 18 of the act * * * and have resisted the adjudication before it was made. That clause of the section clearly gives any creditor the right equally with the alleged bankrupt to do this. It reads as follows: 'The bankrupt, or any creditor, may appear and plead to the petition within five days after the return day, or within such further time as the court may allow.' The court finds the fact to be that before the adjudication W. H. Netherland and the Continental National Bank of Louisville, Ky., each had full knowledge of the

7. In re Western Investment Co., 21 A. B. R. 367, 170 Fed. 677 (D. C. Okla.). Compare, Day v. Beck & Gregg Hdw. Co., 8 A. B. R. 175, 114 Fed. 834 (C. C. A. Ala.), where the court held that "an involuntary adjudication of bankruptcy may be made before the expiration of the time allowed for filing an answer." But in this case the bankrupt was not consenting to the adjudication but was opposing it and had, indeed, filed an answer of denial and demand for a jury, which had been stricken off for lack of verification. He had all of the day on which the adjudication actually was rendered in which he might by law have filed his answer correctly. Also compare, In re Elmira Steel Co., 5 A. B. R. 487, 109 Fed. 456 (Ref. N. Y.). For an instance of such premature adjudication, see, In re Woods, 13 A. B. R. 340, 133 Fed. 82 (D. C. Pa.).

pendency of the petition in this case which sought to have the company adjudicated a bankrupt, and that they acquired this knowledge in ample time to have pleaded to the petition under the clause of the act just referred to, but that each of them failed to do so. Having this knowledge and this right under the act, they became quasi parties to the proceeding at least sufficiently to make it the duty of each then, or within five days thereafter, to intervene or be foreclosed of the right to do so. Too much importance cannot be attached to the fact that they had this previous knowledge; for that, coupled with their rights under clause 'b,' supra, gave them, respectively, their day in court, but, instead of availing themselves of it, they made default. Like others in default in judicial proceedings, they cannot now be heard, unless upon a strong showing which will move the discretion of the court in the direction of granting what they ask."

§ 428. Adjudication on Pleadings.—Adjudication may be had on the pleadings themselves, where attempted opposition fails to be sufficiently pleaded, in the same manner and under the same circumstances, in general, as in other cases. Such motion admits all the averments of the answer, properly pleaded;[8] and the respondents are entitled to a final decree dismissing the petition if such a motion is overruled.[9]

DIVISION 2.

VACATING OF ADJUDICATION.

§ 429. Jurisdiction to Vacate Adjudication.—Jurisdiction to vacate adjudication exists; and the adjudication of bankruptcy, whether on voluntary or involuntary petition may be vacated on proper proceedings and for sufficient cause.[10]

§ 430. Application to Judge, Not Referee.—The application for the vacating of the adjudication must be made to the judge, not to the referee.[11]

The referee simply has charge of the administration of the estate, *after* adjudication, and is not a competent court to declare an adjudication void. Nevertheless, if the record itself shows affirmatively that jurisdiction *does not* exist—not merely that it fails to set forth jurisdictional facts—then, possibly, being void on its face it might be disregarded even by the referee. But, in that event the referee would simply pause and refer the whole matter back to the judge; so, even in that event, it would still be true that the vacating would not be done by the referee but by the judge only.

---

8. In re Waugh (Caskey), 13 A. B. R. 187, 133 Fed. 281 (C. C. A. Wash.).
9. In re Waugh (Caskey), 13 A. B. R. 187, 133 Fed. 281 (C. C. A. Wash.).
Date of Adjudication.—The date of adjudication is the date of the entry of the decree that the defendant is a bankrupt; or, if such decree is appealed from, then the date when such decree is finally confirmed. Bankr. Act, § 1 a (2); In re Lee, 22 A. B. R. 820, 171 Fed. 266 (D. C. Pa.).

10. Impliedly, In re Ives, 7 A. B. R. 692, 113 Fed. 911 (C. C. A. Mich.); impliedly, In re Hudson River Electric Co., 21 A. B. R. 915, 173 Fed. 934 (D. C. N. Y.).
11. In re Imperial Corp'n, 13 A. B. R. 199, 133 Fed. 73 (D. C. N. Y.). Apparently contra, In re Scott, 7 A. B. R. 37 (Ref. Mass.). Apparently contra, In re Clisdell, 2 A. B. R. 424 (Ref. N. Y.).

§ 431. May Vacate "After Term."

§ 431. May Vacate "After Term."—The adjudication may be vacated after the expiration of the term of court wherein entered, for there are no terms of court in bankruptcy.[12]

In re Ives, 7 A. B. R. 694, 111 Fed. 495, 113 Fed. 911 (C. C. A. Mich., reversing 6 A. B. R. 653): "The petition shows that several terms of court intervened between the adjudication sought to be vacated and the filing of the petition, and it is urged that an adjudication in bankruptcy is under the control of the court only during the term at which it is made, and can be set aside or modified only during that term; that it, like all other judgments, passes beyond the power of the court when the term at which it was made closes, unless steps are taken during that term to vacate or correct it. The Supreme Court of the United States has, in strong language, expressed this view in all cases coming within the principle of the cases it was considering, when the expressions were made, and that view is not open to question. Bronson v. Schulton, 104 U. S. 410, 26 L. Ed. 797; Phillips v. Negley, 117 U. S. 665, 29 L. Ed. 1013. But, in § 2, the Bankruptcy Act seems to contemplate that from the filing of the petition to the closing of the estate, the proceeding shall be continuous, and a court of bankruptcy always open, like surrogate and probate courts, where estates are administered and which have no terms. It provides that matters arising in bankruptcy proceedings may be heard in vacation or term time, and orders allowing or disallowing claims may be reconsidered, closed estates reopened, and compositions and discharges set aside. It has been held by the Supreme Court that under the Bankruptcy Act of 1867, the District Court for all purposes of its bankruptcy jurisdiction, is always open, and has no separate terms; that the proceedings in a pending suit are, therefore, at all times open for re-examination upon application therefor in appropriate form, and that any order made in the progress of the case may be subsequently set aside and vacated upon proper showing, provided rights have not become vested under it,. which will be disturbed by its vacation; and it is held that application for such re-examination will not have the effect of a new suit, but of a proceeding in an old one. Sandusky v. National Bank, 23 Wall. 289, 23 L. Ed. 155. This language used in reference to the Act of 1867 was said by this court to be applicable to the present Bankruptcy Act in Re Lemon and Gale Co., 7 Am. B. R. 291, 112 Fed. 296. We are of opinion, therefore, that the question presented by the petition was open and the court below had power to determine it, although several terms of the District Court had expired since the adjudication."

And when jurisdiction is challenged, it should be inquired into as soon as possible.[13]

But, in general, the court may consider lack of jurisdiction, at any time, and however brought to its attention.

In re Columbia Real Estate Co., 4 A. B. R. 411, 101 Fed. 965 (D. C. Ind., affirmed in 7 A. B. R. 441): "Want of jurisdiction is a question that the court

---

12. In re Jemison Mercantile Co., 7 A. B. R. 588, 112 Fed. 966 (C. C. A. Ala.). Compare, as to there being no terms in bankruptcy, In re Worcester Co., 4 A. B. R. 496, 102 Fed. 808 (C. C. A. Mass.). In re Tucker, 18 A. B. R. 378; 153 Fed. 91 (C. C. A. Mass); In re Lemmon & Gale Co., 7 A. B. R. 291, 112 Fed. 296 (C. C. A. Tenn.); In re Henschel, 8 A. B. R. 201, 114 Fed. 968 (D. C. N. Y.); (1867) Sandusky v. National Bank, 23 Wall. 289. Also, see post, § 858, note.

13. See ante, § 414. Also see In re King, 24 A. B. R. 606, 179 Fed. 874 (C. C. A. Ills.), quoted at § 412. In re Waxelbaum, 3 A. B. R. 392, 98 Fed. 589 (D. C. N. Y.).

should consider whenever or however raised, even if the parties forbear to make it or consent that the case may be considered on its merits."

This has been held as to a referee's order fixing in advance the trustee's extra compensation for conducting the business.

In re Russell Card Co., 23 A. B. R. 300, 174 Fed. 202 (D. C. N. J.): "The doctrine of laches, which is insisted on by counsel for the trustee, is not applicable to a motion to vacate an order made without jurisdiction, especially where no rights have become vested under the order sought to be vacated."

The Circuit Court of Appeals may correct errors of the courts of bankruptcy, but it is not itself a court of bankruptcy, and the doctrine that "there are no 'terms of court' in bankruptcy" does not seem to be applicable to its decrees; and such a decree rendered on an appeal, even if the matter were not appealable, cannot be vacated after term, and is not a nullity.[14]

§ 432. Who May Move to Vacate—Court Sua Sponte.

The court, of its own motion, should vacate the adjudication and dismiss the proceedings, if it discovers it has been acting without jurisdiction.[15]

In re Garneau, 11 A. B. R. 679, 127 Fed. 677 (C. C. A. Ills.): "But, aside from that, it would be the duty of the court sua sponte, when it is led to suspect that its jurisdiction has been imposed upon, to inquire into the facts by some appropriate form of proceeding, and, for its own protection against fraud or imposition, to act as justice may require. Morris v. Gilmer, 129 U. S. 329."

And one not entitled to be heard as matter of right, may, nevertheless, be heard by the court, ex gratia, as amicus curiæ, where there is allegation of lack of jurisdiction over the subject-matter.[16]

In re New York Tunnel Co., 21 A. B. R. 531, 166 Fed. 284 (C. C. A. N. Y.): "Although we think these objections are good [that the parties are tort claimants and therefore not holders of provable claims] still if the appellants and petitioners have called our attention to a jurisdictional defect which makes the adjudication a nullity, we feel bound to consider it. * * * But they are strangers to the bankruptcy proceedings, having no right to prove their claims, to defend or to appeal. The most they can do is to call the attention of the court as amici curiæ to a want of jurisdiction of the subject-matter appearing on the face of the record."

§ 433. Any Party in Interest Competent.

Objection to the jurisdiction on the ground that the defendant is not of a class subject to bankruptcy

---

14. Loeser v. Bank & Trust Co., 20 A. B. R. 845, 163 Fed. 212 (C. C. A. Ohio), quoted on other points at § 2888½.

15. In re Columbia Real Estate Co., 4 A. B. R. 411, 101 Fed. 965 (D. C. Ind., affirmed in 7 A. B. R. 441); In re Waxelbaum, 3 A. B. R. 395, 98 Fed. 589 (D. C. N. Y.).

16. In re Columbia Real Estate Co., 4 A. B. R. 411, 101 Fed. 965 (D. C. Ind., affirmed in 7 A. B. R. 441); In re Garneau, 11 A. B. R. 679, 127 Fed. 677 (C. C. A. Ills.); impliedly, In re New England Breeders' Club, 21 A. B. R. 349, 165 Fed. 517 (D. C. N. H.), quoted ante, § 30.

may ordinarily be brought to the attention of the court by any party in interest at any stage of the proceedings.[17]

But see In re Urban & Suburban, 12 A. B. R. 687 (D. C. N. J.): "The unexplained delay of creditors asking leave to intervene for the sole purpose of moving to set aside an adjudication in involuntary proceedings, disentitles them as matter of right to any vacation of the adjudication, but where want of jurisdiction is asserted, the court may consider their objections ex gratia.

"An adjudication will not be set aside as matter of favor upon petition of an intervening creditor to consider the objection that the bankrupt is not such a corporation as may be adjudged bankrupt, where it does not appear upon the face of the petition for adjudication whether or not the corporation was engaged principally in any of the pursuits mentioned in § 4 B."

Compare, also, In re Mason, 3 A. B. R. 599, 99 Fed. 256 (D. C. N. Car.): "Entire want of jurisdiction over the res may be taken advantage of at any time and attacked collaterally. But where objection goes only to the jurisdiction over the person, it must be taken promptly. A creditor cannot prove his debt, participate in election of trustee and distribution of assets, and then, upon application for discharge, object to jurisdiction on account of bankrupt's non-residence."

§ 434. And Only Such as Have Present Interest.

—The only person who may move to vacate an adjudication is one who has an existing interest, not a mere possibility or probability of a future title.[18] Thus, as to creditors, only creditors owning provable claims may move to vacate adjudication.

§ 435. Thus, Creditors Proper Parties.

—Creditors, although in general bound by the adjudication, may, unless guilty of laches, attack the adjudication on the ground of lack of jurisdiction.[19]

---

17. Obiter, In re Niagara Contracting Co., 11 A. B. R. 645, 127 Fed. 782 (D. C. N. Y.). Compare, also, In re Columbia Real Estate Co., 4 A. B. R. 411, 101 Fed. 965 (D. C. Ind.).

18. In re Columbia Real Estate Co., 4 A. B. R. 411, 101 Fed. 965 (D. C. Ind., affirmed in 7 A. B. R. 441).

19. In re Garneau, 11 A. B. R. 679, 127 Fed. 677 (C. C. A. Ills.); In re Scott, 7 A. B. R. 39, 111 Fed. 144 (D. C. Mass.); also, 7 A. B. R. 35 (Ref. Mass.); obiter, In re Hintz. 13 A. B. R. 721, 134 Fed. 141 (D. C. Mass.). Instance, In re Altonwood Park Co., 20 A. B. R. 31, 160 Fed. 448 (C. C. A. N. Y.); instance, In re Hudson River Electric Co., 21 A. B. R. 915, 173 Fed. 934 (D. C. N. Y.).

And it has been held, that the burden of proof still rests upon the bankrupt to establish that he was a resident within the district. In re Scott, 7 A. B. R. 39, 111 Fed. 144 (D. C. Mass.). This holding is to be criticised because, where lack of jurisdiction is not apparent on the face of the petition, the burden of the attack assuredly rests on the attacking party.

The referee, it has been held, has jurisdiction to entertain an application for dismissal of petition after adjudication for lack of jurisdiction. In re Scott, 7 A. B. R. 35, 111 Fed. 144 (Ref. Mass.). Inferentially, In re Clisdell, 2 A. B. R. 424 (Ref. N. Y., reversed, on other grounds, in 4 A. B. R. 95). These holdings are to be criticised, for the attack is one upon a judgment and for matters dehors the record and it should be made either before the court originally rendering the judgment or before a court of competent equity jurisdiction to set aside judgments, the adjudication not being on its face so absolutely void as to permit it to be disregarded. The referee's jurisdiction is derivative and dependent wholly upon the adjudication and he has no business to go back of the adjudication until the order of reference is recalled or a court of competent jurisdiction has annulled the adjudication. But compare, as to collaterally attacking discharges filed after expiration of

Obiter, In re New England Breeders' Club, 22 A. B. R. 128, 169 Fed. 586 (C. C. A. N. H.): "The trustee urged before us that the Hub Company had shown no interest in the vacation of the adjudication, but we hold that its interest as a creditor, without more, was sufficient for that purpose." Quoted further at § 436.

§ 435½. **Whether Tort Claimants Proper Parties.**—It would seem, on principle, that tort claimants, although not holding provable debts, might nevertheless be parties in interest.

But compare, In re New York Tunnel Co., 21 A. B. R. 531, 166 Fed. 284 (C. C. A. N. Y.): "It must be admitted that tort claimants who see the property of a person against whom they make claim, seized and administered in bankruptcy to their own exclusion for the benefit of contract creditors, have an interest which should be protected and are in bad case if the law afford no remedy. We are, however, clear that they can have no relief in this case in the proceedings they have adopted." Quoted further at §§ 30, 432.

§ 436. **Laches Bars Right.**—But laches may bar the objector's right to a vacating of the adjudication, at least if lack of jurisdiction is not apparent on the face of the pleading and must be proved by evidence dehors the record. The application to vacate the adjudication must be promptly made.[20]

In re Worsham, 15 A. B. R. 672, 142 Fed. 121 (C. C. A. Okla.): "When a bankrupt and all of his creditors have recognized the validity and regularity of proceedings in a court of bankruptcy, have participated therein, and sought the benefit thereof, one of such creditors will not be heard long after the adjudication to object to the jurisdiction of the court upon the ground that the proceedings were instituted in a district in which the bankrupt did not reside or have his domicile or principal place of business for the greater portion of the preceding six months; nor upon the ground that a subpœna to the bankrupt, was not issued, he having voluntarily waived the same and entered his appearance; nor upon the ground that the petition failed to allege that the bankrupt was not a wage-earner or a person engaged chiefly in farming or the tillage of the soil. And, for like reasons, he will not be permitted to otherwise contest the petition upon which the adjudication proceeded."

statutory time, In re Fahy, 8 A. B. R. 354, 116 Fed. 239 (D. C. Iowa). But compare, In re Clisdell, 2 A. B. R. 424 (Ref. N. Y., reversed by D. C.). Also compare, In re Goodale, 6 A. B. R. 495, 109 Fed. 783 (D. C. N. Y.).

The objection that the bankrupt is a nonresident of the State, will not be considered upon an application for discharge. In re Goodale, 6 A. B. R. 495, 109 Fed. 783 (D. C. N. Y.); compare, In re Mason, 3 A. B. R. 599, 99 Fed. 256 (D. C. N. Car.). See post, § 2447, "Discharge—Nature of Opposition."

Receivers, Assignees, etc., as Proper Parties.—It has been held, obiter, that receivers appointed outside of bankruptcy are proper parties. In re Hudson River Electric Co., 21 A. B. R. 935, 173 Fed. 934 (D. C. N. Y.). But in this case the record showed the adjudication to be a nullity, in which event anyone is competent to draw the court's attention to the lack of jurisdiction; moreover, a creditor also was making the motion.

20. Obiter, In re Ives, 7 A. B. R. 692, 111 Fed. 495, 113 Fed 914 (C. C. A. Mich.); In re Billing, 17 A. B. R. 92 (D. C. Ala.); compare, In re Mason, 3 A. B. R. 599 (D. C. N. Car.), quoted ante, § 433; compare, In re Polakoff, 1 A. B. R. 358 (Master's Report, affirmed by D. C.); compare, to same effect, though differently reasoned, In re Hintze, 13 A. B. R. 721, 134 Fed. 141 (D. C. Mass.). Instance, held not laches, In re Altonwood Park Co., 20 A. B. R. 31, 160 Fed. 448 (C. C. A. N. Y.).

In re Niagara Contracting Co., 11 A. B. R. 645, 127 Fed. 782 (D. C. N. Y.): "Objections to the jurisdiction of the court ordinarily may be brought to the attention of the court by any party in interest at any stage of the proceeding. German Savings Bank v. Franklin Co., 128 U. S. 526, 32 L. Ed. 519. In this case the lack of jurisdiction is not apparent upon the face of the petition to have the corporation adjudged bankrupt. Whether the court is without jurisdiction depends entirely upon facts which must first be proved. Under such circumstances, the application to open default in pleading must be promptly made, and upon sufficient cause shown in the moving papers."

In re Urban & Suburban, 12 A. B. R. 687. (D. C. N. Y.): "If creditors sleep upon their right to plead to a petition in involuntary bankruptcy until the time for pleading has expired and an adjudication in bankruptcy has been had, they will not be deemed to have any right to a vacation of the adjudication in order that they may then plead. When a creditor applies for an order to set aside such an adjudication for the mere purpose of pleading to the original petition, he must show satisfactory reasons for his delay. The unexplained delay of the interveners in this case disentitles them, as a matter of right, to any vacation of the adjudication."

In re New England Breeders' Club, 22 A. B. R. 125, 169 Fed. 586 (C. C. A. N. H., reversing S. C., 21 A. B. R. 349, 165 Fed. 517): "The trustee's contention in effect is as follows: He does not dispute the correctness of the master's report concerning the nature of the bankrupt's business, but he contends that the District Court erred in holding its want of jurisdiction to be absolute, and in disregarding the questions of laches, damage to creditors, and the like, which were raised by his petition to dismiss. He does not contend that the District Court was altogether without jurisdiction to vacate the bankruptcy proceedings, but he does contend that the District Court was not obliged to vacate the proceedings as matter of law and without considering the circumstances and consequences. The Hub Company, on the other hand, contends that the finding of the master has shown that the District Court was altogether without jurisdiction to adjudicate the club a bankrupt, and that the court was therefore absolutely required to vacate the proceedings as soon as the nature of the bankrupt's business was established. The action of the learned judge in the District Court was plainly based upon his agreement with the Hub Company's contention as stated above, and not upon consideration of the issues which the trustee sought to raise. The adjudication was vacated solely because of a supposed legal necessity arising from an absolute want of jurisdiction, and not because the petitioning creditors and the trustee failed to make out the allegations of the trustee's petition. Upon this distinction rests the decision of the case at bar. To determine what allegations and facts are necessary to support the jurisdiction of a court, and what go only to establish a plaintiff's right to recover, is sometimes matter of difficulty. It is well settled, for example, that the allegations of diversity of citizenship is necessary to uphold the jurisdiction of the Federal courts in those cases where jurisdiction depends upon diversity of citizenship; and even in the ultimate court of appeal the omission of this allegation may be noticed by the court, and, unless remedied, it will cause a vacation of the entire proceeding. But where the plaintiff's allegation of diverse citizenship is sufficient, the defendant, under ordinary circumstances, loses in time his right to dispute the allegation. Hartog v. Memory, 116 U. S. 588. In the case at bar there was no fraud upon the court. In Denver Bank v. Klug, 186 U. S. 202, 10 Am. B. R. 786, the petition in involuntary bankruptcy contained a sufficient allegation of the nature of the respondent's business. This allegation was traversed, and the jury found that the respondent was 'engaged chiefly in farming' within the meaning of the Bankruptcy Act. The District Court dismissed the petition, and the petitioning creditors took an appeal directly to the Supreme Court as in a case where the jurisdiction of the District Court was in issue. The Supreme Court dismissed the appeal, saying that: 'The District Court had and exercised jurisdiction. The conclusion was, it is true, that Klug could not be adjudged a bankrupt, but the court had jurisdiction to so determine, and its jurisdiction over the subject-matter was not and could not be questioned.' "

But, even then, the court of its own motion might vacate the adjudication if it discovers it has been acting without jurisdiction.[21]

§ 436½. **Whether Proving of Claim Estops.**—It has been held, also, that proving his claim in the bankruptcy proceedings is such an acquiescence as will bar the creditor from the right to move for a vacating of the adjudication for want of jurisdiction.[23]

§ 437. **But Record of Adjudication Imports Jurisdiction and Need Not Recite All Jurisdictional Facts.**—The record of the adjudication need not recite all the requisite jurisdictional facts; the adjudication, when made, imports their existence.[24] For the silence of the record on the jurisdictional facts is different from affirmative showing thereon that the jurisdictional facts *do not* exist.[25]

Thus, default adjudication of a corporation will not be vacated merely because the petition fails to show that it was a corporation of a class subject to bankruptcy, at any rate where the petition does not show that it was *not* of such class.[26]

In re Urban & Suburban, 12 A. B. R. 689 (D. C. N. Y.): "The point of this objection is that it does not appear on the face of the petition that the com-

---

21. In re Garneau, 11 A. B. R. 679, 127 Fed. 677 (C. C. A. Ills.); In re Columbia Real Estate Co., 4 A. B. R. 411, 101 Fed. 965 (D. C. Ind.).

23. In re N. Y. Tunnel Co., 21 A. B. R. 531, 166 Fed. 284 (C. C. A. N. Y.).

24 In re Elmira Steel Co., 5 A. B. R. 487, 109 Fed. 456 (Ref. N. Y.); Edelstein v. U. S., 17 A. B. R. 652, 149 Fed. 636 (C. C. A. Minn.); In re First Nat'l Bk. of Belle Fourche, 18 A. B. R. 271 (C. C. A.), quoted post, this paragraph. Dodge v. Kenwood Ice Co., 29 A. B. R. 586, 189 Fed. 525 (C. C. A. Minn., affirming In re Kenwood Ice Co., 26 A. B. R. 499, 189 Fed. 525). Compare, analogously, Loeser v. Bank & Trust Co., 20 A. B. R. 845, 163 Fed. 212 (C. C. A. Ohio), quoted at § 2888½. See "Jurisdiction to Adjudge Bankrupt," ante, § 30.

25. In re First Nat'l Bk. of Belle Fourche, 18 A. B. R. 271 (C. C. A.).

26. Dodge v. Kenwood Ice Co., 29 A. B. R. 586, 189 Fed. 525 (C. C. A. Minn., affirming In re Kenwood Ice Co., 26 A. B. R. 499, 189 Fed. 525). But compare, In re Altonwood Park Co., 20 A. B. R. 31, 160 Fed. 448 (C. C. A. N. Y.) compare also, In re New York Tunnel Co., 21 A. B. R. 531, 166 Fed. 284 (C. C. A. N. Y.), quoted at §§ 30, 441½; compare also, In re Hudson River Electric Co., 21 A. B. R. 915, 173 Fed. 934 (D. C. N. Y.). Also compare, In re Elmira Steel Co., 5 A. B. R. 487, 109 Fed. 456 (Ref. N. Y.), where a referee held that, under the law as it stood before the Amendment of 1910 had broadened the classification of corporations subject to bankruptcy, that an adjudication was void where it was founded upon a petition that did not allege the corporation to be engaged in one of the classes subject to bankruptcy.

pany is a corporation principally engaged in trading or in any of the other pursuits mentioned in § 4b. * * * But neither does it appear that it is not such a corporation. Whether the petition would have been demurrable before adjudication of bankruptcy for this reason it is not necessary to consider."

In re Columbia Real Estate Co., 4 A. B. R. 417, 101 Fed. 970 (D. C. Ind., affirmed in 7 A. B. R. 441): "If, as insisted by counsel, the bankruptcy court is in a technical sense a court of inferior and limited jurisdiction, every fact essential to its jurisdiction must affirmatively appear on the face of the record. It is true that the bankruptcy court is one of limited jurisdiction, and the constitution describes all courts of the United States, except the Supreme Court, as inferior courts. But the Circuit and District Courts of the United States as courts of bankruptcy are courts of record, and as such they are not inferior courts in the sense that jurisdiction must necessarily appear upon the face of the record. Hays v. Ford, 55 Ind. 52; Bank v. Judson, 8 N. Y. 254; Skillern's Ex'rs v. May's Ex'rs, 6 Cranch 267, 2 L. Ed. 574; Ex parte Watkins, 3 Pet. 193, 7 L. Ed. 650; McCormick v. Sullivant, 10 Wheat 192, 199, 6 L. Ed. 300; Kennedy v. Bank, 8 How. 586, 12 L. Ed. 1209.

"The essentials of a valid judgment are jurisdiction of the parties and of the subject-matter. The latter is conferred by law; the former by service of process or in some other manner authorized by law, as by the voluntary appearance of the party during the progress of the proceedings. It is insisted that this court had no jurisdiction over the subject-matter, because the petition failed to allege that the Columbia Real Estate Company is a corporation 'engaged principally in manufacturing, trading, printing, publishing, or mercantile pursuits,' and because the adjudication was had within 15 days after the petition was filed upon the voluntary appearance and confession of the bankrupt, without service of process upon it. It is not necessary to decide whether the creditors' petition is insufficient upon demurrer or whether it is vulnerable to a direct attack on appeal or otherwise. The question is whether the adjudication of bankruptcy is an absolute nullity for the reasons stated. The power conferred upon the bankruptcy court as a court of record to adjudge a natural person or a corporation a bankrupt necessarily includes the power to determine whether the person or corporation is of the class specified in the act. The creditors' petition in this case follows form 3 of the forms in bankruptcy promulgated by the Supreme Court (18 Sup. Ct. xix.), and contains every essential averment required by that form. The adjudication recites that the petition of Henry A. Taylor and others 'that the Columbia Real Estate Company, a corporation, be adjudged a bankrupt within the true intent and meaning of the acts of Congress relating to bankruptcy, having been heard and duly considered, the said Columbia Real Estate Company is hereby declared and adjudged bankrupt accordingly.' The presumption which attaches to all judgments of courts of record, as well as the direct finding that, upon due consideration had, the Columbia Real Estate Company is adjudged a bankrupt 'within the true intent and meaning of the acts of Congress relating to bankruptcy,' concludes all collateral inquiry as to whether or not the corporation was of a class subject to be adjudicated a bankrupt. It will be presumed that the court heard and determined that question, and it was not necessary to set out upon the face of the record the facts or the evidence upon which its conclusion was reached. * * *

"Nor can there be want of jurisdiction over the subject-matter because the adjudication was had on the same day that the petition and answer were filed. There is nothing in § 18 of the Bankruptcy Act which precludes a waiver of process, a voluntary appearance of the bankrupt, and an answer admitting bankruptcy on the day the petition is filed. An adjudication on a voluntary appearance and an answer admitting the averments of the petition would certainly conclude the bankrupt who entered the appearance and filed the answer. It may be when an adjudication has been made without service of process, and before the expiration of 15 days, that the creditors might, upon seasonable application, procure an order vacating the adjudication so far as to allow them to plead and be heard in opposition to the petition. But such right must be exercised with reasonable promptness after actual or constructive notice of the adjudication. In the present case neither the bankrupt nor any creditor is objecting to the adjudication. Their acquiescence shows that they are content."

In re First Nat'l Bk. of Belle Fourche, 18 A. B. R. 271 (C. C. A.): "The petition contained no statement that the Widell corporation was not engaged principally in a manufacturing pursuit and no showing that the court was without jurisdiction of the case; but it set forth the substance of a good cause of action, and it was impregnable to attack after the adjudication."

Much less will an adjudication be vacated where such allegations are merely defective and not wholly lacking.[27]

And where the allegations are sufficient and the lack of jurisdiction is only provable by evidence dehors the record, it is clear that laches may bar the right to move for a vacating of the adjudication.[28]

And where the lack of jurisdiction does not affirmatively appear on the face of the record but is dependent solely upon questions of fact which have been decided in favor of jurisdiction by the court below, the appellate court will not remand the cause with instructions to dismiss the entire proceeding.[29]

The adjudication of a corporation in voluntary bankruptcy proceedings will not be set aside merely because the petition fails to show the authority of the board of directors to ask for such adjudication.[30]

§ 438. Voluntary Bankrupt May Move to Vacate.

A voluntary bankrupt is a competent party to have his own adjudication vacated. Thus, where there is no estate, no claims proved and no trustee appointed the bankrupt may have adjudication vacated and withdraw his voluntary petition, although subsequent creditors acquiring liens on subsequently earned property may object.[31] But the adjudication should not be vacated and the voluntary petition dismissed on application of the bankrupt without notice to creditors;[32] nor unless all costs and expenses are paid.[33]

---

27. In re Marion Contract & Construction Co., 22 A. B. R. 81, 166 Fed. 618 (D. C. Ky.).

28. In re New England Breeders' Club, 22 A. B. R. 125, 169 Fed. 586 (C. C. A. N. H.).

29. Brady v. Bernard & Kettinger, 22 A. B. R. 342, 170 Fed. 576 (C. C. A. Ky.).

30. In re Kenwood Ice Co., 26 A. B. R. 499, 189 Fed. 525 (C. C. A. Minn.); Dodge v. Kenwood Ice Co., 29 A. B. R. 586, 189 Fed. 525 (C. C. A. Minn., affirming In re Kenwood, 26 A. B. R. 499, 189 Fed. 525).

31. In re Hebbart, 5 A. B. R. 8, 104 Fed. 322 (D. C. Vt.). The court in this case uses the phrase "withdraw the petition" although obviously the adjudication of bankruptcy must first be vacated.

32. See ante, § 419.

33. In re Salaberry, 5 A. B. R. 847, 107 Fed. 95 (D. C. Calif.).

Where a voluntary petition, after being filed, is withdrawn and subsequently amended and refiled, the date of the refiling controls as a basis for adjudication. In re Washburn Bros., 3 A. B. R. 585, 99 Fed. 84 (D. C. Conn.).

§ 438½. Vacating of Adjudication by Consent.—Where an alleged bankrupt appears and consents to an adjudication on an involuntary petition which has been filed against him, such adjudication will only be vacated where it appears that the bankrupt's consent thereto was fraudulently obtained.[34]

§ 439. Who May Oppose Vacating.—Any party in interest may oppose the vacating of the adjudication, even the trustee.[35] But subsequent creditors who have, since the adjudication, obtained liens on new property acquired since the adjudication, may not be heard in opposition to the vacating.[36]

§ 440. Grounds for Vacating—No Provable Debt Sufficient Ground.—That there was no provable debt at the date of the adjudication is a sufficient ground for vacating the adjudication. Only debtors owing *provable* debts are entitled to be adjudged bankrupt.[37]

In re Yates, 8 A. B. R. 69, 114 Fed. 365 (D. C. Calif.): This was a case where the only debt scheduled was a judgment rendered against the bankrupt in an action for willful and malicious injury to the person, from which an appeal was taken before adjudication, the effect of which was to suspend the operation of the judgment. The court held the adjudication should be vacated and the proceedings dismissed because at the date of the filing of his petition there was no existing provable debt. The court says: "The appeal, therefore, from the judgment in the action of Risdon v. Yates suspended its operation, and may result in its reversal; and from this it follows that at the date of the adjudication in bankruptcy there was not, nor is there now, any certainty that the plaintiff in the action referred to will succeed in the recovery of any judgment against Yates. Such being the status of the claim for damages involved in that action, it is clear that Yates was not at the date of the filing of his voluntary petition a bankrupt, within the meaning of the law. Section 4 of the Bankruptcy Act provides that 'any person who owes debts, except a corporation, shall be entitled to the benefits of this act as a voluntary bankrupt.' In subdivision 11 of § 1 of that act the word 'debt' is defined as 'any debt, demand, or claim provable in bankruptcy.'"

§ 441. But That Only Debts Not Dischargeable, Insufficient.—It has been held that where the only debts are nondischargeable debts the adjudication should be vacated;[38] or as stated in another case, be vacated "in the discretion of the court."[39] But, manifestly, it cannot be laid down as a rule that the nonexistence of any dischargeable debt is sufficient ground for vacating. So long as any provable debts exist, although they may not

34. In re Gill, 28 A. B. R. 333, 195 Fed. 643 (D. C. Ga.)

35. Obiter, In re Penn. Consol. Coal Co., 20 A. B. R. 872, 163 Fed. 579 (D. C. Pa.); impliedly, In re New York Tunnel Co., 21 A. B. R. 531, 166 Fed. 284 (C. C. A. N. Y.); In re New England Breeders' Club, 22 A. B. R. 125, 169 Fed. 586 (C. C. A. N. H.).

36. In re Hebbart, 5 A. B. R. 8, 104 Fed. 322 (D. C. Vt.).

37. See ante, § 191.

38. In re Maples, 5 A. B. R. 426, 105 Fed. 919 (D. C. Mont.).

39. In re Cololuca, 13 A. B. R. 292 (D. C. Mass.).

be dischargeable, there may be good reason for the creditor or the bankrupt resorting to the bankruptcy remedies, to avoid preferences or legal liens, or to discover property applicable to the payment of the debts; for the sole object of bankruptcy is not discharge from debts.[40]

§ 441¼. Lack of Jurisdiction Sufficient Ground.

—Lack of jurisdiction is, of course, sufficient ground for vacating the adjudication.[41]

Thus, adjudications on voluntary petitions may be set aside for lack of sufficient residence, domicile, etc.[42]

§ 441½. When Is Adjudication a "Nullity."

—When is a decree of adjudication of bankruptcy a nullity?[43]

In re New York Tunnel Co., 21 A. B. R. 531, 166 Fed. 284 (C. C. A. N. Y.): "If a petition for adjudication were made by only two creditors, the law requiring three, there would be a jurisdictional defect on the face of the record, making any adjudication void. On the other hand, if the aggregate amount of claims were stated to be $500 as required by law, and because of setoffs or other reasons was in point of fact less, an adjudication would be an error to be corrected. So if the petition were against a railroad company there would be on the face of the record such a jurisdictional defect as would make an adjudication void. Whereas, if the corporation might or might not be considered within the act, an adjudication, even if erroneous, would have to be corrected by appeal. At the time the adjudication was made in this case, building companies had been held in two districts of this circuit to be within the act. We have since decided they are not subjects of adjudication. It is, moreover, argued in this case that a tunnel company differs from a building company and is within the act. Lack of jurisdiction cannot be said to have appeared on the face of the record and therefore the adjudication made by the District Court, even if erroneous, is not a nullity."

And mandamus will not lie to compel the District Court to disregard an adjudication as a nullity even though the corporation in fact be of a class not subject to bankruptcy, where the record does not affirmatively show that the corporation does belong to an exempted class, but rather either shows it was alleged to have belonged to a class subject thereto;[44] or omits all allegations in respect thereto.

§ 441¾. Premature Adjudication on Bankrupt's Consent.

—That an adjudication was prematurely had upon the bankrupt's consent would be sufficient ground for vacating the adjudication at the motion of any party

---

40. See ante, "Introduction," § a.
41. Compare, §§ 414, 437, 441½. In re Hudson River Electric Co., 21 A. B. R. 915, 173 Fed. 934 (D. C. N. Y.).
42. In re Tully, 19 A. B. R. 604, 156 Fed. 634 (D. C. N. Y.), where the court, however, immediately re-adjudicated the bankrupt without requiring the

bankrupt to reverify or refile his petition; see also, ante, §§ 30, 414.
43. Compare, Loeser v. Bank & Trust Co., 20 A. B. R. 845, 163 Fed. 212 (C. C. A. Ohio), quoted at § 2888½; compare, also ante, §§ 30, 414.
44. In re Riggs (In re New York Tunnel Co.), 214 U. S. 9, 22 A. B. R. 720. See also, post, § 450.

in interest not estopped nor guilty of laches; but if such motion were not made before the rightful answer day, it would be too late.[45]

§ 442. Voluntary Adjudication Vacated Where Involuntary Petition Pending.—An adjudication on a voluntary petition, before hearing had on a pending involuntary petition, where the four months limit for setting aside fraudulent or preferential or other voidable transfers will have elapsed and rendered the transfers unassailable if administration be had under the voluntary proceedings, will be vacated and precedence be given to the involuntary petition.[46]

§ 443. Disturbing of Vested Rights May Bar Vacating.—The disturbing of vested rights acquired under the adjudication may prevent vacating.[47] This doctrine certainly could not prevail where the record shows on its face affirmatively that jurisdiction did not exist.

DIVISION 3.

EFFECT OF ADJUDICATION IN SUBSEQUENT LITIGATION.

§ 444. Adjudication as Res Adjudicata.[48]—The adjudication is binding upon all the world in subsequent litigations between the same adverse parties or their privies as to the status of the debtor as a bankrupt and perhaps also as to the commission of the act of bankruptcy adjudicated and all essential facts involved in the determination of those two issues; and is also binding upon all adverse parties actually engaged in the litigation and their privies likewise as to other essential facts therein contested, such as the validity and amount of the petitioning creditor's claims, etc.[49]

45. See ante, § 427, also, see In re Marion Contract and Construction Co., 22 A. B. R. 81, 166 Fed. 618 (D. C. Ky.), quoted ante, § 427.

46. See ante, § 301. Also see In re Dwyer, 7 A. B. R. 532, 112 Fed. 777 (D. C. N. Dak.).

47. Obiter, In re Ives, 7 A. B. R. 692, 113 Fed. 611, 11 A. B. R. 643 (C. C. A. Mich.).

Insufficient Grounds for Vacating.—An adjudication of bankruptcy on one act of bankruptcy sufficiently pleaded and proved will not be set aside because other alleged acts were not sufficiently pleaded nor proved. In re Lynan, 11 A. B. R. 466, 127 Fed. 123 (C. C. A. N. Y.).

Default adjudication on written admission by board of directors of inability to pay debts and willingness to be adjudged bankrupt on that ground, where subsequently, new board of directors wish to retract admission: held, too late. In re Imperial Corporation, 13 A. B. R. 199, 133 Fed. 73 (D. C. N. Y.).

1 R B—24

48. See post, §§ 450, 1632, 1776, 1777, 1777½.

49. Obiter, In re Continental Corporation, 14 A. B. R. 538 (Ref. Ohio); compare, In re Skinner, 3 A. B. R. 163, 97 Fed. 190 (D. C. Iowa); compare, In re Columbia Real Estate Co., 4 A. B. R. 411, 101 Fed. 965 (D. C. Ind.); compare, In re Cornell, 3 A. B. R. 172, 97 Fed. 29 (D. C. N. Y.); compare, to same general effect, Bear v. Chase, 3 A. B. R. 746 (C. C. A. S. C.); compare, In re Harper, 13 A. B. R. 430 (D. C. Va.); compare, Pepperdine v. Bk. of Seymour, 10 A. B. R. 573 (St. Louis Court of Appeals). But compare Manson v. Williams, 18 A. B. R. 674, 153 Fed. 525 (C. C. A. Me.); obiter, In re Harper, 23 A. B. R. 918, 175 Fed. 412 (D. C. N. Y.), quoted at § 447. Compare action of court in In re Cleary, 24 A. B. R. 742, 179 Fed. 990 (D. C. Pa.). Compare, to same effect, under former Bankruptcy Acts; [1867] In re McKinley, 7 Ben. 562, Fed. Cas. 8,864; Shawhan v. Wherritt, 7 How. 627; [1867] In re Wallace, Fed. Cas. 17,094;

In re Hecox, 21 A. B. R. 314, 164 Fed. 823 (C. C. A. Colo.): "The radical error in the ruling of the District Court and the vice in the position assumed by counsel for the receiver before this court consist in undertaking collaterally to controvert the ground of adjudication in bankruptcy. That adjudication determined that the bankrupt was insolvent, and while insolvent, within four months of the filing of the petition in involuntary bankruptcy, and because of its insolvency, a receiver had been put in charge of its property by order of the State court. * * * Until avoided in a direct proceeding therefor, that adjudication was binding and conclusive on the bankrupt and creditors, as much so as a judgment, inter partes, on due hearing in a court of competent jurisdiction."

Carter v. Hobbs, 1 A. B. R. 215, 92 Fed. 594 (D. C. Ind.): "The adjudication proceeds in rem, and all persons interested in the res are regarded as parties to the bankruptcy proceedings. These parties include not only the bankrupt and the trustee but also all the creditors of the bankrupt," including lienors.

In re Ulfelder Clothing Co., 3 A. B. R. 425, 98 Fed. 409 (D. C. Calif.): "She was the petitioner in the proceeding to have the Henry Ulfelder Clothing Company adjudged bankrupt, and, the alleged fact having been put in issue by the answer to her petition, it was incumbent upon her to prove that she had a legal demand against the corporation for at least $500 in excess of securities held by her. Bankrupt Act, § 59, subd. b. Without proof of this fact, the corporation and creditor who appeared in opposition to the petition for involuntary adjudication would have been entitled to a dismissal of the proceeding. In re Cornwall, 9 Blatch. 114, Fed. Cas. No. 3,250; Bank v. Moore, 2 Bond, 170, Fed. Cas. No. 10,041; In re Skelley, 2 Biss. 260, Fed. Cas. No. 12,921. The question whether she was a creditor in that amount was therefore a material issue in that proceeding, and the decree therein undoubtedly establishes the fact that she was such creditor. The decree does not show upon its face the particular ground or particular claim of indebtedness upon which this adjudication was made, and in such a case it is competent to show, by extrinsic evidence not inconsistent with the record, the particular matter litigated upon the trial and determined by the judgment. * * * Now, in this case, it appears that upon the trial of the issues in the involuntary proceeding the same promissory note upon which Donie Ulfelder bases her present claim against the bankrupt corporation was offered in evidence to prove that she was a creditor of that corporation, and she relied upon no claim in proof of that fact; and the questions whether such note had been duly executed by the corporation and delivered upon a sufficient consideration were in controversy and litigated upon that trial. The inevitable conclusion from these facts is that the validity of the claim founded upon this promissory note was directly in issue in the proceeding in which the Henry Ulfelder Clothing Company was adjudged bankrupt, and it is equally clear that the decree therein was in favor of its validity, as the court, in adjudging that the petitioner was a creditor of the corporation, could have proceeded upon no other ground than that such note was a valid obligation of the corporation. May the same question be again drawn into controversy in the bankruptcy proceeding in which that decree was given? I think not. In considering the legal effect of this decree,

[1867] In re Banks, Fed. Cas. 958; Morse v. Godfrey, 3 Story 364, Fed. Cas. 9,856; [1867] Rayl v. Lapham, 27 O. St. 452: "The main purpose of the proceedings in bankruptcy is the proper distribution of the estate of the bankrupt among his creditors. Such proceedings are in rem, and actual notice to the creditors is not essential to the jurisdiction of the court." Lewis v. Sloan, 68 N. Car. 557; Thornton v. Hogan, 63 Mo. 143.

there does not seem to be any reason for a departure from the well settled rule that matters which have been once litigated and determined by the judgment of a court cannot again be made the subject of legal contention, as between the parties to such judgment and their privies. The right to prosecute a proceeding in involuntary bankruptcy is one of the remedies which the law in the cases prescribed in the Bankruptcy Act gives to the creditor for the enforcement of his claim against his debtor, and in such a proceeding the question whether the petitioning creditor has a legal demand against the alleged bankrupt in such an amount as entitles him to maintain the action may be put in issue and tried, and the decision of that question in favor of the petitioning creditor is conclusive, as to the particular claim thus litigated, in all subsequent proceedings in the cause having relation to such claim, so long as the judgment remains in force. The law certainly does not contemplate that the petitioning creditor shall be required to establish the validity of a particular claim against the bankrupt more than once in the same proceeding, unless the court shall, upon some legal ground grant a new trial of such issue." This case, In re Ulfelder, is discussed in Ayres *v.* Cone, 14 A. B. R. 743, 750, 751; and in Silvey Co. *v.* Tift, 17 A. B. R. 16, 123 Ga. 804.

To same effect, In re Virginia Hardwood Mfg. Co., 15 A. B. R. 136, 139 Fed. 209 (D. C. Ark.): "The mortgage in controversy was executed on the 26th of January, 1905, and withheld from record until the 13th of February, 1905. A petition in bankruptcy was filed against the bankrupt on the 5th of April, 1905, and on the 17th of May, 1905, it was adjudicated a bankrupt upon a trial before the court, in which the American National Bank, of which the present claimant is president, resisted the adjudication on the ground that the bankrupt was not insolvent at the time the mortgage was executed or at the time the petition was filed. The judgment on which this claim is based was recovered on the 8th day of May, 1905, three days after the petition in bankruptcy was filed. It must be taken, therefore, as res adjudicata that the bankrupt was insolvent when the mortgage was executed."

But compare, obiter, contra, in Neustadter *v.* Chic Dry Goods Co., 3 A. B. R. 98, 96 Fed. 830 (D. C. Wash.): "In this case the original petitioners and the defendant have by their opposition to the petition of the intervenors waived all their rights to assail the judgment, and it is contrary to good practice to permit new parties whose rights are in no way affected to come in now to disturb it. These intervenors are at liberty to commence a new and independent proceeding for the assertion of their rights, and this judgment be pleaded against them, for the reason that as they were not notified, the court did not have jurisdiction to render a judgment binding them."

Compare, to same general effect, In re Hintze, 13 A. B. R. 721, 134 Fed. 141 (D. C. Mass.): "That a creditor, after adjudication upon a voluntary petition, may in some cases move to have the adjudication vacated because of the bankrupt's nonresidence, was decided by this court in In re Scott, 7 A. B. R. 39, 111 Fed. 114. But in that case the court expressly noted that the creditor had moved to vacate the adjudication as speedily as possible, and so had waived none of his rights. Here the creditor, by proving his claim, has assented to the adjudication, and has taken advantage thereof. The motion which he now urges is repugnant to his own action in the case. He contends that the bankrupt's residence so affects the jurisdiction of the court that nonresidence may be set up at any time by any person. But this is not so. Let us suppose that the court now tries the question of residence de novo, decides that the bankrupt resided within the district, and accordingly refuses to vacate the adjudication. The creditor can not thereafter attack the adjudication on the ground of nonresidence, however jurisdictional a matter residence may be. As to him, the bankrupt's residence has become res judicata. So the adjudication in bankruptcy, here rendered upon a petition alleging residence, has made that residence res judicata for the purpose of this proceeding, and, as the proceeding was in rem, has determined the bankrupt's residence as against all the world. The injustice of binding a creditor, who has no notice of the proceeding, requires the court to reopen the question at the instance of such a creditor, who has not, expressly or by implication, assented to the adjudication. In re Scott, 7 A. B. R. 39. Where, however, the creditor, by proving his claim, has acquiesced in the adjudication, it is unjust to permit him to dispute that which the court had adjudged with his implied approval.   As soon might the Circuit Court permit a defendant to deny the plaintiff's citizenship in a suit depending thereon, after judgment rendered upon a declaration containing all suitable allegations." The court in this case speaks of the adjudication being res adjudicata. This seems an unfortunate term to be used in this connection, for it was a motion to vacate an adjudication precisely to prevent its becoming res adjudicata. A better classification, it would seem would be to have based the denial on the laches of the creditor.

In re American Brewing Co., 7 A. B. R. 469, 112 Fed. 752 (C. C. A. Ills.): "But we are of opinion that the decision of the referee was correct, in holding that the adjudication in bankruptcy was binding upon the appellants, and conclusive upon the question of insolvency. The appellants, as well as the brewing company, were essentially parties to the petition. In that petition, as one of the grounds of bankruptcy, it was alleged that the American Brewing Company was insolvent, and was indebted in the sum of over $900,000, and that within four months next preceding the date of the filing of the petition it committed an act of bankruptcy, in that it did on February 27, 1899, suffer or permit, while insolvent, Albert Magnus and August Magnus, partners doing business under the firm name of Magnus' Sons, to obtain a preference through legal proceedings, which preference consisted in the procurement by confession on the date aforesaid by said A. Magnus' Sons of a judgment in the Superior Court of Cook County, Ill., against said American Brewing Company, for the sum of $10,050 and costs of suit; that upon said judgment an execution was issued out of said court to the sheriff, and was levied upon a large amount of personal property of said Brewing company. * * * The appellants had an opportunity of answering this petition, but neither they nor the American Brewing Company made any appearance or answer, and judgment went by default in accordance with the law and forms and practice prescribed by the Supreme Court in such cases. To say now that the judgment is not binding upon the question of insolvency is to run counter to well-established principles of law applicable to judgments. If it were necessary, in order to bind creditors by a judgment in bankruptcy, that they should appear and answer, as they always have a right to do, then an adjudication could be prevented simply by creditors abstaining from appearing in the proceedings. But it is well settled that the proceedings are in a large sense in rem, and are binding whether the bankrupt or creditors appear or not. * * *

"The Bankrupt Act (§ 18b) provides that the bankrupt or any creditor may appear and plead to the petition within ten days after the return day, or within such further time as the court may allow. And it is further provided in subdivision 'd' that, if the bankrupt or any of his creditors shall appear within the time limited and controvert the facts alleged in the petition, the judge shall determine, as soon as may be, the issues presented by the pleadings. And by subdivision 'e' it is further provided that if, on the last day within which pleadings may be filed, none are filed by the bankrupt or any of his creditors, the judge shall on the next day, if present, or as soon thereafter as practicable, make the adjudication or dismiss the petition. From this provision it is quite clear that, in order to bind creditors by an adjudication, it is not essential that they should appear. It is enough that they have the right and opportunity to appear, whether they appear or not. It was clearly the privilege, as well as the duty, of the appellants, if they wished to dispute the allegations in the petition that the confession of judgment on February 27th was an act of bankruptcy, to appear and controvert the facts so alleged. Not having done so, we think the return of the referee was right—that the judgment was binding upon them. They were not interested in several other acts of bankruptcy alleged, but they were interested in that, and it was their duty, as well as privilege, to defend against it.˙ * * *

"A judgment by default is just as conclusive as adjudication between parties of whatever is essential to support the judgment as one rendered after answer and contest, and in such case facts are not open to further controversy if they are necessarily at variance with the judgment on the pleadings. * * * And in Garner v. Bank (C. C.), 89 Fed. 636, it was held, in full accordance with the general doctrine of the cases, that a judgment which determines the right of a party, though by default, is a judgment on the merits, and is conclusive as to such right and all matters which properly belonged to the subject, and which the parties, in the exercise of, reasonable diligence, might have brought forward therein. These cases are in line with the general doctrine on this subject, as appears by the adjudged cases."

Compare, to same effect analogously, Hackney v. Hargreaves Bros., 13 A. B. R. 169, 68 Neb. 624: "The schedule was a part of the pleadings in the bankruptcy proceedings, and defendants in these actions are sought to be charged by the trustee as having been given an unlawful preference as creditors of the bankrupt. All the creditors of the bankrupt were parties to the bankruptcy proceedings. In re Pekin Plow Co., 7 A. B. R. 369, 112 Fed. 309. In re Fraizer, 9 A. B. R. 21, 117 Fed. 746; In re Beerman, 7 A. B. R. 431, 142 Fed. 662." But, although the schedules are part of the pleadings yet perhaps they do not bind creditors. It is simply the adjudications, not the pleadings, that bind parties.

Especially is it binding where the party has actually intervened and contested the issue.[50]

---

50. But see **qualified statements of the rule:**

1. "All creditors are parties and bound by the proceedings."

Bear v. Chase, 3 A. B. R. 751, 99 Fed. 920 (C. C. A. S. C.): "Upon the adjudication of the bankrupt, all creditors became parties to the bankruptcy proceedings by operation of law and particularly these creditors by whose acts the bankruptcy was caused."

2. All creditors seeking to prove claims.

In re Keller, 6 A. B. R. 350, 109 Fed. 118 (D. C. Iowa): "When a person appears in a bankruptcy proceeding for the purpose of proving up a claim, he becomes a party thereto, in such sense that the record in many particulars is evidence against him. Thus, the fact of the adjudication, the existence of claims proved up, and the like, may be shown by the record thereof; but, if issue is taken by the trustee on the right to prove up the claims, then the testimony of witnesses taken before the referee upon other issues, to which the claimant was not in fact a party, and when he was not present and could not exercise the right of cross-examination, is not admissible. In such cases the witnesses, including the bankrupt, must be recalled, unless the claimant consents to the use of the testimony as it appears in the proceedings."

But the creditors are parties irrespective of their appearance and proving of claims.

3. "Adjudication of involuntary bank-

Thus, on the question of insolvency, Savings Bk. *v.* Jewelry Co., 12 A. B. R. 784, 123 Iowa 432: "It is further made to appear that the plaintiff bank entered its appearance in the bankruptcy proceedings, and filed therein an answer to the petition, among other things denying the insolvency of Morgan. The issue thus made was tried, resulting in an adjudication of bankruptcy. Based on the conditions as thus made to appear, and as related to the question of insolvency, counsel for intervenor invoke the doctrine of res adjudicata. Counsel for the bank essay to meet this contention by asserting that the bank was not a party to the bankruptcy proceeding, that the filing of its answer was a mere gratuity, and that it became in no way bound by the adjudication, except for the purpose of such bankruptcy proceedings. We may concede that the bank was not a necessary party to the proceedings, yet there could have been no other purpose in its appearance, save in protection of its mortgage interests. Manifestly, an adjudication of bankruptcy, involving of necessity a finding of insolvency, would be one step gained in an attack on such mortgage interests. By appearing and filing an answer, the bank, in effect, intervened in the proceedings, and its right to do so was not challenged. Having contested in a court of competent jurisdiction, with the other creditors of Morgan the question of his insolvency, we are of the opinion it may not again, in any action involving that identical question, wage a similar contest with a trustee representing such creditors."

Breckons *v.* Snyder, 15 A. B. R. 116, 211 Pa. St. 176: "If it had not been given to the defendant in discharge of a debt, it was the bankrupt's money in the defendant's hands, which the trustee could recover for creditors. The adjudication was evidence of the bankrupt's insolvency at its date, and it was not necessary to prove insolvency at the trial."

Ayres *v.* Cone, 14 A. B. R. 739, 138 Fed. 778 (C. C. A. S. Dak.): "Under the Bankruptcy Act, 1898, any creditor may appear and join in an involuntary petition, or be heard in opposition thereto, and those not appearing are in contemplation of law represented by the alleged bankrupt to the extent of being concluded as to all matters directly in issue and determined by the order of adjudication."

But see Montgomery *v.* McNicholas, 15 A. B. R. 94, 138 Fed. 956 (D. C. Pa.): "The record of the verdict of the jury finding that [the bankrupt] committed an act of bankruptcy in that he transferred this liquor license with intent to hinder, delay and defraud his other creditors when he was insolvent, was offered in evidence by the plaintiff. The objection to its admission was sustained."

§ 445. But Better Rule, Adjudication Not Binding Except on Mere Status of Debtor as Bankrupt, unless Parties Actually Contest.

—Perhaps, indeed, the true rule is that the adjudication of bankruptcy,

ruptcy raises no presumption of insolvency at any time prior to the filing of the petition."

In re Chappell, 7 A. B. R. 608, 113 Fed. 545 (D. C. Va.): This is not a correct statement of the law. Where the adjudication is based on an act of bankruptcy, involving as an essential element insolvency at a previous date, that adjudication conclusively establishes insolvency as of that date. On the other hand the adjudication may not be res adjudicata on the subject of insolvency at all, as where it is not essential to prove insolvency in the proof of the act of bankruptcy relied on.

4. Default adjudication of bankruptcy is a judgment on the merits and is conclusive on all who might by the exercise of proper diligence have defended. In re Gorman, 15 A. B. R. 537 (D. C. Hawaii).

In re Harper, 23 A. B. R. 918, 175 Fed. 412 (D. C. N. Y.), quoted at § 447.

though to be sure it is in a proceedings in rem "binding on the whole world," is not binding on others than those actually engaged in the litigation, except as to the status of the debtor as a bankrupt; that the constructive presence of all creditors does not obtain except as to the subject of the debtor's status; that, therefore, except as to parties who have actually litigated the issues, the adjudication in bankruptcy is not binding in subsequent litigation on the matter of insolvency nor even on the matter of the commission of the very act of bankruptcy on which the adjudication is based; that the doctrine of res adjudicata does not apply, because the subjects of the two proceedings are different; in the proceedings on the bankruptcy petition the subject being the status of the debtor, whilst on the subsequent litigation the subject is the property or a debt entitled to share in the property.[51]

Silvey & Co. v. Tift, 17 A. B. R. 12, 123 Ga. 804: "An adjudication in bankruptcy is in the nature of a proceeding in rem, and the adjudication is in the nature of a decree in rem, so far as it fixes the status of the defendant in the proceeding as a bankrupt. Considered in the light of a proceeding in rem, the res involved is the status of the debtor, and the adjudication determines such status to be that of a bankrupt. All persons are bound by the adjudication to that effect; and this was true under the Act of 1867 as well as under the Act of 1898. If the court rendering the judgment had jurisdiction, such judgment could not be attacked collaterally, but only by a direct proceeding in a competent court, unless it appeared that the decree was void in form, or that due notice was not given. Lamp Chimney Co. v. Brass & Cooper Co., 91 U. S. 656, 23 L. Ed. 336; Chapman v. Brewer, 114 U. S. 158, 5 Sup. Ct. 799, 29 L. Ed. 83; Shawhan v. Wherritt, 7 How. 627, 12 L. Ed. 847 (under the Act of 1841); Hanover Nat. Bank v. Moyses, 186 U. S. 181, 192, 8 Am. B. R. 1, 22 Sup. Ct. 857, 46 L. Ed. 1, 113. Where a proceeding in rem is against a particular piece of property, as a vessel, for charges against it, it is generally taken into possession, and the property itself is treated as the defendant, liable for its own debts or defaults; and, after seizure, subsequent proceedings are had by citation to the world, of which the owner is at liberty to avail himself by appearing in the case. In the present case, however, there was no such proceeding in rem against the goods. The proceeding was to determine the status of Griffin as a bankrupt, and it neither was nor could have been commenced by a seizure of the property claimed by the defendants. Mankin v. Chandler, 2 Brock. 125, Fed. Cas. No. 9,030; The Sabine, 101 U. S. 388, 25 L. Ed. 982; Freeman v. Alderson, 119 U. S. 187, 7 Sup. Ct. 165, 30 L. Ed. 372. To illustrate further, proceedings to appoint an administrator are also in the nature of proceedings in rem, and, where the court has jurisdiction, are not subject to collateral attack. But it will not be contended that if a person applies for administration, and sets out in his petition that the entire estate of the decedent consists of a certain house and lot, the judgment appointing him would establish the title of the estate to the property, if in fact it belonged to

---

51. To same effect, In re Continental Corp'n, 14 A. B. R. 538 (Ref. Ohio). And compare, Manson v. Williams, 18 A. B. R. 674, 153 Fed. 525 (C. C. A. Me.). But that the adjudication conclusively establishes insolvency, see Whitwell, trustee, v. Wright, 23 A. B. R. 747, 136 App. Div. N. Y. 246, but this case is not to be commended for its reasoning. To the same effect, In re Harper, 23 A. B. R. 918, 175 Fed. 412 (D. C. N. Y.), quoted at § 447.

General Principles of Res Judicata. —See Talcott v. Friend, 24 A. B. R. 708, 179 Fed. 676 (C. C. A. Ills.).

another than the decedent. The judgment would establish the status of the applicant as an administrator, and that he was duly appointed, but would not determine the title to the property.

"There are two kinds of actions which are commonly spoken of as proceedings in rem. The first is a proceeding against the property without suit against its owner, treating the property as if it were the defendant, but with monition or notice giving any person claiming to be the owner an opportunity to appear. In this class of actions, which are strictly in rem, the judgment is against the property alone. The other class of proceedings in rem are proceedings to determine the status of some person or subject-matter. Such are judgments of outlawry, appointments of guardians, administrations, etc., where the proceeding is to determine status, not title to property. The res which makes it a proceeding in rem is the status, and the determination of status is not a conclusive judgment against third parties as to title. Sometimes a judgment in rem has been defined generally to be an adjudication pronounced upon the status of some particular subject-matter by a tribunal having competent authority for that purpose. Stroupper v. McCauley, 45 Ga. 74, 78; Childs v. Hayman, 72 Ga. 791, 796, 797; Woodruff v. Taylor, 20 Vt. 65. In the Act of 1898 it is provided that 'the bankrupt or any creditor may appear and plead to the petition within 10 days after the return day, or within such further time as the court may allow.' Act July 1, 1898, ch. 541, § 18b (30 Stat. 551 [U. S. Comp. St. 1901, p. 3429]), 1 Fed. St. Ann., p. 583. The bankrupt and his creditors are those given an opportunity to appear and defend against the adjudication in bankruptcy. The defendants in the present case, however, do not claim to be creditors, or defend as such, but contend that they were defrauded out of certain goods, and upon discovering the fraud rescinded the trade and resumed possession of their own goods. To compel them to admit that they were creditors and received the goods as such would require them to waive their defense before they could make it. In some of the decisions creditors are spoken of as being privies of the bankrupt. Often, however, they claim against the debtor rather than as privies. To hold that creditors could, by the petition in bankruptcy and the adjudication, conclusively subject the property of third parties, and make it a part of the estate of the bankrupt, if in fact it was not so, would be to go far beyond the determination of his status. To put an extreme case, suppose that creditors should seek to have their debtor declared a bankrupt, and in their petition shall allege that he had conveyed a house and lot to a named person, as one among other grounds of the proceeding, when in fact the debtor had never owned the house and lot, and had never transferred it to the person named at any time. Clearly, an adjudication that the debtor was bankrupt would not invest him or his trustee with title to the property, or operate to take away the title of the real owner, who had never been sued or summoned into court, and who, perhaps, never heard of the proceedings. In such a case, to hold that the adjudication of bankruptcy against the debtor would take away the property of a third person and add it to his estate would approximate more nearly confiscation than adjudication. Suppose one should steal the property of another, and upon its discovery the real owner should resume possession; if later creditors of the thief should file a petition in bankruptcy against him, alleging that he had given a preference to the owner, surely an adjudication that the thief was a bankrupt would not vest the stolen property in him or the trustee. The object of the proceeding is to have the debtor adjudged to be a bankrupt, not to recover property from third parties. They can not deny that he is a bankrupt, but they can deny that he owns their property. To adjudge A.'s status is not to adjudge B.'s property. * * *

"A slight consideration of the difference between the issues involved in a proceeding in bankruptcy and a suit to recover property from a person holding it adversely and claiming to be the owner will show that the two proceedings are not identical, and that the former is not conclusive of the latter, except as to determining the status of the bankrupt as such. The issue in the former proceeding is whether the debtor is or is not a bankrupt within the meaning of the Act of Congress. Where it is sought to recover property from one alleged to be a creditor who had received a preference, the proceeding rests upon § 60b of the Bankrupt Act, which reads as follows: * * * The various requisites to recovery under this section of the Act are quite different from the mere determination upon the proceedings in bankruptcy that the debtor is a bankrupt.

"The position may be further illustrated by considering a voluntary proceeding in bankruptcy. While differing from a proceeding in invitum, the adjudication there as to the status of the bankrupt would also be, to some extent, in the nature of a judgment in rem, so as to show that he was a bankrupt, but certainly it would not be pretended that a person voluntarily going into bankruptcy could possess himself of property which did not belong to him, or have the title to property claimed by third parties adjudicated to be his, no matter what allegation he might make in his petition or schedule. The adjudication in bankruptcy, therefore, conclusively determined the status of Griffin as a bankrupt, but did not conclude the defendants from making their defense on a suit by the trustee in bankruptcy against them to recover the property."

Thus, it has been held, though in an obiter, that an adjudication on the ground of a fraudulent transfer will not be binding upon the alleged fraudulent transferee in a subsequent suit to recover the property.[52]

Indeed, it has been held that an order of involuntary adjudication against a partnership is not conclusive, either as to the existence of the partnership or the title to its assets, upon the trustee of one of the alleged partners,[53] such trustee not being entitled to oppose the adjudication.

Obiter (res adjudicata waived), Manson *v.* Williams, 22 A. B. R. 22, 213 U. S. 413, affirming 18 A. B. R. 674, 153 Fed. 525: "The appellee says that the question is concluded by the adjudication putting the company into bankruptcy, that being an adjudication against the two brothers. On the other hand, the record shows that the trustees of Henry, although they had filed a denial and answer, were not heard on that question. The principle of law is plain. The adjudication put the two brothers into bankruptcy for the purpose of administering whatever property there might be, as against all the world. But it did not establish the facts upon which it was founded, no matter how necessary the connection, except as against parties entitled to be heard. Tilt *v.* Kelsey, 207 U. S. 43, 52. * * * If the trustees of Henry were not entitled to be heard, it is because they had no concern with whether the alleged firm was wound up in bankruptcy or not, but only with the facts upon which creditors sought to wind it up—that is to say, the existence of the partnership and

---

52. Obiter, In re Larkin, 21 A. B. R. 711, 168 Fed. 100 (D. C. N. Y.).
53. Whether adjudication is res adjudicata as to respondents, relation being that of partners, query, In re Hudson Clothing Co., 17 A. B. R. 826 (D. C. Me.).

the title to the partnership assets—and these facts would remain open to dispute. As the trustees of Henry were not heard, it would come with bad grace from one who might have urged the foregoing consideration, to argue here that they are bound to admit anything except that Henry and his brother are in bankruptcy as partners. Furthermore, we gather from the opinion of the district judge that all parties requested him to examine the evidence, and that the defense of res judicata really was waived. But, as the partnership might have been a partnership in profits only, leaving the title to the capital in Henry alone, the adjudication, even if it established that there had been a partnership, could not conclude anything as to the title to the assets, the matter with which we now are concerned."

§ 446. Adjudication on Ground of Preference Not Binding on Issue of Reasonable Cause for Belief.

—An adjudication on the ground of a preference, at any rate, is not binding in subsequent litigation to recover the preference, on the issue of the existence of reasonable cause for belief on the creditor's part,[54] for such issue is immaterial on the hearing upon the petition for adjudication.

Hussey v. Dry Goods Co., 17 A. B. R. 516 (C. C. A. Kas.): "It is contended that the adjudication which followed on that petition is res adjudicata of the present claim of the dry goods company. There is no merit in that contention. Conceding that under the authority of In re American Brewing Co., 7 Am. B. R. 463, 112 Fed. 752, and Ayres v. Cone, 14 Am. B. R. 739, 138 Fed. 778, the dry goods company would be estopped from again litigating the issues raised by the creditors' petition, namely, whether Sowers was in fact insolvent, or whether he made the alleged transfer with intent to prefer the dry goods company, there is yet left the issue involved in the present case, whether at the time the transfer was made the dry goods company had reasonable cause to believe it was intended by Sowers as a preference, or, as simplified in this case, whether it then had reasonable cause to believe Sowers was insolvent. The giving of a preference by an insolvent as defined by § 60 (a) affords sufficient ground for an adjudication of bankruptcy against him, but is not sufficient to avoid the transfer constituting a preference as against the person receiving it. To accomplish the latter, it must be shown, additionally, that the one receiving it had reasonable cause to believe it was a preference. An issue of that kind was not and could not properly have been presented or tried in the petition for adjudication. In re Rome Planing Mill (D. C.), 3 Am. B. R. 123, 96 Fed. 812. The general rule is that the estoppel of a judgment extends only to those material matters in issue or to those without proof of which it could not properly have been rendered."

§ 446½. Adjudication in General Terms Where Several Distinct Acts Alleged.

—An adjudication in general terms, where several distinct acts are alleged, is not res adjudicata as to any one act.

In re Leston, 19 A. B. R. 506, 157 Fed. 78 (C. C. A. Okla.): "But there were five other distinct acts of bankruptcy charged in the creditors' petition, and the record does not show upon which the adjudication proceeded; therefore the matter is at large. Russell v. Place, 94 U. S. 606, 24 L. Ed. 214; Ætna

---

54. Compare action of court In re Cleary, 24 A. B. R. 742, 179 Fed. 990 (D. C. Pa.).

Life Ins. Co. *v.* Board of Com'rs, 117 Fed. 82, 54 C. C. A. 468. The adjudication in bankruptcy was in general terms, and it might well have been authorized by proof of any one or more of the other acts charged. The controversy here is not that in the original proceeding. The adjudication in bankruptcy stands admitted and uncontested, and, for aught the record shows, it may have proceeded upon a ground wholly disconnected from the acquisition of the homestead."

§ 447. Adjudication Not Binding as to Petitioning Creditors' Claims When Presented for Allowance.

—But the adjudication is not binding upon those not actually parties to the litigation as to the amount nor validity of the petitioning creditors' claims when subsequently presented in the administration of the estate for allowance to share in dividends.[55]

See dissenting opinion in Ayres *v.* Cone, 14 A. B. R. 748, 138 Fed. 778 (C. C. A. S. Dak.): "Did the adjudication of bankruptcy estop the objecting creditors and the trustee who represents them from contesting the allowance of the claim of the appellees and their right to share in the estate of the bankrupt? It is not material whether or not the adjudication estopped the bankrupt, and for that reason it is conceded that on March 28th, 1904, when Gentle was adjudged a bankrupt, 25 days after the filing of the petition in bankruptcy, the issue whether or not he was indebted to the appellees in the sum of $5,861 became res adjudicata between the petitioning creditors and the bankrupt. The estoppel of that adjudication, however, did not arise until that day, which was 25 days after the rights of all creditors in the estate had become fixed, and it did not bind any one who was not a party to the litigation of the issues which that judgment determined.

"Although the bankrupt was thus debarred from subsequently contesting the claim, the adjudication against him gave the owners of that claim no right to any share in his estate or to any dividend from its proceeds. Their right to that share and to that dividend was conditioned by the express terms of the Bankruptcy Act by a subsequent proof of their claim by a written statement under oath (§ 57a) and by its allowance by the referee or by the court, and the trustee and other creditors were expressly granted the right to object to and to contest that allowance after the proof had been filed. Sections 57c, 57k, 30 Stat. 560, 561 (U. S. Comp. St. 1901, pp. 3443, 3444). Not only this, but the duty still rested upon the bankrupt to 'examine the correctness of all proofs of claims filed against his estate' (§ 7 [3], 30 Stat. 548 [U. S. Comp. St. 1901, p. 3425]), and, 'in case of any person having to his knowledge proved a false claim against his estate, disclose that fact immediately to his trustee' (§ 7 [7]), and the duty was imposed upon the trustee to defeat such a claim if possible. Chatfield *v.* O'Dwyer, 4 Am. B. R. 313, 101 Fed. 797, 799, 42 C. C. A. 30, 32.

"Identity of parties is as essential to an estoppel by res adjudicata as identity of causes of action. Fowler *v.* Stebbins, 136 Fed. 365 (decided at the last term). The objecting creditors were not named as defendants. They did not appear, answer, or take any part in the litigation which resulted in the adjudication of bankruptcy. Upon familiar principles, that litigation was therefore res inter alios acta as to them, and they were not bound by the determination of the issues which the parties might present in it, and which the Bankruptcy Act required to be litigated at another time and place. This rule is invoked

---

55. In re Continental Corporation, 14 A. B. R. 538 (Ref. Ohio).

and applied by the express provisions of that Act that the creditors may exercise the option to appear in and be barred by the adjudication (§ 18b-d, 30 Stat. 551 [U. S. Comp. St. 1901, p. 3429]), or to refrain from taking part in it and be free from it, and that they may object to and contest the allowance of claims of all other creditors, without exception (§ 57d). Since no exception of the claims of petitioning creditors from this right of other creditors to contest them was made by the Congress, the conclusive legal presumption arises that it intended to make none, and it is not the province of the courts to do so. Webber *v.* St. Paul City Ry. Co., 38 C. C. A. 79, 82, 97 Fed. 140, 143; Madden *v.* Lancaster Co., 12 C. C. A. 566, 573, 65 Fed. 188, 195; McIver *v.* Ragan, 2 Wheat. 25, 29, 4 L. Ed. 175; Bank of State of Alabama *v.* Dalton, 9 How. 522, 528, 13 L. Ed. 242; Vance *v.* Vance, 108 U. S. 514, 521, 2 Sup. Ct. 854, 27 L. Ed. 808.

"Moreover, the Bankruptcy Act has provided a time, a place, and a tribunal where all claims to share in the estate must be heard and allowed upon proofs of claims, and has given the right to all creditors to contest them there. From this provision the presumption necessarily arises that this time, place, and tribunal were to be exclusive, and that all creditors are relieved from the necessity of contesting claims to share in the estate at any other time or place. Petitioning creditors, like all others, are required to prove and secure an allowance of their claims in the face of the objections of other creditors, notwithstanding the adjudication of bankruptcy in their favor. The litigation upon their petition is not the time nor the place prescribed by the law for the trial of the question whether or not, or to what extent, their claims may share in the distribution of the estate of the bankrupt. The logical and inevitable conclusion from these considerations appears to me to be that, when the validity and extent of a petitioning creditor's claim is determined in the litigation upon the petition which results in the adjudication of bankruptcy, the bankrupt and those creditors, and those only who either voluntarily or involuntarily become parties to that litigation, are estopped by the determination there of the petitioner's claim, while all other creditors and the trustee who represents them, when the petitioning creditor's claim to share in the estate is subsequently presented to the referee or the court for allowance, are free to contest it upon its merits as it stood at the time of the filing of the petition in bankruptcy, regardless of the subsequent adjudication.

"Nor is this conclusion without authority to support it. The only direct decision upon the question sustains it. That is the decision of Judge DeHaven in In re Henry Ulfelder Clothing Co. (D. C.), 3 Am. B. R. 425, 98 Fed. 409, cited by the majority. There is an obiter dictum in the opinion in that case, which will be subsequently considered, to the effect that the bankrupt is the representative of all the creditors in a litigation upon a petition for an adjudication in bankruptcy, and that the determination of any material issue between the petitioning creditor and the bankrupt in that litigation estops all the creditors, whether they are parties to the proceeding or not. The decision in the case, however, repudiates this novel theory, and sustains the position that the determination of the validity and extent of claims in such a proceeding binds only those creditors who are in their own persons parties to the litigation. The case was this: Donie Ulfelder filed a petition in bankruptcy against the Henry Ulfelder Clothing Company, a corporation in which she alleged that the corporation owed her $2,000, that it was insolvent, and that it had committed an act of bankruptcy. The corporation and one of its creditors, Bernard Lowenstein, appeared and filed answers to this petition, in which they denied that the petitioner was a creditor of the corporation and that the corporation was insolvent. Upon the trial of these issues the petitioner introduced in evidence a promissory note of the corporation to her for $2,200, to prove that she was its creditor, and two other promissory notes of the corporation, one to Henry Ulfelder for $1,800 and one to A. Levy for $1,440, for the purpose of proving its insolvency. The corporation and Lowenstein introduced evidence tended to show that the three notes were never executed by the corporation and were without consideration. The court found the issues for the petitioner, and adjudged the corporation a bankrupt. Thereafter the three claims were presented to the referee for allowance by Donie Ulfelder, Henry Ulfelder and A. Levy, respectively, and the bankrupt and Bernard Lowenstein objected to their allowance, upon the same grounds which they had urged at the trial upon the petition in bankruptcy. Neither the trustee nor any other creditor made any objection. The court decided that the issue over the validity of the claim of the petitioner, Donie Ulfelder, was res adjudicata between these parties, because the bankrupt and Lowenstein were both parties to the suit on the petition and to the trial of that issue in that litigation and denied them permission to contest that claim upon its merits. But the court also decided that the issues over the validity of the claims of Henry Ulfelder and A. Levy were not res adjudicata even against the corporation and Lowenstein, notwithstanding the fact that they were material issues and had been carefully tried and determined in the litigation upon the petition, because neither Henry Ulfelder nor A. Levy were parties to the litigation. The court accordingly reversed the order of the referee and directed him to try these issues upon the merits, regardless of the adjudication in bankruptcy. In re Henry Ulfelder Clothing Co. (D. C.), 3 Am. B. R. 425, 98 Fed. 409-411, 413, 414.

"It is obvious that this decision was a direct repudiation of the proposition that the estoppel of the bankrupt was the estoppel of the creditors, because under that theory the estoppel of the bankrupt to contest the claims of Levy and Henry Ulfelder must have estopped them although they were not parties to the litigation. The theory that after the filing of the petition the bankrupt is the representative of the creditors, and that his subsequent estoppel affects the rights of creditors, in the property which he owned at the time the petition was filed, is fallacious, because the status of claims of creditors and the status of the property at the time of filing the petition, and at that time alone, fixes the rights of the parties, and because the power of disposition and application of the property at will, and hence the power to bind it and the creditors, its beneficial owners, is divested from the bankrupt by the law, and vested in the creditors and the court, when the petition in bankruptcy is filed. It is for this reason that the decision in Candee v. Lord, 2 N. Y. 269, 52 Am. Dec. 294, is neither controlling nor persuasive here. In that case Russell Lord, a debtor, confessed a judgment in August, 1843, for $1,400, in favor of Henry Lord, and a second judgment, during the same month, for $1,250, in favor of Champlin. On March 29, 1844, Candee recovered a judgment against Russell Lord for $1,142.90. He brought a suit upon this judgment to avoid the prior judgments for fraud, and Henry Lord and Champlin answered that his judgment was founded upon a forged note. The court rightly held that in the absence of fraud they were bound by the judgment against their debtor, because at the time it was rendered he had the right and the power to sell, to dispose of, to charge with liens, and to apply his property to the payment of his debts as he chose, so that any deed, assurance, or judgment of their debtor estopped his creditors as well as himself. In the case at bar the bankrupt, Gentle, was deprived of his right and power of disposition 25 days before the estoppel by the adjudication in bankruptcy arose, and for that reason his deeds, assurances, and estoppels after the filing of the petition in bankruptcy bound neither his creditors nor the property, which had vested in the court in trust for the creditors when the petition was first deposited. The condition of this property and of the parties after the filing of the petition will more clearly appear by a brief consideration of the effect of that filing upon the rights of the bankrupt and the creditors."

Compare suggestive reasoning in In re Plymouth Cordage Co., 13 A. B. R. 670, 135 Fed. 1000 (C. C. A. Okla.): "The fact that there is no averment that the creditors are less than twelve cannot be more fatal to the right of the petitioner to an adjudication in bankruptcy than the fact that he has made such an averment, which, upon the trial, proves to be without foundation in fact. The truth is that the contention of counsel for the respondent fails to distinguish between the averments essential to jurisdiction over the subject-matter and the parties and those requisite to invoke a favorable adjudication upon the petition. Jurisdiction of the subject-matter and of the parties is the right to hear and determine the suit or proceeding in favor of or against the parties to it. The facts essential to invoke this jurisdiction differ materially from those essential to constitute a good cause of action for the relief sought. A defective petition in bankruptcy or an insufficient complaint at law, accompanied by proper service upon the defendants, gives jurisdiction to the court to determine the questions it presents, although it may not contain averments which entitle the complainant to any relief; and it may be the duty of the court to determine either the question of its jurisdiction or the merits of the controversy against the petitioner or plaintiff. Allegations indispensable to a favorable adjudication or decree include all those requisite to state a complete cause of action, and they comprehend many that are not requisite to the jurisdiction of the suit or proceeding. The averment that all the creditors of Smith were less than twelve was not of the former, but of the latter, class. It was not essential to invoke the jurisdiction of the court over the parties to the proceeding and the property it involved, because the act of Congress gave that court, upon the filing of the petition of the creditor, jurisdiction to hear and determine the questions it presented, whether they were questions of jurisdiction or upon the merits. Not only this, but the averment that the creditors were less than twelve was not even essential to a favorable adjudication upon the petition, because the Bankruptcy Law provided that if two other creditors, whose claims were sufficient in amount, joined in the petition of the cordage company, the court might proceed to adjudicate the issue of bankruptcy upon the merits, although the creditors exceeded twelve in number."

In re Harper, 23 A. B. R. 918, 175 Fed. 412 (D. C. N. Y.): "The allegation in the involuntary petition, the Peninsular Company being one of the petitioning creditors, that such company was a creditor of said Harper, the alleged bankrupt, to the amount stated, and the failure to answer the petition and to controvert the allegation, did not make it res adjudicata as to the creditors or as to the trustee. The Peninsular Company must still file its proof of claim and procure its allowance. Any creditor, or the trustee, may contest it. Matter of the Continental Corporation, 14 Am. B. R. 538, 542, 543; In re Cleveland Ins. Co. (C. C.), 22 Fed. 204; Aspden v. Nixon, 4 How. (U. S.), 467, 498. I agree with the dissenting opinion of Sanborn, C. J., in Ayres v. Cone et al. (C. C. A.), 14 Am. B. R. 739, 138 Fed. 778. Quite probably a creditor, who appears in the proceeding and contests the adjudication on the ground a petitioning creditor is not a creditor of the alleged bankrupt, would be concluded by the adjudication. Not so of those who do not appear or contest. That is not the time or place for presenting and contesting claims as such. There is no privity between the creditors, or between the alleged bankrupt and his creditors, which will bind them on the question referred to."

Contra, Ayres v. Cone, 14 A. B. R. 739, 138 Fed. 778 (C. C. A. S. Dak.): "Where in a proceeding to have a debtor adjudged bankrupt, the validity of the claim of a petitioning creditor is put in issue by the pleadings and adjudged valid, the creditor cannot be required to establish it again before the referee when presented for allowance, at the suggestion of the bankrupt and other creditors, not parties to the petition." But see the dissenting opinion in this case, which, in the author's opinion, states the truer rule.

But the adjudication is binding upon parties or their privies who have actually litigated the same issue in the hearing upon the petition for adjudication.[56]

The adjudication is not, however, binding as to collateral matters not directly brought in issue.[57]

Inferentially, Pepperdine v. Bank, 10 A. B. R. 573 (St. Louis Ct. Appeals): "Appellant urges that the adjudication in bankruptcy is conclusive upon respondent, asserting that the question in issue in the present case was the identical question decided by the bankruptcy court. The bankruptcy court had no lawful authority to pass upon any but the sole issue before it—whether within four months next before the petition Good committed an act of bankruptcy by suffering defendant to obtain judgment against him on March 24, 1899—and no adjudication upon any other issue was sought or rendered in the proceeding."

Nor will the adjudication on an act of bankruptcy committed at one time revert to an earlier date to prove insolvency.[58] But of course it would be admissible whenever proof of a later condition of insolvency would be competent as tending to prove insolvency at an earlier period.

§ 448. Refusal to Adjudge Bankrupt, after Hearing Merits, Res Judicata as to All; and Second Petition Not Maintainable.

—It has been held, obiter, that the refusal to adjudge bankrupt is not res adjudicata binding upon other and different creditors as to the same acts of bankruptcy.[59]

Obiter, In re Lavoc, 13 A. B. R. 400, 134 Fed. 237 (C. C. A. N. Y.): "Reference is made in the brief to the circumstance that the answer avers that the acts of bankruptcy now alleged were set forth in a former petition brought by three other creditors, were denied, and the issues thereon raised considered by the judge who determined them in the bankrupt's favor. It is not contended that there cannot be another trial of the same issues, when different petitioning creditors appear."

But these decisions seem to be of doubtful authority. Bankruptcy proceedings are proceedings in rem, binding on all the world as to the com-

---

56. In re Ulfelder Clothing Co., 3 A. B. R. 425, 98 Fed. 409 (D. C. Calif.).

57. In re Ulfelder Clothing Co., 3 A. B. R. 425, 98 Fed. 409 (D. C. Cal.).

58. Martin v. Bigelow, 7 A. B. R. 220 (Sup. Ct. N. Y.).

59. Obiter, Neustadter v. Chic. Dry Goods Co., 3 A. B. R. 96, 96 Fed. 830 (D. C. Wash.).

mission or noncommission of the acts of bankruptcy therein alleged. After refusal to adjudicate a debtor bankrupt, other creditors may *not* file a new petition upon the same acts of bankruptcy and relitigate the issues; the first adjudication is binding in the bankrupt's favor as to all the world.

§ 448½. **Denying Adjudication but Holding Assets to Aid Reorganization Scheme.**—It is the duty of the bankruptcy court, if it intends to administer the property, promptly to determine the question of adjudication, and to proceed with the selection of a trustee and the administration and distribution of the estate, as required by the act. It cannot deny an adjudication, and then hold jurisdiction over the property for the purpose of allowing some of the creditors to effect a reorganization and distribution of the property.[60]

§ 449. **Laches Bars.**—Laches will bar the creditors' right to interpose the defense of lack of jurisdiction to adjudge bankrupt.[61]

In re Mason, 3 A. B. R. 599, 99 Fed. 256 (D. C. N. Car.): "Creditors, when bankruptcy proceedings have been commenced, must promptly, by motion or petition to vacate the adjudication, object to the jurisdiction of the court, or the objection is waived. A creditor cannot prove his debt and file the same, as in this cause, participate in the election of a trustee, distribute the estate, use the proceeds for his benefit, and then, on the application of the bankrupt for a final discharge, for the first time object to the jurisdiction. Entire want of jurisdiction over the subject-matter may be taken advantage of at any time, and it is never too late to make the objection, and it may be collaterally attacked. Freem. Judgm. 120-117, et seq. But, where objection goes merely to a want of jurisdiction of the person or the thing, there may be a waiver of the objection, or restriction as to the manner and time of making it."

§ 450. **Collateral Attack on Adjudication.**—Adjudication (unless it is void on its face) may not be collaterally attacked.[62]

In re Hecox, 21 A. B. R. 314, 164 Fed. 823 (C. C. A. Colo.): "The radical error in the ruling of the District Court and the vice in the position assumed

---

60. Acme Harvester Co. *v.* Beekman Co., 27 A. B. R. 262, 122 U. S. 300.

61. In re Polakoff, 1 A. B. R. 358 (Master, affirmed by D. C. N. Y.). Compare, ante, § 436, as to laches barring creditor's right to move for vacating of adjudication. Inferentially, compare, In re Altonwood Park Co., 20 A. B. R. 31, 160 Fed. 448 (C. C. A. N. Y.).

Jurisdiction is not affected by failure to file the petition or schedules at the time of their verification. In re Berner, 3 A. B. R. 325 (Ref. Ohio).

62. In re Columbia Real Estate Co., 4 A. B. R. 411, 101 Fed. 965 (D. C. Ind.); In re Goodale, 6 A. B. R. 493, 109 Fed. 783 (D. C. N. Y.). Nonresidence of the bankrupt is not a ques-

tion that can be considered on discharge hearing, In re Clisdell, 4 A. B. R. 95 (D. C. N. Y.), reversing, on this point, 2 A. B. R. 424 (Ref. N. Y.). Compare, quære, In re Berner, 3 A. B. R. 325 (Ref. Ohio). Compare, In re Mason, 3 A. B. R. 599, 99 Fed. 256 (D. C. N. Car.); (1867) In re Fallon, Fed. Cas. No. 4,628; Edelstein *v.* U. S., 17 A. B. R. 649 (C. C. A. Minn.); In re Dempster, 22 A. B. R. 751, 172 Fed. 353 (C. C. A. Mo.), although not correctly stating the rule as to ancillary jurisdiction. But compare, on the facts, apparently, Whitwell, trustee, *v.* Wright, 23 A. B. R. 747, 136 N. Y. Sup. Ct., App. Div. 246. Moore Bros. *v.* Cowan, 26 A. B. R. 902 (Sup. Ct. Ala.).

by counsel for the receiver, before this court consist in undertaking collaterally to controvert the ground of adjudication in bankruptcy. That adjudication determined that the bankrupt was insolvent, and, while insolvent, within four months of the filing of the petition in involuntary bankruptcy and because of its insolvency, a receiver had been put in charge of its property, by order of the State court. * * * Until avoided in a direct proceeding therefor, that adjudication was binding and conclusive on the bankrupt and creditors, as much so as a judgment, inter partes, on due hearing in a court of competent jurisdiction."

Wilson v. Parr, 8 A. B. R. 230 (Ga. Sup. Ct.): "It is claimed, by the answer of some of the defendants to the petition filed by the creditors of the bankrupts, that the adjudication in bankruptcy was fraudulent and void in so far as those respondents were concerned, for reasons set forth by them. It is enough for us to say, in reply to this contention, that, when an adjudication in bankruptcy has in fact been had by the bankruptcy court, such an adjudication will be respected by the State court, and the latter court will not, after a regular adjudication has been had, enter into an inquiry as to whether such adjudication was fraudulent or void. Mr. Black, in the first volume of his work on Judgments (§ 248), citing the case of Chapman v. Brewer, 114 U. S. 158, 5 Sup. Ct. 799, 29 L. Ed. 83, which upon examination seems to support his text, declares: 'An adjudication in bankruptcy, having been made by a court having jurisdiction of the subject-matter, upon the voluntary appearance of the bankrupt, and being correct in form, is conclusive of the fact decreed, and cannot be attacked collaterally in a suit brought by the assignee against a person claiming an adverse interest in the property of the bankrupt,' and Mr. Freeman, in his work on Judgments (volume 2, § 337), declares that discharges in bankruptcy and other orders and decrees of courts of bankruptcy cannot be collaterally impeached by proving them to be irregular, for which proposition he cites a number of cases found in note 1 of page 612. See, also, Brady v. Brady, 71 Ga. 71. Many other authorities could readily be cited to prove that, where an adjudication in bankruptcy has been made by a court of competent jurisdiction, such adjudication will be respected by the State Court, and the question whether it was erroneously made or not, will not be entertained by such court, but the whole matter will be relegated to the proper bankruptcy court in which such adjudication was had, and there the parties complaining may and can have all objections to the regularity of the proceedings of such court considered and passed on."

Thus, lack of jurisdiction to adjudicate bankrupt will not be considered on the hearing upon the bankrupt's petition for discharge.[63] Nor upon trial for the crime "False Oath."[64] Nor upon trial for the crime of "concealment of assets."

Gilbertson v. United States, 22 A. B. R. 32, 168 Fed. 672 (C. C. A. Wis.): "Hence the reference to and adjudication by the referee in the case at bar, however erroneous and avoidable on review, are neither void, nor subject to collateral attack, for contradiction or impeachment of the record. This doctrine is fundamental in reference to adjudications of courts of general juris-

---

63. In re Goodale, 6 A. B. R. 493, 109 Fed. 783 (D. C. N. Y.); In re Mason, 3 A. B. R. 599, 99 Fed. 256.

As, for example, that the bankrupt was an infant. In re Walrath, 24 A. B. R. 541 (D. C. N. Y.).

64. Edelstein v. U. S., 17 A. B. R. 649, 149 Fed. 636 (C. C. A. Minn.).

diction—see Van Fleet on Collateral Attack, §§ 16, 17, 526; 1 Freeman on Judgments, c. 8; 23 Cyc. 1055—and is alike applicable, as we believe, to the adjudication of the District Court in bankruptcy, having unlimited and exclusive jurisdiction in the matters thereof."

Nor upon the trial of a trustee's action to set aside a preferential or fraudulent transfer.

Huttig Mfg. Co. v. Edwards, 20 A. B. R. 349, 160 Fed. 619 (C. C. A. Iowa): "The manufacturing company attacks the validity of the adjudication that D. Winter was a bankrupt, upon the ground that one of the three petitioners in the involuntary proceedings was not a creditor; but since the attack was made in a proceeding by the trustee to annul a preference, it is a collateral, not a direct one. An adjudication of bankruptcy is entitled to the same verity and is no more to be impeached collaterally than other judgments or decrees of competent jurisdiction. It cannot be assailed by the defendant in a suit by the trustee to recover or ávoid a preference upon the ground that one of the petitioners was not in fact a creditor of the bankrupt. When the record shows jurisdiction the adjudication of bankruptcy is subject to impeachment only by a direct proceeding in a competent court."

But where the adjudication is absolutely void on its face, of course it may be disregarded. But, in this connection the distinction is to be noted between an adjudication, the record of which shows affirmatively that jurisdiction does not exist, and an adjudication whose record simply omits to show jurisdictional facts. An adjudication whose record simply omits to show jurisdictional facts may be helped out by the presumption of law that the court did find jurisdictional facts to exist, although the record may be silent. Jurisdiction is imported. Of course such presumption of law could not exist where the record affirmatively declares that such jurisdictional facts did not exist.[65]

And mandamus is improper as a method of obtaining an indirect review of an erroneous adjudication of a corporation which in reality belongs to a class not subject to bankruptcy.[66]

In the case of In re Riggs, it is to be observed that the record in the case did not show affirmatively that the corporation did not belong to a class subject thereto, but, on the contrary, that the pleadings affirmatively declared it to be of a class subject thereto, and the court below was therefore presumed to have had sufficient evidence to sustain its findings. Had the record of the adjudication shown on its face, affirmatively, lack of jurisdiction, it would have been void.

---

65. See further, as to this distinction, ante, § 437, et seq., and post, § 1777 1/7.

Adjudication Based On Service by Publication Precisely as Effective as On Personal Service; Trustee Not Limited in Recovery of Property to District of Bankrupt's Domicile.—In one case the point was sought to be made that the trustee was confined to the district of the bankrupt's domicile in suits for the recovery of property, where the adjudication of bankruptcy was based on service by publication, but the court declared the idea absurd. Hills v. McKinniss Co., 26 A. B. R. 329, 188 Fed. 1012 (D. C. Ohio). See ante, § 308.

66. In re Riggs, 22 A. B. R. 720, 214 U. S. 9. Compare, analogously, § 472.

§ 451. Contractual Relations Not Affected unless Merged in Provable Debts.

—Adjudication in bankruptcy does not sever contractual relations as such.[67]

In re Davis, 25 A. B. R. 1, 180 Fed. 148 (D. C. N. Y.): "I think it fair and just and within the terms of the contract and general rules of law applicable to say that, on the involuntary bankruptcy of a borrowing member of the Homestead Aid Association of Utica and the failure of the trustee to continue the payments: (1) The right to impose and collect fines ceases; (2) such bankruptcy does not operate as a voluntary withdrawal and gives to the association no right to retain profits theretofore actually earned and duly credited; and (3) the trustee of the bankrupt's estate has no claim and is not entitled to credit for profits or interest on the dues paid for the time between the last apportionment and credit of profits and the bankruptcy."

Watson v. Merrill, 14 A. B. R. 453, 136 Fed. 363 (C. C. A. Kas.): "An adjudication in bankruptcy does not dissolve or terminate the contractual relations of the bankrupt, notwithstanding the decisions to the contrary in In re Jefferson (D. C.), 2 Am. B. R. 206, 93 Fed. 448; Bray v. Cobb (D. C.), 3 Am. B. R. 788, 100 Fed. 270; and in In re Hays, Foster & Ward Co. (D. C.), 9 Am. B. R. 144, 117 Fed. 879. Its effect is to transfer to the trustee all the property of the bankrupt except his executory contracts, and to vest in the trustee the option to assume or to renounce these. It is the assignment of the property of the bankrupt to the trustee by operation of law. It neither releases nor absolves the debtor from any of his contracts or obligations, but, like any other assignment of property by an obligor, leaves him bound by his agreements, and subject to the liabilities he has incurred. It is the discharge of the bankrupt alone, not his adjudication, that releases him from liability for provable debts in consideration of his surrender of his property, and its distribution among the creditors who hold them. Even the discharge fails to relieve him from claims against him that are not provable in bankruptcy, and since his obligation to pay rents which are to accrue after the filing of the petition in bankruptcy may not be the basis of a provable claim, his liability for them is neither released nor affected by his adjudication in bankruptcy, or by his discharge from his provable debts. One agrees to pay monthly rents for the place of residence of his family or for his place of business, or to render personal services for monthly compensation for a term of years; he agrees to purchase or to convey property; and he then becomes insolvent and is adjudicated bankrupt. His obligations and liabilities are neither terminated nor released by the adjudication. He still remains legally bound to pay the rents, to render the services, and to fulfill all his other obligations, nothwithstanding the fact that his insolvency may render him unable immediately to do so. Nor are those who contracted with him absolved from their obligations. If he or his trustee pays the stipulated rents for his place of residence or for his place of business, the lessors may not deny to the payor the use of the premises according to the terms of the lease. If he renders the personal services, he who contracted to pay for them may not deny

---

67. In re Brew Co., 16 A. B. R. 110 (D. C. Mo.), quoted ante, § 444. Contra, Bray v. Cobb, 3 A. B. R. 791, 91 Fed. 102 (D. C. N. Car.), reversed in Cobb v. Overman, 6 A. B. R. 324, 109 Fed. 65; Colman Co. v. Withoft, 28 A. B. R. 328, 195 Fed. 250 (C. C. A. Cal.); In re Morgantown Tin Plate Co., 25 A. B. R. 836, 184 Fed. 109 (D. C. W. Va.); In re Boschelli, 25 A. B. R. 528, 183 Fed. 864 (D. C. Pa.).

Compare, where court held a life insurance policy which had no express surrender value to be merely a contractual relation and not transferable property, though the bankrupt died before adjudication. In re Judson, 27 A. B. R. 704, 188 Fed. 702 (D. C. N. Y.), quoted at § 1015.

his liability to discharge this obligation. His trustee does not become liable for his debts, but he does acquire the right to accept and assume or to renounce the executory agreements of the bankrupt, as he may deem most advantageous to the estate he is administering, and the parties to those contracts which he assumes are still liable to perform them. And so throughout the entire field of contractual obligations the adjudication in bankruptcy absolves from no agreement, terminates no contract, and discharges no liability. In re Curtis (La.), 9 Am. B. R. 286; In re Ells (D. C.), 3 Am. B. R. 564, 98 Fed. 967, 968; Witthaus v. Zimmerman, 11 Am. B. R. 314, 316, 86 N. Y. Supp. 315; White v. Griffing, 44 Conn. 437, 446, 447; In re Pennewell, 9 Am. B. R. 490, 119 Fed. 139, 55 C. C. A. 471."

Unless, of course, such contractual relations have become merged in provable claims, and even then it is not the contractual relation that is severed but the claim into which it is merged that is discharged.

Impliedly, In re Adams, 12 A. B. R. 368, 370 (D. C. Mass.): "The creditors seek also to prove their damages for breach of the executory contract. If the contract was broken at or before bankruptcy, they can prove. In re Stern, 8 A. B. R. 569, 116 Fed. 604. It seems that this contract was broken by bankruptcy as of the date of filing the petition."

But contracts for liens as security for debts upon property to be acquired in the future will not affect property acquired after adjudication; as, for instance, contracts for liens on future earned wages where the State law holds such wages to be future acquired property and not simply future accruals under presently possessed property.[68]

In re West, 11 A. B. R. 782, 128 Fed. 205 (D. C. Ore.): "The theory of a lien upon the earnings of future labor is not that it attaches to such earnings from the moment of contract of pledge or assignment, but from the moment of their existence. It is needless to say that there can be no lien upon what does not exist. A pledge or assignment of future wages under an existing employment is said to create an equitable interest in such wages. Stott v. Franey, 20 Ore. 410, 23 Am. St. Rep. 132. This is true of wages earned upon a general employment, as well as those earned upon a definite contract. In this case the railroad company was under no obligation to employ the bankrupt, nor he to work for the company. If future earnings in such a case can be said to have a potential existence, they are the subject of an agreement for a lien; but the lien, or the so-called equitable interest, does not attach until the wages come into existence, and until the lien does attach there is no lien. The discharge in bankruptcy operated to discharge these obligations as of the date of the adjudication, so that the obligations were discharged before the wages intended as security were in existence. The law does not continue an obligation in order that there may be a lien, but only does so because there is one. The effect of the discharge upon the prospective liens was the same as though the debts had been paid before the assigned wages were earned. The wages earned after the adjudication became the property of the bankrupt clear of the claims of all creditors. These debts cannot escape the operation of the Bankruptcy Law by an agreement for a lien upon what the debtor expected to earn, but did not earn until after the adjudication of bankruptcy."

68. In re Karns, 16 A. B. R. 841 (D. C. Ohio). See post, § 2678. Compare, collaterally, In re Sims, 23 A. B. R. 899, 176 Fed. 645 (D. C. N. Y.), quoted at § 2678½.

In re Home Discount Co., 17 A. B. R. 180 (D. C. Ala.): "The effect of the assignment, without regard to its infirmities under the local statute, is avoided by the provisions of the bankruptcy law as to wages earned after the filing of the petition. The power or ability of the debtor to earn wages in the future under a subsisting contract, standing apart from anything which it has brought into existence as property, is the mere right of the debtor to create property in the future. One dominant purpose of the bankruptcy statute is to prevent creditors from seizing, directly or indirectly, upon this right of the bankrupt, after his adjudication, by applying its subsequent fruits to anterior obligations. This right of the bankrupt falls neither under the head of lands, chattels nor choses in action, and it is not vendible. It is not subject to seizure on execution at law, or equitable attachment, and equity will not appoint a receiver to intercept the expected fruits of its exercise. Specific performance of a contract as to future personal services will not be decreed. In a broad sense, the right of a man to render personal services under an existing contract may be said to be his property; but the nature of the right is such that no one can compel him to exercise it, or get title to or lien upon it. The law, except as a punishment for crime, can never take this right away from a man, or confer any property in the right itself upon another man. It can affect the right only by dealing with the property it brings into existence. Whether it can then be taken depends upon the man's status at the time, and whether the law then gives a remedy for the enforcement of his contract concerning the thing his labor has brought into existence. The debtor's right to earn wages in the future and to dispose of the fruits of his labor is not 'property' in any sense in which the bankruptcy statute uses the term, but constitute rather rights and privileges which go to make up a man's liberty and freedom. The plain purpose of the statute is that the title and right to all things and rights which do not fall within the vesting words of § 70 of the bankruptcy statute (30 Stat. 565 [U. S. Comp. St. 1901, p. 3451]) shall remain in the bankrupt, and that as to the rights or things thus saved to him he shall be released from all liability to answer for prior debts and contracts, with certain exceptions not here material. The right of the debtor to work and contract for future service is not mentioned, directly or inferentially, in the rights or things required to be sold, appraised or scheduled, or which pass to the trustee for the benefit of creditors. The studied enumeration of the particular rights and things which the bankrupt is required to surrender takes all other rights and things not named without the definition, thus fixed, of the 'property' which the statute intends to take from the bankrupt or to pass to his creditors. Whatever he is not required to surrender is his absolutely, freed from the enforcement of the obligation of his prior contracts, unless at the time of the filing of the petition it has taken the form of property, upon which a lien has fastened. In that event only does he take it subject to the performance of prior contracts concerning it. If a debtor should solemnly contract for a present valuable consideration not to avail himself of the benefit of a discharge against the enforcement of a contract as to wages to be earned when they do actually come into existence his undertaking would be void on grounds of public policy. Nelson v. Stewart, 54 Ala. 115, 25 Am. Rep. 660. Equity, therefore, cannot import into the obligation of the assignment any promise of the assignor, upon which to build an equity to the lien, that the power will be exercised after the adjudication, to bring wages into existence to satisfy the terms of a prior assignment, or that the bankrupt will not avail himself of a release from the obligation, when it is sought to enforce it after his discharge. The adjudication of a debtor, followed by a discharge, takes away all remedy for the enforcement of the obligation of the contract

concerning wages earned after his bankruptcy, precisely as the discharge releases
the debtor from the performance of the obligation of his promissory note
made prior to the adjudication."

In re Lineberry, 25 A. B. R. 164, 183 Fed. 338 (D. C. Ala.): "An assignment
of wages to be earned in the future is at most an executory agreement to transfer them when earned. It creates no lien on them, except when and as they
come into existence by being earned. At the date of the adjudication, subsequent wages of the bankrupt had not been earned and were not in existence,
and the creditor had no lien on or title to them by virtue of his assignment,
which the bankruptcy law could preserve. The bankruptcy law does not continue a dischargeable debt for the purpose of permitting a lien to be created
after the adjudication, but only to preserve and enforce a lien in existence at
the date of the adjudication. The discharge, when granted, relates back to the
date of adjudication, and property acquired by the bankrupt, intervening the
filing of the petition and the granting of the discharge, is not appropriated to
payment of his debts."

But where, by the state law, an assignment of a contract to be performed
by the assignor in the future will pass future accruals thereunder as of the
date of the original assignment, undoubtedly the future accruals resulting
from the continued performance of the contract will pass to the assignee
thereof and the assignor's trustee in bankruptcy will take no title thereto,
except, of course, in so far as the original assignment might or might not
itself be defeasible as being a preference or a fraudulent transfer, etc., at
the time it was made.[69]

An interesting example arises in cases of assignments of wages to be
earned in the future under a contract of employment existing at the time of
the bankruptcy. Two questions are involved in such cases: First, is the
assignment void as to the trustee in bankruptcy? Second, is it discharged
as to the bankrupt himself? The assignment certainly is not void as to the
trustee, for the contract of employment, being a contract for personal
services would not be an asset of the estate as to future earnings thereunder
even if not previously assigned.[70] It is not dischargeable as to the bankrupt,
because at the time of the bankruptcy it was merely a contract and not a
debt (discharge barring "provable debts" and "debts" only); nor is it a
contract that had become, by virtue of the bankruptcy itself, merged in a
provable debt. This is so, obviously, because, at the time of the bankruptcy,
suit could not have been brought thereon, nor by virtue of the bankruptcy
did the assignor become incapable of carrying out his contract. In fact, the
hypothesis itself is that he did in fact continue to carry it out after the
bankruptcy.[71]

---

69. In re DeLong Fur. Co., 26 A. B.
R. 469, 188 Fed. 686 (D. C. Pa.).

70. Compare, to this effect, In re
Driggs, 22 A. B. R. 621, 171 Fed. 897
(D. C. N. Y.).

71. Mallin v. Wenham, 13 A. B. R.
210, 209 Ills. 252. For this entire subject, see post, § 2662, et seq., "Dis-

charge;" "Effect of Discharge on the
Rights of the Parties." Also, see post,
§ 1150.

Employer, as also Assignee. Adverse Claimants as to Assigned Wages,
Not to Be Proceeded against Summarily.—See post, §§ 1678, 1683.

Johnson *v.* Donahue, 83 N. W. 360 (Tenn. 1906): "Where an insolvent prior to bankruptcy assigns a right to receive certain funds from a railway company thereafter to accrue under a contract in consideration of a pre-existing debt the assignee of said claim is entitled to enforce his right to such subsequently accruing fund."

Citizens Loan Ass'n *v.* Boston & Maine R. R., 19 A. B. R. 650, 196 Mass. 528: "The single question presented by this appeal is whether an assignment of wages to be earned in an existing employment, given before bankruptcy, without fraud, and upon sufficient consideration, to secure a valid subsisting debt, and duly recorded, can be enforced, after the discharge in bankruptcy of the assignor, as to wages earned in the course of the original employment, by the creditor, who has not proved his debt in bankruptcy. A debt is not extinguished by a discharge in bankruptcy. The remedy upon the debt, and the legal, but not the moral, obligation to pay, is at an end. The obligation itself is not cancelled. * * * An assignment of future earnings, which may accrue under an existing employment, is a valid contract and creates rights, which may be enforced both at law and in equity, whichever may in a particular case be the appropriate forum. * * * These cases proceed upon the theory that the worker under contract for service, though indefinite as to time and compensation and terminable at will, has an actual and real interest in wages to be earned in the future by virtue of his contract. He may recover for an unjustifiable interference with such an employment, as for an injury to any other vested property right. * * * It is plain that one may sell wool to be grown upon his own sheep or a crop to be produced upon his own land, but not that to be grown or produced upon the sheep or land of another. No more can one assign wages, where there is no contract for service. * * * But profitable employment is a reality. Wages to be earned by virtue of an existing employment are no more shadowy or unsubstantial than the fleece of next spring or the crop of the following autumn. Money to accrue from such service is not a bare expectancy or mere possibility, but a substance capable of grasp and delivery. It constitutes a present, existing, right of property, which may be sold or assigned as any other property. Although not in the manual possession of the assignor, it is in his potential possession. The transfer of this potential possession, creates the assignee a lienor upon the property right. The holder of such an assignment stands upon a firmer plane than the mortgagee of future acquired property, who has only the right by contract to act betimes in the future for his protection. * * * The assignee of wages to be earned under an existing contract gets a present right, perfect in itself, requiring no future action on his part. * * * It may be taken for granted that the right to future wages to be earned under such a contract does not pass to the trustee in bankruptcy. * * * It is possible that an agreement to execute an assignment, falling short of the creation of a lien, is, when the wages have been actually earned, enforceable in equity, even after a subsequent bankruptcy, or insolvency. We do not decide this, however. * * * At lowest the assignment in question became 'a specific equitable lien on the fund' or was 'an independent collateral agreement given by way of guaranty or other security' for the main debt, and there is no reason why such an agreement should not outlive the remedy upon the debt, to secure which it was given. In either event it was not dissolved by the bankruptcy."

However, statutes providing for an effective levy upon salary to the extent of a certain per cent in favor of certain classes of creditors have been held not to give such a lien upon the entire contract of employment as to appropriate to the judgment salary earned after adjudication, notwithstanding the statutes provide that the levy shall continue until the entire judgment be satisfied.[72]

§ 451½. Adjudication of Corporation Not a "Dissolution" of It.—
The adjudication of a corporation is not a "dissolution" of it.

Nat'l Surety Co. *v.* Medlock, 19 A. B. R. 654, 2 Ga. App. 665: "A corporation by being adjudicated bankrupt, is not thereby civilly dead. It is not thereby dissolved. Holland *v.* Heyman, 60 Ga. 181. To use the sententious language of Judge Bleckley in the case just cited: '"Your money," not "your life," is the demand made by the Bankruptcy Act.'"

---

72. See § 1035; also § 2678½. See post, § 2678½; In re Sims, 23 A. B. R. 899, 176 Fed. 645 (D. C. N. Y.), quoted at § 2678½.

CHAPTER XV.

The Bankrupt—His Duties and Rights of Protection From Arrest and for Stay of Suits.

Synopsis of Chapter.

§ 452. Adjudication Establishes Status of Debtor as Bankrupt.—

By the adjudication, then, the status of the debtor as a bankrupt becomes established.

§ 453. When Begins and When Ceases to Be a "Bankrupt."—The

term "bankrupt," however, may include a debtor against whom a petition is pending, before adjudication thereon.[1]   The term "bankrupt" is applicable to a debtor so long as his bankruptcy proceedings are pending in any of their branches.[2]   After discharge has been granted, at any rate if the estate also be wound up, the debtor properly ceases to be a "bankrupt."   But if a petition to revoke a discharge or set aside a composition is pending he is still a bankrupt.[3]

Elsewhere, under appropriate titles, but not as a connected subject, are considered the different relations the bankrupt sustains to his creditors and their trustee, to third parties and to the court, and certain of the duties devolving upon him by virtue thereof.

DIVISION 1.

DUTIES OF THE BANKRUPT.

§ 454. Statutory Duties of Bankrupt.—The Act itself has attempted in § 7 to summarize the duties of the bankrupt and to specify them; and it is apprehended that the terms used by the statute in so doing are so broad that they embrace most, although not all, the duties growing out of those relations.[4]   These statutory duties are eight in number.

§ 455. First Statutory Duty—Attendance.—The bankrupt must attend the first meeting of his creditors, if directed by the court or a judge thereof to do so; and the hearing upon his application for a discharge, if filed.[5]

§ 456. Corporation Officers "Bankrupts."—In cases of corporation bankrupts, the officers and members of the corporation are for certain purposes at any rate, "the bankrupts;" thus, for the purpose of preparing schedules and as being subject to summary jurisdiction.[6]

§ 457. Order Requisite to Procure Attendance at Creditors' Meetings but Not on Discharge Hearing.—It is requisite that an order be made for his attendance at the first meeting as well as at all other meetings of creditors.[7]   But such prior order is not requisite to procure his attendance at the hearing on his discharge.[8]

---

1. Bankr. Act, § 1 (4): "'Bankrupt' shall include a person against whom an involuntary petition or an application to set a composition aside or to revoke a discharge has been filed, or who has filed a voluntary petition or who has been adjudged a bankrupt." In re Larkin, 21 A. B. R. 711, 168 Fed. 100 (D. C. N. Y.).   See post, § 473.

2. Impliedly, In re Chandler, 13 A. B. R. 614 (D. C. Ills.).   See post, §§ 473, 2497.

3. In re Chandler, 13 A. B. R. 614 (D. C. Ills.).   See post, § 473.

4. In re Dow, 5 A. B. R. 401, 105 Fed. 889 (D. C. Iowa).

5. Bankr. Act, § 7 (a) (1); In re Eagles & Crisp, 3 A. B. R. 734, 99 Fed. 695 (D. C. N. Car.).

6. In re Alphin & Lake Cotton Co., 12 A. B. R. 653, 131 Fed. 824 (D. C. Ark.).

7. Obiter, Inferentially, In re Shanker, 15 A. B. R. 109, 138 Fed. 862 (D. C. Pa.).

8. In re Shanker, 15 A. B. R. 109, 138 Fed. 862 (D. C. Pa.).   Ante, § 455.

§ 458. Second Statutory Duty—Obedience.—The bankrupt must comply with all lawful orders of the court.[9] Disobedience of this duty is ground for barring the bankrupt's discharge.[10]

§ 459. Third, Sixth and Seventh Statutory Duties—Examination of Claims and Reporting of Frauds, etc.—The bankrupt must examine the correctness of all proofs of claim filed against the estate; must immediately inform his trustee of any attempt, by his creditors or other person, to evade the provisions of this act, coming to his knowledge; and in case any person. has to his knowledge proved a false claim against his estate, must disclose that fact immediately to his trustee.[11]

§ 460. Fourth and Fifth Statutory Duties—Execution of Papers. —The bankrupt must execute and deliver such papers as shall be ordered by the court; and must execute to his trustee transfers of all his property in foreign countries.[12]

§ 461. Eighth Statutory Duty—Schedules.—The bankrupt must prepare and file his schedules.[13] The requirements of this duty are considered elsewhere under the subjects of the Schedules[13a] and of Discharge, "Due Scheduling"[13b] and "Concealment" and "False Oath" by omissions from schedules.[13c]

Amendment of 1910—Compositions before Adjudication.—By the Amendment of 1910, permitting compositions before adjudication of bankruptcy, it is made the duty of the bankrupt, in such cases, to file schedules, precisely as in cases of adjudication.[13d]

§ 462. Ninth Statutory Duty—Submission to Examination.—The bankrupt must submit to examination, when present at the first meeting of creditors and at such other times as the court shall order, concerning the conducting of his business, the cause of his bankruptcy, his dealings with his creditors and other persons, the amount, kind and whereabouts of his property, and in addition, all matters which may affect the administration and settlement of his estate.[14]

---

9. Bankr. Act, § 7 (a) (2).

10. See post, subject of the bankrupt's discharge, § 2580.

11. Bankr. Act, § 7 (3) (6) (7). Inferentially. In re Carton. 17 A. B. R. 250, 148 Fed. 63 (D. C. N. Y.).

12. Bankr. Act, § (7), (a). (4) and (5). See post, §§ 969, 1009, 1115, 1835.

13. Bankr. Act, § 7 (a) (8). Obiter, In re Goodman, 23 A. B. R. 504, 174 Fed. 644 (C. C. A. Ala.).

13a. See post, § 476, et seq.

13b. See post, § 2761, et seq.

13c. See post, §§ 2502, 2542.

13d. Bankr. Act, § 12a: "* * * in compositions before adjudication, the bankrupt shall file the required schedules, etc." Also, see §§ 482½, 593½, 2358, et seq.

14. Bankr. Act, § 7 (a) (9). Compare, also, Bankr. Act, § 21 (a).

Habeas Corpus ad Testificandum.—See post, §§ 1568½, 1570.

DIVISION 2.

PROTECTION OF BANKRUPT FROM ARREST.

§ 463. Protection of Bankrupt from Arrest.—A bankrupt is exempt from arrest upon civil process except: First, when issued from the court of bankruptcy itself for contempt or disobedience of its lawful orders; and, second, when issued from a state court upon a claim which would not be released by his discharge in bankruptcy, and even then he shall be exempt from arrest whilst in attendance on the court of bankruptcy or engaged in the performance of a duty imposed by the bankruptcy act.[15]

In re Adler, 16 A. B. R. 416, 144 Fed. 659 (C. C. A. N. Y.): "It is the obvious scheme of the law to protect the bankrupt during the pendency of the proceedings from being harassed by process issuing from the State courts in civil actions. His presence may be required at any time before the court or referee, and § 7 (30 Stat. 548 [U. S. Comp. St. 1901, p. 3424]), defining the duties of bankrupts, directs him to perform acts which practically require his presence within call of the court at all times during the pendency of the proceedings. It is manifest that it will be impossible for him to comply with 'all lawful orders of the court' if he be required at the same time to obey the orders of the State court, and, a fortiori, if he be actually imprisoned on civil process, issued out of the State court. The Bankruptcy Act could not be administered under such conditions."

§ 464. Protected if Debt Dischargeable—Otherwise, Not.—Where the debt is dischargeable he is exempt from arrest.[16] Where the debt is not dischargeable, however, the bankrupt is not exempt, and may be arrested in

---

15. Bankr. Act, § 9 (a). Compare, as to practice, Gen. Order No. 30. And compare, Ex rel Mansfield v. Flynn, 23 A. B. R. 294, 179 Fed. 316 (D. C. N. Y.), quoted at § 470.

Arrest Permissible on Process in State Insolvency Proceedings Where Debtor Not Adjudged Bankrupt, unless State Insolvency Law Superseded by Bankruptcy Act.—In re Crawford, 18 A. B. R. 618, 154 Fed. 769 (C. C. A. Pa., affirming Johnson v. Crawford, 18 A. B. R. 608, 154 Fed. 761); Johnson v. Crawford, 18 A. B. R. 608, 154 Fed. 761 (C. C. Pa., affirmed sub nom. In re Crawford, supra).

16. In re Baker, 3 A. B. R. 101, 98 Fed. 710 (D. C. Kas.); In re Houston, 2 A. B. R. 107, 94 Fed. 119 (D. C. Ky., affirmed sub nom. Wagner v. U. S., 4 A. B. R. 596, 104 Fed. 133, C. C. A.); In re Wenman, 16 A. B. R. 690, 153 Fed. 910 (D. C. N. Y.), which was a case of conversion of proceeds of sale of tickets by passenger ticket agent. In re Fife, 6 A. B. R. 258, 109 Fed.

880 (D. C. Pa.), which was an arrest on a judgment for breach of promise to marry. In re Adler, 16 A. B. R. 416, 144 Fed. 659 (C. C. A. N. Y.); People v. Erlanger, 13 A. B. R. 197, 132 Fed. 883 (D. C. N. Y.).

Barrett v. Prince, 16 A. B. R. 64, 143 Fed. 302 (C. C. A. Ills.). This was a case of a stockholder's alleged conversion of stock for failure to follow instruction—not "embezzlement," "fraud nor fiduciary capacity."

Compare, In re Lorde, 16 A. B. R. 201, 144 Fed. 320 (D. C. N. Y.), where a judgment against a landlord for bite of tenant's vicious dog was held dischargeable and the bankrupt protected.

Also compare, Wagner v. U. S., 4 A. B. R. 596, 104 Fed. 133 (C. C. A. Ky., affirming In re Houston, 2 A. B. R. 107), where habeas corpus was granted in arrest for contempt for failure to pay alimony. This was, however, before the rule was definitely settled that alimony was not a dischargeable debt.

cases where arrest is allowed by State law on civil process where there is no bankruptcy.[17]

§ 465. Arrest before Bankruptcy—Protection Equally Available.

—But one arrested for debt is entitled to his liberty, upon filing subsequently a petition in bankruptcy. The protection of the statute applies to arrest before as well as after the filing of the bankrupcty petition and prevents a continuance of the detention.[18]

§ 466. Duty of Court to Protect.

—And it is the duty of the court to issue the stay if the debt is dischargeable.[19]

§ 467. May Be Arrested upon Criminal Charge.

—The bankrupt may be arrested at any time upon a criminal charge.[20]

§ 468. No Exemption from Arrest for Contempt of Bankruptcy Court Itself.

—The bankrupt may be arrested for contempt of the bankruptcy court or for disobedience of its lawful orders.[21] Thus, a bankrupt may be fined for contempt for surrendering property to a creditor after his petition is filed.[22]

§ 469. Whether Arrest for Contempt of Other Courts within Protection.

—It is a question whether the bankrupt is exempt from arrest for

17. Kavanaugh v. McIntyre, 27 A. B. R. 279 (Sup. Ct. N. Y.); In re Marcus, 5 A. B. R. 365 (C. C. A. Mass., affirming 5 A. B. R. 19, 104 Fed. 331); In re Baker, 3 A. B. R. 101, 96 Fed. 954 (D. C. Kas.). Judgment for support of illegitimate child. Distinguished, In re Lewensohn, 3 A. B. R. 598, 99 Fed. 73 (D. C. N. Y.). Judgments for libel, Thompson v. Judy, 22 A. B. R. 151, 169 Fed. 553 (C. C. A. Ky.). Compare, Peters v. U. S. ex rel. Kelley, 24 A. B. R. 206, 177 Fed. 885.
Subsequent discharge of judgment debtor in bankruptcy is no defense to a pending action against the sheriff for permitting the escape of the judgment debtor who had been arrested on body execution. Baer v. Grell, 6 A. B. R. 428 (Mun. Ct. N. Y.).
18. People v. Erlanger, 13 A. B. R. 197, 132 Fed. 883 (D. C. N. Y.); [1867] In re Seymour, 1 Ben. 348, Fed. Cases 12,684; compare, to same effect. In re Grist. 1 A. B. R. 89 (Ref. N. Y.); contra, In re Claiborne. 5 A. B. R. 812, 109 Fed. 74 (D. C. N. Y.); [1867] also contra, In re Walker, Fed. Cases 17,060; [1867] also contra, Minon v. Van Nostrand, 1 Low 458, Fed. Cases 9,642. Turgeon v. Emery, 25 A. B. R. 694, 182 Fed. 1016 (D. C. Me.).
19. In re Adler, 16 A. B. R. 416, 144 Fed. 659 (C. C. A. N. Y.).

Whether Conditions May Be Imposed on Granting the Protection.—It has been held, that the Bankruptcy Court may, in granting such protection from arrest impose conditions on the bankrupt, such as that he shall not leave the jurisdiction and shall give bond to that effect. In re Lewensohn, 3 A. B. R. 594, 99 Fed. 73 (D. C. N. Y.). Contra, and that no bond may be required, Ex rel Kelley v. Peters, 22 A. B. R. 777, 166 Fed. 613 (D. C. Ill.), reversed on other grounds. Peters v. U. S. ex rel Kelley. 24 A. B. R. 206, 117 Fed. 885 (C. C. A. Ills., reversing U. S. ex rel. Kelley v. Peters, 22 A. B. R. 177, 166 Fed. 613), wherein the appellate court held a judgment against a school teacher for assault not to be dischargeable and the teacher not to be within the protection of the act.
20. Compare, as to arrest for fraudulent insolvency proceedings under State insolvency law superseded by the Bankrupt Act. U. S. ex. rel. Scott v. McAleese, 1 A. B. R. 650 (C. C. A. Penn.).
21. In re Arnett, 7 A. B. R. 522, 112 Fed. 770 (D. C. Tenn.). See also, post, subject of ordering bankrupts to surrender property, § 1813, et seq.
22. In re Arnett, 7 A. B. R. 522, 112 Fed. 770 (D. C. Tenn.).

contempt of other courts;[23] whether arrest for contempt of court is within the "civil process" meant by this provision of the Bankruptcy Act. It has been held that he may be arrested for contempt for failing to appear in proceedings supplementary to execution.[24]

§ 470. Protected While Attending Bankruptcy Court or Performing Statutory Duties, Whether Debt Dischargeable or Not.

—But a bankrupt may not be arrested, in any event, upon civil process issued upon a debt, where he is at the time in attendance upon the bankruptcy court or engaged in the performance of a statutory duty imposed by the Bankruptcy Act.[25] And this protection applies even where the debt is not dischargeable.[26]

Ex rel Mansfield v. Flynn, 23 A. B. R. 294, 179 Fed. 316 (D. C. N. Y.): "The order was valid regardless of the dischargeability of the debt under § 9 a (2), since the relator was arrested while in attendance on the court and while engaged in the performance of a duty imposed by the act."

§ 471. Whether Protection Applies to Arrest on Process from Federal Court.

—It has been held, that the bankrupt will be protected from arrest upon process issuing from the United States Circuit Court equally as well as when issued from the State Court.[27]

§ 472. Habeas Corpus and Injunction Available to Effect Protection.

—Habeas corpus in the Federal Court will lie to make effective the protection of the bankrupt under this provision.[28]

---

23. Not protected from arrest for contempt of state court's order, instance, In re Hall, 22 A. B. R. 49, 170 Fed. 721 (D. C. N. Y.).

24. In re Fritz, 18 A. B. R. 244 (D. C. N. Y.).

Arrest of Bankrupt for Contempt for Failure to Pay Alimony.—Before the Supreme Court of the United States declared alimony not dischargeable, it was held, in some cases proper to release on habeas corpus a bankrupt imprisoned for contempt in failing to pay alimony. In re Houston, 2 A. B. R. 107, 94 Fed. 119 (D. C. Ky., affirmed in 4 A. B. R. 596, rejected in 3 A. B. R. 70, and in 5 A. B. R. 834).

25. In re Lewensohn, 3 A. B. R. 594, 98 Fed. 576 (D. C. N. Y., affirmed in 104 Fed. 1006); In re Dresser, 10 A. B. R. 270, 124 Fed. 915 (D. C. N. Y.); In re Chandler, 13 A. B. R. 614, 135 Fed. 893 (D. C. Ills.); In re Grist, 1 A. B. R. 89 (Ref. N. Y.). Obiter, inferentially, In re Marcus, 5 A. B. R. 365, 105 Fed. 907 (C. C. A. Mass.), Instance, In re Lewensohn, 3 A. B. R. 594, 98 Fed. 576 (D. C. N. Y.), where he was held exempt pending application for discharge.

26. In re Dresser, 10 A. B. R. 270, 124 Fed. 915 (D. C. N. Y.); In re Grist, 1 A. B. R. 89 (Ref. N. Y.); Obiter, inferentially, In re Marcus, 5 A. B. R. 365, 105 Fed. 907 (C. C. A. Mass.).

27. In re Wenman, 16 A. B. R. 961, 153 Fed. 910 (D. C. N. Y.).

28. In re Houston, 2 A. B. R. 107, 94 Fed. 119 (D. C. Ky., affirmed sub nom. Wagner v. U. S., 4 A. B. R. 596). Although occasion for its exercise was doubtful, alimony not being dischargeable. Wagner v. U. S., 4 A. B. R. 596, 104 Fed. 133 (C. C. A. Ky., affirming In re Houston, 2 A. B. R. 107, 94 Fed. 119, D. C. Ky.); In re Fife, 6 A. B. R. 258, 109 Fed. 880 (D. C. Pa.); In re Baker, 3 A. B. R. 101, 96 Fed. 954 (D. C. Kas.); Ex rel. Mansfield v. Flynn, 23 A. B. R. 294, 179 Fed. 316 (D. C. N. Y.), instance, In re Wenman, 16 A. B. R. 690, 153 Fed. 910 (D. C. N. Y.); instance, Ex rel Kelley v. Peters, 22 A. B. R. 177, 166 Fed. 613 (D. C. Ill., reversed, on ground debt not dischargeable, sub nom. Peters v. U. S., ex rel Kelly, 24 A. B. R. 206, 177 Fed. 885 (C. C. A.). But compare, contra, In re Lewensohn, 3 A. B. R. 594, 99

Habeas corpus may not be used as an indirect method of review.[28a]

Peters v. U. S. ex rel. Kelley, 24 A. B. R. 206, 177 Fed. 885 (C. C. A. Ill., reversing U. S. ex rel. Kelley v. Peters, 22 A. B. R. 177, 166 Fed. 613): "And so he was; for a writ of habeas corpus cannot lawfully be used as a means of bringing the original parties into court to relitigate their original controversy —it cannot even be used lawfully to review and revise alleged errors of law or fact in the original litigation. 'No court may properly release a prisoner under conviction and sentence of another court, unless for want of jurisdiction of the cause or person, or for some other matter rendering its proceedings void. Where a court had jurisdiction, mere errors which have been permitted in the course of the proceedings cannot be corrected upon a writ of habeas corpus, which may not in this manner usurp the functions of a writ of error.' Kaizo v. Henry, 211 U. S. 146."

Injunction also will lie to enforce the protection.[29] And the referee may issue the restraining order, if directed against a party and not against a court or officer.[30]

§ 472½. Bond by Bankrupt Not Requisite.

—Where a bankrupt makes application, under Gen. Ord. No. 30 for his release from arrest, the court, neither under § 2 (15) nor under § 9 (b), is authorized to require the bankrupt to give bail.[31]

§ 473. "Bankrupt" for Purposes of Protection, as Long as Any Proceedings Pending.

—For the purpose of this protection one is a "bankrupt" as long as any proceedings in bankruptcy in his case are pending;[32]

Fed. 73 (D. C. N. Y.), impliedly, Barrett v. Prince, 16 A. B. R. 64, 143 Fed. 302 (C. C. A. Ills.); Ex rel. Tarante v. Erlanger, 13 A. B. R. 197, 132 Fed. 883 (D. C. N. Y.); obiter, In re Grist, 1 A. B. R. 89 (Ref. N. Y.). Compare, U. S., ex rel. Scott v. McAleese, 1 A. B. R. 650 (C. C. A. Pa.).

Gen. Order No. 30: "IMPRISONED DEBTOR.—If, at the time of preferring his petition, the debtor shall be imprisoned, the court, upon application, may order him to be produced upon habeas corpus, by the jailor or any officer in whose custody he may be, before the referee, for the purpose of testifying in any matter relating to his bankruptcy; and, if committed after the filing of his petition upon the process in any civil action founded upon a claim provable in bankruptcy, the court may, upon like application discharge him from such imprisonment. If the petitioner, during the pendency of the proceedings in bankruptcy, be arrested or imprisoned upon process in any civil action, the district court upon his application, may issue a writ of habeas corpus to bring him before the court to ascertain whether such process has been issued for the collection of any claim provable in bankruptcy, and if so provable he shall be discharged; if not, he shall be remanded to the custody in which he may lawfully be. Before granting the order for discharge the court shall cause notice to be served upon the creditor or his attorney, so as to give him an opportunity of appearing and being heard before the granting of the order."

28a. Compare, analogously, § 450.

29. In re Adler, 16 A. B. R. 414, 144 Fed. 659 (C. C. A. N. Y.); In re Grist, 1 A. B. R. 89 (Ref. N. Y.).

30. In re Grist, 1 A. B. R. 89 (Ref. N. Y.). Gen. Order XII. In re Siebert, 13 A. B. R. 348, 133 Fed. 781 (D. C. N. J.).

31. Ex rel. Kelley v. Peters, 22 A. B. R. 177, 166 Fed. 613 (D. C. Ill., reversed on ground that debt not dischargeable, sub nom. Peters v. U. S. ex rel. Kelley, 24 A. B. R. 206, 177 Fed. 885, C. C. A.).

32. Impliedly, In re Chandler, 13 A. B. R. 614, 135 Fed. 893 (D. C. Ills.). See ante, § 453.

even after a petition for the revocation of his discharge has been refused, if
review proceedings are pending.[33]

§ 474. **Infliction of Penalty or Forfeiture for Taking Benefit of
Act Prohibited.**—Neither penalty nor forfeiture may be inflicted upon a
debtor for taking the benefit of the Bankrupt Act.[34]

DIVISION 3.

STAYING SUITS AND PROCEEDINGS TO PERMIT BANKRUPT TO PROCURE AND
INTERPOSE DISCHARGE.

§ 475. **Staying Suits to Permit Procuring and Interposing of Discharge.**—The subject of staying lawsuits and proceedings pending the hearing upon the bankrupt's petition for discharge, in order to afford opportunity
for the bankrupt to procure his discharge and to plead it, is considered later,
under the general subject of Discharge.[35]

33. In re Chandler, 13 A. B. R. 614,
135 Fed. 893 (D. C. Ills.). Compare,
collaterally, §§ 453, 2497.
34. In re Hicks, 13 A. B. R. 654, 133
Fed. 739 (D. C. N. Y.), which was
the case of a member of city fire department filing petition in bankruptcy
—proceedings under city ordinance to
collect debt being enjoined.
35. See post, § 2690.

CHAPTER XVI.

SCHEDULES.

Synopsis of Chapter.

§ 476. After Adjudication Voluntary and Involuntary Proceedings Alike Except as to Time of Filing Schedules.—After adjudication of bankruptcy, the subsequent proceedings are precisely alike in both voluntary and involuntary bankruptcies, excepting that the schedules are filed after adjudication in involuntary bankruptcies and before adjudication in voluntary cases; that is to say, the voluntary bankrupt must file his schedules with his petition while the involuntary bankrupt has ten days time after his adjudication within which to file them; otherwise the proceedings are precisely alike.

§ 477. Duty of Bankrupt to File Schedules of Assets, Liabilities and Exemption Claim.—By § 7, clause 8, of the statute, as noted (ante, § 461), it is made one of the duties of the bankrupt to prepare, make oath to and file in court within ten days, unless further time is granted, after the adjudication, if an involuntary bankrupt, and with the petition if a voluntary bankrupt, a schedule of his property, showing the amount and kind of property, the location thereof, its money value in detail, and a list of his creditors, showing their residences if known, if unknown, that fact to be stated, the amounts due each of them, the consideration thereof, the security held by them, if any, and a claim for such exemptions as he may be entitled to, all in triplicate, one copy of each for the clerk, one for the referee and one for the trustee.[1] It is the bankrupt's duty to file them without being ordered to do so.

Obiter, In re Philip Brady, 21 A. B. R. 364, 169 Fed. 152 (D. C. Ky.): "And besides, the Bankruptcy Act expressly requires him to file his schedules without being ruled in the premises."

And failure of the bankrupt to file schedules may be punished as a contempt.[2] But the bankrupt can not be compelled to insert in his schedules matters which may incriminate him.[3]

§ 477½. Individual Schedules Where Firm Alone Bankrupt.—It

has been held that there is no requirement that the individual schedules of each member of the partnership should be filed where the firm alone is adjudicated bankrupt.[4]

But the contrary is the true rule; and non-bankrupt members must file schedules as well as the bankrupt partnership and its bankrupt members.

In re Ceballos & Co., 20 A. B. R. 459, 161 Fed. 445 (D. C. N. J.): " 'Defenses which any debtor proceeded against is entitled to take by the provisions of the act; and in case an adjudication of bankruptcy is made upon the petition, such copartner shall be required to furnish to the marshal, as messenger, a schedule of his debts and an inventory of his property, in the same manner as is required by the act in cases of debtors against whom adjudication of bankruptcy shall be made.' General Order 8 * * *, under the Act of 1898 * * *: 'Any member of a partnership, who refuses to join in a petition to have the partnership declared bankrupt, shall be entitled to resist the prayer of the petition in the same manner as if the petition had been filed by a creditor of the partnership, and notice of the filing of the petition shall be given to him in the same manner as provided by law and by these rules in the case of a debtor petitioned against; and he shall have the right to appear at the time fixed by the court for the hearing of the petition, and to make proof, if he can, that the partnership is not insolvent or has not committed an act of bankruptcy, and to make all defenses which any debtor proceeded against is entitled to take by the provisions of the act; and in case an adjudication of bankruptcy is made upon the petition, such partner shall be required to file a schedule of his debts and an inventory of his property in the same manner as is required by the act in cases of debtors against whom adjudication of bankruptcy shall be made.' Under the Act of 1867 a partnership was not re-

---

1. Haack v. Theise, 16 A. B. R. 700, 51 Misc. (N. Y.) 3.
2. In re Fetterman, 17 A. B. R. 785 (D. C. N. Y.); In re Schulman & Goldstein, 20 A. B. R. 707, 164 Fed. 440 (D. C. N. Y.).
3. In re Podolin, 29 A. B. R. 406,

193 Fed. 1020 (C. C. A. Pa.) quoted at § 482¼.
4. Compare, §§ 65, 2231; also, In re Blanchard & Howard, 20 A. B. R. 422, 161 Fed. 797 (D. C. N. C.); to same effect, In re Bertenshaw, 19 A. B. R. 577, 157 Fed. 363 (C. C. A.).

garded as a legal entity in the sense in which the courts regard it under the Act of 1898. Although General Order 18 referred to the procedure in a case where one or more members of a copartnership refused to join a petitioning partner in a petition to have 'the firm declared bankrupt,' the only way of obtaining an adjudication against a 'firm' under the Act of 1867 was by having all the copartners so adjudged. This is clearly shown by the provisions of that act. Section 11 provided that in a voluntary case the petitioner should annex to his petition a verified schedule of his debts and an inventory of his property; § 42 provided that in an involuntary case the bankrupt should file such schedule and inventory; and § 36 provided that where two or more persons being partners in trade should be adjudged bankrupt 'all the joint stock and property of the copartnership, and also all the separate estate of each of the partners,' should be taken, excepting the parts by that act exempted from seizure. General Order 18 provided a method for enforcing the act in partnership cases, where a petition was filed by less than all the partners. It required each non-joining partner, where the 'firm'—that is, all the partners—were adjudged bankrupt, to furnish 'a schedule of his debts and an inventory of his property in the same manner as is required by the act in cases of debtors against whom adjudication of bankruptcy shall be made.' I think General Order 8 has the same effect."

In re Junck & Balthazard, 22 A. B. R. 298, 169 Fed. 481 (D. C. Wis.): "He must file his schedules of individual property and individual debts as provided by General Order No. 8. This is not an arbitrary regulation, but is inherent in the very nature of the case. Neither is it new. General Order No. 18, under the Act of 1867, was substantially the same. If Balthazard has a surplus of assets after the discharge of his individual liabilities, such surplus must be devoted to the payment of the firm liabilities if the firm assets are insufficient for that purpose. In other words, such surplus must be, considered an asset of the firm, and no settlement can be complete without the information sought to be derived from the individual schedules contemplated by General Order No. 8. The objecting partner may prevent his own adjudication, but he cannot escape an accounting which is necessary to facilitate the jurisdiction of the court over the partnership case."

§ 478. If Bankrupt Fails to File, Petitioning Creditors or Referee to Prepare.

—If the bankrupt is out of the jurisdiction or his whereabouts is unknown or he refuses or fails to prepare schedules, the court may order the petitioning creditors to prepare schedules, or the referee may prepare them himself.[5]

So, since the Amendment of 1910, the bankruptcy court may enter an order directing the institution of ancillary proceedings to compel one residing outside the district to file the required schedules.[6]

§ 479. Duty of Referee to Examine Schedules and Require Amendment.

—It is the duty of the referee to examine the schedules of property and lists of creditors and to cause such as are incomplete or de-

---

5. In case the bankrupt fails to prepare schedules within the ten days limited and the referee himself prepares them in consequence, the bankrupt must not complain that all creditors were not notified of the first meeting. In re Schiller, 2 A. B. R. 704, 96 Fed. 403 (D. C. Va.).

6. Compare post, §§ 1570, 1709½; also see In re Brockton, etc., Co., 29 A. B. R. 76, 200 Fed. 745 (C. C. A. Mass.).

fective to be amended.[7] And it is the referee's duty to require amendment
of defective schedules whether any creditor moves to that effect or not.[8]

§ 480. Officers of Corporation to Prepare Schedules.

—In cases of
bankrupt corporations, the officers and members of the corporation are "the
bankrupts" for the purpose of preparing the schedules, etc., and must prepare the schedules.[9] And should such officers reside outside of the district,
they may be reached by ancillary proceedings.[10]

§ 481. Schedules to Be Filed with Petition, in Voluntary Cases.

—
In voluntary cases the bankrupt must file his schedules with his petition.[11]

§ 482. Within Ten Days after Adjudication, in Involuntary Cases.

—In involuntary cases the bankrupt must file his schedules within ten days
after the adjudication, unless longer time is granted by the court.[12]

§ 482¼. Contempt for Failure to File.

—It may be contempt for the
bankrupt to fail to file his schedules.[13] But the failure to set out matter which
might incriminate the bankrupt is not a contempt.

In re Podolin, 29 A. B. R. 406, 193 Fed. 1021 (C. C. A. Pa.): "As a general proposition, the referee's ruling that the bankrupts must file schedules, so far as they can do so without incriminating themselves, is obviously correct. But, until an effort is made to comply with his order, it is
practically impossible for the court to decide whether a particular fact is
to be included or omitted. To decide that a bankrupt is not bound to put
his hand to a declaration of fact that may incriminate him, does not advance
a particular dispute very much; what is required is an effort in good faith by
the bankrupt to file a schedule that obeys the Act up to the point where the
court can see that further obedience would violate the constitutional protection. When the bankrupts present such schedules as they can conscientiously declare to be a compliance with the order (saving their constitutional
rights), the referee will then be able, either to order them to do specific acts
or to approve the refusal to do them; and in either event the District Court
will then have something definite to rule upon. Until such a situation is
presented, the discussion is almost wholly academic."

§ 482½. Compositions before Adjudication—Amendment of 1910.

—The Amendment of 1910, permitting compositions before adjudication of
bankruptcy, provides that in such cases the bankrupt shall file schedules as
a basis upon which action may be taken by creditors.[13a]

---

7. Bankr. Act, § 39 (a) (2). In re
Mackey & Co., 1 A. B. R. 593 (Ref.
N. Y.). See post, § 508.
8. In re Mackey, 1 A. B. R. 593 (Ref.
N. Y.).
9. Bankr. Act, § 1 (19). In re Alphin & Lake Cotton Co., 12 A. B. R.
654, 131 Fed. 824 (D. C. Ark.).
10. Compare post, § 1705, et seq.;
also see In re Brockton, etc., Co., 29 A.
B. R. 76, 200 Fed. 745 (C. C. A. Mass.).
11. Bankr. Act, § 7 (8). See ante,
§ 476.

12. Bankr. Act, § 7 (8). See ante,
§ 476.
13. In re Schulman & Goldstein, 20
A. B. R. 707, 164 Fed. 440 (D. C. N.
Y.); In re Fetterman, 19 A. B. R. 785
(D. C. N. Y.).
13a. Bankr. Act, § 12a: "A bankrupt
may offer, either before or after adjudication, terms of composition to his
creditors after, but not before, he has
been examined in open court or at a
meeting of his creditors, and has filed

§ 483. Importance of Schedules in Bankruptcy.—The schedules play an important part in bankruptcy. Oftentimes the bankrupt's right to his discharge turns upon the point whether he has or has not made a full and truthful exposition of his assets and liabilities in his schedules. The schedules are supposed to be the statement of the bankrupt to his creditors, and he runs great risk of forfeiting his opportunity to get released from his debts if he makes omissions or misstatements in them.[14]

However, it must not be understood that the scheduling of an asset is essential to the passing of its title to the trustee, nor that the scheduling of a liability is essential to the right of the creditor to participate in the proceedings. The scheduling is merely a part of the most important duty devolving upon the bankrupt, namely, that of giving full information concerning his assets and liabilities. Therefore, assets that ought to have been scheduled by the bankrupt as belonging to the estate, nevertheless pass to the trustee although not scheduled, and the bankrupt does not retain title to them by omitting them from his schedules.[15]

§ 484. Requirements in General.—The statute provides for three different things: 1st, A schedule of assets; 2nd, a list of creditors; and 3rd, a claim for exemptions. Section 30 of the statute provides that all necessary rules, forms and orders as to procedure and for carrying the Act into force and effect shall be prescribed and may be amended from time to time, by the Supreme Court of the United States. In conformity with this command, the Supreme Court has prescribed various orders and official forms; and whilst these orders and forms are not held. to be parts of the statute, for of course Congress could not thus delegate its lawmaking power, yet they are in effect, held to be, virtually, interpretations of the Statute; decisions in advance, as it were, as to what the statute means by its various regulations of procedure.

Thus, as to the prescribed schedule of assets, called Schedule "B" in the forms (for the official forms are not lettered in the same order in which the statutory requirements occur, else it would be schedule "A"), there are only four requisites mentioned in the statute itself; which are that the schedule shall show, 1st, the kind of property; 2nd, its quantity (or as the statute puts it, its amount); 3rd, the location of the property; 4th, its money value in detail; but, while these are the only things required by the words of the statute to be shown by the bankrupt on his schedule of property, yet the official form of this schedule, called Schedule "B," requires a great partic-

---

in court the schedule of his property and the list of his creditors required to be filed by bankrupts. In. compositions before adjudication the bankrupt shall file the required schedules, etc."

14. Whether Schedules Are "Pleadings."—See Johnson v. United States, 20 A. B. R. 724, 163 Fed. 30 (C. C. A. Mass.), quoted at § 2323.

15. Rand v. Iowa Central Railway Co., 12 A. B. R. 164, 96 App. Div. 413 (N. Y. Sup. Ct. App. Div.), instance, In re Kranich, 23 A. B. R. 550, 174 Fed. 908 (D. C. Pa.). See post, § 1113.

ularity of statement in complying with the statutory requirements. Thus, Schedule "B" of assets is subdivided into Schedule B (1), taken up with a statement of the real estate; B (2), with personal property; B (3), with choses in action; B (4), with property in reversion, remainder or expectancy, including property held in trust for the debtor, etc.; B (5) is concerned with the bankrupt's claim for exemptions; and B (6) with books, papers, documents, etc. And each of these subdivisions is again subdivided, so as to require in the end a full and complete statement by the bankrupt of his property. A proper idea of the requirements of Schedule "B" of assets, is best obtained by an inspection of the blank form itself.

Likewise with the "list of creditors" which the bankrupt is required to supply. This list of creditors is named Schedule "A" in the official forms, and is subdivided into Schedule "A" (1), which is taken up with priority claims, such as taxes, wages of workmen and the like; Schedule "A" (2), taken up with a list of secured creditors; Schedule "A" (3), covering creditors whose claims are unsecured; Schedule "A" (4), which contains a list of claims on notes and bills of third parties which the bankrupt has discounted and which the third parties ought to pay, such as customer's paper discounted at bank; and Schedule "A" (5), for accommodation paper signed by the bankrupt.

Securities held by creditors should be scheduled in Schedule "B" of assets, as well as in Schedule "A" of secured debts.[16] Exempt property should be scheduled both as assets and also in Schedule "B" (5) as property claimed to be exempt.

The following points are useful for the practitioner to observe; and are required either by the law or rules, or by the dictates of good practice:

§ 485. Notation to Be Made against Each Item.—Each separate item in the printed schedules should contain some sort of notation against it, to make sure that there has been no unintentional omission, for it will not do simply to make entries under the appropriate headings and opposite the items for the particular species of property owned or kind of debt actually owed, leaving the remaining headings and items without entries. Where there is none of a particular kind of property or debt called for by a particular item, the entry "none" or some similar entry should be made.

§ 486. Ditto Marks and Abbreviations to Be Avoided.—Ditto marks should be avoided.[17] Likewise, abbreviations except such as are in common use.[18]

Obiter, Sutherland v. Lasher, 11 A. B. R. 780, 41 Misc. 249 (Sup. Ct. N. Y.): "If it were necessary to pass upon the point it would also have to be

16. See inferentially, Jacquith v. Rowley, 9 A. B. R. 525, 188 U. S. 620, wherein the court holds, that property held as security is to be considered as part of the assets in ascertaining the solvency of the bankrupt.

17. In re Mackey, 1 A. B. R. 593 (Ref. N. Y.).

18. Gen. Ord. V. Frame of Petitions.—"All petitions and the schedules filed therewith shall be printed or written out plainly, without abbrevi-

held that the words 'residence, 135 Bway,' are not a sufficient designation of any residence, being in plain violation of the rules established by the United States Supreme Court governing the form of petitions and schedules."

§ 487. Signature and Oath.

—Each page must be signed by the bankrupt; and an oath must be made at the end of Schedule "A" and one at the end of Schedule "B," to the effect that the schedules contain all the bankrupt's debts and all his assets respectively; the form of which oath is also prescribed by the Supreme Court.

Perhaps the oath need not be signed by the bankrupt. It has been held that the oaths to the schedules in a voluntary petition need not be signed by the bankrupt, if the petition itself is properly verified and the officer before whom the oath is taken certifies that it is taken by the bankrupt.[19]

§ 488. To Be Filed in Triplicate, Both in Voluntary and in Involuntary Cases.

—These schedules must be prepared in triplicate, one for the clerk to keep on file, one for the referee, and one for the trustee, who will need it in his work. Of course there need be only one petition in the case of a voluntary bankrupt and only two, as we have seen, in the case of an involuntary bankrupt, but in both voluntary and involuntary bankruptcies the number of copies of the schedules is always the same—three.

§ 489. Names and Addresses of Creditors to Be Given.

—The names and addresses of all creditors must be given as accurately as possible;[20] and if the addresses are not known, that fact must be stated.[21]

Where the addresses of none of the creditors are known, some showing should be made to the court that diligent effort has been made to ascertain the same.

In re Dvorak, 6 A. B. R. 66, 68, 107 Fed. 76 (D. C. Iowa): "The act requires the bankrupt to furnish a list of creditors and their addresses, and in cases like the present, when the bankrupt gives a list of creditors, but states that their addresses are unknown, the referee should require the addresses to be furnished, or satisfactory proof to be made that the same cannot be ascertained after due search had been made."

Where any address is unknown the fact must be stated.

Sutherland v. Lasher, 11 A. B. R. 781 (Sup. Ct. N. Y.): "From this it is quite apparent that the schedule was defective. According to the defendant's statements now made, the address of the plaintiff was unknown to him but

ation or interlineation, except where such abbreviation and interlineation may be for the purpose of reference." In re Mackey, 1 A. B. R. 593 (Ref. N. Y.). The case In re Mackey is extreme in its holding as to common abbreviations.

19. In re McConnell, 11 A. B. R. 418 (Ref. N. Y.).

20. See post, subject of "Debts Not Duly Scheduled," not discharged, § 2761, et seq.

21. In re Dvorak, 6 A. B. R. 66, 107 Fed. 76 (D. C. Iowa); In re Mackey, 1 A. B. R. 593 (Ref. N. Y.). See post, § 2487, "Discharge—Opposition on Ground of Failure to Duly Schedule." Sutherland v. Lasher, 11 A. B. R. 782 (Sup. Ct. N. Y.).

instead of so stating in the schedule, as the law requires, an incorrect as well as· indefinite and unauthorized address was given."

§ 490. **Exempt Property to Be Scheduled.**—Exempt property must be scheduled as well as other property.[22]

§ 491. **And Claim for Exemptions to Give Particular Description.** —The claim for exemption must describe with particularity the precise articles and property claimed as exempt. It will not do simply to·say "the bankrupt is a married man," etc., etc., "resident of Ohio," etc., etc., "and claims under section so and so of the statutes," "$500.00 in lieu of a homestead," when perhaps there is no cash money in the estate at all but only unsold merchandise. In other words, the identical property in the form in which it existed at the date of adjudication, or at any rate at the date when the schedules are presumed to be filed, must be described as the property claimed as exempt; thus, if there be cash money at that time, then it may be claimed as money; if there be none, then $500.00 worth of goods or accounts or other property, may be claimed—in goods, in accounts and in other property. It will not do to claim money unless there was money at the time; the property actually in existence at that time to the value of the exemption allowed in lieu of homestead, however, may ·be claimed and must be so described that the trustee may be able to set it off ·at once to the bankrupt and separate it from the assets belonging to the creditors.[23]

§ 492. **Amendment Allowed.**—Amendment may be allowed to the schedules, but the originals must not be altered in any particular. Amendment by interlineation will not be permitted. The amendment must be made out and sworn to precisely like the original schedules. In the application for leave to amend, the cause of the failure to have the original schedules correct must be stated.[24]

§ 493. **Omitted Creditors Added by Amendment.**—Omitted creditors may be added by amendment.[25] And such amendment in its effect reverts to the date of the filing of the petition;[26] subject, probably to whatever exception from the operation of the discharge the creditor's claim might possess by reason of lack of "due scheduling," "due" scheduling doubtless implying scheduling in time for the creditor to participate in all the essential steps of the proceedings and to avail himself of all substantial remedies, such as opposition to discharge, etc.[27]

§ 494. **But Not after Expiration of Year for Filing Claims.**—But it has been held that omitted creditors may not be added by amendment

22. In re Todd, 7 A. B. R. 770, 112 Fed. 315 (D. C. Vt.).
23. See post, subject of "Exemptions," § 1052, et seq.
24. See rule XI of the Supreme Court's General Orders in Bankruptcy.

25. In re Beerman, 7 A. B. R. 434 (D. C. Ga.). Impliedly, In re McKee, 21 A. B. R. 306, 165 Fed. 351 (D. C. N. Y.).
26. In re Beerman, 7 A. B. R. 434 (D. C. Ga.). But compare post, § 2780.
27. See post, § 2780.

after the expiration of the year from the date of the adjudication within which the creditor could file his claim;[28] nor where the bankrupt has delayed asking for leave to make such amendment until within a few days of the end of the year.[29]

However, on principle, creditors, whenever discovered, might be added; such right being properly distinguishable from the effect of lack of "due scheduling" on the discharge, as to which latter matter, see post, "Debts Excepted from the Operation of Discharge" through lack of "Due Scheduling," § 2761, et seq.[30]

---

28. In re Hawk, 8 A. B. R. 71, 114 Fed. 916 (C. C. A.); impliedly, In re Spicer, 16 A. B. R. 802, 145 Fed. 431 (D. C. N. Y.). Compare, analogously, In re Schaffer, 4 A. B. R. 730, 104 Fed. 982 (D. C. N. Car.).

As to whether the omitted creditor should have notice of the application for leave to amend, see In re Hawk, 8 A. B. R. 73, 114 Fed. 916 (C. C. A.). Ordinarily such notice is not necessary where the amendment is sought for within the year limited for proving claims and sufficiently in time to enable the creditor to participate in the distribution of assets.

Stockholder's Liability for Debts of the Corporation—Who to Be Scheduled as the Creditor.—Doubtless, all the creditors of an insolvent corporation, where an action against the bankrupt would lie to enforce "double" liability, might be listed, although the receiver appointed in the stockholder's liability suit would also be a sufficient "agent"

for that purpose. Compare, Dight v. Chapman, 12 A. B. R. 743 (Sup. Ct. Ore.). Also, compare, In re Rouse, 1 A. B. R. 393 (Ref. Ohio, affirmed by D. C.).

Schedules as Evidence.—As to the admissibility of the schedules in evidence, see post, "Pleadings and Practice in Actions by Trustees," § 1745.

Also compare germane subject of the effect of lack of "Due Scheduling," post, § 2761, et seq. Impliedly, In re Walker, 21 A. B. R. 132, 164 Fed. 680 (C. C. A. Calif.). Also, see post, "Schedules Not to Be Used in Criminal Proceedings against Bankrupt," § 2323.

29. In re Kittler, 23 A. B. R. 585, 176 Fed. 655 (D. C. Pa.).

30. When Amendment Too Late for "Due Proof" and Ineffective to Bar Discharge.—Compare post, § 2780.

Use of Schedules in Criminal Prosecution.—See post, §§ 1556, 2323.

PART III.

ADMINISTRATION OF THE ESTATE AFTER ADJUDICATION.

§ 495. Administration of Estate Distinguished from Proceedings for Adjudication.

—Another branch of bankruptcy is now reached, separate, in theory at least, from that which heretofore has been considered. Heretofore have been considered the proceedings leading up to the adjudication of bankruptcy, those which determine the status of the debtor in the community as a bankrupt, the affairs of his estate having only incidentally been considered, as the same may or may not have been in need of attention during the pendency of the petition for adjudication. It being now determined, however, that the debtor is a bankrupt, the consequence follows that his estate comes into court for administration. The administration of the estate is a separate and distinct branch of bankruptcy jurisprudence. It is founded upon the adjudication of bankruptcy, to be sure, but it is distinct from the proceedings leading up to the adjudication. The administration of the estate is a proceedings in rem, like the proceedings leading up to the adjudication, but the res involved in the two proceedings are quite different. The status of the debtor in the community was the res involved in the hearing upon the petition. But that status is now settled; the petition is functus officio, it has become merged in the "adjudication." And we now pass to the proceedings that involve the assets of the debtor as the res.[1]

These latter proceedings—the administration of the bankrupt estate—owing to their complicated nature and the detail work entailed, are mostly carried on before a subsidiary officer, known under the present law as the referee in bankruptcy.

---

1. Compare, In re Continental Corp'r, 14 A. B. R. 588 (Ref. Ohio).
Receivership before adjudication, not part of "Administration of Estate."

Skubinsky v. Bodek, 22 A. B. R. 689, 172 Fed. 332 (C. C. A. Pa.), quoted at §§ 385, 1544.

CHAPTER XVII.

REFEREES IN BANKRUPTCY.

Synopsis of Chapter.

§ 496. History.—Originally, as appears from the bankruptcy statute of King Henry VIII, the administration of the bankrupt's estate was conducted directly by the Lord Privy Seal, Lord High Chancellor, etc., who were, by that Act, created courts of bankruptcy. And with the small population of those days and comparatively little commerce and trading, such few courts were undoubtedly sufficient.

The bankruptcy laws of the United States, however, have generally created inferior judicial officers whose functions have been to relieve the judge himself from the consideration of the numberless legal questions that necessarily arise in the course of the administration of the bankrupt estate. Under the old law of 1867 this officer was called a register and there was not one for each county, as now, but generally only two or three for an entire district. Their fees were high and the two or three had a monopoly of all the cases of a big district.

Under the present law the fees are purposely made very low and the law contemplates that there shall be at least one referee for each county, so each referee receives not only smaller fees but fewer fees than the old registrars received. These improvements in the line of economy and in bringing the courts to the homes of the people played an important part in the arguments that finally induced Congress to pass the present law.

DIVISION 1.

APPOINTMENT, TERM, DISTRICTS, QUALIFICATIONS OF REFEREES.

§ 497. The "Referee."—The present law creates an inferior judicial officer and denominates him "referee."[2]

§ 498. Appointment, and Term of Office.—Referees are appointed by

_____

2. Bankr. Act, § 33. "Creation of two offices—(a) The offices of referee and trustee are hereby created."

the judge of the district court. They are not temporary officers appointed for each case as the occasion arises, as in cases of referees in chancery generally, but are appointed for a term of two years, and have charge of all cases referred to them.[3]

§ 499. Removal.—Referees may be removed because their services are not needed or for other cause, in the discretion of the court.[4]

§ 500. Referees' Districts.—The district court designates the limits of the districts of the referee and may change the same from time to time.[5] The territorial jurisdiction of the referee, is limited, and official acts done outside the limits of his district are undoubtedly void. And the referee's jurisdiction does not extend to cases outside of the district of his appointment.[6]

§ 501. At Least One Referee for Each County.—It is intended by the Act that there shall be at least one referee for each county where any referee is needed at all.[7]

In re Steuer, 5 A. B. R. 214, 104 Fed. 976 (D. C. Mass.): "The Court of Bankruptcy will thus be brought nearer to the residence of suitors as there is a referee in every county."

And the referee must reside or have his office in his own district.[8] These latter two provisions are in the interest of bringing the bankruptcy courts home to the people, thus correcting one of the hardships of previous bankruptcy laws. The spirit of these provisions, however, if not their letter, has been violated in many districts by naming one referee for several counties, who, however, nominally has an office in each.

Such number of referees are to be appointed as may be necessary to assist in expeditiously transacting the bankruptcy business.[9]

§ 502. Qualifications.—Individuals are not eligible to appointment as referees unless they are respectively (1) competent to perform the duties of

---

3. Bankr. Act, § 34 (a): "Courts of bankruptcy shall, within the territorial limits of which they respectively have jurisdiction, (1) appoint referees, each for a term of two years, and may, in their discretion, remove them because their services are not needed or for other cause; and (2) designate, and from time to time change, the limits of the districts of referees, so that each county, where the services of a referee are needed, may constitute at least one district."

General Subject of Jurisdiction to Appoint Referees.—Birch v. Steele, 21 A. B. R. 539, 165 Fed. 577 (C. C. A. Ala.); In re Steele, 20 A. B. R. 446, 161 Fed. 886 (D. C. Ala.), quoted ante,

§ 29; In re Steele, 19 A. B. R. 671, 156 Fed. 863 (D. C. Ala.). Compare, ante, § 29.

4. Bankr. Act, § 34 (a).

5. Bankr. Act, § 34 (a) (2): "* * * designate, and from time to time change, the limits of the district of referees."

6. In re Engineering & Construction Co., 17 A. B. R. 279, 147 Fed. 868 (D. C. N. Y.).

7. Bankr. Act, § 34 (a) (2): "* * * so that each county, where the services of a referee are needed, may constitute at least one district."

8. Bankr. Act, § 35 (a) (4).

9. Bankr. Act, § 37.

the office; (2) not holding any office of profit or emolument under the laws of the United States or of any State other than commissioners of deeds, justices of the peace, masters in chancery, or notaries public; (3) not related by consanguinity or affinity, within the third degree as determined by the common law, to any of the judges of the courts of bankruptcy or circuit courts of the United States, or of the justices or judges of the appellate courts of the districts wherein they may be appointed; and (4) residents of, or have their offices in, the territorial districts for which they are to be appointed.[10]

§ 503. Oath of Office and Bond.—The referee takes the same oath of office as that prescribed for judges of United States Courts;[11] and he is required to give bond in such sum as the court may fix, not to exceed five thousand dollars, conditioned for the faithful performance of his duties.[12] This bond undoubtedly covers merely ministerial duties. Perhaps the instances coming under Bankruptcy Act § 30 (a), "Duties of Referees," would, in general, be covered by the bond.

§ 504. Not to Act Where Interested.—Referees must not act in cases in which they are directly or indirectly interested.[13] But that the referee is a debtor of the bankrupt is no disqualification if the debt is admitted and can not be affected as a liability by the bankruptcy proceedings.[14] And that the referee receives compensation based upon amounts disbursed to creditors does not make him "interested" within the meaning of this section.[15]

§ 505. Not to Practice in Bankruptcy nor Purchase Bankrupt Assets.—Referees must not act as attorneys nor counselors in any bankruptcy proceedings; nor may they purchase, directly or indirectly, any property of an estate in bankruptcy.[16]

DIVISION 2.

STATUTORY AND MISCELLANEOUS DUTIES OF THE REFEREE.

§ 506. Statutory Duties of Referee.—Besides the referee's duties as a branch of a court of equity performing the functions usually to be performed by such courts in the administration of estates, certain special duties are laid upon him by the provisions of the Bankruptcy Act itself, such duties being generally partly or wholly ministerial in their nature.

10. Bankr. Act, § 35 (a).
11. Bankr. Act, § 36 (a). Also, White v. Schloerb, 4 A. B. R. 181, 178 U. S. 542.
12. Bankr. Act, § 50 (a): "Referees, before assuming the duties of their offices, and within such time as the district courts of the United States having jurisdiction shall prescribe, shall respectively qualify by entering into bond to the United States in such sum as shall be fixed by such courts, not to exceed five thousand dollars, with such sureties as shall be approved by such courts, conditioned for the faithful performance of their official duties."
13. Bankr. Act, § 39 (b) (1).
14. Bray v. Cobb, 1 A. B. R. 153, 91 Fed. 102 (D. C. N. Car.).
15. In re Abbey Press, 13 A. B. R. 11, 134 Fed. 51 (C. C. A. N. Y.).
16. Bankr. Act, § 39 (b) (3).

§ 507. First Statutory Duty—To Declare Dividends and Prepare Dividend Sheets.—It is a duty of the referee to declare dividends and prepare and deliver to trustees dividend sheets showing the dividends declared and to whom payable.[17] This section entails ministerial duties of considerable responsibility upon the referees for the accurate preparation of such dividend sheets.

§ 508. Second Statutory Duty—To Examine Schedules.—It is the duty of the referee to examine lists of creditors and schedules of property and to require such as are incomplete or defective to be amended.[18] And it is the referee's duty to require such correction whether any creditor asks for it or not.[19]

§ 509. Third Statutory Duty—To Furnish Information.—It is the duty of the referee to furnish such information concerning the estates in process of administration before him as may be requested by the parties in interest.[20]

Probably such duty would not require the referee to do more than answer questions asked personally and to afford opportunity to inspect records. It may not require him to write elaborate letters of explanation to every inquiring creditor though perhaps Congress meant he should make reasonable written response when reasonably asked, but at any rate courtesy at least would require the referee to give information by letter, if the request be reasonable.

§ 510. Fourth Statutory Duty—To Give Notice to Creditors.—It is the duty of the referee to give notices to creditors that are hereafter discussed.[21]

§ 511. Fifth Statutory Duty—To Make Up Records and Findings for Review.—It is the duty of the referee to make up records and findings for review.[22]

And referees should so conduct their proceedings and make up their records that a full and fair review may be made of their actions.[23]

§ 512. Sixth Statutory Duty—To Cause Schedules to Be Prepared Where Bankrupt Derelict.—It is the duty of the referee either himself to prepare and file the schedules of property and list of creditors or to cause the same to be prepared and filed, when the bankrupt fails, neglects or refuses to do so;[24] and the bankrupt will not be heard to complain that notices of a first meeting called thereon were not sent to all his creditors.[25]

---

17. Bankr. Act, § 39 (a) (1).
18. Bankr. Act, § 39 (a) (2). In re Mackey, 1 A. B. R. 593 (Ref. N. Y.).
19. In re Mackey, 1 A. B. R. 593 (Ref. N. Y.).
20. Bankr. Act, § 39 (a) (3).
21. See next following chapter.
22. Bankr. Act, § 39 (a) (5). Cunningham v. Bank, 4 A. B. R. 195, 103 Fed. 932 (C. C. A. Ky.). This subject is treated post, under the subject of "Review."

23. In re Romine, 14 A. B. R. 788, 138 Fed. 837 (D. C. W. Va.).

24. Bankr. Act, § 39 (a) (6). Impliedly, In re Schiller, 2 A. B. R. 704, 96 Fed. 400 (D. C. Va.).

25. In re Schiller, 2 A. B. R. 704, 96 Fed. 400 (D. C. Va.).

§ 513. Seventh Statutory Duty—To Keep, Perfect and Transmit Records.—It is the duty of the referee to safely keep, perfect, and transmit to the clerk when the cases are concluded the records required to be kept by him.[26]

§ 514. Eighth Statutory Duty—To Transmit to Clerk Papers on File, etc.—It is the duty of the referee to transmit to the clerk such papers as may be on file before him whenever the same are needed in any proceedings in court, and in like manner secure the return of such papers after they have been used, or, if it be impracticable to transmit the original papers, transmit certified copies thereof by mail.[27]

§ 515. Ninth Statutory Duty—To Preserve Evidence.—It is the referee's duty, upon application of any party in interest, to preserve the evidence taken, or the substance thereof as agreed upon by the parties before them when a stenographer is not in attendance.[28]

§ 516. Tenth Statutory Duty—To Get Papers from Clerk.—It is the duty of the referee, whenever his office is in the same city or town where the court of bankruptcy convenes, to call upon and receive from the clerk all papers filed in the court of bankruptcy which have been referred to him.[29]

§ 517. Statutory Duty to Audit Trustee's Accounts.—It is the duty of the referee to audit the accounts of the trustee;[30] and to do so whether creditors except to the accounts or not.[31]

In re Fullick, 28 A. B. R. 634, 201 Fed. 463 (D. C. Pa.): "The whole policy of the law with respect to bankrupt estates is that they shall be economically administered, and it is the duty of referees, as well as of receivers and trustees, none of whom are entitled to receive greater compensation than is fixed by the bankruptcy law, to see that estates are administered with the strictest economy. But the law imposes specially upon referees the settlement and distribution of estates. They must pass upon the accounts of receivers and trustees and be satisfied as to their correctness. It is not proper for a referee to assume that an account is correct or that payments made by an accountant are proper simply because no person interested files an exception thereto."

§ 518. Duty to Audit Receiver's Accounts.—It is also the duty of the referee to audit receiver's accounts where adjudication ultimately is had

---

26. Bankr. Act, § 39 (a) (7).
27. Bankr. Act, § 39 (a) (8).
28. Bankr. Act, § 39 (a) (9).
29. Bankr. Act, § 39 (a) (10).
30. Bankr. Act, § 62. Gen. Order No. XVII. "All accounts of trustees shall be referred as of course to the referee for audit, unless otherwise specially ordered by the court."
A practice has grown up in some districts of referring to special masters various matters that form part of the regular duties of referees, thus putting estates to additional and unnecessary expense. The practice is to be repre-

hended in view of the manifest spirit of economy in which the present law was framed.
For an instance where a district judge appears to have been guilty of this practice, see, In re Hoyt & Mitchell, 11 A. B. R. 784, the district judge there having referred to a special master the matter of auditing the trustee's reports, a duty clearly enjoined on the referee by the statute and General Orders in Bankruptcy as well.
31. In re Baginsky, 2 A. B. R. 243 (Ref. La.).

although such duty is not specifically enjoined upon him by the statute or rules of court.[32] And the failure of the receiver to pay a sum with which his account has been surcharged, will render him liable to punishment for contempt.[33]

§ 518¼. Duty to Allow or Disallow Claims.—It is, of course, the duty of the referee to allow or disallow claims of creditors for sharing in dividends.[34]

§ 518½. No "Certificate of Conformity" under Present Act.—It is no part of a referee's duty to make "certificates of conformity," as was the registrar's duty under the former act, and such certificates are unauthorized, except where specifications of opposition to discharge have been referred to him as special master.[35]

DIVISION 3.

REFERENCE TO REFEREE.

§ 519. Judge May Dispense with Referee and Retain Charge Himself.—Immediately upon adjudication, the case is referred to the proper referee to take charge of the administration of the estate. The judge, however, may, if he so desire, retain direct charge of the case after the adjudication, as he must do before adjudication, and may dispense with the referee.[36]

This power to retain control of the administration of bankrupt estates is seldom, if ever, exercised by the judge; and, indeed, to exercise it would defeat one of the best features of the present law, which is that of having a referee for each county, whereby suitors have the bankruptcy courts brought directly to their own homes and need not seek the distant federal court where the judge himself sits. In fact, since the meeting of creditors must be held at the county seat of the county where the bankrupt resides or at some

---

32. In re Fullick, 28 A. B. R. 634, 201 Fed. 463 (D. C. Pa.), set out under § 517.
Compare evident practice, In re Reliance Storage, etc., Co., 4 A. B. R. 49, 100 Fed. 619 (D. C. Pa.).

33. In re Reliable, etc., Co., 29 A. B. R. 371, 183 Fed. 116 (C. C. A. N. Y.).

34. In re Goble Boat Co., 27 A. B. R. 48, 190 Fed. 92 (D. C. N. Y.), quoted at § 814.

35. In re Randall, 20 A. B. R. 305, 159 Fed. 298 (D. C. Pa.).

36. Bankr. Act, § 22 (a), "After a person has been adjudged a bankrupt the judge may cause the trustee to proceed with the administration of the estate, or refer it (1) generally to the referee or specially with only limited authority to act in the premises or to consider and report upon specified issues; or (2) to any referee within the territorial jurisdiction of the court, if the convenience of parties in interest will be served thereby, or for cause, or if the bankrupt does not do business, reside, or have his domicile in the district."
Ordering Sale Free of Liens and Appointing Commissioners to Make Sale, Instead of Trustee under Referee's Order.—In one case the judge ordered a sale free of liens directly by commissioners instead of referring it to the referee. Sturgis v. Corbin, 15 A. B. R. 543, 141 Fed. 1 (C. C. A. W. Va.); In re [Morgantown] Tin Plate Co., 25 A. B. R. 836, 184 Fed. 109 (D. C. W. Va.).

other place convenient to the litigants, the judge would be obliged to leave his usual court room in all bankruptcies from other counties in order to preside at the different meetings of creditors, even if, as to other matters, he might conduct hearings at the regular court room of the United States District Court.

§ 520. Reference.—Reference is accomplished by the making and entry of an order by the judge, or in the name of the judge by the District Clerk, referring the case to the referee; and the sending of the papers, with a certificate of the order of reference, to the referee.[37]

§ 521. Reference after Adjudication, General or Special; before Adjudication, Special.—The reference after adjudication may be general or special.[38] If the order of reference is not restricted, it will be taken to be a general reference.

References before adjudication are presumably always special, taking up simply the specific duty then at hand which can not be performed by the judge himself because of absence or inability to act. Such special reference, of course, is superseded by the general reference.[39]

§ 521½. References in Compositions before Adjudication.—By the Amendment of 1910, permitting compositions before adjudication of bankruptcy, provision is made for the calling of a meeting of creditors before adjudication, at which the judge or referee is to preside.[39a]

§ 522. Reference to Another Referee.—Reference may be made to another referee than the one regularly having jurisdiction, if the greater convenience of the parties will thus be subserved or cause be shown, or if the bankrupt does not reside or have his principal place of business in the

---

37. Deputy Clerk May Make Reference.—The deputy of the district clerk may sign the order of reference. Gilbertson v. United States, 22 A. B. R. 32, 168 Fed. 6722 (C. C. A. Wis.): "The only objection raised upon its introduction was the order or reference—that it was signed by a deputy, and not by the clerk personally; and such objection impresses us to be without merit, in any view of the effect to be given the adjudication. The appointment of a deputy clerk is expressly authorized by § 558, Rev. St. * * * in general terms, and the powers of a deputy, as recognized at common law, are thereby implied. The appointee in such case is empowered to perform all ministerial acts of the clerk, as his principal (Throop on Public Officers, § 583, 7 Cyc. 248), and thus to make the order of reference. as the statute directs to be made of course, when the petition is filed in the absence of

the District Judge. The clerk is given no discretion nor authority to pass upon the sufficiency of the petition, and performance of the statutory duty is thus made ministerial, and not judicial."

38. Bankr. Act, § 22 (a): "* * * or refer it (1) generally to the referee or specially with only limited authority to act in the premises or to consider and report upon specified issues."

39. In re Ruos (No. 2), 21 A. B. R. 257. 164 Fed. 749 (D. C. Pa.).

39a. Bankr. Act, § 12a, as amended in 1910: "* * * In compositions before adjudication the bankrupt shall file the required schedules, and thereupon the court shall call a meeting of creditors for the allowance of claims, examination of the bankrupt, and preservation or conduct of estates, at which meeting the judge or referee shall preside." Also, see §§ 593¼, 2358, et seq.

district.[40] But the other referee must be in the same district; and a district judge may not refer a bankruptcy case to a referee in another district.[41]

§ 522½. Appointing "Special Master" to Perform a Duty of Referee, Improper.

—It is improper and an abuse of power to appoint either the referee or another person as "special master" to perform duties rightly devolving upon the referee by virtue of his office. It is the clearly expressed intent of the act to entrust the administration of bankrupt estates, where the judge himself does not retain the administration, to the certain judicial officer termed the "referee," whose duties are clearly defined and whose compensation has been carefully limited by congress, in the interest of economy. In many districts the practice prevails of referring, either to such referees or to others, as "special masters," various matters which the act clearly includes among the duties of the referee. In this way additional expense is unnecessarily saddled upon bankrupt estates, and the statutory provision violated which prohibits "any other or further compensation" "in any form or guise" than that "expressly authorized and prescribed by the act."[42]

In re Sweeney, 21 A. B. R. 866, 168 Fed. 612 (C. C. A. Tenn.): "The issues presented by the intervention were properly referred by the court to the referee for the purpose of hearing the evidence and making a report. The referee afterwards filed a report as special master. This was doubtless an inadvertence. There is no authority for converting the referee into a special master. * * * For the most part the duties of a referee are those of a special master, and we know of no authority for the appointment of a special master to do the proper business of the referee. Nor do we know of any power to allow a referee the compensation of a special master. The fees and compensation of that officer were enlarged by the amendment of the act passed February 5, 1903. By § 72 added by that amendatory act it is provided, etc."

Indeed, one Circuit Court of Appeals has undertaken to hold judicially that the bankruptcy court may appoint a "special master" to pass upon petitions for reclamation, going even to the length of suggesting that the Supreme Court correct the act of Congress in this regard.[43] When one considers the multitude of reclamation petitions frequently filed in many small bankruptcies, to recover goods, perhaps a cash register, left on conditional

---

40. Bankr. Act, § 22 (a) (2): "* * * to any referee within the territorial jurisdiction of the court, if the convenience of parties in interest will be served thereby, or for cause, or if the bankrupt does not do business, reside, or have his domicile in the district." In re Western Investment Co., 21 A. B. R. 367, 170 Fed. 677 (D. C. Okla.).

41. In re Engineering & Construction Co., 17 A. B. R. 279, 147 Fed. 868 (D. C. N. Y.).

42. See ante, § 24; post, § 2011. Apparent instances, In re Hoyt & Mitch-

ell, 11 A. B. R. 784, 127 Fed. 968; Laffoon v. Ives, 20 A. B. R. 174. 159 Fed. 861 (C. C. A. Wash.); In re Huntenberg, 18 A. B. R. 697, 153 Fed. 768 (D. C. N. Y.); In re Wilcox Co., 19 A. B. R. 91, 156 Fed. 685 (D. C. N. Y.); In re Allert, 23 A. B. R. 101, 173 Fed. 691 (D. C. N. Y.); In re Photo Engraving Co., 19 A. B. R. 94, 155 Fed. 684 (D. C. N. Y.); In re Strobel, 19 A. B. R. 109, 160 Fed. 916 (D. C. N. Y.).

43. In re Tracy, 24 A. B. R. 539, 185 Fed. 1006 (C. C. A. N. Y.).

sale or on consignment, as well as to recover goods bought under misrepresentation, or otherwise belonging to third parties, it would rather appear that the court itself failed to grasp the true situation in respect to reclamation petitions in bankruptcy proceedings. To allow reference to a special master in such cases would be to load the bankrupt estates to the brim with expense and defeat that purpose of economy in administration apparent throughout the act, besides giving to the referees in bankruptcy in many districts incomes much greater than those of the District Judges. And in any event, as was said in one case, it is not to be forgotten that referees always have the power of resignation from office if they are dissatisfied with its emoluments. It would be well to bear in mind the appropriate warning of the same Circuit Court of Appeals in the case In re Oakland Lumber Co., 23 A. B. R. 181, 174 Fed. 643: "Nothing contributed so much to bring about the repeal of the Act of 1867 as the large expense of administration, the small estates being entirely absorbed in fees. The more economical the administration of the present act the longer will it continue as an important adjunct to trade and commerce."

In determining when the referee may and when he may not be appointed special master, there is no true line of demarkation to be found in the distinction, noted post at § 2864, between "Bankruptcy Proceedings" proper and "Controversies arising in the course of bankruptcy proceedings," allowing his appointment as special master at additional expense to the estate in the latter instances; for such rulings would permit the appointment of the referee as special master in the following instances, each one of which has been held not to be a "proceedings in bankruptcy" but to be a "controversy," to wit: Trustee's petition to marshal liens on property in his possession and to enjoin interference therewith; trustee's petition for a summary order upon the bankrupt to surrender concealed assets; determination of extent of assignees' or receivers' liens on property being surrendered by the state court to the trustee; making of a call or assessment upon the stockholders of a bankrupt corporation; as well as petitions of third parties for reclamation; so that were such rulings to prevail it would seem pertinent to inquire rather what are the duties which the referee is to perform as referee. Nor is there force in the position that the third party is seeking the forum of the bankruptcy court himself, for he does not seek it: he is obliged to resort to it and would be in contempt of court if he attempted to sue in replevin or trover. The true line of demarkation is that noted post, at § 2107½, that the referee is not to be appointed special master at additional expense to the estate in any matters arising in the course of the administration of the bankrupt estate before him over which he would have jurisdiction without any reference as special master, whether they be "Bankruptcy Proceedings Proper" or "Controversies Arising, etc." He may, then, under such ruling be appointed special master only in cases of contested adjudications of bankruptcy and of oppositions to discharge or composition, none of which are concerned with the administration of assets at all, but simply with the determining of the status of the debtor as a bankrupt, and all of which are specially reserved to the judge and consequently forbidden to the referee by the act itself. Of course, the referee may also be appointed special master to take and report evidence and conclusions in independent plenary actions brought in the District Court by the trustees under favor of the Amendment of 1903, to recover assets, as well as in petitions for injunction against a state court or an officer thereof, over which the referee would have no jurisdiction whatsoever. Such clearly is the line of demarkation intended by Congress in the act.

DIVISION 4.

FUNCTIONS AND JURISDICTION OF REFEREES.

§ 523. The Referee, upon Reference, Becomes "The Court."— The referee under the present law is also an officer with more extensive functions than the old registrar possessed.

In re McGill, 5 A. B. R. 155, 106 Fed. 57 (C. C. A. Ohio): "It is to be remembered that under the present act, subject to review by the court, the referee is given broader powers than were conferred upon the register under the Act of 1867. Under the latter act the register could make no decision, but must certify disputed questions to the court for determination."

The referee, in fact, becomes to all intents and purposes the court of bankruptcy, as soon as the case is referred to him. Indeed, the definition in the law itself, in § 1, is that "Courts shall mean the court of bankruptcy in which the proceedings are pending and may include the referee."[44]

In re Simon & Sternberg, 18 A. B. R. 205, 151 Fed. 507 (D. C. Ga.): "The bankruptcy law authorizes the appointment by the court of a tribunal especially qualified to dispose of such conflicts of fact as those which are here presented on review. The referee is a court, and a court of very great importance in the administration of bankrupt assets, and the determination of conflicting rights arising thereunder. This court has attempted to be very careful in the appointment of men of acumen, experience, and character to these positions, and it would be, I think, quite unjustifiable, in view of the facts which are palpably apparent on this record—conflicting as they are—for the court to disturb the finding of the referee.

"The finding of the referee is entitled to the same consideration as that of a district judge upon conflicting evidence, as in an admiralty case, or in any other case where the judges pass upon the facts, if that finding is under review by an appellate tribunal."

In re McIntyre, 16 A. B. R. 85, 142 Fed. 593 (D. C. W. Va.): "Referees in their hearings within the scope of their powers are clothed with the authority of judges, and their orders and decrees are to be reviewed, reversed or annulled under the same rules and conditions as those governing other courts of equity, subject always to the express provisions of the Bankrupt Act."

---

44. In re Tilden, 1 A. B. R. 302, 91 Fed. 501 (D. C. Iowa); In re Sonnabend, 18 A. B. R. 120 (Ref. Mass.);   In re Knopf, 16 A. B. R. 439, 144 Fed. 245 (D. C. S. C.).

White v. Schloerb, 4 A. B. R. 178, 178 U. S. 542: "* * * exercise much of the judicial authority of that court."

Gilbertson v. United States, 22 A. B. R. 32, 168 Fed. 672 (C. C. A. Wis.): "The office of referee, created by the act as an arm of the bankruptcy court, is invested with certain judicial powers (§ 38), 'subject always to a review by the judge,' and his proceedings, after the court acquires jurisdiction, are those of the court."

And the referee takes the same oath of office as that prescribed for judges of the United States Courts.[45]

White v. Schloerb, 4 A. B. R. 181, 178 U. S. 542: "Under §§ 33-43 of the Bankruptcy Act of 1898 and the 12th General Order in Bankruptcy, referees in bankruptcy are appointed by the Courts of Bankruptcy, and take the same oath of office as judges of United States Courts, each case in bankruptcy is referred by the Court of Bankruptcy to a referee and he exercises much of the judicial authority of that Court."

The referee is a judicial officer and his orders are entitled to the credit and respect due to officers who act judicially.[46]

In re Covington, 6 A. B. R. 373, 110 Fed. 143 (D. C. N. Car.): "That they sometimes err is to be expected—so do the ablest judges of all the courts—but they should not be reversed except upon clear and convincing proof of error, especially as to the findings of fact when they have seen the witnesses and heard them testify."

In re Abbey Press, 13 A. B. R. 11, 134 Fed. 51 (C. C. A. N. Y.): "The referee to whom the proceeding in bankruptcy has been referred generally constitutes a court with all the powers of the court for the purposes of the examination of the witnesses."

In re Romine, 14 A. B. R. 788, 138 Fed. 837 (D. C. W. Va., on review, Bank v. Johnson, 16 A. B. R. 206, 143 Fed. 463): "Referees are judicial officers, clothed with judicial powers. They are, however, subordinate to the court above them, and should so conduct their proceedings, and make up their records that a full and fair review may be made of their actions. Their decisions will not be lightly treated, but given the consideration due to conclusions reached by conscientious officers seeking to discharge their duties to the best of their ability."

Thus, a referee's order allowing a claim without surrender of an alleged preference over objection, is res adjudicata in a subsequent suit by the trustee in a state court to recover the alleged preference.[47]

Clendening v. Red River Valley N. Bank, 11 A. B. R. 245 (Sup. Ct. N. Dak.): "Referees are judicial officers clothed with power to adjudicate in the first instance over the allowance or disallowance of claims presented against the

---

45. Bankr. Act, § 36.

46. Clendening v. Red River Valley N. Bk., 11 A. B. R. 245 (Sup. Ct. N. D.). On Review, Referee's Findings on the Facts Not Disturbed unless Manifestly against Weight of Evidence.— See post, § 2839, subject. "Review."

47. Contra, Buder v. Columbia Distilling Co., 9 A. B. R. 331, 70 S. W. 508. This case, however, proceeds not on the theory that the referee's order is not entitled to respect as res iudicata, but that his order of allowance of a claim, where preferences are not attacked and the issue not raised, is not res judicata.

bankrupt's estate, and their findings are entitled to the respect and credit given to officers acting judicially. * * * It is unnecessary to say that we have no supervisory or appellate jurisdiction over referees in bankruptcy or over the decisions of courts of bankruptcy.

"The question which the plaintiff seeks to have us determine has been judicially determined by a tribunal having jurisdiction, and is therefore binding upon us. Smith v. Walker, 77 Ga. 289, 3 S. E. 256. Whether the referee intended to decide these questions is not material. As we have seen, they were necessarily involved, and were in fact determined by his adjudication. Whether his decision was right or wrong we need not discuss. It is sufficient for the purpose of this case to say that the question has been adjudicated by the order of allowance made by the referee, and that the same has not been reconsidered by him or reversed by the judge upon a petition for review. If the trustee was dissatisfied with the adjudication made by the referee, he had a speedy remedy in the bankruptcy court upon a petition for review, and also by appeal from the order of the bankruptcy court if adverse to him."

Likewise, a mortgagee of a bankrupt's real estate, to whom, after due hearing, has been awarded the amount of his lien from the proceeds of sale, is protected by the order of the referee, which established his right to the money, until the order is set aside by proceedings directly taken for that purpose.[48]

Section 38 in clause (4) describes in a nutshell the jurisdiction of referees. It says:

"Referees respectively are hereby invested, subject always to a review by the judge, within the limits of their districts as established from time to time (that is to say, not outside their county), with jurisdiction to perform such part of the duties, except as to questions arising out of the applications of bankrupts for compositions or discharges, as are by this Act conferred on courts of bankruptcy and as shall be prescribed by rules or orders of the courts of bankruptcy of their respective districts."[49]

In re Scott, 7 A. B. R. 36, 37, 111 Fed. 144 (Ref. Mass.): "Under the present act the referee takes the oath of office under 'Title XIII—The Judiciary.' Revised Statutes, §§ 712, 1756, 4995. The functions of the referee have been somewhat inaccurately likened to those of a master in chancery or a United States commissioner, and such latter officers have been sometimes erroneously spoken of as judicial officers. It would be more accurate to designate them as officers of the court, just as an attorney at law is an officer of the court, though clearly not a judicial officer. The distinction between such officers and the magistrates of a court was clearly considered in the case of Todd v. United States, 158 U. S. 278, 282, 284. It may be urged in opposition that the referee, not being a technical constitutional judge, cannot perform judicial functions. In the latter case of Todd v. United States, Mr. Justice Brewer quotes an opinion of Mr. Justice Story, in which he says: 'A court is not a judge, nor a judge a court. A judge is a public officer who, by virtue of his office, is clothed with judicial authorities. A court is defined to be a place in which justice is judicially ad-

---

48. In re Wilkesbarre Furniture M'f'g Co., 12 A. B. R. 472 (D. C. Pa.).
49. In re Drayton, 13 A. B. R. 602, 135 Fed. 883 (D. C. Wis.); Mueller v.
Nugent, 7 A. B. R. 224, 184 U. S. 1; Love v. Export Storage Co., 16 A. B. R. 171, 198, 143 Fed. 1 (C. C. A. Tenn.).

ministered. It is the exercise of judicial power, by the proper officer or officers, at a time and place appointed by law.'

"That Congress determined to confer upon the referee the right and authority to assist the district judge in discharge of the functions of the court is plainly seen by the following provisions of the Act. Section 1 (7), §§ 37, 38 (4). Under these provisions and throughout the act the referee is frequently alluded to as the 'court,' and is spoken of as an assistant of the judge 'in expeditiously transacting the bankruptcy business pending in the various courts of bankruptcy.'

"In a speech of Senator Nelson, he refers to the referee as 'practically a judge in chambers.' Cong. Rec. 55th Cong., 2nd Sess., p. 6298.

"It may be urged as a further objection that the referee has, while exercising his functions, no power to commit for contempt. In answer to this it is to be observed that the English registrar in bankruptcy has likewise no power to commit for contempt, yet such registrar is a judicial officer appointed for life or during good behavior. In addition, a clerk, officer in attendance and seal are provided for by General Order XXVI and III, and the act requires, in § 42, that records of proceedings before referees shall be kept in the same manner 'as records are now kept in equity cases in Circuit Courts of the United States.' "

In re Huddleston, 1 A. B. R. 574 (Ref. Ala.): "Subdivision 7 of § 1 of the act, in defining the word 'court,' says 'and may include the referee.' I take it that it does necessarily include the referee whenever a case is referred to him generally and without limitations. That for all purposes, excepting as to matters of composition and discharge, the referee stands in the place of the judge. It certainly never was intended by the act, that after a case was referred to a referee, every interlocutory motion necessary in the administration of the estate should be heard before the judge, and every order made by him. Such a construction of the act would be an obstruction merely, to the administration of the law, and practically prevent that prompt execution of the act, which, by its very terms, is contemplated."

Knapp & Spencer v. Drew, 20 A. B. R. 355, 160 Fed. 413 (C. C. A. Neb.): "The claim that the referee had no power to entertain the proceeding in question, make an investigation, and report his result to the court for its action is without merit. By § 38 of the Bankruptcy Act of 1898 the referee is empowered to 'perform such part of the duties, except as to questions arising out of the applications of bankrupts for compositions or discharges, as are by this act conferred on courts of bankruptcy, and as shall be prescribed by rules or orders of the courts of bankruptcy of their respective districts.' By general order No. 12 prescribed by the Supreme Court pursuant to the power conferred by the Bankruptcy Act upon it, after a case has been referred to a referee, 'all the proceedings, except such as are required by the act or by these general orders to be had before the judge, shall be had before the referee.' These provisions with the provision for review by the judge on certificate from the referee as contemplated by § 39 (6) and general order No. 27, not only conferred jurisdiction upon the referee to entertain the proceeding now under consideration, but afforded ample provision for review of his decision by the judge of the District Court from whose action alone an appeal to this court can be prosecuted."

However, wherever the act uses the term judge it excludes the referee in bankruptcy: the referee may be the "court" but he is never the "judge."

In re Bloodworth Stembridge Co., 24 A. B. R. 156, 178 Fed. 372 (D. C. Ga.): "'Now, wherever in the Bankruptcy Act the term 'judge' is used, it means the judge of the District Court, and not the referee in bankruptcy."

The other clauses of § 38 of the Act are merely corollary to this clause.

§ 524. May Adjudge Bankrupt on Default, or Dismiss Petition.—

Before adjudication, by clause (1.) referees are given jurisdiction to consider all petitions referred to them by the Clerk of the United States District Court, and to make the adjudication or dismiss the petitions, thus even having jurisdiction to adjudge debtors bankrupt.[50]

But they have no jurisdiction to dismiss the proceedings in bankruptcy after adjudication.[51] It is only the judge who may do so, and not even then until first the adjudication be itself vacated.

§ 525. May Issue Warrants and Orders for Seizing and Releasing Property.—

By clause (3) they are also vested with jurisdiction to

"exercise the powers of the judge for the taking possession and releasing of the property of the bankrupt in the event of the issuance by the clerk of a certificate showing the absence of the judge from the judicial district, or the division of the district, or his sickness or inability to act."[52]

Thus, the warrant to the marshal for the provisional seizure of the bankrupt's property, heretofore mentioned, may be issued by the referee before adjudication, in case the clerk sends him a certificate to the effect that the judge is absent or unable to act.[53]

Thus, also, before adjudication, he may appoint a receiver, if the judge is absent or unable to act, upon receipt of a certificate from the District Clerk to that effect;[54] and, upon receipt of such certificate, may order such receiver to sell assets.[55]

§ 526. After Adjudication and General Reference All Proceedings to Be before Referee.—

After adjudication and reference (unless the reference is restricted) all the proceedings are conducted before the referee, even to the appointment of receivers to take charge of the property until the election of the trustee, precisely same as if they were before the judge himself.[56] By the reference the judge divests himself, to the extent at least of the authority conferred by the order of reference, of control over the proceedings except by way, virtually, of a court to review the orders made by the referee.

Nevertheless the referee's relation to the judge is not precisely that of a trial court to an appellate court.[57]

---

50. Bankr. Act, § 38 (1). See ante, § 425.

51. In re Elby, 19 A. B. R. 734, 157 Fed. 935 (D. C. Iowa).

52. See ante, § 337.

53. See Bankr. Act, § 38 (3).

54. In re Kelly Dry Goods Co., 4 A. B. R. 528, 102 Fed. 747 (D. C. Wis.).

55. In re Kelly Dry Goods Co., 4 A. B. R. 528, 102 Fed. 747 (D. C. Wis.).

56. And a previous special reference is superseded. In re Ruos (No. 2), 21 A. B. R. 257, 164 Fed. 749 (D. C. Pa.).

57. In re DeGottardi, 7 A. B. R. 744, 114 Fed. 328 (D. C. Calif.). Compare, however, In re McIntyre, 16 A. B. R. 85, 142 Fed. 593 (D. C. W. Va.), quoted at § 523.

In re Pettingill & Co., 14 A. B. R. 760, 137 Fed. 840 (C. C. A. Mass.): "The fundamental difficulty about these propositions is that, under § 24b of the Act of July 1, 1898, ch. 541, 30 Stat. 553 (U. S. Comp. St. 1901, p. 3432), the proceedings of the District Court are before us, and not the proceedings of the referee. Although in a loose sense parties who are dissatisfied with the conclusions of the referee are said to appeal to the District Court, yet the action of that court on the findings of the referee did not assume the formalities of an appellate tribunal. Neither, according to the usual practice, are the proceedings before the referee brought before the court on exceptions, and thus made a part of the record, as in the case of a master in chancery. The relations between the court and the referee are usually of an informal character. Section 38 of the Act of July 1, 1898, ch. 541, 30 Stat. 555 (U. S. Comp. St. 1901, p. 3455), and General Order 27 (89 Fed. xi; 32 C. C. A. xxvii), provide for review by the court, of orders of referees in the most general terms, and are far from limiting the court to the rules which govern a chancery suit. Therefore, according to the common practice, the District Court was authorized to disregard the findings of the referee entirely, if it saw fit so to do, and proceed de novo, or reject them for reasons of law, or refuse to accept them in whole or in part, without assigning reasons therefor. The position of the petitioner in this particular would require this court to be bound conclusively by the findings by the referee of the preliminary and ultimate facts, although the District Court was not so bound, a proposition which defeats itself on its very face."

Coal Fields Co. v. Caldwell, 17 A. B. R. 139, 147 Fed. 475 (C. C. A. W. Va.): "The District Courts in the several districts of the United States are, by law, the courts of bankruptcy. The referee is not the District Court. He is only an elemental part of the court; one of the instrumentalities of the court, created by the law for the purpose of carrying out the provisions and purposes of the Bankruptcy Act. He occupies, in many respects, the relation to the bankruptcy court that the master does to the court of chancery. Such orders and proceedings as are had before the referee in any case, after the same is concluded by him and the proceedings certified, become a part of the record of the case and as such belong in the office of the clerk of the court in the district and territory in which the referee acts. The clerk of the District Court, being also a clerk of the bankruptcy court, can alone, therefore, certify to the appellate court the proceedings had in a bankruptcy case, either on appeal or on petition to superintend and revise. He, and he alone, has the authorized seal of the court.

"Certain judicial powers are vested in the referee and also certain administrative duties devolved upon him, but these he exercises, as before stated, as an instrumentality to carry into effect the Bankruptcy Act and as an essential of the court designated by law for that purpose. But these do not constitute him the keeper of the records or authorize him to certify records directly to a Circuit Court of Appeals." This was a case of Special Master on Adjudication, however.

And undoubtedly the judge may revoke a reference before it is completed;[58] or may modify it.

§ 527. Referee May Issue Injunctions.—The referee has power to issue restraining orders and injunctions.[59]

---

58. Bankr. Act, § 40 (c): "In the event of the reference of a case being revoked before it is concluded, and when the case is specially referred, the judge shall determine what part of the fee and commissions shall be paid to the referee."

59. In re Northrop, 1 A. B. R. 427 (Ref. N. Y.). This case goes too far

In re Adams, 14 A. B. R. 23, 134 Fed. 142 (D. C. Conn.): "In his injunctive order, I do not think that the referee exceeded the power which the Act confers upon him. It would be a sad state of things if in such emergencies the referee should be compelled to discover the judge in time to save the situation. The matter in hand was peculiarly within the knowledge of the referee, and the court will, in advance, thank all like officers who shall relieve it from an unnecessary burden."

But the question whether or not the referee has jurisdiction to issue a restraining order in any particular instance becomes immaterial where the district court, on its own motion, issues the injunction anew.[60]

§ 528. But May Not Restrain Courts or Officers Thereof.—But
the referee may not enjoin proceedings of a court or officer.[61] Only the judge may do so. The power of a federal court to restrain a state court or an officer thereof is only exercisable in a few carefully guarded instances, of which bankruptcy is one.

§ 529. May Appoint Receiver.—The referee has power, after receipt
of the order of reference, to appoint a receiver.[62]

in authorizing injunction against court officers. See next section following.

In re Steuer, 5 A. B. R. 209, 104 Fed. 976, 980 (D. C. Mass.); In re Martin, 5 A. B. R. 423, 105 Fed. 753 (D. C. N. Y.); impliedly, In re Wilkes, 7 A. B. R. 574, 112 Fed. 975 (D. C. Ark.); In re Huddleston, 1 A. B. R. 572 (Ref. Ala.); In re White, 10 A. B. R. 799 (Ref. Ala.); In re Mustin, 21 A. B. R. 147, 165 Fed. 506 (D. C. Ala.); In re Lawrence, 20 A. B. R. 698, 163 Fed. 131 (D. C. Ala.).

Quære, In re Benjamin, 15 A. B. R. 352, 140 Fed. 320 (D. C. Pa.): "The right of a referee to award an injunction cannot be regarded as finally settled. For while it is sustained by some of the leading works on bankruptcy (Collier, 5th Ed., p. 132; Brandenburg, 3d Ed. 663), it is denied by rule in certain jurisdictions (In re Siebert, 13 A. B. R. 348), and limited in others (Collier, p. 132, note 52) and is materially restricted, if not taken away, by the general orders promulgated by the Supreme Court. General Order XII. It is not questioned, however, here, and I only refer to it, so that in confirming the action of the referee I may not be committed to it as a precedent. The parties have submitted the question at issue between them to the referee for disposition, and as the court might have referred it to him in the first instance, this must be regarded as an equivalent, by which they are bound. In re Steuer, 5 A. B. R. 209."

The case In re Siebert, however, as well as Rule XII referred to, is solely concerned with the referee's lack of jurisdiction to restrain a court or an officer thereof, a power that is not granted even to the District or Circuit Courts of the United States themselves except in bankruptcy cases. The mention of the restriction in Rule XII, furthermore, would seem to imply authority in the referee to issue injunctions in other cases.

Obiter, In re Berkowitz, 16 A. B. R. 254, 143 Fed. 598 (D. C. Pa.). Instance, In re De Long, 1 A. B. R. 66 (Ref. N. Y.).

60. In re Roger Brown Co., 28 A. B. R. 336, 196 Fed. 758 (C. C. A.).

61. Gen. Order No. XII. In re Siebert, 13 A. B. R. 348, 133 Fed. 781 (D. C. N. J.); In re Berkowitz, 16 A. B. R. 251, 143 Fed. 598 (D. C. Pa.); impliedly, In re Lesser, 5 A. B. R. 325 (C. C. A. N. Y., reversed, on other grounds, sub nom. Metcalf v. Barker, 9 A. B. R. 36, 187 U. S. 165); impliedly, In re Globe Cycle Wks., 2 A. B. R. 447 (Ref. N. Y.). But see contra, In re Sabine, 1 A. B. R. 315 (Ref. N. Y.); contra, In re White, 10 A. B. R. 799 (Ref. Ala.); contra, In re Grist, 1 A. B. R. 89 (Ref. N. Y.); contra, In re Northrop, 1 A. B. R. 427 (Ref. N. Y.); apparently contra, In re Huddleston, 1 A. B. R. 572 (Ref. Ala.). Compare, apparently contra, obiter, Smith v. Belford, 5 A. B. R. 294, 108 Fed. 658 (C. C. A. Ohio).

62. In re Florcken, 5 A. B. R. 802, 107 Fed. 241 (D. C. Cal.); inferentially, In re Moody, 12 A. B. R. 718, 131 Fed. 555 (D. C. Ia.).

§ 530. Even before Adjudication.—The referee has power before adjudication, upon receipt of a certificate of the District Clerk of the absence or disability of the District Judge, to appoint a receiver;[63] but not without notice upon the bankrupt, except in cases where the giving of notice is impossible or would defeat the object of the appointment.[64]

§ 530¼. May Order Trustee to Intervene in Pending Action.—The referee has power to authorize the trustee to intervene in an action which was pending at the time the bankruptcy petition was filed.[65]

§ 530½. May Order Preservation of Lien for Benefit of Estate.— And he may order the preservation of liens, otherwise annulled, for the benefit of the estate.[66]

§ 531. May Marshal Liens.—The referee has power to marshal liens on property in the custody of the bankruptcy court and to determine their validity and priority[67]

In re Rochford, 10 A. B. R. 608 (C. C. A. S. Dak.): "A referee in bankruptcy has jurisdiction to draw to himself by summary process or notice, and in the first instance to determine, the question of the validity of the claim of a third party to a lien upon, or an interest in, property or the proceeds of property lawfully in the custody of a trustee in bankruptcy."

§ 532. May Order Sale of Assets.—The referee has power to order the sale of assets;[68] and may appoint appraisers.[69]

§ 533. And May Sell Free from Liens.—The referee has power to order the sale of assets free of liens.[70]

---

63. In re Kelly Dry Goods Co., 4 A. B. R. 528, 102 Fed. 747 (D. C. Wis.).
64. See ante, §§ 346, 381.
65. Conti v. Sunseri, 18 A. B. R. 891 (Pa. Com. Pleas Court).
66. Conti v. Sunseri, 18 A. B. R. 891 (Pa. Com. Pleas Court).
67. See post, § 1888; also Mound Mines Co. v. Hawthorne, 23 A. B. R. 242, 173 Fed. 882 (C. C. A. Colo.), quoted at § 1796; In re Kellogg, 10 A. B. R. 7, 121 Fed. 332 (C. C. A. N. Y., affirming 7 A. B. R. 623); In re Murphy (note Shutts v. Bank), 3 A. B. R. 505, 98 Fed. 720 (Ref. Mass.). Also, see cases under following sections relative to selling free from liens.
68. In re Sanborn, 3 A. B. R. 54, 96 Fed. 551 (D. C. Vt.); In re Styer, 3 A. B. R. 424, 98 Fed. 290 (D. C. N. Y.); In re Mathews, 6 A. B. R. 96, 109 Fed. 603 (D. C. Ark., affirmed in Chauncey v. Dyke Bros., 9 A. B. R. 444, 119 Fed. 1); inferentially, In re Kellogg, 10 A. B. R. 7, 121 Fed. 333 (C. C. A. N. Y., affirming 7 A. B. R. 623, 113 Fed. 120, 122); inferentially,

In re Rochford, 10 A. B. R. 608 (C. C. A. S. Dak.); impliedly, In re Columbia Iron Wks., 14 A. B. R. 528, 142 Fed. 234 (D. C. Mich.); instance, In re Littlefield, 19 A. B. R. 18, 155 Fed. 838 (C. C. A. N. Y.).
69. In re Fisher & Co., 14 A. B. R. 368, 135 Fed. 223 (D. C. N. J.); In re Styer, 3 A. B. R. 424, 98 Fed. 290 (D. C. N. Y.); inferentially, In re Columbia Iron Wks., 14 A. B. R. 528, 142 Fed. 234 (D. C. Mich.).
70. In re Waterloo Organ Co., 9 A. B. R. 427, 118 Fed. 904 (D. C. N. Y.); In re Styer, 3 A. B. R. 424, 98 Fed. 290 (D. C. N. Y.); In re Mathews, 6 A. B. R. 96, 109 Fed. 603 (D. C. Ark., affirmed in Chauncey v. Dyke Bros., 9 A. B. R. 444, 119 Fed. 1); inferentially, In re Kellogg, 10 A. B. R. 7 (C. C. A. N. Y., affirming 7 A. B. R. 623, 113 Fed. 120, 122); In re Pittelkow, 1 A. B. R. 422, 92 Fed. 901 (D. C. Wis.); In re Granite City Bank, 14 A. B. R. 404, 137 Fed. 818 (C. C. A. Iowa, affirming In re Wilka, 12 A. B. R. 727); inferentially, In re Saxton Furnace

In re Sanborn, 3 A. B. R. 54, 96 Fed. 551 (D. C. Vt.): "That the referee has power to order and approve a sale free of encumbrances of property in possession by the trustee on notice to the encumbrancer seems to be clear."

§ 534. May, on Reference in Judge's Absence or Disability, Order Sale before Adjudication Same as Judge.—And he has power to order a sale on reference to him in the judge's absence or disability before adjudication under such circumstances as would warrant the judge to order a sale.[71]

§ 535. May Tax Costs.—The referee may tax costs.[72]

§ 535½. May Liquidate Claims.—The referee may, of course, liquidate claims, upon proper occasions.[73]

§ 536. May Order Payment of Priority Claims and Order Distribution.—The referee may order the payment of priority claims, and, in general, may order distribution; thus, as to taxes.[74]

§ 537. May Order Witnesses to Appear for Examination.—The referee has full discretion to order witnesses to appear for examination.[75]

§ 538. May Pass on Intervening Petition Claiming Property.—The referee has power to pass upon an intervening petition claiming property or its proceeds in the custody of the bankruptcy court.[76]

§ 539. May Order Surrender of Property Held by Bankrupt.—The referee has power to order the surrender of property held by the bankrupt.[77]

§ 540. Also by Agent of Bankrupt or Person Not Claiming Adversely.—The referee has power to order the surrender of property held

Co., 14 A. B. R. 483 (D. C. Pa.); instance, McNair v. McIntyre, 7 A. B. R. 638, 136 Fed. 697 (C. C. A. N. Car.). See post, subject of "Selling Property Free from Liens," § 1963, et seq. Instance, In re Keller, 6 A. B. R. 351, 109 Fed. 131 (D. C. Iowa); instance, In re Prince & Walter, 12 A. B. R. 675 (D. C. La.); instance, In re New England Piano Co., 9 A. B. R. 767 (C. C. A. Mass.); instance, Carriage Co. v. Solanas, 6 A. B. R. 221, 108 Fed. 532 (D. C. La.); instance, In re Rosenberg, 8 A. B. R. 624, 116 Fed. 402 (D. C. Pa.); In re Miners Brew. Co., 20 A. B. R. 717, 162 Fed. 327 (D. C. Pa.); In re Littlefield, 19 A. B. R. 18, 155 Fed. 838 (C. C. A. N. Y.).

71. In re Kelly Dry Goods Co., 4 A. B. R. 528, 102 Fed. 747 (D. C. Wis.).

72. In re Scott, 7 A. B. R. 710 (D. C. Mass.); inferentially, In re Todd, 6 A. B. R. 88, 109 Fed. 265 (D. C. N. Y.).

Under what circumstances he may tax attorneys' fees as part of the costs, see post, §§ 861½, 1996, 2004.

73. See post, § 712. Also see In re Du Quesne Incandescent Light Co., 24 A. B. R. 419, 176 Fed. 785 (D. C. Pa.).

74. In re Tilden, 1 A. B. R. 302, 91 Fed. 501 (D. C. Iowa).

75. In re The Abbey Press, 13 A. B. R. 11, 134 Fed. 41 (C. C. A. N. Y.).

76. In re Drayton, 13 A. B. R. 602, 135 Fed. 883 (D. C. Wis.).

77. In re Miller, 5 A. B. R. 184, 105 Fed. 57 (D. C. Iowa); In re Rosser, 4 A. B. R. 153, 101 Fed. 462 (C. C. A. Mo.); In re Oliver, 2 A. B. R. 783, 96 Fed. 85 (D. C. Calif.); impliedly, In re Purvine, 2 A. B. R. 787, 96 Fed. 192 (C. C. A. Tex.); In re Mayer, 3 A. B. R. 533, 98 Fed. 839 (D. C. Wis.). See post, § 1816, et seq.

by agents of the bankrupt, or by persons not claiming adverse interests therein.[78]

§ 541. Also Property by Assignees.

—Also property held by assignees under void assignments for the benefit of creditors.[79]

§ 542. Also Property in Hands of Garnishees.

—Also property held by garnishees, where the legal proceedings are void under § 67 "f";[80] but not where it is a mere debt owing by the garnishee to the debtor.

§ 543. Also Property Taken Out of Bankrupt's Possession after Filing of Bankruptcy Petition.

—The referee has power to order the surrender of property taken out of the bankrupt's possession after the filing of the bankruptcy petition;[81] or wrongfully paid out by the bankrupt after the filing,[82] and to order its seizure by the marshal upon warrant of seizure.[83]

§ 544. No Jurisdiction to Order Surrender of Property Held Adversely.

—But the referee has no power to order the surrender of property held adversely by third persons at the time of the adjudication.[84]

§ 545. No Jurisdiction to Entertain Plenary Actions.

—And the referee has no jurisdiction to entertain plenary suits against third parties to recover property adversely held or debts due the estate;[85] for the referee, though included within the term "the court" by clause (7) of § 1 of the act, has not the machinery at hand for the conducting of a plenary suit, with its

---

78. Mueller *v.* Nugent, 7 A. B. R. 224, 184 U. S. 1. See post, §§ 1474, 1823, et seq.

79. But compare, contra, Smith *v.* Belford, 5 A. B. R. 294 (C. C. A. Ohio), on doctrine of overruled case of In re Nugent, 5 A. B. R. 176, reversed in Mueller *v.* Nugent, 184 U. S. 1.

See post, § 1828, et seq.

But that the taking of property out of one's possession and the restraining of such one's use of it as owner are but different acts of the exercise of the same jurisdiction, see In re Ward, 5 A. B. R. 215, 104 Fed. 985 (D. C. Mass.).

80. In re Beals, 8 A. B. R. 639, 116 Fed. 530 (D. C. Ind.).

81. In re Huddleston, 1 A. B. R. 572 (Ref. Ala.).

82. Knapp & Spencer *v.* Drew, 20 A. B. R. 355, 160 Fed. 413 (C. C. A. Neb.), quoted at §§ 523, 1800.

83. Impliedly, but obiter, In re Rochford, 10 A. B. R. 608, 124 Fed. 782 (C. C. A. S. D.).

84. In re Grohs, 1 A. B. R. 465 (Ref.

Ohio); In re Cohn, 3 A. B. R. 421 (D. C. N. Y.); In re Walsh Bros., 21 A. B. R. 14, 163 Fed. 352 (D. C. Iowa), quoted post, at § 1652; In re Peacock, 24 A. B. R. 159, 178 Fed. 851 (D. C. N. Car.), quoted at § 548; contra, In re Shults and Marks, 11 A. B. R. 690 (Ref. N. Y.). See ante, §§ 355, 391; post, § 1652, et seq.

85. Compare post, § 1695; Horskins *v.* Sanderson, 13 A. B. R. 102, 132 Fed. 415 (D. C. Vt.); In re Scherber, 12 A. B. R. 616, 131 Fed. 121 (D. C. Mass.); In re Grohs, 1 A. B. R. 465 (Ref. Ohio); In re Walsh Bros., 21 A. B. R. 14, 163 Fed. 352 (D. C. Iowa), quoted at § 1652; In re Overholzer, 23 A. B. R. 10 (Ref. N. Dak.); compare, In re Steuer, 5 A. B. R. 209, 104 Fed. 976 (D. C. Mass.); quære, In re Goldberg, 1 A. B. R. 385 (Ref. Utah); In re Cohn, 3 A. B. R. 421 (D. C. N. Y.); contra, In re Shults & Marks, 11 A. B. R. 690 (Ref. N. Y.). Compare, apparently contra, In re O'Brien, 21 A. B. R. 11 (Ref. Mass.). Compare, In re Peacock, 24 A. B. R. 159, 178 Fed. 851 (D. C. N. Car.), quoted at § 548.

requirements of formal service of process, rule days, pleadings, trial and verdicts.

A plenary suit brought by a trustee in bankruptcy is not a proceedings in bankruptcy although it may be an action or proceedings growing out of a bankruptcy proceedings. Referees are restricted in their jurisdiction to purely "proceedings in bankruptcy," and also to such controversies arising out of bankruptcy proceedings as concern property within the possession or control of the bankruptcy court.

§ 545½. **Nor to Render Judgment in Personam.**—And the referee has no jurisdiction to render judgment in personam.[86] He proceeds solely by "orders."

§ 545¾. **No Jurisdiction over Discharge Matters.**—The act expressly excludes from the referee's jurisdiction matters pertaining to the discharge of the bankrupt.[87] The petition for discharge is not to be filed with him;[88] and there is no power in the district court to grant him this function by "local rule." The Bankruptcy Act is intended to be uniform in its procedure, throughout the United States, one of the objects of its passage and one of the economic reasons for its existence being precisely the necessity for uniform procedure and remedies throughout the United States.

§ 546. **May Not Vacate Adjudication.**—The referee has no power to pass upon an application for the vacating of the adjudication;[89] nor to dismiss the proceedings after adjudication.[90]

§ 547. **May Disapprove Election of Trustee.**—The referee has authority to disapprove of the trustee elected by creditors.[91]

DIVISION 5.

PLEADINGS AND PRACTICE BEFORE REFEREES.

§ 548. **Proceedings before Referee Summary.**—Proceedings before the referee are summary, not plenary. By this is not meant that the proceedings are ex parte, nor that they are conducted without pleadings; for the power of the court is invoked in bankruptcy as in other branches of jurisprudence, by the filing of pleadings, and, as in other branches, is in

---

86. See post, § 548. Also, see Knapp & Spencer v. Drew, 20 A. B. R. 355, 160 Fed. 413 (C. C. A. Neb.).

87. In re Taylor, 26 A. B. R. 143, 188 Fed. 479 (D. C. Ala.) quoted at § 2430¼.

88. In re Taylor, 26 A. B. R. 143, 188 Fed. 479 (D. C. Ala.) quoted at § 2430¼.

89. In re Imperial Corp., 13 A. B. R. 199 (D. C. N. Y.); In re Elby, 19 A. B. R. 734, 157 Fed. 935 (D. C. Iowa).

But see, contra, In re Scott, 7 A. B. R. 37 (Ref. Mass.). And, also, see, apparently contra, In re Clisdell, 2 A. B. R. 424 (Ref. N. Y.). See ante. § 430.

90. In re Elby, 19 A. B. R. 734, 157 Fed. 935 (D. C. Iowa).

91. See post, § 878, et seq. In re McGill, 5 A. B. R. 155, 106 Fed. 57 (C. C. A. Ohio); In re Sitting, 25 A. B. R. 682. 182 Fed. 917 (D. C. N. Y.); In re Clay, 27 A. B. R. 715, 192 Fed. 830 (C. C. A. Mass.).

general to be exercised only upon notice. But by being "summary" is meant that they proceed by mere notice and by orders upon persons to do or abstain from doing, and not, as in plenary actions, by way of summons or subpœna, by way of stated rule days for pleading in answer and reply, or by way of judgment leviable out of property.

The remedies before the referee are perhaps more drastic than those before a court which proceeds by way of judgment or decree, for the orders of the referee are enforceable by imprisonment for contempt.[92] But for this precise reason they are more limited, for when a remedy is enforceable by depriving the individual of liberty the court is bound to proceed with the utmost caution and only upon clear proof that the person ordered has the present capacity to perform what is ordered. This principle undoubtedly partly lies at the basis of the rule that the orders of the referee may, in general, be made only concerning property in the custody of the court or its officers or of the bankrupt himself, and not concerning property in the custody of third persons, as to whom plenary action alone will lie.

Nor has the Amendment of 1903, giving to the bankruptcy courts jurisdiction over suits for the recovery from third parties of property of the estate fraudulently or preferentially conveyed, enlarged, in this particular, the jurisdiction of the referee. No more now than formerly may the referee proceed by judgment or decree leviable out of the property of the defeated party, nor by order against a third party concerning property not in the custody of the bankruptcy court or of its officers or of the bankrupt. The Amendatory Act of 1903 conferred power on the bankruptcy courts to recover property of the estate from the possession of third parties, to be sure, but such jurisdiction is to be exercised only by plenary action—formal bill or petition, with regular rule days for pleading, hearing and trial—in the ordinary manner of lawsuits; and not merely upon such notice and hearing as may appear to be reasonable, enforceable solely by order upon the person to do or abstain from doing particular acts. There is no more machinery provided now, than formerly, for the carrying on of plenary actions before the referee—no rule days for pleadings prescribed, no juries obtainable.[93]

Quære, In re Mullen, 4 A. B. R. 224, 101 Fed. 413 (D. C. Mass.): "I doubt if the forms of pleading at common law and in equity are applicable to such

---

92. See In re De Gottardi, 7 A. B. R. 741, 114 Fed. 328 (D. C. Calif.).

93. Contra, obiter, that the referee possessed and possesses plenary jurisdiction. In re Murphy (Shults v. Bk.), 3 A. B. R. 505, 98 Fed. 720 (Ref. Mass.).

Contra, obiter, that possibly the referee might call a jury to pass upon the allowability of a claim. In re Rude, 4 A. B. R. 319, 101 Fed. 805 (D. C. Ky.).

Demurrers to Petitions before Referees.—It is doubtful whether demurrer will lie to a summary petition before a referee, whether the objection should not be taken by answer. Inferentially, In re Mullen, 4 A. B. R. 224, 101 Fed. 413 (D. C. Mass.).

Referees should so conduct their proceedings and make up their records that a full and fair review of their acts may be had. In re Romine, 14 A. B. R. 785, 138 Fed. 437 (D. C. W. Va.).

summary proceedings. It may well be that the objections raised by the demurrer should have been presented, as they certainly might have been, in an answer to the merits."

In re Peacock, 24 A. B. R. 159, 178 Fed. 851 (D. C. N. Car.): "To confer upon the referee the jurisdiction to pass upon and decide controversies regarding the title to property between the trustee and third parties, frequently and, as in this case, involving questions and issues of fact, would be to deprive the parties of trial by jury as secured by the Constitution. The mere fact that a person has been adjudged a bankrupt does not deprive other persons owning or claiming purely legal rights to property claimed by the trustee of having such rights adjudicated in the courts and by procedure guaranteed to them by the Constitution."

§ 548½. **Process.**—The Supreme Court's General Order No.'3 provides that "All process, summons and subpœnas shall issue out of the court, under the seal thereof, and be tested by the clerk; and blanks, with the signature of the clerk and seal of the court, may, upon application, be furnished to the referees."[94]

§ 549. **But Not on Plane of Depositions before Notaries nor of Hearings before Masters in Chancery.**—Although the referee is not possessed of jurisdiction to entertain plenary actions, yet he is more than a notary public or master in chancery; he is, when exercising the functions of his office, "the court."[95]

§ 549½. **Notices and "Orders to Show Cause."**—There are two methods of bringing parties before the court of the referee for determination of their rights: notices by mail to creditors (considered post, at § 564, et seq.), and orders to show cause upon parties claiming interests in property or upon whom summary orders to surrender assets or perform some other acts are demanded.[95a] There is, of course, no need of a notice of the granting of the "order to show cause"—it is itself merely a notice.[96]

§ 550. **Hearings Governed by United States Equity Rules, Where Act or Rules Silent.**—Hearings before referees are governed by the United States equity rules, where the special provisions of the Bankruptcy Act or the rules and forms prescribed by the General Orders in Bankruptcy of the Supreme Court or by local rules, are silent.[97]

§ 551. **Competency of Witnesses Whether Governed by United States Statutes, or by State Statutes.**—The competency of witnesses

---

94. See ante, preceding division of this chapter. But compare, In re Covington, 6 A. B. R. 373, 110 Fed. 143 (D. C. N. Car.).

95. See post, § 1537. Compare, Cohen v. American Surety Co., 22 A. B. R. 909, 132 App. Div. (N. Y.) 917.

95a. See post, §§ 1838, 1890, 1980.

96. In re Philip Brady, 21 A. B. R. 364, 169 Fed. 152 (D. C. Ky.). Compare, collaterally, Morehouse v.

Pacific Hardware, etc., Co., 24 A. B. R. 178, 177 Fed. 337 (C. C. A. Nev.): "An order to show cause is but the means prescribed by law for bringing the defendant into court to answer the plaintiff's demands. It is in the nature of process."

97. Dressel v. North State Lumber Co., 9 A. B. R. 541, 119 Fed. 531 (D. C. N. Car.). Compare Gen. Ord. No. 37.

to testify is, to be sure, governed by the United States statutes and not by the state law;[98] but, the federal statutes themselves prescribe that the competency of witnesses in civil proceedings in the federal court is to be determined by the law of the state in which the court is held;[98a] except that, regardless of state law, a party may not testify to transactions with a deceased person where the opposite party is the executor or administrator.

§ 552. Referee to Rule on Evidence and Admit or Exclude.—A referee in bankruptcy, in hearings before him, should rule upon the admissibility and competency of evidence, and may exclude evidence deemed by him inadmissible.[99]

In re Wilde's Sons, 11 A. B. R. 714, 131 Fed. 142 (D. C. N. Y.): "This motion involves the question whether a referee in bankruptcy has any power to exclude evidence. As I understand it, an officer appointed to simply take testimony for the use of the court, as, for instance, an examiner in an equity suit, has no jurisdiction to exclude or pass upon testimony. Unless the parties refer any question of the admission of testimony to the court, he is obliged to take all that is offered. But I think that whenever any officer is appointed whose duty it is to take evidence and also to exercise any judicial duty in regard to it, as to decide issues or to state the facts or law in an opinion or report, it is his right and his duty to exclude inadmissible evidence upon objection. Why should he admit evidence which it would be his duty to disregard if admitted? Substantially all the cases in which evidence is taken by referees in bankruptcy, either in their character as referees or as special commissioners, are cases in which they either decide questions outright or draw conclusions from the evidence in the shape either of a report or an opinion; and I think that in all such cases the referee has the right to exclude evidence which he deems inadmissible. If error is committed by such exclusion, any party interested can take up the matter immediately on a certificate, or can urge the alleged error on final hearing."

In re Ruos, 20 A. B. R. 281, 164 Fed. 749 (D. C. Pa.): "Where a question arises concerning the competency of a witness or the admissibility of evidence, the referee should decide the point himself in the first instance, instead of turning the matter over to the court. It will be time enough to certify the question when he is asked to do so in a proper manner. Very often his ruling will be acquiesced in, and the delay of referring the dispute to the court will be thus avoided."

In re De Gottardi, 7 A. B. R. 723, 114 Fed. 328 (D. C. Calif.): "The first proposition stated in the bankrupts' argument, that a referee is clothed with important powers, among them that of determining objections to testimony, has

---

98. Smith v. Township, 17 A. B. R. 748 (C. C. A. Mich.). Compare, however, before Amendment of 1903, In re Josephson, 9 A. B. R. 345, 121 Fed. 142 (D. C. Ga., on review sub nom. Myers v. Josephson, 10 A. B. R. 687). Compare, post, § 1567. Compare, contra, In re Horne, 22 A. B. R. 269 (Ref. Miss.), where the bankrupt was held disqualified to object to the claim of a decedent's administrator under a State statute forbidding a party so testifying even where claim "assigned." Bankruptcy transfers title by operation of law, not by "assignment," however, even if State statute applicable. Quoted at § 1567.

98a. Compare post, § 1567; see also U. S. Revised Statutes, § 858 as amended June 27, 1906, 34 Stat. L. 618 (Fed. Stat. Annot. Supp. 1909, p. 708). Thus, as to wife testifying to transactions with husband. In re Hoffman, 28 A. B. R. 680, 199 Fed. 448 (D. C. N. J.).

99. In re Kaiser, 3 A. B. R. 767, 99 Fed. 689 (D. C. Minn.). In re Harrison Bros., 28 A. B. R. 293, 197 Fed. 320 (D. C. Pa.), quoted later in this section. See also, post, § 1554.

been approvingly adopted by text writers, and is unquestionably sound. Jurisdiction to hear and determine issues of fact necessarily implies power to pass upon the admissibility of testimony."

It has, however, been held, apparently contra, that the referee must take down all the evidence, simply noting the objections thereto and his ruling thereon.[1]

Mock *v.* Stoddard, 24 A. B. R. 403, 177 Fed. 611 (C. C. A. Idaho): "The objection to this evidence was sustained by the referee, but in accordance with equity procedure the evidence was taken out and certified to the court by the referee as part of the record of the proceedings."

Compare, to same effect, obiter, Bank *v.* Johnson, 16 A. B. R. 208, 143 Fed. 463 (C. C. A. W. Va., reversing, on this point, In re Romine, 14 A. B. R. 785): "We cannot concur in the decision of the District Court that a referee 'acting in his character as referee or as special commissioner has the right to exclude evidence which he deems inadmissible.' For this holding In re Wilde's Sons, 11 Am. B. R. 714, 131 Fed. 142, is cited, and the learned judge states there are many cases to the contrary. Even if the conflicting decisions are considered, the general orders passed by the Supreme Court are controlling; they have the force of the statute, are made pursuant to express authority in the statute. The same question was raised in In re Sturgeon, 14 Am. B. R. 681, 139 Fed. 608. * * *

"No amount of argument could make the matter plainer. Any one who will can understand."

Mo.-Am. Elec. Co. *v.* Hamilton & Brown Co., 21 A. B. R. 270, 165 Fed. 283 (C. C. A. Mo.): "A proceeding in bankruptcy is a proceeding in equity, and it is the duty of examiners, masters, referees, and the court, when taking evidence in controversies therein in the absence of a jury, to take, record, and, in case of an appeal, to return to the reviewing court, all the evidence offered by either party, that which they hold to be incompetent or immaterial as well as that which they deem competent and relevant, to the end that, if the appellate court is of the opinion that evidence rejected should have been received, it may consider it, render a final decree, and thus conclude the litigation without remanding the suit to procure the rejected evidence. From this rule evidence plainly privileged, the testimony of privileged witnesses, and evidence which clearly and affirmatively appears to be so incompetent, irrelevant, and immaterial that it would be an abuse of the process or power of the court to compel its production or permit its introduction, are excepted."

But the contra holding, though strongly supported, certainly can not be the true rule. If referees are without power to exclude questions and an-

---

1. Compare, post, §§ 2554, 2855; National Bank *v.* Abbott, 21 A. B. R. 436, 165 Fed. 852 (C. C. A. Mo.); In re Rauchenplat, 9 A. B. R. 763 (D. C. Porta Rica).

Compare, In re Lipset, 9 A. B. R. 32, 119 Fed. 379 (Ref. N. Y.). Referee Wise held in this case that the referee, acting as special commissioner on discharge, although he might rule upon the admissibility, nevertheless, should take down all the evidence.

Also compare, Dressel *v.* North State Lumber Co., 9 A. B. R. 541, 119 Fed. 531 (D. C. N. Car.). In this case it was held, that on simple objection the referee must not excuse a witness from answering, but must note the objection and take the answer.

Compare, to same effect, In re Sturgeon, 14 A. B. R. 681, 139 Fed. 608 (C. C. A. N. Y.); compare, to same effect, Blease *v.* Garlington, 92 U. S. 1.

swers, license will run riot in the referee's hearings and very bedlam be let loose.[2] It is easy enough to say all questions and answers are to be taken down and objections be simply noted—all for the convenience of possible review, the exceptional case—but the carrying out of the doctrine would lead to insufferable abuses. A reasonable construction of the rule simply is that the referee should admit or exclude evidence, as the case may be, but in cases of exclusion should take down, if requested, the answer the proponent says he expected, which, undoubtedly, the witness himself might be asked to frame. Such rule is sensible, appropriate and long established, and sufficiently conveniences the reviewing courts and protects the rights of all parties.

And it is true that the referee should take the answer, so that the district judge on review may be able to rule without sending the matter back to the referee.[3]

In re Romine, 14 A. B. R. 785, 138 Fed. 437 (D. C. W. Va.): "It is clear to me that in taking testimony the referee must have it taken down, preferably in narrative form, but, upon objection raised, it is his duty to require the matter to be presented by question to which the objection and reason thereof is to be clearly but briefly noted; then to enter his ruling thereon as to whether proper or not, and although he may rule it to be improper, yet allow it to be answered."

Undoubtedly the taking down of the answer after objection sustained under Rule XXII is no more cumbersome than the familiar practice, in other courts, of counsel stating in the record, after objection has been sustained to the question, what it is expected the answer to the question would have been, thus exhibiting to the reviewing court the materiality of the answer and the prejudice resulting from its exclusion.[4] It is doubtful whether the answer should be taken however unless, after objection is sustained, exception is taken to the ruling. Any less strict rule would simply lead to license and interminable confusion and prolonged examination, such as perhaps was the situation in the case In re Romine, above cited, the remedy for which, suggested in the court's opinion, would hardly be adequate.

But, in any event, the referee may absolutely exclude repetitions of the same questions and answers.

In re Romine, 14 A. B. R. 789, 138 Fed. 437 (D. C. W. Va.): "I am persuaded, however, that he is not called upon to suffer and allow counsel * * * to ask and permit witnesses to answer the same question, over and over again, whereby time is unnecessarily consumed and costs incurred; but that upon his noting the fact that the question has been once answered, or the demand to answer has once been positively refused, the court will justify him in preventing vain repetition."

---

2. In re Harrison Bros., 28 A. B. R. 293, 197 Fed. 320 (D. C. Pa.), quoted in text at end of this section.
3. Gen. Order XXII.
4. See, to same effect, In re Lipset, 9 A. B. R. 32, 119 Fed. 379 (Ref. N. Y.); also, to same effect, Dressel v. North State Lumber Co., 9 A. B. R. 541, 119 Fed. 531 (D. C. N. C.).

And in any event, also, the referee may exclude evidence where it is so clearly and plainly incompetent, irrelevant and immaterial that it would have been an abuse of the process or power of the court to have compelled its production.[5]

And it is to be noted that almost all the cases holding the referee's function to be limited to merely noting the objections and nevertheless taking the answers, have been cases where the referee has not been acting as such in contested cases before him, but where he has been acting as special master on discharge or as master commissioner taking depositions for use elsewhere.

In re Harrison Bros., 28 A. B. R. 293, 197 Fed. 320 (D. C. Pa.): "It is true that some courts have reached a contrary conclusion, requiring the referee to hear and record everything that is offered, regardless of how relevant he may consider it. A careful examination of these cases, however, will disclose the fact that in most every instance, where this ruling was made, the referee was acting as a commissioner, or special master, to take testimony to report to the court. In re Lipset (D. C. N. Y.), 9 A. B. R. 32; In re Romine (D. C., W. Va.), 14 A. B. R. 789, 138 Fed. 840; In re Isaacson (D. C. N. Y.), 23 A. B. R. 665, 175 Fed. 292; Bank of Ravenswood v. Johnson (C. C. A., 4th Cir.), 16 A. B. R. 206, 143 Fed. 463. It must be conceded that there is a vast difference in the authority of the referee, in a judicial capacity, vested and clothed with the duties conferred by the act on courts of bankruptcy, and, as such, sitting in his capacity as a commissioner to take testimony or as a special master. He is sitting in the former capacity when he is presiding in any proceeding which was originally instituted before him in the course of bankruptcy after reference—such as a general examination, a proceeding to turn over concealed assets, proceedings to allow, or reject, or expunge a claim, etc. He is sitting in the latter capacity when in the course of bankruptcy a specific proceeding, instituted before another referee or before the district judge and the matter is referred to him to take the testimony and report. Such is his capacity when he is taking testimony upon objections to a discharge, and when he is taking testimony as a commissioner to be read in evidence in a case pending before another referee. When acting in the former capacity his duties are judicial, clothed with judicial power, while under the latter they are but ministerial. When acting in this judicial capacity he is regarded as a judicial officer, invested with the same powers and duties in bankruptcy matters as a district judge, having full power, no doubt, to exclude irrelevant testimony. If this is not the law, to use the language of Remington on Bankruptcy, vol. 1, p. 336, 'If referees are without power to exclude questions and answers, license will run wild in the referees' hearings, and very bedlam be let loose. It is easy enough to say all questions and answers are to be taken down and objections be simply noted, all for the convenience of possible review, the exceptional case, but the carrying out of the doctrine would lead to insufferable abuses.' And the same answer says, on page 929: 'A rule compelling the referee on general examination of bankrupts and witnesses, to take down answers although the question be incompetent and the answers improper, would lead to interminable confusion, and would practically give over such examinations into the absolute control of the examiner, leading to the possibility of intolerable abuse.'

---

5. In re Clark, 21 A. B. R. 776 (Ref. Calif.); obiter, Mo.-Am. Elec. Co. v. Hamilton & Brown Co., 21 A. B. R. 270, 165 Fed. 283 (C. C. A. Mo.), quoted supra.

But it is contended by all the reported cases that hold a contra view that the proposition is controlled by General Order No. 22, as follows: 'The examination of witnesses before the referee may be conducted by the party in person or by his counsel or attorney, and the witnesses shall be subject to examination and cross-examination, which shall be had in conformity with the mode now adopted in courts of law. A deposition taken upon an examination before a referee shall be taken down in writing by him, or under his direction, in the form of a narrative, unless he determines that the examination shall be by question and answer. When complete it shall be read over to the witness and signed by him in the presence of the referee. The referee shall note upon the deposition any question objected to, with his decision thereon, and the court shall have power to deal with the costs of incompetent, immaterial, or irrelevant depositions, or parts of them, as may be just.' A careful analysis of this order is convincing that it does not sustain the conclusion. The first clause relates to the examination of witnesses before the referee acting as a judicial officer and prescribes how that examination shall be conducted, viz., 'by examination and cross-examination,' and then provides how and in what order and manner this examination and cross-examination shall be conducted, viz., 'in conformity with the mode now adopted in courts of law.' This part only relates to the examination of witnesses in open court orally; and in this there is nothing inconsistent with our conclusion. The remainder of the order relates to 'depositions.' Now, a deposition, says Cyc., vol. 13, p.. 832, is 'Testimony taken out of court under authority which will enable it to be read as evidence in court, and has no relation to oral testimony taken in court or before a master.' To the same effect is Factory v. Corning, 7 Blatchford, 16. It does.not relate to testimony taken before the court or tribunal where the proceedings were instituted and conducted. To adopt a contrary conclusion would imply that the Supreme Court had been exceedingly lax in the use of technical legal words and terms and this we will not assume."

§ 552½. Ground of Objection to Be Stated.

The general rule is that the ground of objection must be stated, else the objection, though duly excepted to, will not be available on review.[6]

However, where there can be but one possible ground for the objection and such ground is sufficiently obvious, it may be noticed on review.[7]

§ 553. Referee to Hear Evidence.

The referee must be present and hear the evidence, whenever he is to decide upon the weight of it;[8] but in purely formal hearings his presence may be waived. The referee is to decide each controversy on the evidence introduced on the hearing thereof. Thus, he is not to consider a previous examination of the bankrupt or of a witness, as

---

6. Equity Rule II, 150 Fed. XXVII. Also, compare post, § 2844.

7. Analogously, Johnson v. United States, 20 A. B. R. 724, 158 Fed. 69 (C. C. A. Mass.).

8. In re Wilde's Sons, 11 A. B. R. 714, 131 Fed. 142 (D. C. N. Y.).

As to manner of taking exceptions to the referee's rulings and as to review of same, see post, § 2839, "Review of Referee's Orders."

As to procedure in the general examination of the bankrupt and witnesses, see post, "General Examination of Bankrupt and Witnesses," § 1525, et seq.

As to proper parties in hearings before referee, see various subjects concerned.

As to right to inspect documents, etc., see post, § 915.

being in evidence, unless the same is introduced into evidence or stipulated in.[9]

§ 553¼. **Necessity of Pleadings.**—No pleadings are requisite to bring on a "general examination" of the bankrupt or of witnesses;[10] but in contested matters before the referee, pleadings are requisite; as, for instance, on objection to, or re-examination of, a claim[11] petition and answer are requisite, and leave to plead out of time will be granted only for due cause.[12]

§ 553½. **Reopening of Case for Further Testimony.**—After a party has had an opportunity to call and examine his witnesses and the matter is closed, he should not be permitted to re-open the case for the introduction of evidence which he subsequently concludes would have been an advantage to him.

In re Booss, 18 A. B. R. 658, 154 Fed. 494 (D. C. Pa.): "We approve the conclusions of the referee in this case. While we think every facility and opportunity should be afforded parties interested in bankrupt estates to present their evidence in support of contentions in which they may be interested, there is a limit beyond which it would be impracticable and imprudent to go. After a party has had an opportunity to call and examine his witnesses and the matter is closed, unless there is some especial reason for it, the referee should not be expected to again open the case. A party cannot be permitted to re-open a case whenever he finds that he has not produced some evidence which he subsequently concludes would have been an advantage to him. Like all other litigation, there must be an orderly manner of proceeding as well before a referee as before a jury."

Unless for special reasons.[13]

§ 553¾. **State Regulations of Right to Maintain Suit Not Binding.**—State laws requiring certain partnerships, etc., to file certificates of members, etc., and other local regulations upon the right of a party to maintain a suit, are not binding upon the bankruptcy court.[14]

SUBDIVISION "A."

CREDIBILITY OF WITNESSES AND EVIDENCE ON HEARINGS IN BANKRUPTCY.

§ 554. **Untrustworthy, Though Uncontradicted, Testimony May Be Rejected.**—Oral admissions, denied and uncorroborated, may be not sufficient to support a claim.[15] And the bankrupt's uncorroborated testimony as to the precise time of his becoming insolvent should be received with caution.[16] Even uncontradicted testimony in support of a claim may be so unsatisfactory that it may be rejected and the claim be disallowed, al-

---

9. See post, § 1555½.
10. See post, § 1525, et seq.
11. See post, § 830, et seq.
12. See post, § 841.
13. Compare, Geo. Carroll & Bros. Co. v. Young, 9 A. B. R. 643.

14. In re Farmers' Supply Co., 22 A. B. R. 460, 170 Fed. 502 (D. C. Ohio).
15. In re Kaldenberg, 5 A. B. R. 6, 105 Fed. 232 (D. C. N. Y.).
16. In re Linton, 7 A. B. R. 676 (Ref. Tex.). To same effect, see post, § 2650.

though the objectors may have been under the burden of rebutting the prima facie case made by the deposition for proof of the claim.[17]

Ohio Valley Bank v. Mack, 20 A. B. R. 919, 163 Fed. 155 (D. C. Ohio): "The bankrupt though doing a large business kept no books and it was his practice to destroy all notes and other evidence of indebtedness as soon as the debts were paid or settled. The petitioning (claiming) creditors are members of the family. The answer given to a majority of the questions put to the bankrupt while under examination was 'I don't remember,' and the testimony of the other members of the family who were witnesses was not much more satisfactory."

To same effect, In re Domenig, 11 A. B. R. 555, 128 Fed. 146 (D. C. Pa.): "Much will necessarily depend on the manner of the witness while under examination, and referees should feel themselves obliged to consider of their own motion the credibility of the witness and of the story that is told, even if there should be no opposing testimony. The mere fact that the witness has not been contradicted does not require the acceptance of the testimony."

But where the only evidence adduced on either side is the testimony of the claimant, it has been suggested that, as to any defense of new matter, such as preference, the trustee's case also must fail if the testimony is to be rejected as untrustworthy.

Neumann v. Blake, 24 A. B. R. 575, 178 Fed. 916 (C. C. A. Mo.): "Conceding, for the sake of the argument, that the referee had the right to reject her testimony, yet, if he did reject it, then there was no evidence before him showing that the bankrupt had ever paid her $300, or any other sum. Her testimony was the only testimony in the case, and she testified that the sum of $300 was paid to and used by her for living expenses for herself and children only, and not in part payment of the debt."

But this argument overlooks the common experience that one may well believe a party's admissions against interest whilst doubting what he may say when he thinks he is supporting his own case. Notwithstanding any rule as to vouching for the truthfulness of one's own witnesses, human nature does not sustain the contention that all parts of a party's own testimony is of equal credibility or incredibility.

§ 554½. **Failure to Call Accessible Witnesses.**—Likewise, uncontradicted but uncorroborated testimony of an adverse claimant to property in the trustee's possession may be insufficient, if witnesses are not called who might have substantiated the claim.

In re Mayer, 19 A. B. R. 480, 156 Fed. 432 (D. C. Pa.): "It would be dangerous to accept such testimony as is now before the court without corroboration, save in exceptional cases. The bankrupt, who must have known as much about the matter as his brother, was not called as a witness; there is not a scrap of written evidence to support the claim, directly or indirectly; it is not even

---

17. Compare post, §§ 852, 2650. In re Cannon, 14 A. B. R. 114, 133 Fed. 837 (D. C. Pa.); In re Baumhauer, 24 A. B. R. 750, 179 Fed. 966 (D. C. Ala.); In re Friedman, 21 A. B. R. 213, 164 Fed. 131 (D. C. Wis.), quoted at § 852; similarly, In re Mayer, 19 A. B. R. 480, 156 Fed. 432 (D. C. Pa.), quoted at § 554½.

proved that the property in dispute ever belonged to the partnership, although the merchants, who are said to have sold it to the firm, were easily accessible; and, in a word, the whole statement rests absolutely upon the claimant's uncorroborated account, to which it would be almost impossible for the trustee to reply. I do not decide that in no case can a claim be made out by the unsupported testimony of the creditor, but simply that, under the circumstances of the present case, I do not find such testimony to be sufficient. I therefore hold, that the evidence offered by Max Mayer does not establish his claim to be the owner of the goods in dispute, and that he has not overcome the prima facies of the bankrupt's ownership, due to possession of the property at the time the petition was filed."

Yet, where, on objections to a claim, the deposition for proof of debt is presented as making a prima facie case for the claimant and with it the claimant appears in court in person, the mere fact that the claimant does not go upon the stand in his own behalf was held in one case not to be taken as amounting to a failure to call accessible witnesses.

Baumhauer v. Austin, 26 A. B. R. 385, 186 Fed. 260 (C. C. A. Ala.): "The verification of the proof of debt is in no true sense an ex parte affidavit. In case of contest, as here, the claimant is subject to call by the court or the contestant for explanations in the nature of a cross-examination and would not be permitted to decline to answer any proper question propounded by the court or referee or by the contestant. The claimant was present to answer such a call. He was not called. And this failure to call him more than answers the inference sought to be drawn from the claimant's so-called, but miscalled, silence.

"We conclude that the District Court erred in rejecting any part of the appellant's claim, for which error the decree of that court must be reversed and this case remanded to the court below, with instructions to allow the full claim, and award the costs in that court and in this court in favor of the claimant and against the contestants."

§ 555. But Mere Circumstances of Suspicion Insufficient for Rejection.—But uncontradicted testimony is to be given weight as proof of the facts testified to although circumstances of suspicion may exist, so long as such circumstances fall short of making the testimony incredible.[18]

Thus, the mere facts that the only testimony as to the validity of an assignment of book accounts comes from the bankrupt and the assignee and that they are relatives, are not sufficient to warrant rejection.

In re McCauley, 18 A. B. R. 459, 158 Fed. 322 (D. C. Mich.): "It must be conceded that an agreement resting for its support upon the testimony of the two parties to it, is suggestive of bias and open to suspicion, especially where the amount at stake is large and there is no written evidence of the fact in controversy. But when it is not opposed by any evidence—except the considerations suggested by the interest of the petitioner and his relationship to the bankrupt which the referee rejected as factors in his judgment—and undisputed facts tend to corroborate it, the referee's denial of the petition must be referred to the competency of the evidence accepting its truthfulness."

18. Inferentially, Union Trust Co. v. Bulkley, 18 A. B. R. 42, 150 Fed. 510 (C. C. A. Mich.).

Thus, where a wife presented a claim for money loaned her husband which had come from her father's estate, and claimed that some three hundred dollars paid to her by her husband within the four months period had not been in repayment of the loan but for family expenses though she could not remember the items thereof, the reviewing court held it improper to reject her testimony, though it was the only testimony produced; the court further suggesting that if her testimony were to be rejected, it should be rejected in toto, which would leave the trustee without any proof of the alleged preference.[19]

However, it can not be tolerated as a rule of evidence in the re-examination of claims in bankruptcy, that the court is bound either to reject or to accept all the testimony of the claimant. The rule that one vouches for the witnesses he places on the stand ought not, as a matter of human nature, to prevail in respect to adverse parties, who might readily be believed as to any admissions they might make against interest and yet be disbelieved as to testimony they might think in their own favor; and the rule, it is thought, does not prevail on the re-examination of claims in bankruptcy, at any rate from the deduction to be drawn from the special provisions of the Supreme Court's Rule XXI providing that the referee shall take the testimony of the claimant.

§ 556. Dealings between Near Relatives to Be Scrutinized with Care.

—The rules governing the dealings between near relatives apply to contests over the allowance of claims in bankruptcy. They are to be scrutinized with care.[20]

Yet, the honest or dishonest character of a debt is not to be determined by any mere test of relationship.[21]

In re Domenig, 11 A. B. R. 555, 128 Fed. 146 (D. C. Pa.): "Undoubtedly contracts of this kind between husband and wife ought to be scrutinized with the utmost vigilance, and should never be allowed unless the evidence is clear and convincing in every particular. Ordinarily, there is little evidence to support them, except the testimony of the husband and the wife themselves, and the husband is usually interested nearly as much as the wife in favor of her claim." Inferentially, but obiter, Union Trust Co. v. Bulkeley, 18 A. B. R. 43, 150 Fed. 510 (C. C. A. Mich.): "It is subject to some criticism, such as that the parties were related by marriage, * * * "

§ 557. Also, Obligations Given by Bankrupts on Eve of Bankruptcy.

—Likewise, written obligations and acknowledgments of indebtedness given by bankrupts during the period of insolvency immediately pre-

---

19. Compare post, §§ 852, 2650, and Newmann v. Blake, 24 A. B. R. 575, 178 Fed. 916 (C. C. A. Mo.), quoted at § 554.

20. In re Wooten, 9 A. B. R. 247, 118 Fed. 670 (D. C. N. Car.); In re Kyte, 25 A. B. R. 337, 189 Fed. 531 (D.

C. Pa.), quoted at § 800. Compare similar proposition post, §§ 800, 854.

21. Ohio Valley v. Mack, 20 A. B. R. 40, 163 Fed. 155 (C. C. A. Ohio); Baumhauer v. Austin, 26 A. B. R. 385, 186 Fed. 260 (C. C. A. Ala.).

ceding bankruptcy are to be subjected to close scrutiny and should not be upheld where they are not supported by good and sufficient consideration.[22]

§ 558. Schemes to Charge Partnership Assets with Individual Liabilities.

—Any scheme or device resorted to by persons in contemplation of bankruptcy for the purpose of charging partnership assets with the individual liabilities of the partners is violative of the provisions of the act.

In re Jones & Cook, 4 A. B. R. 141 (D. C. Mo.): "The physical and undisputed facts surrounding the case are also in my opinion, sufficient to stamp the transaction as fraudulent within the meaning of the Bankruptcy Act. The two endorsements were made at the time the firm was in an embarrassed financial condition. They were also made without any new consideration moving from the individual creditor to the firm, and they were made within four months prior to the time when the members of the firm petitioned voluntarily to be adjudicated bankrupts. The endorsements were also made in favor of relatives. Under this state of facts, it is impossible to believe that the parties intended anything less than to gain an unconscionable and unlawful advantage over partnership creditors in violation of the spirit and meaning of the Bankruptcy Act. If authority for the conclusion reached in this case were needed, it can be found in In re Lane, 10 Bank Reg. 135, 14 Fed. Cas. 1070 (No. 8044)."

§ 558⅓. Conspiracy to Defraud Creditors.

—A mere tacit understanding between parties to work to a common unlawful purpose is all that is necessary to constitute a conspiracy to defraud; and it may be proved by circumstantial evidence even in the face of uncontradicted testimony.[23]

§ 558¼. Omission of Items from Books, Destruction of Papers, etc., as Badges of Fraud.

—The omission of items from books of account, the destruction or mutilation of books, checks, stubs or papers may be badges of fraud.[24]

§ 558½. Unusual Manner of Doing Business a Badge or Fraud.

—The conducting of business in an unusual manner, is a badge of fraud; as, for instance, selling job lots to peddlers, failing to enter sales in the books. etc.[25]

§ 558¾. Evasive or Self-Contradictory Testimony.

—Of course, evasive, or self-contradictory testimony of the witness affects his credibility, and may indicate fraud.

In re Friedman, 21 A. B. R. 213, 164 Fed. 131 (D. C. Wis.): "The inference of fraud is strengthened by systematic evasion and contradictory statements of these parties on the witness stand."

Block, trustee, v. Rice, trustee, 21 A. B. R. 691, 167 Fed. 693 (D. C. Pa.): "This,

---

22. See post, § 800. Also see In re Brewster, 7 A. B. R. 436 (Ref. N. Y.). Instances, Ohio Valley Bank v. Mack, 20 A. B. R. 919, 163 Fed. 155 (D. C. Ohio); In re Sanger, 22 A. B. R. 145, 169 Fed. 722 (D. C. W. Va.).

23. In re Friedman, 21 A. B. R. 213, 164 Fed. 131 (D. C. Wis.).

24. In re Friedman, 21 A. B. R. 213, 164 Fed. 131 (D. C. Wis.), quoted at § 856½.

25. In re Friedman, 21 A. B. R. 213, 164 Fed. 131 (D. C. Wis.), quoted at § 856¾.

together with Rice's shifty, evasive, and unreliable manner as a witness, is sufficient to warrant the jury in finding, as they did, that Rice had appropriated the $750 trust fund to his own use."

Thus, repetitions of "I don't know" or "I don't remember" as to matters undoubtedly within the witness' knowledge or memory may indicate falsehood and fraud.[26]

§ 558⅞. Conviction of Crime.

—Of course, conviction of crime affects the credibility of a witness, if it be crimen falsus. It has been held, however, that a witness who has been convicted of misuse of the mails is competent, though the conviction may be taken into account as affecting credibility.[27]

§ 559. Agent's Admission Not Binding unless within Scope.

—The admissions of an agent are not binding on his principal, unless within the scope of his authority. Thus, the husband's admissions of his wife's insolvency, while acting as manager of her business, have been held not competent.[28]

DIVISION 6.

RECORDS OF BANKRUPTCY PROCEEDINGS AND ORDERS OF REFEREE.

§ 560. Records and Files in Bankruptcy.

—The manner of recording cases by copying into one book all papers in the case and all orders entered does not prevail in bankruptcy proceedings in the administration of the estate. A very much looser but much more economical system prevails. Under the old law of 1867 it seems that the records of bankruptcy cases were even less permanent than under the present law.

Under the old law of 1867 there was very little writing into books: the orders of the court and of the registrar and the accounts of the officers, proofs of claims, etc., were simply filed with a red tape around them in the archives of the District Court and there allowed to moulder. Incalculable confusion thus resulted in subsequent years, in the search of titles, etc.; and so the framers of the present Act sought carefully to guard against the recurrence of a similar condition. The present law makes no provision for recording the proceedings in one docket, except that the appearances before the District Judge and the filing of pleadings and orders and their transmission to and return from the referee in charge are noted on the record. No pleadings are copied into the record even yet, but under the present law provision is made that the referee shall keep a little

---

26. Ohio Valley Bank v. Mack, 20 A. B. R. 919, 163 Fed. 155 (D. C. Ohio), quoted at § 554. Also, see post, §§ 1851, 2331.

27. Compare post, § 855½; Morris v. Tannenbaum, 26 A. B. R. 368 (Ref. N. Y.).

28. Duncan v. Landis, 5 A. B. R. 652, 106 Fed. 839 (C. C. A. Pa.).

Res Judicata and Collateral Attack. —As to questions of res judicata and collateral attack arising before referees, compare post, § 1771, et seq.

record book or books—a separate book or books—for each case, in which the filing of papers shall be entered and orders made by him be copied.[29]

Inferentially, In re Carr, 8 A. B. R. 635 (D. C. N. Car.): "A final settlement of the bankrupt's estate will not be ordered until a full and complete record of the proceedings is made, showing that they have been conducted in accordance with the requirements of the statute and the general orders of the Supreme Court and the district rules, and a balance sheet is presented which can be understood, and from which the bankrupt and his creditors can see what has been done with the money."

§ 561. **Orders of Referees.**—Referees act through orders. They do not render "judgments" nor "decrees:" they enter "orders." Without the entry of an order, neither the judge nor the upper courts will review the decision of a referee.[30]

Even notice to parties (other than the ten days' statutory notice to creditors) is ordinarily given by service upon them of an "order to show cause."[31]

§ 562. **Order to Recite Notice, Appearance and Hearing, etc.**— In all orders made by a referee, it shall be recited, according as the facts may be, that notice was given and the manner thereof; or that the order was made by consent; or that no adverse interest was represented at the hearing; or that the order was made after hearing adverse interests.[32]

Faulk v. Steiner, 21 A. B. R. 623, 165 Fed. 861 (C. C. A. Ala.): "The twenty-third General Order in Bankruptcy provides that: 'In all orders made by a referee it shall be recited, according as the fact may be, that notice was given and the manner thereof; or that the order was made by consent; or that no adverse interest was represented, at the hearing; or that the order was made after hearing adverse interest.' The referee, in the appointment [of a receiver] disregarded

29. Bankr. Act, § 42.

Records of Referees.—(a) "The records of all proceedings in each case before a referee shall be kept as nearly as may be in the same manner as records are now kept in equity cases in circuit courts of the United States."

(b) "A record of the proceedings in each case shall be kept in a separate book or books, and shall, together with the papers on file, constitute the records of the case."

(c) "The book or books containing a record of the proceedings shall, when the case is concluded before the referee be certified to by him, and together with such papers as are on file before him, be transmitted to the court of bankruptcy and shall there remain as a part of the records of the court."

Referees should so conduct their proceedings and make up their records that a full and fair review may be

made of their actions. In re Romine, 14 A. B. R. 788 (D. C. W. Va.).

Practice in Southern and Eastern Districts of New York.—This section 42 is wholly disregarded in the Southern and Eastern Districts of New York, and perhaps elsewhere; and the discarded practice under the old law of 1867 there prevails notwithstanding the statute.

30. See post, § 2825, et seq., "Appeals and Error." And also, § 2850.

31. See ante, § 549½.

32. Supreme Court's General Order, No. XXIII. Compare, inferentially, In re Abbey Press, 13 A. B. R. 16, 134 Fed. 51 (C. C. A. N. Y.).

Mere Calendar Entries of Papers Filed Not Sufficient.—Compare, Scofield v. United States ex rel. Bond, 23 A. B. R. 259, 174 Fed. 1 (C. C. A. Ohio). Also, compare In re (James) Dunlap Carpet Co., 22 A. B. R. 788, 171 Fed. 532 (D. C. Pa.).

this order. This rule is prescribed by the Supreme Court by authority of § 30 of the Act, and it is the duty of referees to make their orders conform to it."

In re Saxton Furnace Co., 14 A. B. R. 483 (D. C. Pa.): "A general statement by a referee that notice of an application for the sale of assets free from liens was given to each and every general creditor and lien creditor is insufficient, the record must disclose affirmatively that every creditor whose lien will be discharged by the sale has received due notice of the application."

Compare as to what, if any, recitals are to be made [in District Court, at any rate] In re Fischer, 23 A. B. R. 427, 175 Fed. 531 (C. C. A. N. Y.): "The practice in bankruptcy is similar to that in equity. The 86th Equity Rule provides that there shall be no recitals in decrees or orders. Although in modern practice this is not always strictly adhered to when some useful purpose would be subserved by departing from it, it cannot be held error in the bankruptcy court when such rule is followed."

The order should not be indefinite.

Gillespie v. Piles, 24 A. B. R. 502, 178 Fed. 886 (C. C. A. Iowa): "No railroad company was a party to this proceeding, and the order that the trustee pay out of the proceeds of the sales of these hogs to the respective railroads transporting said nine (9) cars of hogs all unpaid freight thereon, without naming the companies or specifying the amounts was erroneous."

§ 563. Referee May Vacate or Modify Orders or Findings.—The referee has jurisdiction to modify his findings.

In re Hawley, 8 A. B. R. 629 (D. C. Iowa): "I can see no good reason why the referee, before he completed his record and after the evidence had been written out, might not review the same. Undoubtedly it would have been the better practice, had the referee given notice to the counsel, so that they might be reheard, before making the change in the valuation placed upon the land; but that fact does not sustain the position taken by counsel for creditors that the referee is bound by the first conclusion reached upon the question of the value of the land, and cannot modify the same to accord with his conclusion after a review of the evidence, when written out for his consideration."

The referee has jurisdiction, also, to vacate or modify his orders.[33] But it is a question whether the referee has jurisdiction to vacate or modify his orders after the case has been carried up for review.

In re Greek Mfg. Co., 21 A. B. R. 111, 164 Fed. 211 (D. C. Pa.): "It follows, also, that an order once entered is not subject to be reviewed or altered by the referee himself. To permit this would be to enlarge General Order 27 so as to include what the Supreme Court did not see fit to insert—namely, 'the referee' as well as 'the judge'—and I need not say that such enlargement is beyond the power of a District Court. The practice (which has, to some extent, grown up in this district) of filing exceptions to a referee's order, which are thereupon

---

33. Compare, First Nat'l Bk. v. State Bk., 12 A. B. . 440 (C. C. A. Mont.). Also compare,Ranalogously, In re Orman, 5 A. B. R. 698 (C. C. A. Ala.). Compare, Bernard v. Abel, 19 A. B. R. 383, 156 Fed. 649 (C. C. A. Wash.),

quoted at § 422, note. Matter of Brenner, 26 A. B. R. 646, 190 Fed. 209 (D. C. Pa.).

Referee May Not Impeach Own Orders.—Compare post, § 1773.

argued and determined at such time as may be fixed, is merely a method of having the referee review his own ruling, and finds no warrant either in the general order or in the rule of the District Court. The general order requires that the petition for review shall '(set) out the error complained of,' and by this means the same result is reached as by filing exceptions. Occasionally, such practice may conveniently afford the referee the opportunity of correcting an inadvertence or a plain mistake, but even when this is true the correction may ordinarily be made by the judge with as much convenience and as little loss of time. In the great majority of cases, the filing of exceptions is followed by a rehearing that does not change the referee's opinion, and a review by the court is therefore delayed without any corresponding advantage. But in any event the practice appears to be irregular and should be discontinued."

Yet, since the case is not carried up from the referee on appeal, it would seem the "whole case" is not taken away and is still pending before the referee. After the filing of the petition for review, the referee still has jurisdiction to dismiss an application on request of the applicant.[34] Rehearing need not be granted unless for a proper cause.[35] The referee may sua sponte let in additional evidence in the interests of justice.[36] But the referee may not review his own order on exceptions thereto.[37]

34. Inferentially. In re Orman, 5 A. B. R. 698 (C. C. A. Ala.).

35. Instance, In re Royal, 7 A. B. R. 636 (D. C. N. C.), where no newly-discovered evidence was produced and no exceptions had been filed to the findings of fact. See further, on this subject, § 553½.

36. Geo. Carroll & Bro. Co. v. Young, 9 A. B. R. 643. But compare ante, § 553½.

Trustee Not to Execute Order of Referee for Payment of Money until Opportunity for Appeal or Review Given.—In re Nichols, 23 A. B. R. 216, 166 Fed. 603 (D. C. N. Y.).

Litigants to Be Notified of Referee's Decision.—In re Nichols, 22 A. B. R. 216, 166 Fed. 603 (D. C. N. Y.).

37. In re Marks, 22 A. B. R. 568, 171 Fed. 281 (D. C. Pa.). Also, In re Greek Mfg. Co., 21 A. B. R. 111, 164 Fed. 211 (D. C. Pa.), quoted supra.

CHAPTER XVIII.

NOTICES TO CREDITORS.

Synopsis of Chapter.

§ 564. Notices to Creditors, Valuable Feature of Act.—The next step in the proceedings is the fixing of the time and place for the first meeting of creditors and the issuance and mailing of notices to them, and the publication of notice thereof in the newspapers; all which bring up naturally the subject of notices to creditors. Before the passage of the bankruptcy law, one of the greatest abuses in the ordinary administration of insolvent estates was the rushing through of improper sales of assets and of improper distributions of the proceeds.[1] Thus, repeatedly it would happen that the insolvent debtor, on the eve of assignment, would make a preferential mortgage or conveyance to some favored creditor, frequently a relative or friend, and would make the assignment itself moreover, to his attorney or to some relative or friend who would be most likely to act in the debtor's interest and then, after the assignment was made and this assignee placed in charge, all parties, except the unpreferred and unsecured and unfortunate general creditors, forthwith would conspire together to work through some secret sale, usually at needless sacrifice, to some one acting in the debtor's interest or in the interest of some special clique. Frequently, indeed, the debtor himself would thereupon be hired as agent or manager and would go on with the business as formerly, his frustrated general creditors looking on without recourse and watching the proceeds of their own goods thus being dealt out under the guise of court proceedings to the favored creditors and relatives.

Thus it is that one of the most valuable features of the present Bankruptcy Act is its requirement that notice by mail be given to all creditors of virtually every important step in the proceedings.

---

1. Compare, In re Beutels Sons Co., 7 A. B. R. 768 (Ref. Ohio). Also, see post, § 1944.

Compare, Columbia Bank *v.* Birkett, 9 A. B. R. 481 (N. Y. Court of Appeals, affirmed sub nom, Birkett *v.* Columbia Bank, 12 A. B. R. 691, 195 U. S. 345): "In my opinion there are features in the present Bankruptcy Act, which differentiate it from preceding acts and which indicate a legislative intent that greater strictness shall prevail in notifying the creditor of the various proceedings in bankruptcy."

§ 565. Ten Days' Notice by Mail to Creditors.—Creditors are to be given at least ten days' notice by mail, to their respective addresses as they appear in the list of creditors of the bankrupt, or as afterwards filed with the papers in the case by the creditors;[2] unless they waive notice in writing, of

(1) All examinations of the bankrupt;[3]

(2) All hearing upon applications for the confirmation of compositions; or the discharge of bankrupts;[4]

(3) All meetings of creditors;[5]

(4) All proposed sales of property;[6]

(5) The declaration and time of payment of dividends;[7]

(6) The filing of the final accounts of the trustee, and the time when and the place where they will be examined and passed upon;[8]

(7) The proposed compromise of any controversy;[9]

(8) The proposed dismissal of the proceedings.[10]

It is readily seen that if a creditor would file away these various notices as he receives them he would have a fair history of the case as it progresses, without the necessity of personally attending court at all or of having a representative in attendance; and seldom are complaints heard, where the requirements of notice of the present law are observed by the courts, that creditors have been kept in the dark as to the important steps in the progress of the administration of insolvent estates.

Notices should also be given of petitions to redeem from liens.[11]

However, a creditor who is also a lienholder waives lack of notice by appearing at a sale, and cannot excuse himself from failing to ask for a separate sale of the property covered by his lien by pleading lack of ten days' notice as a creditor.[12]

§ 565¼. Thirty Days' Notice of Bankrupt's Discharge Petition.—Amendment of 1910.—By the Amendment of 1910 the length of notice

---

2. Bankr. Act, § 58 (a).

3. See post, § 1535.

4. See post, §§ 2345, 2414, subjects of "Composition" and "Discharge."

5. Death of trustee elect before qualifying while first creditors' meeting still in session will not require new notice. In re Wright, 2 A. B. R. 497, 95 Fed. 807 (Ref. N. Y.).

6. See post, § 1931, et seq., subject of "Sale of Assets."

7. See post, § 2206, et seq., subject of "Dividends."

8. See post, § 2295, et seq., "Final Meetings of Creditors."

9. See post, § 926.

10. See ante, § 419.

11. See post, § 1869. Also see In re Grainger, 20 A. B. R. 166, 173, 160 Fed. 69 (C. C. A. Calif.).

12. See post, § 1987; also see In re Caldwell, 24 A. B. R. 495, 178 Fed. 377 (D. C. Ga.).

of the hearing of the bankrupt's application for a discharge has been extended from ten days to thirty days.[12a]

The object of such extension, is, obviously, to afford opportunity for creditors to hold their meeting called for the purpose of determining whether they shall oppose the bankrupt's discharge.[12b]

§ 565½. **Notices of Composition Meeting before Adjudication.**— By the Amendment of 1910, authorizing compositions before adjudication of bankruptcy[12c] it is provided that the bankrupt, in such cases, shall file the required schedules and thereupon the court shall call a meeting of creditors for the allowance of claims, examination of the bankrupt and preservation or conduct of the estate. The notice of such meeting is already provided for in Bankruptcy Act, § 58 (a) (3), wherein ten days' notice is required of "all meetings of creditors." The notice of the petition for confirmation of composition made before adjudication is likewise already provided for in § 58 (a) (2).

§ 565¾. **Notices of Applications for Compensation of Receiver, Trustee, etc.**—By the Amendment of 1910 to § 48, ten days' notice must be given creditors of all applications of receivers and marshals for allowance of compensation and of all applications of trustees, receivers and marshals for allowance of additional compensation for conducting the business, such notices to specify the amounts asked.[12d]

§ 566. **Notices by Mail Postage Free.**—Some of the forms of notices sent to creditors in conformity with this provision are given in the appendix. The notices are inclosed in penalty envelopes and sent by mail, for the government gives the freedom of the mails to bankruptcy proceedings.

Nothing illustrates more forcibly that bankruptcy proceedings are proceedings in rem than the provisions relative to notices. Were the proceedings not in rem it would be doubtful whether notice by mail would constitute "due process of law." Being in rem it is to be conceded that only such notice as the statute provides for is necessary and that the statute could provide for no notice at all to creditors, as indeed was the case with our preceding Bankruptcy Acts.

§ 567. **Notice to All Scheduled and to All Filing Claims.**—Notice must be sent to all creditors who have been scheduled or who have filed

---

12a. Bankr. Act as amended 1910, § 53 (a): " * * * (9) there shall be thirty days' notice of all applications for the discharge of bankrupts."
12b. See report No. 691 of Senate Judiciary Committee of the 61st Congress, 2nd Session, quoted at § 2431½.
12c. See post, §§ 2358½ et seq.

12d. Bankr. Act, as amended 1910, § 48 (d) and (e): "Provided, further, that before the allowance of compensation notice of application therefor, specifying the amount asked, shall be given to creditors in the manner indicated in section fifty-eight of this act." See post, § 2119 (b).

claims although not scheduled. Notices must be sent to those who are scheduled but who have not filed their claims although the year within which to file proofs of claim has elapsed and such creditors could not participate in the dividends. This is so because, although such creditors are debarred from participation in the estate, yet they are still "parties in interest," entitled to oppose the discharge, and, as such, entitled to participate in the examination of the bankrupt for discovery of facts preventing his discharge, and also to be notified of other matters that they may see to it that the estate is duly and economically administered and the bankrupt's other indebtedness reduced as much as possible. Moreover, the statutory words are explicit and without exception.[13]

It has been held that even those not scheduled nor filing claims must be notified where they have already participated in the bankruptcy proceedings under claim of being creditors and no final determination has been had that they are not creditors, and that an election held without notice to them may be set aside.

In re Evening Standard Pub. Co., 21 A. B. R. 156, 164 Fed. 517 (D. C. N. Y.): "The assumption of the referee and attorneys for the trustee and others, in not notifying Tyner of the first meeting, was that, as he was not scheduled by the bankrupt corporation as a creditor, he was not entitled to notice; but they had notice that he claimed to be a creditor, and that the court had decided that, until his claim was presented in the regular way and offered for allowance and disallowed, he was to be treated as a creditor or alleged creditor. He was entitled to notice of the first meeting of creditors, and entitled to attend and file his claim. If his claim was not then objected to by a creditor and valid on its face, he was entitled to have it allowed, and then to take part in the selection of a trustee. If objected to by creditors, and such objections were verified, then it was the duty of the referee either to adjourn the meeting and try out the merits of the claim, or, if that would unduly postpone the election of a trustee, to proceed on the votes of those whose claims were allowed. Tyner had the right at the first meeting as an alleged creditor to file verified objections to the claims of other alleged creditors." Quoted further at §§ 575, 579½.

§ 568. **Notice by Publication.**—The Act also provides for the publication of notices.[14] Indeed, it is mandatory to publish notice of the first meeting of creditors at least once, and the last publication must be not later

---

13. Apparently, contra, obiter, Clark v. Pidcock, 12 A. B. R. 315 (C. C. A. N. J.), where the court evidently assumes (obiter) that, after the expiration of the statutory year for proving claims, only those creditors who have proved their claims are entitled to notice of the appointment of trustee. Yet, in that instance, the bankrupt never received his discharge, and a creditor who had not proved his claim was nevertheless interested in the proper administration of the estate so that he himself might have the fewer creditors with whom to share future assets of the bankrupt.

14. Bankr. Act, § 58 (b): "Notice to creditors of the first meeting shall be published at least once and may be published such number of additional times as the court may direct; the last publication shall be at least one week prior to the date fixed for the meeting. Other notices may be published as the court shall direct."

than one week before the meeting time.[15]   Other notices are to be published as the court may direct.[16]

§ 569. **Notices to Be Given by Referee.**—All notices are to be given by the referee unless otherwise ordered by the judge.[17]

§ 570. **Notice to State Object, Time and Place.**—Naturally, the notice should state the matter in hand and the time and place of considering the same.

15. Bankr. Act, § 58 (b), supra.   17. Bankr. Act, § 58 (c).
16. Bankr. Act, § 58 (b), supra.

CHAPTER XIX.

MEETINGS OF CREDITORS.

Synopsis of Chapter.

§ 571. Creditors' Meetings Valuable Feature of Modern Bankruptcy Law.

—Another distinguishing and valuable feature of modern bankruptcy law is its provision for calling creditors together in meetings for the purposes of electing a trustee to administer the estate, of examining the bankrupt and other witnesses, of hearing reports of receivers and trustees, and in general of consulting together for the care and protection of the estate, § 55, clause C, providing that:

"The creditors shall at each meeting take such steps as may be pertinent and necessary for the promotion of the best interests of the estate and the enforcement of this Act."

Under the old regime the insolvent debtor, through his appointee, the assignee, usually controlled the administration, and general creditors had little voice in it and usually felt their presence not desired; and it seemed frequently that the assignee and the preferred creditor or creditors were in a tacit understanding to slight and thwart the unfortunate general creditor. In bankruptcy it is quite different. Not only do the creditors elect their own trustee, but he is elected by the creditors whose claims are not secured nor preferred; the administration is essentially an administration by general creditors, by the unprotected creditors.[1]

In re Etheridge Furn. Co., 1 A. B. R. 115, 92 Fed. 329 (D. C. Ore.): "To allow the bankrupt to select the trustee to administer upon his estate, instead of the creditors, as provided in the Bankrupt Act, or to allow the State to take jurisdiction of the estate of the bankrupt and administer and distribute it, would effectually destroy the efficiency of any bankrupt act that might be enacted by Congress, and thus effectually destroy the power granted to Congress to pass a bankrupt act."

In re Henschel, 6 A. B. R. 29, 109 Fed. 861 (Ref. N. Y.): "I am also convinced, and it will hardly be gainsaid, that the enactment of the present bankrupt law is due to the greater extent of the evils which existed under the former systems of state assignments, bills of sale and deeds of trust, whereby the insolvent debtor could select his own assignee or trustee to dispose of his assets, among a favored few of his creditors, and thereby discriminate against the main body of creditors or against any number of creditors; and it is merely the statement of a self-evident truth, to hold that if by any means whatsoever the bankrupt would be able to control the selection of his trustee in bankruptcy, that the true intent and spirit of the bankrupt law would be thereby violated in a very important direction, and its usefulness impaired, if such an evil were allowed to be tolerated, and thereby established as part of the procedure, in bankruptcy."

Obiter In re Gutwillig, 1 A. B. R. 391, 92 Fed. 337 (C. C. A.): "The general purpose of bankrupt laws, and of the present act is not only to administer the assets of insolvent debtors on the basis of equality but to secure that result by giving to the creditors, and not to the debtor, the selection of the person to be entrusted with the administration."

But it must not be thought that bankruptcy proceedings to any considerable extent are conducted by vote of creditors. The conclusion must not be jumped at that they are a species of town meeting, where creditors get together and pass upon rights by the ballot, nor that creditors are like a jury, receiving instruction from the court and then going into session by themselves. In practice, it will be found that bankruptcy proceedings are conducted like any other judicial proceedings, and that the court passes upon the rights of the litigants after due consideration of the evidence and arguments of counsel, upon pleadings properly filed; and that creditors ordinarily will not be asked to vote, nor be allowed to vote, nor even to be heard, except in the usual manner of court proceedings; and that ordinarily

---

1. Compare disadvantages of the rule, In re Columbia Iron Wks., 14 A. B. R. 529, 142 Fed. 234 (D. C. Mich.).   Also compare, as to disadvantages of rule, In re Sumner, 4 A. B. R. 123, 101 Fed. 224 (D. C. N. Y.).

their vote is not conclusive but merely advisory, except in cases of the election of trustee, etc.[2]

Compare, In re Columbia Iron Wks., 14 A. B. R. 529, 530, 142 Fed. 243 (D. C. Mich.): "These differences seem to be due in part to a misconception of the powers of creditors and of trustees, and to conflict of interests and judgment in regard to matters, the disposition of which belongs to the court. * * *

"This controversy, and that relative to the question whether the property should be sold in bulk or in parcels, are matters for determination by the court and not by vote of creditors."

Nevertheless it is a valuable right, that at such meetings creditors may be heard in making suggestions for the practical administration of the estate for the benefit of the trustee. And yet, even as to that, they may not dictate to him, their rights being simply advisory at best.

In actual practice there are only two things over which creditors have control as matter of right, namely, the election of a trustee and the fixing of the amount of his bond. This is as far as the absolute right of creditors to conduct proceedings extends. They have not even the right to vote on the question as to whether an adjournment should be had; the court will rule on that question. Nor may they pass on the qualifications of the surety after they have fixed the bond; the court will rule on that also. Their right extends no further than to vote for a trustee and to fix his bond.

The fact that notices to creditors of the pendency of a petition to sell or compromise, etc., etc., have been issued and that "creditors shall at each meeting take such steps as may be pertinent and necessary for the promotion of the best interests of the estate and the enforcement of this Act" does not place them above the court, but simply operates to give them standing to speak in court and a right there to assemble and confer together.[3] But even the right to vote for trustee and name the bond are of greatest value, and, for the exercise of those rights, the whole trend of the administration of insolvent estates is made to differ in bankruptcy from what it is generally in State Courts, where, in practice, the assignee or receiver, as the case may be, is not the choice of general creditors but is the choice either of the debtor or of the preferred creditors or of both together.[4] And the right of creditors to select a trustee is a substantial right.[5]

By the Amendment of 1910, meetings of creditors are provided for in cases of composition before adjudications of bankruptcy;[5a] and also for

2. In re Heyman, 5 A. B. R. 808, 104 Fed. 677 (D. C. N. Y.).

3. In re Heyman, 5 A. B. R. 808, 104 Fed. 677 (D. C. N. Y.).

4. Inferentially, In re Etheridge Furn. Co., 1 A. B. R. 115, 92 Fed. 329 (D. C. Ore.).

5. In re Henschel, 7 A. B. R. 662, 109 Fed. 869 (C. C. A. N. Y.); In re Malino, 8 A. B. R. 205, 206, 118 Fed. 368 (D. C. N. Y.); In re Kelly Dry Goods Co., 4 A. B. R. 268, 102 Fed. 747 (D. C. Wis.); impliedly, In re Evening Standard Publishing Co., 21 A. B. R. 156, 164 Fed. 517 (D. C. N. Y.), quoted at §§ 567, 870½; In re Kaufman, 24 A. B. R. 117, 176 Fed. 93 (D. C. Ky.).

5a. Bankr. Act, § 12; also see post, § 593¼.

the authorization of the trustee to enter opposition to the bankrupt's discharge.[5b]

§ 572. How Creditors Pass upon Matters at Meetings.—Creditors

pass upon matters submitted to them at their meetings by a majority vote in number and amount of claims of all creditors whose claims have been allowed and are present.[6]

The authorization of the trustee to oppose the bankrupt's discharge at the expense of the estate, provided for by the Amendment of 1910, is to be conferred by such a vote.

§ 573. Only "Creditors" to Vote—Who Are "Creditors."—Only

creditors may vote at creditors' meetings in bankruptcy. "Creditors," as the term is defined in bankruptcy, is any one who owns a demand or claim provable in bankruptcy.[7] The term "creditor" is used in somewhat different senses in different parts of the statute.[8] Thus, when it refers to examinations of bankrupts and witnesses, it includes creditors who have not proved their claims.[9] But, when it refers to voting for trustee or receiving dividends or otherwise participating, it includes only those whose claims have been allowed.[10]

§ 574. Several Claims Assigned to One Person, but One Vote.—

Where a claim has been assigned after proof the real owner alone can vote. And where one person holds several assigned claims he is entitled to but one vote. He is one creditor holding several claims.[11] Thus, where many creditors have assigned their claims to a trustee or committee for the pur-

---

5b. See post, § 593½.

6. Bankr. Act, § 56 (a).
For general discussion of the method of procedure at creditors' meetings, see, obiter, In re Eagles & Crisp, 3 A. B. R. 733, 99 Fed. 695 (D. C. N. Car.). Also, see In re Lazoris, 10 A. B. R. 31, 120 Fed. 716 (D. C. Wis.); In re Henschel, 7 A. B. R. 662, 109 Fed. 869 (C. C. A. N. Y.).

7. Bankr. Act, § 1 (g).
Receiver in Stockholders' Liability Suit a "Creditor" of Bankrupt Stockholder.—A receiver appointed by the State Court to collect the judgment is the duly authorized agent of the corporation and may make the deposition for proof of their claim against a bankrupt stockholder. Dight v. Chapman, 12 A. B. R. 748, 44 Ore. 265 (Sup. Ct. Ore.).
Undischarged Bankrupt Proving Claim Acquired after His Own Adjudication.—An undischarged bankrupt may prove a claim acquired after his own adjudication against another bankrupt. In re Smith, 1 A. B. R. 37 (Ref. N. Y.).

8. In re Walker, 3 A. B. R. 35, 96 Fed. 550 (D. C. N. Dak.).

9. In re Walker, 3 A. B. R. 35, 96 Fed. 550 (D. C. N. Dak.); In re Jehu, 2 A. B. R. 498, 94 Fed. 638 (D. C. Iowa).

10. In re Walker, 3 A. B. R. 35, 96 Fed. 550 (D. C. N. Dak.); In re Ogles, 2 A. B. R. 514 (Ref. Ala.).

11. In re Messengill, 7 A. B. R. 669, 113 Fed. 366 (D. C. N. Car.); (1867) In re Frank, Fed. Cas. No. 5,050, 5 N. B. Reg. 194; compare, inferentially, Leighton v. Kennedy, 12 A. B. R. 229, 129 Fed. 707 (C. C. A. Mass.); In re Columbia Iron Wks., 14 A. B. R. 537, 142 Fed. 243 (D. C. Mich.).
Acceptance of Composition by Majority of Creditors.—The assignee of a large number of creditors can only be counted as one creditor. In re Messengill, 7 A. B. R. 669, 113 Fed. 366 (D. C. N. C.).

pose of controlling the election of trustee and of purchasing the assets, they, may have but one vote.[12]

§ 575. Creditors Not to Vote Whose Claims Not Allowed.

—Creditors whose claims have not been "allowed" may not vote.[13]

Obiter, In re Walker, 3 A. B. R. 35, 96 Fed. 550 (D. C. N. Dak.): "The general principle to be deduced from the entire act would seem to be that only those creditors whose claims have been proved and allowed can participate either in the management of the estate or in the dividends derived therefrom, but as to all other matters any person having a provable claim is entitled to be heard."

Obiter, In re Evening Standard Publishing Co., 21 A. B. R. 156, 164 Fed. 517 (D. C. N. Y.): "Claims should not be voted where duly verified legal objections are filed thereto." Quoted further at §§ 567, 579½.

§ 576. Thus, Secured and Priority Creditors.

—Thus, creditors holding security on the bankrupt's property or entitled to priority of payment from the general assets before other creditors, may not vote except to the amount of their probable deficits after application upon their claims of the security or priority;[14] unless they surrender their securities or priorities.[15] But where a claimant, entitled to priority, inadvertently participates in the election of the trustee, precisely as if his claim were not entitled to priority, it will not be held that he is estopped or has waived his priority.[16]

§ 577. Preliminary Estimate of Values for Voting Purposes.

—Such claims may be allowed to enable the creditors to participate in the proceedings at creditors' meetings held prior to the determination of the value of their securities or priorities, but are to be allowed only for such sums as seem to the court to be owing over and above the value of the securities or priorities.[17] This statutory provision seems to be the only

---

12. In re E. T. Kenney & Co., 14 A. B. R. 611, 136 Fed. 451 (D. C. Ind.).

A combination of creditors for the control of judicial proceedings in their own interests, as distinguished from the interests of the general creditors is against public policy. In re E. T. Kenney Co., 14 A. B. R. 611, 136 Fed. 451 (D. C. Ind.).

13. In re Henschel, 7 A. B. R. 662 (C. C. A. N. Y., reversing In re Henschel, 6 A. B. R. 305); In re Eagles & Crisp, 3 A. B. R. 734, 99 Fed. 695 (D. C. N. Car.); obiter, In re MacKellar, 8 A. B. R. 669, 116 Fed. 547 (D. C. Penna.).

14. See as to the "provability" and "allowability" of such claims, §§ 632 and 748.

Bankr. Act, § 56 (b): "Creditors holding claims which are secured or have priority shall not, in respect to such claims, be entitled to vote at creditors' meetings, nor shall such

claims be counted in computing either the number of creditors or the amount of their claims, unless the amounts of such claims exceed the values of such securities or priorities, and then only for such excess."

In re Eagles & Crisp, 3 A. B. R. 735, 99 Fed. 695 (D. C. N. Car.); In re Columbia Iron Wks., 14 A. B. R. 527, 142 Fed. 234 (D. C. Mich.).

15. In re Eagles & Crisp, 3 A. B. R. 735, 99 Fed. 695 (D. C. N. Car.). Instance, Brown v. City National Bank, 26 A. B. R. 638 (Sup. Ct. N. Y.). Compare, impliedly, In re Milne, Turnbull & Co., 20 A. B. R. 248, 159 Fed. 280 (D. C. N. Y.).

16. In re Ashland Steel Co., 21 A. B. R. 834, 168 Fed. 679 (C. C. A. Ky.). See also, post, § 2139.

17. Bankr. Act, § 57 (c). In re Milne, Turnbull & Co., 20 A. B. R. 248, 159 Fed. 280 (D. C. N. Y.).

Allowing to Vote for Deficit Instead

exception to the established rule against the "provisional" allowance of a claim.

§ 578. Thus, Creditors Holding Voidable Preferences.—Thus, creditors holding voidable preferences may not vote until they have surrendered their preferences.[18]

§ 579. Or, Holding Liens by Legal Proceedings, Nullified by § 67f.—Likewise, creditors holding liens obtained by legal proceedings upon the bankrupt's property while he was insolvent during the four months preceding the bankruptcy, and which, on that account, are nullified by the adjudication under § 67 (f), may vote.[19] But this would be only on the theory that he has abandoned his lien or that the lien has been adjudicated to be void. If still insisting on the validity of his lien, where the validity is still disputable, of course, a different holding would prevail. He would have to surrender such advantage.[20]

§ 579½. Objections So Numerous That Determination of Validity Would Unduly Delay Appointment of Trustee.—Where so many claims are objected to, in apparent good faith, that the determination of their validity would unduly delay the appointment of a trustee, it has been held that the referee may appoint, or may permit an election by those creditors whose claims have been allowed.[21]

In re Evening Standard Pub. Co., 21 A. B. R. 156, 164 Fed. 517 (D. C. N. Y.): "Whether the referee will or will not postpone the election of a trustee, where claims are objected to, is a matter of sound discretion. If such a number of claims are duly objected to that an election by a majority in number and amount cannot be had, then, if circumstances demand, he may and should himself appoint. All this is settled by the weight of well-considered authorities. Claims should not be voted where duly verified legal objections are filed thereto. Of course, the referee may proceed to take proof, and, if the objecting party cannot produce sufficient evidence to sustain them, he will allow the claim. If the objecting party shows legal cause for delay for the purpose of producing evidence not at hand, the referee may in some cases allow the claim for voting purposes; but a better practice is to proceed to an election on the allowed claims, if the condition of the estate demands prompt action. If so many verified objections, apparently valid, are filed that an election by creditors is impossible, let the referee appoint." Quoted further at §§ 567 and 575.

But this is doubtful practice.

---

of Requiring Surrender of Security as Preference—When Not Prejudicial Error.—In re Milne, Turnbull & Co., 20 A. B. R. 248, 159 Fed. 280 (D. C. N. Y.).

18. Bankr. Act, § 57 (g). See, "Allowability of Claims Where the Creditor Holds a Preference," § 768, et seq. Also see, In re Columbia Iron Wks., 14 A. B. R. 527, 142 Fed. 234 (D. C. Mich.); In re Malino, 8 A. B. R. 205, 118 Fed.

638 (D. C. N. Y.); In re Conhaim, 3 A. B. R. 249, 97 Fed. 924 (D. C. Wash.).

19. In re Scully, 5 A. B. R. 716, 108 Fed. 372 (D. C. Pa.).

20. See, "Allowability of Claims Where the Creditor Holds Lien Acquired by Legal Proceedings," § 776, et seq.

21. In re Syracuse Paper & Pulp Co., 21 A. B. R. 174, 164 Fed. 275 (D. C. N. Y.), quoted at §§ 817, 828, 831, 838.

§ 580. For Other Participation than Voting, Claim Need Not Be Allowed.—As to any other matter than participation in voting at creditors meetings, any creditor having a provable claim, whether he proves it or not, is entitled to be heard.

In re Walker, 3 A. B. R. 35, 96 Fed. 550 (D. C. N. Dak.): "The general principle to be deduced from the entire act would seem to be that only those creditors whose claims have been proved and allowed can participate either in the management of the estate or in the dividends derived therefrom, but as to all other matters any person having a provable claim is entitled to be heard."

Thus, a creditor need not actually have filed proof of his claim in order to examine the bankrupt or witness.[22] But prima facie proof of such person's interest may be required;[23] and the listing of the person by the bankrupt in his schedules is sufficient prima facie proof that he is a creditor.[24]

§ 581. Majority Required, Majority Both in Number and Amount of Allowed Claims Present.—The majority required is not a majority of all claims nor of all allowed claims, but is simply a majority of all claims that have been allowed and the creditors holding which, or their proxies, are present.[25] Nor is the majority required a simple majority in numbers of the creditors, nor a simple majority in value, but the majority must be both in number of creditors and amount of the claims.[26]

§ 582. Creditors Not Present, Not to Vote.—Absent creditors may not vote.[27]

In re MacKellar, 8 A. B. R. 669, 116 Fed, 547 (D. C. Pa.): "There is nothing whatever to sustain the position that those who are not present are to be taken into consideration."

§ 583. May Act by Proxy or Attorney and Be Considered "Present."—The creditor may act by proxy or attorney, for § 1 of the Act making certain definition, states in clause (9) that the term "creditor" shall include any one who owns a demand or claim provable in bankruptcy and may include his duly authorized agent, attorney or proxy. Two forms have been prescribed by the Supreme Court, one called "Special Letter of Attorney in Fact," to authorize another to act for one in some special proceedings or in one special day; the other called a "General Letter of Attorney in Fact When Creditor Is Not Represented by Attorney at Law." But proxies of

22. See post, § 1532; In re Walker, 3 A. B. R. 35, 96 Fed. 550 (D. C. N. Dak.). In re Kuffler, 18 A. B. R. 587, 153 Fed. 667 (D. C. N. Y.); In re Jehu, 2 A. B. R. 498, 94 Fed. 638 (D. C. Iowa), quoted at § 1532.
23. In re Walker, 3 A. B. R. 35, 96 Fed. 550 (D. C. N. Dak.).
24. See post, § 1532; In re Kuffler, 18 A. B. R. 587, 153 Fed. 667 (D. C. N. Y.); In re Jehu, 2 A. B. R. 498, 94 Fed.

638 (D. C. Iowa), quoted at § 1532; In re Walker, 3 A. B. R. 35, 96 Fed. 550 (D. C. N. Dak.).
25. In re Henschel, 7 A. B. R. 662, 113 Fed. 443 (C. C. A. N. Y., reversing 6 A. B. R. 305).
26. In re MacKellar, 8 A. B. R. 669, 116 Fed. 547 (D. C. Pa.).
27. In re Henschel, 7 A. B. R. 662, 113 Fed. 443 (C. C. A. N. Y., reversing 6 A. B. R. 305).

absent creditors which are improperly authenticated are not to be considered as constituting the creditor "present."[28]

§ 584. Written Power of Attorney Requisite to Vote.

—The Courts have almost uniformly held, whenever called on to pass upon the question, that even attorneys at law, admitted to practice in the United States Courts, and in good standing, must have written power of attorney in order to vote, although there would be no such requirement in order to act in other respects for clients.[29]

In re Blankfein, 3 A. B. R. 165, 91 Fed. 191 (D. C. N. Y.): "In bankruptcy, this question can hardly be treated as a new one. Under similar provisions of the Act of 1867 the practice was definitely settled, that an attorney could not vote for an assignee merely by virtue of his general authority as attorney-at-law. He must prove his authority by letter of attorney, or by the oath of some one, showing him to be a duly-constituted attorney, i. e., an attorney in fact, for that purpose. See Bump. Bankr. (10th Ed.) 667, note; In re Purvis, 1 N. B. R. 163, Fed. Cas. No. 11,476; In re Knoepfel, 1 N. B. R. 23, 1 Ben. 330, Fed. Cas. No. 789; Id., 1 N. B. R. 70, Fed. Cas. No. 7,892. The latter case was decided in this district by Mr. Justice Blatchford, wherein Mr. Seixas, though he was the attorney and proctor for the parties, and showed a special authority from one Kutter, the attorney in fact of the foreign creditors, was held to have no right to vote for an assignee in their behalf, his special authority to vote being defective. In the case of Martin v. Walker, 1 Abb. Adm. 579, 16 Fed. Cas. 911, Betts, J., held that under a retainer as attorney at law, the proctor could not claim to be attorney in fact.

"'One cannot, by virtue of his retainer as attorney at law, assume to act in the cause in the character of attorney in fact.' Id., 1 Abb. Adm. 584, 16 Fed. Cas. 913.

"I find no sufficient reason for any different rule under the present act. As I have said, there is no substantial difference on this point in the language of the two acts. The Act of 1867 (Rev. St., § 5095) provided:

"'Any creditor may act at all meetings by his duly constituted attorney the same as though personally present,' and this was held to mean an attorney in fact, as above stated.

"In the present act, §§ 56 and 44 authorize creditors to appoint a trustee by vote; and § 1, subd. 9, provides:

"'"Creditor" * * * may include his duly authorized agent, attorney or proxy.'

"The words 'duly authorized' here apply to 'attorney' and 'proxy' as well as to 'agent.' This phrase in effect is, 'his duly authorized attorney,' and this requires the production and exhibition or proof of the authority. Such phraseology would not be used where an attorney at law is intended, since his au-

---

28. In re Henschel, 7 A. B. R. 662, 113 Fed. 443 (C. C. A. N. Y.).

29. Obiter, In re Eagles & Crisp, 3 A. B. R. 733, 99 Fed. 696 (D. C. N. Car.); In re Lazoris, 10 A. B. R. 31, 120 Fed. 716 (D. C. Wis.); In re Scully, 5 A. B. R. 716, 108 Fed. 372 (D. C. Pa.); In re Henschel, 6 A. B. R. 305, 109 Fed. 861 (impliedly, on appeal), 7 A. B. R. 662, 113 Fed. 443 (D. C. N. Y.); In re Sugenheimer, 1 A. B. R. 425, 91 Fed. 744 (D. C. N. Y.); In re Richards, 4 A. B. R. 631, 103 Fed. 849 (D. C. N. Y.); In re Finlay, 3 N. B. N. & R. 78, 3 A. B. R. 738 (D. C. N. Y.). But compare reasoning, analogously, of In re Gasser, 5 A. B. R. 32 (C. C. A. Minn.), and cases cited therein. Contra, In re Crocker Co., 27 A. B. R. 241 (Ref. Mass., affirmed by D. C.).

thority is legally presumed, and is not ordinarily required to be shown. The connection with the word 'proxy' is also some indication that an attorney in fact is meant, who must be 'duly authorized' and in due form; that is, as in case of a proxy, unless proved by oath, as an agent's authority may be proved, to be legally substantiated by some writing that is self-proving or can be proved by oath, and filed with the referee.

"As the present act uses substantially the same language as the Act of 1867, the practice and rulings under that act, in the absence of any contrary indication, ought, I think, to be deemed controlling, as intended to be continued under the present law. The reasons for the rule are the same as under the former act.

"Such seems also to be the intent of the Supreme Court rule 21, subd. 5 (18 Sup. Ct. vii), in providing for a representation of the creditor through a letter of attorney. This clause provides:

"'The execution of any letter of attorney to represent a creditor may be proved,' etc.

"Voting for a trustee, is 'representing' the creditor in a very special sense; and not being a right belonging to an attorney at law as such, the intimation is strong that a letter of attorney is his proper, if not his exclusive, authority. * * *

"The ordinary presumption of an attorney's authority holds, I think, in bankruptcy proceedings, as in other suits; but in my judgment it does not apply at all to acts of the special nature referred to, or to others of a kindred character, which have never been deemed incident to the rights or the duties of an attorney at law, but which have always been performed by the creditors themselves, except when another person has been specifically authorized to perform them.

"In the present case the vote was not offered by either of the attorneys of record, but only by their clerk. This is but a single illustration of the loose practice that would at once arise, if the claim here made were allowed in favor of a mere attorney at law."

However, it seems a wholly unnecessary requirement, in cases of attorneys duly admitted to practice before the court. For in fact, if there is one particular thing a creditor wants of his attorney in a bankruptcy proceeding it is to vote for trustee. That is usually the first duty; and being so it would seem a strong implication would arise from the employment itself that the creditor expects his attorney to vote for him. Certainly it is precisely as appropriate as it would be for attorneys to suggest names of receivers for other courts to appoint. Because there are forms for use in appointing proxies and attorneys in fact is not conclusive that such forms are to be used when the right of attorneys at law to act is brought in question.

Compare In re Crooker Co., 27 A. B. R. 241 (Ref. Mass.): "It is to be observed that no special letter of attorney in fact is required under the bankruptcy practice when a creditor is represented by an attorney at law."

It would be a great convenience on all sides if the requirement in cases of duly admitted attorneys at law were dispensed with. However, in any event, only the attorney actually engaged by the creditor should be allowed to vote—not his clerk nor office boy—for at any rate, the attorney may not delegate his authority, though if a written power of attorney provides for such delegation or substitution, he may so delegate the power.

§ 585. But Not Requisite, for Attorney at Law in Other Matters than Voting.

—But an attorney need not present written power of attorney in order to act for clients in other matters in bankruptcy proceedings; thus, not to withdraw a client's claim altogether.[30]

§ 586. Only Attorneys Admitted to United States Court to Practice.

—Only attorneys admitted to practice in the United States District Court should be allowed to practice in bankruptcy.[31] But appearance by attorney not admitted to practice in the United States District Court will not warrant dismissal of the proceedings, but simply no recognition of the attorney.[32]

§ 587. Powers of Attorney for Corporations and Partnerships to Contain Oath of Official Capacity.

—Powers of attorney to represent partnerships or corporations must contain the oath of the person executing the instrument that he is a member of the partnership, or a duly authorized officer of the corporation on whose behalf he acts.[33]

§ 588. Who May Take Oaths and Acknowledgments.

—Oaths, except on hearings in court, may be administered by (1) referees; (2) officers authorized to administer oaths in proceedings before the courts of the United States, or under the laws of the State where the same are to be taken; and (3) diplomatic or consular officers of the United States in any foreign country.[34]

Justices of the peace are competent to take oaths, and also they may take acknowledgments of powers of attorney, where competent by State law, notwithstanding they be not expressly included in the enumeration of proper officers in the Supreme Court's General Order XXI, Subd. 5, for the power to take oaths granted by the Bankruptcy Act itself, in § 20 (a), includes the lesser power to take acknowledgments.[35]

§ 589. Meetings to Be Held in Conformity with Notices.

—Meetings of creditors must be held at the precise time and place specified in the notices to creditors.

§ 590. May Be Adjourned.

—Meetings of creditors may be adjourned from time to time[36] and the different adjournments will not constitute each

---

30. In re Pauly, 2 A. B. R. 333 (Ref. N. Y.).

31. In re Kindt, 3 A. B. R. 546, 98 Fed. 867 (D. C. Iowa).

32. In re Kindt, 3 A. B. R. 546, 98 Fed. 867 (D. C. Iowa).

33. Gen. Ord. XXI (5). In re Finlay, 3 A. B. R. 738 (D. C. N. Y.).

34. Bankr. Act, § 20 (a).
Acknowledgments in foreign countries may be made before a diplomatic or consular officer although not specifically mentioned in Gen. Ord. XXI (5). In re Suggenheimer, 1 A. B. R. 425, 91 Fed. 744 (D. C. N. Y.).
Compare Gen. Ord. XXI (5).

35. In re Roy, 26 A. B. R. 4, 185 Fed. 550 (D. C. N. Y.); [1867] In re Butterfield, Fed. Cas. No. 2,248; [1867] In re McDuffee, Fed. Cas. No. 8,778.

36. Compare, § 863. Also, see obiter, In re Eagles and Crisp, 3 A. B. R. 733, 99 Fed. 696 (D. C. N. C.); obiter, In re Syracuse Paper & Pulp Co., 21 A. B. R. 174, 164 Fed. 275 (D. C. N. Y.).

a separate meeting of creditors, but each will constitute a session of the same meeting of creditors.[37] But each adjournment should be to a definite time, in order that the prescribed notices may not lapse.

And postponement for "surprise" will not be granted where the "surprise" consists in the overlooking of a plain provision of the law relative to proof of claims.[38]

Nevertheless, adjournment may be granted to enable creditors to amend proofs of debt to state the consideration more properly.[39]

§ 591. First Meeting—Time of Holding.

—The first meeting of creditors must not be held earlier than ten days nor later than thirty days after the adjudication, save and except it may be held later than thirty days thereafter if by any mischance it is not held within the thirty days.[40]

What constitutes "mischance" has not been decided. "Mischance" of course, excludes the idea of design; so, where some of the creditors at the beginning wish the meeting not to be held until after the thirty days, the court should refuse the request. "Mischance" only should stand in the way.

§ 592. First Meeting—Place of Holding.

—The first meeting must be held at the county seat of the county where the bankrupt resides or is domiciled or has his principal place of business. This provision is an advance over all former laws, and is in line with the principle of the present law bringing the bankruptcy courts home to the people, no longer obliging litigants to travel to distant points to get to the federal court, as was the case under the old law. In order still further to carry out this idea, it is also provided that the meeting may be held at even some more convenient place.[41]

§ 593. First Meeting—Referee or Judge to Preside, Allow Claims, Examine Bankrupt.

—At the first meeting of creditors the referee (or if the judge so desires, the judge himself) presides, and, usually, before pro-

---

37. Obiter, In re Eagles & Crisp, 3 A. B. R. 733, 99 Fed. 696 (D. C. N. C.).

38. In re Finlay, 3 A. B. R. 738 (D. C. N. Y.).

39. Obiter, In re Morris, 18 A. B. R. 826, 159 Fed. 591 (D. C. Pa.), quoted at § 863.

40. Bankr. Act, § 55 (a): "The Court shall cause the first meeting of creditors of a bankrupt to be held, not less than ten nor more than thirty days after the adjudication, * * *. If such meeting should by any mischance not be held within such time, the Court shall fix the date, as soon as may be thereafter, when it shall be held."

Failure to Hold First Meeting Cause for Dismissing Discharge Petition, by Local Rule.—The failure to hold the first meeting is, in some jurisdictions, sufficient cause for dismissing an application for discharge. In re Wollowitz, 27 A. B. R. 558, 192 Fed. 105 (C. C. A. N. Y.), decided under a rule of the Southern District. See also, § 2480.

41. Bankr. Act, § 55 (a): "The court shall cause the first meeting of creditors of a bankrupt to be held * * * at the county seat of the county in which the bankrupt has had his principal place of business, resided or had his domicile; or if that place would be manifestly inconvenient as a place of meeting for the parties in interest, or if the bankrupt is one that does not do business, reside or have his domicile within the United States, the Court shall fix a place for the meeting which is the most convenient for parties in interest."

As to notices of such meeting, see preceding chapter.

ceeding with the other business, may allow or disallow the claims of creditors there presented, and may publicly examine the bankrupt or cause him to be examined at the instance of any creditor.

The first thing usually done at the first meeting of creditors is the allowing and disallowing of claims. By § 7, clauses (1) and (3), it is made the duty of the bankrupt to attend the first meeting of his creditors, if an order be entered to that effect, and to assist the court in examining the correctness of all proofs of claims filed against his estate. Generally, then, with the bankrupt's assistance, the court, by which usually is meant the referee since the judge seldom if ever takes advantage of the statutory permission to preside, proceeds to the allowance and disallowance of claims, and then the creditors take up the voting for a trustee.[42]

§ 593¼. Meeting to Consider Composition before Adjudication.—Amendment of 1910.

—By the Amendment of 1910, permitting compositions before adjudication, it is provided that in such cases the bankrupt shall file the required schedules before adjudication, and that thereupon the court shall call a meeting of creditors for the allowance of claims, the examination of the bankrupt, and for the consideration of the conduct of the estate, at which meeting the judge or referee shall preside.[43]

§ 593½. Meeting to Consider Opposition to Discharge.—Amendment of 1910.

—The Amendment of 1910, making the trustee a competent party to oppose the discharge of the bankrupt, only permits him to oppose the discharge when authorized so to do at a meeting of creditors called for such purpose.[44]

Such meeting of creditors is to be called on the ordinary ten days' notice by mail, and it takes action in the ordinary manner.[45]

---

42. Compare, general duty to elect trustee at the first meeting. In re Syracuse Paper & Pulp Co., 21 A. B. R. 174, 164 Fed. 275 (D. C. N. Y.).

43. Bankr. Act, § 12 (a) as amended in 1910: "A bankrupt may offer, either before or after adjudication, terms of composition to his creditors after, but not before, he has been examined in open court or at a meeting of his creditors, and has filed in court the schedule of his property and the list of his creditors required to be filed by bankrupts. In compositions before adjudication the bankrupt shall file the required schedules, and thereupon the court shall call a meeting of creditors for the allowance of claims, examination of the bankrupt, and preservation or conduct of estates, at which meeting the judge or referee shall preside; and action upon the petition for adjudication shall be delayed until it shall be determined whether such composition shall be confirmed."

44. Bankr. Act, § 14 (b): "The judge shall hear the application for a discharge and such proofs and pleas as may be made in opposition thereto by the trustee or other parties in interest, at such times as will give the trustee or parties in interest a reasonable opportunity to be fully heard, and investigate the merits of the application and discharge the applicant unless he has (1) committed an offense.........

....

"Provided, That a trustee shall not interpose objections to a bankrupt's discharge until he shall be authorized so to do at a meeting of creditors for that purpose."

45. See ante, § 565¼.

CHAPTER XX.

Proofs of Claims.

Synopsis of Chapter.

§ 594. Proof of Claim—What Is It?—The term proof of claim is the technical term used in bankruptcy for the formal affidavit of the creditor setting forth his claim. Thus, § 57, clause "A", defines a proof of claim, saying: "Proof of claim shall consist of a statement under oath in writing, signed by a creditor," etc.

Proof of claim, then, consists of a statement, under oath, in writing, signed by a creditor, setting forth the claim, the consideration therefor, and whether any and if so, what securities are held therefor and whether any, and if so what payments have been made thereon, and that the sum claimed is justly owing from the bankrupt to the creditor.[1]

The Supreme Court has prescribed certain further requirements in its General Orders and Forms in Bankruptcy; chiefly to be found in General Order No. XXI and the forms for proofs of debts, secured and unsecured, by individuals, partnerships, corporations and agents respectively—being Forms Nos. 31 to 37 inclusive.

§ 595. "Proof" and "Allowance" Different Terms, Likewise "Filing."

—The proof and the allowance of claims are distinct terms.[2] The "proof" is the sworn statement by which a creditor presents his claim to the court's consideration; allowance is the judicial action by which the validity and amount of a claim is established for participation in the distribution of dividends. Care and particularity are required in the preparation of a proof of claim in bankruptcy, for it is both the creditor's pleading and his evidence and makes for him a prima facie case.[3] And it must be made as provided in the Bankruptcy Act and the forms prescribed by the Supreme Court, and a proof made in the form of ordinary pleadings, although setting up a good cause of action, is insufficient.[4] But the defect is not "fatal" as the court in the case, In re Dunn Hardware Co., 13 A. B. R. 147, 132 Fed. 719 (D. C. N. Car.), seems to indicate. It may be cured by amendment.

The court, by which is meant the referee, for the judge, as heretofore stated, seldom exercises his power of dispensing with the referee and attending to the details of the administration himself, apparently has no authority to allow any claims except such as have been "duly proved,"[5] as will appear from the later clauses of this same § 57, and only creditors whose claims have been allowed may share in dividends or vote for trustee or participate in the proceedings—except perhaps to examine the bankrupt, if necessary to do so in establishing the validity of their own particular claims —and it is therefore of importance to ascertain what statements are essential to constitute the affidavit of the creditor "due" proof of his claim.

There are three steps to be taken. First, the creditor must "prove" his claim—that is the creditor's act. He must then present it to the proper officer, who thereupon performs the ministerial duty of "filing" it. Thereafter, the court allows or disallows it, this latter act being a judicial act.

In re Two Rivers, etc., Co., 29 A. B. R. 518, 199 Fed. 877 (C. C. A. Wis.): "Three steps are necessary to complete the allowance of a claim. Section 57a shows how a claim shall be 'proved.' This is the claimant's act. Section 57c provides that proved claims 'may, for the purpose of allowance, be filed.' Filing is the ministerial act of the clerk or referee. That filing is not allowance is

---

1. Bankr. Act, § 57 (a).

2. In re Fairlamb Co., 28 A. B. R. 515, 199 Fed. 278 (D. C. Pa.).

3. See post, "Pleadings and Procedure on Objection to Claims," § 830, et seq.

4. In re Dunn Hardware Co., 13 A. B. R. 147, 132 Fed. 719 (D. C. N. C.).

5. Post, § 813; also compare, In re (James) Dunlap Carpet Co., 22 A. B. R. 788, 171 Fed. 532 (D. C. Pa.).

established by the language that the claim is filed 'for the purpose of allowance.' It may be that the command of § 57d, 'shall be allowed upon receipt by or upon presentation to the court,' would entitle a claimant to an order of allowance instanter unless objections were at once interposed, or unless the court upon its own motion should postpone consideration. But 'allowance,' different from the party's act of 'proving' and the ministerial act of 'filing,' is a judicial act. This is found, not only by comparing with each other the several provisions of § 57, but also by recurring to § 2 (2), relating to the powers and duties of bankruptcy courts, wherein the acts of allowing, disallowing, and reconsidering claims are all given the same quality. In practice it may be common to forego formal orders of allowance, and to treat as allowed, for purposes of distributing dividends, all claims to which objections have not been filed. But the inclusion of proved and filed claims in an order of distribution may be considered as an indirect order of allowance. Until a direct or indirect order of allowance is made, objections may properly be filed. And, until a direct or indirect order of allowance is made, it is not necessary to proceed under §§ 57k and 57l, for a reconsideration of a claim and a recovery of dividends already paid. It was, therefore, error to strike out the trustee's objections to appellee's claim unless Conant's offer was to treat as 'allowed' all claims 'proved' and 'filed,' or unless the trustee had no standing to object."

§ 595½. Agreeing to Treat Informal Papers as "Proofs of Claim."

—Attempt is sometimes made to have informal papers not containing sufficient allegations "by which to amend" treated as claims, this fault most commonly arising in cases of claims that have not been properly filed within the year.[6]

§ 596. Caption and Title.

—The affidavit, or as it is technically called, the "deposition," for proof of claim must be correctly entitled in the case and must have the court wherein the case is pending correctly designated in the caption.[7] But the failure properly to entitle the cause is not a fatal defect.[8]

Then follows the body of the affidavit, the opening clause of which designates the place where the affidavit is made.

§ 597. "Claim" to Be Set Forth and Alleged to Be "Justly Owing."

—The affidavit must set forth the claim, that is to say, must *make claim to a debt* and must aver the debt to be justly owing from the bankrupt.[9] There must be a specific amount claimed, and the nature of the claim must be given.[10]

There seems to be no particular form for proving unliquidated claims. Damages might be claimed in a specific amount though the claim be unliquidated. Perhaps a mere written application to the Court setting up the facts of the existence of the unliquidated claim, together with a brief description

---

6. See post, §§ 618, 729 and 735. See In re Kessler, 25 A. B. R. 512, 186 Fed. 127 (C. C. A. N. Y., reversing 23 A. B. R. 901, 176 Fed. 647).

7. Gen. Ord. XXI.

8. In re Blue Ridge Packing Co.,

11 A. B. R. 36, 125 Fed. 619 (D. C. Penn.).

9. Bankr. Act, § 57 (a).

10. As to unliquidated claims, see post, § 704, et seq.

of its nature, accompanied by a request for an order of the court to direct the manner of liquidation, would be the proper practice.

§ 598. **Due Date and Interest.**—In interpreting the statutory requirement that the affidavit must set forth the claim, the Supreme Court has prescribed, in its General Order No. XXI and in its forms, that the average due date shall be stated in case of an account.[11]

If the due date or average due date is not given, nor the computed interest stated, the officers of the court need not compute the interest on the claim and dividends will be paid only on the principal. Interest is to be computed to the date of the filing of the bankruptcy petition, if the instrument draws interest. If it does not draw interest and falls due later, then interest must be rebated to the date of the filing of the bankruptcy petition.[12]

Where the debt is secured the creditor is entitled to compute interest to the date of realizing on the security.[13]

Interest on secured claims ceases on the filing of the petition in bankruptcy; and a creditor selling his security thereafter cannot apply the proceeds first to the payment of the interest accruing since the filing of the petition, then to the principal, and prove a claim for the balance that might be due.[14] But interest and dividends which have accrued on securities may be applied by the creditor to the after accruing interest on his debt.[15]

But the rule that interest ceases at the date of the filing of the petition, does not apply to solvent estates.[16]

§ 599. **Debts Owing but Not Yet Due.**—Debts on written instruments absolutely owing at the time of bankruptcy, but not yet due, may be proved;[17] with interest to the date of bankruptcy if bearing interest, or a rebate of interest to the same date, if not bearing interest.[18]

---

11. Gen. Ord. XXI: "Depositions to prove debts existing in open account shall state when the debt became or will become due; and if it consists of items maturing at different dates the average due date shall be stated, in default of which it shall not be necessary to compute interest upon it."

In re Goble Boat Co., 27 A. B. R. 48, 190 Fed. 92 (D. C. N. Y.).

12. Bankr. Act, § 63 (a) (1): "* * * with any interest thereon which would have been recoverable at that date or with a rebate of interest upon such as were not then payable and did not bear interest."

Whether interest to be given on allowed claims where trustee in bankruptcy ordered to pay over to trustees in liquidation, In re John Osborne's Sons & Co., 24 A. B. R. 65, 177 Fed. 184 (C. C. A. N. Y.).

13. Obiter, Coder v. Arts, 18 A. B. R. 513, 152 Fed. 943 (C. C. A. Iowa);

Coder v. Arts, 22 A. B. R. 1, 213 U. S. 223, quoted at §§ 758½, 1997½; In re Stevens, 23 A. B. R. 239, 173 Fed. 842 (D. C. Ore.), quoted at § 758½.

14. Sexton v. Dreyfus, 25 A. B. R. 363, 219 U. S. 339 (reversing 24 A. B. R. 287, 171 Fed. 751, and also reversing In re Kessler, 22 A. B. R. 607, 171 Fed. 751), quoted at § 758½.

15. Sexton v. Dreyfus, 25 A. B. R. 363, 219 U. S. 339 (reversing 24 A. B. R. 287, 171 Fed. 751, and also reversing In re Kessler, 22 A. B. R. 607, 171 Fed. 751), quoted at § 758½.

16. Johnson v. Norris, 27 A. B. R. 107, 190 Fed. 459, 466 (C. C. A. Tex.); Sexton v. Dreyfus, 25 A. B. R. 363, 219 U. S. 339, quoted supra, reversing, In re Kessler, 24 A. B. R. 287, 180 Fed. 979 (C. C. A.), and also reversing, In re Kessler, 22 A. B. R. 607, 171 Fed. 751.

17. Bankr. Act, § 63 (a) (1).

18. Bankr. Act, § 63 (a) (1).

§ 600. Must State Whether Judgment Taken.—The affidavit must state whether any judgment has been taken on the claim.[19] If judgment has been taken therefor, the judgment must be aptly described.

§ 601. Must State Whether Note Given.—The affidavit must state whether any note has been given for the claim or for a part of the claim.[20]

§ 602. If Instrument in Writing Given, Original to Be Attached.—If any note or other instrument in writing has been given, the original must be attached to the affidavit and left in the files until the claim is allowed. After allowance or disallowance of the claim, the original note or other written instrument may, upon order of the referee, be withdrawn, upon substituting a copy therefor.[21] This requirement undoubtedly applies not only to commercial paper but to all cases of written instruments including written contracts.[22] But a judgment or transcript of the record of a judgment is not a "written instrument" and need not be filed.[23]

Compare, analogously, Cox *v.* Farley, 2 W. L. M. (Ohio) 315: "A record is undoubtedly the evidence of an indebtedness; but is it a 'written instrument'?

19. Gen. Ord. XXI (1). In re Goble Boat Co., 27 A. B. R. 48, 190 Fed. 92 (D. C. N. Y.).

20. Gen. Ord. XXI (1). In re Goble Boat Co., 27 A. B. R. 48, 190 Fed. 92 (D. C. N. Y.).

21. Bankr. Act, § 57 (b): "Whenever a claim is founded upon an instrument of writing, such instrument, unless lost or destroyed, shall be filed with the proof of claim. If such instrument is lost or destroyed a statement of such fact and of the circumstances of such loss or destruction shall be filed under oath with the claim. After the claim is allowed or disallowed, such instrument may be withdrawn by permission of the court upon leaving a copy thereof on file with the claim."

It has been held, but probably incorrectly, that where the bankrupt's liability is that of an endorser, notice of dishonor and any other facts necessary to fix such liability must be stated. In re Stevens, 5 A. B. R. 11, 104 Fed. 323 (D. C. Vt.).

But query, whether any more allegations are necessary than are directly prescribed by the statute, general orders and forms.

Where the claim is for balances due on various collateral notes upon which the bankrupt is either maker or endorser, and which were in part to become due after discount, the date of discount, amount advanced and to whom must be stated in the proof of claim. In re Stevens, 5 A. B. R. 11, 104 Fed. 323 (D. C. Vt.).

But the fact that a written instru-

ment is not filed with the proof of claim raises no presumption against its existence. In re Dresser, 13 A. B. R. 747 (C. C. A. N. Y.).

Where no objection to a claim was made upon the ground that the original notes and mortgages, the basis of the claim, were not attached thereto, it will be presumed that the original securities were present at the trial, and not attached, or may have been attached and copies substituted or their presence waived. In re Carter, 15 A. B. R. 126, 138 Fed. 846 (D. C. Ark.).

Waiving Note and Proving on Original Consideration.—A note may be waived and proof be made on the original consideration.

In re Worcester Co., 4 A. B. R. 504, 102 Fed. 808 (C. C. A. Mass.): "In bankruptcy it is of no consequence whether proof was made of the original account or of the note. Therefore, if the original account belonged to the county, so at its option did the note, and the county claiming the note might prove it, or repudiating it, it might prove the original account." Such waiver, however, does not dispense with the necessity of stating whether such a note was given nor with production of the original.   .

22. Inferentially, In re Dresser, 13 A. B. R. 747, 135 Fed. 495 (C. C. A. N. Y.); obiter and inferentially, In re Big Meadows Gas Co., 7 A. B. R. 697, 113 Fed. 794 (D. C. Pa.).

23. But compare, impliedly, contra, McCabe *v.* Patton, 23 A. B. R. 335, 174 Fed. 217 (C. C. A. Pa.).

* * * Now, from the use of the words 'written instrument,' it is clear that the Code refers to an instrument executed by or between parties. Webster defines the word, as a writing containing the terms of a contract. In this sense, a record is not a written instrument. The judgment of the court is the ground of the action and the record is the mere evidence of that recovery. The record is as accessible to the one party as to the other. It is public property and either party can obtain a copy of it."

§ 603. Consideration to Be Stated.—The affidavit must state the consideration.[24]

In re. Scott, 1 A. B. R. 553 (D. C. Tex.): "Upon the proof in bankruptcy proceedings of a debt due a creditor, the statement of the consideration should be sufficiently specific and full to enable other creditors to pursue proper and legitimate inquiry as to the fairness and legality of the claim. If the proof is so meagre and general in character as not to do this, it must be held insufficient. Where it is not sufficiently specific and full the creditor must amend or the referee will expunge from the record of the case the proof already made."

In re Stevens, 5 A. B. R. 806, 104 Fed. 325 (D. C. Vt.): "The provisions of § 57, a, b, respecting the statement of consideration and payments required something more than would be sufficient in a declaration against the bankrupt upon these causes of action, and extend to the particulars of each for the information of the trustee and those interested in the estate, but not beyond what relates to the claim as it accrued to claimant."

[1867] In re Elder, Fed. Cas. No. 4,326: "But what was the object of the lawmaker in requiring the consideration to be stated in the deposition? The answer to this will help ascertain how particular the statement of it must be. One object, no doubt, was to enable the register to see whether it is legal in its nature, and will support a demand or promise. Another, to show him whether or not the demand is unliquidated, and must be ascertained by assessment before its allowance. Another, to afford the assignee means for comparing the books of the bankrupt with the proof. But the chief object, no doubt, was to put a check upon the proof of fraudulent and fictitious claims, by requiring the claimant to give such a particular and definite statement of the consideration, as would enable other creditors to trace out, discover and expose the fraud or illegality of the claim, if any existed.

"The requirement is intended to be for the benefit of all other creditors of the estate of the bankrupt, and to prevent fraud. If the statement of the consideration is so general and indefinite as to afford no aid to the creditors in their inquiry as to the fairness and legality of the claim, it does not effect the object of the law, and must be held insufficient."

It is not proper to state the consideration merely as being, "for goods, wares and merchandise." The proof ought further to specify the general nature of the goods, wares and merchandise, as, for instance, leather or tinware, etc., etc.[25]

---

24. Bankr. Act, § 57 (a). In re Blue Ridge Packing Co., 11 A. B. R. 36, 125 Fed. 619 (D. C. Pa.); In re Creasinger, 17 A. B. R. 543 (Ref. Calif., affirmed by D. C.); In re Coventry Evans Furniture Co., 22 A. B. R. 272, 171 Fed. 673 (D. C. N. Y.), quoted later at § 603. Compare, In re Watertown Paper Co., 22 A. B. R. 190, 169 Fed. 252 (C. C. A. N. Y.).

25. In re Blue Ridge Packing Co., 11 A. B. R. 36, 125 Fed. 619 (D. C. Pa.). See note to In re Scott, 1 A. B. R. 553 (D. C. Tex.); In re Coventry Evans Furniture Co., 22 A. B. R. 272, 171 Fed. 673 (D. C. N. Y.), quoted further on in this paragraph.

In re Morris, 18 A. B. R. 828, 159 Fed. 591 (D. C. Pa.): "The proofs of debt objected to were clearly defective, most of them being simply stated to be for 'services,' 'mdse., etc.,' 'balance of wages,' 'balance of professional services,' for 'goods sold and delivered,' and the like; none of which meets the law."

[1867] In re Elder, Fed. Cas. No. 4,326: "Looking then at the object of the law, and the reasons for requiring a statement of the consideration in the deposition, I consider that a general statement that the considerations of a demand is goods, wares and merchandise, or hay, barley and board, is not sufficient; that the kinds of goods, the quantity, the price and near the date of sale should be stated; that the quantity of hay, or barley, the price, and the time of delivery, if delivered at one time, or if delivered continuously through a period of time, that period should be stated. If the proof falls short of this, the register ought not to consider it satisfactory, and should withhold his approval."

Even claims founded upon promissory notes and other commercial paper importing consideration should state the consideration.[26]

In re Coventry Evans Furniture Co., 22 A. B. R. 272, 171 Fed. 673 (D. C. N. Y.): "The claim filed is a mere statement that the company is indebted to Darling in the sum of $7,329.90, without any information as to the basis of such indebtedness except that the consideration for such debt is a promissory note of the company to Darling's order for $7,151.13, giving date. The consideration of the note is not stated. That this proof of claim was a compliance with § 57a of the Bankruptcy Act * * * is not seriously contended. If the claim was on the note, an instrument in writing, evidence of indebtedness, the section requires that the consideration for the note be stated. If a note is given for property, or money loaned or advanced, or for work, labor, and services, etc., as the case may be, the proof of claim must so state and give facts in regard thereto which will enable the trustee and creditors to investigate and ascertain the consideration and justice of the claim. If the claim is for a debt for work, etc., or money loaned, or property sold, etc., and no note has been given, the proof of claim should state the consideration and give facts which will enable the trustee and creditors to ascertain the adequacy of the consideration and the justice and legality of the claim. Whether the claim be on a promissory note, other instrument in writing, or on an account, or for money loaned, etc., the proof of claim must state 'the consideration' for the debt. A proof of claim which complies with the requirements of § 57 establishes the claim, entitles it to allowance in the first instance, and throws the burden of overthrowing it on the trustee when appointed, and on the creditors of the bankrupt if they would contest. Whitney v. Dresser, 200 U. S. 532, 15 Am. B. R. 326, * * * and cases there cited. If it fails to do this, it is not entitled to allowance, and, if allowed, the trustee when appointed may have it disallowed and expunged, unless it is corrected by amendment or established by proof. The proof of claim must set forth 'the consideration,' not a general statement that there was a consideration. The claim is 'proved' and entitled to allowance only when it is properly verified and gives 'the consideration' therefor and contains the other statements required. It is not sufficient to say that the bankrupt is indebted to claimant in a certain sum, and then say that the consideration for the debt is a written promise to pay it reciting 'for value received.' True, this written promise also acknowledges a consideration for the promise, but it does not give the consideration as required by § 57a."

---

26. [1867] In re Elder, 3 Bankr. Reg. 670, 1 Sawy. 73, Fed. Cases 4,326. See note to In re Scott, 1 A. B. R. 553 (D. C. Tex.).

The requirement that the consideration must be stated would not, of course, operate to nullify the principle that the instrument imports a consideration. It is simply a statement of fact for the information of creditors and does not deprive the claimant of any of his rights.

And such statement must be sufficiently full and explicit to enable other creditors to investigate the fairness and legality of the claim.[27]

§ 604. Account to Be Itemized.

—In carrying out and interpreting the statutory requirement that the consideration must be stated, the Supreme Court has prescribed in its General Order XXI that if the claim is upon an account the account must be in detail, that is to say, be itemized, and be attached to the affidavit.[28] This is so even with an account for legal services.[29] The items must be dated and described.[30]

The basis of this requirement is probably that creditors, coming together from long distances, should have the claims of other creditors presented in such form that by simple inspection their validity may appear, and creditors be not subjected to the trouble of instituting protracted enquiries at great expense. Thus, it will not fulfill the requirement to attach an account which sets forth as a part of the account the item merely "to account rendered" so much, or "to balance due" so much, in a lump sum.

§ 604½. All Credits to Be Shown.

—All credits are to be shown.[31]

It is the claimant's duty not only to prove the amount due on the obligation but also the payments made thereon.[33]

§ 605. Claims Provable in Name of Real Party in Interest.

—Claims are, in general, to be made in the name of the party substantially in interest.[34]

27. Orr v. Park, 25 A. B. R. 544, 183 Fed. 683 (C. C. A. Ga.), quoted at § 814.

28. Gen. Order XXI. In re Blue Ridge Packing Co., 11 A. B. R. 36, 125 Fed. 619 (D. C. Penn.); In re Scott, 1 A. B. R. 553 (D. C. Tex.); In re Chasnoff, 3 N. B. N. & R. 1 (Ref. Neb.); In re Creasinger, 17 A. B. R. 543 (Ref. Calif., affirmed by D. C.).

Account Stated.—When an "account rendered" becomes an "account stated," see post, § 694, note.

29. In re Scott, 1 A. B. R. 553 (D. C. Tex.); In re Creasinger, 17 A. B. R. 543 (Ref. Calif., affirmed by D. C.).

30. In re Blue Ridge Packing Co., 11 A. B. R. 36, 125 Fed. 619 (D. C. Penn.).

31. Obiter, In re Watertown Paper Co., 22 A. B. R. 190, 169 Fed. 252 (C. C. A. N. Y.).

In one instance, on review, a wife's claim against her husband's estate was disallowed, because an amendment had been had, after expiration of the year, to show undisclosed credits, with the object of taking the claim out of the statute of limitations, the claimant originally having erased the word "except" from the form, as if there were no credits. In re Girvin, 20 A. B. R. 490, 160 Fed. 442 (D. C. Vt.).

33. In re Graves, 25 A. B. R. 372, 182 Fed. 442 (D. C. Vt.).

34. In re Pangborn, 26 A. B. R. 40, 185 Fed. 673 (D. C. Mich.). Compare, inferentially to this effect, Mackey v. Randolph Macon Coal Co., 24 A. B. R. 719, 178 Fed. 881 (C. C. A. Mo.). Bank loaning money to creditor, which creditor in turn lends to bankrupt, is not, on that account, the real party in interest, even though the creditor is one of the bank's trustees. Ohio Valley Bank v. Mack, 20 A. B. R. 40, 163 Fed. 352 (C. C. A. Ohio). See ante, § 203½.

Mortgage Bondholders or Trustee

In re Worcester Co., 4 A. B. R. 504, 102 Fed. 808 (C. C. A. Mass.): "Bankruptcy, however, is governed by the rules of equity proceedings, and takes no cognizance of the technical rules of the common law with reference to parties to litigation, and, like equity, it acts in the names of the parties substantially interested. So that, whether or not the note was indorsed by Dwinell, the debt could be proved by the county, if it owned it (as it was proved), and in no other way. The indorsement by Dwinell was of no effect, except as a matter of convenience, as affording uncontroverted evidence that it belonged to the county."

§ 606. Secured Claims.—If the claim is a secured claim that fact must be stated and the security be described.[35]

But the failure to do so may be corrected by amendment.[36]

§ 607. Priority Claims.—Claims entitled to priority of payment before general creditors out of dividends must be "proved."[37] They are none the less provable debts because of their right to priority of payment before other debts.

To this rule there is of course the usual exception of the claims of the state and federal governments for taxes and other demands. The sovereign is not to be put to the necessity of making proof of debt.[38]

But no special form of proof of a priority claim is prescribed.[39]

In re Jones, 18 A. B. R. 209 (D. C. Mich.): "While the statute expressly provides what the proof of claim shall contain no requirement is made as to the contents of a petition for priority."

Nor need the "proof" contain formal demand for priority of payment.[40]

In re Jones, 18 A. B. R. 209 (D. C. Mich.): "There is no requirement that

for Mortgage, Which Is Proper Party to Prove Claim for Deficiency?—Compare Mackey v. Randolph-Macon Coal Co., 24 A. B. R. 719, 178 Fed. 881 (C. C. A. Mo.).

Tax Collector under Statute Giving Him Right to Sue in Own Name after Three Months, Disqualified When.—In re Corwin Mfg. Co., 26 A. B. R. 269, 185 Fed. 977 (D. C. Mass.).

Legatees Proving Where Executor Refuses.—Thus where an executor refuses to make a claim for a debt owing to the estate which he represents, the legatees may do so. Matter of Lough & Burrows, 25 A. B. R. 597, 182 Fed. 960 (C. C. A. N. Y.).

One of Several Sureties, for Reimbursement Notwithstanding Illegal Transfer to Him.—One of several sureties on the same instrument may prove for reimbursement against the principal's estate, in behalf of all, where all contributed equally to pay the debt, notwithstanding a transfer of property to him on their joint behalf has been set aside as improper. In re [Salvator] Brew. Co., 26 A. B. R. 21, 183 Fed. 910 (D. C. N. Y.).

35. Bankr. Act, § 57 (a).
As to what claims are and what are not provable and allowable, see post, chs. XXI and XXIV.
As to determining value of securities for the purpose of voting and sharing in dividends, see post, ch. XXIV, div. 1, subd. "A," § 763; and for the purpose of sharing in dividends, see post, ch. XXIV, div. 1, subd. "A," § 759, et seq.

36. Maxwell v. McDaniels, 27 A. B. R. 692, 184 Fed. 311 (C. C. A. W. Va.).

37. In re Dunn, 25 A. B. R. 103, 181 Fed. 701 (D. C. N. Y.); In re Hayward, 12 A. B. R. 264, 130 Fed. 720 (D. C. Pa.); instance, claim of county for labor of its convicts, In re Worcester Co., 4 A. B. R. 504, 102 Fed. 808 (C. C. A. Mass.).

38. Thus, as to taxes, see post, § 701. Thus, as to damages on government contract, see post, § 730.

39. In re Worcester Co., 4 A. B. R. 504, 102 Fed. 808 (C. C. A. Mass.).

40. In re Worcester Co., 4 A. B. R. 504, 102 Fed. 808 (C. C. A. Mass.).

priority should be claimed in the petition (deposition) for proof of claim. This priority is matter of administration and may be asserted at any time in connection with or before the payment of dividends.

However, it is good practice to make the proof conform to that prescribed for a secured debt and to insert allegations bringing the claim within those enumerated in § 64 as being entitled to priority of payment.

§ 608. Assigned Claims—Assigned before Bankruptcy.

—If a claim has been assigned before the bankruptcy, of course the assignee makes the proof and makes it in his own name. He is the creditor.[41]

In re Worcester County, 4 A. B. R. 504, 102 Fed. 808 (C. C. A. Mass.): "Even claims assigned before bankruptcy must be proved by the assignee. This was so determined by Judge Lowell in In re Fortune, 1 Low. 384, Fed. Cas. No. 3,586—a decision which was never controverted, and which, on fundamental principles of equity rules of proceeding, can not be. In case of a debt assigned before bankruptcy, the original assignor is not entitled to be recognized, either in a petition for an adjudication of bankruptcy or in a proof of debt; and the assignee necessarily comes in his own name as the only party to the record. All the discussion and doubt about the method of proceeding with assigned debts, whether under the present statute or previous ones, relate to those assigned after the proceedings in bankruptcy are commenced."

§ 609. Assigned after Bankruptcy, but before Proof.

—If a claim has been assigned, however, after the bankruptcy but before it has been proved, the claimant's proof must be supported by an affidavit of the one who was owner of the claim at the time of the commencement of the bankruptcy proceedings. This supporting affidavit must set forth the true consideration of the debt and that it is entirely unsecured, or if it be secured then the security must be described, precisely as in the proof of secured claims.[42]

§ 610. Assigned after Proof.

—Of course claims that have been proved and entered of record, and that are afterwards assigned, do not require any action on the part of the court except to guard against imposition and falsehood as to the fact of the assignment actually having been made. To this end, whenever notice of the assignment of a claim which has already been proved is received, the referee must give ten days notice by mail to the original creditor who made the proof of claim to deny the assignment if it be untrue. No special form of an assignment of a claim is required.[43]

§ 611. Proof by Person Contingently or Secondarily Liable.

—Persons contingently or secondarily liable for a bankrupt's debt as, for instance, a surety or endorser for him, may prove the debt in the name of the creditor,

---

41. In re Worcester County, 4 A. B. R. 502, 102 Fed. 808 (C. C. A. Mass.). See post, § 740.

42. Gen. Order XXI. See post, § 741.

43. See In re Miner, 9 A. B. R. 103, 117 Fed. 953 (D. C. Ore.). See, also, post, ch. XXVII, § 742; instance, In re American Specialty Co., 27 A. B. R. 463, 178 Fed. 106 (C. C. N. Y.).

if the creditor fails to prove it himself.[44]   If the name of the creditor be unknown to the person contingently liable, as is likely to occur in the case of endorsers on negotiable notes, the claim may be proved in the name of the person contingently liable.[45]

Of course, the object of this statutory provision and this general order for permitting the proof of contingent claims is to relieve the surety as much as possible and to prevent the injustice that would be worked upon him were the creditor himself to lie back contented to rely solely upon the security, taking no steps to get any portion of the debt paid by the person primarily obligated therefor.[46]   It is the creditor's claim that is to be thus proved, not the surety's; and the proof therefore must be in the name of the creditor and not in the name of the surety, unless the name of the creditor is unknown.[47]

Livingston v. Heineman, 10 A. B. R. 42, 120 Fed. 786 (C. C. A. Ohio): "The surety, to obtain his distributive share of the bankrupt's estate must proceed

---

44. Bankr. Act, § 57 (i). Obiter, Hayes v. Comstock, 7 A. B. R. 493 (Sup. Ct. Iowa). In re Carter, 15 A. B. R. 126, 138 Fed. 846 (D. C. Ark.); obiter, Phillips v. Dreher Shoe Co., 7 A. B. R. 326, 112 Fed. 404 (D. C. Penna.).

See post, "Rights of Creditors against Third Parties Jointly or Secondarily Liable for Bankrupt," § 1510, et seq.

See, in addition, In re Otto F. Lange Co., 22 A. B. R. 414, 170 Fed. 414 (D. C. Iowa); In re Lyons Sugar Co., 27 A. B. R. 610, 192 Fed. 445 (D. C. N. Y.).

45. Gen. Order XXI (4): "The claims of persons contingently liable for the bankrupt may be proved in the name of the creditor when known by the party contingently liable. When the name of the creditor is unknown, such claim may be proved in the name of the party contingently liable; but no dividend shall be paid upon such claim, except upon satisfactory proof that it will diminish pro tanto the original debt."

46. See Hayes v. Comstock, 7 A. B. R. 493 (Sup. Ct. Iowa).

47. Bankr. Act, § 57 (i). Insley v. Garside, 10 A. B. R. 52, 121 Fed. 699 (C. C. A. Alaska); obiter, Phillips v. Dreher Shoe Co., 7 A. B. R. 326, 112 Fed. 404 (D. C. Penn.); In re Dillon, 4 A. B. R. 63, 100 Fed. 627 (D. C. Mass.); impliedly, Swarts v. Siegel, 8 A. B. R. 696, 117 Fed. 13 (C. C. A. Mo.); impliedly, In re Schmechel, 4 A. B. R. 719, 104 Fed. 64 (C. C. A. Mo.).

So, also, as we will later see, if the creditor has received voidable preferences then the surety must surrender them or their value as a prerequisite to the allowance of his claim for the surety is subrogated to the creditors' claim "cum onere." Livingston v. Heineman, 10 A. B. R. 39, 120 Fed. 786 (C. C. A. Ohio, reversing, on other grounds, In re New, 8 A. B. R. 566); compare, quære, In re Dillon, 4 A. B. R. 63, 100 Fed. 627 (D. C. Mass.); In re Schmechel, 4 A. B. R. 719, 104 Fed. 64 (D. C. Mo.); In re Waterbury Furn. Co., 8 A. B. R. 79, 114 Fed. 255 (D. C. Conn.); Cookingham v. Morgan, Fed. Cas. 3,183; Bartholomew v. Bean, 18 Wall. 635.

Swarts v. Siegel, 8 A. B. R. 696, 117 Fed. 13 (C. C. A. Mo.): "An indorser, an accommodation maker or a surety on the obligation of a bankrupt is a creditor under the act of 1898, and a payment on such an obligation by the principal debtor while insolvent to the innocent holder of the contract within four months before the filing of the petition for adjudication in bankruptcy will constitute a preference which will debar the indorser, accommodation maker, or surety from the allowance of any claim in his favor against the estate of the bankrupt unless the amount so paid is first returned to that estate." Impliedly, Landry v. Andrews, 6 A. B. R. 281, 22 R. I. 597; In re Rea, 82 Iowa 239; Cutler v. Steele, 85 Mich. 632; Dunnigan v. Stevens, 122 Ills. 401, 404; (1867) Ahl v. Thornor, Fed. Cas. No. 103; (1867) Sill v. Solberg, 6 Fed. 474, 477; (1867) Scammon v. Cole, Fed. Cas. 12,432.

in the manner pointed out by the Bankrupt Law; that is, if the creditor fails to prove the claim, he must prove it in the name of the creditor, and he will then be permitted to participate in the distribution to the extent that he has discharged the obligation."

The surety may, of course, prove his own claim for indemnity against the bankrupt if the surety has paid anything or suffered any loss on account of his principal, before the filing of the petition.[48]

§ 612. Creditor Not Obliged to Prove Claim against Principal, Even on Surety's Demand nor to Lend Written Instrument to Surety, unless.

—The creditor is not under any active duty either to prove his claim against the bankrupt principal, nor to let the surety take the written instrument to attach to a proof of claim. The creditor is entitled to its possession, and if the surety desires its possession, he must pay the debt.[49] But, if the surety demands that the creditor either prove or let the surety have the written instrument in order to prove, and offers to fully indemnify the creditor against loss and expense, the creditor's refusal would probably work a pro tanto release, to the extent of the dividends lost thereby.

Obiter, query, Bank v. Sawyer, 6 A. B. R. 154 (Mass. Sup. Jud. Ct.): "We are of opinion that the holder has no such active duty either to prove the note of his own motion, or to tender it to the endorser to enable the latter to make proof, as to make such an omission on the part of the holder a release of the endorser.

"Even equity will not compel a creditor to prove in bankruptcy against his principal debtor for the benefit of a surety, unless the surety himself moves in the matter and requires the creditor to act, furnishing him with suitable indemnity against the consequences of risk and delay, and against expense. Watertown Bank v. Simmons, 131 Mass. 85, and cases cited; Wright v. Simpson, 6 Ves. 714, 734; Ex parte Rushforth, 10 Ves. 414; Mayhen v. Crickett, 2 Swanst. 185, 191; 1 Story, Eq. Jur., § 639. See Bellows v. Lovell, 5 Pick. 307, 311.

"The plaintiff was entitled to the possession of the note until it should be paid. Reynolds could pay it in performance of his promise as endorser, be reinstated in his original title, and then prove his own claim in bankruptcy without help. He made no payment, nor did he request the plaintiff either to prove the note or to allow it to be filed in support of any attempted proof. Whether, if he had requested the plaintiff to prove the note, rendering the expenses of such proof with proper indemnity, or had himself attempted to prove his own claim, requesting the plaintiff under proper indemnity to allow the filing of the note in support of such proof, he would have been released by a refusal on the part of the plaintiff, it is not necessary to consider, and upon those points we express no opinion."

---

48. Boyce v. Guaranty Co., 7 A. B. R. 6, 111 Fed. 138 (C. C. A. Ohio). In this case a surety on defaulting contractor's bond who completed the work at greater cost than contract price, was held to be a creditor for the loss. See, inferentially, Insley v. Garside, 10 A. B. R. 52, 121 Fed. 699 (C. C. A. Alaska); In re Bingham, 2 A. B. R. 223, 94 Fed. 796 (D. C. Vt.). Thus, an endorser paying a note before the maker's bankruptcy may prove for the full amount. In re McCord, 22 A. B. R. 204, 174 Fed. 72 (D. C. N. Y.).

49. Bank v. Sawyer, 6 A. B. R. 154 (Mass. Sup. Jud. Ct.).

§ 613. Surety, on Payment, Subrogated, Pro Tanto, to Creditor's Dividends.

—The surety is subrogated to the creditor's dividends, pro tanto, if he has paid anything thereon either before or *after* the bankruptcy.[50] But where the surety has paid only a part and a contest arises between him and the creditor as to who shall make the proof the creditor will be preferred.[51]

§ 614. Signature and Verification.

—The deposition must be signed by the "creditor;"[52] and must be verified.[53]

It must be signed and sworn to by the claimant in person; except that, for good cause, an agent may make the oath. In the event the agent makes the oath, the affidavit must state the reason why the claimant in person did not make it, and must also show the agent has actual knowledge of the facts.[54] What are sufficient reasons for an agent's making the proof instead of the creditor himself, are varied, as, for instance, that the creditor is sick or is traveling and could not have been reached in time after receipt of the notice for him to have prepared the claim for the first meeting of creditors, and so forth. It is hardly sufficient reason that the creditor himself was merely "absent" from the city, or county, or state, so long as it does not appear that he could not have been reached by proper diligence notwithstanding.

In re Reboulin Fils. & Co., 19 A. B. R. 215 (Ref. N. J.): "When General Order XXI provided that a proof of claim made by an agent should state the reason the deposition was not made by the claimant in person, it would seem as if the provision was for some purpose, and that the reason must be a good, and valid, and sufficient reason and 'such a reason as would satisfy the officer taking the proof that it was proper to dispense with the oath of the claimant in person' or with the oath of the treasurer, etc. The reason given by the attorney for making proof of claim in question does not seem to me to be such a reason. The attorney in fact does not appear to have legal knowledge of the facts set out in the proof of claim; in a court or before the referee he would not be a competent witness to prove sufficient to establish the claim; indeed I do not see how he would be able to testify that any money was advanced on the claim in question at all. The power of attorney attached to the proof of claim was executed in France, December first, 1905. There appears to be no reason why the treasurer, or proper officer, should not have verified the proof of claim in

---

50. Bankr. Act, § 57 (i): "* * * and if he discharge such undertaking in whole or in part he shall be subrogated to that extent to the rights of the creditor."

In re Mason, 2 A. B. R. 60 (Ref. R. I.); In re Carter, 15 A. B. R. 126, 138 Fed. 846 (D. C. Ark.); Livingston v. Heineman, 10 A. B. R. 42, 120 Fed. 786 (C. C. A. Ohio); inferentially, to same effect, In re Heyman, 2 A. B. R. 651, 95 Fed. 800 (D. C. N. Y.); In re Lange Co., 22 A. B. R. 414, 170 Fed. 114 (D. C. Iowa).

51. In re Heyman, 2 A. B. R. 651, 95 Fed. 800 (D. C. N. Y.).

52. Bankr. Act, § 57 (a). Who are and who are not "creditors" and what claims are "provable," will be later considered. See ch. XXI.

53. Bankr. Act, § 57 (a); Orr v. Park, 25 A. B. R. 544, 183 Fed. 683 (C. C. A. Ga.).

54. Obiter, In re Stradley & Co., 26 A. B. R. 149, 187 Fed. 285 (D. C. Ala.); compare, In re Medina Quarry Co., 24 A. B. R. 769, 182 Fed. 508 (D. C. N. Y.).

this matter, even though he was in France, and it could have been done as well as to execute the power of attorney in France."

Defective verification may be cured by amendment.[55]

If the creditor is a partnership, the proof of claim must show that the affidavit is made by one of the members of the partnership.[56]

If the creditor is a corporation, the proof must be sworn to by the treasurer. In case there be no treasurer, then it is to be made by the officer whose duties most nearly correspond to those of treasurer; as, for instance, the cashier of a national bank.[57]

The signature and oath must be those of a natural person. One of the most common mistakes is to sign the corporate name to the affidavit, as, for instance, "The ————————— Co., by John Doe, Treasurer." This, obviously, is improper, because it purports to be the oath of a corporation, and yet a corporation cannot be sworn, nor can it be put in jail for perjury. It has no "soul" and an oath does not bind it. Therefore, the oath and signature must be those of an individual; who, of course may, and should, describe, in the body of the affidavit, his relation to the corporation which owns the claim.

The verification may be made by oath, or in case of conscientious scruples, by affirmation; and may be made before a referee in bankruptcy, any officer authorized to administer oaths in proceedings before the courts of the United States, or under the laws of the State where the same are to be taken; or before any diplomatic or consular officer of the United States in any foreign country.[58]

The same rules, so far as concerns the proper officer before whom acknowledgments may be taken and as to oaths to capacity, apply to acknowledgments of powers of attorney.[59]

The verification may be made before the attorney of the claimant.[60]

A notary public's official character, even in another State than the one wherein the bankruptcy proceedings are pending, needs no certification of its authenticity in the first instance, other than the signature and seal that purport to be his.[61]

§ 615. Several Claims by Same Creditor.—Different claims of the same creditor need not be included in one proof.[62]

55. In re Stevens, 5 A. B. R. 806, 107 Fed. 243 (D. C. Vt.); In re Medina Quarry Co., 24 A. B. R. 769, 182 Fed. 508 (D. C. N. Y.).

56. Gen. Order No. XXI.

57. Gen. Order No. XXI.

58. Bankr. Act, § 20.

59. In re Sugenheimer, 1 A. B. R. 425, 91 Fed. 744 (D. C. N. Y.).

60. In re Kimball, 4 A. B. R. 144, 100 Fed. 177 (D. C. Mass.).

61. In re Pancoast, 12 A. B. R. 275, 129 Fed. 643 (D. C. Penn.).

62. In re Goldstein, 29 A. B. R. 301, 199 Fed. 665 (D. C. Mass.).
Claims against Several Bankrupts on Same Instrument.—May be presented against each estate and receive dividends thereon from each, not to exceed total amount due. B'd of Comm'rs Kan. v. Hurley, 22 A. B. R. 209, 169 Fed. 92 (C. C. A. Kans.). Also, see post, § 1519.

In re Ball, 10 A. B. R. 564, 123 Fed. 164 (D. C. Vt.): "She had previously proved an unsecured claim, and that is insisted to be a waiver of all not there included. But the law does not seem to require that all claims should be brought into one. No good reason .appears for holding ·that one should be barred by not being combined with the others, and there may be good reasons why secured and unsecured claims should not be put together."

But it is usual, and the better practice, to include all in one proof.

§ 616. Single Claim Not to Be Split.—And a single claim may not be split, else allowance or disallowance of one part will be res adjudicata as to all.

In re Drumgoole, 15 A. B. R. 261 (D. C. Pa.): "But, assuming the correctness of the claimant's position, and conceding that the contract was not as Mr. Etting has found it, I think the claimant cannot now succeed because he has split his cause of action, and therefore is forbidden to recover more than he claimed before Mr. Hunter. He could have had all the whiskey reguaged at that time, and presented his full claim for damages. Instead of doing this, he chose to confine himself to the loss on two of the barrels only, and on familiar principles he cannot sue again for the loss on the others."

§ 617. Proofs of Claim Amendable.—Proofs of claim may be amended.[63]

In re Stevens, 5 A. B. R. 806, 107 Fed. 243 (D. C. Vt.): "Amendments are allowed for the correction of misstatements and minor inaccuracies, including verification."

In re Myers & Charni, 3 A. B. R. 760, 99 Fed. 601 (D. C. Ind.): "This is a motion in behalf of James McCormick, one of the creditors of the bankrupt, to amend his proof of claim heretofore filed, by adding thereto a statement of a security in the nature of a claim to an equitable lien upon certain real estate under a notice of lis pendens in a suit pending against the bankrupt and his wife prior to the adjudication in bankruptcy, no mention of which was made in the proof of claim filed. The reason assigned for asking leave to amend is, in order that the complainant in that suit may not be embarrassed in its prosecution by the contention that the complainant had waived his lien by the filing of his claim in bankruptcy as a wholly unsecured claim. * * *

"There is no doubt of the power of the court to allow the amendment asked for; but in the administration of the bankruptcy law, its fundamental principle of equal distribution among creditors seems to me to forbid the exercise of this discretionary power in the interest of one creditor to the prejudice of others, where there is no perfected lien or established security in the creditor's favor,

---

63. Hutchinson v. Otis, 10 A. B. R. 135, 190 U. S. 552; In re Creasinger, 17 A. B. R. 540 (Ref. Calif., affirmed by D. C.); In re Roeber, 11 A. B. R. 464 (C. C. A. N. Y.); inferentially, McCallum & McCallum, 11 A. B. R. 448, 127 Fed. 768 (D. C. Pa.); inferentially, In re Pettingill, 14 A. B. R. 763, 137 ·Fed. 840 (Ref. Mass.); inferentially, In re Thompson's Sons, 10 A. B. R. 581, 123 Fed. 174 (D. C. Pa.); inferentially, In re Scott, 1 A. B. R. 553 (D. C. Tex.); impliedly, In re Robinson, 14 A. B. R. 626, 136 Fed. 994 (D. C. Mass.); In re Faulkner, 20 A. B. R. 542, 161 Fed. 900 (C. C. A. Kans.), quoted at § 734; In re Schiebler, 21 A. B. R. 309, 163 Fed. 545. (D. C. N. Y.); In re Horne & Co., 23 A. B. R. 590 (Ref. Miss.); obiter, In re Stradley & Co., 26 A. B. R. 149, 187 Fed. 285 (D. C. Ala.); Maxwell v. McDaniels, 27 A. B. R. 692, 184 Fed. 311 (C. C. A. W. Va.).

but only a contingent and inchoate lien, in the effort to secure a preference by litigation. (See In re Lesser, 3 Am. B. R. 758, 99 Fed. 913.) The equities of the general creditors through the trustee should be preferred.

"If the omission of the creditor to disclose the existence of his suit and the lien claimed thereby, would have the effect of disabling him from obtaining a judgment for his own benefit alone, the court should not aid the creditor in securing a preference by granting the present application."

In re Morris, 18 A. B. R. 828, 159 Fed. 591 (D. C. Pa.): "The proofs of debt objected to were clearly defective, most of them being simply stated to be for 'services'; 'mdse., etc.,' 'balance of wages,' 'balance of personal services,' 'for goods sold and delivered' and the like; none of which meets the law. * * * They were of course capable of correction in this respect, and the referee cannot be said to have gone out of the way to allow it."

And they may be amended where mistake has been made, either of fact or law, so long as there is no fraud, and when all the parties can be placed in the same situation that they would have been in had the error not occurred.[64]

§ 618. Amendment to Be Based on an Original Proof Filed.—An amendment must be based upon an original claim filed. And the power of permitting amendment must not be perverted to let in dilatory creditors who have failed to file any proof of claim within the statutory year limited for filing claims.[65]

It has been held, however, that an amendment may be allowed even though no formal proof of claim has been presented; as, for instance, where the existence of the claim is shown by the record;[66] but "hard cases make bad law" and the ruling that no claim need be filed by the creditor in order to support amendment, if the record shows its existence otherwise, followed to its logical conclusion would lead to unbearable laxity in the filing of claims; and it cannot be denied that Congress meant to require creditors to file definite claims and that, promptly, so that estates could be speedily wound up.

But, at any rate, the original proof need not be formal in order to support an amendment.[67] Thus, an agreement to accept a settlement, signed by the creditor and setting forth the amount and nature of his claim, will be sufficient to support an amendment.[68] Again, a mere letter mentioning the claim, received by the receiver and acknowledged by him to the creditor, has been held a sufficient basis.[69]

And it is sufficient filing to have filed it with the trustee.[70]

64. In re Myers & Charni, 3 A. B. R. 760, 99 Fed. 601 (D. C. Ind.).

65. See post, subject, "Year's Limitation for Filing Claims, Amendment of Claims after Expiration of Year," ch. XXII, § 734, et seq.

66. In re Salvator Brew. Co., 28 A. B. R. 56, 193 Fed. 989 (C. C. A. N. Y.).

67. See §§ 595½, 735; In re Kessler & Co., 25 A. B. R. 512, 186 Fed. 127 (C. C. A. N. Y., reversing 23 A. B. R. 901, 176 Fed. 647).

68. In re Fairlamb Co., 28 A. B. R. 515, 199 Fed. 278 (D. C. Pa.).

69. In re Kessler, 25 A. B. R. 512, 186 Fed. 127 (C. C. A. N. Y., reversing In re Kessler, 23 A. B. R. 901, 176 Fed. 647).

70. See post, § 729. The original claim need not be formal. In re Kessler, 25 A. B. R. 512, 186 Fed. 127 (C. C. A. N. Y.), reversing In re Kessler, 23 A. B. R. 901, 176 Fed. 647.

§ 619. **Amendment Changing Legal Nature of Cause of Action.**—
The amendment may allege the facts to make a different case, but the facts
must be substantially the same.[71]

§ 620. **Conditions May Be Imposed.**—The court may impose conditions upon granting leave to amend.[72]

§ 621. **Amendment May Be Refused.**—The court may refuse to permit amendment;[73] as, for instance, where the amendment proposed would
change the claim into one not provable.

Impliedly, In re Robinson, 14 A. B. R. 626, 136 Fed. 994 (D. C. Mass.): "A
creditor sought to prove a note made in New York at a usurious rate of interest. On due objection the claim was disallowed, and the creditor has moved
to amend his original proof by substituting therefor a claim 'for money fraudulently obtained by said bankrupt and received to the deponent's use.' The frauds
alleged were representations of fact concerning the bankrupt's business, his assets, and his intended application of the money borrowed. The referee refused
to permit the amendment, on the ground that the claim as amended would not
be provable. If provable as amended, it should be allowed. The law of New
York so taints with illegality a usurious contract that money borrowed thereby
cannot be recovered as money had and received. * * * The creditor cannot
recover upon the usurious contract itself, nor yet upon the common counts, since
any implied contract to pay money advanced is merged in the express usurious
contract actually made. If, however, the creditor can establish a provable claim
apart from the usurious contract, and unaffected by it, he will prevail. * * *
If a creditor can prove for money had and received without regard to a non-
usurious note, he can here prove without regard to the usurious note."

Also, for instance, where the amendment would prejudice general creditors.[74]

§ 622. **Amendment Permissible after Expiration of Year for
"Proving" Claims.**—Proofs of claim may be amended after the expiration
of the year limited by statute for filing (proving) claims.[75]

---

71. Inferentially, In re ₁Robinson,
14 A. B. R. 626, 136 Fed. 994 (D. C.
Mass.).

72. Note to In re Friedman, 1 A. B.
R. 510.

73. In re Wilder, to be found in
note to 3 A. B. R. 761 (D. C. Ind.).

74. In re Wilder, 3 A. B. R. 761 (D.
C. Ind.). This decision seems to be
treading on doubtful ground. If the
failure to allege the security, originally, was purposeful or operated to
mislead creditors to their hurt the
claimant may be estopped, of course.
Otherwise, leave to amend should not
be refused.

75. Hutchinson v. Otis, 10 A. B. R.
135, 190 U. S. 550; In re Faulkner, 20
A. B. R. 542, 161 Fed. 900 (C. C. A.

Kans.), quoted at § 734. See, also, In
re Horne & Co., 23 A. B. R. 590 (Ref.
Miss.); contra, In re Moebins, 8 A. B.
R. 590, 116 Fed. 47 (D. C. Pa.).

But for further discussion of the
subject of amendment of proofs of
claim after expiration of the statutory
year for proving claims, see post, ch.
XXII, § 734, et seq.

Although the effect of such amendment may be that formal proof of
claim is thereby made after the one-
year limitation period. In re Kessler, ·25 A. B. R. 512, 186 Fed. 127
(C. C. A. N. Y., reversing 23 A. B. R.
901, 176 Fed. 647), quoted post, § 735;
instance, In re Fairlamb Co., 28 A. B.
R. 515, 199 Fed. 278 (D. C. Pa.); In re
Standard, etc., Co., 26 A. B. R. 601,
186 Fed. 586 (D. C. Wis.).

§ 623. Withdrawal of Proofs of Claim.—Proofs of claim may be withdrawn.[76]

In re Strickland, 21 A. B. R. 734, 167 Fed. 867 (D. C. Ga.): "The only question before the court is the propriety of the referee's order allowing a creditor to withdraw his debt and intervention before the final determination of the cause. Now, the right to dismiss legal proceedings has long inured to parties in all jurisdictions, State and National. * * * The only limitation upon that right is that the party dismissing shall pay all costs, and that the dismissal shall not violate any substantial right, nor render it unavailable. That is the law in Georgia and obtains almost universally. * * * Can the withdrawal of a proof of debt be said to violate any substantial right of the bankrupt, or place him in a position more prejudicial than that which he occupies before the proof was filed? An examination of the precedents shows that all the recent cases sanction a withdrawal or amendment, under ordinary circumstances, of proceedings in bankruptcy."

Thus, they may be withdrawn as unsecured and new proofs be made as secured.[77] Or they may be withdrawn and a petition for reclamation or a petition for the tracing of trust funds be substituted.[78]

The right of withdrawal is an absolute right of the claimant and is not subject to the discretion of the court.

In re Stewart, 24 A. B. R. 474, 178 Fed. 463 (D. C. N. Y.): "I do not think it within the power of the court, or referee, to prevent such withdrawal or abandonment of the claim presented. The withdrawal is a matter of right in the creditor and not a matter of discretion with the referee or judge." Quoted further at § 639.

But though "withdrawn," yet the deposition for proof of debt itself should remain in the files.

The filing of a proof of claim is not necessarily an "election of remedies,"[79] as where made in ignorance of facts.[80]

It has been held that a claim may be withdrawn from an individual estate and filed against firm assets, after the expiration of the year for filing the claim.[82]

§ 624. Attorney at Law Competent to Withdraw without Written Power.—An attorney at law duly admitted to practice in the United States District Court need not present written power of attorney for the purpose of withdrawing a client's claim.[83]

---

76. In re Friedman, 1 A. B. R. 510 (Ref. N. Y.); In re Stewart, 24 A. B. R. 474, 178 Fed. 463 (D. C. N. Y.), quoted at § 739; In re Loden, 25 A. B. R. 917, 184 Fed. 965 (D. C. Ga.).

77. See post, "Secured Claims," ch. XXIV, div. 1, § 765.

78. In re Stewart, 24 A. B. R. 474, 178 Fed. 463 (D. C. N. Y.), quoted at § 639.

79. In re Stewart, 24 A. B. R. 474, 178 Fed. 463 (D. C. N. Y.), quoted at § 639; In re Strickland, 21 A. B. R. 734, 167 Fed. 867 (D. C. Ga.).

80. In re Stewart, 24 A. B. R. 474, 178 Fed. 463 (D. C. N. Y.), quoted at § 639.

82. In re Horne & Co., 23 A. B. R. 590 (Ref. Miss.). But compare, post, § 737.

83. In re Pauley, 2 A. B. R. 333 (Ref. N. Y.).

CHAPTER XXI.

PROVABLE DEBTS.

Synopsis of Chapter.

§ 625. Only Such Are "Provable" Debts as Statute Declares.—

Only such claims are provable debts as the statute declares to be such. Thus, as to costs.

In re Marcus, 5 A. B. R. 19, 104 Fed. 331 (D. C. Mass., affirmed in 5 A. B. R. 365): "To be provable, they must be included within the definition of § 63."

In general, only contract claims, judgments, taxes and court costs are capable of being proved in bankruptcy and of being allowed to participate in dividends.[1]

The reason of this is plain—bankruptcy is concerned with business obligations. It is the law concerned with traders and merchants chiefly.

Brown & Adams *v.* Button Co., 17 A. B. R. 566 (C. C. A. Del.): "Bankruptcy is supposedly concerned only with commercial matters and was early confined to traders. And while it has been gradually extended and enlarged, the original idea has not been altogether departed from. Its purpose is to free a person from his debts, or to subject him to proceedings on account of them. This may not be controlling but it is suggestive; and a construction which goes outside of it has certainly to be justified."

Moreover, other kinds of claims are too indefinite, such as damages for torts, etc., etc., until they are reduced to judgment.

DIVISION 1.

MEANING OF "DEBT" AND "PROVABILITY."

§ 626. "Debt."—By "debt" is meant any debt, demand or claim provable in bankruptcy.[2]

§ 627. Includes Demands and Claims Not Technically "Debts."—It includes not only "debts," as the term technically is used, but also demands or claims.[3]

In re Gerson, 6 A. B. R. 12, 107 Fed. 897 (C. C. A. Penna.): "The indorser's engagement is to pay a sum certain at a fixed date, to-wit, the amount of the bill

---

1. Bankr. Act, § 63 (a): "Debts of the bankrupt may be proved and allowed against his estate which are,

"1st. A fixed liability, as evidenced by a judgment or an instrument in writing, absolutely owing at the time of the filing of the petition against him (or by him) whether then payable or not, with any interest thereon which would have been recoverable at that date or with a rebate of interest upon such as were not then payable and did not bear interest.

"2d. Due as costs taxable against an involuntary bankrupt who was at the time of the filing of the petition against him plaintiff in a cause of action which would pass to the trustee and which the trustee declines to prosecute after notice.

"3d. Founded upon a claim for taxable costs incurred in good faith by a creditor before the filing of the petition in an action to recover a provable debt.

"4th. Founded upon an open account or upon a contract express or implied.

"5th. Founded upon provable debts reduced to judgments after the filing of the petition and before the consideration of the bankrupt's application for a discharge, less costs incurred and interest accrued after the filing of the petition and up to the time of the entry of such judgments."

2. Bankr. Act, § 1 (11). In re Harper, 23 A. B. R. 918, 175 Fed. 412 (D. C. N. Y.); In re Chandler, 25 A. B. R. 865, 185 Fed. 1006 (C. C. A. Ills.); Germania Savings & Trust Co. *v.* Loeb, 26 A. B. R. 238, 188 Fed. 285 (C. C. A. Tenn.); In re Wyoming Valley Assoc., 28 A. B. R. 462, 198 Fed. 437 (D. C. Pa.).

That a loan reached the bankrupt's treasury through several hands does not render it any the less provable or allowable. In re American, etc., Co., 27 A. B. R. 463, 178 Fed. 106 (C. C. A. N. Y.).

3. Bankr. Act, § 1 (11). Compare, to this effect, Clarke *v.* Rogers, 26 A. B. R. 413, 183 Fed. 518 (C. C. A. Mass.), quoted post at § 1308.

or note at its maturity, if it is not paid upon due presentment by the party primarily liable, upon due notice of its dishonor being given to the indorser. If it can be affirmed that such an unmatured liability is not a 'debt,' in a technical sense, certainly it is a 'demand' or 'claim,' and comes it seems to us, within the scope of the fourth subdivision of § 63 of the act. The primary purpose of the Bankrupt Act was to relieve insolvent debtors from their pecuniary liabilities, and to secure ratable distribution of their estates among their creditors."

In re Mahler, 5 A. B. R. 457, 105 Fed. 428 (D. C. Mich.): "The general intent of Congress in the enactment of the statute was to make every debt and demand existing against the bankrupt at the time of his adjudication which was recoverable, either at law or in equity, provable in bankruptcy."

Likewise, by "debt" is not meant the certain, liquidated sum which the technical term implies.[4] And by "debt" is not meant merely obligations that could be reduced to judgments in personam. Obligations enforceable only in equity against particular property, as contracts of a married woman enforceable only against her separate estate, are "debts" within the meaning of the Bankruptcy Act;[5] likewise, obligations arising not by direct contract but by implication of law, as subrogation in favor of a wife, in States where the wife and husband may not contract directly with each other.[6] Also, even where not enforceable at all, either in law or in equity, claims and demands have been held "provable" in bankruptcy; as a wife's claim for money loaned to her husband, in Massachusetts.[7]

And the fact that a debt is payable in merchandise, after a certain time, on the creditor's demand, does not render it any the less a provable debt.[8]

Thus, "debt" has been held to include damages for false representation, inducing the entering into a contract of sale, whereby loss has occurred.[9]

But it has been held, that, where by state statute, attachment costs are a priority claim against the debtor's property but not against him personally, they lack an essential element of a provable debt in bankruptcy.

In re The Copper King, 16 A. B. R. 150 (D. C. Calif.): "This definition leaves open the question as to the meaning of the word 'debts' in the particular clause under consideration; and, in my opinion, it is there used in its technical sense, and refers only to such debts as are based upon contract, express or implied, or to personal obligations for the payment of money imposed upon the bankrupt by statute. The insolvency law of California does not make the insolvent upon the contingency therein named, personally liable for the costs in-

4. MacDonald v. Tefft-Weller Co., 11 A. B. R. 800, 128 Fed. 381 (C. C. A. Fla.); inferentially, In re Talbott, 7 A. B. R. 29, 110 Fed. 924 (D. C. Mass.).

5. MacDonald v. Tefft-Weller Co., 11 A. B. R. 800, 128 Fed. 381 (C. C. A. Fla.); compare, In re Talbott, 7 A. B. R. 29, 110 Fed. 924 (D. C. Mass.); compare, In re Gerson, 6 A. B. R. 12, 107 Fed. 897 (C. C. A. Penna.); In re Mahler, 5 A. B. R. 45, 105 Fed. 428 (D. C. Mich.).

6. In re Nickerson, 8 A. B. R. 707 (D. C. Mass.).

7. James v. Gray, 12 A. B. R. 573 (C. C. A. Mass., declining to follow In re Talbott, 7 A. B. R. 29, 110 Fed. 924 (D. C. Mass.).

8. In re Spot Cash Hooper Co., 23 A. B. R. 546, 188 Fed. 861 (D. C. Tex.).

9. In re Harper, 23 A. B. R. 918, 175 Fed. 412 (D. C. N. Y.).

curred by his creditor, in an action in which a writ of attachment has been issued. The liability is not personal, but is against his estate. The liability for such costs, therefore, even if considered as a debt, is not a debt 'owing' by the bankrupt."

§ 628. What Is "Provable" Debt.

—A provable debt means an obligation susceptible of being presented in such form as to come within some one or more of the classes of debts designated in § 63 (a) as "provable" debts, whether actually so presented or not.

Crawford v. Burke, 12 A. B. R. 666, 195 U. S. 176: "Under this section, whether the discharge of the defendants in bankruptcy shall operate as a discharge of plaintiff's debt, it not having been reduced to judgment, depends upon the fact whether that debt was 'provable' under the bankruptcy act, that is, susceptible of being proved.

"We are clear that the debt of the plaintiff * * * might have been proved under § 63 (a) had plaintiff chosen to waive the tort and take his place with the other creditors of the estate."

Thus, claims may be "provable" although not permitted to be "proved" because of the expiration of the year's time limited for "proving" claims.[10]

§ 629. Whether "Provable" or Not Depends on Status at Date of Filing Bankruptcy Petition.

—The question whether or not a debt is provable turns upon its status at the time of the filing of the petition.[11]

In re Neff, 19 A. B. R. 23, 157 Fed. 57 (C. C. A. Ohio, affirming 19 A. B. R. 911): "The status of a claim must depend upon its provability at the time the

---

10. Norfolk & W. R'y Co. v. Graham, 16 A. B. R. 616 (C. C. A. W. Va.); Morgan v. Wordell, 6 A. B. R. 167, 178 Mass. 350.

11. Williams & Co. v. U. S. Fidelity Co., 28 A. B. R. 802 (Ct. App. Ga.); impliedly, In re Lough & Burrows, 25 A. B. R. 597, 182 Fed. 961 (C. C. A. N. Y.); Slocum v. Soliday, 25 A. B. R. 460, 183 Fed. 410 (C. C. A. Mass.), quoted post at § 658; In re Roth & Appel, 24 A. B. R. 588, 181 Fed. 667 (C. C. A. N. Y.), quoted at § 654; Germania Saving & Trust Co. v. Loeb, 26 A. B. R. 238, 188 Fed. 285 (C. C. A. Tenn); In re Bingham, 2 A. B. R. 223, 94 Fed. 796 (D. C. Vt.); Swarts v. Fourth Nat'l Bk., 8 A. B. R. 673, 117 Fed. 1 (C. C. A. Mo.); Swarts v. Siegel, 8 A. B. R. 689, 117 Fed. 13 (C. C. A. Mo.); Bray v. Cobb, 3 A. B. R. 790, 100 Fed. 270 (D. C. N. Car., reversed, on other grounds, in Cobb v. Overman, 6 A. B. R. 324, 109 Fed. 65); In re Graff, 8 A. B. R. 745, 117 Fed. 343 (D. C. N. Y.); Steinhardt v. Nat'l Bk., 18 A. B. R. 87, 52 Misc. (N. Y.) 465; Steinhardt v. Nat'l Bk., 18 A. B. R. 87, 52 Misc. (N. Y.) 465, reversed, on other grounds, Steinhardt v. National Bank, 19 A. B. R. 72, 120 A. D. 255; In re Reading Hos-

iery Co., 22 A. B. R. 562, 171 Fed. 195 (D. C. Pa.); In re Garlington, 8 A. B. R. 602, 115 Fed. 999 (D. C. Tex.); obiter, Ruhl-Koblegard Co. v. Gillespie, 22 A. B. R. 643, 61 W. Va. 554. See post, "Contingent Claims," § 640, et seq. See post, "Claims Not Owing at Time of Filing of Petition," § 668, et seq.

However, a surety on a redelivery bond given to secure release of the bankrupt's property from an attachment or other lien which itself would be dissolved by the adjudication, has been held not to have a provable debt, though, at the time of the filing of petition, the lien would not yet have been dissolved. Compare § 648½; In re Windt, 24 A. B. R. 536, 177 Fed. 584 (D. C. Conn.), quoted at § 648½.

Premiums on Fire Insurance Policy.—Premiums on a fire insurance policy which has not been assumed by the trustee and has become void for change of title are only allowable against the estate for the premium due at the time of the filing of the bankruptcy petition. In re Hibbler Mach. Sup. Co., 27 A. B. R. 612, 192 Fed. 741 (D. C. N. Y.).

bankrupt petition was filed. At that time it must come within the definition of § 63 of the Bankruptcy Act; it cannot be benefited by its status at a later date." Quoted further at § 674.

Board of Commissioners *v.* Hurley, 22 A. B. R. 209, 169 Fed. 92 (C. C. A. Kans.): "Indeed, the condition at the time of the filing of the petition measures the extent of the estate and the rights of all creditors of the bankrupt and all parties interested in the property, throughout all the provisions of the law." Quoted further at §§ 1519, 1521.

In re Pettingill & Co., 14 A. B. R. 728, 137 Fed. 840 (D. C. Mass.): "The provability of a claim under the Bankrupt Act of 1898 depends upon its status at the time the petition in bankruptcy is filed: if then 'provable' within the definition of § 63, it may be proved; otherwise not."

In re Swift, 7 A. B. R. 374, 112 Fed. 315 (C. C. A. Mass.): "The trustee maintains that the form of proof prescribed by the Supreme Court requires that it should state that the debt proved existed 'at and before the filing' of the petition for adjudication of bankruptcy; but in view of the statute, this must be construed, as is commonly done, to give such effect to the word 'and' that it may read either 'or' or 'and,' as circumstances may require. That part of the present Bankruptcy Act which describes what debts may be proved does not repeat at all points the words 'owing at the time of the filing of the petition,' but it is impossible to consider it other than as though it did thus repeat them. There can be no question that it is sufficient if the debt existed at the point of time of the filing of the petition in bankruptcy.

Slocum *v.* Soliday, 25 A. B. R. 460, 183 Fed. 410 (C. C. A. Mass.): "In order that the claim may be proved it must have existed at or before the filing of the petition in bankruptcy which the adjudication follows."

§ 630. "Provability" and "Validity" Different Terms.

—The provability of a claim is not dependent upon its validity. Provability and validity are different terms. The claim may be wholly false and improper in fact and yet it will be a provable claim if on its face it comes within any of the classes mentioned.[12]

Hargardine-McKittrick Dry Goods Co. *v.* Hudson, 10 A. B. R. 225, 122 Fed. 232 (C. C. A. Mo.): "The plaintiff's judgment was a provable debt, and the fact that a recovery upon it might be defeated by the plea of payment or a plea of the Statute of Limitations or any other plea in bar, did not take it out of the class of provable debts. The term 'provable debts' does not mean only such debts as are valid and against the allowance of which no defense can be successfully interposed."

§ 631. Whether a "Debt," "Claim" or "Demand," Dependent on State Law.

—Nevertheless, whether it be a "debt," "claim" or "demand" is determined by state law;[13] and a claim, which in its nature is such that,

---

12. See note to Morgan *v.* Wordell, 6 A. B. R. 167, 59 N. E. 1037 (Mass. Sup. Jud. Ct.); obiter, In re Grant Shoe Co., 12 A. B. R. 349, 130 Fed. 881 (C. C. A. N. Y.). Also, see In re Dillon, 4 A. B. R. 63, 100 Fed. 627 (D. C. Mass.); (1867) In re Kingsley, Fed. Cas. 7,819, 1 N. B. Reg. 329.

For cases where this distinction seems to have been lost sight of, see

In re Burlington Malting Co., 6 A. B. R. 369, 109 Fed. 777 (D. C. Wis.); In re Farmer, 9 A. B. R. 19, 116 Fed. 763 (D. C. N. Car.), wherein a judgment barred by the statute of limitations was held not "provable."

13. In re Brown, 21 A. B. R. 123, 164 Fed. 673 (C. C. A. Calif.); In re Talbot, 7 A. B. R. 29, 110 Fed. 924 (D. C. Mass.).

by the law of the state, it is not enforceable, is not provable, although elsewhere it might be enforceable; thus, as to wife's claims in Massachusetts and elsewhere.[14]

Thus, as to alleged claims against a corporation which, under the local law, is prohibited from incurring debts.[15] So, as to the right of a creditor to prove a balance due after crediting an allowance made to him, as a priority claimant, under the local law.[16]

So, a claim recoverable under the law of the state may be allowed in bankruptcy, notwithstanding an objection thereto on principles of general law. Thus, under a Massachusetts statute a customer may recover margins paid to a bucket shop proprietor; and, therefore, a claim therefor will be allowed in bankruptcy.[17]

But it has been held that the bankruptcy courts are not bound by local law as to stipulations for attorney's collection fees in notes and mortgages.[18]

§ 632. "Provability" and "Allowability" Different Terms.—"Provability' and "allowability," likewise, are different terms. Likewise different are the "proof" and "allowance" of claims.[19]

Steinhardt v. National Bank, 19 A. B. R. 72, 120 App. Div. N. Y. 255: "Proof of the claim is one thing, and its allowance is quite another."

"Provability" refers to the nature of the obligation, whether a contract obligation, etc., while "allowability" refers to its right to share in dividends. "Allowability" implies not only "provability," but also "validity."[20] If for any reason the claim is improper—if it be too large, if it be fraudulent, if it has been paid, if it be founded upon illegal consideration or if there be no consideration at all for it or if it be barred by the statute of limitations or incapable of proof because of the statute of frauds, or if for any other of the thousand and one defenses that may be made to claims the claim be improper—it is not "allowable," that is to say, will not be allowed to participate in the estate, yet all the time it may be a "provable" claim notwithstanding, as the term is used, for its provability is to be determined by its face and form and is not affected by what it may be proved to be in substance.

Allowability perhaps implies even more than provability and validity. A claim may be a claim on contract and a valid one at that and yet not be "allowable" because "secured" to its full amount. Allowability refers to

---

14. In re Talbott, 7 A. B. R. 29, 110 Fed. 924 (D. C. Mass.).

15. In re Wyoming Valley Assoc., 28 A. B. R. 462, 198 Fed. 436 (D. C. Pa.).

16. In re Floyd & Bohr Co., 29 A. B. R. 149, 200 Fed. 1016 (D. C. Ky.).

17. Streeter v. Lowe, 25 A. B. R. 774, 184 Fed. 263 (C. C. A. Mass.).

18. Mechanics' Amer. Nat. Bank v. Coleman, 29 A. B. R. 386, 204 Fed. 24 (C. C. A. Mo.), quoted post at § 671.

19. See ante, § 595. Also see In re Two Rivers, etc., Co., 29 A. B. R. 518, 199 Fed. 877 (C. C. A. Wis.), quoted ante at § 595; In re Mertens & Co., 16 A. B. R. 829 (C. C. A. N. Y.).

20. Williams & Co. v. U. S. Fidelity Co., 28 A. B. R. 802 (Ct. App. Ga.).

the right to share in the general dividends; claims are "allowed,' to share in dividends.

Hence, for instance, "secured" claims may be provable although "allowable" only for the amounts found owing over and above the value of any securities held therefor.[21]

However, it would seem on principle that a priority claim should nevertheless be "allowable," it being simply granted priority in the distribution of the estate out of the assets not appropriated to particular creditors 'before the bankruptcy; yet § 57 (e) places priority claims and secured claims in the same class, and grants them "allowability" only to the extent of the deficit thereon.[22]

Likewise, preferred claims and claims upon which the creditor holds a lien, obtained on the insolvent's property by legal proceedings within four months, may be "provable" and be "proved," although not "allowable" nor "allowed" except upon surrender of the preference.[23]

In re Hornstein, 10 A. B. R. 308, 122 Fed. 266 (D. C. N. Y.): "The distinction between 'proved' and 'allowed' is always made apparent throughout the Bankruptcy Act, and the term 'provable claims,' in § 59 B, providing that three or more creditors who have provable claims against any person, etc., may file a petition to have him adjudged a bankrupt, is not to be given the same meaning as allowable claims."

"A creditor with an unsurrendered preference should always be allowed to 'prove' his claim and may be a petitioner in bankruptcy but the claim will be 'allowed' only upon condition that the preference is surrendered."

Stevens v. Nave-McCord Co., 17 A. B. R. 610, 150 Fed. 71 (C. C. A. Colo.): "A creditor who holds a voidable preference has a claim that is provable in the sense that formal written proof of it may be made and filed, but which he may not procure an allowance of, nor vote at a creditors' meeting nor obtain any advantage by, under the bankruptcy law, until he has surrendered his preference."

§ 633. "Provability" Not Dependent on "Dischargeability."—

Nor is provability dependent on dischargeability.[24] A claim may be a provable claim and be allowed to participate in dividends and yet not be affected by the bankrupt's discharge. This is illustrated by the instance of debts for property obtained by false representations or pretenses;[25] or property willfully and maliciously injured.[26]

---

21. Compare, impliedly, to this effect, Bankr. Act, § 57 (e). See Steinhardt v. National Bank, 19 A. B. R. 72, 120 App. Div. N. Y. 255.

22. In re Eagles & Crisp, 3 A. B. R. 735, 99 Fed. 695 (D. C. N. Car.); In re Columbia Iron Wks., 14 A. B. R. 527, 142 Fed. 234 (D. C. Mich.); obiter, In re Pettingill & Co., 14 A. B. R. 765 (Ref. Mass.).

23. Bankr. Act, § 57 (g). In re Richard. 2 A. B. R. 512, 94 Fed. 633 (D. C. N. Car.); In re Clover Creamery

Ass'n (Evans v. Claridge), 23 A. B. R. 884, 176 Fed. 907 (C. C. A. Wis.).

24. Though compare, In re Roth & Appel, .24 A. B. R. 588, 181 Fed. 667 (C. C. A. N. Y.): "With a few exceptions not applicable here that which is not dischargeable in bankruptcy is not provable in bankruptcy."

25. Instance, Katzenstein v. Reid, 16 A. B. R. 740 (Ct. App. Tex.).

26. Kavanaugh v. McIntyre, 21 A. B. R. 327, 128 App. Div. 722, 112 N. Y. Supp. 897.

§ 634. Nor on Right to Share in Dividends in Any Particular Order of Priority.

—Nor is provability dependent on the right to share in the dividends in any particular order of priority. Provability depends upon the nature of the liability—not upon whether there are any assets applicable thereto. Thus, a partnership debt is also a provable debt against the individual estate of a bankrupt member though entitled to share in dividends therefrom only after individual debts are satisfied.[27]

However, "allowability" may be thus dependent; for a priority claim— for example, a claim for the wages of a workman, clerk or servant, rendered within the prescribed time—is "provable," though "allowable" only for any deficit remaining after application of the priority.[28]

DIVISION 2.

CLAIMS EX DELICTO.

§ 635. Claims "Ex Delicto" for Money Not Provable unless in Judgment.

—Claims ex delicto, for money cannot be proved as such.[29] Thus, an unliquidated claim for damages for personal injury is not a provable claim, and is not susceptible of being made into a provable claim.[30]

In re Yates, 8 A. B. R. 70, 114 Fed. 365 (D. C. Calif.): "But a cause of action against him for unliquidated damages for a personal tort, such as is involved in the action of Risdon v. Yates, before referred to, is not within either of the classes named."

In re Ostrom, 26 A. B. R. 273, 185 Fed. 988 (D. C. Minn.): "It is admitted that the claim for personal injuries as it existed before the verdict was not provable or allowable, but it is said that, when the verdict was rendered, the liability became fixed and it then became provable and allowable. * * * Even if it can be said, in accordance with those decisions, [67 Minn. 420 and 104 Minn. 1] that a verdict created a fixed liability, yet it is not a fixed liability evidenced by a judgment or instrument in writing, conditions which must by the present act, be complied with before even a fixed liability can become a provable debt."

Nor is a claim for damages for mere destruction of property a provable debt.

Obiter, Clarke v. Rogers, 26 A. B. R. 413, 183 Fed. 518 (C. C. A. Mass.): "On the other hand, a mere tort, for example, a trespass involving a mere destruction of property, does not lay the foundation for a proceeding under this section."

---

27. See post, § 2230, et seq., subject of "Distribution in Partnership Cases."

28. Bankr. Act, § 56 (b) and §§ 57 (e), 57 (h). See ante, § 632.

29. In re Dorr, 21 A. B. R. 752 (Ref. Calif.).

30. Beers v. Hanlin, 3 A. B. R. 745, 99 Fed. 695 (D. C. Ore.); In re Brinckmann, 4 A. B. R. 551, 103 Fed. 65 (D. C. Ind.); In re Wigmore, 10 A. B. R. 661 (D. C. Calif.); In re Ostrom, 26 A. B. R. 273, 185 Fed. 988 (D. C. Minn.); [1867] Block v. McClelland, Fed. Cas. No. 1,462.

Thus, damages for wrongful death are not provable. In re New York Tunnel Co., 20 A. B. R. 25, 159 Fed. 688, and 21 A. B. R. 531, 166 Fed. 284 (C. C. A. N. Y.).

Even though the plaintiff was under contract of employment with the bankrupt.[31]

It is doubtful whether damages for the infringement of a patent are provable.[32]

And Bankruptcy Act, § 17 (a) (2), excepting from the operation of discharge "liabilities for obtaining property by false pretenses or false representations, or willful and malicious injuries to the person or property of another," does not enlarge the classes of provable debts so as to include injuries to the person, not yet reduced to judgment.

> In re New York Tunnel Co., 20 A. B. R. 25, 159 Fed. 688 (C. C. A. N. Y): "In 1903, § 17 was amended in various ways. One change was the substitution of the word 'liability' in place of the word 'judgments.' And the provision as it now stands affords some basis for the claim that the exception from the operation of the discharge of particular liabilities for tort implies that such liabilities in general are [not] discharged [and hence are provable debts]. But this implication does not carry far. The amendment was to an exception in the discharge statute which states what debts shall not be discharged rather than what shall be. A negative provision that liabilities for certain torts shall not be discharged, does not of itself, make all other tort liabilities provable debts. It is apparent that Congress by the amendment intended to preclude the possibility of claims for certain torts being discharged whether reduced to judgment or not. Having this object in view it used language not wholly in harmony with the other sections of the act. But we see nothing to indicate an intention to enlarge the classes of provable debts. Certainly no intention is evidenced to bring in claims for torts which were never provable under the earlier bankrupt acts."

But if the claim be reduced to judgment before the filing of the bankruptcy petition, it may be proved as a judgment,[33] though not if not reduced to judgment until after the filing of the petition.[34]

§ 636. But Provable Where Tort Waivable and Claim Presentable as in Contract.

—However, in cases where the tort may be waived and suit be brought in contract, the claim may be proved in bankruptcy; but may not be so proved where the tort cannot be waived and suit be brought in contract.[35]

---

31. In re Crescent Lumber Co., 19 A. B. R. 112, 154 Fed. 724 (D. C. Ala.).

32. Graphophone Co. v. Leeds & Catlin, 23 A. B. R. 337, 174 Fed. 158 (U. S. C. C.).

33. Burnham v. Pidcock, 5 A. B. R. 590, 68 N. Y. Supp. 1007 (affirming 5 A. B. R. 45).

34. Impliedly, In re Crescent Lumber Co.. 19 A. B. R. 112, 154 Fed. 724 (D. C. Ala.).

35. Brown & Adams v. Button Co., 17 A. B. R. 565, 149 Fed. 48 (C. C. A. Del., affirming In re United Button Co., 15 A. B. R. 391); Machel v. Rochester, 14 A. B. R. 431, 135 Fed. 904

(D. C. Mont.); In re Wigmore, 10 A. B. R. 661 (Ref. Calif.); In re Filer, 5 A. B. R. 834, 125 Fed. 261 (D. C. N. Y.); In re Brinckmann, 4 A. B. R. 551, 103 Fed. 65 (D. C. Ind.); (1867) Dusar v. Murgatroyd, Fed. Cas. 4,199; (1867) Duggett v. Emerson, Fed. Cas. 3,962; (1867) In re Hennocksburgh, Fed. Cas. 6,367; (1867) In re Schuchardt, Fed. Cas., No. 12,483; (1867) Black v. McClelland, Fed. Cas. 1,462; inferentially, obiter, In re Mertens, 16 A. B. R. 825, 147 Fed. 177 (C. C. A. N. Y.). In re Southern Steel Co., 25 A. B. R. 358, 183 Fed. 498 (D. C. Ala.), quoting entire text statement. Compare, inferentially, Maxwell v.

In re United Button Co., 15 A. B. R. 391, 140 Fed. 495 (D. C. Del., affirmed sub nom. Brown & Adams v. Button Co., 17 A. B. R. 566, 149 Fed. 48): "A claim for unliquidated damages resulting from injury to the property of another, not reduced to judgment and unaccompanied and unconnected with any contractual or quasi contractual liability is not susceptible of liquidation under § 63b of the Bankruptcy Act of 1898."

Crawford v. Burke, 12 A. B. R. 666, 195 U. S. 176: "We are clear that the debt of the plaintiff was embraced within the provision of paragraph a, as one 'founded upon an open account, or upon a contract, express or implied,' and might have been proved under § 63a had plaintiff chosen to waive the tort, and take his place with the other creditors of the estate."

In re Hirschman, 4 A. B. R. 715, 104 Fed. 69 (D. C. Utah): "Section 63, subsection 'a,' does not authorize the proof of any claim arising ex delicto, unless a recovery may be had quasi ex contractu."

Clarke v. Rogers, 26 A. B. R. 413, 183 Fed. 518 (C. C. A. Mass): "A claim based on a tort as known at common law is undoubtedly provable whenever it may be resolved into an implied contract. For example, it is a settled rule that where a tort feasor by conversion of personal property has sold the property converted, and received cash therefor, the true owner may sue him for money had and received as on an implied contract. This, of course, is a mere fiction of law; but, like all other such fictions, it is effectual when it will accomplish the ends of justice. So that, in that case, the owner of the property may proceed for a tort, or, at his option, on an implied contract which would entitle him to make proof under § 63."

Not every tort is of such a nature that it may be waived and suit be brought on an implied contract. Only those torts that have resulted in the enrichment of the wrongdoer[35a] are such, for the measure of the enrichment is the measure of the implied contract. Thus, one who has converted the property of another, or has obtained goods under false pretenses, has thereby enriched himself to the extent of the value of the goods so obtained, and their value will be the measure of the implied contract to pay for goods "had and received," in case the tort be waived.[36]

Martin, 22 A. B. R. 93 (N. Y. Sup. Ct. App. Div.):

Thus, as to conversion of stock pledged to bankrupt stockbroker. In re Dorr (Allen v. Forbes), 26 A. B. R. 408, 186 Fed. 277 (C. C. A. Mont.).

35a. Or of someone else in his stead.

36. Inferentially, In re Heinsfurter, 3 A. B. R. 113, 97 Fed. 198 (D. C. Iowa). See able and interesting discussion, to same general effect, in In re Wigmore, 10 A. B. R. 661 (Ref. Calif.). See discussion in In re Cushing, 6 A. B. R. 22 (Ref. N. Y.). Instance, conversion of car load of eggs, sold for cash, by getting the carrier to deliver them without payment of the draft attached to the bill of lading. Clingman v. Miller, 20 A. B. R. 360, 160 Fed. 326 (C. C. A. Kans.). Instance, conversion of proceeds of sale by agent on commission. In re

Hale, 20 A. B. R. 633, 161 Fed. 387 (D. C. Conn.).

Reynolds v. New York Trust Co., 26 A. B. R. 698, 188 Fed. 611 (C. C. A. Mass.).

Thus, to pay over money received, even though reserved upon an illegal gambling contract. In re Dorr (Allen v. Forbes), 26 A. B. R. 408, 186 Fed. 277 (C. C. A. Mont.).

Instance, conversion of proceeds of sale of goods held by bankrupt in trust for bank which had advanced the purchase price and taken trust receipts from bankrupts in exchange for bills of lading. In re Coe, 26 A. B. R. 352, 185 Fed. 522 (C. C. A. N. Y.).

Conversion of Goods Held in Trust by Partnership Giving Rise to Two Claims, Both Provable.—Where a partnership fails to turn over trust

In re United Button Co., 15 A. B. R. 396 (D. C. Del.): "On the facts as alleged no contract on the part of the bankrupt can be implied in fact, and no circumstances are disclosed giving rise to a contract implied in law or quasi contract. It does not appear that the tort feasor obtained or derived from the petitioners through the commission of the tort any property for the value or proceeds of which it could be held liable under any quasi contractual obligation. It is not like the case of a wrongful conversion of personal property, where there is an election of remedies. The alleged claim is for damages for a tort pure and simple. No election between a remedy ex delicto and one ex contractu was or is possible. Keener on Quasi Contracts, 159, 160. The doctrine of 'waiver of tort' can have no application."

But no enrichment could be predicated of the tort, assault and battery, or of the tort, personal injury. Therefore, the waiving of such torts does not entitle one to prove in bankruptcy his claim for the damages resulting from the assault and battery or the personal injury, for no such claim can be brought within any of the classes of provable debts.[37]

In accordance with the principles above stated a transfer to make good a defalcation committed in the capacity of an administrator, executor or other trustee may be a preference because the defalcation could be presented in form ex contractu and thus make of it a "debt."[38]

The bankruptcy court may resort to common law principles in determining whether the tort may be waived, and a suit on the contract brought, in any particular case; the local decisions not being binding in this respect.[39]

---

money the proceeds of sale held for the account of a bank which had advanced the moneys to pay the purchase price, two claims arise, one against the partnership on its acceptance of the drafts, the other against the partners individually as joint tort feasors, for the conversion, both provable at same time. In re Coe, 26 A. B. R. 352, 185 Fed. 522 (C. C. A. N. Y.).

37. In re United Button Co., 15 A. B. R. 391, 140 Fed. 495 (D. C. Del.); In re Wigmore, 10 A. B. R. 661 (Ref. Calif.); In re Filer, 5 A. B. R. 582, 125 Fed. 261 (Ref. N. Y.); compare, In re Hirschman, 4 A. B. R. 715, 104 Fed. 69 (D. C. Utah).

See interesting article upon "The Provability of Tort Claims in Bankruptcy," by Stanley Folz, Esq., in the American Law Register for August, 1904.

Compare, also, where tort appears to have been insisted on but referee allowed the claim evidently as a contract debt notwithstanding, In re Lazarovic, 1 A. B. R. 478 (Ref. Kas.), distinguished in 6 A. B. R. 23.

Compare, also, the following instances of waiving tort and proving

in contract; (1) fraudulent scheme for inducing persons to deposit money to be used in gambling, In re Arnold & Co., 13 A. B. R. 320, 133 Fed. 789 (D. C. Mo.); (2) child's funds held in trust by father but converted to his own use, he giving a note to himself therefor, as child's guardian, In re Upson, 10 A. B. R. 602, 123 Fed. 807 (D. C. N. Y.); (3) broker converting stock of customer (bought on margin but exceeding in value the customer's debt) by pledging the stock to a third person, In re Swift, 9 A. B. R. 385, 114 Fed. 947 (D. C. Mass.); broker's relation to customer for whom he buys and sells stock on margin is that of debtor and creditor and not fiduciary and beneficiary, and a payment on a money account between them may be a preference, In re Gaylord, 7 A. B. R. 577 (D. C. Mo.). But, even if that of fiduciary and beneficiary, yet the claim would be provable.

38. Clarke v. Rogers, 26 A. B. R. 413, 183 Fed. 518 (C. C. A. Mass.). See post, "'Preference' Implies Transfer to a 'Creditor,'" § 1304.

39. Reynold v. New York Trust Co., 26 A. B. R. 698, 188 Fed. 611 (C. C. A. Mass.).

Damages for loss arising on a contract of sale or purchase entered into through fraudulent misrepresentations, are, of course, a provable debt.[40]

§ 637. Claimant Must Elect.

—The claimant must elect whether he will retain his claim as one ex delicto, in which event it will be not provable, or will waive the tort and file the claim as upon an implied contract.[41]

§ 638. Not to Waive Tort as to Part and Affirm It as to Balance of Same Transaction.

—A claimant may not affirm contractual relations as to part of the property and claim as a creditor thereon, and, as to the remainder, involved in the same transaction, repudiate contractual relations and sue in tort for the recovery of specific property.[42]

In re Heinsfurter, 3 A. B. R. 113, 97 Fed. 198 (D. C. Iowa): "Precedents are not wanting in which the owner of property converted by another to his own use has been permitted to waive the tort and sue upon an implied contract that the party so converting the property is impliedly held as thereby promising to pay the value thereof. But no case has been cited by counsel for claimant, nor have I found any case in the limited time at my disposal for the search, wherein a party rescinding, or attempting to rescind, a contract of purchase for fraud on the part of the purchaser, has been permitted to retain part of the property obtained by him under his attempted rescission and then elect to sue for the remainder of the property as upon an implied contract to pay therefor because of the vendee's having converted it to his own use."

Varnish Wks. v. Haydock, 16 A. B. R. 287, 143 Fed. 318 (C. C. A. Ohio): "* * * it was open to the petitioner, the purchase having been procured by fraud, to elect whether to confirm the sale notwithstanding, and maintain the position of a creditor for the price, or to repudiate the sale and recover the goods. But the vendor must make his election promptly on discovery of the fraud. This is the settled law. Upon this principle Judge Ray held, in In re Hildebrant (D. C.), 120 Fed. 992, that a vendor could not affirm the contract of sale as to part of the goods, and claim the price, and disaffirm as to another part, and recover the goods in specie. * * * And having made his election in such circumstances, the vendor makes it once for all."

Nevertheless, to petition the bankruptcy court for an order for the return of property obtained by the bankrupt's fraudulent misrepresentations and

---

40. In re Harper, 23 A. B. R. 918, 175 Fed. 412 (D. C. N. Y.).

41. Compare, In re Mertens & Co., 16 A. B. R. 827 (C. C. A. N. Y.). See cases cited, next paragraph following, § 638. Compare, as to the effect on dischargeability of the proving of a claim in bankruptcy created by the bankrupt's fraud, § 2750½; also, Standard Sewing Machine Co. v. Kattell, 22 A. B. R. 376, 132 App. Div. 539, 107 N. Y. Supp. 32. Compare, to this effect, Atherton v. Green, 24 A. B. R. 650, 179 Fed. 806 (C. C. A. Ills.), quoted at § 1307½.

42. But compare, apparently contra, In re Lewensohn, 3 A. B. R. 594, 99 Fed. 73 (D. C. N. Y., distinguished in

6 A. B. R. 23), to the effect that proof of a debt before the referee in no way prejudices the creditors' remedy under the state law by arrest on account of the fraud by which sale and delivery of the goods were obtained. Also, In re Kenyon, 19 A. B. R. 194, 156 Fed. 836 (D. C. Ohio); (1867) Parmalee v. Adolph, 28 Oh. St. 10; (1841) Everett v. Derby, 5 Law Rep. 227; obiter (ignorance held to excuse apparent election), In re Stewart, 24 A. B. R. 474, 178 Fed. 463 (D. C. N. Y.). Compare, impliedly, and obiter yet valuable as throwing sidelight, Talcott v. Friend, 24 A. B. R. 708, 179 Fed. 676 (C. C. A. Ills.), quoted at §§ 2662, 2750½, 2753½.

still in the possession of the court, and at the same time to present a claim for the portion already sold before bankruptcy, have been held not to be inconsistent; that the original contract was disaffirmed in both instances, but that the implied contracts to return the property remaining and to pay for that converted, are affirmed.[43]

In re Hildebrant, 10 A. B. R. 184, 120 Fed. 992 (D. C. N. Y.): "While it is undoubtedly true that a party cannot both affirm and disaffirm a contract, when induced by fraud; that an election to proceed on the contract is an affirmance thereof, and waives the fraud—still it cannot be doubted that, when a party is induced to part with his property by fraudulent representations, he may, on discovery of the fraud, retake, by replevin or other appropriate proceedings, such of the property as he can find, and recover in an appropriate action the value of the goods not found, or, more properly speaking, damages for the fraud. But such claim and action for the damages could not be based on the contract, and the action would not be for the contract price, but simply for the damages, measured by the value of the goods not found. This court knows of no decision or rule of law that will deprive a person of the right to retake such of his property, fraudulently obtained, as he can find in the possession of the wrongdoer, and then maintain an action against such wrongdoer for the value of that part disposed of. This is not an election of remedies, nor is it pursuing two inconsistent remedies nor is it both an attempted affirmance and disaffirmance of the contract in toto, and such acts are not open to any other construction. See Welch v. Seligman, 72 Hun 138, 25 N. Y. Supp. 363; Abb. N. Y. Cyc. Dig. 542. So in this proceeding in bankruptcy the petitioner had the right to demand a return of such of the goods fraudulently obtained as it found in the hands of the trustee, and, by any proper proceeding, to compel such return, and also present and prove its claim for the value of the goods not found as damages, first, however, having the amount liquidated in the manner provided by the Bankrupt Act. The question is, did the petitioner put its claim in such form and take such proceedings as to indicate a purpose to affirm the contract and proceed thereunder? It is certain that this petitioner could not split its demand and affirm the contract as to a part of the goods delivered on certain days, and repudiate as to the other part.",

To same effect, Silvey & Co. v. Tift, 17 A. B. R. 9, 123 Ga. 804, 51 S. E. 748: "If a vendor in reliance upon material misrepresentations has made a sale, and has rescinded it on discovery of the fraud, but all of the property sold is not in the possession of the purchaser, and some of it has been sold or disposed of by him so as to be beyond the reach of the vendor, the latter may reclaim all the property which can be recovered. As to that which he cannot recover, he may have a right of action against the purchaser, not upon the contract, but based on the theory of the conversion of the goods not found, or an action based upon the contract implied by law where a vendee has disposed of the goods for money and the seller has waived the tort. * * * He cannot, however, proceed both under the contract of sale and against it. He cannot take back such of the goods as remain on hand as part payment of the indebtedness arising from the

---

43. In re Hirschman, 4 A. B. R. 715, 104 Fed. 69 (D. C. Utah); inferentially, to same general effect, In re Wilcox & Wright, 1 A. B. R. 544 (Ref. Tenn.); compare, analogously, apparently to same general effect, In re Lewensohn, 3 A. B. R. 594, 99 Fed. 73 (D. C. N. Y.). Compare, also, analogously, apparently to same general effect, Maxwell v. Martin, 22 A. B. R. 93 (N. Y. Sup. Ct. App. Div.); obiter, In re A. O. Brown, 23 A. B. R. 423, 175 Fed. 469 (C. C. A. N. Y.). Compare post, § 1882, note 149.

contract of sale, and retain a claim or seek payment for the balance of the purchase price. These two positions would be inconsistent."

Thus, a debtor obtained by fraudulent misrepresentations certain goods just before filing his petition in bankruptcy. Some of the goods he himself sold before going into bankruptcy. The rest were found in the trustee's possession. The seller asked for an order on the trustee for the redelivery to him of the goods still in the trustee's hands and for the allowance of his claim against the estate for the value of those sold by the bankrupt beforehand. The court held these demands were not inconsistent—that both rested on the rescission of the original sale, the waiving of the tort and the claim upon an implied contract, to-wit: Upon the debtor's contract, as trustee by implication, to turn over the property still unsold and the proceeds of the property sold, to his principal. This was the reasoning in the case In re Hirschman, 4 A. B. R. 716, 104 Fed. 69.

The reasoning of that case does not appear sound. In that case the proof of claim was *not* a petition for the recovery of the proceeds of the converted property; it was not a petition for the recovery of the property itself nor its proceeds but was a petition to share in *dividends,* whether such dividends were the proceeds of the property converted or not—an *affirmance* of the contract relation which the claimant had expressly disaffirmed in his other application for surrender of the property in specie.

Likewise, in the case In re Hildebrant, "damages for the fraud" are not a provable claim in bankruptcy, and the only way such damages can be placed in provable form is to *affirm* a contract to pay for the goods. The courts in the cases In re Hirschman and In re Hildebrant and other cases similarly reasoned seem to fail to retain consistency throughout. In effect, these cases disaffirm the contractual relations to the extent of reclaiming the property that can be come at and affirm contractual relations for the purpose of sharing in dividends for the value of the property that could not be come at—inconsistent positions, surely. The decisions proceed on the theory that there is no inconsistency in waiving the tort and claiming on a contract so long, as the contract is an implied contract and not the actual express contract originally existing between the parties. But this distinction ought not in reason to prevail. The affirmance of contract relations, whether based on the fiction of an implied contract or on an actual express contract, is alike inconsistent with a claim ex delicto. Whether implied or express, it is a *contract relation* that is affirmed, and the inconsistency consists in affirming and disaffirming contractual relations at the same time.

However, it cannot be doubted that the proving of the claim in bankruptcy and the receipt of dividends thereon, if there was an actual contract in existence, is no bar to a subsequent action for deceit in inducing the claimant to enter into the contract.

Talcott *v.* Friend, 24 A. B. R. 708, 179 Fed. 676 (C. C. A. Ills.): "Filing the claim was an affirmance of the contract of sale and constituted an election not to rescind and attempt to recover what plaintiff had delivered to defendants in pursuance of the contract. But an action for deceit is not based on rescission. It, too, nullifies an affirmance. It means that plaintiff has elected to abide by the contract, to retain and make the best of what he received thereunder, and to recover the difference between what he received and what he parted with as his damages in being misled." Quoted further at §§ 2570½, 2662, 2751, 2753½.

§ 639. After Election, Claimant Foreclosed.—Where the claimant has elected to waive the tort and claim upon implied contract and has prosecuted the elected remedy to judgment, he is foreclosed from any other remedy.[44]

Varnish Wks. v. Haydock, 16 A. B. R. 286 (C. C. A. Ohio): "Not only did the petition make no claim that the petitioner was ignorant at the time of proving its claim of the facts in regard to the representations of the bankrupt and of its intention in making the purchase, but the facts stated by the referee are sufficient, prima facie, to support the conclusion that the petitioner had knowledge of the essential facts when it voted for the trustee. In these circumstances the election of the petitioner to prove its claim as a general creditor was final. * * * The assumption of the position of a general creditor toward the assets would naturally be a strong inducement to the other creditors in pursuing the bankruptcy proceedings, for this would imply a sharing of the assets, and this result would be defeated if their associates were permitted to turn about and reclaim the assets in specie."

Lynch v. Bronson, 20 A. B. R. 409, 160 Fed. 139 (D. C. Conn.): "As already suggested, the parties chiefly interested have offered themselves to this court as creditors of the estate. By filing their claims against the bankrupt they have waived their right to dispute the passing of the title in their goods to him, prior to bankruptcy. They have done more than that. They have, by affirmative action, ratified the original purchase, sale and delivery of those goods, as constituting a valid title thereto in the bankrupt."

Compare, Thomas v. Taggart, 19 A. B. R. 710, 209 U. S. 385: "In the proof of his claim, Hall sets forth the following statement relative thereto: 'Said deponent hereby stipulates that by filing notice of this claim he does not waive any right of action that he now has to recover possession of said certificates or the value thereof against either of the bankrupts or any person in whose possession they may be found, or any right of action that he has against either or both of said bankrupts for the conversion of said certificates to their own use, * * *' In this claim, the essential question is as to the effect of Hall's proof of his claim in bankruptcy as a waiver of his right to recover the shares of stock covered by the receipt. We are of the opinion that, in view of the reservation just made, there was nothing in Hall's conduct amounting to an election to pursue his claim as a creditor in bankruptcy, which now prevents his recovery of the certificates of stock in question. It is true that he voted at the first meeting of the creditors on December 19, 1904, upon an informal ballot for trustee in bankruptcy, and at the formal election of trustees on December 21, 1904, Mr. Hall did not vote, though the referee finds that he participated

---

44. In re Hirschman, 4 A. B. R. 715, 104 Fed. 69 (D. C. Utah); Reynolds v. New York Trust Co., 26 A. B. R. 698, 188 Fed. 611 (C. C. A. Mass.); In re Berry & Co., 23 A. B. R. 27, 174 Fed. 409 (C. C. A.). Other instances of election of remedies, see index; also instance, attempting to obtain security after bankruptcy which was rejected before bankruptcy, In re Reading Hosiery Co., 22 A. B. R. 562, 171 Fed. 195 (D. C. Pa.).

actively at the meetings held for the election of trustee. We are of the opinion that the reservation of Hall evidenced his intention to hold on to whatever rights he had in his shares of stock, and there is nothing in his conduct which should preclude him, after he had discovered that the shares had been returned to the trustee in bankruptcy from reclaiming them as his own property."

But the election must have been knowingly made, else it will not be binding.[45]

In re Stewart, 24 A. B. R. 474, 178 Fed. 463 (D. C. N. Y.): "He claims that he has never made a legal election to pursue his remedy by proving his claim as a debt for the reason he was ignorant of the facts and of his rights, and that his right to withdraw the claim proved is one of which the court cannot deprive him; that he has neither received a dividend nor done any act since informed of the facts which can be construed as a waiver of his right to stand on the fraud or as an election to stand on the claim presented and allowed; and that nothing has been done by him at any time that in any way prejudices the rights of other creditors or that has misled them or the trustee. I do not think it in accord with equity or good conscience to hold that a creditor of a bankrupt who has been in fact deprived of his property by the fraudulent acts of the bankrupt of which the creditor was ignorant, and who presents his claim as for goods sold and delivered at the first meeting of creditors, and then on a full examination of the bankrupt discovers the fraud, and that he is entitled both in law and equity to a return of his property, is estopped from withdrawing his claim as proved and allowed and proceeding to reclaim the property itself.

And the right of the claimant to withdraw his claim for the debt in order to present it for reclamation, or for the tracing of trust funds, has been held to be an absolute right, not dependent on the discretion of the court.

In re Stewart, 24 A. B. R. 474, 178 Fed. 463 (D. C. N. Y.): "I do not think it within the power of the court, or referee, to prevent such withdrawal or abandonment of the claim presented. The withdrawal is a matter of right in the creditor, and not a matter of discretion with the referee or judge."

Yet it must not be inferred that the question of the effectiveness of the facts to bind the claimant by election may not be raised on defense to the subsequently filed petition for reclamation or for the tracing of trust funds.

§ 639½. Claims Ex Contractu Provable, Though Also Presentable in Tort.—Claims ex contractu are of course provable, though also presentable in tort.

Grant Shoe Co. v. Laird Co., 21 A. B. R. 484, 212 U. S. 445: "Again it has been suggested that a cause of action for a breach of warranty really is for deceit and sounds in tort, claims for torts not being mentioned among the 'Debts which may be proved' in § 63a. In re Morales, 5 Am. B. R. 425, 105 Fed. 761. No doubt at common law a false statement as to present facts gave rise to an action of tort, if the statement was made at the risk of the speaker, and led to harm. But ordinarily the risk was not taken by the speaker unless the statement was fraudulent, and it was precisely because it was a warranty, that is, an absolute undertaking by contract that a fact was true, that if a warranty

45. Obiter, In re Berry, 23 A. B. R. 27, 174 Fed. 409 (C. C. A.).

was alleged it was not necessary to lay the scienter. Schuchardt *v.* Allen, 1 Wall. 359; Norton *v.* Doherty, 3 Gray, 372. In other words, a claim on a warranty as such necessarily was a claim arising out of a contract, even if in case of actual fraud there might be an independent claim purely in tort."

DIVISION 3.

CONTINGENT CLAIMS INCLUDING CLAIMS OF SURETIES.

§ 640. Contingent Claims Not "Provable."—Contingent claims are not provable.[46]

§ 641. Test of Contingency.—The test as to whether a claim is really contingent or is simply unliquidated or unascertained by legal proceedings would seem to be this: Have all the facts necessary to be proved to fasten liability already occurred? If so, the claim is not contingent, although the liability and the extent of damages may not yet have been ascertained by the consideration of a court as evidenced by judgment or decree, nor even the full extent of damages arising been already suffered. The contingency, in other words, is a contingency of facts necessary to fasten liability at all, not a contingency of the court's judgment on the facts nor a contingency as to the extent of the damages resulting from the injury. Again, so long as it remains uncertain whether a contract or liability will ever give rise to an actual duty or liability, and there is no means of removing the uncertainty by calculation, it is too contingent to be a provable debt.[47]

---

46. Compare discussions: In re Ells, 3 A. B. R. 564, 98 Fed. 967 (D. C. Mass.); In re Pettingill & Co., 14 A. B. R. 728, 137 Fed. 143 (D. C. Mass.); In re Swift, 7 A. B. R. 381, 112 Fed. 315 (C. C. A. Mass.); In re Mahler, 5 A. B. R. 457, 105 Fed. 428 (D. C. Mich.); In re Arnstein, 4 A. B. R. 246, 101 Fed. 706 (Ref. N. Y.); In re Collignon, 4 A. B. R. 250 (Ref. N. Y.); Watson *v.* Merrill, 14 A. B. R. 453, 136 Fed. 359 (C. C. A. Kans.); Phœnix National Bank *v.* Waterbury, 20 A. B. R. 140, 108 N. Y. Supp. 391, quoted at § 690; In re Roth & Appel, 24 A. B. R. 588, 181 Fed. 666 (C. C. A. N. Y.), quoted at §§ 641, 653, 654, 656, 659; In re American Vacuum Cleaner Co., 26 A. B. R. 621, 192 Fed. 939 (D. C. N. J.).

Instance, In re Hartman, 21 A. B. R. 610, 166 Fed. 766 (D. C. Pa.), in which the court held that where upon the dissolution of a partnership composed of a bankrupt and his father, they execute a written instrument by which the bankrupt agrees to pay his father a certain sum with interest during his lifetime, or his heirs five years after his death, reserving the right to pay any part or all of the amount to his father, or in the event of his death before full payment to pay any part or all, to his heirs any time before the expiration of the five years, and the father agrees to make no disposition of his estate or any part thereof by will or otherwise, the father's claim against the bankrupt is a contingent liability and under § 63a (1) cannot be proved in the bankruptcy proceedings.

Stockholders' Double Liability.—See post, "Unliquidated Claims," § 709, et seq.

Contracts to Buy Stock in Future.—See post, §§ 689, 690.

47. Compare post, § 659. Colman Co. *v.* Withoft, 28 A. B. R. 328, 195 Fed. 250 (C. C. A. Cal.); Williams & Co. *v.* U. S. Fidelity Co., 28 A. B. R. 802 (Ct. App. Ga.). (1841) Riggins *v.* Magwire, 15 Wall. 549.

The English Bankrupt Act (1869) includes almost all kinds of contingent claims among provable debts. The 31st section of that act makes every kind of debt or liability provable in bankruptcy except demands in the nature of unliquidated damages arising otherwise than by reason of contract or promise, so long as the

Obiter, Dunbar v. Dunbar, 10 A. B. R. 145, 190 U. S. 340: "We do not think that by the use of the language in § 63 (a) it was intended to permit proof of contingent debts or liabilities or demands, the valuation or estimation of which it was substantially impossible to prove."

The subject of contingent claims is an abstruse subject and one that has not been clearly analyzed in the decisions. On the one hand, it is to be borne in mind that neither the adjudication of bankruptcy nor the discharge affects merely *contractual relations,* unless such relations at the time of bankruptcy, or by virtue of the bankruptcy, have become merged in a "debt, demand or claim," as noted heretofore in the discussion of the effect of adjudication in bankruptcy upon the rights of parties.[48]

On the other hand, it is equally to be borne in mind that if it has become thus merged at the time of bankruptcy, whether it amounts to the certain, liquidated and definite money demand technically. known as a "debt" or constitutes merely a "claim" or "demand" against the debtor, it constitutes a "provable debt" as the term is used in bankruptcy.[49]

Again, so long as it remains uncertain whether a contract or liability will ever give rise to an actual duty or liability, and there is no means of removing the uncertainty by calculation, it is too contingent to be a provable debt.

In re Roth & Appel, 24 A. B. R. 588, 181 Fed. 666 (C. C. A. N. Y.), affirming 22 A. B. R. 504, 174 Fed. 640: "Indeed, looking at the claim as it existed either at the time of the petition or the adjudication, it was altogether contingent in its nature: (1) It was uncertain, as just pointed out, whether the lessor would re-enter and terminate the lease: (2) In case the lease were terminated it was uncertain whether there would be any loss in rents. If the rent received by the

value of the liability is capable of being ascertained by fixed rules or assessable only by a jury, or as matter of opinion. Ex parte Neal, 14 Chancery Div. 579.

The Acts of 1841 and 1867 were each different from that of 1898 on the subject of the provability of contingent claims. Section 5 of the Act of 1841 provided in terms for the holders of uncertain or contingent demands coming in and proving such debts under the act. The Act of 1867, § 19, provided expressly for cases of contingent debts and contingent liabilities contracted by the bankrupt, and permitted application to be made to the court to have the present value of the debt or liability ascertained and liquidated, which was to be done in such manner as the court should order and the creditor was then to be allowed to prove for the amount so ascertained. Dunbar v. Dunbar, 10 A. B. R. 150, 190 U. S. 340.

Some claims are called "contingent" that are merely unliquidated, for an instance of which see In re [James] Dunlap Carpet Co., 20 A. B. R. 882,

163 Fed. 541 (D. C. Pa.). Compare, Loeser v. Alexander, 24 A. B. R. 72, 176 Fed. 265 (C. C. A. Ohio).

But even under the Bankruptcy Acts of 1841 and 1867, which, unlike the present act, expressly permitted the proof of contingent demands, claims for unaccrued rent were not provable, In re Roth & Appel, 24 A. B. R. 588, 181 Fed. 667 (C. C. A. N. Y.); [1841] Bosler v. Kuhn (Pa. Sup. Ct.), 8 Watts & S. 183; [1867] Ex parte Houghton, 1 Lowell 554, Fed. Cas. No. 6,725; In re May, 9 N. B. Reg. 419, Fed. Cas. No. 9,325; Bailey v. Loeb, 11 N. B. Reg. 271, Fed. Cas. No. 739.

48. Ante, § 451. Compare, impliedly to same effect, Phœnix Nat. Bank v. Waterberry, 20 A. B. R. 140, 108 N. Y. Supp. 391, quoted at § 690.

49. Ante, § 627.

Section 57 (n) is not operative to let in contingent claims becoming fixed within the year. In re Roth & Appel, 22 A. B. R. 504, 174 Fed. 64 (D. C. N. Y.), affirmed, but this point not adverted to, 24 A. B. R. 588, 181 Fed. 666 (C. C. A.).

landlord from the new tenant equalled or exceeded that stipulated in the lease there would be no loss, and, consequently, no foundation for any claim upon the indemnity covenant."

§ 642. Endorsers, Sureties, etc., for Bankrupt Impliedly Excepted by Statute.—The principal difficulties have arisen in regard to indorsements of commercial paper and obligations of sureties and others similarly situated, before maturity and default have made the obligations absolute; and have arisen in the endeavor to reconcile the rule that contingent claims are not provable in bankruptcy, with the apparently inconsistent rulings that obviously contingent claims on commercial paper and other similar obligations are nevertheless provable.

Distinctions are made to show that indorsements of commercial paper and similar obligations are nevertheless contracts, and hence provable debts before default has fixed the indorsers or surety's liability. But such distinctions, while doubtless valid, evade the point at issue, which is: Are such obligations not contingent? And if so, while so, are they not for that reason not provable? That they are provable is not to be denied. That they are contingent ought, also, not to be denied. It would be better frankly to place their provability upon the fact that the statute, by force of its special provisions allowing proofs by those secondarily liable in the name of the creditor, places such persons, sub modo, in the shoes of the creditor, though their own obligation is contingent. Such, really, is the basic trouble.

By virtue of the statutory provisions those secondarily liable to a creditor are made to stand in the creditor's shoes.[50]

§ 643. Bankrupt Surety, Guarantor or Endorser.—The liability of the bankrupt as endorser or surety, upon his contract of endorsement of suretyship, is a provable debt although default has not been made by the principal until after the filing of the petition or until after adjudication. It constitutes a "demand" or "claim" even if not a "debt." Most of the decisions in support of the proposition add the qualification "provided it become fixed and absolute within the statutory period of one year from the date of adjudication limited for proving claims."[51]

---

50. Compare, In re Smith, 17 A. B. R. 112 (D. C. R. I.). Snow *v.* Dalton, 28 A. B. R, 240, 203 Fed. 843 (C. C. A. N. Car.); In re Elletson Co., 28 A. B. R. 434, 174 Fed. 859 (D. C. W. Va); Kelsey *v.* Munson. 28 A. B. R. 520, 198 Fed. 841 (C. C. A. Colo.); In re T. A. McIntyre & Co., 28 A. B. R. 459, 189 Fed. 46 (C. C. A. N. Y.).

51. In re Gerson (Moch *v.* Market St. Bk.), 6 A. B. R. 11, 107 Fed. 897 (C. C. A. Penn., affirming In re Gerson, 5 A. B. R. 89); In re Rothenberg. 15 A. B. R. 485, 140 Fed. 798 (D. C. N. Y.); In re Smith, 17 A. B. R. 112 (D. C. R. I.), in which case the liability became absolute by default after adjudication but before proof. In re Stout, 6 A. B. R. 505, 109 Fed. 794 (D. C. Mo.). In re Marks & Garson, 6 A. B. R. 641 (Ref. N. Y.); contra, Morgan *v.* Wordell, 6 A. B. R. 167, 59 N. E. 1037, 178 Mass. 350 (Mass. Sup. Jud. Ct.); also, contra, Goding *v.* Rosenthal. 6 A. B. R. 641, 180 Mass. 43, 61 N. E. 222 (Mass. Sup. Jud. Ct.); also, contra, In re Chambers, Calder & Co., 6 A. B. R. 707 (Ref. R. I.); impliedly, In re O'Donnell, 12 A. B. R. 621, 131 Fed. 150 (D. C. Mass.); impliedly, In re Pettingill & Co., 14 A. B. R. 733, 137 Fed. 143 (D. C. Mass.).

Claims against Several Bankrupts in

In re Ph. Semmer Glass Co., 14 A. B. R. 25, 135 Fed. 77 (C. C. A. N. Y.): "The appellant seeks to differentiate the case at bar on the ground that the notes held by the First National Bank were not due at the date of adjudication (they have since matured), and that the bankrupt was not the maker, but the endorser, wherefore the notes did not constitute a 'debt' of the bankrupt. His argument is interesting and ingenious, but entirely disregards § 1, subd. 11, Bankruptcy Act, which provides that the word 'debt,' when used in said Act, 'shall include any debt, demand, or claim provable in bankruptcy.' * * *

"We concur with the Court of Appeals for the Third Circuit (Moch v. Market St. Nat. Bank, 6 Am. B. R. 11, 107 Fed. 897) in the conclusion that the liability of a bankrupt indorser of commercial paper which did not become absolute till after the filing of the petition is a debt provable in bankruptcy."

In re Simon, 28 A. B. R. 611, 197 Fed. 102 (D. C. N. Y.): "It is true that, to enable a claimant to share in the distributive part of the bankrupt estate, the debt must be a fixed liability absolutely owing at the time the petition against the bankrupt is filed; but it is not thought material as to when the debt or liability is payable. At the time of filing the petition in bankruptcy promissory notes previously made or indorsed by the bankrupts, and discounted at a bank, though they are payable at some future time, nevertheless constitute an absolute liability, and there is vested in each creditor an equitable right or interest in the assets of the bankrupt."

It has even been held that where the bankrupt is a guarantor on an oral guaranty, the guaranty is a provable debt and the one to whom the guaranty is made is a "creditor," the fact that the guaranty is not written going merely to the proof.[52]

Huttig Mfg. Co. v. Edwards, 20 A. B. R. 349, 160 Fed. 619 (C. C. A. Iowa): "A surety or endorser for a bankrupt has been held to be a creditor within the meaning of the bankruptcy law; and, upon the same principle a guarantor liable upon a fixed liquidated demand as this was, is a debtor to him who holds it, and his liability is to be counted in determining his financial status. That the guaranty may have been oral and therefore within the statute of frauds of Iowa where the transaction occurred, is immaterial. The Iowa statute relates merely to the evidence or proof of the undertaking and not to its validity."

A fortiori, it is a provable debt if default and protest have been duly made before bankruptcy.

Different Bankruptcies on Same Instrument.—The creditor is entitled to prove against each for the full amount due on the instrument at the date of the filing of the bankruptcy petition and to receive dividends from each state up to amount of entire debt. Board of Commissioners v. Hurley, 22 A. B. R. 209, 169 Fed. 92 (C. C. A. Kans.). See ante, § 615; post, § 1519.

Firm Obligations on Which Partner Individually Endorser Provable against Individual Estate.—Firm obligations on which one of the partners is an endorser, may be proved against the individual estate of such endorser, see post, § 2258, et seq.; also see In re White, 25 A. B. R. 541, 183 Fed. 310 (C. C. A. Ills.).

52. Creditor Consenting to Bankrupt's Composition Releases Surety. —Although the statute declares that "discharge" shall not release those secondarily liable for a bankrupt's debt, and although the confirmation of a composition is in effect a discharge, yet a creditor who voluntarily consents in writing to accept the bankrupt's offer of composition probably thereby releases the surety, since he has himself directly contributed voluntarily to the principal debtor's release. In re Benedict, 18 A. B. R. 604 (Ref. N. Y.), quoted at § 1513½.

Obiter, Whitwell, trustee, v. Wright, 23 A. B. R. 747 (N. Y. Sup. Ct. App. Div.). But it is difficult to see precisely how the question could properly have arisen in this case, the suit being one brought by the trustee to recover a preference, after adjudication, and the question of the provability of the indorsement being wholly collateral, as well as being conclusively established by the adjudication. Also, see, Cohen v. Pecharsky, 23 A. B. R. 754, 121 N. Y. Supp. 602.

§ 644. Bankrupt as Principal—Surety Is Creditor before Default, and from Date of Signing.—The indebtedness of a bankrupt principal to his surety who subsequently discharges the obligation in whole or in part, takes effect from the date the surety signs the obligation.[53]

In re Stout, 6 A. B. R. 508, 109 Fed. 794 (D. C. Mo.): "As between the principal and surety, Potter's undertaking was contingent upon Stout's default. The implied contract or obligation was therefore, raised by law between the surety and the principal that the latter should indemnify the former, and this implied contract took effect from the date of the surety's signing the note, and not merely from the time he paid the money; the payment in such case relating to the inception of the implied liability."

Livingston v. Heineman, 10 A. B. R. 39, 120 Fed. 787 (C. C. A. Ohio, reversing In re New, 8 A. B. R. 566, D. C.): "A surety, when he assumes the relation, becomes contingently the creditor of the debtor and the debtor of the creditor."

Swarts v. Siegel, 8 A. B. R. 694, 695, 117 Fed. 13 (C. C. A. Mo.): "There is another reason why Siegel & Bro. are not entitled to the allowance of their claim unless the $14,600 is repaid. It is that they were creditors of the dry goods company when the amount was paid to the bank. A creditor is 'one who gives credit in business transactions.' Cent. Dict., p. 1341, tit. 'Creditor.' Siegel & Bro. gave credit to the dry goods company in a business transaction. They signed its notes, became absolutely' liable to pay them, and thereby gave it credit. If they had simply indorsed them, and thus become only contingently liable, the same result would have followed. One who loans his credit to another is as much his creditor as one who loans his money to him. A creditor is 'one who has the right to require the fulfillment of an obligation or contract.' Bouv. Law Dict., p. 435. An indorser, an accommodation maker, or a surety on an obligation of a debtor has a right to require the fulfillment of the obligation or contract of that debtor. '"Creditor" shall include any one who owns a demand or claim provable in bankruptcy.' Section 1, subd. 9, Bankr. Law 1898. 'Debts of a bankrupt may be proved and allowed against his estate which are

---

53. Inferentially, Swarts v. Fourth Nat. Bk., 8 A. B. R. 673, 117 Fed. 1 (C. C. A. Mo.); impliedly, In re Lyon, 10 A. B. R. 25, 121 Fed. 723 (C. C. A. N. Y., affirming 7 A. B. R. 412); Crandall v. Coats, 13 A. B. R. 712, 133 Fed. 965 (D. C. Iowa); In re Mathews & Rosenkraus, 15 A. B. R. 72 (Ref. Mass.); inferentially, Landry v. Andrews, 6 A. B. R. 281 (Sup. Ct. R. I.). Compare, to same effect, under law of 1841, Mace v. Wells, 7 How. 272, and under law of 1867, Hunt v. Taylor, 108 Mass. 508; McAtee v. Shade, 26 A. B. R. 151, 185 Fed. 442 (C. C. A. Mo.), quoted at § 1310; In re Salvator Brew.

Co., 28 A. B. R. 56, 193 Fed. 989 (C. C. A. N. Y.); Kobusch v. Hand, 19 A. B. R. 379, 156 Fed. 660 (C. C. A. Mo.); In re Farmers' Supply Co., 22 A. B. R. 460, 170 Fed. 502 (D. C. Ohio); Brown v. Streicher, 24 A. B. R. 267, 177 Fed. 473 (D. C. R. I.).

Indorser Paying Note before Maker's Bankruptcy Entitled to Prove for Full Amount.—In the absence of an express agreement to the contrary, of course, an indorser paying a note before the maker's bankruptcy is entitled to prove the claim for its full amount. In re McCord, 22 A. B. R. 204, 174 Fed. 72 (D. C. N. Y.).

(1) a fixed liability * * * (4) founded upon an open account or upon a contract express or implied.' Section 63. Provision is here made for the proof of two classes of debts—those which evidence fixed liabilities of the debtor, and those founded upon contracts, which evidence contingent or uncertain liabilities. The debt of a principal debtor to his indorser, his accommodation maker, or his surety before the latter has paid the obligation is a contingent liability founded upon contract, and falls directly within the terms and meaning of subdivision 4 of this section. To make assurance doubly sure, however, Congress expressly provided that 'whenever a creditor, whose claim against a bankrupt estate is secured by the individual undertaking of any person, fails to prove such claim, such person may do so in the creditor's name, and if he discharge such undertaking in whole or in part he shall be subrogated to that extent to the rights of the creditor.' Section 57i. An indorser, an accommodation maker, or a surety on the obligation of a bankrupt is a person whose individual undertaking secures the claim against the bankrupt estate of the holder of that obligation, and by the terms of this section he may prove that claim whenever the creditor fails to do so. The language is broad, comprehensive, and without exception. He has the same right to prove it before as after he discharges the obligation in whole or in part, and if he is an indorser he has the same right to make his proof before as after his liability ceases to be contingent and becomes fixed. The last clause of the paragraph, 'and if he discharge such undertaking in whole or in part he shall be subrogated to that extent to the rights of the creditors,' neither limits the class who may prove their claims under this paragraph to those who have discharged their undertakings entirely or partly, nor in any way restricts the class which the earlier portion of the paragraph permits to establish their demands against the estate of the bankrupt. On the other hand, it adds emphasis and certainty to the patent meaning of the earlier portion of the paragraph that the indorser or surety may prove the claim in the name of the holder of the bankrupt's obligation whenever the creditor fails to do so, and before, as well as after, the surety discharges his undertaking, because, while such proof in the name of the creditor would send the dividends to the original holder of the claim, the latter portion of the paragraph adds the provision that if the surety discharges his undertaking he shall then be subrogated to the rights of the original holder, and hence to the right to receive the dividends. Sections 57i and 63 (4) were obviously intended to prevent the injustice that would be inflicted upon indorsers and sureties for the bankrupt whenever the holders of their obligations should elect to make no proof of their claims against the bankrupt estates, and to reply exclusively upon the liabilities of the sureties if the latter were not allowed to prove the claims. These sections have accomplished their purpose. The remedy they provided is as broad and comprehensive as the evil which they were passed to prevent, and an indorser or a surety has a provable claim against the estate of a bankrupt, and is his creditor under the act of 1898 before, as well as after, his liability becomes fixed."

In re O'Donnell, 12 A. B. R. 621, 131 Fed. 150 (D. C. Mass.): "Was Reichenbacher a creditor preferred by the assignments? He was then an indorser of the respondents' paper. His liability was contingent. In re Moch v. Market Bank, 6 Am. B. R. 11, 107 Fed. 897, a noteholder was held to have a provable claim against a bankrupt indorser, and in Swarts v. Siegel, 8 Am. B. R. 689, 117 Fed. 13, 54 C. C. A. 399, it was said that an accommodation indorser, even before payment, is a creditor of the bankrupt debtor whose paper he has indorsed. See pages 696, 697, Am. B. R., and pages 17, 18, 117 Fed. Reichenbacher was, therefore, the bankrupt's creditor at the time of both assignments. If the assignments stand, Reichenbacher will receive a greater percentage of his debt than other creditors. Whether he can hold the assignments by paying to the estate the amount he has preferred, need not now be determined."

Smith *v.* Wheeler, 5 A. B. R. 46 (C. C. A. N. Y. Sup. Ct. App. Div.): "If the claim of the plaintiff was a provable debt within the meaning of the Bankrupt Act, then the discharge is a bar. By subdivision 'i' of § 57 of the act it is provided as follows:

"'Whenever a creditor, whose claim against a bankrupt is secured by the individual undertaking of any person, fails to prove such claim, such person may do so in the creditor's name, and if he discharge such undertaking in whole or in part he shall be subrogated to that extent to the rights of the creditor.' * * * It must be held, I think, that the claim of the plaintiff was provable under the Bankrupt Act, and that, therefore, the discharge is a bar."

Obiter, In re Dillon, 4 A. B. R. 64, 100 Fed. 627 (D. C. Mass.): "There is difficulty in holding that the present Bankrupt Act allows the proof of contingent claims in general but the contingent claims of sureties are specially provided for by § 57 (i). * * *

"The provisions of the two acts, though quite differently worded, yet reach in most respects the same result. Under both acts the surety can get nothing by way of dividend unless he pays the original debt in whole or in part. If he discharges the whole debt, then, under the first clause above quoted of § 19 of the Act of 1867, and under § 57i of the Act of 1898, he stands in the place of the original creditor, or is subrogated to his rights. This is true whether the payment is made before or after the bankruptcy. Plainly the words, 'if he discharge such undertaking,' in § 57i, are not limited to the time before adjudication. If the surety pays only a part of the original debt, then, by the express provisions of § 57i of the Act of 1898, the surety is subrogated to the original creditor 'to that extent.'"

But compare, Goding *v.* Rosenthal, 6 A. B. R. 641, 61 N. E. 222 (Mass. Sup. Jud. Ct.): "By the execution of the bond of March 29th, 1898, to August, in which the present plaintiff was a surety for the present defendant the latter incurred an obligation to the present plaintiff to reimburse him any amount which he might be compelled as surety to pay upon the bond. This obligation was in force when, on February 13, 1900, the present defendant's petition in bankruptcy was filed. It was an obligation founded upon an implied contract, and it was evidenced by an instrument in writing and in one sense it was a fixed liability. But no debt was absolutely owing at the time of the petition. The obligation was contingent upon the happening of a breach of the bond and a payment by the surety. The payment by the surety was not until June 12, 1900, and there seems to have been no breach of the bond before that date. Therefore, neither the obligee in the bond nor the surety could prove in the bankruptcy proceedings a claim founded upon the bond, unless merely contingent claims are provable under the Bankruptcy Act of 1898."

§ 645. Surety Paying Principal's Debt after Principal's Bankruptcy.

—Thus, even where the surety pays his principal's debt after the principal has been adjudged bankrupt, the surety holds a claim for indemnity that had its origin before the bankruptcy and is therefore a provable and dischargeable debt.

This rule has for its basis the peculiar provisions of the Bankruptcy Act permitting proof of claims in the name of the creditor by sureties and others secondarily liable therefor even before payment by the sureties, where the creditor fails or refuses to make the proof himself; and also subrogating pro tanto such persons, thus secondarily liable, to the creditor's dividends in so far as such persons shall discharge the obligations (§ 57i) making, in short, such persons thus secondarily liable, quasi "owners" of the claims, hence qualified "creditors;" "creditors" including not only owners of "debts" but those owning "demands or claims provable in bankruptcy."[54]

Compare similar reasoning, In re Gerson, 5 A. B. R. 89 (D. C. Pa., affirmed sub nom. Moch v. Market St. Bk., 6 A. B. R. 11, 109 Fed. 897): "A debt is defined by § 1 of the act to be 'any debt, demand or claim provable in bankruptcy,' and § 63 sets forth in detail the classes of provable debts. There are: (1) certain fixed liabilities, (2) and (3) certain liabilities for costs, (4) any debt, claim or demand founded upon an open account or upon a contract express or implied; and (5) provable debts reduced to judgment after the filing of the petition. It is the scope of clause 4 that is now in controversy, and this I think is broad enough to include a claim founded upon the contract of endorsement even before the liability under such a contract has become fixed. The endorser's engagement may not be a 'debt,' strictly so called, until there has been demand and notice of non-payment but even before demand and notice there is certainly a contingent liability, and this may be clearly embraced within the words 'demand or claim.' I did not consider this clause of the section when I decided Schaefer's case, but, now that it has been brought to my attention, I cannot avoid the conclusion that clause 4 ought to have been applied in that decision, and if applied, should have brought me to the conclusion that a contract of endorsement is a provable debt even if the note does not fall due until after the petition is filed. It is provable not under clause 'A' (1), but under clause 'A' (4). The contract of indorsement is an express contract (Martin v. Cole, 104 U. S. 37), and the holder of the note has a demand or claim founded thereon, which may ripen into a debt or fixed liability, or may be defeated by his failure

---

54. Bankr. Act, § 1 (9): "'Creditor' shall include any one who owns a demand or claim provable in bankruptcy, and may include his duly authorized agent, attorney, or proxy." Swarts v. Siegel, 8 A. B. R. 694, 695, 117 Fed. 13 (C. C. A. Mo.); Livingston v. Heineman, 10 A. B. R. 39, 120 Fed. 787 (C. C. A. Ohio). Compare, similar reasoning, In re Gerson (Moch v. Market St. Bk.), 6 A. B. R. 11, 109 Fed. 897 (C. C. A. Penn., affirming 5 A. B. R. 89). Compare, contra, Goding v. Rosenthal, 6 A. B. R. 641, 180 Mass. 43, 61 N. E. 222 (Mass. Sup. Jud. Ct.); Morgan v. Wordell, 6 A. B. R. 167, 59 N. E. 1037 (Mass. Sup. Jud. Ct.); also, apparently contra, In re Marks & Gerson, 6 A. B. R. 641 (Ref. N. Y.); also, contra, In re New, 8 A. B. R. 566, 116 Fed. 116 (D. C. Ohio, reversed sub nom. Livingston v. Heineman, 10 A. B. R. 39, 120 Fed. 787, C. C. A. Ohio); compare, also, Swarts v. Fourth Nat'l Bk., 8 A. B. R. 673, 117 Fed. 1 (C. C. A. Mo.). Inferentially, In re Lange Co., 22 A. B. R. 414, 170 Fed. 114 (D. C. Iowa).

Under the laws of 1841 and 1867, "contingent and uncertain" claims were provable by express provision. In re Brew. Co., 16 A. B. R. 110, 115, 143 Fed. 579 (D. C. Mo.): "It is a noteworthy fact that under the Bankrupt Act of 1841 and 1867 the right was given to prove 'uncertain and contingent demands' against the estate. This provision was omitted from the present Bankrupt Act of 1898."

Solvent Partner's Claim against Bankrupt Partner for Liquidation of Firm Affairs.—Where a solvent partner has undertaken the liquidation of the partnership affairs instead of having them administered in the individual bankruptcy of the other partner, his claim (where the bankrupt partner was not indebted to the firm nor to the solvent partner at the date of adjudication), is not a provable debt. In re Walker, 23 A. B. R. 805, 176 Fed. 455 (D. C. Ala.), quoted at § 2259. See also, post, § 711, note. Also, see § 2259.

to take certain steps. But it is a contingent right of some sort founded upon the contract, and is, I think, embraced in words of such excessive scope as 'demand or claim.'"

Hayer v. Comstock, 7 A. B. R. 495, 115 Ia. 187 (Sup. Ct. Iowa): "This debt was a fixed liability evidenced by an instrument in writing, and absolutely owing by the defendant at the time of the filing of the petition in bankruptcy, and therefore might be proved against the estate as it was. It is the fact that the bankrupt absolutely owed this fixed liability, evidenced in writing, at the time of the filing of the petition, that made it provable, regardless of the person to whom it was owing. If the creditor had failed to prove the claim, the plaintiff could have done so in its name, not because the debt was then due to him, but because it was a fixed liability, evidenced in writing, and absolutely owing by the defendant. Being proved as it was by the creditor, it was not required that the surety should take any further steps. We do not overlook the distinctions that exist as between liability of the debtor to the creditor and his liability to his surety, but we emphasize the fact that it was the fixed liability, evidenced in writing, 'absolutely owing' by the defendant, that made this a provable claim against his estate. Said paragraphs in § 57 and in the general orders of the Supreme Court recognize the right of the surety to protect himself before payment, and when his liability is contingent, and to share in the dividends of the estate after payment."

In re Schmechel Co., 4 A. B. R. 719, 104 Fed. 64 (D. C. Mo.): "Congress having thus by statute made an express provision (§ 57i) on this subject, under well-settled rules of construction, it is conclusive of any other rule or method. The claim of the creditor being 'secured by the individual undertaking of' the guarantor, if the creditor fail to prove up the debt against the estate, the guarantor could 'do so in the creditor's name,' or having as he claims discharged 'such undertaking' by executing to the creditor his individual note for the balance thereof, 'he shall be subrogated to that extent to the rights of the creditor.' Unquestionably, had he pursued the first course, of presenting the debt 'in the creditor's name' for allowance, he could have done so only by bringing to the estate the amount of the preferred payment. Having chosen, after the adjudication in bankruptcy, to discharge his collateral undertaking, he can only 'be subrogated to that extent to the rights of the creditor.'"

Contra, Phillips v. Dreher Shoe Co., 7 A. B. R. 326, 112 Fed. 404 (D. C. Pa.): "No one has any rights under the Bankrupt Law outside of what it gives him, and those of a surety are defined by this section, beyond which he cannot go. By it he has the right to prove, in case the principal creditor fails to do so. He does not indeed have to discharge the obligation in order to have his privilege, but in case he does do so, in whole or in part, he becomes entitled to that extent to the right of subrogation, and in any event, when he proves the debt, he proves it not in his own name, but in that of the original holder. In re Christensen, 2 N. B. N. 1094. The particular point to be noticed in the present connection with regard to the position of the surety, is that he only has a right to prove, in case the principal creditor fails to do so; and the latter cannot be said to fail until he has had an opportunity and passed it by, which can only occur when, by proceedings duly instituted, the estate of the debtor has been drawn into the bankruptcy court to be there administered, and all parties have been called upon to make known their claims. When that has been done, and he neglects to act, the surety, so as not to be prejudiced, may himself prove the debt in his stead. This, so far as I can see, is all the relief given by the act, and whether adequate or inadequate, it must suffice. It follows from this that at the outstart, the surety who has not taken up the obligation, has no provable claim, and therefore has no standing to petition."

The statutory provision of § 57i giving sureties the status of quasi owners of provable claims prevents any new debt arising against the bankrupt by the sureties making payment after bankruptcy. Being made thereby quasi owners of provable claims their "demands" and "claims" are pro tanto discharged.

§ 646. Where Principal's Liability Not Provable in Favor of Creditor, Not Provable in Favor of Surety.

—Where the principal debtor's liability is not a "provable" claim in favor of the creditor at the time of the principal debtor's bankruptcy, of course, it is not a provable claim in favor of the surety.

§ 647. Sureties for Bankrupt's "Faithful Discharge of Duty," etc., Where No Default Till after Petition Filed, Not "Provable."

—But would a bankrupt be considered as discharged from his liability to a surety upon a bond given for the performance of a duty and not for the payment of money, where the bankrupt's default does not occur until after bankruptcy? Contractual obligations are not severed by the discharge unless claim thereunder (at any rate in the creditor's name) can be made at the time of bankruptcy. Thus, the rule probably would be different in cases of sureties on official and other similar bonds from what it would be in cases of sureties and endorsers on commercial paper. Creditors themselves upon bonds given merely for the faithful performance of duty or for other obligations than the payment of money have not provable claims at the date of bankruptcy as to defaults occurring afterwards and are not therefore "creditors," even within the meaning of the Bankrupt Act; therefore, much less would the sureties on such bonds be creditors and have provable claims.

Thus, a bankrupt's liability upon a redelivery bond, given by him before bankruptcy to the sheriff to obtain repossession of property taken on replevin, is too contingent to be provable where the judgment in favor of the plaintiff against him is not rendered until after discharge.[55]

§ 648. Obtaining of Judgment Prerequisite to Liability on Bond.

—A judgment itself may be a fact without which no liability can arise, in which event, if the judgment be not obtained until after the surety's bankruptcy, it is not a provable debt.

Thus, it was held, in the lower court, that the liability of a bankrupt as surety on the bond of an administrator who was charged with and found liable for misappropriation of funds but who, by order of the orphan's court, was directed to retain the funds until further order, was not "absolutely owing," because the court had not yet ordered the fund turned over at the time of bankruptcy; but the reviewing court reversed the holding on

55. Clemmons v. Brinn, 7 A. B. R. 714 (Sup. Ct. N. Y. App. Term).

1 R B—33

the ground that the prior adjudication of the orphan's court finding the amount due from the administrator had fixed the surety's liability.[56] Thus, also the right of a wife by statute on divorce to one third of personalty, in Arkansas, is not, before divorce, a provable claim.[57]

It is not upon this principle that a surety on an appeal bond is released by the bankruptcy of the principal. The suretyship obligation is still existent but the cause of action thereon is dependent on the obtaining of a judgment against the principal, whose discharge prevents such judgment being obtained.[58]

§ 648½. Surety on Redelivery Bond Where Attachment or Other Lien Dissolved by Adjudication.

—It has been held that the surety on a redelivery bond given to effect release from an attachment or other lien which itself would be dissolved by the adjudication, is not a provable debt.

In re Windt, 24 A. B. R. 536, 177 Fed. 584 (D. C. Conn.): "The adjudication * * * would dissolve the attachment lien. With such dissolution would disappear also the obligation of the administrator's decedent to respond to the officer on the receipt, and the mortgage note given to secure him from loss thereby would fail for lack of consideration. I do not think one can force another into bankruptcy by the use of alleged debts, which, by operation of law will be extinguished, and therefore not provable, the instant the adjudication exists."

But it is a "provable" debt because it is, in its nature, a debt on contract. The mere fact that something may occur to defeat the obligation is not sufficient to destroy its provability. Moreover, under the doctrine of § 2712, post, it is within the discretion of the court to permit the suit to proceed to judgment precisely in order to permit the plaintiff to fix the surety's liability. The property, having been released to the bankrupt as was intended by the giving of the bond, may have been disposed of by the bankrupt or may have passed to the trustee; nevertheless the surety's liability remains if the court permits, and the surety after payment, will be subrogated to the creditor's claim or have a claim for indemnity.

§ 649. Cosurety's Claim for Contribution for Payments after Bankruptcy.

—The liability of a cosurety or comaker for contribution it would seem would follow the same rule as that of a principal to a surety; such cosurety simply being subrogated to the rights of the creditor against the other cosurety in case he has discharged the obligation in the proportion in which he is cosurety.

In re Bingham, 2 A. B. R. 223, 94 Fed. 796 (D. C. Vt.): "The bankrupt was impliedly bound to save him harmless from this part of that debt, and has not

56. See in re Wiseman & Wallace, 10 A. B. R. 545, 123 Fed. 185 (D. C. Pa., reversed sub nom. Hibbard v. Bailey, 12 A. B. R. 104, 129 Fed. 575, C. C. A. Pa.).

57. Hawk v. Hawk, 1 A. B. R. 563, 102 Fed. 679 (D. C. Ark.).

58. As to staying discharge and refusal to stay creditors' actions, in order to permit creditors to perfect rights against sureties, see post, §§ 1524, 1914, 2446, 2712.

done so; but the detriment has occurred since the filing of the petition; and till that occurrence Hartshorn had no provable claim on that account. By this Bankruptcy Act all claims turn upon their status at the time of the filing of the petition; and decisions upon statutes having different provisions in this respect will not afford safe guides for the construction of this. It affords relief for a surety when the creditor does not prove the claim by allowing the surety to prove it for subrogation, but nothing more. The relief is the same that the surety would have if the creditor should prove the claim, and get what could be had upon it, voluntarily. The creditor has no right to anything more than payment; and the surety who has borne the burden is entitled to the benefit. These rights arise, not from the original contract of suretyship, but from the equities of the subsequent transactions. Miller v. Sawyer, 30 Vt. 412. Subrogation of the surety to the rights of the creditor does not enlarge them. They extend only to such dividends as the creditor can have. Here Hartshorn should pay the balance due between him and the bankrupt to the trustee, now, for administration; and the trustee should pay the dividends on the bankrupt's half of the note, when declared, to Hartshorn."

In settling the question of contribution between cosureties, those who are insolvent or without the jurisdiction will be excluded from the computation.[59]

§ 650. Bankrupt's Guaranty of Dividends Not Yet Declared nor Due.

—The bankrupt's guaranty of dividends to the holder of stock is not a provable claim as to dividends not falling due until after bankruptcy.[60]

§ 651. Bond for Annuity, Annuitant Still Living.

—A bond to secure the payment of an annuity, the annuitant still living, has been held to be a provable debt; that it is a liability fixed and absolutely owing although the extent of the future damages is not yet fully suffered. The court avoids the obviously contingent nature of the claim by saying that damages are ascertainable by computation on the basis of the tables of mortality.

Cobb v. Overman, 6 A. B. R. 324, 109 Fed. 65 (C. C. A. N. Car.): "It is hard to see what sum was evidenced by the bond as absolutely owing except the penalty itself. The claim would seem provable more easily under Clause 4." This case is criticized in In re Pettingill & Co., 14 A. B. R. 733, 137 Fed. 143 (D. C. Mass.).

Thus, a husband's liability on a contract to support a divorced wife as long as she lives is a provable debt, the contingency being sure to occur and the expectancy being a subject of calculation.

Obiter, Dunbar v. Dunbar, 10 A. B. R. 139, 190 U. S. 340: "A simple annuity which is to terminate upon the death of a particular person may be valued by reference to the mortality tables."

A contract to support her until she remarries, however, is not a liability provable in bankruptcy, for the contingency may never happen or may hap-

---

59. Gaddy v. Witt, 27 A. B. R. 457 (Tex. Cir. App.).

60. In re Pettingill & Co., 14 A. B. R. 728, 137 Fed. 143 (D. C. Mass.).

pen to-morrow and there is no basis of experience, as in cases of annuities for life.[61]

Dunbar *v.* Dunbar, 10 A. B. R. 139, 190 U. S. 340: "* * * if the contract had come within the category of annuities and debts payable in future, which are

61. Annuity to wife contingent on not remarrying is a provable claim under the English Act. Dunbar *v.* Dunbar, 10 A. B. R. 139, 190 U. S. 340: "It is true that this has been done in England under the English Bankruptcy Act of 1869. In Ex parte Blakemore (1877), 5 Chan. Div. 372, 22 Eng. Rep. 139, it was held, by the court of appeal, that the value of the contingency of a widow's marrying again was capable of being fairly estimated, and that proof must be admitted for the value of the future payments as ascertained by an actuary. That decision was made under the thirty-first section of the Bankruptcy Act of 1869. James, Lord Justice, said:

"'No doubt it is uncertain whether the appellant will marry again, just as the duration of any particular life is uncertain. But, though the duration of any particular life is uncertain, the expectation of life at a given age is reduced to a certainty when we have regard to a million of lives. The value of the expectation of life is arrived at by an average deduced from practical experience.'

"Although the English Statute makes it necessary to arrive at a conclusion upon this point, yet there is no 'practical experience' as to the chances of continuance of widowhood, such as may be referred to where the probable continuance of life is involved. In the latter case we have the experience tables in regard to millions of lives, and under such circumstances there is, as Lord Justice James said, almost a certainty as to the valuation to be put on such a contingency. But under the English Statute, the thirty-first section makes every kind of debt or liability provable in bankruptcy except demands in the nature of unliquidated damages arising otherwise than by reason of a contract or promise, so long as the value of the liability is 'capable of being ascertained by fixed rules, or assessable only by a jury, or as matter of opinion.' So under the Act, in Ex parte Neal, 14 Chan. Div. 579, there was a separation deed between husband and wife, and the husband was to pay an annuity to the wife, which was terminable 'in case the

wife should not lead a chaste life; in case the husband and wife should resume cohabitation; and in case the marriage should be dissolved in respect of anything done, committed or suffered by' the other party, after the date of the deed. The annuity was also to be proportionately diminished in the event of the wife's becoming entitled to any income independent of the husband, exceeding a certain amount a year. After the execution of the deed the husband went through bankruptcy, and it was held that the value of the annuity was capable of being fairly estimated, and was provable in the liquidation. In that case, speaking of the thirty-first section of the Act of 1869, it was stated that 'words more large and general it is impossible to conceive; they cover every species of contingency.' It was also stated that it was 'difficult to see how any case could arise which would not come within' the language of this act. Bramwell, Lord Justice, said: 'But for the present Bankruptcy Act our decision must have been the same as that in Mudge *v.* Rowan' (1868), 3 Ex. 85; but he said that the present Bankruptcy Act was very different in its terms from the act which was in force when that case was decided.

"In the case of Mudge *v.* Rowan, supra, there was a deed of separation between husband and wife, in which the husband covenanted to pay an annuity to his wife by quarterly installments, the annuity to cease in the event of future cohabitation by mutual consent. It was held that this was not an annuity provable under the Bankruptcy Act of 1849, 12th and 13th Vic., ch. 106, § 175; nor a liability to pay money under the 24th and 25th Vic., ch. 134, § 154.

"The 175th section of the Act of 1849 expressly provided that the creditor might prove for the value of any annuity, which value the court was to ascertain. Kelly, Chief Baron, said:

"'The annuity seems to me to be so uncertain in its nature as to be impossible to be valued. In many cases the commissioner of bankruptcy may have to deal with contingencies the value of which depends upon a variety of circumstances, and where the valuation is very difficult. But here I am

absolute and existing claims, that the value of the wife's probability of survivorship after death of her husband might have been calculated on the principles of life annuities.

"But how can any calculation be made in regard to the continuance of widow-

at a loss to see any single circumstance upon which a calculation of any kind could be based.'

"Martin, Baron, said:

" 'This contingency depends upon an infinite variety of circumstances, into which it is idle to suppose a commissioner could inquire.'

"Channell, Baron, concurring, said: " 'The tendency of recent legislation, and the course of recent decisions, has been to free a debtor who becomes a bankrupt, from all liability of every kind; but I do not think an order of discharge a bar to such a claim as the present. * * * I quite admit that, to bring annuity within the Act of 1849, it is not necessary to have any actual pecuniary consideration. I also feel that in many cases the difficulty of calculating the present value of contingencies may be very great, and yet they may be within the acts. But here it appears to me that the difficulty is insuperable.'

"In Parker v. Ince (1859), 4 Hurl & Norm. 52, there was a bond conditioned to pay an annuity during the life of the obligor's wife, provided that if the obligor and his wife should at any time thereafter cohabit as man and wife the annuity should cease, and it was held that the annual sum thus covenanted to be paid by the defendant was not an annuity within the 175th section of the Bankruptcy Law or Consolidation Act of 1849, nor a debt payable upon a contingency within the 175th section, nor a liability to pay money upon a contingency within the 178th section, and consequently the discharge in bankruptcy was no bar to an action for recovery of a quarterly payment due on the bond.

"Martin, Baron, said:

" 'That cannot be such an annuity as would fall within the one hundred and seventy-fifth section, because a value can not be put upon it. How is it possible to calculate the probability of a man and his wife who are separated living together again? Their doing so depends upon their character, temper and disposition, and it may be a variety of other circumstances. Then is it money payable upon a contingency within the one hundred and seventy-eighth section? I think it is not.'

"It is only, therefore, by reason of the extraordinary broad language contained in the 31st section of the English Bankruptcy Act of 1869 that the English courts have endeavored to make a fair estimate of the value of a contract based on the continuance of widowhood, even though the value was not capable of being ascertained by fixed rules, nor assessable by a jury, but was simply to be estimated by the opinion of the court or of some one intrusted with the duty.

"In the Blakemore case, 5 Cha. Div. 372, 22 Eng. Rep. 139, after the announcement of the judgment, the report states that it was then arranged that it should be referred to an actuary to ascertain the annuity as a simple life annuity, and to deduct from that value such a sum as he should estimate to be the proper deduction for the contingency of widowhood. In other words, it was left to the actuary to guess the proper amount to be deducted."

As to claims for installments of rent to accrue in the future, which involve somewhat the subject of contingency, see, next succeeding, Division "4."

Other Instances of Contingency and Not Contingency.—Subcontractor not to be paid by head contractor until owner pays contractor for same work and materials.

In re Ellis, 16 A. B. R. 225 (C. C. A. Ohio): "The contract governs, and under its terms he agrees to pay only for the labor and material for which he is paid. He assents to become the medium of payment to the subcontractor, but he assumes no independent liability. His obligation, his debt, is altogether dependent upon the payment to him by the owners."

Liability of directors and officers for misappropriation of corporate funds held to be contractual and provable. In re Brown, 21 A. B. R. 123, 164 Fed. 673 (C. C. A. Calif.).

Stockholder's liability for corporate debts also provable. In re Walker, 21 A. B. R. 132, 164 Fed. 680 (C. C. A. Calif.).

Future taxes and insurance covenanted to be paid as part of rent by tenant, not matured by provision maturing future installments of rent upon default in present installment. In re Pittsburg Drug Co., 20 A. B. R. 227, 164 Fed. 482 (D. C. Pa.).

hood when there are no tables and no statistics by which to calculate such contingency? How can a valuation of a probable continuance of widowhood be made? Who can say what the probability of remarrying is in regard to any particular widow? We know that some of the factors might be in the question; inclination, age, health, property, attractiveness, children. These would at least enter into the question as to the probability of continuance of widowhood, and yet there are no statistics which can be gathered which would tend in the slightest degree to aid in the solving of the question.

"In many cases where actions are brought for the violation of contracts, such as Pierce v. Tennessee Coal, etc., R. Co., 173 U. S. 1; Rochm v. Horst, 178 Id. 1, and Achell v. Plumb, 55 N. Y. 592, it is necessary to come to some conclusion in regard to the damages which the party has sustained by reason of the breach of the contract, and in such cases resort may be had to the tables of mortality and to other means of ascertaining as near as possible what the present damages are for a failure to perform in the future, but we think the rules in those cases are not applicable to cases like this under the Bankruptcy Act.

"Taking the liability as presented by the contract, if the mortality tables were referred to for the purpose of ascertaining the value so far as it depended upon life, the answer would be no answer to the other contingency of the continuance of widowhood; and if having found the value as depending upon the mortality tables you desire to deduct from that the valuation of the other contingency, it is pure guesswork to do it."

DIVISION 4.

CLAIMS FOR RENT.

§ 652. Provability of Rent Involved in Provability of Contingent Claims.—The subject of the provability of claims for rent is somewhat involved in the subjects of the provability of contingent claims and of claims not owing at the time of the filing of the bankruptcy petition; but it is better treated separately as an entirety.[62]

There has been an apparent divergency of opinion among the decisions on the subject, arising chiefly as to the provability of claims for future installments of rent.

§ 653. Does Bankruptcy Sever Relation of Landlord and Tenant?—The question whether or not installments of rent accruing in the future are provable debts in bankruptcy, hinges a good deal (although not wholly, Atkins v. Wilcox, 5 A. B. R. 319, 105 Fed. 595) upon the further question, whether or not the bankruptcy of the tenant operates to sever the relation of landlord and tenant—itself a branch of the subject previously considered, "The Effect of the Adjudication upon the Rights of the Parties."[63]

---

62. Compare discussions post as to Rent, Leaseholds, etc., and Unliquidated Claims and ante, Contingent Claims. In re Ells, 3 A. B. R. 594, 98 Fed. 967 (D. C. Mass.); In re Arnstein, 4 A. B. R. 246, 101 Fed. 706 (Ref. N. Y.); In re Collignon, 4 A. B. R. 250 (Ref. N. Y.); Watson v. Merrill, 14 A. B. R. 453, 136 Fed. 359 (C. C. A. Kan.); In re Pettingill & Co., 14 A. B. R. 332, 137 Fed. 143 (D. C. Mass.); impliedly, In re Roth & Appel, 24 A. B. R. 588, 181 Fed. 667 (C. C. A. N. Y., affirming 22 A. B. R. 504, 174 Fed. 64).

63. See interesting article in 39 Am. Law Reg. (N. S.) 656 on the subject, "Does the Relation of Landlord and

That it is severed, see [64]

In re Jefferson, 2 A. B. R. 213, 93 Fed. 951 (D. C. Ky., rejected in In re Ells, 3 A. B. R. 566, 98 Fed. 967, D. C. Mass.): "And yet the court sees no way to avoid the conclusion that the relation of landlord and tenant in all such cases ceases, and must, of necessity, cease, when the adjudication is made. If the relation does cease, the landlord afterwards has no tenant and the tenant has no landlord. At the time of the adjudication the bankrupt is clearly absolved from all contractual relations with, and from all personal obligations to, the landlord growing out of the lease, subject to the remote possibility that his discharge may be refused—a chance not worth considering. After the adjudication there is no obligation on the part of the tenant growing out of the lease. He not only owes no subsequent duty, but any attempt on his part to exercise any of the rights of a tenant would make him a trespasser. His relations to the premises and to the contract are thenceforth the same as those of any other stranger. He can not use nor occupy the premises. No obligation upon his part to pay rent can arise when he can neither use nor occupy the property. The one follows the other, and it seems clear that no provable debt, and, indeed, no debt of any sort against the bankrupt, can arise for future rent. No rent can accrue after the adjudication in such a way as to make it the debt of the bankrupt, and future rent had not, in any just sense, accrued before the adjudication. This result grows unavoidably out of the peculiar relations of landlord and tenant, and the peculiar contract between them, by which rent accrued monthly as the occupation and use of the property progressed."

In re Hays, 9 A. B. R. 144, 117 Fed. 879 (D. C. Ky.): "Under these circumstances there is no 'fixed liability' for a demand 'absolutely owing' to the landlord at the time of the adjudication, except for the rent which had accrued or been earned up to that date; and certainly, in the nature of the case, no such debt can accrue against the bankrupt after the adjudication, and, if not, it cannot be proved against his estate as one of his debts. Section 63. There is no just reason why the bankrupt's estate should bear any such burden. The landlord cannot have every advantage while other creditors are probably losing most of their demands. Other creditors irremediably lose their debts. The landlord losses only his tenant, and may recoup that loss by reletting the premises.

"The trustee succeeds to the legal title in the assets and property of the bankrupt, but does not succeed to the duty of performing any of his obligations. They are discharged by the proceeding in bankruptcy, leaving no one bound to perform them further than the distribution of the assets under the orders of the referee will do it. A leasehold or term bought and paid for in advance would be an asset, but a mere right to use real estate upon the condition of paying full current rent for it, if property or an asset at all (unless in cases too rare to

Tenant Become Severed by the Operation of the Bankrupt Law?" Also, see note to In re Jefferson, 2 A. B. R. 208 (D. C. Ky.); compare, Atkins v. Wilcox, 5 A. B. R. 317, 105 Fed. 598 (C. C. A.). Ante, § 451. Compare, In re Inman & Co., 22 A. B. R. 524, 171 Fed. 185 (D. C. Ga.), quoted at § 686. Compare, In re Rubel, 21 A. B. R. 566, 166 Fed. 131 (D. C. Wis.), quoted at § 656.

64. In re Hinckel Brew. Co., 10 A. B. R. 484, 123 Fed. 942 (D. C. N. Y.); Bray v. Cobb, 3 A. B. R. 788, 100 Fed. 270 (D. C. N. Car., reversed in Cobb v. Overman, 6 A. B. R. 324, 109 Fed. 65, C. C. A.; Cobb v. Overman itself criticised in In re Pettingill & Co., 14 A. B. R. 733, 137 Fed. 143, D. C. Mass.); compare, under law of 1867, Bailey v. Loeb, 11 N. B. R. 271, Fed. Cases 739, 2 Fed. Cas. 376; In re Webb, 29 Fed. Cases 494; In re Breck, 4 Fed. Cases 43.

change the result), is so in a sense so attenuated as not to be worth considering in practical affairs, and so unimportant as not to affect the common sense rule followed in the Jefferson case.

"As pointed out in the opinion in the Jefferson case, rent and use or occupation, or the right or opportunity to occupy, are dependent and correlative terms. Rent cannot accrue without a tenant. The bankrupt himself manifestly ceases to be such at the adjudication, and the trustee is not authorized by law to become such in his stead. * * * The Bankruptcy Act, however, dissolves and discharges the liability of a tenant to his landlord, as well as every other, and makes it legally impossible for him, after the adjudication, to continue the liability to pay rent, unless there is a new contract."

However, all the cases holding that the tenant's bankruptcy severs the relation of landlord and tenant, further hold (where the question is adverted to) that the landlord's bankruptcy does not so operate.

Obiter, In re Hays, 9 A. B. R. 144, 117 Fed. 879 (D. C. Ky.): "To avoid any misconception, it may be advisable to add that it is entirely possible that different reasons would require a different result in case a landlord should become bankrupt. In that case, where the legal title to the real estate would devolve upon the trustee in bankruptcy, and who would then be the substituted but temporary landlord by operation of law, the land itself might be regarded as performing such duties to the tenant as his needs required. He would doubtless have rights to the use of the land, which could not and need not be taken from him because of a mere change of ownership of the naked legal title to the premises. Change of ownership of real estate never affects the rights of the tenant. It is a matter with which, in normal cases, he has no concern. The act clearly authorizes the trustee to sell the remainder interest of the bankrupt in the land. But this does not require the destruction of the tenant's rights therein. His interest in the premises depends upon his obligation and ability to pay rent for the use. So long as this obligation and ability continue, his rights continue. When they cease, his rights end. With his bankruptcy both obligation and ability to pay rent terminate. But when the landlord becomes bankrupt the land still remains to serve all the purposes of the tenant. It may be sold quite as well with as without a paying tenant, though, if there be a tenant in possession, he thereafter becomes the tenant of the purchaser. In short, when the tenant is adjudged bankrupt the landlord no longer has one, inasmuch as § 47 does not authorize the trustee to become such, and the relations of the landlord with the tenant cease by virtue of the adjudication; but when a landlord is adjudged bankrupt the tenant by operation of law still has a landlord in the trustee, who, under § 70, holds the legal title to the premises, and in such case the relation of landlord and tenant may continue. This may clearly mark the distinction between the two cases. In one there is both a landlord and a tenant, each capable of performing his respective duties, while in the other there is not. Upon these considerations it may be that, the reason for the rule stated in the Jefferson case ceasing, the rule would not apply to the case of a bankrupt landlord. The question does not, of course, arise in this case, but I am glad of the opportunity of pointing out what may be a marked difference."

But the better and more logical rule is that *the bankruptcy of the tenant, even, does not sever the relation of landlord and tenant,* and that the tenant and his surety remain liable, and that the rent obligation is not discharged as to future rent, unless the trustee elects to retain the lease as an asset.[65]

Watson *v.* Merrill, 14 A. B. R. 458, 136 Fed. 359 (C. C. A. Kas.): "An adjudication in bankruptcy does not dissolve or terminate the contractual relations of the bankrupt, notwithstanding the decisions to the contrary in In re Jefferson (D. C.), 2 A. B. R. 206, 93 Fed. 448; Bray *v.* Cobb (D. C.), 3 A. B. R. 788, 100 Fed. 270; and In re Hays, Foster & Ward Co. (D. C.), 9 A. B. R. 144, 117 Fed. 879. Its effect is to transfer to the trustee all the property of the bankrupt except his executory contracts, and to vest in the trustee the option to assume or to renounce these. It is the assignment of the property of the bankrupt to the trustee by operation of law. It neither releases nor absolves the debtor from any of his contracts or obligations, but, like any other assignment of property by an obligor, leaves him bound by his agreements, and subject to the liabilities he has incurred. It is the discharge of the bankrupt alone, not his adjudication, that releases him from liability for provable debts in consideration of his surrender of his property, and its distribution among the creditors who hold them. Even the discharge fails to relieve him from claims against him that are not provable in bankruptcy, and, since his obligation to pay rents which are to accrue after the filing of the petition in bankruptcy, may not be the basis of a provable claim, his liability for them is neither released nor affected by his adjudication in bankruptcy, or by his discharge from his provable debts. One agrees to pay monthly rents for the place of residence of his family or for his place of business, or to render personal services for monthly compensation for a term of years; he agrees to purchase or to convey property; and he then becomes insolvent and is adjudicated a bankrupt. His obligations and liabilities are neither terminated nor released by the adjudication. He still remains legally bound to pay the rents, to render the services, and to fulfill all his other obligations, notwithstanding the fact that his insolvency may render him unable immediately to do so. Nor are those who contracted with him absolved from their obligations. If he or his trustee pays the stipulated rents for his place of residence or for his place of business, the lessors may not deny to the payor the use of the premises according to the terms of the lease. If he renders the personal services, he who contracted to pay for them may not deny his liability to discharge this obligation. His trustee does not become liable for his debts, but he does acquire the right to accept and assume or to renounce the executory agreements of the bankrupt, as he may deem most advantageous to the estate he is administering, and the parties to those contracts which he assumes are still liable to perform them. And so throughout the entire field of contractual obliga-

---

65. Also, In re Curtis, 9 A. B. R. 286, 109 Fed. 171 (Sup. Ct. La.); Witthaus *v.* Zimmerman, 11 A. B. R. 314, 91 App. Div. 202 (Sup. Ct. N. Y.); obiter, In re Adams, 12 A. B. R. 368, 130 Fed. 788 (D. C. Mass.); In re Ells, 3 A. B. R. 564, 98 Fed. 967 (D. C. Mass., distinguished in Atkins *v.* Wilcox, 5 A. B. R. 319, 105 Fed. 595, C. C. A.); In re Roth & Appel, 22 A. B. R. 504, 174 Fed. 64 (D. C. N. Y.), quoted post, § 653; Shapiro *v.* Thompson, 24 A. B. R. 91 (Ala.); In re Koester, 17 A. B. R. 391 (Ref. Ohio). Compare discussion, In re Pettingill & Co., 14 A. B. R. 728, 137 Fed. 143 (D. C. Mass.); compare, analogously, In re Brew. Co., 16 A. B. R. 110, 143

Fed. 579 (D. C. Mass.).

Compare, under law of 1867, Ex parte Houghton, Fed. Cases 6,725: "The earlier law of England, which we have adopted in this country, was that the assignees of a bankrupt have reasonable time to elect whether they will assume a lease which they find in his possession; and, if they do not take it, the bankrupt retains the term on precisely the same footing as before, with the right to occupy, and the obligation to pay rent. If they do take it, he is released, as in all other cases of valid assignment, from all liability, excepting on his covenants; and from these he is not discharged in any event."

tions the adjudication in bankruptcy absolves from no agreement, terminates no contract, and discharges no liability."

In re Pennewell, 9 A. B. R. 490, 119 Fed. 139 (C. C. A. Mich.): "The adjudication of a tenant as a bankrupt does not ipso facto terminate his lease and put an end to his estate in the leased premises, so as to give a subtenant a claim for damages against the bankrupt's assets." Yet, see the later remark in the court's opinion in this case: "It may be true that if the trustee had elected not to adopt the lease and realized its value to the estate, the lease would have come to an end."

In re Roth & Appel, 24 A. B. R. 588, 181 Fed. 667 (C. C. A. N. Y., affirming 22 A. B. R. 504, 174 Fed. 64): "The authorities are not entirely in accord upon the question whether a lease containing the usual provisions, is terminated by bankruptcy. In some cases it has been held that bankruptcy destroys the relation of landlord and tenant and practically annuls the lease. * * * In other cases it is held that bankruptcy does not sever such relation; that the tenant remains liable, and that the obligation to pay rent is not discharged as to the future unless the trustee elect to retain the lease as an asset. * * * In our opinion the latter view is the correct one. We think the early law as stated in Ex parte Houghton, supra, is the law under the present bankruptcy statute applicable in the case of leases having the usual covenants and conditions. In that case the court said:

" 'The earlier law of England, which we have adopted in this country, was that the assignees of a bankrupt have a reasonable time to elect whether they will assume a lease which they find in his possession; and, if they do not take it, the bankrupt retains the term on precisely the same footing as before, with the right to occupy and the obligation to pay rent. If they do take it he is released, as in all other cases of valid assignment, from all liability, excepting on his covenants; and from these he is not discharged in any event.'

"This reasoning leads by another course to the same conclusion already reached. If the lessee remain liable upon the lease, after his bankruptcy in cases where it is not assumed by the trustee, it necessarily follows that 'his estate is not liable thereon."

Thus, bankruptcy and the bankrupt's subsequent discharge not operating to sever the relation, then the bankrupt remains liable for rent accruing after adjudication, where the trustee rejects the lease.[66]

In re Roth & Appel, 22 A. B. R. 504, 174 Fed. 64 (D. C. N. Y., aff'd, see quotation, supra): "It appears to me plain that this situation as between lessor and lessee is not altered by any bankruptcy on the part of the lessee. Bankruptcy does not terminate the lease. This must be so from the very nature of bankruptcy, which does not destroy but conserve property, and the leasehold estate is property which may (and frequently does) become the property of the trustee and inure to the benefit of creditors. It is impossible to conceive of a trustee in bankruptcy selling a lease if bankruptcy destroy the same lease. If the lease survives adjudication and is rejected by the trustee (i. e., not appropriated as belonging to the estate), it is necessarily an existing and continuing contract—and such contract requires parties thereto. Who are these parties? The landlord is one. The trustee in bankruptcy, not having appropriated the lease, is not the other; therefore that other must be the bankrupt lessee. Such being the case, does the bankrupt's continu-

---

66. Watson v. Merril, 14 A. B. R. 453, 136 Fed. 359 (C. C. A. Kas.); obiter. In re Collignon, 4 A. B. R. 251 (Ref. N. Y.).

ing liability on a lease which has survived adjudication and been abandoned by the trustee—give rise to a provable debt? There are obvious reasons of expediency and equity why such claims should not be provable. A landlord is a species (speaking very loosely) of preferred or secured creditor, in that his rent is presumed to be no more than a fair measure of the value of the use of his land, and that land he can always recover if his rent is not paid. If the trustee pays his rent (as rent) he has appropriated the lease. If no one pays that rent the presumption of law is that the landlord on getting back his land can obtain from other tenants the value of its use. It is therefore inequitable to permit a landlord not only to recover and re-let the demised premises, but to share pari passu with other creditors not so favorably situated. In the second place, the admission of landlords' claims arising and continuing to arise after adjudication and after condition of the lease broken, tends to delay the settlement of estates and should not be encouraged unless the law absolutely requires it."

Bankruptcy does not ipso facto sever all contractual relations. To be sure, adjudication in bankruptcy operates as a date of cleavage between the old estate and the new estate of the debtor. On that date all property of the bankrupt (which was itself in existence at the time of the filing of the petition, or its proceeds) passes to creditors in satisfaction of the claims of creditors (owing at the time of the filing of the petition) ; and the discharge of the bankrupt frees (as of the date of adjudication) all property acquired subsequently to the adjudication from all subsequently incurred indebtedness ; but all this is far different from saying that bankruptcy dissolves all contractual relations, or that the discharge releases the debtor therefrom. Bankruptcy affects property and debts ; it passes title to the property and divides it among the debts. It is not concerned with contractual relations nor obligations but with *"debts, claims and demands"* and "provable" debts, claims and demands at that. Liabilities and obligations that are neither "debts, claims nor demands," or that are not by the statute itself specifically given the attributes of provable debts, claims or demands, are not dissolved nor discharged. Where a contractual relation exists which has not become merged in a right of action provable as a debt, claim or demand in bankruptcy, such contractual relation continues to exist unimpaired. If the contractual relation is such as may be assumed by another, the trustee may assume it, assuming at the same time all the contractual obligations not already merged into "provable" claims. If the contractual relation is not such, or if the trustee refuses to assume it, then the original parties remain bound on it for all future obligations arising therefrom, though *not for any obligations arising therefrom that had already become crystallized or merged into provable debts;* so that, if all obligations arising therefrom are so merged, then the original parties are no longer bound at all.[67]

Now, some contractual relations are, by virtue of the bankruptcy itself, absolutely terminated. The obligations thereon, ipso facto, terminate—are

---

67. In re Brew. Co., 16 A. B. R. 111, 143 Fed. 579 (D. C. Mo.); In re Mahler, 5 A. B. R. 457, 105 Fed. 428 (D. C. Mich.).

merged in the breach of the contract, which becomes thereupon a "provable" claim in bankruptcy. Such contractual relations are, therefore, rightly said to be dissolved by the bankruptcy, but it is so not because they are contractual relations but because they have become completely and absolutely absorbed and merged in a right of action for breach of contract.[68]

Other contractual relations there are of a continuing and recurrent nature, giving rise, not to one single obligation, but to recurring obligations arising from time to time. Of such nature is the relation of landlord and tenant. It is a contract, or rather a relation, with intermitted or recurrent obligations. It is a series of obligations connected by a contract. The particular obligation may or may not be broken as it comes and thus may or may not be a provable debt; but the contract itself—unless by its terms bankruptcy is a breach of it as an entirety—still subsists, unmerged.

Historically, also, this theory of the nature of the relation of landlord and tenant, is borne out. The tenant's rights were not themselves a debt but a mere relation, giving rise at regular and stated intervals to separate and distinct obligations—knight service, rent service, etc., etc.—whose respective breaches, as the defaults occurred, would occasion separate debts to arise.[69]

Bosler v. Kuhn (Act of 1841), 8 Watts & S. 183: "A rent service is not a debt, and a covenant to pay it is not a covenant to pay a debt. It is a security for the performance of a collateral act. The annual payments spring into existence, and for the first time become debts, when they are demandable; for, while they are growing due, the landlord has no property in anything distinct from the corpus of the rent or the realty of which they are the product; and the fruit must be severed from the tree which bears it before it can become personal property and a chose in action. A debt is an entire thing although it be payable by installments; and to admit it to be proved when thus constituted would require the installment to be combined with a penalty, such as formerly was called in aid of an annuitant, or else to be consolidated by the contract. To whatever length the law may go for the purpose of liquidating a contingent demand, it must necessarily stop short when the demand is not only uncertain in itself, but incapable of being reduced to a certainty."

In re Mahler, 5 A. B. R. 457, 105 Fed. 428 (D. C. Mich., affirming 2 N. B. N. & R. 70): "A covenant to pay rent quarterly creates no debt until it becomes due. * * * It is not an unliquidated claim, capable of valuation, which may be proved and allowed after its amount has been ascertained."

In re Arnstein, 4 A. B. R. 247, 101 Fed. 706 (Ref. N. Y.): "A contract of lease is peculiar in its nature, and differs in many respects from other contracts. Rent, as such, is an incident to, and grows out of, the use and occupancy, and is the consideration therefor. Unaccrued rent cannot be said, therefore, to be a fixed liability then absolutely owing, payable in the future, or, indeed a 'debt' of any kind, as that word seems to be used in the act. It is only an unmatured obli-

---

68. In re Pettingill & Co., 14 A. B. R. 733, 137 Fed. 143 (D. C. Mass.).
69. In re Mahler, 2 N. B. N. & R. 70 (Ref. Mich., affirmed in 5 A. B. R. 453). Compare, to same effect, the following decisions under the law of 1867: Ex parte Houghton, Fed. Cas. 6,725; In re Dreck, 12 N. B. Reg. 215, Fed. Cas. 1,822; Bailey v. Loeb, 11 N. B. Reg. 271, Fed. Cas. 739; In re May, 9 N. B. Reg. 419, Fed. Cas. 9,325.

gation to pay in the future a consideration for future enjoyment and occupancy. This cannot be said to be, properly speaking, a present debt, demand or claim at all, as these words are apparently used in the foregoing provisions, due regard being had to the context, and cannot come within either the clause as to fixed liability then owing or a debt founded on contract. The authorities, both under the earlier act in 1841, and the last act, and the present one, seem unanimous to this effect. Ex parte Houghton, 1 Low. 554, Fed. Cas. No. 6,725; In re Breck, 12 N. B. R. 215, Fed. Cas. 1,822; Bailey *v.* Loeb, 11 A. B. R. 271, Fed. Cas. No. 739; In re May, 9 N. B. R. 419, Fed. Cas. No. 9,325. The above are under the late act."

In re Roth & Appel, 24 A. B. R. 588, 181 Fed. 667 (C. C. A. N. Y.): "Rent is a sum stipulated to be paid for the use and enjoyment of land. The occupation of the land is the consideration for the rent. If the right to occupy terminate, the obligation to pay ceases. Consequently, a covenant to pay rent creates no debt until the time stipulated for the payment arrives. The lessee may be evicted by title paramount or by acts of the lessor. The destruction or disrepair of the premises may, according to certain statutory provisions, justify the lessee in abandoning them. The lessee may quit the premises with the lessor's consent. The lessee may assign his term with the approval of the lessor so as to relieve himself from further obligation upon the lease. In all these cases the lessee is discharged from his covenant to pay rent. The time for payment never arrives. The rent never becomes due. It is not a case of *debitum in præsenti solvendum in futoro.* On the contrary, the obligation upon the rent covenant is altogether contingent."

§ 654. Rent Accrued Up to Date of Filing Bankruptcy Petition, Provable.

—Rent accrued up to the date of the filing of a petition in bankruptcy is provable, like any other debt.[70]

The date of the filing of the petition determines the status of the claim.[70a]

In re Roth & Appel, 24 A. B. R. 588, 181 Fed. 667 (C. C. A. N. Y., affirming S. C., 22 A. B. R. 504, 174 Fed. 64): "The inquiry then is as to the status of the lessor's demand upon this indemnity covenant at the time when the petition in bankruptcy was filed, for it is held that that is the time when the provability of claims against the estate of a bankrupt is fixed."

But the claim must, of course, be a bona fide one for rent; thus the landlord cannot be allowed, as rent, a sum for which a mechanic's lien has been filed against the premises, for repairs made by the tenant under a covenant to repair.[71] And a covenant requiring the tenant to pay water and gas rentals, and giving the landlord the right to distrain therefor if he pays them, does not authorize the allowance of such items as rent, especially where the landlord has not paid them.[72]

§ 655. Rent Due and Payable before Such Filing but for Occupancy to Occur Afterwards, Provable.

—Rent due and payable before

70. In re Arnstein, 4 A. B. R. 246, 101 Fed. 706 (D. C. N. Y.); In re Roth & Appel, 22 A. B. R. 504, 174 Fed. 64 (D. C. N. Y.), quoted at § 653; Impliedly, Slocum *v.* Soliday, 25 A. B. R. 460, 183 Fed. 410 (C. C. A. Mass.).

Fraudulent transferee's claim for rent. In re Hurst, 23 A. B. R. 554 (Ref. W. Va).

70a. See ante, § 629.

71. In re O'Malley & Glynn, 27 A. B. R. 143, 191 Fed. 999 (D. C. Pa.).

72. In re Family Laundry Co., 27 A. B. R. 517, 193 Fed. 297 (D. C. Pa.).

the filing of the petition but for occupancy to occur in the future, is also a provable debt.[73]

Wilson v. Penna. Trust Co., 8 A. B. R. 169, 114 Fed. 742 (C. C. A. Pa.): "The rent for the entire residue of the term would be provable as an unpreferred debt, entitled only to a pro rata dividend and the unexpired portion of the term would become an asset of the bankrupt's estate, to be disposed of by the trustee in bankruptcy for the benefit of the estate."

§ 656. Installments Accruing after Adjudication, for Occupancy Thereafter, Not Provable.

—Rent accruing after adjudication of bankruptcy and not due before adjudication, is not provable against the estate,[74] except so far, of course, as it may constitute part of the expense of administration.

In re Rubel, 21 A. B. R. 566, 166 Fed. 131 (D. C. Wis.): "The text books and the authorities all seem to concur in the proposition that rent upon such a lease [three years leave at annual rental payable monthly, having one year more to run] which has not accrued at the time of adjudication cannot be proven as a claim in bankruptcy. * * * These authorities are not in accord as to the method of reasoning by which the conclusion is reached. Some of them hold that the adjudication destroys the relation of landlord and tenant, and practically annuls the lease. Others hold that the claim, not being provable in bankruptcy, is not affected by the discharge; that the bankrupt remains bound by his covenant, but that the trustee is not bound thereby. It is con-

---

73. In re Mitchell, 8 A. B. R. 327, 110 Fed. 87 (D. C. Del.); obiter, inferentially, English v. Key, 29 Ala. 115.

But the bankruptcy act of 1867 contained a provision not found in the act of 1898: "Where the bankrupt is liable to pay rent or other debt falling due at fixed and stated periods, the creditor may prove for a proportionate part thereof, up to the time of the bankruptcy, as if the same grew from day to day and not at such fixed and stated periods. § 19." See also, Atkins v. Wilcox, 5 A. B. R. 317, 105 Fed. 595 (C. C. A.).

74. In re Hays, 9 A. B. R. 144, 117 Fed. 879 (D. C. Ky.); In re Jefferson, 2 A. B. R. 206, 93 Fed. 948 (D. C. Ky.); Atkins v. Wilcox, 5 A. B. R. 313, 105 Fed. 595 (C. C. A.); In re Hinckel Brewing Co., 10 A. B. R. 484, 123 Fed. 942 (D. C. N. Y.); In re Mahler, 2 N. B. N. & R. 70 (Ref. Mich., affirmed by D. C., 5 A. B. R. 453); In re Curtis, 9 A, B. R. 286, 109 La. Ann. (Sup. Ct. La.); In re Roth & Appel, 22 A. B. R. 504, 174 Fed. 64 (D. C. N. Y.), quoted at § 653; Shapiro v. Thompson, 24 A. B. R. 91 (Ala.). Obiter, In re Adams, 12 A. B. R. 368, 130 Fed. 788 (D. C. Mass.); quære, In re Arnstein, 4 A. B. R. 246, 101 Fed. 706 (Ref. N. Y.); compare, In re Ells, 3 A. B. R. 654, 98 Fed.

967 (D. C. Mass.); Bray v. Cobb, 3 A. B. R. 788, 100 Fed. 270 (reversed, on other grounds, in Cobb v. Overman, 6 A. B. R. 324, 109 Fed. 65 (C. C. A. N. Car.); contra, In re Mitchell, 8 A. B. R. 324, 156 Fed. 87 (D. C. Del.); Colman Co. v. Withoft, 28 A. B. R. 328, 195 Fed. 250 (C. C. A. Cal.); In re Abrams, 29 A. B. R. 590, 200 Fed. 1005 (D. C. Iowa).

Likewise under the law of 1841. Bosler v. Kuhn, 8 Watts & S. 183; Savory v. Stocking. 4 Cush. 607; In re Roth & Appel, 24 A. B. R. 588, 181 Fed. 667 (C. C. A. N. Y.).

Likewise under the law of 1867. In re Webb, 6 N. B. Reg. 302, Fed. Cases 17,315; Bailey v. Loeb, 11 N. B. Reg. 271, Fed. Cas. 739; Ex parte Houghton. Fed. Cas. 6,725; In re Breck, 12 N. B. Reg. 215, Fed. Cas. 1,822; In re Roth & Appel, 24 A. B. R. 588, 181 Fed. 667 (C. C. A. N. Y.).

Likewise under English Bankruptcy Law: 1 H. B. L. 433, 4 Term Reps. 94; Aurrol v. Mills, 8 East 318; S. P. Cotterell v. Hook, Dog. 97; Marks v. Upton, 7 Term Rep. 305.

Contra, In re Caloris Mfg. Co., 24 A. B. R. 609, 179 Fed. 722 (D. C. Pa., disapproving In re Roth & Appel, supra).

ceded on all hands that the trustee has a reasonable time after his appointment to determine whether he will adopt the lease as an asset of the estate,
and offer the same for sale, or whether he will ignore it entirely. For practical purposes, it makes no difference in the instant case which line of authority is adopted, for either is fatal to a recovery of rent, as such, for the unexpired term."

In re Collignon, 4 A. B. R. 250 (Ref. N. Y.): "In principle and on authority
a rent charge to accrue is not a present debt (Lansing *v.* Prendergast, 9 Johns.
127). Nor is it contingent, like the liability of an endorser on an insolvent's
note not yet due, which is capable of valuation and would probably be admitted
to proof at any time before the winding up of the estate. * * *

"Entirely apart, therefore, from the question of the provability of the rent
to accrue at the time of the first meeting, I hold that this claimant in now proving up a claim which has been 'liquidated' by her reletting the premises, is not
within the intendment of § 63. Her debt is a new debt, due to new acts on her
part, for which she can doubtless hold the lessee, but which should not be recognized here to the detriment of other creditors."

Watson *v.* Merrill, 14 A. B. R. 453, 136 Fed. 359 (C. C. A. Kas.): "Rents
which the bankrupt had agreed to pay at times subsequent to the filing of the
petition in bankruptcy do not constitute a provable claim under the Bankruptcy
Law of 1898, because they are not a 'fixed liability * * * absolutely owing
at the time of the filing of the petition against him,' and because they do not
constitute an existing demand, but both the existence and the amount of the
possible future demand are contingent upon future events, such as default of
lessee, re-entry of lessor, and assumption by trustee, so that they neither form
the basis of an unliquidated nor a liquidated provable claim."

In re Roth & Appel, 24 A. B. R. 588, 181 Fed. 667 (C. C. A. N. Y., affirming
S. C., 22 A. B. R. 504, 174 Fed. 64): "It follows from these principles that rent
accruing after the filing of a petition in bankruptcy against the lessee is not
provable against his bankrupt estate as 'a fixed liability * * * absolutely
owing at the time of the filing of the petition,' within the meaning of § 63 (a)
(1) of the Bankruptcy Act of 1898. It is not a fixed liability, but is contingent
in its nature. It is not absolutely owing at the time of the bankruptcy, but is
a mere possible future demand. Both its existence and amount are contingent
upon uncertain events. * * * Even under the Bankruptcy Acts of 1841 and
1867, which, unlike the present act, expressly permitted the proof of contingent
demands, claims for unaccrued rent were not provable."

And the rule is not different where the claim is wholly liquidated within
the year.[75]

§ 657. Rent Accruing before Adjudication but after Filing of Petition.

—Whether rent accruing before adjudication, but after the petition has been filed, is provable, has been variously decided.[76]

That it may not be proved, see obiter, In re Adams, 12 A. B. R. 368, 130 Fed.
788 (D. C. Mass.): "That a landlord, as an ordinary creditor, can prove against
the bankrupt estate for rent falling due between the filing of the petition and

---

75. Contra, In re Caloris Mfg. Co.,
24 A. B. R. 609, 179 Fed. 722 (D. C.
Pa.).

76. That it may be proved, see In
re Hinckel Brew. Co., 10 A. B. R. 484,

123 Fed. 942 (D. C. N. Y., distinguished In re Adams, 12 A. B. R. 368, 130
Fed. 788, D. C. Mass.); and In re Mahler, 5 A. B. R. 453, 105 Fed. 428 (D. C.
Mich.).

adjudication, I do not believe. The cases cited do not support the proposition, and as adjudication, ipso facto, does not ordinarily terminate a lease, the latter part of the argument is not applicable."

§ 658. Bankruptcy Stipulated to Terminate Lease, Future Rents Not Provable.

—Where the lease contains a condition that the tenant's bankruptcy may terminate the lease, neither future rent nor damages for loss upon such termination, may be proved.[77]

Slocum v. Soliday, 25 A. B. R. 460, 183 Fed. 410 (C. C. A. Mass.): [The lease contained the provision " * * * if the lessee shall petition to be or be declared bankrupt or insolvent, etc., * * * the lessor lawfully may, immediately or at any time thereafter and without demand or notice, enter into and upon the demised premises, etc."] The court said: "It does not clearly appear from the record whether the lessors rest their claim for any rentals subsequent to the filing of the petition in bankruptcy, or the equivalent thereof, on the demand arising out of the ordinary relations of landlord and tenant holding under an unexpired lease, as readjusted by statutes in bankruptcy, or whether they rely on the special provisions of the lease which we have cited. If the former, the rule that rent, as such, arises out of the occupation of the leased premises, or, as in support therefor, the rule that there is no certain liability, because non constat the tenant may not continue to occupy the premises, are too well established to require any discussion by us so far as this case is concerned. If the lessors rely on the peculiar provisions of the lease, it seems to us emphatically demonstrable that no claim arises therefrom provable here. In order that a claim may be proved, it must have existed at or before the filing of the petition in bankruptcy which the adjudication follows. * * * This proposition does not seem to be contested; but the lessors maintain that the status of the parties, out of which their present claim under the peculiar provisions of this lease arises, was fixed simultaneously with the filing of the petition in bankruptcy, if not prior thereto. The provision in the lease contemplates several alternatives. The one relied on by the lessors is '(b).' ['b' provided for payment at time of 'termination,' of difference between rental value and residue of term.] This alternative has relation to the time of 'such termination.' Indeed, the whole of this special provision of the lease has no operation, except from the time when the lessors enter into or upon the premises as provided therein. This entry clearly could not be made in a case in bankruptcy, except on the condition that the lessee had already been petitioned into bankruptcy, or declared bankrupt. To the common apprehension, the entry could not occur, either in fact or in theory of law, until after the petition in bankruptcy, had been filed; and the order of things in the law is the same. Therefore no claim based on the particular provision referred to could have had existence, except in the possible undisclosed or disclosed intention of the lessors, prior to the filing of the petition in bankruptcy or at the time of such filing. Any mere such intention, whether disclosed or undisclosed, would not be of effect to create a claim which the law would regard as provable. Whatever the intention may have been, there was no existing claim which could be proved in bankruptcy, until the lessors had exercised their option to enter, and had actually entered in accordance therewith. Until that time there was simply a

77. In re Shaffer, 10 A. B. R. 633, 124 Fed. 111 (D. C. Mass.). Compare In re Roth & Appel, 24 A. B. R. 593, 181 Fed. 667 (C. C. A. N. Y.), quoted at § 659.

contingency that there might be a claim; but neither under the present statutes in bankruptcy nor under any prior statutes was there anything in such a contingency which was capable of being proved against a bankrupt's estate."

§ 659. Bankruptcy or Default in Payment Maturing Future Installments.

—There are leases which provide that upon the lessee becoming bankrupt or defaulting in the payment of any one installment, all the remaining installments of rent for the unexpired term shall at once become due and payable.[78] Nevertheless such rent for the unexpired term has been held not provable,[79] or at least doubtfully so.[80]

In re Winfield Mfg. Co., 15 A. B. R. 25, 137 Fed. 984 (D. C. Pa.) and 15 A. B. R. 257, 40 Fed. 185 (D. C. Pa.): "'The lease contained the following provision: "The said lessees further agree in case of their insolvency, or the entering of a judgment against them in any court of record, or the filing of a petition by or against them or any of them, in bankruptcy, or insolvency, that the entire rent reserved for the term of this lease shall immediately become due and payable. * * *"' The present claimant accepted a surrender of the premises on May 10th and has since that date been in exclusive possession. He has been paid in full all the rent that was due when the petition in bankruptcy was filed, and has been allowed compensation at the rental rate for the receiver's use and occupation. By accepting the surrender he assented to the position that the lease had been brought to an end by the proceedings in bankruptcy, and I am unable to see, therefore, in what essential respect his situation differs from the situation of the landlord whose claim was rejected in Wilson v. Trust Co. As the court there said, and I may now repeat:

"'The contract was not divisible. If the claimant desired to avail himself of the stipulation as to bankruptcy for the purpose of securing a preference for one year's rent, he was bound to conform to the contract as a whole. But this he declined to do.'"

But compare, obiter, inferentially contra, Atkins v. Wilcox, 5 A. B. R. 316, 105 Fed. 965 (C. C. A.): "The lease does not provide in express terms that the bankruptcy of the lessee would have the effect to mature the notes and render them exigible."

The reasoning by which the conclusion is reached that such maturing

---

78. See Wilson v. Penna. Trust Co., 8 A. B. R. 169, 114 Fed. 742 (C. C. A. Penna.); In re Winfield Mfg. Co., 15 A. B. R. 24, 137 Fed. 984 (D. C. Pa.), and 15 A. B. R. 257, 140 Fed. 185 (D. C. Pa.). Whether condition for forfeiture upon bankruptcy is legal, quære. Wilson v. Penna. Co., 8 A. B. R. 169, 114 Fed. 742 (C. C. A. Penna.). In re Pittsburg Drug Co., 20 A. B. R. 227, 164 Fed. 482 (D. C. Pa.).

But if a lien upon the bankrupt's property is reserved which, under the State law, is good against levying creditors, would it not be good in bankruptcy, the trustee simply taking the leasehold as an asset? Compare, In re Goldstein, 2 A. B. R. 603 (Ref. Pa.); compare impliedly, In re Pittsburg Drug Co., 20 A. B. R. 227, 164 Fed. 482 (D. C. Pa.).

79. Compare, inferentially, In re Shaffer, 10 A. B. R. 633, 124 Fed. 111 (D. C. Mass.); In re Cress-McCormick Co., 25 A. B. R. 464 (Ref. Miss.).

80. Obiter, in Wilson v. Penn. Trust Co., 8 A. B. R. 169, 114 Fed. 742 (C. C. A. Penn.). In the case of Wilson v. Penna. Trust Co. occurs an interesting discussion of the situation in law where the bankrupt's lease provided that on bankruptcy all remaining installments for the term should become due at once; where three months were already in arrears; where the trustee occupied for two months; and a third party for three months; and where the State law gave the landlord a lien on the goods on the premises for one year's rent.

of future installments cannot create provable debts is not always clear; but perhaps at bottom it rests on the duty that the landlord has of reducing the damage as much as possible by procuring a new tenant to take the bankrupt's place, and that so there is no amount that is absolutely owing at the time of the bankruptcy—that other facts may later occur to change the entire amount. It is not that the claim simply is unliquidated, as appears to be the reasoning in the case In re Collignon, 4 A. B. R. 250; for the claim is not simply unliquidated, but furthermore all the facts have not at the time of bankruptcy occurred that will fix the liability, for the landlord may succeed in getting a tenant who will pay the same or even better rent, thus eliminating all damage, and then there would be nothing "absolutely owing" nor "fixed."[81]

In re Shaffer, 10 A. B. R. 633, 124 Fed. 111 (D. C. Mass.): "The liability is contingent, not only upon re-entry by the lessor, but upon loss of rent or other damage occurring."

In re Ells, 3 A. B. R. 564, 98 Fed. 969 (D. C. Mass.): "If the lessor permitted the lease to continue or if the rent subsequently obtained by him equalled or exceeded that provided in the lease, the claim would not arise."

Yet it is obvious that a tenant could make a lease whereby the entire rent for the term would be payable at once in the very beginning. In such event, should the tenant pay the rent in one lump sum and afterwards go into bankruptcy, all there would be to it would be that the leasehold would be an asset of the estate, fully paid for. Suppose he had agreed to pay the entire sum at once at the very beginning, but had failed to do so, and the landlord sought to prove the amount in one lump sum against the bankrupt estate. All there would be to it, then, would be that the leasehold would be an asset of the estate, not fully paid for. It is indeed difficult to see how this situation differs in principle from the case of a lease where all the remaining installments at once become due on default in paying one installment or on bankruptcy. The remainder of the rent is a claim against the estate and the leasehold itself is an asset of the estate.[82]

Wilson v. Penn. Trust Co., 8 A. B. R. 169, 144 Fed. 742 (C. C. A. Penna.): "The rent for the entire residue of the term would be provable as an unpreferred debt, entitled only to a pro rata dividend and the unexpired portion of the term would become an asset of the bankrupt's estate, to be disposed of by the trustee in bankruptcy for the benefit of the estate."

Obiter, In re Roth & Appel, 24 A. B. R. 593, 181 Fed. 667 (C. C. A. N. Y.): "As we have seen, it expressly provides that in case the lessee is declared bankrupt the lease shall terminate and the lessor shall have the right to re-enter. Under such a lease as this the trustee could not adopt the lease against the lessor's objection. The lessor had the right to terminate it and did terminate it by re-entry. And when he terminated it the obligation of the bankrupts as

---

81. In re Roth & Appel, 24 A. B. R. 588, 181 Fed. 667 (C. C. A. N. Y.), quoted at § 641 and later at § 659.

82. In re Keith-Gara Co., 29 A. B. R. 466, 203 Fed. 585 (D. C. Pa.).

lessees terminated. * * * Undoubtedly the parties to a lease may agree that bankruptcy shall terminate it and that upon such termination all future installments of rent shall at once become due and payable. In such a case the installments may be regarded as consolidated by the contract, or perhaps as falling due by way of penalty. Not improbably claims based upon such leases are provable in bankruptcy."

And such remainder of rent might even become entitled to priority under § 64 (b) (5).[83]

§ 660. Even Where Notes Given for Future Rent, Notes Not Provable.

—It has been held even that notes given for future rent are not provable claims against the estate.[84]

Atkins *v.* Wilcox, 5 A. B, R. 313, 105 Fed. 595 (C. C. A.): "In the absence of an express provision that the bankruptcy of the lessee would have the effect to mature the rent notes given and render them exigible, the amount of rent as yet to accrue should not be allowed as against other creditors.".

But are enforceable against the surety and are not discharged by the bankruptcy.

The attitude of the court in the case, In re Curtis, well illustrates the conflict in the rulings. The question there was whether the surety for future rent was released by the tenant's bankruptcy. Upon the original hearing the court held the bankruptcy put an end to the lease as of the date of the adjudication and that therefore no rent could accrue thereafter, and consequently that notes given therefor failed of consideration, and that the surety could avail himself of the failure. Upon rehearing, the court held the bankruptcy did not put an end to the lease, that the claim for rent thereafter accruing was contingent, was not provable against the estate, was not barred by the discharge and that the surety was still liable therefor.

The latter conclusion was correct. Although the claim for the rent was in the form of notes, secured by endorsement, yet the facts in the case undoubtedly were that either the notes were nonnegotiable, or that the contest arose between the original parties and therefore the notes amounted to no more than the covenant in the lease itself to pay rent in installments. Such claim for rent, as already noted, would have been contingent since all the facts had not occurred prior to the bankruptcy that would have fixed the liability. So the claim was not provable against the estate because contingent. The leasehold was not terminated, but the trustee might accept it or reject it: if he accepted it he would be bound by its covenants; if he rejected it then the bankrupt would be bound by

---

83. In re Pittsburg Drug Co., 20 A. B. R. 227, 164 Fed. 482 (D. C. Pa.).

84. In re Hays, 9 A. B. R. 144, 117 Fed. 879 (D. C. Ky.). See In re Curtis, 9 A. B. R. 286 (Sup. Ct. La.); analogously, Watson *v.* Merrill, 14 A. B. R. 453, 136 Fed. 359 (C. C. A. Kas.); In re Stern & Levi, 26 A. B. R. 535, 190 Fed. 70 (D. C. Tex.).

its covenants, precisely as he would by any other contingent claim not provable and hence not dischargeable in bankruptcy.

§ 661. But Provable if Negotiable and in Hands of Innocent Holders, or Taken as Payment.

—Undoubtedly, in case the tenant has given his negotiable notes and these notes are in the hands of bona fide holders, there would be a different result, for they would amount to a payment in full in advance.

§ 662. Sureties for Future Rent Not Released by Principal's Bankruptcy.

—At any rate, sureties for rent to accrue in the future are not released by the bankruptcy of the principal.[85]

Witthaus v. Zimmerman, 11 A. B. R. 314 (Sup. Ct. N. Y. App. Div.): "I am also of the opinion that even though it be held that the lease by the adjudication was so far terminated as to release the tenant from thereafter paying rent, that this did not of itself affect the defendant's guaranty or relieve him from liability thereunder. The act, § 16, provides that: 'The liability of a person who is a codebtor with or guarantor, or in any manner a surety for a bankrupt, shall not be altered by the discharge of such bankrupt.' This language seems to negative the idea that the adjudication had any effect upon the defendant. Not only this, but to hold otherwise would destroy the benefit sought to be accomplished by the guaranty—which was the payment of the rent reserved—if the tenant did not choose to, or by reason of insolvency, could not pay. The plaintiff took no part in the bankruptcy proceeding and I am unable to see upon what principle of law a binding contract can be destroyed by an act of a third party in which a party to the contract did not participate and over whom he had no control."

§ 663. Likewise, Liens for Future Rent Not Released.

—And if liens exist upon the bankrupt's property as security for rent to become due in the future, or for installments of future rent becoming due at once on default, such liens will be unimpaired in bankruptcy, if good against levying creditors under state law.[86]

Thus, where the landlord, both by a contract in writing, and also by force of State statute, has a lien for future rent, such lien is unimpaired in bankruptcy.

Martin v. Orgain, 23 A. B. R. 454, 174 Fed. 772 (C. C. A. Tex.): "This lien is good and valid in cases like the present for rent due and to become due. * * * Under the agreed statement of facts, the appellant has by contract in writing a lien for the amount of rent due and to become due, and she also has such lien by force of the statutes of the State of Texas."

85. Bankr. Act, § 16 (a): "The liability of a person who is a codebtor with, or guarantor or in any manner a surety for, a bankrupt shall not be altered by the discharge of such a bankrupt." In re Curtis, 9 A. B. R. 286 (Sup. Ct. La.).

86. In re Goldstein, 2 A. B. R. 603 (Ref. Penna.); Martin v. Orgain, 23 A. B. R. 454, 174 Fed. 772 (C. C. A. Tex.), quoted at § 663. Compare, Shapiro v. Thompson, 24 A. B. R. 91 (Ala. Sup. Ct.).

§ 664. But Mere Re-Entry Clause Gives No Lien, on Sale of Leasehold.

—But no lien for overdue rent attaches to the proceeds of the trustee's sale of a leasehold belonging to the bankrupt by virtue of a mere re-entry clause.[87]

§ 665. Landlord Forfeiting Lease or Accepting Surrender Waives Claim for Unexpired Term.

—If the landlord accepts the surrender of the leasehold[88] or forfeits the residue of the term upon the bankruptcy, he waives his right to a claim for the rent for the unexpired portion of the term.[89]

Wilson v. Penna. Trust Co., 8 A. B. R. 169, 114 Fed. 742 (C. C. A. Pa.): "Notwithstanding the ruling in Platt v. Johnson, 168 Pa. 47, 31 Atl. 935, 47 Am. St. Rep. 877, upholding as valid a provision in a lease that the entire rent for the balance of the term should become due if the lessee should become embarrassed, or make an assignment for the benefit of creditors, or be sold out by sheriff's sale, it may well be doubted whether the stipulation here making the whole rent for the whole term due and payable if the lessee 'shall become bankrupt' is enforceable as against the provisions of the Bankrupt Act. But the court below did not pass upon that question, and we do not find it necessary to consider it. Assuming the validity of the stipulation where the lessee is adjudged a bankrupt, these consequences would follow its enforcement. In the first place, under the Pennsylvania Act of 1836 the landlord would be entitled to priority of payment out of the proceeds of sale of the tenant's goods upon the demised premises to the extent of one year's rent. Longstreth v. Pennock, 20 Wall. 575, 22 L. Ed. 451. Secondly, the rent for the entire residue of the term would be provable as an unpreferred debt, entitled only to a pro rata dividend, and the unexpired portion of the term would become an asset of the bankrupt's estate, to be disposed of by the trustee in bankruptcy for the benefit of the estate. The latter result, however, this claimant repudiated altogether. He sought a partial and one-sided enforcement of the stipulation. He attempted to secure a preference for one year's rent, and at the same time retain his interest as landlord unimpaired in the residue of the term. He took that position at the start, and held it to the end. His proof was only for a single year's rent as a preferred debt, and then, at the expiration of the year, he took, and has since maintained, exclusive possession of the leased premises. The court held—and we think rightly—that the claimant could not split up the term in that way. The contract was not divisible. If the claimant desired to avail himself of the stipulation as to bankruptcy for the purpose of securing a preference for one year's rent, he was bound to conform to the contract as a whole. But this he declined to do. We are therefore of opinion that the action of the court was right."

And cannot insist on enforcing the provision making all future rent fall

87. In re Ruppel, 3 A. B. R. 233 (D. C. Pa.).

88. Raising rent and making repairs which the tenant is obligated for, is evidence of acceptance of surrender, even where the landlord pretends he is doing so in behalf of the tenant. In re Piano Forte Mfg. Co., 20 A. B. R. 899, 163 Fed. 413 (D. C. Pa.).

89. In re Winfield Mfg. Co., 15 A. B. R. 24, 137 Fed. 984, and 15 A. B. R. 257, 140 Fed. 185 (D. C. Pa.); analogously, In re Shaffer, 10 A. B. R. 633, 124 Fed. 111 (D. C. Mass.); South Side Trust Co. v. Watson, 29 A. B. R. 446, 200 Fed. 50 (C. C. A. Pa.), following Wilson v. Pennsylvania Trust Co., which is quoted in the text; In re Desmond & Co., 28 A. B. R. 456, 198 Fed. 581 (D. C. Ala.).

due upon bankruptcy;[90] nor insist on the restoration of the property to its original condition by the tenant, under a covenant so to do at the end of the term.[91] And a reletting of the premises, even to the trustee in bankruptcy, will be deemed a forfeiting of the term, unless done expressly to mitigate damages.[92] But if he does not accept such surrender yet he may not prove for the balance of the term, under a clause making all future rent due on bankruptcy.[93]

Likewise, damages under a covenant to indemnify for loss of rent cannot be allowed where the landlord has re-entered under a clause permitting re-entry on bankruptcy.[94]

In re Shaffer, 10 A. B. R. 633, 124 Fed. 111 (D. C. Mass.): "The bankrupt was tenant under a lease which provided that upon his bankruptcy the lessor might terminate the lease and re-enter, and 'in case of such termination the lessee shall be liable to the lessor for all losses and damage sustained by the lessor on account of the premises remaining unleased or being left for the remainder of the term for a less rent than that herein reserved.' The lessor has duly re-entered, and seeks to 'prove for damages sustained on account of breach of condition of a lease.' In re Ells (D. C.), 3 Am. B. R. 564, 98 Fed. 967, this court held that the lessor could not prove for a breach of a covenant by the lessee that he would after re-entry indemnify the lessor against all the loss of rents and other payments which might occur by reason of the termination of the lease. In effect the covenant in the case at bar is the same. The liability is contingent, not only upon re-entry by the lessor, but upon loss of rent or other damage occurring. 'If the lessor permitted the lease to continue, or if the rent subsequently obtained by him equalled or exceeded that provided in the lease, the claim would not arise.' 98 Fed. 969. The covenant here is not like that suggested by Judge Lowell in Ex parte Lake, 2 Low. 544, 546, Fed. Cas No. 7,991, 'to pay any loss or damage consequent upon the diminished value of the premises.' The diminished value would be a fact to be proved as of the date of bankruptcy or re-entry. But in the case at bar damages could not be ascertained until the arrival of the term of the lease as originally limited, or until there had been a reletting at a reduced rent."

Likewise, damages, under a covenant to restore the premises to its original condition at the end of the term, cannot be allowed where the landlord has re-entered.[95]

And it has been held that where the purchaser of a bankrupt's stock agreed, as part of his bid, to pay certain taxes and water rates, which were due as rentals on the premises wherein the bankrupt had conducted his business, and did so pay them, the landlord, having accepted the purchaser as his ten-

---

90. Wilson v. Penna. Trust Co., 8 A. B. R. 169, 114 Fed. 742 (C. C. A. Penna.); In re Piano Forte Mfg. Co., 20 A. B. R. 899, 163 Fed. 413 (D. C. Pa.).

91. In re Arnstein, 2 N. B. & R. 106 (Ref. N. Y., affirmed by D. C.).

92. In re Arnstein, 2 N. B. & R. 106 (Ref. N. Y., affirmed by D. C.).

93. In re Winfield Mfg. Co., 15 A. B. R. 25, 137 Fed. 984, and 15 A. B. R. 257, 140 Fed. 185 (D. C. Pa.).

94. To same effect, In re Ells, 3 A. B. R. 564, 98 Fed. 967 (D. C. Mass.).

95. In re Arnstein, 2 N. B. N. & R. 106 (Ref. N. Y.).

ant, cannot maintain a claim against the bankrupt estate for the said taxes and water rates.[96]

§ 666. Bankruptcy of Tenant No Breach of Subtenant's Covenant of Quiet Enjoyment.

—The adjudication of a tenant as a bankrupt does not ipso facto terminate his own lease and put an end to his estate so as to give a subtenant a claim for damages against the bankrupt's assets.[97]

§ 667. Rent for Occupation after Filing of Petition and before Adjudication, Recoverable at Stipulated Rate.

—Rent of premises occupied by the bankrupt or the officer of the court in charge of the estate after the filing of the petition and before adjudication, is recoverable at the rate stipulated for in the lease,[98] or on a quantum valebat.[99]

DIVISION 5.

CLAIMS NOT OWING AT TIME OF FILING BANKRUPTCY PETITION.

§ 668. Subject of Claims "Not Owing" Involves That of Contingent Claims.

—The subject of the provability of claims not owing at the time of the filing of the bankruptcy petition somewhat involves the subject of contingent claims,[1] but is better treated separately, although undoubtedly the same ground thereby will be partially retraversed.

§ 669. Claims Not Owing at Time of Filing Bankruptcy Petition, Not Provable.

—Claims not owing at the time of the filing of the bank-

---

96. Ellis v. Rafferty, 29 A. B. R. 192, 199 Fed. 80 (C. C. A. Pa.).

97. In re Pennewell, 9 A. B. R. 490, 119 Fed. 139 (C. C. A. Mich.).

Subtenant's Eviction Must Occur before Tenant's Bankruptcy, Else No Provable Claim.—Where a subtenant has not been disturbed before the bankruptcy in his quiet enjoyment, his subsequent eviction by the trustee of the tenant does not give him a provable claim against the bankrupt estate. In re Pennewell, 9 A. B. R. 490, 119 Fed. 139 (C. C. A. Mich.).

Subtenant No Damages Where No Right of Forfeiture Reserved Even Where Tenant Stipulated against Subletting.—Where a lease contains a stipulation against subletting without the landlord's consent but no clause of forfeiture therefor a subtenant has no provable claim for his damages for false representations on the tenant's covenant that he had good right to sublease, for there being no clause of forfeiture the subtenant can not be dispossessed by the landlord and the latter has merely a personal action against the tenant for breach of the

stipulation. In re Pennewell, 9 A. B. R. 490, 119 Fed. 139 (C. C. A. Mich.).

98. In re Hinckel Brew. Co., 10 A. B. R. 489, 123 Fed. 942 (D. C. N. Y.). See post, §§ 985, 2034, 2035.

99. In re Adams, etc., Co., 28 A. B. R. 923, 199 Fed. 336 (D. C. Mass.).

1. Impliedly, Phœnix National Bank v. Waterbury, 20 A. B. R. 140, 108 N. Y. Supp. 391, quoted post, § 690.

Instances Held to Be "Fixed Liability Absolutely Owing."—Liability of directors for misappropriation of corporate funds. In re Brown, 21 A. B. R. 123, 164 Fed. 617 (C. C. A. Calif.).

Surety on Redelivery Bond Where Attachment or Other Lien Not Dissolved until Adjudication.—The surety on a redelivery bond given to dissolve an attachment or other lien by legal proceedings nullified, eventually, by the adjudication of bankruptcy, is not a provable debt though the lien be not yet dissolved at the time of the filing of the bankruptcy petition. In re Windt, 24 A. B. R. 536, 177 Fed. 584 (D. C. Conn.), quoted and discussed at § 648½.

ruptcy petition are not provable, whether the claims be on judgments or written instruments, or upon open accounts or contracts express or implied.[3]

Thus, a claim for money loaned the bankrupt, after the filing of the bankruptcy petition though before the adjudication, is not allowable.[4]

§ 670. Judgments and Written Instruments Must Be "Absolutely Owing" to Be "Provable."

—It is specifically provided by the statute as to claims upon judgments and written instruments that such claims must be "absolutely owing" at the time of the filing of the bankruptcy petition.[6]

§ 671. Attorney's Collection Fee Stipulated in Note or Mortgage.

—Claims on stipulations for attorneys' collection fees contained in written instruments are not provable where no attorney is employed to collect or enforce the obligation until after bankruptcy. They are not "absolutely owing" at the time of the filing of the bankruptcy petition.[7]

Nor where they have not matured until after bankruptcy, even though the attorney was employed and performed services before bankruptcy.[8]

Nor are they "absolutely owing at the time of the filing of the bankruptcy petition" even where reduced to judgment before the bankruptcy, if a transcript of the judgment is not filed with the proof, it has been held in one case;[9] although it would hardly seem requisite, on principle, to file such a transcript.[10]

But they are provable where such services are rendered before bankruptcy, if otherwise valid.[11]

---

3. Compare §§ 629, 654, 694½. In re Rome, 19 A. B. R. 820, 162 Fed. 971 (D. C. N. J.); In re Stern & Levi, 26 A. B. R. 535, 190 Fed. 70 (D. C. Tex.). Also In re Roth & Appel, 24 A. B. R. 588, 181 Fed. 667 (C. C. A. N. Y.), quoted at § 694½.

4. In re Rome, 19 A. B. R. 820, 162 Fed. 971 (D. C. N. J.).

6. Bankr. Act, § 63 (a) (1). Instance (leases), Bray v. Cobb, 3 A. B. R. 789, 100 Fed. 270 (D. C. N. Car., reversed, on other grounds, in Cobb v. Overman, 6 A. B. R. 324); instance, annuities, Bray v. Cobb, 3 A. B. R. 789, 100 Fed. 270 (D. C. N. Car., reversed, on other grounds, in Cobb. v. Overman, 6 A. B. R. 324); instance, annuities, Dunbar v. Dunbar, 10 A. B. R. 139, 190 U. S. 340.

7. In re Gebhard, 15 A. B. R. 381, 140 Fed. 571 (D. C. Pa.); In re Garlington, 8 A. B. R. 602, 115 Fed. 999 (D. C. Tex.); In re Keeton, Stell & Co., 11 A. B. R. 367, 126 Fed. 429 (D. C. Tex.); In re Hersey, 22 A. B. R. 863, 177 Fed. 1004 (D. C. Iowa); Mc-

Cabe v. Patton, 23 A. B. R. 335, 174 Fed. 217 (C. C. A. Pa.); In re Jenkins, 27 A. B. R. 860, 192 Fed. 1000 (D. C. S. C.); Mechanic's-A m e r i c a n Nat. Bank v. Coleman, 29 A. B. R. 396, 204 Fed. 24 (C. C. A. Mo.), quoted later at this same section.

8. In re Milling Co., 16 A. B. R. 456 (D. C. Tex.).

9. McCabe v. Patton, 23 A. B. R. 335, 174 Fed. 217 (C. C. A. Pa.).

10. See ante, § 602.

11. Merchants' Bk. v. Thomas, 10 A. B. R. 299, 121 Fed. 306 (C. C. A.); obiter, In re Milling Co., 16 A. B. R. 456 (D. C. Tex.); In re Edens & Co., 18 A. B. R. 643, 151 Fed. 940 (D. C. S. C.). See post, § 796½. But compare, In re Hersey, 22 A. B. R. 863, 171 Fed. 1004 (D. C. Iowa). Matter of Ferreri, 26 A. B. R. 658, 188 Fed. 675 (D. C. La.). Compare analogously, where allowed as part of lien on selling free from liens, In re Holmes Lumber Co., 26 A. B. R. 119, 189 Fed. 178 (D. C. Ala.); compare, In re Torchia, 26 A. B. R. 188, 185 Fed. 576 (D. C. Pa.).

And in some states the attorney's collection fee will not necessarily be allowed at the stipulated rate, especially not at any usurious rate, but will be cut down to what is reasonable.

Bank v. Walker, 20 A. B. R. 840, 163 Fed. 510 (C. C. A. Md.): "It is undoubtedly true that in a number of States it is held legal for creditor and debtor to contract that in case the debtor fail to pay upon maturity that then the creditor may recover, in addition to his debt, interest and costs, a reasonable sum for attorney's fees for collection. And this has been held to be the law in Maryland. Bowie v. Hall, 69 Md. 434, 16 Atl. 64; Gaither v. Tolson, 84 Md. 638, 36 Atl. 449. It is also true that in other States such contracts are held void, and in no State where usury laws are in effect are they permitted to be enforced, if such charges are either unreasonable or made a subterfuge for usurious exactions. A creditor would not, for instance, under the law of Maryland, under such a contract be permitted to exact a commission of $500 for collecting a $100 debt. Nor would it be permitted to collect a commission of $1,400 'for collecting' a debt of $28,000, which the debtor came forward, an hour after it was due, to pay and before any attorney had been employed to collect it, for, as said in Bowie v. Hall, supra, the purpose of such a provision 'is clearly not to put any money above the legal rate of interest into the pocket of the lender, but merely to enable him to get back his money with legal interest, and nothing more.'"

But it has been doubted, in one case, whether any attorney's fees are allowable, in bankruptcy, at all, as part of the allowance of a claim.[12]

The same rules prevail of course as to stipulated fees for the collection of mortgages. Thus, where, under the local law, such fees are "not owing" until suit is brought on the mortgage, they cannot be proved in bankruptcy, even though the mortgagee is obliged to collect his claim in the bankruptcy court, because the very intervention of bankruptcy prevents the right to collection fees from becoming complete.[13]

It has been held that the federal courts are not bound by the local laws, or the construction thereof by the state courts, in matters of this kind.

Mechanics-Amer. Nat. Bank v. Coleman, 29 A. B. R. 386, 204 Fed. 24 (C. C. A. Mo.).

"The position of counsel for appellant is that a clause in a note stipulating for an attorney's fee, provided the note is placed in the hands of an attorney for collection, is valid, enforceable, and conclusive as to amount; that such is the law of the State of Missouri, in which this contract was made, and, therefore, binding upon this court. The proposition, as stated, cannot be accepted in its entirety. The question here presented is one which falls within the domain of general or commercial law. It involves simply the construction and effect of recitals in negotiable instruments, and no question of right under the constitution and statutes of a state. In such matters the decisions of the state court are not controlling in the federal tribunals. 'It is not only the privilege, but the duty of the federal courts, imposed upon them by the constitution and statutes of the United States, to consider for themselves, and to form their independent opinions and decisions upon, questions of commercial or general law presented in cases in which they have jurisdiction, and it is a duty whch they cannot justly

---

12. In re Hersey, 22 A. B. R. 863, 171 Fed. 1004 (D. C. Iowa).

13. In re Weiland, 28 A. B. R. 620, 197 Fed. 116 (D. C. Ga.).

renounce or disregard. Independent School Dist. *v.* Rew, 111 Fed. 1. The doctrine thus announced by this court finds abundant confirmation in the decisions of the Supreme Court of the United States. The 34th section of the Judiciary Act of 1789 (Act Sept. 24, 1789, c. 20, § 34, 1 Stat. 92, U. S. Comp. St. 1901, p. 581), declaring that the laws of the several states shall be regarded as rules of decision in trials at common law in the courts of the United States in cases where they apply, is limited in its application to State laws strictly local. It does not extend to contracts or other instruments of a commercial nature, the true interpretation and effect whereof are to be sought, not in the decisions of the local tribunals, but in the general principles and doctrines of commercial jurisprudence. In such cases it is the right and duty of the national courts to exercise their own judgment."

§ 672. Open Accounts and Contracts Express or Implied Must Be Likewise Owing.

—Although the statute fails expressly so to require, yet the decisions are that claims founded on open accounts or upon contracts, express or implied, must likewise be owing at the time of the filing of the bankruptcy petition, in order to be provable.[14]

In re Swift, 7 A. B. R. 382, 112 Fed. 315 (C. C. A. Mass.), affirming 5 A. B. R. 335: "That part of the present Bankruptcy Act which describes what debts may be proved does not repeat at all points the words 'owing at the time of the filing of the petition,' but it is impossible to consider it other than as though it did thus repeat them. There can be no question that it is sufficient if the debt existed at the point of time of the filing of the petition in bankruptcy."

In re Bingham, 2 A. B. R. 223, 96 Fed. 796 (D. C. Vt.): "By this Bankruptcy Act, all claims turn upon their status at the time of the filing of the petition."

In re Adams, 12 A. B. R. 368, 130 Fed. 788 (D. C. Mass.): "But a creditor cannot prove for an indebtedness arising between the filing of an involuntary petition and the adjudications of his debtor as a bankrupt. This appears from the analogy of § 63 (a) (1) (2) (3) & (5) as applied to the interpretation of clause (4). In clauses (1) and, for example, the limit of time must be the same, inasmuch as the clause (4) includes clause (1) and, if clause (4) were less limited in point of time the limit imposed upon clause (1) would become nugatory. * * * The same result is indicated by the analogy of § 59 (b) (d) & (f)."

Thus, also, attorney's fees rendered after the filing of the bankruptcy petition and before the adjudication, for services not related to the bankruptcy are not provable.

In re Burka, 5 A. B. R. 12, 107 Fed. 674 (D. C. Mo.): "Only such debts are provable as were in existence at the time of filing the petition. The fact that the fourth subdivision contains no words of limitation is considered by claim-

---

14. Obiter, In re Coburn, 11 A. B. R. 212, 126 Fed. 218 (D. C. Mass., affirmed sub nom. Moulton *v.* Coburn, 12 A. B. R. 553); In re Garlington, 8 A. B. R. 602, 115 Fed. 999 (D. C. Tex.); In re Pettingill & Co., 14 A. B. R. 728, 137 Fed. 143 (D. C. Mass.); (1867) In re Patterson, Fed. Cas., No. 10,815; (1867) In re Crawford, Fed. Cas., No. 3,363; In re Ward, 12 Fed. 325 (D. C. Tenn.); (1867); In re Nounnan, 7 N. B. Reg. 15; Zavelo *v.* Reeves, 29 A. B. R. 493, 227 U. S. 625; In re Roth & Appel, 24 A. B. R. 593, 181 Fed. 667 (C. C. A. N. Y.), quoted at § 694½. But compare, contra ("Where liquidated within the year!"), In re Caloris Mfg. Co., 24 A. B. R. 609, 179 Fed. 722 (D. C. Pa.).

ant's counsel a warrant for his contention that his claim, which is founded on an open account, is provable, notwithstanding the fact that it was not in existence when the petition was filed. It is not apparent why this subdivision is inserted without words of limitation as to the time the claim should have accrued. Especially is this so when there seems to have been a studied effort to insert such words in relation to all the other provable claims. But I cannot construe this omission into a general provision for allowance of demands against the estate of a bankrupt, irrespective of the time when they accrued. If such construction be given to the statute, there would be no limitation even to such claims as existed at the date of the adjudication. The general language would cover any claim that might accrue during the pendency of the proceedings, even up to the final discharge. In the absence of express provision to the contrary, I think that debts provable under the act must be such as existed at the date of the filing of the petition. That date is one to which many general provisions are referable. For instance, it is enacted in chapter 1, § 1, subdivision 10, that the words 'date of bankruptcy,' 'time of bankruptcy,' 'commencement of proceedings' or 'bankruptcy,' when used in the act with reference to time, 'shall mean the date when the petition is filed.' Moreover, the conclusion reached is in clear analogy with the general rule of procedure in courts charged with the administration of trust estates. According to my observation and experience, the rights of creditors of insolvent estates administered in equity generally relate to the time of the institution of the proceedings which ultimately result in the sequestration of the property which is to be administered.

"It is argued by claimant's counsel that because the trustee is vested with the title not only to property which the bankrupt had at the time of the filing of the petition against him, but also to such property as he may have acquired after that, and prior to the date of adjudication, and because all such property goes into the funds for creditors, therefore all creditors having claims which originated at any time prior to the actual adjudication should participate in the fund; in other words, that, as the property which the bankrupt acquires after the filing of the petition enhances the fund for the benefit of creditors, all creditors whose rights accrued at any time before actual adjudication should participate in it. This is a plausible argument, and I presume it would be true that, if the property acquired by the bankrupt after the filing of the petition and before the adjudication did vest in the trustee, creditors whose rights accrued between those dates should share in the property of the bankrupt, like other creditors; but the argument, in my opinion, is based on false premises. Section 70 of the Bankruptcy Act, which is relied on by claimant's counsel in support of the argument, contains the following provisions:

"The trustee of the estate of a bankrupt upon his appointment and qualification * * * shall be vested by operation of law with the title of the bankrupt, as of the date he was adjudged a bankrupt, * * * to all * * * (5) property which prior to the filing of the petition, he could, by any means, have transferred * * * !"

"After a careful consideration of the provisions of this section, I am persuaded that there are two separate subjects treated of: First, the time at which the title to something vests in the trustee; second, the 'something' or property the title of which is to vest in the trustee. Inasmuch as the trustee, by the provisions of the act, cannot be chosen or qualified until some time after the date of the filing of the petition, and in fact until some time after the date of adjudication, it is appropriate and fit that some time should be fixed, to which his title to whatever he gets should relate; and such, in my opinion, is the subject-matter of the first part of the section in question. Properly interpreted, the trustee is by operation of law vested with the title as of the date the bankrupt was adjudged to be a bankrupt. The further provisions of the section, already quoted, undertake to point out the property of which by operation of law he is to become the owner, namely, all property which prior to the filing of the petition the bankrupt could have transferred. In other words, the property which the trustee acquires must have been property or rights which so existed prior to the filing of the petition that the bankrupt might have transferred them. This clearly means the property or rights of property which existed at the time. Such being the true interpretation of § 70, it affords no ground for the argument made by the claimant's counsel. Inasmuch as no property which the bankrupt may have acquired after the filing of the petition and before the date of adjudication is taken by the trustee, there is no ground for the argument that the claimant, holding a claim accrued since the filing of the petition, and before adjudication, should participate in the assets. His claim is neither provable, nor is the bankrupt discharged by the final judgment of the court from the obligation to pay such a claim."

Compare, In re Gerson (Moch *v.* Market St. Bk.), 6 A. B. R. 11, 107 Fed. 897 (C. C. A. Penn.): "The first and fourth subdivisions of § 63 are distinct provisions, and are, we think, independent of each other. We are unable to agree to the proposition that subdivision 1 qualifies and is to be carried down and read into subdivision 4." This was in a case where the court held a contract of endorsement is a provable debt although it does not become fixed and absolute until after the filing of the bankruptcy petition.

Compare, In re Smith, 17 A. B. R. 114 (D. C. R. I.): "It is argued that, because subdivision 1 specifies a fixed liability absolutely owing, it excludes all liabilities which were contingent at the time of filing the petition from proof under other subdivisions. The logical fault is obvious. While contingent liabilities are excluded from class 1 (defined by subdivision 1), it does not at all follow that liabilities now or formerly contingent are excluded from other distinct classes. The specification of certain characteristics for class 1, is no indication that cases comprehended in other classes may not have entirely different characteristics. Assuming that, so long as it is uncertain whether a contract or engagement will ever give rise to an actual liability, and that so long as the demand is contingent, it is not provable, it by no means follows that a demand which has ceased to be contingent before proof should be rejected because it had been contingent before the date of filing the petition. While the language, 'Debts of the bankrupt · * * * which are * * * founded upon an open account, or upon a contract express or implied' may not include contingent obligations, it does include obligations no longer contingent, though they were contingent at the date of filing the petition."

Thus, for instance, work done under a building contract after a petition in bankruptcy is filed, is not a provable debt on quantum meruit, but is provable if for breach of contract.[15]

Thus, where by peculiar contract arrangements a contractor's obligation to pay his subcontractor for materials was conditioned on the owner's pay-

---

15. In re Adams, 12 A. B. R. 368, 130 Fed. 788 (D. C. Mass.): In this case the court held, that where, in ignorance of a pending petition in bankruptcy against one party to a building contract, the other party furnished material and labor, under the contract, his claim therefor was not a provable debt against the bankrupt estate, but that the damages for breach of contract were provable.

ments, the debt was held insufficient to qualify the subcontractor, to file a petition in bankruptcy against the head contractor.[16]

Whether one "import" the clause "absolutely owing at the time of the filing of the petition," into the subsequent classes or not, nevertheless, from the nature of things, it is a necessary qualification of all the subsequent classes. The date of the filing of the petition is the date of cleavage; contractual relations not then merged into provable debts are not dissolved, and in the absence of the statutory provisions permitting the proof of claims by those secondarily liable for their payment, doubtless claims upon indorsements before maturity and default would be held to be contingent and not provable. But the statute, by thus permitting one who is secondarily liable for the bankrupt's debt to prove the debt in the name of the creditor (which may be done even before the maturity of the debt by proper rebate of interest), makes the debt of the one secondarily liable quasi provable, and therefore dischargeable, thus protecting the rights of the surety and of the bankrupt as well. But all this is done by way of exception, necessarily implied, to the rule that contingent claims are not provable. Based upon their provability being by way of exception, the criticisms and distinctions pointed out In re Gerson, supra, and in In re Smith, supra, become immaterial.

The case In re Lyons Sugar Co., 27 A. B. R. 610, 192 Fed. 445 (D. C. N. Y.), apparently holds that a claim, in order to be provable as one founded upon a contract express or implied need not be a fixed liability absolutely owing at the time of the filing of the bankruptcy petition and that Bankruptcy Act § 63 (a) (4) is not limited by § 63 (a) (1); but on analysis that case will be found to come clearly within the next section, § 673, since it relates to the claim of a surety of the bankrupt for costs accruing after bankruptcy. Manifestly the surety's liability was fixed and was absolutely owing at the time of the bankruptcy though his damages were not all liquidated until later.

§ 673. But to Be "Owing" Not Necessarily to Be "Due" nor Damages Liquidated.—But in order that the debt be "owing," it is not necessary that it be "due"[17] nor that the damages be liquidated.[18]

---

16. In re Ellis, 16 A. B. R. 225, 143 Fed. 108 (C. C. A. Ohio).

17. In re Simon, 28 A. B. R. 611, 197 Fed. 102, 105 (D. C. N. Y.); In re Percy Ford Co., 28 A. B. R. 919, 199 Fed. 334 (D. C. Mass.).

Thus, costs accruing and paid by a surety of the bankrupt after the bankruptcy are a "fixed" liability and are absolutely owing, also, at the time of the filing of the bankruptcy petition, though they be not yet "due" nor "liquidated." See In re Lyons Sugar Co., 27 A. B. R. 610, 192 Fed. 445 (D. C. N. Y.), wherein the court, however, seems

to think it necessary to deny that Bankr. Act, § 63 (a) (1), limits Bankr. Act, § 63 (a) (4).

18. Compare post, § 685, et seq. See Phœnix National Bank v. Waterbury, 20 A. B. R. 140, 108 N. Y. Supp. 391, quoted at § 690; Germania Savings & Trust Co. v. Loeb, 26 A. B. R. 238, 188 Fed. 285 (C. C. A. Tenn.).

In re Lyons Sugar Co., 27 A. B. R. 610, 192 Fed. 445 (D. C. N. Y.), wherein the court held costs accruing and paid after bankruptcy by a surety of the bankrupt were provable.

§ 674. Bankruptcy Operating as Anticipatory Breach.

—But the obligor's bankruptcy may itself operate as an anticipatory breach.[19]

Obiter, In re Duquesne Incandescent Light Co., 24 A. B. R. 419, 176 Fed. 785 (D. C. Pa.): "So, in the case at bar upon the filing of the petition in bankruptcy,. and the adjudication thereon, it was impossible for the bankrupt to accept a delivery of the goods and make payment for them. A breach of the contract therefor occurred upon the filing of the petition, and the claimant was relieved upon making tender of the goods."

In re Pettingill, 14 A. B. R. 733, 137 Fed. 143 (D. C. Mass.): "For admission to proof, however, the claim need not arise before bankruptcy, nor need the contract be broken theretofore. It is sufficient for proof if the breach of contract and bankruptcy are coincident. To some extent bankruptcy operates as a breach of the bankrupt's contracts. This has been deemed true of the bankrupt's commercial paper, even though that paper is made payable after bankruptcy. It is true that the trustee in bankruptcy in some cases may elect to keep the bankrupt's contracts alive and to carry them out. In other cases, the creditor may be able to ignore the breach arising from bankruptcy and to keep a contract alive against the bankrupt. With these limitations upon the rule we need not deal here. If the trustee desires to keep the contract alive, he must manifest his election within a reasonable time. Where he does not do this, and where the creditor, by seeking to prove, manifests his election to treat the contract as broken, the court of bankruptcy may permit proof of claims arising from a breach of contract, which breach did not occur before bankruptcy, but was caused constructively by the adjudication of bankruptcy itself. See Ex parte Swift, 112 Fed. 315, 50 C. C. A. 263; Ex parte Pollard, 2 Lowell 411, Fed. Cas. No. 11,252. Bankruptcy itself may be treated as a breach of the bankrupt's contracts, analogous to that complete repudiation of the contract before the time of performance which was shown in Hochster v. Delatour, 2 E. & B. 678, and in Roehm v. Horst, 178 U. S. 1, 20 Sup. Ct. 780, 44 L. Ed. 953, or to a complete disenablement of performance of the contract, as in Forst v. Knight, 7 Exch. 111.

"It seems, therefore, that the test of provability under the Act of 1898 may be stated thus: If the bankrupt, at the time of bankruptcy, by disenabling himself from performing the contract in question, and by repudiating its obligation, could give the proving creditor the right to maintain at once a suit in which damages could be assessed at law or in equity, then the creditor can prove in bankruptcy on the ground that bankruptcy is the equivalent of disenablement and repudiation. For the assessment of damages proceedings may be directed by the court under § 63b."

In re Adams, 12 A. B. R. 368, 130 Fed. 788 (D. C. Mass.): "It seems that this contract was broken by bankruptcy as of the date of filing the petition."

In re Swift, 7 A. B. R. 379, 122 Fed. 315 (C. C. A. Mass., affirming 5 A. B. R. 335): "As we have already said, the solution of the proper relations of the parties in this case growing out of the assignment, or out of the filing of the petition in bankruptcy, is fixed by the law; and the simple rule, based on fundamental principles, and traceable in the text writers and decisions of the courts for fully a century, must be applied to the effect that, 'where a man has dis-

---

19. Compare, § 690. Inferentially, In re Stern, 8 A. B. R. 569, 116 Fed. 604 (C. C. A. N. Y.). Goods of peculiar or special make, rule of damages. In re Duquesne Incandescent Light Co., 24 A. B. R. 419, 176 Fed. 785 (D. C. Pa.), quoted at § 687.

abled himself from performing his contract, it is unnecessary to make any request or demand for performance.' * * *

"These propositions may be made somewhat clearer by comparing the position of a banker with that of a stockbroker. A banker has not, ordinarily, on hand sufficient funds to meet the checks of all his depositors if they should all draw simultaneously, and he is not expected to do so. A like rule applies to stockbrokers. In the one case as well as in the other, so long as either remains solvent, he is presumed to be able to meet his contracts; and no action can be maintained against a banker by a depositor without first drawing a check or making some other proper demand, nor, in the case of a stockbroker, without a tender by his customer of the balance due him, and a demand of his stock. On the other hand, when either has made a voluntary assignment for the benefit of creditors, or gone into bankruptcy, or perhaps, when he has committed some other notorious act of insolvency, he has parted with the control of his assets, and the law assumes, as is the fact, that his ability to perform his contracts has terminated, and that a demand and tender would be futile, and, ordinarily, an action may at once be brought. All this, of course, is subject to the rights which we have already stated, of a trustee in bankruptcy, or other representative of an insolvent, to rehabilitate the contract within a reasonable time, if it is for the interest of the estate so to do. These are the simple principles which, in the absence of a demand or tender by either party, the law necessarily applies to the case at bar, and the only doubt is whether the disenabling of the present bankrupts to perform their contract arose at the time of the voluntary assignment or out of the proceedings in bankruptcy. * * *

"However, we need not go into the troublesome questions that are raised by this omission, because we have already seen that in the case at bar the proceedings in bankruptcy render unnecessary a demand and tender, and, like the great mass of matters affected by such proceedings, we must hold that this proof of debt relates to the time when they were commenced. From that time the stocks in question were put beyond the power of the stockbrokers to deliver effectually. The contract ripened simultaneously with the beginning of the proceedings in bankruptcy, as the consequence thereof in connection with the adjudication which followed. Of course, as everything related back to the filing of the petition, the ripening of the claim did not occur before it was filed, nor afterwards, but simultaneously with it, as already said. Consequently, by necessary effect, there was created and existed, when the proceedings commenced a provable claim." Citing also, Carr *v.* Hamilton, 129 U. S. 256; In re Northern Counties of Eng. Fire Ins. Co., 17 Ch. Div. 341, and Ex parte Stapleton, 27 Monk's Eng. Rep. 128, 10 Ch. Div. 590.

In re Neff, 19 A. B. R. 23, 157 Fed. 57 (C. C. A. Ohio, affirming 19 A. B. R. 911): "The defense is that these claims were not 'fixed liabilities,' 'absolutely owing' at the time of the filing of the petition against the bankrupt. This is based upon the fact that the liability of the bankrupt is made dependent upon the surrender of the stock certificates at a date which had not then arrived and that it was optional with the promisees to surrender or keep the stock until that time and that the liability of the promisor was undetermined and contingent until such surrender at the time named. That the promisor might refuse performance until the time named is true. But, if before the time of performance, one absolutely repudiate liability and disavow unequivocally any purpose to perform at any time, the other party may treat such repudiation, at his election, as a breach of the agreement and sue for his damages. So if one of the parties absolutely disables himself from performing the contract by putting performance out of his power the other party may treat that as a repudiation and bring his action to recover damages then or wait the time of performance at his election. This aspect of the question of an anticipatory breach is well put by Fuller, Chief Justice, in Roehm v. Horst, cited above, when he says: 'It is not disputed that if one party to a contract has destroyed the subject matter, or disabled himself so as to make performance impossible, his conduct is equivalent to a breach of the contract although the time of performance has not arrived; and also that if a contract provides for a series of acts, and actual default is made in the performance of one of them, accompanied by a refusal to perform the rest, the other party need not perform, but may treat the refusal as a breach of the entire contract, and recover accordingly.' Bankruptcy is a complete disablement from performance, and the equivalent of an out and out repudiation, subject only to the right of the trustee, at his election, to rehabilitate the contract by performance." Quoted further at § 629.

But bankruptcy has been held not to operate as an anticipatory breach of a continuing contract to buy, as to future installments of goods.[20] And where a tenant had deposited a fund with his landlord to secure the faithful performance of the covenants of the lease during its entire term, the same eventually to be applied, in case of such faithful performance, upon the last six months' rent, the landlord's bankruptcy will not entitle the tenant to apply the security to rents accruing after bankruptcy and before the last six months of the term of the lease.[21]

As a legal proposition, of course, bankruptcy alone does not constitute a breach of a contract, or authorize a rescission thereof where it does not involve personal skill, etc., and may be fully performed by the bankrupt's trustee, or by others who succeed to his rights.

In re [Morgantown] Tin Plate Co., 25 A. B. R. 836, 184 Fed. 109 (D. C. W. Va.): In short, it would seem the only thing required by the contract of it, which was not fully performed, was a five years' operation of the mill at a capacity to employ about 500 people. It was prevented from doing this because of financial embarrassment and bankruptcy. As a legal proposition insolvency or bankruptcy alone does not, in a contract of this kind, constitute either breach or authorize its rescission or abandonment, for it may be finally and fully performed by others who may be acting, for instance, as trustee or as successors or purchasers of the bankrupt's property and rights involved therein or affected thereby."

§ 675. Bankruptcy Operating by Contract to Mature Future Installments.

—Bankruptcy, likewise, may, by contract, be made to mature future installments of debt.[22]

20. In re Brew Co, 16 A. B. R. 110, 143 Fed. 579 (D. C. Mo.); In re Inman & Co., 23 A. B. R. 566, 171 Fed. 185 (D. C. Ga.), quoted at § 690½.

21. In re Banner, 18 A. B. R. 62 (D. C. N. Y.).

22. See, subject of "Claims for Rent," ante, div. 4, § 659.

Liquidation within Year of Rent Claims for Future Occupancy.—Merely that rent claims for future occupancy are liquidated within the year will not make them any the less contingent or more provable. Compare, ante, §§ 656, 672. Contra, In re Caloris Mfg. Co., 24 A. B. R. 609, 179 Fed. 722 (D. C. Pa.).

Division 6.

Judgments and Written Instruments.

§ 676. Judgments and Written Instruments "Absolutely Owing," Provable.—A fixed liability as evidenced by a judgment or an instrument in writing, absolutely owing at the time of the filing of the bankruptcy petition, whether then payable or not, is a provable debt in bankruptcy.[23]

§ 677. Must Be for Money.—Only judgments, and written instruments, the damages for the breach of which can be estimated in money, are provable.

§ 678. Must Be "Absolutely Owing" at Time of Bankruptcy Petition but Need Not Be Due.—The written instrument must be fixed and absolutely owing at the time of the filing of the bankruptcy petition, else it will not be a provable claim.[24] Thus, liability upon bonds may be a "fixed liability" absolutely owing.[25] Thus, claims where the liability is contingent are not provable.[26] Likewise, claims otherwise not "absolutely owing" are not provable.[27] But the claim need not be due yet.[28]

---

23. Bankr. Act, § 63 (a) (1). Instance, judgment, In re Adler, 16 A. B. R. 417, 144 Fed. 659 (C. C. A. N. Y.); instance, written instrument, Hibbard v. Bailey, 12 A. B. R. 104, 129 Fed. 575 (C. C. A. Pa., reversing Wiseman v. Wallace, 10 A. B. R. 545); instance, written instrument, Cobb v. Overman, 6 A. B. R. 324, 109 Fed. 65 (C. C. A. N. Car., reversing Bray v. Cobb); instance, written instrument, Bray v. Cobb, 3 A. B. R. 790, 100 Fed. 270 (D. C. N. Car., reversed, on other grounds, sub nom. Cobb v. Overman, 6 A. B. R. 324, 109 Fed. 65).

Proof necessary for judgments as well as for any other claim: Judgments will not be allowed to share in distribution any more than other claims unless due "proof" is made, In re Rosenburg, 16 A. B. R. 465 (D. C. La.). But this case seems to hold that the lien of the levy will also be lost if due "proof" be not made. Such would not be the case, however, for lienholders can not be deprived of their security until they have been notified to set up their rights and have had a chance to defend. Instance, In re Randolph, 26 A. B. R. 623, 187 Fed. 186 (D. C. W. Va.). Instance, lease as written instrument, obiter, Martin v. Orgain, 23 A. B. R. 454, 174 Fed. 772 (C. C. A. Tex.).

Whether attaching of transcript to proof of claim on a judgment requisite, see ante, § 602.

Damages for Breach of Covenant to Pay Rent to Accrue in Future Whether "Fixed Liability" Where Proved within Year.—See post, §§ 694½, 707.

24. In re Neff, 19 A. B. R. 23, 157 Fed. 57 (C. C. A. Ohio), quoted, on other point, at § 674; Phœnix National Bank v. Waterbury, 23 A. B. R. 250 (N. Y. Ct. App., affirming 20 A. B. R. 140, 108 N. Y. Supp. 391, quoted at § 690), quoted at § 2731.

In re O'Neil, 27 A. B. R. 5, 189 Fed. 1010 (D. C. N. Y.), wherein the court held that a note given by the bankrupt after his adjudication will not support a prima facie claim against his estate.

25. Loeser v. Alexander, 24 A. B. R. 75, 176 Fed. 265 (C. C. A. Ohio), wherein a bond taken by a county treasurer from a deputy not authorized by statute, was held a provable debt.

26. See ante, "Contingent Claims," § 640.

27. See ante, "Claims Not Absolutely Owing," § 668, et seq.

28. Bankr. Act, § 63 (a) (1). Hibbard v. Bailey, 12 A. B. R. 104, 129 Fed. 575 (C. C. A. Penn., reversing Wiseman v. Wallace, 10 A. B. R. 545). Bray v. Cobb, 3 A. B. R. 790, 100 Fed. 270 (D. C. N. Car.).

§ 679. Interest.—Interest, if any would have been recoverable at the date of the filing of the bankruptcy petition, will be provable;[29] but not interest to accrue;[30] although in applying security upon a claim, interest may be computed to the date of payment.[31] And a rebate of interest will be required, if the instrument is not yet due and does not bear interest.[32]

§ 680. Judgments for Personal Injuries and Similar Torts Provable, Though Torts Themselves Not.—Judgments for personal injury and other similar torts, not capable of being presented in form ex contractu, are provable although the unliquidated claims for the torts themselves would not be provable;[33] but are not provable where not rendered before the filing of the bankruptcy petition,[34] even though verdict has been rendered.[35] A fortiori, they are not provable where the suits for their recovery are not brought until after adjudication.[36]

§ 681. Judgments Provable, Though Not Dischargeable.—A judgment for fraud, conspiracy or deceit, although it be not released by the bankrupt's discharge, may be provable.[37]

§ 682. Judgments, Though Rendered within Four Months, Provable.—A judgment itself, although rendered within the four months preceding the filing of the petition, and while the bankrupt was insolvent, is a provable claim, notwithstanding § 67 (f) declares such judgments "void," the voidability referring merely to the lien created thereby and not to the judgment itself.[38]

Doyle v. Heath, 4 A. B. R. 705 (Sup. Ct. R. I.): "Literally construed, again § 67f avoids 'all judgments' against a bankrupt rendered within four months of the filing of the petition, irrespective of the time of the institution of the suit in which the judgment was rendered, and all such judgments are avoided, although no lien or preference was created thereby, for the language is without

---

29. Bankr. Act, § 63 (a) (1). Bray v. Cobb, 3 A. B. R. 788, 790, 100 Fed. 270 (D. C. N. Car.).
30. See ante, § 598. Bray v. Cobb, 3 A. B. R. 790, 100 Fed. 270 (D. C. N. Car.). But compare, In re Osborne's Sons & Co., 24 A. B. R. 65, 177 Fed. 184 (C. C. A. N. Y.).
31. See §§ 598, 758½, 1997½.
32. Bankr. Act, § 63 (a) (1). See ante, § 598.
33. In re Lorde, 16 A. B. R. 201 (D. C. N. Y.), wherein a judgment against a landlord for the bite of a vicious dog kept by a tenant was held **dischargeable.** Obiter and inferentially, Beers v. Hanlin, 3 A. B. R. 745, 99 Fed. 695 (D. C. Ore.); obiter, Burnham v. Pidcock, 5 A. B. R. 45 (affd. in 5 A. B. R. 490); (1867) Manning v. Keyes, 9 R. I. 224; (1867) Howland v. Cason, 16 N. B. Reg. 372.

34. In re Ostrom, 26 A. B. R. 273, 185 Fed. 988 (D. C. Minn.), quoted ante, § 635; [1867] Block v. McClelland, Fed. Cas. No. 1,462.
35. In re Ostrom, 26 A. B. R. 273, 185 Fed. 988 (D. C. Minn.), quoted ante, § 635; [1867] Block v. McClelland, Fed. Cas. No. 1,462.
36. In re Crescent Lumber Co., 19 A. B. R. 112, 154 Fed. 724 (D. C. Ala.). Also, see post, § 697.
37. Under law of 1867, In re Van Buren, 19 N. B. Reg. 149; compare, In re Lorde, 16 A. B. R. 201 (D. C. N. Y.).
38. In re Pease, 4 A. B. R. 547 (Ref. N. Y.). Also, see cases cited under the subject "Liens by Legal Proceedings Nullified by Bankruptcy," post, § 1448, et seq.; especially, § 1487. Instance, In re Scully, 5 A. B. R. 716, 108 Fed. 372 (D. C. Pa.).

limitation or exception. But the difficulty and unreasonableness of adopting a literal construction of the words 'all judgments' appear upon considering the effect produced upon other sections of the act, and upon other provisions of the United States statutes concerning judgments. In the first place, the words are found in the act under the subtitle 'Liens,' and they are conjoined with 'levies, attachments or other liens.' Again, under § 63a of the act the debts which may be proved against a bankrupt are defined as including '(1) a fixed liability, as evidenced by a judgment or an instrument in writing absolutely owing at the time of the filing of the petition against 'him;' and this without restriction as to the date of entry of the judgment. And § 63 (5) also includes debts 'founded upon provable debts reduced to judgment after filing of the petition.' Under § 17, among debts not affected by a discharge are '(2) judgments in actions for fraud or obtaining property by false pretenses or false representations, or for willful and malicious injury to the person or property of another'—a manifest inconsistency if the words 'all judgments' are to be taken literally. Again, § 905, Rev. St. U. S., provides, that 'the record and judicial proceedings of the courts of any State or Territory when duly authenticated as therein specified, shall have such faith and credit given to them in every court in the United States as they have by law or usage in the courts of the state from which they are taken.' And it is hardly to be supposed that this general provision of federal legislation, first substantially enacted in 1790, was intended to be repealed by the single addition of the word 'judgments' in this clause of the bankrupt act of 1898. And, if the words 'all judgments' are to be literally construed, they must include judgments rendered in the courts of foreign countries, irrespective of treaty stipulations, and even the judgments of the very court in which the estate of the bankrupt is being administered. We decline to adopt such a construction of the language of the act, and we construe the words 'all judgments' to be qualified and defined by their context, and to be limited to the lien or preference created by such a judgment."

The judgment, when offered for proof, may be attacked only for fraud, collusion or want of jurisdiction,[39] under the usual rules.

§ 683. Judgments for Penal Fines, Alimony, Support, etc., Not Provable.

—But even certain classes of judgments have been construed not to be claims provable in bankruptcy, such as judgments by way of penal fines,[40] for alimony, and judgments and agreements for the support of a wife or children or of a bastard child.[41] The reasoning appears to be that bankruptcy is concerned only with civil debts and judgments and that

39. In re Pease, 4 A. B. R. 547 (Ref. N. Y.); contra, see erroneous decision, St. Cyr. v. Daignault, 4 A. B. R. 638 (D. C. Vt., rejected in 5 A. B. R. 373).

40. In re Southern Steel Co., 25 A. B. R. 358, 183 Fed. 498 (D. C. Ala.), statutory penalty for cutting trees.

41. McKittrick v. Cahoon, 95 N. W. 223 (Minn.); Wetmore v. Wetmore, 13 A. B. R. 1, 196 U. S. 68. See Dunbar v. Dunbar, 10 A. B. R. 139, 190 U. S. 340, wherein the court held, that a husband's obligation to support his divorced wife under an agreement to pay her an annuity "during her life or until she remarries" is not a liability provable under the Bankruptcy Act and his discharge in bankruptcy does not release him therefrom. Also that a father's liability under an agreement with his divorced wife to pay to her for the support of their minor children until they respectively become of age is not a provable nor dischargeable debt.

In re Moore, 6 A. B. R. 590, 111 Fed. 145 (D. C. Ky.). Fine imposed upon conviction for crime was held not to be a provable debt, declining to follow

these judgments are police regulations to compel obedience to police laws, in which the state itself is an interested party, and as such they are not within the purview nor intent of the Act:[42] and in the case of alimony decrees that they also are not "fixed liabilities."[43]

But even in these cases there seems to have been a looseness of thought and a confusion in the minds of the courts between the term "provability" and the term "dischargeability," the court holding in one instance that because the fine was not "dischargeable" it was not "provable"—a clear non sequitur.[44]

§ 683½. Penalties and Forfeitures Due State, etc.

—Section 57j of the Bankruptcy Act expressly declares that a debt owing to the United States, a state, county, district or municipality as a penalty or forfeiture shall only be allowed for the amount of the pecuniary loss sustained by the act, transaction or proceeding out of which the penalty or forfeiture arises," with actual costs and interest.[45]

An obligation is penal, within the meaning of § 57j, when its amount is measured neither by the obligee's loss, nor by the valuation placed by him on what he has given in exchange; thus a recovery on a recognizance given in a criminal case is essentially a penalty and a forfeiture, and will not be allowed in bankruptcy. But the costs awarded may be proved.[46]

§ 684. Dormant Judgments.

—Whether dormant judgments are provable or not will depend somewhat on local law. Nevertheless, it would

---

In re Alderson, 3 A. B. R. 544, 98 Fed. 583 (D. C. W. Va.).

In re Baker, 3 A. B. R. 101, 96 Fed. 954 (D. C. Kas.). Judgment for support of bastard child.

In re Hubbard, 3 A. B. R. 528, 98 Fed. 710 (D. C. Ills.). Support of minor child.

42. See Audubon v. Shufeldt, 5 A. B. R. 829, 181 U. S. 575; In re Baker, 3 A. B. R. 101, 96 Fed. 954 (D. C. Kas.); In re Hubbard, 3 A. B. R. 528, 98 Fed. 710 (D. C. Ills.).

43. In re Smith, 3 A. B. R. 67 (Ref. N. Y.).

Provability of Alimony before the Amendment of 1903.—That it was not provable: Audubon v. Shufeldt, 5 A. B. R. 829, 181 U. S. 575; Lynde v. Lynde, 181 U. S. 183; Barclay v. Barclay, 184 Ills. 375 (51 L. R. A. 351); Welty v. Welty, 63 N. E. (Ills.) 161; Young v. Young, 7 A. B. R. 171 (Sup. Ct. N. Y., C. C. A. N. Y.); Turner v. Turner, 6 A. B. R. 289, 108 Fed. 785 (D. C. Ind.); Maisner v. Maisner, 6 A. B. R. 295 (Sup. Ct. N. Y. App.); In re Shepard, 97 Fed. 187 (D. C.); In re Anderson, 97 Fed. 321 (D. C.); In re Smith,

3 A. B. R. 67 (Ref. N. Y.). This case bases its rule upon the fact that the alimony was not a "fixed liability." In re Newell, 3 A. B. R. 837, 99 Fed. 931 (D. C. Mass.).

That is was provable if a final decree: Arlington v. Arlington, 10 A. B. R. 103 (Sup. Ct. N. Car.). See, also, Arlington v. Arlington, 13 A. B. R. 89 (D. C. N. Car.).

That it was provable as to such portion as had accrued before bankruptcy: Fite v. Fite, 5 A. B. R. 461, 61 S. W. 26 (Ky.); In re Challoner, 3 A. B. R. 442, 98 Fed. 82 (D. C. Ills.).

That it was provable even if payable in installments at so much per month during life: In re Van Orden, 2 A. B. R. 801, 96 Fed. 86 (D. C. N. J.), rejected by U. S. Sup. Ct. in Audubon v. Shufeldt, 5 A. B. R. 829, 181 U. S. 575. Contra, In re Smith, 3 A. B. R. 67 (Ref. N. Y.).

44. See In re Moore, 6 A. B. R. 590, 104 Fed. 869 (D. C. Ky.).

45. In re York Silk Mfg. Co., 27 A. B. R. 525, 188 Fed. 735 (D. C. Pa.).

46. In re Caponigri, 27 A. B. R. 513, 193 Fed. 291 (D. C. N. Y.).

seem that such judgments are "provable," although by virtue of the statute limiting their operation, etc., they may not be "allowable."[47]

DIVISION 7.

CONTINUING CONTRACTS AND CONTRACTS OF SALE AND OF EMPLOYMENT.

§ 685. Damages for Breach of Contracts of Sale, Employment and Continuing Contracts, Provable.

—Damages for breach of contracts of sale or of purchase and for breach of continuing contracts and perhaps also of contracts of employment are provable debts, although the time of performance has not expired (if there has been a repudiation or renunciation of the obligation by the bankrupt or if the bankruptcy operates as an anticipatory breach), so long as the amount is ascertainable that is necessary to be expended to complete the contract or the future profits of the contract or the wages are ascertainable that can be earned during the period contracted for.[48] They may be unliquidated claims, but they are nevertheless provable.[49]

Where goods are of special or peculiar make, or where there is no open market for them, the difference between the contract price and the cost of manufacture, rather than the difference between the contract price and the market price, may be the rule of damages;[50] and any actual sales made on the open market will be for the buyer to prove in mitigation of damages;[51] and if there is no reasonable market for them the "Uniform Code of Sales" adopted in many of the states permits recovery of the full price if the goods have been duly manufactured and tendered to the buyer.

§ 686. Contracts of Employment.

—Thus, it has been held that damages for breach of a contract of employment are provable, although the term of employment has not expired:

In re Silverman Bros., 4 A. B. R. 83, 101 Fed. 219 (D. C. Mo.) : "There can be no question but what if, on the 9th day of January, 1899, there was a breach of the contract between Silverman Bros. and Rosenberg by his discharge from their service, or by their voluntary act, which rendered the performance of the contract on their part impossible, a cause of action at once arose in favor of Rosenberg against Silverman Bros. for damages, and it is equally clear that the subsequent adjudication of bankruptcy in February, 1899, did not put an end to the cause of action, as it was then an existing right, which the mere adjudication in

---

47. Compare, instance, In re Rebman, 17 A. B. R. 767, 150 Fed. 759 (C. C. A. Calif.).

48. Instance, damages for repudiation of contract to sell by receivers in State court, on subsequent bankruptcy. In re National Wire Corp., 22 A. B. R. 186, 66 Fed. 631 (D. C. Conn.).

49. Pratt v. Auto, etc., Co., 28 A. B. R. 483, 196 Fed. 495 (C. C. A. Mass.).

Compare post, § 707, "Damages on Contract Accruing after Bankruptcy."

50. In re Du Quesne Incandescent Light Co., 24 A. B. R. 419, 176 Fed. 785 (D. C. Pa.), quoted on analogous points ante, § 674.

51. In re Du Quesne Incandescent Light Co., 24 A. B. R. 419, 176 Fed. 785 (D. C. Pa.), quoted on analogous subject ante, § 674.

bankruptcy could not destroy. So, the real question in this case is not whether an adjudication in bankruptcy against the employer would put an end to a contract with an employee, like the one in question, so that the discharge of the employee would be under the operation of the bankrupt law, and not by reason of the voluntary act of the employer, but it is whether or not the act of Silverman Bros. in making the deed of trust, and placing Swift in absolute charge of the store and its business, whereby Rosenberg was displaced as manager and employee, did not constitute a breach of the contract, and create a subsisting cause of action, three weeks before the adjudication in bankruptcy. * * *

"On the discharge of Rosenberg without his fault or consent, a cause of action at once arose in his favor against Silverman Bros. He would not have to wait until the expiration of the year covering the term of his employment before he could institute the action. In such action he would be entitled to recover the amount that would have been due him if he had continued to work for Silverman Bros. under the contract from the date of his discharge until the expiration of the contract, after allowing credit for anything which he may have earned from services rendered to others, or under other contracts, after allowing further credit for what the court or jury hearing the case may believe, from the facts and circumstances in evidence, he will be able to earn between the time of trial and the termination of the year."

But not where a corporation employer reserves the right to cancel the contract in case it winds up its affairs.[52] And probably the claim could not be successfully liquidated until the end of the term.

Some of the decisions seem to make the provability dependent upon the term of employment expiring within the year limited for proving claims.[53] But such qualification seems hardly necessary; for the deposition for proof of debt might be filed within the year and later be amended if later the liquidated amount be found to be different from that claimed in the proof of claim[54] and, also, § 57 (n) is not to be construed as enlarging the classes of debts to be considered "provable."[55]

But, on the other hand, well considered cases take the opposite view and deny, altogether, such provability.[56]

In re Inman & Co., 22 A. B. R. 524, 171 Fed. 185 (D. C. Ga.): "The liability here on the part of the employers was certainly contingent. It was contingent upon the life, health, and ability to render services on the part of the employee in the future, and contingent also upon the life of the members of the firm of Inman & Co. The death of one member would have dissolved the firm and necessitated the winding up of its affairs. * * * It will be seen from the foregoing that the conclusion reached in this case of Watson v. Merrill was that claims for future rent, and probably, from the language used in the opinion, for future personal services, are not provable in bankruptcy, though the reason given therefor is entirely different from that given in the other cases. According to this last opinion contracts such as those in question here will remain of force and unaffected by the bankruptcy proceedings. Bailey v. Loeb, 2 Fed. Cas. 376,

52. In re Sweetser, Pembroke & Co., 15 A. B. R. 650, 142 Fed. 131 (C. C. A. N. Y.).

53. In re (James) Dunlap Carpet Co., 20 A. B. R. 882, 163 Fed. 541 (D. C. Pa.).

54. Compare, § 722.

55. Compare, § 641, note, and § 737¾.

56. In re American Vacuum Cleaner Co., 26 A. B. R. 621, 192 Fed. 939 (D. C. N. J.), holding the liability to be "contingent."

was decided under the Act of 1867 by Circuit Judge Wood, afterwards a justice of the Supreme Court. An extract from the opinion in that case will show the view that Judge Wood entertained of the matter, as follows: 'For instance a business man has a manager or bookkeeper hired by the year, at a salary payable quarterly. At the end of two months he is adjudicated bankrupt. His manager or bookkeeper may prove for a proportionate part of his salary up to the time of the bankruptcy, but he cannot prove for any part that may accrue and fall due after the bankruptcy. The clear purpose of the Bankruptcy Act is to cut off all claims for rent to accrue, or for services to be rendered, after the date of the bankruptcy.' The fact that this decision by Judge Wood was under the Bankruptcy Act of 1867 strengthens it as an authority, because it is generally conceded that the Bankruptcy Act of 1867 was more liberal as to the proof of claims for contingent liabilities than is the present act. In Malcomson v. Wappoo Mills et al. (C. C.), 88 Fed. 680, Judge Simonton held that: 'Damages are not recoverable against a corporation for its failure to perform a contract for the sale and delivery of merchandise, where performance was prevented solely by the action of a court in appointing a receiver for the corporation, and enjoining all others from interfering with its business or property. In such cases the breach of contract is damnum absque injuria.' It seems clear to me that adjudication in bankruptcy ends contracts for rent, and for personal services, and I agree with the views expressed in the opinions in In re Jefferson, supra, Bray v. Cobb, supra, In re Hayes, Foster & Ward Company, supra, and Malcomson v. Wappoo Mills et al., supra. The case of James Dunlap Carpet Co. (D. C.), 20 Am. B. R. 882, 163 Fed. 541, is a case favorable to the contention of the claimants here to the extent of allowing proof of claim. The difficulty about the case to my mind is that the learned judge based his decision on Moch v. Market Street National Bank, 6 Am. B. R. 11, 107 Fed. 897 * * * In the case of Moch v. National Bank the person seeking to prove had indorsed for the bankrupt and the paper matured after the bankruptcy proceedings were instituted. The indorser paid the paper, and then proposed to prove it as a debt against the bankrupt in the bankruptcy proceedings. I can see no similarity at all between such a case and the case of an employee seeking to prove for salary to be earned by services to be rendered in the future. The indorsement in the Moch Case was a definite and fixed liability which the indorser had undertaken for the bankrupt, and it was in existence before the bankruptcy proceedings commenced. It matured, and the indorser was compelled to pay the debt pending the bankruptcy proceedings. This is entirely different from a contract to render personal services. Such services depend upon the life, health, and ability otherwise of the employee to render the services, and also upon the life, certainty, and perhaps other contingencies as to the employer. But it is a partnership in bankruptcy here, and whatever is true as to individual cases there would seem to be no doubt, first, that a partnership is dissolved by the bankruptcy proceedings (22 Am. & English Cyclopedia of Law [2d Ed.] 202, and 30 Cyc. 654, and cases cited in both); and, second, if the firm is dissolved by operation of law, then certainly the contracts of that firm are ended. In Griggs v. Swift, 82 Ga. 392, 9 S. E. 1062, * * * it is held in the opinion by Chief Justice Bleckley: 'From the very nature of a contract for the rendering of personal services to a partnership in its current business, where nothing is expressed to the contrary, both parties should be regarded as having by implication intended a condition dependent on the one hand upon the life of the employee, and, on the other, upon the life of the partnership, provided the death in either case was not voluntary.' Wood on Master and Servant, § 163, is then quoted with approval to the following effect: 'Where a servant is em-

ployed by a firm, a dissolution of the firm dissolves the contract, so that a servant is absolved therefrom; but, if the dissolution results from the act of the
parties, they are liable to the servant for his loss therefrom, but, if the dissolution results from the death of a member of the firm, the dissolution resulting
by operation of law, and not from the act of the parties, no action for damages will lie. * * * So, if a firm consists of two or more persons, and one
or more of them dies, but the firm is not thereby dissolved, the contract still
subsists, because one or more of his partners is still in the firm, and this is so
even though other persons are taken into the firm. The test is whether the
firm is dissolved. So long as it exists, the contract is in force, but, when it is
dissolved, the contract is dissolved with it, and the question as to whether damages can be recovered therefor will depend upon the question whether the
dissolution resulted from the act of God, the operation of law, or the act of
the parties.' None of the cases cited from the United States courts seems to
bear directly upon the question immediately involved here—that is, of the right
of an employee to prove for future services—except, perhaps, the case of James
Dunlap Carpet Company, supra, and with the utmost respect for the learned
judge deciding the case I am, for the reason stated above, unable to agree with
his conclusion. I have, perhaps, cited authorities at unnecessary length, but the
question is an interesting one, and is presented in its present shape for the first
time in this district. I do not believe that it was the intention and purpose of the
Bankruptcy Act that contracts extending into the future for rent and personal
services should be left hanging over the bankrupt to embarrass and harass
him after his discharge in bankruptcy. It is said that if this is not true, and
he is relieved of such liability by the Bankruptcy Act, it follows that claims
for such rent and personal services should be admitted to proof in the bankruptcy proceedings. I do not think this follows at all. The adjudication in
bankruptcy ends all such contracts. Of course, proof may be allowed for any
amount due prior to the institution of the proceedings in bankruptcy. It is
provided by the Bankruptcy Act that for most personal services the employee
would have priority for any amount due him for as much as three months
preceding the bankruptcy proceedings. This fact of priority of payment for
three months extending to so large a class of employees is another reason
why I believe it was the intention, in passing this act, that such contracts
should terminate with the adjudication in bankruptcy. All this is certainly true
as to a partnership. The adjudication dissolves it by operation of law, and
that dissolution ends all its liabilities except such as are expressed in the act.
My conclusion is that the referee in bankruptcy correctly decided that this
claim should not be admitted to proof." Compare, however, quotation at § 690½.

The true rule would seem to be that stated in § 685, namely, that such
damages are provable but only in the event that there has been a repudiation or renunciation of the obligation or that the bankruptcy operates as
an anticipatory breach. The cases differ in their conclusions simply on
the question as to whether or not, in the particular instance, a breach had
been committed before bankruptcy or the bankruptcy had operated itself
as a breach of the contract.

§ 687. **Continuing Contracts to Supply Goods.**—Thus damages
for breach of a continuing contract to supply goods are provable.[58]

---

58. Instance, In re National Wire
Corporation, 22 A. B. R. 186, 166 Fed.
631 (D. C. Conn.). As to what constitutes breach and damages, ibid.

In re Stern, 8 A. B. R. 569, 116 Fed. 604 (C. C. A. N. Y., affirming In re Manhattan Ice Co., 7 A. B. R. 408): "But in the case at bar, the question is not necessarily whether the claims are liquidated or unliquidated, but whether they are 'provable.' The statute provides that the petitioning creditors shall have 'provable claims.' Counsel for defendant corporation contends that damages to accrue in the future are not provable because they are uncertain in amount, and because not having yet accrued they are not yet in existence. But in actions for personal injuries, or for breaches of warranty in the sale of seeds, or for failure to deliver goods which have no recognized market value, the injured party is entitled to recover compensation for such elements of damage as are shown to be reasonably certain or provable, or such as naturally result in such cases and may be supposed likely to occur in the given case. * * *

"The authorities are conflicting as to whether an action will lie for damages for the breach of an executory contract before the stipulated time of such performance has arrived." The court citing, Roehm v. Horst, 178 U. S. 1; Pierce v. R. R. Co., 173 U. S. 1; Norrington v. Wright, 115 U. S. 188; United States v. Behan, 110 U. S. 338, and others.

Where the goods are not yet manufactured the rule has been laid down that the measure of damages is the difference between the cost of manufacture and the contract price, although the entire lot of goods has not been yet manufactured nor are ready for delivery.

In re Du Quesne Incandescent Light Co., 24 A. B. R. 419, 176 Fed. 785 (D. C. Pa.): "Under the facts of this case, we are also of the opinion that the true measure of damages is the difference between the cost of manufacture and the contract price, and this although the entire lot of goods were not manufactured and ready for delivery. The rule in Pennsylvania, the place of the contract, is well settled." This case further quoted at § 674.

§ 688. Uncompleted Building Contracts.—Thus, damages for breach of a partly finished building contract are provable, but not quantum valebat or quantum meruit for materials and labor furnished thereunder after the filing of the petition and before adjudication.

In re Adams, 12 A. B. R. 368, 130 Fed. 788 (D. C. Mass.): "Before bankruptcy the creditors here seeking to prove had contracted with the bankrupt to build for him certain houses, at a price to be paid from time to time during construction. No work had been done under the contract before the petition in bankruptcy was filed. Thereafter, and before adjudication, the creditors, in ignorance of the pending petition, furnished materials and labor under the contract. For this they seek to prove. But a creditor cannot prove for an indebtedness arising between the filing of the involuntary petition and adjudication. * * * The creditors seek also to prove their damages for breach of the executory contract. If the contract was broken at or before bankruptcy, they can prove. It seems that this contract was broken by bankruptcy as of the filing of the petition."

§ 689. Continuing Contracts to Buy.—Thus, also, a claim upon the bankrupt's contract to buy at a fixed date or at fixed dates, occurring after his bankruptcy, may be proved, if the bankrupt has repudiated the obligation or if the bankruptcy may operate as an anticipatory breach and

the trustee does not assume the contract.[59] Likewise, damages for breach of warranty in contracts of sale are provable, although the amount is undetermined.[60] Thus, also, margins on purchases of marketable commodities for future delivery are provable.[61]

§ 690. **But Not Provable, unless Obligation Renounced or Bankruptcy Itself Operates as Breach.**—But unless there has been a repudiation or renunciation of the continuing obligation by the bankrupt, or unless the bankruptcy itself operates as an anticipatory breach, the claim is not provable.[62]

In re Brew. Co., 16 A. B. R. 111, 143 Fed. 579 (D. C. Mo.): "It may be conceded as the law of this jurisdiction that where a party is bound from time to time, as expressed in the contract, to deliver articles to be manufactured or products to be grown, each parcel as delivered to be paid for at a certain time and in a certain way, a refusal by the vendee to be further bound by the terms of the contract or to accept further deliveries constitutes a breach of the contract as a whole, and gives the vendor a right of action to recover the damages he may sustain by reason of such refusal. In such case the positive refusal of the vendee to perform when tender is made, or notice by him to the vendor before maturity of the time for delivery that he will not carry out the contract, will release the vendor from making any tender, and entitle him to an action in advance of the fixed period for delivery on his part to recover damages as for breach of the whole contract. Roehm v. Horst, 178 U. S. 1. * * *

"The sole reliance of the claimant to bring it within this rule for such breach is predicated on the adjudication in an involuntary proceeding in bankruptcy against the vendee, I am unable to consent to the proposition that such an adjudication in bankruptcy, ex vi termini, is in law tantamount to a refusal of the bankrupt to perform, or that it hereby permanently disabled itself from performance, to bring the claim asserted by petitioner within the operation of the rule laid down in Roehm v. Horst, supra. * * *

"Why should a rule be applied to a corporation—a legal entity—different in this respect from a natural person? Section 1, cl. 19, of the Bankruptcy Act (Act July 1, 1898, ch. 541, 30 Stat. 544 [U. S. Comp. St. 1901, p. 3418]), declares that 'persons' shall include corporations, except where otherwise specified. An adjudication in bankruptcy of a corporation does not work a dissolution of the

---

59. Obiter, In re Brew. Co., 16 A. B. R. 110 (D. C. Mo.); compare, In re Pettingill, 14 A. B. R. 735, 137 Fed. 143 (D. C. Mass.), where the rule is stated without the qualification. In re Neff, 19 A. B. R. 23, 157 Fed. 57 (C. C. A. Ohio), quoted at §§ 629, 674; In re Du Quesne Incandescent Light Co., 24 A. B. R. 419, 176 Fed. 785 (D. C. Pa.), quoted at § 674. Compare post, § 707, "Damages on Contracts Accruing after Bankruptcy."

Damages where goods are of special or peculiar make and have no market value. In re Du Quesne Incandescent Light Co., 24 A. B. R. 419, 176 Fed. 785 (D. C. Pa.), quoted ante, § 674, on another point. For rules, see ante, § 685.

60. In re Grant Shoe Co., 12 A. B. R. 349, 130 Fed. 881 (C. C. A. N. Y., affirming 11 A. B. R. 48).

61. Compare, In re Knott, 6 A. B. R. 749, 109 Fed. 626 (D. C. Vt.); Grant Shoe Co. v. Laird Co., 21 A. B. R. 484, 212 U. S. 445.

62. In re Morgantown Tin Plate Co., 25 A. B. R. 836, 184 Fed. 109 (D. C. W. Va.); Impliedly, In re Spittler, 18 A. B. R. 425, 151 Fed. 942 (D. C. Conn.), quoted, on other point, at § 690½. In re Neff, 19 A. B. R. 23, 157 Fed. 57 (C. C. A. Ohio), quoted at §§ 629, 674; also, In re Neff, 19 A. B. R. 911 (D. C. Ohio, affirmed in 19 A. B. R. 23, 157 Fed. 57).

corporation or a forfeiture or loss of its franchise. The very policy of the bankrupt law is that by the adjudication and the surrender to the trustee of all assets of the bankrupt then owned he may thereby be manumitted from the burden of existing debts, and by his unimpeded energies and industry the better be enabled to prosecute his business and earn a livelihood and a competency. Why should any different rule be applied to a corporation coerced into bankruptcy, which but represents the aggregate co-operation and capital of a number of individual stockholders? Its stockholders may decide to infuse new life into it by assessments or otherwise, and its directors resume business, go ahead, and perform any executory contract. And if they had an advantageous contract with the vendor for providing it with hops in its business, why should it not be left in position to avail itself of the yet unexecuted contract?

"In Lovell v. St. Louis Life Insurance Company, 111 U. S. 264, the court held that where an insurance company had terminated its business and transferred its assets and policies to another company, whereby it totally abandoned the performance of its contracts by transferring all of its assets and obligations to the new company, it thereby authorized the insured to treat the contract as at an end and to sue to recover back the premiums already paid, although the time for performance of the obligation, to-wit, the death of the insured, had not arrived. For, as said by Mr. Justice Bradley, referring to a life insurance company which had gone into liquidation, in Car v. Hamilton, 129 U. S. 252, 256, 9 Sup. Ct. 295, 32 L. Ed. 669:

"'By that act the company becomes civiliter mortuus, its business is brought to an absolute end, and the policyholders become creditors to an amount equal to the equitable value of their respective policies, and entitled to participate pro rata in its assets.'

"In re Swift, 7 Am. B. R. 374, 112 Fed. 315, a broker had made a contract to deliver certain stock to a customer. It was held that he made it impossible to fulfill his agreement to deliver the stock by his adjudication in bankruptcy, for the reason that it took the stock from him and vested it, with all his property, in his trustee. But that is clearly not this case.

"As to In re Pettingill & Co. (D. C.), 14 Am. B. R. 728, 137 Fed. 143, relied upon by the petitioner, I may say that I can concur in the syllabus of that case that under the Bankrupt Act the provability of a claim depends upon its status at the time of the filing of the petition in bankruptcy. If not then a provable debt, as defined in the Act, it cannot be proved, although it may thereafter come within such definition. 'If a bankrupt, at the time of bankruptcy, by disenabling himself from performing a particular contract, and by repudiating its obligation, could give the other party the right to maintain at once a suit in which damages could be assessed at law or in equity, then such party may prove as a creditor in bankruptcy, on the ground that bankruptcy is the equivalent of disenablement and repudiation.'

"If, however, it was intended to hold that, as applied to an executory contract for the sale of annual crops to be raised in successive years, where no breach had occurred at the time of an involuntary adjudication in bankruptcy, the mere act of such declared statutory insolvency constituted such a breach of the contract as to enable the vendor to prove up against the estate the contingent damages, as on a repudiation of the contract by the vendee, I cannot consent thereto. There was no renunciation by the vendee company of the contract after the commencement of performance or renunciation before the time for performance had arrived. Nor has the vendee deliberately incapacitated itself or rendered performance of the contract impossible within the rule laid down in Roehm v. Horst, 178 U. S. 18."

Phœnix National Bank *v.* Waterbury, 20 A. B. R. 140, 108 N. Y. Supp. 391 (affirmed in 23 A. B. R. 250), which see quoted, post, § 2731: "The question is whether the sum was 'absolutely owing at the time of the filing of the petition.' An examination of the contract shows that it is essentially an agreement for a sale and purchase in the future, and as we construe it cannot be regarded as in any sense a present sale with a postponement of payment. The language is that the defendants 'agree to purchase * * * on the first day of May, 1900.' Until that time the whole title remained in plaintiff. Before May 1, 1900, the plaintiff could not call upon defendants to take the stock, and consequently could not put defendants under a present obligation to pay the purchase price. In other words, the plaintiff could not prior to that date put the defendants in the position of debtors to it. The fact that the amount to be paid when the agreement to purchase should be consummated was to be the sum of $25,000 with interest from a stated date, does not characterize the transaction as one creating a debt presently owing, but payable in the future. That method of fixing the amount to be paid resulted from the option given by the contract to defendants, not to plaintiff, to complete the purchase on an earlier date than May 1, 1900, and was only another way of saying that the purchase price should be a sum equivalent to $25,000, with interest from April 2, 1894, to the date of purchase. We are unable to find in the contract any words indicating that the transaction amounted to a present sale of the stock, with the date of payment deferred. If, for instance, the plaintiff had sold the stock to a third person, before the time came for the completion of the purchase, it is difficult to see how plaintiff could have been sued in conversion, or, if on the date of the filing of the petition in bankruptcy, the defendants had been seeking to reduce the assessment of their personal property for the purposes of taxation, they would not have been permitted to deduct the agreed purchase price of the stock as a debt which they then owed. The provability of a debt under the present Bankruptcy Act is specifically referred to the date of filing the petition. If it is owing then, it may be proved. If it becomes due after the filing of the petition, even if before the adjudication, it may not be proved and will not be discharged. Herein the present Bankruptcy Act differs from its predecessors. Both the Act of 1841 and that of 1867, besides providing for the proving of debts presently owing, but not presently payable, expressly provided that contingent debts and liabilities might be proven, and payment thereon made out of the bankrupt's assets. (Bankruptcy Act of 1867, § 19; Bankruptcy Act of 1841, § 5.) Both the Act of 1867 and that of 1841 carefully observed and preserved the distinction between contingent liabilities that were not due and might never become due, and debts which were owing but not payable until a future day. The present act has provided that the latter may be proved, but has made no provision for the former. In regard to other omissions in the present act of provisions contained in the former acts, the rule has obtained that the omissions must be deemed to have been deliberate and intentional, and should not be supplied by construction (Bardes *v.* Hawarden Bank, 178 U. S. 524, 4 Am. B. R. 163; Pirie *v.* Chicago Title & Trust Co., 182 U. S. 438, 5 Am. B. R. 814), and in at least one case this omission has been held to forbid the proof of contingent liabilities. (Matter of Marks, 6 Am. B. R. 641.) And even if we were permitted to make the attempt to read into the act by construction, that which the Congress had omitted, we should find ourselves confronted with the positive declaration that in order to be provable, a debt must be 'absolutely owing.' Clearly that which is only contingent, cannot be said to be 'absolutely' owing. The defendants' liability is not of that class of claims referred to in subdivision 4 of rule 21 of the United States Supreme Court General Orders in Bankruptcy which is limited to persons who may be contingently liable for some debt or default of the bankrupt. That the defendants' liability under their contract was contingent cannot, we think, be disputed. Such liability was not to become absolute until May 1, 1900, long after the petition in bankruptcy was filed. Up to that time the defendants owed plaintiff nothing, and there was nothing which plaintiff had a right to demand of defendants. Before that time, many things might happen in consequence of which no debt would become owing from defendants to plaintiff. In our view, therefore, whatever obligation the contract imposed upon defendants was merely contingent when the petition in bankruptcy was filed, was not provable in that proceeding, and was not discharged as a result of that proceeding."

§ 690½. Renunciation of Executory Contracts in General.—A

trustee is under no obligation to assume an executory contract of the bankrupt, and if the same be burdensome he may renounce it, in which event the other party may be entitled to prove his damages for the breach.[63]

Similarly, if the bankrupt before the bankruptcy has renounced the contract, the other party may prove his claim for the damages caused by the breach.

In re Spittler, 18 A. B. R. 425, 151 Fed. 942 (D. C. Conn.): "On behalf of himself and his corporation, he stated, in no uncertain terms, the fact that the existing situation precluded and eliminated any possibility of performing the contract on their part. The referee allowed the claim with much hesitation The doubts which assailed him do not trouble me. He thinks that the decided cases rather carry the idea that the refusal to perform, or the inability to perform, must be a wrongful refusal, or an inability growing out of a disposition to commit a wrongful act. I do not so read the cases. An absolute inability to perform, which is of such a nature that there is no reasonable probability that thereafter a situation will arise which will make performance possible, is enough. If to such inability is added a statement that it exists, then the party so informed is in a position to treat the contract as broken and to pursue his remedy." Referred to in In re Nat. Wire Corp., 22 A. B. R. 186, 166 Fed. 631 (D. C. Conn.).

But it has been held that involuntary bankruptcy proceedings are not to be considered an anticipatory breach of a contract of sale.

In re Inman & Co., 23 A. B. R. 566, 175 Fed. 312 (D. C. Ga.): "It is agreed that there had been no breach of the contract prior to the filing of the petition in bankruptcy proceedings. It is also agreed that there has been no tender since the commencement of the bankruptcy proceedings by S. Lesser of any of the goods to the receiver or trustee. He relies upon an anticipatory breach of the contract caused by the bankruptcy proceeding. I do not believe that, where involuntary proceedings in bankruptcy are instituted, and the bankrupt's business and effects are taken charge of by the court, and administered for the benefit of creditors, it constitutes such a breach of an executory contract as to authorize proof in bankruptcy for the amount of damages claimed to have been caused by the failure to carry out the contract, nor do I think that any of the cases cited go to this extent." Compare, however, quotation at § 686.

---

63. See post, §§ 932, 1144½.
What Does Not Constitute Breach of Bankrupt's Contract to Buy.—In re

National Wire Corporation, 22 A. B. R. 186, 166 Fed. 631 (D. C. Conn.).

DIVISION 8.

CLAIMS FOR COSTS.

§ 691. Costs as Provable Claims.—Costs taxable against an involuntary bankrupt, who was at the time of the filing of the petition against him, plaintiff in a cause of action which would pass to the trustee and which the trustee declines to prosecute after notice, are provable against the bankrupt estate.[64] And taxable costs incurred in good faith by a creditor before the filing of the bankruptcy petition, in an action to recover a provable debt, are provable debts against the bankrupt estate.[65]

But to sue or levy execution when the creditor suspects his debtor of being insolvent is not "bad faith" and costs incurred therein are nevertheless provable; nor is it necessary that the action or proceedings should have accrued to the benefit of the estate, unless it is sought to give the costs priority of payment out of the estate under § 64 (b) (2).

Obiter, In re Harnden, 29 A. B. R. 504, 200 Fed. 172, 175 (D. C. New Mex.): "It is said, however, on behalf of the referee's ruling, that the claimants manifestly acted in bad faith, because they knew that Harnden was insolvent, or at least in a failing condition, when they levied their execution. There is no proof to sustain the referee's finding that claimants knew he was insolvent. The mere fact that they believed him to be in financial straits did not preclude their proceeding to assert their legal rights. The law favors the vigilant, and certainly cannot impute bad faith because creditors, believing those indebted to them to be in close circumstances financially, proceed to attempt a collection of what is due them. Indeed, proceedings to collect a debt are usually the result of a conviction by the creditor that he is otherwise in danger of losing his claim. The referee seems also to have been influenced in his decision by the fact that these costs did not inure to the benefit of the estate. This, however, is no part of the requirements of statute making such costs a provable debt. Such a consideration is germane if there be an attempt to give such a claim priority in the administration of the assets (In re Beaver Coal Co., supra); but here there is no such attempt. The relief sought is simply that these costs may be received as provable claims."

§ 692. Part Incurred before Filing of Petition, Part Afterward.—Where part of the costs were incurred before and part after the filing of the petition against the debtor, the part incurred before the filing is provable against the estate and is discharged by the bankrupt's discharge.[66] And the part incurred afterwards is neither provable nor dischargeable and the bankrupt remains liable thereon.[67]

---

64. Bankr. Act, § 63 (a) (2). But compare, In re Marcus, 5 A. B. R. 19, 104 Fed. 331 (D. C. Mass.).

65. Bankr. Act, § 63 (a) (3); In re Harnden, 29 A. B. R. 504, 200 Fed. 172 (D. C. N. Mex.), quoted supra; In re Amoratis, 24 A. B. R. 565, 178 Fed. 919 (C. C. A. Calif.), quoted on other points as § 2197.

Costs on Recognizance Given in Criminal Case.—In one case it has been held that the costs on a recovery on a recognizance given in a criminal case may be proved, though the recovery itself be not provable since it is a penalty within the meaning of Bankr. Act § 57 (j). In re Caponigri, 27 A. B. R. 513, 193 Fed. 291 (D. C. N. Y.).

66. Aiken, Lambert & Co. v. Haskins, 6 A. B. R. 46 (N. Y. Sup. Ct.).

67. Aiken, Lambert & Co. v. Haskins, 6 A. B. R. 46 (N. Y. Sup. Ct.).

In re Marcus, 5 A. B. R. 365, 105 Fed. 907 (C. C. A. Mass.): "The bankrupt was adjudicated such on his own petition, filed before the judgment for costs was rendered, as already said. Therefore the costs were not provable against the estate.. * * *

"Section 63a directs specifically what taxable costs are provable, and its provisions with reference thereto must be held to cover that entire subject-matter." This decision says "after adjudication," but it was a case of voluntary bankruptcy and therefore the date of the filing of the petition and of the adjudication were likely the same.

The ruling that costs accruing and paid after the bankruptcy by a surety of the bankrupt are provable[68] does not militate against the doctrine of this section; for such costs are provable as part of the damages, unliquidated at the time of the filing of the bankruptcy petition, accruing by virtue of the suretyship, the suretyship being a liability both fixed and absolutely owing at the time of the bankruptcy though damages thereunder were not liquidated until afterwards, under the doctrine of § 673, ante.

§ 693. Costs Where Attachment or Execution Dissolved.—Costs incurred in good faith prior to the filing of the bankruptcy petition on attachment or execution, where the lien of the attachment or execution is dissolved by the subsequent bankruptcy within four months, are provable claims.[69]

DIVISION 9.

OPEN ACCOUNTS AND CONTRACTS EXPRESS OR IMPLIED.

§ 694. Open Accounts and Contracts Express or Implied, Provable.—Debts founded upon open accounts or upon contracts express or implied are provable.[70]

This class of provable claims is the most extensive of all classes, but the discussion of the different points involved is taken up in other Divisions of

---

68. In re Lyons Sugar Co., 27 A. B. R. 610, 192 Fed. 445 (D. C. N. Y.), discussed ante at § 672 and § 673.

69. Bankr. Act, § .63 (a) (3). In re Allen, 3 A. B. R. 38, 96 Fed. 512 (D. C. Calif.); In re Thompson Mercantile Co., 11 A. B. R. 579 (Ref. Minn.); In re Amoratis, 24 A. B. R. 565, 178 Fed. 919 (C. C. A. Calif.), quoted on other points at § 2197.

Where, however, the lien is preserved for the benefit of the estate under § 67f, the lien for costs is also preserved, Receivers v. Staake, 13 A. B. R. 281, 133 Fed. 717 (C. C. A. Va.). Obiter, In re Thompson Mercantile Co., 11 A. B. R. 579 (Ref. Minn.); inferentially, In re Goldberg Bros., 16 A. B. R. 522, 144 Fed. 566 (D. C. Me.). See post, § 1490.

Some cases have also seemed to lead to the inference that in some instances —probably where the attachment proceedings have operated to the benefit of all creditors—the court would consider the costs to be an equitable lien on the property. In re Francis-Valentine Co., 2 A. B. R. 522, 94 Fed. 793 (C. C. A. Calif.). See ante, § 400; also, see post, §§ 2001, 2063, et seq., "Costs of Administration," "Expenses of Petitioning Creditors."

Attachment Costs as a Priority Claim under § 67 (b) (5).—See post, §§ 2196, 2197, 2198.

70. Bankr. Act, § 63 (a) (4); In re Big Cahaba, etc., Co., 25 A. B. R. 761, 183 Fed. 662 (D. C. Ala.); Sturgiss v. Meurer. 26 A. B. R. 851, 191 Fed. 9 (C. C. A. W. Va.).

this chapter and elsewhere in the treaties in paragraphs too numerous even to refer to in detail.

It has been held that there is no implied promise of reimbursement to be drawn from the use of the words "represent and warrant" except in cases of conveyances of real estate, transfers of personal property, or contracts of insurance, and then only as between the opposite parties; and that where one of several joint purchasers uses those words towards his co-purchasers no right of action for their failure to be true will arise against him in their favor on the basis of any implied contract of reimbursement.[71]

§ 694½. Claims "Not Owing," or "Contingent," etc., Not Provable as "on Contract Express or Implied.—Claims that are "contingent" or not "owing at the time of the filing of the bankruptcy petition" and hence not provable, are not made provable by the clause permitting proof of claims "on contract express or implied."

In re Roth & Appel, 24 A. B. R. 588, 181 Fed. 667 (C. C. A. N. Y.): "It is urged, in effect, that the claim whether regarded as a demand for rent or as based upon the indemnity provision, is 'a debt founded upon an express contract' and provable under the fourth clause of § 63 (a), irrespective of the question whether it is of such character as to be provable under the first clause. * * * All claims upon instruments in writing not provable under the first clause, because not absolutely owing at the time of the petition, might be proved as claims founded upon a 'contract express or implied' under the fourth clause if no limitations are attached to the latter. We cannot regard this interpretation as tenable. We think that the different clauses of § 63 (a) should not be considered as independent, but should be read together, and that the said limitation in the first clause should be considered as repeated in the fourth clause."

Not even where liquidated within the year limited for proof of claims.[72]

DIVISION 10.

PROVABLE DEBTS REDUCED TO JUDGMENT AFTER BANKRUPTCY PETITION FILED AND BEFORE DISCHARGE.

§ 695. Provable Debts Reduced to Judgment after Bankruptcy but before Discharge, Provable.—Debts founded upon provable debts reduced to judgment after the filing of the petition and before the consideration of the bankrupt's application for a discharge are provable, less costs incurred and interest accrued after the filing of the petition and up to the time of the entry of such judgment.[73]

---

71. Switzer & Johnson *v.* Henking, 19 A. B. R. 300, 158 Fed. 784 (C. C. A. Ohio).

Partners for Contributory Share.— See post. §§ 2247½. 2259.

Accounts Stated.—What constitutes an "account stated;" also when an "account rendered" becomes an "account stated." Little, Trustee, *v.* Mc-

Clain, 22 A. B. R. 837, 118 N. Y. Supp. 917.

72. Contra (rent claim), In re Caloris Mfg. Co., 24 A. B. R. 609, 179 Fed. 722 (D. C. Pa.).

73. Bankr. Act, § 63 (a) (5). In re McBryde, 3 A. B. R. 729, 99 Fed. 686 (D. C. N. Car.).

§ 696. Object—To Prevent Effect of Merger.—The object of this provision appears to be the avoidance of the injustice both to creditors and debtors of the doctrine that judgments operate as mergers of original causes of action so that original causes of action are lost in the judgments and yet the judgments are not provable nor dischargeable debts because not rendered until *after* the filing of the petition.

In re Pinkel, 1 A. B. R. 333 (Ref. N. Y.): "This is the old question of the effect of the entry of a judgment on a provable debt between the filing of the petition in bankruptcy and the discharge, the action having been begun prior to the filing of the petition. The numerous and contradictory District Court decisions on this point under the Law of 1867 would be amusing were an examination of them productive of anything better than confusion. Under the Acts of 1800 and 1841, there seems to have been little question; and the Federal courts so far modified the doctrine of a merger resulting from a reduction of a contract debt to a judgment, as to permit the proving of a debt in bankruptcy even after it had been merged in a judgment for all other purposes. But the Law of 1867 (§ 21, or R. S. 5106) both prohibited a creditor having a provable debt from prosecuting the same to judgment before the bankrupt's right to a discharge should be determined, and gave the bankrupt the right to a stay to prevent such prosecution at any time. Arguing from this that no judgment between the filing of the petition and the granting of the discharge could have validity, if attacked, and that after the discharge was granted it could be pleaded in bar, many of the District Courts settled back on the old doctrine of merger, and held that the debt which antedated the application in bankruptcy was gone and that the judgment when obtained was a new debt, which, being after the filing of the bankrupt's petition, could not be proven and therefore was not discharged. Typical cases holding this doctrine are: Re Williams, 2 N. B. R. 229; Re Gallison, 5 N. B. R. 353; Re Mansfield, 6 N. B. R. 388. Other district judges, notably Judge Blatchford, in the Southern District of New York, early insisted that such a ruling would be unjust to the creditor in preventing him from sharing in dividends to which he seemed entitled, and equally unjust to the bankrupt in permitting some of his creditors to begin actions and, by withholding the entry of judgments until after a petition in bankruptcy was filed, to preserve their claims undischarged and thus subsequently collect them out of after-acquired property. This view led to a series of decisions (Re Brown, 3 N. B. R. 585; Re Rosey, No. 12,066, Fed. Cases; Re Vickery, No. 16,930, Fed. Cases; Re Stansfield, No. 13,294, Fed. Cases) which held that the debt was not merged in the judgment, and that therefore the debt or claim as it stood at the time of filing the petition in bankruptcy and not the judgment entered thereafter should be proved. There were also cases betwixt and between, notably that of Re Crawford, 3 N. B. R. 385, and Monroe *v.* Upton, 50 N. Y. 593, who held so far to the doctrine of merger as to compel the proof of the judgment not as a new debt, but as the old debt in a new form. * * *

"The exact question did not come before the United States Supreme Court until 1887. In the case of Boynton *v.* Ball, 121 U. S. 457, Mr. Justice Miller writing the opinion, that court, in a case which arose under the Law of 1867, lays down the broad doctrines that, notwithstanding the change in the form of the debt from that of a simple contract by merger into a judgment, it in bankruptcy still remains the same debt, the existence of which was provable in bankruptcy. This is tantamount to saying that the doctrine of merger does not apply in bankruptcy, but no more.

"The law of 1898 agrees with the law of 1867 in giving the bankrupt the right to stay pending suits, and, though it does not in so many words prohibit the prosecution of suits on provable debts, the right to stay puts the question in much the same form as that which led to such confusion under the former law. Boynton *v.* Ball would therefore settle the question, were there not a new clause in the present statute which must now be interpreted. Section 63 of the Law of 1898 provides: 'Debts of the bankrupt may be proved and allowed against his estate which are * * * (5) founded upon provable debts reduced to judgments after the filing of the petition and before the consideration of the bankrupt's application for discharge, less costs incurred and interests accrued after the filing of the petition and up to the time of the entry of such judgments.' "

The object, also, is to permit judgment to be taken after bankruptcy, where judgment is necessary to fix the liability of those secondarily liable for the bankrupt, without destroying the bankrupt's right of discharge therefrom.

By the operation of this Class V, judgments obtained after the filing of the bankruptcy petition, but before the discharge hearing, are themselves discharged, if founded on a debt itself provable, whether stay is granted or not.

By the operation of this Class V, on the other hand, opportunity may be given to creditors to obtain judgment where the obtaining of a judgment is necessary to take advantage of certain remedies, as, for instance, where creditors levying execution on exempt property may have special rights in the exempt property denied to creditors without judgments; and also where judgment is necessary to fix the liability of a surety on an appeal bond conditioned to pay any "judgment" that might be rendered against the debtor; and also where a mechanic's lien is dependent upon suit being started in a particular way within a limited time.

§ 697. Original Obligation Must Have Been "Provable."—The original obligation must itself have been a provable debt; that is to say, must have been a judgment, or written instrument, or costs, or taxes, or an open account or a contract, express or implied; and it must also have been in existence at the time of the filing of the bankruptcy petition.[74]

Thus, a judgment for personal injury rendered before discharge but after the filing of the petition, is not a provable debt.[75]

The nature of the liability, rather than the remedy by which it was enforced, determines its provability.[76]

---

74. In re Pinkel, 1 A. B. R. 333 (Ref. N. Y.).
75. In re Crescent Lumber Co., 19 A. B. R. 112, 154 Fed. 724 (D. C. Ala.). Also, see ante, § 680.
76. In re Southern Steel Co., 25 A. B. R. 358, 183 Fed. 498 (D. C. Ala.).

§ 698. Original Debt, Not the Judgment, to Be Proved.—Evidently it is the original debt, not the judgment, that is to be proved;[77] and claims thus reduced to judgment retain the character of the indebtedness out of which they arise.[78]

§ 699. Whether Judgment Itself Still Valid, for Other Purposes. —It has been held that the judgment itself is not annulled, simply its lien.[79]

In re Richard, 2 A. B. R. 513, 94 Fed. 633 (D. C. N. Car.): "Respondents have received, and can receive no preference, lien or advantage by reason of, or under the judgments of the magistrate's court. They are nullities in this court to this extent, but they establish the claim. Section 63, in prescribing what debts may be proved, provides '(5) for provable debts reduced to judgment after the petition is filed, etc.' "

Probably it is still valid as res adjudicata.

§ 700. Does Not Enlarge Time for Proving Claims nor Confer Lien, etc.—On the other hand, class 5 does not enlarge the time for proving claims in bankruptcy;[80] nor does it confer a lien in bankruptcy or otherwise confer additional rights therein.[81]

DIVISION 11.

TAXES.

§ 701. Taxes.—Taxes also are "provable" in their nature.[82]

§ 702. Taxes Not to Be Proved in Form of Other Debts.—Taxes do not need to be proved in the form prescribed for other claims, the treasurer's receipt therefor being sufficient.[83]

§ 703. Trustee to Search Out Taxes.—And there is no obligation upon the tax officers to present the claim at all, the obligation resting upon the trustee to search out and pay the taxes.

And the trustee may be surcharged where his failure to pay taxes subjects the estate to interest and penalties.[84]

---

77. In re Pinkel, 1 A. B. R. 333 (Ref. N. Y.).

78. In re McBryde, 3 A. B. R. 729, 99 Fed. 686 (D. C. N. Car.).

79. Apparently, but not really, contra, St. Cyr. v. Daignault, 4 A. B. R. 638 (D. C. Vt.).

80. In re Leibowitz, 6 A. B. R. 268, 108 Fed. 617 (D. C. Tex.).

81. In re McBryde, 3 A. B. R. 729, 99 Fed. 686 (D. C. N. Car.).

82. Taxes Considered under Subject of "Distribution."—As to what are and what are not taxes within the purview of this section, and the duties of the trustee in relation thereto, see post, subject of "Distribution," § 2133, et seq.

83. Bankr. Act, § 64 (a). Compare, In re Cleanfast Hosiery Co., 4 A. B. R. 702 (Ref. N. Y.); In re United Button Co., 15 A. B. R. 400, 140 Fed. 495 (D. C. Del.).

84. In re Monsarrat (No. 2), 25 A. B. R. 820 (D. C. Hawaii).

DIVISION 12.

UNLIQUIDATED CLAIMS.

§ 704. Claim May Be "Provable" Though "Unliquidated."—A claim may be "provable" even if "unliquidated."[85]

In re Du Quesne Incandescent Light Co., 24 A. B. R. 419, 176 Fed. 785 (D. C. Pa.): "The claim under consideration was founded upon an express contract in writing, the damages for the breach of which were unliquidated. The claim was therefore a provable claim, and under Section 63 (b) could be liquidated upon application to the court in such manner as it should direct."

Thus, damages for breach of contract to marry are "provable," though unliquidated.[86] On the other hand a claim for moneys loaned is a liquidated and not an unliquidated claim.[87] But unliquidated claims must be liquidated before being allowed.[88] The statute says "proved and allowed," but it is obvious that some sort of "proof" must be filed before the court may "direct" the manner of liquidation, and doubtless such proof is sufficient to base an amendment upon, the amendment likely being the "proved" claim here meant.[89]

§ 705. "Unliquidated Claims" Do Not Enlarge Classes of "Provable" Debts.—Clause (b) of § 63 does not enlarge the classes of provable debts but simply provides for reducing into form in which they may be proved those debts which if liquidated (that is to say, made certain and definite in amount), could be proved under clause (a) as being either judgment debts, contract debts, taxes or costs.[90]

---

85. Bankr. Act, § 63 (b). In re Stern, 3 A. B. R. 569, 116 Fed. 604 (C. C. A. N. Y., affirming In re Manhattan Ice Co., 7 A. B. R. 408, 114 Fed. 400); In re Grant Shoe Co., 11 A. B. R. 48 (D. C. N. Y., affirmed in 12 A. B. R. 349, 130 Fed. 881, C. C. A.); Grant Shoe Co. v. Laird Co., 21 A. B. R. 484, 212 U. S. 445, affirming In re Grant Shoe Co., supra. In re Hilton, 4 A. B. R. 774, 104 Fed. 981 (D. C. N. Y.). Contra, In re Big Meadows Gas Co., 7 A. B. R. 697, 113 Fed. 974 (D. C. Penn.).

86. In re Fife, 6 A. B. R. 258, 109 Fed. 880 (D. C. Pa.); In re Crocker, 3 A. B. R. 188 (Ref. N. Y.); In re McCauley, 4 A. B. R. 122, 101 Fed. 223 (D. C. N. Y.); Finnegan v. Hall, 6 A. B. R. 648 (N. Y. Sup. Ct.); impliedly (because dischargeable), Bond v. Milliken, 17 A. B. R. 811, 109 N. W. 774 (Iowa); Desler v. McCauley, 7 A. B. R. 138 (N. Y. Sup. Ct., App. Div., reversing 6 A. B. R. 491).

87. In re Halsey Elec. Generator Co., 20 A. B. R. 738, 163 Fed. 118 (D. C. N. J.).

88. Bankr. Act, § 63 (b). In re Cushing, 6 A. B. R. 22 (Ref. N. Y.); In re Silverman Bros., 4 A. B. R. 83, 101 Fed. 219 (D. C. Mo.).

89. Suggestively, In re Mertens, 16 A. B. R. 829 (C. C. A. N. Y.); Inferentially, Grant Shoe Co. v. Laird Co., 21 A. B. R. 484, 212 U. S. 445.

90. In re Marcus, 5 A. B. R. 19 (D. C. Mass., affirmed in 5 A. B. R. 365, 105 Fed. 907); In re Hirschman, 4 A. B. R. 715, 104 Fed. 69 (D. C. Utah); In re Wigmore, 10 A. B. R. 664 (Ref. Calif.); compare, Crawford v. Burke, 12 A. B. R. 659, 195 U. S. 176; compare, Beers v. Hanlin, 3 A. B. R. 745, 99 Fed. 695 (D. C. Ore.), where the court seems to hold the doctrine that the bankruptcy court might permit suit to be maintained upon a purely personal tort in order that it might become "provable" as a judgment. However, the court in fact does not go to that extent. See, in addition, In re Inman & Co., 22 A. B. R. 524, 171 Fed. 185 (D. C. Ga.); In re Southern Steel Co., 25 A. B. R. 358, 183 Fed. 498 (D. C. Ala.); Clarke v. Rogers, 26 A. B. R. 413, 183 Fed. 518 (C. C. A. Mass.).

Dunbar *v.* Dunbar, 10 A. B. R. 139, 190 U. S. 349: "This paragraph (b), however, adds nothing to the class of debts which might be proved under paragraph (a) of the same section. Its purpose is to permit an unliquidated claim, coming within the provisions of § 63a to be liquidated as the court shall direct."

Brown & Adams *v.* Button Co., 17 A. B. R. 565, 149 Fed. 48 (C. C. A. Del., affirming In re United Button Co.): "The first of the two paragraphs into which it is divided is given up to an enumeration of the debts which are entitled to be proved against the estate, among which is to be found everything in the way of a fixed obligation, or which, as being of a commercial character, a bankrupt could expect to be relieved from; and, complete in itself, it is not to be added to. The other paragraph plainly has to do with a mere matter of procedure; how unliquidated claims founded upon open account or contract, specified in the preceding paragraph, may be liquidated or settled."

In re Yates, 8 A. B. R. 69, 114 Fed. 365 (D. C. Calif.): "This subdivision is not to be construed as authorizing the proof of claims not declared in subdivision (a) to be provable. Its object is simply to provide that unliquidated claims which fall within the scope of subdivision (a) are to be liquidated in such manner as the court shall direct."

In re United Button Co., 15 A. B. R. 397, 140 Fed. 496 (D. C. Del., affirmed sub nom. Brown & Adams *v.* Button Co., 17 A. B. R. 565, 149 Fed. 48): "There is no legitimate ground for an assumption that Congress intended by so providing for the liquidation, proof and allowance of 'unliquidated claims' to add to the classes of provable demands mentioned in § 63a. Such an assumption would be not only uncalled for, but wholly inadmissible. For, unless the 'unliquidated claims' of § 63b be restricted to those made provable by § 63a, there is no limitation upon the provability of unliquidated demands of whatsoever nature against a bankrupt. Such a result would be repugnant to the express enumeration contained in § 63a, and, further, would, as hereinafter appears, involve a wide departure from the settled policy of every system of bankruptcy heretofore in force in the United States."

In re New York Tunnel Co., 20 A. B. R. 25, 159 Fed. 688 (C. C. A. N. Y.): "This paragraph evidently relates to procedure. It provides for the liquidation of such of the claims enumerated in the preceding paragraph, e. g., for breach of contract, as might require such process. The one paragraph particularly enumerating the debts which are provable, we see no ground for holding that the other opens the door to unliquidated demands of every nature."

Inferentially, In re Grant Shoe Co., 12 A. B. R. 350, 130 Fed. 881 (C. C. A. N. Y., affirming 11 A. B. R. 48, and affirmed sub nom. Grant Shoe Co. *v.* Laird Co., 21 A. B. R. 484, 212 U. S. 445): "To hold. as is contended by the alleged bankrupt, that a claim is not provable because the amount of the claim itself is not determinable, or its validity is disputed, would defeat the involuntary provisions of the Bankrupt Act. The court below has found that the claim, although unliquidated is a provable one and under the provisions of § 63 (b) of said Act, has provided for its liquidation. * * * The order of the District Court is affirmed."

In re Roth & Appel, 24 A. B. R. 588, 181 Fed. 667 (C. C. A. N. Y.): "Section 63 (b) adds nothing to the class of debts provided under 63 (a). It merely permits the liquidation of an unliquidated claim provable under the latter provision."

The words "liquidated by litigation" are not confined to litigant creditors; thus they have been held to extend to a surety on an appeal bond for costs in a suit pending when the petititon in bankruptcy was filed, where part of the costs did not accrue until after the filing of the bankruptcy petition.[91]

§ 706. Only Contract Claims and Tort Claims Capable of Presentation as if on Implied Contracts, Liquidatable.—Inasmuch as all classes under clause (a) save and except contract debts are, from their very nature already liquidated—as judgments, taxes and costs—clause (b) simply provides for the liquidation of unliquidated contract debts, as, for instance, for determining the amount of damages for a breach of contract, etc., etc.;[92] including tort claims when the tort has been waived.[93]

§ 707. Damages on Contracts Accruing after Bankruptcy.—Thus, as to unliquidated contract debts: Damages for breach of continuing contracts to supply goods or render services or pay money may be liquidated, even before the expiration of the term, if the future damages are ascertainable.

Thus, as to continuing contracts to sell or buy goods;[94] as to annuity bonds;[95] as to contracts for annual salary, where dismissal occurs before the end of the term.[96] Thus, also, as to breach of contract to marry, which, it has been held, may be liquidated by the bankruptcy court (the referee).[97] Thus, likewise, as to the prospective profits lost by breach of contract to furnish goods;[98] as well as damages for refusal to receive goods contracted for.[99]

Annuity installments accruing after bankruptcy may be liquidated and the claim proved.[1] Again, damages for breach of contract to supply the government with goods can be liquidated, and the claim is provable;[2] likewise damages for breach of contract to supply customers with goods.[3]

---

91. In re Lyons Sugar Co., 27 A. B. R. 610, 192 Fed. 445 (D. C. N. Y.). See also ante, §§ 672, 673, 692.

92. See cases cited under the subject "Damages for Breaches of Continuing Contracts and of Contracts of Sale and of Employment," ante, Div. 7. See also, instances hereinafter cited. And for liquidating such unliquidated claims for tort as are capable of being presented as implied contracts, see ante, "Claims Ex Delicto," Div. 2, this chapter. See also, Clarke v. Rogers, 26 A. B. R. 413, 183 Fed. 518 (C. C. A. Mass.).

93. Clarke v. Rogers, 26 A. B. R. 413, 183 Fed. 518 (C. C. A. Mass.).

94. In re Stern, 8 A. B. R. 569, 116 Fed. 604 (C. C. A. N. Y.); In re Manhattan Ice Co., 7 A. B. R. 408, 114 Fed. 400 (D. C. N. Y., affirmed sub nom. In re Stern, 8 A. B. R. 569, 116 Fed. 604 (C. C. A. N. Y.). Also compare, to same effect, In re Pettingill & Co., 14 A. B. R. 728, 137 Fed. 143 (D. C. Mass.); also compare, to same effect,

In re Stoever, 11 A. B. R. 345, 127 Fed. 394 (D. C. Pa.).

95. Compare, to same effect, Cobb v. Overman, 6 A. B. R. 324, 109 Fed. 65 (C. C. A. N. Car.).

96. In re Silverman Bros., 4 A. B. R. 83, 101 Fed. 219 (D. C. Mo., reversing 2 A. B. R. 15).

97. In re Crocker, 8 A. B. R. 188 (D. C. N. Y.).

98. In re Structural Steel Car Co., 13 A. B. R. 373 (Ref. Ohio); In re Saxton Furnace Co., 15 A. B. R. 445, 142 Fed. 293 (D. C. Pa.), including commissions paid to an agent by the seller.

99. In re Structural Steel Car Co., 13 A. B. R. 385 (Ref. Ohio).

1. In re Cobb v. Overman, 6 A. B. R. 324, 109 Fed. 65 (C. C. A. N. Car.).

2. In re Stoever, 11 A. B. R. 345, 127 Fed. 394 (D. C. Pa.).

3. See ante, §§ 674, 685, 689. Also see In re Du Quesne Incandescent Light Co., 24 A. B. R. 419, 176 Fed. 785 (D. C. Pa.), quoted, but on other points, §§ 674, 685, 712; In re Manhattan Ice

And for breach of contract of a stockbroker with his customer to purchase shares on margin.[4]

And a subscription to a mercantile agency, is a provable claim, although the period has not elapsed.

> In re Mirror & Beveling Co., 15 A. B. R. 122 (Ref. N. Y.): "A contract between a mercantile agency and a customer, whereby, in consideration of an annual subscription fee, such agency agrees to supply such customer with its reference book and detailed report during the year, is an enforceable contract against the bankrupt; and even though at the time of the bankruptcy a large portion of the contract year has yet to elapse, such mercantile agency has a provable debt for the full subscription price."

And damages for breach of warranty of goods has been held likewise provable, though the damages were not ascertained at the time of bankruptcy.[5]

The query arises, however, in case the term were of long duration, how could the damages be liquidated within the statutory time since the employee is bound to use his best efforts to get employment meantime and thus to reduce the damages, and it cannot be known until the end of the term what his damage will amount to? The same reasoning probably would apply here as in the case of rent, as to which, see ante, "Claims for Rent," Div. 4, this chapter, § 652, et seq.

Liquidation within the year will not, however, make an otherwise contingent claim, or claim not owing at the time of the filing of the bankruptcy petition, any the more provable;[6] as, for example, damages for breach of covenant to pay rent in the future are.[7]

But where the bankruptcy does not, in and of itself, disable the bankrupt from the performance of the contract it is difficult to see how the debt is provable for possible future failure to meet its obligations as they accrue from time to time.[8]

Where the goods contracted for are of special or peculiar make, the value of damages against a defaulting buyer may be the difference between the contract price and the cost of manufacture, rather than the contract price and the market price[9] and any actual sales are for the buyer to prove, in mitigation.[10] The Uniform Code of Sales, adopted in many of the states, provides that where there is no reasonable market for such goods

---

Co., 7 A. B. R. 408, 114 Fed. 400 (D. C. N. Y., affirmed sub nom. In re Stern, 8 A. B. R. 569, 116 Fed. 604, C. C. A. N. Y.).

4. In re Swift, 7 A. B. R. 374, 112 Fed. 315 (C. C. A. Mass.); In re Swift, 3 N. B. N. & R. 271 (D. C. Mass.); In re Hurlbutt Hatch Co., 16 A. B. R. 198 (C. C. A. N. Y.).

5. In re Morales, 5 A. B. R. 425, 105 Fed. 761 (D. C. Fla.). In this case the claim was held to sound in tort, not in contract.

6. But compare, contra, In re Cal-

oris Mfg. Co., 24 A. B. R. 609, 179 Fed. 722 (D. C. Pa.), cited ante at §§ 656, 672, 675.

7. But compare, contra, In re Caloris Mfg. Co., 24 A. B. R. 609, 179 Fed. 722 (D. C. Pa.).

8. In re Brew Co., 16 A. B. R. 110, 143 Fed. 579 (D. C. Mo.).

9. In re Du Quesne Incandescent Light Co., 24 A. B. R. 419, 176 Fed. 785 (D. C. Pa.).

10. In re Du Quesne Incandescent Light Co., 24 A. B. R. 419, 176 Fed. 785 (D. C. Pa.).

the manufacturer may claim for the entire price, notifying the buyer that the goods are being held on his account.

§ 708. Liquidated Amount Stipulated in Contract.—Where a liquidated amount is stipulated in a contract as damages for its breach, such stipulated amount may or may not be regarded as the true amount of the claim, according to circumstances; and where the actual damages sustained are clearly much less than the sum stipulated, the stipulated sum will be regarded as a mere penalty to secure performance.[11]

But unearned installments of rent, although liquidated by a written lease, can not be proven.[12]

§ 709. Stockholders', Officers' and Directors' Liabilities.—Stockholders' secondary liability for debts of the corporation in some of the states is not only a debt created by the statute, but is also one founded upon an implied contract, and it is provable in bankruptcy if the circumstances are such that the claimant could have maintained a suit to enforce the stockholders' liability.[13] It is fixed and not contingent, for all the facts necessary to fix it have already occurred. It is simply unascertained and unliquidated and upon liquidation being made, it becomes provable and allowable.[14]

It has been held that, in California, the statutory or constitutional liability of officers and directors to creditors for funds embezzled or misappropriated is contractual and self-operating, and a provable debt.[15]

The construction put upon such constitutional or statutory provision by the highest court of the state will govern in determining the nature of the liability in bankruptcy.[16]

A bankrupt's liability for his unpaid stock subscription also is a provable debt.[17]

11. Northwest Fixture Co. *v.* Kilbourne & Clark, 11 A. B. R. 725 (C. C. A. Wash.). Compare, to similar effect, In re Bevier Wood Pavement Co., 19 A. B. R. 462, 156 Fed. 583 (D. C. N. Y.).

12. In re Rubel, 21 A. B. R. 566, 166 Fed. 131 (D. C. Wis.).

13. Compare post, § 978.

14. In re Rouse. 1 A. B. R. 393 (Ref. Ohio); In re Remington Automobile & Motor Co., 9 A. B. R. 533, 119 Fed. 441 (D. C. N. Y.); In re Walker, 21 A. B. R. 132, 164 Fed. 680 (C. C. A. Calif.).

Dight *v.* Chapman, 12 A. B. R. 743, 65 L. R. A. 793 (Ore.): A judgment determining the amount to be contributed by the stockholders of an insolvent corporation for the payment of its debts under constitutional and statutory provisions making stockholders liable for debts to the amount of the par value of the stock held by them

was held in this case to render the amount due from each stockholder a debt provable in bankruptcy proceedings, against him so as to be cancelled by a discharge although he did not appear in the proceedings against the corporation, where the judgment therein is binding upon him.

In some of the States it is. however, in the nature of a penalty and not a contract.

The receiver appointed to collect the judgment on the stockholder's liability may prove the claim against the bankrupt stockholders. Dight *v.* Chapman, 12 A. B. R. 743 (Sup. Ct. Ore.).

15. In re Brown, 21 A. B. R. 123, 164 Fed. 673 (C. C. A. Calif.).

16. In re Brown, 21 A. B. R. 123, 164 Fed. 573 (C. C. A. Calif.); In re Walker, 21 A. B. R. 132, 164 Fed. 680 (C. C. A. Calif.).

17. Impliedly, In re Watkinson, 16 A. B. R. 245 (D. C. Pa.). But it is due

§ 710. Liquidation of Claims Ex Delicto Not Authorized, unless.—

This clause does not authorize the liquidation of claims ex delicto, unless they are of such nature that the claimant may waive the tort and sue on the implied contract.[18]

§ 711. Contingent Claims Not to Be Liquidated and Proved under § 63 (b).—

Contingent claims, not being provable, may not be liquidated and then proved under § 63 (b) ; thus, as to claims for rent to accrue after bankruptcy.[19]

In re Rubel, 21 A. B. R. 566, 166 Fed. 131 (D. C. Wis.): "We have seen that the unearned installment of rent, although liquidated by a written lease, cannot be proven under § 63 (a), so that the proceeding to liquidate would have been unavailing in the instant case."

Thus, as to claims of a solvent partner liquidating the firm assets himself rather than permitting them to be administered in the individual bankruptcy of his partner, where the bankrupt partner was not indebted either to the firm or the solvent partner at the time of adjudication.[20]

But claims for rent to accrue in the future, or damages for breach of covenant to pay rent in the future, are not made provable by their becoming liquidated within the year.[21]

§ 712. Manner of Liquidation.—

The court will direct the manner of the liquidation upon the claimant making application to that end.[22]

to the corporation or its receiver and not to a purchaser of a debt of the corporation, In re Watkinson, 16 A. B. R. 245 (D. C. Pa.).

18. In re United Button Co., 15 A. B. R. 396, 140 Fed. 495 (D. C. Del.); see In re Hirschman, 4 A. B. R. 716, 104 Fed. 69 (D. C. Utah); In re Wigmore, 10 A. B. R. 664 (Ref. Calif.); In re Filer, 5 A. B. R. 582, 835 (D. C. N. Y.); In re Yates, 8 A. B. R. 69, 4 Johns 317, 9 Johns 395; In re Morales, 5 A. B. R. 425, 105 Fed. 761 (D. C. Fla.); In re New York Tunnel Co., 20 A. B. R. 26, 159 Fed. 688 (C. C. A. N. Y.), quoted, on other point, at § 705. Compare, In re Cushing, 6 A. B. R. 22 (Ref. N. Y.); compare, Crawford v. Burke, 12 A. B. R. 659, 195 U. S. 176; compare, Hawk v. Hawk, 4 A. B. R. 463, 102 Fed. 679 (D. C. Ark.). See ante, this ch., Div. 2, "Claims Ex Delicto."

Apparently contra, by inference, Beers v. Hanlin, 3 A. B. R. 745, 99 Fed. 695 (D. C. Ore.): "An unliquidated claim is not a provable debt in bankruptcy, and when arising out of tort must be reduced to judgment, or, pursuant to application to the court be liquidated as the court shall direct in order to be proved."

19. In re Arnstein, 4 A. B. R. 246 (Ref. N. Y.); In re Collignon, 4 A. B. R. 250 (Ref. N. Y.); In re Roth & Appel, 24 A. B. R. 588, 181 Fed. 667 (C. C. A. N. Y.), quoted at § 694½. Contra, ("where liquidated within the year") In re Caloris Mfg. Co., 24 A. B. R. 609, 179 Fed. 722 (D. C. Pa.). See ante, this ch., "Contingent Claims," Div. 3. Also, ante, this ch., "Claims for Rent," Div. 4.

20. In re Walker, 23 A. B. R. 805, 164 Fed. 680 (D. C. Ala.), quoted at § 2259.

21. Contra, In re Caloris Mfg. Co., 24 A. B. R. 609, 179 Fed. 722 (D. C. Pa.).

22. In re Silverman Bros., 4 A. B. R. 84, 101 Fed. 219 (D. C. Mo.); instance, In re Faulkner, 20 A. B. R. 542, 180 Fed. 900 (C. C. A. Kans.), quoted at § 734. Obiter, In re Du Quesne Incandescent Light Co., 24 A. B. R. 419, 176 Fed. 785 (D. C. Pa.), quoted on other points at § 674. As to the corresponding provisions of the preceding bankruptcy acts of 1800, 1841 and 1867 and discussion of the same, see In re United Button Co., 15 A. B. R. 394, 140 Fed. 495 (D. C. Del.).

In re United Button Co., 15 A. B. R. 390, 140 Fed. 495 (D. C. Del.): 'Under the power conferred on the court by § 63b, to direct the manner in which unliquidated claims against a bankrupt may be liquidated, ample authority exists to adopt any procedure appropriate to the particular case, whether it be submission to a jury on an issue framed, or production of evidence before the referee or some other method."

But application to that end should be made.

Obiter, In re Rubel, 21 A. B. R. 566, 166 Fed. 131 (D. C. Wis.): "The damages which he claims are entirely unliquidated, and under the provisions of § 63 (b) would not be ripe for presentation or allowance until they had been liquidated by such means as the court might direct upon a petition to that effect. It appears that no application had been made to liquidate this claim. Under these circumstances it would not be necessary to go further in order to justify the ruling of the referee."

But if no application is made and yet the referee takes evidence and determines the amount, it is a sufficient liquidation.

In re Du Quesne Incandescent Light Co., 24 A. B. R. 419, 176 Fed. 785 (D. C. Pa.): "The claim was therefore a provable claim, and under § 63b could be liquidated upon application to the court in such manner as it should direct. As no application was made to the court, and there is no standing order or rule providing a method of procedure by jury trial upon issue framed or by an adjudication upon evidence before the referee or judge, and as the parties submitted themselves to the referee, who after a full hearing and careful consideration of all the evidence adjudicated the claim, which in our opinion was a most satisfactory and appropriate method for the proper liquidation of the damages, we see no reason why the claim is not to be considered as having been proved and liquidated in accordance with §§ 63a and b of the Act."

A proceedings on an issue joined before the referee to determine the validity of an alleged mortgage lien has been held to be a liquidation by litigation.[23]

§ 713. Bankruptcy Court Itself May Liquidate.—The bankruptcy court may itself undertake the liquidation.[24]

And it was held, in one case, that the bankruptcy court might call in a jury to aid in assessing the damages.

---

23. In re Standard, etc., Co., 26 A. B. R. 601, 186 Fed. 586 (D. C. Wis.).

24. Obiter. In re Rouse, 1 A. B. R. 394 (Ref. Ohio, affirmed by D. C.); obiter, In re United Button Co., 15 A. B. R. 392, 140 Fed. 495 (D. C. Del.); In re Buchan's Soap Corporation, 22 A. B. R. 380, 169 Fed. 1017 (D. C. N. Y.). Compare, In re Harper, 23 A. B. R. 918, 175 Fed. 412 (D. C. N. Y.), quoted, on another point § 2259. In re Du Quesne Incandescent Light Co., (Pa.), quoted at §§ 704, 712. And a proceeding on an issue joined before the referee to determine the validity of an alleged mortgage lien has been held to be a liquidation by litigation. In re Standard, etc., Co., 26 A. B. R. 601, 186 Fed. 586 (D. C. Wis.); Matter of Hirth, 26 A. B. R. 666, 189 Fed. 926 (D. C. Minn.).

Thus, where, without formal application, the parties submit the question of liquidation to the referee. In re Du Quesne Incandescent Light Co., 24 A. B. R. 417, 176 Fed. 785 (D. C. Pa.), quoted at § 712.

Obiter, In re United Button Co., 15 A. B. R. 395, 140 Fed. 495 (D. C. Del.):
"A jury constitutes part of the machinery of a district court of the United
States, and the ascertainment of the amount of unliquidated damages is, in
general, a function appropriate to a jury. The power of the court under the
Act of 1867 to cause unliquidated damages for which the bankrupt was liable
'to be assessed in such mode as it may deem best' and under the Act of 1898 to
'direct' the 'manner' in which unliquidated claims against a bankrupt may 'be
liquidated' was and is broad enough to include authority to provide for their
submission to a jury."

But a claim arising under a contractor's bond given to the United States,
in accordance with the act of February 24, 1905, can not be liquidated in
the Bankruptcy Court, as the statute prescribes the exclusive method by
which such claims may be enforced.

In re Hawley, 28 A. B. R. 58, 194 Fed. 751 (D. C. Wash.): "The rights of
the parties are defined by the statute which exacted the bond, and by that
statute suppliers of materials used in the prosecution of contract work for
the government, claiming the right to have recourse upon the bond, must proceed in a prescribed manner; that is to say, they must either intervene in a
suit prosecuted by the government, or, if the government does not sue on the
bond, they must within a limited time commence an independent suit upon
the bond in the United States Circuit Court for the district in which the contract was to be performed and executed. The jurisdiction of that court is by
an express provision of the statute made exclusive, and the statute also provides that only one action upon the bond shall be maintainable, and it must
be so conducted that all demands against the obligors may be litigated and
adjusted, and that the money recoverable shall be distributed pro rata, if the
amount thereof shall be insufficient to pay the full amount of all the claims
which may be proved."

§ 714. Liquidation by Litigation.

—The Court may direct litigation to
be instituted, or if already instituted, to be maintained.[25]

And this is usually done in cases of stockholder's double liability, where
the facts are complex and the usual procedure has been in the State
Courts.[26] Where only creditors with judgments may enforce stockholders'
liability on unpaid subscriptions, the bankruptcy court will permit them to
reduce their claims to judgment after the adjudication of bankruptcy, but
will thereupon permit only one subsequent proceeding in behalf of all, to
marshal the conflicting claims.[27] But even in stockholders' liability cases,
if the facts are few and simple, as they likely would be were the corporation itself penniless and all its stockholders insolvent, the court will itself
liquidate the claim.[28]

---

25. In re Rouse, 1 A. B. R. 394 (Ref.
Ohio); In re United Button Co., 15 A.
B. R. 390, 140 Fed. 495 (D. C. Del.);
In re Buchan's Soap Corporation, 22
A. B. R. 380, 169 Fed. 1017 (D. C.
N. Y.).
26. In re Rouse, 1 A. B. R. 394 (Ref.
Ohio). Obiter, Graphophone Co. v.

Leeds & Catlin, 23 A. B. R. 337, 174
Fed. 158 (U. S. C. C.).
27. In re Remington Automobile &
Motor Co., 9 A. B. R. 533, 119 Fed.
441 (D. C. N. Y.).
28. Obiter, In re Rouse, 1 A. B. R.
393 (Ref. Ohio).

And amendment of proof may be allowed, after expiration of the year.[29]

§ 714½. Suffering Pending Action in State Court to Proceed to Judgment, as Liquidation.—It has been held that where an action upon an unliquidated claim is pending in a state court when the defendant is adjudicated bankrupt, and the trustee permits the case to go to judgment by default, the claim is thereby liquidated, and that if the trustee be dissatisfied with the judgment rendered in the state court action, his remedy is to move to open the default, and in case of his failure so to do that the proof of claim upon the judgment stands.[30]

But such cannot be the correct rule unless the claimant shall first have obtained the direction of the bankruptcy court to so maintain the action for the purpose of liquidation, for the bankruptcy court has exclusive jurisdiction to determine the validity of claims presented for sharing in dividends, and, as to unliquidated claims, is given authority to direct the manner of liquidation. A contrary rule would result in the tying up of estates indefinitely and in the necessity of the trustee's defending every pending suit in personam against the bankrupt. If the claimant has a right to bind the bankruptcy trustee by a subsequently rendered judgment in personam against simply the bankrupt, then he has the right to proceed to such judgment and may not be stayed. The fallacy of the court's reasoning seems to consist in confusing a proceedings against the bankrupt for a personal judgment with a proceedings against the trustee for a share in dividends—two different rights with different defendants and different defenses.

§ 715. Original Proof Not Necessarily Formal.—But the original proof need not have been formal,[31] and may have lacked some of the usual allegations and even may not have been verified.[32] Thus, the claim of a mechanic's lienholder to a lien upon a special fund paid into the bankruptcy court, made by way of petition, may, after expiration of the year, be amended to conform to the regular proof of claim as prescribed by the Supreme Court's forms and be then, for the first time, verified.[33] And it has been held, that where a wife succeeds in an action against her husband and his trustee in bankruptcy, commenced within the year after the adjudication to enforce a resulting trust in certain land about to be sold as part of the

29. See ante, § 622; post, § 722.
30. In re Buchan's Soap Corporation, 22 A. B. R. 380, 169 Fed. 1017 (D. C. N. Y.).
31. In re Faulkner, 20 A. B. R. 542, 161 Fed. 900 (C. C. A. Kans.), quoted, on other point, at § 734. In re [Salvator] Brew Co., 26 A. B. R. 21, 183 Fed. 910 (D. C. N. Y.), although this case states extreme doctrine. But compare, § 595½, "Agreeing to Treat Informal Papers as 'Proofs of Claim.'"
32. Compare, to similar effect, In re Mertens, 16 A. B. R. 825 (C. C. A. N.

Y.). But compare, In re Dunn Hdw. Co., 13 A. B. R. 147, 132 Fed. 719 (D. C. N. Car.), where the court held a claim set up by way of a pleading was "fatally" defective. This decision states the law too extremely. The claim was certainly amendable if, as stated, it contained allegations sufficient for a good pleading.
Compare analogous proposition as to year's limitation for filing claims, at § 735.
33. In re Roeber, 11 A. B. R. 464, 127 Fed. 122 (C. C. A. N. Y.).

bankrupt estate, her claim is "proven" within the limitation of §§ 57 and 57 (n).[34] Similarly, where an assignment of a claim has been duly filed within the year, it has been held to be a sufficient filing to permit of an amendment, after the expiration of the year, though the deposition for proof of debt itself is not filed until after the year.[35]

If all the facts necessary to establish a *bona fide* indebtedness are in the record, the proof may be amended.[36]

§ 716. Whether, after Trustee's Recovery of Preference, etc., in Independent Suit after Expiration of Year, Defeated Party's Pleadings to Be Considered Proofs Filed within Year, or Litigation "a Liquidation."—A preferred creditor from whom a preference has been recovered after the expiration of one year from the date of the adjudication, in a suit filed by the trustee within the year, and who now seeks to prove his claim for the debt, is held not to be presenting his claim too late.[37]

Indeed, it does not appear that the suit need even have been begun within the year,[38] perhaps the theory being that the dividend would be a permissible offset in any event and would be taken into account as such in the State court regardless of any bankruptcy limitation of time for the presentation of claims for sharing in dividends, and that therefore, by grace, instead of delaying the judgment in the State court to permit of the ascertainment of the dividend, the whole matter should be left to the bankruptcy court as a matter outside of § 57 (n) ; or perhaps, the theory being that § 57 (g) and not § 57 (n) is controlling.[39]

Likewise, where an attaching creditor, under advice of counsel, failed to file his claim but litigated the matter up to the Supreme Court, on his final defeat, after the expiration of the year, it was held that his claim might be filed.[42]

And a proof, duly filed within the year, may be amended after the year, by striking out a credit which was a preference and which the trustee had meanwhile recovered by litigation.[43]

Again, it has been held that a contest with the trustee, carried on within the year, over the validity of an assignment of securities by a bankrupt

34. Buckingham *v.* Estes, 12 A. B. R. 182 (C. C. A. Tenn.).

35. Bennett *v.* Am. Credit Indemnity Co., 20 A. B. R. 258, 159 Fed. 624 (C. C. A. Ky.).

36. In re Standard, etc., Co., 26 A. B. R. 601, 186 Fed. 586 (D. C. Wis.).

37. See post, § 727½ and § 1770½. Also see In re Keyes, 20 A. B. R. 183, 160 Fed. 763 (D. C. Mass.); In re Coventry Evans Furniture Co., 22 A. B. R. 623, 171 Fed. 673 (D. C. N. Y.); In re Lange Co., 22 A. B. R. 414, 170 Fed. 114 (D. C. Iowa), quoted at § 727½; In re Fagan, 15 A. B. R. 522, 140 Fed. 758 (D. C. S. Car.); In re

Noel, 18 A. B. R. 11, 150 Fed. 89 (C. C. A. N. H.); contra, In re Damon, 14 A. B. R. 809 (Ref. N. Y.).

38. See post, § 727½.

39. See post, § 727½. Also see In re [Baker] Notion Co., 24 A. B. R. 808, 180 Fed. 922 (D. C. N. Y.).

42. In re Baird, 18 A. B. R. 655, 154 Fed. 215 (D. C. Pa., reversing 18 A. B. R. 228).

43. See post, § 737¼. Contra, In re Kemper, 15 A. B. R. 675, 142 Fed. 210 (D. C. Iowa). This case denies that the claim was the same, yet, on the facts it was the same claim. Merely a credit was cut out.

corporation to its directors to secure them for individually endorsing corporate obligations, wherein the validity of the endorsements and assignments was proved, as also the payment by the directors, was sufficient proof within the year to support a liquidation after the year.[44]

§ 716½. Likewise as to Unsuccessful Litigation over Property in Custody of Bankruptcy Court.

—Similarly, after the termination of unsuccessful litigation over property in the custody of the bankruptcy court, the claimant may prove up for the amount due him even though the year has expired.[45]

§ 717. If Liquidated by Litigation within Thirty Days before or after Expiration of Year, Then Sixty Days Longer Granted.

—Where the claim is liquidated by outside litigation and the final judgment in the litigation is rendered within thirty days before or after the expiration of the year, then the claimant has sixty days from the date of the final judgment to file his claim.[46] And "litigation" here undoubtedly means litigation outside of the bankruptcy proceedings themselves, for if an unliquidated claim be duly filed within the year, the delay in its liquidation by means other than outside litigation is within the control of the court, hence the reason for the limitation disappears.[47] But this litigation must have been directed by the court;[48] and must have been directed to the liquidation of the creditor's claim itself and not concern, exclusively, collateral matters, the amount of the claim itself being undisputed.

In re Thompson's Sons, 10 A. B. R. 581, 123 Fed. 174 (D. C. Pa.): "I see no escape from the positive declaration of this clause. It cannot be successfully contended that the claim was in process of liquidation in the sense borne by that word in the foregoing paragraph. If the litigation there referred to means litigation between the claimants and the bankrupt, no such dispute existed; and, assuming it to include litigation between the claimants and third parties, by which the bankrupt estate may be affected, although it is not represented therein, the object of the contest between the owner and the claimants was not to liquidate a claim. The amount was not in dispute. The sole question was whether E. O. Thompson's estate was liable, and it was not 'liquidation' to determine that controversy."

44. In re [Salvator] Brew Co., 26 A. B. R. 21, 183 Fed. 910 (D. C. N. Y.).

45. In re Landis, 19 A. B. R. 420, 156 Fed. 318 (D. C. Pa.). Also, see post, § 727¾. Obiter, In re [Baker] Notion Co., 24 A. B. R. 808, 180 Fed. 922 (D. C. N. Y.). Compare (although it does not appear whether the property was, or was not, in the custody of the bankruptcy court, yet the bankruptcy court was evidently the forum of the "liquidation") In re [Salvator] Brew Co., 26 A. B. R. 21, 183 Fed. 910 (D. C. N. Y.); In re Salvator Brew Co., 28 A. B. R. 56, 193 Fed. 988 (C. C. A. N. Y.).

46. Bankr. Act, § 57 (n); In re Noel (Powell v. Leavitt), 18 A. B. R. 10, 150 Fed. 89 (C. C. A. N. H.); In re Keyes, 20 A. B. R. 183, 160 Fed. 763 (D. C. Mass.); In re Baird, 18 A. B. R. 655, 154 Fed. 215 (D. C. reversing same court 18 A. B. R. 228); In re Standard, etc., Co., 26 A. B. R. 601, 186 Fed. 586 (D. C. Wis.).

47. Inferentially, In re Mertens & Co., 16 A. B. R. 829, 147 Fed. 137 (C. C. A. N. Y.).

48. Bankr. Act, § 63 (b). Compare, § 714. But see § 716.

It is a possible and perhaps reasonable construction of the statute that a claim may be liquidated at any time the court may direct, whether before or after the expiration of the year, so long as the claim is filed within the year (or in cases of pending litigation, within the sixty days mentioned in § 57 (n)).[49]

In re Mertens & Co., 16 A. B. R. 829, 147 Fed. 177 (C. C. A. N. Y.): "From these various sections we deduce the following propositions: That proof and allowance of claims are two separate and distinct steps; that a clear statement of a claim in writing duly verified and filed with the referee, if made within a year, is sufficient to take the claim out of the statutory limitations, even though it may be allowed, or liquidated and allowed, afterwards.

"We think that § 63b must be interpreted in the light of the other sections of the law and that to construe it as meaning that no proof of unliquidated claims can be filed until the precise amount due thereon is established will, in practical operation, make the allowance of such claims impossible, for the reason that a hostile trustee or creditor can easily delay the liquidation until after the expiration of the year. A more reasonable and sensible construction is that the filing of the proof, like the filing of a declaration at common law, if made within the time, takes the claim out of the statute of limitations, and that after such proof is made the claim is before the court to be dealt with as the interest of the bankrupt and the creditors may require. No hard and fast rule can be made for the guidance of the referee in such matters; much is left to his discretion; and if the best interests of the estate require, he may withhold action on the claim or postpone the dividend thereon until the status of the claim is fully determined. * * *

"It may be pertinent to inquire how a claim can be liquidated as the court shall direct, unless a statement of the claim is filed with or brought to the attention of the court."

And a still more liberal construction is that, if the liquidation be not accomplished until after the beginning of the thirty days preceding the expiration of the year, then it will be sufficient if proof of claim be filed within sixty days after the liquidation is accomplished by final judgment, no matter when such final judgment be rendered, whether within the zone of thirty days before, or at any time after the expiration of the year.[50]

In re Noel (Powell v. Leavitt), 18 A. B. R. 11, 150 Fed. 89 (C. C. A. N. H.): "It has been suggested that, in order to bring a claim within the exception, final judgment in the litigation must be rendered within thirty days of the expiration of the year, either before or after. In re Keyes [20 A. B. R. 183, 160 Fed. 763], decided in the District Court of Massachusetts, November 8, 1906. If we depended altogether upon the grammatical construction of the sentence, and disregarded altogether the nature of the injustice against which the exception was intended to guard, this construction might not be unreasonable. But to limit to thirty or to sixty days the time during which litigation will suspend the

---

49. But compare, In re Noel (Powell v. Leavitt), 18 A. B. R. 10, 150 Fed. 89 (C. C. A. N. H.), quoted post.
50. In re [Baker] Notion Co., 24 A. B. R. 808, 180 Fed. 922 (D. C. N. Y.); impliedly, Page v. Rogers, 211 U. S.

575, 21 A. B. R. 496; In re Baird, 18 A. B. R. 655, 154 Fed. 215 (D. C. Pa.). Compare, In re Lange Co., 22 A. B. R. 414, 170 Fed. 114 (D. C. Iowa), quoted at § 727½.

operation of the statute of limitations, and to exclude from proof claims liquidated by litigation fourteen or fifteen months after adjudication, is to establish a serious distinction, with only a fantastic difference. That a creditor whose claim was in litigation might, by an unqualified statute of limitations, be deprived of his just share of the bankrupt's estate, was the 'mischief felt,' the 'occasion and necessity' of the exception. To save the rights of such a creditor was 'the object and the remedy in view,' and the intention of the legislature is to be ascertained accordingly. 1 Kent Com. 462; 1 Plow. 205; Potter's Dwarris, 194. We therefore interpret the exception as if it read:

"'If the final judgment therein is rendered within thirty days before the expiration of such time, or at any time thereafter.'

"We have to determine if the proceeding here had in the State Court was a liquidation by litigation of the creditor's claim, within the meaning of the Bankrupt Act.

"This is the creditor's contention. The trustee, on the other hand, contends that the exception in clause 'n' refers only to a suit brought under § 63b (30 Stat. 563, c. 541 [U. S. Comp. St. 1901, p. 3447]) to fix the face value of a claim due from the bankrupt's estate, which otherwise by reason of its indefinite amount would not be provable. Upon a consideration of the clause already quoted, as its meaning is illustrated by the whole Bankrupt Act, we agree with the contention of the creditor. In re Keppel v. Tiffin Savings Bank, 197 U. S. 356, 13 Am. B. R. 552, the Supreme Court decided that the enforced surrender of a preference by a creditor did not necessarily deprive him of his right to prove thereafter. In that case formal proof was offered within a year of the adjudication; but the court expressly repudiated that construction of the law which would hold that the creditor's 'right to prove (his) lawful claims against the bankrupt estate was forfeited simply because of the election to put the trustee to proof in a court of the existence of the facts made essential by the law to an invalidation of the preference.' On the contrary, it held that 'whenever the preference has been abandoned or yielded up and thereby the danger of inequality has been prevented, such creditor is entitled to stand on an equal footing with other creditors and prove his claims.' Pages 363, 364 of 197 U. S.; page 557 of 13 Am. B. R. The phrase 'liquidated by litigation' is general, and the object of the exception which is made to the statutory limit of time is plainly to allow the proof of a claim after the expiration of a year by a creditor who during that time was engaged in litigation with the bankrupt's estate concerning its liability to him. In a sense, the debt evidenced by the promissory notes held by Powell had already been liquidated apart from bankruptcy proceedings, Powell could have sued Noel at law for their face value. It may be that, pending the litigation, he could have proved his claim in bankruptcy as a secured claim, leaving his proof to be amended, in case his mortgage was avoided. Hutchinson v. Otis, 8 Am. B. R. 382, 115 Fed. 937, 941; on appeal, 190 U. S. 552, 10 Am. B. R. 135. But to prove during litigation a claim which cannot be allowed unless the creditor fails in the litigation is but an empty formality. If the security is as large as the debt, it is a formality which can hardly be accomplished under the rules and with the forms which have been provided. Notice of the claim is given in effect by the litigation, and, if the preferred creditor is not to be deprived of his proof altogether, there seems no good reason why he should not offer it immediately after the litigation is ended. The substantial amount of Powell's claim, the amount for which he could seek allowance and upon which he could demand a dividend, here remained uncertain until the validity of the mortgage had been settled. To hold that Powell's claim was 'liquidated by litigation' in the proceeding which, for some purposes, determined the amount for which it should be allowed, is not, we think, a forced construction of the language of the Act. It is rather that 'honest and practical interpretation' which we declared should be applied to statutes in bankruptcy."

Concerning the ruling of In re Noel, these criticisms seem appropriate. First, it disregards the plain words of the statute. The statute does not say "If the final judgment therein is rendered within thirty days before the expiration of such time, or *at any time thereafter.*" On the contrary the wording is absolutely unambiguous, "Or if they are liquidated by litigation and the final judgment therein is rendered within thirty days before or after the expiration of such time, then within sixty days after the rendition of such judgment." We are not to disregard the plain wording of a statute. Second, such permission might defeat the very purpose of § 57 (n) limiting the proving of claims to one year. It is concededly the purpose of § 57 (n) to hasten the winding up of bankrupt estates. The long drawn out administrations possible under the old law of 1867 (some of which were still pending at the time the Act of 1898 was passed) were deprecated by the framers of the Act of 1898. Section 57 (n) is a new provision, appearing in no former act, and the mischiefs aimed at are real. Yet, under the ruling in In re Noel, if the claimant but hold an unliquidated claim he is placed on a higher footing than other claimants and may be as leisurely as he pleases in getting it liquidated, for the trustee has notice and must withhold sufficient dividends to cover the claim. Under such ruling the mere serving of notice by the holder of an unliquidated claim would suspend indefinitely the closing of the estate, for his "dividend" must be held until his claim is liquidated and there is *no statutory provision prescribing when he shall begin his liquidating litigation.*

Yet, on the other hand, it is true that such liquidation by litigation is not an absolute right of the creditor perhaps; but may be within the option of the bankruptcy court in directing the manner of liquidation under § 63 (b); and if the bankruptcy court directs liquidation to be accomplished by litigation it would be a hardship to make the claimant lose his rights because of such order of the court or by the slowness of the court wherein the litigation is pending. At any rate, if the rule in In re Noel is to be adopted as the final rule of law, the qualification of § 63 (b) should be kept in mind and the distribution of the estate not be delayed, unless the court shall have directed the litigation. In that event, the application of the claimant for the court's direction might amount, in effect, to an informal filing capable of later amendment into "due" proof.

But after all no real hardship would be put upon the creditor by adhering to the rule that an actual, written proof of claim must be filed within the year. There is no obstacle to prevent the creditor from filing his proof of claim at any time within the time fixed by the act, without surrendering his preference. True, he cannot secure its allowance until it is liquidated, and until he has surrendered the preference, nor can he until then be permitted to vote at a meeting of creditors, yet there would be all the time a pending claim, and by thus making his formal proof he would have brought himself within the statutory requirements as to time.[51]

In conformity with the rule laid down in In re Noel it has been held that, after a preference has been set aside or recovered by litigation, the defeated creditor will be in time if he files proof of his claim within sixty days after the final judgment is rendered.[52] Thus, also, it has been held that he will be in time, after unsuccessful appeal from court to court until final defeat in the Supreme Court, the claimant being an attaching creditor within four months.[53] But if he fails to file proof of his claim within sixty days after final judgment is rendered, he will be barred.[54]

And it has been held to be a "liquidation by litigation," such that the failure to file a formal proof of claim until after the expiration of the year was not fatal, where directors of a bankrupt corporation were unsuccessful in litigation with the trustee over security which had been transferred to them on becoming sureties for certain debts which they had afterwards paid.[55]

So it would seem now that the prohibitions of § 57 (n) have been so relaxed by judicial construction that almost any litigation with the trustee is sufficient to amount to a "liquidation" and to remove the bar of the year's limitation.

It has been held however, that litigation between third persons is not sufficient.

In re Daniel, 29 A. B. R. 284, 193 Fed. 772 (D. C. Ga.): "These provisions, it will be observed, fully protect the holders of secured claims from the very incipiency of the bankruptcy, affording them an opportunity to participate with the excess of their claims over and above their securities in the proceedings, and providing ways and means of determining that excess by a valuation of the securities by them and the trustee 'by agreement, arbitration, compromise or litigation, as the court may direct.' This claimant might have invoked at any time after the adjudication the benefit of the provision for the purpose of ascertaining the amount for which it could file an unsecured claim, but, believing itself amply secured, it elected to reduce the collateral to money independently of the bankruptcy proceedings. Having met with disappointment in realizing thereon, it now takes the position that it has been engaged in liquidating its demand by litigation, and therefore comes within the saving clause of § 57n. But, the term 'liquidated,' as used in the Act, implies a dispute as to the validity or amount of the claim, and here there was no dispute or contention as to the bank's claim. It was a definite amount—a fixed liability of the

51. In re [Baker] Notion Co., 24 A. B. R. 808, 180 Fed. 922 (D. C. N. Y.); In re Clover Creamery Ass'n (Evans v. Claridge), 23 A. B. R. 884, 176 Fed. 907 (C. C. A. Wis.).
52. In re Noel (Powell v. Leavitt), 18 A. B. R. 10, 150 Fed. 89 (C. C. A. N. H.), quoted supra; In re Keyes, 20 A. B. R. 183, 160 Fed. 763 (D. C. Mass.).

53. In re Baird, 18 A. B. R. 655, 154 Fed. 215 (D. C. Pa.).
54. In re Clover Creamery Ass'n (Evans v. Claridge), 23 A. B. R. 884, 176 Fed. 907 (C. C. A. Wis.), quoted, on other points, at § 717½.
55. In re [Salvator] Brew. Co., 26 A. B. R. 21, 183 Fed. 910 (D. C. N. Y.).

bankrupt—unchallenged and unquestioned by bankrupt, his trustee or any party in interest. The litigation in which claimant was involved was altogether with third parties—strangers to the record herein—and was not for the purpose of liquidating the claim, but to determine the title or right to property as between it and persons claiming adversely to it. In the cases cited by counsel for the bank in support of its contention that its claim is one liquidated by litigation, the litigation in each instance originated between the claimant and the bankrupt, or occurred between the claimant and the trustee, presenting a state of facts very different from that at bar. The litigation intended in § 57n is not litigation between third parties."

§ 717½. Date of "Final Judgment."—Since, in all events, the claim must be filed within sixty days after the rendition of final judgment, it becomes important to determine the date of final judgment. Negotiations between the parties, after the entry of the final judgment in the action, will not suffice to prolong the time, notwithstanding the negotiations might be entered on the court records, as for instance, by the offsetting of judgments by the stipulation of the parties.

In re Clover Creamery Ass'n (Evans v. Claridge), 23 A. B. R. 884, 176 Fed. 907 (C. C. A. Wis.): "While not entirely clear, it may be conceded that it appears from the stipulation of facts that on January 26, 1909, in pursuance of a stipulation between the parties, the Supreme Court entered an order offsetting the two judgments for costs against each other, leaving a judgment for costs in appellee's favor on that date of $119.70. Whether or not this latter order was a part of the liquidation proceedings contemplated by the statute may be doubted. Nor is it important, as we view it. Certainly, after this was done and the several amounts of the two judgments thus definitely ascertained, there remained nothing more that the State courts could do in liquidating appellee's claim. Between themselves, they proceeded very leisurely—i. e., from January 26, 1909, to April 16, 1909—to offset one judgment against the other and satisfy the balance due the trustee. Surely this transaction, covering the period from March 29, 1909, to April 16, 1909, was in no sense a part of the liquidation by litigation described in said § 57n of the statute. It was simply the negotiations of the parties, which might have been long or short, as they chose. It never has been held that, in the absence of fraud, delays so caused would avail to suspend any statute of limitation, much less the exception of § 57n aforesaid."

CHAPTER XXII.

Year's Limitation for Filing Claims.[1]

Synopsis of Chapter.

§ **718. Despatch in Administration.**—One of the complaints urged against the passage of any bankruptcy law at the time the bill for the present one was before Congress was that the bankruptcy courts were slow in winding up estates. Indeed, at the time the bill was under discussion, one member of the opposition brought the fact to the attention of Congress that there were several cases even then still undisposed of that had been begun under the old law, more than twenty years beforehand. This fact in the history

---

1. See "Unliquidated Claims," ante, §§ 704, et seq.

of the legislation explains the appearance in different sections of the present law of repeated provisions intended to hasten the administration of bankrupt estates.[2] One of these provisions is the limitation of time for proving claims.[3] It is a new provision, appearing for the first time in the Bankruptcy Act of 1898.[3a]

§ 719. Year's Limitation for Filing Claims.

—Claims may not be filed in bankruptcy after the end of a year from the adjudication, except that unliquidated claims have a somewhat longer time.[4]

In cases of appeal or review, the year does not begin to run until the date of entry of the dismissal of the appeal,[5] or of the affirmance of adjudication.

§ 719½. Subject Involved in That of Provability of "Unliquidated Claims."

—The subject of the year's limitation for the proof of claims is somewhat involved in the preceding subject of the "Provability of Unliquidated Claims."[5a]

But § 59 (n) does not operate to make claims provable which otherwise would not be so.[6]

§ 720. "Proving" Means Filing Here.

—The statute uses the word "proved" in § 57 "n." In this section the word "proved" does not mean the written proof of claim itself, but the filing of such proof of claim.

In re Ingalls Bros., 13 A. B. R. 513, 514, 137 Fed. 517 (C. C. A. N. Y., reversed on the ground that filing with the trustee is sufficient, sub nom. Olcutt v. Green, 17 A. B. R. 75, 204 U. S. 96): "Briefly stated, the argument for the first proposition is that § 57a defines a proof of claim as 'a statement under oath, in writing, signed by a creditor, setting forth the claim,' etc.; that subsec. e provides that 'claims after being proved may, for the purpose of allowance, be filed by the claimants—before the referee;' that subsec. d provides that 'claims which have

---

2. In re Muskoka Lumber Co., 11 A. B. R. 761, 127 Fed. 886 (D. C. N. Y.). Also, compare ante, § 23. Obiter, In re Faulkner, 20 A. B. R. 542, 161 Fed. 900 (C. C. Kans.), quoted at § 734. See also, § 387.

3. For general discussion of the nature of the limitation of time for proving claims, see In re Peck, 20 A. B. R. 629, 161 Fed. 762 (D. C. N. Y.).

3a. Norfolk & W. R. v. Graham, 16 A. B. R. 613, 145 Fed. 809 (C. C. A. W. Va.).

4. Bankr. Act, § 57 (n): "Claims shall not be proved against a bankrupt subsequent to one year after the adjudication; or, if they are liquidated by litigation and the final judgment therein is rendered within thirty days before or after the expiration of such time, then within sixty days after the rendition of such judgment; provided that the rights of infants and insane persons without guardians, without no-

tice of the proceedings, may continue six months longer."

See "Unliquidated Claims," ante, § 704, et seq. See discussion of this provision in In re Damon, 14 A. B. R. 809 (Ref. N. Y.); Steinhardt v. National Bank, 19 A. B. R. 72, 122 App. Div. N. Y. 55; In re Basha & Son, 27 A. B. R. 435, 193 Fed. 151 (D. C. N. Y.).

5. In re Lee. 22 A. B. R. 820, 171 Fed. 266 (D. C. Pa.). Also, Bankr. Act, § 1, a, (2): "Adjudication shall mean the date of the entry of a decree that the defendant in a bankruptcy proceeding is a bankrupt, or, if such decree is appealed from, then the date on which such decree is finally confirmed."

5a. See ante, § 704, et seq.

6. Steinhardt v. Nat'l Bank, 19 A. B. R. 72, 122 A. D. 55; In re Clover Creamery Ass'n (Evans v. Claridge), 23 A. B. R. 884, 176 Fed. 907 (C. C. A. Wis.), quoted, on other point, at § 717½; In re Roth & Appel, 22 A. B. R. 504, 174 Fed. 64 (D. C. N. Y.).

been duly proved shall be allowed, upon receipt by or upon presentation to the court (referee), etc.;' that subsec. n provides that 'claims shall not be proved against a bankrupt estate subsequent to one year after adjudication;' that a 'proof' is a claim 'proved;' that the word 'proved' must be assumed to have been employed in but a single sense and with a single meaning in the same section, and was not designed and cannot be construed to have in subsec. n any larger meaning than in a, c or d; in short, that no logical or necessary construction of subsec. n imposes any limitation upon the time of filing, but the contrary; and, finally, applying the section to the facts on the case, that the three claims in issue, having been 'proved' within the year, may be filed at any time.

"As a matter of first impression the construction urged seems almost conclusively reasonable. Pursued further, however, the proposition is perhaps reduced to the absurd when it is seen that the prohibition against 'proving' in its literal effect would not prohibit—would simply forbid an act which per se would be not only utterly harmless but utterly foolish, unless logically related to some further act designed to render it effective. If 'proved' in subsec. n is the mere equivalent of 'proof' in subsec. a and 'proved' in subsec. c and d, there seems to be nothing better than some purely speculative reason for subsec. n, since practically the time of verification can make no possible difference to parties in interest, except as involved in the time of filing. 'Proof' under subsec. a involves nobody save the creditor himself; filing—'proved'—under subsec. n involves notice to all parties in interest. That the presumably logical and consistent use of language is opposed by the practically illogical and inconsistent consequences involved, seems to have been the decision or assumption of every court before which the interpretation of subsec. n has arisen, although most of the decisions are somewhat general, rather than specific, and none of them specifically appears to have been predicated upon the precise state of facts disclosed here, i. e., upon proofs verified within the year, but offered for filing thereafter, which squarely raises the question of construction. However, their purpose cannot be doubted, and being unbroken in point of their conclusion, they must be accepted as conclusive against the petitioners."

§ 721. Claim "Allowed" after Expiration of Year if Filed within Year.

—And a claim may be "allowed" after the expiration of the year, if filed within the year.[7]

§ 722. May Be "Liquidated" after Expiration of Year, if "Filed" within.

—And a claim may be "liquidated" after the expiration of the year, if "filed" within the year.[8]

§ 722½. Priority May Be Claimed for It Afterwards.

—Similarly, priority over other claims in the distribution of the assets may be asserted after the expiration of the year.

---

7. In re Mertens, 16 A. B. R. 825, 147 Fed. 177 (C. C. A. N. Y.); In re Pettingill & Co., 14 A. B. R. 766, 137 Fed. 143 (Ref. Mass.); In re [Salvator] Brew. Co., 26 A. B. R. 21, 183 Fed. 910 (D. C. N. Y.).

8. See post, § 2139. Also see In re Mertens & Co., 16 A. B. R. 829, 147 Fed. 177 (C. C. A. N. Y.), quoted ante, § 717; In re Faulkner, 20 A.

B. R. 542, 161 Fed. 900 (C. C. A. Kans.), quoted at § 734. Instance, In re [Salvator] Brew. Co., 26 A. B. R. 21, 183 Fed. 910 (D. C. N. Y.).

Inferentially, though claim filed too late because not filed within sixty days after final judgment in the liquidation, In re Clover Creamery Ass'n (Evans v. Claridge), 23 A. B. R. 884, 176 Fed. 907 (C. C. A. Wis.), quoted at § 717½.

In re Ashland Steele Co., 21 A. B. R. 834, 168 Fed. 679 (C. C. A. Ky.): "We think that the substantive claims having been proven within the time allowed by the act, it was within the power of the court to allow the claim priority and give them the preference to which by law they were entitled, notwithstanding no definite claim of the kind had been made within the year."

§ 723. Court's Power Absolutely Ceases.—Section 57 (n) is an absolute termination of the court's power to allow claims that are presented after the expiration of one year.[9]

Bray v. Cobb, 3 A. B. R. 788, 100 Fed. 272 (reversed, on other grounds, in Cobb v. Overman, 6 A. B. R. 324, 109 Fed. 65): "The section is more than a limitation of the time within which claims may be proved. It is a prohibition. The language used was intended to limit the time absolutely, and the reasons for thus limiting the time may be seen from an examination of other sections. * * * The general purpose of the Act seems to be to settle the estate within a reasonable time."

In re Paine, 11 A. B. R. 351, 127 Fed. 246 (D. C. Ky.): "The language of the clause is plain and unequivocal. There is no ambiguity about it and it admits of no construction. The decisions are clear to the effect that no proof of debt can be made after the expiration of one year from the adjudication except in those instances" specially excepted.

In re Muskoka Lumber Co., 11 A. B. R. 761, 127 Fed. 886 (D. C. N. Y.): "The entire theory of the Bankrupt Act as stated by the cases, would seem to be the settlement of the estate in bankruptcy within a reasonable time. Congress, in its wisdom, has said 'claims shall not be proved against the bankrupt estate subsequent to one year.' This provision must be strictly construed against the creditor, in order to carry out the liberal spirit shown by other provisions of the Act, toward the debtor."

In re Prindle Pump Co., 10 A. B. R. 405 (Ref. N. Y.): "The provision is new under our bankruptcy system. Under former acts proofs could be made and filed at any time, even after many years. As all proofs, whenever made related back to the commencement of the bankruptcy proceedings, the bankrupt estate becoming thus impressed with a trust for the benefit of creditors, even the various statutes of limitation did not apply and any claim not barred at the time of the inception of the bankruptcy proceedings, could, if just and sustained by adequate proof, be proved, apparently without any limitation of time. The pro-

---

9. In re Shaffer, 4 A. B. R. 728, 104 Fed. 982 (D. C. N. Car.); In re Hawk, 8 A. B. R. 71, 114 Fed. 916 (C. C. A.); In re Hilton, 3 N. B. N. & R. 104, 104 Fed. 981, 4 A. B. R. 774 (D. C. N. Y.); In re Damon, 14 A. B. R. 809 (Ref. N. Y.); compare, In re McCallem, 11 A. B. R. 447 (D. C. Penn.); In re Rhodes, 5 A. B. R. 197, 105 Fed. 231 (D. C. Penn.); In re Leibowitz, 6 A. B. R. 268, 108 Fed. 617 (D. C. Tex.); In re Moebius, 8 A. B. R. 590, 116 Fed. 47 (D. C. Penn.); In re Kemper, 15 A. B. R. 675, 142 Fed. 210 (D. C. Iowa); to same effect in composition cases, see In re Brown, 10 A. B. R. 588, 123 Fed. 336 (D. C. Colo.); In re Ingalls Bros.,

13 A. B. R. 512, 137 Fed. 517 (C. C. A. N. Y.); In re Baird & Co., 18 A. B. R. 288 (D. C. Pa.); In re Pettingill & Co., 14 A. B. R. 763 (Ref. Mass.).

Contra, where the only estate for distribution was precisely the preferential transfer to the creditor whose claim it is being sought to prove: In re Fagan, 15 A. B. R. 522, 140 Fed. 758 (D. C. S. Car.). This point was not involved in Keppel v. Tiffin Sav. Bk., cited in the opinion as precedent.

Also, compare contra observations (obiter) in In re Peck, 20 A. B. R. 629, 161 Fed. 762 (D. C. N. Y.); In re French, 25 A. B. R. 77, 181 Fed. 583 (D. C. Mass.).

vision in the Act of 1898 was clearly intended, in conformity with the general purpose of the Act, to aid in compelling the prompt distribution of bankrupt estates among diligent creditors and prompt closing of the proceedings and there is no warrant for giving its mandatory language any other than its plain meaning."

In re Sanderson, 20 A. B. R. 396, 160 Fed. 278 (D. C. Vt.): "It is useless here to consider whether the court is not ordinarily vested with sufficient equity powers to grant relief where it is equity so to do, because this statute cuts out any common law equity powers vested in the court, for such allowance. The courts have construed this statute literally. The claim in question cannot be allowed as it is barred by this statute. In re Stein, 1 Am. B. R. 662, 94 Fed. 124. * * * Some courts have gone so far as to hold that a creditor not named in the schedule and having received no notice, directly or indirectly, is barred in one year from proving or having his claim allowed."

In re Peck, 21 A. B. R. 707, 161 Fed. 762 (C. C. A. N. Y., affirming 20 A. B. R. 629): "The latter clause of this paragraph (§ 57n) is somewhat ambiguous, and has been construed in cases which are relied upon by the petitioner. Such are In re Noel, 18 Am. B. R. 10, 150 Fed. 89, 80 C. C. A. 43; In re Baird (D. C.), 18 Am. B. R. 655, 154 Fed. 215; Keppel v. Tiffin Savings Bank, 197 U. S. 356, 13 Am. B. R. 552, * * * . But the first clause of the paragraph is unobscure and specific; it prescribes a period of limitations, and there is nothing in the act which relieves any creditor from its operation, except in the case where claims are being liquidated by litigation. Whether or not there may be exceptional cases which would not fall within the statute is a question on which we now express no opinion; but to hold that this clear and imperative provision is to be disregarded whenever a creditor may assert that he was misled because the bankrupt's schedules stated that some particular asset was of little or no value, seems to us to be legislation, not construction."

In re Meyer, 25 A. B. R. 44, 781 Fed. 904 (D. C. Ore.): "This provision has been repeatedly construed by the courts, and they are practically agreed that it is more than a limitation, but is prohibitory, and that the courts have no power or discretion to extend the time therein specified, or permit the proof of claims after the expiration of the year, even if the claimant has been misled by the fraudulent concealment of assets of the bankrupt."

This proposition however is to be taken subject to the qualifications introduced by the doctrines with regard to unliquidated claims and to the sufficiency of a filing with the trustee and to what basis is requisite to support amendment of a claim; the conjoint effects of which qualifications seriously impair the strength of the proposition.

§ 724. Claims Presented Afterwards, Refused or Stricken from Files.

—Claims presented too late should be refused filing, or, if filed notwithstanding, should be stricken from the files by the court of its own motion.[10] And where a claim has been rejected because not presented within the year, although an undisputedly just claim, it cannot be got in by afterwards bringing suit on it and taking judgment thereon. This is not the liquidating by litigation contemplated by § 57 (n).[11]

---

10. In re Pettingill & Co., 14 A. B. R. 766 (Ref. Mass.).

11. In re Prindle Pump Co., 10 A. B. R. 405 (D. C. N. Y.).

According to the practice in most parts of the country the "striking from the files" is not a physical act. The actual paper containing the proof of claim is not cast out, nor refused a place among the court papers or files. The paper rests in the files, though a formal order be entered "striking" it "from the files" or refusing it allowance; in either of which events the injured claimant has his remedy by review. Every litigant is entitled at any rate to file his papers and the referee does not refuse them a physical place in his files, if proper in size, shape, etc., and not scurrilous. However, if the referee does refuse, mandamus will doubtless lie to bring up the issue and in some jurisdictions the practice is to refuse the offer of filing or to return the paper, physically, if inadvertently filed.[12]

§ 725. Limitation Applies Even Where Creditor Not Notified, etc.

—The limitation applies even as to claims where the creditor has not had the requisite notice, nor knowledge, or has been misled by erroneous statements of assets in the schedules;[13] and although the bankrupt is a corporation and not likely ever to have assets again.[14]

§ 726. Applies Though Assets Not Distributed, or New Assets Discovered.

—This limitation applies, although assets still remain in the trustee's hands undistributed;[15] and although the estate has been reopened on the discovery of the new assets;[16] and although new assets have been discovered which the bankrupt innocently had failed to schedule.[17]

---

12. Compare, In re [Baker] Notion Co., 24 A. B. R. 808, 180 Fed. 922 (D. C. N. Y.), where the court appears to have approved the practice of the referee in absolutely refusing to allow the physical filing of the claim.

13. In re Peck, 21 A. B. R. 707, 161 Fed. 762 (C. C. A. N. Y.), quoted supra. But compare, In re Peck, 20 A. B. R. 629, 161 Fed. 762 (D. C. N. Y.). Also compare, In re Pierson, 23 A. B. R. 58, 174 Fed. 160 (D. C. N. Y.).

14. In re Muskoka Lumber Co., 11 A. B. R. 761, 127 Fed. 886 (D. C. N. Y.). The only remedy of such a creditor is to sue the bankrupt, the debt not being discharged.

One case holds that the bankrupt may be estopped from making the objection where he intentionally and in bad faith failed to schedule property so as to induce creditors not to file claims. In re Towne, 10 A. B. R. 284, 122 Fed. 313 (D. C. Mass.). But this decision seems to overlook the fact that § 57 n, operates as an absolute termination of the court's power to act and is not dependent on objection being filed by any one; the court itself should refuse to act in such cases without waiting for any one to file objec-

tions. Moreover, was not the creditor himself guilty of neglect? This case was distinguished and explained in In re Pettingill & Co., 14 A. B. R. 775, and is rejected in In re Damon, 14 A. B. R. 809 (Ref. N. Y.).

Another case seeming to present a relaxation of the rule is In re Brinberg, 9 A. B. R. 601, criticised in In re Damon, 14 A. B. R. 809 (Ref. N. Y.).

15. In re Muskoka Lumber Co., 11 A. B. R. 761, 127 Fed. 886 (D. C. N. Y.); contra, In re Fagan, 15 A. B. R. 522, 140 Fed. 758 (D. C. S. Car.).

16. In re Shaffer, 4 A. B. R. 728, 104 Fed. 982.

Contra, where no claims had originally been presented, no meeting of creditors ever called and no trustee appointed, In re Pierson, 23 A. B. R. 58, 174 Fed. 160 (D. C. N. Y.), which, as a precedent, is hardly to be approved, or, at best, is to be confined strictly within the facts therein displayed—of apparent dereliction on the part of the bankruptcy referee in the original proceedings.

In re Meyer, 25 A. B. R. 44, 181 Fed. 904 (D. C. Ore.), disapproving In re Towne, criticised, supra, § 725, note 8.

17. In re Peck, 20 A. B. R. 629, 161.

§ **727. Applies Though Litigation Pending.**—The limitation applies, although litigation is pending over the validity of a lien held for the claim;[18] or where it is pending for the recovery of assets,[19] thus, where pending over the validity of an attachment lien levied within the four months.[20]

§ **727¼. Except Where Litigation Be for Liquidation.**—Except that, where litigation is pending involving the liquidation of the claim, and such litigation is not ended before eleven months after the adjudication, the creditor may file his claim at any time within sixty days after final judgment has been rendered therein.[21]

§ **727½. Or Perhaps Where Litigation Be Over a Preference, Fraudulent Transfer, etc., Where Claim Would Be Reduced if Transferee Successful.**—Perhaps even judgments in suits brought by trustees to recover preferences or other improper transfers may be considered to be liquidation by litigation, such as to permit the creditor, within sixty days after the final judgment, to file his claim for the balance due him.[22]

And the same ruling has been held applicable upon the recovery of a fraudulent transfer.

[Perhaps, obiter] In re Clark, 24 A. B. R. 388, 176 Fed. 954 (D. C. N. Y.): "Could the claimants Smith file their claim on this bond and the notes mentioned therein within 60 days of the termination of that litigation by the stipulation mentioned; the litigation not having been instituted by the trustee until more than one year from the date of adjudication? If a preferential mortgage is annulled and set aside at the suit of the trustee, the creditor, so preferred, may thereafter prove his claim to secure which the mortgage was given and have it allowed. Keppel v. Tiffin Savings Bank, 197 U. S. 356, 13 Am. B. R. 552; Page v. Rogers, 211 U. S. 575, 581, 21 Am. B. R. 496. In view of these decisions, I do not see why a creditor may not prove his claim and have it allowed in a case where his mortgage is set aside and annulled on the ground that it was executed and delivered with intent to hinder, delay, and defraud creditors. If in such suit the court should adjudge that the bond to secure which the mortgage was given was wholly without consideration, that would be binding and a

---

Fed. 762 (D. C. N. Y., affirmed in 21 A. B. R. 717, 161 Fed. 762). Contra, In re Pierson, 23 A. B. R. 58, 174 Fed. 160 (D. C. N. Y.), wherein, however, the facts would seem to display woeful neglect by the bankruptcy referee in the original case.

18. But compare analogous propositions under subject of "Unliquidated Claims," § 716, et seq.

19. In re Havens, 25 A. B. R. 116, 182 Fed. 367 (D. C. N. Y.).

20. In re Baird & Co., 18 A. B. R. 228 (D. C. Pa.).

21. In re Keyes, 20 A. B. R. 183, 160 Fed. 763 (D. C. Mass.). Such is the doctrine of the case In re Noel (Powell v. Leavitt), 18 A. B. R. 10, 150 Fed. 89 (C. C. A. N. H.), discussed ante,

§ 717; In re [Baker] Notion Co., 24 A. B. R. 808, 180 Fed. 922 (D. C. N. Y.); In re [Salvator] Brew. Co., 26 A. B. R. 21, 183 Fed. 910 (D. C. N. Y.).

22. In re Noel (Powell v. Leavitt), 18 A. B. R. 10, 150 Fed. 89 (C. C. A. N. H.), quoted at § 717; In re Coventry Evans Furniture Co., 22 A. B. R. 623, 171 Fed. 673 (D. C. N. Y.). But see discussion ante, §§ 716, 717; In re [Baker] Notion Co., 24 A. B. R. 808, 180 Fed. 922 (D. C. N. Y.).

Thus, where a transfer to the directors of a bankrupt corporation, as security for becoming sureties for corporate debts (afterwards paid by them), was set aside. In re [Salvator] Brew. Co., 26 A. B. R. 21, 183 Fed. 910 (D. C. N. Y.).

complete answer to the claim when filed. But such is not this case. We have no adjudication that Clark did not owe Smith the amount of the notes, or some part thereof. * * * I find nothing in the bankruptcy act to the effect that, where claims are liquidated by litigation, the suit or litigation must be commenced within one year after the adjudication in order that the claimant may thereafter prove his claim in case the litigation goes against him. Clearly the trustee may institute suit at any time before the statute of limitations has barred his right so to do. * * * This judgment was rendered after the expiration of one year from the date of adjudication. It is immaterial when the litigation, in which the liquidation as to the validity of the mortgage was had, was commenced. It was commenced; the creditor stood upon the mortgage as valid, as he had the right to do without incurring any penalty or forfeiture, as none is prescribed in the bankruptcy act; and, when defeated and compelled to surrender his security, he had the right to prove his claim, and, if established, to have it allowed. * * * If the creditor with a preference may stand on his security until driven therefrom by a judgment in a litigation, and then prove his claim, it is quite clear that the trustee cannot, in the absence of some express provision of law, deprive him of the right to prove his claim in such event by delaying the bringing of suit. The trustee cannot penalize the creditor by any such action. Suppose the appointment of a trustee is delayed one year and three months after adjudication, and he thereafter successfully attacks a mortgage held by a secured creditor on the ground it was a preference, can or cannot the creditor then prove his claim? Where is the statute saying he cannot? Subdivision n of § 57, quoted, as construed by the Supreme Court, says he can; that is, it imposes no time limitation on the commencement of the proceedings wherein the claim was 'liquidated by litigation.' * * * Counsel for the trustee urges that it is apparent from the decision of the Supreme Court of the State of New York—and the opinion constituting the only decision filed is handed up—that the mortgage was tainted by fraud, and that therefore it was absolutely void, and that the claimants cannot have advantage or benefit in any manner growing out of such fraudulent transaction. Section 57g provides: 'The claims of creditors who have received preferences, voidable under section sixty, subdivision b, or to whom conveyances, transfers, assignments, or incumbrances, void or voidable under section sixty-seven, subdivision e, have been made or given, shall not be allowed unless such creditors shall surrender such preferences, conveyances, transfers, assignments, or incumbrances.' This section has been so fully considered by the Supreme Court in Keppel v. Tiffin Savings Bank (supra), that nothing important can be added. Reading the sections therein referred to with § 57g, and we find that this case is within the provisions and cases referred to. Section 57g does not refer to preferences alone, but to conveyances, transfers, assignments, and incumbrances also, and the claims of creditors to whom voidable preferences and voidable conveyances and transfers have been given are not to be allowed unless such preferences, conveyances, transfers, etc., are surrendered. The decisions of the Supreme Court referred to apply to the whole of § 57g, and not to the language referring to preferences alone."

Although such a liberal doctrine is fraught with many dangers and seems to the author not to be wholly consistent with other provisions of the act.[23]

In re Keyes, 20 A. B. R. 183, 160 Fed. 763 (D. C. Mass.): "The referee's certificate recites the history of the litigation in the State courts to set aside the conveyance of property which the bankrupt had made to these petitioners before

23. Compare §§ 716, 717.

adjudication. It further states that, if the bill of sale had been held to be good, the claims of the petitioners would have been satisfied, and they would not have presented any claims against the bankrupt estate. They sought to hold the property covered by the bill of sale as security for these very claims now presented. Their claims were satisfied or unsatisfied, according as the bill of sale was held good or bad in the result of the litigation. Although the litigation did not in terms relate to the amounts due these creditors, yet, since the question litigated necessarily involved the determination of the net amount for which their claims should be finally allowed, I think the claims are to be considered as 'liquidated by litigation,' within the meaning of § 57n."

Indeed, some courts say that the United States Supreme Court's holdings mean that § 57 (n) of the act, prohibiting proof of claims after the expiration of a year, is not applicable at all to claims arising through the surrender of preferences, one court holding it not to be applicable even to claims arising upon the enforced surrender of fraudulently transferred property,[24] all such claims coming rather under § 57 (g), which permits the allowance of claims on surrender of preferences voidable under § 60 (b) and of transfers voidable under § 67 (e) and which is held to modify and control § 57 (n).[25]

In re Lange Co., 22 A. B. R. 414, 170 Fed. 114 (D. C. Iowa): " * * * the Supreme Court does not regard the claims of creditors who have been deprived of merely voidable preference as falling within the provision of § 57n, but as claims accruing under § 57g at the time the preference is surrendered or the creditor is deprived thereof by the judgment of the court, and that they may be proved and allowed thereafter before the estate is finally settled. Page *v.* Rogers was not referred to upon the argument of this case, and the opinion had not been published at the time the suit of the trustee against this bank was determined."

And, whatever be the reasoning whereby the apparently strict wording of § 57 (n) is obviated, the rule seems to be thoroughly established that the section does not apply to the presentation of claims of a creditor from whom a preference has been recovered by suit.

In re Coventry Evans Furniture Co., 22 A. B. R. 623, 171 Fed. 673 (D. C. N. Y.): "The facts are that the note was paid by the bankrupt, prior to the filing of the petition; that suit was brought by the truste to recover the amount, the claim being that it was a preferential payment; and that in such suit as to such note the Citizens Trust Company was defeated and compelled to pay back the amount. Thereupon, and more than one year after the adjudication, the note was duly proved and presented for allowance, and rejected by the referee, for the reason [that it was] not proved and presented within the year or time fixed by § 57 (n) of the act. This was erroneous. Keppel *v.* Tiffin Savings Bank, 197 U. S. 356, 13 A. B. R. 552. That case is decisive of the question. The claim must be allowed."

---

24. In re Clark, 24 A. B. R. 388, 176 Fed. 954 (D. C. N. Y.), quoted supra, § 727½.

25. In re Clark, 24 A. B. R. 388, 176 Fed. 954 (D. C. N. Y.), quoted at § 727½.

§ 727¾. Litigation Over Property in Custody of Bankruptcy Court, Sufficient Filing.—Where litigation is carried on over property in the custody of the bankruptcy court, the papers filed in the case will be sufficient to prevent the bar of the statute; thus, after the unsuccessful termination of the claimant's contest over the question of the ownership of property in possession of the court, he is not too late to claim on contract even though the year has expired.[26]

It has even been held unnecessary to file a formal deposition for proof of debt in such cases.[27]

But such ruling is unnecessary—the papers in the original litigation should be treated as informal claims and the formal proof subsequently filed be considered as being by way of amendment.

§ 728. Applies Also to Secured Claims, as to Deficit.—The limitation applies to secured claims, as to the deficit, the same as to unsecured claims.[28]

In re Sampter, 22 A. B. R. 357, 170 Fed. 938 (C. C. A. N. Y.): "In this state of things Marks filed August 16, 1907, more than two years after the adjudication, his claim against the individual estate of Arnold Sampter for the deficiency resulting in the foreclosure actions above mentioned, amounting to $8,866.36. * * * Under §§ 57a and 57e, of the Bankruptcy Act, Marks could have proved his claim, though it was secured, and not liquidated. Besides this, it was liquidated within a year of the adjudication. Service of copies of the complaints in the foreclosure actions on the trustee was not a proof of claim in bankruptcy. There is no ground for holding, assuming the power to do so, that the peremptory requirements of § 57n should be disregarded."

§ 729. Filing with Trustee Sufficient.—Filing with the trustee will suffice, for it is to be inferred from Rule XXI (1), providing that "Proofs of debt received by any trustee shall be delivered to the referee to whom the cause is referred;" also from subsection "c" of § 57 providing that "claims after being proved may, for the purpose of allowance, be filed by the claimants in the court where the proceedings are pending or before the referee, if the case has been referred," that the referee is not the sole officer of the court with whom a claim may be sufficiently filed to take it out of the limitations of § 57 (n).[29]

Orcutt v. Green, 17 A. B. R. 75, 204 U. S. 96 (reversing In re Ingalls Bros., 13 A. B. R. 512, 137 Fed. 517, C. C. A. N. Y.): "We are of opinion, taking into consideration the various provisions of the fifty-seventh section of the Bank-

---

26. C o m p a r e § 716½; also see In re Landis, 19 A. B. R. 420, 156 Fed. 318 (D. C. Pa.). In re Strobel, 20 A. B. R. 884, 160 Fed. 916 (D. C. N. Y.).
27. In re Strobel, 20 A. B. R. 884, 160 Fed. 916 (D. C. N. Y.).
28. In re Baird & Co., 18 A. B. R. 228 (D. C. Pa.); Steinhardt v. National Bank, 19 A. B. R. 72, 122 App. Div. (N. Y.) 55; inferentially, In re Clover

Creamery Ass'n (Evans v. Claridge), 23 A. B. R. 884, 176 Fed. 907 (C. C. A. Wis.).
29. But a trustee may not escape the limitations of Bankr. Act, § 57 (n), by filing his own claim with himself. Orcutt v. Green, 17 A. B. R. 75, 204 U. S. 96; In re Kessler, 25 A. B. R. 512, 186 Fed. 127 (C. C. A. N. Y.), reversing 23 A. B. R. 901, 176 Fed. 647.

ruptcy Act, in connection with No. 21 of the General Orders in Bankruptcy, adopted by this court, that the presentation and delivery of proofs of claim to the trustee in bankruptcy within the year after the adjudication is filing within the statute and the general order above mentioned.

"The General Orders of this court are provided for by § 30 of the Bankruptcy Act, which enacts that 'All necessary rules, forms, and orders as to procedure and for carrying this Act into force and effect shall be prescribed, and may be amended from time to time, by the Supreme Court of the United States.' Under that section this court had the power to provide, as it has done in Order 21, that 'Proofs of debt received by any trustee shall be delivered to the referee to whom the cause is referred.' There is nothing in that provision inconsistent with, or opposed to anything stated in the bankruptcy law upon the subject, and we must therefore take the statute and the order and read them together, the order being simply somewhat of an amplification of the law with respect to procedure, but nothing which can be construed as beyond the powers granted to the court by virtue of the law itself. The question is not whether any one but the court or referee can pass upon a claim and allow it or disallow it. That must be done by the court or referee, but it is simply whether a delivery of a claim, properly proved, to the trustee is a sufficient filing. The law provides, subsection c of § 57, that the claims, after being proved, may, for the purpose of allowance, be filed by the claimants in the court where the proceedings are pending, or before the referee, if the case has been referred; but that does not prohibit their being filed somewhere else prior to their allowance, and the order in bankruptcy in substance provides that they may be filed after being proved, with the trustee. Such order is equivalent to saying that proofs of debt (or claim) may be received by the trustee. When they are so received by him they are in legal effect received by the court, whose officer the trustee is. Having been received by the trustee, under authority of law, the proofs of debt are thereby sufficiently filed so far as the creditors are concerned, and it is the duty of the trustee to deliver them to the referee. If the trustee inadvertently neglects to perform that duty it is the neglect of an officer of the court, and the creditors are in no way responsible therefor. The presentation and filing have been made within the time provided for and with one of the proper officers, and his failure to deliver to the referee can not be held to be a failure on the part of the creditor to properly file his proofs."

And the filing of pleadings by the creditor in a suit brought by the trustee may be considered sufficient "presentation" to the trustee.[30] But it is not sufficient to deliver the proof to a mere employee of the trustee. If, however, it is made to appear that the employee is in charge of the trustee's office, or business, such delivery might present at least *prima facie* evidence of filing.[31]

It has been held that filing with the receiver is sufficient.[32]

§ 730. Limitation Not Applicable to United States Government nor to Taxes.—The limitation of § 57 (n) does not apply to claims of

---

30. In re [Salvator] Brew. Co., 26 A. B. R. 21, 188 Fed. 522 (D. C. N. Y.); also compare ante, §§ 716, 716½, 727¼, 727½.

31. In re Lathrop, etc., Co., 28 A. B. R. 756, 197 Fed. 164 (C. C. A. N. Y.).

32. In re Kessler. 25 A. B. R. 512, 186 Fed. 127 (C. C. A. N. Y., reversing 23 A. B. R. 901, 176 Fed. 647).

the United States government; thus, it does not apply in the bankruptcy of a contractor under contract to supply paper to the government.[33]

Nor does § 57 (n) apply to taxes.

In re Cleanfast Hosiery Co., 4 A. B. R. 702 (Ref. N. Y.): "Assuming, however, for the purposes of the argument, that taxes are provable claims, § 64 of the act relates specifically to taxes, and provides a special method for their payment, to-wit, that the court shall order the trustee to pay them, and that the receipt of the proper officer shall entitle the trustee to a credit for the amount paid. A formal proof of claim, as in case of provable debts generally, is not specifically required; in fact, the latter provision as to a receipt by the proper officer would seem to imply that none is necessary, and no time limit is imposed. I think this section should in these respects control, rather than § 57, subdivision 'n,' above mentioned, prescribing the rule as to provable debts as a class, under the familiar rule of construction, that a statutory provision as to a general class must give way to a special provision relating to one of the class. The provisions as to the special case will be held an implied exception to the clause relating to the general class, and effect be thus given to both clauses."

§ 731. Withholding of Dividend Until Expiration of Year Not Required.

—Section 57 (n) does not operate to enlarge a procrastinating creditor's rights so as to require the trustee to withhold until the close of the year the paying out of dividends, when ready, on proved and allowed claims; but it is, on the contrary, a curtailment of the creditor's rights, so that, even if money be still in the estate after the expiration of the year, yet it can not be shared in by one who does not prove his claim until the expiration of the year.[34]

§ 732. Claims Capable of Liquidation but Not Liquidated, Nevertheless Discharged.

—Claims that might have been liquidated but were not liquidated are nevertheless barred by the bankrupt's discharge.[35]

§ 733. Claims Not Proved within Year, Nevertheless Available as Offsets.

—Where a claim is provable in its nature, but has not been proved within the year, it is nevertheless available as an offset in an independent suit brought by the trustee against the claimant, if otherwise a valid offset.[36]

§ 734. Amendment of Claim after Expiration of Year.

—A proof of debt may be amended after the close of the year, for the amendment, like all amendments, reverts to the time of the original filing and takes effect from that time, and should in all respects be considered the same, as if it had been already filed then.[37]

---

33. In re Charles M. Stover, 11 A. B. R. 345, 127 Fed. 394 (D. C. Penn.).

34. Compare post, § 2214. Also see In re Stein, 1 A. B. R. 662, 94 Fed. 124 (D. C. Ind.); In re Bell Piano Co., 18 A. B. R. 185 (D. C. N. Y.).

35. In re Hilton, 4 A. B. R. 774, 104 Fed. 981 (D. C. N. Y.).

36. See post, § 1178; ante, § 716. Also

see Norfolk & Western Ry. Co. v. Graham, 16 A. B. R. 615 (C. C. A. W. Va.). But compare, limitation of rule, In re Clover Creamery Ass'n (Evans v. Claridge), 23 A. B. R. 884, 176 Fed. 907 (C. C. A. Wis.).

37. Hutchinson v. Otis, 10 A. B. R. 135, 190 U. S. 552, 555 (affirming 8 A. B. R. 382). In this case, the Supreme

In re Faulkner, 20 A. B. R. 542, 161 Fed. 900 (C. C. A. Kans.): "It matters not what the paper filed with the referee on July 5, 1905, was styled. Scrutiny of it discloses that it contained every essential statement required by § 57 to constitute proof of a claim, and fully and accurately informed the court of the amount of petitioner's claims and the securities held for their payment. The referee by his order made a finding of the exact sums due the petitioner, as well as the amount of interest thereon, and ordered the collateral sold and the proceeds to be applied on 'said indebtedness,' and that report of sale be made to him for confirmation. All this was done within the year following the date of the adjudication, and it cannot be denied that it constituted a complete scheme by the execution of which the balance due the petitioner after application of the proceeds of sale of the collateral could be ascertained from the court records. No further act on the part of the petitioner was necessary to definitely fix the balance due him. Notwithstanding this, however, he, after the year expired, out of abundant precaution made a resumé of the proceedings taken and the result thereof, and definitely stated the same, and formally asked for an allowance of the balance so found to be due him, in order that he might participate pro rata with other unsecured creditors in the assets of the bankrupt's estate. This was denied, and his claim was expunged. We think this was wrong. The limitation of time within which proofs of claim should be made must necessarily be observed. Such disposition of bankruptcy cases that creditors may expeditiously realize what they may is important and necessary; but the substance of things, and not the forms merely, should be observed. Bankruptcy proceedings are equitable in their nature, and should be as far as possible conducted on broad lines to accomplish the ultimate purpose of distributing the assets of a bankrupt pro rata among his creditors. Atchison, T. & S. F. Ry. Co. v. Hurley, 18 Am. B. R. 396, * * * 153 Fed. 503, 508. In this case everything necessary to determine the balance due the petitioner was done before the year expired within which proof of claims could be made. All the statements required by § 57 had been made, the debt had been judicially determined and stated, the collateral had been ascertained, an upset price fixed, a sale ordered, and provision had been made for the application of the proceeds of sale to the satisfaction of the debt pro tanto. The working out of this scheme necessarily and accurately resulted in the amount due the petitioner. 'Id certum est quod certum reddi potest.' Assuming, however, but not deciding, that the proceedings taken and orders made did not constitute technical proof of petitioner's claims within the year, as required by § 57, we have no doubt they constituted

Court of the United States held, that where the proof of debt originally filed is defective, a substituted proof by consent of the trustee may be filed more than a year after adjudication and the clause (n) of § 57 forbidding proof of claims subsequent to one year after adjudication can not be taken to exclude amendments. It had been held contra, In re Moebins, 8 A. B. R. 590, 116 Fed. 47 (D. C. Pa.).

See, in addition, Bennett v. Am. Credit Indemnity Co., 20 A. B. R. 258, 159 Fed. 624 (C. C. A. Ky.); In re Horne & Co., 23 A. B. R. 590 (Ref. Miss.); In re [Salvator] Brew. Co., 26 A. B. R. 21, 188 Fed. 522 (D. C. N. Y.). Instance,

amendment of wife's claim, to show credit to obviate statute of limitations, refused, evidently for fraud, In re Given, 20 A. B. R. 490, 160 Fed. 199 (D. C. N. Y.). Contra, where, by amendment after the year a creditor from whom a preference has been recovered by litigation, seeks to add to his claim the value of the preference recovered. In re Kemper, 15 A. B. R. 677, 142 Fed. 210 (D. C. Iowa), although on the facts, this case seems to have been wrongly decided: the claim was not a new one nor a distinct one —it was the old claim with a former credit excluded.

such substantial showing of it as warranted the amendment of the original proof of claim as made by the petitioner in his affidavits filed July 18, 1906."

§ 735. But an Original Claim Must Exist, Filed within Year.—Of course, there must have been an original proof duly filed within the year; otherwise there would be nothing by which to amend; and the power of amendment is not to be distorted to let in dilatory creditors who have filed no proof within the limited year.[38]

In re Pettingill & Co., 14 A. B. R. 763, 137 Fed. 143 (Ref. Mass.): "The word 'proved' in § 57n must be read to include filing the claim with the referee; consequently no claim can be allowed against a bankrupt estate unless it has not only been verified but also filed with the referee within one year after the date of the adjudication."

In re McCallum & McCallum, 11 A. B. R. 448 (D. C. Pa.): "With every disposition to be liberal in the allowance of amendments, there is, nevertheless a limit to the power of the court in this regard. If the year within which claims may be proved is unexpired, amendments are largely a matter of course, but after the expiration of the year a different situation is presented. The rights of creditors are then fixed by the act itself, and no new right can be introduced. If the proof of a right that had already been asserted in substance should thereafter be found to lack form or precision, ordinarily, I suppose such defect might still be remedied."

But the original claim need not have been styled "proof of debt;"[39] and the creditor's pleadings in a suit by the trustee may be sufficient.[40]

And the filing of an informal claim with the receiver or trustee may be sufficient.

In re Kessler, 25 A. B. R. 512, 186 Fed. 127 (C. C. A. N. Y., reversing 23 A. B. R. 901, 176 Fed. 647): "On October 30, 1907, the firm of Kessler & Co. made an assignment for the benefit of creditors to William Williams, who next day sent out a printed circular to the creditors. Heine & Company, bankers in Paris, received a copy, and promptly on such receipt sent (Nov. 12, 1907), to Williams' assignee an account in detail of their transactions with Kessler & Company showing a balance owing to Heine & Company. The account was accompanied with a letter stating that it was an extract of account of the firm showing a debit balance of Fr; 140720, and adding that Heidelbach, Ickelheimer & Company, of New York, were authorized to represent Heine & Co. in this matter. There was no verification under oath, nor any statement of consideration (except perhaps inferentially) nor any statement whether any securities were held as collateral therefor. On Nov. 8, 1907, petition in bankruptcy was filed, and on Nov. 11 a receiver was appointed, who on Dec. 30, 1907, was elected trustee. The books and records of the bankrupts including the letter and account received from Heine & Company were turned over by Williams to the

---

38. Also, In re Mowery, 22 A. B. R. 239 (D. C. Ohio); In re Basha & Son, 27 A. B. R. 435, 193 Fed. 151 (D. C. N. Y.); In re Lathrop, etc., Co., 28 A. B. R. 756, 197 Fed. 164 (C. C. A. N. Y.); In re Daniel, 29 A. B. R. 284, 193 Fed. 772 (D. C. Ga.).

39. In re Faulkner, 20 A. B. R. 542, 161 Fed. 900 (C. C. A. Kans.), quoted at § 734. Compare ante, §§ 622, 729. In re [Salvator] Brew. Co., 26 A. B. R. 21, 188 Fed. 522 (D. C. N. Y.).

40. In re [Salvator] Brew. Co., 26 A. B. R. 21, 188 Fed. 522 (D. C. N. Y.).

receiver and have since remained in his possession as receiver or as trustee. Shortly thereafter and about Nov. 30, 1907, Mr. Delos McCurdy, a member of the bar, at the request of Heidelbach, Ickelheimer & Company, called on the receiver and asked him if he had received from the assignee a claim of Heine & Company in Paris against the bankrupt estate. The receiver stated that the papers that had come over were still in confusion, but that if he would come in a day or two afterwards he would tell him accurately about it. A day or two afterwards Mr. McCurdy called again and asked the receiver if that claim was received from the assignee. He said it was. Mr. McCurdy asked him if it was all right and he said it was. The witness says: 'He asked some person there with respect to the matter, and the person made the reply, and he turned to me and said, "It is all right."' It may fairly be presumed that Heidelbach, Ickelheimer & Company communicated the result of Mr. McCurdy's interview to Heine & Company; it would seem from statements in one of their letters that subsequently they received from time to time communications emanating from the District Court, Southern District of New York. There seems no reason to doubt that they, in good faith, supposed that they had duly filed a proper claim until they were advised by the trustee, in the summer of 1909, that no claim filed by them was found upon the list. The trustee had sént out a circular to 'all creditors and parties in interest, in September, 1908, asking them to examine and see if their claims were filed with the referee.' It was held by the Supreme Court in I. B. Orcutt Company v. Green, 204 U. S. 96, 17 Am. B. R. 72, that presentation and delivery of claims to the trustee is sufficient. * * * It would be harsh and inequitable to refuse them relief upon the statement of facts above recited, if there were power to grant it. It is not disputed that the papers sent to the assignee and by him turned over to the receiver do not comply with the requirements of the statute; but it has been repeatedly held that 'a proof of claim' which is defective in some substantial particular may be amended, and that such amendment may be made subsequent to the expiration of one year after adjudication, although the effect of such amendment may be that 'proof of claim' is thereby effectively made only after the year limited by section 57n."

Where an assignment of a claim was filed within the year, but the deposition for proof of debt itself was not filed until after, it has been held a sufficient filing of the claim;[41] and to be amendable thereafter.[42]

And the rule has been so relaxed by recent decisions that it has finally come to be held in one circuit that a failure to file within the year owing to a "pardonable mistake" will warrant the allowance of a *nunc pro tunc* order, especially where it also appears that the claim was recognized by the court and the creditors as one entitled to share in composition proceedings.[43]

§ 736. Power of Amendment Not to Be Distorted to Let in Dilatory Creditors Who Have Withdrawn Proofs.—The power of amendment is not to be distorted to let in dilatory creditors who have withdrawn their proofs.[44]

41. In re Bennett, 18 A. B. R. 320, 153 Fed. 673 (C. C. A. Ky.).

42. Bennett v. Am. Credit Indemnity Co., 20 A. B. R. 258, 159 Fed. 624 (C. C. A. Ky.).

43. In re Basha & Son, 29 A. B. R. 225, 200 Fed. 951 (C. C. A. N. Y.).

44. In re Thompson Sons, 10 A. B. R. 581, 123 Fed. 174 (D. C. Penna.).

§ 737. Dilatory Creditors Filing Claims against Firm, Amending to File Claims against Separate Partners.

—And it has been held that the power of amendment is not to be distorted to enable creditors who hold firm notes with an individual partner's endorsement, and who have proved their claims solely against the partnership estate, to amend, after the expiration of the year, by adding proof against the individual partner's estate also.

In re McCallum & McCallum, 11 A. B. R. 447 (D. C. Penn.): "The contract entered into by the maker of a promissory note, and the contract entered into by the indorser, are entirely distinct and separate undertakings. It does not affect this conclusion that the contract of endorsement is made by a member of the firm that has previously made the other contract. The same man has made two contracts in different characters one as a partner and the other as an individual."

But this rule is perhaps too strict, and it has been held on the other hand that, after the expiration of the year, a creditor may withdraw a claim filed against an individual estate and file it against the partnership estate.[45]

§ 737¼. Amending after Year on Surrender of Preference or Fraudulent Transfer.

—A claim may be amended after the expiration of the year by adding thereto the amount covered by a preferential transfer that has meanwhile been surrendered,[46] or the amount covered by a fraudulent transfer that has meanwhile been surrendered, even though the surrender thereof may have been compulsory.[47] The claim is not increased—merely a credit is stricken out.

§ 737½. Increasing Claim or Adding New Claim.

—It is probably permissible by amendment after the expiration of the year to increase the amount of the claim already filed;[48] otherwise, too, than by the mere striking out of surrendered preferences, although the question is not free from doubt. But it would seem, on principle, to be wholly improper, at any rate, to permit an entirely new and distinct claim to be added after expiration of the year by way of an amendment to a claim already duly filed.[49]

§ 737¾. Section 57 (n) Does Not Enlarge Classes of Provable Debts.

—Section 57 (n) does not operate to enlarge the classes of debts to be considered "provable";[50] thus, not to make provable a claim that was

45. In re Horne & Co., 23 A. B. R. 590 (Ref. Miss.).

46. See ante, §§ 715, 716, 716½, 727¼, 727½, 727¾; In re Sheibler, 21 A. B. R. 309, 163 Fed. 545 (D. C. N. Y.); contra, In re Kemper, 15 A. B. R. 677, 142 Fed. 210 (D. C. Iowa).

47. Necessarily impliedly, In re Clark, 24 A. B. R. 388, 176 Fed. 955 (D. C. N. Y.), quoted at § 727½.

48. Contra, obiter, In re Mowery, 22 A. B. R. 239 (D. C. Ohio).

49. In re Mowery, 22 A. B. R. 239 (D. C. Ohio).

50. Compare, §§ 641, 685.

contingent at the time of the filing of the bankruptcy petition, but which has become fixed within the year after the adjudication.

In re Roth & Appel, 22 A. B. R. 504, 174 Fed. 64 (D. C. N. Y.): "Nor can I think that § 57 (n) affects the matter at all. That 'claims shall not be proved' subsequent to a 'year after the adjudication' is not an enlargement of the class of provable claims, but merely a restriction of the time wherein provable claims may be presented."

CHAPTER XXIII.

ASSIGNMENT OF CLAIMS.

Synopsis of Chapter.

§ **738. Assignment of Claims.**—Claims may be assigned before or after bankruptcy, and before or after the filing of the formal deposition for proof of debt.[1]

§ **739. Several Assigned to One Person—Claims Merge for Voting, etc.**—If several claims of different creditors are assigned to one person, such person becomes but a single creditor, although holding, to be sure, several claims;[2] even though assigned "in trust."[3]

§ **740. Assigned before Bankruptcy.**—A claim assigned before the debtor's bankruptcy as already noted (ante, ch. XX, § 608, et seq.), may be proved in the name of the assignee, he being the "owner" of the claim. No special form of proof is requisite, of course. And all that is necessary is to prove such a state of facts as will estop the assignor from making the same claim.[4]

In re Miner, 9 A. B. R. 100 (D. C. Ore.): "The form of assignment of a claim is immaterial, and the proof of the claim need only be such as will estop the assignor from making the same claim."

1. Compare, general discussion, In re Finley, 3 A. B. R. 738 (D. C. N. Y.). **Assignment of Claim Not Payment of It.**—An arrangement with a corporation buying in all a bankrupt's assets and business, to pay to a claimant a quantity of goods "in liquidation" of the claimant's claim, the claim, however, to be presented against the estate, amounts to a purchase of the claim and not to a payment of it, and the claim is not extinguished although the words used were in the form of payment. Haas-Baruck Co. v. Portu-

ondo, 15 A. B. R. 130, 138 Fed. 949 (D. C. Pa.).

2. In re Massengill, 7 A. B. R. 669, 113 Fed. 366 (D. C. N. Car.); Leighton v. Kennedy, 12 A. B. R. 229, 129 Fed. 737 (C. C. A. Mass.); In re Burlington Malting Co., 6 A. B. R. 369, 109 Fed. 777 (D. C. Wis.); (1867) In re Frank, Fed. Cas. No. 5,050.

3. In re E. T. Kenney Co., 14 A. B. R. 611, 136 Fed. 451 (D. C. Ind.).

4. In re Miner, 8 A. B. R. 248, 114 Fed. 998 (D. C. Ore.).

§ 741. Assigned after Bankruptcy, but before Filing Proof.—
Claims assigned after the bankruptcy of the debtor but before the filing
of formal proof, must be accompanied by an affidavit of the one who owned
the claim at the time the bankruptcy petition was filed. This affidavit must
state the true consideration of the debt, and that it is entirely unsecured, or,
if secured, the security, as is required in proving secured claims.[5]

§ 742. Assigned after Filing.—Where claims are assigned after proof,
ten days notice must be sent to the original claimant to give him time and
opportunity to deny the assignment, at the expiration of which time, if no
denial of the assignment be made, and satisfactory proof be made of the
assignment, the assignee's name is formally substituted on the court's records for the original claimant's name, and thereafter the assignee stands in
the place of the original claimant.[6]

§ 743. Ten Days Notice to Original Claimant.—Notice by mail must
be immediately given the original claimant. Presumably it is a ten days
notice, since such is the usual length of notice prescribed in bankruptcy, and,
moreover, ten days time by the General Order XXI (3) is allowed for filing objections to the claim of assignment. The notice may be given by mail.
Undoubtedly, personal service of notice would be proper, and of course notice may be waived. Notice by mail can not be taken to be the exclusive
manner of notice. The notice is to be given by the referee, or, at any rate,
it is to run in his name.

§ 744. "Satisfactory Proof" of Assignment to Be Filed.—Satisfactory proof of the assignment is to be filed, as a prerequisite to entry of
the order of substitution. Such "proof" refers here, naturally, to a sworn
statement alleging the assignment. It certainly does not refer to the filing
of any original papers themselves, constituting the assignment; for assignments of claims, it is conceivable, may be verbal and are not always in form
for "filing," General Order XXI (5) further providing how "an assignment
of claim after proof," may be "proved."[7]

---

5. Gen. Ord., XXI (3). See ante,
ch. XX, § 609.

6. Gen. Ord. XXI (3): "Upon the
filing of satisfactory proof of the assignment of a claim proved and entered
on the referee's docket, the referee
shall immediately give notice by mail
to the original claimant of the filing
of such proof of assignment; and if no
objection be entered within ten days,
or within further time allowed by the
referee, he shall make an order subrogating the assignee to the original
claimant. If objection be made, he
shall proceed to hear and determine
the matter." See ante, ch. XX, § 610.

**Subrogation of Sureties Paying
Claim, Assignees, etc.—**Sureties who
pay claims after the bankruptcy, also
assignees, may be subrogated to the
claimant's rights, even the right of rescission of sale. Sessler *v.* Paducah
Dist. Co., 21 A. B. R. 723, 168 Fed. 44
(C. C. A. La.).

7. As to the effect of the assignment of a priority claim upon the
priority, see post, § 2133, et seq., subject of "Distribution."

§ 744½. Assignment Filed within Year, Though Deposition for Proof of Debt, Not.—Where an assignment of a claim has been filed within the year, though the deposition for proof of debt is not filed until after, it has been held a sufficient filing to avoid the prohibition of Bankruptcy Act, § 57 (n).[8]

---

8. Bennett *v.* Am. Credit Indemnity Co., 20 A. B. R. 258, 159 Fed. 624 (C. C. A. Ky.).

CHAPTER XXIV.

ALLOWABLE CLAIMS.

Synopsis of Chapter.

§ 745. "Allowability" Distinguished from "Provability."

—As we have seen, there is a difference between a claim that is allowable and one that is merely provable. Of course no claim that is not provable may be considered by the court; the court itself will cast out a claim that is not provable, for it has jurisdiction to allow or disallow only provable claims and claims that are "duly proved"—claims, that is to say, that are of correct nature and of essentially correct form. The question still remains, after it has been determined that a claim is in proper form (i. e., "duly proved") and belongs to some one of the classes of debts which in their nature are "provable," whether the particular debt is one that should be "allowed" to participate in the dividends; whether, in short, the claim is "allowable."

§ 746. Only "Provable" Claims "Allowable."

—No claim, of course, is allowable unless it be provable.[1]

§ 747. Converse Not True—All "Provable" Claims Not Necessarily "Allowable."

—The converse of the proposition is not true, for all provable claims are not necessarily allowable claims. There may exist incorrectness, illegality, offsets, counterclaims, securities held, and a thousand and one other things that will, if brought to the Court's attention in a legal way, bar the claim in whole or reduce it in part and to such extent render it incapable of sharing in dividends.

Thus we come to consider "secured" and "preferred" claims, as to their "allowability," likewise claims outlawed by the Statute of Limitations, and

---

1. As to the "allowability" of claims as affected by their "provability," see preceding chapter, and cases cited therein.

those subject to offset, counterclaim and the many other defences affecting the validity and amount of claims in general.

DIVISION 1.

ALLOWABILITY AS AFFECTED BY THE HOLDING OF SECURITIES, PREFERENCES AND LEGAL LIENS.

SUBDIVISION "A".

ALLOWABILITY OF SECURED CLAIMS.

§ 748. Meaning of "Secured" Claim.—A "secured" claim, within the meaning of bankruptcy law, is a claim against the bankrupt where the creditor owning it, or a surety, indorser, or other person secondarily liable for the debt, holds security upon property of the bankrupt of a kind that would pass to the trustee in bankruptcy.[2]

§ 749. Distinguished from "Provable" Claim.—A secured claim may, of course, be "provable" if the nature of the debt brings it within one of the classes of § 63; and it may be "proved." Forms Nos. 32 and 36 have been prescribed by the Supreme Court for proof of secured claims.[3]

§ 750. Distinguished from "Preferred" Claim.—A "secured" claim is to be distinguished from a "preferred" claim, in bankruptcy parlance.[4]

§ 751. "Allowable" Only after Deduction of Securities.—Secured claims, although valid and "provable," are not "allowable" to share in dividends, except to the extent of any deficit left after deduction of the value of the securities from the debt.[5]

---

2. Definition of "secured" creditor, Bankr. Act, § 1 (23): "'Secured creditor' shall include a creditor who has security for his debt upon the property of the bankrupt of a nature to be assignable under this act or who owns such a debt for which some indorser, surety or other persons secondarily liable for the bankrupt has such security upon the bankrupt's assets."

Original owner's acceptance of trustee's quitclaim deed to land purchased, but afterwards declined, by bankrupt, specific performance having been meanwhile decreed by court, held to prevent claim for deficit between decree for purchase price and value of property. In re Davis, 24 A. B. R. 667, 179 Fed. 871 (D. C. Pa.).

3. Steinhardt v. National Bank, 19 A. B. R. 72, 122 App. Div. N. Y. 55; instance, In re Keep, etc., Co., 28 A. B. R. 765, 200 Fed. 80 (D. C. N. Y.). See ante, ch. XXI, "Provable Debts," Div. 1, § 628, et seq.

4. Impliedly, In re Busby, 10 A. B. R. 650, 124 Fed. 469 (D. C. Pa.).

Question of Surrender of Preference to Be Determined before Determination of Value of Securities.—In re Quinn, 21 A. B. R. 264, 165 Fed. 144 (C. C. A. Ill.). See post, § 767½.

5. Bankr. Act, § 57 (e): "Claims of secured creditors and those who have priority may be allowed to enable such creditors to participate in the proceedings at creditors' meetings held prior to the determination of the value of their securities or priorities, but shall be allowed for such sums only as to the courts seem to be owing over and above the value of their securities or priorities."

Bankr. Act, § 57 (h): "The value of securities held by secured creditors shall be determined by converting the same into money according to the terms of the agreement pursuant to which such securities were delivered to such creditors or by such creditors and the trustee, by agreement, arbitra-

In re Stevens, 23 A. B. R. 239, 173 Fed. 842 (D. C. Ore.): "There seems to be no provision for the allowance of any claim fully secured. The allowance can go only to any balance that may remain of the claimant's demand after applying the value of the property incumbered by the claim." Compare, Flint v. Chaloupka, 18 A. B. R. 293, 78 Neb. 594.

Kohout v. Chaloupka, 11 A. B. R. 265 (Sup. Ct. Neb.): "But in this connection it is important to keep in mind that a secured creditor is not, under the Bankruptcy Law, forced to the alternative of either relying wholly on his security, or, abandoning that, prove his claim with other creditors. It is, we think, settled by a number of authoritative adjudications that a creditor who has security for his debt, if that security is insufficient, may prove his claim for the overplus, and does not abandon his security if he makes a full disclosure of it and the value thereof. Under such circumstances he may vote upon the choice of an assignee upon such overplus. In re Bolton, Fed. Cas. No. 1,614. So, where a creditor proves for the full amount of his claim, specifying the securities held by him for the debt, he may participate in the dividends to the extent that his claim is greater than the value of the security."

Thus, subcontractors' claims are allowable only for the deficit after deduction of the funds appropriated to them by the attested accounts which they have filed.[6]

Indeed, a claim may be entirely "disallowed" where amply secured.[7]

§ 752. Thus, Notes (Not Accommodation) of Third Parties, Endorsed by Bankrupt as Collateral, Deducted.

—Thus, notes of third persons payable to the bankrupt, not made for the bankrupt's accommodation, and by him endorsed as collateral to his own debt, are securities held on the property of the bankrupt and must be deducted.

§ 753. No Double Proof on Original Note and on Indorsement of Collateral.

—There may be no double proof of the same debt, once on the original note and again on the indorsement of collateral.[8]

tion, compromise, or litigation, as the court may direct, and the amount of such value shall be credited upon such claims, and a dividend shall be paid only on the unpaid balance.'' Compare also, ante, § 220.

Inferentially, Flint v. Chaloupka, 18 A. B. R. 293, 78 Neb. 594; In re Hines, 16 A. B. R. 496, 144 Fed. 543 (D. C. Pa.); In re Little, 6 A. B. R. 681, 110 Fed. 62 (D. C. Iowa); instance, In re Hurlbutt, Hatch & Co., 16 A. B. R. 198, 135 Fed. 504 (C. C. A. N. Y.); impliedly, In re Milne, Turnbull & Co., 20 A. B. R. 248, 159 Fed. 280 (D. C. N. Y.).

Election between deducting as collateral and surrendering as without consideration, In re Waterloo Organ Co., 20 A. B. R. 110, 159 Fed. 426 (C. C. A. N. Y.).

Mortgage Bondholders or Trustee for Mortgage, Which to Prove for Deficit.—Mackey v. Randolph Macon Coal Co., 24 A. B. R. 719, 178 Fed. 881 (C. C. A. Mo.).

6. In re Grive, 18 A. B. R. 737, 153 Fed. 597 (D. C. Conn.).

7. In re Kenney, 10 A. B. R. 452 (Ref. Mass.); In re Stevens, 23 A. B. R. 239, 173 Fed. 842 (D. C. Ore.), quoted supra.

8. First Nat'l Bk. v. Eason, 17 A. B. R. 593 (C. C. A. Tex.).

Also, see post, "Rights of Creditors against Third Parties Jointly or Secondarily Liable;" "But Bankrupt Estate Not to Pay Two Dividends on Same Claim," § 1520.

Paper obligations issued as security and being held as collateral but in reality not being liens on anything and constituting mere additional promises to pay without additional consideration will not be permitted to increase the actual indebtedness. John Matthews

§ 754. Likewise, Orders on Third Parties by Bankrupt, Deducted.

—Likewise, orders drawn by the bankrupt in favor of the creditor on third parties indebted to the bankrupt, are securities held on the bankrupt's property, and are to be deducted.[9]

§ 755. Securities on Exempt Property, Deducted.

—Securities held on the bankrupt's exempt property are to be deducted.[10]

In re Cale, 25 A. B. R. 367, 182 Fed. 439 (D. C. Minn.): "It seems to be settled, until the United States Supreme Court shall decide differently, that the right of the general creditors to the general assets will be protected, and that the creditor with an enforceable lien or claim against exempt property can collect only the deficiency from the general assets."

In re Lantzenheimer, 10 A. B. R. 720, 124 Fed. 716 (D. C. Iowa): "If the bankrupt proceedings had not been instituted in this case, the creditor would have had the full right to enforce her mortgage security upon the piano, without exhausting the nonexempt property of the debtor; and the exemption privileges secured to the bankrupt by the state statute are not restricted or lessened by holding that the creditor can prove up her claim, and receive a dividend only on the difference between the value of the security and the full amount of her claim.

"The rule contended for by the creditor would result, in the great majority of the cases, in giving to the creditor a greater share in the estate of the debtor, without really benefiting the bankrupt; and I can see no good reason why the court should interpolate into clause 'h' of § 57 an exception not named therein to-wit, that if the security held by the creditor is upon exempt property, the creditor can prove his claim for the whole amount due. * * * The institution of the proceedings in bankruptcy did not change the rights of the mortgagor and mortgagee in this particular. The latter still retained the right to enforce the mortgage against the property, and in requiring the mortgagee to credit upon her claim the value of the mortgage security, as provided for in § 57 of the Bankrupt Act, no burden was cast upon the exempt property other or different in its results than would have been the case had the proceedings in bankruptcy not been brought. The effect upon the exemptions of the bankrupt, whatever it may be, of enforcing the mortgage lien is the result, not of any special provisions of the act, but of the act of the debtor in creating a special lien upon the exempt property; and there is nothing in the act which requires the ruling that greater protection must be extended to exempt property in the administration of estates in bankruptcy than would be afforded under the provisions of the State law in case the debtor had not been adjudged a bankrupt."

In re Little, 6 A. B. R. 681, 110 Fed. 621 (D. C. Iowa): "From the facts shown on the record, it appears that Coonley held security upon the horses

Inc. v. Knickerbocker Trust Co., 27 A. B. R. 629, 192 Fed. 557 (C. C. A. N. Y.). But if in the hands of a bona fide holder for value the rule might be different.

But it is not "double proof of the same indebtedness" where both an individual partner has endorsed the firm's note and also the firm has transferred as collateral security for the same debt a certain trust deed of real estate of the partner given to the firm for loans from the firm to him. In re White, 25 A. B. R. 541, 183 Fed. 310 (C. C. A. Ills.), quoted on other points at § 756. Compare § 796 1/10, "Several Obligations for Same Debt."

9. In re Hines, 16 A. B. R. 496, 144 Fed. 142 (D. C. Pa.).

10. See Finley v. Poor, 10 A. B. R. 377, 121 Fed. 739 (C. C. A. Ky.).

Whether Holder of Waiver of Ex-

for the unpaid portion of the purchase price, and therefore, under the provisions of clause 'h' of § 57 of the Bankrupt Act, he is only entitled to a dividend upon the amount of his claim after deducting the value of his security, to be ascertained as provided for in such clause. The fact that the bankrupt and the creditor agreed to a different disposition of the matter cannot defeat the right of other creditors to insist that the claims, being secured, can be proved only as provided for in § 57; and the fact that the property was set aside as exempt does not release it from the special lien existing against it."

The contrary also has been held, namely, that exempt property should not be deducted because "not of a nature to be assignable under the act," although the meaning of the term in this connection is at least obscure.[11]

It was similarly apparently held, under the law of 1867, that securities on the bankrupt's exempt homestead should not be deducted, since the homestead was property in which creditors would have had no interest, in any event.[12]

And there is considerable apparent logic in the position that the value of exempt property held as security should not be deducted, since such liens do not diminish the fund otherwise belonging to the trustee. Yet, in most instances, such a rule would be difficult of application in practice, to say the least; besides which there seems no sound warrant for it, since the property, though exempt, is, nevertheless, property of the bankrupt.

§ 756. No Deduction Where Securities Not on Bankrupt's Property.

—Where the property held as security is not the property of the bank-

emption Note a "Secured" Creditor? —It has been held, that the holder of a note containing a waiver of exemptions is a secured creditor, the value of whose security must be deducted before allowance of his claim. In re Meredith, 16 A. B. R. 331, 144 Fed. 230 (D. C. Ga.).

Suggestion, obiter, Lockwood v. Exch. Bk., 10 A. B. R. 107, 190 U. S. 294: "As in the case at bar, the entire property which the bankrupt owned is within the exemption of the State law, it becomes unnecessary to consider what, if any, remedy might be available in the court of bankruptcy for the benefit of general creditors, in order to prevent the creditor holding the waiver as to exempt property from taking a dividend on his whole claim from the general assets, and thereafter availing himself of the right resulting from the waiver to proceed against exempt property."

Obiter, Bell v. Dawson Grocery Co., 12 A. B. R. 159, 120 Ga. 130: "The waiver becomes in the nature of a security in that the debt may be made out of any property owned by the debtor, without regard to any exemption rights which the debtor would have had but for the waiver."

Obiter (1867), In re Bass, 3 Woods 382, Fed. Cas. 1,091: "What equities might arise if there were several creditors, and some of them had a lien or claim against the homestead property, and others not, it is not necessary to decide. Those who have no such claim might, perhaps, properly object to those having such a claim being allowed to come in for a dividend against the general assets until they had first exhausted their remedy against the exempted property, on the principle of marshaling assets. This would depend on the question whether the equity of the general creditors is superior to that of the bankrupt and his family in reference to the right of homestead and exemption. In some cases, at least, the equities might perhaps be equal, in which case the court would not require the assets to be marshaled."

11. In re Bailey, 24 A. B. R. 201 (D. C. Utah).

12. (1867) In re Stillwell, 7 Nat. B. Reg. 225.

rupt, the claim should be allowed without deduction for the value of the securities.[13]

In re Mertens, 15 A. B. R. 362, 142 Fed. 445 (C. C. A. N. Y., reversing on other grounds, 14 A. B. R. 226, and itself affirmed sub nom. Hiscock v. Varick, 18 A. B. R. 9): "If the securities were not the property of the partnership when they were pledged to the bank as collateral for the payment of the indebtedness, the bank was entitled to have its claim against the partnership allowed, and allowed at its face without any reduction. If they were not part of the partnership assets, they were not part of the joint estate in bankruptcy, and as to that estate the bank was under no obligation to apply or realize their value in reduction of its claim. If they were the property of Jacob M. Mertens individually, and were pledged by him, the bank would have been at liberty upon selling them to apply the proceeds to the payment of his individual debt; and no application having been made at the time, the settled rule of equity and of the courts of bankruptcy required the application of the proceeds in exoneration of the individual estate. * * *

"Many other authorities might be cited to the same effect, but the doctrine is so well established that it would be superfluous to refer to them. The provisions of the present Bankrupt Act requiring secured creditors to surrender preferences, and when the security is not preferential to have its value determined as a condition precedent to the allowance of the claim, have no application to cases in which the security was not the property of the bankrupt."

In re Noyes Bros., 11 A. B. R. 506, 127 Fed. 286 (C. C. A. Mass.): "It is too late to go to the reason of the rule which permits a creditor whose claim is secured or partly paid by an accommodation endorser to prove his claim to its full amount and exclude from the bankrupt estate the avails of such security or part payment, because the authorities in this country and England establishing that rule are such that we feel we ought to be governed by them."

To same effect, Swarts v. Fourth Nat. Bk. of St. Louis, 8 A. B. R. 673, 117 Fed. 1 (C. C. A. Mo.): "A creditor who holds the obligations of a bankrupt which have been partly paid by an accommodation maker, an indorser, or a surety, may prove and have his claim allowed, against the estate of the bankrupt, for the full amount owing by the bankrupt on the obligations. If the dividends on those obligations, plus the amount previously paid by the surety, amount to more than the obligations, the creditor will hold the surplus in trust for the surety."

Thus, property of individual members of a partnership held as security for a firm debt need not be deducted in the allowance of the claim against the partnership estate.[14]

---

13. In re Graves, 20 A. B. R. 818, 163 Fed. 358 (D. C. Vt.); In re Lange, 22 A. B. R. 414, 170 Fed. 114 (D. C. Iowa).

14. In re Coe, Powers & Co., 1 A. B. R. 275 (Ref. Ohio, affirmed by D. C.). In this case it was held, that the value of the individual accommodation endorsements of the members of a bankrupt partnership should not be deducted from the amount due on the partnership note, the endorsements not being the property of the firm. In re Mertens, 15 A. B. R. 364 (C. C. A. N. Y., reversing, on other grounds, 14 A.

B. R. 226); Hiscock v. Varick Bank, 18 A. B. R. 6, 206 U. S. 28 (affirming In re Mertens, 15 A. B. R. 364, C. C. A. N. Y.).

But notes appearing on their face to be pledged by the bankrupt partnership will be assumed, until the presumption is rebutted, to belong to the bankrupt firm. Inferentially, In re Mertens, 14 A. B. R. 226 (D. C. N. Y.).

Creditor's Secret Renewal of Security in His Own Name without Bankrupt's Knowledge, Security Still "Bankrupt's Property."—But where a creditor who

[1867] Ex parte Whiting, 14 N. B. Reg. 307: "When one partner has pledged his shares for the debts of the firm, proof may be made in full against the assets of the firm, because it is only when the proof is against the same estate which furnished security, that a sale and application of the security is required by the Bankrupt Law."

In re Plummer, 1 Phillips 56: "In administration under bankruptcy, the joint estates and separate estates are considered as distinct estates, and accordingly it has been held that a joint creditor having a security upon the separate estate is entitled to prove against the joint estate without giving up his security, upon the ground that it is a different estate."

Wilder v. Keeler, 3 Paige 167: "A creditor of a joint estate is always entitled to whatever he may obtain out of the fund in the hands of the surviving partner, without relinquishing his security against the separate estate of the deceased partner." In re Howard Cole & Co. (Under law of 1867), 4 N. B. Reg. 571.

In re White [Cummings v. Day], 25 A. B. R. 541, 183 Fed. 310 (C. C. A. Ills.): "But White, being an indorser individually upon the indebtedness due from the firm of George E. White & Company to Lusch, amounting to $40,000, it is said that these notes, put up as collateral, are 'double evidence' of the same indebtedness. We think not. The obligation that was put up as collateral, is the obligation of White to the firm, wholly independent of the obligation of White as endorser of the firm to Lusch—as wholly independent as if the notes had been the notes of a stranger to the firm—a collateral that the creditor had the right to ask, that the debtor had the right to give, and that, in the asking and giving, increased the security of the original debt of the firm to Lusch. True, the collateral could not have been used to an extent beyond the debt to which it was collateral, and the debt cannot be allowed except to the extent that the collateral has not paid it, but the sale of the collateral having amounted to but a small proportion of the debt, and the question here being the responsibility of White individually and not of his firm, these questions do not arise."

And a merely additional obligation of the bankrupt for the same debt may not be allowed as a separate claim except in so far as the law of negotiability may protect an innocent holder nor, if it be sold, may its proceeds be applied on the original debt and the debt be allowed for the difference; for there is but *one* debt, no matter how many writings may have been signed by the bankrupt to evidence the debt, and unless some security on

was holding the bankrupt's lease as security, procured secretly a renewal of it in his own name, the lease is still to be regarded as security on the bankrupt's property.

Fitch v. Richardson, 16 A. B. R. 836, 147 Fed. 196 (C. C. A. Mass.): "On fundamental principles of equity, there can be no question that the renewal by the creditor of the lease of the stall inured to the benefit of the debtor, subject to a liquidation of his debt, and that the new lease was held by the creditor merely as security for the claim offered in proof. Also according to settled rules of courts of equity, the fact that his debtor apparently acquiesced in a claim that the creditor had re-

newed the lease for his own sole benefit is of no effect. Especially is that true in the present case, where the creditor admits that he obtained the renewal behind the back of the debtor, and without consulting him. Even if he had consulted him, equity looks at the relative positions of creditor and debtor, and holds that, in view of the fact that the debtor is, at least theoretically, more or less under compulsion, all dealings by a creditor with securities which he has received are regarded as involuntary on the part of the debtor, and as subject to the original relation in which they stood, unless a new and adequate consideration passes between the parties."

the bankrupt's property be bound thereby, there is nothing to deduct.[15] Thus, where "debenture bonds" were made by the bankrupt and delivered as "collateral security" to its note but not secured by mortgage or in any other way, the court held that the "debenture bonds" amounted, in effect simply to another promise to pay the same debt and need not be deducted and that they might not be sold and their proceeds applied.[16]

§ 757. No Deduction for Amounts Paid by Surety.

—There should be no deduction for the amounts paid in on the debt by the surety. The creditor should prove for the entire debt as if no part thereof had been paid by the surety;[17] and if the dividend plus the payments made by the surety exceed the total amount due, then the creditor holds the excess in trust for the surety.[18]

§ 758. No Deduction for Property of Principal Held as Security by Creditor Where Surety Bankrupt.

—Collateral belonging to the principal debtor need not be deducted from the claim sought to be proved against the bankrupt surety or endorser; it is not security on the property of the bankrupt.[19]

Gorman v. Wright, 14 A. B. R. 135, 136 Fed. 164 (C. C. A. N. Car., reversing In re Matthews, 13 A. B. R. 91): "That the claim of P. H. Gorman was properly proven as an 'unsecured' claim against the estate of the bankrupt Matthews is entirely clear. The security held by said Gorman was the property of the maker of the note, in which the bankrupt had no interest, and, therefore, under subsection 23 of § 1 of the Bankruptcy Act, the claim was properly allowed against the estate of the bankrupt indorser for the full amount due, regardless of said security."

Obiter, In re Headley, 3 A. B. R. 272, 97 Fed. 765 (D. C. Mo.): "That the N. Y. judgment creditors also held judgments against W. W. Coover, as co-defendant, under which there had been a levy upon the stock of said Coover * * * such fact does not make the judgment creditors secured creditors within the meaning of the Act." •

But, of course, if the collateral has been realized upon, it must be deducted.

---

15. [John] Matthews Inc. v. Knickerbocker Trust Co., 27 A. B. R. 629, 192 Fed. 557 (C. C. A. N. Y.), affirming In re Matthews, 26 A. B. R. 19, 188 Fed. 445; In re Matthews, 26 A. B. R. 19, 188 Fed. 445 (D. C. N. Y.), affirmed sub nom. [John] Matthews Inc. v. Knickerbocker Trust Co., 27 A. B. R. 629, 192 Fed. 557 (C. C. A. N. Y.).

16. In re Matthews, 26 A. B. R. 19, 188 Fed. 445 (D. C. N. Y., affirmed sub nom. [John] Matthews Inc. v. Knickerbocker Trust Co., 27 A. B. R. 629, 192 Fed. 557 C. C. A.); [John] Matthews Inc. v. Knickerbocker Trust Co., 27 A. B. R. 629, 192 Fed. 557 (C.

C. A. N. Y., affirming In re Matthews, 26 A. B. R. 19, 188 Fed. 445).

17. Swarts v. Fourth Nat'l Bk. of St. Louis, 8 A. B. R. 673, 117 Fed. 1 (C. C. A. Mo.); In re Noyes Bros., 11 A. B. R. 506, 127 Fed. 286 (C. C. A. Mass.).

18. Swarts v. Fourth Nat'l Bk. of St. Louis, 8 A. B. R. 673, 117 Fed. 1 (C. C. A. Mo.).

19. To same effect under law of 1867, In re Anderson, 12 N. B. Reg. 502, Fed. Cas. 350; and In re Dunkerson, Fed. Cas. 4,157. Apparently contra, obiter, analogously, In re McCoy, 17 A. B. R. 760 (C. C. A. Ind.).

In re Graves, 20 A. B. R. 818, 163 Fed. 358 (D. C. Vt.): "Mr. Clement was entitled to prove his claim for the amount due thereon, but having foreclosed on the property of another and obtained full and complete title thereto, he should have dividends only on the balance after deducting the value of the mortgaged property which he has received from said corporation, which is his principal debtor."

In such case it has been held that the actual value, and not the amount realized on the security, will be deducted; and if that value exceeds the amount due, that the claim will be disallowed.[20]

§ 758½. Interest, after Deduction.—Interest is to be computed on the lien to the date of payment, or of readiness to pay, so far as the lien is paid from the fund derived from such property.

Coder v. Arts, 22 A. B. R. 1, 213 U. S. 223, affirming 18 A. B. R. 513, 152 Fed. 943: "Nor do we think the Circuit Court of Appeals erred in holding that, inasmuch as the estate was ample for that purpose, Arts was entitled to interest on his mortgage debt."

In re Stevens, 23 A. B. R. 239, 173 Fed. 842 (D. C. Ore.): "Thus is evinced a purpose of fixing the date of the filing of the petition as a time with reference to which all claims shall be computed with a view to ascertaining their amounts, and thus is a basis established for striking and paying dividends. The estate pays no accruing interest thereafter. In re Haake, 11 Fed. Cas. 134, No. 5,883. The rule is convenient, fair and equitable to all concerned, and affords a ready and indubitable basis for distribution of the assets under the provisions of the act among the creditors of the estate. By § 67d it is declared that liens given and accepted in good faith shall not be affected by the act. A lien in the usual course of business is given to secure interest accruing, as well as the principal of a demand, and it needs no argument to demonstrate the fact that, if the act should declare that interest shall cease upon secured demands at a given date, whether the demands are paid or not, it would affect the lien constituting such security. Another proposition is true also,— that, while the Bankruptcy Act contemplates that a secured creditor shall prove his claim, he may, notwithstanding, decline to make proof, and he does not thereby waive or lose his lien upon the property pledged. In re Goldsmith (D. C.), 9 Am. B. R. 419, 118 Fed. 763. His lien is yet simply unaffected by the Bankruptcy Act. * * * Now, if the secured claimant is entitled to his interest when he omits to make proof of his claim, it would not seem that it was the purpose of the act to cut off the running of his interest at the time of the filing of the petition in bankruptcy when his claim is proved. Indeed, § 67d is indicative of the opposite intendment, in declaring that good faith liens shall not be affected by the act. The act, otherwise construed, would result in the impairment of the lienor's contract, and could not stand under the Federal Constitution. Of course, the lienor may waive his security, and, if that is done, he comes in as one of the general creditors, and will share their rights and none other. But, if there be no waiver of the security, the estate is encumbered with the entire demand, including principal and interest. The next inquiry is, then, when does the interest cease to run upon a secured claim? The manifest answer to this is, when the money is realized from the property pledged. That is the end of the proceedings, we might say, for foreclosing the lien, and the duty

20. In re Graves, 25 A. B. R. 372, 182 Fed. 443 (D. C. Vt.).

then devolves upon the trustee to pay the claimant his debt. The estate ought not to be burdened with the payment of interest subsequent to that time. Sturgis was, therefore, entitled to interest on his demand to the time the realty covered by his mortgage was sold and the money realized therefor with which to pay such demand.

It was held at one time by the Circuit Court of Appeals,[21] upholding the decision of the District Court, that in determining the amount of the deficit to be "allowed" for sharing in dividends, the security might be marshalled first against the interest computed to the date of realizing thereon, the remainder to be the allowable deficit; however, a contrary rule prevails in England, established by a long line of authorities,[22] which permits, to be sure, the marshalling of securities against interest first, and furthermore against interest as computed to the date of the marshalling, but which, thereafter, in computing the deficit for sharing in dividends along with other claims, requires that the interest on the debt be computed regardless of the security and merely to the date of filing of the petition, the security then to be deducted, this contrary rule having much to be said in its favor, for in this way the secured creditor would be given the benefit of a full proportion of his security and at the same time the *debt* itself would not be enlarged, nor would the creditor, as to the deficit, be given dividends on a debt computed in effect differently from the claims of other creditors. The Supreme Court of the United States finally settled the question practically in favor of the English rule, holding that the interest on secured claims, as well as on other claims, ceases on the filing of the petition in bankruptcy and a creditor selling his security thereafter can not apply the proceeds first to the payment of interest accruing since the filing of the petition, then to the principal, and prove a claim for the balance that might be due, although interest and dividends which have accrued on the security may be applied by the creditor to after accruing interest on his debt.

Sexton *v.* Dreyfus, 25 A. B. R. 363, 219 U. S. 339, reversing In re Kessler, 24 A. B. R. 287, also reversing In re Kessler & Co., 22 A. B. R. 607, 171 Fed. 751: "In both of these cases, secured creditors, selling their security some time after the filing of the petition in bankruptcy, and finding the proceeds not enough to pay the whole amount of their claims, were allowed by the referee to apply the proceeds first to interest accrued since the filing of the petition, then to principal, and to prove for the balance. The referee certified the question whether the creditors had a right to the interest. The district judge answered the question in the affirmative, giving the matter a very thorough and

21. In re Kessler, 24 A. B. R. 287, 180 Fed. 979 (C. C. A. N. Y.) sustaining, though by a divided court, In re Kessler & Co., 22 A. B. R. 687, 171 Fed. 751.

22. Ex parte Wardell, 1 Cooke's Bankr. Law, p. 181; Ex parte Hersey, 1 Cooke's Bankr. Law, p. 181; Ex parte Badger, 4 Vesey 165; Ex parte Ramsbottom, 2 Mont. & Ayrton, 80; In re Penfield, 4 J. DeG. & Sm. 282; In re Savin, 7 Chan. 760; In re Talbott, 39 Chanc. 567; Quartermaine's Case L. R. 1 Chanc. 639; In re Bonacino, 1 Manson 59.

persuasive discussion, and declining to follow the English rule. Re Kessler, 22 Am. B. R. 606, 171 Fed. 751. On appeal, his decision was affirmed by a majority of the Circuit Court of Appeals. 24 Am. B. R. 287, 180 Fed. 979. The argument certainly is strong. A secured creditor could apply his security to interest first when the parties were solvent (Story v. Livingston, 13 Pet. 359, 371, 10 L. Ed. 200, 206), the liens are not affected by the statute. Sec. 67d (30 Stat. at L. 564, chap. 541, U. S. Comp. Stat. 1901, p. 3449). The law is not intended to take away any part of the security that a creditor may have, as it would seem at first sight to do if the course adopted below were not followed. Some further countenance to that course is thought to be found in § 57, which provides that the value of securities shall be determined by converting them into money 'according to the terms of the agreement,' for it is urged that, by construction, the right to apply them to interest is as much part of the agreement as if it had been written in. Nevertheless, it seems to us that, on the whole, the considerations on the other side are stronger and must prevail. For more than a century and a half the theory of the English bankrupt system has been that everything stops at a certain date. Interest was not computed beyond the date of the commission. Ex parte Bennet, 2 Atk. 527. This rule was applied to mortgages as well as to unsecured debts (Ex parte Wardell, 1787; Ex parte Hercy, 1702, 1 Cooke, Bankruptcy Laws, 4th Ed. 181 [1st Ed. Appx.]); and notwithstanding occasional doubts, it has been so applied with the prevailing assent of the English judges ever since (Ex parte Badger, 4 Ves. Jr. 165; Ex parte Ramsbottom, 2 Mont. & A. 79; Ex parte Penfold, 4 De G. & S. 282; Ex parte Lubbock, 9 Jur. N. S. 854; Re Savin, L. R. 7 Ch. 760, 764; Ex parte Bath, L. R. 22 Ch. Div. 450, 454; Quartermaine's Case [1892], 1 Ch. 639; Re Bonacino, 1 Manson, 59). As appears from Cooke, supra, the rule was laid down not because of the words of the statute, but as a fundamental principle. We take our bankruptcy system from England, and we naturally assume that the fundamental principles upon which it was administered were adopted by us when we copied the system, somewhat as the established construction of a law goes with the words where they are copied by another State. No one doubts that interest on unsecured debts stops. See § 63 (1). Shawnee County v. Hurley (C. C. A., 8th Cir.), 22 Am. B. R. 209, 94 C. C. A. 362, 169 Fed. 92, 94. The rule is not unreasonable when closely considered. It simply fixes the moment when the affairs of the bankrupt are supposed to be wound up. If, as in a well known illustration of Chief Justice Shaw's (Parks v. Boston, 15 Pick. 198, 208), the whole matter could be settled in a day by a pie-powder court, the secured creditor would be called upon to sell or have his security valued on the spot, would receive a dividend upon that footing, would suffer no injustice, and could not complain. If, under § 57 of the present act, the value of the security should be determined by agreement or arbitration, the time for fixing it naturally would be the date of the petition. At that moment the creditors acquire a right in rem against the assets. Chemical Nat. Bank v. Armstrong, 28 L. R. A. 231, 8 C. C. A. 155, 16 U. S. App. 465, 59 Fed. 372, 378, 379; Merrill v. National Bank, 173 U. S. 131, 140, 43 L. Ed. 640, 643, 19 Sup. Ct. 360. When there is delay in selling because of the hope of getting a higher price, it is more for the advantage of the secured creditor than of anyone else, as he takes the whole advance, and the others only benefit by a percentage, which does not seem a good reason for allowing him to prove for interest by indirection. Whenever the creditor proves, his security may be cut short. That is the necessarily possible result of bankruptcy. The rule under discussion fixes the moment in all cases at the date which the petition is filed; but beyond the fact of being compelled to realize his security and look for a new investment, there is no other invasion of the secured creditor's contract rights, and that invasion is the same in kind whatever moment may be fixed. It is suggested that the right of a creditor having security for two claims, one provable and the other unprovable, to marshal his security against the unprovable claim (see Hiscock *v.* Varick Bank, 206 U. S. 28, 37, 18 Am. B. R. 1, 51 L. Ed. 945, 951, 27 Sup. Ct. 681), is inconsistent with the rule applied in this case. But that right is not affected by fixing a time for winding up, and the Bankruptcy Law does not touch securities otherwise than in this unavoidable particular. The provision in § 57h for converting securities into money according to the terms of the agreement has no appreciable bearing on the question. Apart from indicating. in accordance with § 67d that liens are not to be affected, it would seem rather to be intended to secure the right of the trustees and general creditors in cases where the security may be worth more than the debt. The view that we adopt is well presented in the late Judge Lowell's work on bankruptcy, § 419; seems to have been entertained in Coder *v.* Arts (C. C. A., 8th Cir.), 18 Am. B. R. 513, 152 Fed. 943, 950, 15 L. R. A. (N. S.) 372, 82 C. C. A. 91 (affirmed without touching this point, 213 U. S. 223, 22 Am. B. R. 1, 53 L. Ed. 772, 29 Sup. Ct. 436, 16 A. & E. Ann. Cas. 1008), and is somewhat sustained by analogy in the case of insolvent banks (Merrill *v.* National Bank, *supra*, White *v.* Knox, 111 U. S. 784, 787, 28 L. Ed. 603, 604, 4 Sup. Ct. 686). Interest and dividends accrued upon some of the securities after the date of the petition. The English cases allow these to be applied to the after-accruing interest upon the debt. Ex parte Ramsbottom; Ex parte Penfold; and Quartermaine's Case—*supra*. There is no more reason for allowing the bankrupt estate to profit by the delay beyond the day of settlement than there is for letting the creditors do so. Therefore to apply these subsequent dividends, etc., to subsequent interest, seems just."

§ 759. Determination of Value of Securities.

—The value of securities for deduction may be determined; 1st, by converting them into money according to the terms of the agreement pursuant to which such securities were delivered to the creditor; or 2nd, by agreement between the creditor and the trustee; or 3rd, by arbitration; or 4th, by compromise; or 5th, by litigation.[23]

If, under § 57, the value is determined by agreement or arbitration, the time for fixing it will be the date of the filing of the petition in bankruptcy.[24]

§ 760. Creditor Entitled to Pursue Method Stipulated in Contract.

—If the agreement under which the securities were delivered provides the method for converting them into money, the creditor holding the securities

---

23. Bankr. Act, § 57 (h): "Value of securities held by secured creditors shall be determined by converting the same into money according to the terms of the agreement pursuant to which such securities were delivered to such creditors or by such creditors and the trustee, by agreement, arbitration, compromise. or litigation, as the court may direct, and the amount of such value shall be credited upon such claims, and a dividend shall be paid only on the unpaid balance." Hiscock *v.* Varick Bk., 18 A. B. R. 8, 206 U. S. 28 (affirming In re Mertens, 15 A. B. R. 362, and reversing 14 A. B. R. 226).

24. Sexton *v.* Dreyfus, 25 A. B. R. 363, 219 U. S. 339, *reversing* 24 A. B. R. 287, 171 Fed. 751, quoted ante, § 758½.

has the right to have the securities converted into money according to such method, provided he follow such method.[25]

Hiscock v. Varick Bk., 18 A. B. R. 9, 206 U. S. 28 (affirming In re Mertens, 15 A. B. R. 362): "It is only when the securities have not been disposed of by the creditor in accordance with his contract that the court may direct what shall be done in the premises."

In re Mertens, 15 A. B. R. 362, 142 Fed. 445 (C. C. A. N. Y., reversing 14 A. B. R. 226, and itself affirmed sub nom. Hiscock v. Varick Bk., 18 A. B. R. 9): "The decision of the court below proceeded not only upon the ground that the sale was unwarranted by the terms of the pledge, but also upon the ground that having been after the filing of the petition in bankruptcy it was inoperative and subject to the supervision and control of the court, because the act suspends the exercise of the pledgee's remedy pending the adjudication of bankruptcy.

"By the present Act, the title of the trustee is vested in the estate of the bankrupt 'as of the date he was adjudged a bankrupt.' We are of opinion that until the date of the adjudication a lienor or pledgee is at liberty to perfect any title which the nature of the lien permits. Under the Act of 1867, no lien could be acquired after the filing of the petition in bankruptcy, because the title of the assignee vested as of the commencement of the proceeding in bankruptcy. Now the trustee takes the property of the bankrupt in the condition in which he finds it at the date of the adjudication, unless it has been encumbered fraudulently or in contravention of some of the provisions of the Act. Under the former Act there are many decisions that a lien previously acquired could not be enforced subsequent to the commencement of the proceeding, except with the permission of the bankruptcy court. The Supreme Court, however, refused to sanction these decisions, and held that the lienor was entitled to perfect his title and enforce his rights as though no proceeding had been commenced. Eyster v. Gaff, 91 U. S. 521; Jerome v. McCarter, 94 U. S. 734. The change in the present Act, by which the trustee's title is that only which exists at the date of the adjudication, removes any uncertainty which arose under the Act of 1867. It was intended, we think, to permit all legitimate business transactions between a debtor and those dealing with him to be carried out and consummated as freely until he has been adjudicated a bankrupt as though no proceeding were pending. In many cases the proceeding against an alleged bankrupt is unfounded, and for this and other reasons never culminates in an adjudication. While the filing of a petition in bankruptcy is a caveat to all the world, the notice ought not to have the effect of paralyzing all business dealings with the debtor, or to prevent lienors or pledgees from enforcing their contracts. This is its practical effect if the rights and remedies of all concerned are in suspense until it can be ascertained whether an adjudication is or is not to follow the commencement of the proceeding. That Congress did not intend that lienors or pledgees should be prejudiced in enforcing their rights by the commencement of the proceedings in bankruptcy is indicated by the change made in the present Act with respect to the proof of claims by secured creditors. By the former Act, it was provided that a secured creditor should be admitted as a creditor only for the balance of his debt after deducting the value of the

25. Inferentially, obiter, In re Castle Braid Co., 17 A. B. R. 149, 145 Fed. 224 (D. C. N. Y.); In re Mayer, Leslie & Baylis, 19 A. B. R. 356, 157 Fed. 836 (C. C. A. N. Y.); In re Peacock, 24 A. B. R. 159, 178 Fed. 851 (D. C. N. Car.); obiter, In re Davison, 24 A. B. R. 460, 179 Fed. 750 (D. C. N. Y.); instance, In re White, 25 A. B. R. 541, 183 Fed. 310 (C. C. A. Ills.), quoted on other point at § 756.

pledged property ascertained by an agreement between him and the assignee in bankruptcy, or by a sale under the direction of the court. Under that provision, if a pledgee sold the pledged property prior to the appointment of the assignee, or without the permission of the court, he was precluded from proving his claim or obtaining any share of the bankrupt's estate to which he would otherwise have been entitled. The present Act provides that the value of his security may be determined, among other methods, by converting it into money, pursuant to his contract rights, and thus if he has enforced it as the contract with the debtor allowed, he is permitted to prove the unsatisfied balance of his claim. Section 57, subdivision h, prescribes several modes of valuation, and the one referred to is exclusive of the others and is superfluous and useless unless it is intended to authorize the creditor without interference by the trustee or the court to value his own security, provided he turns it into money, 'according to the terms of the agreement pursuant to which' it was delivered to him.

"We conclude that the claim against the individual estate should have been allowed for the balance claimed."

At any rate, in the absence of oppression or fraud.[26]

In re Brown, 5 A. B. R. 220 (D. C. Penn.): "I do not pass upon the question, whether the court may interfere to prevent a fraudulent or oppressive exercise of such a right. No such exercise is threatened in the present case. It is agreed that the creditors intend to deal fairly with the property pledged, and will make an honest effort to sell for the best prices that can be obtained. This being so, I am of opinion that the Bankrupt Act gives the court no authority to intervene between these creditors and their exercise of the right to sell given by the collateral notes. Each of these creditors has a lien, which I must assume, in the absence of evidence to the contrary, was given and accepted in good faith for a present consideration, and not in contemplation of, or in fraud upon, the statute; and such liens are declared by clause 'd' of § 67 to be unaffected by the act. The phrase 'unaffected by the act' may perhaps be too broad. Other sections do affect such liens in some respects not now material, but the general meaning of the phrase is clear. Such liens are left as the act finds them, and (passing the question whether the court may interfere in the case of a fraudulent or oppressive enforcement) they may be proceeded upon according to their terms.

"It was argued that clause 'h' of § 57 gives the necessary power to restrain and regulate the creditors' right to sell. * * *

"Assuming that this clause intends to do something more than provide for a method of determining the value of securities held by secured creditors, if such creditors desire to ascertain and to prove a possibly unsecured balance of their claims, I cannot avoid the conclusion that the court is only permitted to intervene when the agreement between the bankrupt and the creditor fails to provide a method by which the value of the securities may be ascertained—again reserving the question of the court's power in the case of a fraudulent or oppressive conversion. This clause seems to me to be explicit. The value of such securities is to be ascertained 'by converting the same into money according to the terms of the agreement pursuant to which such securities were delivered to such creditors.' If there be no such agreement, the clause then goes on to

26. Hiscock v. Varick Bk., 18 A. B. R. 8. 206 U. S. 28 (affirming In re Mertens, 15 A. B. R. 362, and reversing 14 A. B. R. 226); In re Peacock, 24 A. B. R. 159, 178 Fed. 851 (D. C, N. Car.).

say that the value is to be ascertained by such creditors and the trustee, by agreement, arbitration, compromise or litigation, as the court may direct. The supervision of the court is thus confined to the ascertainment of value where the bankrupt and his creditor have themselves failed to deal with this subject. In such an event the court may direct how the value is to be ascertained, and may choose among the methods of 'agreement, arbitration, compromise, or litigation,' supervising and controlling either form of proceeding.

"Clause 7 of § 2, giving the court power to 'cause the assets of bankrupts to be collected, reduced to money and distributed, and determine controversies in relation thereto, except as herein otherwise provided,' and clause 15 of the same section, giving power to 'make such orders, issue such process and enter such judgments, in addition to those specifically provided for, as may be necessary for the enforcement of the provisions of this act,' must, of course, be read in connection with the rest of the statute, and are necessarily qualified by such provisions as are to be found in clause 'd' § 67, concerning liens, and by clause 'h' of § 57, concerning the method of ascertaining the value of securities held by creditor."

And the court will not enjoin the exercise of the right to sell.[27]

It is not necessary to ask the direction, or permission, of the court to realize on the security where it is realized on according to the terms of the contract, nor need a proof of debt be filed as preliminary thereto.

Ward v. First Nat. Bk., 29 A. B. R. 312, 202 Fed. 609 (C. C. A. Ohio): "It is contended that the court below erred in not holding, as was there insisted, that the Bank should have made a formal proof of its claims against the bankrupt's estate. There is no requirement that a creditor holding a security shall do this, although he may do so at his option. He can rely upon his security and enforce it otherwise. Besides, in this instance each of the claims made by the Bank in its intervening petition was, in a specific sense, against the trustee, as such, and not against the bankrupt except in a general way. Under these circumstances the Bank filed its petition before the referee and prayed for an order directing the trustee to pay directly to it certain moneys held by him, but to which, upon the facts it stated, the Bank claimed to be entitled. We think this was a convenient and proper way to secure a determination of the questions involved, and that a formal proof of debt against the bankrupt was not necessary to that end."

Although the preliminary filing of a proof of debt is the better practice.

§ 761. Unless Oppressively or Unfairly Exercised.—But the court will interfere with or declare void any oppressive, unfair, or fraudulent exercise of the power given by the terms of the agreement.[28]

Obiter, Hiscock v. Varick Bk., 18 A. B. R. 9, 206 U. S. 28: "Of course where there is fraud or a proceeding contrary to the contract the interposition of the court might properly be invoked."

---

27. In re Brown, 5 A. B. R. 220 (D. C. Pa.). But compare, contra, In re Cobb, 3 A. B. R. 129, 96 Fed. 281 (D. C. N. Car.); In re Mayer, Leslie & Baylis, 19 A. B. R. 356, 157 Fed. 836 (C. C. A. N. Y.). See post, § 1913.

28. In re Mertens, 14 A. B. R. 226 (D. C. N. Y., reversed on the facts, in 15 A. B. R. 362); compare, In re Jersey Island Packing Co., 14 A. B. R. 689, 138 Fed. 625 (C. C. A. Calif.).

Obiter, In re Mertens, 15 A. B. R. 368 (C. C. A. N. Y., affirmed sub nom. Hiscock v. Varick Bk., 18 A. B. R. 9, 206 U. S. 28): "Doubtless the pledgee cannot avail himself of his authority, however unlimited, to sacrifice the property wantonly, or to purchase it himself at a valuation so inadequate as to suggest a fraudulent purpose."

But the burden of proving the unfairness or oppression rests on the trustee.[29]

Impliedly, Hiscock v. Varick Bk., 18 A. B. R. 9, 206 U. S. 28: "The trustee did not offer to prove that others were prepared to purchase and might have done so but for want of information, or that the policies had a greater value than was realized at the sale, or that he was prepared to redeem the pledge for the benefit of the estate, nor did he offer to do so. There was nothing in the evidence tending to show a wanton sacrifice or an intention to buy in at so inadequate a price as to justify the inference of a fraudulent purpose. * * * Clearly there is nothing on the face of the record to justify a charge of fraud on account of inadequacy."

And sales, unfairly or oppressively made thereunder, even if made before adjudication (perhaps if after the petition is filed), may be declared ineffectual for determining the value of securities, when the creditor later presents his claim for allowance.[30]

The trustee also may sue the creditor for an accounting,[31] and the State law is to determine the propriety of the stipulated method.

Hiscock v. Varick Bk., 18 A. B. R. 6, 206 U. S. 28: "The questions of the extent and validity of the pledge were local questions, and the decisions of the courts of New York are to be followed by this court. * * * Here there was an absolute power of sale, coupled with an interest. The bank had had both title and possession of the policies for a period of more than two years before the filing of the petition. It had a valid debt against both the copartnership and individual estates, which is not questioned. It could, therefore, make a sale under the power granted, and transfer title in its own name. Numerous decisions of the Court of Appeals of the State of New York sustain contracts of pledge waiving the right of the pledgor to exact strict performance of the common-law duties of a pledgee. In the absence of fraud, the pledgee may buy at his own sale held without notice, or demand, or advertisement, when power so to do is expressly granted by the pledgor."

§ 762. Which of Remaining Four Methods, Left to Court's Discretion.

—Which one of the four remaining methods should be adopted is left to the discretion of the court.[32]

---

29. In re Mertens, 15 A. B. R. 368, 142 Fed. 445 (C. C. A. N. Y., affirmed sub nom. Hiscock v. Varick Bk., 18 A. B. R. 9, 206 U. S. 28).

30. In re Mertens, 14 A. B. R. 226 (D. C. N. Y., reversed, on the facts, in 15 A. B. R. 362).

In re Davis, 23 A. B. R. 446, 174 Fed. 556 (C. C. A. Pa.); In re Dix, 23 A. B. R. 889, 176 Fed. 582 (D. C. Pa.), which, though cases of determination of value by litigation, e. g., by foreclosure sale, rather than by pursuing the contract method, yet were cases where the bidding was merely formal and afforded no test of real value and was disregarded as unfair.

31. Obiter, In re Peacock, 24 A. B. R. 159, 178 Fed. 851 (D. C. N. Car.).

32. Bankr. Act, § 57 (h). Instance, agreeing with trustee, In re Grive, 18 A. B. R. 737, 153 Fed. 597 (D. C. Conn.); impliedly, In re Davison, 24 A. B. R. 460, 179 Fed. 750 (D. C. N. Y.).

§ 762¾. Value Not Necessarily That at Date of Bankruptcy.—It is not necessary that the value be determined as of the date of the bankruptcy. It is sufficient that it be the amount actually realized or be the value at the time of the determination.[35]

§ 762½. Determination by Litigation.—The value of securities may be determined by litigation.[36] But where the creditor buys in the property at foreclosure sale at a nominal figure, although its actual value is vastly greater and perhaps enough to pay the principal and interest, such foreclosure sale price has been disregarded as a "determination by litigation," and the bankruptcy court has taken evidence of actual value.[37]

The court held in one case that the sum bid at the sheriff's sale not being conclusive evidence of such value under the State law would not be held to be such in the bankruptcy court, although conceding, obiter, that had the State law made such price realized at sheriff's sale conclusive evidence of value, the bankruptcy court might have followed it.[38]

§ 763. Preliminary Determination of Values for Voting Purposes. —For the purpose of permitting the creditor to participate in creditors' meetings held prior to the determination of the values of their securities in the above manner, the claims of secured creditors may be allowed—temporarily, so to speak—in such amounts as the court may estimate to be the deficit.[39] This is an exception to the rule that any "provisional" allowance of a claim is ineffective in bankruptcy.

§ 764. No Judgment in Bankruptcy Proceedings against Claimant for Excess of Security.—Where the value of the security is determined to be greater than the amount of the debt secured, no judgment for the excess may be entered in the bankruptcy proceedings in favor of the estate against the claimant: he is an adverse claimant in possession who may be reached only by plenary action.[40]

§ 765. Withdrawing Claims Filed as Unsecured and Refiling as Secured.—A creditor may withdraw the proof of his claim as unsecured

---

35. Impliedly, Steinhardt v. National Bank, 19 A. B. R. 72, 122 App. Div. N. Y. 55.

36. Bankr. Act, § 57 (h). Instance, In re Davis (Winter's Appeal), 23 A. B. R. 446, 174 Fed. 556 (C. C. A. Pa.).

Thus, the value of insurance policies held as security, though containing no clause of cash surrender value, In re Davison, 24 A. B. R. 460, 179 Fed. 750 (D. C. N. Y.).

37. In re Davis (Winter's Appeal), 23 A. B. R. 446, 174 Fed. 556 (C. C. Pa.); In re Dix, 23 A. B. R. 889, 176 Fed. 582 (D. C. Pa.); In re Davis, 23 A. B. R. 157 (Ref. Pa.).

38. In re Davis (Winter's Appeal), 23 A. B. R. 446, 174 Fed. 556 (C. C. A. Pa.).

39. Bankr. Act, § 57 (e); In re Stevens, 23 A. B. R. 239, 173 Fed. 842 (D. C. Ore.); instance, In re Milne, Turnbull & Co., 20 A. B. R. 248, 159 Fed. 280 (D. C. N. Y.).

40. In re Peacock, 24 A. B. R. 159, 178 Fed. 851 (D. C. N. Car.); Fitch v. Richardson, 16 A. B. R. 835 (C. C. A. Mass.); see post, "Conflict of Jurisdiction, Adverse Claimants," § 1679. Compare, post, § 1694; compare, also, §§ 1187, 1188.

and may substitute one as secured;[41] but leave so to do may, in proper cases, be refused.[42]

§ 766. Proof of Secured Debt as Unsecured, Waiver or Not.—

Proof of a secured debt as unsecured may,[43] but does not necessarily, amount to a waiver of the security.[44]

Kohout v. Chaloupka, 11 A. B. R. 267 (Neb. Sup. Ct.): "The rule invoked by plaintiff in error to sustain his position is, of course, well settled, namely, that a creditor of a bankrupt may either directly or indirectly waive his security, and prove his claim as unsecured; as where a creditor, by judgment execution, attachment, or creditor's suit, proves his claim without disclosing his lien, in which event he will not subsequently be permitted to enforce it, but will be deemed to have waived it."

(1867) White v. Crawford, 9 Fed. 371 (C. C.): "A creditor waives any lien he may have upon the property of his debtor by proving up his debt as an unsecured claim."

(1867) Shoorten v. Booth, 32 La. Ann. 397: "A creditor who proves his whole debt as one without security, or against a bankrupt's estate, thereby releases any mortgage he may have."

It is a waiver of the security if made with knowledge of the facts; but even an express relinquishment of securities made in ignorance of facts may not be a waiver.[45] And where no one has been caused to change his position thereby the claim may be withdrawn and one proving the debt as secured be substituted.[46] And the creditor may be re-instated in the security so relinquished, where the estate will be left no worse off than if the security had not been originally relinquished. And a relinquishment made in ignorance or mistake of law also is not necessarily a waiver,[47] thus, the relinquishment of a seat on the stock exchange, where it was relinquished under misapprehension of law as to such property passing.[48]

But such proof is a waiver only as to the trustee; and it has been held in

---

41. In re Friedman, 1 A. B. R. 510 (Ref., since, D. C. N. Y.). See ante, ch. XX, "Proof of Claims," "Withdrawal of Claims," § 623.

42. In re Wilder, 3 A. B. R. 761, 101 Fed. 104 (D. C. N. Y.), in note. See ante, ch XX, "Proof of Claims." § 621.

43. Dunn, Salmon Co. v. Pillmore, 19 A. B. R. 172, 106 N. Y. Supp. 546.

44. In re Friedman, 1 A. B. R. 510 (Ref., since, D. C. N. Y.); instance, held waiver, obiter, In re Downing, 15 A. B. R. 425 (D. C. Ky.); instance held not waiver to assert "vendor's privilege" under Civil Code of Louisiana, Sessler v. Paducah Distilleries Co., 21 A. B. R. 723, 168 Fed. 44 (C. C. A. Ala.); inferentially, In re Loden, 25 A. B. R. 917, 184 Fed. 965 (D. C. Ga.).

45. Hutchinson v. Otis, 8 A. B. R. 382, 115 Fed. 937 (C. C. A. Mass., affirmed in 10 A. B. R. 135): Where,

within four months before the filing of a bankruptcy petition, a nonresident creditor brought two garnishee suits against the bankrupt in other States; and collected his judgments; but afterwards had to return them to the trustee, the creditor meanwhile voluntarily relinquishing his garnishment security under misapprehension as to bankruptcy. Analogously as to priority claims, In re Ashland Steel Co., 21 A. B. R. 834, 168 Fed. 679 (C. C. A. Ky.). See post, § 2139.

46. In re Friedman, 1 A. B. R. 510 (Ref., since, D. C. N. Y.).

47. In re Swift, 7 A. B. R. 117, 111 Fed. 507 (D. C. Mass.); obiter, Hutchinson v. Otis, 8 A. B. R. 382, 115 Fed. 937 (C. C. A. Mass., affirmed in 10 A. B. R. 135).

48. In re Swift, 7 A. B. R. 117, 111 Fed. 503 (D. C. Mass.).

one case that where a creditor had instituted a fraudulent conveyance suit more than four months before the debtor's bankruptcy, and thereafter had filed his claim in the bankruptcy proceedings as an unsecured claim, without disclosure of the security, the debtor's subsequent discharge in bankruptcy was not pleadable as a bar, since the suit was one in rem and not in personam, and that even if it had been in personam, the fraudulent grantee could not take advantage of the waiver, the court in that case, however, in obiter affirming the main proposition of this section, § 766.

Flint v. Chaloupka, 18 A. B. R. 293, 78 Nebr. 594: "Plaintiff herein filed proof of her claim with the referee in bankruptcy and participated in the election of a trustee. She did not disclose to the court of bankruptcy that she had or claimed a lien upon the land here in controversy by virtue of the institution of this suit. Defendants contend that, by the filing of the claim with the bankruptcy court without reference to the security claimed, plaintiff abandoned such security, and the subsequent discharge of the elder Chaloupka operates as a bar to this suit. Had plaintiff remained out of the bankruptcy court, no doubt would arise as to her right to prosecute her creditor's bill. Had the bankrupt listed with the trustee the land in controversy and a disposition thereof made by the trustee, no doubt would exist but that the plaintiff, not having disclosed nor claimed under her lien, would have been estopped from the prosecution of this suit. And, further, in an action properly brought by the trustee in bankruptcy against the plaintiff herein, we think that, under the existing facts, the trustee would have prevailed, and the land in controversy would have been subjected to the payment of all claims against the bankrupt. But none of these propositions exist here. Can the bankrupt, or his fraudulent grantee of the land which was never in the jurisdiction of the bankruptcy court, plead a discharge in bankruptcy as a bar to a creditor's suit against a creditor who wrongfully failed to disclose his security to the bankruptcy court? * * * Cases directly in point are few, but the weight of authority, we believe, and the rule more in harmony with justice, will not permit a fraudulent grantee to plead the subsequent discharge of his grantor as a defense in a creditor's suit brought more than four months prior to the institution of the bankruptcy proceeding, and which pertains to land which was never brought within the jurisdiction of the bankruptcy court."

And the fact that a creditor, after the adjudication of bankruptcy, filed his claim as a general creditor has been held not to constitute a waiver of his right to attach, nor estop him as against the debtor from subsequently attaching property in an action for its purchase price as to which there could be no exemptions, after the same had been set apart as exempt.[49]

And, in short, the fact that a claim has been proved as a general debt against the estate, does not waive the creditor's right to proceed, under the local laws, for its collection as against property which has been set apart as exempt, if such remedy is otherwise available.[50]

---

49. See post, § 1108. Also see Northern Shoe Co. v. Cecka, 28 A. B. R. 935 (Sup. Ct. N. Dak.), quoted at § 1108.

50. Northern Shoe Co. v. Cecka, 28 A. B. R. 935 (Sup. Ct. N. Dak.). See post, § 1108.

§ 767. Security Surrendered, Claim Allowed without Deduction.

—If the security is surrendered, the claim may be allowed without deduction.[51]

Thus, sub-contractors waiving their attested accounts may share pari passu.[52]

§ 767¾. Security Need Not Be Surrendered as Prerequisite to Allowance of Deficit.

—The security in the creditor's hands need not be surrendered as prerequisite to the allowance of the deficit, nor will the payment of a dividend vest a right to the possession thereof in the trustee.

In re Davison, 24 A. B. R. 460, 179 Fed. 750 (D. C. N. Y.): "The contention seems to be that having procured the present value of the securities to be determined and having received that value to apply on the debt and having also taken a dividend, pro rata, with the others, on the balance of the debt, the interest of the bank in such securities has ceased and the equity, if any, belongs to the estate. But the bank has the policies as securities for the entire debt and must pay therefore their present value by crediting the amount on the debt before having a dividend on the balance. Sections 57a, 57e, 57h. The law does not provide that on crediting the value of the security on the debt and being allowed a dividend on the balance the secured creditor is to surrender the security, even if tendered the value thereof as fixed by the court. The secured creditor has the right to retain the policies as security, for any balance and any premiums it may pay to keep them alive. In the absence of something in the Bankruptcy Act to the contrary I am of the opinion that, in cases where the value of the security is determined by agreement, arbitration or litigation as the court directs, it is contemplated that the secured creditor is to retain such securities, after receiving the dividends, subject to such claims as others may have therein or thereon when finally converted into money."

§ 767½. Question of Preference Settled before Value of Securities Determined.

—It is the proper practice that any question as to whether or not the security is a preference should be determined before the security is converted into money.

In re Quinn, 21 A. B. R. 264, 165 Fed. 144 (C. C. A. Ill.): "The District Court and the referee in bankruptcy, upon the presentation by a creditor of

---

51. In re Eagles & Crisp, 3 A. B. R. 735, 99 Fed. 695 (D. C. N. Car.); In re Hurlbutt, Hatch & Co., 16 A. B. R. 198 (C. C. A. N. Y.); instance, Lacey v. Citizens Bank, 28 A. B. R. 433, 198 Fed. 484 (C. C. A. Mo.).

Proving Debt as Secured but Allowance Made without Deduction, No Waiver of Security in Subsequent Sale and Marshaling of Liens.—Where a creditor has duly proved his claim as secured, but the order of allowance allows it at its face without deduction for the value of securities it will not effect a waiver of the security in the subsequent marshaling of the assets and their sale. It will be presumed

the referee recognized the existence of the security but determined its value, for the purpose of participation in creditors' meetings, to be nothing. Bassett v. Thackara, 16 A. B. R. 787, 72 N. J. L. 81, 60 Atl. 39. This decision should have referred to Bankr. Act, § 57 (e), rather than § 57 (h). The sale was itself a compliance with § 57 (h).

Signing Subsequent "Liquidation Agreement," Whether Waiver of Security.—In re Cyclopean Co., 21 A. B. R. 679, 167 Fed. 971 (C. C. A. N. Y.).

52. In re Grive, 18 A. B. R. 737, 153 Fed. 597 (D. C. Conn.).

the customary proof of a secured debt which is objected to by the trustee on the ground that the security claimed constitutes a voidable preference, may hear and decide the issue and allow the claim as a secured or an unsecured debt before the alleged security is converted into money, under the provisions of § 57h * * *, and this is the preferable practice because it enables parties to know the extent of their interests before the property is sold."

SUBDIVISION "B."

ALLOWABILITY OF CLAIMS OF CREDITORS HOLDING VOIDABLE PREFERENCES.

§ 768. Surrender of "Preferences" Prerequisite to Allowance.—

Claims of creditors holding voidable preferences are not "allowable" unless the preferences are surrendered.[53]

One of the most important features of bankruptcy law is its treatment of creditors who have received preferences. The questions relating to this subject are so complex, varied and withal so very important that their consideration will be postponed until consideration of the general subject of preferences is reached.[54]

If a creditor or his agent has received a preference within four months preceding the bankruptcy and has received it when he has had reasonable cause for believing that a preference would thereby be effected,[55] such creditor's claim shall not be allowed until the preference has been surrendered.[56]

The "surrender" must be to the trustee, not to the bankrupt nor to any other person.[57]

But a preference which is not voidable does not prevent the creditor from proving his claim for any balance due after applying the property preferentially transferred.[58]

§ 768½. Whether Preferential Liens on Exempt Property to Be Surrendered.—

It has also been held that liens upon or other transfers of

---

53. Bankr. Act, § 57 (g): "The claims of creditors who have received preferences shall not be allowed unless such creditors shall surrender their preferences."

In re Columbia Iron Wks., 14 A. B. R. 527, 142 Fed. 234 (D. C. Mich.); In re Eagles & Crisp, 3 A. B. R. 735, 99 Fed. 605 (D. C. N. Car.); In re Malino, 8 A. B. R. 205, 118 Fed. 368 (D. C. N. Y.); In re Conhaim, 3 A. B. R. 249, 97 Fed. 924 (D. C. Wash.); In re Rice, 21 A. B. R. 212, 164 Fed. 589 (D. C. Pa.); In re Thomas Deutschle & Co. (No. 2), 25 A. B. R. 348, 182 Fed. 435 (D. C. Pa.); In re Feinberg & Sons, 26 A. B. R. 587, 187 Fed. 283 (D. C. Mass.).

54. Post, § 1271, et seq. Such claims may be "provable" although not "allowable," ante, § 632. And demand upon the creditor to surrender the preference is not essential. Obiter, Eau Claire Nat'l Bk. v. Jackman, 17 A. B. R. 682.

55. Before the Amendment of 1910 it read "reasonable cause for believing that the debtor intended thereby to give a preference."

56. Practice on Hearing of Objections to Allowance.—See post, §§ 811, 830, et seq.

Deposition for Proof of Debt Makes Prima Facie Case against Objections on the Ground of Preference, When.— In re Milne, Turnbull & Co., 20 A. B. R. 248, 159 Fed. 280 (D. C. N. Y.).

Question of Preference to Be Settled before Security Converted into Money. —See ante, § 767½.

57. In re Bailey, 24 A. B. R. 201, 176 Fed. 990 (D. C. Utah).

58. In re Carlisle, 20 A. B. R. 373, 199 Fed. 612 (D. C. N. Car.).

exempt property need not be surrendered, because they do not constitute preferences, the title to exempt property in no event passing to the trustee.[58a]

§ 769. Preference Surrendered, Claim "Allowable."—Such claim may be allowed if the preference is surrendered.[59]

§ 770. Not Voluntarily Surrendered but Only on Litigation, Yet Allowable.—If the preference is not voluntarily surrendered but only after litigation has ended by recovery of the preference, yet it may then be "allowed."[60]

Keppel v. Tiffin Sav. Bk., 13 A. B. R. 552, 197 U. S. 356: "On the one hand, it is insisted that a creditor who has not surrendered a preference until compelled to do so by the degree of a court cannot be allowed to prove any claim against the estate. On the other hand, it is urged that no such penalty is imposed by the Bankrupt Act, and hence the creditor, on an extinguishment of a preference, by whatever means, may prove his claims. These contentions must be determined by the text, originally considered, of § 57g of the Bankrupt Act, providing that 'the claims of creditors who have received preferences shall not be allowed unless such creditors shall surrender their preferences.' We say by the text in question, because there is nowhere any prohibition against the proof of a claim by a creditor who has had a preference, where the preference has disappeared as the result of a decree adjudging the preferences to be void, unless that result arises from the provision in question. We say also from the text as originally considered, because, although there are some decisions, under the Act of 1898, of lower Federal Courts, which are referred to in the margin, denying the right of a creditor to prove his claim, after the surrender of a preference by the compulsion of a decree or judgment, such decisions rest not upon an analysis of the text of the Act of 1898 alone considered, but upon what were deemed to have been analogous provisions of the Act of 1867 and decisions thereunder. We omit, therefore, further reference to these decisions, as we shall hereafter come to consider the text of the present act by the light thrown upon it by the Act of 1867 and the judicial interpretation which was given to that Act. * * *

"We think it clear that the fundamental purpose of the provision in question was to secure an equality of distribution of the assets of a bankrupt estate. This must be the case, since, if a creditor having a preference retained the preference, and at the same time proved his debt and participated in the distribution of the estate, and advantage would be secured, not contemplated, by the law. Equality of distribution being the purpose intended to be affected by the provisions, to interpret it as forbidding a creditor from proving his claim after a surrender of his preference, because such surrender was not voluntary, would frustrate the object of the provision, since it would give the bankrupt estate the benefit of the surrender or cancellation of the preference, and yet

---

58a. In re Bailey, 24 A. B. R. 201, 176 Fed. 990 (D. C. Utah). Also, compare ante, § 755.

59. Bankr. Act, § 57 (g); Ohio Valley Bank v. Mack, 20 A. B. R. 40, 163 Fed. 155 (C. C. A. Ohio); In re Chaplin, 8 A. B. R. 121, 115 Fed. 162 (D. C. Mass.). In this case there occurs an instance of the confusion of terms "proved" and "allowed."

60. Eau Claire Bk. v. Jackman, 17 A. B. R. 683, 204 U. S. 522; In re Oppenheimer, 15 A. B. R. 267, 140 Fed. 51 (D. C. Iowa); Ohio Valley Bank v. Mack, 20 A. B. R. 40, 163 Fed. 155 (C. C. A. Ohio); Page v. Rogers, 21 A. B. R. 496, 211 U. S. 575, quoted at § 1770¼; In re Lange, 22 A. B. R. 414, 170 Fed. 114 (D. C. Iowa); In re Elletson Co., 28 A. B. R. 434. 193 Fed. 84 (D. C. W. Va.).

deprive the creditor of any right to participate, thus creating an inequality. But it is said, although this be true, as the statute is plain, its terms can not be disregarded by allowing that to be done which it expressly forbids. This rests upon the assumption that the word 'surrender' necessarily implies only voluntary action, and here excludes the right to prove where the surrender is the result of a recovery compelled by judgment or decree.

"The word 'surrender,' however, does not exclude compelled action, but, to the contrary, generally implies such action. That this is the primary and commonly accepted meaning of the word is shown by the dictionaries. Thus, the Standard dictionary defines its meaning as follows:

" '1. To yield possession of to another upon compulsion or demand, or under pressure of a superior force, give up, especially to an enemy in warfare; as, to surrender an army or a fort.'

"And in Webster's International Dictionary the word is primarily defined in the same way. The word, of course, also sometimes denotes voluntary action. In the statute, however, it is unqualified, and generic, and hence embraces both meanings. The construction which would exclude the primary meaning, so as to cause the word only to embrace voluntary action, would read into the statute a qualification, and this in order to cause the provision to be in conflict with the purpose which it was intended to accomplish—equality among creditors. But the construction would do more. It would exclude the natural meaning of the word used in the statute, in order to create a penalty, although nowhere expressly or even by clear implication found in the statute. This would disregard the elementary rule that a penalty is not to be readily implied, and, on the contrary, that a person or corporation is not to be subjected to a penalty unless the words of the statute plainly impose it. Tiffany v. National Bank, 18 Wall. 409, 410, 21 L. Ed. 862, 863. If it had been contemplated that the word 'surrender' should entail upon every creditor the loss of power to prove his claims if he submitted his right to retain an asserted preference to the courts for decision, such purpose could have found ready expression by qualifying the word 'surrender' so as to plainly convey such meaning. Indeed, the construction which would read in the qualification would not only create a penalty alone by judicial action, but would necessitate judicial legislation in order to define what character and degree of compulsion was essential to prevent the surrender in fact from being a surrender within the meaning of the section.

"It is argued, however, that courts of bankruptcy are guided by equitable considerations, and should not permit a creditor who has retained a fraudulent preference until compelled by a court to surrender it, to prove his debt, and thus suffer no other loss than the cost of litigation. The fallacy lies in assuming that courts have power to inflict penalties, although the law has not imposed them. Moreover, if the statute be interpreted as it is insisted it should be, there would be no distinction between honest and fraudulent creditors, and therefore every creditor who in good faith had acquired an advantage which the law did not permit him to retain would be subjected to the forfeiture simply because he had presumed to submit his legal rights to a court for determination. And this accentuates the error in the construction, since the elementary principle is that courts are created to pass upon the rights of parties, and that it is the privilege of the citizen to submit his claims to the judicial tribunals—especially in the absence of malice and when—acting with probable cause—without subjecting himself to penalties of an extraordinary character. The violation of this rule, which would arise from the construction, is well illustrated by this case. Here, as we have seen, it is found that the bank acted in good faith, without knowledge of the insolvency of its debtor and of wrongful intent on his part, and yet it is asserted that the right to prove its lawful claims against the bankrupt estate was forfeited simply because of the election to put the trustee to proof, in a court, of the existence of the facts made essential by the law to an invalidation of the preference.

"We are of opinion that, originally considered, the surrender clause of the statute was intended simply to prevent a creditor from creating inequality in the distribution of the assets of the estate by retaining a preference, and at the same time collecting dividends from the estate by the proof of his claim against it, and consequently that whenever the preference has been abandoned or yielded up, and thereby the danger of inequality has been prevented, such creditor is entitled to stand on an equal footing with other creditors and prove his claims."

§ 771. Allowable if Not Surrendered until Adverse Ruling by Referee When Presented for Allowance.

—The rule is the same whether the compulsory surrender be accomplished by independent action outside of the bankruptcy proceedings or by orders made in the bankruptcy proceeding themselves by the referee disallowing the claim.[61]

In re Oppenheimer, 15 A. B. R. 267, 140 Fed. 51 (D. C. Iowa): "A creditor does not lose the right to prove his claim by submitting to the judgment of the court the question of the validity of alleged preferential payments."

§ 772. If Disallowed in Bankruptcy Proceedings Order to Fix Time for Surrender and Allowance.

—If the claim is disallowed in the bankruptcy proceedings themselves on the ground of a preference received, the order of disallowance should fix a time within which the creditor might surrender his preference and have his claim allowed; and it is error to fail to give the creditor an opportunity to surrender the preference.

In re Oppenheimer, 15 A. B. R. 267, 140 Fed. 51 (D. C. Iowa): "The referee, on finding that the payments were in fact voidable preferences, because made within the four months immediately preceding the filing of the petition in bankruptcy, should have fixed a reasonable time within which the petitioners might surrender the preferences and have their claims allowed, and, if the preferences were not so surrendered, then reject the claims, as provided by Bankruptcy Act. It was error, therefore, to reject the claims without giving the petitioners an opportunity to surrender the preferences, if in fact the payments are such."

And the prospective dividend may be applied on the preference to be surrendered.[62]

§ 773. But Surrender Not Requisite to Validity of Different Lien on Marshaling Liens for Sale—Requisite Only When Allowance to Share in Dividends Sought.

—But the requirement of surrender of prefer-

---

61. Instance, Ohio Valley Bank *v.* Mack, 20 A. B. R. 40, 163 Fed. 155 (C. C. A. Ohio).

A fortiori, Page *v.* Rogers, 21 A. B. R. 496, 211 U. S. 575. Also, see post, § 1770¼.

62. Page *v.* Rogers, 21 A. B. R. 496, 211 U. S. 575, quoted at § 1770¼.

ences as a pre-requisite applies simply when allowance to share in dividends is sought; and liens, themselves not preferences, will not be denied validity in the marshaling of assets or distribution of proceeds of sale because of the fact that the lienholder may have received, on a distinct transaction, a preference which he does not surrender.[63]

§ 773½. Distinct Claims, and Preference on One Only, Yet to Be Surrendered before Any Allowed.

—The operation of § 57 (g), requiring the surrender of preferences as a prerequisite to allowance, cannot be avoided by showing the payment claimed to be a preference to have been made on a different debt of the creditor than the one presented for allowance. The total indebtedness between the parties is the basis for the determination of a preference, regardless of the form and number of the component debts.[64]

In re Mayo v. Contracting Co., 19 A. B. R. 551, 157 Fed. 469 (D. C. Mass.): "The petitioner contends that his two claims are distinct and independent, and that in any case, whether the $2,000 be surrendered or not, his claim of $2,131.18, which did not arise under the contract of May 13, 1905, and was not included in his suit in equity wherein the decree of January 12, 1906, was entered, ought to be allowed. I do not think the two claims can be considered distinct and independent in such a sense as to require this result. Both were due at the time of the preference. The suit in equity might have been brought upon both as well as upon one only. The only difference between them in the nature of the indebtedness claimed is that one claim arose under an implied contract, the other under an express contract. Both might have been included in one and the same proof of claim."

§ 774. Surrender Where Not Void under Act but under General Equity Principles.

—The rule has been announced in one case where a creditor received a secret preference in a composition agreement made with creditors before bankruptcy that, on ordinary principles of equity and not by virtue of any express provision of the Bankruptcy Act, such preference must be surrendered before allowance of the claim.[65]

§ 774½. Surrender of Fraudulent Transfers.

—It is doubtless also true that the claim of one who has received a transfer which is not merely preferential but is actually fraudulent may be refused allowance until the transferred property is surrendered.[66]

§ 775. Allowability of Claims of Fraudulent or Preferential Transferee after Setting Aside or Surrender of Transfers.

—After a transfer has been set aside in the State court at the suit of the trustee as

---

63. In re Franklin, 18 A. B. R. 218 (D. C. N. Car.).
64. See post, § 1421; also, Swartz v. Fourth National Bank, 8 A. B. R. 673, 117 Fed. 1 (C. C. A. Mo.); In re Beswick, 7 A. B. R. 395 (Ref. Ohio); Dunn v. Gans, 12 A. B. R. 316, 129 Fed. 750

(C. C. A. Pa.), quoted post at § 1421; In re Meyer, 8 A. B. R. 598, 115 Fed. 997 (D. C. Tex.), quoted at § 1421.
65. In re Chaplin, 8 A. B. R. 121, 115 Fed. 162 (D. C. Mass.).
66. Compare, In re Bloch, 15 A. B. R. 748, 142 Fed. 676 (C. C. A. N. Y.).

preferential or fraudulent, the claim of the transferee for reimbursement of consideration is allowable against the transferror's bankrupt estate, if he be not guilty of actual fraud but only of constructive fraud.[68]

By the same course of reasoning by which has been derived the rule permitting the allowance of claims of preferred creditors on the surrender of preferences, whether such surrender be compulsory or voluntary, made within the year or afterwards, it has been held that a fraudulent transferee may be entitled to allowance of his claim, so far as the debt which it secures or which was its consideration be itself valid, upon surrender of the fraudulent transfer, the basis of the ruling being that the Supreme Court has established that § 57 (g) controls § 57 (n) and impliedly permits such allowance in cases of the surrender of preferences and that the same rules would apply to the surrender of fraudulent transfers since they are associated together in § 57 (g).[69]

In re Elletson Co., 28 A. B. R. 434, 193 Fed. 84 (D. C. W. Va.): "In considering this question a distinction is to be recognized, it seems to me, between a fraudulent and void debt and a fraudulent and void conveyance executed to secure a valid debt. Generally speaking in the first instance no remedy is afforded the creditor to collect the debt. In the second instance, under the laws of this State, the valid debt by reason of the taking of a fraudulent conveyance to secure it will not be denied payment, but will be postponed in payment to at least all debts existing at the time of such fraudulent conveyance. The Bankruptcy Act recognizes no principle whereby a valid debt may be postponed in payment of another, both being unsecured, for 'the primary object of the bankrupt law is to secure the equal distribution of the property of the bankrupt of every kind among his creditors.' Trimble v. Woodhead, 102 U. S. 650; In re Hurst, 26 A. B. R. 781, 188 Fed. 707 (D. C. W. Va.) * * * In Keppel v. Tiffin Sav. Bank, 197 U. S. 356, 13 A. B. R. 552, the same court has substantially, it seems to me, laid down the principles that must govern here. In that case the question propounded by the Circuit Court of Appeals was 'Can a creditor of a bankrupt, who has received a merely voidable preference and who has in good faith retained such preference until deprived thereof by the judgment of a court upon a suit of the trustee, thereafter prove the debt so voidably preferred?' The answer to this question was in the affirmative."

Indeed, the alleged preferential transferee may, by cross-bill, offset his claim for dividends in the trustee's suit to set aside the preference.[70]

And this especially is true where the consideration was an honest and

---

68. Barber v. Coit, 16 A. B. R. 419, 144 Fed. 381 (C. C. A. Ohio), quoted at § 1734½; Jackson v. Sedgwick, 26 A. B. R. 836, 189 Fed. 508 (C. C. N. Y.); In re Medina Quarry Co., 24 A. B. R. 769, 182 Fed. 508 (D. C. N. Y.), where the court held that a committee of bondholders of an insolvent corporation conniving to transfer assets to a reorganized corporation composed of old bondholders and old directors were not debarred from proving the bonds held by them for the bondholders.

Whether Reimbursement of Transferee for Care, etc., of Property Meanwhile Allowable.—Compare, In re Nechamkes, 19 A. B. R. 189, 155 Fed. 867 (D. C. N. Y.). Compare ante, §§ 716, 717, 717½, 733; post, § 1179½.

69. Compare §§ 770, 771, 774½, 1227 and 1734½. In re Clark, 24 A. B. R. 388, 176 Fed. 955 (D. C. N. Y.), quoted at §§ 727½ and 1227½.

70. Ommen, trustee, v. Talcott, 23 A. B. R. 570, 175 Fed. 259 (D. C. N. Y.).

undisputed debt.[71] But it is doubtful whether such a rule prevails where the fraud was actual; and certainly it cannot prevail where the debt itself, to secure or pay which the fraudulent transfer was made, or the entire transaction itself was in its inception contrived to hinder, delay or defraud creditors, even though value may have passed to the transferee.

§ 775½. **Burden of Proof.**—The burden of proof is on the trustee to establish that the transaction amounted to a preference and that the property was received with "reasonable cause for belief."[72]

SUBDIVISION "C."

ALLOWABILITY OF CLAIMS WHERE CREDITOR HOLDS LIEN BY LEGAL PROCEEDINGS.

§ 776. **Allowability Where Lien by Legal Proceedings within Four Months.**—Claims of creditors for which a lien has been obtained on the bankrupt's property by legal proceedings within four months of the bankruptcy and while the debtor was insolvent may be, nevertheless, allowed upon surrender of the lien.[73]

In re Richard, 2 A. B. R. 512, 513, 94 Fed. 633 (D. C. N. Car.): "There is no denial of respondents' 'debt,' as defined in § 1 (11), nor allegation that there was any actual fraud in obtaining the judgments—only such fraud of the Bankrupt Law as vitiates any lien acquired. The debts are due. Respondents have received and can receive no preference, lien, or advantage by reason of or under the judgments of the magistrate's court. They are nullities in this court to this extent, but they establish the debt. * * * The respondents must pay the cost in the State court, and refund what has been collected under these proceedings. They are still creditors of the bankrupt, after a fruitless fight. They have gained no advantage and acquired no lien, but are still creditors unsecured. Should they be punished by a loss of their debts because they were vigilant? The law does not so provide. * * * They are creditors, and, on a surrender of the amount collected of the bankrupt estate, are entitled to prove their claims as other unsecured creditors."

Such claims may be "provable."[74]

The subject of the rights of parties where liens have been obtained upon the property of the bankrupt, by legal proceedings within four months of the bankruptcy, and while the bankrupt was insolvent, is one of the most important subjects in bankruptcy.[75] Suffice it to say here, such claims are provable, if in their nature they belong to any of the classes of debts men-

---

71. In re Hurst, 26 A. B. R. 781, 188 Fed. 707 (D. C. W. Va.).

72. See post, §§ 1403½, 1768. Also see, In re Pfaffinger, 18 A. B. R. 807, 154 Fed. 528 (D. C. Ky.).

73. In re Scully, 5 A. B. R. 716, 108 Fed. 372 (D. C. Pa.).. In this case, surrender of the lien was not adverted to as a prerequisite.

74. See ante, ch. XXI, "Provable Claims," Div. 1, § 632. Also, ante, part II, ch. II, "Parties and Petition in Involuntary Bankruptcy," Div. 1, "Proper Parties," § 234.

75. It will be later more fully discussed, see post, "Liens by Legal Proceedings Nullified by Bankruptcy," § 1429, et seq.

tioned in § 63. They are also "allowable," because it is the lien that is rendered null and void by the bankruptcy, and the claim itself is not barred from allowance.

§ 777. Judgments, Whose Liens Null under § 67 "f," Nevertheless "Allowable."—Thus, judgments, whose liens are rendered null and void under § 67 (f) as operating to create such liens, are nevertheless themselves allowable, it being the judgment lien and not the judgment itself that is affected.[76]

§ 778. Judgment Remains and Is Res Judicata.—Indeed, the judgment remains res judicata, so far as it determines the validity of the claim, although its lien is dissolved by the bankruptcy adjudication.[77]

Impliedly, Pepperdine v. Bk. of Seymour, 10 A. B. R. 575 (Mo. Ct. App.): "A proper construction of the Bankrupt Act makes it evident that the preferential lien of a judgment, where a lien is obtained as the effect of a judgment, was intended to be destroyed by the adjudication in bankruptcy, but the purpose of the law was not to render void the judgment itself as such."

§ 779. Nevertheless, Lien to Be Surrendered before Claim Allowable.—It seems, furthermore, that the creditor should formally relinquish his lien obtained by the legal proceedings before his claim should be allowed.[78]

Division 2.

Allowability of Claims as Affected by Their Validity.

§ 780. Validity of Claims Determined, in General, by State Law. —Unless repugnant to the peculiar provisions of the Bankrupt Act, the validity of claims is to be determined by the law of the State.[79]

In re Worth, 12 A. B. R. 570, 130 Fed. 927 (D. C. Iowa): "The notes * * * being Iowa contracts, and payable in Iowa, are to be governed by the laws of that state relating to usury."
In re Talbott, 7 A. B. R. 29, 110 Fed. 924 (D. C. Mass.): "The provability of a wife's claim must depend upon its enforceability, either at law or in equity in the courts of the State."

---

76. In re Richard, 2 A. B. R. 512, 94 Fed. 633 (D. C. N. Car.); impliedly, Pepperdine v. Bk. of Seymour, 10 A. B. R. 575 (Mo. Ct. App.); In re Smith, 23 A. B. R. 864, 176 Fed. 426 (D. C. N. Y.), quoted ante, § 234.
77. In re Richard, 2 A. B. R. 512, 94 Fed. 633 (D. C. N. Car.).
78. In re Richard, 2 A. B. R. 512, 94 Fed. 633 (D. C. N. Car.); inferentially (as to such creditors' right to maintain involuntary petition without offer to surrender), see "Parties and Petition in Involuntary Bankruptcy," § 234. Even though the lien was obtained in a foreign country. In re Knight,

etc., Co., 36 A. B. R. 787, 190 Fed. 893 (C. C. Ala.).
79. First Nat'l Bk. v. Altman, Miller & Co., 12 A. B. R. 12 (Ref. Ohio); In re Tucker, 12 A. B. R. 594, 131 Fed. 64 (D. C. Mass.); In re Trombly, 16 A. B. R. 599 (Ref. Vt.). But compare, contra, as to wife's claims in Massachusetts, James v. Gray, 12 A. B. R. 573, 131 Fed. 401 (C. C. A. Mass.), refusing to follow In re Talbott, 7 A. B. R. 29, 110 Fed. 924 (D. C. Mass.); impliedly, In re Elletson Co., 23 A. B. R. 530, 174 Fed. 859 (D. C. W. Va.), quoted at § 1896. Also compare similar propositions post, §§ 1140, 1896.

As interpreted by its highest tribunal.[80]

In re Worth, 12 A. B. R. 572 (D. C. Iowa): "The construction of a local statute by the highest court of the State is, under the familiar rule, controlling upon the federal courts in such State."

Except upon matter of general law the state decisions will be followed. But upon questions of common law and not of statute, the state decisions may not be followed.[81]

Likewise, the measure of damages for breach of contract is determined by State Law, as, for example, for breach of contract of manufacture of goods of special make where the entire lot contracted for has not been manufactured.[82]

§ 781. Judicial Notice of State Law.—And the bankruptcy court will take judicial notice of the State law.[83]

§ 782. Trustee Entitled to All Objections Bankrupt Might Have Urged, but Not Limited to Such.—The trustee is entitled to urge all the objections the bankrupt might have urged. But the right of the trustee to object to a creditor's claim is not limited to objections which the bankrupt might himself have raised, but includes those where the transaction contravenes the peculiar provisions of the bankruptcy act relative to preferences and void legal liens obtained within the four months of bankruptcy, and where the transaction would be void against creditors had there been no bankruptcy proceedings, or had the trustee been a levying creditor or a creditor holding an unsatisfied execution. Otherwise, however, the trustee is restricted to objections which the bankrupt himself might have raised.[84]

Thus, he may urge lack of consideration.[85]

The trustee is entitled to counterclaim for damages suffered by the bankrupt in carrying out a contract involved in the claim, which he was induced to enter into by the claimant's false representations.[86]

Thus, it may be shown that the claimant released the bankrupt from the claim after the commencement of the bankruptcy proceedings.[87]

§ 783. Creditors and Trustee Bound by Bankrupt's Contracts and Acts.—The trustee is bound by the bankrupt's contracts and acts;[88]

---

80. But compare, James v. Gray, 12 A. B. R. 573, 131 Fed. 401 (C. C. A. Mass.); In re Brown, 21 A. B. R. 123, 164 Fed. 673 (C. C. A. Calif.).
81. In re Hess, 14 A. B. R. 559, 134 Fed. 109 (Ref. Pa., affirmed by D. C.).
82. In re Duquesne Incandescent Light Co., 24 A. B. R. 419, 176 Fed. 785 (D. C. Pa.), quoted at § 687.
83. In re Trombly, 16 A. B. R. 599 (Ref. Vt.).
84. In re Arnold & Co., 13 A. B. R. 320, 133 Fed. 789 (D. C. Mo.), in which the rule is stated too broadly.
Thus, as to measure of damage for

breach of contract of manufacture where all goods not yet manufactured, In re Duquesne Incandescent Light Co., 24 A. B. R. 419, 176 Fed. 785 (D. C. Pa.).
85. [Merchants & Manufactures] National Bank of Columbus v. Galbraith, 19 A. B. R. 319, 157 Fed. 208 (C. C. A. Ohio).
86. In re Harper, 23 A. B. R. 918, 175 Fed. 412 (D. C. N. Y.).
87. In re Norris, 26 A. B. R. 945, 190 Fed. 101 (D. C. Minn.).
88. In re Edson, 9 A. B. R. 505 (D. C. Vt.). Instance, commissions of

except where fraud exists or special rights are given by the provisions of the Bankruptcy Act to the trustee.

Thus, the trustee "stands in the bankrupt's shoes" as to claims against a bankrupt stockbroker for money left for the purchase of stock, but wrongfully converted by the broker to his own use.

West v. McLaughlin Co., 20 A. B. R. 654, 162 Fed. 124 (C. C. A. Mich.): "The testimony leaves no doubt that the money was paid to the bankrupt for the purpose of buying the 350 shares of stock in the Virginia, etc., Company; and, this being true, we think the court below proceeded upon an erroneous theory of the principles of law upon which the case was to be tried and determined. The trustee represented the bankrupt, stood in his shoes, and the burden of proof rested upon him, precisely as it would have rested upon the bankrupt, had there been no adjudication, and it devolved upon appellee to show that the purchase had in fact been made by the bankrupt in order to defeat the claim. If the purchase had not been made, the bankrupt held the $5,000 for appellant's use, and as money which, in equity and good conscience, he ought not to retain. The burden was not upon the creditor to show that there was no actual purchase of stock, and it was error to disallow and reject the claim upon the contrary assumption."

Thus, the trustee is bound by the bankrupt's assumption of debts.[89]

And by his assumption of liens, where such assumption is binding by State law; for example, where a partnership buys out a corporation and assumes its debts.[90]

But, since the Amendment of 1910 to § 47 (a) (2) the trustee is bound thereby only to the extent a creditor "armed with process" would be bound.

---

agent paid by seller as part of seller's claim where bankrupt repudiated contract of sale effected by agent, In re Saxton Furn. Co., 15 A. B. R. 445, 142 Fed. 293 (D. C. Pa.). See post, subject of "Title to Assets," § 1144, et seq.

Effect of Adjudication of Bankruptcy on Contract Claims.—The subject of the effect of the adjudication of bankruptcy upon contractual rights and rights of property has already been discussed herein under the titles, "Adjudication as Res Adjudicata" (§ 444); "Contractual Relations Not Affected unless Merged in Provable Debts" (§ 451); "Damages for Breach of Contracts of Sale, Employment and Continuing Contracts," (§ 685, et seq.); "Damages on Contracts Accruing after Bankruptcy," (§ 707); "Does Bankruptcy Sever Relation of Landlord and Tenant," (§ 652); and is also discussed later under the general subjects of "Leaseholds" (§ 981), etc. The subject of "Bankruptcy as an Anticipatory Breach of Contract" is discussed at §§ 674, 675, 685, et seq.

Estoppel Where Notes Secured by Accounts Are Themselves Repledged as Collateral under Representation—In re Milne, Turnbull & Co., 26 A. B. R. 10, 185 Fed. 244 (C. C. A. N. Y.).

Thus, as to measure of damages for breach of contract of manufacture where entire lot of goods not yet manufactured. In re Duquesne Incandescent Light Co., 24 A. B. R. 419, 176 Fed. 785 (D. C. Pa.).

Instance [stockholder's claim for endorsing corporate obligations upheld notwithstanding issue of stock to him for an insolvent partnership business taken over by the corporation, the corporation being bound by the contract of taking over, third parties rights not intervening and old firm's creditors all being paid]. In re Alleman Hardware Co., 25 A. B. R. 331, 181 Fed. 810 (C. C. A. Pa.), reversing 22 A. B. R. 871, quoted at § 976.

89. Instance, In re Sickman & Glenn, 19 A. B. R. 232, 155 Fed. 508 (D. C. Pa.).

90. Instance, In re Sickman & Glenn, 19 A. B. R. 232, 155 Fed. 508 (D. C. Pa.).

ALLOWABILITY AS AFFECTED BY STATUTE OF LIMITATIONS.

§ 784. Statute of Limitations as Defense to Allowance.—The statute of limitations may be interposed against the allowance of a claim.[91]

§ 785. Trustee's Duty to Interpose It.—It is the trustee's duty to interpose it.[92]

§ 786. As to Creditor Interposing It.—Any creditor otherwise qualified to defend, it has been held, may also plead it: it is not such a personal defense of the debtor that a creditor in bankruptcy is not also entitled to make it.[93] A claim barred by the statute of limitations is nevertheless "provable" in bankruptcy;[94] although such a claim when proved may be expunged or disallowed.[95]

§ 787. Scheduling Does Not Revive Outlawed Debts.—The fact that the bankrupt has put in his list of claims, in Schedule A, a debt that is barred by the statute of limitations will not operate to revive the debt as against the other creditors. It is not such a written acknowledgment as will take away the bar of the statute, at least as to the trustee or the other creditors.[96] But it has been held that should the estate prove to be solvent, the scheduling of a barred debt will revive it as against the bankrupt, even though he did not know he was solvent when he made the schedule.[97]

---

91. In re Wooten, 9 A. B. R. 247, 118 Fed. 670 (D. C. N. Car.); In re Lipman, 2 A. B. R. 46, 94 Fed. 353. (D. C. N. Y.), and notes; In re Hargardine-McKittrick Co. v. Hudson, 10 A. B. R. 225, 122 Fed. 232 (C. C. A. Mo., affirming 6 A. B. R. 637); obiter, In re Kuffler, 19 A. B. R. 181, 155 Fed. 1018 (D. C. N. Y.), instance, In re Watkinson, 16 A. B. R. 245, 143 Fed. 602 (D. C. Pa.); instance, dormant judgment, In re Rebman, 17 A. B. R. 767 (C. C. A. Calif.). As to dormant judgments, see In re Rebman, 17 A. B. R. 767 (C. C. A. Calif.).

Amendment of Wife's Claim Apparently Outlawed, to State Credit to Remove the Bar, Refused under Circumstances of Bad Faith.—In re Girvin, 20 A. B. R. 490, 160 Fed. 197 (D. C. N. Y.).

92. In re Wooten, 9 A. B. R. 247, 118 Fed. 670 (D. C. N. Car.).

93. See In re Lafferty & Bro., 10 A. B. R. 290, 122 Fed. 558 (D. C. Pa.); compare, In re Lipman, 2 A. B. R. 46, 94 Fed. 353 (D. C. N. Y.).

94. In re Hargardine-McKittrick Co. v. Hudson, 10 A. B. R. 225, 122 Fed. 232 (C. C. A. Mo.). Compare, ante, § 747.

95. In re Hargardine-McKittrick Co.

v. Hudson, 10 A. B. R. 225, 122 Fed. 232 (C. C. A. Mo.); In re Lipman, 2 A. B. R. 46, 94 Fed. 353 (D. C. N. Y.).

96. In re Wooten, 9 A. B. R. 247, 118 Fed. 670 (D. C. N. Car.); In re Lipman, 2 A. B. R. 46, 94 Fed. 353 (D. C. N. Y.); In re Resler, 2 A. B. R. 166, 95 Fed. 804 (Ref. Minn., affirmed by In re Resler, 2 A. B. R. 602); [1867] In re Doty, 16 N. B. Reg. 202, Fed. Cases, No. 4,017. But see, In re Gibson, 69 South Western 974.

Each item of an account for money loaned is severable so that some may be barred by the statute and others not. In re Wooten, 9 A. B. R. 247, 118 Fed. 670 (D. C. N. Car.).

97. In re Currier, 27 A. B. R. 597, 192 Fed. 695 (D. C. N. Y.).

Whether Order of Allowance a "Judgment" Sufficient to Toll Statute.—It has not been determined whether the order of allowance of a claim in bankruptcy amounts to such a "judgment" as to toll the statute, in future actions against the bankrupt where discharge has been refused, see post, "Effect of Discharge."

Statute Suspended During Bankruptcy, as to Subsequent Actions against Bankrupt.—It is well settled,

§ 788. What Statute of Limitations Governs.—The Statute of Limitations that governs federal courts in the particular district where the bankruptcy proceedings are pending, governs in the allowance of claims. It is the law of the forum that governs.[98] It is the statute of the State where the proceedings are pending,[99] or where an action could be brought on the claim.[1]

SUBDIVISION "B".

ALLOWABILITY AS AFFECTED BY RES ADJUDICATA.

§ 789. Res Adjudicata Binding.—Res judicata is binding in bankruptcy, as elsewhere.[2]

Handlan v. Walker, 29 A. B. R. 4, 200 Fed. 567 (C. C. A. Mo.): "The controlling question is whether the judgment of the State court concludes the controversy and bars the further prosecution of the claim in the court of bankruptcy. We think it does. The contract was the foundation of Handlan's right. No liability for the cost of restoration appears save by its provisions. His action in the State court was upon the contract and for all his disbursements; the judgment was upon the merits. The claim there was not for damages to the premises by the negligence of the bankrupt or the trustee, but was specially upon the contract for the cost of putting the premises in their condition before the bankrupt installed its machinery; and likewise the present claim, except that it is for 'a balance' alleged to be due. The rule as to the conclusiveness of an adjudication when the same matter again comes up between the same parties is too familiar to require much restatement. It covers questions of both law and fact upon which their rights depend and those which might have been determined as well as those which were."

Where the judgment itself is not void it is binding in bankruptcy.[3] The adjudication in bankruptcy has been held to be conclusive upon at least all parties to the bankruptcy proceedings of the facts necessarily proved.[4] Thus

however, that where the bankrupt's discharge is refused, the period of the bankruptcy preceding the refusal is not to be counted in as part of the period constituting the bar. See post, "Effect of Discharge."

98. In re Resler, 2 A. B. R. 116, 95 Fed. 804 (Ref. Minn., affirmed by In re Resler, 2 A. B. R. 602).

99. Hargardine-McKittrick Dry Goods Co. v. Hudson, 10 A. B. R. 225, 122 Fed. 232 (C. C. A. Mo., affirming 6 A. B. R. 657); inferentially, In re Farmer, 9 A. B. R. 19, 116 Fed. 763 (D. C. N. Car.); In re Stoddard Bros. Lumber Co., 22 A. B. R. 435, 169 Fed. 190 (D. C. Idaho).

1. In re Lipman, 2 A. B. R. 46, 94 Fed. 353 (D. C. N. Y.). Compare, In re Dunavant, 3 A. B. R. 41, 96 Fed. 542 (D. C. N. Car.).

2. General Principles of Res Judi-

cata.—See Talcott v. Friend, 24 A. B. R. 708, 179 Fed. 676 (C. C. A. Ills.).

Mortgage Bondholders Individually or Trustee of Mortgage, Which to Prove for Deficiency, and Whether Bondholders Bound by Deficiency Decree in Foreclosure by Mortgage Trustee.—Mackey v. Randolph Macon Coal Co., 24 A. B. R. 719, 178 Fed. 881 (C. C. A. Mo.).

Merger and Res Judicata Distinguished.—Mackey v. Randolph Macon Coal Co., 24 A. B. R. 719, 178 Fed. 881 (C. C. A. Mo.).

3. In re Chase, 13 A. B. R. 294, 133 Fed. 79 (D. C. Mass.).

4. Ayers v. Cone, 14 A. B. R. 739, 138 Fed. 778 (C. C. A. S. Dak.). But compare, In re Continental Corp'n, 14 A. B. R. 538 (Ref. Ohio). Also, compare, Whitney v. Wenman, 14 A. B. R. 591 (D. C. N. Y.).

it would be conclusive as to the insolvency of the bankrupt at the date of the commission of the act of bankruptcy on which the adjudication was based, where insolvency was necessarily involved. But there is doubt upon this point, for the relief sought in the two proceedings is wholly different —in the one, the adjudication is concerning the status of a person, in the other, concerning a right to share in that person's assets.[4a] And in involuntary bankruptcies the adjudication of bankruptcy is not at any rate conclusive of insolvency at any time prior to the adjudication.[5]

§ 790. Adjudication Not Res Adjudicata as to Amount or Validity of Petitioning Creditor's Claim.

—But the decree of adjudication in involuntary bankruptcy is not res adjudicata at any rate as to the amount nor validity of one of the petitioning creditors' claims, when subsequently presented for allowance to share in dividends.[6]

§ 791. Order of Allowance or Disallowance, Res Adjudicata.

—An order of allowance or of disallowance of a claim, not appealed from, nor reversed, is a bar, as res judicata, to a suit on the same cause of action in another jurisdiction;[7] also in subsequent proceedings in the bankruptcy proceedings themselves.[8]

§ 792. Trustee's Failure to Contest Allowance, Bar to Suit to Recover Preference.

—The trustee's failure to contest a claim, otherwise valid, because of voidable preferences received thereon, is a bar to his subsequent suit to recover the preferences.[9]

§ 793. "Provisional" Allowance Improper.

—A claim may not be allowed "provisionally" to enable a creditor to participate in creditors' meetings. The "provisional" qualification has been held void and the claim to be res adjudicata in subsequent litigation.[10]

SUBDIVISION "c".

ALLOWABILITY OF COMMERCIAL PAPER.

§ 794. Negotiability Unimpaired by Bankruptcy.

—The attributes

4a. Compare ante, § 447.

5. Inferentially, In re Linton, 7 A. B. R. 676 (Ref. Penn.).

6. In re Continental Corp'n, 14 A. B. R. 538 (Ref. Ohio); compare, also, the Court's reasoning in Whitney v. Wenman, 14 A. B. R. 591 (D. C. N. Y.). See dissenting opinion in Ayres v. Cone, 14 A. B. R. 739, 138 Fed. 778 (C. C. A. S. Dak.); contra, Ayres v. Cone, 14 A. B. R. 739 (C. C. A. S. Dak.). See, also, "Effect of Adjudication or Rights of Parties," § 447.

7. Hargardine-McKittrick Dry Goods Co. v. Hudson, 10 A. B. R. 225, 122 Fed. 232 (C. C. A. Mo.); obiter, In re Heinsfurter, 3 A. B. R. 109, 97 Fed. 198 (D. C. Iowa); Clendening v. Nat'l Bk., 11 A. B. R. 245 (Sup. Ct. N. Dak.).

8. Compare, In re Drumgoole, 15 A. B. R. 261 (D. C. Pa.).

9. Clendening v. Nat'l Bk., 11 A. B. R. 245 (Sup. Ct. N. Dak.); contra, Buder v. Columbia Distilling Co., 9 A. B. R. 331, 70 S. W. 508 (St. Louis Ct. App.). Compare analogous proposition post, § 1751½.

10. Clendening v. Nat'l Bk., 11 A. B. R. 245 (Sup. Ct. N. Dak.); compare, In re Malino, 8 A. B. R. 205, 118 Fed. 368 (D. C. N. Y.).

of negotiability are unimpaired by bankruptcy; and the rights and immunities of bona fide holders, granted by the law merchant, are protected in bankruptcy.[11]

In re Wyly, 8 A. B. R. 604, 116 Fed. 38 (D. C. Tex.): "The rights of a purchaser or holder of a negotiable instrument who has taken it bona fide, for a valuable consideration, in the ordinary course of business, before due, without notice are not affected by the equities existing between the antecedent parties. This proposition is too well settled to need the citation of authorities for its support. The Bankruptcy Act does not by its term alter the rights for its indorsee of negotiable instruments, and so they exist just as before its enactment."

Thus, as to accommodation paper. Accommodation paper of a corporation, although ultra vires, may be proved against it in bankruptcy by an innocent holder for value who took it, before maturity, in the usual course of business.[12]

But where the endorsee and holder had knowledge that it was accommodation paper, it is not an allowable claim if ultra vires.[13] Likewise, where accommodation paper has been diverted from the purpose for which it was originally given, only innocent purchasers for value in the due course of business will be protected against the defense,[14] and the burden of proof of bona fides is on the holder.[15]

Thus the ordinary rules prevail as to whether an endorsement is as a guaranty for one's own benefit or is for accommodation, where one corporation owns another corporation's stock and endorses the latter's notes.[16] Likewise, the accommodation paper of a partnership, although the partner who signed the firm name was acting beyond the scope of his actual authority, will bind the firm in the hands of a bona fide purchaser.[17]

---

11. Impliedly, In re Levi, 9 A. B. R. 176, 121 Fed. 198 (D. C. N. Y., rev'g 8 A. B. R. 244); instance, In re Car Wheel Wks., 14 A. B. R. 595, 139 Fed. 421 (D. C. N. Y.), a case wherein corporate paper was affected with bad faith but held by an innocent endorser.

The bankrupt corporation for whose benefit the ultra vires accommodating was done by the other corporation is estopped from urging the ultra vires of the accommodation and the ultra vires is not available defense to the trustee. Farmers & Merchants' Bk. v. Akron Mach. Co., 12 A. B. R. 6 (Ref. Ohio); compare, Wollerstein v. Ervin, 7 A. B. R. 256 (C. C. A. Penna.).

12. In re Akron Twine & Cordage Co., 11 A. B. R. 321 (Ref. Ohio).

13. In re Prospect Worsted Mills, 11 A. B. R. 502 (D. C. Mass.). The syllabus of this case sets forth the propositions decided, as follows: "One manufacturing corporation can not pledge its credit for the price of goods sold to another corporation. The guaranty of the debt of one manufacturing corporation by the unanimous consent of the stockholders of another is subject to the claims of the creditors of the latter. Consent of wife and daughter of president of corporation where president and his sons manage the whole corporation can not be presumed to accommodation endorsement merely from fact that the president and his sons were managing the corporation."

14. In re Hopper-Morgan Co., 19 A. B. R. 518, 158 Fed. 351 (D. C. N. Y.).

15. In re Hopper-Morgan Co., 19 A. B. R. 539, 158 Fed. 351 (D. C. N. Y.).

16. In re Car Wheels Wks., 15 A. B. R. 571 (D. C. N. Y.).

17. Union Nat'l Bk. v. Neill, 17 A. B. R. 848, 149 Fed. 720 (C. C. A. Tex.).

Thus, as to claims of sureties for the bankrupt;[18] and as to stipulations for attorney's collection fees in notes;[19] and as to the rights of parties where the maker endorses his own notes.[20]

Thus, the ordinary rules of commercial paper apply in bankruptcy as to showing the true relation, where a surety signs first and his principal second.[21] Also the ordinary rules as to each endorser having recourse against prior parties, prevails in the absence of agreement among them to the contrary.[22]

Thus, the ordinary rules of commercial paper apply as to filling in blanks and altering the place of payment, etc.[23]

Thus, the ordinary rule of commercial paper that the burden of proof of the bona fide holding is upon the claimant, applies.[24]

Thus, the delivery of a negotiable instrument by the trustee in bankruptcy to the purchaser thereof is sufficient to pass the title thereto, where previously endorsed by the bankrupt. It is not necessary, in such cases, for the trustee to endorse it.[25]

§ 794½. Transfer of Notes, Transfers Also Right to Securities.—
The doctrine that a transfer of a debt carries with it the equitable right to the securities held therefor applies in bankruptcy.[26]

Thus, where a banking firm pledged with a bank certain notes of a merchant which it had taken under an arrangement whereby it paid the merchant's debts from time to time and took assignments of his accounts therefor, it was held that the pledge of the notes carried the equitable right to the accounts.[27]

§ 795. Nonnegotiable Paper Subject to Same Defenses as Elsewhere.—
Likewise, nonnegotiable paper is subject to the same defenses in bankruptcy as elsewhere.[28]

§ 796. Disregarding Note and Claiming on Original Consideration.—
Claim may be made upon the original obligation and a note given therefor be disregarded under the same circumstances and with the same qualifications available had there been no bankruptcy.[29]

---

18. See ante, ch. XXI, "Provable Claims," div. 3; "Contingent Claims," § 642, et seq. Also, see post, under the general subject of "Preferences."

19. See ante, ch. XXI, "Provable Debts," div. 5; "Claims Not Owing at Time of Bankruptcy," § 671.

20. In re Edson, 9 A. B. R. 505 (D. C. Vt.).

21. In re Carter, 15 A. B. R. 126, 138 Fed. 846 (D. C. Ark.).

22. In re McCord, 22 A. B. R. 204 (Ref. N. Y.).

23. First National Bank of Wilkesbarre v. Barnum, 20 A. B. R. 439, 160 Fed. 245 (D. C. Pa.).

24. In re Hill & Sons, 26 A. B. R. 132, 187 Fed. 214 (D. C. Pa.).

25. Wade v. Elliott, 28 A. B. R. 888 (Ct. App, Ga.).

26. In re Milner, Turnbull & Co., 26 A. B. R. 10, 185 Fed. 244 (C. C. A. N. Y.).

27. In re Milne, Turnbull & Co., 26 A. B. R. 10' 185 Fed. 244 (C. C. A. N. Y.).

28. In re Goodman Shoe Co., 3 A. B. R. 200, 96 Fed. 949 (D. C. Pa.).

29. Instance, Du Vivier v. Gallice, 17 A. B. R. 557, 149 Fed. 118 (C. C. A. N. Y.).

§ 796⅛. Several Obligations for Same Debt.—A merely additional obligation of the bankrupt for the same debt may not be allowed as a separate claim and the total indebtedness of the bankrupt be thus multiplied, except in so far, of course, as the law merchant may protect an innocent holder for value before maturity; and doubtless its negotiation may be enjoined, or the claim of the original creditor be reduced pro tanto. Thus, where "debenture bonds" were issued by the bankrupt as collateral security to its notes but not secured by mortgage or in any other way, the court held that the "debenture bonds" amounted, in effect, simply to another promise to pay the same debt and that they might not be sold and their proceeds applied.[30]

§ 796¼. Note Allowed in Full Though Another Also Liable.—Where a bankrupt, for a valuable consideration, has assumed the payment of promissory notes, his estate is liable for their full amount, though another party is also liable thereon.[31]

§ 796½. Stipulation for Attorney's Fees.—Notes containing stipulations as to attorney's fees for collection have been allowed in bankruptcy, including the fee stipulated.[32] But the validity and extent of such claims are to be determined by the local law.

§ 796¾. Miscellaneous Defenses to Commercial Paper.—A note given in consideration of a "clearing check" has been upheld as being upon valuable consideration.[33] A note given for a gambling debt is subject to the ordinary rules.[34]

Where a corporation was organized on the failure of another corporation but had different stockholders and did not assume the former corporation's debts nor take over all of its assets, a note which it gave to take up one of the old corporation's debts was held to be without consideration and to be ultra vires.[35]

---

30. In re Matthews, 26 A. B. R. 19, 188 Fed. 445 (D. C. N. Y.), affirmed sub nom. Matthews v. Knickerbocker Trust Co., 27 A. B. R. 629, 192 Fed. 557. Compare, analogous doctrine, § 753 [John] Matthews Inc. v. Knickerbocker Trust Co., 27 A. B. R. 629, 192 Fed. 557 (C. C. A. N. Y.), affirming In re Matthews, 26 A. B. R. 19, 188 Fed. 445.

31. In re Girvin, 20 A. B. R. 320, 160 Fed. 197 (D. C. N. Y.).

32. See ante, § 671. Also see In re Edens & Co., 18 A. B. R. 643, 151 Fed. 940 (D. C. S. C.); Merchant's Bank v. Thomas, 10 A. B. R. 299, 121 Fed. 306 (C. C. A.); obiter, In re Milling Co., 16 A. B. R. 456 (D. C. Tex.). But compare, obiter, In re Hersey, 22 A.

B. R. 863, 171 Fed. 1004 (D. C. Iowa). Compare, In re Torchia, 26 A. B. R. 188, 185 Fed. 576 (D. C. Pa.). Compare, analogously, where allowed as part of lien on selling free from liens, In re Holmes Lumber Co., 26 A. B. R. 119, 189 Fed. 178 (D. C. Ala.).

33. [Merchants and Manufacturers] National Bank of Columbus v. Galbraith, 19 A. B. R. 319, 157 Fed. 208 (C. C. A. Ohio).

34. Gambling debt, note given for, whether enforceable in hands of innocent holder for value. Compare, obiter (held not holder for value), In re William Hill & Sons, 26 A. B. R. 133, 187 Fed. 214 (D. C. Pa.).

35. In re Stanford Clothing Co., 26 A. B. R. 124, 187 Fed. 172 (D. C. Ala.).

§ 797. Allowability of Claims of Relatives, Stockholders, etc.— Claims of relatives are allowable in bankruptcy if valid by State law and not in contravention of the provisions of the Bankruptcy Act.[36]

Ohio Valley Bank Co. v. Mack, 20 A. B. R. 40, 163 Fed. 155 (C. C. A. Ohio): "The fact that the bankrupt is closely related to a creditor is a circumstance which justifies a more rigid scrutinizing than would be the case if no such relation existed. Nevertheless the honest or dishonest character of a debt is not to be determined by any mere question of relationship." Citing Davis v. Schwartz, 155 U. S. 638; Estes v. Gunter, 122 U. S. 456.

Likewise are the claims of stockholders.[37] But preferred stockholders, holding property of the corporation under trust deed as security for their preference, are, nevertheless, not creditors but stockholders, the preference relating merely to distribution in the event of winding up whilst solvent, not in the event of insolvency.

Spencer v. Smith, 29 A. B. R. 120, 201 Fed. 647 (C. C. A. Col.): "The certificate of preferred stock evidenced a contract between the stockholders of the corporation. Stockholders may make such contracts between themselves as are not contrary to law or against public policy. The contract which the stockholders intended to make in issuing the stock in question must be determined from the language of the stock itself, taken in connection with the articles of incorporation. As the corporation made no profits, the present holders of the preferred stock have no claim for dividends. The only claim they have arises from that provision of the certificate of stock which provides that in the event of a distribution of the assets of the corporation, the preferred stock outstanding at that time shall first be paid at eleven dollars per share, and the remainder of the corporate assets shall be divided ratably among the holders of the common stock. The question now presented is, are the present holders of outstanding preferred stock creditors of the corporation, or are they simply preferred stockholders? If they are creditors they have a secured claim against the bankrupt estate; if they are preferred stockholders then the above provision is laid as against the holders of common stock, for the preference in the distribution of assets was a matter concerning which the stockholders could lawfully agree as between themselves. If, however, the provision giving a preference in the distribution of assets to the preferred stockholders is sought to be upheld as against creditors of the corporation, it must fail as being against public policy and therefore void.

"The assets of a corporation represented by its capital stock are a trust fund for the payment of its debts, and the law will not permit stockholders to agree among themselves that this trust fund shall be appropriated by them or some of them as against the claims of creditors. We are therefore of the opinion that the present holders of the preferred stock of the corporation are not creditors

---

36. Instance, In re Macauley, 18 A. B. R. 459, 158 Fed. 322 (D. C. Mich.).
37. In re Bennett Shoe Co., 20 A. B. R. 704, 162 Fed. 691 (D. C. Conn.).

Endorsement of corporate obligations. In re L. M. Alleman Hardware Co., 25 A. B. R. 331, 181 Fed. 810 (C. C. A. Pa.), reversing 22 A. B. R. 871, quoted at § 976.

thereof, but stockholders; that the provision contained in the certificate of preferred stock, giving a preference of eleven dollars per share to the holders thereof refers only to the distribution of assets as between stockholders, and has no reference to the distribution of assets for the payment of the debts of the corporation; that if by any interpretation it could be construed as referring to the distribution of assets to pay debts then it is void as being against public policy."

§ 798. Thus, Wife's Claims.—A wife's claim against her bankrupt husband's estate is allowable, if valid by state law.

In re Novak, 4 A. B. R. 311, 101 Fed. 800 (D. C. Iowa): "Under the provisions of the Code of Iowa, a wife may become the creditor of the husband. * * * This being the settled rule in Iowa, I can see no ground for holding that the wife, being an actual creditor in good faith, may not exercise the right conferred by the Bankrupt Act upon creditors to initiate proceedings in bankruptcy when cause therefor exists."

Thus, as to her claims for services to husband rendered outside of domestic duties they are allowable in bankruptcy in States where she may make contracts directly with her husband;[38] but are not allowed in New York;[39] nor in Wisconsin, for her services as bookkeeper;[40] nor in Vermont, for clerking in her husband's restaurant and store.[41]

And her claims may be allowable notwithstanding the state statute forbids a wife suing her husband except for divorce or recovery of her separate estate.[42] And she is competent to testify in support of her own claim although the statute forbids husband and wife testifying "against each other;" for her suit is not "against" him.[43]

A wife's claim for an annuity against her husband, based upon an alimony judgment later converted into an annuity secured by deed of trust, is allowable, even though they subsequently re-marry.[44]

So, also, obligations arising not by direct contract between husband and wife but by implication of law, as, for instance, subrogation, are allowable in Massachusetts, although in that State husband and wife may not contract with each other.[45] A wife's claim not registered as her separate property in accordance with state law in Oregon has been held nevertheless allowable.[46]

A wife who has gone on her bankrupt husband's note and given a mortgage on her separate property to secure his debt has been held to be a surety and not the principal, although she signs first; and she has been held entitled to prove the claim in the creditor's name.[47] She would, on payment be

---

38. In re Domenig, 11 A. B. R. 552, 128 Fed. 146 (D. C. Penn.); In re Cox, 29 A. B. R. 456, 199 Fed. 952 (D. C. N. Mex.).

39. In re Kaufman, 5 A. B. R. 104 (D. C. N. Y.); Obiter, In re Suckle, 23 A. B. R. 861, 176 Fed. 828 (D. C. Ark.).

40. In re Winkels, 12 A. B. R. 696 (D. C. Wis.).

41. In re Trombly, 16 A. B. R. 599 (Ref. Vt.).

42. In re Domenig, 11 A. B. R. 552, 128 Fed. 146 (D. C. Penn.).

43. In re Domenig, 11 A. B. R. 552, 128 Fed. 146 (D. C. Penn.).

44. Savage v. Savage, 15 A. B. R. 599 (C. C. A. Va.).

45. In re Nickerson, 8 A. B. R. 707, 116 Fed. 1003 (D. C. Mass.).

46. In re Miner, 9 A. B. R. 100, 117 Fed. 953 (D. C. Ore.).

47. In re Carter, 15 A. B. R. 126, 138 Fed. 846 (D. C. Ark.).

subrogated to the mortgagee's lien.[48] But a wife's claim upon a loan of corporate stock to her husband has been held not a provable [allowable] debt in Massachusetts.[49]

In one case a wife's claim for money loaned at different times, aggregating $10,000 and more, was disallowed on review because of the bar of the statute of limitations, although the referee had found that there had been a payment on account of some $1,000 sufficient to revive the debt, the wife's proof having failed originally to show such credit, and amendment having been allowed after the expiration of the year for filing claims, the court considering the testimony not worthy of credit.[50]

A note given by a corporation to the wife of its principal stockholder (she herself being also a stockholder) for money loaned to effect a proposed composition with creditors, has been held to be an allowable claim against the corporation when later adjudged bankrupt.[51]

And the wife's claim for money loaned out of her separate estate has been held allowable in Pennsylvania,[52] likewise in Vermont.[53]

In Arkansas a wife's claim for salary as clerk for her bankrupt husband is held, on the ground of public policy, not to be allowable, notwithstanding the Married Women's Act of that State.[54] Nor can the wife form a mercantile partnership with her husband in that state, although a married woman may form a partnership with any other person.[55] Likewise, a promissory note of a married woman, not for the benefit of her separate estate, is not allowable in Arkansas.[56]

Yet, on the other hand, the wife's claim for money loaned her husband out of her separate estate, although under State law not enforceable in Massachusetts, has been held nevertheless allowable in bankruptcy;[57] and, in Wisconsin, to be enforceable, and her claim therefor to be a provable debt against her husband's estate;[58] likewise in Maine.[59] A wife's claim has been held invalid in Illinois, where it was based on an unconsummated gift.[60]

Money given by the bankrupt to his wife to defray family expenses has been held not to be a preference, upon her bona fide claim for money loaned

48. In re Carter, 15 A. B. R. 126, 138 Fed. 846 (D. C. Ark.).

49. In re Tucker, 12 A. B. R. 594, 131 Fed. 647 (D. C. Mass.). But, compare her right to recover proceeds of sale thereof, Tucker v. Curtin, 17 A. B. R. 354 (C. C. A. Mass.).

50. In re Girvin, 20 A. B. R. 490, 160 Fed. 197 (D. C. N. Y.).

51. In re Bennett Shoe Co., 20 A. B. R. 704, 162 Fed. 691 (D. C. Conn.).

52. In re Kyte, 21 A. B. R. 110, 164 Fed. 302 (D. C. Pa.).

53. In re Hill, 27 A. B. R. 146, 190 Fed. 390 (D. C. Vt.).

54. In re Suckle, 23 A. B. R. 861, 176 Fed. 828 (D. C. Ark.).

55. In re Suckle, 23 A. B. R. 861, 176 Fed. 828 (D. C. Ark.).

56. In re Suckle, 23 A. B. R. 861, 176 Fed. 828 (D. C. Ark.).

57. James v. Gray, 12 A. B. R. 573, 131 Fed. 401 (C. C. A. Mass.); contra, In re Talbott, 7 A. B. R. 29, 110 Fed. 924 (D. C. Mass.).

58. In re Neiman, 6 A. B. R. 329, 109 Fed. 113 (D. C. Wis.). But see, inferentially contra, In re Winkels, 12 A. B. R. 696 (D. C. Wis.), where the court refused to allow a wife's claim for services as husband's bookkeeper in his store.

59. In re Foss, 17 A. B. R. 439 (D. C. Me.).

60. In re Chapman, 5 A. B. R. 570, 105 Fed. 901 (D. C. Ills.).

out of her own estate, the reviewing court reversing the referee for rejecting her uncontradicted testimony.[61]

§ 799. Child's Claim and Parent's Claim.

—A child's claim against a bankrupt parent's estate, as also a parent's claim against a bankrupt child's estate, is allowable where valid by State law.[62]

§ 800. But Ordinary Rule of Close Scrutiny Prevails.

—But the ordinary rule that the claims of relatives against an insolvent estate should be closely scrutinized before allowance, prevails in bankruptcy.[63]

Ohio Valley Bank Co. v. Mack, 20 A. B. R. 40, 163 Fed. 155 (C. C. A. Ohio): "The fact that the bankrupt is closely related to a creditor is a circumstance which justifies a more rigid scrutiny than would be the case if no such relation existed."

In re Rider, 3 A. B. R. 192 (D. C. N. Y.): "In the present instance the principal accusation against the claim is based upon the relationship of father and son existing between the bankrupt and the creditor. This fact demanded closer scrutiny than is required in the case of ordinary claims, and such an examination appears to have been given by the referee."

In re Wooten, 9 A. B. R. 249 (D. C. N. Car.): "Being the claim of a son against his father, aside from other circumstances, the rule governing the dealings between near relations applies. This rule is familiar learning—well settled—and need not be here discussed or any of the abundant authorities cited."

Obiter, In re Grandy & Son, 17 A. B. R. 214 (D. C. S. C.): "All transactions between a wife and a husband, who afterwards proves to be in failing circumstances, ought to be subject to the closest scrutiny by the courts, and no claim by her upon his estate, unless sustained by abundant testimony, ought to be allowed; but in this case there is no question of the absolute good faith of the transaction."

Instance, In re Kyte, 25 A. B. R. 337, 182 Fed. 166 (D. C. Pa.): "Two sons of a bankrupt father, who clerk for him, and know perfectly well his financial extremity, a day or two before he executes an assignment for the benefit of creditors, buy up mechanics' liens against his real estate to the amount of over $2,000 against which, if directly settled between the original claimants and the

<hr>

61. Neumann v. Blake, 24 A. B. R. 575, 178 Fed. 916 (C. C. A. Mo.), quoted at § 554. And compare, §§ 554, 852.

62. Ohio Valley Bank Co. v. Mack, 20 A. B. R. 40, 163 Fed. 155 (C. C. A. Ohio), quoted at § 797; In re Miller, 13 A. B. R. 87, 132 Fed. 414 (D. C. Vt.); In re Rider, 3 A. B. R. 192, 96 Fed. 811 (D. C. N. Y.); In re Wooten, 9 A. B. R. 247, 118 Fed. 670 (D. C. N. Car.); In re Brewster, 7 A. B. R. 486 (Ref. N. Y.). In re Upson, 10 A. B. R. 602, 123 Fed. 807 (D. C. N. Y.), in which case the bankrupt held money in trust for daughter, but loaned it to his own business giving to himself as guardian, a note for the amount, the court holding the note provable and allowable. Embry v. Bennett, 20 A. B. R. 651, 162 Fed. 139 (C. C. A. Ky.), in which case

it was held the trustee could not offset against the childrens' claims. (for loss of their money which the bankrupt had held as their guardian) the sums expended by him for their education at college.

63. In re Brewster, 7 A. B. R. 486 (Ref. N. Y.). Compare, to same effect, analogously, Horner-Gaylord Co. v. Miller & Bennett, 17 A. B. R. 267 (D. C. W. Va.). In re Domenig, 11 A. B. R. 555, 128 Fed. 146 (D. C. Pa.), quoted ante, § 556; inferentially, but obiter, Union Trust Co. v. Bulkeley, 18 A. B. R. 43, 150 Fed. 510 (C. C. A. Mich.), quoted ante, § 556; also, In re Kyte, 21 A. B. R. 110, 164 Fed. 302 (D. C. Pa.); impliedly, In re Sanger, 22 A. B. R. 145, 169 Fed. 722 (D. C. W. Va.). Compare ante, § 556, and post, § 854.

bankrupt, there would be set-offs on book accounts, amounting to nearly $1,800, the mechanics' liens, however, in the hands of the sons, being good against the real estate, and having been got out of the road in this way, the father is enabled to realize on the book accounts, which are thus abstracted from what would otherwise be available for the benefit of creditors. It goes beyond the range of human credulity to believe that this was not a collusive scheme between the bankrupt and his sons, arranged for this very purpose. That was the natural effect of it, and the presumption is that it was so intended."

Yet the claimant's own uncontradicted testimony in support of the claim may not be rejected because of the relationship, unless it is intrinsically unbelievable or otherwise incredible,[64] and the honest or dishonest character of a debt is not to be determined by any mere test of relationship.[65]

SUBDIVISION "E".

ALLOWABILITY OF MISCELLANEOUS CLAIMS—CLAIMS AFFECTED BY ULTRA VIRES—ILLEGALITY—USURY—FRAUD—CLAIMS FOR MONEY LOST IN GAMBLING—CLAIMS AGAINST BANKRUPT STOCKBROKER—CLAIMS FOR UNPAID STOCK SUBSCRIPTION—CLAIMS FOR COMMISSIONS—CLAIMS ON ANNUAL SUBSCRIPTION, ETC.

§ 801. In General.—In general, claims are allowable in bankruptcy if they be provable, and if they be by state law valid.[66]

64. Compare, inferentially to this effect, Neumann v. Blake, 24 A. B. R. 575, 178 Fed. 916 (C. C. A. Mo.), quoted at §§ 554, 852.

65. Ohio Valley v. Mack, 20 A. B. R. 40, 163 Fed. 155 (C. C. A. Ohio); Baumhauer v. Austin, 26 A. B. R. 385, 186 Fed. 260 (C. C. A. Ala.).

66. In re Benedict, etc., Co., 27 A. B. R. 409, 192 Fed. 1011 (D. C. Ky.).

Various Defenses to Allowance of Claims Passed on in Bankruptcy Reports.—1. Secret partner against firm. Rush v. Lake, 10 A. B. R. 455, 122 Fed. 561 (C. C. A.), reversing 7 A. B. R. 96.

2. Firm note claimed to be for individual partner's debt. Rush v. Lake, 10 A. B. R. 445, 122 Fed. 561 (C. C. A.), reversing 7 A. B. R. 96.

3. Stipulation for attorney's fee in note. See ante, §§ 671-794.

4. Corporate note in the hand of the payee given for a purchase of its own stock that rendered the company insolvent, is not an allowable claim. In re Smith Lumber Co., 13 A. B. R. 123, 132 Fed. 618 (D. C. Tex.).

5. Original debts revived on failure to pay composition notes. In re Carton, 17 A. B. R. 343, 148 Fed. 63 (D. C. N. Y.).

6. Claims of president of bankrupt corporation who, shortly before bankruptcy, overstated assets, to the loss of a creditor relying thereon, should not be allowed until he has satisfactorily accounted for the discrepancy: he should be held to the truth of his statement. In re Royce Dry Goods Co., 13 A. B. R. 257, 133 Fed. 100 (D. C. Mo.).

7. Notes given to officer of corporation by corporation. In re Castle Braid Co., 17 A. B. R. 143, 145 Fed. 224 (D. C. N. Y.).

8. Compensation of officer of corporation is said not to be allowable unless prior to the services the compensation was fixed by by-law or by formal resolution of the board of directors duly entered on the minutes, so as to contain the elements of a contract. In re Grubbs-Wiley Grocery Co., 2 A. B. R. 442 (D. C. Mo.).

9. Salary of business manager. Mason v. St. Arbans Furniture Co., 17 A. B. R. 868, 149 Fed. 898 (D. C. Vt.).

10. Release of debt. In re Howard, 4 A. B. R. 69, 100 Fed. 630 (D. C. Calif.).

11. Statute of frauds. In re Pettingill & Co., 14 A. B. R. 728, 135 Fed. 218 (D. C. Mass.).

12. Rebate upon creditor's claim. In re Douglass & Sons Co., 8 A. B. R. 113, 114 Fed. 772 (D. C. Conn.).

13. Proof of claim not filed until after bankrupt's death although claim-

§ 802. Thus, Claims Alleged to Be Ultra Vires.

—Claims upon alleged ultra vires contracts are allowable in bankruptcy if valid by State law, and are not allowable if invalid by State law. Thus, as to that of a corporation which has attempted to be partner of a firm.[67] Likewise, as to accommodation ultra vires negotiable paper.[68]

Farmers & Merch. Bk. *v.* Akron Mach. Co., 12 A. B. R. 6 (Ref. Ohio): "Where accommodation paper is made by one corporation for the benefit of another corporation which negotiates the same and uses the proceeds thereof and the former is compelled to pay the same at maturity and the latter corporation becomes bankrupt, the corporation which has so accommodated the bankrupt company may prove its claim against the bankrupt and participate in dividends."

So, also, as to a resolution of the board of directors of a corporation fixing the salary of its officers.[69]

And as to the claim where a corporation has bought in its own stock to settle dissensions among stockholders.[70] And agreements by corporations to repurchase their own stock from withdrawing or dissatisfied stockholders are beyond their powers.[71]

And bonds of a corporation issued not for money, labor or property actually received for lawful use as required by New York statute, are not allowable;[72] although such corporate bonds issued as security for credit are valid.[73]

Likewise, the giving of a note and mortgage by a corporation to secure an individual debt of its managing officer and principal stockholder has been held ultra vires, and the note has been held not allowable.[74]

Likewise, as to sales and other transactions between corporations and their

ant present at bankruptcy proceeding before, no evidence of the debt appearing on the bankrupt's books; claim rejected. In re Shaw, 7 A. B. R. 458 (D. C. Penn.).

14. **Infant's claim upon repudiation of contract.** In re Huntenberg, 18 A. B. R. 698, 153 Fed. 768 (D. C. N. Y.).

15. **Unauthorized contract by officer of corporation may not be ratified by him.** In re Roanoke Furnace Co., 21 A. B. R. 597, 166 Fed. 944 (D. C. Pa.).

16. **Release of Security by Liquidation Agreement.**—No release of security is caused by the signing of a "liquidation agreement" before the bankruptcy. In re Cyclopean Co., 21 A. B. R. 679, 167 Fed. 971 (C. C. A. N. Y.).

17. **Partnership—When Claim Is Allowable against Partnership, When Not.**—See post, § 2230, et seq.

18. **Forged endorsement.** In re Lamon, 22 A. B. R. 635, 171 Fed. 516 (D. C. N. Y.).

19. Vendor under land contract accepting quit claim from vendee's trustee in bankruptcy, waives claim

for unpaid purchase price. Kenyon *v.* Mulert, 26 A. B. R. 184, 184 Fed. 825 (C. C. A. Pa.).

67. Wallerstein *v.* Ervin, 7 A. B. R. 256, 112 Fed. 124 (C. C. A. Penn.).

68. In re Akron Twine & Cordage Co., 11 A. B. R. 321 (Ref. Ohio).

69. In re McCarthy, 28 A. B. R. 45, 196 Fed. 247 (D. C. N. J.).

70. In re Castle Braid Co., 17 A. B. R. 143, 145 Fed. 224 (D. C. N. Y.).

71. Compare, § 803. Also, see Allen *v.* Com'l Nat. Bk., 27 A. B. R. 33, 191 Fed. 97 (C. C. A. Mich.); In re Tichenor-Grand Co., 29 A. B. R. 409, 203 Fed. 720 (D. C. N. Y.) quoted at § 805½; In re Sapulpa Produce Co., 26 A. B. R. 900 (Ref. Okla.).

72. In re Waterloo Organ Co., 13 A. B. R. 466, 134 Fed. 341 (C. C. A. N. Y.).

73. In re Waterloo Organ Co., 13 A. B. R. 477, 134 Fed. 345 (C. C. A. N. Y., distinguishing 13 A. B. R. 466).

74. Am. Mach. Co. *v.* Norment, 19 A. B. R. 679, 157 Fed. 801 (C. C. A. N. Car.).

officers, directors or stockholders, the ordinary rules will prevail; thus, when the president of an insolvent furnace company and the principal owner of its stock, made an assignment to it of his rights as the lessee of certain coal mines owned by claimant, which assignment without authority of the corporation contained a provision that it should indemnify him against liability thereon, and claimant's bills for ore mined and delivered on his order were paid by him until the adjudication of himself and the company, the claimant was held not to be a creditor of the company, and its claim for a balance due was held to be provable only against the bankrupt estate of the president.[75]

The guaranty or payment by a corporation, without benefit to itself, of the debt of another, in which it has no interest, is beyond its powers;[76] thus, the note of a newly-organized corporation was held invalid where it was made to take up the note of another corporation that had failed and whose assets had, in great part though not entirely, been taken over by it, the two sets of stockholders being different and the debts of the original corporation not having been assumed.[77]

And the guaranty by a bankrupt corporation whose business had been that of supplying saloons, of the notes of a saloon corporation for money borrowed from a brewery has been held invalid as ultra vires notwithstanding a resolution passed that it was done to "extend business" nor that one man was the principal stockholder in both the debtor and guarantor corporations.[78]

The endorsement by one corporation of the notes of another corporation whose stock is largely owned by the first corporation has been held to create a guaranty and not an accommodation and to be not ultra vires.[79] But where the charter of a corporation has been amended so as to validate a claim which, without such amendment, would not have been allowable, the claim so validated may be proved and allowed in bankruptcy.[80]

§ 803. Claims Tainted with Illegality or Fraud.

§ 803. Claims Tainted with Illegality or Fraud.—Claims are not allowable in bankruptcy that are invalid under State law because of illegality or fraud. Thus, as to claims tainted with usury.[81]

---

75. In re Roanoke Furnace Co., 21 A. B. R. 597, 166 Fed. 944 (D. C. Pa.).

76. Mapes v. German Bank of Tilden, 23 A. B. R. 713, 176 Fed. 89 (C. C. A. Neb.).

77. In re Stanford Clothing Co., 26 A. B. R. 124, 187 Fed. 172 (D. C. Ala.).

78. In re Liquor Dealers Supply Co., 24 A. B. R. 399, 177 Fed. 197 (C. C. A. Ills.).

79. In re Car Wheel Wks., 15 A. B. R. 571, 141 Fed. 430 (D. C. N. Y.).

80. In re Benedict, etc., Co., 27 A. B. R. 409, 192 Fed. 1011 (D. C. Ky.).

81. Instance, In re Robinson, 14 A. B. R. 626, 136 Fed. 430 (D. C. Mass.): In this case amendment was allowed to avoid the illegality. The reasoning of the court, however, seems somewhat sophistical. The court says as long as the claim is based upon implied contract the express contract will prevail over any implied contract and so the charge of usury will remain; so the court suggests that the claim be changed to one for obtaining money by fraud and then that the tort be waived and claim be made again upon the implied contract for money had and received. This seems like juggling with names. If the claim can be proved at all it can only be proved in the form of a contract, express or implied, for tort claims, as such, are not provable in bankruptcy, of course: then if proved as a contract the express and usurious con-

In re Worth, 12 A. B. R. 566, 130 Fed. 927 (D. C. Iowa): "Under the Iowa statute, however, the usurious contract is not void, but voidable only to the extent of the interest in excess of the legal rate, and as construed by the Supreme Court of that State, the right to interpose such a defense is the privilege of the borrower only, and if he does not avail himself of the privilege so granted the statute is no longer applicable. Carmichael v. Bodfish, 32 Iowa, 418. The construction of the local statute by the highest court of the State is, under the familiar rule, controlling upon the federal courts in such State. The objecting creditors in the present case are in no manner parties or privies to the alleged usurious contract of the Sheldon State Bank, in no manner connected therewith, and cannot therefore be heard to interpose the objection of usury thereto."

But an agreement whereby a certain percentage in addition to legal rate is charged, not as interest, but for services to be rendered by the lender, is not usurious.[82] Thus, as to the validity of contracts for the sale of liquors.[82a] Thus, as to claims in restraint of trade or contrary to public policy.[83]

Thus, as to gambling contracts.[84] Thus, as to the claim of a customer where there has been gambling on margins.[85] Claims against the bankrupt for money lost in a gambling scheme are allowable although the money is knowingly used for gambling purposes, if fraudulent misrepresentations exist, making the parties not in pari delicto.[86] But a contract for future delivery of merchandise where there is no evidence to show that, instead of the delivery of the articles purchased, there was to be a mere payment of the difference between the contract price and the market price, is not a gambling contract and a claim upon it is not invalid.[87] Even though the original transaction may itself have been illegal as a gambling contract yet after it is closed and the money has been received a new obligation arises to pay over the money.[88] But the mere fact that money was given to the bankrupt in pursuance of a gambling contract will not constitute a defense to a claim for money had and received, as to such sums thereof as were in the bankrupt's possession at the time the petition was filed.[89]

Thus, as to claims where a secret advantage has been given to the claim-

---

tract will prevail over any implied contract.

Compare, analogously (commissions for procuring loan allowed, as part of lien on selling free of liens), In re Holmes Lumber Co., 26 A. B. R. 119, 189 Fed. 178 (D. C. Ala.).

82. In re Mesibovsky, 29 A. B. R. 235, 200 Fed. 562 (C. C. A. N. Y.).

82a. Compare, where held valid as not contrary to State statute, In re Fenn, 24 A. B. R. 130, 177 Fed. 334 (C. C. A. Vt., reversing In re Fenn, 22 A. B. R. 833, 172 Fed. 620, D. C. Vt.).

83. Held not contrary to public policy nor in restraint of trade. In re Clark, 21 A. B. R. 776 (Ref. Calif.).

84. In re Ætna Cotton Mills, 22 A. B. R. 629, 171 Fed. 994 (D. C. S. Car.); In re [William] Hill & Sons (plea of innocent holder for value held not proved), 26 A. B. R. 133, 187 Fed. 214 (D. C. Pa.).

85. Cleage v. Laidley, 17 A. B. R. 598, 149 Fed. 346 (C. C. A. Mo.).

86. In re Arnold & Co., 13 A. B. R. 320, 133 Fed. 789 (D. C. Mo.).

87. In re Dorr (Allen v. Forbes), 26 A. B. R. 408, 186 Fed. 276 (C. C. A. Mont.).

88. In re Dorr (Allen v. Forbes), 26 A. B. R. 408, 186 Fed. 276 (C. C. A. Mont.).

89. In re Norris, 26 A. B. R. 945, 190 Fed. 101 (D. C. Minn.).

ant in a former composition arrangement made before bankruptcy.[90] Likewise, as to a fraudulent claim where money was paid to the bankrupt on a pretended sale.[91]

Claims of those engaged with the bankrupt in a conspiracy to defraud creditors, of course are not to be allowed;[92] and are not allowable for any part.[93] And the proof of such conspiracy may be made from circumstantial evidence, even against positive affirmative testimony where such testimony is inherently improbable; and, to prove the existence of the conspiracy, it is only necessary to show, from circumstantial evidence, a mere tacit understanding among the parties to work to a common purpose.[94] A fraudulent transferee's claim for the rent of fraudulently conveyed property, upon the transfer being set aside, has been disallowed.[95] So, also, as to a mortgage given for the purpose of hindering, delaying, or defrauding the bankrupt's creditors under circumstances which are sufficient to put the mortgagee on inquiry.[97] So, as to claims purchased for the purposes of perpetrating a fraud on the rights of the creditors.[98]

Nor may the creditor recover on quasi contract, the contract itself being illegal.[99]

An agreement whereby a corporation promised to repurchase its capital stock in violation of local law, to refund to the claimant the purchase price of the stock bought by him should he wish to withdraw from the corporation, will not sustain a claim against the corporation's estate in bankruptcy.[1] So, as to a claim for the price of stock illegally purchased by a corporation.[2]

90. Instance, Batchelder & Lincoln Co. v. Whitmore, 10 A. B. R. 641, 122 Fed. 355 (C. C. A. Mass.): instance, In re Chaplin, 8 A. B. R. 121, 115 Fed. 162 (D. C. Mass.).

91. In re Lanshaw, 9 A. B. R. 167, 118 Fed. 365 (D. C. Mo.).

92. In re Friedman, 21 A. B. R. 213, 164 Fed. 131 (D. C. Wis.).

93. In re Friedman, 21 A. B. R. 213, 164 Fed. 131 (D. C. Wis.).

94. In re Friedman, 21 A. B. R. 213, 164 Fed. 131 (D. C. Wis.). Instance of proof of conspiracy to defraud, Pratt v. Columbia Bank, 18 A. B. R. 406, 157 Fed. 137 (D. C. N. Y.).

95. In re Hurst, 23 A. B. R. 554 (Ref. W. Va.).

97. In re Thoratt, 29 A. B. R. 84, 199 Fed. 319 (D. C. Ga.).

98. In re Kyte, 25 A. B. R. 337, 182 Fed. 166 (D. C. Pa.), quoted at § 800.

99. In re Tichenor-Grand Co., 29 A. B. R. 409, 203 Fed. 720 (D. C. N. Y.): "However, the creditor asserts that even though the contract was illegal he may recover in quasi-contract. This I must say seems to me quite impossible. The very purpose of making the contract illegal is to prevent the shareholder from taking money out of the corporate treasury. It would be an absurd result to allow him to do it in another way. All cases which allow a recovery by contract implied in law, do so for reasons of equity, to prevent the defendant from unjustly retaining what should go to the plaintiff. It would be quite paradoxical to declare illegal a contract because the corporation should in justice retain its capital for its creditors and not distribute it among shareholders, when in the next breath one directed the corporation to pay over the same capital to shareholders because it was unjust for the corporation longer to retain it. No authority based upon a transaction between a corporation and third parties has any application when the real question turns upon the priority of creditors to shareholders, as here."

1. Allen v. Commercial Nat. Bank, 27 A. B. R. 33, 191 Fed. 97 (C. C. A. Mich.); In re Tichenor-Grand Co., 29 A. B. R. 409, 203 Fed. 720 (D. C. N. Y.) quoted at § 805½.

2. In re Sapulpa Produce Co., 26 A. B. R. 900 (Ref. Okla.).

So, as to claims for compensation for alleged services rendered to a corporation by one of its officers.[3]

The fact that the claimant loaned the bankrupt money which belonged to the claimant's minor children, does not affect the validity of the claim.[4]

§ 803½. Non-Compliance with Statutory Prerequisites for "Doing Business" or "Maintaining Suit."

—It has been held that a claim of a foreign corporation which has failed to comply with certain statutory requirements before "doing business" within the State will not be allowed.[5]

On the other hand, it has also been held that State statutes prohibiting parties from instituting or maintaining suits until they have complied with certain registry or deposit requirements, have no applicability to suits in the federal courts; the federal court accepting the substantive rights of parties as it finds them by State law, but itself determining what shall be prerequisite to the maintenance of suits in its own forum.[6]

§ 804. Claims by Customers against Bankrupt Stockbroker.

—Claims by customers against a bankrupt stockbroker buying and selling stock on margins, are provable and the relation is held in some cases not to be fiduciary but to be that of debtor and creditor, and to be on implied contract;[7] and in other cases to be that of pledgor and pledgee,[8] or bailor and bailee, and the latter seems now to be the established rule.[8a]

---

3. In re McCarthy, etc., Co., 28 A. B. R. 45, 196 Fed. 247 (D. C. N. J.).

4. In re American Specialty Co., 27 A. B. R. 463, 191 Fed. 807 (C. C. A. N. Y.).

5. In re Montello Brick Works, 20 A. B. R. 855, 163 Fed. 621 (D. C. Pa.); In re Montello Brick Works, 23 A. B. R. 374, 375, 174 Fed. 498 (C. C. A. Pa.).

6. See post, § 1753¾. Also, see In re Dunlop, 19 A. B. R. 361, 156 Fed. 945 (C. C. A. Minn.).

7. In re Gaylord, 7 A. B. R. 577, 113 Fed. 131 (D. C. Mo.).

And preferences must be surrendered, as in case of other creditors. In re Gaylord, 7 A. B. R. 577, 113 Fed. 131 (D. C. Mo.); impliedly, but obiter, In re Topliff, 8 A. B. R. 141, 114 Fed. 323 (D. C. Mass.); contra, Richardson v. Shaw, 16 A. B. R. 842, 147 Fed. 659 (C. C. A. N. Y.).

And the right of set-off also exists. In re Topliff, 8 A. B. R. 141, 114 Fed. 323 (D. C. Mass.).

And the contract may be broken by the bankruptcy of the broker. In re Pettingill & Co., 14 A. B. R. 729, 137 Fed. 143 (D. C. Mass.); In re Swift, 7 A. B. R. 374, 112 Fed. 315 (C. C. A. Mass., affirming 5 A. B. R. 335), the court saying "where a man has disabled himself from performing his contract,

it is unnecessary to make any request or demand for performance."

And the date of the filing of the bankruptcy petition fixes the amount of damages. In re Pettingill & Co., 14 A. B. R. 729, 131 Fed. 143 (D. C. Mass.); In re Swift, 7 A. B. R. 374, 112 Fed. 315 (C. C. A. Mass., affirming 5 A. B. R. 335); In re Graff, 8 A. B. R. 745, 117 Fed. 343 (D. C. N. Y.). Compare In re Neff, 19 A. B. R. 23, 157 Fed. 57 (C. C. A. Ohio).

8. In re Bolling, 17 A. B. R. 399 (D. C. Va.); Richardson v. Shaw, 16 A. B. R. 842, 147 Fed. 659 (C. C. A. N. Y.); In re Berry & Co., 17 A. B. R. 467, 149 Fed. 176 (C. C. A. N. Y.).

Conversion of Shares of Stock by Broker.—In re Graff, 8 A. B. R. 744, 117 Fed. 343 (D. C. N. Y.); In re Floyd, Crawford & Co., 15 A. B. R. 277 (Ref. N. Y.); In re Swift, 9 A. B. R. 385, 118 Fed. 348 (D. C. Mass.); In re Bolling, 17 A. B. R. 399 (D. C. Va.); In re Berry & Co., 17 A. B. R. 467, 149 Fed. 176 (C. C. A. N. Y.).

Claims on Contracts to Purchase Stock Where Buyer Becomes Bankrupt.—Phenix Nat. Bank v. Waterbury, 20 A. B. R. 140, 123 App. Div. 453, 108 N. Y. Supp. 391, quoted at § 690.

8a. Compare post, § 1313; also see Richardson v. Shaw, 209 U. S. 365, 19 A. B. R. 717 (affirming 16 A. B. R. 876, 147 Fed. 59); also see Thomas v. Tag-

Claims for money left with brokers, who later become bankrupt, for the purchase of shares of stock, but which the brokers wrongfully convert, are valid claims; and probably are such though left for the purpose of buying stock on margin, since any illegality attaching to the contract would simply excuse nonperformance of the contract and would not permit the detention of the money itself from its rightful owner.[9]

And the burden rests on the trustee to prove illegality, not on the claimant to prove legality; especially, "strict proof" is not to be required of the claimant.[10]

So, a claim for margins paid to the proprietor of a bucket shop may be recovered where such recovery is permitted by local law.[11]

§ 805. Unpaid Stock Subscriptions.—Claims against a bankrupt stockholder for unpaid stock subscription are valid in bankruptcy.[12]

§ 805½. Rescission of Stock Subscription or Purchase Where Corporation Is, or Becomes, Bankrupt.—After bankruptcy of a corporation it has been held to be too late, as against creditors, to rescind a subscription for fraud and misrepresentation and to prefer a claim for moneys paid, even though the fraud be not discovered before.

Scott v. Abbott, 20 A. B. R. 335, 160 Fed. 573 (C. C. A. Mo.): "From the foregoing summary of the main and essential facts we find ourselves confronted with the following question of law: Whether persons who have been induced by false statements of the officers of a corporation to innocently purchase some of its preferred stock, and who for a year or more have accepted dividends declared quarterly upon the stock purchased by them, may, after discovering the falsity of the statements made, and after a state of insolvency and actual bankruptcy of the corporation has supervened, repudiate their purchases, and participate in the assets of the insolvent estate pro rata with general creditors who innocently contracted their debts on the strength of the validity of the increase of stock and of the additional resources which appellants and others similarly situated have reasonably caused them to believe the corporation possessed? Ordinarily it is true that any person who has been deceived by false and material statements of another into making a contract with him may, by timely action and observance of other equitable principles, rescind the same and recover back money paid in its performance. And this is ordinarily true when individuals make contracts with corporations. The executive officers of the corporations, acting within the scope of their general authority, may so misrepresent material facts as to entitle persons dealing with them to rescind their contracts. But is there nothing in the present case which differentiates it from such cases? Appellants have admittedly been for some time and now are prima facie stockholders of the shoe com-

gart, 209 U. S. 385, 19 A. B. R. 710 (affirming In re Berry, 17 A. B. R. 468, C. C. A. N. Y.).

9. West v. McLaughlin Co., 20 A. B. R. 654, 162 Fed. 124 (C. C. A. Mich.); In re Dorr (Allen v. Forbis), 26 A. B. R. 408, 186 Fed. 276 (C. C. A. Mont.).

10. West v. McLaughlin Co., 20 A. B. R. 654, 162 Fed. 124 (C. C. A. Mich.).

11. Streeter v. Lowe, 25 A. B. R. 774, 184 Fed. 263 (C. C. A. Mass.).

12. Hays v. Wagner, 18 A. B. R. 163 (C. C. A. Ohio).

Bankruptcy as Breach of Contract to Purchase Corporate Stock.—In re Neff, 19 A. B. R. 23, 157 Fed. 57 (C. C. A. Ohio).

pany, and nothing else. They have from the beginning allowed themselves to be held out as such. The real party against which they are seeking relief is the body of general creditors of their corporation. Whatever relief may be granted to them in this case will reduce the percentage which the general creditors will ultimately realize upon their claims. Although a corporation is in law treated as an entity separate from its component stockholders, the latter are, in substance, all there is to a corporation. They, by their duly chosen agents, conduct all its business. They enjoy the net earnings which is the final object and purpose of a manufacturing and business corporation. They own all the assets, but own the same subject to a well-recognized prior right of creditors thereto. * * * In view of the foregoing facts and principles the rights of the innocent general creditors are superior to those of the deceived stockholders. It is a familiar, general principle of law, as well as of morals, that when one of two innocent parties must suffer by the fraud of another, the one who has enabled such third party to commit the fraud ought to sustain the loss. * * * ' While it is there assumed, without commitment, however, that a stockholder may, by proper proceedings, instituted in good faith and in due time before the suspension of a bank, secure a rescission of his contract of subscription for fraud practiced upon him by the officers, yet the case affords direct authority for what we deem to be a just and practical general rule: That when one has for a considerable period of time prior to the failure of a corporation occupied the position of one of its stockholders, and exercised and enjoyed the rights, privileges, and fruits of that relation, including the chance of enhanced value of his holdings, when fortune frowns, and the chances turn against him, it is too late to assert, as against creditors of the corporation, the right to rescind his contract of stock subscription on the ground of false representations after a state of insolvency has supervened, and after proceedings to wind up the corporation for the benefit of creditors have been or are about to be instituted. * * * A case involving the foregoing elements inevitably discloses such want of diligence, such delay or inactivity, or such counter-equities in favor of creditors as within well-recognized principles precludes resort to a court of equity for redress by a defrauded stockholder. The rule just announced has not been established without opposition and vigorous dissent, but we think it is now so firmly fixed as to command general obedience."

Nor may a stockholder exercise his right under a secret agreement made by the corporation at the time of the purchase of the stock to repurchase it.[13]

In re Tichenor-Grand Co., 29 A. B. R. 409, 203 Fed. 720 (D. C. N. Y.): "It is no doubt quite true that courts have at times enforced contracts for the re-purchase of corporate stock when the condition or option was part of the original subscription as here, Ophir Consolidated Mines v. Bryntesen, 143 Fed. 829. The trustee says that the case involved only treasury stock, but there is no evidence that it was paid up, nor did the court in any sense rely upon such an assumption. Moreover, if a corporation which supposes itself solvent may buy its own stock (In re Castel Braid Co. [D. C. N. Y.], 17 Am. B. R. 143, 145 Fed. 224), I can see no reason why it may not buy it from an original subscriber under an option of re-sale originally reserved to him. I must say that all such rights appear to me to be quite contrary to a reasonable protection of creditors unless they are limited to purchases which leave the original capital intact, i. e., purchases from surplus, because they necessarily

13. In re Owen Pub. Co., 20 A. B. R. 639 (Ref. N. Y.).

result in keeping up the appearance of a capital which has been actually depleted. If a corporation has received property into its treasury of the value of its authorized shares, that is no doubt subject to the vicissitudes of its enterprises, which will be represented by public knowledge of its success or of the value of its shares. If, however, it purchases its own shares, this affects neither the value of the other shares, the success of its enterprises, nor the amount of its apparent share capital. It is merely a method of secret distribution against the deceit of which its creditors have absolutely no means of protection. The fund which they have the right to rely upon has been surreptitiously taken from them. It seems to me very little relief against the evils which such a right causes to limit it to cases where the corporation is thought to be solvent. It is a strange thing, I think, that there have been cases which permit the practice, which seems to me to be inevitably mischievous commercially." Quoted further at § 803.

But, of course, a purchaser of corporate stock, who, prior to the bankruptcy of the corporation, has repudiated the sale, offered to surrender his certificates, and demanded the purchase price paid therefor, may prove a claim against the corporation's estate in bankruptcy for such purchase price with interest thereon from the date of the rescission; providing, of course, that such rescission was, because of the corporation's fraud, justified.[14]

§ 806. Also Claims for Money Deposited with Bankrupt Banks.—
Also claims of the public for moneys deposited with the bankrupt.[15]

§ 807. Claims for Commissions for Taking Orders.—
The claims of agents for commissions for taking orders are allowable in bankruptcy, if valid by the State law.[16]

§ 808. Claims by County for Hire of Convict Labor.—
Claims by the county for the hire of convict labor are allowable against the estate of a bankrupt contractor.[17]

§ 809. Annual Subscription to Mercantile Agency Reports.—
Annual subscriptions to mercantile agencies' reports are allowable claims even though a large portion of the unexpired year still remains.[18]

§ 810. Claims on Old Concern's Debts Where Business Taken Over.
—A corporation organized for the purpose of taking over the assets of a partnership, and carrying on its business at the same place and composed of the same persons, to whom all its stock is issued, is liable for the debts of the partnership, even though they were not expressly assumed by the writings transferring the assets to it.[19]

---

14. Davis *v.* Louisville Trust Co., 25 A. B. R. 621, 181 Fed. 10 (C. C. A. Ky.).

15. In re Salmon & Salmon, 16 A. B. R. 626 (D. C. Mo.); In re Smart, 14 A. B. R. 672, 136 Fed. 974 (D. C. Ohio).

16. In re Ladue Tate Mfg. Co., 14 A. B. R. 235, 135 Fed. 910 (D. C. N. Y.).

17. In re Wright, 2 A. B. R. 592, 95 Fed. 807 (D. C. Mass., affirmed in 4 A. B. R. 496).

18. In re Buffalo Mirror & Beveling Co., 15 A. B. R. 122 (Ref. N. Y.); In re Glick, 25 A. B. R. 871, 184 Fed. 967 (D. C. N. Y.).

19. Du Vivier *v.* Gallice, 17 A. B. R. 557, 149 Fed. 118 (C. C. A. N. Y.). Sale by insolvent corporation to re-

On the other hand, where a corporation which had been organized upon the failure of another corporation and had taken over its assets in great part, though not entirely, gave a note to take up a note of the old corporation, the note was held in one case invalid for lack of consideration, the two sets of stockholders not being identical and no assumption of debts having been made.[20]

§ 810⅓. **Corporations with Same Stockholders.**—That the stockholders of two separately chartered corporations are identical; that one is a shareholder in the other, and that they have mutual dealings, will not, as a general rule, merge them into one corporation, or prevent the enforcement by one of an otherwise valid claim against the other.[21]

§ 810¼. **Partner's Claim for Excess Contribution.**—A partner's claim for excess of contribution to the partnership enterprise is both a provable debt and an allowable claim; [22] although it is not entitled to share in partnership assets until after satisfaction of firm debts, on the marshaling of firm and individual estates in bankruptcy.[23]

§ 810⅜. **Claims of One Bankrupt Estate against Another.**—The Act in § 57 (m) provides that "the claim of any estate which is being administered in bankruptcy against any like estate may be proved by the trustee and allowed by the court in the same manner and upon like terms as the claims of other creditors."[24]

§ 810½. **Offsets.**—Claims against which the trustee holds valid offsets are allowable only for the balance due. This is the converse of the proposition that the "Right of Offset and Counterclaim" is unimpaired, discussed post, § 1170, et seq., for of course the claim of the trustee against the claimant is pro tanto an asset. But it has been held that where a stockholder in a bankrupt corporation owes a balance on his stock at the time of the bankruptcy and has also a claim against the bankrupt for money loaned,

organized corporation composed of bondholders and directors held fraudulent. In re Medina Quarry Co., 24 A. B. R. 769, 182 Fed. 508 (D. C. N. Y.).

20. In re Stanford Clothing Co., 26 A. B. R. 124, 187 Fed. 172 (D. C. Ala.).

21. In re Watertown Paper Co., 22 A. B. R. 190, 169 Fed. 252 (C. C. A. N. Y.). But compare, on analogous proposition, "Consolidation of Partnership, Corporation and Individual Petitions," ante, § 304½. Also, compare germane proposition, "Ignoring Fiction of Corporate Entity," § 1225½.

Officers Pledging Bonds as Collateral—Rights of Subsequent Purchaser of Secured Debt.—In re Watertown Paper Co., 22 A. B. R. 190, 169 Fed. 252 (C. C. A. N. Y.).

22. In re Rice, 21 A. B. R. 205, 164 Fed. 509 (D. C. Pa.); In re Pangborn, 26 A. B. R. 40, 185 Fed. 673 (D. C. Mich.).

Presented by Administrator of Deceased Partner. In re Pangborn, supra.

23. In re Rice, 21 A. B. R. 205, 164 Fed. 509 (D. C. Pa.).

24. Instance, In re Milne, Turnbull & Co., 26 A. B. R. 10, 185 Fed. 244 (C. C. A. N. Y.); instance (trustee himself becoming bankrupt, preference charged in later bankruptcy against former estate as creditor). Block, Tr. v. Rice, Tr., 21 A. B. R. 691, 167 Fed. 693 (D. C. Pa.). Compare also, § 1313½.

for which he holds notes of the bankrupt, he cannot be permitted to share in a dividend until he pays his liability for the balance of the stock issued to him.[25]

§ 810¾. **Miscellaneous Claims.**—Claims for royalties, where not in the nature of penalties but for liquidated damages have been held allowable.[26]

A claim for expenses and commissions incurred by a trustee under a deed of trust before the bankruptcy, has been refused allowance as not coming within the enumeration of § 63.[27] But this is doubtful law if the trustee was appointed under a valid deed of trust executed by the bankrupt; for it was then surely a claim upon a contract.

A claim for goods sold to the bankrupt for cash, but wrongfully obtained by the bankrupt from the carrier without payment, is for conversion and is provable.[28]

A note given for a loan of money with which to effect a composition with creditors before the bankruptcy, is a valid claim.[29]

A bankrupt declined to carry out a contract to purchase land and the owner obtained a decree for specific performance, whereupon the bankruptcy occurred; later the trustee quitclaimed the land to the original owner, who, though accepting the deed, subsequently presented his claim for the deficit of his decree for the purchase price after deduction of the value of the land, but the court disallowed the claim on the ground that the acceptance of the quitclaim deed effected a union of the legal and equitable estates in the original owner and extinguished the claim.[30]

Fire insurance premiums, where the policy has not been assumed by the trustee and has terminated at the filing of the bankruptcy petition are only allowable for the amount owing at the date of filing.[31]

25. In re Standard Dairy & Ice Co., 20 A. B. R. 321 (Ref. D. C.). Also, see post, § 1185.

26. In re Bevier Wood Pavement Co., 19 A. B. R. 462, 156 Fed. 583 (D. C. N. Y.).

27. In re Standard Dairy & Ice Co., 20 A. B. R. 321 (Ref. D. C.).

28. Clingmam v. Miller, 20 A. B. R. 360, 160 Fed. 326 (C. C. A. Kans.).

29. In re Bennett Shoe Co., 20 A. B. R. 704, 162 Fed. 691 (D. C. Conn.).

30. In re Davis, 24 A. B. R. 667, 179 Fed. 871 (D. C. Pa.).

31. In re Hibbler Mach. Sup. Co., 27 A. B. R. 612, 192 Fed. 741 (D. C. N. Y.).

CHAPTER XXV.

Allowance, Disallowance and Re-Examination of Claims.

Synopsis of Chapter.

DIVISION 1.

DIVISION 1.

JURISDICTION AND PARTIES.

§ 811. Allowance, Disallowance and Reconsideration of Claims.
—Claims may be allowed, disallowed and reconsidered.[1]

§ 812. "Provisional" Allowance, for Voting, etc.—It would seem,
on principle that claims may not be allowed "provisionally" to permit credit-

---

1. Bankr. Act, § 2 (2): "That the courts of bankruptcy * * * are hereby invested * * * with such jurisdiction * * * to * * * (2) allow claims, disallow claims, reconsider allowed or disallowed claims, and allow or disallow them against bankrupt estate."

Bankruptcy Act, § 57 (k): "Claims which have been allowed may be reconsidered for cause and reallowed or rejected in whole or in part, according to the equities of the case, before, but not after, the estate has been closed."

In re Syracuse Paper and Pulp Co., 21 A. B. R. 174, 164 Fed. 275 (D. C. N. Y.), quoted at § 817. In re Harst, 23 A. B. R. 555 (Ref. W. Va.).

ors to vote;[2] that they must either be allowed or disallowed absolutely; at any rate, that the annexing of the term "provisionally" to the order of allowance is without legal effect.

Clendening *v.* Nat'l Bk., 11 A. B. R. 245 (Sup. Ct. N. Dak.): "The contention that the allowance was temporary, and merely to enable the defendant to vote at the creditors' meetings, likewise contradicts the legal effect of the order of allowance.'

To same effect, In re Malino, 8 A. B. R. 205, 118 Fed. 368 (D. C. N. Y.): "The referee overruled the objections, offering to consider them later, and accepted the proofs of claims objected to as presented and a trustee was elected thereupon. I think the proceedings were erroneous. The right of creditors to select a trustee is a substantial one, and it does not rest in the discretion of the referee to allow claims as voting bases when objections are made, which are apparently genuine. While the selection of a trustee can not be tied up indefinitely by obstructive tactics, which are obviously for the purpose of delay, and in proper cases provisional allowances or disallowances may be made in order that a trustee may be expeditiously selected; nevertheless, the proceeding should not be so summary as to exclude the consideration of all objections. Objecting creditors, and the bankrupt are entitled to a hearing upon the objections for the purpose of determining, at least, whether they are honestly made and there is reasonable ground for their consideration. These facts being established, the claims should not be allowed for the purpose of voting."

Compare obiter, In re Evening Standard Pub. Co., 21 A. B. R. 156, 164 Fed. 517 (D. C. N. Y.): "Claims should not be voted where duly verified legal objections are filed thereto. Of course, the referee may proceed to take proof, and if the objecting party cannot produce sufficient evidence to sustain them he will allow the claim. If the objecting party shows legal cause for delay for the purpose of producing evidence not at hand, the referee may in some cases allow the claim for voting purposes; but a better practice is to proceed to an election on the allowed claims, if the condition of the estate demands prompt action. If so many verified objections, apparently valid are filed, that an election by creditors is impossible, let the referee appoint."

But there is quite a line of authorities to the contrary, holding that an allowance may be made, temporarily, where a hearing on the objections would unduly prolong the election of a trustee.[3]

In re Milne, Turnbull & Co., 20 A. B. R. 248, 159 Fed. 280 (D. C. N. Y.): "This argument raises the very vexed question as to how far the referee is bound to go in the liquidation and allowance of claims before proceeding to the election of a trustee. In this case he did proceed so far as to ascertain that the proofs left him in doubt as to whether the largest creditor of the bankrupt was a preferred creditor. The only decision in this district is In re Malino (D. C.), 8 Am. B. R. 205, 118 Fed. 368, and it is there held that 'in proper cases provisional allowances or disallowances may be made in order that a trustee may be expeditiously selected.' This ruling is hardly consistent with that in Re Columbia Iron Works (D. C.), 14 Am. B. R. 526, 142 Fed. 242. If such provisional allowances cannot be made by a referee in doubt after the objecting creditor has had an opportunity of examining the bankrupt

---

2. See post, § 865.

3. In re Kelly Dry Goods Co., 4 A. B. R. 528, 102 Fed. 747 (D. C. Wis.),

quoted at § 865. Instance, In re Harper, 23 A. B. R. 918, 175 Fed. 412 (D. C. N. Y.). Also see ante, § 579½.

(as is the case here), the only other possible course where the largest claim in the estate is attacked is to defer the election of a trustee until intricate questions both of fact and law have been settled before the referee and by the District Court. It seems to me that such practice would be intolerable, and the necessary evil of receiverships unnecessarily increased. In this case the burden was upon the objecting creditors to establish by a fair preponderance of testimony that Kessler & Co. were preferred creditors. They were unable to do this to the satisfaction either of the referee or myself after a prolonged hearing. They have only succeeded in suggesting a series of questions which will require for elucidation an exhaustive examination of transactions between the Milne firm and the Kessler firm extending over many months, if not several years; and I think the referee was right, after twice adjourning the election and then affording an opportunity to the objecting creditors to examine the bankrupt in support of their objection, in provisionally allowing the Kessler vote for an amount much smaller than the probable deficit in collateral, and in holding that because the objection of preference had not been sustained by a fair preponderance of evidence it should be provisionally overruled. The election is confirmed, and the petition of review dismissed."

§ 813. Procedure Where Claim "Duly Proved" and Not Objected to.

—If the claim is "provable," that is, belongs to one of the classes mentioned in § 63, of the Act, as being "provable" claims, and is also "duly proved," that is, correct in form, the court (in practice, the referee) must, upon its presentation or receipt, "allow" the claim, that is, enter an order, permitting it to share in dividends, unless it is objected to by proper parties or unless, for good cause, the referee of his own motion postpones the allowance.[4]

Compare, In re (James) Dunlop Carpet Co., 22 A. B. R. 788, 171 Fed. 532 (D. C. Pa.): "Was the bank's claim 'duly proved?' Not, was it definitely and finally proved, but was it sufficiently proved, prima facie, so as to require its allowance unless objection * * * be made by parties in interest."

It is good practice to make these allowances at some creditors meeting, so that interested parties might be present.

Obiter, In re (James) Dunlop Carpet Co., 22 A. B. R. 788, 171 Fed. 532 (D. C. Pa.): "Ordinarily—I do not say necessarily—it (the order of allowance) should be performed at some meeting of creditors, when the act may be done with a certain degree of publicity."

Of course, a claim may be allowed in part, and disallowed in part, where that action is warranted by the proofs.

In re Goldstein, 29 A. B. R. 301, 199 Fed. 665 (D. C. Mass.): "The petitioner for review contends that the referee ought to have disallowed the proof altogether, but that, instead of doing so, he 'amended it of his own volition

---

4. Bankr. Act, § 57 (d): "Claims which are duly proved shall be allowed, upon receipt by or upon presentation to the court, unless objection to their allowance shall be made by parties in interest, or their considera-

tion be continued for cause by the court upon its own motion."
Of course, in cases of secured claims the court will first determine the value of the securities held, see ante, § 759, et seq.

and reduced it to the amount of $1,700,' and that he had no right to allow it for $1,700 without requiring it to be resworn. If this contention is sound, a proof of claim must be regarded as an entirety, which the court must either accept in full or reject altogether. I find nothing in the Act which requires me so to regard it. There are express provisions in § 57, cls. 'k' and 'l,' for the reallowance or rejection 'in whole or in part' of a claim reconsidered after allowance. But it is not only upon reconsideration that objections to a claim, either by parties in interest or by the court of its own motion, may be dealt with. Clauses 'd' and 'f' of § 57 provide for the hearing and determination of such objections before allowance, and I am unable to believe it a necessary result of clauses 'k' and 'l' that the original allowance of a claim can only be for its full amount, and may not be for a part of that amount. To say that this is what the act requires, and that a claim, of which a part, but not the whole, is sustained by the proof, must be amended and resworn before it can be allowed at all, would be, in my opinion, a departure, unwarranted by anything in the act, from the recognized principle that the practice regarding proof of claims is to be liberal and free from technicalities."

Obiter, In re (James) Dunlop Carpet Co., 22 A. B. R. 788, 171 Fed. 532 (D. C. Pa.): "Ordinarily—I do not say necessarily—it (the order of allowance) should be performed at some meeting of creditors, when the act may be done with a certain degree of publicity."

§ 814. Where Claim Not "Duly Proved."

§ 814. Where Claim Not "Duly Proved."—If the claim is not "duly proved," that is to say, if the affidavit for proof of debt be not correct in form,[5] or if the claim on its face is not a provable claim, that is to say, if it be not one of those mentioned in § 63, the referee should not "allow" the claim.

Orr v. Park, 25 A. B. R. 544, 183 Fed. 683 (C. C. A. Ga.): "If the allegations of the proof do not set forth all the necessary facts to establish a claim, or are self contradictory, the claim may be disallowed; or the referee may unquestionably order proper and legitimate inquiries into the fairness and legality of such claim, that he may be enabled to pass on it intelligently and judicially."

And the referee should not allow it even though no party in interest objects.[5a]

In re Goble Boat Co., 27 A. B. R. 48, 190 Fed. 92 (D. C. N. Y.): "A referee is not justified in allowing a claim against an estate in bankruptcy when the proofs do not comply with the statute or general orders promulgated by the Supreme Court, whether creditors or the trustee raise specific objections to the sufficiency of the proofs filed or not. It is the duty of the referee to examine the proofs filed and see that they are sufficient. As a rule a majority of the creditors of a bankrupt cannot afford to go to the expense of employing an attorney to attend and examine the claims filed, and the duty rests on the referee before allowing a claim to see that the proofs filed comply with the statute and general orders."

5. In re Coventry Evans Furn. Co., 22 A. B. R. 272, 171 Fed. 673 (D. C. N. Y.), quoted at § 603; In re Goble Boat Co., 27 A. B. R. 48, 190 Fed. 92 (D. C. N. Y.).

5a. Compare post, § 830, Also see, inferentially In re Cannon, 14 A. B. R. 114, 133 Fed. 837 (D. C. Pa.).

On the contrary, the court should disallow the claim, without prejudice to a refiling when "duly proved," or the proof may be withdrawn by the claimant.

In re Sumner, 4 A. B. R. 124, 101 Fed. 224 (D. C. N. Y.): "The meaning of this subdivision is that, if objection be interposed, or the court be not satisfied with the prima facie case thus made, the claim shall not be accepted as proven, until disposition shall have been made of such objection, or, if the court continue the consideration, until the court shall be convinced of its validity."

And, if a claim which has not been "duly proved," has, nevertheless, been allowed, the order of allowance may be vacated.[6]

§ 815. To Be "Allowed" on Presentation or Receipt—No Motion nor Pleading Requisite.

—The claim, if on its face provable and duly proved, and if it be not objected to by parties nor be postponed by the court, must be "allowed" upon "presentation" or "receipt," and no further motion nor pleading is requisite than the mere presentation or receipt of the deposition for proof of debt, the deposition being itself both the pleading and the evidence, and other pleading being unauthorized.[7]

In re Sumner, 4 A. B. R. 124, 101 Fed. 224 (D. C. N. Y.): "This section provides both the method of presenting the claim and the evidence necessary, in the first instance, to sustain it. The 'statement under oath,' if it contain the matter pointed out, is at once the claimant's pleading and his evidence, and makes for him a prima facie case."

§ 816. Court on Own Motion, Postponing Allowance.

—The court (referee) may, however, even though no party objects and the claim be "duly proved," postpone the allowance, "for cause."[8] What will constitute "cause" under this section is not defined.[9]

§ 816½. Allowance in Compositions before Adjudication.

—The Amendment of 1910, permitting compositions before adjudication of bankruptcy, provides for a meeting of creditors for the allowance of claims, thus impliedly authorizing the allowance of claims before adjudication of bankruptcy.[9a]

§ 817. Reconsideration of Claims.

—Claims which have been allowed may be reconsidered, for cause, and reallowed or rejected, in whole or in

---

6. In re Coventry Evans Furn. Co., 22 A. B. R. 272, 171 Fed. 673 (D. C. N. Y.), quoted at § 603.

7. In re Carter, 15 A. B. R. 126, 138 Fed. 846 (D. C. Ark.); In re Shaw, 6 A. B. R. 499, 109 Fed. 780 (D. C. Pa.).

8. Bankr. Act, § 57 (d).

9. Compare ante, § 579½.

9a. Bankr. Act 12a, as amended in 1910: "* * * in compositions before adjudication, the bankrupt shall file the required schedules and thereupon the court shall call a meeting of creditors for the allowance of claims, etc." See also, §§ 593½, 2358, et seq.

part.[10]   And a petition for re-examination may be presented at any time prior to the closing of the estate.[11]

In re Syracuse Paper and Pulp Co., 21 A. B. R. 174, 164 Fed. 275 (D. C. N. Y.): "But the allowance of a claim is not final; for if, at a later time, it is desired to open it and try out its validity, it can be done." Quoted further at § 838.

§ 818. Objection and Disallowance.—Claims may be objected to by parties in interest and be disallowed.[12]

In re Sully & Co., 18 A. B. R. 124 (C. C. A. N. Y.): "It is true that the trustee in bankruptcy was about to bring an action against them to recover a considerable sum of money, and it is argued that their defense will be seriously prejudiced by the adjudication in the bankruptcy proceeding, fixing the amount of the claims of the Cotton Exchange creditors. However this may be, they are not parties in interest in the proceeding itself in any legal sense, or within the meaning of the Bankruptcy Act. It is not enough that their rights may be incidentally affected by the proceeding. The term 'parties in interest' applies to those who have an interest in the res which is to be administered and distributed in the proceeding and does not include those who are merely debtors or alleged debtors of the bankrupt."

Objections may be filed at any time before the allowance of the claim.[13]

§ 818½. Counterclaim and Offset.—The trustee is entitled to file objections by way of counterclaim or offset.[14]

§ 819. Before Election of Trustee, Either Bankrupt or Creditor Proper Party.—Before the election of a trustee, either the bankrupt or any creditor may object to a claim, or may petition for its re-examination.[15] Thus, any creditor may object;[16] or the bankrupt may object.

In re Ankeny, 4 A. B. R. 72, 100 Fed. 614 (D. C. Iowa): "I concur in the ruling of the referee that the bankrupt may move to set aside and expunge the

---

10. Bankr. Act, § 57 (k): "Claims which have been allowed may be reconsidered for cause and reallowed or rejected in whole or in part, according to the equities of the case, before but not after the estate has been closed."
Bankr. Act, § 57 (k) and Gen. Order No. XXI (6) have reference to claims against the bankrupt that were in existence when the petition was filed and not to claims against the estate for expenses of administration, such as a receiver's account. Such expenses, if objectionable, should be promptly objected to and exception filed when the question is raised before the referee. In re Reliance Storage & Warehouse Co., 4 A. B. R. 49, 100 Fed. 619 (D. C. Penna.).
In re Hurst, 23 A. B. R. 554 (Ref. W. Va.); In re Effinger, 25 A. B. R. 924, 184 Fed. 725, 728 (D. C. Md.).
Thus, the court may diminish or expunge an allowed claim unless the claimant pays to the trustee the value of certain property of the estate which the claimant wrongfully converted to his own use. In re W. A. Paterson Co., 25 A. B. R. 855, 186 Fed. 629 (C. C. A. eighth circuit).

11. In re Globe Laundry, 28 A. B. R. 831, 198 Fed. 365 (D. C. Tenn.); In re Canton, etc., 28 A. B. R. 791, 197 Fed. 767 (D. C. Md.).

12. Bankr. Act, § 57 (d); In re Greenfield, 27 A. B. R. 427, 193 Fed. 98 (D. C. Pa.).

13. In re Two Rivers, etc., Co., 29 A. B. R. 518, 199 Fed. 877 (C. C. A. Wis.).

14. See post, § 1203; In re Harper, 23 A. B. R. 918, 175 Fed. 412 (D. C. N. Y.).

15. Bankr. Act, § 57 (d) and (k).

16. Impliedly, In re Lafferty, 10 A. B. R. 290, 122 Fed. 558 (D. C. Pa.).

allowance of an alleged claim. In the absence of any enactment in the statute, it might well be held that it was the duty of the bankrupt to object to the allowance of unjust or fictitious claims against his estate, which, if allowed, would decrease the dividend coming to the creditors. The theory of the act is that the bankrupt entitled himself to a discharge by yielding up his non-exempt property to be divided among his creditors, but a bankrupt would not be acting in good faith, nor would he be carrying out the true spirit of the act, if he knowingly permitted false or unjust claims to be allowed, to the injury of his actual creditors. By clause 7 of § 7 of the act, it is declared to be the duty of the bankrupt, in case any person proves a false claim against his estate, to disclose the fact immediately to his trustee. In the present case no trustee has been appointed. This fact precludes giving notice to the trustee, but it does not justify the allowance of the false claim, nor prevent the bankrupt from objecting to the proof thereof."

§ 820. **Others May Not Object.**—Parties, other than the bankrupt, who are not creditors may not be heard on the hearing of contested claims against the estate;[17] and it has been held that a creditor, before his standing as such has been established by the allowance of his own claim, may not object to the allowance of others;[18] although the true rule would seem to be simply that he must prove he is a creditor, and that this proof may be supplied either by the order of allowance or otherwise, it being remembered always that the deposition for proof of debt is itself to be taken as prima facie proof.[19]

The rule, whatever may be its limitations, does not exclude the bankrupt, for it is one of the bankrupt's duties to object to erroneous claims.[20]

§ 821. **Thus, Neither Receiver nor Debtor of Bankrupt.**—The rule enunciated in the preceding paragraph would exclude the receiver. And would also exclude debtors of the bankrupt.[21]

§ 822. **Creditors' Motive in Objecting Immaterial.**—But simply that a creditor is making the objection in reality for the benefit of a debtor or other person not himself entitled to make the objection, is immaterial. The creditor has a clear legal right and his motive is of no consequence.[22]

---

17. Dressel v. North State Lumber Co., 9 A. B. R. 541, 119 Fed. 531 (D. C. N. Car.); In re Pittsburg Zinc Co. Consol., 28 A. B. R. 880, 198 Fed. 316 (D. C. Mo.).

18. Dressel v. North State Lumber Co., 9 A. B. R. 541, 119 Fed. 531 (D. C. N. Car.).

19. Compare inferentially, and obiter [claim of objecting creditor not yet allowed], In re Evening Standard Pub. Co., 21 A. B. R. 156, 164 Fed. 517 (D. C. N. Y.): "Tyner had the right, at the first meeting, as an alleged creditor to file verified objections to the claims of other alleged creditors."

20. Bankr. Act, § 7 (a) (3). Also see In re Ankeny, 4 A. B. R. 72, 100 Fed.

614 (D. C. Iowa); compare analogously, Griffin v. Mutual Life Ins. Co., 11 A. B. R. 622, 119 Ga. 664 (Sup. Ct. Ga.); contra, In re Levy, 7 A. B. R. 56 (Ref. N. Y.).

21. In re Sully, 15 A. B. R. 304, 142 Fed. 895 (D. C. N. Y., reversed on the facts in 18 A. B. R. 123).

22. Before the election of a trustee it has been held creditors may not raise the defense of usury, for such defense is purely personal to the bankrupt: the trustee, however, may make the defense, for he succeeds to all the bankrupt's rights. In re Worth, 12 A. B. R. 566, 130 Fed. 927 (D. C. Iowa). But this is doubtful law, for the trustee's title reverts to the adjudication.

In re Sully & Co., 18 A. B. R. 125 (C. C. A. N. Y.): "The petitioners are creditors to the amount of over $3,700, and their interest in the result of a re-examination is clear. It is doubtless true that they would not have intervened merely in order to protect themselves, and that they were mainly, and perhaps solely, influenced by a desire to assist Hawley and Ray. But if they had reasonable grounds for asserting the rights secured to them by the Bankrupt Act, whether they chose to do so for their own advantage or for that of third persons is quite immaterial. The element of motive cannot prejudice the assertion of a clear legal right or statutory privilege. They have been deprived of the right reserved to them by § 57, merely because they would have been willing to forego it, or would not have asserted it, if they had not been moved by friendly consideration for Hawley and Ray. This was a matter which concerned only themselves. There was nothing censurable in the motive which induced them to proceed. Indeed, if they believed that unfounded or exaggerated claims of certain other creditors were to be used by the trustee and those creditors to the harm of Hawley and Ray, they were commendable in lending the latter their assistance. As their application was a legitimate one, we see no reason why it should be denied upon a consideration of motive"

§ 823. Expense of Contesting Claims to Control Election of Trustee, Not Chargeable against Estate.

—The expense of the contest of a claim made in the effort to control the election of a trustee are not chargeable against the estate.[23]

§ 824. After Trustee Elected, All Objections, etc., to Be by Him or in His Name.

—After the election and qualification of the trustee, all objections and applications for re-examination of claims should be taken by the trustee or in the trustee's name.[24]

In re Lewensohn, 9 A. B. R. 368, 121 Fed. 538 (C. C. A.): "* * * The act is silent as to the party by whom a re-examination may be moved.

"The trustee represents every creditor. The orderly conduct of the administration requires that a proceeding for the re-examination of the claims should be taken in the interests of all the creditors, and not be permitted at the instance

---

23. In re Worth, 12 A. B. R. 566, 130 Fed. 927 (D. C. Ia.); compare, to same effect, In re Fletcher, 10 A. B. R. 398 (D. C. N. Y.); Inferentially, In re Mercantile Co., 2 A. B. R. 419, 95 Fed. 123 (D. C. Mo.).

24. See dissenting opinion in Ayres v. Cone, 14 A. B. R. 739, 138 Fed. 783 (C. C. A. S. Dak.), the dissenting opinion undoubtedly stating the correct rule. See analogously, as to summary order on bankrupt, In re Rothschild, 5 A. B. R. 587 (Ref. Ga.); apparently contra, obiter, In re Carter, 15 A. B. R. 126, 138 Fed. 846 (D. C. Ark.); impliedly, In re Sully & Co., 18 A. B. R. 123 (C. C. A. N. Y.); In re Koenig v. Van Hoogenhuyze, 11 A. B. R. 619, 127 Fed. 891 (D. C. Tex.); obiter, In re Carton & Co., 17 A. B. R. 349 (D. C. N. Y.); analogously (plenary suit to recover property), In re Bailey, 18 A. B. R. 226 (D. C. Pa.); inferentially, Chatfield v. O'Dwyer, 4 A. B. R. 313, 101 Fed. 797 (C. C. A. Ark.); compare, In re Little River Lumber Co., 3 A. B. R. 682, 101 Fed. 558 (D. C. Ark.); compare, In re McCallum, 11 A. B. R. 447, 127 Fed. 768 (D. C. Pa.); compare facts in In re Stover, 5 A. B. R. 250, 105 Fed. 355 (D. C. Pa.), and in In re Linton, 7 A. B. R. 676 (Ref. Penn.). Here, however, it does not appear whether a trustee had been elected or not nor (in the case, In re Linton, at any rate) whether the applications were for re-examination of claims already allowed or objections thereto before allowance. Contra, inferentially, McDaniel v. Stroud, 5 A. B. R. 689, 106 Fed 486 (C. C. A. S. Car.). Obiter, In re Roadarmour, 24 A. B. R. 49, 177 Fed. 379 (C. C. A. Ohio).

of any one creditor unless demanded by the interests of all. If the trustee should without sufficient reason refuse to proceed, the court by its order could compel him to do so, or remove him for disobedience. It has been held under the present act that a creditor cannot prosecute an appeal from the judgment of a court of bankruptcy allowing the claim of another creditor, and that the trustee is the only party who can do so. Chatfield *v.* O'Dwyer, 4 Am. B. R. 313, 101 Fed. 797; Foreman *v.* Burleigh, 6 Am. B. R. 230, 109 Fed. 313. The provision allowing such appeals does not designate the party by whom they may be prosecuted, and these decisions proceeded upon the ground that the trustee is the proper party and the only proper party, because he represents the interests of all creditors in the estate. There is such a close analogy between the two proceedings of a re-examination and a review that these decisions are apposite.

"The court below was of the opinion that the proceeding was authorized by General Order 21, clause 6. That part of Order 21, which is pertinent, reads as follows:

" 'When the trustee or any other creditor shall desire the re-examination of any claim filed against the bankrupt's estate, he may apply by petition to the referee to whom the case is referred for an order for the re-examination, and thereupon the referee shall make an order fixing a time for hearing the petition, of which due notice shall be given by mail addressed to the creditor.'

"This regulates the procedure for re-examination without regard to the party by whom or the time when it may be pursued, and does not purport to confer any right or privilege beyond these expressly or impliedly given by the act. The court below seems to have construed the language as though it were intended to permit the trustee or any creditor to apply by petition 'whenever he may desire to do so.' Thus read it would permit a re-examination after the estate had been closed, and this clearly could not have been intended because it is forbidden by clause k of § 8. It may be given due effect by reading it as authorizing a petition by a creditor at the appropriate stage of the proceeding when it may be desirable for the creditor to intervene. The word 'desire' is used in the sense of 'intend.' It may become desirable and necessary to re-examine a proved claim prior to the qualification of the trustee, as delays frequently ensue in the election and qualification of this officer, and it might be that evidence would be lost in the meantime. This probably was within the contemplation of the General Order, but we cannot believe it was within its intention to permit the trustee and creditors concurrently to pursue a re-examination of a claim, or to permit a creditor to do so when the trustee for sufficient reasons does not approve, or when in the interests of all it is desirable that the trustee should conduct the proceeding."

In re (Narciso) Ferrer, 22 A. B. R. 785, 162 Fed. 139 (D. C. Porto Rico): "We think, though, that after the trustee is appointed, he is the proper person to contest all claims against the estate because he represents all of the creditors in representing the estate."

In re Sully & Co., 15 A. B. R. 321, 142 Fed. 895 (D. C. N. Y.): "The trustee alone is authorized to institute proceedings for the re-examination and expunging of claims."

In re Mexico Hardware Co., 28 A. B. R. 736, 197 Fed. 650 (D. C. N. Mex.): "The trustee for the estate, although duly selected and qualified at the date of these several proceedings, does not appear in either instance. Can either of these proceedings be prosecuted by a general creditor? The authorities are all to the effect that this cannot be done, but that a proceeding either for a reconsideration of a claim by the referee or a review of the referee's rulings by the court must be prosecuted by the trustee. This rule may seem technical. and yet it is based on the soundest principles of procedure. If it be conceded that any creditor aggrieved by the referee's ruling may move against it, either before him or before the court, the result may be such a succession of motions or petitions as to be practically interminable. The policy of the Bankruptcy Act, which is designed to speedy conclusion of insolvency cases, is that any such proceeding shall be prosecuted by the trustee, who represents all of the creditors, rather than by such individual creditors."

Contra, inferentially, In re Roche, 4 A. B. R. 369, 101 Fed. 956 (C. C. A Tex.): "Under this statute (1867) there was strong reason for contending that an appeal from a judgment allowing a claim could only be made by an assignee dissatisfied therewith. The Act of 1898 is silent as to the party who may take an appeal on the allowance or disallowance of the claim. The omission of the provision above quoted from the Act of 1867 is significant, and we are of opinion that the intention of the lawmakers was, not to restrict the right of appeal, but to leave in force the general rule that, where an appeal lies from any judgment or decree, the same may be taken by any party or person injured or affected by the decree or judgment. The record in this case shows that the appellant, as a creditor of the bankrupt, is directly interested in the judgment complained of, not only as a general creditor of the bankrupt, but as having a special lien on the sum in the hands of the trustee."

Contra, In re Hatem, 20 A. B. R. 470, 161 Fed. 895 (D. C. N. Car.): "The only question argued here is, 'Can an unsecured creditor object to the proof of claim by another unsecured creditor?' there being a receiver and a trustee in bankruptcy, and it not being shown the trustee has been applied to and refused to act. The general doctrine is that, where there is a trustee, cestui que trust must act through or by the trustee, and when they assume to act in propria personæ they must show the trustee has, upon application duly made to him, refused to act. This is not 'new' law, but old, well-settled law. It has been so held time out of memory. Where a trustee or any creditor shall desire the examination of a claim filed against the bankrupt estate, he may apply by petition to the referee for an order for such examination. Where a trustee has been appointed, he must file the petition for re-examination of a creditor's claim, and not another creditor. * * * But does this rule obtain in bankruptcy? Is there not a statutory provision to the contrary? Section 57d * * * provides: 'Allowance of Claims—Claims which have been duly proved shall be allowed, upon receipt by or upon presentation to the court, unless objection to their allowance shall be made by parties in interest,' etc. True, the trustee is a party in interest; but this provision for objection to their allowance by parties in interest clearly indicates the purpose of Congress to abrogate the rule as to proceedings in bankruptcy, and provides for objections being made by parties in interest, other creditors."

And prior objections filed by creditors are superseded by those of the trustee.[25]

§ 825. Creditor May Not Have Re-Examination of His Own Claim on Disallowance, Though Rehearing Not Forbidden.

—And a creditor probably is not permitted to apply for a re-examination of his own claim

---

25. In re Harper, 23 A. B. R. 918, 175 Fed. 412 (D. C. N. Y.); and the proper practice is to have the trustee substituted for the creditor therein.

upon disallowance, his proper practice being to petition for review of the order of disallowance.[26] But of course the court has the discretion to grant him a rehearing, under the usual rules.

§ 826. On Trustee's Refusal, He May Be Ordered, etc., or Creditor or Bankrupt May Proceed.

—On refusal of the trustee for insufficient reasons to proceed, he may be ordered to do so.[27]

Obiter, Ohio Valley Bank v. Mack, 20 A. B. R. 40, 163 Fed. 155 (C. C. A. Ohio): "This appeal is by a creditor who was, upon application, allowed to appeal, the trustee refusing to appeal though requested to do so. This practice seems admissible in the sound discretion of the district judge when the trustee refuses to appeal, though the better practice would be to order the trustee to appeal or to allow the dissatisfied creditor to appeal in his name, being indemnified in either case against costs by such creditors."

Obiter, In re Syracuse Paper & Pulp Co., 21 A. B. R. 174, 164 Fed. 275 (D. C. N. Y.): "True, the trustee represents the creditors, and this reopening of a claim is done by the trustee; but if a creditor, one or more, makes a prima facie case, and asks the trustee to take measures for the opening of the claim, and he refuses, an appeal to the referee or court would effect the desired result, and perhaps result in the removal of the trustee."

And the trustee may be removed for noncompliance with the order.[28]

In re Stern, 16 A. B. R. 513, 144 Fed. 956 (C. C. A. Iowa): "* * * if he refuses to oppose a claim or to move for its reconsideration when he ought to do so, he may be compelled to act or to permit the objecting creditors to act in his name."

Or the creditor may himself proceed;[29] or the bankrupt may proceed;[30] in which events it is proper that the reasonable expense of a successful resistance should be paid out of the estate.[31]

---

26. Obiter, In re Chambers, Calder & Co., 6 A. B. R. 707 (Ref. R. I.); In re Mexico Hardware Co., 28 A. B. R. 736, 197 Fed. 650 (D. C. N. Mex.).

27. McDaniel v. Stroud, 5 A. B. R. 685, 106 Fed. 486 (C. C. A. S. Car.); Chatfield v. O'Dwyer, 4 A. B. R. 313, 101 Fed. 797 (C. C. A. Ark.); analogously, In re Lewensohn, 9 A. B. R. 368, 121 Fed. 538 (C. C. A.); obiter, In re Carton & Co., 17 A. B. R. 349 (D. C. N. Y.); analogously, In re Bailey, 18 A. B. R. 226 (D. C. Pa.); In re (Narciso) Ferrer, 22 A. B. R. 785, 162 Fed. 139 (D. C. Porto Rico). Obiter, In re Roadarmour, 24 A. B. R. 40, 177 Fed. 379 (C. C. A. Ohio).

For an instance where the court refused to entertain a motion made by the bankrupt for an order upon the trustee to institute such proceedings, see, In re Levy, 7 A. B. R. 56 (Ref. N. Y.). But compare, inferentially,

contra, Griffin v. Mut. Life Ins. Co., 11 A. B. R. 622, 119 Ga. 664.

28. In re Lewensohn, 9 A. B. R. 368, 121 Fed. 538 (C. C. A.); In re Syracuse Paper and Pulp Co., 21 A. B. R. 174, 164 Fed. 275 (D. C. N. Y.), quoted at § 826.

29. In re Sully & Co., 18 A. B. R. 120 (C. C. A. N. Y.); In re Little River Lumber Co., 3 A. B. R. 682 (D. C. Ark.); McDaniel v. Stroud, 5 A. B. R. 685, 106 Fed. 486 (C. C. A. S. C.); analogously, In re Bailey, 18 A. B. R. 226 (D. C. Pa.); Ohio Valley Bank Co. v. Mack, 20 A. B. R. 40, 163 Fed. 155 (C. C. A. Ohio), quoted, supra. Obiter, In re Roadarmour, 24 A. B. R. 49, 177 Fed. 379 (C. C. A. Ohio).

30. Obiter, In re Carton & Co., 17 A. B. R. 349 (D. C. N. Y.).

31. In re Little River Lumber Co., 3 A. B. R. 682, 101 Fed. 558 (D. C. Ark.).

And the court may require the creditor to indemnify the trustee against costs and expenses.[32]

But compare, In re Baird, 7 A. B. R. 448, 112 Fed. 960 (D. C. Pa.): "It is certainly not the duty of a trustee to litigate every question that may be called to his notice by the creditors, however frivolous or apparently lacking in support it may be. On the other hand, he should not be permitted, by requiring indemnity in every instance against the costs and expenses of a suit to cast the risk of controversy upon the particular creditor who may request to undertake it."

Or to pay the costs if unsuccessful.[33]   And, of course, this rule does not require the trustee to contest claims unless he believes the objections to be proper.

In re Ferrer, 22 A. B. R. 785, 162 Fed. 139 (D. C. Porto Rico): "It is not intended by the views herein expressed that the trustee or referee shall be obliged at the instance of contentious counsel or contentious bankrupts or individual creditors, to contest or move for reconsideration of any or every claim against the estate unless such officers believe that the application has merit."

It is the duty of the referee to enquire into the merits of any application by a creditor or the bankrupt for an order on the trustee to contest a claim.[34]

§ 827. If Creditor Proceeds, Should Use Trustee's Name.

—In such cases, however, the proper practice would be for the creditor to use the trustee's name, by leave of court;[35] although he has been held entitled to reimbursement in a case where it appears he did not use the trustee's name but proceeded in his own name.[36]   And a creditor and the trustee may, by formal entry, adopt the objections filed by the bankrupt before the election of a trustee and need not file new objections.[37]

---

32. In re Bailey, 18 A. B. R. 226, 151 Fed. 953 (D. C. Pa.); obiter, Ohio Valley Bk. Co. v. Mack, 20 A. B. R. 40, 163 Fed. 155 (C. C. A. Ohio), quoted, supra. Obiter, In re Roadarmour, 24 A. B. R. 49, 179 Fed. 377 (C. C. A. Ohio).
33. In re Sully & Co., 18 A. B. R. 126 (C. C. A. N. Y.); Chatfield v. O'Dwyer, 4 A. B. R. 313, 101 Fed. 797 (C. C. A. Ark.).
34. In re (Narciso) Ferrer, 22 A. B. R. 785, 162 Fed. 139 (D. C. Porto Rico).
35. McDaniel v. Stroud, 5 A. B. R. 685, 106 Fed. 486 (C. C. A. S. C.); In re Sully & Co., 18 A. B. R. 126 (C. C. A. N. Y.); In re Bailey, 18 A. B. R. 226 (D. C. Pa.).
36. In re Little River Lumber Co., 3 A. B. R. 682, 101 Fed. 558 (D. C. Ark.).
37. Contra, Ayres v. Cone, 14 A. B. R. 739, 138 Fed. 778 (C. C. A. S. Dak.), but the able and dissenting opinion

of Sanborn, J., in this case undoubtedly states the true rule.
It has been held, that a trustee and also a creditor might institute a joint proceeding, upon a joint petition against several creditors. As to trustee, see In re Lyon, 7 A. B. R. 61 (D. C. N. Y.); as to creditor, In re Linton, 7 A. B. R. 676 (Ref. Penn.).
This practice is improper and leads to confusion, since different defenses are involved and creditors are entitled to separate hearings. It does not save a "multiplicity of suits" but provokes a multiplicity of objections for the consideration of a court of review. The rule laid down by Chancellor Kent is clearly distinguishable. Different preferences received by different creditors at different times and different places and in different amounts are not "connected" within the meaning of Chancellor Kent. The only connection is the uniformity of legal principles in-

§ 828. Though but One Creditor in Position to Object, Yet Trustee May Object.—Where only one or less than all of the creditors is in a position to object to the claim, nevertheless the trustee succeeds to such creditor's defense and may urge it, even if the creditor himself does not urge it.

Instance, In re Royce Dry Goods Co., 13 A. B. R. 267, 133 Fed. 100 (D. C Mo.): "When this claim was presented for allowance, the wronged creditors unquestionably had the right to object thereto on the ground that the claimant was estopped to deny the truth of his representations. If so why may not the trustee for them?"

But it hardly seems correct to hold that where a claim is good as against all the other creditors and is bad only as to the one, yet that it may be thrown out altogether. A better rule it would seem would be to make it the subject of a special order in the distribution, and adjust the priorities in the dividends in accordance with the respective equities;[38] and postpone such claimant's dividend, or subject it to such creditor's claims.[39]

§ 829. Creditor Holding Special Defense, Yet May Not Object in Own Name.—It is doubtful whether the creditor holding the special defense may object to the allowance of the claim, but at any rate he may, on distribution, have the dividend on such claim subjected to his own claim.[40]

DIVISION 2.

PLEADING AND PROCEDURE ON OBJECTIONS TO CLAIMS AND ON RE-EXAMINATION OF ALLOWED CLAIMS.

§ 830. Objections for Lack of Form or "Provability," Not Necessarily in Writing.—Objections to claims on the ground that they are not provable as being not among the enumerated classes of provable debts or that they are not duly "proved," as being defective in the form of affidavit, need not be made in writing, if the proof of claim shows the fault on its face. An oral intimation to the court is sufficient and the court may and should act without any motion.[41]

§ 831. Objections for Substance Properly in Writing.—Objections to claims for matters of substance ought, by the better practice, to be in writing, although there is no statutory requirement to that effect, nor any rule nor form of the Supreme Court requiring it.[42]

---

volved and the necessity of proving the bankrupt's insolvency in each case. These do not constitute a connected series of acts.

38. See post, § 2133, et seq., subject of "Marshaling of Priorities in Dividends."

39. Obiter, In re Royce Dry Goods Co., 13 A. B. R. 627, 133 Fed. 100 (D. C. Mo.).

40. But compare, In re Royce Dry Goods Co., 13 A. B. R. 267, 133 Fed. 100 (D. C. Mo.).

41. Compare ante, § 814. Also see In re Goble Boat Co., 27 A. B. R. 48, 190 Fed. 92 (D. C. N. Y.), quoted ante, § 814. Inferentially, In re Cannon. 14 A. B. R. 114, 133 Fed. 837 (D. C. Pa.).

42. See, inferentially, In re Wooten, 9 A. B. R. 247, 118 Fed. 670 (D. C. N.

In re Royce Dry Goods Co., 13 A. B. R. 257, 133 Fed. 100 (D. C. Mo.): "There is nothing in the Act or rules in bankruptcy directing the form of such objections. They should be in writing."

Compare, to same effect, In re Linton, 7 A. B. R. 676 (Ref. Penn.): "Objections to proofs of claims should be set forth in the form of a petition for review."

Compare, inferentially to same effect, In re Syracuse Paper & Pulp Co., 21 A. B. R. 174, 164 Fed. 275 (D. C. N. Y.): "The objections were not verified or reduced to writing. Evidently they were made at random and for purposes of delay. * * * The referee, in the absence of verified objections, and in the absence of any offer of evidence to sustain the oral objections made, overruled the objections in most instances and proceeded to obey the statute, which is imperative that the trustee shall be elected or appointed by the creditors at their first meeting. * * * I do not doubt that it is competent for the referee to adjourn this first meeting of creditors for a reasonable time, and from time to time when necessary, and in a proper case it is his duty so to do. But when it is apparent, as it was here, that certain attorneys in their own interest take it upon themselves to orally object to all, or substantially all, claims presented which may be voted against their nominee for trustee, and fail to file written and verified objections, or to offer then and there some evidence tending to support those made, and it is apparent that to try out the validity of such unsupported oral objections would unduly postpone the election of a trustee or trustees, it is the duty of the referee to obey the spirit and letter of the law and proceed with the election of a trustee. Any other course in such a case should not be tolerated. It is quite true that the creditors are to elect the trustee; but it is also true that at the first meeting they are to perform this duty, and that they should come prepared to act with reasonable expedition, and that these matters should not be dragged along on mere oral objections to verified claims apparently valid, and which are conceded by the bankrupt to be valid. And verified claims, presumptively valid, and which are entitled to probative force, which in effect prove themselves, should not be held up or denied allowance or participation in the election of trustees on mere oral objections in any case, unless some written evidence is placed before the court tending to impeach their validity, or some oral evidence is offered at the time having that tendency, or it is made to appear that such evidence exists, but cannot be then obtained and presented."

Compare, In re Cannon, 14 A. B. R. 114, 133 Fed. 837 (D. C. Penna.): "A preliminary question is raised by the refusal of the referee to sustain the objection of the claimants' counsel to the examination of the witnesses, 'because no formal exception to the claim has been filed by the trustee.' This position is based upon the assumption that the trustee must put his objections in writing before the claim can be attacked by testimony or other evidence. No doubt it is desirable that the trustee's objections shall be clearly and distinctly stated in advance of the investigation, so far as this may be possible in order that the claimant may know what he is called upon to meet. But this information may be communicated to him in several ways; the trustee's objections may be noted by the stenographer, as was the case in In re Shaw, 6 Am. B. R. 499, 109 Fed. 780; or they may be stated orally, as was done in the

Car.); Orr v. Park, 25 A. B. R. 544, 183 Fed. 683 (C. C. A. Ga.), quoted on other points at § 814. But compare, contra (where "precise amount disputed from the first") Embry v. Bennett, 20 A. B. R. 651, 162 Fed. 139 (C. C. A. Ky.).

instance now under consideration, if the referee permits this course to be pursued; or they may be filed in writing, this being the method which the claimants insist upon as the exclusive method. Undoubtedly, the last-named practice has obvious advantages, and should be followed as a rule, wherever practicable, but the Bankrupt Act does not require objections to be always in writing, § 57d directing the allowance of claims that have been duly proved, 'unless objection to their allowance should be made by parties in interest, or their consideration be continued for cause by the court upon its own motion.' The manner of making such objections is thus left open, and should, I think, be largely committed to the discretion of the referee. It is conceivable, that while a trustee might have enough information to justify him in entering objection to a particular claim upon a ground which he might be able to state in general terms, he might not have information sufficiently precise to permit him to file specific objections in advance of the hearing; and I think it would be going too far to require him to make an attempt that could only result in failure. Whatever will give sufficient preliminary information to the claimant concerning the character of the trustee's objection, is, I think, all that can fairly be required, especially when this is afterwards supplemented, as in the present case, by specific objections in writing."

It has been held in some cases that the objections need not be under oath;[43] and that, in the discretion of the court, need not even be in writing, but may be stated orally;[44] but the better rule is that they should be under oath,[45] and be in writing.

§ 832. Each Claim, Properly, to Be Separately Objected to.—It is undoubtedly the better practice not to join in one pleading objections to different claims.

Impliedly, Ohio Valley Bank Co. v. Mack, 20 A. B. R. 40, 163 Fed. 155 (C. C. A. Ohio): "Neither are the six claims in question to be treated en masse. Each claim must stand upon its own bottom and is to be judged by the evidence which tends to prove or disprove it."

The same objections may not be applicable to all; the same evidence may not be requisite; and on review the record would be inconveniently voluminous.

Yet it has been held that objections to different claims may be set forth in one pleading.

In re Linton, 7 A. B. R. 676 (Ref. Penn.): "Any number of creditors can properly be named in the same petition, but each should be served with a copy of the petition, and a copy of the order made to appear and show cause why their claims should not be reduced in amount or expunged." This may have been a case of re-examination of claims already allowed rather than objection thereto before allowance.

Objections may be by way of off-set or counterclaim.[46]

43. In re Wooten, 9 A. B. R. 247, 118 Fed. 670 (D. C. N. C.).
44. In re Cannon, 14 A. B. R. 114, 133 Fed. 837 (D. C. Penna.); Embry v. Bennett, 20 A. B. R. 650, 162 Fed. 139 (C. C. A. Ky.).

45. Impliedly, In re Evening Standard Pub. Co., 21 A. B. R. 156, 164 Fed. 517 (D. C. N. Y.), quoted at § 812.
46. Compare post, § 1203. In re Harper, 23 A. B. R. 918, 175 Fed. 412 (D. C. N. Y.), quoted at § 837.

§ 833. Objections to Be Specific.

—The objections should be specific;[47] and undoubtedly should follow the usual rules of pleading—pleading and denying allegations of fact, and not being indefinite.

§ 834. Amendment of Objections Permissible.

—Amendment of objections may be permitted.[48] The proper practice is for the proposed amendment to be presented along with the application;[49] and if it fails to allege facts sufficient to constitute a valid objection to the claim, leave to file the amendment may be refused.[50]

§ 835. Overruling Trustee's Motion to Dismiss Claim for Failure to Make Prima Facie Case.

—On overruling the trustee's motion, made at the close of the claimant's case, to disallow the claim on the claimant's own proof, it is error to proceed as if the case had been entirely submitted and to allow the claim. Opportunity should then be given to the trustee to support his objections with evidence;[51] nor should the reviewing court allow the claim upon reversal of the referee's order of disallowance made at the close of the claimant's case, but should remand with instructions to hear trustee's evidence in support of the objections.

In re Livingston Co., 16 A. B. R. 385, 144 Fed. 971 (C. C. A. N. Y.): "We think this was error, because by such disposition of the cause the claim was allowed without any opportunity to the trustee to put in what proof he might be able to produce tending to controvert the case made by the claimant."

§ 836. Petition for Re-Examination.

—Where the re-examination of a claim once allowed is desired, a petition for an order expunging the claim should be filed.[52]

But where objections to the allowance of claims have been filed by creditors, and are treated as a petition for re-consideration, the proceedings

---

47. In re Royce Dry Goods Co., 13 A. B. R. 257, 133 Fed. 100 (D. C. Mo.): "Should be sufficiently explicit to indicate to the claimant the nature and character thereof."

48. In re Royce Dry Goods Co., 13 A. B. R. 257, 133 Fed. 100 (D. C. Mo.). Here to conform the objections to the proof.

49. Analogously, Knapp & Spencer v. Drew, 20 A. B. R. 355, 160 Fed. 413 (C. C. A. Neb.).

50. Compare, analogously, to this effect Johnson v. Anderson, 11 A. B. R. 294, 70 Neb. 233, quoted at § 1770½.

51. Inferentially, In re Livingston Co., 16 A. B. R. 385, 144 Fed. 971 (C. C. A. N. Y.).

52. Rule XXI (6) of the Supreme Court's General Orders in Bankruptcy: "When the trustee or any creditor shall desire the re-examination of any claim filed against the bankrupt's estate, he may apply by petition to the referee to whom the case is referred for an order for such re-examination, and thereupon the referee shall make an order fixing a time for hearing the petition, of which due notice shall be given by mail addressed to the creditor. At the time appointed the referee shall take the examination of the creditor, and of any witness that may be called by either party, and if it shall appear from such examination that the claim ought to be expunged or diminished, the referee may order accordingly."

Compare, to same effect, In re Linton, 7 A. B. R. 676 (Ref. Penn.); inferentially, and obiter, In re Docker-Foster Co., 10 A. B. R. 584, 123 Fed. 190 (D. C. Pa.).

thereon will not be disturbed for irregularity, unless, possibly, it should appear that prejudice resulted.[53]

§ 837. To Be Specific, and Sufficiency Tested in Usual Way.—The

petition for re-examination should be specific. The sufficiency or insufficiency of the allegations may be tested in the usual manner of procedure.

In re Harper, 23 A. B. R. 918, 175 Fed. 412 (D. C. N. Y.): "These objections must be tested by the same rules as would apply to a complaint, setting up a cause of action."

Thus, a motion for a more specific statement is proper to cure indefiniteness in the pleading.[54]

§ 838. Good Cause to Be Shown.—Good cause must be shown, however, for setting aside an order of allowance before the court will reconsider the claim.[55]

Compare, inferentially, to same effect, In re Smith, 2 A. B. R. 648 (Ref. N. Y.): "The better practice, when application is made to increase or decrease the sum at which a claim has previously been allowed, is to vacate the former order of allowance, and allow the claim at the new amount as if then moved for the first time."

What is necessary to constitute good cause in such cases is not clear. At any rate facts sufficient to obtain a rehearing in accordance with the Federal Equity rules would, of course, be sufficient here.

In re George Watkinson Co., 12 A. B. R. 370 (D. C. Pa.): "Neither the terms of the act, nor the general orders, require the petitioner to aver facts which, if proved, would defeat the claim. It is only necessary, in my judgment, to aver facts which, if true, are a sufficient cause for the re-examination of the claim."
In re Syracuse Paper & Pulp Co., 21 A. B. R. 174, 164 Fed. 275 (D. C. N. Y.): "And it is the duty of the referee and judge to afford such a rehearing on a prima facie case." Quoted at §§ 817, 826.

In other words, the petition for re-examination need not be the final statement of the complete case, although of course probability of the existence of facts sufficient to defeat it must be shown in order to show "good cause."

§ 839. Creditor to Be Given Due Notice.—The creditor whose claim is attacked should be given due notice of the petition.[56] But such notice may

---

53. In re Canton, etc., Co., 28 A. B. R. 791, 197 Fed. 767 (D. C. Md.).
54. In re Ankeny, 4 A. B. R. 72, 100 Fed. 614 (D. C. Iowa).
55. In re Lorch & Co., 28 A. B. R. 784, 199 Fed. 944 (D. C. Ky.); In re Pittsburg Zinc Co. Consol., 28 A. B. R. 880, 198 Fed. 316 (D. C. Mo.).
Bankr. Act, § 57 (k): "* * * may be reconsidered for cause." In re Doty, 5 A. B. R. 58 (Ref. N. Y.).

But Perhaps Petition Should Set Up Facts Sufficient to Defeat Claim as Well as Merely to Show Good Cause. —The petition for re-examination, perhaps, should set up facts which, if proved, would defeat the claim; otherwise the re-examination would be vain.
56. In re Linton, 7 A. B. R. 676 (Ref. Penn.). Compare practice, as described in In re Doty, 5 A. B. R. 58 (Ref. N. Y.).

be waived by an appearance and participation in the proceedings.[57]

· § 840. Notice by Referee, and May Be by Mail.—The notice is to be given by the referee, not by the creditor nor trustee (unless otherwise ordered by the judge).[58] The notice may be by mail and notice by mail would be "due notice."[59]

§ 841. Creditor to File Answer.—The creditor should file an answer thereto, else the claim may be expunged pro confesso.

In re Docker-Foster Co., 10 A. B. R. 584, 123 Fed. 190 (D. C. Penn.): "Under the provisions of General Order No. 37, which extends the equity rules of the Supreme Court to proceedings in equity instituted for the purpose of carrying into effect the provisions of the Bankrupt Act, or for enforcing the rights and remedies given by it, failure to file an answer to a petition seeking to expunge a claim justifies a decree pro confesso under Rule 18, carrying the ordinary incidents and consequences of such a decree."

And where the time allowed a claimant to file an answer to a petition to expunge his claim expires without an answer being filed, an application for leave to file an answer, made after the trustee has presented all his testimony, is properly denied.[60]

In re (Lewis) Eck & Co., 18 A. B. R. 657, 153 Fed. 495 (D. C. Pa.): "It will be observed that the precise question before the court is, whether the referee was right in deciding that upon the facts stated he had no authority to allow the claimants to file an answer at the time when they asked leave so to do. In my opinion, this decision of the referee was correct. The claimants had ample opportunity to make defense to the petition; for, if the fifteen days originally allowed for this purpose had for any reason been insufficient, further time would no doubt have been granted upon cause shown either to the referee or to the court. It was only necessary that a prompt application should be made, but it was too late to ask for leave after the trustee's case had been put in, and the claimants were thus fully advised of the evidence which they were obliged to meet. To grant leave now—no unusual excuse being offered— would give them an undue advantage, which the court, no more than the referee, is disposed to allow them."

§ 842. Reconsideration Refused for Laches.—Reconsideration of an allowed claim will be refused where the trustee is guilty of laches.[61] The creditors laches in this respect may also be considered.[62] But, except for laches, a petition for re-examination may be presented at any time prior to the closing of the estate.[63]

---

57. Orr v. Park, 25 A. B. R. 544, 183 Fed. 683 (C. C. A. Ga.), quoted at § 814.

58. In re Stoever, 5 A. B. R. 250, 105 Fed. 355 (D. C. Pa.).

59. Rule XXI (6).

60. Compare, analogously, ante, § 553½ and post, § 858½.

61. In re Hinckel Brew Co., 10 A. B. R. 484, 123 Fed. 942 (D. C. N. Y.). In re Hamilton Furn. Co., 8 A. B. R.

588, 116 Fed. 115 (D. C. Pa.). In this case claims had been allowed and dividends paid thereon. Compare facts, In re Geo. Watkinson, 12 A. B. R. 370 (D. C. Pa.).

62. In re Pittsburg Zinc Co. Consol., 28 A. B. R. 880, 198 Fed. 316 (D. C. Mo.).

63. In re Globe Laundry, 28 A. B. R. 831, 198 Fed. 365 (D. C. Tenn.); In re Canton, etc., Co., 28 A. B. R. 791, 197 Fed. 767 (D. C. Md.).

§ 843. Burden of Proof—Original Order of Allowance, Prima Facie Case.

—The burden of proof rests on the party desiring the reconsideration of an order of allowance, for the original order of allowance establishes a prima facie case.[64] Before allowance the proof of debt makes a prima facie fase for the creditor.[65]

§ 844. Deposition for Proof of Debt Prima Facie Case for Claimant.

—The mere presentation of the duly verified and filed deposition for proof of debt makes a prima facie case, even when objected to, and must stand until the objector adduces evidence which authorizes the referee to expunge or reduce it.[66]

Whitney *v.* Dresser, 15 A. B. R. 326, 200 U. S. 535: "The only question warranting the appeal is whether the sworn proof of claim is prima facie evidence of its allegations in case it is objected to. It is not a question of the burden of proof in a technical sense—a burden which does not change whatever the state of the evidence—but simply whether the sworn proof is evidence at all.

"The Circuit Court of Appeals observed that the proof of claim warrants the payment of a dividend in the absence of objection, and, therefore, must have some probative force. In reply it is argued that what is done in default of opposition is no test of what is evidence when opposition is made; that a judgment may be entered on a declaration for want of an answer, yet a declaration is not evidence; that it is contrary to analogy to give effect to an ex parte affidavit, and that on general principles it is the right of any party against whom a claim is made to have it proved, not only upon oath, but subject to cross-examination.

"Notwithstanding these forcible considerations we agree with the Circuit

---

64. In re Howard, 4 A. B. R. 69, 100 Fed. 630 (D. C. Calif.); In re Doty, 5 A. B. R. 58 (Ref. N. Y.); In re Pittsburg Zinc Co. Consol., 28 A. B. R. 880, 198 Fed. 316 (D. C. Mo.). Compare, In re Osborne's Sons, 24 A. B. R. 65, 177 Fed. 184 (C. C. A. N. Y.).

65. Obiter, In re Doty, 5 A. B. R. 58 (Ref. N. Y.).

66. In re Doty, 5 A. B. R. 58 (Ref. N. Y.); In re Cannon, 14 A. B. R. 114, 133 Fed. 837 (D. C. Pa.); compare, In re Shaw, 6 A. B. R. 499, 109 Fed. 730 (D. C. Pa.); compare, inferentially, In re Wooten, 9 A. B. R. 247, 118 Fed. 670 (D. C. N. Car.); In re Creasinger, 17 A. B. R. 546, 145 Fed. 224 (Ref. Calif.); obiter, In re Jones, 18 A. B. R. 208 (D. C. Mich.); (1867) In re Saunders, 2 Lowell 441, 446, Fed. Cases 12,371; (1867) In re Felter, 7 Fed. 906; In re Harper, 23 A. B. R. 918, 175 Fed. 412 (D. C. N. Y.); In re McIntyre & Co., 24 A. B. R. 1, 174 Fed. 627 (C. C. A. N. Y.), quoted in this paragraph, on another point; In re C. M. Montgomery, 25 A. B. R. 431, 185 Fed. 955 (D. C. Tex.); Baumhauer *v.* Austin, 26 A. B. R. 385, 186 Fed. 260 (C. C. A. Ala., reversing on the facts In re

Baumhauer, 24 A. B. R. 750, 179 Fed. 966), quoted on other points at § 554½; obiter, In re Baumhauer, 24 A. B. R. 750, 179 Fed. 966 (D. C. Ala. reversed on the facts Sub. Nom. Baumhauer *v.* Austin, 26 A. B. R. 385, 186 Fed. 260, C. C. A.).

Some cases seem to indicate that the ordinary rules as to the introduction and weight of evidence and the conduct of trials prevail in the hearing of the objections to claims in bankruptcy. Thus it has been held that, in Pennsylvania, a claimant against the estate of a deceased bankrupt is not competent to testify in support of his claim although he is called by the trustee to testify concerning a transfer of property made to him by the bankrupt within four months preceding the adjudication. In re Shaw, 6 A. B. R. 499, 109 Fed. 780 (D. C. Penn.).

Thus it has been held that every creditor must establish his claim by a preponderance of the evidence if it is denied. In re Wooten, 9 A. B. R. 247, 118 Fed. 670 (D. C. N. C.); inferentially, In re Ladue Tate Mfg. Co., 14 A. B. R. 235, 135 Fed. 910 (D. C. N. Y.).

Court of Appeals. The prevailing opinion, not only in the Second Circuit, but elsewhere, seems to have been that way. * * * The alternative would be that the mere interposition of an objection by any party in interest, § 57d, would require the claimant to produce evidence. For if the formal proof is no evidence a denial of the claim must have that effect. If it does not, then the formal proof is some evidence even when there is testimony on the other side. The words of the statute suggest, if they do not distinctly import, that the objector is to go forward, and thus that the formal proof is evidence even when put in issue. The words are: 'Objections to claims shall be heard and determined as soon,' etc. Section 57f. It is the objection, not the claim, which is pointed out for hearing and determination. This indicates that the claim is regarded as having a certain standing already established by the oath. Some force also may be allowed to the word 'proof' as used in the Act. Convenience undoubtedly is on the side of this view. Bankruptcy proceedings are more summary than ordinary suits. Judges of practical experience have pointed out the expense, embarrassments and delay which would be caused if a formal objection necessarily should put a creditor to the production of evidence or require a continuance. Justice is secured by the power to continue the consideration of a claim whenever it appears there is good reason for it. We believe that the understanding of the profession, the words of the Act and convenient and just administration all are on the side of treating a sworn proof of claim as some evidence even when it is denied."

In re Dresser, 13 A. B. R. 747, 135 Fed. 495 (C. C. A. N. Y.): "We are dealing here with a statute, the primary object of which is to collect the property of the bankrupt speedily and divide it equally among his creditors. Analogies drawn from pleadings in actions at common law and in equity furnish little assistance in the interpretation of such a law. If the doctrine be once established that a proof of claim in bankruptcy is entitled to no greater weight than a complaint in an ordinary action at law the most serious results will follow. Any vindictive or contumacious creditor can, by filing objections, compel creditors to come from distant states and even from foreign countries to testify in support of their claims before a word of testimony impeaching their validity has been adduced. No one disputes that in the absence of objection the proof of claim stands as sufficient warrant for the payment of a dividend based thereon. It is not then a mere pleading, confessedly it possesses some probative force. This being so it is not easy to approve the logic which deprives it of all weight, as evidence upon the mere filing of an objection. If the appellant's contention be sustained an efficient administration of the law might, as we have seen, be made difficult, if not impossible. We see no reason or necessity for such an interpretation of the law. On the other hand a construction which requires the objector to offer some proof before subjecting the creditor to the expense and annoyance of presenting sustaining evidence seems to be in accord with the intent and purpose of the act and to present a simple, efficient and perfectly fair rule of procedure. In a vast majority of instances the claims of creditors are susceptible of the most simple verification. The trustee has the bankrupt's books at his disposal and can at any time call upon the bankrupt for assistance. In cases where exaggerated or fraudulent claims are filed there is no difficulty in ascertaining and proving facts sufficient to establish the true character of the claim, thus putting the claimant upon his proof.

"The subject was carefully examined in In re Sumner (D. C.), 4 Am. B. R. 123, 101 Fed. 224, and the conclusion was reached that under § 57 'a,' 'b,' 'd' and 'f' of the Act the objector, though not required to disprove the claim, must produce 'evidence whose probative force shall be equal to, or greater than, the evidence offered in the first instance by the claimant.' This, we think, is a correct statement of the law and is in accord with General Order 21 (6), 89 Fed. x, which seems to indicate that the claim must stand until evidence has been adduced which authorizes the referee to expunge or reduce it. See, also, In re Shaw (D. C.), 6 A. B. R. 499, 109 Fed. 780; In re Felter (D. C.), 7 Fed. 904, affirmed sub nom. Whitney v. Dresser, 15 A. B. R. 326, 200 U. S. 535."

In re Sumner, 4 A. B. R. 123, 101 Fed. 224 (D. C. N. Y.): "It is apparent from subdivision 'f' that the statute contemplates that, after the claimant has presented his claim in the prescribed manner, objection may be made, and that thereafter the question of the objection shall be taken up and decided. This does not mean that the burden of proof is upon the objector to disprove the claim, but that he shall produce evidence whose probative force shall be equal to, or greater than, the evidence offered in the first instance, by the claimant. The burden of proof is always upon the claimant, but the statute points out how he may meet it for the purpose of making a prima facie case; and further provides that a creditor, or other person entitled, may, by interposing objection, so relate himself to the record as to be able to give evidence in opposition to the claim. Therefore, if the creditor shall have complied with § 57a, by filing with the referee a statement under oath, he shall be entitled to have his claim accepted, unless from some circumstance the referee demands further evidence from him, or unless an objection is interposed, and such objection is followed by evidence offered by the objector, which shall overthrow the presumptive case made by the claimant."

In re Castle Braid Co., 17 A. B. R. 148 (D. C. N. Y.): "If they set forth all the necessary facts to establish the claim, and are not self-contradictory, prima facie, they establish the claim, even in the presence of objections, and the objector is then called upon to produce evidence and show facts tending to defeat the claim of probative force equal to that of the allegations of the proof of claim. The burden of proof is always on the claimant, but, as probative force is given to the allegations of the proofs of claim, and no probative force is given to the objections, this must be met, overcome, or at least equalized, by the objecting party. In short, if the proofs of claim state facts sufficient to make a prima facie case, and it is stated that there is no security, the referee is bound to allow the claim, unless evidence controverting such facts is given by the objecting party, or an offset or counterclaim thereto is proved or established, or it appears that security is held for the claim."

In re Carter, 15 A. B. R. 126, 138 Fed. 846 (D. C. Ark.): "The presentation of a claim in proper form duly verified except as to particulars which the court treats as waived presents a prima facie case in favor of the claimant upon which he has a right to rest and the burden of proof is upon the objectors."

In re Syracuse Paper & Pulp Co., 21 A. B. R. 174, 164 Fed. 275 (D. C. N. Y.): "The claims stood proved, and were entitled to allowance, unless met and overthrown by proof." Quoted, on other points, at §§ 826, 831.

In re Milne, Turnbull & Co., 20 A. B. R. 248, 159 Fed. 280 (D. C. N. Y.): "It is to be remembered that some probative force is to be given the sworn proof of claim. That proof negatived a preference, and the burden of proving a preference is therefore upon the creditors objecting on that ground to the voting power of the claim. To sustain that burden there was introduced in evidence an agreement," etc.

At any rate the probative effect of the deposition rests, without doubt, upon the rule that requires the claimants' personal presence for cross-examination, and it would seem proper to deny such deposition the effect of prima facie proof unless, with it, the claimant in person presents himself.[67]

At least if the prima facie case is overcome, then the claimant must proceed to establish his claim.

In re Baumhauer, 24 A. B. R. 750, 179 Fed. 966 (D. C. Ala., reversed on other points in Baumhauer *v.* Austin, 26 A. B. R. 385, 186 Fed. 260, C. C. A. Ala.): "If there be proof of facts sufficient to rebut the prima facie proof the referee should disallow the claim unless the claimant produces further evidence sufficient to establish his claim."

This rule in practical administration throws a great burden upon creditors and the trustee in bankruptcy, in objecting to claims. They are obliged thereby frequently to prove a negative—that goods, for instance, were never sold, or never delivered or never paid for; thus reversing the usual rules of evidence in the trial of cases and making bankruptcy procedure unnecessarily peculiar and perplexing.

Let the instance of the claim of a relative for money borrowed be taken. The claimant introduces his deposition into evidence and rests. Now, what must the trustee or objecting creditors do? Their oath to their written objections is not, apparently, as weighty as the claimant's oath to his deposition, for *they* must proceed further; they must "introduce evidence" "to overthrow the presumptive proof." Now, what facts does the deposition for proof of claim allege? For if *facts* are not deposed to in the claimant's proof, how will the trustee or creditors be able to know what *facts* they must, under the rule, "rebut?" No facts are deposed to; the proof of claim states simply legal conclusions. Of course, it would be different were the claimant bound to introduce all his evidence in the first instance—not only the deposition for proof of the claim but all his other evidence in chief. In that instance there would, be no difficulty; for if he rested his case on the deposition, then, after the objecting creditor or trustee had introduced evidence, the case would be closed except for rebutting evidence from the claimant. But such a procedure is obviously not what the rule contemplates, for there would be no material change from the ordinary method of procedure thereby. If the rule contemplates that the claimant may, for the first time, introduce his witnesses to substantiate his case in chief, *after* his opponent has concluded his defense, the rule would work inequitably, for the objecting creditors or trustee would have to deny every conceivable adverse circumstance while the claimant might sit by and put in his own case in chief afterwards. The rule is peculiar, unnecessary and vexatious and is not altogether practicable. It has generally been found that deviation from the time honored order of pro-

---

67. Compare post, § 846. Also compare suggestively, Baumhauer *v.* Austin, 26 A. B. R. 385, 186 Fed. 260 (C. C. A. Ala., reversing on the facts In re Baumhauer, 24 A. B. R. 750, 179 Fed. 966), quoted on other points at § 554½.

cedure is unwise. This instance would seem to be no exception. It would seem sufficient to give the deposition for proof of debt simply the effect of evidence *when no objections are filed to the claim*, or at any rate to require the claimant to put in all his proof along with it, except such as is mere rebuttal. The courts have introduced the rule for the protection of claimants against unfounded objections; but it would seem that the oath of the objectors and the penalty of costs ought to be sufficient guaranties of good faith, and that, in the effort to protect claimants from unfounded objections, bankruptcy practice should not be thrown into confusion and be made a new and strange procedure for lawyers to learn.

In any event, the claimant must rely and stand upon the deposition as proof of debt and not go ahead with his proof aliunde in the first instance.

*In re McIntyre & Co., 24 A. B. R. 1, 176 Fed. 552 (C. C. A. N. Y.): "There would, therefore, be much force in the claimant's contention if he had taken the same position before the referee. He might properly have stood upon his proof of claim and have insisted that the objections should go forward. But he did not do so. He offered to establish the allegations of his proof of claim by the entries in the stock record book and contended that the inference to be drawn therefrom supported the charge of conversion. Having thus attempted to establish the allegations in his proof of claim, he cannot be permitted to use those very allegations to supply the deficiencies in his testimony. A proof of claim may have some probative force but it certainly should not be regarded as self-proving unless relied upon."

And if the claimant does not rely on his proof of claim, and introduces additional evidence, the matter will then be decided in accordance with the combined effect of the "proof" and the evidence so offered, even though it results in a disallowance or reduction of the claim.[68]

§ 845. But, at Any Rate, Prima Facie Case for Allowance as Priority Claim, Not So Established.

But, at any rate, a prima facie case for the allowance of the claim as a priority claim is not established by the mere presentation of the deposition containing allegations which, if true, would establish such priority. The effect of the deposition as prima facie proof goes no further than merely to establish prima facie the provability and allowability of the claim, not the order of its priority in the distribution of the assets.[69]

In re Jones, 18 A. B. R. 208 (D. C. Mich.): "It is contended by the petitioner that, as the petition was sworn to, the truth of the allegation in question is prima facie established upon the principle that the sworn proof of claim against the bankrupt is prima facie evidence of its allegations, even if objected to. This is undoubtedly the rule, as applied to the proof of the claim itself as a general claim, considered apart from the question of priority. * * * These decisions do not, to my mind, support the proposition that allegations

68. In re Greenfield, 27 A. B. R. 427, 193 Fed. 98 (D. C. Pa.).
69. Whether Prima Facie Proof, **Also of Ownership of Claim.**—In re (James) Dunlop Carpet Co., 22 A. B. R. 788, 171 Fed. 532 (D. C. Pa.).

relating to alleged priority are to be taken as prima facie true, for the purpose of establishing such priority, in the absence of evidence for or against the fact. The proof of claim, as such, is governed by § 57 of the Bankrupt Act (30 Stat. 560 [U. S. Comp. St. 1901, p. 3443]). The subject of priorities is governed by § 64. The question presented in the Dresser Case related entirely to the proof of claim as a general claim, under § 57 of the Bankrupt Act, and had nothing to do with the question of priority, under § 64 of the Act. * * * The reasons for the rule of prima facies applicable to proofs of claims do not apply to petitions for priority. In my opinion the allegations relating to priority were not prima facie evidence of their truth."

§ 845½. Nor Prima Facie Case for Reclamation of Converted Property.

—And it would certainly be improper to give the proof of debt any probative force in support of a claimant seeking to recover converted property or its proceeds, as was the apparent, though obiter, holding in one case.[70]

Indeed, whatever probative force such deposition could have would rather be against such a claimant, as being an admission that the relation of debtor and creditor existed, rather than that of bailee and bailor.

§ 846. Claimant Must Present Himself for Examination.

—Opportunity should be given to examine the claimant where hearing is had upon a petition to re-examine a claim already allowed.[71]

In re Sumner, 4 A. B. R. 123, 101 Fed. 224 (D. C. N. Y.): "An opportunity should be given to examine the claimant and other witnesses, if the attendance of the same can be procured seasonably and without embarrassing delay, and it may be that in suitable cases the referee should suspend a determination of the matter until evidence can be taken by deposition. But a suspension of the proceedings for the purpose of obtaining the evidence of witnesses not within the jurisdiction of the court should only be exercised where the referee is convinced that there is not only formal objection to the claim interposed in good faith, but also that there is substantial reason for believing that such evidence is necessary for the just administration of the estate."

Indeed, it is doubtless by virtue of the rule requiring the presence of the claimant in person for cross-examination that the deposition for proof of debt is itself given probative effect in making a prima facie case.[72]   And

---

70. Obiter, In re McIntyre & Co., 24 A. B. R. 1, 176 Fed. 552 (C. C. A. N. Y.), quoted at § 1883.

71. Impliedly, Gen. Order 21 (6): "At the time appointed, the referee shall take the examination of the creditor, etc." Obiter, In re Doty, 5 A. B. R. 58 (Ref. N. Y.); Impliedly, Laffoon v. Ives, 20 A. B. R. 174, 159 Fed. 861 (C. C. A. Wash.).

Nonresident Creditor Exempt from Service of Summons While So in Attendance.—And while he is so in attendance he is exempt from service of summons upon him in another action by the trustee, in case he be a nonresident.

Morrow v. Dudley & Co., 16 A. B. R. 459 (D. C. Pa.): "Of the right of a party to attend a judicial hearing away from the place of his residence, without being subjected to the service of process, there is, of course, no question, and hearings before the referee are no exception."

72. Suggestively, Baumhauer v. Austin, 26 A. B. R. 385, 186 Fed. 260 (C. C. A. Ala.), quoted at § 554½, and reversing In re Baumhauer, 24 A. B. R.

the examination is in the nature of a cross-examination.[73] But it seems that the referee has no authority to require the claimant to appear, the denial of any probative effect to the deposition for proof of debt probably being the only penalty, except as the ordinary rules of practice might prescribe.[74]

§ 847. Place for His Examination.—The place of the re-examination of a nonresident creditor on a reconsideration of his claim may be either in the district where the proceedings are pending or where he resides, as the referee may order.[75]

§ 848. Nonresident Claimant Entitled to Reimbursement.—A nonresident creditor is entitled to reimbursement of reasonable traveling fees and hotel expenses, but not counsel fees, when ordered to appear on re-examination of his claim.[76]

§ 849. Jury Trials Not to Be Had.—Jury trials can not be had before the referee. There is no machinery adequate therefor and, such proceedings being equitable in their nature, a jury could not be demanded as of right.

But compare, In re Rude, 4 A. B. R. 319, 101 Fed. 805 (D. C. Ky.): "Bankruptcy proceedings are equitable in their nature, and while the court and possibly the referee, might have had a jury to pass upon the amount of the attorney's fee (lien claimed by attorney on client's dividend) that was a matter of discretion and not of right. The court does not understand that in equitable proceedings parties have a right to have an issue tried out of chancery by a jury."

§ 850. Variance between Claim and Proof.—Material variance between the statement of the claim, in the formal deposition for proof of debt, and the evidence, is fatal, unless remedied in the usual manner.

In re Lansaw, 9 A. B. R. 167, 118 Fed. 365 (D. C. Mo.): "The rule of law obtains everywhere, under every system of pleading, that the party must establish 'by evidence the case made in his pleading; and he is not entitled to recover on evidence which shows a different right of recovery.' * * *

"The Bankrupt Law, which proceeds much upon principles of equity jurisprudence and practice, requires that the claimant, in presenting his claim to the referee for allowance against the bankrupt estate, must make a statement of what his claim is, and he must purge himself by presenting his claim under oath. He cannot present for allowance a claim for $700, alleged to have been advanced by him to the bankrupt, and which was put into the business of the mercantile store of the bankrupt, and undertake to sustain it by proof that his mother requested the bankrupt to pay the claimant $800 on a debt he owed her, and which was afterwards compromised at $700. The claim should have been rejected by the referee on this ground, without more."

But an inconsequential variance between the allegations of a claimant as

73. In re Castle Braid Co., 17 A. B. R. 150, 145 Fed. 224 (D. C. N. Y.).

74. In re Goble Boat Co., 27 A. B. R. 48, 190 Fed. 92 (D. C. N. Y.).

75. In re Geo. Watkinson Co., 12 A. B. R. 370 (D. C. Pa.). Compare, Laffoon v. Ives, 20 A. B. R. 174, 159 Fed. 861 (C. C. A. Wash.).

76. In re Geo. Watkinson Co., 12 A. B. R. 370 (D. C. Pa.).

to when his debt against the bankrupt arose, and his testimony upon that point, does not require a reversal of the allowance of his claim by the referee.[77]

§ 851. Trustee's Attorney Not to Act as Claimant's Attorney.

—A claimant should not be represented by the trustee's attorney. Professional ethics would forbid the practice.[78]

§ 852. Untrustworthy, Though Uncontradicted, Testimony May Be Rejected.

—Oral admissions denied and uncorroborated may be not sufficient to support a claim.[79] And the bankrupt's uncorroborated testimony as to the precise time of his becoming insolvent should be received with caution.[80]

Uncontradicted testimony in support of a claim may be so unsatisfactory that it may be rejected and the claim be disallowed.[81]

In re Friedman, 21 A. B. R. 213, 164 Fed. 131 (D. C. Wis.): "Louis Friedman and E. M. Rieselbach testified unequivocally that they had no knowledge of the financial condition of the bankrupt at any time. The bankrupt corroborated them in this regard, and there was slight positive evidence to the contrary. Counsel therefore argues that the court must, as matter of law, find their contention established. But such is not the law. If the positive evidence is inherently improbable, the court may reach a conclusion based upon the circumstantial evidence in the case which is more convincing. Quock v. Ting, 140 U. S. 417."

In re Rome, 19 A. B. R. 820, 162 Fed. 971 (D. C. N. J.): "These statements and facts certainly call for satisfactory evidence on the part of Fleischman to support his claim. He has sought to support it by the testimony of himself and his wife and of the bankrupt and his daughter. Notwithstanding the testimony of these four witnesses, the referee has rejected the claim. He has filed an opinion which is a sad commentary on the credibility of these four witnesses. The claim can not be rejected on any other theory than that they are unworthy of belief. It is a serious matter to reject the claim on such a ground. But their statements bear such marks of inherent improbability, and

---

77. In re Stout, 6 A. B. R. 505, 103 Fed. 618 (D. C. Mo.).

78. In re Stern, 16 A. B. R. 513, 144 Fed. 956 (C. C. A. Iowa); Ohio Valley Bank v. Mack, 20 A. B. R. 919, 163 Fed. 155 (D. C. Ohio). So, also, it has been held improper for the bankrupt's attorney to represent the claimant. In re Wooten, 9 A. B. R. 247. The reasoning of the court, however, in this case is not free from objections. The bankrupt could not make admissions to bind the estate anyway, no matter whether his attorney was the claimant's attorney or not.

79. In re Kaldenberg, 5 A. B. R. 6, 105 Fed. 232 (D. C. N. Y.).

80. In re Linton, 7 A. B. R. 676 (Ref. Tex.).

81. Compare ante, §§ 554, 555, and post, § 2650. Also, see instance Ohio Valley Bank v. Mack, 20 A. B. R. 919. 163 Fed. 155 (D. C. Ohio), quoted at § 554.

In re Baumhauer, 24 A. B. R. 750, 179 Fed. 966 (D. C. Ala., reversed on the facts, sub nom., Baumhauer v. Austin, 26 A. B. R. 385, 186 Fed. 260, C. C. A.): "While it is true that the positive testimony of an uncontradicted witness can not be disregarded by the referee or the court arbitrarily or capriciously, yet there may be such a gross or such an inherent improbability in the statements of the witness in reference to the fact testified to as to discredit him, and to induce the court or referee to disregard his evidence in the absence of any direct conflicting testimony."

in some respects are so inconsistent with one another, that I have been forced to a conclusion in accord with that expressed by the referee."

And this is true, although the objectors may have been under the burden of rebutting the prima facie case made by the deposition for proof of the claim.[82]

However, if such testimony be also the only evidence in support of the trustee's own affirmative defenses, the question at once arises whether the trustee likewise has not failed in his proof.

> Neumann v. Blake, 24 A. B. R. 575, 178 Fed. 916 (C. C. A. Mo.): "Conceding, for the sake of argument, that the referee had the right to reject her testimony, then there was no evidence before him showing that the bankrupt had ever paid her $300 or any other sum. Her testimony was the only testimony in the case, and she testified that the sum of $300 was paid to and used by her for living expenses for herself and children only, and not in part payment of the debt."

Yet testimony is not to be taken as inseparable. One may well believe admissions against interest made by a party, and at the same time doubt what he says in support of his claim. The actual credibility of the different parts of a witness' testimony is apart from the arbitrary rule of evidence that a party vouches for the truthfulness of the witnesses he produces. Moreover, in view of the Supreme Court Rule XXI (6) providing that the referee shall take the testimony of the claimant in the re-examination of claims in bankruptcy, it is doubtful that the rule of vouching for credibility applies.

§ 853. But Uncontradicted Testimony, Not Incredible, to Be Given Weight, Notwithstanding Suspicious Circumstances.

—But uncontradicted testimony is to be given weight as proof of the facts testified to, although circumstances of suspicion may exist, so long as such circumstances fall short of making the testimony incredible.[83]

§ 854. Dealings between Near Relatives to Be Closely Scrutinized.

—The rules governing the dealings between near relatives apply to contests over the allowance of claims in bankruptcy: they are to be scrutinized with care.[84]

Nevertheless, the honest or dishonest character of a debt is not to be determined by any mere test of relationship.[85]

§ 855. Also, Written Obligations Given by Bankrupts on Eve of Bankruptcy.

—Likewise, written obligations and acknowledgments of in-

---

82. In re Cannon, 14 A. B. R. 114, 133 Fed. 837 (D. C. Pa.). To same effect, In re Domenig, 11 A. B. R. 555, 128 Fed. 146 (D. C. Pa.).

83. Inferentially, Union Trust Co. v. Bulkeley, 18 A. B. R. 42, 150 Fed. 510 (C. C. A. Mich.).

84. In re Wooten, 9 A. B. R. 247, 118 Fed. 670 (D. C. N. Car.); In re Domenig, 11 A. B. R. 555, 128 Fed.

146 (D. C. Pa.); inferentially, but obiter, Union Trust Co. v. Bulkeley, 18 A. B. R. 42, 150 Fed. 510 (C. C. A. Mich.). Compare, same proposition ante, §§ 556, 800.

85. Ohio Bank v. Mack, 20 A. B. R. 40, 163 Fed. 155 (C. C. A. Ohio); Baumhauer v. Austin, 26 A. B. R. 385, 186 Fed. 260 (C. C. A. Ala.).

debtedness given by bankrupts during the period of insolvency immediately preceding bankruptcy, are to be subjected to close scrutiny, and should not be upheld where they are not supported by good and sufficient consideration.[86]

§ 856. Schemes to Charge Partnership Assets with Individual Liabilities.

—Any scheme or device resorted to by persons in contemplation of bankruptcy, for the purpose of charging partnership assets with the individual liabilities of the partners, is violative of the provisions of the Act.

In re Jones & Cook, 4 A. B. R. 141 (D. C. Mo.): "The physical and undisputed facts surrounding the case are also in my opinion, sufficient to stamp the transaction as fraudulent within the meaning of the Bankruptcy Act. The two endorsements were made at the time the firm was in an embarrassed financial condition. They were also made without any new consideration moving from the individual creditor to the firm, and they were made within four months prior to the time when the members of the firm petitioned voluntarily to be adjudicated bankrupts. The endorsements were also made in favor of relatives. Under this state of facts, it is impossible to believe that the parties intended anything less than to gain an unconscionable and unlawful advantage over partnership creditors in violation of the spirit and meaning of the Bankruptcy Act. If authority for the conclusion reached in this case were needed, it can be found in In re Lane, 10 N. B. R. 135, 14 Fed. 1070 (No. 8,044)."

§ 856⅓. Omission of Items from Books, Destruction of Papers, etc., as Badges of Fraud.

—The omission of items from books, the destruction or mutilation of books, checks or other papers, are also badges of fraud.[88]

§ 856¼. Conspiracy to Defraud Creditors.

—A mere tacit understanding between parties to work to a common unlawful purpose is all that is necessary to constitute a conspiracy; and it may be proved by circumstantial evidence, even in the face of uncontradicted, if incredible, testimony.

In re Friedman, 21 A. B. R. 213, 164 Fed. 131 (D. C. Wis.): "Books are intended to show a correct history of all business transactions. A dishonest set of books is the surest earmark of fraud, while the destruction or mutilation of books of account amounts practically to a confession. Not only were two of the bankrupt's books destroyed, but those that remained were made to conceal the debts to the family aggregating nearly $30,000. The books of claimants were produced, and were equally defective and unsatisfactory. There are numerous checks from the bankrupt to Rieselbach, amounting to $2,600, that were not the subject of entry anywhere. The checks of the bankrupt to Louis, produced by the trustee, would more than balance all loans made by Louis that found their way into the bank account of the bankrupt. Yet the books on both sides omit all reference to such checks. The stubs in Rieselbach's check books covering the critical period were unfortunately destroyed, which would have thrown light upon his participation in the purchase of the original stock of goods. The volume of business thus concealed, and the number of transactions thus hidden by concerted action, leave little doubt that the parties were pursuing a common purpose. In contemplation of law this amounts

---

86. In re Brewster, 7 A. B. R. 436 (Ref. N. Y.).

88. In re Friedman, 21 A. B. R. 213, 164 Fed. 131 (D. C. Wis.). Quoted at § 856¼.

to confederation. A mere tacit understanding between conspirators to work to a common purpose is all that is essential to constitute a guilty actionable combination. Patnode *v.* Westenhaver, 114 Wis. 460, 90 N. W. 467."

So, also, is the omission of items from the books of account a badge of fraud.

In re Friedman, 21 A. B. R. 221, 164 Fed. 131 (D. C. Wis.): "To further discredit the bankrupt's good faith it appeared in evidence that many of the sales made at wholesale to peddlers and others were not entered in any book, and never passed through the hands of the cashier, but the proceeds of such sales were pocketed by the bankrupt."

§ 856⅜. Unusual Manner of Conducting Business, as Badge of Fraud.

—The conducting of the business in an unusual manner is a badge of fraud; as, for instance, a retailer selling at less than cost, or selling job lots, or selling without entering the items in the books, étc.

In re Friedman, 21 A. B. R. 213, 164 Fed. 131 (D. C. Wis.): "It further appears that shortly before the failure six cases of goods were shipped by the bankrupt to the Friedman Mercantile Company, of St. Louis, in the original packages of the consignors, for which that company were to pay the bankrupt the cost price in cash, to furnish him ready money. It further appears that similar shipments were made to the claimants, Rieselbach and Louis Friedman, to an amount which cannot now be ascertained. As bearing upon the extent of this back-door trade, the expert accountants testified that according to the books there should have been on hand at the time of the failure goods to the amount of $81,000, whereas in truth and in fact such goods inventoried at cost price about $38,000. The bankrupt can make no explanation of this deficit of over $40,000, and the books throw no light upon the subject. The books do' not show the advances made and money loaned by the several relatives of the bankrupt which are the subjects of these claims. Again, the fraudulent purpose of the bankrupt is disclosed by the fact that shortly before the failure, and when he was owing over $56,000 to merchandise creditors, he distributed $7,600 in cash among his relatives."

§ 856½. Similar Fraudulent Transactions.

—Evidence of similar fraudulent transactions is admissible on the proof of intent, and to show the same parties to be associated.[89]

§ 856⅝. Money Actually Advanced in Furtherance of Conspiracy Not Refunded nor Allowed, on Disallowance of Claim.

—Money actually advanced by conspirators in furtherance of their scheme to defraud will not be allowed as a debt nor refunded on disallowance.

In re Friedman, 21 A. B. R. 213, 164 Fed. 131 (D. C. Wis.): "It is urged however, with great confidence that, inasmuch as the evidence shows that the several sums of money represented by the notes were in fact advanced to the bankrupt, therefore these claims must be allowed. It would be a new doctrine, indeed, if a court of equity were called upon to hand back conspirators money which they have embarked in a fraudulent scheme and by means of

89. In re Friedman, 21 A. B. R. 213, 164 Fed. 131 (D. C. Wis.).

which the fraudulent purpose has been effectuated. It has been repeatedly held that, where a fraudulent conveyance is set aside by a court of equity, no accounting is to be taken of the money which the fraudulent grantee has actually invested to secure the fraudulent conveyance. This contention of claimants is disposed of by the following authorities: Ferguson v. Hillman, 55 Wis. 181, 190, 12 N. W. 389, is a leading case, where a large number of authorities to the same effect are collated and cited in the opinion. This doctrine was adhered to in Bank of Commerce v. Fowler, 93 Wis. 241, 245, 67 N. W. 423. See, also, In re Flick (D. C.), 5 Am. B. R. 465, 105 Fed. 503; Burt v. Gotzian, 102 Fed. 937, 43 C. C. A. 59, and Lynch v. Burt, 132 Fed. 417, 67 C. C. A. 305, both of which were decisions of the Circuit Court of Appeals of the Eighth Circuit. The theory of these cases is that when a creditor participates in a scheme to defraud other creditors, and in furtherance thereof advances money or incurs expense, the entire transaction is contaminated by the fraud, and a court of equity will not practically pay a bonus upon the fraud by returning such advance or expense."

§ 856¾. Great Latitude in Admission of Evidence in Cases Where Fraud Claimed.

—In the investigation of questions of fraud, great latitude is allowed in the admission of evidence. Questions of fraud can scarcely ever be proved by direct evidence, hence the necessity for the admission of all the circumstances fairly connected with the transaction.[90]

§ 856⅞. Conviction of Crime.

—A witness who has been convicted of misuse of the mails is competent, though the conviction may be taken into account as affecting his credibility.[90a]

§ 857. Agent's Admissions Not Binding unless within Scope.

—The admissions of an agent are not binding on his principal unless within the scope of his authority. Thus, the husband's admissions of his wife's insolvency, while acting as manager of her business, have been held not competent.[91]

Likewise, a corporation is not bound by the admissions or declarations of its officers unless in the performance of some duty.[92]

§ 858. Vacating of Allowance or Disallowance after Expiration of Current Term.

—Vacating of an order of allowance [93] or of disallow-

---

90. In re Luber, 18 A. B. R. 476, 152 Fed. 492 (D. C. Pa.).

90a. Compare ante, § 558⅞; Morris v. Tannenbaum, 26 A. B. R. 368 (Ref. N. Y.).

91. Duncan v. Landis, 5 A. B. R. 652, 106 Fed. 839 (C. C. A. Pa.).

92. In re Coventry Evans Furn. Co., 22 A. B. R. 272, 171 Fed. 673 (D. C. N. Y.).

93. Bankr. Act, § 2; compare, inferentially, In re Ives, 7 A. B. R. 692, 113 Fed. 911 (C. C. A. Mich.); In re Worcester Co., 4 A. B. R. 496, 102 Fed. 811 (C. C. A. Mass.).

No Terms of Court, in Bankruptcy. —That there are no terms of court in bankruptcy, see In re First Nat'l Bk., of Belle Fourche, 18 A. B. R. 274 (C. C. A.): "A proceeding in bankruptcy is a continuous suit. There are no terms of the bankruptcy court. It is always open, and until the termination of the pending suit that court has the power to re-examine its orders therein upon a timely application in an appropriate form. Sandusky v. National Bank, 90 U. S. 289, 293, 23 L. Ed. 155; Lockman v. Lang, 132 Fed. 1, 4, 65 C. C. A. 621, 624."

In re Keyes, 20 A. B. R. 183, 160 Fed. 763 (D. C. Mass.): "The terms of the court within which its decision was made came to an end before this petition for rehearing was filed; but I think I am justified in holding that, in bank-

ance [94] may be had after the expiration of the current term of the United States District Court, for there are no terms in bankruptcy proceedings.

Obiter, In re Tucker, 18 A. B. R. 386 (C. C. A. Mass.): "It must be regarded as well settled that the rule relating to the powers of ordinary judicial tribunals, limiting summary proceedings to the term at which judgment is entered, does not apply to proceedings in bankruptcy."

But will not modify its order where there has been laches.

In re Hoyt & Mitchell, 11 A. B. R. 784 (D. C. N. Car.): "An order made upon the affirmance of the report of a special master disallowing payments made by a trustee, in violation of the district rules, is final, and will not be set aside or modified, upon a motion made more than a year afterwards."[94a]

The district court cannot modify or vacate its orders, or grant rehearings, in matters where an appeal is pending, for the matter is no longer before it and it has no further jurisdiction.

First Nat'l Bk. v. State Bk., 12 A. B. R. 440 (C. C. A. Mont.): "The overwhelming weight of authority of the State courts is that an appeal, properly perfected, absolutely removes the case from the trial court, and places it in the appellate tribunal. The case must, of necessity, either be in the appellate or lower court. It cannot very well be in both courts at the same time. Such a course would lead to endless confusion. Under all the ordinary rules of practice, the appellate court alone would have the jurisdiction. After the cause leaves the lower court, it is deprived of taking any action upon any question involved in the appeal. Many of the authorities in the state courts upon this point are collected and cited in Elliott's App. Proc., § 541. The Federal authorities are substantially to the same effect.

"The precise point here raised has not been discussed in the national courts, because the practice adopted by appellant in this case is virtually unknown; but it has been incidentally referred to in several decisions to the effect that the decree in the District or Circuit Courts, when an appeal has been taken therefrom, is suspended until the appeal is disposed of. This rule is frequently stated in admiralty and other causes."

But it retains jurisdiction where the review is by petition for review and not by appeal.[95]   On dismissal of an appeal, the district court may hear a

ruptcy proceedings, the court's power to reconsider and revise its orders and decrees does not expire with the term at which they were made." Also, compare ante, § 431, note.

In re Henschel, 8 A. B. R. 201, 114 Fed. 968 (D. C. N. Y.); In re Lemmon & Gale Co., 7 A. B. R. 291, 112 Fed. 300 (C. C. A.); In re Mercur, 10 A. B. R. 505, 122 Fed. 384 (C. C. A., affirming 8 A. B. R. 275, 116 Fed. 655); Sandusky v. Nat'l Bk., 23 Wall. 289; contra, In re Hawk, 8 A. B. R. 71, 114 Fed. 300 (C. C. A.); inferentially and obiter, In re Riggs Restaurant Co., 11 A. B. R. 509 (C. C. A. N. Y.): "There can be no doubt that a court has power if reasonably exercised to resettle an order, imperfectly phrased, so as to conform its text to the decision it was intended to embody." In re Kaufman,

14 A. B. R. 387 (D. C. N. Y.); In re Tucker, 18 A. B. R. 378, 153 Fed. 91 (C. C. A. Mass.).

94. In re Keyes, 20 A. B. R. 183, 160 Fed. 763 (D. C. Mass.).

94a. It might pertinently be inquired here, however, how it comes that the district judge in the case quoted from, was having a "special master" pass upon the trustee's reports, presumably at an additional expense to the estate, when there was a referee who was the duly constituted officer to pass upon trustee's reports, performing this duty as part of the duties of his office without additional expense to creditors. See ante, §§ 24, 522½; post, § 2011.

95. In re Orman, 3 A. B. R. 698 (C. C. A. Ala.).

petition for a rehearing, and its order will be appealable.[96]

§ 858½. Reopening of Case for Further Testimony.

—After a party has had an opportunity to call and examine his witnesses and the matter is closed, he should not be permitted to reopen the case for the introduction of evidence which he subsequently concludes would have been an advantage to him, unless for special reason.[97]

§ 859. Rehearing Where Mere Pretence to Revive Right of Appeal.

—It has been held that rehearing will be denied where it is applied for upon the pretense of reconsidering the merits, but in reality for the purpose of reviving the petitioner's right of appeal, which had been lost by laches.[98]

But it would seem that the application for rehearing should be decided on its merits, and not on the motives of the applicant. If ground for rehearing exists, the motive should not interfere with the granting of the application. If ground does not exist, then the motive of the applicant is immaterial.

§ 860. Review of Referee's Order Refusing to Reopen Hearing.

—Ordinarily, the judge will uphold a referee in refusing to reopen the case to allow creditors who have shown laches in presenting their claims to be heard, but where there is manifest error the judge will look into the record and correct the error.[99]

§ 861. Claims Not Re-Examined after Closing of Estate.

—Re-examination of an allowed claim cannot be had after the estate is closed.[1] Whether § 57 (k) of the Act is meant to prohibit the re-examination of a claim after a closed estate has been reopened is not certain. There appear to be no decisions directly on the point.

But a petition for re-examination may be presented at any time before the closing of the estate;[2] unless there be laches.[3]

§ 861½. Costs on Disallowance.

—The costs may be taxed against the unsuccessful claimant.[4] It has been held, that on disallowance of a claim, there cannot be taxed an attorney's fee for the trustee.[5] However, there are no "costs" in bankruptcy except commissions and expenses outside of the filing fees, so it is difficult to see what costs ever can be taxed against an unsuccessful claimant other than the expenses of the trustee incurred by reason of the litigation, and assuredly the trustee's attorney's fees are precisely such expense.

96. Obiter, First Nat. Bk. v. State Bk., 12 A. B. R. 443 (C. C. A. Mont.).

97. In re Booss, 18 A. B. R. 658, 154 Fed. 494 (D. C. Pa.), quoted at § 553½. Also, see §§ 553½, 841.

98. In re Girard Glazed Kid Co., 12 A. B. R. 295, 129 Fed. 841 (D. C. Penna.); compare, In re Chambers, Calder & Co., 6 A. B. R. 707 (Ref. R. I.).

99. Compare, in general, "Review of Referee's Orders," §§ 2861, et seq. Also see In re Wood, 2 A. B. R. 695, 95 Fed. 946 (D. C. N. Car.).

1. Bankr. Act, § 57 (k).

2. In re Globe Laundry, 28 A. B. R. 831, 198 Fed. 365 (D. C. Tenn.); In re Canton, etc., Co., 28 A. B. R. 791, 197 Fed. 767 (D. C. Md.).

3. See ante, § 842.

4. See ante, § 535; post, § 2004.

5. In re Rome, 19 A. B. R. 820, 162 Fed. 971 (D. C. N. J.).

CHAPTER XXVI.

Trustees.

Synopsis of Chapter.

DIVISION 1.

ELECTION, APPOINTMENT AND QUALIFYING OF TRUSTEES.

§ 862. Appointment of Trustee at First Meeting, etc.—We have now, as the result of our following the usual course of a bankruptcy proceedings thus far, arrived at the subject of the appointment of a trustee.

The creditors at their first meeting after the adjudication or after a vacancy has occurred in the office of trustee, or after an estate has been reopened, or after a composition has been set aside or a discharge revoked, or if there is a vacancy in the office of trustee, appoint one trustee or three trustees. If the creditors do not appoint a trustee or trustees, the court appoints.[1]

§ 863. Election May Be Postponed.—The election of a trustee may be postponed, for cause; thus, upon the bankrupt's announcement that he is going to offer terms of composition;[2] or upon unanimous request of creditors for an adjournment to compose their differences where there has been no choice on the first ballot; creditors not being restricted to one ballot.[3]

---

1. Bankr. Act, § 44 (a). In re Syracuse Paper & Pulp Co., 21 A. B. R. 174, 164 Fed. 275 (D. C. N. Y.). For general discussion, see In re Eagles & Crisp, 8 A. B. R. 734, 99 Fed. 696 (D. C. N. Car.); also, In re Henschel, 7 A. B. R. 662, 113 Fed. 443 (C. C. A.); also, In re Lewensohn, 3 A. B. R. 299, 98 Fed. 576 (D. C. N. Y.).
2. In re Rung Bros., 2 A. B. R. 620 (Ref. N. Y.).
3. In re Nice & Schreiber, 10 A. B. R. 639 (D. C. Pa.).

And, whether the referee will or will not postpone the election of a trustee, where claims are objected to, is a matter of sound discretion.[4]

Thus, it is, after all, discretionary to postpone it for the purpose of enabling creditors to amend their proofs of claims.

In re Morris, 18 A. B. R. 828, 154 Fed. 211 (D. C. Pa.): "There can be no question of the right of a referee, under ordinary circumstances to postpone a meeting of creditors, for the purpose of allowing a restatement or perfecting of a proof of debt as was apparently the intention here. However inadvisable, as a rule, this may be, it is a matter of discretion, which is not to be interfered with except for abuse."

But the selection of a trustee may not be tied up indefinitely by obstructive tactics, obviously for the purpose of delay.[5]

But it has also been held not erroneous to refuse to postpone it and for the referee to appoint, where neither side has the requisite majority of claims both in number and amount and where reasonable opportunity has been given creditors to make choice at the appointed hour.

In re Goldstein, 29 A. B. R. 301, 199 Fed. 665 (D. C. Mass.): "The creditors' vote, taken after allowance of the claim as above, showed no choice of trustee. One candidate had a majority in number; the other, a majority in amount. The petitioner for review thereupon asked an adjournment to the next regular court day, two weeks distant. The request was refused by the referee, on the ground, as he reports, 'of expense to the estate, and that, if a new vote was taken, it would result then in a disagreement.' The supporters of both candidates had informed him, as he also states, that an agreement was hopeless. It would seem, although his report does not expressly so state, that he thereupon appointed a trustee under the last clause of § 44. The remaining question certified is: Did he err in refusing to adjourn the meeting for the purpose of allowing the creditors to vote again? No unanimous request was made for an adjournment. There is nothing to show that reasonable opportunity for choice by the creditors at the regular time had not been afforded, or that the refusal to adjourn can be regarded as having abridged the creditor's right to such reasonable opportunity. If all the claims proved had been objected to and continued for consideration, the referee might lawfully have proceeded to appoint a trustee himself, as Judge Lowell held in this court, in In re Cohen (D. C. Mass.), 11 Am. B. R. 439, 131 Fed. 391. I must hold that there was no error in his refusal to adjourn the meeting."

It has been held that a postponement should be allowed where the majority of claims are in the hands of persons who are not entitled to vote thereon, as, for instance, where they were solicited by the bankrupt's attorney, in order that the creditors who were apparently innocent of complicity might select proper representatives.[6]

4. In re Evening Standard Pub. Co., 21 A. B. R. 156, 164 Fed. 517 (D. C. N. Y.); impliedly, In re Syracuse Paper & Pulp Co., 21 A. B. R. 174, 164 Fed. 275 (D. C. N. Y.).

5. In re Malino, 8 A. B. R. 205, 206, 118 Fed. 368 (D. C. N. Y.); In re Sumner, 4 A. B. R. 123, 101 Fed. 224 (D. C. N. Y.).

6. In re Walker & Co., 29 A. B. R. 499, 176 Fed. 455 (D. C. Ala.), quoted on this point at § 892; In re Kaufman, 24 A. B. R. 117, 179 Fed. 287 (D. C. N. Y.), quoted at § 893½.

§ 864. Allowance of Claims May Be Postponed.—If claims are objected to, their allowance may be postponed, if the result would not affect the election of the trustee, that is to say, if with or without the claim on either side the election would be the same. Whether a claim will be postponed or the objections to it heard without delay and before the election, are questions resting in the sound discretion of the Court.[7]

§ 865. "Provisional" Allowance for Voting Purposes.—It would seem that claims objected to may not be allowed for voting purposes and the consideration of the objections thereto postponed. The creditor's right to vote and to exclude improper claims from being voted is a substantial right.[8]

In re Malino, 8 A. B. R. 205, 118 Fed. 368 (D. C. N. Y.): "The right of creditors to select a trustee is a substantial one (In re Henschel, 7 A. B. R. 662), and it does not rest in the discretion of the referee to allow claims as voting bases when objections are made which are apparently genuine." But in this case the Court modifies the rule and says provisional allowances are permissible in "proper cases." Evidently where the ground of objection is that the claimant has been preferred it is not a "proper case."

Clendenning v. Nat'l Bank, 11 A. B. R. 245 (N. Dak. Sup. Ct.): "The contention that the allowance was temporary, and merely to enable the defendant to vote at the creditor's meetings, likewise contradicts the legal effect of the order of allowance."

But there is a line of authorities to the contrary, holding that an allowance may be made, temporarily, where a hearing on the objections would unduly prolong the election of a trustee.[9]

Contra, obiter, In re Kelly Dry Goods Co., 4 A. B. R. 528, 102 Fed. 747 (D. C. Wis.): "Surely no construction is admissible which would permit other creditors, through the mere filing of objection to a claim, to exclude a bona fide claimant from voting on the election of a trustee."

There may, of course, however, be a preliminary determination of the value of securities held by a secured creditor, for the purposes of voting.[10]

§ 866. Only Partnership Creditors to Vote in Partnership Bankruptcies.—In partnership bankruptcies, it is only the partnership creditors who may vote for trustee; and this is so, even where the individual partners are also adjudicated bankrupts as individuals in the same proceedings and their individual estates in process of administration therein.[11]

---

7. See In re Eagles & Crisp, 3 A. B. R. 733, 99 Fed. 696 (D. C. N. C.); In re Columbia Iron Works, 14 A. B. R. 527, 127 Fed. 99 (D. C. Mich.); In re Malino, 8 A. B. R. 205, 118 Fed. 368 (D. C. N. Y.). See ante, § 816.

8. See ante, § 812.

9. See ante, § 812. In re Evening Standard Pub. Co., 21 A. B. R. 156, 164 Fed. 517 (D. C. N. Y.), quoted at § 812; In re Milne-Turnbull Co., 20 A. B. R. 248, 159 Fed. 280 (D. C. N. Y.), quoted at § 812.

10. See ante, § 763.

11. Bankr. Act, § 5 (b): "The creditors of the partnership shall appoint the trustee; in other respects so far as possible the estate shall be administered as herein provided for other estates."

Obiter, In re Eagles & Crisp, 3 A. B. R. 733, 99 Fed. 696 (D. C. N. Car.). But the provision that the "creditors

§ 867. Conversely, Individual Creditors to Vote in Individual Bankruptcies.

—In individual bankruptcies, the individual creditors are entitled to vote for trustee, although all the assets belong to the partnership and there is but one joint creditor.[12]

§ 867½. Partnership Trustee, Trustee Also of Individual Estates.

—The partnership trustee is trustee also of the individual estates.[13]

In re Coe, 18 A. B. R. 715, 154 Fed. 162 (D. C. N. Y.): "Section 5 of the Bankrupt Act provides that the creditors of a partnership in bankruptcy shall appoint the trustee, and that such trustee shall keep separate accounts of the partnership property and of the property belonging to the individual partners. There is no specific provision in the act authorizing a different trustee for the separate estate of individual partners, and I think that § 5 contemplates that the partnership trustee shall be the trustee of the individual partners. There are obvious advantages in such a practice, and there would be serious objections to having different trustees for the partnership assets and the individual assets. It is claimed in this case that the partnership has a large claim against the estate of Coe, and that the trustee elected by the partnership creditors would presumably act in the interests of the firm creditors. It is his duty not to do so, but to be strictly impartial as between the creditors of the partnership and of each individual partner. I think, under such circumstances, that it would be proper for the referee to permit any creditors either of the individual partners or of the firm to appear and contest the claim of the partnership estate against the individual estate of the partner Coe, notwithstanding the general rule that a trustee only can contest claims. But I think that there is no authority for appointing separate trustees."

§ 868. Majority in Number and Amount, Present, Whose Claims Allowed, Requisite,

—The election of a trustee is to be accomplished in general in the same manner in which creditors take action in other matters at their meetings. Thus, a majority in number and amount must coincide in their choice.[14]

§ 869. No Such Majority, Court to Appoint.

—Where there is no majority on the election by the creditors, the court, that is to say, in practice, the referee, makes the appointment. This the statute prescribes in so many words.[15]

Neither the statute nor rules limit the creditors to one balloting. If there

---

of the partnership shall appoint, etc.," applies only in the case of a joint petition. In re Beck, 6 A. B. R. 554, 110 Fed. 140 (D. C. Mass.). As to what claims are provable against the partnership as distinguished from the individuals, see post, § 2230, et seq., "Distribution in Partnership Cases."

12. In re Beck, 6 A. B. R. 554, 110 Fed. 140 (D. C. Mass.).

13. See ante, § 65; post, § 2233; also obiter, In re Eagles & Crisp, 3 A. B. R. 733, 99 Fed. 696 (D. C. N. Car.); In re Stokes, 6 A. B. R. 262, 106 Fed. 312 (D. C. Pa.).

14. See ante, "Creditors' Meetings," § 581, et seq. There can not be any official trustee appointed by the court, nor any general trustee to act in classes of cases. See Supreme Court's General Order in Bankruptcy, No. XIV. See criticism of this provision, In re Cobb, 7 A. B. R. 202, 112 Fed. 655 (D. C. N. Car.).

15. Bankr. Act, § 44 (a). In re Kuffler, 3 A. B. R. 162, 97 Fed. 187 (D. C. N. Y.); In re Brooks, 4 A. B. R. 50, 100 Fed. 432 (D. C. Pa.); In re Richards, 4 A. B. R. 631, 103 Fed. 849 (D. C. N. Y.); In re Morris, 18 A. B. R. 828, 154 Fed. 211 (D. C. Pa.).

is no choice on the first vote, the request of the creditors for an adjournment for a reasonable time to compose their differences should be granted.[16] It has been held that if at the first meeting all claims offered are in dispute and it is impracticable at the time to settle the dispute, it is within the proper discretion of the referee to make the appointment.[17] This, however, is doubtful practice. Rather the referee should sit down and try out the objections vigorously. Then the atmosphere will soon clear away. When the court (referee) makes the appointment, it is the better practice not to appoint either of the opposing candidates.[18]

§ 870. Court Also to Appoint Where Creditors Fail Altogether to Act.

—Where no creditors (with allowed claims) appear at all, the court also may appoint the trustee.[19]

It has been held that the court has not authority to appoint a trustee unless the creditors have failed to act.[20]

In re Newton, 6 A. B. R. 52, 107 Fed. 439 (C. C. A. Mo.): "When they fail to do so, either at the first meeting, or afterwards in case of a reopening of the estate, and not till then, power is conferred upon the court to make such appointment."

§ 870½. Also, Whether to Appoint Where Disputed Claims So Numerous That Determination Would Unduly Delay Administration.

—On the other hand, it has been held, that where all or so many of the claims are disputed that a determination of their validity before the appointment of a trustee would unduly delay the administration of the estate, the court may appoint.[21]

Obiter, In re Evening Standard Pub. Co., 21 A. B. R. 156, 164 Fed. 517 (D. C. N. Y.): "Whether the referee will or will not postpone the election of a trustee is a matter of sound discretion. If such a number of claims are duly objected to that an election by a majority in number and amount cannot be had, then, if the circumstances demand, he may and should himself appoint. All this is settled by the weight of well-considered authorities. * * * If so many verified objections, apparently valid, are filed that an election by creditors is impossible, let the referee appoint."

Yet the right of creditors to participate in the election of a trustee is a substantial right.[22]

And the power to appoint the trustee where claims are excluded from vot-

16. See In re Nice & Schreiber, 10 A. B. R. 639, 123 Fed. 987 (D. C. Penn.); inferentially, In re Kuffler, 3 A. B. R. 162, 97 Fed. 187 (D. C. N. Y.).

17. In re Cohen, 11 A. B. R. 439, 131 Fed. 391 (D. C. Mass.).

18. Instance, In re Cohen, 11 A. B. R. 441, 131 Fed. 391 (D. C. Mass.); instance, contra (noting the trouble resulting therefrom), In re Richards, 4 A. B. R. 631, 103 Fed. 849 (D. C. N. Y.).

19. Bankr. Act, § 44 (a): "If the creditors do not appoint a trustee or trustees as herein provided, the court shall do so."

20. Obiter, In re Fisher & Co., 14 A. R. B. 366, 370, 135 Fed. 223 (D. C. N. Y.); Fowler v. Jenks, 11 A. B. R. 255, 90 Minn. 74 (Sup. Ct. Minn.).

21. In re Cohen, 11 A. B. R. 439, 131 Fed. 391 (D. C. Mass.).

22. See ante, §§ 597, 865, 812. Compare, also, collaterally, In re Van De Mark, 23 A. B. R. 760, 175 Fed. 287 (D. C. N. Y.).

ing merely because disputed, is doubtful, and, at best, is to be exercised only in extreme cases.

§ 871. Dispensing with Trustee Where No Assets, and No Creditors Present.

—Where no assets are shown by the schedules and no creditor appears at the first meeting, the court (referee) may by order setting forth the facts dispense with the appointment of a trustee altogether.[23]

In re Levy, 4 A. B. R. 108, 101 Fed. 247 (D. C. Wis.): "In the absence of substantial assets, either appearing from the schedules or discoverable, the appointment of a trustee is not indispensable."

Thereafter, the court, without notice to creditors, at almost any length of time, may appoint a trustee if deemed advisable, even though the referee has long since returned the files in the case to the clerk, for the estate is not technically closed and "reopening" is not necessary in order to authorize the appointment.[24]

§ 872. But if Assets Shown, Trustee to Be Appointed, Though No Creditor Appears.

—But if any assets are shown, even if they be exempt, a trustee should be appointed; for no one but the trustee has the power to set apart exempt property to the bankrupt, and the scope of General Order No. 15 cannot be extended.[25]

And in any case, even where no assets are shown and no creditor appears, it is the better practice to appoint a trustee to make an investigation. The deposit of $5.00 to cover the trustee's fee must not be returned to the bankrupt, because it belongs to his estate; so there is no economy in omitting to appoint a trustee. Moreover, if no trustee is appointed and the estate is closed, in whom is the title to property that the bankrupt has concealed? Title to property does not vest until the appointment and qualification of a trustee;[26] and concealment is not a ground for refusing a discharge unless it is concealment from the "trustee."[27] For an example of such situation, see

In re Toothacker, 12 A. B. R. 100, 101, 128 Fed. 187 (D. C. Conn.): "There appearing to be no assets, a trustee was not appointed * * *. By omitting

---

23. General Order XV; impliedly, Clark v. Pidcock, 12 A. B. R. 315, 129 Fed. 745 (C. C. A. N. J.); obiter, In re Eagles & Crisp, 3 A. B. R. 734 (D. C. N. Car.).

24. Clark v. Pidcock, 12 A. B. R. 315 (C. C. A. N. J.): In this case it appeared that at the first meeting of creditors called by the referee on the 21st. day of November, 1899, no creditors were present, and no trustee was appointed and that but one creditor proved his debt, and that the schedule of the bankrupt disclosed no assets, and that it was ordered by the referee that "until further order of the court no trustee be appointed and no other meeting of the creditors be called." On the 28th day of January, 1902, the referee made the final report above re-

cited, and that "the estate of the bankrupt has been fully administered and so far as referred to me it has been closed," the court held that after the lapse of more than a year, it had jurisdiction under § 44 and Gen. Order 15 to appoint a trustee, upon the petition of the assignee of the creditor alleging that the bankrupt had died leaving various properties which he had fraudulently disposed of with intent to defraud creditors. However, this decision is qualified by the fact that the only creditor whose claim was allowable was the one asking the appointment.

25. Compare, to same effect, In re Smith, 2 A. B. R. 190 (D. C. Tex.).

26. See § 70.

27. See § 29 (b) (1).

to place it in the schedules, he was enabled to escape a trustee from whom to conceal it."

Rand v. Iowa Central Ry. Co., 12 A. B. R. 164, 96 App. Div. (N. Y.) 413 (reversed, however, in Rand v. Ry. Co., 16 A. B. R. 692, 186 N. Y. 58, but illustrative of the point, notwithstanding): "The plaintiff contends that the title and right to maintain the action remained in him until the appointment of a trustee in bankruptcy, and since one was not appointed his title and right have not been divested. This contention on the part of the plaintiff seems so extraordinary and fraught with consequences so disastrous to the rights of creditors that a court should hesitate to so declare the law unless there be no avenue of escape."[28]

§ 873. Trustee Elected, Not Compelled to Act.—There is no power to compel a person who has been elected trustee to accept the trust.

And it has been held, in one case, that if there be no substantial assets he may demand compensation as a condition of acceptance and that if creditors insist upon his acceptance, they will have to furnish him his fees or otherwise arrange with him.[29]

But there is no power in the court to allow him any other or different compensation than that prescribed in the Act.[30]

§ 874. Either One Trustee or Three to Be Elected, Not Merely Two.—Creditors may elect one trustee or three trustees. They may not elect merely two trustees. There must be one or three; no other number will do.[31]

But there is no requirement that all three be elected at once, and an election and appointment of merely two trustees is not necessarily void, the inference arising that the third trustee will later be elected.

In re Fisher & Co., 14 A. B. R. 369, 135 Fed. 223 (D. C. N. J.): "The point made by the objecting creditor is that, as the creditors at their first meeting elected two trustees and not one trustee or three trustees, the appointment was absolutely void. I am not willing so to hold, especially in view of what was done in this case."

And a petition for leave to sell assets filed by two trustees before a third trustee is elected is not void, the third trustee being elected before the sale was made and joining in the petition therefor.[32]

Presumably the creditors themselves determine the question as to whether there shall be one trustee or three, determining it in the same manner they determine other questions at creditors' meetings.

§ 875. Whether Number May Be Subsequently Increased.—Whether, after one trustee has been elected, the creditors may, at a subsequent meeting, vote to increase the number to three and thereupon elect

28. Rand v. Railway Co., 16 A. B. R. 692, 186 N. Y. 58 (reversing 12 A. B. R. 164, 96 App. Div. 413).

29. In re Levy, 4 A. B. R. 108, 101 Fed. 247 (D. C. Wis.).

30. Bankr. Act, § 44. Also, see post, § 2029.

31. Bankr. Act, § 47 (b); In re Fisher & Co., 14 A. B. R. 366, 135 Fed. 223 (D. C. N. J.).

32. In re Fisher & Co., 14 A. B. R. 366, 135 Fed. 223 (D. C. N. J.).

two more trustees to act with the one already appointed, is not decided under the present law. Probably the wording of § 44 would imply that such change could not be made unless the existing trustee had been "removed" or the office had been "vacated;" in which events, of course, the creditors would be entirely free to determine whether he should be succeeded in the office by one or by three. Under the law of 1867, by petition to the court, an additional trustee could be appointed.[33]

§ 876. Concurrence of Two Requisite, Where Three Appointed.— Of course where three trustees are appointed, it requires a concurrence of two of the trustees to act in any matter.[34]

§ 877. Qualifying of Trustees.—Trustees are required to enter into bond for the faithful performance of duty before entering on the duties of their office.

It is the referee's duty at once to notify the trustee of his appointment; whereupon it becomes the trustee's duty in turn at once to notify the referee of his acceptance or rejection of the trust.[35] No oath of office is expressly required, although, by general rules, such oath is appropriate. A trustee must qualify within ten days from the day of his appointment. The court may by order give him a longer period, however, but not to exceed five days extra, making fifteen days in all.[36] If he has not qualified by the end of that time, the delay is fatal; the office becomes ipso facto vacant and a new election must be held.[37]

Inferentially, Breckons v. Snyder, 15 A. B. R. 112, 211 Pa. St. 176: "Although it does not appear of record that the trustee obtained an extension of time for the filing of a bond, the presumption is in favor of the regularity of all proceedings before the referee, and that the trustee complied with all the requirements of the law, and was qualified to act."

The creditors are to fix the trustee's bond in each instance and the amount of it is to be fixed by the majority in number and amount of creditors present whose claims have been allowed, in accordance with the usual rules as to creditors' actions at their meetings. The amount of the bond may be increased by them at any time;[38] and presumably may also be decreased by them.

---

33. (1867) In re Overton, 5 N. B. Reg. 366.

34. Bankr. Act, § 47 (b): "Whenever three trustees have been appointed for an estate the concurrence of at least two of them shall be necessary to the validity of their every act concerning the administration of the estate."

35. Gen. Order XVI.

36. Bankr. Act, § 50 (b): "Trustees, before entering upon the performance of their official duties, and within ten days after their appointment, or within such further time, not to exceed five days, as the court may permit, shall respectively qualify by entering into bond to the United States, with such sureties as shall be approved by the courts, conditioned for the faithful performance of their official duties."

37. Bankr. Act, § 50 (k): "If any trustee fail to give bond as herein provided and within the time limited, he shall be deemed to have declined his appointment and such failure shall create a vacancy in his office."

38. Bankr. Act, § 50 (c).

If the creditors fail to fix the amount of the bond, the referee must fix it.[39] There must be at least two sureties on the trustee's bond;[40] (except when a surety corporation is surety), and each surety must be proved to be worth the full amount of the bond over and above all his debts and exemptions.[41] Corporations, that is to say surety companies, may be sureties on the trustee's bond;[42] in which event two sureties will not be necessary.[43]

Suits upon trustee's bonds properly are brought in the name of the United States and no leave of court is necessary. If brought in any other name, leave of court must, at least, be had.[44]

It has been held that such action may be brought in the United States District Court.[45]

An order on the trustee to account is not a prerequisite to a suit against the sureties on the bond, where the trustee has absconded.[46]

DIVISION 2.

APPROVAL AND DISAPPROVAL OF CREDITORS' ELECTION.

§ 878. Approval and Disapproval of Creditors' Election.—The creditor's selection of a trustee is subject to the approval or disapproval of the judge or referee.[47]

In re Henschel, 6 A. B. R. 25, 109 Fed. 861; 6 A. B. R. 305 (D. C. N. Y., rev'd on other grounds 7 A. B. R. 662, 113 Fed. 443): "This provision of course means something; it means that a supervisory power is vested in the court to meet contingencies which could not be definitely provided for in the act, and which must appeal to the good judgment and conscience of the court, and whereby the court would be armed with the power to prevent the selection of a person, who, in its judgment, and notwithstanding the expressed desire of the majority

---

39. Bankr. Act, § 50 (c).
40. Bankr. Act, § 50 (e).
41. Bankr. Act, § 50 (f).
42. Bankr. Act, § 50 (g).
43. In re Kalter, 2 A. B. R. 590 (Ref. Penna.). As to whether the premium for the bond is chargeable against the estate, see analogously, In re Hoyt, 9 A. B. R. 574, 119 Fed. 987 (D. C. N. Car.).
44. Alex Union Surety & Guaranty Co., 11 A. B. R. 32, 89 N. Y., App. Div. 3 (N. Y. Sup. Ct.).
45. U. S. ex rel. v. Union Surety Co., 9 A. B. R. 114, 118 Fed. 482 (D. C. N. Y.). In re Kajita, 13 A. B. R. 19 (D. C. Hawaii). Trustee's bonds do not become void on the first recovery but continue in force for two years after the estate is closed, unless the amount thereof is previously exhausted.
46. Scofield v. U. S. ex rel. Bond, 23 A. B. R. 259, 174 Fed. 1 (C. C. A. Ohio).

47. Gen. Order No. XIII: "The appointment of a trustee by the creditors shall be subject to be approved or disapproved by the referee or by the judge and he shall be removable by the judge only." In re Hare, 9 A. B. R. 522 (D. C. N. Y.).
The Bankruptcy Act of 1867 contained a similar provision in the statute itself. U. S. Rev. Stats., § 5034: "All elections or appointments of assignees shall be subject to the approval of the judge, and when in his judgment, it is for any cause needful or expedient, he may appoint additional assignees or order a new election."
See, in addition, In re Hanson, 19 A. B. R. 237, 156 Fed. 717 (D. C. Minn.); In re Van De Mark, 23 A. B. R. 760, 175 Fed. 287 (D. C. N. Y.), quoted at § 882; In re Clay, 27 A. B. R. 715, 192 Fed. 831 (C. C. A. Mass.); In re Stradley & Co., 26 A. B. R. 149, 187 Fed. 285 (D. C. Ala.).

in number and amount of the creditors, or even of all the creditors, would not be a proper selection, and whose appointment might result in a defeat of the proper, just and equitable administration of the bankrupt law in that particular case; but the emergency should not be a trivial one; it should be one of grave character and due weight, and unless such an emergency appears in the present case, it would become the duty of the referee to approve the selection, always subject of course, to a review of such action by the learned district judge."

In re Eastlack, 16 A. B. R. 533, 145 Fed. 68 (D. C. N. J.): "The present Bankrupt Act contains no provision like the one quoted above the Act of 1867 but the Supreme Court has promulgated an order, Gen. Ord. 13 * * * It is evident that the Supreme Court intended by this order to establish a rule concerning the approval or disapproval of elections by creditors similar to that which existed under the Act of 1867. The decisions under the present law on this point show that such has been the understanding of our federal courts."

Scofield v. United States ex rel. Bond, 23 A. B. R. 259, 174 Fed. 1 (C. C. A. Ohio): "It appears that the creditors were not summoned to elect a new trustee [on absconding of old one] and it is urged that the court could only appoint the trustee in case the creditors failed to elect one. But the appointment of a trustee is finally subject to the approval of the court, and in some conditions the court might itself make the appointment. The whole matter of appointing trustees is subject to the power and superintendence of the court. If the court ought to have summoned the creditors to elect a trustee, its failure to do so was a mere irregularity, and cannot be taken advantage of collaterally, certainly not by those who are not creditors or otherwise interested in the appointment."

In fact, the theory of the law is that creditors simply recommend the trustee and that the court appoints him;[48] for § 2 in clause 17 provides that courts of bankruptcy shall have power "Pursuant to the recommendation of creditors, or when they neglect to recommend the appointment of trustees, appoint trustee, and upon complaints of creditors, remove the trustees for cause upon hearings and after notice to them."

§ 879. Statutory Qualifications of Trustee.—The only statutory qualifications of the trustee are that he have actual competency and have actual residence or an office in the district; either individuals or corporations being competent.[49]

The statute requires that the trustee be "competent to perform the duties of that office." Competency ought not to be limited to capability, but should exclude as well those whose relations to the estate are such as to make them unfit. It is with the question of what constitutes competency or incompetency that the courts have been mostly concerned.[50]

In re Henschel, 6 A. B. R. 25 and 305, 109 Fed. 861 (Ref. and D. C. N. Y., rev'd on other grounds 7 A. B. R. 662, 113 Fed. 443): "To my mind the selection of a

48. To such general effect, Scofield v. United States ex rel. Bond, 23 A. B. R. 259, 174 Fed. 1 (C. C. A. Ohio), quoted supra, § 878.

49. Bankr. Act, § 45: "Trustees may be individuals who are respectively competent to perform the duties of that office, and reside or have an office in the judicial district within which they are appointed, or corporations authorized by their charters or by law to act in such capacity and having an office in the judicial district within which they are appointed."

50. In re Margolies, 27 A. B. R. 398, 191 Fed. 369 (D. C. N. Y.).

proper and competent person as a trustee, in a case of the importance of the present one, should be regarded not as a merely perfunctory matter, but as a matter to be treated in the interest of all the creditors, and when I say 'all the creditors,' I do not mean a majority, but all the creditors, and that presents the fact that the minority of creditors have also some rights which the court will recognize and respect; and to secure such a proper trustee, the person to be nominated and elected, and who shall be installed in the office, should be like Cæsar's wife, entirely above suspicion; that is to say, not only above suspicion, in so far as personal character or personal capacity are concerned, but also above the suspicion of having any undue affiliations or connections with the bankrupt; one holding no interest which is favorable to the bankrupt, and above the suspicion of having made anti-election bargains, pledges or promises with any clique or set of creditors, or with any number of attorneys representing certain interests.

"This is my view of what should be found in the proper trustees; it is not an ideal or fanciful creation, but it is what every trustee should be in order to properly execute the bankrupt law, according to its true spirit and intent."

§ 880. Neither Residence nor Citizenship Requisite, if Office in District.

—Neither residence nor citizenship is required, but merely that the proposed trustee have an office or residence within the judicial district; that is to say, in this respect it is sufficient if the trustee have an office or residence anywhere in the district.[51] It must be an actual residence or office.[52] An alien is competent, if capable of performing his duties, and if he have an office or residence within the district.[53] But it is no disqualification that a nonresident trustee would cause additional expense to the estate for traveling expenses; especially is it true that the referee should not refuse to confirm the creditor's election on that ground.[54]

§ 881. Corporations Competent.

—A surety company may act as a trustee.[55]

§ 881½. Referee to Be Impartial.

—The referee must be impartial, not even indicating his preference for one candidate over another.

In re Jacobs & Roth, 18 A. B. R. 728, 157 Fed. 988 (D. C. Pa.): "The whole aspect of the case gives one the impression that the referee was taking too active an interest in the selection of a trustee. It is not the part of a referee to identify himself in any manner with the interests of either the bankrupt, or his creditors, or the counsel interested in the case. His duty is to keep himself entirely free from any interest or any manifestation of interest in the case one way or the other, and the more perfectly he can accomplish this the better can he perform the duties of his position."

§ 882. Creditors' Choice Not to Be Lightly Interfered with.

—The choice of the creditors should not be interfered with on slight grounds; and, unless there be shown incompetency—either personal, as want of

---

51. As to effect of subsequent removal of residence from district, see post, § 943.

52. Obiter, In re Seider, 20 A. B. R. 709, 163 Fed. 139 (D. C. N. Y.).

53. In re Coe, 18 A. B. R. 715, 154 Fed. 162 (D. C. N. Y.).

54. In re Jacobs & Roth, 18 A. B. R. 723, 157 Fed. 988 (D. C. Pa.).

55. Bankr. Act, § 45.

capacity or lack of integrity, or because of the trustee's relation towards the bankrupt or of his having adverse interests towards the estate, or, of course, because of his lack of an office or residence within the district,—his appointment should be approved.[56]

In re Van De Mark, 23 A. B. R. 760, 175 Fed. 287 (D. C. N. Y.): "The statute plainly and unequivocally provides that the creditors shall have the power to appoint a trustee or trustees, subject to the approval or disapproval of the referee; and this statutory right without adequate cause cannot be taken from them by the bankruptcy court."

In re Lloyd, 17 A. B. R. 98, 148 Fed. 92 (D. C. Wis.): "It must be remembered, however, that, by the terms of the Act the creditors are empowered to select a trustee. It is a serious matter to disfranchise creditors and deprive them of rights expressly conferred by the Bankruptcy Act."

In re Lazoris, 10 A. B. R. 32, 120 Fed. 716 (D. C. Wis.): 'Their selection is subject to approval or disapproval by the referee for cause only.'

In re Eastlack, 16 A. B. R. 535, 145 Fed. 69 (D. C. N. J.): "These cases establish the rule that the election of a trustee by the creditors is not to be disapproved, unless there is good reason for believing that the election has been directed, managed or controlled by the bankrupt or his attorney or by some influence opposed to the creditors' interest."

§ 883. Candidate May Be Creditor.

—Merely that the candidate is a creditor, or even is the largest creditor, is no disqualification in itself, no antagonistic relation being shown, and his claim not being disputed.[57]

Nor is the trustee rendered incompetent because of representing creditors as their attorney prior to his election.[58]

§ 884. Hostility Toward Bankrupt No Disqualification.

—The trustee's hostility to the bankrupt is not a valid objection to the approval of his election, unless perhaps in extreme cases. It is not the trustee's duty to be unbiased toward the bankrupt.[59]

§ 885. Solicitation of Office No Disqualification nor Solicitation of Claims Illegal.

—Solicitation of the office is not in itself a disqualification, unless done in the interest of the bankrupt or at his request.[60]

56. In re Lewensohn, 3 A. B. R. 299, 99 Fed. 73 (D. C. N. Y.); compare, to same effect, In re Gordon Supply & Mfg. Co., 12 A. B. R. 94 (D. C. Pa.), in which case, however, the court set aside the election because of possible adverse relations. In re Blue Ridge Packing Co., 11 A. B. R. 36, 125 Fed. 619 (D. C. Penna.). Compare, to same effect, under law of 1867, In re Smith, 1 N. B. Reg. 243, 247, 2 Ben. 113, 22 Fed. Cas. 261; In re Clairmont, 1 N. B. Reg. 276, Fed. Cas. 810; In re Funkenstein, Fed. Cas. 1,004; In re Barrett, 2 N. B. Reg. 533, Fed. Cas. 909; (1867) In re Grant, 2 N. B. Reg. 106, 10 Fed. Cas. 973; In re Margolies, 27 A. B. R. 398, 191 Fed. 369 (D. C. N. Y.); In re Kreuger, 27 A. B. R. 440,

196 Fed. 704 (D. C. Ky.); compare, on facts, to same effect, In re Jacobs & Roth, 18 A. B. R. 728, 157 Fed. 988 (D. C. Pa.); In re Hare, 9 A. B. R. 520, 119 Fed. 246 (D. C. N. Y.).

57. In re Lazoris, 10 A. B. R. 31, 120 Fed. 716 (D. C. Wis.).

58. In re Margolies, 27 A. B. R. 398, 191 Fed. 369 (D. C. N. Y.).

59. In re Lewensohn, 3 A. B. R. 299, 98 Fed. 576 (D. C. N. Y.); In re Mangan, 13 A. B. R. 303, 133 Fed. 1000 (D. C. Pa.).

60. In re Brown, 2 N. B. N. & R. 590 (Ref.); [1867] In re Haas, 8 N. B. Reg. 189. But see [1867] In re "A Bankrupt," 2 N. B. Reg. 100; In re Crocker Co., 27 A. B. R. 241 (Ref. Mass.).

Nor is the solicitation of claims illegal.

Compare, In re Lloyd, 17 A. B. R. 98 (D. C. Wis.): "It is not professional, but is not unlawful, for lawyers to solicit claims. The ethics and best thought of the profession are opposed to any solicitation of business. But there is no doubt that the practice is common, and perhaps more prevalent in bankruptcy than in other departments. The habit is not to be commended, but matters of taste or etiquette must be left largely to the good sense of the individual attorney."

Thus, it has been held that the election of a trustee should not be disapproved merely because he, as the representative of a majority of the creditors, voted for himself.[61]

§ 886. Undischarged Bankrupt Incompetent.—A bankrupt who himself has not yet been discharged should not be appointed trustee over another bankrupt's estate.[62]

§ 887. Trustee Elected in Bankrupt's Own Interest Incompetent.
—The election of a trustee in the bankrupt's own interest should be disapproved. It is the policy of the bankruptcy law to take the management of bankrupt estates out of the hands of the bankrupts themselves. The bankrupt has no right to influence the choice of a trustee and he has no voice in the election. Accordingly, interference by the bankrupt, the voting of claims in his interest or at his direction, should be discountenanced and held to invalidate the choice of a trustee thus secured.[63]

---

61. In re Margolies, 27 A. B. R. 398, 191 Fed. 369 (D. C. N. Y.).

62. In re Smith, 1 A. B. R. 37 (Ref. N. Y.).

63. In re McGill, 5 A. B. R. 155, 106 Fed. 57 (C. C. A. Ohio), where the Circuit Court of Appeals decided that since the referee presiding at the first meeting of creditors must determine the qualifications of voters, he is right in refusing to permit one to vote who acts under a power of attorney nominally executed by certain creditors but in fact procured by the bankrupt himself in order to vote for his choice for trustee.

Falter v. Reinhard, 4 A. B. R. 782, 104 Fed. 292 (D. C. Ohio, affirmed sub. nom. In re McGill, 5 A. B. R. 155, 106 Fed. 57, C. C. A.); to same effect, see In re Dayville Woolen Co., 8 A. B. R. 85, 114 Fed. 674, in which case one attorney, it appears, held the majority of the claims and was about to vote them. He had been attorney for the bankrupt before the bankruptcy. He refused to answer the question asked by some of the other creditors present whether any of the claims he was intending to vote were held in the in-

terest of the bankrupt, claiming that there was no right to ask the question. The reviewing court held that it was the duty of the referee to have put the question and to have permitted a full investigation into the relations of the voter to the bankrupt and the creditors, and if there had appeared to be reasonable cause to believe any collusion existed that the referee should have declined either to receive the collusive votes or to approve the election. In re Lewensohn, 3 A. B. R. 299, 98 Fed. 576 (D. C. N. Y., cited, with approval, in In re McGill, 5 A. B. R. 155, 106 Fed. 57, C. C. A. Ohio). Also, obiter, In re Mabrie & Brown, 11 A. B. R. 449, 128 Fed. 316 (D. C. Pa.): "The votes cast upon proxies that had been solicited by the bankrupts were properly rejected. (1867) In re Houghton, Fed. Cases, 6,729. But compare, In re Gordon Supply & Mfg. Co., 12 A. B. R. 94, 129 Fed. 622 (D. C. Pa.); In re Walker, 29 A. B. R. 499, 176 Fed. 455 (D. C. Ala.), quoted at § 892; In re Henschel, 6 A. B. R. 25 and 305, 109 Fed. 865 (Ref. and D. C. N. Y., reversed on other

In re Lloyd, 17 A. B. R. 97, 148 Fed. 92 (D. C. Wis.): "No attorney should be permitted to vote any claim that has come to him through the instrumentality of the bankrupt. * * *

"It appeared in evidence that it has been customary for bankrupts to furnish lists of creditors to some certain lawyer before the schedules are filed. The referee, in his opinion, denounces this practice as reprehensible. I fully concur in that opinion. By applying to the bankruptcy court, the bankrupt voluntarily surrenders all control over his estate, and the same passes to the officers of the law, under the Act. Any effort on his part to control the selection of a trustee, or to shape any of the proceedings of the court, must be resented and rebuked. It is a pernicious intermeddling which cannot be too strongly condemned. Referees should be vigilant to detect, and take all lawful means to prevent, any such interference by the bankrupt in court proceedings. * * *

"If it appears that any disclosure of the contents of the schedules has been made before the same are filed, the presumption arises that the bankrupt is seeking thereby to accomplish some ulterior purpose, and any claims secured through such illicit practice should not be allowed any part in the selection of a trustee."

In re Hanson, 19 A. B. R. 235, 156 Fed. 717 (D. C. Minn.): "At an adjourned session of the first meeting of creditors at the office of the referee on March 18, 1902, Mr. Byrnes appeared as attorney for the bankrupts, and also as attorney for a large number of the creditors, having powers of attorney authorizing him to represent them in making proofs of their claims and in the appointment of trustee. Among the creditors so represented by Mr. Byrnes was Hannah Hanson, the mother of the bankrupts, whose claim was upon a promissory note made to her by the bankrupts jointly July 16, 1901, for $4,893.85, payable on demand, with 8 per cent. interest, on which note was endorsed $2,450, as paid February 7, 1902, one day before the date of the petition in bankruptcy. On the objection of other creditors that it appeared that said Hannah Hanson had received an unlawful preference, proof of her claim was not allowed. On proceeding to the appointment of trustee, Thomas H. Green was nominated by the attorney in fact of certain creditors, and John S. Anderson was nominated by said John T. Byrnes on behalf of the creditors represented by him, although other creditors then objected that said Byrnes, because he was the attorney of record of the bankrupt and then acting as such, was disqualified from participating in the appointment of trustee. Pending the appointment of trustee, the meeting of creditors was adjourned until the next day; and in the interim, by the advice of said Byrnes, and through the active personal exertions of the bankrupts, most of the creditors represented by said Byrnes revoked their powers of attorney to him and executed like powers of attorney to L. E. Covell, with the understanding that said Covell should as their representative vote for said John S. Anderson for trustee. On the next day a majority of the creditors in number and amount, including the creditors so represented by said Covell, voted for said John S. Anderson, although other creditors objected to the appointment of said Anderson, on the ground that he was the choice of the bankrupts, and that his majority vote was the result of the proxies and powers of attorney procured from creditors by the active interference of the bankrupts and

grounds 7 A. B. R. 662, 113 Fed. 443). Obiter, In re Van De Mark, 23 A. B. R. 760, 175 Fed. 287 (D. C. N. Y.); instance, In re Fletcher W. Ployd, 25 A. B. R. 194, 183 Fed. 791 (D. C. Pa.); In re Sitting, 25 A. B. R. 682, 182 Fed. 917 (D. C. N. Y.). Compare ante, § 384½.

their attorney. * * * As even the objecting creditors freely admit that Mr. Anderson is a man of responsibility, integrity, and high standing, it seems unfortunate that his appointment was brought about by such improper interference on the part of the bankrupts as should have caused it to be disapproved. But it is well settled by all the authorities that the trustee represents the creditors, and not the bankrupt, in the administration of the estate; and that it is improper that the bankrupt shall actively interfere with the matter of his selection and appointment; and that, if he does interfere and the person aided by him is appointed by votes procured by such interference, the appointment should for that reason be disapproved. * * * The rule is a salutary one, and based on obviously sound reason. It often happens that it becomes the duty of the trustee to actively antagonize the bankrupt by efforts to discover secreted assets, or to set aside conveyances as fraudulent, or to recover preferences. There should be no color of basis for suspicion of any partiality or sense of obligation on the part of the trustee toward the bankrupt. Hence, however high the character of a proposed trustee may be, the active interference of the bankrupt in favor of his appointment will render him practically ineligible to appointment as trustee in that bankruptcy."

[1867] In re Wetmore, Fed. Cas. 17,466: "While the choice of an assignee is vested by law in a majority in number and amount of the creditors, it is subject, nevertheless, to the approval of the district judge—a provision which implies a discretionary power to disapprove a choice so made. While the judge ought not arbitrarily, capriciously, or from dislike or partiality, to overrule the decision of the creditors, he is bound to see that the rights of the minority are properly protected, and to refuse confirmation, where he has good reason to suspect the assignee had been chosen in the interests of the bankrupts."

[1867] In re Bliss, Fed. Cas. 1,543: "It is certainly against the policy of the act that a bankrupt should select his assignee, as, by electing a fraudulent person or person disposed to favor him, the rights of the creditors might suffer. It is true that, if the creditors do not care sufficiently for the matter to attend the meeting, they ought not to complain. But still the law is no less brought into contempt. A fraudulent discharge of a debtor, or the discharge of a debtor who does not surrender all his assets, is precisely what those charged with the execution of the law are bound to guard against. If the court could be advised that in any particular case the bankrupt had brought in one or more of his friends, although bona fide creditors, and had by them chosen an assignee who was also his friend and in his interest, it is clear that the court would withhold its approval."

In re Columbia Iron Wks., 14 A. B. R. 527, 142 Fed. 234 (D. C. Mich.): "Mr. Moore, it is shown by the report of the trustee, holds, with one of the bankrupt's attorneys, the power of attorney of Bennett, trustee, and also several powers of attorney running to himself jointly with another of the bankrupt's attorneys, and this does not appear to be denied. He was disqualified from voting for a trustee upon those claims (In re Wetmore, 16 N. B. R. 514; In re McGill, 5 A. B. R. 155, 106 Fed. 57-62), and his vote should have been rejected."

And the furnishing of a list of creditors in advance of the filing of the schedules is a reprehensible practice;[64] although it is not improper where such advance list of creditors is furnished at the solicitation of creditors

---

64. In re Lloyd, 17 A. B. R. 97, 148 Fed. 92 (D. C. Wis.).

and for their aid and not at the instigation of the bankrupt nor in his interest.[65]

Thus, likewise, the trustee should not even be nominated by the bankrupt or his attorneys.

In re Rekersdres, 5 A. B. R. 811, 108 Fed. 206 (D. C. N. Y.): "Mr. Mintz also produced powers of attorney from three creditors to vote for a trustee, and these were a majority in number and amount of the creditors in attendance. Objection was made in behalf of another creditor to the nomination of a trustee by Mintz, and the referee refused to appoint the candidate so named, because his business association with Harvey, the attorney of the bankrupt, raised the presumption that the person nominated for trustee was nominated in fact by the bankrupt or his attorney, and therefore not a suitable person to act in the interest of the creditors, since the trustee should be the free and unbiased choice of the creditors, and not be influenced by any other interest. Falter v. Reinhard, 4 Am. B. R. 782; In re McGill, 5 Am. B. R. 155, 106 Fed. 57.

"The referee's ruling is approved. A trustee should be wholly free from all entangling alliances or associations that might in any way control his complete independence and responsibility. For this reason I disallow the appointment of attorney's clerks or other employees as trustees or receivers, under the practical control of other interests not directly responsible.

"For substantially similar reasons, proxies presented under circumstances of evident collusion with the bankrupt should be disallowed. It would be intolerable if the bankrupt by such means should be enabled to prevent or embarrass necessary investigation into his conduct or estate."

Neither the bankrupt nor his attorney should be permitted to have any influence in the election of the trustee.[66] And a former attorney of the bankrupt is an improper person.[67]

A stockholder and legal adviser of the bankrupt corporation is an improper person for trustee.

In re Gordon Supply & Mfg. Co., 12 A. B. R. 94, 129 Fed. 622 (D. C. Pa.): "There can be no objection personally to the trustee who has been chosen by a majority of those interested in the estate, at the creditors' meeting; and the right to such majority under ordinary circumstances to control the matter must be conceded. The trustee is the representative of creditors and they are the ones to decide who he shall be, subject only to the right of the court to supervise the choice where it is objected to. In the present instance the trustee chosen is not only a stockholder in the bankrupt corporation against which the proceedings were instituted, but he has been admittedly associated closely

---

65. In re Turner, 20 A. B. R. 646 (Ref. Mass.).

· 66. Obiter, In re Cooper, 14 A. B. R. 320, 135 Fed. 196 (D. C. Penna.); In re Lloyd, 17 A. B. R. 97, 148 Fed. 92 (D. C. Wis.); In re Sitting, 25 A. B. R. 682, 182 Fed. 917 (D. C. N. Y.); In re Morris, 18 A. B. R. 828, 154 Fed. 211 (D. C. Pa.).

67. Inferentially, In re Gordon Supply & Mfg. Co., 12 A. B. R. 94, 129 Fed. 622 (D. C. Penn.). Compare cases cited in In re Rung, 2 A. B. R. 620

(D. C. N. Y.). It has been held that the attorney for the bankrupt should not even be allowed to appear for a creditor. In re Kimball, 4 A. B. R. 144, 100 Fed. 177 (D. C. Mass.). But such a broad rule is hardly proper. There may be occasions when such an appearance would be proper and again when it would not be proper. At any rate the creditor's claim itself should not on that account be disallowed. Obiter, In re Kimball, 4 A. B. R. 144, 100 Fed. 177 (D. C. Mass.).

as attorney and legal adviser with those who have been hitherto in control, and their management is not only the subject of criticism, but may call for action on the part of the trustee to hold them personally responsible. To approve of the trustee now selected comes too near, therefore, to a continuation of previous conditions to be warranted. With so many others who would be fully as efficient and entirely acceptable, the majority have no right to impose their present choice on the objecting minority.

"The election is therefore set aside and a new election ordered"

But where the circumstances preclude the inference of acting in the bankrupt's interests, it may not be improper to allow the bankrupt's former attorney to vote claims and even to be voted for as trustee. Thus, an attorney employed only for the special purpose of preparing and filing a bankrupt's petition, for which he is paid no fee, may vote for trustee upon claims of creditors sent to him without his solicitation or the procurement of the bankrupt, specially where the bankrupt had disappeared.[68] And where uninfluenced, the votes for a former attorney of the bankrupt are not to be rejected as nullities.[69]

And it has been held, apparently, that some showing of actual influence effected must be made, and that only such votes as were so proved to have influenced should be rejected.

In re Eastlack, 16 A. B. R. 536, 145 Fed. 168 (D. C. N. J.): "There is no evidence whatever tending to show that any one of these persons was influenced in his vote either by the bankrupt or his attorney. It is true that, as the letter set forth in the referee's certificate was sent 'to substantially all the creditors,' some, and possibly all, of these 32 creditors received copies of it. But not one of them was called as a witness on the question as to whether he was influenced by it. For aught that appears in the case, they may have made inquiry concerning Dr. Grace and, independently of the letter they received, have satisfied themselves that he was the best available man for the trusteeship. The situation was altogether different from what it would have been had these 32 creditors, or any considerable portion of them, been brought to the referee's office by the bankrupt or his attorney."

Compare, In re Lloyd, 17 A. B. R. 98 (D. C. Wis.): "I do not think the referee had power to disqualify the 13 creditors who appear to have employed Bouck & Hilton in the regular way, and who had no concern with the bankrupts in the matter, simply because Bouck & Hilton had received certain other claims through the instrumentality of the bankrupt. This would in effect be to punish creditors who were innocent in the premises."

And that the mere existence of such relation is not, in and of itself, a disqualification.

In re Kaufman, 24 A. B. R. 117, 179 Fed. 552 (D. C. Ky.): "We should by no means approve a practice which would permit an attorney to act at the same time for a bankrupt and for the bankrupt's creditors, and especially at the first meeting of creditors. Such disapproval would be much empha-

68. In re Cooper, 14 A. B. R. 320, 135 Fed. 196 (D. C. Penn.).
69. In re Machin & Brown, 11 A. B. R. 449, 128 Fed. 316 (D. C. Penn.);
In re Syracuse Paper and Pulp Co., 21 A. B. R. 174, 164 Fed. 275 (D. C. N. Y.).

sized if the creditors, in making their selection of an agent, were influenced by the bankrupt himself and in his interest. But the relation of attorney for the bankrupt may have ceased in this case with the filing of the consent to the adjudication, or the creditors may have appointed their attorney and agent entirely upon their own desire and without any thought or suggestion of the interest of the bankrupt. These matters could hardly be fairly settled upon the mere oral suggestion at the meeting of the fact that the same man was the attorney who had appeared for the bankrupt and who now appeared for the creditors. The creditors did not do an unlawful thing but they did a thing which, under circumstances such as we have indicated, might meet with judicial disapproval. But those circumstances ought first to be inquired into before they could be the basis of a fair decision. Upon consideration of the matter, and upon reading * * * authorities * * * we have reached the conclusion that the proper practice in such contingencies as arose in this case would be to postpone an election for a day or two in order to get at the exact facts instead of assuming anything to be true upon the mere fact alone that the same person appeared to be the attorney both for the bankrupt and for creditors. Peradventure, his relations with the bankrupt may have ceased when the consent was filed. Prompt inquiry would develop the real facts, and if necessary the creditors might be given an opportunity to authorize a new agent. The attainment of a fair expression of the wishes of the creditors as to the control and management of a business which became theirs when the adjudication was made, is abundantly worth the short time it will take to get it."

But if the cases In re Eastlack, In re Kaufman and In re Loyd are to be interpreted as so laying down the rule, they are not to be approved. Such proof would be almost impossible to produce, and the cleverer and more dangerous the collusion, the more difficult would it be to disqualify the particular voters or candidates who have colluded.[70] And the mere existence of such dual relation is at any rate sufficient to cast the burden of rebuttal upon such attorney.

In one case it was held not improper to elect a director of a bankrupt corporation as one of three trustees.

In re Syracuse Paper & Pulp Co., 21 A. B. R. 174, 164 Fed. 275 (D. C. N. Y.), quoted further at § 888: "As stated, two of those elected and confirmed by the referee are men of the highest probity and business ability, and entirely disinterested; and the inclusion of Driscoll, familiar with all the books and affairs of the company, was wise and proper. Should he attempt to hide or cover the transactions, or balk proper legal proceedings, it would be ground of removal, and the referee should not hesitate to report the facts, and this court would speedily remove him. It was suggested on the argument that there is a possibility that it will became the duty of the trustees to bring action against some or all the directors, including Driscoll, and that he, as trustee, cannot sue himself as director, or as an individual. There will be ample

70. See In re Morton, 9 A. B. R. 508 (D. C. Mass.), for a peculiar state of facts: All unsecured and unpreferred creditors had been paid in full; a new trustee was to be selected to distribute the assets amongst preferred creditors who might thereafter have their claims allowed; some of these unpreferred creditors voted at the bankrupt's solicitation for a certain trustee; held, that the court would not disturb the selection, the bankrupt's solicitation not being shown to be by way of improper inducement.

1 R B—45

opportunity to cross that bridge when reached, if it ever is; but I am of opinion that a trustee as such may be party complainant or plaintiff as such, and also defendant as an individual. In this case Hakes and Bosworth may prosecute all necessary actions, making Driscoll as director or personally or even as trustee, a party defendant, stating the necessity for such action."

But the decision in the case In re Syracuse Paper & Pulp Co. was undoubtedly based on the fact that there were three trustees elected, two of whom were in no way occupying inconsistent positions, the third trustee being chosen merely as a convenience because of his familiarity with the details of the bankrupt's business. To extend the doctrine enunciated in that case to cases where only one trustee is elected would be subversive of proper administration and be a shock to the moral sense as well; for that "one cannot serve two masters" is both sound sense and good law. It would be worse than kneeling to "socialistic doctrine" which the court in that case, obiter, seems to consider involved. And the question, after all, is one largely of the facts of each particular case.[71]

There is no statutory provision, either in the Bankruptcy Act, or elsewhere, which forbids a creditor having as his attorney or agent the person who has acted as attorney for the bankrupt in the preparation of his consent to an adjudication, but judicial policy greatly discourages the practice of attorneys at law acting as attorneys at the same time both for the bankrupt and for his creditors, because such a practice might lead to conduct and results which would be strongly condemned.[72] Indeed, an attorney who takes such inconsistent positions surely lays the foundation of future trouble for himself.

However, it has been held that if, by want of proper advice, creditors exercise their right to name and do name as their agent to act for them a person whom mere judicial policy discourages from so doing, the creditors should not, for that reason alone, be absolutely denied a voice in the selection of a trustee.[73]

§ 888. Votes Cast by Relatives, Stockholders, Directors and Employees.

—It would seem that votes cast by relatives of the bankrupt should be closely scanned, before allowing the election to turn on them.[73a] And the same rule should apply to those cast by employees or by stockholders or directors of a bankrupt corporation.[74]

In re Day & Co., 23 A. B. R. 56, 176 Fed. 377 (D. C. N. Y.): "* * * that Wodiska was a director of the company and a brother-in-law of the president,

---

71. Instance where facts held insufficient to warrant disapproval, In re Ketterer Mfg. Co., 19 A. B. R. 225, 155 Fed. 987.

72. Obiter, In re Kaufman, 24 A. B. R. 117, 179 Fed. 552 (D. C. Ky.), quoted supra.

73. In re Kaufman, 24 A. B. R. 117, 179 Fed. 552 (D. C. Ky.).

73a. In re Sitting, 25 A. B. R. 682, 182 Fed. 917 (D. C. N. Y.).

74. Obiter (vote allowed because no collusion), In re Stradley & Co., 26 A. B. R. 149, 187 Fed. 285 (D. C. Ala.): "Where there is reason to apprehend collusion or improper influence, as the result of such action, the referee may refuse a vote to such claimant."

and that his subdivision of the claims, although bona fide, was with the aim of controlling the appointment of the trustee. With this admitted, the case comes within Re McGill, 5 A. B. R. 155, 106 Fed. 57 and all those votes should not have been counted * * * If the referee had known these facts he would doubtless have thrown out the votes, and declared elected the rival candidate. * * * The situation therefore is that not only has there never been an election in fact, but the creditors have never had a fair opportunity for an election— by which I mean an opportunity without the interference of the bankrupt's officers. This they should have. I believe I might throw out the votes illegally cast, and now declare the other candidate elected, but that course does not seem to be as satisfactory. * * *"

Yet directors, stockholders and employees of bankrupt corporations are entitled to vote.[75]

In re Syracuse Paper & Pulp Co., 21 A. B. R. 174, 164 Fed. 275 (D. C. N. Y.), quoted further at § 887: "A vote on the claim of Mr. Latterner was objected to on the ground that the claimant was an employee of the bankrupt company, and therefore not a proper person to vote for the election of a trustee. No such disability is imposed by the Bankruptcy Act or by common sense. It might be that two-thirds of the creditors of the bankrupt company were employees of the concern. Are they to be debarred from voting on the suspicion that they may have a friendly feeling for the company that has given them employment? * * * were objected to on the same ground, with the addition that he was also a director. The law imposes no such disability on the creditor of such a corporation who happens to be a stockholder or director therein, and there is no valid reason why he should be debarred from voting for trustee. To be a stockholder in or attorney for a corporation may be a bar to his holding political office in the minds of those who would strike down corporate industries, or in the minds of political demagogues; but this socialistic doctrine has not yet been applied by the Congress of the United States to creditors of bankrupt corporations who have been so unfortunate or unwise as to become stockholders therein. Political preferment may be denied by the people to stockholders in corporations, and laws may be hereafter enacted which will deny property rights to that, now unfortunate, class of our citizens, as a punishment for association with corporations; but such disabilities are not yet written upon the statute books of these United States of America. This court declines to anticipate legislation in that regard. Cases may arise where the directors of a bankrupt corporation, also creditors thereof, may seek to control the election of the trustee in the interest of the bankrupt itself, and in opposition to the interests of the general creditors. In such a case I do not doubt that the referee or judge has the power to set aside such an election, if made; but it would be on other grounds than that the directors were not entitled to vote for the appointment of the trustee. In this case there was no combination of directors; no attempt to elect trustees in the interest of the bankrupt corporation."

And the evil of permitting the action of a majority in number of creditors to be controlled by the vote of an officer or stockholder having a large claim, can be sufficiently guarded against by the discretion vested in

75. In re Stradley & Co., 26 A. B. R. 149, 187 Fed. 285 (D. C. Ala.), quoted further in this same section. Compare, ante, § 215.

the referee to refuse a vote to such a claimant in cases of collusion or improper influence.

In re Stradley & Co., 26 A. B. R. 149, 187 Fed. 285 (D. C. Ala.): "The evil of permitting the action of a majority in number of creditors to be controlled by the vote of an officer or stockholder of the bankrupt corporation having a large claim, can be corrected by the discretion vested in the referee in cases of collusion, improper influence or unfit candidate."

However, there is nothing to prevent an officer or director or attorney of a bankrupt corporation nor any relative of a bankrupt from voting on his own allowed claim, even though the votes of others procured by him may be invalidated.

Obiter, In re Day & Co., 24 A. B. R. 252, 178 Fed. 545 (C. C. A. N. Y., affirming 23 A. B. R. 56): "As to so much of the order, however, which forbids an officer of the corporation, or its attorney or Wodiska from themselves voting on any allowed claims of their own we are not inclined to assent to the proposition that they may thus summarily be deprived of the right to vote secured by them by § 56 of the Bankruptcy Act. No question of irregular or improper proxy is presented, as in the case relied on. * * * We are satisfied from the record that the claims which Wodiska turned over, without consideration therefor, to persons from whom he obtained proxies to vote for trustee should have been excluded from voting, and concur with the district judge in his disposition of them."

§ 889. Prior Assignee or Receiver as Candidate.—A receiver or assignee for creditors in charge of the property under orders of a State Court, and who has been acting as such, is generally to be considered an improper person for trustee, because he holds adverse interests and may have to be required to account for and to surrender property to the bankruptcy court, and thus be called upon to hold antagonistic and inconsistent positions.[76]

In re Clay, 27 A. B. R. 715, 192 Fed. 831 (C. C. A. Mass.): "The petitioner urges that an assignee selected by the bankrupt is not necessarily and at all events disqualified to become a trustee in bankruptcy, citing In re Blue Ridge Packing Co. (D. C. Pa.), 11 Am. B. R. 36, 125 Fed. 619, and contends that, unless something else appears, his appointment should be approved, even if objected to by a minority of creditors. While the fact that the person chosen by the creditors is the bankrupt's assignee, whose accounts are unsettled, may not amount to an absolute disqualification in point of law, and while the choice of such person by creditors, under special circumstances, may be properly approved by the referee or judge, we are of the opinion that no special or additional circumstances are necessary to justify the disapproval of an assignee who is accountable to the bankrupt's estate. There is both a practical and a legal presumption against the propriety of such an appointment, for the reason that as assignee he is an accounting party to the estate, and as trustee

---

76. Instance, where precisely this situation occurred. Loveless v. Southern Grocer Co., 20 A. B. R. 180, 159 Fed. 415 (C. C. A. La.). But see contra, In re Blue Ridge Packing Co., 11 A. B. R. 36, 125 Fed. 620 (D. C. Penn.). Also, contra, instance, In re Byerly, 12 A. B. R. 186 (D. C. Penn.).

will have to investigate his own account. In Williams on Bankruptcy (9th ed.), p. 85, it is said: 'It is a good objection that the trustee is an accounting party to the estate, and will as trustee have to investigate his own account.' The brief of the trustee cites in support of his contention upon this point: Remington on Bankruptcy, § 889; Stuyvesant Bank, 6 N. B. R. 272, Fed. Cas. No. 13,581; Williams on Bankruptcy (9th ed., 1908), p. 85; Baldwin on Bankruptcy (10th ed., 1910), p. 196; Griffith's Law of Bankruptcy (1867), p. 829; In re Mardon, 1 Q. B. (1896) 140; In re Martin, 21 Q. B. D. 29; In re Stovold, 6 Morrell's Bankruptcy Reports, 7; Ex parte Mendell, 4 Deacon & Chitty's Eng. Bank Rep. 725; McFarlane v. Grieve, 10 Murray & Young, 551."

However, in some instances where such receiver or assignee has taken no important steps under the receivership or assignment and has practically been simply holding the property until bankruptcy proceedings could be instituted, and where he is not otherwise disqualified, such receiver or assignee has sometimes been appointed receiver or trustee in the bankruptcy proceedings also. Especially does the practice prevail where no objection is made.

Of course one who has been acting as receiver in the bankruptcy court is not for that reason disqualified.[77]

§ 890. Creditor with Disputed Claim Incompetent.

—A creditor whose claim is disputed and between whom and the estate contest is likely to arise and who from the circumstances is likely to be antagonistic to the estate, should not be approved.[78]

So a trustee selected by, and apparently in the interest of such a creditor, will be disapproved.[79]

§ 891. Candidate Interested in Scheme of Composition Incompetent.

—A candidate who is interested in a scheme of composition with the creditors is an improper person for trustee.[80]

§ 892. Votes Improperly Obtained from Innocent Creditors or Cast for Disqualified Candidates Not Nullities.

—Votes on proxies improperly obtained from innocent creditors or cast for a disqualified or incompetent candidate are not absolute nullities so as to give the election to the other candidate, who has not received the votes of a majority of creditors

---

77. In re Crocker Co., 27 A. B. R. 241 (Ref. Mass.).

78. In re Law, 13 A. B. R. 650 (Ref. Ills., affirmed by D. C.): In this case the court held that powers of attorney obtained through the influence of the attorneys for creditors who have received alleged preferences may not be used in the selection of a trustee, especially in a case where the unsecured creditors have no possible way of realizing on their claims unless the trustee is able to recover the alleged preference. See (impliedly) In re Lazoris, 10 A. B. R. 31, 120 Fed. 716 (D. C. Wis.); compare, to same effect, cases cited in In re Rung, 2 A. B. R. 620 (D. C. N. Y.).

79. In re Anson Mercantile Co., 25 A. B. R. 429, 185 Fed. 993 (D. C. Tex.).

80. In re Wrisley Co., 13 A. B. R. 193 (C. C. A. Ills.). Analogously, In re E. T. Kinney Co., 14 A. B. R. 611 (D. C. Ind.).

present, both in number and amount whose claims have been allowed, for the creditor is still "present" with an "allowed" claim.[81]

In re Machin & Brown, 11 A. B. R. 449, 128 Fed. 316 (D. C. Pa.): "Conceding for present purposes that he could not be approved because of his previous relation, it does not follow that the votes voluntarily cast for him are not to be regarded at all. The creditors who cast them were exercising 'a legal right in a legal and proper manner,' to use the language of the referee, and even if they were voting for a candidate who could not be approved by the court, this did not make their votes a nullity so that the opposing candidate must be declared elected."

In re Walker & Co., 29 A. B. R. 499, 176 Fed. 455 (D. C. Ala.): "At a creditors' meeting it appeared to the referee that the claims of a large majority in number and amount were represented by the attorneys who had filed the voluntary petition for the bankrupt but who had ceased to represent the bankrupt after the date of the filing of the petition, and that this firm of attorneys, during their representation of the bankrupt, had solicited a part of the claims held by them. It also appeared that they were going to vote them for a person as trustee who was put forward in the interest of or with the desire of the bankrupt. The referee determined that the claims were improperly represented and that the person to be voted for by them was an inappropriate person to act as trustee. Thereupon the attorneys who represented such claims asked leave to vote them for another and suitable person, which was denied them upon the ground that they could not with propriety represent the claims by reason of their former connection with the bankrupt and the manner in which they had acquired the claims. The attorneys thereupon asked the referee to defer the creditors' meeting for a reasonable time to enable the creditors they represented to obtain other proper representation. No improper conduct was charged to the creditors, nor does it appear that they were in collusion with the bankrupt or his former attorneys or had any improper motive in seeking the election of such person as trustee, nor did it appear that they knew of any conduct on the part of the bankrupt or his former attorneys that would preclude the former attorneys from representing them at the meeting. The referee held that the claims represented by the firm of attorneys, being improperly represented, could not be held as being present at the meeting at all, and declined to defer the meeting in order to enable them to obtain proper representation, but permitted a minority in number and amount of the proven claims to proceed with the election of a trustee, who was unsatisfactory to the majority. The creditors whose votes were disallowed filed a petition for review to the district judge. The conclusion of the referee is concurred in so far as it determines that the attorneys holding the proxies of the majority in number and amount were not proper persons to vote their claims, and in so far as it determines that the candidate put in nomination by these attorneys was not a suitable person to act as trustee. In view of the fact that the majority creditors were not in fault in being improperly represented by such attorneys and in voting their claims for an ineligible trustee, it seems fair that they should have had a reasonable opportunity to acquire proper representation and to vote their claims for a suitable candidate, no injury to the estate being made to appear as a result of the delay to the meeting."

But where the votes are by proxies and the proxies are not duly executed,

81. If the incompetent candidate has received the majority in number and the other candidate the majority in amount, the referee may appoint. In re Lazoris, 10 A. B. R. 31, 120 Fed. 716 (D. C. Wis.).

the creditors are not to be considered as "present" and their proxy votes are not to be counted.[82] Collusive votes where the creditor is in complicity are, on the other hand, to be held as nullities, and the other candidate may be considered elected.

§ 893. Question of Collusion to Be Definitely Disposed of before Approval.

—The question as to whether there is any collusion with the bankrupt or preferred creditor is one which should be definitely disposed of before the appointment, and, if there appears to be reasonable cause to believe such collusion exists, the referee should either decline to receive the collusive votes or to approve the election until the question is settled.[83]

§ 893½. Improper Votes Not to Be Counted.

—The proper practice, perhaps, is that the improper votes should be excluded when offered to be cast.[84]

In re Van De Mark, obiter, 23 A. B. R. 760, 175 Fed. 287 (D. C. N. Y.): "It is true, votes for trustee may be rejected on the ground that they are in the interest of the bankrupt and were cast for a trustee who presumably would assist in carrying out a fraud upon the creditors. * * * It is contended that counsel for the bankrupt had solicited proxies of creditors authorizing him to vote for trustee, and that such votes for Mr. Storrs should not be considered or counted. The practice of counsel for the bankrupt of soliciting proxies from creditors and voting them to control the election of a trustee is not viewed with favor by the bankruptcy law, and the referee would have been justified in excluding such votes or proxies as being manifestly in the interest of the bankrupt; but no such order was made, and the objection to certain creditors voting for trustee was overruled."

Compare, In re Kaufman, 24 A. B. R. 117, 179 Fed. 552 (D. C. Ky.): "Here the majority creditors in fact voted through their attorney for one person for trustee and the minority creditors voted for another. When the referee passed upon the objections he held that the majority creditors could not be represented by the attorney they had named. He did so upon the ground indicated, and thereupon excluded their votes. Those creditors were not in fact present at the meeting and were not otherwise represented thereat. But the referee held that the majority creditors, though not permitted to be represented by the attorney of their choice, nevertheless had to be taken into the estimate when it came to be determined whether the person voted for by the minority creditors had received the votes of a majority in number and value of the creditors who were present and whose claims had been allowed. In this ruling he must have regarded the majority creditors as being present for the count but not present for the voting. The result was that he declared

---

82. In re Henschel, 7 A. B. R. 662, 11 Fed. 443 (C. C. A. N. Y., reversing 6 A. B. R. 305). See ante, § 582, et seq.

83. In re Dayville Woolen Co., 8 A. B. R. 85, 114 Fed. 674 (D. C. Conn.).

84. Obiter and inferentially, In re Stradley & Co., 26 A. B. R. 149, 187 Fed. 285 (D. C. Ala.), quoted at § 888. In re Day & Co., 23 A. B. R. 56, 176 Fed. 377 (D. C. N. Y.).

that there had been no election, and himself appointed another person as trustee. This result is not maintainable upon any ground. If the majority were present, then the minority creditors who were present had the right to conduct the meeting, and as their candidate did receive the votes of the majority in number and value of the creditors present, the referee was without power to disregard that result, and especially was he without power to disregard it upon the grounds upon which he acted. The creditors are not to be counted as present simply because their claims have been allowed. In order to be present they must attend in person or by duly authorized agent or attorney, and those creditors who do so attend constitute the meeting, whether they constitute a majority in number and value of the claims allowed or not."

Distinctions are to be noted between, first, the throwing out of votes because improper on account of collusion, etc.; second, the refusal of votes under certain proxies because of having been improperly obtained, and postponement of the election for new proxies, the creditors themselves being innocent of complicity;[84a] third, the refusal of votes because of defective proxies; and, fourth, the disqualification of the candidate himself. Votes on defective proxies may be thrown out and yet the candidate for whom they would be voted not be disqualified. On the other hand, a candidate may be disqualified though the votes be legal. Also, undoubtedly, a candidate may be refused approval precisely because he has been elected through improper or collusive votes or votes improperly obtained in the interest of the bankrupt or of some other adverse person.

§ 894. When Referee Disapproves, Order of Disapproval to Be Entered and Opportunity for Review Given.

—When the referee disapproves of the creditor's choice, it is his duty to make an order to that effect, and the parties then may carry it up for review by the judge as in case of any other order made by the referee.[85]

In re Hare, 9 A. B. R. 520, 119 Fed. 246 (D. C. N. Y., Ray, J.): "This they proceeded to do. The creditors having appointed a trustee, there was nothing for the referee to do in that regard except approve or disapprove such appointment. * * *

"It is plain that, the appointment by the creditors having been actually made, the referee was called upon to approve or disapprove the appointment. This he could not do by mental action or words alone. It was his duty to make an order in writing disapproving the appointment, if he disapproved, and on this the parties had a right to be heard before the judge, as 'he (the trustee) shall be removed by the judge only.' This general order confers no power on a referee to announce, as was done in this case, that he will not appoint the trustee already appointed by the creditors. It does authorize him to disapprove such appointment by order, and should this be done at the time the appointment is made by the creditors it is probable that the creditors might proceed at once to appoint some other person, as this would be an acquiescence in such disapproval; but should they not do this the matter should be reported to the

84a. Compare, In re Walker & Co., 29 A. B. R. 499, 176 Fed. 455 (D. C. Ala.), quoted at § 802.
85. Instance, In re Clay, 27 A. B.

R. 715, 192 Fed. 830 (C. C. A. Mass.); In re Anson Mercantile Co., 25 A. B. R. 429, 185 Fed. 993 (D. C. Tex.).

judge, who may remove the trustee appointed by the creditors, and order another appointment by the creditors."

§ 895. Upon Final Disapproval, Another Election Requisite, Referee Not to Appoint.

—But if creditors do not carry up the order of disapproval or if, after it has been carried up, the judge affirms it, then *the creditors should hold another election;* and the referee has at no time the right, upon disapproval of the creditors' choice, at once and summarily to appoint a trustee himself; the creditors must be given an opportunity again to vote.[86]

In re Hare, 9 A. B. R. 520, 119 Fed. 246 (D. C. N. Y.): "In no event can the referee ignore the appointment made by the creditors, and proceed summarily to appoint the trustee without holding another election, as was done in this case. He cannot compel the creditors to vote, but he can give them an opportunity. If they do not vote, they have neglected to appoint or recommend."

In re Lewensohn, 3 A. B. R. 299, 98 Fed. 576 (D. C. N. Y.): "If upon the referee's disapproval of an elected trustee or upon a trustee's refusal to accept or failure to qualify, there is a vacancy in the office of trustee, the case falls within § 44 of the Bankruptcy Act and a further election by the creditors must be had where such an election is practicable. The court may not, as a rule, appoint until after opportunity is afforded creditors for a new election where that is practicable."

In re MacKellar, 8 A. B. R. 669, 116 Fed. 547 (D. C. Penn.): "The right of a referee to disapprove or veto the choice made by the creditors is quite different from the right to himself name. The act expressly vests in the creditors the right to say who shall represent them in administering the bankrupt's estate (§ 44); and it is only when they make no choice that the court or referee is authorized to do so for them (Ibid). That is to say, where there has been no action on the part of creditors, the duty devolves upon the court of supplying it. It is not authorized to intervene, however, simply because the choice is one which cannot be approved; an unworthy choice is not the same as no choice at all; the creditors by actually acting having indicated their intention to avail themselves of the privilege given them by the law, which is not exhausted by a single exercise of it. The section which we are considering gives them the right to meet and appoint a trustee whenever and so often as there is a vacancy; and this occurs as is pointed out in In re Lewensohn, 3 Am. B. R. 299, 98 Fed. 576, when they have chosen someone whom the referee declines to approve. It therefore became the duty of the referee, not to name a trustee, as he did, but to call another meeting of the creditors and let them do so."

---

86. In re Mangan, 13 A. B. R. 303, 133 Fed. 1000 (D. C. Penn.); In re Jacobs & Roth, 18 A. B. R. 728, 157 Fed. 988 (D. C. Pa.); Contra, obiter, In re Day, 23 A. B. R. 56, 176 Fed. 377 (D. C. N. Y.). And compare, where trustee had abandoned his trusteeship. Scofield v. United States ex rel. Bond, 23 A. B. R. 259, 174 Fed. 1 (C. C. A. Ohio), quoted at § 878. See also, In re Van De Mark, 23 A. B. R. 760, 175 Fed. 287 (D. C. N. Y.). In re Margolies, 27 A. B. R. 398, 191 Fed. 369 (D. C. N. Y.).

Where Election of Trustee Set Aside and New Election Ordered, Intervening Sales Not Invalidated.—In re Evening Standard Pub. Co., 21 A. B. R. 156, 164 Fed. 517 (D. C. N. Y.).

But the new trustee's appointment may not be collaterally attacked for such failure to call another election.[87]   And if the creditors fail to act after such reasonable opportunity has been given, the referee may make the appointment.[88]

DIVISION 3.

TRUSTEE'S RELATION TO CREDITORS AND COURT.

§ 896. Occupies Dual Position—Official Custodian for All—Also Party Litigant.

—The trustee occupies a dual position. He is both an officer of the court, like a receiver or marshal, protecting and administering the property in the interests of all, and also is the owner of an interest, a party litigant, as having the title to the general assets in trust for unsecured creditors.[89]

McLean v. Mayo, 7 A. B. R. 116, 113 Fed. 106 (D. C. N. Car.): "While the Bankruptcy Act creates the office of trustee in bankruptcy, such trustee is a quasi officer of the court in a qualified sense; he is in reality elected by and represents the creditors of the bankrupt under the provisions of the Bankruptcy Act. The bankruptcy court will protect the trustee in the discharge of his quasi official duties, but as the representative of the creditors his duties as such representative must be discharged, not as an officer of the court, strictly speaking, but as provided in the Bankrupt Act."

Compare, Goldman v. Smith, 2 A. B. R. 104 (Ref. Ky.): "But it would violate the main purpose of the Bankruptcy Law which is to distribute the property of the bankrupt equally among his creditors, to hold that the trustee represented lien claims, or would or could do anything to perfect or preserve a lien against his estate."

Compare, In re Smith, 9 A. B. R. 603 (D. C. N. Y.): "A trustee in bankruptcy is defined by the Bankrupt Act as an officer (§ 1) and is, in a certain restricted sense, an officer of the Court—but he is not an officer of the court in any such sense as a receiver. He takes the legal title to the property, and in respect to suits stands in the same general position as a trustee of an express trust, or an executor."

For these reasons, while representing secured creditors in his capacity as custodian, he does not represent them in any other capacity, his capacity as a party litigant or party in interest being confined to representing unsecured creditors.[90]

<hr>

87. Scofield v. United States ex rel. Bond, 23 A. B. R. 254, 174 Fed. 1 (C. C. A. Ohio), quoted at § 878.

88. In re Clay, 27 A. B. R. 715, 192 Fed. 830 (C. C. A. Mass.), quoted on another point at § 889.

89. In re Baber, 9 A. B. R. 406, 110 Fed. 520 (D. C. Tenn.); impliedly, Taylor v. Taylor, 4 A. B. R. 215, 45 Atl. 440 (N. J. Ch.). Thus, notice to the trustee is notice to all creditors, In re Hanson, 5 A. B. R. 747, 107 Fed. 252 (D. C. Ore.).

90. Goldman v. Smith, 2 A. B. R. 104 (Ref. Ky.), in which case it was held the trustee cannot perfect liens for secured creditors.

When asking for allowance out of the estate for his own compensation and for expenses, he does not represent creditors, but represents simply himself. But see, apparently contra, but obiter, Gray v. Mercantile Co., 14 A. B. R. 780, 138 Fed. 344 (C. C. A. N. Dak.): "The trustee is not their representative. He is seeking to strike

Taylor *v.* Taylor, 4 A. B. R. 215 (N. J. Ch.), 45 Atl. 440: "The point, however, made by the counsel for Mr. Murphy, is that the trustee represents all the creditors, and that, inasmuch as this is a suit brought by a creditor to reach the property of his bankrupt debtor, the right to sue for such assets upon bankruptcy passed to the trustee. In respect to general creditors of a bankrupt, the trustee is undoubtedly their representative. In gathering in the assets of a bankrupt, he can, as such representative of the general creditors, seek to uncover property fraudulently conveyed or concealed by the debtor. The right of a trustee to pursue and recover by suit any property which legally or equitably belongs to the estate of a bankrupt cannot be doubted. A receiver, as the representative of an insolvent corporation, may file a bill to set aside illegal or fraudulent transfers of the property of a corporation. Smith, Rec., pp. 397-406; Button Co. *v.* Spielman, 50 N. J. Eq. 120, 24 Atl. 571; Spielman *v.* Knowles, 50 N. J. 796, 27 Atl. 1033. So an assignee, under our assignment act, and executors and administrators of an insolvent estate, as the representatives of the general creditors, may, for the benefit of the creditors, set aside conveyances of the assignor or decedent made in fraud of their creditors, to the extent that such property is needed for the payment of debts. Pillsbury *v.* Kingdon, 33 N. J. Eq. 287. But while the trustee so represents general creditors, and while the entire right of such creditors to pursue the property of the bankrupt passes to the trustee, who thus obtains an exclusive right to bring such suits (McCartin's Ex'rs *v.* Perry's Ex'r, 39 N. J. Eq. 198), such officer does not succeed to the rights of secured creditors. A creditor who has a lien upon the property of the bankrupt is his own representative, so far as concerns his security."

Compare, In re Ducker, 13 A. B. R. 769, 134 Fed. 43 (C. C. A. Ky.): "The trustee is the hand of the court. He stands as its agent to liquidate the assets to protect them and bring them before the court for final distribution. He is not, in fact, more representative of one creditor or claimant than another. The trustee, in the procedure, because he has the legal title to the assets and is charged with the duty of saving and protecting them, represents the general fund. He is not a purchaser, but as the title of his office imports, he is trustee for all who have interests, and according to those interests. He himself has no interest and there is nothing in his representation which stands between the court and those who have interests for the recognition and protection of which they appeal to its authority. We have thus explained our views upon this subject founded as they are upon what we conceive to be fundamental and controlling principles."

§ 897. Occupies Fiduciary Relation—A trustee stands to creditors in a fiduciary relation.[91]

In re Wrisley Co., 13 A. B. R. 193, 133 Fed. 388, 390 (C. C. A. Ills.): "A trustee in bankruptcy is an officer of the court chosen by vote of the creditors. He stands to creditors in a fiduciary relation. He holds the estate in trust

down the allowance of their claims, and in this is the representative of the general creditors of the estate. Chatfield *v.* O'Dwyer, supra. Of course he cannot represent or speak for both sides to the controversy."

91. Compare, to same effect, In re Royce Dry Goods Co., 13 A. B. R. 267 (D. C. Mo.).

Before the election of a trustee, if no receiver is appointed, the bankrupt is the quasi trustee of the property, In re Wilson, 6 A. B. R. 287, 289 (D. C. W. Va.); obiter and inferentially, Blake *v.* Valentine, 1 A. B. R. 378, 89 Fed. 691 (D. C. Calif.); ante, § 383.

primarily for creditors; secondarily, if there be a surplus, for the benefit of the bankrupt. He should have no interest to serve except to conserve the estate. He should not be interested in any scheme of composition. In all matters between creditors and bankrupt he, should stand indifferent. His sole care should be to make the most out of the estate, and that primarily in the interest of the creditors. When he goes beyond that, and seeks to aid the bankrupt at the expense of the creditors, and by concealment or by false representations induces creditors to act contrary to their interest, he violates his duty, and should be removed from the trust to which he has been false."

He is chosen to represent *all* creditors.[92]

In re Baird, 7 A. B. R. 448, 112 Fed. 960 (D. C. Pa.): "It may be safely said, however, that if a trustee bears in mind that he is the representative of the estate considered as a whole, is bound to be vigilant and attentive in advancing its interests, and is under obligation to seek to carry out in the strictest good faith the provisions of the Bankrupt Act where they seem to apply plainly to the estate committed to his charge, he is not likely to go far wrong in doing or refusing to do, what may be asked of him by the creditors."

He should not be interested in any scheme of composition.[93]

He should have no interest to serve except to conserve the estate.[94]

In re Frazin & Oppenheim, 24 A. B. R. 598, 183 Fed. 28 (C. C. A. N. Y.): "The one thing, more than all others, which creditors and bankrupt alike have the right to expect from those having official duties to perform relating to the property of the estate is disinterestedness in its disposition and liquidation."

Amicable relations between the trustee and creditors are much to be desired.[95]

§ 898. Trustee Not to Be Dictated to by Creditors.—He is not to be dictated to by creditors and he should follow his best judgment.[96]

In re Columbia Iron Wks., 14 A. B. R. 526, 142 Fed. 234 (D. C. Mich.): "Equally removed from the interference of the creditors is the action of the trustee so long as that officer shall act with fidelity to his trust. He is chosen to represent all the creditors, not a majority, however great. * * * Subject to the control of the court and statutory limitations, the entire administration of the trust estate is in his hands. He cannot, therefore, yield his judgment to that of a majority of the creditors, merely because they are a majority, without a breach of his trust. To thus abdicate his duties is to make himself a mere passive trustee. It is proper that he should consult with the creditors upon important matters and get the benefit of their knowledge and experience, but the responsibility of decision rests upon him. Finance Co. v.

---

92. In re Lewensohn, 9 A. B. R. 368, 121 Fed. 539 (D. C. N. Y.); In re Columbia Iron Wks., 14 A. B. R. 530 (D. C. Mich.); In re MacDougall, 23 A. B. R. 762, 175 Fed. 400 (D. C. N. Y.); In re Kreuger, 27 A. B. R. 440, 196 Fed. 704 (D. C. Ky.).

93. In re Wrisley Co., 13 A. B. R. 193 (C. C. A. Ills.).

94. In re Wrisley Co., 13 A. B. R. 193 (C. C. A. Ills.).

95. McPherson v. Cox, 96 U. S. 404; May v. May, 167 U. S. 310.

96. (1867) In re Dewey, 4 N. B. Reg. 412, 414; inferentially, In re Baber, 9 A. B. R. 406, 119 Fed. 525 (D. C. Tenn.): inferentially, In re Baird, 7 A. B. R. 448, 112 Fed. 960 (D. C. Pa.).

Warren, 82 Fed. 528. The 43rd section of the act of 1867 made provision for superseding the ordinary bankruptcy proceedings by a vote of three-fourths of the creditors and the conveyance to trustees of the estate of the bankrupt to wind up and settle the same under the direction of a committee of the creditors. * * * The present Bankruptcy Law has no corresponding provision. The strong inference from its absence is that the trustee must discharge his duties according to his best judgment, subject only to the control of the court. He has been held a quasi officer of the court. * * * It is equally objectionable, it would seem, for him to attempt to serve the body of the creditors represented by the trustee and his own clients, who have claims against the estate. Ex parte Arrowsmith, 14 Ves. 209. While thus far in the case at bar no conflict between his duty to the trustee and that owing to his clients seems to have arisen, such a conflict is not unlikely and should be forestalled."

But of course the trustee may, if he so desires, submit questions concerning the administration of estates to the creditors for their advice, and it has even been held in one case that the court may order him to do so.[97]

And the court may appoint special counsel to advise the trustee.[98]

He should not ask the court for instructions, but should act on his own responsibility, under the advice of counsel if necessary.   •

In re Baber, 9 A. B. R. 406, 119 Fed. 525 (D. C. Tenn.): "Nor can this practice be resorted to for the purpose of carrying on litigation between himself and adverse parties in such an informal and irregular way as has been done in this case. Trustees in bankruptcy are sui generis. * * *
"He is not, like a receiver, a mere caretaker and manager of the estate to execute the orders of the court in the progress of administration, but he is the agent of the creditors, selected by them as a man of affairs to conduct the business of collecting the assets and distributing the proceeds among the creditors. The statute invests him with the title of the bankrupt, and makes him not only quasi owner, but the owner pro hac of all the property and rights of action belonging to the bankrupt. The management of the estate is committed to his discretion, and he is expected to exercise his powers and discharge his duties with the same intelligence that an owner would do, subject, of course, primarily, to the supervision of the creditors in their meetings called for the purpose, and the whole administration subject to the supervision of the court of bankruptcy. The proceedings are not conducted, like insolvency proceedings in the chancery courts of Tennessee, by a receiver, under the constant orders of the court, and who can do nothing, scarcely, without the previous direction of the chancellor; but the proceedings in bankruptcy are to be conducted according to the specific directions of the bankruptcy statutes and the rules and the forms prescribed by the Supreme Court. It is a comprehensive scheme of administration by the creditors through their trustee, with which the court interferes as little as possible."

Thus, as to whether the trustee should employ counsel or not, the trustee must exercise reasonable judgment; and it is held in some jurisdictions that the court will not undertake to give any direction, but will pass upon the propriety of the employment of counsel and the payment of a reasonable

---

97. In re Arnett, 7 A. B. R. 522, 112 Fed. 770 (D. C. Tenn.). Compare also, to such effect, In re Harper, 23 A. B. R. 918, 175 Fed. 412 (D. C. N. Y.), quoted at § 933.

98. In re Arnett, 7 A. B. R. 522, 112 Fed. 770 (D. C. Tenn.).

value for his services after such services have been rendered;[99] although in other jurisdictions it is held that the court must approve in advance the necessity of employment of counsel and also the counsel selected.[99a]

In re Abram, 4 A. B. R. 575, 103 Fed. 273 (D. C. Calif.): "The trustee of an estate in bankruptcy is entitled to the advice and assistance of counsel when necessary for the proper discharge of his duties as such trustee, and the reasonable expense incurred by him for such a purpose may be allowed as a charge against the estate; but the court will not, ordinarily, in the first instance, undertake to give any direction to the trustee in the matter of the employment of an attorney. The trustee must exercise a reasonable judgment in that matter; that is, he must exercise a reasonable judgment as to the necessity for securing the assistance of counsel—such judgment as a man of ordinary prudence would use in the transaction of his own business. When professional services have been rendered by an attorney to the trustee in his official capacity, the court will, in a proper proceeding, determine whether the employment of such an attorney was necessary, and, if found necessary, the reasonable value of his services."

But see, obiter, contra, In re Baird, 7 A. B. R. 448, 112 Fed. 960 (D. C. Pa.): "In doubtful cases the referee and the court will solve his perplexities."

The true rule might be that, except perhaps as to the employment of counsel, he should not ask the court's advice when acting simply as the representative of the general creditors, but might do so when acting simply as an impartial officer of the court, in custody of property belonging to different contestants.[1]

§ 898¼. **Trustee, in Administrative Matters, Not to Be Controlled by Outside Courts.**—The trustee, in the exercise of his discretion, as well as in the carrying out of orders of the bankruptcy court in the administration of the estate, is not to be interfered with nor controlled by proceedings brought in other courts.[2]

§ 898½. **But Not to Oppose Bankrupt's Discharge unless Authorized by Creditors.**—However, by the Amendment of 1910, making the trustee a competent party to oppose the bankrupt's discharge, the qualification is imposed that he shall only do so when authorized by creditors at a meeting called for that purpose.[3]

§ 899. **Approval of Court before Starting Litigation Not Necessary, Except Where Substituted in Pending Suit.**—The trustee need not obtain the approval of the court in advance of starting a suit for the

---

99. (1867) In re Mallory, 4 N. B. Reg. 157, 159.

99a. Thus, in the Southern and Eastern Districts of New York; in New Jersey, etc.

1. Compare, McLean v. Mayo, 7 A. B. R. 115, 113 Fed. 106 (D. C. N. C.).

2. See post, §§ 1788½, 1910½. Also, see In re Kranich, 23 A. B. R. 550, 174

Fed. 908 (D. C. Pa.); also compare, In re Leeds & Catlin Co., 23 A. B. R. 679, 175 Fed. 309 (D. C. N. Y.). Graphophone Co. v. Leeds & Catlin Co., 23 A. B. R. 337, 174 Fed. 158 (U. S. C. C.), quoted at § 1806¼.

3. Bankr. Act, as amended in 1910, § 14B; see ante, §§ 565¼, 572; also, see post, §§ 940½, 2458, et seq.

recovery of property or debts. It is his general duty to collect the assets, and he is responsible for failure to do so.[4]

Traders' Ins. Co. *v*. Mann, 11 A. B. R. 272 (Sup. Ct. Ga.): "The fact that this is to be 'under the direction of the court' no more requires a preliminary order to sue than it would necessitate a special order to authorize him to go in person and present a note and demand payment. The money, when collected after suit or without suit, and the use to be made, thereof, was to be 'under the direction of the court.' But being bound to collect he was not obliged to secure a special order to bring a suit necessary to collect. As to actions by or against the bankrupt pending at the time of the adjudication, the act requires him to obtain instructions from the court before intervening. But the express requirement that he must obtain an order in such instances, while being silent as to the necessity therefor in cases like this, is conclusive that special permission was not necessary where he had to sue in order to collect a debt due the estate."

But the trustee must obtain the approval of the court before he may be substituted for the bankrupt in a pending case.[5]

§ 900. Creditors Not to Elect "Supervising Committee."

—Creditors will not be allowed to nominate or elect a committee to supervise the trustee. He is, upon appointment, vested with discretion commensurate with his responsibility, and cannot be trammelled by any supervising committee.[6]

§ 901. Nor to Elect Attorney for Trustee.

—Nor should creditors be allowed to nominate and elect an attorney for the trustee; he should not be thus controlled by indirection; and it would not be fair to the minority.[7]

In re Columbia Iron Wks., 14 A. B. R. 526, 142 Fed. 234 (D. C. Mich.): "He has a right generally to choose his own counsel, and that right will not be controlled unless it is plainly abused. The majority of creditors have no more power to dictate whom he shall employ as counsel than the beneficiaries, under a deed of trust or a will, have to determine that matter by the vote of the greater number."

[1867] In re Mallory, 4 N. B. Reg. 157, 159: "The assignee's attorney is a minister of the court, and his duty is to the estate, even to the prejudice of his own claim, and it is considered inconsistent with his duties if he acts also as attorney for the bankrupt."

---

4. Callahan *v*. Israel, 186 Mass. 383; contra, obiter, In re Ryburn, 16 A. B. R. 515, 145 Fed. 662 (D. C. Conn.). Compare In re Harper, 23 A. B. R. 918, 175 Fed. 412 (D. C. N. Y.), quoted at § 933; In re Monsarrat (No. 2), 25 A. B. R. 820 (D. C. Hawaii).

5. Bankr. Act, § 11 (e): also see post, § 1641; also see In re Price, 1 A. B. R. 606, 92 Fed. 987 (D. C. N. Y.); Bear *v*. Chase, 3 A. B. R. 746 (C. C. A. S. C.); impliedly, Traders' Ins. Co *v*. Mann, 11 A. B. R. 272 (Sup. Ct.

Ga.); impliedly, Callahan *v*. Israel. 186 Mass. 383; impliedly, Hahlo *v*. Cole, 15 A. B. R. 591, 112 App. Div. 686 (N. Y.); Kessler *v*. Herklotz, 22 A. B. R. 257 (N. Y. Sup. Ct. App. Div.).

6. (1867) In re Stillwell, 2 N. B. Reg. 104.

7. In re Arnett, 7 A. B. R. 522, 112 Fed. 770 (D. C. Tenn.); contra, In re Smith, 1 A. B. R. 37 (Ref. N. Y.); contra, obiter, In re Little River Lumber Co., 3 A. B. R. 682, 101 Fed. 558 (D. C. Ark.).

§ 902. But Trustee Not to Employ Counsel Representing Adverse Interests.—However, the trustee should not be allowed to engage counsel representing interests adverse to the general estate.[8]

In re Stern, 16 A. B. R. 513, 144 Fed. 956 (C. C. A. Iowa): "* * * from the inception of these proceedings he was represented and presumably advised by counsel who was also representing the creditor whose claim was challenged. Of course, this ought not to have been, no matter what may have been the belief of counsel respecting its propriety. The interests of the creditor were adverse to the bankrupt estate, with the protection of which the trustee was charged and were in conflict with the interests of others who were represented by the trustee."

In re Columbia Iron Wks., 14 A. B. R. 527, 142 Fed. 234 (D. C. Mich.): "It is equally objectionable, it would seem, for him to attempt to serve the body of the creditors represented by the trustee and his own clients, who have claims against the estate. Ex parte Arrowsmith, 14 Ves. 209. While thus far in the case at bar no conflict between his duty to the trustee and that owing to his clients seems to have arisen, such a conflict is not unlikely and should be forestalled."

But in a composition, the bankrupt's attorney may not, necessarily, be occupying such an adverse position.

Keyes v. McKirrow, 9 A. B. R. 322, 180 Mass. 261 (Sup. Jud. Ct. Mass.): "The only questions argued by the defendant are those that grow out of the fact that the plaintiff acted also as attorney for the bankrupt, the defendant's contention being that the contract for services between the plaintiff and the defendant was so far against public policy that the plaintiff cannot now have this money. The answer to this contention is that the services rendered to the trustee were in the collection of debts due the estate and that there were no adverse or conflicting interests between the bankrupt and the trustee in regard to this business. Although in general it is doubtless better that the trustee should not employ in the settlement of the estate the same counsel whom the bankrupt employs, and although the rule since adopted by the United States District Court forbidding such an employment is a good one, there may be matters, like the collection of debts, in which the bankrupt's attorney might serve the trustee without impropriety."

And there is no legal objection to permitting the attorney of the trustee to make out and present the formal proof of a creditor's claim, where the interests of the bankrupt estate are not prejudiced thereby.[9] And an attorney who represents litigants will be presumed to be rendering such services as he performs in their interest and at their expense, unless actually engaged by the trustee.[10]

§ 903. Trustee Liable for His Attorney's Misfeasance.—The trus-

---

8. In re Rusch, 5 A. B. R. 565, 105 Fed. 608 (D. C. Wis.); In re Teuthorn, 5 A. B. R. 767 (D. C. Mass.), wherein it was held that the bankrupt's attorney may not act for the trustee in the examination of the bankrupt. In re Smith, 29 A. B. R. 628, 203 Fed. 369 (C. C. A. Mich.).

9. In re McKenna, 15 A. B. R. 4, 137 Fed. 611 (D. C. N. Y.).

10. Inferentially, In re Kelly Dry Goods Co., 4 A. B. R. 530, 102 Fed. 747 (D. C. Wis.).

tee is liable for the misfeasance of his attorney, although he has a right to employ counsel and has not been negligent in his selection.[11]

In re Howard, 12 A. B. R. 462, 130 Fed. 1004 (D. C. Calif.): "That this court has jurisdiction in this summary proceeding to require the trustee to make restitution of all moneys received by him under the decree of the Circuit Court subsequently reversed by the decree of the Circuit Court of Appeals, I entertain no doubt. The trustee is an officer of the court, and as such is subject to its direction in all matters concerning money or property which may have come into his possession by virtue of his office. It is claimed, however, by the trustee, that he is only responsible for so much of the money as actually came into his hands under such reversed decree; that in the action referred to he was the representative of the estate of the bankrupt, and as such had a right to employ an attorney; that he was not guilty of any negligence in the matter of the employment of such attorney, and cannot, therefore, be made personally responsible for the wrongful act of the attorney in appropriating a part of the moneys received on said judgment in payment of the fee claimed by him. It may be conceded that such would be the rule if the question were presented upon the settlement of the trustee's account in the estate in bankruptcy, but, as between the trustee and his petitioner, a stranger, the trustee cannot be permitted to avoid compliance with the final decree of the United States Circuit Court directing him to make restitution of moneys received by him under the reversed decree by a plea that a portion of such moneys was unlawfully appropriated by his attorney in the action in which such decree was rendered. The money received by his attorney was, in judgment of law, received by the trustee, and must be restored by him to the petitioner."

§ 904. Trustee within Summary Jurisdiction of Bankruptcy Court.

—The trustee is an officer of the court, and is subject to the direction of the court in all matters concerning money or property, which may have come into his possession by virtue of his office.[12]

Thus, he may be restrained from consummating a sale.[13]

DIVISION 4.

DUTIES AND POWERS OF TRUSTEE.

§ 905. Statutory Duties and Those Not Statutory.

—The statute in § 47 lays down certain duties for the trustee to perform. While this section lays down certain duties, it is not to be taken as excluding other duties not explicitly named. Presumably it touches mostly upon such duties as might otherwise be left in doubt. Thus, the first duty, that of accounting

---

11. Analogously (receiver), Mason v. Wolkowich, 17 A. B. R. 712 (C. C. A. Mass.).

12. In re Howard, 12 A. B. R. 462, 130 Fed. 1004 (D. C. Calif.). See post, subject of "Summary Jurisdiction to Order Trustee to Surrender Property to Rightful Owners," § 1872, et seq.

See post, subject of "Summary Jurisdiction over Trustee and Receiver to Prevent Their Interference, etc.," § 1900.

13. Instance, United Wireless Tel. Co. v. National El. Sig. Co., 28 A. B. R. 889, 189 Fed. 727 (C. C. A. Me.).

for and paying over interest received has not always been clearly considered as a duty of an officer receiving public funds, or funds in litigation, where the statute has been silent upon the point. Likewise, there are certain of these enumerated duties that arise from the peculiarities of the bankruptcy law itself. Nevertheless, there are certain other duties of the trustee, very essential to the proper administration of the bankruptcy act, that are not specifically mentioned at all in this section. Thus, it is undoubtedly a most important duty of the trustee to oppose the allowance of all improper claims against the estate, as it likewise is a most important duty of the bankrupt as laid down in § 7 (7) "in case of any person having to his knowledge proved a false claim against his estate" to "disclose that fact immediately to his *trustee*;" it being furthermore ruled, that all proceedings on review of an order allowing or disallowing a claim, must be taken by the trustee or in his name.[14] Yet this very important duty of the trustee is not specifically mentioned in the enumeration of his duties in § 47, nor is it mentioned in the General Orders in Bankruptcy.

§ 906. **Trustee to Account for Interest.**—The trustee must account for and pay over to the estate in his control all interest received by him upon property of the estate.[15]

§ 907. **To Collect Assets and Reduce Them to Money.**—The trustee must collect the property of the estate and reduce it to money, under the direction of the court.[16]

And he must use due diligence in collecting the assets and may be charged with the value of assets lost by failure to discharge such duty.

In re Reinboth, 19 A. B. R. 15, 157 Fed. 672 (C. C. A. N. Y.): "The referee misconceived the law. A trustee may be charged with the value of assets which never came into his possession if he fail in his duty to get them into his possession. Trustees in bankruptcy, like executors and administrators, are bound to use due diligence to get in the assets of the estate—to secure possession of the tangible property and collect the debts. If they fail in their duty they may be charged in their accounts with the value of the assets thereby lost. If they take no steps to secure property or collect debts, of which they have knowledge, they are presumptively negligent. The burden is upon them to explain their failure to act."

§ 908. **To Close Estate Expeditiously.**—The trustee is to close the estate as expeditiously as is compatible with the best interests of the par-

---

14. See ante, § 824, and post, subject of "Appeals and Error," § 2864, et seq.

15. Bankr. Act, § 47 (a) (1).

16. Bankr. Act, § 47 (a) (2); Bankr. Act, § 2 (7): "* * * cause the estate of bankrupts to be collected, reduced to money and distributed, and determine controversies in relation thereto, except as herein otherwise provided." In re MacDougall, 23 A. B. R. 762, 175 Fed. 400 (D. C. N. Y.).

Trustee Presenting Claim as Creditor in Another Bankruptcy.—In re Milne, Turnbull & Co., 26 A. B. R. 10, 185 Fed. 244 (C. C. A. N. Y.); In re Monsarrat (No. 2), 25 A. B. R. 820 (D. C. Hawaii).

ties in interest.[17]

§ 909. To Deposit Moneys in Depository.—All moneys received by the trustee must be deposited in an officially designated depository.[18]

This order is mandatory, and may not be evaded even by another order of the District Court, unless such order amount to a "designation" under § 61, and such designated depository give bond in accordance therewith.

Huttig Mfg. Co. v. Edwards, 20 A. B. R. 349, 160 Fed. 619 (C. C. A. Iowa): "The remaining matter necessary to be considered arises on the appeal of the trustee. The District Court directed him to withdraw the proceeds of the sale of D. Winter's property from the depository of funds in bankruptcy and to deposit them in some national bank in the district, taking a certificate of deposit, payable six months from date, and bearing the highest current rate of interest. The objection to this order is well made. Section 61 of the Bankruptcy Act * * * makes it the duty of courts of bankruptcy to designate by order banking institutions as depositories of funds of bankrupt estates, and to require of them bonds for the safe-keeping and forthcoming thereof. It was from such a depository the court directed the funds to be taken. Section 47a (3) * * * makes it the duty of a trustee to deposit all money received by him in one of the designated depositories, and general order 29 * * * prescribes the method of withdrawals. These provisions of the act and the general order are mandatory in form, and were designed to insure the safety of the funds rather than an increment by way of interest while they were idle. The funds were those of litigants and the risk which always attends the making of profit should not be incurred unless the right is clear. Doubtless consent by all parties interested would justify a departure from the prescribed rule. Rev. Stat., § 5504 * * *. But such consent was not obtained."

It is possible, perhaps, that such depository be designated for a special case and not generally.

§ 910. Failure to So Deposit—Bond Liable on Loss.—Failure to so deposit them renders the trustee's bond liable in the event of loss.[19] Also the referee's bond if done by his order.[20]

---

17. Bankr. Act, § 47 (a) (2); Boyd v. Glucklich, 8 A. B. R. 393, 116 Fed. 131 (C. C. A. Iowa); obiter, In re Paine, 11 A. B. R. 354, 127 Fed. 246 (D. C. Ky.); obiter, In re Koenig, 11 A. B. R. 618, 127 Fed. 891 (D. C. Tex.). Ante, § 23.

18. Bankr. Act, § 47 (3); Bankr. Act, § 61: "Courts of bankruptcy shall designate, by order, banking institutions as depositories for the money of bankrupt estates, as convenient as may be to the residences of trustees and shall require bonds to the United States, subject to their approval, to be given by such banking institutions, and may, from time to time, as occasion may require, by like order increase the number of depositories. or the amount of any bond, or change such depositories."

In re Carr, 8 A. B. R. 637, 116 Fed. 556, 9 A. B. R. 58, 117 Fed. 572 (D. C. N. Car.), where the court says they should be deposited to the trustee as such, designating the estate. In re Hoyt, 9 A. B. R. 574, 119 Fed. 987 (D. C. N. Car.); In re Cobb, 7 A. B. R. 202, 112 Fed. 655 (D. C. N. Car.); In re Hoyt & Mitchell, 11 A. B. R. 784, 127 Fed. 968 (D. C. N. Car.).

19. In re Hoyt, 9 A. B. R. 574, 119 Fed. 987 (D. C. N. Car.); In re Hoyt & Mitchell, 11 A. B. R. 784, 127 Fed. 968 (D. C. N. Car.); obiter, In re Cobb, 7 A. B. R. 232, 112 Fed. 655 (D. C. N. Car.).

20. In re Hoyt, 9 A. B. R. 574, 119 Fed. 987 (D. C. N. Car.).

· According to the holdings of one court, a trustee will not be allowed for his disbursements, unless the fund from which the same are checked has been deposited in the designated depository.[21]

Obiter, In re Hoyt, 9 A. B. R. 574, 119 Fed. 987 (D. C. N. Car.): "Amounts paid out by trustees otherwise than is allowed in the Bankrupt Act will not be allowed in the settlement of the estate. The manifest purpose of Congress in requiring trustees, referees and designated depositories to give bonds was to protect estates in bankruptcy from (among other acts) paying out funds otherwise than the law and rules permit."

But this is probably an unwarranted deduction from the rule.

§ 911. Disbursements Only on Order of Court.—Disbursements must be made only on the order of the court, and the trustee takes his own risk in paying out funds of the estate without order of the court.[22]

In re Rude, 4 A. B. R. 319, 101 Fed. 805 (D. C. Ky.): "The trustee made the distribution in this case without any order or judgment as a basis for it, and this action of his cannot defeat the rights of the attorney if they otherwise existed. There was no legal warrant for the distribution, and the trustee, when making it, took the chances of disapproval in whole or in part. The fund must be regarded as still in the hands of the trustee, and under the control of the court, to be paid out according to its order."

And it has been held by one court that the trustee will not be allowed for unauthorized disbursements, although the court, upon application, might have authorized them originally.[23]

§ 912. Disbursements to Be by Check, Countersigned.—All disbursements by the trustee must be by check, and the checks must be countersigned by the judge or referee, etc.[24]

21. In re Hoyt. & Mitchell, 11 A. B. R. 784, 127 Fed. 968 (D. C. N. Car.).

22. Impliedly, In re Hoyt & Mitchell, 11 A. B. R. 784, 127 Fed. 968 (D. C. N. Car.); impliedly, In re Cobb, 7 A. B. R. 202, 112 Fed. 655 (D. C. N. Car.). But the apparent ruling in In re Cobb, 7 A. B. R. 202, 112 Fed. 655 that the referee cannot make the order for distribution is "hæret in cortice." Without exception, unless in North Carolina, the referee makes the order of distribution and a contrary practice would lead to interminable confusion in large commercial districts.

23. In re Hoyt & Mitchell, 11 A. B. R. 784, 127 Fed. 965 (D. C. N. Car.).

But see In re Cobb, 7 A. B. R. 202, 112 Fed. 655 (D. C. N. Car.), where Judge Purnell seems to have relaxed his somewhat rigid rules.

24. Bankr. Act, § 47 (a) (4): "* * * disburse money only by check or draft on the depositories in which it has been deposited."

Gen. Order XXIX: "No moneys deposited as required by the act shall be drawn from the depository unless by check or warrant, signed by the clerk of the court, or by a trustee, and countersigned by the judge of the court, or by a referee designated for that purpose, or by the clerk or his assistant under an order made by the judge, stating the date, the sum and the account for which it is drawn; and an entry of the substance of such check or warrant, with the date thereof, the sum drawn for, and the account for which it is drawn; shall be forthwith made in a book kept for that purpose by the trustee or his clerk; and all checks and drafts shall be entered in the order of time in which they are drawn, and shall be numbered in the case of each estate. A copy of this general order shall be furnished to the depository, and also the name of any referee or clerk authorized to countersign said checks."

§ 913. Depository Liable for Payment of Improperly Drawn Orders.

—And a depository will be liable for paying out funds on orders not drawn in accordance with General Order No. 29.[25]

§ 914. Trustee to Furnish Information.

—The trustee must furnish such information concerning the estate and its administration as may be requested by parties in interest.[26]

Furthermore, he is also subject to appear under subpœna, as a witness or to produce documents or books, in outside suits.[27]

§ 915. His Accounts and Papers Open to Inspection.

—The accounts and papers of the trustee are to be open to the inspection of officers and all parties in interest.[28]

In re Sauer, 10 A. B. R. 353, 122 Fed. 101 (D. C. N. Y.): "A trustee defending a reclamation proceeding apparently occupies quite a different relation toward the reclaiming creditor from what he does toward the body of general creditors. But I think upon consideration that the provisions of §§ 47 and 49 of the Bankrupt Act give any person interested in any bankrupt estate an absolute statutory right to the inspection of all accounts and papers of the trustee and to be furnished with any information concerning the bankrupt estate which the bankrupt has."

Obiter, In re Sully, 15 A. B. R. 323, 142 Fed. 895 (D. C. N. Y.): "Ordinarily creditors have an absolute right under the Act to examine all the books and papers relating to the estate, in the possession of the trustee."

Impliedly, In re Sully, 18 A. B. R. 126 (C. C. A. N. Y.): "But if they had reasonable grounds for asserting the right secured to them by the Bankrupt Act, whether they chose to do so for their own advantage or for that of third persons is quite immaterial. The element of motive cannot prejudice the assertion of a clear legal right or statutory privilege."

Even adverse claimants are entitled to such inspection.

In re Sauer, 10 A. B. R. 353, 122 Fed. 101 (D. C. N. Y.): "It might often happen that the bankrupt's papers would furnish the only evidence to support the reclaiming creditor's claim. It is not the duty of a trustee to resist every reclamation proceeding. It is his duty to investigate every such claim and to resist those that ought to be resisted, and I think that a reclaiming creditor has the same rights as any other creditor in a bankruptcy proceeding to inspect all the accounts and papers."

But the right to such inspection may be denied to mere debtors of the estate.[29]

It was held in one case that inspection might be denied the creditors who

---

25. Obiter, In re Cobb, 7 A. B. R. 202, 112 Fed. 655 (D. C. N. Car.); In re C. M. Burkhalter & Co., 25 A. B. R. 378, 182 Fed. 353 (D. C. Ala.), quoted at § 389.

26. Bankr. Act, § 47 (a) (5); In re Sauer, 10 A. B. R. 353, 122 Fed. 101 (D. C. N. Y.).

27. Obiter, Graphophone Co. v. Leeds & Catlin Co., 23 A. B. R. 337, 174 Fed. 158 (U. S. C. C. N. Y.), quoted at § 1806¼.

28. Bankr. Act, § 49 (a).

29. In re Sully, 18 A. B. R. 125 (C. C. A. N. Y., affirming 15 A. B. R. 323, supra).

were not acting in good faith.[30] But this case was reversed on a related point on review. The creditor has an absolute legal right to such inspection and his particular motive is immaterial.[31] And this right of inspection applies to the general examinations of bankrupts or witnesses already taken.

In re Samuelsohn, 23 A. B. R. 528, 174 Fed. 911 (D. C. N. Y.): "This is a petition for the review of an order made by the referee in bankruptcy herein, denying the petition of Simon M. Shimberg, a creditor herein, for an order directing the trustee to file with the referee, or with the clerk of this court, the testimony of the bankrupts, given upon their examination, or to permit said Shimberg to have access to the same. The question submitted for review is in principle controlled by In re Sauer (D. C.), 10 Am. B. R. 353, 122 Fed. 101. In that case, it is true, the claim had been proven and allowed; but such fact is not a material distinction from this case, in which the petitioner for review was scheduled by the bankrupts as a creditor, had received notice of the meeting of creditors, and had duly filed his claim. Under § 7a (9) of the Bankruptcy Act * * *, the petitioner had the unquestionable right to examine the bankrupts before the referee, even though his claim was not filed or formally proven (In re Price [D. C.], 1 Am. B. R. 419, 91 Fed. 635; In re Jehu [D. C.], 2 Am. B. R. 498, 94 Fed. 638; In re Walker [D. C.], 3 Am. B. R. 35, 90 Fed. 550); and under § 39 (9) a party in interest has the right to apply to the referee to preserve the evidence taken. The petitioner for review was a party in interest within the meaning of §§ 47 and 49, and § 39, subds. 3, 9, even though he may not have formally proved his claim. This would seem to be the effect of the decision of the Circuit Court of Appeals for the Second Circuit in Matter of Sully, 18 Am. B. R. 123, 152 Fed. 619. The testimony taken, as authorized by the referee, is a part of the record in the proceedings, and creditors generally have access to it while it remains in the custody of the referee. * * * It is urged in opposition to permitting the petitioner to examine the testimony of the bankrupts that the interests of the petitioner and the trustee are antagonistic, and that he intends to bring suit against such petitioner to recover preferences given him by the bankrupts, and therefore a disclosure of the testimony of the bankrupts, who are hostile to the interests of the bankrupt estate, may result prejudicially to the creditors. This contention, however, is not maintainable, in view of the absolute right which a party in interest has to examine a bankrupt, and the right which he has to be informed concerning the estate by the trustee or referee. The trustee is not wholly at a disadvantage; for, if his surmise prove correct, there is nothing to prevent the impeachment of the bankrupts on the trial, if they should materially vary their former testimony."

And applies, even though the one asking for the inspection be a creditor who has not proved his claim;[32] or is a creditor against whom the trustee contemplates bringing suit and where such inspection might hamper the trustee in such suit.[33] And such inspection should be allowed to State officers carrying on criminal prosecution.

---

30. In re Sully, 18 A. B. R. 125 (C. C. A. N. Y.).

31. Inferentially, In re Sully, 18 A. B. R. 125 (C. C. A. N. Y.), quoted supra.

32. In re Samuelsohn, 23 A. B. R. 528, 174 Fed. 911 (D. C. N. Y.), quoted supra.

33. In re Samuelsohn, 23 A. B. R. 528, 174 Fed. 911 (D. C. N. Y.), quoted supra.

In re Tracy, 23 A. B. R. 438, 177 Fed. 532 (D. C. N. Y.): "The petitioner insists that the trustee's duties are confined to the administration of the estate, and it is no part of those duties to assist in the prosecution of the bankrupt. I do not mean to say that the trustee has any such duties, or that he is delinquent when he does not aid a prosecution. It is one thing, however, to say that he has no such positive duties and another to say that it is an abuse of his powers so to assist. If the trustee proposed to show the books to trade rivals of the bankrupts so as to prejudice them in re-establishing themselves in business, it would clearly be a wanton and illegal misuse of power. However, the trustee is an officer of this court, and this court cannot remain impartial, a disinterested spectator, when the issue is of the detection and prosecution of crime. It cannot, and of course it does not, assume that this petitioner or anyone else is guilty of any crime, but when the responsible authorities of a State institute lawful proceedings to inquire into acts which may be criminal, in due course of law, that is a public purpose to which no court can remain indifferent, whether the prosecution be before the tribunals of the United States or of the State of New York. Any documents which are in our possession and to show which is not illegal, will, I hope, always be open to the inspection of any public officer charged with the prosecution of crime."

§ 916. Trustee to Keep Accounts.

—The trustee must keep regular accounts showing all amounts received and from what sources, and all amounts expended and on what accounts.[34]

§ 917. To File Reports.

—The trustee must file written reports with the court of the condition of the estate and the amount of money on hand, and such other details as may be required by the court, within the first month after his appointment and every two months thereafter, unless otherwise ordered by the court.[35]

The trustee may be ordered to file a final report;[36] and disobedience of the order may be contempt.[37]

He must lay before the final meeting of creditors a detailed statement of the administration of the estate, and must file his final report and account fifteen days before the time fixed for the final meeting of creditors.[38]

§ 917½. Exceptions to Trustee's Reports.

—Of course exceptions may be filed to trustee's reports. Thus, exceptions were filed in one case because the trustee had allowed the bankrupt to occupy a sawmill and to use horses, wagons, etc., without adequate rent;[39] again, where the trustee had

---

34. Bankr. Act, § 47 (a) (6). As to auditing same, see ante, § 517, "Referee's Duties."

35. Bankr. Act, § 47 (a) (10).

36. O'Conor v. Sunseri, 26 A. B. R. 1, 184 Fed. 712 (C. C. A. Pa.).

37. O'Conor v. Sunseri, 26 A. B. R. 1, 184 Fed. 712 (C. C. A. Pa.).

Contempt Proceedings Dismissed.—A contempt proceedings was dismissed where the district judge, in approving the referee's certificate, extended the time for filing the report,

no supplemental proceedings being instituted to cover disobedience of the extended time. O'Conor v. Sunseri, 26 A. B. R. 1, 184 Fed. 712 (C. C. A. Pa.).

38. Bankr. Act, § 47 (a) (7) (8). See post, subject of "Final Meeting of Creditors." For forms, see No. 48, "Trustee's Return of No Assets," and Nos. 49 and 50. "Account of Trustee" and "Oath to Account."

39. Bank of Clinton v. Kondert, 20 A. B. R. 178, 159 Fed. 703 (C. C. A. La.).

failed to contest a right of property, after being ordered by the court to contest, and had finally allowed a redelivery bond given therefor to be canceled.[40]

And the burden of proof may shift to the trustee under some circumstances.[41]

§ 918. To Pay Dividends within Ten Days.—The trustee must pay dividends within ten days after they are declared by the referee.[42]

§ 919. To Set Apart Exempted Property.—The trustee must set apart the bankrupt's exemptions.[43]

§ 920. Where Real Estate, Trustee to File Certificate with Recorder.—The trustee must, within thirty days after the adjudication, file a certified copy of the decree of adjudication in the office where conveyances of real estate are recorded in every county where the bankrupt owns real estate not exempt from execution, and pay the fee for such filing, and he will receive a compensation of fifty cents for each copy so filed, which, together with the filing fee, will be paid out of the estate of the bankrupt as part of the costs and disbursements of the proceedings.

But the statutory provision to this effect is directory only; and it does not interfere with the passing of the title to the trustee by operation of law.[44]

§ 921. Trustee to Deliver to Referee Claims Filed with Him.—Proofs of debt received by the trustee must be delivered to the referee to whom the cause is referred.[45]

From this statutory provision has been deduced the rule that filing with the trustee will toll the year's limitation for filing claims.[46]

§ 922. Arbitration of Controversies.—The trustee may, pursuant to the direction of the court, submit to arbitration any controversy arising in the settlement of the estate.[47]

§ 923. Allegations of Application to Arbitrate.—The application must clearly and distinctly set forth the subject matter of the controversy, and the reasons why the trustee thinks it proper and most for the interest

40. In re Reinboth, 19 A. B. R. 15, 157 Fed. 672 (C. C. A. N. Y.).

41. In re Reinboth, 19 A. B. R. 15, 157 Fed. 672 (C. C. A. N. Y.).

42. Bankr. Act, § 47 (9). See post, subject of "Dividends."

43. See post, subject of "Exemptions," § 1073.

"**L i s Pendens**" — **Cancellation of, Duty of Trustee in Relation Thereto.** —In re Miller, 22 A. B. R. 759 (N. Y. Sup. Ct).

44. Hull v. Burr, 26 A. B. R. 897 (Sup. Ct. Fla.).

45. Instance, In re Kessler, 25 A. B. R. 512, 186 Fed. 127 (C. C. A. N. Y.); Rule XXI (1); Orcutt v. Green, 17 A. B. R. 75, 204 U. S. 96 (reversing, on other grounds, In re Ingalls Bros., 13 A. B. R. 512, 137 Fed. 517, C. C. A. N. Y.). As to compensation of trustees, see post, subject of "Costs of Administration," § 2108. As to other matters pertaining to the trustee's duties, see respective titles.

46. Ante, § 729.

47. Bankr. Act, § 26 (a).

of the estate that the controversy should be settled by arbitration or agreement.[48]

§ 924. Manner of Procedure on Arbitration.

—Three arbitrators are to be chosen by mutual consent, or one by the trustee, one by the other party to the controversy, and the third by the two so chosen, or if they fail to agree in five days after their appointment, the court is to appoint the third arbitrator.[49]

§ 925. Findings of Arbitrators Have Force of Verdict, and Reviewable.

—The written findings of the arbitrators, or a majority of them, as to the issues presented, may be filed in court and shall have like force and effect as the verdict of a jury.[50] And such findings are reviewable by the court and may be set aside or adjudged upon as a verdict of a jury.[51]

§ 926. Compromise of Controversies.

—The trustee may, with the approval of the court, compromise any controversy arising in the administration of the estate upon such terms as he may deem for the best interests of the estate.[52]

But it has been held that a receiver in bankruptcy has no authority to compromise claims against the bankrupt estate.[53]

A proposed compromise which is not for the creditors' best interests will not be approved.[54]

§ 927. Allegations of Application to Compromise.

—The application must clearly and distinctly set forth the subject matter of the controversy and the reasons why the trustee deems it for the best interests of the estate that the same be settled by agreement.[55] It should also, by good practice, state the terms on which the controversy can be settled.

§ 928. Ten Days Notice by Mail Requisite.

—Ten days notice by mail to all creditors is requisite.[56]

---

48. Rule XXXIII: "Whenever a trustee shall make application to the court for authority to submit a controversy arising in the settlement of a demand against a bankrupt's estate, or for a debt due to it, to the determination of arbitrators, or for authority to compound and settle such controversy by agreement with the other party, the application shall clearly and distinctly set forth the subject matter of the controversy, and the reason why the trustee thinks it proper and most for the interest of the estate that the controversy should be settled by arbitration or otherwise."

49. Bankr. Act, § 26 (b).

50. Bankr. Act, § 26 (c).

51. In re McLam, 3 A. B. R. 245, 97 Fed. 922 (D. C. Vt.).

52. Bankr. Act, § 27 (a); In re Linderman, 22 A. B. R. 131, 166 Fed. 593 (D. C. Pa.); Instance, In re Kranich, 23 A. B. R. 550, 174 Fed. 908 (D. C. Pa.).

53. Southern, etc., Co. v. Hichman & W. Co., 27 A. B. R. 203, 190 Fed. 888 (D. C. Ala.), quoted ante, § 394½.

54. Riley v. Pope, 26 A. B. R. 618, 186 Fed. 851 (D. C. Ga.); In re Geiselhart, 25 A. B. R. 318, 181 Fed. 622 (D. C. La.).

55. Rule XXXIII, supra.

56. Bankr. Act, § 58: "Creditors shall have at least ten days notice by mail * * * of (7) the proposed compromise of any controversy."

See In re Greeman, 9 A. B. R. 68, where the ten days notice does not appear to have been given. Yet the

§ 929. Creditors Entitled to Be Heard, but Vote Not Conclusive.
—Creditors are entitled to be heard and even to vote, but their action is not conclusive upon the court but merely advisory.[57]

§ 930. What Claims May Be Compromised.
—Demands against the estate and debts due it both may be compromised.[58]

Thus, a judgment against the trustee in the State Court for conversion of another's property where the time for appeal has not yet expired may be compromised and an accord and satisfaction made during the meantime be approved.[59] Thus, claims against third parties for alleged preferences may be compromised.[60] Thus, the trustee has been permitted to compromise an action of replevin brought against the debtors, prior to his bankruptcy, to recover property procured on materially false statements; but, in such case it was held that, if the creditors objecting to such compromise indemnified the estate as to costs and expenses, the proposed compromise would not be approved.[61] Thus, a claim against the bankrupt's wife for cash and bonds in her possession, claimed by the trustee to belong to the estate, may be compromised, where any attempt at recovery thereof might not only be tedious and expensive, but also might fail.[62]

Of course a proposed compromise that is not for the best interests of the creditors will not be approved by the court.[63]

And it is not within the power of the court to approve of a proposed compromise which would compel dissenting creditors to accept stock in a new corporation, put such stock in a voting trust, consent to the creation of debts, give up their existing claims on certain assets, and give their assent to other plans usually contained in a contract of reorganization.[64]

The court will not sanction a compromise, even where assets be brought into the estate thereby, if it is based on a promise to stifle a criminal prosecution of the bankrupt.[65]

---

failure to give such notice could, it would seem only be available to the creditors, not to the party making the settlement. Query, but suppose the creditors dissented, would the compromise be valid? and if not, would it be binding on the other party?

57. In re Heyman, 5 A. B. R. 808, 108 Fed. 207 (D. C. N. Y); impliedly, In re Linderman, 22 A. B. R. 131, 166 Fed. 593 (D. C. Pa.). Inferentially, In re Meadows, Williams & Co., 25 A. B. R. 100, 181 Fed. 911 (D. C. N. Y.) wherein creditors opposing a compromise were ordered to file a bond indemnifying the estate against costs, expenses, and counsel fees; In re Kearney Bros., 25 A. B. R. 757, 184 Fed. 190 (D. C. N. Y.).

58. Bankr. Act, § 27 (a); Rule XXXIII.

59. In re Freeman, 9 A. B. R. 63 (D. C. N. Y.).

60. In re Linderman, 22 A. B. R. 131, 166 Fed. 593 (D. C. Pa.).

61. In re Kearney Bros., 25 A. B. R. 757, 184 Fed. 190 (D. C. N. Y.); compare, inferentially, In re Meadows, Williams & Co., 25 A. B. R. 100, 181 Fed. 911 (D. C. N. Y.).

62. In re Kranich, 23 A. B. R. 550, 174 Fed. 908 (D. C. Pa.).

63. In re Geiselhart, 25 A. B. R. 318, 181 Fed. 622 (D. C. Pa.); Riley v. Pope, 26 A. B. R. 618, 186 Fed. 857 (D. C. Ga.).

64. In re Northampton, etc., Co., 25 A. B. R. 565, 185 Fed. 542 (D. C. Pa.).

65. In re Rosenblatt, 18 A. B. R. 663, 153 Fed. 335 (D. C. Pa.); Mulford v. Fourth St. Nat. Bank, 19 A. B. R. 742, 157 Fed. 897 (C. C. A. Pa.).

It has been held under the facts in one case that the court had nothing
to do with the part of the compromise agreement which dealt with the
raising of funds to make payments outside and which did not come into the
estate as an asset for distribution.[67]

§ 931. Rights of Lienholders Not to Be Prejudiced.

—The rights
of lienholders may not be prejudiced thereby and the interests of all parties
must be considered.[68]

It has been held that in matters of this nature it would be inequitable to
permit the trustee to have rights greater than those of the bankrupt.[69]

But such can not be the rule, since the Act designs he should have greater
rights under some circumstances.

§ 932. Abandonment of Worthless or Burdensome Assets.

—The
trustee may decline to accept, or may abandon, property or contracts that
are burdensome because worthless, encumbered with liens in excess of value
or charged with burdens, or otherwise unprofitable.[70]

Atchison, etc., R. Co. *v.* Hurley, 18 A. B. R. 396, 153 Fed. 503 (C. C. A. Kans.):
"It is well settled that trustees in bankruptcy are not bound to accept property or take over contracts which are onerous and unprofitable, and which would
burden rather than benefit the estate. In the execution of their trust they are
confronted at the outset with the duty of electing whether to assume an existing
executory contract, continue its performance, and ultimately dispose of it for
the benefit of the estate or to renounce it and leave the injured party to such
legal remedies, for the breach, as the case affords. [Cases cited.] If they elect

---

67. In·re Linderman, 22 A. B. R.
131, 166 Fed. 593 (D. C. Pa.).
**Minority Stockholders Need Not
Accept Trustee's Settlement of Action
against Directors of Bankrupt Corporation, if They Indemnify.**—And minority stockholders will not be compelled
to accept an unprofitable settlement of
an action by the trustee in bankruptcy
of a bankrupt corporation against the
directors and certain stockholders of
the corporation, where they are willing to protect the estate from loss. In
re Woodbury, etc., Inst., 27 A. B. R.
497, 191 Fed. 319 (C. C. A. N. Y.).

68. In re Adamo, 18 A. B. R. 181,
151 Fed. 716 (D. C. N. Y.).

69. In re Geiselhart, 25 A. B. R.
318, 181 Fed. 622 (D. C. Pa.).

70. Watson *v.* Merrill, 14 A. B. R.
454, 136 Fed. 359 (C. C. A. Kans.),
quoted at § 982; Kessler *v.* Herklotz,
22 A. B. R. 257 (N. Y. Sup. Ct. App.
Div.), quoted at § 1640; Equitable
Loan & Security Co. *v.* Moss, 11 A.
B. R. 111 (C. C. A.); In re Jersey Island Packing Co., 14 A. B. R. 689,
138 Fed. 625 (C. C. A. Calif.); In re
Cogley, 5 A. B. R. 731, 107 Fed. 73
(D. C. Iowa); In re Rose, 26 A. B. R.
752, 193 Fed. 815 (D. C. Ky.). Abandonment may be granted at the cost
of the lienholder or other party benefited thereby. Equitable Loan & Security Co. *v.* Moss, 11 A. B. R. 111 (C.
C. Ala.).
**Trustee Quitclaiming to Vendor of
Land after Decree of Specific Performance, Vendor's Claim Extinguished.**—
The original owner's acceptance of a
quitclaim deed from the trustee in
bankruptcy, quitclaiming land purchased, but afterwards declined by
the bankrupt, where specific performance had meanwhile been decreed before the bankruptcy, wherein the state
court had passed title of the property
to the bankrupt and ordered him to
pay the purchase price, extinguishes
the original owner's claim for the balance of the purchase price. In re
Davis, 24 A. B. R. 667, 179 Fed. 871
(D. C. Pa.).

to assume such a contract, they are required to take it 'cum onere,' as the bankrupt enjoyed it, subject to all its provisions and conditions in the same plight and condition that the bankrupt held it." Quoted further at §§ 1144, 1145.

Oldmixon v. Severance, 18 A. B. R. 823, 104 N. Y. Supp. 1042: "A trustee in bankruptcy is not bound to take property which may involve him in litigation."

Thus, a trustee has been authorized to abandon the bankrupt's interest in real estate purchased under a land contract, upon which the bankrupt had made a comparatively small payment.[71]

In re Zehner, 27 A. B. R. 536, 193 Fed. 787 (D. C. La.): "It is well settled that the trustee is not required to administer property burdened with liens or mortgages and he may abandon same to the secured creditor. In fact, it is his duty to do so whenever it is certain the general estate will derive no benefit from the sale of such property."

§ 933. Is Matter of Discretion.—The question as to whether or not the trustee shall elect to take burdensome property is not one of jurisdiction or right, but of discretion.[72] Thus, as to unliquidated claims.

Compare, In re Harper, 23 A. B. R. 918, 175 Fed. 412 (D. C. N. Y.): "Trustees in bankruptcy are not justified in rushing the estates of bankrupts into doubtful or unproductive litigations. It is not their privilege to use the estates committed to their charge to settle questions of law which may arise. If success is doubtful in the case of a claim alleged to be due the estate and the fruits of success will not pay the expense of cultivating the field, it is their duty, as a general rule, to abandon the claim, unless the creditors, or a substantial majority of them, desire the litigation to proceed. Referees in bankruptcy should and must see to it that estates are administered in accordance with this rule, and should exercise their supervisory power over trustees accordingly."

§ 934. Manner of Effecting Abandonment.—It would appear that the trustee may either file a formal petition for leave to abandon, which would be the only proper practice where the property is already in his custody; or, where the property is not in his custody, simply refuse to accept it, unless he desires the formal action of the court by petition to abandon.

Probably, notice to creditors is not necessary, since there is no mention of it in § 58; but, inasmuch as an abandonment of property is not different in its nature from other parting with title thereto. it is good practice for notice to creditors to be given.[72a]

---

71. Kenyon v. Mulert, 26 A. B. R. 184, 184 Fed. 825 (C. C. A. Pa.).
And Where Vendor of Land Accepts Quitclaim Deed from Trustee Rescission Will Be Complete.—Kenyon v. Mulert, 26 A. B. R. 184, 184 Fed. 825 (C. C. A. Pa.).
72. In re Cogley, 5 A. B. R. 731, 107 Fed. 73 (D. C. Iowa); Instance, In re Linderman, 22 A. B. R. 131, 166 Fed. 593 (D. C. Pa.).
72a. No "Abandonment to" a Particu-

lar Person.—It is incorrect to make the order of abandonment read "abandon to" any particular person. An abandonment is a going away and leaving a thing. The moment it is an abandonment "to" a particular person it becomes a transfer to such person of whatever rights are thus sought to be "abandoned." The distinction is more than verbal; it denotes an entirely different method of procedure with consequent different rights.

§ 935. Declining, or Failing after Notice to Accept, Abandonment.

—If the trustee, with knowledge and after a reasonable time, declines to accept property of an onerous or unprofitable character, the bankrupt may reassert title.[73]

[1867] Dushane v. Beall, 161 U. S. 513: "If, with knowledge of the facts, or being so situated as to be chargeable with such knowledge, an assignee, by definite declaration or distinct action, or forbearance to act, indicates in view of the particular circumstances, his choice not to take certain property, or if, in the language of Ware, J., in Smith v. Gordon, 6 Law Rep. 313, he, with such knowledge, 'stands by without asserting his claim for a length of time, and allows third persons in the possession of their legal rights to acquire an interest in the property,' then he may be held to have waived the assertion of his claim thereto."

[1867] Sessions v. Romadka, 145 U. S. 29: "In this case the assignee had taken a year to wind up the estate, and had given no sign of his wish to assume this property, if indeed he knew of its existence. On being asked with reference to it by the proposed purchaser, he replied that the estate was all settled up, that he had no power to do anything in the matter, and that Poinier (the bankrupt) was the only one who could give a title. A plainer election not to accept can hardly be imagined. Granting that up to that time he had known nothing about the happening, it was his duty to inquire into the matter if he had any thoughts of accepting them, and not to mislead the plaintiff's agent by referring him to the bankrupt as the proper person to apply. Under the circumstances plaintiff could do nothing but purchase of Poinier. Bearing in mind that no claim to this property is now made by the assignee, but that this alleged title to it is set up by a third person who confessedly has no interest in it himself, it is entirely clear that the defendants ought not to prevail as against a purchaser who bought it of the bankrupt after the assignee had disclaimed any interest in it. Had the existence of this patent been concealed by the bankrupt or the assignee had discovered it subsequently—after his discharge—and desired to take possession of it for the benefit of the estate, it is possible that the bankruptcy court might reopen the case and vacate the discharge for that purpose. Clark v. Clark, 17 How. 315. But it does not lie in the mouth of an alleged infringer to get up the right of the assignee as against a title from the bankrupt acquired with the consent of such assignee. It is quiet evident from the facts stated that this patent, which seems to have been the cause of Poinier's insolvency, was thought to be of little or no value, that the assignee so regarded it, and that its real value was only discovered when the plaintiff had brought to bear upon the manufacture of the device, his own skill and enterprise."

But such declining will not so operate unless done with knowledge or notice of all essential facts.[74] And abandonment implies, generally, some affirmative act.

First Nat. Bank v. Lasater, 13 A. B. R. 698, 196 U. S. 115: "The question then presented is, whether this right of action, having once passed to the trustee in bankruptcy, was retransferred to J. L. Lasater upon the determina-

---

73. First Nat'l Bank v. Lasater, 13 A. B. R. 698, 196 U. S. 115; Amer. File Co. v. Garrett, 110 U. S. 288; 295; Sparhawk v. Yerkes, 142 U. S. 1; Sessions v. Romadka, 145 U. S. 29; Dushane v. Beal, 161 U. S. 513.

74. First Nat'l Bk. v. Lasater, 13 A. B. R. 698, 196 U. S. 115, quoted supra.

tion of the bankruptcy proceedings, he having returned no assets to his trustee, and having failed to notify him or the creditors of this claim for usury, and beginning this action within less than two months after the final discharge of the trustee. We have held that trustees in bankruptcy are not bound to accept property of an onerous or unprofitable character, and that they have a reasonable time in which to elect whether they will accept or not. If they decline to take the property the bankrupt can assert title thereto. American Fire Company *v.* Garrett, 110 U. S. 288, * * * Sparhawk *v.* Yerkes, 142 U. S. 1, * * * Sessions *v.* Romadka, 145 U. S. 29, * * * Dushane *v.* Beall, 161 U. S. 513. * * * But that doctrine can have no application when the trustee is ignorant of the existence of the property, and has had no opportunity to make an election. It cannot be that a bankrupt, by omitting to schedule and withholding from his trustee all knowledge of certain property, can, after his estate in bankruptcy has been finally closed up, immediately thereafter assert title to the property on the ground that the trustee had never taken any action in respect to it. If the claim was of value (as certainly this claim was, according to the judgment below), it was something to which the creditors were entitled, and this bankrupt could not, by withholding knowledge of its existence, obtain a release from his debts, and still assert title to the property."

In re Wiseman & Wallace, 20 A. B. R. 293, 150 Fed. 236 (D. C. Pa.): "In my opinion, neither refusal nor abandonment can be properly established by mere silence or inaction under the circumstances disclosed by the foregoing statement of facts. When there is a duty to act, either actually known to exist or legally imposed by reason of such notice as is the equivalent of knowledge in fact, failure to stir may be significant; but when no such duty exists, mere inaction furnishes ordinarily an unsafe basis for the inference that doing nothing should be held to be as weighty as conduct."

§ 936. Once Abandoned, Not Afterwards Reclaimable.—Property abandoned may not be reclaimed by the trustee if afterwards found valuable.[75]

§ 937. Redeeming from Liens.—The trustee may redeem property encumbered by liens or held under charges.[76]

§ 938. Selling Subject to Liens.—The trustee may sell property subject to liens.[77]

§ 939. Selling Free from Liens.—The trustee may sell property free from liens.[78]

---

75. Instance, Meyers *v.* Josephson, 10 A. B. R. 687, 124 Fed. 734 (C. C. A. Ga.), which was a case where a life insurance policy was abandoned by the trustee, the bankrupt subsequently dying before the estate was closed. Rugsley *v.* Robinson, 19 Ala. 404.

76. Impliedly, Supreme Court's Official Form No. 43. In re Bacon, 12 A. B. R. 730, 132 Fed. 157 (D. C. N. Y.). Post, "Redemption of Property from Liens and Charges," § 1868, et seq.

77. Supreme Court's Official Form No. 44.

78. See post, § 1963, et seq., "Selling Property Subject to and Free from Liens."

In one case the district judge ordered a sale by commissioners under his direct order rather than by the trustee under order of the referee. Sturgiss *v.* Corbin, 15 A. B. R. 543, 141 Fed. 1 (C. C. A. W. Va.).

§ 940. Free from Some, Subject to Others.—The trustee may sell property free from some liens and subject to others.[79]

§ 940¼. May Oppose Bankrupt's Discharge.—Amendment of 1910.—By the Amendment of 1910, the trustee may, if authorized by creditors, at a meeting of creditors called for that purpose, oppose the bankrupt's discharge, and at the expense of the estate.[79a]

The object and effect of this amendment are obvious. It tends to distribute the expense of opposition to a bankrupt's discharge over the entire body of creditors, all of whom are supposed to receive the benefit thereof, rather than to impose it upon the individual creditor, who, theretofore, had been the party qualified to oppose such discharge; and at the same time it tends to prevent improvident and oppressive oppositions to discharge, by requiring authorization of the trustee at a meeting of creditors called for the purpose.[79b]

§ 940½. But Only When Authorized by Creditors at Meeting.—The trustee may not, of his own discretion, oppose the bankrupt's discharge, but only when authorized by the creditors at a meeting called for that purpose.[80]

There must be ten days' notice given of this meeting of creditors, for § 58 provides that there shall be ten days' notice of "all meetings of creditors." The notice should definitely state the object of the meeting to be that of determining whether the trustee should oppose the bankrupt's discharge, for the proviso to amended Section 14 (b) requires that the meeting shall be "called for that purpose." By a corresponding amendment of § 58, the time of notice of the bankrupt's application for discharge has been extended from ten days to thirty days, thus affording time for the meeting of creditors to be held in the meanwhile.[81]

---

79. See post, § 1965, "Selling Free from Liens."

79a. Bankr. Act, as amended 1910, § 14b: "The judge shall hear the application for a discharge and such proofs and pleas as may be made in opposition thereto by the trustee or other parties in interest at such time as will give the trustee or parties in interest a reasonable opportunity to be fully heard, and investigate the merits of the application and discharge the applicant unless, etc. * * * Provided, That a trustee shall not interpose objections to a bankrupt's discharge until he shall be authorized to do so at a meeting of creditors called for that purpose."

79b. See Report No. 691 of the Senate Judiciary Committee of the 61st Congress, Second Session: "The first of these changes, making the trustee a competent party to oppose a bankrupt's discharge, is a desirable change, as thereby the expense of the proceedings in opposition to discharge will be spread over all of the creditors, and not be borne by a single creditor who may file objections. Moreover, it lessens the danger of improper oppositions to discharge by single creditors for the purpose of forcing settlements."

80. Bankr. Act as amended in 1910, § 14b, quoted at § 940¼.

81. See Report No. 691 of the Senate Judiciary Committee of the 61st Congress, Second Session: "The second change, namely, that the trustee can only oppose discharge when authorized to do so at a meeting of creditors, is also desirable, affording a proper check upon improvident and improper opposition to discharge."

The authority for the trustee to oppose the discharge is to be conferred by a majority vote, in number and amount of claims, of all creditors whose claims have been allowed and are present at the meeting.[82] If they do not authorize him, the court is powerless to do so, and the absence of all creditors is not to be taken as permitting the court of its own volition to authorize the opposition. Manifestly, the object of the Amendment is to give creditors an opportunity to oppose a discharge at the common expense of all and it does not involve a judicial act. If any creditor is aggrieved by the refusal of the majority he is at liberty alone to oppose the discharge.

Division 5.

Removal and Death, and Other Vacancies in Trusteeship.

§ 941. Removal of Trustees.—Courts of bankruptcy have the power upon complaint of creditors to remove trustees for cause, upon hearing and after notice to them.[83]

In re Syracuse Paper & Pulp Co., 21 A. B. R. 174, 164 Fed. 275 (D. C. N. Y.): "The creditors and all of them are at liberty to examine the directors, including Driscoll, and if it shall develop that he is an improper person to act as trustee, or that his presence as such interferes with the due and proper administration' of the estate he can be removed."

§ 942. Judge Alone May Remove.—The judge, in contradistinction from the referee, has sole power of removal, and the referee has no power of removal.[84]

§ 943. Good Cause to Be Shown.—Good cause must be shown for the removal. What is good cause may be discovered by the holdings in analogous cases, but to attempt a definition of it would be as unwise and impolitic, as it is said to be to attempt to define "fraud" in terms that would cover all its numerous forms.[85]

Mere removal of residence from the district will not warrant removal from office, where the change neither makes it impossible for him to perform his duties as trustee, nor difficult for creditors to locate and communicate with him.[86]

---

82. Bankruptcy Act, § 56 (a): "Creditors shall pass upon matters submitted to them at their meetings by a majority vote in number and amount of claims of all creditors whose claims have been allowed and are present, except as herein otherwise provided." Also, see ante, § 572.

83. Bankr. Act, § 2 (17); obiter, In re Jamaica, etc., Co., 28 A. B. R. 763, 197 Fed. 240 (D. C. N. Y.). Also see cases cited under subsequent sections of this Division.

84. Sup. Court's Gen. Ord. XIII.

85. (1867) In re Blodgett, 5 N. B. Reg. 772; (1867) In re Perkins, 8 N. B. Reg. 56. Obiter, In re Wrisley Co., 13 A. B. R. 193, 133 Fed. 388 (C. C. A. Ills.). This was a case of a trustee who was interested in a scheme of composition with creditors; and who, by concealment and false representations in aid of the bankrupt, induced creditors to act contrary to their interest. Also, see Bankr. Act, § 2 (17); In re Carothers & Co., 27 A. B. R. 603, 192 Fed. 691 (D. C. Pa.).

86. In re Seider, 20 A. B. R. 703, 163 Fed. 139 (D. C. N. Y.).

But a mere attitude of unfriendliness towards measures instituted to compel the bankrupts to turn over property appears to have been considered sufficient cause for removal where, at any rate, despite his lethargy, other creditors have gone ahead and by vigorous action secured the surrender of the property.[87]

§ 944. Notice and Due Hearing Requisite.

And the trustee must have been given notice in order to have time fairly to prepare himself, and due hearing must be had.[88]

It has been held that the trustee may not, on the hearing, collaterally impeach the complaining creditor's status, where the creditor's claim has not been disallowed.[89] But where the claim has not been allowed, it would hardly seem proper to give the mere filing of it the effect of res adjudicata, simply because the debt is prima facie proof.

§ 945. Hearing Should Be on Petition.

The creditor seeking the removal should prepare a petition and file it before the judge, setting up the grounds upon which the removal is asked.[90]

Upon this petition, rule to show cause should be issued upon the trustee.[91]

§ 946. But Referee to Report Derelict Trustee for Removal Though No Creditor Petitions.

Even without complaint of creditors, the referee may report the trustee for removal; and it is his duty to do so, if the trustee fails to file a report or perform an order required by law for five days after the same shall have become due.[92]

§ 947. Death, Removal or Resignation Not to Abate Pending Suits.

The death or removal of a trustee will not abate pending suits.[93] So as to the trustee's resignation.[94]

§ 947½. Expenses and Compensation of Trustee on Removal.

On removal for misconduct, the court has discretion to refuse all compensation.[95]

---

87. In re Fidler & Son. 23 A. B. R. 16; 172 Fed. 632 (D. C. Pa.).
88. Bankr. Act, § 2 (17).
89. In re Roanoke Furnace Co., 18 A. B. R. 661, 152 Fed. 846 (D. C. Pa.).
90. (1867) In re Hicks, 19 N. B. Reg. 449.
91. Instance, In re Roanoke Furnace Co., 18 A. B. R. 661, 152 Fed. 846 (D. C. Pa.).
92. Gen. Ord. No. XVII.
93. Bankr. Act, § 46 (a): "Death or removal of a trustee shall not abate any suit or proceedings which he is prosecuting or defending at the time of his death or removal, but the same may be proceeded with or defended by his joint trustee or successor in the same manner as though the same had been commenced or was being defended by such joint trustee alone or by such successor."
Death before Adjournment of Meeting.—Where the trustee elect dies before qualifying it is proper at a continuation of the meeting at which he was chosen, to allow the creditor who named him to name his successor. No new notice to creditors is necessary. In re Wright, 2 A. B. R. 497, 97 Fed. 187 (Ref. N. Y.).
94. Hull v. Burr, 28 A. B. R. 837 (Sup. Ct. Fla.).
95. See post, § 2113; obiter, In re Fidler & Son. 23 A. B. R. 16, 172 Fed. 632 (D. C. Pa.).

In re Leverton, 19 A. B. R. 434, 155 Fed. 931 (D. C. Pa.): "That the referee, under the circumstances, properly denied the accountant's claim for commissions, there can be no question. It is specifically provided by the Bankruptcy Act (§ 48c) that: 'The court may, in its discretion, withhold all compensation from any trustee who has been removed for cause.' But without this, upon the general principles which prevail with regard to the administration of trusts, compensation is to be withheld, where there is either fraud or willful misconduct. 28 Am. & Eng. Encycl. Law, 2d Ed. 1038."

And, perhaps, also, expenses, under some circumstances.

In re Leverton, 19 A. B. R. 434, 155 Fed. 931 (D. C. Pa.): "Nor do the expenses of the accountant stand any better. Hanna v. Clark, 204 Pa. 145. These, in the present instance, are made up of railroad fares, hotel bills, etc., made necessary because the bankrupt's estate was at Dushore, while the accountant lived at Scranton, seventy-five miles distant. Had a trustee been selected from the vicinity, as should have been done, in the interest of economy, this expense would have been entirely obviated. And as the accountant, through the solicitation of claims, not to say interest in the bankrupt, pushed himself forward into the place, now that occasion has been found to remove him, he must bear the brunt of it."

And where a trustee has resigned, to avoid removal, he may be denied compensation.[96]

§ 948. Creditors to Elect New Trustee on Death, Removal, etc.— Creditors may elect not only at the first meeting, but also after a vacancy has occurred in the office of trustee, as by failure to qualify, final disapproval by the court, death, resignation, removal[97] or abandonment.[98]

§ 949. Also on Reopening of Estate.—Also, after an estate once closed has been reopened for further proceedings, creditors should elect a new trustee.[99]

---

96. Instance, where denied in part, In re Fidler & Son, 23 A. B. R. 16, 172 Fed. 632 (D. C. Pa.).

Attorneys' Fees Allowed Creditors' Attorney Who Have Effected Removal of Improper Trustee.—See, In re Fidler & Son, 23 A. B. R. 16, 172 Fed. 632 (D. C. Pa.).

97. Bankr. Act, § 44 (a). In re Lewensohn, 3 A. B. R. 299, 98 Fed.

576 (D. C. N. Y.); Hull v. Burr, 28 A. B. R. 837 (Sup. Ct. Fla.).

98. Abandonment of Trust by Absconding Trustee.—Scofield v. United States ex rel. Bond, 23 A. B. R. 259, 174 Fed. 1 (C. C. A. Ohio), quoted at § 878.

99. Bankr. Act, § 44 (a). Fowler v. Jenks, 11 A. B. R. 255, 90 Minn. 74 (Minn. Sup. Ct.).

PART IV.

Assets and Title to Assets.

§ 950. In Orderly Progress, Subject of Assets Reached.—In the usual course of a bankruptcy case, after the election of the trustee, comes naturally a more particular consideration of the question of assets—as to what assets pass to the creditors and what title creditors take to them. Of course the question of assets has already been touched upon more or less as incidental to a discussion of the provisional remedies available to creditors pending the hearing upon the petition for adjudication, but the place for a more complete consideration of the subject comes at the stage of the proceedings immediately following the election of the trustee, for it is only upon the trustee's election and qualification, as will be later noted, that the complete title of creditors vests and it is only then, also, that all the remedies become available for collecting in the assets for creditors. And first comes the consideration of the question of what kinds and classes of property pass to the trustee in bankruptcy.

CHAPTER XXVII.

KINDS OF PROPERTY PASSING AND NOT PASSING TO THE TRUSTEE BY VIRTUE OF THE BANKRUPTCY.

Synopsis of Chapter.

§ 951. Kinds of Property Passing and Not Passing to Trustee.—

All kinds of property .(save such as is exempt) which, before the filing of the bankruptcy petition, was capable of being transferred by any means by the bankrupt, or of being levied on by creditors or otherwise seized by judicial process and sold thereunder, pass to the trustee in bankruptcy, likewise certain powers and rights and documents, not always considered strictly as transferable or leviable property, pass to the trustee.[1]

Section 70 states not only the time the title vests but also the manner of its vesting, the kinds of property vesting, and the nature of the title to the property that passes to the trustee.

Compare, In re Burke, 5 A. B. R. 14, 104 Fed. 326 (D. C. Mo.): "After a careful consideration of the provisions of this section I am persuaded that there are two separate subjects treated of: First, the time at which the title to something vests in the trustees; second, the 'something' or property the title to which is to vest in the trustee."

Thus the title vests on the trustee's appointment and qualification, but reverts to the date of adjudication; the title vests by operation of law; title vests to all kinds of property that was capable of being levied on and sold by judicial process or of being transferred, by any means, at the time of the

---

1. Bankr. Act, § 70 (a): "The trustee of the estate of a bankrupt, upon his appointment and qualification, and his successor or successors, if he shall have one or more, upon his or their appointment and qualification, shall in turn be vested by operation of law with the title of the bankrupt, as of the date he was adjudged bankrupt, except in so far as it is to property which is exempt, to all (1) documents relating to his property; (2) interests in patents, patent rights, copyrights, and trade marks; (3) powers which he might have exercised for his own benefit, but not those which he might have exercised for some other person; (4) property transferred by him in fraud of his creditors; (5) property which prior to the filing of the petition he could by any means have transferred or which might have been levied upon and sold under judicial process against him; provided, that when any bankrupt shall have any insurance policy which has a cash surrender value payable to himself, his estate, or personal representatives, he may, within thirty days after the cash surrender value has been ascertained and stated to the trustee by the company issuing the same, pay or secure to the trustee the sum so ascertained and stated, and continued to hold, own, and carry such policy free from the claims of the creditors participating in the distribution of his estate under the bankruptcy proceedings, otherwise the policy shall pass to the trustee as assets; and (6) rights of action arising upon contracts or from unlawful taking or detention of, or injury to, his property."

Compare, Insolvency Statute of Massachusetts, In re Littlefield, 19 A. B. R. 18, 155 Fed. 838 (C. C. A. Mass.). Partially, Hansen Mercantile Co. v. Wyman, Partridge & Co., 22 A. B. R. 877, 105 Minn. 491, 117 N. W. 926.

filing of the petition, as well as certain other property; and finally, the title that passes is that of the bankrupt and also that of creditors.

In re Pease, 4 A. B. R. 578 (Ref. N. Y.): "Section 70a, providing that a trustee in bankruptcy shall be vested by operation of law with the title of the bankrupt, as of the date he was adjudged a bankrupt, is not antagonistic to § 70a (5), providing that the trustee shall be vested with property which prior to the filing of the petition the bankrupt could have transferred, etc. The former refers to the time the title vests; the latter to what title."

By the operation of § 47 (a) (2) of the Act, as amended in 1910, as well as other sections of the Act, the trustee is vested with the rights and remedies of creditors, in addition to the title of the bankrupt which is given him by § 70 of the Act.

§ 952. Distinct Scope to Each Class.—Of course, by far the widest of the classes of assets passing to the trustee by virtue of § 70 of the Act is class (5) "property which * * * he could by any means have transferred or which might have been levied upon, etc." And, in many instances, this class will be found to include assets usually considered likewise to belong to some of the other classes. Nevertheless, doubtless, the other classes are added to clear up all uncertainty and to cover instances of powers, rights, documents, etc., not usually classed as "property," much less as "transferable" or "leviable" property. Thus, it is evident, the lawmakers intended to give the trustee in bankruptcy most extensive ownership.

These different classes must be given distinct scope.

Cleland v. Anderson, 11 A. B. R. 605 (Neb. Sup. Ct.): "If a right of action in tort, upon which an action is pending may, under our statute, be classed in any sense as property, it does not follow that it is included in the fifth subdivision of the federal statute in question. That statute classified these matters for itself. It specifies, first, documents; second, interests; third, powers; fourth and fifth, property; and sixth, rights of action. Upon such a classification, it will not do to say that rights of action are property. The plain intention of the statute is to otherwise classify them, and to distinguish, for the purpose of this classification, between property and rights of action. The sixth subdivision, therefore, must be taken to specify all rights of action that pass to the trustee in bankruptcy; and, as the right of action involved in this case is not included, it follows that it did not pass."

In re Dann, 12 A. B. R. 27, 129 Fed. 495 (D. C. Ills.): "As stated by Judge Jenkins in In re Rouse-Hazzard & Co., 1 A. B. R. 234, the principle of construction is elementary that 'specific provisions relating to a particular subject' must 'govern in respect to that subject as against general provisions contained in the same act.' * * * Section 70 thus provides specifically for vesting in the trustee the interest of the bankrupt in patents and patent rights, and the presumption arises therefrom when followed by clause 5 in reference to general property, that it was so provided in recognition of the distinction of this class of interests from the general classification of property, as pointed out in the foregoing citations. Under the rule of interpretation referred to I am of opinion that the interest of the bankrupt in the alleged invention cannot be reached through the general terms of clause 5 in the face of this specific provision for patent interests."

§ 953. Local Law Determines Whether Particular Property within Classification.—Whether the property is of such a nature that its title passes, or not, is in general, to be determined by local law.[2]

DIVISION 1.

DOCUMENTS.

§ 954. Documents Pass.—The title to all documents relating to the bankrupt's property passes to the trustee in bankruptcy.[3]

§ 955. "Documents" Include Books, Deeds, Instruments, Papers, Relating to Business.—Not only "documents" as the term is popularly used, but also all books, deeds, instruments and papers relating to the bankrupt's property, pass to the trustee.[4]

In re Hess, 14 A. B. R. 559, 136 Fed. 988 (D. C. Penna.): "Under § 70, clause 1, the trustee of a bankrupt is vested by operation of law with the title to all "documents relating to the bankrupt's property." Section 1, clause 13, defines a 'document' to include any books, deed or instruments of writing, and includes deeds, all other muniments of title, contracts, securities, bills receivable, notes, bank books, bills of exchange, account books, and all papers and books relating to his business. These books and papers of the bankrupt, which come within the designation of documents, are regarded by the Bankrupt Act as personal property, the title to which, by operation of law, is vested in the trustee."

§ 956. Title Itself Passes—Trustee Becomes Owner.—The title itself passes, so the trustee owns the documents and does not simply have the right to inspect them.[5]

And the trustee is entitled to their possession even though they contain incriminating matter.

2. In re Shenberger, 4 A. B. R. 487, 102 Fed. 978 (D. C. Ohio).

Instance, Lease for Ten Years a Chattel Real Not Subject to Chattel Mortgage under New York Law.—In re Fulton, 18 A. B. R. 591, 153 Fed. 664 (D. C. N. Y.).

And where the status of the property has already been passed upon by the state court, it will be considered res judicata in the bankruptcy court. In re Seavey, 27 A. B. R. 373, 195 Fed. 825 (D. C. N. Y.).

3. Bankr. Act, § 70 (a) (1); In re Hess, 14 A. B. R. 559, 136 Fed. 988 (D. C. Penna.); In re Madden, 6 A. B. R. 614 (C. C. A. N. Y.); Kerrch v. United States, 22 A. B. R. 544, 171 Fed. 366 (C. C. A. Mass.); Babbitt v. Dutcher, 216 U. S. 102, 23 A. B. R. 519.

4. Bankr. Act, § 1 (13): "'Document' shall include any book, deed, or instrument in writing." Babbitt v. Dutcher, 216 U. S. 102, 23 A. B. R. 519; inferentially, In re Hyman J. Herr (No. 1), 25 A. B. R. 141, 182 Fed. 715 (D. C. Pa.).

5. In re Madden, 6 A. B. R. 614, 110 Fed. 348 (C. C. A. N. Y.). Kerrch v. United States, 22 A. B. R. 544, 171 Fed. 366 (C. C. A. Mass.); Babbitt v. Dutcher, 216 U. S. 102, 23 A. B. R. 519; In re Harris, 26 A. B. R. 302, 221 U. S. 274. Nevertheless it is doubtful whether the bankrupt can be compelled to deliver them over, if he claims his privilege not to give incriminating evidence against himself. In re Hess, 14 A. B. R. 559, 136 Fed. 988 (D. C. Pa.); compare, In re Rosenblatt, 16 A. B. R. 308 (D. C. Pa.). Also, see post, subject, "Discovery of Assets, Incriminating Evidence," § 1558.

In re Harris, 221 U. S. 274, 26 A. B. R. 302: "If a trustee had been appointed, the title to the books would have vested in him by the express terms of § 70, and the bankrupt could not have withheld possession of what he no longer owned, on the ground that otherwise he might be punished. That is one of the misfortunes of bankruptcy if it follows crime. The right not to be compelled to be a witness against oneself is not a right to appropriate property that may tell one's story."

§ 957. Documents, Books and Papers Not Relating to Bankrupt's Property Do Not Pass.

—It is only to the documents relating to the bankrupt's property that title passes. His purely personal papers, not relating to his property, do not pass to the trustee.

DIVISION 2.

PATENTS, COPYRIGHTS AND TRADE MARKS.

§ 958. Patents, Copyrights and Trade Marks Pass.

—The title to all interests in patents, patent rights, copyrights and trade marks passes to the trustee in bankruptcy.[6]

In re Howley Dresser Co., 13 A. B. R. 94, 132 Fed. 1002 (D. C. N. Y.): "Upon an absolute assignment of a copyright the property therein vests in the assignee and passes to the assignee's trustee in bankruptcy."

Thus, licenses to sell patented articles will pass, subject to the conditions of the license.[7]

§ 959. Pending Applications Do Not Pass.

—But no title passes to mere pending applications for patents, although after adjudication the patent is actually issued.[8]

In re Dann, 12 A. B. R. 27, 129 Fed. 495 (D. C. Ills.): "The term is in no sense applicable to the incorporeal interest of an inventor in an alleged invention for which no patent has issued, though application is pending. It would be

6. Bankr. Act, § 70 (a) (2). Compare, In re McBride & Co., 12 A. B. R. 81, 132 Fed. 285 (D. C. N. Y.), where it was held, that a contract between a publisher and an author whereby the former undertook to publish and market literary productions of the latter, was a personal engagement involving trust and confidence and could not be assigned or delegated to another by the trustee in bankruptcy of the publisher without the author's consent; and that this rule obtains even though the publisher is a corporation; and that where, in pursuance of such a contract, the copyrights had been acquired in the name of the publisher, the District Court had jurisdiction to entertain a summary proceeding by the author to compel the trustee in bankruptcy of the publisher to assign the copyrights.

7. In re Spitzel, 21 A. B. R. 729, 168 Fed. 156 (D. C. N. Y.).

8. In re McDonald, 4 A. B. R. 92, 101 Fed. 239 (D. C. Iowa).

Contra, In re Cantelo Mfg. Co., 26 A. B. R. 57, 185 Fed. 276 (D. C. Me.); but this case is extreme; not only is it doubtful whether title passes to pending applications and also doubtful whether an employment to invent passes ownership of the resulting patent though perfected on the employer's money, but it especially is doubtful that the inventor was not an "adverse claimant" entitled to plenary action before being required to execute an assignment; yet the "estoppel" was very strong in this case.

a misnomer if employed in the latter sense, for no right to a patent exists except as provided by statute and upon allowance thereunder. Without such allowance of an application the applicant has no interest which can be denominated a 'patent right' whatever may be his interest in the invention claimed."

DIVISION 3.

POWERS.

§ 960. "Powers" Pass.—The title to all powers which the bankrupt might have exercised for his own benefit passes to the trustee in bankruptcy.[9]

§ 961. But Not Powers Not Exercisable for Bankrupt's Own Benefit.—But not powers which he could only have exercised for some other person.

As to what is probably meant by the word "powers" as here used, see Fisher v. Cushman, 4 A. B. R. 654, 103 Fed. 860 (C. C. A. Mass.): "In behalf of the trustee in bankruptcy, reference is made to the paragraph of § 70 of the Bankrupt Act which provides that the trustee shall be vested with certain 'powers;' and it is claimed that this applies at bar, because the bankrupt had the power to realize from the license. However, we prefer not to attempt to rest the case on this expression, because we doubt whether so popular a signification can be given to the word, and whether, on a careful examination of the English statutes from which this was drawn, and of the decisions of the English courts in regard thereto, we might not be required to determine that it is to be construed technically, as known to the common law."

Hesseltine v. Prince, 2 A. B. R. 600, 95 Fed. 802 (D. C. Mass.): "Section 70 (3) was relied upon in argument by counsel for the trustee; but, however, the husband's right in his wife's real estate should be described, it certainly is not a power."

DIVISION 4.

PROPERTY FRAUDULENTLY CONVEYED.

§ 962. Fraudulently Transferred Property Passes.—The title to all property transferred by the bankrupt in fraud of his creditors passes to the trustee in bankruptcy.[10]

Now, while this kind of property could not "by any means be transferred by the bankrupt," already having once been fraudulently transferred by

---

9. In re Kellogg, 10 A. B. R. 10, 112 Fed. 52 (C. C. A. N. Y., affirming 7 A. B. R. 623). To plead usury.

The right to change the beneficiary of a life insurance policy would be such a "power." See post, § 1007. Also, In re Orear, 24 A. B. R. 343, 178 Fed. 632 (C. C. A. Mo.).

10. In re Kohler, 20 A. B. R. 89, 159 Fed. 871 (C. C. A. Ohio); impliedly, Ruhl-Koblegard Co. v. Gillespie, 22 A. B. R. 643, 61 W. Va. 554;

In re Hurst, 23 A. B. R. 554 (Ref. W. Va.); In re Duggan, 25 A. B. R. 479, 183 Fed. 405 (C. C. A. Ga.), affirming 25 A. B. R. 479.

Barnes Mfg. Co. v. Norden, 7 A. B. R. 553 (Sup. Ct. N. J.). And a creditor cannot maintain a fraudulent conveyance suit therefor for his own benefit. For full discussion of fraudulently conveyed property, see post, § 1216, et seq.

him, and therefore could not come under the one branch of class 5, "property which he could by any means have transferred," yet it precisely fits under the other branch; for fraudulently conveyed property can be "levied upon and sold under judicial process against the debtor," although it cannot be again transferred by him. So, in theory, this is merely an instance under class 5, rather than a distinct class by itself. Yet, by its separate mention, it is made clear that, at least as to fraudulently conveyed property, the trustee was not limited to standing precisely in the "bankrupt's" shoes even before the Amendment of 1910 to § 47 (a) (2) endowed him with the rights, powers and remedies also of a creditor "armed with process."

DIVISION 5.

TRANSFERABLE PROPERTY AND PROPERTY CAPABLE OF SUBJECTION BY LEGAL PROCESS.

§ 963. Property Transferable, or Capable of Subjection by Legal Process, Passes.—By far the most extensive class of assets passing to the trustee in bankruptcy is class 5.

Property which prior to the filing of the petition, the bankrupt could by any means have transferred or which might have been levied upon and sold under judicial process against him (with the exception of exempt property and with certain qualifications relative to life insurance policies) passes to the trustee.[11]

Compare, In re Judson, 27 A. B. R. 704, 188 Fed. 702 (C. C. A. N. Y., affirmed sub nom. Everett v. Judson, 228 U. S. 474, 30 A. A. B. 1): "Referring to the language of the provision in question as shown in the footnote [§ 70(a)] it seems clear that a trustee in bankruptcy takes title as of the date of the adjudication, not to the property owned by the bankrupt at that time, but to the property owned at the time of the filing of the petition. The trustee's title vests, it is true, as of the date of the adjudication, but the title which vests is limited to the property belonging to the bankrupt at the time of the commencement of the proceedings—the filing of the petition. The one date determines when the title vests; the other, the property to which the title vests. Property acquired by the bankrupt after the filing of the petition is not—to

---

11. Bankr. Act, § 70 (a) (5). In re Harris, 2 A. B. R. 359, 99 Fed. 71 (Ref. Ills.); In re Russie, 3 A. B. R. 6, 96 Fed. 608 (D. C. Ore.); Brown v. Barker, 8 A. B. R. 450 (N. Y. Sup. Ct. App. Div.); In re Rennie, 2 A. B. R. 182 (Ref. Ind. Ter.); In re Rasmussen, 13 A. B. R. 466, 136 Fed. 704 (D. C. Ore.); obiter, In re Burka, 5 A. B. R. 12, 104 Fed. 326 (D. C. Mo.); In re Coffin, 16 A. B. R. 686, 146 Fed. 181 (D. C. Conn.); In re Burtis, 26 A. B. R. 680, 188 Fed. 527 (D. C. N. Y.); In re Matschke, 27 A. B. R. 770, 193 Fed. 284 (D. C. N. Y.); obiter, Board of Commrs. Kans. v. Hurley, 22 A. B. R. 209, 169 Fed. 92 (C. C. A. Kan.), quoted on other points at §§ 629, 1519, 1521; In re Perkins, 19 A. B. R. 134, 155 Fed. 237 (D. C. Me.); Hansen, Mercantile Co. v. Wyman, Partridge & Co., 22 A. B. R. 877, 105 Minn. 491, 117 N. W. 926. For the general subject of the title taken by the trustee, see post, § 1144, et seq.

No Similar Clause under Act of 1867.—Hansen v. Wyman, 21 A. B. R. 398, 117 N. W. 926.

Instances Not Elsewhere Classified —Land under Water.—In re Bailey, 19 A. B. R. 470, 156 Fed. 691 (D. C. N. Y.).

use the language of the act—property which 'prior to the filing of the petition he could by any means have transferred.' We think it clear that the time of the filing of the petition in this case should be taken as the date of the cleavage determining the property passing to the trustee and through him to the creditors."

Gould v. N. Y. Life Ins. Co., 13 A. B. R. 235, 132 Fed. 927 (D. C. Ark.): "It will be noticed that this subdivision 5, § 70 (a), provides for the vesting in the trustee of the title not only of all property subject to seizure or sale under judicial process, but also all property which prior to the filing of the petition the bankrupt might have transferred. This practically covers everything the bankrupt might own, and from which by sale some funds could be realized by the trustee for the benefit of the estate."

In re Jersey Island Packing Co., 14 A. B. R. 692, 138 Fed. 625 (C. C. A. Calif.): "And the beneficial interest of a bankrupt in property held in trust passes, also, in all cases where that interest might have been transferred to another by the bankrupt or might have been levied upon under judicial proceedings against him."

In re Howland, 6 A. B. R. 495, 109 Fed. 869 (D. C. N. Y.): "In this State, where merchandise is sold on a conditional contract, but with the understanding that it is to be dealt with in the same manner as other property owned by the vendee, such sale is inconsistent with the continued ownership of the vendor and the property may be seized and sold on execution by the creditors of the vendee. The property sold to the bankrupt by the Mishawaka Company falls within this rule. It was placed in the general stock of the bankrupt and a portion was sold at retail over his counter. The merchandise in question, therefore, passed to the trustee pursuant to the provisions of Bankr. Act, § 70 (5) as property 'which might have been levied upon and sold under judicial process against the bankrupt.' Neither this section nor § 67a, which is also in point, is found in the act of 1867."

But this means property which the bankrupt could lawfully have transferred, not property which he could have transferred in violation of law.[12]

In re Dunlop, 19 A. B. R. 361, 156 Fed. 545 (C. C. A. Minn.): "The 'property which prior to the filing of the petition he [the bankrupt] could by any means have transferred' within the meaning of this clause of § 70, is property that he could by any means have transferred to another lawfully under the same terms that he transfers it by law to the trustee; that is to say, without consideration. It does not include the property of another, which the bankrupt is authorized to transfer only on the condition that he sells it for value, or sells it and holds its proceeds for its owner."

§ 964. If Capable Either of Transfer or of Being Levied on.—If it was capable either of being transferred or of being levied upon, it will pass.[13]

---

12. But see, apparent disregard of the qualification, In re Burke, 22 A. B. R. 69, 168 Fed. 994 (D. C. Ga.): "Subd. 5 of § 70 of the Bankruptcy Act vests in the trustee the title of the bankrupt to all property which prior to the filing of the petition he could by any means have transferred, etc. If, then, these cultivators and implements could have been the subject of transfer by the express authority of the instrument of sale, it seems clear that the title of the trustee is good against the vendor."

13. O'Dell v. Boyden, 17 A. B. R. 757, 150 Fed. 731 (C. C. A. Ohio); Rosenbluth v. DeForest, etc., 27 A. B. R. 359 (Sup. Ct. Conn.).

The mere fact that the bankrupt conducted his business under a firm

Page *v.* Edmunds, 9 A. B. R. 281, 187 U. S. 596: "Was the seat in the stock exchange property which could have been by any means transferred, or which might have been levied upon and sold under judicial process? If the seat was subject to either manner of disposition, it passed to the trustee of the appellant's estate.

"We think it could have been transferred within the meaning of the statute. The appellant could have sold his membership, the purchaser taking it subject to election by the exchange, and some other conditions. It had decided value. The appellant paid for it in 1880, $5,500, and he testified that the last price he had heard paid for a seat was $8,500. One or the other of these sums, or, at any rate, some sum, was the value of the seat. It was property and substantial property to the extent of some amount, notwithstanding the contingencies to which it was subject. In other words, the buyer took the risk of the contingencies. And they seem to be capable of estimation. The appellant once estimated them and paid $5,500 for the seat in controversy; another buyer estimated them and paid $8,500 for a seat. A thing having such vendible value must be regarded as property, and as it could have been transferred by some means by appellant (one of the conditions expressed in § 70), it passed to and vested in his trustee."

Thus, also, a lease providing for forfeiture on attempted assignment cannot be "transferred" by the debtor but may be levied on and sold under judicial process against him.[14]

Again, it has been held that where an elevator company or other company having goods in possession, for which elevator certificates or warehouse receipts have been issued, becomes bankrupt, the fact of outstanding certificates against the flour and grain in its storage tanks or goods in its warehouse is not sufficient to prevent title passing to the trustee in bankruptcy, since the property could have been levied upon by creditors.[15]

In re Milbourne Mills Co., 20 A. B. R. 746, 162 Fed. 988 (D. C. Pa.): "As we read the cases of York Mfg. Co. *v.* Cassel, supra, and Davis *v.* Crompton, supra, the court in both held that the bankrupt never had title to property covered by a conditional sale and was not included in the property to which a trustee in bankruptcy took title under subdivision 5 of § 70a, because that subdivision not only requires that the property to which the trustee takes title shall be property which would have been liable to be levied upon and sold under judicial proceedings against the bankrupt by the creditors, but that the bankrupt must have had some previous title to it, or the rights of the creditors fixed by a previous lien placed upon it by levy or attachment. But neither of these cases go so far as to say that property upon which a creditor could have levied, concededly belonging to the bankrupt, to which it had title and possession before the bankruptcy proceedings and of which title it had never been divested, although covered by a certificate or pledge as collateral security for a loan, belongs to the pledgee as against the trustee

name, does not prevent it from passing to the trustee as his individual property, if, in fact, it was such. In re Gibson, 27 A. B. R. 401, 191 Fed. 665 (D. C. S. D.).

14. See post, subject of "Leaseholds," § 979, et seq.

15. See post, § 1884; compare, perhaps (Security) Warehousing Co. *v.* Hand, 19 A. B. R. 291, 206 U. S. 415 quoted at § 1146.

in bankruptcy. The pledge is no doubt good as between the pledgor and pledgee in Pennsylvania as against creditors who have never levied, but as the title still remained in the pledgor, who is the bankrupt when it is so adjudged, its title passed to the trustee. It is property, the title to which passes to the trustees under subdivision 5, § 70a of the act, as property 'which might have been levied upon and sold under judicial proceedings against him.' * * * The facts in this case are nearly similar to those under consideration by the Supreme Court in the case of Security Warehousing Co. v. Hand [19 A. B. R. 291, 206 U. S. 415], and there the trustee held the property for the general creditors. In that case it was in effect held that where there was no delivery or change of possession, such certificates as those given did not operate as a delivery of the property mentioned therein. It was also held that the general law of pledge requires possession, and it cannot exist without it."

However, it is to be observed that if, under the law of the State, such certificates or receipts were sufficient to pass title to the property itself, they would doubtless be likewise sufficient in bankruptcy. Indeed, such seems to be the qualification imposed by the Supreme Court in the case of Security Warehousing Co. v. Hand, 19 A. B. R. 291, 206 U. S. 415.

§ 965. If Transferable "by Any Means," or Leviable, It Passes, Otherwise, Not.—If capable of being disposed of or its possession parted with by any means, and either absolutely or conditionally, it passes to the trustee; but if not so capable it does not pass, unless leviable upon or coming within some one of the other classes of § 70 (a).[16]

§ 966. Broad Scope of Class 5.—The broadest possible scope is given to this class 5 of assets. Not only is "transfer" a word of widest content by the definition of the Bankruptcy Act itself, including all possible interests of the bankrupt in property, but also in class 5 of assets it is further provided that such interests pass if "by any means" they can be made to pass. Thus, conditional and contingent interests pass, even if, in addition to being conditional or contingent, the assistance of the bankrupt or of some one else over whom the bankruptcy court has control is requisite in order to consummate the "disposing of" the property.[17]

SUBDIVISION "A."

MEMBERSHIP IN STOCK EXCHANGES, CLUBS, ETC., LICENSES AND OTHER PRIVILEGES.

§ 967. Thus, Memberships in Stock Exchanges, Clubs, etc., Licenses and Personal Privileges, Pass.—A good example of the broad scope of this class 5 of assets is furnished by memberships in stock exchanges. The transferability of such memberships is wholly contingent upon the purchaser being elected a member by the exchange. Again, its transfer commonly is not to be effected by any of the ordinary and usual means

---

16. Bankr. Act, § 1 (25): "'Transfer' shall include the sale and every other and different mode of disposing of or parting with property or the possession of property, absolutely or conditionally, as a payment, pledge, mortgage, gift or security."

17. Gould v. N. Y. Life Ins. Co., 13 A. B. R. 235, 132 Fed. 930 (D. C. Ark.).

of transferring property—neither by sale, assignment, pledge, mortgage, etc.—but only by the holder making written request upon the exchange to transfer the membership. Thus, membership in stock exchanges illustrate, most aptly, the broad inclusiveness of class 5. Such property not only is capable merely of contingent transfer, but also is capable of transfer only by peculiar means.

Personal privileges, if in any way they can be sold, even conditionally and though they require peculiar means for consummating the transfer, thus pass to the trustee, as memberships in clubs and in stock exchanges and licenses. Thus, a membership in a chamber of commerce will pass.[18]

And the money value of a seat in the stock exchange belonging to a bankrupt member passes to the trustee, in the absence of any forfeiture clause in the constitution or by-laws.[19]

O'Dell v. Boyden, 17 A. B. R. 758, 150 Fed. 731 (C. C. A. Ohio): "Though possessing none of the qualities of a negotiable or even a nonnegotiable instrument, this membership has a pecuniary market value and constitutes a property right which, under the settled principles of the law, is capable of passing by will or inheritance. In re Hellman, 174 N. Y. 254. Though its sale and transfer are clogged with onerous conditions and the property one of a narrow character, these conditions and characteristics go only to the reduction of the pecuniary market value and do not deprive it of its character as property. Powell v. Waldron, 89 N. Y. 328. As a valuable property right, incorporeal in character, it may be reached and subjected as property by a creditor through the flexible remedies of equity. A court of chancery through a decree in personam may compel the co-operation of the number in steps necessary to consummate a sale and transfer under the rules of the association. * * * Such a seat constitutes a property right which is not only descendable, taxable and assignable, but is one which passes to the trustee of a bankrupt member, and the bankrupt court may compel the bankrupt to sign all transfers, or consents essential to bring about its sale under the rules of the exchange. * * * That an assignee or transferee, in pledge or otherwise, would obtain such an equitable right as would enable him through the aid of equity to bring about its transfer through the co-operation of the member, cannot be doubted. If a creditor, having no equitable lien by contract, might obtain one by aid of equity, there is no reason why an assignee or transferee might not also."

Subject however to liens of creditor members, under the rules of the stock exchange.[20]

---

18. In re Neimann, 10 A. B. R. 739, 124 Fed. 738 (D. C. Wis.).

19. Page v. Edmonds, 9 A. B. R. 281, 187 U. S. 596, quoted at § 964; In re Gaylord, 7 A. B. R. 195, 111 Fed. 717 (D. C. Mo.); In re Hurlbutt, Hatch & Co., 13 A. B. R. 50, 135 Fed. 504 (C. C. A. N. Y.); In re Gregory, 23 A. B. R. 270, 174 Fed. 629 (C. C. A. N. Y.).

But the proceeds of a sale of the seat will not be ordered paid to the trustee where supplementary proceedings had been instituted prior to four months. Wrede, receiver, v. Clook, trustee, 21 A. B. R. 821 (N. Y. Sup. Ct. App. Div.).

Lien of Correspondent of Bankrupt Stockbroker on Stock Exchange Seat. —Where a customer has paid the bankrupt for stock purchased through a correspondent, but the bankrupt fails to remit purchase price, see post, § 1882; also, see In re Meadows, Williams & Co., 23 A. B. R. 124, 177 Fed. 1004 (D. C. N. Y.).

20. In re Gregory, 23 A. B. R. 270, 174 Fed. 629 (C. C. A. N. Y.).

And subject also to the decision of the stock exchange tribunal establishing the order and validity of such liens.[21]

In re Currie (Austin), 26 A. B. R. 345, 185 Fed. 263 (C. C. A. N. Y.): "The proposition that a bankrupt's seat in the New York Stock Exchange is property or assets passing to his trustees may be admitted. I think it must be admitted, but am unable to perceive how it advances the petitioner's case. A seat in this Stock Exchange is property of such a nature that it can never become available to the assignee, legal representative, receiver or trustee of a Stock Exchange member, until the claims of other members of this unincorporated association have been settled by the sole tribunal entitled to pass upon the same according to the laws of the exchange, which are no more than the contractual engagements entered into by every person joining the organization, and therefore binding upon all those successors in interest who claim by, through, or under a Stock Exchange member."

Conditioned of course upon the usual rules regulating the binding force of tribunals outside of the regularly constituted courts.

A liquor license will pass, or not pass, according to local law.[22]

Thus, it will pass in Minnesota.

In re May, 5 A. B. R. 1 (Ref. Minn. affirmed D. C.): "Without undertaking to make nice discriminations between what may properly be classified as property, and what clearly appears to be a mere personal privilege, it is held that whatever has a money value in the hands of a trustee, so that some person may be willing to buy from him at a price, even though it partake of the qualities of a personal privilege, in the sense of being not legally assignable, passes to the trustee, except such property as is expressly exempted by law. * * *

"The village liquor license now in the possession of the bankrupt, is in some sense property. It represents the investment of a large amount of money, and will be deemed to have a money value. The trustee in bankruptcy is entitled to said license, and is bound to realize upon it, whatever he may be able to sell it for. The question as to what title he may be able to give, is for the consideration of an intending purchaser."

And in Virginia.[23]

But a liquor license will not pass in Georgia, because it is not a contract nor a property right.[24] And it has been variously held in Pennsylvania; one case holding that a liquor license will not pass since it is peculiarly a

21. In re Currie (In re Austin), 26 A. B. R. 345, 185 Fed. 263 (C. C. A. N. Y.).

Creditor Member Holding Other Security Besides Lien on Stock Exchange Seat.—For a case where a creditor member holding other security besides his lien on the bankrupt stock broker's seat, was yet not required to exhaust his other security first, see In re Currie (Austin), 26 A. B. R. 345, 185 Fed. 263 (C. C. A. N. Y.).

22. Instance where benefits of license held to pass. In re Baumblott, 18 A. B. R. 496, 156 Fed. 422 (D. C. Pa.).

License to Sell Patented Article.—Will pass subject to the conditions of the license, In re Spitzel & Co., 21 A. B. R. 729, 168 Fed. 156 (D. C. N. Y.); see ante, § 958.

23. In re Flaherty, 25 A. B. R. 943, 184 Fed. 962 (D. C. Va.).

24. In re Keller, 16 A. B. R. 727 (D. C. Ga.).

personal privilege,[25] whilst other cases hold that it will pass,[26] whilst in Massachusetts it will pass,[27] conditioned, however, on the assent of the public authorities to the transfer.[28] But even in Massachusetts if the public authorities refuse assent to the mortgaging of the liquor license by the bankrupt, the proceeds of the sale of the liquor license will not be turned over to satisfy the mortgagee.[29]

And the right of a bankrupt to apply for a renewal of a liquor license has been held to pass to the trustee and the bankrupt has been required to make application therefor.[30]

Likewise, a market stall license passes to the trustee under the same ruling.[31]

§ 968. **Though Subject to Contingency of Election or of Approval of Public Authorities.**—This is so notwithstanding the membership may be a subject of election : the purchaser buys subject to the contingency that he may not be elected. Also, notwithstanding such personal privileges cannot be levied on and sold, they may be transferred by the bankrupt, for "transfer" includes *conditional* sales and "any and every mode of parting with property or the possession of it," according to the definition of the term "transfer" contained in § 1.[32]

---

25. In re Olewine, 11 A. B. R. 40, 125 Fed. 840 (D. C. Penna.); Instance, In re Comer & Co., 22 A. B. R. 558, 171 Fed. 261 (D. C. Pa.); instance, In re Miller, 22 A. B. R. 580, 171 Fed. 263 (D. C. Pa.); In re Wiesel & Knaup, 23 A. B. R. 59, 173 Fed. 718 (D. C. Pa.).
26. In re Becker, 3 A. B. R. 412, 98 Fed. 407 (D. C. Penna.): "No doubt there is a clearly visible distinction between a right to property and a mere personal privilege; but I see no abstract reason why some personal privileges may not also come to have qualities belonging usually to property rights alone—such, for example, as capacity to be transferred, and sufficient attractiveness to make other persons willing to pay money for the opportunity to acquire them. Where, as in the case of a license to sell liquor, these qualities are found to exist in fact, it seems to me that the privilege has ceased to be a privilege merely, and has become, in some sense and in some degree, property also. It can' hardly be correct to hold that a bankrupt's creditors may not avail themselves of the fact that money can be had for the chance of stepping into the licensee's place, but that the bankrupt himself may make the same bargain, and put the money safely into his pocket. The license court may or may not accept the buyer as the bankrupt's successor. That is the buyer's affair, and is not decisive upon the point now being considered. He buys a contingency, and buys it with his eyes open; but, in my opinion, the trustee has the contingency to sell, and the bankrupt is bound to execute the instruments necessary to carry out the sale."
27. In re Fisher, 3 A. B. R. 406, 98 Fed. 89 (D. C. Mass.); In re Brodbine, 2 A. B. R. 53, 93 Fed. 643 (D. C. Mass.).
28. Fisher v. Cushman, 4 A. B. R. 646, 103 Fed. 860 (C. C. A. Mass., affirming In re Fisher, 3 A. B. R. 406, 98 Fed. 89, affirming 1 A. B. R. 557).
29. In re McArdle, 11 A. B. R. 358, 126 Fed. 442 (D. C. Mass.).
30. In re Wiesel & Knaup, 23 A. B. R. 59, 173 Fed. 718 (D. C. Pa.).
31. In re Emrich, 4 A. B. R. 89, 101 Fed. 231 (D. C. Ga.).
32. Page v. Edmunds, 9 A. B. R. 277, 187 U. S. 596 (affirming In re Page, 5 A. B. R. 707, and 4 A. B. R. 467, 102 Fed. 746); In re Neinmann, 10 A. B. R. 739, 124 Fed. 738 (D. C. Wis.); In re May, 5 A. B. R. 1 (Ref. Minn.); In re Hurlbut, et al., 13 A. B. R. 50, 135 Fed. 504 (C. C. A. N. Y.); In re Gaylord, 7 A. B. R. 195, 111 Fed. 717 (D. C. Mo.); O'Dell v. Boyden, 17 A. B. R. 757, 150 Fed. 731 (C. C. A. Ohio); In re Emrich, 4 A. B. R. 89,

§ 969. And Though "Transferable" Only by Peculiar and Unusual Means.—And this is so, also, though the privilege is transferable only by peculiar and unusual means.[33] Thus, where transferable only on the former owner's written application, the bankrupt may be compelled to sign an application to the stock exchange for a sale and transfer of the seat and a payment of the proceeds to the trustee in bankruptcy;[34] and may be compelled to execute the instruments conferring upon the trustee the right to sell.[35] And the bankrupt also may be compelled to execute an assignment of a license to the trustee.[36]

O'Dell *v.* Boyden, 17 A. B. R. 759 (C. C. A. Ohio): "Only through a court of equity can the pecuniary value of such an asset be realized to creditors or assignees. Only by decree in personam compelling the bankrupt member, can such a transfer of membership be effectuated as will put the buyer in the place of Henrotin as a member. Over him for that purpose the bankrupt court has exclusive control, and, in this sense, also, may it be said, that the 'seat' or 'membership' was in custodia legis when the trustee sought the aid of the court to adjudicate the claims and liens asserted by O'Dell."

And the bankrupt has also been compelled to aid in effecting a sale of a renewal of a liquor license applied for.[37]

§ 969½. Rewards.—It has been held that government rewards earned before bankruptcy but not awarded until afterward, do not pass to the trustee;[38] but do pass if both earned and awarded before bankruptcy.[39]

SUBDIVISION "B."

EXPECTANCIES AND POSSIBILITIES OF ACQUIRING PROPERTY; INCHOATE INTERESTS; VESTED AND CONTINGENT INTERESTS; LEGACIES; REMAINDERS; LIFE ESTATES AND REVERSIONARY INTERESTS.

§ 970. Property Rights Must Exist in Bankrupt.—Although the property may consist of a contingent or conditional interest and be transferable only by peculiar "means," yet there must at least be something there which the law would denominate a property right.[40]

Thus, mere expectancies and bare possibilities of acquiring property do

101 Fed. 231 (D. C. Pa.); In re Olewine, 11 A. B. R. 40, 125 Fed. 840 (D. C. Pa.); In re Becker, 3 A. B. R. 412, 98 Fed. 407 (D. C. Pa.). But compare, In re Ghazal, 22 A. B. R. 119, 169 Fed. 147 (D. C. N. Y.).

33. Compare principles enunciated in In re Wright, 19 A. B. R. 454, 157 Fed. 544 (C. C. A. N. Y.), quoted post, § 994.

34. In re Hurlbut, 13 A. B. R. 50, 135 Fed. 504 (C. C. A. N. Y.). Ante, § 460; post, §§ 1009, 1115, 1835.

35. In re Becker, 3 A. B. R. 412, 96 Fed. 407 (D. C. Pa.).

36. In re Emrich, 4 A. B. R. 89, 101 Fed. 231 (D. C. Pa.); In re Wiesel & Knaup, 23 A. B. R. 59, 173 Fed. 718 (D. C. Pa.); similarly as to insurance policies, post, § 1009.

37. In re Wiesel & Knaup, 23 A. B. R. 59, 173 Fed. 718 (D. C. Pa.).

38. In re Ghazal, 20 A. B. R. 807, 163 Fed. 602 (D. C. N. Y.).

39. In re Ghazal, 22 A. B. R. 119, 169 Fed. 147 (D. C. N. Y.).

40. In re Wetmore, 6 A. B. R. 214, 108 Fed. 210 (C. C. A. Pa., affirming 4 A. B. R. 335).

not pass. They do not constitute property nor title to property, nor can they be transferred or levied on, therefore they do not pass to the trustee.[41]

In re Wetmore, 6 A. B. R. 214, 108 Fed. 210 (C. C. A. Penna., affirming 4 A. B. R. 335): "A bare possibility or mere expectation of acquiring property does not constitute property or a title to property; nor can it be transferred or levied upon. While the right of enjoyment may be uncertain and contingent, it is necessary that an interest or title of some kind be vested in the bankrupt in order that it may pass by operation of law to the trustee."

Thus, where a father died before his son's adjudication and the mother died afterward, it was held there was no vested interest to pass to the trustee of the son, notwithstanding the wish and confidence expressed in the father's will that his widow, to whom he had left everything, would make a bequest to the son, among others.[42]

Thus, as to a claim of alimony existing at the time of filing the petition, where the alimony is not awarded until subsequently thereto.

In re LeClaire, 10 A. B. R. 733, 124 Fed. 654 (D. C. Iowa): "Certainly, at the date of the adjudication in this case, the mere claim or possible right to alimony asserted by the bankrupt in the divorce proceedings could not have been levied on and sold under judicial process, nor was it a property right which could be made the subject of barter and sale with third parties by the bankrupt himself. Prior to the entering of the decree of divorce in the District Court of Clay county, which was not done until some days after the date of adjudication, it could not be known whether a divorce would be granted to the bankrupt, or whether any alimony would be allowed her; and, if allowed, it could not be known whether it would be in the form of stated amounts of money to be paid by the husband, or by setting apart specific property to her, both of which methods are permissible under the statute of Iowa. * * * It seems clear that a claim for alimony asserted in a suit for divorce is not a property right that can be sold and transferred by the claimant, or that can be levied on by judicial process."

Thus, a stockholder's lien upon customer's securities.

In re Berry, 15 A. B. R. 360, 146 Fed. 623 (D. C. N. Y.): "The stock was the customers' property. If the bankrupts had what is called a special property in it, in the way of a lien upon it, I do not think that that is what is referred to in the Bankrupt Act as the bankrupt's property."

Thus, government rewards for the detection of smugglers, which have not been awarded by the Secretary of the Treasury until after the informer's adjudication, will not pass to the informer's trustee in bankruptcy, even though the services were performed before the filing of the petition in bankruptcy.

41. In re Hogan, 28 A. B. R. 166, 194 Fed. 846 (C. C. A. Wis.); In re Gardner, 5 A. B. R. 432 (D. C. N. Y.); In re Woods, 13 A. B. R. 240, 133 Fed. 82 (D. C. Pa.); In re Braeutigam, 3 N. B. N. & R. 461 (Ref. N. J.); In re Hoadley, 3 A. B. R. 780, 101 Fed. 233 (D. C. N. Y.); In re Freeman, 2 N. B. N. & R. 569 (Ref. Tenn.); In re Ehle, 6 A. B. R. 476 (D. C. Vt.); apparently, contra. In re Twaddell, 6 A. B. R. 539, 110 Fed. 145 (D. C. Del.).

42. In re Harper, 18 A. B. R. 741, 155 Fed. 105 (C. C. A. N. Y.).

In re Ghazal, 23 A. B. R. 178, 169 Fed. 147 (C. C. A. N. Y.): "Until he (Secretary of the United States Treasury) acts, the informer has merely an expectation of reward."

But, of course, such rewards as have been awarded before the bankruptcy will pass to the trustee.[43]

So, in some jurisdictions, the common-law rule that property held by husband and wife jointly is held in entirety without possibility of severance still prevails; each has only an expectancy, for, upon the death of one, the other takes the estate; and although the husband's trustee in bankruptcy is undoubtedly clothed with the husband's interest, whatever that may be, his right to it must await the contingency of the husband surviving the wife.[44]

§ 971. Mere Inchoate Interests Do Not Pass.

—Nor would a mere inchoate interest pass,[45] and this would be so although the bankrupt by joining in a deed or otherwise might be able to estop himself from afterwards claiming title to the property when the inchoate interest actually should become consummate and vested. Yet this ability to estop one's self does not amount to an ability to transfer the title and so such property does not pass to the trustee.[46] Thus inchoate dower interests do not pass;[47] nor do estates by curtesy initiate.[48] But estates by curtesy consummate do pass.[49]

§ 972. Vested Interests Pass.

—If the interest actually is a vested interest, it passes to the trustee, as for instance vested remainders and inheritances, legacies and devises, if the death of the ancestor or testator occurs before the adjudication of the heir, legatee or devise.[50]

---

43. In re Ghazal, 22 A. B. R. 119, 169 Fed. 147 (D. C. N. Y.).

44. In re Beihl, 28 A. B. R. 310, 197 Fed. 870 (D. C. Pa.).

45. In re Hogan, 28 A. B. R. 116, 194 Fed. 846 (C. C. A. Wis.).

46. In re Twaddell, 6 A. B. R. 539; 110 Fed. 145 (D. C. Del.); In re Russell, 13 A. B. R. 24 (Ref. Ohio); Hesseltine v. Prince, 2 A. B. R. 600, 95 Fed. 802 (D. C. Mass.).

47. In re Russell, 13 A. B. R. 24 (Ref. Ohio).

Release of dower in preferential mortgage does not remain available to the mortgagee upon the setting aside of the mortgage as a preference, even though a conveyance of a wife's dower right can not be a preference since it is not a transfer of the bankrupt's property, but because the release is a mere incident, falling with the fall of the conveyance itself. In re Lingafelter, 24 A. B. R. 656, 181 Fed. 24 (C. C. A. Ohio).

48. Hesseltine v. Prince, 2 A. B. R. 600, 95 Fed. 802 (D. C. Mass.).

49. In re Marquette, 4 A. B. R. 623, 103 Fed. 777 (D. C. Vt.).

50. Impliedly, In re Roosa, 9 A. B. R. 531, 119 Fed. 542 (D. C. Iowa); In re Wood, 3 A. B. R. 572, 95 Fed. 946 (D. C. N. Y.); In re Schenberger, 4 A. B. R. 487 (D. C. Ohio); In re McHarry, 7 A. B. R. 83, 111 Fed. 408 (C. C. A. Ills.); In re Twaddell, 6 A. B. R. 539, 110 Fed. 145 (D. C. Del.); In re May, 5 A. B. R. 1 (Ref. Minn., affirmed by D. C.); Churchman's Appeal (Pa.), 12 Atl. 600; In re St. John, 5 A. B. R. 190, 105 Fed. 234 (D. C. N. Y.); In re Mosier, 7 A. B. R. 268, 112 Fed. 138 (D. C. Vt.); Osman v. Galbraith Admr., 9 A. B. R. 339 (Sup. Ct. Mich); In re Arden, 26 A. B. R. 684, 188 Fed. 475 (D. C. N. Y.); In re Judson, 26 A. B. R. 775, 188 Fed. 702 (D. C. N. Y.); In re Seavey, 27 A. B. R. 373, 195 Fed. 825 (D. C. N. Y.).

In re McKenna, 15 A. B. R. 4, 137 Fed. 611 (D. C. N. Y.): "The facts in this case are somewhat peculiar. Isaac Bradt died at the city of Albany, N. Y., on the 29th day of December, 1902, at 8 o'clock and 45 minutes a. m., leaving a last will and testament, in and by which he left a general legacy of $25,000 to said Edward J. McKenna, of the city of Troy, N. Y. Said Edward J. Mc-Kenna, said legatee, filed a voluntary petition in bankruptcy in the Northern District of New York on the same day, December 29th, 1902, at ten o'clock in the forenoon, and on the same day, at 2:30 o'clock p. m., he was duly adjudi-cated a bankrupt. His petition and schedules were verified December 27th, 1902; and the circumstances, sickness of Bradt, very frequent visits of McKenna to him, etc., are such that it is not unreasonable to think that McKenna knew he was a legatee in the will, and was seeking to obtain a discharge in bank-ruptcy prior to coming into such legacy, that he might enjoy it without impair-ment. * * * There is no question that, on the appointment of Andrew P. McKean as trustee, the title to the legacy vested in him as such, and he was entitled to receive it."

As, for instance, reversionary interests, such as the reversionary interest of creditors in property set apart as a homestead upon the abandonment or other expiration of the homestead.

In re Woodard, 2 A. B. R. 339, 95 Fed. 260 (D. C. N. Car.): "It will be seen from these authorities that creditors have some rights, shadowy and de-ferred it may be, against debtors, even under the homestead provisions of the State constitution. They may obtain judgments and acquire liens—liens they may not live to realize, but which may benefit their heirs or estate when the exemption terminates under the law."

And the interest, if vested, will pass, although the extent of the interest may be undetermined; such as annuities.[51] But it has been held, that an-nuities do not pass where alienation is restricted.[52] The undetermined interest of a bankrupt in a decedent's estate will pass;[53] even the distributive share in personalty where the decree, though entered subsequently to the adjudication of bankruptcy, takes effect as of a date prior thereto.[54]

And fire insurance money will pass where the fire occurs after adjudica-tion and settlement is made without disclosure of the trustee's rights in the decedent's estate.[55]

---

51. Brown v. Barker, 8 A. B. R. 450 (Sup. Ct. N. Y., App. Div.), S. C., 74 N. Y. Sup. 43, wherein the court held, that the surplus income of a trust fund left by bankrupt's father for bankrupt's support, beyond the sum necessary for the bankrupt's support is an asset liable to claims of cred-itors and passes to the trustee as being property transferable and levia-ble upon. To same effect, In re Tif-fany, 13 A. B. R. 310, 147. Fed. 314 (D. C. N. Y.). In re Baudouine. 3 A. B. R. 55, 96 Fed. 536 (D. C. N. Y., reversed, on jurisdictional grounds, in 3 A. B. R. 651, C. C. A. N. Y.). In re Burtis, 26 A. B. R. 680, 188 Fed. 527 (D. C. N. Y.).

52. Munroe v. Dewey, 4 A. B. R. 264 (Mass. Sup. Jud. Ct.).

53. In re Mosier, 7 A. B. R. 268, 112 Fed. 138 (D. C. Vt.); Osman v. Galbraith Admr., 9 A. B. R. 339 (Sup. Ct. Mich.); In re Kane, 20 A. B. R. 66, 161 Fed. 633 (D. C. N. Y.); In re Crouse, 28 A. B. R. 540, 196 Fed. 907 (D. C. N. Y.).

54. McNaboe v. Marks, 16 A. B. R. 767 (N. Y. Sup. Ct.).

Growing crops in land before severance, cultivated by the bankrupt as a tenant farmer on shares, will pass.[56]

And the interest will pass although it may be subject to a contingency; such as the contingency that the remainderman, to take, must survive the life tenant;[57] or that the interest be terminable upon death;[58] such as life estates in real property.

It has been held, in accordance with State law, that when an insolvent contests his father's last will, he may abandon or settle the contest at any stage of the litigation upon any terms he pleases, and his creditors have no cause of complaint, and that his subsequent adjudication in bankruptcy will not give the trustee any cause of action growing out of such settlement or abandonment, unless it be to recover some consideration which the bankrupt may have received and afterwards may have transferred in derogation of the bankruptcy law.[59]

SUBDIVISION "C."

PROPERTY HELD IN TRUST FOR BANKRUPT AND BY BANKRUPT AND IN-ALIENABLE PROPERTY.

§ 973. Property Held in Trust for Bankrupt Passes.—The beneficial interest of the bankrupt in property held in trust for him passes to his trustee in bankruptcy.[60] Thus, the beneficial interest of the bankrupt in property held in trust for the bankrupt and others, the beneficiaries to share profits and losses, passes to the trustee.[61] Likewise, property held by another on a resulting trust for the bankrupt, would pass to the trustee.[62]

---

55. In re Kane, 20 A. B. R. 616, 161 Fed. 633 (D. C. N. Y.).

56. In re Barrow, 3 A. B. R. 414, 98 Fed. 582 (D. C. Va.); compare, In re Luckenbill, 11 A. B. R. 455, 127 Fed. 984 (D. C. Pa.).

57. In re Twaddell. 6 A. B. R. 539. 110 Fed. 145 (D. C. Del.); contra, In re Hoadley, 3 A. B. R. 780 (D. C. N. Y.). In this case the distinction was drawn between contingency of person and contingency of event.

58. Obiter, In re Force, 4 A. B. R. 116 (Ref. Mass.).

59. Edington v. Masson, 24 A. B. R. 183, 177 Fed. 209 (C. C. A. Ala.).

60· In re Jersey Island Packing Co., 14 A. B. R. 962, 138 Fed. 625 (C. C. A. Calif.); In re Burtis, 26 A. B. R. 680, 188 Fed. 527 (D. C. N. Y.).

61. In re Alden, 16 A. B. R. 362 (Ref. Ohio).

62· Instance Held Not a Resulting Trust.—Real estate bought with bank-rupt's money but put in wife's name when the bankrupt solvent. In re Foss, 17 A. B. R. 439 (D. C. Me.): "Where, upon the purchase of property, the consideration is paid by one. and the legal title conveyed to another, a resulting trust is thereby raised, and the person named in the deed will hold the property as trustee of the party paying the consideration. The burden is on the party who alleges the trust."

But compare, Evans v. Staalle, 11 A. B. R. 182 (Minn.), where a judgment creditor, suing in the State Court after adjudication of the debtor, was permitted to appropriate property held in secret trust to his own judgment. Undoubtedly the trustee of the debtor had the title but evidently he never sought to assert.

Also compare, where resulting trust held not to exist in favor of wife, In re Teter, 23 A. B. R. 223, 173 Fed. 798 (D. C. W. Va.).

§ 974. Property Held by Bankrupt as Trustee of Resulting Trust, Not.

—Property held by the bankrupt as trustee of a resulting trust does not pass.[63]

§ 975. Spendthrift Trusts and Restrictions on Alienation.

—As to the effectiveness of restrictions upon the alienation of property held in trust for spendthrifts, there have been various rulings, all of which are in conformity with the rules heretofore laid down.[64]

Brown v. Barker, 8 A. B. R. 459 (Sup. Ct. N. Y. App. Div.): "The surplus income of this trust fund, if such surplus is established, is, beyond dispute, a species of property—an asset—which is liable to the claims of creditors. * * * Such claims are not limited for their satisfaction to any surplus which may exist at a given date when proceedings are instituted, but their payment may be enforced out of the surplus arising in the future, as the income accrues and becomes payable. The right to such future surplus is not indefinite and uncertain, even though the surplus itself may be subject to the fluctuations and uncertainties of securities and of the continuance of the beneficiary's life. Williams v. Thorn, 70 N. Y. 270. It is not impossible to conceive of cases where, if the right to follow and secure for the benefit of creditors the surplus of such an income does not pass to the assignee in bankruptcy, it will be lost to creditors entirely, through the discharge of the bankrupt from his debts."

---

63. In re Davis, 7 A. B. R. 258 (D. C. Mass.); compare, where resulting trust held not to exist, Merrill v. Hussey, 16 A. B. R. 816, 64 Atl. (Me.) 819; Phillips v. Kleinman, 27 A. B. R. 195 (Sup. Ct. Pa.); Silling v. Todd, 27 A. B. R. 127 (Sup. Ct. Va.).

In re Coffin, 18 A. B. R. 127, 146 Fed. 171 (C. C. A. Conn., reversing 16 A. B. R. 687). In this case a corporation had borrowed money pro rata from all its stockholders and given a trust deed on its property to secure them. Afterwards having great confidence in the bankrupt, who was one of the stockholders, all the stockholders had the trustee deed the property to the bankrupt absolutely and thereafter by suit the title was quieted in the bankrupt. The court below held the decree was binding and that the bankruptcy trustee took title free from any trust; but the reviewing court reversed this holding and declared that the trust persisted notwithstanding the decree, since the trust relation had been subsequently recognized by the trustee.

64. In re Baudouine, 3 A. B. R. 55, 95 Fed. 536 (D. C. N. Y., reversed on question of jurisdiction, in 3 A. B. R.

651, 101 Fed. 574, C. C. A. N. Y.); In re Tiffany, 13 A. B. R. 310, 138 Fed. 192 (D. C. N. Y.); Munroe v. Dewey, 4 A. B. R. 264 (Sup. Jud. C't Mass.); In re McKay, 16 A. B. R. 238 (D. C. N. Y.); McNaboe v. Marks, 16 A. B. R. 50, 135 Fed. 504 (C. C. A. N. Y.); Butler v. Baudouine, 16 A. B. R. 238, note 84 App. Div. (N. Y.) 215, affirmed in 177 N. Y. 530. As to validity of conditions restricting the passing of property to a trustee in bankruptcy, see note to In re Baudouine, 3 A. B. R. 56 (D. C. N. Y.). Excuse of creditor for failing to recover judgment, that bankruptcy court had enjoined him, held insufficient. Brown v. Barker, 8 A. B. R. 450 (Sup. Ct. N. Y. App. Div.); S. C., 74 N. Y. Sup. 43. However, it was sufficient because the Bankrupt Act specifically provides for precisely the restraining order granted in the case. See Bankr. Act, § 11.

Other Inalienable Property.—Indian lands where, until the expiration of a term of twenty-five years, the Indian could not sell or transfer the land nor could the land be levied on, In re Russie, 3 A. B. R. 6, 96 Fed. 608 (D. C. Ore.).

UNPAID STOCK SUBSCRIPTIONS.

§ 976. Unpaid Stock Subscriptions Pass.—Unpaid stock subscriptions in a bankrupt corporation pass to the trustee.[65]

Babbitt *v.* Read, 23 A. B. R. 254, 173 Fed. 712 (U. S. C. C. N. Y.): "This right of the corporation to enforce the liability of stockholders for the purpose of paying its debts passed to the trustee, under § 70 a (6) of the Bankruptcy Act, and while he is ready to enforce it, no one else can."

Allen *v.* Grant, 14 A. B. R. 349 (Sup. Ct. Ga.): "The trustee in bankruptcy of an insolvent corporation may sue for the recovery of unpaid subscription, not only where the subscription is payable in cash, but also where it is expressly made payable in specifics, fraudulently overvalued.

"A subscription to stock, payable in specifics, worth not more than 10 per cent. of the face of the shares, is a legal fraud upon subsequent creditors of the corporation, who may look to the authorized capital stock as a trust fund for the payment of their debts.

"A transferee, who takes such shares with knowledge that they have been improperly issued, as fully paid-up, becomes liable for the unpaid subscription.

"This liability can be enforced by the trustee in bankruptcy. For while he represents the corporation in a sense, he also represents the creditors."

Impliedly, In re Alleman Hardware Co., 22 A. B. R. 871, 172 Fed. 611 (D. C. Pa.): "The capital stock of a corporation, as has been many times declared, is a trust fund for the benefit of creditors, which can not be juggled with. Handley *v.* Stutz, 139 U. S. 417, 427. A stock subscription is primarily payable in

---

65. Compare ante, § 709. Also see In re Crystal Springs Bottling Co., 3 A. B. R. 194, 96 Fed. 945 (D. C. Vt.); inferentially, In re Miller Electrical Maintenance Co., 6 A. B. R. 701, 111 Fed. 515 (D. C. Pa.); In re Automobile & Motor Co., 15 A. B. R. 214 (D. C. N. Y.); inferentially, In re Morris Arc Lamp Co., 10 A. B. R. 569 (D. C. Pa.).

That a stockholder who is also a creditor may not offset his claim against his liability for unpaid stock subscription, see post, subject "Set-Off and Counterclaim," ch. 30, div. 1, subd. "E," § 1185. In re Goodman Shoe Co., 3 A. B. R. 200, 96 Fed. 949 (D. C. Pa.).

In re Remington Automobile Co., 18 A. B. R. 389, 153 Fed. 345 (C. C. A. N. Y., affirming 15 A. B. R. 214); In re Beachy & Co., 22 A. B. R. 538, 170 Fed. 825 (D. C. Wis.); In re Automobile & Motor Co., 15 A. B. R. 214 (D. C. N. Y., affirmed In re Remington Automobile Co., 18 A. B. R. 389, 153 Fed. 345, C. C. A. N. Y.); inferentially, In re Morris Arc Lamp Co., 10 A. B. R. 569 (D. C. Pa.). Compare, Firestone Co. *v.* Agnew, 21 A. B. R. 292 (N. Y.); compare, In re

Flood-Pratt Dairy Co., 23 A. B. R. 148 (Ref. Ohio), as to corporation selling its stock at less than par. Babbitt *v.* Read, 23 A. B. R. 254, 173 Fed. 712 (U. S. C. C. N. Y.); In re Newfoundland Syndicate, 28 A. B. R. 119, 196 Fed. 443 (D. C. N. J.).

But, under the New York statute, if the stock has not been formally subscribed, an issue of it as paid up, at inadequate prices, gives no right of action to the corporation itself, but only to certain classes of persons, to whose rights it has been held the trustee in bankruptcy of the corporation does not succeed. In re Jassoy Co., 23 A. B. R. 622, 178 Fed. 515 (C. C. A. N. Y.). And, from a reading of the decision it would not appear that the Amendment of 1910, giving the trustee the rights and remedies of creditors holding execution, etc., would affect the holding.

Bankrupt Corporation Engaged in Illegal Lottery, Whether Defence.—Roney *v.* Crawford (Ga.), 24 A. B. R. 638; In re Alleman Hdw. Co., 22 A. B. R. 871, 172 Fed. 611 (D. C. Pa.), reversed on facts, 25 A. B. R. 331, 181 Fed. 810 (C. C. A. Pa.).

money, but by arrangement may also be paid in property, contributed and accepted in good faith, at a fair valuation. This is expressly allowed by statute in Pennsylvania (Act of April 29, 1874, § 17, P. L. 81), but would be good without that (Coit v. Gold Amalgamating Co., 119 U. S. 343), and is not open to objection, unless there is such a discrepancy as to be practically fraudulent (American Tube Co. v. Baden Gas Co., 165 Pa. 489; Pennsylvania Tack Works v. Sowers, 2 Walk. (Pa.) 416; Coit v. Gold Amalgamating Co., 119 U. S. 343). Nor does the holder become liable, as for unpaid stock, because the statutory formalities have not been complied with. Sternburgh v. Duryea Power Co., 20 A. B. R. 219. It is not open to creditors to take advantage of this, whatever may be said as to the State, or other stockholders. As between corporation and stockholder, also, a valuation, however extravagant, all parties consenting, is binding. But not as to creditors, who have the right to assume that the capital stock stands for property of a substantial value, and who presumptively deal with it on the strength of that. The corporation has no right to give away stock, without getting a fair equivalent, and where creditors are concerned an agreement that it should be treated as fully paid or non-assessable, or otherwise limiting liability thereon, is invalid. Handley v. Stutz, 139 U. S. 417; Camden v. Stuart, 144 U. S. 104. The Constitution of Pennsylvania expressly prohibits a fictitious issue of stock (Art. XVI, § 7), as does the General Corporation Act following it (Act April 29, 1874, P. L. 81). And it offends against the law, where everything is problematical and prospective, and there is nothing to sustain the stock but an extravagant estimate of benefits to come. In re Wyoming Valley Ice Co., 153 Fed. 187, 158 Fed. 608. A formal subscription is not necessary to create a liability or stock. Whoever accepts shares allotted to him undertakes to pay for them, if necessary, to meet the demands of creditors, and when the only payment that can be shown, is by properly fraudulently over-valued, it is the same as no payment whatever. Handley v. Stutz, 139 U. S. 417; Camden v. Stuart, 144 U. S. 104; Elyton Land Co. v. Birmingham Warehouse Co., 92 Ala. 407. And this is true, because of the fraud, in bankruptcy, as well as elsewhere. Applying these principles, which are well settled, the liability of Gitt for the $25,000 of stock which he got without paying for it, is not open to question. The hollowness of the transaction, by which there was an apparent payment, appears upon the most casual consideration. It was not merely a case of excessive valuation, in which the parties were led away by an oversanguine view of the situation, if this would excuse it. * * * Here the transaction was not fair. There was no value contributed for the stock received and the parties knew it, there being a mere shuffling off of the affairs of an insolvent concern to escape further individual responsibility."

And its trustee in bankruptcy may maintain suit for the same in the State court;[66] and the petition of a creditor in a similar action is demurrable.[67]

But where the corporation had no right to enforce the liability, its trustee in bankruptcy has none; as, for instance, where it had, in good faith, issued the stock in payment for a patent or for a building site in a State where such consideration is sufficient, although the actual value thereof might be less than the par value of the stock.[68]

---

66. Instance, Roney v. Crawford (Ga.), 24 A. B. R. 638.

67. Thrall v. Union Maid Tobacco Co., 22 A. B. R. 288, 54 O. Law Bull. 732 (Com. Pleas Court).

68. Also compare, In re Reming-

Sternbergh *v.* Power Co., 20 A. B. R. 625, 161 Fed. 540 (C. C. A. Pa.): "On this company becoming bankrupt its trustee acquired no higher rights than the bankrupt possessed * * *, and it is clear that company had no right of action against Sternbergh. * * * Having taken these patents at a valuation to which every person in interest agreed, and having enjoyed them for all these years while they were running, it is clear this company cannot question nor repudiate the transaction, and assess or collect on the full-paid stock which it issued for them. This is not the case of an uncollected or unpaid assessment or of a subscription. It is an indirect attempt to invalidate an executed transaction, which has stood unchallenged and ratified by six years' acquiescence and enjoyment of the consideration paid therefor."

Or, for another instance, where it turns out that a partnership was insolvent at the time it was taken over by a corporation organized for that purpose and stock issued to the partners therefor.

In re Alleman Hdw. Co., 25 A. B. R. 331, 181 Fed. 810 (C. C. A. Pa.): "Now, in the present case, it is alleged the firm was insolvent when its property was taken over by the company, and the $25,000 in stock which Gitt and Johns received in payment therefor, and all of which Gitt now owns, was issued without consideration and in violation of the provisions of the Pennsylvania act of April 29, 1874 (P. L. 81) as amended by the act of April 17, 1876 (P. L. 32) which provides: 'Every corporation created under the provisions of this Act or accepting its provisions, may take such real and personal estate, mineral rights, patent rights, and other property, as is necessary for the purpose of its organization and business and issue stock in the amount of the value thereof, in payment thereof.'

"Now, granting that subsequent events show the partnership was then insolvent, we then have the question: How was any party now before us affected thereby, or how could that issue be involved in this distribution? This company came into existence, and its whole corporate business was based on the stock of goods it obtained from this firm. Its whole business existence and the assets here distributed are founded on the affirmance, ratification, and enjoyment of the contract for the sale of the property of Gitt and Johns to the corporation. It sold these goods and mixed the proceeds up in its operations, and the present fund had its origin in property of the old firm. How does it lie in the mouth of the company to at the same time enjoy the property it received and allege the illegality of its reception? We are not here dealing with a fraud, we are not dealing with a subscription to stock, we are not dealing with the rights of any creditor who was misled; but we are dealing with a case where no party who might have been injured thereby is concerned, where all the creditors of the old firm have been paid, and where there is no proof that any creditor of the new corporation has been deceived or misled by the stock issue complained of. If, then, the rights of no individual creditor are here involved or sought to be enforced, it follows that Gitt's claim cannot be rejected unless the bankrupt company itself has a counterclaim against him. And how can it be said it has? It is true capital stock is a trust fund for the benefit of creditors, and, if stock is ficticiously and fraudulently issued, it may be collected for the benefit of creditors (Coit *v.* Gold Co. [C. C.] 14 Fed. 16; Hand-

ton Automobile Co., 18 A. B. R. 389, 153 Fed. 345 (C. C. A. N. Y.); similarly, In re Beachy & Co., 22 A. B. R. 538, 170 Fed. 825 (D. C. Wis.); In re Alleman Hardware Co., 22 A. B. R. 871, 172 Fed. 611 (D. C. Pa.).

ley v. Stutz, 139 U. S. 436, 11 Sup. Ct. 530, 35 L. Ed. 227); but when, as here, the value of the consideration of the stock was fairly debatable, and the corporation enjoyed, used, and did its entire corporate business for several years on the property conveyed to it, and where the property cannot be restored or the contract rescinded, and where no person here interested was in any way induced to act or was misled or wronged by the maintenance of that status, we think the corporation has not such right or claim against Gitt as prevents his unquestioned debt from participating in its distribution. Under these facts, it is clear that this corporation had, prior to the bankruptcy, no right of action against Gitt to recover on this stock which was issued to him for his merchandise. And, if such be the case, the status of the parties is not changed by bankruptcy, for, as was said in Thompson v. Fairbanks, supra. 'Under the present Bankruptcy Act, the trustee takes the property of the bankrupt, in case unaffected by fraud, in the same plight and condition that the bankrupt himself held it, and subject to all the equities imposed upon it in the hands of the bankrupt.'"

A stockholder who is also a creditor of the bankrupt corporation may not offset his claim against the claim upon the unpaid stock subscription, because the supervening insolvency has destroyed such right;[69] but, he doubtless may offset the dividend coming to him thereon from the bankrupt estate,[70] and he certainly will not be permitted to offset a claim for a dividend wrongly declared by the bankrupt corporation when insolvent or otherwise not earned.[71]

§ 977. Bankruptcy Court May Make "Call."

—And the bankruptcy court has jurisdiction in the bankruptcy proceedings themselves, to make the assessment prerequisite to the institution of suits to collect the unpaid stock subscriptions.[72]

Sawyer v. Upton, 17 Wall. 620: "The trustee is the proper one to make the call."

Clevenger v. Moore, 12 A. B. R. 738 (N. J. Sup. Ct.): "It is contended that the refusal to nonsuit was error because the trustee made no assessment, but simply demanded the whole amount due upon the stock. The answer to this is that the trustee followed the direction of the order of the United States District Court, which had jurisdiction of the matter, which was to make the assessment for 'the whole amount remaining unpaid on said stock.' The decree recites that the defendant was duly notified of the proceeding. The propriety or validity of that assessment cannot be questioned collaterally."

In re Remington Automobile Co., 18 A. B. R. 389, 153 Fed. 345 (C. C. A. N. Y.): "Had the corporation not become bankrupt, it could have laid an

69. See post, § 1185.
70. See post, § 1185.
71. Roney v. Crawford (Ga.), 24 A. B. R. 638.
72. In re Miller El. Maint. Co., 6 A. B. R. 701, 111 Fed. 515 (D. C. Penna.); Hawkins v. Glenn, 131 U. S. 328; In re Crystal Spring Bottling Co., 3 A. B. R. 194, 96 Fed. 945 (D. C. Vt.); inferentially, Allen v. Grant, 14 A. B. R. 349 (Sup. Ct. Ga.); inferentially,

In re Morris Arc Lamp Co., 10 A. B. R. 569 (D. C. Pa.); Impliedly, In re Hutchinson Co., 20 A. B. R. 307 (Ref. Mich.); In re Eureka Furniture Co., 22 A. B. R. 395, 170 Fed. 485 (D. C. Pa.); (1867) Wilbur v. Stockholders of the Corporation, 18 Nat. Bankr. Reg. 179; In re Newfoundland Syndicate, 28 A. B. R. 119, 196 Fed. 443 (D. C. N. J.), quoted further along in this section.

assessment upon such of its stockholders as were liable for further calls to make up full payment, and the right to make an assessment and call passed by the bankruptcy to the trustee. The Supreme Court, in Scovill *v.* Thayer, 105 U. S. 143, 26 L. Ed. 968, holds that the proper practice in such cases is for the trustee to file petition in the bankruptcy court for an order directing him to make an assessment and call upon the unpaid stock of the corporation for the purpose of paying its debts. In order to determine whether such an order should be made, it is necessary for the court to examine into and decide certain questions of fact, e. g., whether at the time of the issue of any particular share the full value was or was not paid in, whether any subsequent payments were made on account of it, whether the corporation was indebted in excess of assets, and what is the amount of its indebtedness. We are unanimously of the opinion that the practice followed in this case was correct, and that the decision of the District Court as to any question the decision of which was necessary to the making of the order will be res adjudicata in any subsequent proceeding between the trustee and any stockholder who received notice of the proceeding. Thus, in a plenary action against a stockholder to enforce assessment, he cannot be heard to question the findings made in this proceeding as to the amount paid for the stock, as to the indebtedness of the corporation, or as to the amount of the assessment, but he may present and make proof of any individual defense which he may have to such action. In this connection it may be noted that the phraseology of the order is such that it might be contended that execution for the respective amounts might be issued against the individuals named. This should be corrected. The writer is further of the opinion that, inasmuch as the stockholder is to be concluded as to the amount of corporation indebtedness by the finding in the bankruptcy court, he is entitled to have that amount proved by the best evidence, if he appears and asks for it. In the case at bar the indebtedness was proved merely by presentation of the proofs of claim. To this counsel for stockholders objected, and claimed the right to cross-examine whoever might swear to the debt. His contention was overruled and exception reserved. The writer is of the opinion that this was reversible error, but the majority does not think so."

In re Monarch Corporation, 24 A. B. R. 428, 196 Fed. 252 (D. C. Conn.): "The trustee in bankruptcy has all the powers originally invested in the board of directors. He can ask for an assessment upon the capital stock to such an amount as shall be needed to pay debts and expenses, provided the stock shall be found to be in fact partly unpaid for, no matter what the original terms of issue were."

Jurisdiction to make the call exists though some of the stockholders are non-resident, for the jurisdiction to make the call depends on jurisdiction over the corporation and its affairs, not over its stockholders personally.

In re Monarch Corp., 24 A. B. R. 428, 196 Fed. 252 (D. C. Conn.): "Two objections are urged against it: First, Lack of jurisdiction over the stockholders who reside in other states. * * * The first objection is easily disposed of. The bankrupt corporation is within the jurisdiction of this court and its officers, directors and stockholders, in so far as their dealings with the bankrupt are concerned, must to that extent, surely, be amenable to its authority.

"But the property here in controversy was in the possession of the bankrupt when the petition was filed and when the adjudication was made, and it then passed within the jurisdiction of the District Court below. The second section of the Bankruptcy Law invests the District Court sitting in bankruptcy with power to (7) 'cause the states of bankrupts to be collected, reduced to money and distributed and determine controversies in relation thereto except as otherwise provided,' and the exception is of cases involving those controversies between trustees in bankruptcy and adverse claimants specified in § 23, which relate to property which was not in the possession of the bankrupt when the petition for adjudication was filed and in which the defendants do not consent to suits in the district courts. The District Court sitting in bankruptcy has jurisdiction to determine by summary proceedings after a reasonable notice to claimants to present their claims to it, controversies between the trustee and adverse claimants over liens upon and the title and possession of (1) property in the possession of the bankrupt when the petition in bankruptcy is filed (2) property held by third parties for him (3) property lawfully seized by the marshal as the bankrupt's under Clause 3 of § 2 of the Bankruptcy Law and (4) property claimed by the Trustee which has been lawfully reduced to actual possession by the officers of the court. Such controversies are controversies in proceedings in bankruptcy under § 2, and they are not controversies at law or in equity, as distinguished from proceedings in bankruptcy within the meaning of § 23."

Upon this assessment hearing it would seem to be proper for the court to take into account, in determining the extent of the call, evidence tending to show that stock issued as fully paid up is not so in fact.

In re Monarch Corp., 24 A. B. R. 428, 196 Fed. 252 (D. C. Conn.): "It is alleged that the stockholders have obtained full-paid, nonassessable stock by paying a trifle in cash and agreeing to pay the entire balance in patents, and that the patents have not been delivered to the corporation.

"Whether or not, by reason of such failure to deliver the patents, that portion of the stock which the patents were to pay for remains unpaid, is a question of law to be settled when the report from a master on the facts comes in."

The proceeding is an equitable one, and the trustee must present such facts as will warrant the court to the exercise of its equitable powers in making the call.

In re Monarch Corp., 28 A. B. R. 382, 196 Fed. 252 (D. C. Conn.): "The real case is in a nutshell. The stock was issued as full paid in consideration of the patents referred to. It turns out that full title to the two patents was not vested in the corporation. It is conceded that, if such title had been vested in the corporation, there would be no substantial basis for the present motion. But it appears that the sole and exclusive right to make the articles which the patents monopolized was turned over to the corporation as payment for the stock, and was accepted by the corporation, and under such protection the patented articles were made and sold in large quantities. There is no question of fraud before the court. It is not claimed that the promoters were palming off patents known by them to be worthless. In truth, all the facts lead to the inevitable conclusion that the promoters had implicit faith in the invention. Now, the appeal here made by the trustee is addressed to a court of equity. The trust fund theory which he invokes has no standing in any other court, but the conscience of the court is shocked when it listens to the present appeal, founded, as it is, upon the most attenuated of all technicalities. The corporation got and used all the rights which the patents granted, but because it did not get those rights *verbatim et literatim,* as written in the contract, the poor stockholder must be held up and forced to pay debts which he did not dream he was responsible for. The lack of equity in the trustee's position is intensified when it appears that the bulk of the indebtedness outstanding is due to the very stockholders who are to be mulcted by this process. It does not strike me as a case in which the directors took property of less value than the corporation expected to get. They took the property relied upon, but they did not take it with the formalities and particularities which would have been exercised if they had been more careful and painstaking."

No personal judgment, however, can be entered against the stockholder in the proceedings on the assessment in the bankruptcy court,[73] much less any order on him to pay.[74] Judgment against the stockholder is to be had later, in plenary action.[75]

The findings in the bankruptcy court, at any rate if made upon due notice to the stockholder, are conclusive upon him in the later plenary action to recover the personal judgment upon the questions of the amount of debts, the amount of deficit of the corporate assets and the necessity for the call, and, also, upon the question as to the actual amount paid in by other stockholders. It has also apparently been held binding upon each particular stockholder as to the amount and validity of the claim against himself.[76]

But such last mentioned rule is doubtful, for each stockholder is entitled to his day in court in a plenary action,[76a] and a plenary action is necessary to enforce the payment of unpaid stock subscription.[77]

Compare, In re Munger Vehicle Tire Co., 21 A. B. R. 395, 168 Fed. 910 (C. C. A. N. Y.): "We are of the opinion that the District Court had jurisdiction to make a call upon the stockholders of the Munger Vehicle Tire Company if the facts warranted the court in taking such action. We think, however, that the hearing before the referee should be expressly limited to the determination of this issue alone. It being conceded at the argument that the prayer of the petition is too broad, it follows that the reference to determine whether the relief prayed for in the petition should be granted, is also too broad and opens a field of inquiry which may possibly be prejudicial to the interests of the Rubber Company. The issue before the referee should be confined solely to the question, should there be a call upon the shareholders of unpaid stock, and if so, to what amount? With the controversy thus narrowed, we fail to see how the Rubber Company will be prevented from making any defense it may have

73. In re Remington Automobile Co., 18 A. B. R. 389, 153 Fed. 345 (C. C. A. N. Y.), quoted supra.

74. But compare, In re Eureka Furn. Co., 22 A. B. R. 395, 170 Fed. 485 (D. C. Pa.).

75. In re Remington Automobile Co., 18 A. B. R. 389, 153 Fed. 345 (C. C. A. N. Y.), quoted supra.

76. In re Remington Automobile Co., 18 A. B. R. 389, 153 Fed. 345 (C. C. A. N. Y.), quoted supra. Compare, In re Eureka Furn. Co., 22 A. B. R. 395, 170 Fed. 485 (D. C.

Pa.). Also, see post, "Res Judicata in Actions by and against Trustees," § 1777 3-7.

Res judicata of order of bankruptcy court in subsequent plenary action, compare rules in analogous actions to recover from bankrupt's attorneys of prepaid fees after re-examination in bankruptcy court, post, § 2099.

76a. Compare, In re Hutchinson & Wilmoth, 19 A. B. R. 313, 158 Fed. 74 (C. C. A. Mich.).

77. Kiskadden v. Steinle, 29 A. B. R. 346, 203 Fed. 375 (C. C. A. Ohio).

to an action brought against it as a stockholder, whether it appears before the special master or fails to do so."

Babbitt *v.* Read, 23 A. B. R. 254, 173 Fed. 712 (U. S. C. C. N. Y.): "It will be noticed that the referee in bankruptcy has not found the amount due by the stockholders, or even expressly that there is any amount due. The defendants contend that such a finding is a necessary preliminary to a plenary suit against stockholders, and cite In re Remington (C. C. A.), 18 Am. B. R. 389, 153 Fed. 345, to that effect. All the proceedings in that case were in the bankruptcy court, and the stockholders were apparently residents and parties. This court held the proceedings there taken to be regular, and referred to Scovill *v.* Thayer, 105 U. S. 143, 26 L. Ed. 968. But, where plenary proceedings are necessary against stockholders, I see no reason why the bankruptcy court may not leave the question of the amount due by them to the courts in which the plenary proceedings are instituted. The authority given by the referee in bankruptcy to the trustee to collect such amount as may be owing from stockholders seems to me an authorized demand for payment within the language of Mr. Justice Woods in Scovill *v.* Thayer, at page 155 of 105 U. S., 26 L. Ed. 968: 'But under such circumstances, before there is any obligation upon a stockholder to pay without an assessment and call by the company, there must be some order of a court of competent jurisdiction, or at the very least some authorized demand upon him for payment.' The stockholders would certainly have no reason to complain of such a course. Be this as it may, the stockholders have the right to set up in a plenary suit such personal defenses as are now to be considered."

But in most states it is likely the bankruptcy court would confine itself to directing the trustee to institute or maintain the ordinary statutory suits in the state court in the nature of equitable actions wherein all stockholders are brought into one suit, and the requisite assessment therein ordered.

One case holds the order directing the trustee to bring suit is a sufficient "call."

Allen *v.* Grant, 14 A. B. R. 349 (Sup. Ct. Ga.): "The order of the bankruptcy court directing the trustee to bring suit for the recovery of the unpaid subscriptions is sufficiently in the nature of a call or assessment to authorize the maintenance of a suit against the stockholders, as for unpaid subscriptions."

Some cases hold, but erroneously, that the Bankruptcy Court has jurisdiction to entertain such suits.[78] This is clearly contrary to the law, even as it stands since the Amendment of 1903, conferring jurisdiction on the District Courts over suits brought by trustees to set aside or recover preferential or fraudulent transfers, such suits not concerning "transfers."

In re Hutchinson & Wilmoth, 19 A. B. R. 313, 158 Fed. 74 (C. C. A. Mich.): "It will be observed that it was not a petition which simply demands an assessment and call upon the stock of the bankrupt corporation, as in the case of Scovill *v.* Thayer, 105 U. S. 143. It is clear from a reading of the petition that Hutchinson and Wilmoth, who organized the corporation and held all

---

78. In re Crystal Springs Bottling Co., 3 A. B. R. 194, 96 Fed. 945 (D. C. Vt.); Skillen *v.* Magnus, 19 A. B. R. 397, 162 Fed. 689 (D. C. N. Y.). Also, see § 1692. Also compare (1867) Wilbur *v.* Stockholders of the Corporation, 18 Nat. Bankr. Reg. 179.

the stock except one share, are bankrupts, and that the attempt of the trustee is to bring in Carrie W. Haley, a non-resident, the mother-in-law of Wilmoth, who it seems paid substantially all of the money which went into the concern, as a defendant and compel her to answer averments which charge her with being a party to certain fraudulent acts which it is alleged, subjected her to liability for the debts of the corporation. We do not think this can be done without serving her personally and giving her the opportunity of defending herself in the forum where she is subject to suit. Toland *v.* Sprague, 12 Pet. 300, 328. In the ordinary case, where an assessment and call is made on the stock of a bankrupt corporation, the order to show cause demands an investigation by the court in charge of the bankrupt, into the necessity and propriety of making the assessment and call; and afterwards, when a suit is brought to collect the assessment, the stockholder has the opportunity of presenting his defense in the court in which it is necessary, in order to obtain jurisdiction, to serve him personally. But in the present case, as we have suggested, and as the abstract we have made of the petition shows, there is presented against Carrie W. Haley, a suit in equity which she ought not to be compelled to answer, except in the proper forum and after that personal service which the law accords her as a means of protecting her rights. A court of bankruptcy has no jurisdiction of a suit at law or in equity brought by a trustee to recover property or collect debts, or to set aside transfers of property alleged to be fraudulent, except by consent of the defendant. * * * By the Amendment of February 5, 1903, such court was given jurisdiction of suits for the recovery of property under § 60b, § 67c and § 70e. * * * But this is not a case of a preferential or fraudulent transfer under those sections. The suit outlined in the bill is therefore one of a plenary nature of which the bankruptcy court has no jurisdiction except by consent of the defendant, of which there is no pretense here."

In re Newfoundland Syndicate, 28 A. B. R. 119, 196 Fed. 443 (D. C. N. J.): "To ascertain whether there are insufficient corporate assets, and whether capital stock has been issued at less than par value, are administrative matters, not involving any personal judgment affecting such stockholders in their individual capacity. Their personal presence is therefore not necessary when such ascertainment and assessment is made; nor are they entitled to any other notice than the constructive one had by operation of law by the institution of such bankruptcy proceedings. The enforcement of said assessment against the stockholders alleged to be liable thereto, however, is plenary in its nature, and, except with their consent, cannot be made in the bankruptcy court. (Section 23b, Bankruptcy Act.) In the suit to collect such assessment, the defendant is entitled to make all defenses that relate to him in his individual, as distinguished from his corporate capacity, such as that he is not a stockholder, or that he has fully paid for the stock taken."

§ 978. Statutory Secondary Liability of Stockholders Not an Asset.

—But the statutory secondary liability of directors and stockholders is not an asset of the corporation.[79] And such liability is not enforceable by the trustee in bankruptcy of the corporation.

---

79. In re Crystal Springs Bottling Co., 3 A. B. R. 194, 96 Fed. 945 (D. C. Vt.); In re Beachy & Co., 22 A. B. R. 538, 170 Fed. 825 (D. C. Wis.).

Compare, also, ante, § 709.
Offsetting stockholder's claim against unpaid stock subscription, see post, § 1185.

In re Beachy & Co., 22 A. B. R. 538, 170 Fed. 825 (D. C. Wis.): "It seems clear, therefore, that this statutory cause of action belongs exclusively to creditors. It is a secondary security which is not an asset of the estate and does not pass to the trustee. Such a claim may be enforced by the creditor in any court having jurisdiction quite independently of the bankruptcy proceedings."

SUBDIVISION "E."

LEASEHOLDS.

§ 979. Bankrupt as Landlord.—Of course, leaseholds where the bankrupt is the lessor pass to his trustee.[80] The lessor's adjudication as bankrupt does not sever the relation of landlord and tenant.[81]

§ 980. Bankrupt as Tenant.—Leaseholds owned by the bankrupt as tenant at the time of the filing of the petition, and which contain no express prohibition upon the transfer of the title, pass to the trustee.[82]

§ 981. Tenant's Bankruptcy Not Ipso Facto Termination of Lease.—The tenant's adjudication as a bankrupt does not ipso facto terminate the lease, nor put an end to his estate in the leased premises.[83]

§ 982. Trustee Not Bound to Accept Lease as Asset.—The trustee need not accept the lease.[84]

Watson v. Merrill, 14 A. B. R. 454, 136 Fed. 359 (C. C. A. Kans.): "The trustee in bankruptcy has the option to assume or renounce the leases and other executory contracts of the bankrupt, as he may deem for the best interest of the estate."

But, if he accepts it, he is bound by its terms.[85]

The title to the lease vests as of the date of the adjudication but is subject to divestiture by the trustee's subsequent rejection. The title, it has been held, vests at once on the trustee's appointment and qualification, and does not hang in suspense, but vests subject to divestiture by the trustee's subsequent action in rejecting it.

In re Frazin & Oppenheim, 23 A. B. R. 289, 174 Fed. 713 (D. C. N. Y.): " * * * but, in my opinion, the title to the lease does not remain in the air

---

80. Instance, In re Fulton, 18 A. B. R. 591, 153 Fed. 664 (D. C. N. Y.).
81. Obiter, In re Hays, 9 A. B. R. 114, 117 Fed. 879 (D. C. Ky.).
82. Crowe v. Baumann, 27 A. B. R. 100, 190 Fed. 399 (D. C. N. Y.). Instance (oral, indefinite term is lease for year in South Carolina), In re Schwartzman, 21 A. B. R. 885, 167 Fed. 399 (D. C. S. C.).
83. See ante, § 653.
84. In re Ells, 3 A. B. R. 564, 98 Fed. 967 (D. C. Mass.); Bray v. Cobb, 3 A. B. R. 788, 100 Fed. 270 (D. C. N. Car., reversed, on other grounds,

in Cobb v. Overman, 6 A. B. R. 324, C. C. A.); Atchison, etc., R. Co. v. Hurley, 18 A. B. R. 396, 153 Fed. 503 (C. C. A. Kans.), quoted at §§ 1144, 1144½, 1145, 1150½; In re Roth & Appel, 22 A. B. R. 504, 174 Fed. 64 (D. C. N. Y.); In re Frazin & Oppenheim, 23 A. B. R. 289, 174 Fed. 713 (D. C. N. Y.); In re Roth & Appel, 24 A. B. R. 588, 181 Fed. 667 (C. C. A. N. Y., affirming S. C., 22 A. B. R. 504, 174 Fed. 64).
85. Atchison, etc., R. Co. v. Hurley, 18 A. B. R. 396, 153 Fed. 503 (C. C. A. Kans.).

until the trustee affirmatively takes action to assume the lease. The true view, in my opinion, is that the trustee, upon his appointment, is vested with the lease, subject to the right to decline to accept it, within a reasonable time, if his acceptance of it will not be advantageous to the estate."

§ 983. Entitled to Time to Accept or Reject.

—The trustee has a reasonable time within which to make up his mind whether he will accept or reject the lease.[86] This is so from the peculiar nature of a lease, it possessing as an incident the burden of a periodical charge for the payment over to the landlord of the rent issuing out of it. To accept the lease then might founder the entire estate. Accordingly, the trustee has a reasonable time after the adjudication in which to make his election. What constitutes a reasonable time varies of course with the facts of each case. And if the trustee does not assume the lease, some cases hold the bankrupt remains liable thereon.[87]

At any rate, if the trustee does not assume the lease, the bankrupt estate, it has been held in some cases, is not liable for rent thereafter.[88]

§ 984. Trustee's Right to Occupy Premises for Reasonable Period.

—The trustee may continue to occupy and use the premises for a reasonable period, sufficient to enable him to remove the bankrupt's property, such right being analogous to the similar right of a tenant of a contingent term upon termination of the term. He may stay there long enough to remove the property by selling it, if thereby the landlord is not unduly prejudiced.[89]

In re Schwartzman, 21 A. B. R. 885, 167 Fed. 399 (D. C. S. C.): "* * * there can be no doubt that it was the right and duty of the court to grant the restraining order prayed for. The petitioner, but a few days before had been selected by the creditors as trustee of an estate consisting of a stock of merchandise valued at $25,000, stored in a building specially built for the bankrupt with fittings especially adapted, at considerable expense, for their proper display and he was notified that the owner of the building would require him to remove the same within two or three days. It was obvious that great loss

---

86. In re Ells, 3 A. B. R. 564, 98 Fed. 967 (D. C. Mass.); Matter of Sterm & Levi, 26 A. B. R. 535, 190 Fed. 70 (D. C. Tex.); In re Rubel, 21 A. B. R. 566, 166 Fed. 131 (D. C. Wis.), quoted on other points at § 656; In re Schwartzman, 21 A. B. R. 885, 167 Fed. 399 (D. C. S. C.), quoted on other points at § 984; In re Frazin & Oppenheim, 23 A. B. R. 289, 174 Fed. 713 (D. C. N. Y.), quoted at § 982.

Value of Lease, the Difference between Rent Obtainable and Rent Reserved.—In re Ketterer Mfg. Co., 20 A. B. R. 694, 156 Fed. 638 (D. C. Pa.).

87. In re Ells, 3 A. B. R. 564, 98 Fed. 967 (D. C. Mass.).

88. Bray v. Cobb, 3 A. B. R. 788, 100 Fed. 270 (D. C. N. Car., reversed in Cobb v. Overman, 6 A. B. R. 324, C. C. A.).

And where the trustee rejects the lease, the landlord's claim for the expense of changing the premises back to their original use cannot be charged against the bankrupt's estate under a clause merely covenanting that the tenant shall restore the premises "in good condition." In re International Mailing Co., 23 A. B. R. 664, 175 Fed. 308 (D. C. N. Y.).

89. Impliedly, In re Stanton Co., 20 A. B. R. 549, 162 Fed. 169 (D. C. Conn.). Compare, inferentially to this effect, In re Rubel, 21 A. B. R. 566, 166 Fed. 131 (D. C. Wis.).

and damage would follow precipitate removal. In these circumstances it was the duty of this court as a court of equity, while giving full recognition to the legal right to the landlord to so regulate the time and manner of its enforcement as not to cause unnecessary loss to others. Immediate ejection from the premises would have entailed great depreciation of the value of the bankrupt's estate, and, if the bankrupt had a lease of the premises for twelve months, as averred in the petition, it was the duty of the trustee to determine whether or not it was for the benefit of the creditors to assume said lease. If a sale upon the premises was necessary to avoid great loss, it was obviously the duty of the trustee to conduct the sale there, and it seems equally clear that it was the duty of the court to relieve him from the coercion of a situation where precipitate action might have resulted in irreparable damage, and such delay as might be reasonably necessary seems clearly within the power of a court of equity to grant. The bond of a $1,000 [restraining order bonds] etc."

§ 985. Whether Bound to Pay Rent Stipulated, or Only for Use and Occupation.

—The trustee does not thereby become bound to the lease, and will be liable for merely the reasonable rent for the use of the premises [subject to his right to occupy free of charge for any unexpired portion of a term for which the landlord may hold a provable claim, in accordance with the principles stated post, § 992] whilst so occupying them and will not become liable for the rent stated in the lease itself, for to make him liable for the stated rent would be to bind him to the lease.[90]

Inferentially, Bray v. Cobb, 3 A. B. R. 788, 100 Fed. 270 (D. C. N. Car.): "Under such circumstances it would be chargeable to the estate, not as rent under bankrupt's contract but as costs and expenses of administrating the same. * * * If he did so use the bank he or the estate would be chargeable with the rent for the time it was used." This case was reversed, but on other grounds, in Cobb v. Overman, 6 A. B. R. 324 (C. C. A.).

In re Foundry Co., 21 A. B. R. 509, 166 Fed. 381 (D. C. N. Y.), the court, however, in this case dissenting from the proposition enunciated at § 992: "This court has held in a number of instances that if a receiver is actually in possession, for the purpose of preserving his estate, during a certain number of days, he should pay as part of the expenses of maintaining the estate, the pro rata rents, at a reasonable value, for that time, and in the same way this court has held in a number of instances that the receiver is entitled to the benefit of being compelled to pay only a reasonable value for the property, if the rental value happens to be greater because of some contract liability which will result in a claim against the estate in the hands of the trustee, or against the bankrupt himself if he should subsequently continue the lease."

In re Jefferson, 2 A. B. R. 206, 93 Fed. 948 (D. C. Ky.): "The duties of the trustee of the bankrupt are clearly defined by § 47 of the act, and can in

---

90. Compare ante, § 667, and post, § 2034; also see In re Adams, 28 A. B. R. 923, 199 Fed. 337 (D. C. Mass.); In re Luckenbill, 11 A. B. R. 455, 127 Fed. 984 (D. C. Pa.); In re Stanton Co., 20 A. B. R. 549, 162 Fed. 169 (D. C. Conn.); In re Foundry Co., 21 A. B. R. 509, 166 Fed. 381 (D. C. N. Y.), although in this case the court expressly dissents from the proposition contained in § 992. Nevertheless, the rent stipulated in the lease should be accepted as the measure of the reasonable worth of the use and occupation, in the absence of clear showing of unreasonableness. See post, "Costs of Administration," § 2135.

no way be construed as making him the tenant, nor as authorizing the estate to be a tenant of the landlord under the lease, however much the trustee may become such by express or implied agreement with the landlord for the short time he may be compelled to occupy the premises in the discharge of the duties of trustee. He should, of course, for that time pay rent, and it should be treated as part of the expense of administering the trust estate."

A like rule applies where the premises are occupied by the receiver.[91]

And the trustee may perhaps be bound to make good, as part of the rent for the use and occupation, damage accruing to the landlord through loss of prospective tenants, etc.[92]

§ 986. Previous Forfeiture Not Nullified by Tenant's Bankruptcy.

—The landlord's previous exercise of the right to forfeit the lease is not avoided by the tenant's bankruptcy;[93] except of course where the subsequent bankruptcy operates to nullify or remove the ground of forfeiture itself.[93a]

Nor, on principle would any right of forfeiture after bankruptcy be taken away from the landlord; so, that, if such right or forfeiture was given in the lease and was exercised after the bankruptcy by the landlord, the trustee would become a mere trespasser thereafter.[94]

These rights of forfeiture are always subject, however, to the usual allowance of a reasonable time for effecting a removal, under the doctrine of the preceding section, § 985.

In re Hunter, 18 A. B. R. 477, 151 Fed. 904 (D. C. Pa.): "It is conceded that the claim is not provable against the estate under the provisions of § 63 of the Bankrupt Act, but it is contended that a wrong was done by the refusal to yield possession of the premises upon April 1, for which an action would lie against the trustee personally; and further, that, as the wrong was done in the interest of the bankrupt estate, and to its actual profit, by saving the cost of removing the goods and by obtaining better prices at the sale upon the bankrupt's premises, the trustee would have a valid claim against the estate to be reimbursed whatever damages it might be compelled to pay in an action by the landlord, and therefore to prevent circuity of action, the damages may be allowed in the first instance against the estate. I believe this position to be sustained by the authorities. Undoubtedly the trustee was a trespasser after April 1. It was bound to know that it had no right to remain on the premises after that date, except by agreement with the landlord; and especially is this true, after the landlord had given express notice that possession was desired on April 1, and that he had secured a tenant for a term beginning on that

---

91. In re Adams Cloak, etc., House, 28 A. B. R. 923, 199 Fed. 337 (D. C. Mass.).

92. Compare, impliedly to this effect, In re Hunter, 18 A. B. R. 477, 151 Fed. 904 (D. C. Pa.).

93. Lindeke v. Associates Realty Co., 17 A. B. R. 215, 146 Fed. 630 (C. C. A. Minn.). Covenant in long term lease, to build, on penalty of forfeiture; forfeiture declared before bankruptcy.

93a. As, where the ground of forfeiture was an assignment without the landlord's written consent, which is itself avoided by the subsequent bankruptcy within four months, see post, § 987.

94. See post, § 992½. But compare, inferentially contra, In re Rubel, 21 A. B. R. 566, 166 Fed. 131 (D. C. Wis.).

day. The fact that the notice was not given until March 24 is of little or no importance. The trustee knew exactly when the bankrupt's lease expired, and it was bound to know that, if it continued to occupy the premises after April 1, without the landlord's express agreement, it would do so at its own risk. If, therefore, it made arrangements to hold a sale on the premises upon April 4, it did so with constructive knowledge that such an arrangement was subject to be defeated by notice to vacate, and when the notice was received its duty was to give up the premises before April 1. Six days afforded ample time to remove the goods, and, if an adjournment of the sale or a new order to sell was thereby rendered necessary, the delay was of slight consequence, and no one was to blame except the trustee. The landlord having, therefore, been entitled to the possession of his property on April 1, and the trustee having refused to surrender, the latter became a trespasser and was liable in damages. The direct and immediate consequence of its refusal was that the new tenant threw up the lease, and, as the landlord was not able to find another tenant within the term, he lost the rent for three months. For this sum I think the trustee would be directly and personally liable to be sued."

But the forum for enforcing the landlord's rights of ejectment after the forfeiture would be the bankruptcy court, probably by petition for an order upon the trustee to quit the premises; certainly not by ejectment or forcible detainer proceedings in the State court.[95] And notice to quit, served upon the receiver, has been held insufficient in one case.[96]

But doubtless he may sue the trustee personally for damages.[97] In the event the trustee be thus sued personally, the bankrupt estate would be bound to indemnify the trustee, if it had benefited by the detention.[98]

In accordance with the above rules it has been held that where, prior to bankruptcy, proceedings for restitution of possession have been determined against the bankrupt tenant, which neither he nor his trustee attempts to review, the trustee has no interest in the leasehold which may be disposed of as an asset of the estate.[99]

§ 987. Covenants of Forfeiture for Assigning or Subletting, Not Violated by Bankruptcy.

—The trustee will get the title, although the lease itself may contain conditions against subletting or assigning the leasehold or may contain the right of forfeiture or re-entry therefor. Such conditions refer to the voluntary acts of the lessee in subletting and assigning the lease; and, even if an assignment for the benefit of creditors might break the condition, bankruptcy itself certainly would not so operate, for the title in bankruptcy passes purely by operation of law and not by voluntary act, as it does in the case of a voluntary assignment. The trustee is vested with the title, but not by "assignment."[1]

95. See post, § 1799.
96. In re Rubel, 21 A. B. R. 566, 166 Fed. 131 (D. C. Wis.).
97. In re Hunter, 18 A. B. R. 477, 151 Fed. 904 (D. C. Pa.). See post, § 1780.
98. In re Hunter, 18 A. B. R. 477, 151 Fed. 904 (D. C. Pa.).

99. In re Van Da Grift, etc., Co., 27 A. B. R. 474, 192 Fed. 1015 (D. C. Ky.).
1. In re Thiessen, 2 N. B. N. & R. 628; also, 625 (D. C. Neb., and Ref. Neb.); In re Gose, 3 N. B. R. & R. 840 (Ref. Ohio). Covenants against assignment and underletting contained

Gazlay v. Williams, 20 A. B. R. 18, 210 U. S. 41: "The passage of the lessees' estate from Brown, the bankrupt, to Williams, the trustee, as of date of the adjudication, was by operation of law and not by the act of the bankrupt, nor was it by sale. The condition imposed forfeiture if the lessee assigned the lease or the lessee's interest should be sold under execution or other legal process without lessors' written consent. A sale by the trustee for the benefit of Brown's creditors was not forbidden by the condition and would not be in breach thereof. It would not be a voluntary assignment by the lessee, nor a sale of the lessee's interest, but of the trustees' interest held under the bankruptcy proceedings for the benefit of creditors. Jones in his work on Landlord and Tenant lays it down (§ 466) that 'an ordinary covenant against subletting and assignment is not broken by a transfer of the leased premises by operation of law, but the covenant may be so drawn as to expressly prohibit such a transfer, and in that case the lease would be forfeited by an assignment by operation of law.'"

In re Bush, 11 A. B. R. 415, 126 Fed. 878 (D. C. R. I.): "The clause in question is not the equivalent of an express provision declaring the lease void in case of bankruptcy, and it is not applicable to assigns by operation of law, or to their immediate vendees."

Doe v. Bevan, 3 Maule & Selw. 353: "Lord Ellenborough said: 'The courts have construed it to mean voluntary assigns as contradistinguished from assigns by operation of law and further than that, that the immediate vendee from the assigns in law is not within the proviso; the reason of which is that the assignee in law cannot be incumbered with the engagements belonging to the property he takes, such as in this case the carrying on the bankrupt's trade in the public house, which is a strong instance. In such cases, therefore, the law must allow the assignee to divest himself of the property and convert it into a fund for the benefit of creditors.'

"Le Blanc, J., said: 'There can be no doubt that the lessee might have relieved himself from all inconvenience by expressly providing in the lease that if the lessee should become bankrupt or shall deposit the lease with any one then the lease should be void.'

"And again: 'It is clear that there has been no assignment by the lessee himself; it is also clear that the lessee's becoming bankrupt is not a breach, but the assignees under the commission have assigned. They were bound to assign because they took only as trustees for the purpose of disposing of the property to the best advantage for the benefit of creditors; and they are compelled under the order of the court of chancery to sell it in discharge of the debt of Whitbread & Co.'

"Bayley, J., said: 'It has never been considered that the lessee's becoming bankrupt was an avoiding of the lease within this proviso; and if it is not, what

in leases having the force of conditions are not favored by the courts. Gazley v. Williams, 17 A. B. R. 253 (C. C. A. Ohio); In re Frazin & Oppenheim, 23 A. B. R. 289, 174 Fed. 71" (D. C. N. Y.), quoted at § 989; Gazley v. Williams, 17 A. B. R. 253 (C. C. A. Ohio), affirmed in 20 A. B. R. 18, 210 U. S. 41; In re Gutman, 28 A. B. R. 643, 197 Fed. 472 (D. C. Ga.).

This attitude of disfavor, however, does not permit resort to sophistical reasoning to read out of such a covenant that which it really contains. It simply requires that what is claimed to be within it shall be clearly and manifestly so and that if there is a felt doubt as to its being within it, that it be excluded therefrom. The cases go very far towards holding that the mere letter of the covenant is controlling. Gazley v. Williams, 17 A. B. R. 253 (C. C. A. Ohio).

Rights of landlord may be determined in advance of sale of lease. Gazley v. Williams, 17 A. B. R. 253 (C. C. A. Ohio).

act has the lessee done to avoid it? All that has followed upon the bankruptcy is not by his act, but by operation of the law transferring his property to his assignees. Then shall the assignees have capacity to take it and yet not to dispose of it; shall they take it only for their own benefit or be obliged to retain it in their hands to the prejudice of the creditors for whose benefit the law originally cast it upon them? Undoubtedly that can never be.'"

Impliedly, In re Adams, 14 A. B. R. 23, 143 Fed. 142 (D. C. Conn.): "The trustee takes the premises by operation of law, and the bankrupt has in no sense violated the provisions of the lease by his proceedings. He assigned nothing, transferred nothing, conveyed nothing."

This is so, even though a general assignment preceded the bankruptcy, for the trustee does not take under the assignment, but in denial of its validity.

In re Bush, 11 A. B. R. 417, 126 Fed. 878 (D. C. R. I.): "Counsel for the lessor concedes that, where an involuntary bankrupt is tenant under a lease containing a covenant against assignment, an adjudication in bankruptcy is not a breach, and that the lease passes to the trustee. He makes the distinction that the transfer is effected by operation of law, and not by the voluntary act of the bankrupt. But the title to this lease which the creditors seek to preserve is not a title arising under the voluntary act of the bankrupt—that is, the general assignment—but a title which, by operation of law, vests in the trustee despite the general assignment. To constitute a breach of covenant not to assign, a valid assignment carrying the legal estate is required. If the assignment is void as an act of bankruptcy, it will not constitute a breach."

Besides which, if the general assignment occurred within the four months preceding the bankruptcy, it is itself nullified by the bankruptcy, and the ground of forfeiture is thus removed or rendered nugatory and unavailing, equity not favoring forfeitures.

§ 988. Leasehold Liberated from Forfeiture Clause.

—Where the title to the leasehold thus passes by operation of law, it passes freed from the clause of forfeiture, and may thereafter be sold and assigned by the trustee and perhaps, also, by the purchaser who buys it from the trustee.[2]

Compare, suggestively, although not directly in point, Lindeke v. Associates Realty Co., 17 A. B. R. 227 (C. C. A. Minn.): "The purchaser of the leasehold interest under the sale by the trustees in bankruptcy would not be liable for any antecedent breach of the covenant to build; and if the claim for damages therefor were liquidated and allowed in the bankruptcy proceedings, in any view the purchaser would take the property unburdened of the building covenant."

Compare, Gazley v. Williams, 17 A. B. R. 252 (C. C. A. Ohio, affirmed by Supreme Court, 210 U. S. 41, 20 A. B. R. 18, quoted ante, § 987): "The appellee maintains, on several grounds, that a sale by him of the leasehold estate for

---

2. Goodbehere v. Bevan, 3 M. & S. 383; obiter, Bemis v. Wilder, 100 Mass. 446 (1868); In re Bush, 11 A. B. R. 417, 126 Fed. 878 (D. C. R. I.); obiter, inferentially, In re Frazin & Oppenheimer, 23 A. B. R. 289, 174 Fed. 713 (D. C. N. Y.); In re Gutman, 28 A. B. R. 643, 197 Fed. 472 (D. C. Ga.). **Arrears of Rent—Rights of Purchaser and Landlord.**—In re Ketterer, 20 A. B. R. 694, 156 Fed. 638 (D. C. Pa.).

the benefit of creditors will not work a forfeiture thereof. He contends that this case comes within the rule laid down in Dumpor's Case, 4 Coke 119b (1 Smith's Lead. Cases 15). That rule is that where a lease is upon a proviso that the lessee, shall not alien without the special license of the lessors, if the license is once given, the condition is annulled, removed or destroyed, that is, has spent its force, so that it can have no effect on a subsequent alienation. Here the interest of Kueny, the original lessee, was sold to said Brown by the procurement of appellants. This, it is urged, exhausts the condition and brings the case within the rule stated."

§ 989. Bankruptcy Works Forfeiture, if Specifically Provided.—

A distinct and unequivocal condition of the lease forfeiting the residue of the term, in case the lessee become a bankrupt, will cause a forfeiture,[3] provided steps be taken to declare the forfeiture.

Obiter, In re Frazin & Oppenheim, 23 A. B. R. 289, 174 Fed. 713 (D. C. N. Y.): "There can be no doubt, under the authorities, that a covenant by the lessee, in a lease not to assign, mortgage or pledge the lease or underlet without the lessor's consent, is not violated by the lessee's bankruptcy. * * * The covenant, however, providing that, in the case of the lessee's insolvency, or the institution of bankruptcy proceedings by or against him or the appointment of a receiver or trustee of the lessee's property or the devolution upon any person, by operation of law, or the lessee's occupancy, the lessor may re-enter, is violated by the occurrence of any of the acts specified. The rule is well stated in Jones on Landlord and Tenant, § 466, cited with approval in Gazlay v. Williams, 210 U. S. 41, 20 Am. B. R. 18, where it is said that 'an ordinary covenant against subletting and assigning is not broken by a transfer of the leased premises by operation of law, but the covenant may be so drawn as to expressly prohibit such a transfer, and in that case the lease would be forfeited by an assignment by operation of law.' "

But such forfeiture may be waived; as, for instance, by the acceptance of rent under the lease from the trustee.[4]

In re Frazin & Oppenheim, 23 A. B. R. 289, 174 Fed. 713 (D. C. N. Y.): "It is equally well settled that the acceptance of rent by a landlord, after a breach of a covenant in a lease authorizing re-entry, waives the right of re-entry, and the right thus waived is dispensed with forever. * * * The landlord, in this case, by accepting rent from the trustee, waived all the provisions in the lease authorizing re-entry, and the result is, in my opinion, that the trustee can sell this lease and give a perfect title to it, and the purchaser can take the prem-

---

3. Impliedly, In re Ells, 3 A. B. R. 564, 98 Fed. 967 (D. C. Mass.). But quære, Wilson v. Penna. Trust Co., 8 A. B. R. 196, 114 Fed. 742 (C. C. A. Penna.): "Notwithstanding the ruling in Platt v. Johnson, 168 Pa. 47, 31 Atl. 935, 47 Am. St. Rep. 877, upholding as valid a provision in a lease that the entire rent for the balance of the term should become due if the lessee should become embarrassed, or make an assignment for the benefit of creditors, or be sold out by sheriff's sale, it may well be doubted whether the stipulation here making the whole rent for the whole term due and payable if the lessee 'shall become a bankrupt' is enforceable as against the provisions of the Bankrupt Act."

Impliedly, Gazlay v. Williams, 20 A. B. R. 18, 210 U. S. 31. Instance, but forfeiture waived by acceptance of rent, In re Montello Brick Wks., 20 A. B. R. 859, 163 Fed. 624 (D. C. Pa.).

4. In re Montello Brick Wks., 20 A. B. R. 859, 163 Fed. 624 (D. C. Pa.).

ises for the term of the lease, not subject to re-entry so long as the purchaser complies with the provisions of the lease."

§ 990. But if Specific Method Stipulated, Such Method Alone Effective.

—But if the lease provides that the forfeiture shall be declared in a certain way, as, by re-entry, that method must be pursued, and if the landlord is prevented from enforcing his rights in the manner prescribed, the lease cannot be forfeited.[5]

§ 991. Where Future Rent Already Paid, Leasehold Passes.

—Where the future rent is already paid the leasehold of course passes at once.[6] So, it seems that a sum paid to a landlord for an extension of the term, may be set-off against a claim for rent.[7]

§ 992. Receiver or Trustee Occupy Free, for Any Period for Which Landlord Holds Provable Claim.

—Where the future rent is payable in advance and falls due before the bankruptcy, but is not paid, and the tenant and receiver or trustee if any, have continued the occupancy without the landlord having taken any steps to declare a forfeiture, the use of the premises for the period covered by the installment thus falling due, nevertheless, likewise passes to the trustee free of charge, the landlord simply having his provable claim against the estate for the rent thus due before bankruptcy.[8]

But where all the remaining rent is to become due upon default or bankruptcy and where at the same time default and bankruptcy are stipulated to forfeit the lease, the landlord cannot insist upon his claim or lien for the future rent, and at the same time declare a forfeiture or make re-entry.

---

5. In re Ells, 3 A. B. R. 564, 98 Fed. 967 (D. C. Mass.).

6. Obiter, In re Ells, 3 A. B. R. 564, 98 Fed. 967 (D. C. Mass.).

7. In re Abrams, 29 A. B. R. 590, 200 Fed. 1005 (D. C. Ia.).

8. In re Mitchell, 8 A. B. R. 324, 116 Fed. 87 (D. C. Cal.); compare, impliedly, Wilson v. Penna. Trust Co., 8 A. B. R. 169, 114 Fed. 742 (C. C. A. Pa.). Contra, In re Foundry Co., 21 A. B. R. 509, 166 Fed. 381 (D. C. N. Y.).

Re-entry clause gives no lien on proceeds of sale of leasehold: And the landlord has no lien for such over due rent upon the proceeds of the trustee's sale of the leasehold by virtue of any mere re-entry clause in the lease itself. In re Ruppel, 3 A. B. R. 233, 97 Fed. 778 (D. C. Penna.).

Trustee of Bankrupt Tenant Cannot Perfect Landlord's Lien.—Trustee in bankruptcy of tenant cannot perfect lien in favor of landlord: he does not represent secured creditors except in

the capacity of mere custodian. Goldman v. Smith, 2 A. B. R. 104 (Ref. Ky.).

Trustee has right to have crops under a lease on shares where tenant becomes bankrupt. In re Luckenbill, 11 A. B. R. 455, 127 Fed. 984 (D. C. Penna.); In re Barrow, 3 A. B. R. 414, 98 Fed. 582 (D. C. Va.).

Landlord's Claim under Covenant to Restore Premises in "Good Condition."—In re International Mailing Co., 23 A. B. R. 664, 175 Fed. 308 (D. C. N. Y.).

Rule in England, under Statute.—By statute, in England, where a bankruptcy takes place between two periods fixed for payment of rent, the landlord is not entitled to be paid in full for the quarter's rent accruing due after the bankruptcy, notwithstanding that the assignee in bankruptcy takes and keeps possession of the premises until the quarter day. De Buisson, ex parte Caston, 10 L. T. 792 (England).

Wilson *v.* Penna. Trust Co., 8 A. B. R. 169, 114 Fed. 742 (C. C. A. Penna.): "Assuming the validity of the stipulation where the lessee is adjudged a bankrupt, these consequences would follow its enforcement. In the first place, under the Pennsylvania act of 1836 the landlord would be entitled to priority of payment out of the proceeds of sale of the tenant's goods upon the demised premises to the extent of one year's rent. Longstreth *v.* Pennock, 20 Wall. 575, 22 L. Ed. 451. Secondly, the rent for the entire residue of the term would be provable as an unpreferred debt, entitled only to a pro rata dividend and the unexpired portion of the term would become an asset of the bankrupt's estae, to be disposed of by the trustee in bankruptcy for the benefit of the estate. The latter result, however, this claimant repudiated altogether. He sought a partial and one-sided enforcement of the stipulation. He attempted to secure a preference for one year's rent, and at the same time retain his interest as landlord unimpaired in the residue of the term."

§ 992½. Forfeiture While in Custody of Bankruptcy Court.—

Neither the landlord nor the trustee gain or lose any rights by the bankruptcy; the trustee succeeds merely to the bankrupt's rights. If the lease contains a forfeiture clause, it may, in proper cases, be forfeited after bankruptcy, as well as before, though the forum for the assertion of rights consequent thereon will be the bankruptcy court and not the State court.

In the event of forfeiture after the trustee has assumed possession, the bankruptcy court will permit the trustee to continue to occupy the premises only on equitable conditions, such as that of payment of rent for the period after the forfeiture; for, from that time, the trustee is no longer occupying under the lease, for the lease has been forfeited. If there be no forfeiture clause or right of re-entry, the trustee succeeds of course to whatever right of continued possession the bankrupt himself would have possessed.[9]

However, of course if the bankruptcy operates itself to remove or nullify the ground of forfeiture, as in cases of general assignments within four months of the bankruptcy, the right of forfeiture can not be exercised.[9a]

§ 993. Rents of Mortgaged Premises, Uncollected or Accruing after Bankruptcy.—

Rents of mortgaged property accruing after bankruptcy, also rents accruing beforehand but uncollected at the time of bankruptcy, or collected but still in the bankrupt's hands, all pass to the trustee of the bankrupt mortgagor, in the absence of any clause in the mortgage including the rents, or of any other contract giving the mortgagee the right thereto, unless and until the mortgagee has taken steps to sequester the rents by the appointment of a receiver, or otherwise, in the bankruptcy court.[10]

---

9. **Raising Rent and Making Tenant's Repairs Evidence of Landlord's Acceptance of Surrender of Lease.—** In re Piano Forte Manf'g Co., 20 A. B. R. 899, 163 Fed. 413 (D. C. Pa.). See ante, § 986.

9a. Compare ante, §§ 986, 987.

10. In re Cass, 6 A. B. R. 722 (Ref.

Ohio); In re Dole, 7 A. B. R. 21, 110 Fed. 926 (D. C. Vt.); Elmore *v.* Symonds, 183 Mass. 321, 67 N. E. 314; impliedly, In re Hollenfeltz, 2 A. B. R. 499 (D. C. Iowa); obiter, In re Force, 4 A. B. R. 116 (Ref. Mass.); (1867) In re Shedaker, 4 N. B. Reg. 168; (1867) Foster *v.* Rhodes, 10 N.

In re Chase, 13 A. B. R. 294, 124 Fed. 753 (D. C. Mass.): "Ordinarily the mortgagor is entitled to rents and profits accrued up to the time that the mortgagee enters or brings his right of entry or his bill to foreclosure, and this right inheres in a trustee in bankruptcy. * * * There may be exceptional cases where a court of bankruptcy, proceeding upon equitable considerations, will treat some informal attempt by the mortgagee to obtain possession of the mortgaged property as the equivalent of a bill in equity and the appointment of a receiver."

In re Banner, 18 A. B. R. 64, 149 Fed. 936 (D. C. N. Y.): "I therefore follow Freedman's Sav. Co. v. Shepherd, 127 U. S. at page 502, holding that it is 'competent for the parties to provide in the mortgage for the payment of rents and profits to the mortgagee while the mortgagor remains in possession. But when the mortgage contains no such provision, and even where the income is expressly pledged as security for the mortgage debt, with the right in the mortgagee to take possession upon the failure of the mortgagor to perform the conditions of the mortgage, the general rule is that the mortgagee is not entitled to the rents and profits of the mortgaged premises until he takes actual possession, or until possession is taken in his behalf by a receiver, or until in proper form he demands and is refused possession.' This I believe is the true view. That a mortgagee out of possession can, upon the instant of a default in mortgage interest, become to all intents a landlord of the mortgaged building, seems to me something not to be encouraged. The form of words used in this mortgage operated merely as a pledge of the rents, to which the pledgee does not become entitled until he asserts his right and in some legal form endeavors to reduce the pledge to possession. An application for a receivership, followed by due demand, is such an appropriate form; and this form was followed within a few days after the appointment of the State court receiver, to wit, on or about September 1, 1906."

In re Torchia, 26 A. B. R. 188, 185 Fed. 576 (D. C. Pa.): "It is a rule of law that a mortgagee out of possession is not entitled to rents. An emphatic pronouncement of this principle with references to ancient and modern authorities, may be found in Teal v. Walker, 111 U. S. 242. Many of the cases cited state the principle in various ways, but all to the one end that a mortgagor of real estate is not liable for rent while in possession. He contracts to pay interest, not rent. And, further, that a mortgagee must recover the possession

---

B. Reg. 523; (1867) In re Bennett, Fed. Cases 1,313, 12 N. B. Reg. 257. Draft drawn by landlord on agent for future rents to be collected by agent and discounted at bank has been held to be an equitable assignment of the rents and to be good against landlord's trustee in bankruptcy. In re Oliver, 12 A. B. R. 694, 132 Fed. 588 (D. C. Tex.).

Under a mortgage, which, after the usual provision giving the holder a right to a receiver of the rents and profits of the premises, provided "And the said rents and profit are hereby, in the event of any default or defaults in the payment of said principal or interest assigned to the holder of this mortgage," the holder is a mere pledgee of the rents, to which he does not become entitled until after

his application for a receiver has been granted and the receiver has made demand. In re Banner, 18 A. B. R. 61, 149 Fed. 936 (D. C. N. Y.).

Fraudulent transferee's claim for rent, on setting aside fraudulent transfer. In re Hurst, 23 A. B. R. 554 (Ref. W. Va.).

Similarly, Trustee Using Property Held on Conditional Sale Pending Reclamation.—It has been held that the trustee cannot be bound to pay the rental value of machines sold on conditional sale, for his use thereof whilst continuing the business, pending reclamation proceedings, unless the conditional vendors take some positive step to charge the trustee therewith. In re Daterson Pub. Co., 26 A. B. R. 582, 188 Fed. 64 (C. C. A. Pa.), quoted at § 2035½.

by regular entry by suit before he is entitled to the rents and profits. * * * The mortgagee is no nearer to the possession of the mortgaged premises after the election of the trustee than he was before. He could not have higher rights against the trustee than he had against the bankrupt. If the trustee be required to pay the rents to the mortgag.·e, the mortgagee to that extent has higher rights than he had before the proceedings were started. If the bankrupt be not required to pay the rents and profits to the mortgagee prior to possession by the mortgagee, the trustee certainly ought not to be required to do so."

§ 993½. **Sale of Leasehold Where Landlord Has Lien.**—Where the landlord has a lien for his rent upon the property on the premises, under certain circumstances the landlord has been relegated to his rights against the purchaser of the leasehold where such purchaser has given sufficient bond for the further payment of rent.[11]

SUBDIVISION "F."

CONTRACTS FOR BANKRUPT'S PERSONAL SERVICES; UNSCHEDULED AND CONCEALED PROPERTY; FIXTURES; ENCUMBERED PROPERTY AND OTHER PROPERTY PASSING AND NOT PASSING.

§ 994. **Uncompleted Contracts Involving Personal Skill or Confidence.**—Uncompleted contracts for personal services or for the exercise of skill, wherein trust and confidence are reposed or reliance had on skill, do not pass.[12]

In re McBride & Co., 12 A. B. R. 83, 132 Fed. 285 (Ref. N. Y.): "After a careful consideration of the terms of the contract and the evidence adduced, I am of the opinion that the claimant is entitled to the copyrights in question because I must find on the facts and law that the contract was a personal engagement between author and publisher, involving trust and confidence which cannot be assigned or delegated to another without the author's consent."

Jetter Brew. Co. v. Scollan, 15 A. B. R. 300 (Sup. Ct. N. Y. App.): "The assignability of a contract, in general, depends upon its nature and the character of the obligation assumed; and when the contract is one for services, or the delivery of manufactured goods requiring science or peculiar qualification the contract will not be held to be assignable without the consent of the party sought to be held thereby." This was a case of a contract for the purchase of goods made by a particular manufacturer, namely, an agreement to buy "landlord's beer."

Thus a contract of agency between an insurance company and its general agent does not pass.[13]

Obiter, In re Wright, 18 A. B. R. 199, 151 Fed. 361 (D. C. N. Y.): "That the contract in question is declaratory of the relations of personal confidence between the bankrupt and the insurance company is undoubted, and that a contract which involves the capacity of either or both parties to perform the conditions imposed cannot be assigned, is well settled."

---

11. In re Varley & Bauman Co., 26 A. B. R. 104, 188 Fed. 761 (D. C. Ala.).

12. Compare, In re McAdam, 3 A. B. R. 417 (D. C. N. Y.).

13. In re Wright, 16 A. B. R. 778 (Ref. N. Y.). See post, § 1131.

But commissions on renewal premiums accruing after the bankruptcy on policies written beforehand, will pass, because they are assignable.

In re Wright, 18 A. B. R. 199, 151 Fed. 361 (D. C. N. Y., reversing 16 A. B. R. 778): "The vital question in this case, however, depends upon another principle, to wit, whether the bankrupt, Wright, can assign his commissions on renewal premiums to accrue annually in the future or the right to compel the insurance company to pay the same when they accrue. Concededly, if the commissions in question are assignable by the bankrupt, or are subject to levy and sale pursuant to judgment and execution against him, they constitute 'property,' as that term is legally defined, and the trustee in bankruptcy is vested by operation of law with the title of the bankrupt. That payment of the commissions, according to the terms of the contract, depended upon the future payment of renewal premiums by policy holders, and in a sense were contingent, is not thought of material importance. Evidence was given to show that customarily about 75 per cent. of the renewal premiums were paid. Hence, notwithstanding the element of contingency, the amount of the commissions to become due is determinable with reasonable certainty. I am unable to conceive upon what basis the confidential character of the contract will be destroyed, if the commissions of renewal premiums were set aside for the benefit of the general creditors, or when payable should be turned over to the trustee instead of to the bankrupt. The contract of employment, as I view it, will be destroyed only in case the bankrupt fails to faithfully discharge his duties or violates a material covenant contained therein."

In re Wright, 19 A. B. R. 454, 157 Fed. 544 (C. C. A. N. Y., affirming 18 A. B. R. 199): "It may be conceded that this contract, as a whole, is based upon personal trust and confidence and is not assignable. Arkansas Valley Smelting Co. v. Belden Mining Co. (127 U. S. 379) But there is a difference between an absolute assignment of a contract and an assignment of rights under a contract. The personal confidence which precludes the transfer of rights arising out of a contract must be involved in the nature of rights themselves. Hearst v. Roehm (84 Fed. 569). It is not ordinarily involved in the right to receive moneys due or to grow due under a contract and this right is generally assignable without the consent of the other party. Fortunato v. Patten (147 N. Y. 277); Knevals v. Blauvelt (82 Me. 458). The right to receive the renewal commission under the present contract which is the right involved in the question certified, seems not to involve personal confidence. The contracts of insurance have already been obtained. The collection of renewal premiums is largely a ministerial act. The contract provides that the insurance company shall appoint a cashier to receive such moneys. Even the bankrupt testified that seventy-five per cent. of the renewal premiums are paid upon mere notice. The collection charge made by the company against an agent's estate is only two and one-half per cent. It is possible that if the interests under the contract are transferred to the trustee the insurance company may defeat the object of the transfer by withholding its consent. It does not appear that it has refused its consent and there is no presumption that it will do so. But the fact that the interest is defeasible does not prevent its transfer. Defeasible and contingent interests of this nature are assignable. In re Becker, 3 Am. B. R. 412, 98 Fed. 407; Fortunato v. Patten, supra. It is urged in the second place that the collection of renewal premiums requires continued service on the part of the bankrupt and that his creditors are not entitled to his future services. This contention may be agreed to without affecting the question whether the renewal interests are assignable. It is true that in case they are transferred, the bankrupt cannot be compelled to render any future services. Collection by means of the cashier alone might or might not prove effective. Some arrangement for procuring the bankrupt's services might be desirable. If no arrangement could be made the insurance company might refuse its consent to the transfer. So it is possible that the bankrupt might cause the forfeiture of the renewal interests by leaving the employment of the company. These contingencies might render the interest to be transferred to the trustee of little value. But they would not render such interest unassignable."

And contracts for future deliveries of personal property, wherein there is no express prohibition of assignment, will pass, if they are not dependent upon future personal dealings between the original parties and if the trustee or receiver in bankruptcy of the vendee stands ready to pay on delivery and relieve the vendor from his obligation to make deliveries on credit.[14]

Exempt wages or salary, if not claimed as exempt will pass to the trustee,[15] though earned under a contract involving personal skill or confidence.

So where the contract, even though uncompleted at the time of the bankruptcy and involving personal skill, has been since completed by the trustee, the trustee will be entitled to the consideration which the bankrupt was to have received therefor if bankruptcy had not intervened.[16]

§ 995. Personal Right to Purchase, Not Transferable.—A personal right to purchase, not transferable, does not pass to creditors.[17]

§ 996. Property Not Scheduled, or Concealed Otherwise, Passes.
—Property belonging to the estate but not scheduled by the bankrupt will nevertheless pass.[18] Thus, in one case, where the death of a child before the bankruptcy threw upon the bankrupt an undivided interest which he failed to disclose to his trustee, and, subsequent to the bankruptcy, a fire occurred and the insurance money for the decedent's share was settled for and paid over to one creditor, without notice to the trustee, the trustee, on discovery of the facts, was held entitled to recover the money.[19] Likewise as to property concealed from the trustee until the estate is closed: its title does not revest in the bankrupt.[20]

§ 996½. Trustee's Failure to Sue, Gives No Right to Individual Creditor to Sue.—The trustee's failure to sue for the recovery of property gives no right to an individual creditor to sue.[21]

14. In re Niagara Radiator Co., 21 A. B. R. 55, 164 Fed. 102 (D. C. N. Y.).
15. In re Driggs, 22 A. B. R. 621, 171 Fed. 897 (D. C. N. Y.).
16. Ford v. State Board of Education, 27 A. B. R. 236 (Sup. Ct. Mich.).
17. In re Hansen, 5 A. B. R. 747, 107 Fed. 252 (D. C. Ore.).
18. Rand v. Iowa Central Ry. Co., 12 A. B. R. 164 (Sup. Ct. N. Y. App.

Div.); Ruhl-Koblegard Co. v. Gillespie, 22 A. B. R. 643, 61 W. Va. 554.
19. In re Kane, 20 A. B. R. 616, 152 Fed. 587 (D. C. N. Y.).
20. Fowler v. Jenks, 11 A. B. R. 255 (Minn.).
21. Ruhl-Koblegard Co. v. Gillespie, 22 A. B. R. 643, 61 W. Va. 554. See ante, § 824.

§ 997. Property Sold on Conditional Sale with Power to Sell in Usual Course.

—Property sold on conditional sale to the bankrupt, with power in the bankrupt to sell the same again in the usual course of trade, passes to the bankrupt's trustee.[22]

§ 998. Property Belonging to Bankrupt by Marital or Parental Right.

—Property belonging to the bankrupt by virtue of marital or parental rights passes to the trustee, as, for instance, the product of a wife's lands, in States where the husband is entitled thereto by virtue of his marital rights.[23]

But the earnings of an emancipated minor child of the bankrupt do not pass.[24]

§ 999. Encumbered Property Passes.

—Property encumbered with liens passes to the trustee, subject to the liens according to their validity.

Thus, money due on building or paving contracts passes, subject to lien;[25] likewise, real estate encumbered with liens.[26]

So as to property transferred by a deed which operates as an equitable mortgage merely.[27] But if, under the local law, the income or product of encumbered property would go to the lien creditors, that rule will be followed in bankruptcy.[28]

§ 1000. Fixtures May Pass.

—Fixtures may or may not pass, according to circumstances.[29]

And it is held that a covenant restricting a tenant's ordinary right to remove a trade fixture, is to be strictly construed and will not be extended by implication.[30]

§ 1001. Stocks, Bonds, Commercial Paper, Mortgages, Merchandise, etc., Pass.

—Stocks,[31] bonds and other securities; also all kinds of merchandise, funds in bank, commercial paper owned by the bankrupt, mortgages, and, in short, any and all the numerous forms of transferable property or property that can be levied on at the time of the filing of the petition, all pass to the trustee.

---

22. In re Howland, 6 A. B. R. 495, 109 Fed. 896 (D. C. N. Y.).

23. In re Rooney, 6 A. B. R. 478, 109 Fed. 601 (D. C. Vt.); compare, In re Marsh, 6 A. B. R. 537 (D. C. Vt.).

24. In re Dunavant, 3 A. B. R. 41, 96 Fed. 542 (D. C. N. Car.).

25. In re Cramond, 17 A. B. R. 22, 145 Fed. 966 (D. C. N. Y.).

26. In re Noel, 14 A. B. R. 915, 137 Fed. 694 (D. C. Md.); In re Roger Brown Co., 28 A. B. R. 336, 196 Fed. 758 (C. C. A. Iowa); In re Zehner, 27 A. B. R. 536, 193 Fed. 787 (D. C. La.). See further, for this subject, the various subjects under the topic of "What Title Does the Trustee Take?" post, ch. XXX.

27. In re Samuel Borg., 25 A. B. R. 189, 184 Fed. 640 (D. C. Minn.).

28. In re Torchia, 26 A. B. R. 579, 188 Fed. 207 (C. C. A. Pa.) quoted on another point at § 993.

29. See post, § 1152. Compare, In re Smith, 9 A. B. R. 590, 121 Fed. 1014 (D. C. R. I.); compare, In re Clark & Co., 9 A. B. R. 252, 118 Fed. 358 (D. C. Pa.).

30. Montello Brick Co. v. Trexler, 21 A. B. R. 896, 163 Fed. 624 (C. C. A. Pa., affirming 20 A. B. R. 859).

31. French v. White, 18 A. B. R. 905, 78 Vt. 89, wherein an ineffective attempt had been made by the bankrupt to pledge the stock. Inferentially, Greenhall v. Carnegie Trust Co., 25 A. B. R. 300, 180 Fed. 812 (D. C. N. Y.).

§ 1001½. **Claims against the Government.**—Claims against the United States government may pass.[33]

Assignments of such claims by the bankrupt will be ineffectual to pass title to the assignee, unless duly witnessed, acknowledged, etc., with all the formalities required by the United States statutes.[34]

SUBDIVISION "G."

LIFE INSURANCE POLICIES AS ASSETS.

§ 1002. **Life Insurance Policies as Assets.**—Among the assets of the bankrupt which might be thought to pass to the trustee in bankruptcy under class 5, of § 70 (a), as being property which, prior to the filing of the petition, the bankrupt could by some means have transferred, or which might have been levied upon and sold under judicial process against him, are life insurance policies wherein the bankrupt, his estate, or personal representative is the beneficiary. Such policies, as also polices wherein he has reserved the right to change the beneficiary at will, constitute property of the bankrupt; and even if his interest or that of his estate or personal representative be merely contingent, conditional or partial, as in cases of certain tontine and endowment policies, etc., such interest, whatever it may be, undoubtedly constitutes property of the bankrupt which, by some means, he could transfer. Certain of such policies might even be subjected to a creditor's claim by legal process. He could sell the policy or his interest therein and in so doing he would not be limited to the mere cash surrender value which the insurance company itself might give him; indeed, the actual value of any particular policy, owing to some change in health, might differ widely from its stated cash surrender value, the latter being based wholly on averages.

However, Congress dealt specially with the subject of life insurance policies, by way of a proviso which follows directly after the enunciation of the broadly inclusive class 5 of assets, the proviso reading as follows: "Provided, that when any bankrupt shall have any insurance policy which has a cash surrender value payable to himself, his estate or personal representatives, he may, within thirty days after the cash surrender value has been ascertained and stated to the trustee by the company issuing the same, pay or secure to the trustee the sum so ascertained and stated, and continue to hold, own and carry such policy free from the claims of the creditors participating in the distribution of his assets under the bankruptcy proceedings, otherwise the policy shall pass to the trustee as assets."

Now the wording of Bankruptcy Act, § 70 (a) (5), and its proviso is

---

33. Bank of Commerce v. Downie, 25 A. B. R. 199, 218 U. S. 345, affirming Nat'l Bk. of Seattle v. Downie, 20 A. B. R. 531, 161 Fed. 839.

34. Nat. B'k of Seattle v. Downie, 20 A. B. R. 531, 161 Fed. 839 (C. C. A. Wash.), affirmed sub nom. Bank of Commerce v. Downie, 218 U. S. 345, 25 A. B. R. 199.

susceptible of the construction that such policies, unless exempt under State law, themselves pass as assets to the trustee, subject only to the right of the bankrupt or his personal representatives to redeem them by paying or securing to the trustee their cash surrender value as the same existed at the date of the filing of the bankruptcy petition.[35]

But Bankruptcy Act, § 70 (a) (5), and its proviso are also susceptible of a different construction, namely, that Congress did not mean the proviso merely as a qualification upon the operation of the broad classification of class 5 of assets, but meant thereby rather to take the entire subject of life insurance policies out of that classification and treat of it separately, although under the form of a mere proviso; and this latter view has been adopted by the Supreme Court of the United States and is therefore the law; so that the proviso exclusively is to be looked to, and it is to be read as if, standing alone, it was the only source of the trustee's title to life insurance policies on the bankrupt's life. And, going further, by judicial construction, the Supreme Court has limited the property rights of the trustee in life insurance policies to what the bankrupt himself, whilst still alive, might have been able at the date of the filing of the bankruptcy petition to have obtained from the insurance company for their surrender, holding that it is not the policy, nor the bankrupt's interest in the policy, that passes subject to the right of redemption, but rather only the surrender value; so that the rule might now be stated as follows: The trustee is entitled to the cash surrender value, and only to the cash surrender value, that would have been obtainable from the insurance company at the date of the filing of the bankruptcy petition, upon all insurance policies on the bankrupt's life that are not exempt by state law and that are payable to the bankrupt, his estate or personal representative.[35a]

§ 1003. Proviso of § 70 (a) (5) Limits and Defines Trustee's Interests—Not Mere Method of Redemption of Policies Passing by Preceding Clause.—The proviso of § 70 (a) (5) then does not provide

35. Bankr. Act, § 70 (a), 70 (a) (5). The complete statement of the rule according to this apparently rejected doctrine would be as follows: Life insurance policies on the bankrupt's life which are not exempted by the State law and which are payable either absolutely, conditionally or contingently, in whole or in part, to the bankrupt himself or to his estate or personal representatives, or in which he has reserved the right to change the beneficiary, pass, to the extent of such absolute, conditional, partial or contingent interest, to the trustee in bankruptcy; but, if they had, at the date of the filing of the bankruptcy petition, either by contract or by negotiation with the insurer a cash surrender value, they are redeemable by the bankrupt or his personal representative or other party in interest by the payment or securing of payment to the trustee of such cash surrender value within thirty days after the trustee is notified by the company of such value.

35a. Everett v. Judson, 228 U. S. 474, 30 A. B. 1 (affirming In re Judson, 27 A. B. R. 704, 192 Fed. 834, C. C. A. N. Y.), quoted at § 1004; Andrews v. Partridge, 228 U. S. 479, 30 A. B. R. 4 (reversing Partridge v. Andrews, 27 A. B. R. 388, 191 Fed. 325, C. C. A. N. J.); Burlingham v. Crouse, 228 U. S. 459, 30 A. B. R. 6 (affirming S. C., 24 A. B. R. 632, 181 Fed. 479 C. C. A. N. Y.), quoted at §§ 1003, 1012, 1016.

a mere method for the bankrupt to redeem policies which otherwise would pass to the trustee, but it is in the nature of later legislation—a later clause[35b] —defining and limiting the trustee's interest in life insurance policies, confining it to the mere cash surrender value and furnishing the exclusive right and title of the trustee.[35c]

Burlingham v. Crouse; 228 U. S. 459, 30 A. B. R. 6 (affirming 24 A. B. R. 632, 181 Fed. 479): "True it is that life insurance policies are a species of property and might be held to pass under the general terms of subdiv. 5, § 70a, but a proviso dealing with a class of this property was inserted and must be given its due weight in construing the statute. It is also true that a proviso may sometimes mean simply additional legislation, and not be intended to have the usual and primary office of a proviso, which is to limit generalities and exclude from the scope of the statute that which would otherwise be within its terms. This proviso deals with explicitness with the subject of life insurance held by the bankrupt which has a surrender value. Originally life insurance policies were contracts in consideration of annual sums paid as premiums for the payment of a fixed sum on the death of the insured. It is true that such contracts have been much varied in form since, and policies payable in a period of years, so as to become investments and means of money saving, are in common use. But most of these policies will be found to have either a stipulated surrender value or an established value, the amount of which the companies are willing to pay, and which brings the policy within the terms of proviso (Hiscock v. Mertens, supra), and makes its present value available to the bankrupt estate. While life insurance is property, it is peculiar property. Legislatures of some of the states have provided that policies of insurance shall be exempt from liability for debt, and in many states provision is made for the protection from such liability of policies in favor of those depending upon the insured. See Holden v. Stratton, supra. Congress undoubtedly had the nature of insurance contracts in mind in passing § 70a with its proviso. Ordinarily the keeping up of insurance of either class would require the payment of premiums perhaps for a number of years. For this purpose the estate might or might not have funds, or the payments might be so deferred as to unduly embarrass the settlement of the estate. Congress recognized also that many policies at the time of bankruptcy might have a very considerable present value which a bankrupt could realize by surrendering its policy to the company. We think it was this latter sum that the act intended to secure to creditors by requiring its payment to the trustee as a condition of keeping the policy alive."

What meaning the Supreme Court would give, under such construction, to the concluding words of the statutory proviso, "otherwise the *policy* shall pass to the trustee as assets," it is, to be sure, difficult to conceive. Such concluding words would seem to be consistent only with the statement of the rule first enunciated in the preceding section, namely, that the policy, or the bankrupt's interest therein, itself passes subject merely to the right of redemption. Again, it is pertinent to inquire in what way the trustee would

35b. Though, in fact, it was not an amendment but was part of the original legislation.
35c. See citations at note 35a. But see, contra, In re Coleman, 14 A. B. R. 461, 136 Fed. 818 (C. C. A. N. Y.), quoted post at § 1008.

realize on his cash surrender value asset in the event of the failure or refusal of the bankrupt or his personal representative to redeem, unless on
the theory that the policy itself might pass to the trustee under certain circumstances. And it is perhaps proper here to observe that the Supreme
Court in the cases of Everett *v.* Judson, Andrews *v.* Partridge and Burlingham *v.* Crouse was concerned with the question of what date should
be taken for the right of redemption and the cash surrender value, the bankrupt in all three cases having died after the filing of the petition; so, that
strictly speaking the question was not before it as to whether the policy itself passed subject merely to the right of redemption, or only the cash surrender value. Moreover, in all three cases the policies had been assigned—
in one, absolutely, in the others, collaterally—before the bankruptcy for valuable consideration and they were therefore no longer "payable to the bankrupt, his estate or personal representatives" and so, even under the rejected
doctrine or any other doctrine enunciated in any of the decisions, they would
not have been assets of the estate, and the entire discussion seems to have
been somewhat unnecessary. Nor is the more recent ruling to be reconciled
with the utterances of the Supreme Court in Holden *v.* Stratton, 198 U. S.
214, 14 A. B. R. 94, wherein the court clearly takes the view that it is the
policy itself that passes unless redeemed by paying in the cash surrender
value, as will appear from the following quotation from that case:

"As § 70 (a) deals only with property which, not being exempt, passes to the
trustee, the mission of the proviso was, in the interest of the perpetuation of
policies of life insurance, to provide a rule by which where such policies passed
to the trustee because they were not exempt, if they had a surrender value their
future operation could be preserved by vesting the bankrupt with the privilege
of paying such surrender value; whereby the policy would be withdrawn out of
the category of an asset of the estate. That is to say the purpose of the proviso
was to confer a benefit upon the insured bankrupt by limiting the character of
the interest in a non-exempt life insurance policy which should pass to the trustee
and not to cause a policy when exempt to become an asset of the estate."

§ 1004. **Date of Filing Petition Controls.**—Although the Supreme
Court expressly holds, as shown in the preceding section, that class
5 of § 70 (a), namely, "property which, prior to the filing of the petition, the bankrupt could by any means have transferred, etc.," does
not concern the subject of life insurance policies; and, further, although Bankruptcy Act, § 70 (a), in its general statement says that the trustee is vested with the title of the bankrupt "as of the date he [the debtor]
was adjudged a bankrupt" yet the Supreme Court holds that as to life insurance policies the date of the vesting of title is not "as of the date he
[the debtor] was adjudged a bankrupt" but rather the date set for determining the kinds of property passing under Class 5, namely, the date
of "the filing of the bankruptcy petition," so holding on the theory that
Congress has manifested in other sections of the statute not specifically

treating of the subject, a general intent to vest title as of the date of the filing.[35d]

Everett v. Judson. 228 U. S. 474, 30 A. B. R. 1 (affirming In re Judson, 27 A. B. R. 704, 119 Fed. 834, C. C. A. N. Y.): "The present case has, however, a feature not directly involved in the case of Burlingham v. Crouse, because Judson, the insured, committed suicide before the adjudication in bankruptcy, although after the filing of the petition, and it is the contention of the petitioner that the Bankruptcy Act vested the title of the property in the trustee as of the time of the adjudication, and that the death of the bankrupt between the filing of the petition and the date of the adjudication made the proceeds of the policies assets in the hands of the trustee. While it is true that § 70a provides that the trustee, upon his appointment and qualification, becomes vested by operation of law with the title of the bankrupt as of the date he was adjudged a bankrupt, there are other provisions of the statute which, we think, evidenced the intention to vest in the trustee the title to such property as it was at the time of the filing of the petition. This subject was considered in Acme Harvester Co. v. Beekman Lumber Co., 222 U. S. 300, 27 Am. B. R. 262, 56 L. Ed. 208, 32 Sup. Ct. Rep. 96, wherein it was held that, pending the bankrupt proceedings and after the filing of the petition, no creditor could obtain by attachment a lien upon the property which would defeat the general purpose of the law to dedicate the property to all creditors alike. Section 70a vests all the property in the trustee, which, prior to the filing of the petition, the bankrupt could by any means have transferred, or which might have been levied upon and sold under judicial process against him. The bankrupt's discharge is from all provable debts and claims which existed on the day on which the petition for adjudication was filed. Zavelo v. Reeves, 227 U. S. 625, 630, 631, 29 Am. B. R. 493, 33 Sup. Ct. Rep. 365. The schedule that the bankrupt is required to file, showing the location and value of his property, must be filed with his petition. We think that the purpose of the law was to fix the line of cleavage with reference to the condition of the bankrupt estate as of the time at which the petition was filed, and that the property which vests in the trustee at the time of the adjudication is that which the bankrupt owned at the time of the filing of the petition. And it is as of that date that the surrender value of the insurance policies mentioned in § 70a should be ascertained. The subsequent suicide of the bankrupt before the adjudication was an unlooked-for circumstance which does not change the result in the light of the construction which we give the statute."

In re Judson, 27 A. B. R. 704, 192 Fed. 834 (C. C. A. N. Y., affirmed sub nom. Everett v. Judson, 228 U. S. 474, 30 A. B. R. 1, quoted supra): "Referring to the language of the provision in question as shown in the footnote, it seems clear that a trustee in bankruptcy takes title as of the date of the adjudication, not to the property owned by the bankrupt at that time, but to the property owned at the time of the filing of the petition. The trustee's title vests, it is true, as of the date of the adjudication, but the title which vests is limited to the property belonging to the bankrupt at the time of the commencement of the proceedings—the filing of the petition. The one date determines when the title vests; the other, the property to which the title vests. Property

---

35d. Andrews v. Partridge, 228 U. S. 479, 30 A. B. R. 4 (reversing Partridge v. Andrews, 27 A. B. R. 388, 191 Fed. 325, C. C. A. N. J.); Burlingham v. Crouse, 228 U. S. 459, 30 A. B. R. 6 (affirming S. C., 24 A. B. R. 632, 181 Fed. 479, C. C. A. N. Y.).

acquired by the bankrupt after the filing of the petition is not—to use the language of the act—property which 'prior to the filing of the petition he could by any means have transferred.' We think it clear that the time of the filing of the petition in this case should be taken as the date of cleavage determining the property passing to the trustee and through him to the creditors. Examining now into the situation of these life insurance policies at the time of the filing of the petition in bankruptcy we find, as already stated, that two of them had a small, and one of them no, cash surrender value. The two policies having a cash surrender value come within the express terms of the proviso of the statute and although the bankrupt died before making his election, we think that his executor had the right to tender the cash surrender value to the trustee and became entitled to the benefit of the policies."

§ 1005. Policies Exempt by State Law Do Not Pass.

—In any event policies exempt by State law do not pass, even if payable to the bankrupt or his estate and though they have cash surrender value and are not redeemed, the State exemption laws, by virtue of § 6 and § 70 (a) of the Bankruptcy Act, controlling all other sections of the act.[36]

Holden v. Stratton, 14 A. B. R. 94, 198 U. S. 202: "As we have said, § 6 of the Act adopts, for the purposes of the bankruptcy proceedings, the exemptions allowed by the laws of the several States. * * *

"It is beyond controversy that if the section just quoted stood alone, the policies in question would be exempt under the Bankrupt Act. The contention that they are not, arises from what is assumed to be a limitation imposed upon the terms of § 6 by a proviso found in § 70a of the act. * * *

"Considering the matter originally, it is, we think, apparent that § 6 is couched in unlimited terms, and is accompanied with no qualification whatever. Even a superficial analysis of § 70a, demonstrates that that section deals not with exemptions but solely with the nature and character of property, title to which passes to the trustee in bankruptcy. The opening clause of the section declares that the trustee after his appointment shall be vested 'by operation of law with the title of the bankrupt, * * * except in so far as it is to property which is exempt,' and this is followed by an enumeration under six headings, of the various classes of property which pass to the trustee. Clearly, the words 'ex-

---

36. Steele v. Buell, 5 A. B. R. 165, 104 Fed. 968 (C. C. A. Iowa, reversing In re Steele, 3 A. B. R. 549); contra, In re Scheld, 5 A. B. R. 102, 104 Fed. 870 (C. C. A.); contra, In re Lange, 1 A. B. R. 189, 91 Fed. 361 (D. C. Iowa, reversing 1 A. B. R. 187). Instance, not exempt; semi-tontine policy payable to wife if bankrupt dies during tontine period, is not exempt to him in New York until expiration of tontine period, In re Phelps, 15 A. B. R. 170 (Ref. N. Y.); In re Booss, 18 A. B. R. 658, 154 Fed. 494 (D. C. Pa.), an endowment policy; In re Pfaffinger, 21 A. B. R. 255, 164 Fed. 526 (D. C. Ky.), policy payable to wife but with change of beneficiary clause; In re Whelpley, 22 A. B. R. 433, 169 Fed. 1019 (D. C. N. H.); ob-iter, In re Moore, 23 A. B. R. 109, 173 Fed. 679 (D. C. Tenn.). Instance not exempt, semi-tontine policy, In re Wolff, 21 A. B. R. 452, 165 Fed. 984 (D. C. N. Y.), quoted at § 1009; instance held not exempt, In re White, 23 A. B. R. 90, 174 Fed. 333 (C. C. A. N. Y.); Allen v. Central Wisconsin Trust Co., 25 A. B. R. (126 Sup. Ct. Wis.); In re Orear, 24 A. B. R. 343, 178 Fed. 632 (C. C. A. Mo.), quoted on other point at § 1007; In re Schaefer, 26 A. B. R. 340, 189 Fed. 187 (D. C. Ohio); In re Carlon, 27 A. B. R. 18, 189 Fed. 815 (D. C. S. D.).

Policy payable to wife but with change of beneficiary clause. In re Johnson, 24 A. B. R. 277, 176 Fed. 591 (D. C. Minn.).

cept in so far as it is property which is exempt,' make manifest that it was the intention to exclude from the enumeration, property exempt by the Act. This qualification necessarily controls all the enumerations, and, therefore, excludes exempt property from all the provisions contained in the respective enumerations. The meaning now sought to be given to the proviso, cannot in reason be affixed to it without holding that the words 'except in so far as it is the property which is exempt,' do not control and limit the proviso. But to say this is to read out of the section the dominant limitations which it contains, and, therefore, to segregate the proviso from its context and cause it to mean exactly the reverse of what, when read in connection with the context, it necessarily implies." Reversing In re Holden, 7 A. B. R. 615 (C. C. A. Wash.).

Pulsifer *v.* Hussey, 9 A. B. R. 657, 97 Me. 434: "By the laws of Maine * * * this insurance is exempt from the claims of creditors, also by the Bankruptcy Act of 1898.

"The Bankrupt Act of 1898 provides, in § 6, that the 'act shall not affect the allowance to bankrupts of the exemptions which are prescribed by the State laws.' And § 70 of the Bankrupt Act provides that the trustee of the bankrupt shall 'be vested by operation of law with the title of the bankrupt * * * except in so far as it is to property which is exempt,' to various enumerated kinds of property and to 'property which prior to the filing of the petition he could by any means have transferred, or which might have been levied upon and sold under judicial process against him.' Held, that this clause must be construed in the light of the terms in the earlier part of the same section which excepts exempted property. Any other construction would annihilate all the exemptions especially provided for in the act."

The exemption of the proceeds of a life insurance policy upon death does not, however, exempt the policy itself during the bankrupt's life.

In re Moore, 23 A. B. R. 109, 173 Fed. 679 (D. C. Tenn.): "Section 2478 * * * provides that: 'Any life insurance effected by a husband on his own life shall, in case of his death, inure to the benefit of his widow and children; and the money thence arising shall be divided between them according to the law of distribution, without being in any manner subject to the debts of the husband, whether by attachment, execution or otherwise.' * * * After careful consideration of the Tennessee statutes and the decisions of the Supreme Court of Tennessee in reference thereto, I am of the opinion that these statutes do not exempt, in favor of the husband, during his life, policies of insurance upon his life, payable either to himself or to his estate, but merely exempt the proceeds of such policies, after his death, for the benefit of his widow and children or next of kin, free from the claims of his creditors. It is apparent from the face of these statutes that they create no exemption in favor of the husband himself, a construction which is emphasized by the fact that the Tennessee statute creating exemptions in favor of the heads of families does not include policies of insurance upon their own lives. Code Tenn., 1858, § 2391 (Shannon's Code, § 3794). Nor is there anything in either of these statutes indicating that it was intended to create any exemption, even in favor of the wife and children, during the life of the husband. On the contrary, § 2478 (Shannon's Code, § 4231) by its terms applies only in case of death of the husband, and provides for the division of the proceeds according to the law of distributions. And while § 2294 (Shannon's Code, § 4030) does not in terms refer to the husband's death, the fact that it was intended to apply only after his death is shown, not merely by its being found in the chapter relating to the administration of estates, but also by the provision that the insurance 'shall inure to the benefit of the widow an I next of kin, to be distributed as personal property;' such provision being manifestly applicable only after the husband's death."

Correspondingly, where the wife is in partnership with her husband, and the husband dies and the partnership becomes bankrupt, the proceeds of insurance policies, taken out by the husband in favor of his wife, are not, in general, exempt from the claims of partnership creditors, since the statute does not attempt to exempt such proceeds from the beneficiary's own debts, but only from the debts of the deceased.[37]

Thus, in some states policies of life insurance which have been taken out for the benefit of dependent relatives, are vested in them exempt from the claims of the creditors of the insured.[38]

The fact that the policy gave the insured certain benefits in his lifetime, and the right to change the beneficiary, does not change its character as exempt, if it is such under the state law.[39]

§ 1006. Policies Payable or Assigned Absolutely to Third Person.

—No title at all passes where the policies are payable absolutely to a wife or husband, or kindred of the insured bankrupt or to other third person.[40]

Obiter, Pulsifer v. Hussey, 9 A. B. R. 657, 97 Me. 434: "Section 70 of the Bankrupt Act does not include policies payable to a wife or kindred of the assured, but only applies to policies payable to the assured or his personal representatives."

Nor where assigned by valid assignment.[41]

Burlingham v. Crouse, 228 U. S. 459, 30 A. B. R. 6 (affirming S. C., 24 A. B. R. 632, 181 Fed. 479): "It is urged, however, that under § 70 (a) the cash surrender value was to be paid by the *bankrupt* when ascertained, and the policies kept alive for his benefit; and as these policies had been assigned by the beneficiary to McIntyre & Co., not as collateral, but absolutely, they would not come within the terms of the proviso, and therefore the proceeds of the policy vested in the bankrupt estate; but we find nothing in the act by which the right of the assignee of a policy to the benefits which would have accrued to the bankrupt is limited. As we have construed the statute, its purpose was to vest the surrender value in the trustee for the benefit of the creditors, and not otherwise to limit the bankrupt in dealing with his policy."

---

37. In re Day, 23 A. B. R. 785, 175 Fed. 1022 (D. C. Tenn.).
Married Woman's Separate Estate. —As to the bearing of the Tennessee statutes upon the married woman's separate estate, where she has embarked it in partnership enterprise, see In re Day, 23 A. B. R. 785 (D. C. Tenn.).
38. South Side Trust Co. v. Wilmarth, 29 A. B. R. 29, 199 Fed. 418 (C. C. A. Pa.). In this case, however, the rights in the policy passed for other reasons.

39. In re Orear, 26 A. B. R. 521, 178 Fed. 632 (C. C. A. Mo.).
40. In re Dews, 2 A. B. R. 483 (D. C. R. I.); In re Steele, 3 A. B. R. 549, 98 Fed. 78 (D. C. Iowa, reversed, on other points, in 5 A. B. R. 165); obiter, In re White, 23 A. B. R. 90, 174 Fed. 333 (C. C. A. N. Y.), quoted at § 1008.
41. In re Steele, 3 A. B. R. 549, 98 Fed. 78 (D. C. Iowa, reversed, on other points, in Steele v. Buell, 5 A. B. R. 165); obiter, South Side Trust Co. v. Wilmarth, 29 A. B. R. 29, 199 Fed. 418 (C. C. A. Pa.).

But where a policy the cash surrender value of which otherwise would have passed has been fraudulently assigned to a third person the trustee may doubtless recover the cash surrender value as the same stood at the date of the filing of the bankruptcy petition.[42]

Similarly, it would seem that an assignment of the policy within the four months preceding the bankruptcy could be a preference only to the extent of the cash surrender value as of the date of the filing of the bankruptcy petition.[42a]

§ 1007. Payable to Bankrupt, His Estate or Personal Representatives.

—The cash surrender values of policies which are payable to the bankrupt, his estate or personal representative and are not exempt—as such cash surrender values existed at the date of the filing of the bankruptcy petition—pass to the trustee in bankruptcy.[43]

Whether such is the complete statement of all the rights the trustee takes in insurance policies, all other interests remaining in the bankrupt or his personal representative, or that, as held formerly in some cases, the trustee takes such policies themselves subject merely to the right of redemption on the part of the bankrupt or his personal representative by paying or securing their cash surrender values, has been discussed ante, in §§ 1002. 1003, and 1004.[43a]

§ 1008. Payable Conditionally, Contingently or Partly to Bankrupt's Estate, as "Endowment" and "Tontine" Policies; Policies Assigned as Security, etc.

—Before the Supreme Court had announced its decision in the cases of Everett v. Judson, Burlingham v. Crouse and Andrews v. Partridge, discussed ante in §§ 1002, 1003, and 1004, wherein it has held that not the policy itself but only its cash surrender value passes to the

---

42. Kirkpatrick v. Johnson, 28 A. B. R. 291, 197 Fed. 235 (D. C. Pa.).

42a. Compare discussion ante, §§ 1002, 1003 and 1004, also Burlingham v. Crouse, 228 U. S. 459, 30 A. B. R. 6 (affirming S. C., 24 A. B. R. 632, 181 Fed. 479, C. C. A. N. Y.).

43. Everett v. Judson, 228 U. S. 474. 30 A. B. R. 1 (affirming In re Judson, 27 A. B. R. 704, 192 Fed. 834. C. C A. N. Y.); Andrews v. Partridge, 228 U. S. 479, 38 A. B. R. 4 (reversing Partridge v. Andrews, 27 A. B. R. 388, 191 Fed. 325, C. C. A. N. J.); Burlingham v. Crouse. 228 U. S. 459, 30 A. B. R. 6 (affirming S. C., 24 A. B. R. 632, 181 Fed. 479), quoted at §§ 1003, 1016; Pulsifer v. Hussey, 9 A. B. R. 657, 97 Me. 434, quoted at § 1005, where the court says not only that it is only cash surrender value that goes to the trustee but that it is only such cash surrender value as the policy possesses by its very terms; and

that if it has no cash surrender value it remains the bankrupt's property. In re McDonnell, 4 A. B. R. 92, 101 Fed. 239 (D. C. Iowa); In re Hernich, 1 A. B. R. 713 (Ref. Md., rejected in In re Boardman, 4 A. B. R. 622, 103 Fed. 783 [D. C. Mass.]).

43a. Holdings before supreme courts' decisions discussed ante, at §§ 1002, 1003 and 1004. In re Moore, 23 A. B. R. 109, 173 Fed. 679 (D. C. Tenn.); Van Kirk v. Slate Co., 15 A. B. R. 239, 140 Fed. 38 (D. C. N. Y.); In re Slingluff, 5 A. B. R. 76, 106 Fed. 154 (D. C. Md.).

See inferentially, Meyers v. Josephson, 10 A. B. R. 687, 124 Fed. 734 (C. C. A. Ga.), where the court intimates that the trustee might sell such policy for what it would bring, reversing In re Josephson, 9 A. B. R. 345, where the court in an obiter dictum had remarked that such a policy would go free to the bankrupt.

trustee, many of the lower courts, following the doctrine that it was the policy itself which passed subject merely to the bankrupt's right of redemption by the paying or securing of the cash surrender value, had ruled that, where the bankrupt's interest in such policies was not absolute or exclusive, that is to say, where an interest in the policies was, to be sure, "payable to the bankrupt, his estate or personal representative" but was so payable only on the happening of some contingency, or only conditionally or partially as in tontine policies, etc., then that such contingent, conditional or partial interest would pass to the trustee, to sell for what it might be worth subject merely to the right of the bankrupt, or his personal representative in the event of his death, to redeem such interest by paying the cash surrender value.

In re Coleman, 14 A. B. R. 461, 136 Fed. 818 (C. C. A. N. Y.): "Section 70, subd. 5, contains a proviso which is intended to modify the right of the trustee to take title to policies by enabling the bankrupt to retain policies that have a cash surrender value by paying the amount thereof to the trustee. This is a privilege conferred upon the bankrupt respecting the class of policies that have an ascertainable cash value. In such case the rights of the parties are specifically stated. The value of such a policy is easily ascertainable, and the bankrupt is given an opportunity to pay the ascertained value and keep the policy. This peculiar favor to the bankrupt is a limitation upon the trustee's right, but the proviso is not to be regarded as the sole grant of power to the trustee to take policies not exempt. The trustee's capacity to take this and other property is found in the portion of the statute, whereby he is vested with the title to all 'property which, prior to the filing of the petition, he (bankrupt) could by any means have transferred or which might have been levied upon or sold under judicial process against him.' This is sufficiently comprehensive to carry to the trustee the policies in question."

Thus, as to policies payable to the wife or if the wife dies first, then to the bankrupt's estate, the bankrupt's contingent interest was held under the now rejected doctrine to pass to the trustee,[44] likewise where the policy contained the added proviso that the bankrupt himself might at any time surrender the policy for "paid up" insurance or other value.

In re White, 23 A. B. R. 90, 174 Fed. 333 (C. C. A. N. Y.): "The district judge was of opinion that the wife of the bankrupt was the legal owner of the policy; that it was her property, and if the insured had the option of terminating her ownership he had not exercised it. But we think the policy is the property of the husband; that the contract is made with him and that the wife's interest depends on the contingency of her surviving him. If the property in the policy were absolutely the wife's, the insurance would be payable upon her death to her estate. Certainly the bankrupt has an interest in the policy. If he survive his wife the insurance will be payable not to her estate, but to him or to his estate or to a beneficiary designated by him. This is a vested future interest. Besides this, though not obliged by the contract to do so, the company is willing, apparently under the option given the insured to surrender the policy for

44. In re Holden, 7 A. B. R. 615, 113 Fed. 141 (C. C. A. Wash., reversed, on other grounds, in Holden v. Stratton, 14 A. B. R. 94, 198 U. S. 202).

paid-up insurance or other value, to pay the sum of $1,804.23 upon its surrender. The situation is exactly the same as if the policy contained a stipulation for a cash surrender value. Hiscock v. Mertens, 205 U. S. 202, 17 Am. B. R. 483, affirming this court in 15 Am. B. R. 701, 142 Fed. 445. These are clearly interests of the bankrupt which go to the trustee under § 70a (5) of the Bankruptcy Act, subject, of course, to the privilege therein reserved to the bankrupt to keep the policy free from the claims of his creditors participating in the distribution of his estate by paying its value, $1,804.23, to the trustee."

Or might change the beneficiary.[45] Thus, as to endowment policies payable to the bankrupt at the end of the endowment period or to his wife if death occurred before the expiration of the endowment period, the bankrupt's defeasible interest was, by this line of cases, held under the rejected rule to pass to the trustee, subject always of course to the right of redemption.[46]

Likewise, *"tontine"* policies payable to the bankrupt, his executors, administrators or assigns on a date named, or if he die before then to his mother or wife or other relative, if living, or if not living then to his heirs, administrators or assigns, having cash surrender value, were held to pass to the trustee subject to the relative's rights, and subject, of course, to the redemption rights.[47]

Likewise, as to a *semi-tontine policy* payable to the wife in case of the bankrupt's death before the end of the tontine period, the bankrupt having the option to receive cash at the end of the tontine period if he survive, the interest of the bankrupt was held under the now rejected doctrine to vest in the trustee.[48]

In re Mertens, 12 A. B. R. 712, 131 Fed. 972 (D. C. N. Y.): "While courts and judges of great learning have differed as to the proper construction of this section, it seems clear to this court that the policies in question here, containing as they do provisions beyond the ordinary life insurance policy, and in the nature of a contract for the investment of earnings under the policy, constitute assets, and have passed to the trustee, unless the bankrupt has prevented such effect by his action. This depends wholly on whether or not these policies have a 'cash surrender value payable to the insured,' J. M. Mertens 'his estate or personal representatives,' within the intent and meaning of § 70, above quoted."

Thus, also, policies in which the bankrupt or his estate had only a partial interest, as in cases of assignment of part, assignment as security, interest of a wife arising in equity by virtue of the payment of premiums, etc.[49]

45. In re Hettling, 23 A. B. R. 161, 175 Fed. 65 (C. C. A. N. Y.).

46. In re Diack, 3 A. B. R. 723, 100 Fed. 770 (D. C. N. Y.); Clark v. Ins. Co., 16 A. B. R. 138, 143 Fed. 175 (U. S. C. C. Pa.); In re Loveland, 27 A. B. R. 765, 192 Fed. 1005 (D. C. Mass.).

47. In re Boardman, 4 A. B. R. 620, 103 Fed. 783 (D. C. Mass.); impliedly Pulsifer v. Hussey, 9 A. B. R. 657, 97 Me. 434; Clark v. Ins. Co., 16 A. B. R. 140, 143 Fed. 175 (U. S. C. C. Pa.);

In re Wolff, 21 A. B. R. 452, 165 Fed. 984 (D. C. N. Y.), quoted at § 1009.

48. In re Phelps, 15 A. B. R. 170 (Ref. N. Y.); In re Slingluff, 5 A. B. R. 76, 106 Fed. 154 (D. C. Md.); In re Welling, 7 A. B. R. 345, 113 Fed. 189 (C. C. A. Ills.); impliedly, In re Becker, 5 A. B. R. 438, 106 Fed. 54 (D. C. N. Y.); In re Churchill, 29 A. B. R. 153, 197 Fed. 111, 114 (D. C. Wis., reversed, 31 A. B. R. 1, 198 Fed. 711, D. C. Wis.).

49. Impliedly, In re Boardman, 4 A.

Impliedly, In re Diack, 3 A. B. R. 723, 100 Fed. 770 (D. C. N. Y.): "It is immaterial here whether the lien of Mrs. Diack for the premiums paid by her be treated as a legal or as a merely equitable lien. In bankruptcy both alike are preserved. In my view Mrs. Diack, under the law of this State, from the moment the policy had any surrender value through the payment of premiums, became entitled by its terms to a contingent legal interest in it, which entitled her to pay the premiums upon it, if necessary, in order to prevent it from lapsing; and on a surrender of the policy, defeating its ultimate provisions, any such payments previously made by her would create in her favor an equitable lien or charge upon her husband's interest for the same proportion of those payments that her husband's interest in the surrender value of the policy bore to the whole surrender value."

Also, subject, of course, to the rights of any pledgee or assignee for other purpose,[50] and also subject to the right of redemption.

But only such conditional, contingent or partial interest was held to pass to the trustee; as, for example, where a policy was payable to the wife absolutely but, in addition, provided for an annuity to the husband at the expiration of twenty years.[51]

However, the above distinctions will be of no importance and the cases will be misleading if the Supreme Court's construction of the life insurance proviso of § 70 (a) (5) means that in no event the policy itself passes but at best only its cash surrender value, as discussed at §§ 1002, 1003 and 1004. As a practical deduction from the holding it would seem of necessity that even the cash surrender value would not pass in cases of partial, contingent or conditional interests but only where the policy is payable entirely, absolutely and unconditionally to the bankrupt, his estate or personal representative.[51a]

§ 1009. Change of Beneficiary.—Policies payable to a wife or husband of the bankrupt or kindred or other person, wherein the insured reserves the right to change the beneficiary at will, are property which the bankrupt could, by some means, have transferred precisely as much as are those which are payable to the insured himself or to his estate. They amount to no more than a direction to pay to a certain one after death a policy that up to the time of death the bankrupt himself could have "transferred" at pleasure.[52]

B. R. 620, 103 Fed. 783 (D. C. Mass.), impliedly, Pulsifer v. Hussey, 9 A. B. R. 657, 97 Me. 434; In re Wolff, 21 A. B. R. 452, 165 Fed. 984 (D. C. N. Y.), quoted at § 1007.

50. In re Wolff, 21 A. B. R. 452, 165 Fed. 984 (D. C. N. Y.), quoted at § 1009. Compare, Clark v. Ins. Co., 16 A. B. R. 138, 143 Fed. 175 (U. S. C. C. A. Pa.).

A fortiori (pledgee also paying premiums, has lien therefor), Burlingham v. Crouse, 24 A. B. R. 632, 181 Fed. 479 (C. C. A. N. Y., affirmed in 228 U.. S. 459, 30 A. B. R. 6), quoted at § 1012.

51. In re Schaefer, 26 A. B. R. 340, 189 Fed. 187 (D. C. Ohio).

51a. In re Churchill, 31 A. B. R. 1, 198 Fed. 711 (D. C. Wis., reversing 29 A. B. R. 153, 197 Fed. 111).

52. Foxhever v. Order of the Red Cross, 2 Ohio C. C. Reports (N. S.) 394. Apparently, but obiter, In re Whelpley, 22 A. B. R. 433, 169 Fed. 1019 (D. C. N. H.); apparently contra, but obiter because exempt, In re Pfaffinger, 21 A. B. R. 255, 164 Fed. 526 (D. C. Ky.); compare, partially pro, though not squarely on the point, In re Hettling, 23 A. B. R. 161, 175 Fed. 65 (C. C. A. N. Y.); In re Hyman J. Herr

Compare, though not placed squarely on the ground, In re Wolff, 21 A. B. R. 452, 165 Fed. 984 (D. C. N. Y.): "The policy was made payable to the wife of the bankrupt, 'if living, if not, then to the assured's executors, administrators or assigns, subject to the right of the assured to change the beneficiary.' * * * The provision for the changing of beneficiaries is as follows: 'This policy is issued with the express understanding that the assured may, provided this policy has not been assigned, change the beneficiary, or beneficiaries, at any time during the continuance of this policy, by filing with the society a written request, duly acknowledged, accompanied by said policy.' It will be seen by this that the consent of the wife was not necessary to a change of beneficiary. Further, an option was given to the assured, if living at the time of the payment of the last premium, to receive a cash dividend, and to draw the entire cash value of the policy according to a certain table, together with this dividend, or to choose any one of several other plans which have nothing to do with this particular case. * * * In the present case, the policy is payable to the wife, if living at the time of the death of the bankrupt. This in terms makes her estate contingent upon survivorship, and the insured, as has been stated above, was given the privilege of changing the beneficiary, or, if he survived the full period, of diverting the payment from the wife by acceptance of certain of the conditions. The policy was therefore in the nature of what is sometimes called a semi-tontine policy, payable to the bankrupt at a certain date, or, if he should die before that time, to the wife if living. The latter form was passed upon in the case of In re Diack, 3 Am. B. R. 723 (D. C.), 100 Fed. 770, and the wife was there held to be entitled only to the proportionate part of the policy represented by the premiums which she had actually paid. The same idea has been expressed in a number of cases (In re Boardman [D. C.] 4 Am. B. R. 620, 103 Fed. 783; In re Phelps, 15 Am. B. R. 170; In re Coleman, 14 Am. B. R. 461, 136 Fed. 818, 69 C. C. A. 496), and has been followed in the courts of the state of New York in Waldron v. Becker, 33 Misc. 182, 68 N. Y. Supp. 402. In those cases it has been stated that the only policies which are entirely exempt under the state statutes, such as the New York domestic relations law above mentioned, are those in which the wife is the sole beneficiary. The result of this would seem to be that the trustee in bankruptcy was entitled to claim as of the date of adjudication the surrender value of whatever portion of the policy in question had been obtained or had accrued from the premiums paid by the bankrupt himself. A loan having been made by the Equitable Life Assurance society, and the policy assigned as security, it makes no difference whether this loan was procured for the benefit of Mr. or Mrs. Wolff, inasmuch as they both joined therein. Inasmuch as the surrender value was at all times security for the loan, the surrender value was thereby reduced to the extent of the principal of the loan with interest, and this should be deducted at the outset. The premiums from the date of the loan to the time of adjudication were all paid by Mrs. Wolff, and she has therefore in equity become entitled to whatever proportion of the surrender value has been acquired through the payment of these premiums."

(No. 2), 25 A. B. R. 142, 182 Fed. 715, 716 (D. C. Pa.); In re Catherine A. Dolan, 25 A. B. R. 145, 182 Fed. 949 (D. C. Pa.); In re Loveland, 27 A. B. R. 765, 192 Fed. 1005 (D. C. Mass.).
Provided, of course, that the policy be not exempt. In re Johnson, 24 A.

B. R. 277, 176 Fed. 591 (D. C. Minn.); Instance, Kirkpatrick v. Johnson, 28 A. B. R. 291, 197 Fed. 235 (D. C. Pa.); Instance, South Side Trust Co. v. Wilmarth, 29 A. B. R. 29, 199 Fed. 418 (C. C. A. Pa.).

In re Orear, 24 A. B. R. 343, 178 Fed. 632 (C. C. A. Mo.): "Subdivision 5 of § 70 specifies as property the title to which will vest in the trustee: 'Property which prior to the filing of the petition he (bankrupt) could by any means have transferred or which might have been levied upon and sold under judicial process against him.'

"Subdivision 25, § 1, of the Bankruptcy Act, provides that 'the word "transfer" shall include the sale and every other and different mode of disposing of, or parting with, property, absolutely or conditionally as a payment, pledge, mortgage, gift or security.' All of the policies of insurance in controversy contained the following provisions: 'The insured may nominate a beneficiary or beneficiaries hereunder, and may also change any beneficiary or beneficiaries nominated by him or named in the policy.'

"Under this provision the insured was unequivocally given the right and power to change the beneficiary in each policy without the concurrence of the beneficiary named in the policy and even against the will of such beneficiary. Not only so, but this power was one which he could exercise for his own benefit. To illustrate: He could have borrowed money and have changed the beneficiary so that the lender would have held the policy as security for the repayment of his money. He also could have exercised this power so ·as to have secured indulgence from an existing creditor. He further could have exercised this power so as to have made the policy payable to his own estate. He still further could have exercised this power by naming as the beneficiary some trustee for all his creditors. See Atlantic Mut. Life Ins. Co. v. Gannon, 179 Mass. 291, 60 N. E. 933.

"Of the case of Central Nat. Bank v. Hume, 128 U. S. 195, it is enough to say that the policies there in question did not empower the insured to change the beneficiary, but contained provisions to the contrary, as is shown by the statement preceding the opinion. Neither did the policy in Gordon v. Ware National Bank, hereinafter cited, so empower the insured.

"In the case of Gordon v. Ware National Bank, 132 Fed. 444, this court in an opinion where all the cases are cited held that the owner of a policy of insurance may lawfully and in good faith assign the same to a creditor who has no insurable·interest in the assignor to secure the payment of a debt, and that on default of payment the creditor may foreclose the pledge and sell the policy at judicial sale. It necessarily results from this state of the law that Jacob W. Derr, prior to the filing of the petition in bankruptcy, could have transferred to one or more of his creditors the insurance policies in question to secure the payment of his debts. This being so, the policies were property which, under § 70, subd. 5, above mentioned, passed to the trustee upon the adjudication of Derr as a bankrupt." In the case In re Orear there were eight policies, in one of which the wife was named as beneficiary, and in three others of which the sister was so named, the four remaining policies having no beneficiary named.

But of course the right to change the beneficiary would not, of itself, vest title in the trustee as to policies which are exempt under local law.[53]

---

53. In re Orear, 26 A. B. R. 521, 178 Fed. 632 (C. C. A. Mo.); In re Johnson, 24 A. B. R. 277, 176 Fed. 591 (D. C. Minn.). See ante, § 1005.
Under the rejected doctrine that the policy itself passed, subject merely to redemption, it had never been decided whether the court should act without notice to the named beneficiary, though in one case the point seemed to have been raised and notice not required,

However, the Supreme Court's ruling, discussed ante, §§ 1002, 1003, and 1004, based as it is on a rejection of the doctrine that life insurance policies themselves pass under class 5 and on an affirmation of the opposite doctrine that the proviso is the sole source of title and must alone be looked to, would seem necessarily to prevent the passing of even the cash surrender value of a change of beneficiary policy.(except of course a policy where the beneficiary is expressly the bankrupt or his estate), since the policy itself does not come within the strict wording of the proviso as being "payable to the bankrupt, his estate or personal representative," being only capable of being made so.

§ 1010. Bankrupt Required to Execute Papers to Realize on Policies.—The bankrupt may be required to execute assignments or other

In re Orear, 24 A. B. R. 343, 178 Fed. 632 (C. C. A. Mo.).

Where Bankrupt the Beneficiary.— Conversely, where it is the bankrupt that is the beneficiary in such a policy containing a change of beneficiary clause—there is no such vested interest as will pass to the trustee, In re Hogan, 28 A. B. R. 166, 194 Fed. 846 (C. C. A. Wis.), quoted at § 1017.

Holdings, before Supreme Court's ruling that policy itself does not pass, but only cash surrender value: In re Hyman J. Herr (No. 2), 25 A. B. R. 142, 182 Fed. 715, 716 (D. C. Pa.).

Clark v. Equitable Life Assur. Soc., 16 A. B. R. 137, 143 Fed. 175 (U. S. C. C. Pa.): "The policy in question was a tontine policy and probably has no cash surrender value, but, even if it had, the bankrupt never availed himself of the privilege given by the proviso, and the policy therefore passed to the trustee as assets of the estate. That policies of life insurance such as this, having an actual value, pass to the trustee, has been directly decided by several of the Federal courts." In re White, 23 A. B. R. 90, 174 Fed. 333 (C. C. A.), quoted ante, § 1006; In re Hettling, 23 A. B. R. 161, 175 Fed. 65 (C. C. A. N. Y.). Obiter, Gould v. N. Y. Life Ins. Co., 13 A. B. R. 237, 132 Fed. 927 (D. C. Ark.): "That Congress did not intend to prevent the vesting in the trustee of the title to life policies which have a cash value but have no surrender value clearly appears from the language used, for, had that been the intention of Congress, there would have been no trouble to express it in terms neither ambiguous nor subject to different constructions.

"Another reason why it is clearly apparent that Congress did not intend to prevent a trustee in bankruptcy from becoming vested with the title to policies which have a cash value, but no surrender value, is that it is a well-known fact that until within the last few years many of the leading life insurance companies did not issue policies which had a cash surrender value at any time before maturity, basing their refusal to do so upon the meritorious ground that the right of surrender would in many instances defeat the beneficent object of life insurance to provide a fund for the family of the assured after his death, as the fact that the money could be obtained at any time by a loan or a surrender of the policy would tempt the assured to avail himself of this privilege whenever his business interests required any moneys which he could not otherwise easily obtain. Many of the tontine policies, when first issued, not only made no provision for a cash surrender value, but contained a special provision for an entire forfeiture of the policy upon the failure of the assured to pay a single premium at maturity, although such premium was the last one to be paid before the maturity of the policy.

"If the contention of the learned counsel for the defendant is correct, such a policy, no matter how great its actual value, or how large a sum could be obtained by a sale thereof, would still remain the property of the bankrupt. It requires no extended argument to show that such a construction would be in conflict with the entire spirit of the Bankruptcy Act. The court is clearly of the opinion that the title to a life policy payable, as this was, to the assured's executors, administrators, or assigns, passes to the trustee upon the adjudication of bankruptcy, even if it had no surrender value, provided it has a real cash value, which could be realized either by sale by the trustee or otherwise."

papers to the trustee to enable the latter to realize upon the policies.[57]

In re Coleman, 14 A. B. R. 461, 136 Fed. 818 (C. C. A. N. Y.): "The trustee is at liberty to sell the husband's interest in the Equitable policy, and the bankrupt should execute an assignment of his interest to the trustee for the purpose of enabling the latter to give title on such sale."

In re Phelps, 15 A. B. R. 170 (Ref. N. Y.): "A bankrupt may not only be required to assign to the trustee his interest in such a policy but also may be required to execute a power of attorney to exercise such options at and after the expiration of the tontine period."

§ 1011. If No Actual Cash Surrender Value, at Date of -Filing Bankruptcy Petition.

—But if there be no cash surrender value, at the date of the filing of the bankruptcy petition, then the policy will remain the bankrupt's property; and nothing will pass to the trustee.[60]

---

57. See post, §§ 1115, 1835; ante, § 460; In re Diack, 3 A. B. R. 723, 100 Fed. 770 (D. C. N. Y.); In re Wolff, 21 A. B. R. 452, 165 Fed. 984 (D. C. N. Y.), quoted on other points at § 1007. Compare same rule as to licenses, In re Wiesel & Knaup, 23 A. B. R. 59, 173 Fed. 718 (D. C. Pa.), and ante, § 969; (on the facts) In re Orear, 24 A. B. R. 343, 178 Fed. 632 (C. C. A. Mo.), quoted on other points at § 1007.

60. Everett v. Judson, 228 U. S. 474, 30 A. B. R. 1 (affirming In re Judson, 27 A. B. R. 704, 192 Fed. 834, C. C. A. N. Y.); Andrews v. Partridge, 228 U. S. 479, 30 A. B. R. 4, reversing Partridge v. Andrews, 27 A. B. R. 388, 191 Fed. 325 C. C. A. N. J.); Burlingham v. Crouse, 228 U. S. 459, 30 A. B. R. 6 (affirming 24 A. B. R. 632, 181 Fed. 479 C. C. A. N. Y.); In re Phelps, 15 A. B. R. 170 (Ref. N. Y.); In re Josephson, 9 A. B. R. 350, 121 Fed. 142 (D. C. Ga., affirmed in Meyer v. Josephson, 10 A. B. R. 987, 124 Fed. 734); (perhaps also) Pulsifer v. Hussey, 9 A. B. R. 659, 97 Me. 434.

Contra holdings before Supreme Court's ruling discussed ante, §§ 1002, 1003, 1004, and post, § 1016. Contra, In re Welling, 7 A. B. R. 345, 113 Fed. 189 (C. C. A. Ills.); contra, In re Slingluff, 5 A. B. R. 76, 106 Fed. 154 (D. C. Md.); contra, In re Steele, 3 A. B. R. 549, 98 Fed. 78 (D. C. Iowa, reversed, on other grounds, in Steel v. Buell, 5 A. B. R. 165, 104 Fed. 968). Also, contra, obiter, Gould v. N. Y. Life Ins. Co., 13 A. B. R. 236, 132 Fed. 927 (D. C. Ark.): "Were it not for the proviso to subdivision 5, the bankrupt would not be entitled to any privilege whatever in relation to his life policies. It is only by virtue of the proviso that he is given the option of becoming the purchaser of the policies upon payment by him of the cash surrender value. and of that he must avail himself within 30 days after the value has been ascertained. The proviso does not control the vesting of the title to the bankrupt's estate. It merely modifies it as to one item, viz: life policies which have a cash surrender value. * * * it is doubtful whether any other policy than that which has a cash surrender value is subject to redemption by the bankrupt."

Also contra In re Mertens, 12 A. B. R. 712, 131 Fed. 972 (D. C. N. Y.): "While courts and judges of great learning have differed as to the proper construction of this section, it seems clear to this court that the policies in question here, containing as they do provisions beyond the ordinary life insurance policy, and in the nature of a contract for the investment of earnings under the policy, constitute assets, and have passed to the trustee, unless the bankrupt has prevented such effect by his action. This depends wholly on whether or not these policies have a 'cash surrender value payable to the insured,' J. M. Mertens, 'his estate or personal representatives,' within the intent and meaning of § 70, above quoted."

Also contra, obiter, Pulsifer v. Hussey, 9 A. B. R. 659, 97 Me. 434: "But for it, in states where life policies are not exempted, and no beneficiary is named, the entire interest in the insurance would pass to the trustee."

Also contra, Clark v. Equit. Life Ass. Soc., 16 A. B. R. 137, 143 Fed. 175. XXXV Ins. Law Journ. 257 (U. S. C. C. Pa.): "The policy in question was a tontine policy and probably has no cash surrender value, but, even if it had, the bankrupt never availed himself of the privilege given by the pro-

Gould *v.* N. Y. Life Ins. Co., 13 A. B. R. 233, 132 Fed. 927 (D. C. Ark.): "But, if the policy has no actual cash value, does the title vest in the trustee? That this policy had no real cash value is apparent from the agreed statement of facts. The policy had been in force only one year. The first premium had not yet been paid, although the policy, having been delivered, was in full force. The assured was, at the time of his death, only 30 years of age, and in good health. The annual premium for the next 19 years was $254.85. Unless the second annual premium was paid on or before the 16th day of June, 1904, the policy would become absolutely worthless on the 16th day of July, 1904. The trustee made no efforts to pay the premium, and it is hardly necessary to state that, had he applied to the court for directions, the court would not only not have authorized him to pay the premium on the policy, but would have directed him to surrender it. It was the unfortunate suicide of the bankrupt less than a month before the policy became absolutely void which made it a valuable asset.

"The general rule is that personalty which has no salable value, such as books of account, private manuscripts, family pictures, and heirlooms, are not subject to levy and sale under execution; for the object of an execution, as is that of bankruptcy proceedings, is to realize something substantial for the benefit of creditors, and not to harass the debtor. If nothing could be realized either by a surrender or a sale of the policy, there was nothing to pass to the trustee. * * * The mere chance that the bankrupt might die, or, as in this case, commit suicide, within the short time the policy was to remain in force, is not a privilege which the law will protect. It would be a mere wager on the life of an unfortunate debtor, and for this reason against public policy. * * * As the policy at the time of the bankrupt's adjudication was practically of no value, for it could not have been surrendered for a cash consideration, nor, in the opinion of the court, could anything have been realized if offered for sale—and that the trustee was of that opinion is evidenced by the fact that he made no efforts to sell the same, or even have it appraised as property of the bankrupt—there was nothing to pass to the trustee except the right to speculate on the bankrupt's life for a short time; and neither the Bankruptcy Act nor any other statute authorizes this."

In re Buelow, 3 A. B. R. 389, 98 Fed. 86 (D. C. Wash.): "They have no cash surrender value, and no value for any purpose except as they may become valuable at the time of the death of the insured, provided the premiums shall be kept paid. Therefore they are not assets of the bankrupt estate." This case was distinguished in In re Coleman, 14 A. B. R. 464 (C. C. A. N. Y.).

In re Judson, 27 A. B. R. 704, 192 Fed. 834 (C. C. A. N. Y., affirmed sub nom. Everett *v.* Judson, 228 U. S. 474, 30 A. B. R. 1): "But we

viso (proviso to clause 5 of § 70 of the Bankrupt Act. 1898) and the policy therefore passed to the trustee as assets of the estate."

Also contra, Van Kirk *v.* Slate Co., 15 A. B. R. 239, 140 Fed. 38 (D. C. N. Y.): "The proviso * * * does not include those policies in which the right to surrender is not provided for therein: they pass to and vest in the trustee as of the date of adjudication."

Also contra, In re Orear, 24 A. B. R. 343, 178 Fed. 632 (C. C. A. Mo.): "We think the District Court fell into error in holding that the policies of insurance

did not pass to the trustee. Its judgment that they did not pass was based upon the erroneous proposition that the proviso in § 70 above quoted, defined and limited what insurance policies should pass. Whereas, the true construction to be given to said proviso requires us to hold that it simply excepts from the property of the bankrupt which would otherwise pass to the trustee under the other provisions of § 70, policies of insurance which have a cash surrender value, either by the term of the policy or by the concession of the insurance company."

do not not place our decision with respect to these policies solely upon the ground that they had a trifling cash surrender value at the time of the filing of the petition and so came expressly within the provision. We place it also upon a broader ground which applied likewise to the policy having no cash surrender value. We think that the statute in question clearly indicates an intention upon the part of Congress to permit bankrupts to retain the advantages of existing life insurance policies provided they will pay to their trustees all that could be obtained by surrendering such policies at the commencement of the proceedings. In the case of policies having a cash surrender value, the proviso covers the case. In the case of policies having no cash surrender value, the proviso does not apply expressly, but reading it in connection with the other provisions we think that such policies are not 'property' within the meaning of the statute, but are in the nature of .personal rights. True, they are 'property' within technical definitions of that term. But they represent nothing more than the right to pay future premiums at a fixed rate. Their value is altogether speculative, and in our opinion it was not the intention of Congress that bankrupts should be deprived of their policies to enable trustees of bankrupt estates to use their funds to speculate with."

$^{\tau}$hey will not pass to the trustee even if the bankrupt dies before the estate is closed ; [61] or after the filing of the bankruptcy petition and before adjudication.[62]

§ 1012. Pledging the Policy or Borrowing upon Cash Surrender Value.

—Likewise, if the policy has been assigned or pledged, or if the bankrupt has borrowed from the company upon it, to its full surrender value or partially, then to that same extent the cash surrender value passing to the trustee is diminished.[63]

Compare Burlingham v. Crouse, 228 U. S. 459, 30 A. B. R. 6 (affirming S. C., 24 A. B. R. 632, 181 Fed. 479): "It is urged, however, that under § 70 (a) the cash surrender value was to be paid by the *bankrupt* when ascertained, and the policies kept alive for *his* benefit; and as these policies had been assigned by the beneficiary to McIntyre & Co., not as collateral, but absolutely, they would not come within the terms of the proviso, and therefore the proceeds of the policy

61. Gould v. N. Y. Life Ins. Co., 13 A. B. R. 233, 132 Fed. 927 (D. C. Ark.), quoted supra.

62. Everett v. Judson, 228 U. S. 474, 30 A. B. R. 1 (affirming In re Judson, 27 A. B. R. 704, 192 Fed. 834, C. C. A. N. Y.), quoted at § 1004; Burlingham v. Crouse, 228 U. S. 459, 30 A. B. R. 6 (affirming 24 A. B. R. 632, 181 Fed. 479, C. C. A. N. Y.); Andrews v. Partridge, 228 U. S. 479, 30 A. B. R. 4 (reversing Partridge v. Andrews, 27 A. B. R. 388, 191 Fed. 325, C. C. A. N. J.).

It was held, before the Supreme Court's rulings discussed ante §§ 1002, 1003, and 1004, that even though the policy had no cash surrender value at the date of adjudication, but a few months later and without further payment would have a paid-up value and could be used as collateral to a loan, it had a substantial value as property, to the benefit of which the trustee was entitled. In re Coleman, 14 A. B. R. 461, 136 Fed. 818 (C. C. A. N. Y.). Also it was formerly held that, even though there be no cash surrender value at the date of adjudication and yet by the payment of a commission the policy might be given a cash surrender value, it might pass. In re Orear, 24 A. B. R. 343, 178 Fed. 632 (C. C. A. Mo.).

63. Everett v. Judson, 228 U. S. 474, 30 A. B. R. 1 (affirming In re Judson, 27 A. B. R. 704, 192 Fed. 834, C. C. A. N. Y.), quoted at § 1004; In re Judson, 27 A. B. R. 704, 192 Fed. 834 (C. C. A. N. Y.), quoted at § 1016; Andrews v. Partridge, 228 U. S. 479, 30 A. B. R. 4 (reversing Partridge v. Andrews, 27 A. B. R. 388, 191 Fed. 325, C. C. A. N. J.).

vested in the bankrupt estate; but we find nothing in the act by which the right of the assignee of a policy to the benefits which would have accrued to the bankrupt is limited. As we have construed the statute, its purpose was to vest the surrender value in the trustee for the benefit of the creditors, and not otherwise to limit the bankrupt in dealing with his policy." Quoted further at § 1003 and § 1010.

Burlingham v. Crouse, 24 A. B. R. 632, 181 Fed. 479 (C. C. A. N. Y. affirmed in 228 U. S. 459, 30 A. B. R. 6): "The meaning and intent of Congress in enacting this proviso is, in the opinion of the majority of the court, very clear when we consider the practice of insurance companies. The original idea of life insurance was to contract with the insurer that if certain yearly premiums were regularly paid during the lifetime of the insured a specified sum of money would upon his death be paid by the insurer to a person named in the policy as beneficiary. Under such a contract nothing would be received from the insurer until the death of the insured, and the insured had no personal interest in the policy. Modified forms of contract have, however, become common. In some instances the policy is made payable to insured's estate so that he retains the power to dispose of its proceeds at will. So, too, sometimes by express stipulation in the contract (as in this case), sometimes by practice of the company, the privilege is given to the insured to surrender his policy at any time (usually after several premiums have been paid) and receive a fixed sum of money in exchange. Such sum is called the 'cash surrender value' of the policy. Unless such a policy passed to the trustee, the bankrupt could surrender it and himself collect the cash. Manifestly Congress 'intended to prevent a debtor from investing in policies of this kind money which equitably belongs to his creditors and reaping the benefit thereof, after he has secured protection against the enforcement of debts due from him through a discharge in bankruptcy.' In re Lange, 91 Fed. 361. It is the object of the statute to place in the hands of the trustee, for distribution among the creditors, every dollar which the bankrupt could collect. Therefore, if he has a policy on which money could be collected by surrendering it, he must turn over such policy to the trustee, who may thereupon surrender and collect. Having done this, there can be, of course, no possible objection to the bankrupt effecting new insurance on his own life, if some friend or relative chooses to assist him to pay the premiums. But his doing so would involve one element of hardship. The old policy may have been taken out many years before, when the assured was a young man and the annual premium low; for the new policy a much higher premium may have to be paid. Indeed his condition of health might be such that he could not pass the examination and secure a new policy at all and thus be unable to secure something for his family in the event of his death. It seems quite apparent from the language of the proviso that Congress was not solicitous to subject the unfortunate bankrupt to any such unnecessary hardship, and so has provided that if there is paid or secured to the trustee for the creditors all that the bankrupt could obtain by surrendering the old policy he may hold and carry such policy. The policies in this case are of the kind referred to as having a cash surrender value; that value at the date when trustees qualified was somewhat less than $15,000. Had the Insurance Company not made a loan to the bankrupts and secured itself by an assignment of the policies, the bankrupt or the trustees could have collected that amount upon surrendering them. But the company did make a loan of $15,370 on the security of the policies, and the propriety of that loan and the validity of the company's lien on the policies are not questioned. Therefore, on the day the title vested in the trustees, the cash which the company had agreed to pay on surrender would, if surrender were claimed have been entirely absorbed in releasing the lien of the company whether the privilege of surrender were exercised by the bankrupt or by the trustees. There was therefore nothing to pay or secure to the trustees to take the place of the money the bankrupt might obtain by surrendering, because he could not obtain anything himself by such surrender, although the policy had a cash surrender value. To hold upon such a state of facts that the policies passed to the trustee as assets, unless the individual insured bankrupt or the bankrupt firm or somebody paid the trustees $15,000 in addition to the $15,000 which the Insurance Company would take in satisfaction of the lien, would, in our opinion, be a clear violation of the intent of Congress as expressed in the section quoted supra."

§ 1013. Retention of Policy by Paying or Securing Cash Surrender Value.

—If the policy thus payable to one's estate or self has a cash surrender value, then the bankrupt, or, if he die, his personal representative, may retain it on paying or securing to the trustee the cash surrender value within thirty days after it has been ascertained and stated to the trustee by the insurance company.[66]

And only the cash surrender value will go to the trustee.[67]

In re Josephson, 9 A. B. R. 345, 121 Fed. 142 (D. C. Ga.): "By § 70 (a) (5) of the Bankruptcy Act of 1898, Congress expressed the purpose that after the payment of the cash surrender value of a policy or where there is no cash surrender value, the bankrupt may be entitled to hold, own and carry such policy free from the claims of creditors."

As to whether the duty is upon the trustee or the bankrupt, in the first instance, to ask for the statement of the cash surrender value from the insurance company, there is some doubt.[68]

§ 1014. Failure of Bankrupt to Pay or Secure Cash Surrender Value.

—As discussed ante, at § 1003, some difficulty results in the practical operation of the rule that it is the cash surrender value alone and not the policy subject to redemption, that passes; for, in the event the bankrupt fails or refuses to "pay or secure" to the trustee the cash surrender value there is no way by which the trustee could realize on the cash surrender asset, unless by declaring that the policy itself shall then pass to the trustee as assets,[69] as a sort of penalty; which would be, however, an abandonment of the doctrine that it is only the cash surrender value that passes.

§ 1015. Cash Surrender Value Not Expressly Provided for in Policy.

—The surrender value need not be an express contract right of surrender, the right of redemption or retention of the policy existing where the insurer

---

66. Bankr. Act, § 70 (a) (5).

67. See cases cited §§ 1002, 1003, 1004, 1016. Also obiter, Pulsifer v. Hussey, 9 A. B. R. 659, 97 Me. 434.

68. Compare, inferentially, Van Kirk v. Slate Co., 15 A. B. R. 239, 140 Fed. 38 (D. C. N. Y.).

69. Compare In re Hyman J. Herr (No. 2), 25 A. B. R. 142, 182 Fed. 715, 716 (D. C. Pa.).

Compare Clark v. Ins. Co., 16 A. B. R. 140 (U. S. C. C. Pa.). Compare In re Orear, 24 A. B. R. 343, 178 Fed. 632 (C. C. A. Mo.), quoted supra.

recognizes, in practice, a cash surrender value although it be not so provided by the express terms of the policy.[73]

Hiscock v. Mertens, 17 A. B. R. 483, 205 U. S. 202 (affirming In re Mertens, 15 A. B. R. 701, 142 Fed. 445, which in turn reversed 12 A. B. R. 712): "We are hence confronted with the problem whether the obiter of Holden v. Stratton shall be pronounced to be the proper construction of § 70 of the Bankrupt Act. We may remark at the commencement that that obiter was not inconsiderately uttered, nor can it be said that it was inconsequent to the considerations there involved. * * * There is no expression in either of the cases (In re McKenney and In re Newlands) that the cash surrender value depended upon contract as distinct from the usage of companies. And § 70 expresses no distinction. At the time of its enactment there were policies which stated a surrender value, and a practice which conceded such value if not stated. If a distinction had been intended to be made it would have been expressed. Able courts, it is true, have decided otherwise, but we are unable to adopt their view. It was an actual benefit for which the statute provided, and not the manner in which it should be evidenced. And we do not think it rested upon chance concession. It rested upon the interest of the companies and a practice to which no exception has been shown. And that a provision enacted for the benefit of debtors should recognize an interest so substantial and which had such assurance was perfectly natural. What possible difference could it make whether the surrender value was stipulated in a policy or universally recognized by the companies. In either case the purpose of the statute would be subserved, which was to secure to the trustee the sum of such value and to enable the bankrupt to continue to hold, own and carry such policy free from the claims of the creditors participating in the distribution of the estate under the bankruptcy proceedings."

Obiter, Holden v. Stratton, 14 A. B. R. 94, 198 U. S. 214: "There has been some contrariety of opinion expressed by the lower Federal courts as to the exact meaning of the words 'cash surrender value' as employed in the proviso, some courts holding that it means a surrender and other courts holding that the words embrace policies, even though a stipulation in respect to surrender value is not contained therein, where the policy possesses a cash surrender of the policy. It is to be observed that this latter construction harmonizes with the practice under the Act of 1867, In re Newland, 6 Ben. 342; In re McKinney, 15 Fed. 535, and tends to elucidate and carry out the purpose contemplated by the proviso as we have construed it. However, whatever influence that construction may have, as the question is not necessarily here involved, we do not expressly decide it."

---

73. Inferentially and obiter, Burlingham v. Crouse, 228 U. S. 459, 30 A. B. R. 6 (affirming 24 A. B. R. 632, 181 Fed. 479); In re Mertens, 15 A. B. R. 701, 142 Fed. 445 (C. C. A. N. Y., reversing 12 A. B. R. 712 and affirmed sub nom. Hiscock v. Mertens, 17 A. B. R. 483, 205 U. S. 202); compare In re Coleman, 14 A. B. R. 461, 136 Fed. 818 (C. C. A. N. Y.); compare obiter, In re Orear, 24 A. B. R. 343' 178 Fed. 632 (C. C. A. Mo.); In re Hyman J. Herr (No. 2), 25 A. B. R. 142, 182 Fed. 715, 716 (D. C. Pa.); In re Churchill, 29 A. B. R. 153, 197 Fed. 111, 114 (D. C. Wis.), reversed on other grounds in 31 A. B. R. 1, 198 Fed. 711 (D. C. Wis.); In re White, 23 A. B. R. 90, 174 Fed. 333 (C. C. A. N. Y.), quoted at § 1008; In re Phelps, 15 A. B. R. 170 (Ref. N. Y.), contra, In re Mertens, 12 A. B. R. 712, 131 Fed. 972 (D. C. N. Y., reversed sub nom. Hiscock v. Mertens, 17 A. B. R. 483, 205 U. S. 202); contra, Pulsifer v. Hussey, 9 A. B. R. 659, 97 Me. 434; contra, In re Welling, 7 A. B. R. 344, 113 Fed. 189 (C. C. A. Ills.); contra, Van Kirk v. Slate Co., 15 A. B. R. 239, 140 Fed. 38 (D. C. N. Y.).

Obiter, Gould v. N. Y. Life Ins. Co., 13 A. B. R. 236, 132 Fed. 927 (D. C. Ark.): "But, in view of the fact that this proviso was enacted solely for the benefit of the unfortunate debtor, and the further fact that the payment by him of the full value of the policy—that is, the payment of all that the trustee could realize by a surrender or sale of the policy—gives the creditors all that they can possibly receive, many of the courts have construed this proviso liberally by applying it to all life policies, whether they have a surrender value or not, if there is a cash value to them which can be obtained by the trustee from a sale of the policy. Such a liberal view can do no harm to the creditors, while, on the other hand, it may prove very beneficial to the bankrupt, who thereby is enabled to continue his life policy at the lower rate, based upon the age when it was first taken out, instead of paying the increased rate necessarily charged at an advanced age, and also enables him to retain a policy even if the state of his present health would prevent him from securing a new policy."

In re Boardmen, 4 A. B. R. 622, 103 Fed. 783 (D. C. Mass.): "In this case I agree with the referee. The policy has a cash surrender value within the intent of the statute. The fact that this value is not stated in the policy is immaterial. If in the ordinary course of business the bankrupt can obtain cash from the company by a surrender of the policy, his creditors are entitled to the cash."

Possibly even though the policy have no cash value by contract nor by recognition obtainable from the company itself, the court, being a court of equity, might follow the analogy of the law and fix, by evidence or otherwise, the cash value of the policy and permit the bankrupt to redeem or retain the policy on payment or securing payment of it to the trustee.[74]

It has been held that a right to the return of unearned premiums is a species of surrender value, and, as such, passes to the trustee.[75]

§ 1016. Death of Bankrupt before Redemption Accomplished.—If the bankrupt die after the filing of the bankruptcy petition, then the bankrupt's legal representative succeeds to his right to retain the policy and its proceeds by payment or securing of payment to the trustee of the cash surrender value, as such surrender value may have existed at the date of the filing of the bankruptcy petition,[76] whether he die before adjudication[77] or after adjudication.

Burlingham v. Crouse, 228 U. S. 459, 30 A. B. R. 6 (affirming S. C., 24 A. B. R. 632, 181 Fed. 479, C. C. A. N. Y.): "Congress recognized also that many policies at the time of bankruptcy might have a very considerable present value which a bankrupt could realize by surrendering his policy to the company.

74. Inferentially, Hiscock v. Mertens, 17 A. B. R. 483, 205 U. S. 202. Compare suggestion, obiter, Holden v. Stratton, 14 A. B. R. 94, 198 U. S. 214.
75. In re Judson, 26 A. B. R. 775, 188 Fed. 702 (D. C. N. Y.).
76. Everett v. Judson, 228 U. S. 474, 30 A. B. R. 1 (affirming In re Judson, 27 A. B. R. 704, 192 Fed. 334, C. C. A. N. Y.); Andrews v. Partridge, 228 U. S. 479, 30 A. B. R. 4 (reversing Partridge v. Andrews, 27 A. B. R. 388, 191 Fed. 325, C. C. A. N. J.); Burlingham v. Crouse, 228 U. S. 459, 30 A. B. R. 6 (affirming S. C., 24 A. B. R. 632, 181 Fed. 479 C. C. A. N. Y.); Van Kirk v. Slate Co., 15 A. B. R. 239, 140 Fed. 38 (D. C. N. Y.).
77. Andrews v. Partridge, 228 U. S. 479, 30 A. B. R. 4 (reversing Partridge v. Andrews, 27 A. B. R. 388, 191 Fed. 325, C. C. A. N. J.).

We think it was this latter sum that the act intended to secure to creditors by requiring its payment to the trustee as a condition of keeping the policy alive. In passing this statute Congress intended, while exacting this much, that when that sum was realized to the estate, the bankrupt should be permitted to retain the insurance which, because of advancing years or declining health, it might be impossible for him to replace. It is the twofold purpose of the Bankruptcy Act to convert the estate of the bankrupt into cash and distribute it among creditors, and then to give the bankrupt a fresh start with such exemptions and rights as the statute left untouched. In the light of this policy the act must be construed: We think it was the purpose of Congress to pass to the trustee that sum which was available to the bankrupt at the time of bankruptcy as a cash asset; otherwise to leave to the insured the benefit of his life insurance."

Van Kirk v. Slate Co., 15 A. B. R. 239, 140 Fed. 38 (D. C. N. Y.): "This policy has never passed to the trustee in bankruptcy as assets of the estate he represents, for the reason that the insurance company issuing the policy has never stated to the trustee the cash surrender value thereof. Therefore the bankrupt in his lifetime was not, and the administrators of his estate since his death have not been, called upon or required to render or pay or secure to the trustee the amount of such cash surrender value. I find no evidence or concession establishing that Hughes or his administrators have waived or lost the right to take and hold this policy on paying or securing to the trustee the cash surrender value thereof. I find no evidence or concession establishing as a fact that the trustee has surrendered the rights of the estate in such policy. It is true that he paid no attention to it until after the death of Hughes, but his neglect, if there was any neglect, did not operate to change title or effect the rights of the estate represented by him. The interest of the trustee in that policy on his appointment was $2,219, and it has never grown to any greater interest. The value to the policy to Hughes, beyond the cash surrender value, was uncertain and contingent. Had Hughes died the day after the adjudication, the right to take and hold the policy on paying the cash surrender value on the day of adjudication would have vested in the administrators of Hughes when appointed. This right to take and hold such a policy is not personal to the bankrupt—not a right that is extinguished by his death, but one that survives to his executors or administrators."

In such cases, the legal representatives will not in all probability be held to forfeit the right by failure strictly to pay the redemption money within the thirty days.[78]

And the rights of the bankrupt as to cash surrender value may redound to the benefit of an assignee of the policy.

Burlingham v. Crouse, 228 U. S. 459, 30 A. B. R. 6 (affirming S. C., 24 A. B. R. 632, 181 Fed. 479, C. C. A. N. Y.): "It is urged, however, that under § 70 (a), the cash surrender value was to be paid by the bankrupt when ascertained, and the policies kept alive for his benefit; and as these policies had been assigned by the beneficiary to McIntyre & Company, not as collateral, but absolutely, they would not come within the terms of the proviso, and therefore the pro-

---

78. Three Cornered Case.—Pledgee of the policy; legal representatives of the deceased bankrupt and the trustee in bankruptcy; pledgee has the first right; trustee has right to cash surrender value; residue goes to the legal representatives. Van Kirk v. Slate Co., 15 A. B. R. 239, 140 Fed. 38 (D. C. N. Y.).

ceeds of the policies vested in the bankrupt's estate; but we find nothing in the act by which the right of the assignee of a policy to the benefits which would have accrued to the bankrupt is limited."

§ 1017. Bankrupt as Beneficiary on Life of Another.

—Where the bankrupt is the beneficiary under a policy on the life of another, his or her interest may or may not pass to the trustee, depending on the terms of the policy.[79]

But where the insured has the right to change the beneficiary at any time, the bankrupt, even though named as the beneficiary, has no such vested interest as will pass to his trustee.

In re Hogan, 28 A. B. R. 166, 194 Fed. 846 (C. C. A. Wis.): "Whatever may be the rule, therefore, in reference to the interest and rights of one named unqualifiedly as the beneficiary under a life insurance policy, we are of opinion that such rule is not applicable to the express terms of the present policy, providing that the insured may 'change the beneficiary at any time,' and that interpretation thereof must rest on the principles of contract law unaffected by special rules in respect of insurance policies which may appear in various jurisdictions, other than the place of the present contract. In the absence of restraint imposed by rule or statute governing the contract, the above stated terms of insurance were plainly open to arrangement between the contracting parties, and are conclusive of rights thereunder. So, if the question presented is one of general law, we are advised of no rule thereof which would establish in the bankrupt, through the fact alone that he had been named, for the time being, as an intended beneficiary, a property right in the contract during the life and volition of the insured (mother), within the meaning of section 70a of the Bankruptcy Act."

§ 1018. Procuring Insurance in Fraud of Creditors.

—Under what circumstances the buying of insurance or the paying of premiums is a fraud on creditors is in general a question of state law and comes more appropriately under the subject of fraudulent transfers, voidable by the trustee.[80] It has been held that the trustee may recover from an insurance company money paid by the bankrupt while insolvent, as the purchase price of an annuity on his own life not to begin until a future time not yet arrived, notwithstanding the bona fides of the insurance company; this being held on the doctrine that the good faith of the transferee is an insufficient defense where the consideration moving from him is wholly executory.[80a]

It has been held that the trustee cannot recover sums of money paid to an insurance company, under the terms of a "deferred annuity contract" of insurance, even though the insured was acting in general bad faith with his creditors, where the transaction was bona fide on the part of the company;

---

79. Carr *v.* Myers, 15 A. B. R. 116, 211 Pa. St. 349; instance, In re Blalock, 9 A. B. R. 269, 118 Fed. 679 (D. C. S. C.). Husband and wife both in bankruptcy, policies of insurance on life of one to the benefit of the other pass to trustee since they represent all the interests. In re Holden, 7 A. B. R. 615, 113 Fed. 142 (C. C. A. Wash., reversed, on other grounds, in Holden *v.* Stratton, 14 A. B. R. 94, 198 U. S. 202).

80. See post, § 1209, et seq.

80a. Smith *v.* Mutual Life Insurance Co., 19 A. B. R. 707, 158 Fed. 365 (D. C. Mass.). Also, see post, § 1218.

but that, in such case, the trustee may seize the contingent right of the insured, or may waive it, should he wish to do so.[80b]

DIVISION 6.

RIGHTS OF ACTION UPON CONTRACTS AND FOR DETENTION OR INJURY TO PROPERTY.

§ 1019. Rights of Action on Contracts and for Injury, etc., to Property Pass.—The title to all rights of action arising upon contracts or from the unlawful taking or detention of, or injury to, the bankrupt's property passes to the trustee.[81]

Such choses in action are assignable and transferable without question, and thus might come under class 5.

Thus, promissory notes and other commercial paper pass to the trustee.[82]

And the trustee may disregard the note and sue on the original consideration precisely as the bankrupt might have done.[83]

And contracts to buy on future delivery pass, where the trustee stands ready to pay cash on delivery, and the contract is not dependent upon future dealings between the vendor and the original vendee.[84]

80b. Mutual Life Ins. Co. v. Smith, 25 A. B. R. 768, 184 Fed. 1 (C. C. A. Mass., reversing Smith v. Mutual Life Ins. Co., 19 A. B. R. 707, 158 Fed. 365 and 24 A. B. R. 514).

81. And the bankrupt does not retain title thereto by failing to schedule such rights. Rand v. Iowa Central Ry. Co., 12 A. B. R. 164 (N. Y. Sup. Ct. App. Div.); First Nat. Bk. v. Lasater, 13 A. B. R. 698, 196 U. S. 115.

Where the bankrupt is the beneficiary in a policy on the life of another the terms of the contract must be looked to, to determine whether any interest exists which may pass to the trustee. Carr v. Myers, 15 A. B. R. 116, 211 Pa. St. 349.

The amount recovered in an action for death by wrongful act is an asset passing to the trustee of a bankrupt beneficiary. In re Burnstine, 12 A. B. R. 597, 131 Fed. 828 (D. C. Mich.).

Unpaid assessment for stock subscription, even though assessed by court and not by the directors, passes to the trustee. Clevenger v. Moore, 12 A. B. R. 738 (N. J. Sup. Ct.).

Instance passing. Claim for usurious interest. First Nat. Bk. v. Lasater, 13 A. B. R. 698, 196 U. S. 115.

Damages for a landlord's negligence in allowing water to get into leased premises passes to the trustee of the tenant. Obiter, In re Becher Bros.,

15 A. B. R. 228, 139 Fed. 366 (D. C. Pa.).

Instance passing, notwithstanding agreement, without new consideration to accept payment of notes in personal services and support. In re Powers, 1 A. B. R. 433 (Ref. Vt.).

Neither claim for alimony nor homestead awarded to bankrupt wife after adjudication of alimony, is property passing to the trustee. In re Le Claire, 10 A. B. R. 753, 124 Fed. 654 (D. C. Iowa).

For the general subject of rights of action on contracts passing and not passing to the trustee, see post, § 1144, et seq.

Instance, judgment for damages notwithstanding claim that such judgment had passed to creditor of bankrupt by levy under statutory provision, prior to bankruptcy. Mining Co. v. R. R. Co., 18 A. B. R. 492.

Inferentially, Greenhall v. Carnegie Trust Co., 25 A. B. R. 300, 180 Fed. 812 (D. C. N. Y.).

Contract to locate and operate a mill. In re [Morgantown], Tin Plate Co., 25 A. B. R. 836, 184 Fed. 109 (D. C. W. Va.), quoted at § 674.

82. Instance, In re Jackson, 2 A. B. R. 50, 94 Fed. 797 (D. C. Vt.).

83. In re Jackson, 2 A. B. R. 50, 94 Fed. 797 (D. C. Vt.).

84. In re Niagara Radiator Co., 21 A. B. R. 55, 164 Fed. 102 (D. C. N. Y.).

A contract of settlement by a debtor with the trustee in bankruptcy of a creditor passes to and binds the trustee in bankruptcy of the debtor.[85]

A right of action for wrongful attachment arising prior to bankruptcy passes to the trustee.[86]

Malicious attachment of corporate property is not a personal tort, but is an injury to property passing to the trustee in bankruptcy of the corporation.[86a]

Damages occasioned by street grading, and accruing prior to bankruptcy, pass to the trustee.[87]

It has been held to be a "right of action for injury to property," passing to the trustee, that a bankrupt has lost money in carrying out a contract induced by false representations.[88]

The statutes and decisions of the state might enlarge class 6 but could hardly restrict it. That is to say, if the law of some state should hold a right of action for slander to be assignable then it might pass to the trustee in bankruptcy, under the general class 5 of the act, namely, property capable of being transferred; although, all the time it is not mentioned in class 6. However, on the other hand, if the law of some state should hold that the right of action for injury to property is not assignable, nevertheless it would pass as being within the express provisions of class 6. In such a case use would be found for specifically classifying the kinds of property, as is done in § 70 (a).[89]

§ 1020. But Not Torts for Injury to Person.

—Rights of action for slander,[90] or libel or malicious prosecution,[91] will not pass to the trustee,

85. In re Baumblatt, 18, A. B. R. 496, 156 Fed. 422 (D. C. Pa.).

86. Hansen v. Wyman, 21 A. B. R. 398, 105 Minn. 491, 117 N. W. 926.

86a. Hansen Mercantile Co. v. Wyman, Partridge & Co., 22 A. B. R. 877, 105 Minn. 491, 117 N. W. 926.

87. In re Torchia, 26 A. B. R. 579, 188 Fed. 207 (C. C. A. Pa.).

88. In re Harper, 23 A. B. R. 918, 175 Fed. 412 (D. C. N. Y.).

89. In Nebraska an interest in a pending suit for a tort seems to be assignable whilst the right of action for the tort itself is not assignable; therefore such an interest would pass to the trustee as "property" under class 5 rather than as a right of action under class 6.

See Cleland v. Anderson, 11 A. B. R. 605 (Nebraska Sup. Ct.), reversing on rehearing 10 A. B. R. 429, the court holding: "A right of action for tort is not 'property' within the meaning of the National Bankruptcy Act; and even though an action is pending thereon such right does not pass to the trustee in bankruptcy.

"An action for conspiracy whereby plaintiff was driven out of business as a dealer in lumber is an action in tort and does not rise 'from the unlawful taking or detention of or injury to his property' within the meaning of the Federal Bankruptcy Act."

The argument of the Court on rehearing is that since class 5 provides for "property" and class 6 for "rights of action," rights of action cannot, in the meaning of the Bankruptcy Act, be included within the class, "property," as to do so would violate the canons of statutory construction; and that therefore all rights of action that pass to the trustee are mentioned in class 6.

90. Dillard v. Collins, 25 Gratt. 343.

91. In re Haensell, 1 A. B. R. 286, 91 Fed. 355 (D. C. Calif.); Noonan v. Orton, 34 Wis. 259, 17 Am. Rep. 441; Francis v. Burnett, 84 Ky. 223; Epstein v. Handverker, 26 A. B. R. 712 (Sup. Ct. Okla.).

for they do not come under class 6 nor do they come under the general rule, namely, property which was capable of being transferred by the bankrupt. Such rights of action are not assignable nor can they be subjected by legal process.

Thus, it has been held that the purely personal tort of fraudulently recommending a person as trustworthy or solvent does not pass to the trustee.[92]

Nor will a right of action for personal injury to the bankrupt, caused by a street car accident, pass to the trustee;[93] nor, in general, for malicious attachment;[94] nor for negligence of an attorney;[95] nor for malicious trespass.[96]

It has been held that a corporation cannot bring an action ex delicto for a purely personal tort, nor can it be awarded purely personal damages, but that malicious attachment of corporate property is not a personal tort, but gives rise to a cause of action for injury to property, which passes to the trustee in bankruptcy of the corporation.[97]

§ 1021. Nor for Personal Services Involving Trust and Confidence.

—Rights of action upon contracts for personal services involving trust and confidence are not assignable nor does subjection thereof by legal process convey any rights;[98] even where the party is a corporation.[99]

But an agreement to accept personal services and support in payment of notes, without new consideration, will not defeat the passing of title to the trustee.[1]

DIVISION 7.

EXEMPTIONS.

§ 1022. Exempt Property Does Not Pass.

—Property exempted to debtors of the bankrupt's class at the time of the filing of the bankruptcy petition, by the laws of the state where the bankrupt has had his domicile for the greater portion of the six months preceding such filing, does not pass to the trustee and may not be administered in bankruptcy if claimed as ex-

---

92. (1867) In re Crockett, 2 Ben. 514, Fed. Cas. No. 3402; obiter, Hansen Mercantile Co. v. Wyman, Partridge & Co., 22 A. B. R. 877, 105 Minn. 491. 177 N. W. 926; Zabriskie v. Smith, 13 N. Y. 322.

93. Sibley v. Nason, 22 A. B. R. 712, 196 Mass. 125.

94. Brewer v. Dew, 11 M. & W. 625.

95. (Eng.) Wetherell v. Julius, 10 C. B. 267.

96. Rogers v. Spence, 12 Cl. & Finn. 700; Rose v. Buckett, 2 K. B. D. 449.

97. Hansen Mercantile Co. v. Wyman, Partridge Co., 22 A. B. R. 877,

105 Minn. 491, 117 N. W. 926. But, compare, Noonan v. Orton, 34 Wis. 259. Compare, Francis v. Burnett, 84 Ky. 23; Slauson v. Schwabacher, 4 Wash. 783, 31 Pacific 329.

98. See ante, "Contracts for Bankrupt's Personal Services," subdiv. "F", § 994. In re D. H. McBride & Co., 12 A. B. R. 81 (Ref. N. Y.).

99. In re D. H. McBride & Co., 12 A. B. R. 81 (Ref. N. Y.). Compare statement of rule where held assignable. In re [Morgantown] Tin Plate Co., 25 A. B. R. 836, 184 Fed. 109 (D. C. W. Va.), quoted at § 674.

1. In re Powers, 1 A. B. R. 432 (Ref. Vt.).

empt, but upon due claim being made, is to be set apart to the bankrupt in the form and manner prescribed by the bankruptcy act.[2]

Steele *v.* Buel, 5 A. B. R. 165, 104 Fed. 968 (C. C. A. Iowa): "The only right or title the trustee has to any of the bankrupt's property is acquired under this section. It vests the title of the property in the trustee, 'except in so far as it is to property which is exempt.' How is it to be known what 'is exempt?' There is but one source of information on that subject, and that is the State law adopted by § 6, and the legal effect of this exception is precisely the same as if it read, 'except property which is exempt under the State law.' This exception must be read into every other clause and provision of the section. The fifth clause of this section shows conclusively that the construction of the proviso contended for by the trustee is wholly inadmissible."

Obiter, Richardson *v.* Woodward, 5 A. B. R. 96, 104 Fed. 873 (C. C. A. Va.): "The intention was to adopt the State laws governing exemptions. Hence, the courts of bankruptcy will look to, and be governed by, the constitutions, statutes and decisions of the several States and Territories, in deciding who is entitled to exemptions, and the amount and species of property to be exempt. A bankrupt is entitled to the same exemptions as if proceeded against as a

---

2. Bankr. Act, § 6: "This Act shall not affect the allowance to bankrupts of the exemptions which are prescribed by the State laws in force at the time of the filing of the petition in the State wherein they have had their domicile for the six months or the greater portion thereof immediately preceding the filing of the petition." Bankr. Act, § 8 (7).

Bankr. Act, § 47 (a) (11): "Set apart the bankrupt's exemptions and report the items and estimated value thereof to the court as soon as practicable after their appointment."

Gen. Order, No. 17, Form, Schedule B-5; Lockwood *v.* Exchange Bk., 10 A. B. R. 110, 190 U. S. 294; Holden *v.* Stratton, 14 A. B. R. 94, 198 U. S. 202; Page *v.* Edmunds, 9 A. B. R. 281, 187 U. S. 596; Lipman *v.* Stein, 14 A. B. R. 30, 134 Fed. 235 (C. C. A. Pa.); In re Wells, 5 A. B. R. 310, 105 Fed. 762 (D. C. Ark.); In re Grimes, 2 A. B. R. 735, 96 Fed. 529 (D. C. N. Car.); In re Hills, 2 A. B. R. 798, 96 Fed. 185 (D. C. Conn.); In re Durham, 4 A. B. R. 762, 104 Fed. 231 (D. C. Ark.); In re Jackson, 8 A. B. R. 594, 116 Fed. 46 (D. C. Pa.); In re Camp, 1 A. B. R. 168, 91 Fed. 745 (D. C. Ga.); In re Seabolt, 8 A. B. R. 57, 113 Fed. 766 (D. C. N. Car.); Ingram *v.* Wilson, 11 A. B. R. 192, 125 Fed. 913 (C. C. A. Iowa); Bell *v.* Dawson Grocery Co., 12 A. B. R. 161 (Sup. Ct. Ga.); In re Little, 6 A. B. R. 681, 110 Fed. 621 (D. C. Iowa); In re Hatch, 4 A. B. R. 350, 102 Fed. 280 (D. C. Iowa); Woodruff *v.* Cheeves, 5 A. B.

R. 303, 105 Fed. 601 (C. C. A. Ga.); obiter, In re Lucius, 10 A. B. R. 653, 124 Fed. 455 (D. C. Ala.); McGahan *v.* Anderson, 7 A. B. R. 643, 113 Fed. 115 (C. C. A. S. C.); In re Mayer, 6 A. B. R. 121, 108 Fed. 599 (C. C. A. Wis.); Cannon *v.* Dexter Broom & Mattress Co., 9 A. B. R. 725, 120 Fed. 657 (C. C. A. S. C.); Smalley *v.* Laugenour, 13 A. B. R. 692, 196 U. S. 93; In re Groves, 6 A. B. R. 728 (Ref. Ohio); In re McClintock, 13 A. B. R. 606 (Ref. Ohio); In re Duffy, 9 A. B. R. 358, 118 Fed. 926 (D. C. Pa.); In re Ogilvie, 5 A. B. R. 374 (Ref. Ga.); McCarty *v.* Coffin, 18 A. B. R. 152, 150 Fed. 307 (C. C. A. Tex.); In re Meriweather, 5 A. B. R. 436, 107 Fed. 102 (D. C. Ark.); In re Woodward, 2 A. B. R. 692, 95 Fed. 955 (D. C. N. Car.); In re Mullen, 15 A. B. R. 275 (D. C. Me.); In re Ellithorpe, 7 A. B. R. 18, 111 Fed. 163 (D. C. N. Y.); In re Kane, 11 A. B. R. 534, 127 Fed. 552 (C. C. A. Ills.); In re Falconer, 6 A. B. R. 558, 110 Fed. 111 (C. C. A. Ark.); In re Wilson, 10 A. B. R. 625 (C. C. A. Calif.); Powers Dry Goods Co. *v.* Nelson, 7 A. B. R. 506 (Sup. Ct. N. Dak.); In re Wood, 17 A. B. R. 93, 147 Fed. 877 (D. C. Wis.); In re Black, 4 A. B. R. 777, 104 Fed. 28 (D. C. Pa.); In re Yeager, 25 A. B. R. 51, 182 Fed. 951 (D. C. Pa.); Cowan *v.* Burchfield, 25 A. B. R. 293, 180 Fed. 614 (D. C. Ala.); In re Goodman (Goodman *v.* Curtis), 23 A. B. R. 504, 174 Fed. 644 (C. C. A. Ala.); The Gregory Co. *v.* Bristol, 26 A. B. R. 938, 191 Fed. 31 (C. C. A. Minn.).

debtor under the State law, and none other. 'Shall not affect' means shall not enlarge or diminish. In determining these exemptions the bankrupt courts will follow the construction given the State laws by the highest courts of the State the statute of which is involved. The decisions to this effect are numerous and uniform."

First Nat'l Bk. of Sayre *v.* Bartlett, 21 A. B. R. 88, 35 Pa. Super. Ct. 593: "We think it very clear that the language 'estate of the bankrupt' as used in the Act of 1898 does not include the exempted property, but only such as passes to the trustee."

But if not claimed as exempt, it will pass.[3]

§ 1023. Not Unconstitutional for Lack of "Uniformity" as to Exemptions.

—The Bankruptcy Act is not unconstitutional for lack of the uniformity required by § 8 of article 1 of the Constitution of the United States, by reason of the adoption of the exemptions prescribed by the several State laws.[4]

Hanover Nat'l Bk. *v.* Moyses, 8 A. B. R. 1, 186 U. S. 181: "The system is, in the constitutional sense, uniform throughout the United States, when the trustee takes in each State whatever would have been available to the creditors if the Bankruptcy Law had not been passed."

In re Deckert, 2 Hughes 183: "The power to except from the operation of the law, property liable to execution under the exemption laws of the several States, as they were actually enforced, was at one time questioned upon the ground that it was a violation of the constitutional requirement of uniformity, but it has thus far been sustained, for the reason that it was made a rule of the law to subject to the payment of debts under its operation only such property as could by judicial process be made available for the same purpose. This is not unjust, as every debt is contracted with reference to the rights of the parties thereto under existing exemption laws, and no creditor can reasonably complain if he gets his full share of all that the law, for the time being, places at the disposal of creditors. One of the effects of a bankrupt law is that of a general execution issued in favor of all the creditors of the bankrupt in reaching all his property subject to levy, and applying it to the payment of all his debts according to their respective priorities. It is quite proper, therefore, to confine its operation to such property as other legal process could reach. A rule which operates to this effect throughout the United States is uniform within the meaning of that term, as used in the Constitution."

In re Rouse, Hazard & Co., 1 A. B. R. 240, 91 Fed. 96 (C. C. A. Wis.): "It is probably true that Congress could constitutionally in the Bankrupt Act recognize the varying systems of the several States with respect to exemptions and with respect to priority of payment of debts."

Thus, the adoption of the exemption laws of the several states is no more violative of the constitutional requirement of uniformity than is the acceptance of the varying limitations upon the kinds and titles of property passing to the trustee in the several states. So long as, in each State, the trustee acquires whatever rights creditors there possess, the law is uniform

3. In re Driggs, 22 A. B. R. 621, 171 Fed. 897 (D. C. N. Y.).
4. See ante, § 11.

within the meaning of the Constitution. Indeed, were exemptions the same in bankruptcy throughout the United States, the law would not be uniform, for in some States creditors would receive more under the bankruptcy law than under State law and in other States would receive less, under precisely the same condition of facts.

One of the cardinal principles of the Bankruptcy Act is to grant to creditors (in addition to the right to recover preferences and the right to annul liens acquired by legal proceedings within four months) only those rights which would have been theirs had bankruptcy not supervened, saving to the bankrupt and his family every right and exemption which would have been theirs as against creditors enforcing their claims by ordinary judicial process.[5]

§ 1024. No Title to Exempt Property Passes.

—No title to exempt property passes to the trustee at all.[6]

Lockwood v. Exchange Bk., 10 A. B. R. 107, 190 U. S. 294: "We think that the terms of the Bankruptcy Act of 1898 above set out, as clearly evidence of the intention of Congress that the title to the property of a bankrupt generally exempted by State laws should remain in the bankrupt and not pass to his representative in bankruptcy, as did the provisions of the Act of 1867, considered in In re Bass."

In re Wells, 5 A. B. R. 308 (D. C. Ark.): "Wells selected and claimed this very property as exempt, and it was set apart to him by the trustee as such. The title to this property did not therefore pass to the trustee. It never be-

---

5. In re Cohn, 22 A. B. R. 761, 171 Fed. 586 (D. C. N. Dak.):

6. Bankr. Act, § 70 (a): "The trustee * * * shall be vested by operation of law with the title of the bankrupt * * * except in so far as it is to property which is exempted." Obiter, In re Royce Dry Goods Co., 13 A. B. R. 268, 133 Fed. 100 (D. C. Mo.); In re Grimes, 2 A. B. R. 735, 96 Fed. 529 (D. C. N. Car.); In re Durham, 4 A. B. R. 760, 104 Fed. 231 (D. C. Ark.); In re Jackson, 8 A. B. R. 594, 116 Fed. 46 (D. C. Ark.); In re Hatch, 4 A. B. R. 350, 102 Fed. 280 (D. C. Iowa); In re Friedrick, 3 A. B. R. 803, 100 Fed. 284 (C. C. A. Wis.); In re Black, 4 A. B. R. 777, 104 Fed. 28 (D. C. Pa.); In re LeVay, 11 A. B. R. 116, 125 Fed. 913 (D. C. Pa.); In re Camp, 1 A. B. R. 165, 91 Fed. 745 (D. C. Ga.); Powers Dry Goods Co. v. Nelson, 7 A. B. R. 506 (Sup. Ct. N. Dak.); In re Castleberry, 16 A. B. R. 160 (D. C. Ga.); In re Seabolt, 8 A. B. R. 57, 113 Fed. 766 (D. C. N. Car.); Ingram v. Wilson, 11 A. B. R. 192, 125 Fed. 913 (C. C. A. Iowa); Bell v.

Dawson Grocery Co., 12 A. B. R. 161 (Sup. Ct. Ga.); compare, In re Mayer, 6 A. B. R. 117, 108 Fed. 599 (C. C. A. Wis.), that the trustee has title "sub modo." Under law of 1867, In re Bass, 3 Woods 384, 2 Fed. Cases 1004.

While the trustee gets no title to exempt property yet the reversionary interest in the property upon the abandonment or other loss of it as a homestead, is an asset of the estate passing to the trustee, who may sell 'it. In re Woodward, 2 A. B. R. 339 (D. C. N. Car.); In re Mayer, 6 A. B. R. 131 (C. C. A. Wis.). But compare, In re Camp, 1 A. B. R. 168 (D. C. Ga.).

See, in addition, Paramore & Ricks, 19 A. B. R. 130, 156 Fed. 211 (D. C. N. Car.); In re Edwards, 19 A. B. R. 632, 156 Fed. 794 (D. C. Ala.); Zumpfe v. Schultz, 20 A. B. R. 916, 35 Pa. Super. Co. 106, quoted at § 1107; Snyder v. Guthrie, 24 A. B. R. 58 (Pa. Court of Common Pleas); In re Carlon, 27 A. B. R. 18, 189 Fed. 815 (D. C. S. D.); Huntington v. Baskerville, 27 A. B. R. 219, 102 Fed. 813 (C. C. A. S. D.).

came vested in him. By the very terms of the Bankruptcy Act the title remained in Wells, or, at least, did not pass to the trustee. It did pass to the possession of the trustee for a specific purpose—that of preparing a complete inventory of the bankrupt's estate, and to set apart the exemptions according to the provisions of the forty-seventh section of the act, with the estimated value of each article (Rule 17 of Supreme Court of General Orders in Bankruptcy). But the title to the exempt property did not change."

In re Hill, 2 A. B. R. 798, 96 Fed. 285 (D. C. Conn.): "All this is no answer to the fact that exempt property is never in the Court of Bankruptcy. The act provides that the title to all property, except such as is exempt, vests in the trustee in bankruptcy. Exempt property never becomes assets in the Bankrupt Court for administration. The title never passes. Only a qualified right of possession is in the trustee. As to property which is exempt, relating back to the adjudication, title remains in the bankrupt, and it is only to be set apart, and otherwise the trustee can exercise no right, and owes no duty. It never gets into the Court of Bankruptcy. Consequently, as to these questions—the effect of waiver notes and the right of creditors holding such obligations—there is no jurisdiction whatever in the Bankrupt Court. If it should undertake to deal with the questions suggested by counsel, it would be dealing with property over which the act provides that the Bankrupt Court could have no jurisdiction and control."

In re Boyd, 10 A. B. R. 342, 120 Fed. 999 (D. C. Iowa): "No title to exempt property passes to the trustee, and, if property is exempt as against the creditors generally, it cannot be well held that a title thereto vests in the trustee simply because a single creditor may have the right to subject the property to the payment of his claim. This right is not a title to the property, nor a lien thereon, but is simply a right or privilege personal to the creditor owning the claim for the unpaid purchase price, which certainly does not vest in the trustee, and therefore the same should be presented by the creditor in his own name."

In re Bailey, 24 A. B. R. 201, 176 Fed. 990 (D. C. Utah): "The title to the homestead property did not pass to the trustee. The fact that it was mortgaged to certain creditors did not make it assets to be administered in bankruptcy."

In re Hastings, 24 A. B. R. 360, 181 Fed. 34 (C. C. A. Mich.): "The title, therefore, to property of a bankrupt which is generally exempt by the law of the state in which the bankrupt resides remains in the bankrupt, and does not pass to the trustee."

It is not that the bankrupt is allowed his maintenance out of the fund belonging to the creditors, as was provided in the old Roman Law of Cessio Bonorum and in the English Bankruptcy Acts and as appears to be the rule under some of the State Insolvency Statutes today (see In re Anderson, 6 A. B. R. 555, D. C. Mass., and In re Lynch, 4 A. B. R. 262, D. C. Ga.), where the bankrupt was allowed a certain per cent. of his assets for his own maintenance. This is not the theory of the present national bankruptcy act at all. The bankrupt's exemptions are not a priority claim to be paid out of the creditors' funds like the claims of workmen, clerks or servants. From the beginning, no title at all passes to exempt property; it was and is and will continue to be the bankrupt's own property and the trustee never takes nor holds any interest in the property whatsoever, except a reversionary interest on abandonment. His only right is as trustee for both the bankrupt and the creditors to hold the property of both until that belonging to the one can be separated and set aside from that belonging to the others.

Indeed, the present Bankruptcy Act seems to confer on the bankrupt, by negation of the trustee's title thereto, an absolute title to exempt property even in States where exemptions partake more of the nature of allowances out of the estate or perhaps of mere rights to use the property during the existence of the family relation and occupancy of the property.[7]

In re Camp, 1 A. B. R. 168, 91 Fed. 745 (D. C. Ga.): "According to the decisions of the Supreme Court of Georgia, property exempted in bankruptcy has a very different status from that of property set apart and allowed by the ordinary of the county as a homestead. In the former case, that of exemption in bankruptcy, the bankrupt gets an absolute title; he may immediately sell it, or he may, according to its character, mortgage or pledge it; on the other hand, the title to a homestead under the State law, is in the head of the family for the benefit of the family; his title is nominal during the existence of the family, the beneficial interest being in it, so that there is very little reason in Georgia, especially, for any action of the State officials when the title vests absolutely in the bankrupt by virtue of the exemption in the bankruptcy proceedings."

In re Ogilvie, 5 A. B. R. 380 (Ref. Ga.): "* * * the Supreme Court of this State has decided that a homestead in bankruptcy constitutes a different estate than one allowed by State law. * * * The estate obtained in bankruptcy is a fee simple, subject, however, to be levied upon and sold for claims superior to the homestead of older date, and also liable to be seized and sold for subsequent debts of bankrupt."

However, compare, Fenley v. Poor, 10 A. B. R. 378, 121 Fed. 739 (C. C. A. Ky.): "In construing the exemption statute, the Court of Appeals of Kentucky, in the case of Gaines v. Casey, 10 Bush 92, draws a distinction between the homestead exemption and the legal title to the fee, and holds that the right to a homestead may be waived by mortgaging it, and that such security would terminate whenever the debtor ceased to be a housekeeper or removed from the premises, although if the mortgage was of the fee, it could not be thus affected. This construction would leave the fee, which is separate and distinct from the homestead exemption, assignable, even under the contention of the appellees. But the definition in the Bankruptcy Act refers to the nature of the property, and, if it is such as to be assignable under the act, the fact that it includes exemptions under the State laws in force at the time of the filing of the petition could not affect its nature and make it nonassignable. The act provides that the bankrupt shall make claim under oath to his exemptions and file the same in triplicate, and also makes it the duty of the trustee to set apart the bankrupt's exemptions, and report the items and estimated value to the court, and makes it the duty of the judge to determine all claims of bankrupts to their exemptions. These provisions clearly indicate that the whole estate of the bankrupt is assigned, under the law, to the trustee, and that then the claim of the bankrupt is to be made for his exemptions, which are to be set apart by the trustee and determined by the court. The fact that the debtor has a homestead right in a tract of land does not change the nature of the property and make it nonassignable. In re Sisler (D. C.), 2 Am. B. R. 760, 96 Fed. 402. The homestead right may be abandoned, or, if there

7. In re Lynch, 4 A. B. R. 262, 101 Fed. 579 (D. C. Ga.). Also, compare remarks in Roden Grocery Co. v. Bacon, 13 A. B. R. 251 (C. C. A. Ala.).

be no objection or application on the part of the bankrupt to have the homestead set apart to him, the property may be sold, and the proceeds distributed among his creditors. The property is of a nature to pass to the trustee, and after it passes it may be either set apart to the bankrupt or converted into money. There are cases in which real estate of greater value than is allowed by the statute as exempt, in which the bankrupt has a homestead right, is converted into money, and the amount of the exemption is paid to the bankrupt, and the balance distributed among his creditors. In re Oderkirk (D. C.), 4 Am. B. R. 617, 103 Fed. 779. When the property is sold by the trustee, or is set apart as exempt, the trustee has no further interest in or control of it; but the security of the mortgagee is not affected thereby, and he is no less a secured creditor because the property covered by his mortgage has been set apart as exempt. In re Little (D. C.), 6 Am. B. R. 681, 110 Fed. 621. The claim should not have been allowed as an unsecured claim. It could only participate in the dividends after the value of the security is deducted from the amount of the debt."

Nevertheless, as to homestead exemptions where the homestead is not exempted to the bankrupt absolutely but only during occupancy, the question is still perplexing, since there always remains a non-exempt reversionary interest likely to become a full title on abandonment of the homestead.[8]

It is immaterial whether the exempt property is separable from other property, or commingled therewith; or even though it is incapable of being separated therefrom. Where, however, immediate severance is not feasible, the bankrupt cannot have his exemptions set apart until the essential separation has been accomplished.[9]

A conversion of exempt property by the trustee renders him personally liable.[10]

§ 1025. What Date Fixes Right to Exemptions.—The date of the filing of the bankruptcy petition fixes the status as to exemptions.[11]

8. In re Mayer, 6 A. B. R. 117 (C. C. A. Wis.); Finley v. Poor, 10 A. B. R. 378, 121 Fed. 739 (C. C. A. Ky.).

9. Bank of Nez Perce v. Pindel, 28 A. B. R. 69, 193 Fed. 917 (C. C. A. Idaho).

10. Compare post, § 1780; also see Southern Irr. Co. v. Wharton Nat. Bank (Civ. App. Tex.), 28 A. B. R. 941.

11. Bankr. Act, § 6: "This act shall not affect the allowance to bankrupts of the exemptions which are prescribed by the State laws in force at the time of the filing of the petition in the State wherein they have had their domicile for the six months or the greater portion thereof immediately preceding the filing of the petition."

Also compare inferentially, §§ 1002, 1003, 1004, 1117, 1126, et seq. Inferentially, In re Elmira Steel Co., 5 A. B. R. 487 (Ref. N. Y.), although in this case the court is not considering the matter of exemptions.

Date of "Adjudication."—Some decisions seem to indicate that the date of the adjudication is the date of cleavage: In re Johnson, 24 A. B. R. 277, 176 Fed. 591 (D. C. Minn.); In re W. R. Rainwater, 25 A. B. R. 419, 191 Fed. 738 (D. C. Miss.).

Suggestively, In re Mayer, 6 A. B. R. 117, 108 Fed. 599 (C. C. A. Wis.): "The intention of this statute is, without doubt, that the creditors shall have all of the estate of a bankrupt which is not exempt, and that the bankrupt shall have the exemptions allowed by the law of his domicile determined by relation to the date of adjudication."

In re Seabolt, 8 A. B. R. 60, 113 Fed. 766 (D. C. Ga.): "The right to the exemption accrued to the debtor when

Compare, discussion, obiter, In re Youngstrom, 18 A. B. R. 572, 153 Fed. 97 (C. C. A. Colo.): "The present case, however, presents the question: At what point of time must the bankrupt be entitled to a particular exemption under the State laws to have it allowed and set apart under the saving and protecting provisions of the Bankruptcy Act? The answer must, of course, be found in that act. Naturally, it would be expected that this point of time would not be later than the date as of which the general estate of the bankrupt is wrested from his dominion and vested in his trustee for the benefit of the creditors. And such, we think, is actually and plainly the effect of the provisions before set forth. Thus it is declared, in § 6, that the exemptions to be allowed are those prescribed by the State laws in force 'at the time of the filing of the petition,' and, in § 70a, that, upon his appointment and qualification, the trustee shall be vested, by operation of law, with the title of the bankrupt, 'as of the date he was adjudged a bankrupt,' to all property, not exempt, which 'prior to the filing of the petition' he could by any means have transferred, or which might have been levied upon and sold under judicial process against him. Other provisions strengthen this view, notably the requirement of § 7, cl. 8, that a voluntary bankrupt shall claim his exemptions at the time of filing his petition, and that an involuntary bankrupt shall claim them within ten days after the adjudication, unless further time is granted. Indeed, we think the statute admits of doubt only in respect of whether the right to any claimed exemption is to be determined as of the time of the filing of the petition or as of the time when the debtor was adjudged a bankrupt. That it is to be determined as of the earlier date is suggested by those provisions of § 6, § 7, cl. 8, and § 70a, cl. 5, which make the time of the filing of the petition of special significance, and that it is to be determined as of the later date is suggested by the provision in § 70a that the trustee shall be vested with the title of the bankrupt as of the date he was adjudged a bankrupt. But, as the facts of the present case do not require that we determine this matter, we pass it, observing, first, that the present act differs from that of 1867 in that by § 14 of the latter the trustee became vested with the title of the bankrupt as of the date of the commencement of the proceedings; and, second, that the Circuit Court of Appeals of the Seventh Circuit seems to regard the date when the debtor was adjudged a

the creditors instituted proceedings in bankruptcy to subject his property to the payment of his debts, and upon the appointment of a trustee in bankruptcy the title of the property reserved by the law as the debtor's exemption did not vest in such trustee, but remained in the debtor, awaiting the mere legal formality of having it appraised and set apart to him."

Inferentially, In re Oleson, 7 A. B. R. 22, 110 Fed. 796 (D. C. Iowa): "The right to hold the land as exempt is not questioned, and, if it be true that it was and is exempt, I can see no ground for holding that the rental therefor contracted for and accruing after the adjudication belongs to the creditors.

"It is also charged that the chattel mortgage to the father is void as to creditors, being given without consideration."

Date of "Claiming" Exemptions.— Other decisions say that the right of a bankrupt to his exemption is to be determined as of the date when it is claimed. In re O'Hara, 20 A. B. R. 714, 162 Fed. 325 (D. C. Pa.); also, In re Donahey, 23 A. B. R. 795, 176 Fed. 458 (D. C. Pa.). These cases thus, apparently, attempt to create a new date of cleavage, that is, the date when the exemption is claimed. Inasmuch as the situation in most of the decided cases has been the same at the time of the filing of the schedules as at the date of the adjudication, these decisions must be taken as obiter dicta so far as concerns the validity of this new date of cleavage. That the mere date of filing a schedule, should be a determining fact for the establishment of rights of property is not to be conceded. A new date of cleavage should not be thus introduced into bankruptcy law.

bankrupt as controlling, as is shown In re Mayer, 6 Am. B. R. 117, 108 Fed. 599, 608."

Compare, inferentially, Smalley *v.* Laugenour, 13 A. B. R. 692, 196 U. S. 93: "And the court held that the order of the District Judge of the United States for the District of Washington, sitting in bankruptcy, awarding the property to Laugenour as property exempt from the claims of his creditors, and which related back to the time of the filing of the petition in bankruptcy, which was prior to the date of the attempted sale, was a judgment conclusive as between the parties that the property was so exempt at that date." This case is not conclusive, however, for the date of the filing of the petition coincided with that of the adjudication, it being a case of voluntary bankruptcy.

Mullinix *v.* Simon, 28 A. B. R. 1, 196 Fed. 775 (C. C. A. Ark.): "The bankrupt's right to such exemptions as are permitted by state laws is referable to the condition of things as they existed, 'at the time of the filing of the petition.' Section 6 of the Bankruptcy Act. At that time the title to his stock of merchandise was in the bankrupt and the property was undoubtedly in his hands as 'vendee.'" But it does not appear in this case but that .the petition was a voluntary petition and hence the adjudication simultaneous with the filing of the petition. Moreover, the precise distinction as between the date of the filing and the date of adjudication as the correct date of severance does not appear to have been raised.

If the bankrupt then was entitled to the exemptions he claimed, the property remains his property, free from the claims of creditors, notwithstanding he may no longer be entitled to exemptions at the time the trustee is ready to set apart exempt property. The date of the filing of the bankruptcy petition is the line of cleavage. That date severs his old estate from his new estate, his old creditors from his new ones. Thus, if then not exempt, the subsequent marriage of the bankrupt will not render it exempt.

In re Fletcher, 16 A. B. R. 491 (Ref. Ohio): "All he gains, earns or acquires subsequent to the filing of his petition is absolutely free from the claims of his prior creditors. The commencement of bankruptcy proceedings marks the division of his old financial condition and his new financial condition. He is supposed to give up everything and to be freed of his debts, and it is not in the spirit of the bankruptcy law to allow him subsequent to the commencement of bankruptcy proceedings to change his status so as to claim any greater rights out of the property than he possessed at the time he commenced the proceedings.

"The very fact that the bankrupt is required to make his claim in the schedules filed with his petition, indicates that the framers of the Bankruptcy Law intended that the bankrupt's exemptions, if he intended to claim any, must be claimed as of the time he filed his petition. At the time Fletcher filed his petition, he was not entitled to any exemptions, and he can not do anything subsequent to that time to change his relation to his property.".

And if then exempt, absolutely exempt, the subsequent death of the bankrupt's wife or loss of his family or other change of his status as to exemptions[11a] will not cause it to revert to his trustee.

11a. Change of debtor's occupation, giving different exemptions, rights re- main same. In re Fly, 6 A. B. R. 550, 110 Fed. 141 (D. C. Calif.).

Likewise, his subsequent death, before the exemptions are set apart to him, will not defeat the exemptions nor cause the exempt property to fall into the general estate; the exemptions will pass to the representatives of the deceased bankrupt free from the claims of the old creditors.[12]

However, it has been held that the mere perfecting of homestead exemption rights by filing a statutory "designation of homestead" may be done after the bankruptcy.[13]

In re Culwell, 21 A. B. R. 614, 165 Fed. 828 (D. C. Mont.): "Yet the act does not make it a precedent to having a homestead allowed to the bankrupt claiming the same in the bankruptcy court, that the homestead shall have been designated pursuant to the State statute, prior to the date of adjudication in bankruptcy. * * * If the bankrupt has expeditiously and in good faith made his declaration, following the claim in the schedule, the property is exempt and cannot be retained for administration."

To be sure, the *title* to the nonexempt property, by § 70 (a), does not rest in creditors until the date of adjudication and so the effectual separation of title does not occur until then, but the *status* of the property is determined as of the date of the filing of the bankruptcy petition, at any rate as to all property in the custody of the bankruptcy court at that date, such, for example, as property in the possession or control of the bankrupt, such property being impounded, so to speak, and held in statu quo so far as the rights of the parties therein may be concerned, until the subsequent adjudication shall vest the title.[13a]

It is a question, as noted in the preceding section, whether, upon the subsequent abandonment of the homestead, after it has been adjudicated that the same should be set apart to the bankrupt as exempt, the title still remains in the bankrupt or reverts to the trustee. It might seem that perhaps the Bankruptcy Act gives the bankrupt absolute title to exempt property even where, under state law, it is exempt only so long as used as a homestead, this being based on the apparent denial, in § 70 (a), to the trustee of any title to exempt property; yet, perhaps the better reasoning is that the homestead is not exempt absolutely but only during user and that there always remains a reversionary interest in the trustee which, perhaps indeed, the trustee might sell as an asset of the estate at any time.[14]

---

12. In re Seabolt, 8 A. B. R. 57, 113 Fed. 766 (D. C. N. Car.); contra, In re Parschen, 9 A. B. R. 389, 119 Fed. 976 (D. C. Ohio).

13. In re Fisher, 15 A. B. R. 652 (D. C. Va.). Compare analogous doctrine, as to perfecting of mechanics' liens pending bankruptcy, § 1155.

13a. Compare, Acme Harvester Co. v. Beekman, 222 U. S. 300, 27 A. B. R. 262, quoted post, § 1126. Also compare reasoning of §§ 1002, 1003, 1004, 1117.

14. In re Mayer, 6 A. B. R. 117, 108 Fed. 599 (C. C. A. Wis., Jenkins, C. J., dissenting): In this case it was held that, after a court of bankruptcy had adjudicated and determined the property which should be set apart to the bankrupt as a homestead under the laws of the State of Wisconsin and there was nothing left to do but to determine the line of boundary of said homestead at the most, and the bankrupt, in order to avoid the consequences of an order adjudging him in contempt had fled the country, that under such circumstances the prop-

JURISDICTION OF THE BANKRUPTCY COURT OVER EXEMPT PROPERTY.

§ 1026. Bankruptcy Court's Jurisdiction over Exemptions Exclusive.—The bankruptcy court has jurisdiction, and the jurisdiction is exclusive, to determine the claims of bankrupts to their exemptions.

Section 2, subd. 11, of the Bankruptcy Act confers the express authority upon courts of bankruptcy to "determine all claims of bankrupts to their exemptions;" and this jurisdiction is exclusive—the State courts cannot pass upon them, although it is true the State laws set the bounds and limits of the right to the exemptions—the exclusive forum where these rights are to be determined being the court of bankruptcy.[15]

In re Lucius, 10 A. B. R. 653, 124 Fed. 455 (D. C. Ala.): "The bankrupt court has jurisdiction to determine all claims of bankrupts to their exemptions, and has exclusive jurisdiction to determine such claims."

McGahan v. Anderson, 7 A. B. R. 641, 113 Fed. 115 (C. C. A. S. C.): "The bankrupt court, as a necessity, must alone deal with the exemptions of the bankrupt. If any other tribunal was to intervene to determine this question, it would be the exercise of a jurisdiction, which might result in a conflict of authority, and deprive the bankrupt court of its rightful power to speedily determine all questions of law and right arising under the Bankrupt Act, which was clearly the intention of Congress when it enacted the law."

In re [Jonas B.] Baughman, 25 A. B. R. 167, 183 Fed. 668 (D. C. Pa.): "It is said that the bankruptcy court has no jurisdiction over exempt property except to set it aside. No doubt to a qualified extent that is true, but it does not apply here. In order to get the benefit of the exemption, it must be claimed and until it is, and specific property has been set off under it, the court has full authority to consider and dispose of whatever is involved. It may deny the bankrupt his exemption where he has waived or forfeited it, or for any reason it cannot be rightly claimed. It is only after the bankrupt has been found entitled to it, and it has been set off to him, that the court loses its hold."

§ 1027. Trustee Entitled to Possession Long Enough to Set Apart. —The trustee has the right to the possession of the property long enough to set it apart.[16]

§ 1028. Court May Enjoin Interference.—And if it is in his posses-

erty set apart as a homestead had been abandoned by the bankrupt, and passed to the trustee, and became property which he might administer as part of the bankrupt estate, and that the court of bankruptcy still had jurisdiction to deal with such property.

15. In re Overstreet, 2 A. B. R. 486 (Ref. Ark.); In re McCrary Bros., 22 A. B. R. 160, 169 Fed. 485 (D. C. Ala.); The Gregory Co. v. Bristol, 26 A. B. R. 938, 191 Fed. 31 (C. C. A. Minn.).

16. In re McClintock, 13 A. B. R. 606 (Ref. Ohio, affirmed by D. C.). Obiter, First Nat'l Bk. of Sayre v. Bartlett, 21 A. B. R. 88, 35 Pa. Super. Ct. 593. Compare, In re Mayer, 6 A. B. R. 117 (C. C. A. Wis.), that the trustee has title thereto "sub modo." Also, compare, In re McCartney, 6 A. B. R. 366 (D. C. Wis.), where the bankruptcy court granted leave to a garnishee to pay into the bankruptcy court exempt wages garnished. But no longer, In re Soper, 22 A. B. R. 868, 173 Fed. 116 (D. C. Neb.). Also, see § 1032.

sion, the bankruptcy court may enjoin the State. Court's officers, or at any rate the parties in the state court, from interfering with the trustee's custody until the property has been thus set apart by him.[17]

§ 1029. **But Will Not Necessarily Order Surrender.**—But the bankruptcy court is not obliged summarily to order the delivery of the property over to the trustee, if it is not already in his possession.[18]

§ 1030. **Nor Authorize Trustee to Intervene in Attachment Case to Obtain Possession.**—And it has been held that the trustee has no right to intervene in an attachment case for the purpose of obtaining possession of the attached property.[19]

§ 1031' **After Obtaining Possession, No Amendment of Claim of Exemptions to Defeat Lienholders as to Whom Property Not Exempt.**—After the trustee has obtained possession of property not claimed as exempt, on the plea ·that the lien thereon is void as to creditors, the bankrupt ·should not be permitted to come in and claim it as exempt and thus assert the creditors' rights to enable him to defraud the lienholder out of property to which, as between the bankrupt and the lienholder, the lienholder is entitled.[20]

§ 1032. **Bankruptcy Court May Not Administer, but Only Determine and Set Apart Exemptions.**—The bankruptcy court is without power to administer exempt property, save and except merely to determine it to be exempt and to set it apart as such; and the bankruptcy court will

---

17. In re Beals, 8 A. B. R. 639, 116 Fed. 530 (D. C. Ind.); inferentially, In re Tune, 8 A. B. R. 285, 115 Fed. 906 (D. C. Ala.). But even in that event the lien of the levy made by the State Court's officers will probably remain good on the property in the trustee's hands and be restored to full vigor as soon as he has set apart the property 'as exempt.

Where the garnishee is aware of the fact that the property or credits in his hands are exempt, it is his duty to disclose such fact. in his answer, where the defendant. is not served with notice or notice is given only by publication; otherwise payment by him into court or a judgment charging him as garnishee will not relieve him from subsequent liability to the bankrupt. In re Beals, 8 A. B. R. 639, 116 Fed. 530 (D. C. Ind.).

Leave ·has been granted in one case to a garnishee (who had been ordered by the State court to pay into the State court) ·to turn ·over exempt wages to the bankruptcy court. In

re McCartney, 6 A. B. R. 366, 109 Fed. 629 (D. C. Wis.):

The referee could not enjoin the State court's officers, the effect being to stay proceedings of a court or officer as to which the referee has no jurisdiction. In re Siebert, 13 A. B. R. 348, 133 Fed. 781 (D. C. N. J.). Compare, § 1918.

18. Sharp v. Woolslare, 12 A. B. R. 396 (Superior Ct. Penna.); Jewett Bros. v. Huffman, 13 A. B. R. 738 (Sup. Ct. N. Dak.); compare, In re Hatch, 4 A. B. R. 350, 102 Fed. 280 (D. C. Iowa).

19. Jewett Bros. v. Hoffman, 13 A. B. R. 738 (Sup. Ct. N. Dak.).

20. See remark to a similar effect, In re J. C. Winship Co., 9 A. B. R. 638, 120 Fed. 93 (C. C. A. Ills.). But compare contra, in principle, In re Soper, 22 A. B. R. 868, 173 Fed. 116 (D. C. Neb.), wherein the court held that, after setting aside a chattel mortgage as a preference the mortgagor bankrupt could claim his exemptions freed from the mortgage lien! Also, compare, § 1061, note.

not undertake to determine the validity, extent nor priority of liens thereon or rights therein.[21]

As soon as the trustee has properly set off the bankrupt's property, all the trustee's rights, even that of mere custody, cease, and after the trustee's report has been finally approved, the bankruptcy court is without control over the property and without power to determine any rights thereto.[22]

Lockwood v. Exch. Bk., 10 A. B. R. 112, 190 U. S. 294: "The fact that the Act of 1898 confers upon the court of bankruptcy authority to control exempt property in order to set it aside, and thus exclude it from the assets of the bankrupt estate to be administered, affords no just ground for holding that the court of bankruptcy must administer and distribute, as included in the assets of the estate, the very property which the act in unambiguous language declares shall not pass from the bankrupt or become part of the bankruptcy assets. The two provisions of the statute must be construed together and both be given

---

21. In re Yeager, 25 A. B. R. 51, 182 Fed. 951 (D. C. Pa.); Newberry Shoe Co. v. Collier, 25 A. B. R. 130 (Sup. Ct. Va.); Instance, In re Loden, 25 A. B. R. 917, 184 Fed. 965 (D. C. Ga.); Bank of Nez Perce v. Pindel, 28 A. B. R. 69, 193 Fed. 917 (C. C. A. Idaho).

22. Powers Dry Goods Co. v. Nelson, 7 A. B. R. 506 (Sup. Ct. N. Dak.); inferentially, In re Bolinger, 6 A. B. R. 171, 108 Fed. 374 (D. C. Penn.); Sharp v. Woolslare, 12 A. B. R. 396 (Superior Ct. Penn.).

In re J. E. Maynard & Co., 25 A. B. R. 732, 183 Fed. 823 (D. C. Ga.). Compare, In re [Jonas B.] Baughman, 25 A. B. R. 167, 183 Fed. 668 (D. C. Pa.), quoted at § 1026; Sullivan v. Mussey, 25 A. B. R. 781, 184 Fed. 60 (C. C. A. Tex.), affirming 25 A. B. R. 91.

In re Camp, 1 A. B. R. 165, 91 Fed. 745 (D. C. N. Car.); In re Hills, 2 A. B. R. 798, 96 Fed. 185 (D. C. Ga.); Ingram v. Wilson, 11 A. B. R. 192, 125 Fed. 913 (C. C. A. Iowa); In re LeVay, 11 A. B. R. 116, 125 Fed. 990 (D. C. Pa.); impliedly, In re Wells, 5 A. B. R. 311, 105 Fed. 762 (D. C. Ark.); obiter, In re Royce Dry Goods Co., 13 A. B. R. 268, 133 Fed. 100 (D. C. Mo.); In re Bender, 17 A. B. R. 895 (Ref. Ohio); In re Ogilvie, 5 A. B. R. 374 (Ref. Ga.); In re Hopkins, 1 A. B. R. 209 (Ref. Ala.); In re Black, 4 A. B. R. 776, 104 Fed. 28 (D. C. Pa.); In re Moore, 7 A. B. R. 285, 112 Fed. 289 (D. C. Ala.); Roden Grocery Co. v. Bacon, 13 A. B. R. 253, 133 Fed. 515 (C. C. A. Ala.); In re Swords, 7 A. B. R. 436, 112 Fed. 661 (D. C. Ga.). Apparently contra, In re Sloan, 14 A. B. R. 435, 135 Fed. 873 (D. C. Pa.), but in this case right

of exemption was lost by assigning it. Instance, contra, Burrow v. Grand Lodge, 13 A. B. R. 542, 133 Fed. 708 (C. C. A. Tex.); instance, contra, In re Stout, 6 A. B. R. 505 (D. C. Mo.); contra, In re Garden, 1 A. B. R. 582, 93 Fed. 423 (D. C. Ala., overruled by In re Moore, 7 A. B. R. 285, 112 Fed. 289); In re Blanchard, 20 A. B. R. 417, 161 Fed. 739 (D. C. N. Car.); In re Paramore & Ricks, 19 A. B. R. 130, 156 Fed. 211 (D. C. N. Car.); In re Blanchard & Howard, 20 A. B. R. 422, 161 Fed. 797 (D. C. N. Car.); In re Edwards, 19 A. B. R. 632, 156 Fed. 794 (D. C. Ala.); In re Maxson, 22 A. B. R. 424, 170 Fed. 356 (D. C. Iowa); In re MacKissic, 22 A. B. R. 817, 171 Fed. 259 (D. C. Pa.); In re Soper, 22 A. B. R. 868, 173 Fed. 116 (D. C. Neb.).

In re Brumbaugh, 12 A. B. R. 204, 128 Fed. 971 (D. C. Penn.), where the court held, in substance, that the only question to be determined upon a bankrupt's claim for exemptions is whether he is entitled thereto as against general creditors, and that it was therefore no ground for opposing a bankrupt's application therefor that in the State courts he would not be able to maintain his claim to the property set apart as exempt against a judgment for breach of promise to marry recovered prior to his adjudication.

Compare, limitations of rule where exemptions involved in marshalling of liens, First Nat'l Bk. of Sayre v. Bartlett, 21 A. B. R. 88, 35 Pa. Super. Ct. 593.

Compare, analogous rule where property found to belong to adverse claimants, In re Smyth, 21 A. B. R. 853 (D. C. Pa.). Also, see post, § 1797.

effect. Moreover, the want of power in the court of bankruptcy to administer exempt property is besides shown by the context of the act, since throughout its text exempt property is contrasted with property not exempt, the latter alone constituting assets of the bankrupt estate subject to administration. The Act of 1898, instead of manifesting the purpose of Congress to adopt a different rule from that which was applied, as we have seen with reference to the Act of 1867, on the contrary exhibits the intention to perpetuate the rule, since the provision of the statute to which we have referred in reason is consonant only with that hypothesis."

In re Little, 6 A. B. R. 681, 110 Fed. 621 (D. C. Iowa): "By the action of the trustee, confirmed by the referee, the exemptions claimed by the bankrupt were allowed, and the particular property was set apart to him, and passed into his possession and control. When thus separated from the general estate, the exempt property ceased to be in the possession of the trustee or of the court, and under the provisions of § 70, the trustee took no title thereto. Under these circumstances the referee rightly ruled that the court of bankruptcy would not entertain jurisdiction over the exempt property at the request of the claimant bank. When the application on behalf of the bank was filed, the exempt property had passed from the possession of the court in bankruptcy. The trustee had no title thereto, and the creditors at large had no equity therein."

In re Jackson, 8 A. B. R. 594, 116 Fed. 46 (D. C. Pa.): "We have nothing further to do with it than to see that the trustee sets it aside, and to dispose of such questions as may arise incident to that process. After the property exempted has been separated and delivered, its subsequent fate does not concern us. If some one of the bankrupt's creditors has already obtained, or should afterwards obtain, a lien upon it, it is not for this court to interfere with his right."

In re Grimes, 2 A. B. R. 730, 96 Fed. 529 (D. C. N. Car.): "After the exempt property has been designated and set apart to the bankrupts by the trustee, it has been administered, and has passed out of the possession and control of the Bankruptcy Court. The trustee has no further concern with it, nor has the court any jurisdiction to defend such property from adverse claims or liens that may or may not be distinguished by the bankruptcy proceedings. It will not entertain a proceeding to enforce a lien upon such property."

In re Hatch, 4 A. B. R. 349, 102 Fed. 280 (D. C. Iowa): "The actual possession of the property is held by the bankrupt, and since the same was segregated from the estate, and assigned to the bankrupt as exempt, it has ceased to be within either the actual or constructive possession of the court of bankruptcy."

In re Durham, 4 A. B. R. 762, 104 Fed. 231 (D. C. Ark.): "* * * he is only entitled to the possession thereof for the purpose of ascertaining * * * whether the value of the property does not exceed that allowed as exempt by the laws of the State. As soon as that is ascertained it is the duty of the trustee to deliver it to the bankrupt."

McKenney & Cheney, 11 A. B. R. 54, 118 Ga. 387: "Under the Bankruptcy Act of 1898 the bankrupt court is without authority or power to administer property set aside as exempt under the Constitution of this State."

Bell v. Dawson Grocery Co., 12 A. B. R. 161, 120 Ga. 628: "It is now well settled both in this and the Federal Courts that the trustee in bankruptcy has no power nor control over the exempted property after it has been set apart to the applicant. The title never passes to him, but remains in the bankrupt. The trustee can set apart the exemption and pass upon such objections as may be made by creditors to his so doing. But he cannot administer the property exempted, nor determine the rights of creditors asserting waivers against it."

In re Hartsell & Son, 15 A. B. R. 177 (D. C. Ala.): "It has been uniformly ruled of late, that the court of bankruptcy has nothing to do with exempt property except to ascertain whether it be exempt, and then to set it aside. It has no authority to enforce even an admitted lien upon the exempt property. Setting aside the property as exempt does not affect the rights of the lienholder, nor does it in any wise prevent a creditor, whose claim is not avoided by the discharge in bankruptcy, from proceeding against the property in the hands of the bankrupt, just as though he had not been adjudged a bankrupt."

In re Lucius, 10 A. B. R. 654, 124 Fed. 455 (D. C. Ala.): "When the exemption has been set apart by the trustee, and he has reported it to the court for its approval, and when approved and the bankrupt's right to it has been finally determined, the property embraced in the exemption ceases to be a part of the assets to be administered by the court in connection with the bankrupt's estate, and the bankrupt court would have no jurisdiction to entertain a plenary suit in equity by a creditor of the bankrupt to reach and subject to his claim such exempt property."

Woodruff v. Cheeves, 5 A. B. R. 303, 105 Fed. 601 (C. C. A. Ga.): "It seems clear to us that this language of the statute leaves no room for argument to show that the exempt property constitutes no part of the estate in bankruptcy subject to administration by the trustee or the court of bankruptcy."

In re Castleberry, 16 A. B. R. 160 (D. C. Ga.): "It is thoroughly settled now that the bankrupt court will not undertake to enforce debts claimed to be good against the homestead exemption."

Nat'l Bk. of Sayre v. Bartlett, 21 A. B. R. 88, 35 Pa. Super. Ct. 593: "It does not seem that the District Court has any control over it, except such as may be necessary to aid in having it appraised and set apart under the State laws. * * * We think it very clear that the language 'estate of the bankrupt' as used in the Act of 1898 does not include the exempted property, but only such as passes to the trustee."

In re Culwell, 21 A. B. R. 614, 165 Fed. 828 (D. C. Mont.): "The authority to control property in order to set it aside, if exempt, and to exclude it from the assets of the bankrupt estate, which are to be administered upon, does not in any way extend authority to the trustee to administer upon exempt property as though it were an asset of the estate."

[1867] In re Bass, 3 Woods 382: "In other words, it is made as clear, as anything can be, that such exempted property constitutes no part of the assets in bankruptcy. The agreement of the bankrupt in any particular case to waive the right to the exemption makes no difference. He may own other debts in regard to which no such agreement has been made. But whether so or not, it is not for the bankrupt court to inquire. The exemption is created by the State law, and the assignee acquires no title to the exempt property. If the creditor has a claim against it he must prosecute that claim in a court which has jurisdiction over the property, which the bankrupt court has not."

Some decisions, while conceding that the bankruptcy court has no jurisdiction to administer exempt property, hold that the rule is not violated when the bankruptcy court undertakes to administer the property in its custody otherwise exempt, for the benefit of those creditors who hold waivers of exemption or as to whom the property is not exempt, as in States where there are no exemptions against claims for purchase price, for torts or for necessaries; the reasoning being in substance that, as to such creditors, the court is *not* administering exempt property, and the court being in possession of the res is competent to determine conflicting claims and interests therein and should not refuse to do so, especially since the creditor is barred by the bankruptcy from asserting his rights by levy in the customary manner. Among such decisions are the following:[23]

In re Gordon, 8 A. B. R. 255, 115 Fed. 445 (D. C. Vt.): "This is not contrary to the cases cited by the bankrupt, that hold waivers of, or liens upon, exemptions to be outside the jurisdiction of the courts of bankruptcy, for here what is reached is not within the exemption. Woodruff v. Cheeves, 5 Am. B. R. 296, 105 Fed. 601. Bankruptcy courts have nothing to do with exemptions but to set them out. Here, as to these prior claims, there is no exemption in this homestead to set out."

In re Sisler, 2 A. B. R. 768, 96 Fed. 402 (D. C. Va.): "These decisions sustain the position of the creditor in this case that his debt, containing a waiver of the homestead exemption, can be enforced in this court against the property claimed by the bankrupt as exempt under the provisions of the homestead law. The court can find no reason for denying the right of the creditor to have the property surrendered by the bankrupt subjected to the payment of his debt. We have seen that this property is not exempt. The debt proved by the creditor is not a lien on this property, and therefore cannot follow it after the discharge of the bankrupt, and be enforced in a State Court. The discharge of the bankrupt could be pleaded in a State Court as a complete bar to its recovery."

In re Bragg, 2 N. B. N. & R. 84 (Ref. Ala.): "The whole argument is based on the assumption of the very fact to be decided, viz: Is the property claimed by the bankrupt, exempt to him? Certainly, if the property claimed by the bankrupt is not exempt to him as against any creditor, then it should not be set apart to him against the protest of such creditor, merely because it is exempt as against other creditors."

In re Boyd, 10 A. B. R. 339, 120 Fed. 999 (D. C. Iowa): "It is not questioned that, if the property had been fully paid for, it would be exempt from the claims of creditors under the provisions of § 4008 of the Code of Iowa, but by § 4015 of the Code it is declared that 'none of the exemptions prescribed in this chapter shall be allowed against an execution issued for the purchase money of property claimed to be exempt, and on which such execution is levied,' and the question for consideration is whether effect can be given to this section of the Code in cases of bankruptcy. According to the statements of counsel, the ruling of the referee was based upon the thought that the benefit of § 4015 was available only to one who had secured a judgment for the unpaid purchase price, and had caused an execution for the collection of the judgment to be levied upon the property. Section 6 of the Bankrupt Act (Act July 1, 1898, 30 Stat. 548 [U. S. Comp. St. 1901, p. 3424]), declares, in substance, that the act shall not affect the allowance to bankrupts of the exemptions prescribed by the law of the State wherein the bankrupt has his domicile. It certainly was not the intent of this section to enlarge the exemptions available to the bankrupt under the law of the State. It is clear that, if the bankrupt had not invoked the benefit of the Bankrupt Act, the property he now claims to be exempt to him would have been liable to be subjected to the payment of the unpaid portions of the purchase price. True, the mode which the creditors would have been compelled to pursue in order to subject the property to the payment of their claims would be to obtain judgment, and cause a levy of execution on the property; but the

---

23. In re Richardson, 11 A. B. R. 379 (Ref. Ala.); impliedly, In re Campbell, 10 A. B. R. 730, 124 Fed. 417 (D. C. Va.).

substance of the right secured by § 4015 of the Code of Iowa is that no property can be held exempt against the debt due for the purchase price, although this right can only be enforced in the State court through the form of a judgment and levy of execution. By instituting the proceedings in bankruptcy, the debtor has brought this property into the custody and under the control of this court, acting as a court in equity. The bankrupt now asks the court to make an order setting apart this specific property to him as exempt under the law of the State. The creditors, B. R. Evans and D. A. Lyon, pray the court for an order declaring the property not exempt as against their claims, and directing the sale thereof for their benefit.

"It is a familiar rule that, when property comes under the control and custody of the court, all parties claiming interests or rights therein or thereto will be permitted to assert such rights before the court having custody of the property. It is equally well settled that in such cases regard will be paid and protection be granted to the substance of the right asserted, even though the court may not be able to adopt and follow the form of the remedy which, under the statutes of the State, would be alone open to the claimant if the property was not in the custody of the court. Thus, in Krippendorf v. Hyde, 110 U. S. 276, 280, 28 L. Ed. 145, it was said:

"'The only legal remedy which can be said to be adequate for the purpose of protecting and preserving his right to the possession of his property was an action in replevin. Of this remedy at law in the State court he was deprived by the fact that the proceedings in attachment were pending in a court of the United States, because the property attached, being in the hands of the marshall, is regarded as in the custody of the court. This was the point decided in Freeman v. Howe, 24 How. 450 (16 L. Ed. 749), the doctrine of which must be considered as fully and finally established in this court. * * * For if we affirm, as that decision does, the exclusive right of the Circuit Court in such a case to maintain the custody of property seized and held under its process by its officers, and thus to take from owners the ordinary means of redress by suits for restitution in State courts, where any one may sue, without regard to citizenship, it is but common justice to furnish them with an equal and adequate remedy in the court itself which maintains control of the property; and, as this may not be done by original suits on account of the nature of the jurisdiction as limited by differences of citizenship, it can only be accomplished by the exercise of the inherent and equitable powers of the court in auxiliary proceedings incidental to the cause in which the property is held, so as to give to the claimant, from whose possession it has been taken, the opportunity to assert and enforce his right. And this jurisdiction is well defined by Mr. Justice Nelson, in the statement quoted, as arising out of the inherent power of every court of justice to control its own process so as to prevent and redress wrong. * * * So the equitable powers of the courts of law over their own process to prevent abuse, oppression, and injustice are inherent and equally extensive and efficient, as is also their power to protect their own jurisdiction and officers in the possession of property that is in the custody of the law; and when, in the exercise of that power, it becomes necessary to forbid to strangers to the action the resort to the ordinary remedies of the law for the restoration of property in that situation, as happens when otherwise conflicts of jurisdiction must arise between courts of the United States and of the several States, the very circumstances appear which give the party a title to an equitable remedy because he is deprived of a plain and adequate remedy at law.'

"Thus is declared the principle that is decisive of the question under consideration. The bankrupt, by instituting proceedings in bankruptcy, placed his property within the custody and control of this court. He now asks the court to set apart to him as exempt certain articles of personal property. Two of his creditors appear, and show to the court that the articles in question were sold by them on credit to the bankrupt, and have not been paid for, and that under the State law the articles remain liable for the unpaid portions of the purchase price. The bankrupt answers thereto that under the State statute the only remedy open to the creditors by which they can enforce their rights against the property is by obtaining judgments and levying executions on the property. To this it is replied that the bankrupt, by his own act in filing his petition in bankruptcy and procuring the adjudication in bankruptcy, has put it out of the power of the creditors to obtain judgments at law against him, and, the property being within the custody of the court, the only remedy now open to them is to invoke the protection of this court. Under these circumstances, it is not open to the bankrupt, while admitting—as he is compelled to do—that the State statute does not exempt this property from liability for the unpaid purchase price thereof, to assert that by bringing the property into the custody of this court and obtaining the adjudication in bankruptcy, he has defeated the rights of the creditors by barring them from following the remedy provided for in the State statute. To justify this court in setting aside this property to the bankrupt as exempt, it must appear that it is exempt under the provisions of the law of Iowa. Under that law the creditors could subject the property to the payment of their claims, the method of so doing being the procuring judgments at law against the debtor and the levy of executions on the property. This method of enforcing the rights of the creditors has been barred to them by the act of the debtor in procuring himself to be adjudged a bankrupt, and in placing the property within the control of this court; but, as held in the cited case of Krippendorf v. Hyde, that is the very reason why this court is in duty bound to furnish an equivalent remedy, which can be readily done by ordering the trustee to sell the articles claimed as exempt, and, after paying the costs of sale, to apply the balance left to the payment of the claims of the named creditors, B. R. Evans and D. A. Lyon, any surplus left to be paid to the bankrupt, as these articles are exempt, under the State statute, from the claims of the general creditors.

"Upon the question of the proper mode of presenting questions of this character, it seems clear that they should be presented by the party specially interested, rather than by the trustee. As against the general creditors, the property is exempt, and the bankrupt is entitled to have the same assigned to him as exempt, except as against the claim of the person from whom the property was purchased on credit. If such creditor does not, in proper time and while the property is in the custody of the court, assert his claim, and invoke the protection of the court, it will be assumed that he waives his right, and, if the property is set apart as exempt, and is delivered to the bankrupt, so that in fact it passes from the custody of the court, it is difficult to see upon what theory the court can afterwards assert a jurisdiction over the same.

"No title to exempt property passes to the trustee, and, if property is exempt as against the creditors generally, it cannot be well held that a title thereto vests in the trustee simply because a single creditor may have the right to subject the property to the payment of his claim. This right is not a title to the property, nor a lien thereon, but is simply a right or privilege personal to the creditor owning the claim for the unpaid purchase price, which certainly does not vest in the trustee, and therefore the same should be presented by the creditor in his own name."

It is possible that there has been a failure to observe the dual capacity of the trustee in bankruptcy; that he is not only a party litigant acting in behalf of general creditors by virtue of the title and rights conferred upon him by §§ 47, 67 and 70 of the Act, but is also the officer of the court, a custodian, holding all property in his possession subject to the determination of the rights of the parties therein, holding property to which the creditors have not title or have only qualified title equally as well as that to which they have absolute title, so holding it until the court shall have determined the various rights to it and liens upon it in favor of the different claimants.[24]

Probably the courts having once so thoroughly committed themselves to the construction that the statutory provision, § 70 (a), reserving title to exempt property to the bankrupt, means that the trustee has no control over exempt property even in his capacity as a mere ministerial officer, except to set it apart, it is fruitless to discuss the ground work of these rulings. Yet were the question to be considered de novo, it would seem that the bankruptcy court ought to administer the exempt property equally as well as the non-exempt property, having actual custody thereof, and that the fact that the trustee *as a party litigant*—the trustee for general creditors—has no *title* to exempt property, ought not to be construed to prevent him from retaining control over it *as the officer of the court,* nor to prevent the rights of the various parties therein being determined by the bankruptcy court.

Nevertheless, the law is settled differently, and seems to be, in brief, that the sole question to be determined by the bankruptcy court is whether or not the property is exempt against creditors in general. If it be so exempt, then it is to be set apart, and further administration of it refused, notwithstanding that, as to some creditors, it might not be exempt.[25]

But where property is only partially exempt, as, for instance, where it exceeds in value the exemption allowances, it seems that it may then be administered in the bankruptcy proceedings so far, at any rate, as to make the excess available as an asset.

First Nat. Bank *v.* Lanz, 29 A. B. R. 247, 202 Fed. 117, 121 (C. C. A. La.): "Ordinarily when a preferential transfer is set aside, the exempt property is restored to the bankrupt's estate, and then becomes subject to his exemptions, and should be set aside as exempt to him by the trustee. In this case the property exceeds in value the bankrupt's exemption, and for that reason, it is necessary that it be administered through the bankruptcy court, in order that the estate may profit by the excess. Upon sale of the property either the appellant or the bankrupt would, as against the trustee in bankruptcy, be entitled to the amount of the homestead exemption out of the proceeds of the sale. As between the appellant and the bankrupt, if controversy arises, their respective rights to the amount of the exemption would have to be worked out in the State court. Lockwood *v.* Exchange Bank, 190 U. S. 294, 10 Am. B. R. 107. If either consents to the payment by the trustee to the other, it

24. See ante, § 896.
25. In re Brumbaugh, 12 A. B. R. 204, 128 Fed. 971 (D. C. Penn.); In re

Maxson, 22 A. B. R. 424, 170 Fed. 356 (D. C. Iowa).

would be proper for the trustee to make payment to such other. In the absence of such consent, it will be the duty of the trustee to hold the amount of the exemption to abide the decision of the State court, and then pay it to the appellant or to the bankrupt according to the award of the State court."

It has been held, however, that the court has no jurisdiction to sell exempt property and administer the proceeds, even though requested to do so by the bankrupt and all other parties in interest.[26]

§ 1033. But Not to Deliver to Bankrupt Simply Because Claimed Exempt, if Third Party Claims Ownership.

—The rule denying jurisdiction over exempt property would not, however, permit the court to give property, once in its custody but belonging to another, over to an irresponsible bankrupt simply because the latter claims it as exempt. And if the bankrupt claims, as exempt, property in the hands of the trustee to which a third party also lays claim of ownership or of right of possession, the bankruptcy court must determine between the two applicants and deliver the property to the person entitled thereto.[27]

Remark, In re Antigo Screen Door Co., 10 A. B. R. 359, 362, 123 Fed. 249 (C. C. A. Wis.): "We take it that any court, whether one of equity, common law, admiralty or bankruptcy, having in its treasury a fund touching which there is a dispute, may, by virtue of its inherent powers, determine the right to the fund thus in its possession. Jurisdiction in that respect is an incident of every court."

Possibly, also, the bankruptcy court would have such jurisdiction where the third party claims even as a lienholder, especially if the bankrupt has not specified the articles he demands as exempt and none have yet been set apart to him.[28]

In a certain sense indeed, it is true that the jurisdiction of the bankruptcy court to determine the rights of bankrupts to their exemptions, which is an exclusive jurisdiction (ante, § 1026), carries with it an implied right to determine all questions of ownership including those of the qualified ownership of lienholders; and on principle it is hard to distinguish between the conceded right and duty of the bankruptcy court to turn the property over to an adverse claimant asserting absolute ownership and to turn over to a lienholder the amount of his qualified ownership.[29]

26. In re Rising, 27 A. B. R. 519 (D. C. Tex.). But this is, of course, extreme doctrine. Consent under such circumstances would undoubtedly confer jurisdiction. Compare, on general subject of consent conferring jurisdiction, post, § 1696.

27. Compare, as to same principle: In re J. C. Winship Co., 9 A. B. R. 641, 120 Fed. 93 (C. C. A. Ills.); Havens & Geddes Co. v. Pierek, 9 A. B. R. 571, 120 Fed. 244 (C. C. A. Ills.); In re Lemmon & Gale Co., 7 A. B. R. 291 (C. C. A. Tenn.); In re McCallum, 7 A. B. R. 596, 113 Fed. 393 (D. C. Penn.); instance, In re Hennis, 17 A. B. R. 889 (Ref. N. Car.); In re Boyd, 10 A. B. R. 337, 120 Fed. 999 (D. C. Iowa), quoted at § 1032.

28. In re Lucius, 10 A. B. R. 653, 124 Fed. 455 (D. C. Ala.); compare, In re Hennis, 17 A. B. R. 889 (Ref. N. Car.).

29. Compare result of reasoning in Lucius v. Cawthorne-Coleman Co., 13 A. B. R. 696, 196 U. S. 149, where the

§ 1033½. And May Determine Priority Where Involved in Marshaling of Liens.—And, unquestionably, where the claim of exemptions is involved with conflicting claims of lienholders, the bankruptcy court must have jurisdiction to determine the priority and extent of such exemption right as against the lienholders and the trustee, although as to the liens on the exempted property itself, after determination of the question as to whether or not it is exempt, the bankruptcy court might not retain jurisdiction.[30]

In re Highfield, 21 A. B. R. 92, 163 Fed. 924 (D. C. Pa.): "But the referee also holds that the court has no authority over property claimed as exempt except to appraise and set it off, leaving it to the State courts to work out and enforce conflicting claims with regard to it. This is no doubt true so far as concerns specific goods or property sought to be retained as exempt by the bankrupt. * * * But even here the court will undertake to inquire and decide whether by reason of fraud he has not forfeited his rights. And if so it is difficult to see why it may not do so, also, where the question is whether for any reason he has not waived or lost them. The distinction would seem to be that while the bankruptcy court has no jurisdiction over the property claimed as exempt once the right to it has been established, it may, preliminary to that, determine whether for any reason the right cannot be asserted."

§ 1033¾. Mortgaging or Assigning Unselected Exempt Property.—In accordance with the laws of some of the states, a debtor may mortgage or assign property to be selected or claimed in the future as exempt but not yet so selected or claimed, giving to the mortgagee or transferee the power to make the selection and claim; and such transfer and power in such states will be recognized in bankruptcy, and will prevail over an express waiver of exemptions made by the bankrupt in his schedules, such mortgage in such states neither being invalid for indefiniteness of description nor being contrary to public policy.

In re Hastings, 24 A. B. R. 360, 181 Fed. 34 (C. C. A. Mich.): "It is clear, under the foregoing decisions, that the bankrupt had the power to convey to petitioner his existing exemptions; and as under the laws of Michigan one may lawfully mortgage or convey property thereafter to be acquired (Curtis *v.* Wilcox, 49 Mich. 425; Loudon *v.* Vinton, 108 Mich. 313, 318-19), it is plain that the lien in question was not rendered invalid from the fact that it was made to apply to the stock as it should exist at the time the lien was sought to be enforced. It is urged by the trustee that the description of the exemptions transferred is inadequate in that the exact property so intended to be exempted was

Supreme Court apparently found the question of the validity of exemption claims might involve the determination of the right of the creditors holding exemption waivers and similar claims.

30. Liens on Exempt and Non-Exempt Property Set Aside as Preferences, Whether Revived as to Exempt Property.—It has been held that where a chattel mortgage covering both exempt and non-exempt property is set aside or surrendered as a preference, it does not retain its validity as against the exempt property but that the bankrupt is entitled to have the exempt property set off to him free therefrom. In re Soper, 22 A. B. R. 868, 173 Fed. 116 (D. C. Neb.). But see contra principle, that preferences have to do simply with property which otherwise would go into the estate, post, § 1292.

not specified, and authorities are cited lending more or less support to this contention. The right of a wife to elect to waive the provisions of her husband's will and to take under the statute of distributions involves a personal discretion, the exercise of which by any one other than the one for whose benefit the right is given, may well be held to offend against public policy. Conceding that there is an analogy between an election to waive the terms of a will and an election to waive the benefit of a statute pertaining to exemptions, we can recognize no such analogy between the first mentioned right of election and the right to select exemptions which have not been waived, but which, on the contrary, have been expressly claimed, by a lawful assignment and transfer. The case before us does not involve the right of some one other than the bankrupt to insist upon or to waive his claim of exemptions, but only the right of the assignee under a valid assignment to make the selection of the exemptions so assigned, under an express authority therefor contained in the instrument of assignment. Had the bankrupt personally made the claim under the bankruptcy proceedings, there can be no doubt that the exemptions would have passed to the petitioner here. The assignment in terms authorizes the petitioner to make the selection in the name of the assignor or otherwise, thus constituting petitioner, to say the least, the agent of the assignor for the purpose.

"It is to be noted that the Michigan statute in express terms permits the selection of exemptions to be made by the debtor 'or his authorized agent.' C. L. Mich. 1897, § 10326. This feature plainly distinguishes the case before us from the case of an assignment of a widow's right to elect whether to waive the terms of a will or to take under the statute of distributions, as well as from a case of a conveyance of unassigned dower, for neither of which acts is there any statutory authority. The personal discretion involved in the selection by an assignee, under power of attorney from a debtor, is of no more importance than in the case of a selection by an agent in the absence of an assignment. It is clear that this lawful authority to select exemptions, given upon a valuable consideration and coupled with an interest, could not be revoked by the failure of the bankrupt to claim the exemptions in his own name, or even by his express waiver thereof; and that the assignor was estopped so to do." This case is quoted further at § 1040.

§ 1034. Waiver of Exemptions in Notes.

—Where the bankrupt has waived exemptions in judgment notes, as he may validly do in certain States, the bankruptcy court cannot administer the exempt property for the benefit of those holding such judgment notes, although as to the holders of such notes exemptions have been waived.[31]

31. Lockwood v. Exchange Bk., 10 A. B. R. 112, 190 U. S. 294, quoted at § 1032; Bell v. Dawson Grocery Co., 12 A. B. R. 161, 120 Ga. 628; Roden Grocery Co. v. Bacon, 13 A. B. R. 253, 133 Fed. 515 (C. C. A. Ala.); Woodruff v. Cheeves, 5 A. B. R. 303, 105 Fed. 601 (C. C. A. Ga.); In re Camp, 1 A. B. R. 165, 91 Fed. 745 (D. C. N. Car.); In re Swords, 7 A. B. R. 436, 112 Fed. 661 (D. C. Ga.); In re Hills, 2 A. B. R. 798, 96 Fed. 185 (D. C. Ga.); In re Ogilvie, 5 A. B. R. 374 (Ref. Ga.); First Nat'l Bk. of Sayre v. Bartlett, 21 A. B. R. 88, 35 Pa. Super. Ct. 593, quoted on other points at §§ 1022, 1032, 1100; In re Brown, 1 A. B. R. 256 (D. C. Pa.); compare, In re Schechter, 9 A. B. R. 729 (D. C. Colo.); In re Hopkins, 1 A. B. R. 209 (Ref. Ala.); contra, In re Richardson, 11 A. B. R. 379 (Ref. Ala.); contra, In re Sisler, 2 A. B. R. 768, 96 Fed. 402 (D. C. Va.); contra, In re Garden, 1 A. B. R. 582, 93 Fed. 423 (D. C. Ala., reversed in In re Moore, 7 A. B. R. 285); contra, In re Renda, 17 A. B. R. 522, 149 Fed. 614 (D. C. Pa., distinguished in Zumpfe v. Schultz, 20 A. B. R. 916, 35 Pa. Super. Ct. 106).

In re Moore, 7 A. B. R. 285, 112 Fed. 289 (D. C. Ala.): "It has been argued that the waiver estopped the bankrupt from claiming the exemption, and that the court of bankruptcy should summarily enforce the estoppel by turning over the exempt property to the creditor who holds the waiver notes. * * * The bankrupt has the right to stand on the law of the land. The law of the land is that the waiver cannot be enforced against him, save after judgment and execution in the mode provided by statute. When he claims exemptions against a mere naked waiver, he neither denies the waiver nor seeks to escape from the legal consequence which the law attaches to the waiver when made. He is merely demanding that the naked waiver shall not have effect beyond the limits which the law assigns it, as long as it remains a mere waiver. When he claims exemptions, and to that extent opposes the waiver, his defense against it is not that he did not make the waiver, nor that the waiver, if it had ripened into a judgment in the statutory mode, ought not to prevail over the right of exemption. His position, admitting all this and the making of the waiver, is that his right of exemption can be defeated only by a judgment and execution conforming in all respects to the statute, and in existence at the time the exemption is claimed. The allowance of his contention that a mere waiver, not reduced to judgment, cannot prevail over the right of exemption, will not defeat any just expectation raised by the taking of the note with the waiver, since the law of the land of its own force incorporated, as a term of the contract made by the waiver, that the right of exemption should not be defeated by such waiver, unless it was enforced by judgment and execution conforming to the statute. The bankrupt has never agreed, by the making of the waiver, that it should be enforced against him or his property, save by due process of law, which in this instance requires that there be judgment and execution before the waiver can be fastened upon the property."

In re Black, 4 A. B. R. 776 (D. C. Pa.): "The fact that one of the creditors of the bankrupt's estate holds notes in which the debtor has, by contract, waived the benefit of such exemption law, does not affect the latter's right to the statutory exemption from the bankrupt estate. This contract right of exemption waiver, personal to the creditor, has never been enforced by him; and the fact that such an unexercised right existed in favor of a certain creditor cannot serve to vest this court, sitting as a court of bankruptcy, with jurisdiction and control over exempt property which Congress has expressly excepted from its jurisdiction."

Contra, In re Bragg, 2 N. B. N. & R. 84 (Ref. Ala.): "Suppose all the creditors held waiver notes, could it be said that the bankrupt was entitled to any exemptions?"

And the rule is the same where actual levy has been made before the bankruptcy.[32]

---

32. Instance, First Nat'l Bk. of Sayre v. Bartlett, 21 A. B. R. 88, 35 Pa. Super. Ct. 593. But the bankruptcy court may not refuse to set apart homestead exemption because of an apparent scheme to prefer certain creditors on the eve of bankruptcy by confessing judgment on some of such waiver notes, In re Batten, 22 A. B. R. 270, 170 Fed. 688 (D. C. Va.).

The claim must have been reduced to judgment, in Alabama, in mode prescribed by statute, and extent of exemption claim ascertained, else waiver is not available. In re Moore, 7 A. B. R. 285, 112 Fed. 289 (D. C. Ala.); In re Hopkins, 1 A. B. R. 209 (Ref. Ala.). Compare, to same effect, in Pennsylvania, inferentially, In re Black, 4 A. B. R. 776, 104 Fed. 28 (D. C. Pa.).

Homestead exemptions will be denied in Virginia where the benefit of the exemption would wholly inure to

However, the holder of such a note cannot proceed against the property until it has been actually set apart as exempt; nor can he compel the bankrupt to claim his exemptions; nor prevent the withdrawal of such a claim where one has been made.[33]

Amendment of 1910.—What effect the Amendment of 1910 to § 47 (a), by which the trustee is to be deemed vested with all the rights, powers and remedies of a creditor holding a lien by legal or equitable process on property in his custody, will have in this regard has not yet been determined. There is some ground for believing that the trustee's custody will be held a sufficient levy in behalf of creditors holding exemption waiver notes and other similar rights, to establish for them their special rights.

§ 1035. Property Not Exempt as to "Necessaries," "Manual Work and Labor," "Unpaid Purchase Price" or Judgments for Torts.—Where, by the law of the State, the property is exempt as to certain creditors and not as to others—as for instance, wages in States where wages are exempt as to all creditors, except that a certain per cent. thereof are not exempt as to creditors for necessaries;[34] and for another instance, where there are no homestead exemptions against claims for manual work and labor; and for still another instance, a levy for the unpaid purchase price of goods in States where there is no exemption from levy in an article, upon a judgment for its unpaid purchase price; and for still another instance, where

the creditors holding such exemption waivers and not to the bankrupt's family. In re Garner, 8 A. B. R. 263, 115 Fed. 200 (D. C. Va.). Compare, to similar effect, Morgan v. King, 7 A. B. R. 176, 111 Fed. 730 (C. C. A. W. Va.).

Statutory exemptions cannot, but constitutional exemptions can, be waived in advance by the debtor in Georgia. In re Reinhart, 12 A. B. R. 78, 129 Fed. 510 (D. C. Ga.).

Even if no discharge be applied for or granted and the statutory time for obtaining discharge has elapsed, yet the bankruptcy court will have no jurisdiction. In re Swords, 7 A. B. R. 436, 112 Fed. 661 (D. C. Ga.).

Waiver of Exemptions in Leases. —The same rule prevails as to waiver of exemptions in leases: if distraint is made before adjudication the lien of the distraint is good and exemptions cannot be claimed in the property distrained exempt as to any surplus over the rent due. In re Hoover, 7 A. B. R. 330, 113 Fed. 136 (D. C. Penn.).

Even if no distraint is made the same rule would prevail if the rent were also a priority claim. In re Sloan, 14 A. B. R. 435, 135 Fed. 873 (D. C. Penn.).

Instance of waiver of exemptions in lease, In re Highfield, 21 A. B. R. 92, 163 Fed. 924 (D. C. Pa.).

Is Holder of Exemption Waiver Note a "Secured Creditor?"—It has been held that the holder of a note containing waiver of exemptions is a "secured" creditor, the value of whose security must be deducted before allowance of his claim. In re Meredith, 16 A. B. R. 331 (D. C. Ga.).

33. Compare, analogously, post, § 1102. Also see In re Jonas B. Baughman, 25 A. B. R. 167, 183 Fed. 668 (D. C. Pa.).

34. Maas v. Kuhn, 22 A. B. R. 91 (N. Y. Sup. Ct. App. Div.).

Ten Per Cent of Salary until Entire Judgment Paid, Whether Effective Levy on Wages Earned after Adjudication.—The New York law providing that ten per cent of the debtor's salary shall not be exempt from levy upon certain judgments, and that the lien of the levy shall continue until the entire judgment is paid, has been held not to cover wages earned after adjudication, though under one continuous employment. See ante, § 451; post, § 2678½. Also see In re Sims, 23 A. B. R. 899, 176 Fed. 645 (D. C. N. Y.), quoted post, § 2678½.

property is not exempt from levy for a tort—a mooted question arises, when the property is in the custody of the court, as to whether or not the bankruptcy court retains it for administration for the benefit of those creditors as to whom it is by law not exempt; some courts having held that the property being in the custody of the court, that court may not shirk the responsibility of turning it over to the rightful party, especially since the creditor is prevented from levying upon it whilst it is in such custody, and holding that the court in so doing is not administering exempt property, for as to such creditors, it is not exempt property.[35]

Some of the courts have gone simply to the extent of holding that it should not be set apart to the bankrupt, but should be held for the benefit of creditors as to whom it is not exempt.

McGahan v. Anderson, 7 A. B. R. 641, 113 Fed. 119 (C. C. A. S. C.): "This action of the referee was not approved by the court, the court holding that only the $75 of the $500 could be set aside, and overruled the action of the referee in setting aside the $425 in cash as a personal exemption. In this conclusion of the court below we concur, for the reason that under the provisions of the constitution of the State of South Carolina, money derived from the sale of merchandise on which purchase money is still due cannot be set aside as an exemption, and it would be unjust to the creditors to do so."

In re Renda, 17 A. B. R. 522, 149 Fed. 614 (D. C. Pa., distinguished in Zumpfe v. Schultz, 20 A. B. R. 916, 35 Pa. Super. Court 106): "* * * but is met by wages claims, against which there is no exemption under the state law; a claim of the landlord for two month's rent amounting to $300, on a lease waiving exemption; and an attachment execution from the Common Pleas on a judgment with waiver, in which the receiver was served as garnishee.

"* * * But having to come into the court to get it, the rights of others who also lay claim to the fund may properly be considered and there is no occasion to send them elsewhere for relief. The case is not like that where goods are set apart to the bankrupt under his exemption, over which, thereafter the

---

35. Cannon v. Dexter Broom & Mattress Co., 9 A. B. R. 724, 120 Fed. 657 (C. C. A. S. C.); In re Campbell, 10 A. B. R. 723, 124 Fed. 417 (D. C. Va.); In re Boyd, 10 A. B. R. 339, 120 Fed. 999 (D. C. Iowa), quoted in full above. Inferentially, In re Schechter, 9 A. B. R. 729 (D. C. Colo.), in which case the court refused to allow the bankrupt to claim property not paid for but apparently did not give it over to the creditor who had sold it to the bankrupt but left it in the general estate. In re Bragg, 2 N. B. N. & R. 84 (Ref. Ala.), quoted, supra; inferentially, In re Stout, 6 A. B. R. 505 (D. C. Mo.); In re Gordon, 8 A. B. R. 255, 115 Fed. 445 (D. C. Vt.), quoted, supra; In re Sisler, 2 A. B. R. 768, 96 Fed. 402 (D. C. Va.), quoted, supra; obiter, In re Durham, 4 A. B. R. 760, 104 Fed. 231 (D. C. Ark.); obiter, In re Wilkes, 7 A. B. R. 574,

112 Fed. 975 (D. C. Ark.). See discussion, ante, § 1032, et seq.

Compare peculiar and apparently erroneous ruling, In re Strickland, 20 A. B. R. 923 (Ref. Ga.), allowing a claim for wages precedence over homestead as a matter of priority in bankruptcy!

Compare remark In re Autigo Screen Door Co., 10 A. B. R. 359, 123 Fed. 249 (C. C. A. Wis.), quoted at § 1033.

"No Exemption against Purchase Price" Does Not Include Lender of Money to Make Purchase.—Where the statute provides that there shall be no exemption against the purchase price, such non-exemptability refers only to the claim of the seller himself and cannot be extended to cover that of one who has made a loan by which the property has been purchased. In re Bailes, 23 A. B. R. 789, 176 Fed. 460 (D. C. S. C.). See post, § 1107.

bankrupt court has no jurisdiction, and liens upon which are therefore to be enforced in the State courts. Lockwood v. Exchange Bank, 190 U. S. 294, 10 Am. B. R. 107. The bankrupt assented to the sale by the receiver by which the fund was produced, and the money being in the latter's hands the court has now to say how it is to be disposed of, necessarily passing upon conflicting claims. In re Rodgers, 11 Am. B. R. 79. If the opposite course were pursued in the present instance, it would work manifest injustice. The bankrupt could put the money into his pocket, and those in whose favor he has waived his right to it would be without redress; and that too, in the case of the landlord, in the face of the fact, that if he had not been restrained by the court from enforcing the distress which he had made, he would have realized his money.

"* * * Disposition will therefore be made of it as follows:

Fund for distribution.....................................	$607.07
Costs:	
Filing fees to be returned to petitioning creditors...........	$30.00
Depositing by same with referee	15.00
	$45.00
Additional fees due referee.................................	22.85
To attorney of petitioning creditors........................	35.00
To attorney of bankrupt...................................	25.00
	$127.85
Wages due:	
William Simmons	$18.75
James Malloy	54.00
	$72.75
Rent due:	
Landlord, two months....................................	$300.00
Balance to bankrupt on his $300 exemption claim.............	106.47
	$607.07."

Others have gone further and held that the same rule should prevail even though no levy has been made on the exempt property;[36] and that the burden of separating the unpaid-for goods from those paid for rests on the bankrupt.[37]

However, even where the ruling is that it should not be set apart, the seller does not appear to have any priority in its proceeds over other creditors.[38]

---

36. In re Campbell, 10 A. B. R. 723, 124 Fed. 417 (D. C. Va.); In re Schechter, 9 A. B. R. 729 (D. C. Colo.); inferentially, In re Tobias, 4 A. B. R. 555, 103 Fed. 68 (D. C. Va.); In re Sloan, 14 A. B. R. 435, 135 Fed. 873 (D. C. Pa.). But in this case the exemption right was abandoned by assignment. Inferentially, In re Renda, 17 A. B. R. 522, 149 Fed. 614 (D. C. Pa.).

37. In re Tobias, 4 A. B. R. 555, 103 Fed. 68 (D. C. Va.); In re Campbell, 10 A. B. R. 723, 124 Fed. 417 (D. C. Va.); In re Schechter, 9 A. B. R. 729 (D. C. Colo.).

38. Cannon v. Dexter Broom & Mattress Co., 9 A. B. R. 724, 120 Fed. 657 (C. C. A. S. C.); contra, In re Boyd, 10 A. B. R. 339, 120 Fed. 999 (D. C. Iowa), quoted in full above.

In re Campbell, 10 A. B. R. 723, 124 Fed. 417 (D. C. Va.): "It is true that under the State law, considered alone, the homestead can be claimed in unpaid-for property as against the claim of everyone except that of the vendor. But the Bankrupt Act, so to speak, consolidates the demands of all the creditors. What is gained for one is gained pro rata for all. The other creditors are in some sense the assignees in part of the claims of the vendor creditors. So far as the bankrupt is concerned, the result is the same whether the objection be made by a vendor creditor or by some other creditor. And since the other creditors have an interest in the matter, the failure or the refusal of the vendor creditor to file objections to an allowance of homestead should not be allowed to prejudice the rights of the other creditors. It follows that the exceptions in the case at bar would not be vitally defective even if they showed that the exceptants were not the vendors of any of the articles set apart by the trustee. The burden of proof having rested on the bankrupt, and as he offered no evidence tending to show that the articles claimed had been paid for, the referee rightly held that he was not entitled to the exemption."

This rule seems unreasonable, as it is only as to him that it is not exempt, as to which compare the analogous doctrine of In re Cannon, 10 A. B. R. 64, 121 Fed. 582 (D. C. S. C.), where the court in setting aside for nonrecord a chattel mortgage void as to subsequent creditors only, divided the fund first among the subsequent creditors and not among all alike.

But the weight of authority since the Supreme Court's announcement of its opinion in the Lockwood case, is that the bankruptcy court could not so retain it for administration; and indeed the contrary rule would, on reason, conflict with the well-established rules prevailing in regard to judgment notes containing waivers of exemptions and in regard to liens on exempt property.[39]

In re Brumbaugh, 12 A. B. R. 204, 128 Fed. 971 (D. C. Penn.): "It is undoubtedly true, under the law of Pennsylvania by which the exemption is given, that it cannot be claimed in cases of tort, but only of contract * * * (but) it affords no ground for opposing the bankrupt's exemption in the present instance, that he would not be able to maintain a claim for it against the judgment of Miss Keim (for breach of promise of marriage). If that be legally true of it, she has simply to issue execution and seize the property set apart to him and the State courts will then determine her rights. But they must be worked out there and not here, the only question which now concerns us being, whether the bankrupt as against general creditors is entitled to his exemption, as to which there can be no doubt."

Ingram v. Wilson, 11 A. B. R. 192, 125 Fed. 913 (C. C. A. Iowa): "In the case in hand, the property which is involved was generally exempt under the laws of the State of Iowa, the same being the bankrupt's homestead. By virtue of those laws (Code Iowa, 1897, § 2976) it could only be sold on execution 'for debts contracted prior to its acquisition,' and even for such debts it could

39.   Inferentially, In re Bolinger. 6 A. B. R. 171, 108 Fed. 374 (D. C. Pa.); In re Durham, 4 A. B. R. 760, 104 Fed. 231 (D. C. Ark.); In re Butler, 9 A. B. R. 539, 120 Fed. 100 (D. C. Ga.); In re Wells, 5 A. B. R. 308, 105 Fed. 762 (D. C. Ark.); In re Castleberry, 16 A. B. R. 160, 133 Fed. 821 (D. C. Ga.); inferentially, Graham v. Richardson, 8 A. B. R. 700 (Sup. Ct. Ga.); inferentially. Maas v. Kuhn, 22 A. B. R. 91 (N. Y. Sup. Ct. App. Div.).

not be sold except 'to supply a deficiency remaining after exhausting the other property of the debtor liable to execution.' No creditor of the bankrupt other than Wilson had, as it seems, any interest in the homestead, inasmuch as the facts which he alleged as a basis for the order only showed a right personal to himself to have this property subjected to the payment of his claim after all the other property of the bankrupt had been exhausted. This right, existing only in favor of one creditor, did not cause the title of the homestead to vest in the trustee in bankruptcy, nor did it confer any greater authority upon the bankrupt court to administer upon it by ordering its sale and the distribution of its proceeds than where, as in the case cited, a single creditor had acquired the right to sell exempt property by force of a private contract which had been entered into in accordance with the laws of the State of Georgia."

In re Maxson, 22 A. B. R. 424, 170 Fed. 356 (D. C. Iowa): "But this does not destroy its character as a homestead nor defeat the general exemption thereof, and whether or not it may be subjected to certain specified debts will not be determined by the court of bankruptcy, for its jurisdiction over exempt property when it determines it to be such is to set it apart to the bankrupt, and, if it is liable for specific debts, the creditor to whom it is so liable must proceed to subject it to the payment thereof by proper proceedings in the State court."

At any rate, where the property has once been turned over to the bankrupt.[40]

Amendment of 1910.—What effect the Amendment of 1910 to § 47 (b) (2), by which the trustee is to be deemed vested with all the rights, powers and remedies of a creditor holding a lien by legal or equitable process on property in his custody, will have in this regard has not yet been determined. There is some ground for holding that such custody may operate as a sufficient levy in behalf of creditors holding labor claims or claims for unpaid purchase price or claims of similar character.

§ 1036. Sales of Merchandise in Bulk, Whether Bankrupt Entitled to Exemptions Out of Unpaid Purchase Price, until Creditors Paid.

—Nevertheless, it has been held in cases of sales of merchandise in bulk where the statute requires notice to creditors, etc., as prerequisites to the validity of the sale, that the bankrupt will not be allowed exemptions from the purchase price until the creditors have been paid in full.

In re O'Connor, 16 A. B. R. 785 (D. C. Wash.): "The bankrupt claims as exempt part of the unpaid purchase price of a stock of merchandise which he sold in bulk previous to the initiation of bankruptcy proceedings. The effect of the statute is to charge the purchase price with a trust in favor of the vendor's creditors, by making the vendee responsible for the application of the money to the payment of their claims. It follows as a legal consequence that the right of the vendor to receive any part of the money is postponed until all of his creditors have been paid in full, and when the fund is insufficient to pay his debts in full he must be deemed to have retained no interest in the matter other than the right of a party to a contract to enforce performance. In such a case performance means payment to the vendor's creditors pro rata. The transaction is inconsistent with any right of the vendor to claim the money

40. In re Little, 6 A. B. R. 686, 110 Fed. 621 (D. C. Iowa).

under the exemption law adversely to creditors, because the statutory obligation of the vendee is necessarily incorporated into the contract, and the vendor
must be deemed to have assented to the application of the purchase money, as
the statute has prescribed. Such assent on his part waived any right which he
might otherwise have asserted to select the purchase money in lieu of other
property which would be exempt from attachment or execution for debt. The
statute does not merely charge the purchase money with a trust in favor of
creditors in substitution for their rights to enforce payment of debts due, by
levying upon the goods in the hands of their debtor, but in unrestricted terms
it imposes an absolute obligation upon the vendee to see to the application of
the whole of the purchase money, if necessary to pay all the debts of the
vendor."

§ 1037. Exempt Property Not in Possession or Already Set Off Not to Be Retaken, for Benefit of Parties as to Whom Not Exempt, nor of Lienholders.

—Where the bankruptcy court has not the possession
of such property, or, having had the possession, has set the property apart
and delivered it to the bankrupt as exempt, the trustee must not retake possession of it in order to administer it for the benefit of certain creditors as to
whom it may not be exempt, as for instance, in states where property is
not exempt as against a levy for the unpaid purchase price thereof,[41] nor
to administer it for the benefit of lienholders.[42]

Obiter, In re Boyd, 10 A. B. R. 337, 120 Fed. 999 (D. C. Iowa): "If such
creditor does not, in proper time and while the property is in the custody of
the court, assert his claim, and invoke the protection of the court, it will be
assumed that he waives his right, and, if the property is set apart as exempt,
and is delivered to the bankrupt, so that in fact it passes from the custody
of the court, it is difficult to see upon what theory the court can afterwards
assert a jurisdiction over the same."

SUBDIVISION "B."

KINDS AND AMOUNTS OF PROPERTY EXEMPTED; PERSONS ENTITLED; AND
LAW GOVERNING SAME.

§ 1038. State Law of Domicile Governs.

—The state exemption law
of the state where the bankrupt has had his domicile during the greater

---

41. In re Seydel, 9 A. B. R. 255, 118
Fed. 207 (D. C. Iowa); In re Little,
6 A. B. R. 681, 110 Fed. 621 (D. C.
Iowa); inferentially, In re Hatch, 4
A. B. R. 349, 102 Fed. 280 (D. C.
Iowa).

In Georgia there is no exemption
against a levy under a judgment for the
purchase price of the property, but
otherwise where the seller has not reduced his claim to judgment; held, the
bankruptcy court will not, in the latter case, deny the bankrupt's exemption in the property. In re Butler, 9
A. B. R. 539, 120 Fed. 100 (D. C. Ga.).
Compare, as to waiver of exemptions

in Alabama, similar rule, In re Moore,
7 A. B. R. 285 (D. C. Ala.). In South
Carolina a different rule prevails. Mc-
Gahan v. Anderson, 7 A. B. R. 642, 113
Fed. 115 (C. C. A. S. C., reversing In
re Anderson, 4 A. B. R. 640).

42. In re Little, 6 A. B. R. 686, 110
Fed. 621 (D. C. Iowa); In re Hatch,
4 A. B. R. 349, 102 Fed. 280 (D. C.
Iowa); In re Bender, 17 A. B. R. 896
(Ref. Ohio); In re Wishnefsky, 24 A.
B. R. 798, 181 Fed. 896 (D. C. N. J.).

A fortiori, on principle, In re Soper,
22 A. B. R. 868, 173 Fed. 116 (D. C.
Neb.). Discussed at § 1031, note, and
§ 1061, note.

portion of the six months preceding the filing of the bankruptcy petition fixes the exemption rights in the bankruptcy proceedings.[43]

It is possible that a debtor may go into bankruptcy in one State and have his exemption rights determined by the laws of another State; for he may have his residence or principal place of business in one state and thus be entitled to go into bankruptcy there and yet have his domicile in another state. It is the law of the State of his domicile alone that fixes his exemption rights.[44]

Obiter, In re Philip Brady, 21 A. B. R. 364, 169 Fed. 152 (D. C. Ky.): "If the bankrupt resides in Tennessee (which by the way was well enough shown to be the fact and so stated in our former opinion) his exemptions, as his response insists should be the case, will most probably be governed by the law of that State, and all questions in that connection can be easily presented and determined when the schedules are filed and exemptions claimed. He was adjudicated a bankrupt in Kentucky because his principal place of business had been in that State and not because of residence here."

And the bankruptcy court will take judicial cognizance of the State exemption laws.[45]

§ 1039. Whether Court of Bankrupt's Domicile May Set Apart Homestead in Real Estate in Another State Having Different Homestead Laws.—But it is a question whether the bankruptcy court of the district of the bankrupt's domicile may set apart a homestead to the bankrupt in real estate located in another State where the homestead laws are different. Such power has been denied.[46] The question is somewhat dependent on the existence of liens or other rights of third parties; also, somewhat on the nature of the homestead right in the particular State as to whether an "estate" or not.

§ 1040. State Law Governs Kind and Amount and Person Entitled.—The State law[47] governs the kind and the amount of property al-

43. Bankr. Act, § 6. Instance, In re Schulz, 14 A. B. R. 319, 136 Fed. 228 (D. C. Ore.); McCarty v. Coffin, 18 A. B. R. 152, 150 Fed. 307 (C. C. A. Tex.); Duncan v. Ferguson-McKinney Co., 18 A. B. R. 155 (C. C. A. Tex.); In re Baker, 24 A. B. R. 411, 182 Fed. 392 (C. C. A. Ky.), quoted at § 1041; In re Irwin, 23 A. B. R. 487, 177 Fed. 284 (C. C. A. Pa.).

44. The burden of proving a change of domicile is on the one asserting the change. In re Grimes, 2 A. B. R. 160, 94 Fed. 800 (D. C. N. Car.); compare, to same effect, In re Waxelbaum, 3 A. B. R. 267, 97 Fed. 562 (D. C. N. Y.); compare, to same effect, In re Berner, 3 A. B. R. 325 (Ref. Ohio); compare, to same effect, In re Clisdell, 2 A. B. R. 424 (D. C. N. Y.); In re Baker, 24

A. B. R. 411, 182 Fed. 392 (C. C. A. Ky.), quoted at § 1041.
As to distinction between "residence" and "domicile," as applied to the allowance of exemptions in bankruptcy, see § 33, footnote, In re Dinglehoef Bros., 6 A. B. R. 242 (D. C. N. Car.); In re Owings, 15 A. B. R. 473, 140 Fed. 739 (D. C. N. Car.). Also, see ante, cognate subject of jurisdiction of the bankruptcy court over insolvent debtors as dependent on residence or domicile, § 30, et seq.

45. In re Reed, 26 A. B. R. 286, 191 Fed. 920 (D. C. Okla.).

46. In re Owings, 15 A. B. R. 472, 140 Fed. 739 (D. C. N. Car.).

47. Or the federal homestead law in cases involving federal homestead, of course. In re Cohn, 22 A. B. R. 761, 171 Fed. 368 (D. C. N. Dak.).

lowed as exempt; the persons entitled thereto and the acts that will forfeit the right.

In re Hastings, 24 A. B. R. 360, 181 Fed. 34 (C. C. A. Mich.): "In applying the exemption laws, the bankruptcy courts are bound to follow the construction of such laws announced by the highest court of the State whose statute is involved." This case is quoted further at § 1033¾.

In re Baker, 24 A. B. R. 411, 182 Fed. 392 (C. C. A. Ky.): "In view of § 6 of the Bankruptcy Act, the validity of the action of the trustee in setting apart the bankrupt's exemptions and the rights of the bankrupt in that behalf, are to be tested by the laws of Kentucky. The Federal Courts are accustomed in such cases to follow the decisions of the court of last resort of the State, whose laws are so drawn in question."

§ 1041. State Law Governs.—The State law governs as to exemptions in bankruptcy.[48]

48. Steele v. Buell, 5 A. B. R. 165, 104 Fed. 968 (C. C. A. Iowa); Lipman v. Stein, 14 A. B. R. 30, 134 Fed. 235 (C. C. A. Pa., affirming In re Bessie Stein, 12 A. B. R. 384, 130 Fed. 629); In re Groves, 6 A. B. R. 728 (Ref. Ohio); In re McClintock, 13 A. B. R. 606 (Ref. Ohio); In re Duffy, 9 A. B. R. 358, 118 Fed. 926 (D. C. Penn.); In re Staunton, 9 A. B. R. 79 (D. C. Penn.); In re Ogilvie, 5 A. B. R. 374 (D. C. Ga.); In re Meriweather, 5 A. B. R. 436, 107 Fed. 102 (D. C. Ark.); In re Camp, 1 A. B. R. 165, 91 Fed. 745 (D. C. N. Car.); In re Woodward, 2 A. B. R. 692, 95 Fed. 955 (D. C. N. Car.); In re Durham, 4 A. B. R. 760, 2 N. B. N. 1101, 104 Fed. 231 (D. C. Ark.); Holden v. Stratton, 14 A. B. R. 94, 198 U. S. 702; In re Mullen, 15 A. B. R. 275, 140 Fed. 206 (D. C. Me.); In re Ellithorpe, 7 A. B. R. 18, 111 Fed. 163 (D. C. N. Y.); In re Haskin, 6 A. B. R. 485, 109 Fed. 789 (D. C. Pa.); Duncan v. Ferguson-McKinney Co., 18 A. B. R. 155, 150 Fed. 269 (C. C. A. Tex.); McCarty v. Coffin, 18 A. B. R. 152, 150 Fed. 307 (C. C. A. Tex.); (1867) Goodall v. Tuttle, Fed. Cases 5,533, 7 N. B. Reg. 193; In re Wood, 17 A. B. R. 93, 147 Fed. 877 (D. C. Wis.); In re Stone, 8 A. B. R. 416, 116 Fed. 35 (D. C. Ark., affirmed sub nom. In re Irvin, 9 A. B. R. 689, 120 Fed. 733); impliedly, In re Irvin, 9 A. B. R. 689 (C. C. A. Ark.); In re Moore, 7 A. B. R. 285, 112 Fed. 289 (D. C. Ala.). But this case states the rule too broadly. Obiter, Richardson v. Woodward, 5 A. B. R. 96, 104 Fed. 873 (C. C. A. Va.; In re Youngstrom, 18 A. B. R. 572, 153 Fed. 97 (C. C. A. Colo.), quoted on other point at § 1025; In re Pfeiffer, 19 A. B. R. 230, 155 Fed. 892 (D. C. Pa.); In re Giles, 19 A. B. R.

306, 158 Fed. 596 (C. C. A. Ohio); impliedly, In re Letson, 19 A. B. R. 506, 157 Fed. 78 (C. C. A. Okla.); In re Wishnefsky, 24 A. B. R. 798, 181 Fed. 896 (D. C. N. J.); In re Mussey, 25 A. B. R. 91, 179 Fed. 1007 (D. C. Tex.); Cowan v. Burchfield, 25 A. B. R. 293, 180 Fed. 614 (D. C. Ala.); In re J. E. Maynard & Co., 25 A. B. R. 732, 183 Fed. 823 (D. C. Ga.); In re Glisson, 25 A. B. R. 911, 182 Fed. 287 (D. C. Ga.); In re Scheier, 26 A. B. R. 739, 188 Fed. 744 (D. C. Wash.); In re Bassett, 26 A. B. R. 800, 189 Fed. 410 (D. C. Wash.); In re Rutland Grocery Co., 26 A. B. R. 942 (D. C. Ga.); In re Carlon, 27 A. B. R. 18, 189 Fed. 815 (D. C. S. D.); In re Andrews & Simonds, 27 A. B. R. 116, 193 Fed. 776 (D. C. Mich.); In re Kolber, 27 A. B. R. 414, 193 Fed. 281 (D. C. Pa.); In re Cochran, 26 A. B. R. 459, 185 Fed. 912 (D. C. Ga.); In re Nicholson, 27 A. B. R. 908 (D. C. Tex.); Mullinix v. Simon, 28 A. B. R. 1, 196 Fed. 775 (C. C. A. Ark.); Bank v. Nez Perce v. Pindel, 28 A. B. R. 69, 193 Fed. 917 (C. C. A. Idaho); In re Hammond, 24 A. B. R. 811, 198 Fed. 574 (D. C. Ky.); In re Vickerman, 29 A. B. R. 298, 100 Fed. 589 (D. C. S. Dak.).

Amendment of Exemption Laws.—Amendment of wages exemption law does not affect right to exemptions in wages earned before the amendment, In re Holden, 12 A. B. R. 96, 127 Fed. 980 (D. C. Wash.).

Statutory Prerequisites of Filing Deed or Declaration of Homestead.—In some States it is requisite to the right of homestead that the debtor file a deed or declaration of homestead. In such States such preliminary deed is also requisite to perfect the exemption right in the bankrupt. But delay

Smalley *v.* Laugenour, 13 A. B. R. 692, 196 U. S. 93: "The rights of a bankrupt to property as exempt are those given him by the State statute, and if such exempt property is not subject to levy and sale under those statutes, then it cannot be made to respond under the Act of Congress."

In re Sullivan, 17 A. B. R. 578, 148 Fed. 815 (C. C. A. Iowa, affirming 16 A. B. R. 87): "If the Supreme Court of Iowa, in construing its statute of exemption has decided that the crops grown on the homestead are, for that reason alone, exempt from liability to creditors of the owner of the homestead, we must follow that interpretation and hold likewise."

In re Manning, 7 A. B. R. 571, 112 Fed. 948 (D. C. Pa.): "* * * and what the law of the State does not give cannot be set aside by the trustee."

In re Wunder, 13 A. B. R. 701, 133 Fed. 821 (D. C. Pa.): "A bankrupt is entitled to the same exemption as if proceeded against under the State law and to none other."

In re Stevenson & King, 2 A. B. R. 230, 93 Fed. 789 (D. C. N. Car.): "It contemplates that the Bankruptcy Law shall not affect the exemptions as allowed under the State law and construed by the courts of the State. Hence the State decisions are paramount in cases like the one at bar."

In re McCrary Bros., 22 A. B. R. 161, 169 Fed. 485 (D. C. Ala.): "In determining what exemptions a person is entitled to, the United States courts will follow the rule as laid down by the State statute and as interpreted by the Supreme Court of the State."

§ 1042. As Construed by Highest State Tribunal.

—The bankruptcy court is bound by the construction put upon exemption laws by the highest courts of the state;[49] if such construction be reasonably clear and even if it is the bankruptcy court's opinion that the State court is likely later to change the rule.[50]

But not necessarily by obiter dicta.[51]

§ 1043. But Where Decisions Not Authoritative or Conflicting, Bankruptcy Court Construes.

—But where there are no State decisions, or where there is a conflict of construction, the court of bankruptcy will

in filing it until after bankruptcy will not forfeit it. In re Fisher, 15 A. B. R. 652 (D. C. Va.); In re Culwell, 21 A. B. R. 614, 165 Fed. 828 (D. C. Mont.), quoted at §§ 1025, 1032.

Federal Homesteads.—Of course, by "State law" is meant law other than the Bankruptcy Act itself. Federal homesteads are, of course, governed by the federal law. In re Cohn, 22 A. B. R. 761, 171 Fed. 568 (D. C. N. Dak.).

49. Holden *v.* Stratton, 14 A. B. R. 94, 198 U. S. 202; In re Stone, 8 A. B. R. 416, 116 Fed. 35 (D. C. Ark.); Richardson *v.* Woodward, 5 A. B. R. 96, 104 Fed. 873 (C. C. A. Va.); In re Stevenson & King, 2 A. B. R. 230, 93 Fed. 789 (D. C. N. Car.); In re Woodard, 2 A. B. R. 692, 95 Fed. 955 (D. C. N. Car.); In re Mullen, 15 A. B. R. 275, 140 Fed. 206 (D. C. Me.); In re Meriweather, 5 A. B. R. 436, 107 Fed. 102 (D. C. Ark.); In re Wood, 17 A. B. R. 93, 147 Fed. 877 (D. C. Wis.); In re Sullivan, 17 A. B. R. 578, 148 Fed. 115 (C. C. A. Iowa); In re Pfeiffer, 19 A. B. R. 230, 155 Fed. 892 (D. C. Pa.); In re Giles, 19 A. B. R. 306, 158 Fed. 596 (C. C. A. Ohio); In re McCrary Bros., 22 A. B. R. 161, 169 Fed. 485 (D. C. Ala.), quoted at § 1041; In re Youngstrom, 18 A. B. R. 572, 153 Fed. 97 (C. C. A. Colo.), quoted on other points at § 1015; In re Hastings, 24 A. B. R. 360, 181 Fed. 34 (C. C. A. Mich.), quoted at § 1041; In re Baker, 24 A. B. R. 411, 182 Fed. 392 (C. C. A. Ky.), quoted at § 1041; In re Thedford, 28 A. B. R. 191 (D. C. Tex.).

50. In re Baker, 24 A. B. R. 411, 182 Fed. 392 (C. C. A. Ky.), quoted at § 1043.

51. In re Sullivan, 17 A. B. R. 578, 148 Fed. 115 (C. C. A. Iowa).

give it a construction to carry out the purport and intention of the Bankruptcy Act.[52]

Richardson *v.* Woodward, 5 A. B. R. 96, 104 Fed. 873 (C. C. A. Va.): "But where there is no construction of a State law by the State courts, or there is a conflict of construction, and a proper case is presented, involving a construction of State constitutions or statutes, the court of bankruptcy will, as other courts of the United States do, give it a construction to carry out the purport and intent of the act of Congress; and § 2, subdivision 11, provides that the courts of bankruptcy shall determine all the claims of bankrupts to their exemptions."

The State decisions will be followed where they are interpretations of the State exemption law, but not where they are mere declarations of general law, mere definitions of property.[53]

However, the mere belief that the State court will eventually change its rule is insufficient to warrant disregard of a reasonably clear rule.

In re Baker, 24 A. B. R. 411, 182 Fed. 392 (C. C. A. Ky.): "We of course agree that where the decisions of the State court are in conflict and point to no definite rule touching the construction of a statute of the State, the Federal courts are quite as much at liberty to place their own construction upon the statute as they would be if the State court had not construed it at all. But if there be a rule of decision which is reasonably clear with respect to a given statute, we think the Federal courts are bound in a case like this to follow the rule rather than to undertake to determine upon their own interpretation whether the State court may not change the rule in the future."

§ 1044. May Select in Kind, Regardless of Impairment of Remainder.

—Where the State law gives the debtor the right to select his exemptions in kind, he may do so as bankrupt, even though his property consists of a stock of goods which cannot be divided without greatly impairing the value, or even rendering practically worthless the balance left.[54]

§ 1045. Whether Wife, or Mortgagee or Other Interested Party, May Claim Exemptions Where Bankrupt Neglects or Refuses, Determined by State Law.

—The State law determines what bankrupts are entitled to exemptions and whether a wife, mortgagee or other third party may claim them when the bankrupt fails or refuses to do so.[55]

Thus, it has been held in accordance with the laws of one State, where the bankrupt, before bankruptcy, has mortgaged or assigned in general terms such existing property as might be exempt to him, without further specification or description, giving also to the mortgagee or assignee the power to

---

52. Jennings *v.* Stannus & Son, 27 A. B. R. 384, 191 Fed. 347 (C. C. A. Wash.).

53. Page *v.* Edmunds, 9 A. B. R. 277, 187 U. S. 596.

54. In re Grimes, 2 A. B. R. 730, 96 Fed. 529 (D. C. N. Car.).

55. See post, §§ 1061, 1062, 1093¾, 1292, 1293. Also In re Youngstrom, 18 A. B. R. 57", 153 Fed. 97 (C. C. A Colo.); compare, instance, In re Jennings & Co., 22 A. B. R. 160, 166 Fed. 639 (D. C. Ga.); In re Hastings, 24 A. B. R. 360, 181 Fed. 34 (C. C. A. Mich.), quoted on other points at §§ 1040, 1061.

make the selection, that such mortgagee or assignee, in the event of subse-quent bankruptcy, is entitled to his lien and can select and claim the exempt property, even though the bankrupt expressly waives exemptions in his schedules.[56]

It has been held in Wisconsin, that a mortgagee may not make the claim where it would validate a mortgage otherwise void as to creditors as a preference.[56a]

§ 1046. Converting Nonexempt Property into Exempt, on Eve of Bankruptcy.

—The conversion of nonexempt property into exempt prop-erty, within the four months preceding bankruptcy, while insolvent or even on the eve of bankruptcy, is not invalid, and will not, in general, bar the bankrupt from claiming the latter as exempt.[57]

In re Letson, 19 A. B. R. 506, 157 Fed. 78 (C. C. A. Okla.): "In the absence of a local rule to the contrary, and there is none in Oklahoma, the mere use by an insolvent of nonexempt funds or assets in acquiring a homestead does not make it subject to the claims of creditors."

Providing, of course, that fraud be absent from the transaction.[57a]

§ 1047. Instances of Exemptions Allowed and Disallowed in Bankruptcy in Accordance with State Law.

—Many instances are to be found in the decisions, of exemptions allowed and disallowed in accord-ance with State law, some of which are referred to in the footnotes hereto.[58]

---

56. In re Hastings, 24 A. B. R. 360, 181 Fed. 34 (C. C. A. Mich.), quoted at § 1061.

56a. In re Schuller, 6 A. B. R. 278, 108 Fed. 591 (D. C. Wis.).

57. Huenergardt v. Brittain Dry Goods Co., 8 A. B. R. 341, 116 Fed. 31 (C. C. A. Kas.); In re Wilson, 10 A. B. R. 525, 123 Fed. 20 (C. C. A. Calif.); In re Irvin, 9 A. B. R. 689 (C. C. A. Ark., affirming In re Stone, 8 A. B. R. 416, 116 Fed. 35); In re Wood, 17 A. B. R. 93 (D. C. Wis.); In re Ham-monds, 28 A. B. R. 811, 198 Fed. 574 (D. C. Ky.); Southern Irr. Co. v. Whar-ton Nat. Bank, 28 A. B. R. 941 (Tex. Civ. App.). In re Kolber, 27 A. B. R. 414, 193 Fed. 281 (D. C. Pa.), where it was held that bona fide severance of partnership relations, and the transfer of all the firm property to one of its members, fourteen days prior to the transferee's bankruptcy, did not de-prive such transferee of his exemption as an individual. Contra, In re Bos-ton, 3 A. B. R. 388 (D. C. Neb.).

Converting Nonexempt Property into Exempt Property on Eve of Bank-ruptcy to Give Preference to Certain Creditors Holding Notes Wherein Ex-emptions Waived.—In re Batten, 22 A. B. R. 270, 170 Fed. 688 (D. C. Va.).

57a. Bankrupt had invested $200 in contract for land: he procured dis-missal of petition in bankruptcy on stipulation that his attorneys would re-turn to him $1800 he had transferred to them and would immediately allow a new petition to be filed against him. Thereupon and before new petition was filed, he paid the $1800 on the land contract and filed a declaration of homestead thereon; the court re-fused to allow the exemption. In re Gerber, 26 A. B. R. 608, 186 Fed. 693 (C. C. A. Wis.).

58. "Tools and Implements of Trade:"

California.—"Tools and implements necessary for carrying on his trade," are not in all cases limited to those the bankrupt personally uses, but may include those used by others neces-sarily assisting him. In re Peterson, 2 A. B. R. 630, 95 Fed. 417 (D. C. Calif.).

Iowa.—Cream separator exempt. In re Hemstreet, 14 A. B. R. 825, 139 Fed. 958 (D. C. Iowa).

Kansas.—"Necessary tools and im-plements and $400 of stock in trade" to "any mechanic, miner or other person" does not include druggist. In re Lynde, 17 A. B. R. 906 (Ref. (Kas.).

"Tool of trade"—in Maine the canoe of a registered guide, but not his rifle, is exempt. In re Mullen, 15 A. B. R. 275, 140 Fed. 206 (D. C. Me.).

Nebraska.—"Tools of business," poultry dealer, entitled in Nebraska to horse and wagon, office furniture, scales, etc. In re Conley, 19 A. B. R. 200, 162 Fed. 806 (D. C. Neb.).

New York.—"Tools and implements" of baker, in New York, exempt. In re Osborn, 5 A. B. R. 111, 104 Fed. 780 (D. C. N. Y.).

"Suitable tools" of candy maker in Vermont. In re Trombly, 16 A. B. R. 599 (Ref. Vt.).

"Professional tools" include "undertakers'" outfits in Maryland. Steiner v. Marshall, 15 A. B. R. 486, 140 Fed. 710 (C. C. A. Md.).

"Head of Family:"

In Arkansas includes unmarried man supporting widowed mother and sixteen year old brother. In re Morrison, 6 A. B. R. 488, 110 Fed. 734 (D. C. Ark.).

Wife, is, when bankrupt has absconded, in Colorado. In re Youngstrom, 18 A. B. R. 572, 153 Fed. 97 (C. C. A. Colo.).

South Carolina.—Husband, living separate from wife by mutual consent, and wife getting property from him for separate support, husband no longer "head of family" in South Carolina. In re Finklea, 18 A. B. R. 738. 153 Fed. 492 (D. C. S. Car.).

Unmarried man paying board and tuition of sister at school, is not. In re McGowan, 22 A. B. R. 469, 170 Fed. 493 (D. C. S. C.).

An individual doing business under a fictitious name resembling a corporate name is nevertheless entitled to exemptions. In re Carpenter, 6 A. B. R. 465, 109 Fed. 558 (C. C. A. Fla.).

Children still living together on land occupied by their parents before death as a family homestead are entitled still to claim it as the homestead of the "family," in Iowa, although the parents have been dead twelve or thirteen years. In re Rafferty, 7 A. B. R. 415 (D. C. Iowa).

"Head of family" in Virginia and South Carolina includes married woman owning property and doing business as a feme sole, although living with husband. Richardson v. Woodward, 5 A. B. R. 94, 104 Fed. 873 (C. C. A. Va.);

In re McCutchen, 4 A. B. R. 81, 100 Fed. 779 (D. C. S. C.).

Wife living with husband on land owned by her is the "head of the family" and entitled to exemptions therein as a homestead, when she becomes bankrupt. In re Hasting, 7 A. B. R. 362 (Ref. Mo.). But compare, In re Jamieson, 6 A. B. R. 601 (D. C. R. I.).

"Head of Family" in Washington. —No "double-headed head of family;" bankrupt wife living with husband who is earning good wages; presumably the husband and not the wife is the "head." In re Herbold, 14 A. B. R. 118 (D. C. Wash.).

"Householder" in Rhode Island.— Married woman may not claim exemptions as such where her husband is in fact the head and support of the family. In re Jamieson, 6 A. B. R. 601 (D. C. R. I.).

"Homestead:"

Kansas.—Homestead exemptions. In re Parker, 1 A. B. R. 708 (Ref. Kas.).

Michigan.—Actual use of homestead, not mere intention to use it as such, requisite. In re Hatch, 2 A. B. R. 36 (Ref. Mich.).

Sale of homestead encumbered with liens in Colorado and allowance of $2000.00 from equity of redemption. In re Nye, 13 A. B. R. 142, 133 Fed. 33 (C. C. A. Colo.).

Iowa.—Homestead exemptions of divorced bankrupt. In re Pope, 3 A. B. R. 525, 98 Fed. 722 (D. C. Iowa).

Kentucky.—Homestead in property coming by descent but not in that by purchase as against prior debts. In re Baker, 24 A. B. R. 411, 182 Fed. 392 (C. C. A. Ky.).

Homestead in general. In re Carmichael, 5 A. B. R. 551, 108 Fed. 789 (D. C. Ky.); In re Downing, 15 A. B. R. 423, 139 Fed. 590 (D. C. Ky.), though acquired within four months by marriage with adulteress. In re Sale, 16 A. B. R. 235, 143 Fed. 310 (C. C. A. Ky.). None to husband where wife has life tenancy and he the remainder in fee upon her death.

Homestead in unimproved lands. In re Baker, 24 A. B. R. 411, 182 Fed. 392 (C. C. A. Ky.).

Minnesota.—The proceeds from the sale of crops raised on homestead property are not exempt. In re Friedrich, 28 A. B. R. 656, 199 Fed. 193 (D. C. Minn.).

Missouri.—Homestead purchased with pension money, not itself exempt under U. S. Rev. Stat. 4747. In re Stout, 6 A. B. R. 505, 109 Fed. 794 (D. C. Mo.).

Homestead of an unborn child in North Carolina is to be allowed from lands of which the father dies seized, exempt from father's debts. In re Seabolt, 8 A. B. R. 57, 113 Fed. 766 (D. C. Ga.).

Divorced man with minor son entitled to homestead in **Ohio.** In re Rhodes, 6 A. B. R. 173, 109 Fed. 117 (D. C. Ohio); likewise, divorced woman. In re Giles, 19 A. B. R. 306, 158 Fed. 596 (C. C. A. Ohio).

Instance, **Oregon,** homestead exemption out of equity of redemption from foreclosure. In re Barrett, 16 A. B. R. 46 (D. C. Ore.).

No homestead in **South Carolina** unless at the time the same was acquired the debtor was in a solvent condition and able to satisfy all claims against him, and the debtor has the burden of proof of these facts and must prove them clearly and conclusively. No exemption in South Carolina in a homestead purchased or built in part with the proceeds of goods unpaid for. McGahan v. Anderson, 7 A. B. R. 641, 113 Fed. 115 (C. C. A. S. C.).

Texas.—Husband and wife may not effectually encumber homestead. Burow v. Grand Lodge, 13 A. B. R. 542, 133 Fed. 708 (C. C. A. Tex.).

Vermont.—In re Libby, 4 A. B. R. 615, 103 Fed. 776 (D. C. Vt.); In re Marquette, 4 A. B. R. 623, 103 Fed. 777 (D. C. Vt.), which was a case of homestead in estate by curtesy.

Washington.—Homestead exemptions. In re Buelow, 3 A. B. R. 389, 98 Fed. 86 (D. C. Wash.).

Homestead in land occupied by bankrupt as tenant by curtesy, in **Wisconsin.** In re Kaufmann, 16 A. B. R. 118, 142 Fed. 898 (D. C. Wis.).

"**Homestead—Abandonment or Change of:**"

Iowa.—Where the State law authorizes a change of homestead, a new homestead, to the extent in value of the former one, is exempt from liability for debts not enforceable against the former homestead, although incurred before the change of homestead was made. In re Johnson, 9 A. B. R. 257 (D. C. Iowa).

No abandonment of homestead by temporary leasing of it for a year. In re Pope, 3 A. B. R. 525, 98 Fed. 722 (D. C. Iowa).

Kansas.—Changing one's homestead within the four months period to one more valuable or eligible is perfectly

legitimate if done in good faith. Huenergardt v. Brittain Dry Goods Co., 8 A. B. R. 341, 116 Fed. 31 (C. C. A. Kas.).

Missouri.—Abandonment of homestead in Missouri. In re Lynch, 1 A. B. R. 245 (Ref. Mo.).

North Dakota.—After living on homestead debtor goes on debauch, ending up in hospital and getting out of hospital too late to work on farm that year, so working as accountant in winter. In re Malloy, 26 A. B. R. 31, 188 Fed. 788 (C. C. A. N. Dak.).

Oregon and Washington.—None where intention to return: none where removal was to another State for purpose of earning money to establish business in place of his homestead that would enable the debtor permanently to maintain his family; and so notwithstanding petition in bankruptcy alleged residence for greater portion of six months in the State to which he had removed. In re Schulz, 14 A. B. R. 317, 135 Fed. 228 (D. C. Ore.); In re Thompson, 15 A. B. R. 283, 140 Fed. 251 (D. C. Wash.).

Abandonment of Business Homestead in Texas.—In re Harrington, 3 A. B. R. 639, 99 Fed. 390 (D. C. Tex.); In re Flannagan, 9 A. B. R. 140 (D. C. Tex.); McCarty v. Coffin, 18 A. B. R. 148, 150 Fed. 307 (C. C. A. Tex.); Duncan v. Ferguson-McKinney Co., 18 A. B. R. 155, 150 Fed. 269 (C. C. A. Tex.); In re Presnall, 21 A. B. R. 905, 167 Fed. 406 (D. C. Tex.).

Texas.—Temporary absence from a homestead, or the temporary renting of it does not destroy its exempt character; that can only be accomplished by disposing of it, or leaving it with the intention of not using it further as a homestead. In re Thedford, 28 A. B. R. 191 (D. C. Tex.).

"**Homestead—Business Homestead:**"

Texas.—No business homestead in rural residence. Burow v. Grand Lodge, 13 A. B. R. 542, 133 Fed. 708 (C. C. A. Tex.).

Homestead—"Designation of:"

Colorado — Designation of Homestead on Margin of Records.—In re Youngstrom, 18 A. B. R. 572, 153 Fed. 97 (C. C. A. Colo.).

Iowa—Failure to Plat Homestead.—In re Eash, 19 A. B. R. 738, 157 Fed. 996 (D. C. Iowa).

Oklahoma.—Particular description of property claimed requisite. In re Mathews, 20 A. B. R. 369 (Ref. Okla.).

Virginia.—Failure to record with recorder of deeds, debtor's declaration of claim of homestead exemptions in accordance with State law, not cured by making "claim" in bankruptcy in accordance with bankruptcy law and forms. In re Gardner, 8 A. B. R. 263 (D. C. Va.); In re Tobias, 4 A. B. R. 555, 103 Fed. 68 (D. C. Va.), wherein the court held that such a recording fixes the right and is more than a mere "claiming" of the right. But delay in filing the declaration until after bankruptcy is not fatal, In re Fisher, 15 A. B. R. 652 (D. C. Va.).

Homestead — Second Allowance— "Double Exemptions:"

Second allowance of homestead, after exhaustion of first, not allowable in Georgia, though several years apart. In re Jeffers, 17 A. B. R. 368 (Ref. Ga.).

No Double Exemption.—Where bankrupt has had set off to him a homestead of forty acres and crops sufficient for a year's support as the Statute prescribes, he may not have the remainder of the crops growing on the homestead on the plea that it is part of the realty. In re Hoag, 3 A. B. R. 290, 97 Fed. 543 (D. C. Wis.).

Partnership Exemptions:

Alabama.—In re McCrary Bros., 22 A. B. R. 161, 169 Fed. 485 (D. C. Ala.).

Georgia.—In re Jennings & Co., 22 A. B. R. 160, 166 Fed. 639 (D. C. Ga.).

North Carolina.—In North Carolina, one of two or more partners may have a portion of the partnership effects set apart to him, as his personal exemption, with the consent of the other partner or partners, and the partnership creditors cannot object to this exemption. In re Grimes, 2 A. B. R. 160, 94 Fed. 800 (D. C. N. Car.); In re Stevenson & King, 2 A. B. R. 230, 93 Fed. 789 (D. C. N. Car.); In re Duguid, 3 A. B. R. 794 (D. C. N. Car.); In re Wilson, 4 A. B. R. 260, 101 Fed. 571 (D. C. N. Car.); In re Camp, 1 A. B. R. 165, 91 Fed. 745 (D. C. N. Car.); In re Seabolt, 8 A. B. R. 57, 113 Fed. 766 (D. C. N. Car.).

But no exemption will be allowed a partner unless his partnership share will at least equal the exemption. In re Camp, 1 A. B. R. 165, 91 Fed. 745 (D. C. N. Car.); In re Gartner Hancock Lumber Co., 22 A. B. R. 898, 173 Fed. 153 (D. C. N. C.).

And consent of the other partners must be shown. In re Monroe & Co.,

19 A. B. R. 255, 156 Fed. 216 (D. C. N. Car.).

Consent of both is shown if both sign partnership petition in bankruptcy. In re Stevenson & King, 2 A. B. R. 230, 93 Fed. 745 (D. C. N. Car.). A surviving partner may have his personal exemption from partnership effects with the consent of the administrator of the deceased partner, In re Seabolt, 8 A. B. R. 57, 113 Fed. 766 (D. C. N. Car.).

But in allowing a personal property exemption out of firm assets, even if both parties consent, it must appear that the members of the firm have no individual personal property exemption exclusive of firm assets; if they have such exemption it cannot be allowed from the firm assets, In re Steed and Curtis, 6 A. B. R. 73, 107 Fed. 682 (D. C. N. Car.).

And after a partner has declared he has retired from the firm and is only working as clerk, he will be denied exemptions from the firm assets. In re Fowler & Co., 16 A. B. R. 580, 145 Fed. 270 (D. C. N. Car.).

The selection from the firm assets must be in kind; allowance of the exemption out of the proceeds of sale is not proper. In re Blanchard, 20 A. B. R. 417, 161 Fed. 793 (D. C. N. Car.).

An infant who, although he contributed to the capital stock of a partnership, assented to being ignored in all firm transactions, is not entitled to a personal property exemption out of the assets of the firm. In re Floyd & Co., 18 A. B. R. 827, 154 Fed. 757 (D. C. N. C.).

Vermont, Maryland, New Jersey, Pennsylvania, South Dakota, Oklahoma and Arkansas.—No exemptions in partnership property as against claim of partnership creditors. In re Mosier, 7 A. B. R. 268, 112 Fed. 138 (D. C. Vt.); In re Meriweather, 5 A. B. R. 435, 107 Fed. 102 (D. C. Ark.); In re Head & Smith, 7 A. B. R. 556, 114 Fed. 489 (D. C. Ark.); In re Beauchamp, 4 A. B. R. 151, 101 Fed. 106 (D. C. Md.); In re Demarest, 6 A. B. R. 232, 110 Fed. 638 (D. C. N. J.); In re Prince & Walter, 12 A. B. R. 675, 131 Fed. 546 (D. C. Pa.); In re Novak, 18 A. B. R. 236, 150 Fed. 602 (D. C. S. Dak.); In re Vickerman, 29 A. B. R. 298, 199 Fed. 589 (D. C. S. Dak.); In re Golden Rule Mercantile Co., 21 A. B. R. 397 (Ref. Okla.).

Wisconsin.—Exemptions in partnership assets allowed by consent of other partners if no individual estate.

In re Nelson, 2 A. B. R. 556 (D. C. Wis.); In re Friedrich, 3 A. B. R. 801, 100 Fed. 284 (C. C. A. Wis.).

Washington.—Partnerships are not entitled to exemptions; and the fact that one of two partners is a minor does not alter the situation. Jennings *v.* Stannus & Son, 27 A. B. R. 384, 191 Fed. 347 (C. C. A. Wash.).

No exemptions in the quasi partnership property of husband and wife in Washington. In re Herbold, 14 A. B. R. 116 (D. C. Wash.).

"Pension Money Exemptions:"

Maine.—Not exempt in Maine. In re Jones, 21 A. B. R. 536, 166 Fed. 337 (D. C. Me.).

New York.—Real estate purchased partly with pension money in New York, but out of which has been withdrawn by mortgage more than the amount of pension money invested, the real estate not being necessary for pensioner's support, held not to be exempt. In re Ellithorpe, 7 A. B. R. 18, 111 Fed. 163 (D. C. N. Y., affirming 5 A. B. R. 681).

Vermont.—Pension money still in bankrupt's hands at time of adjudication, exempt in Vermont. In re Bean, 4 A. B. R. 53, 100 Fed. 262 (D. C. Vt.).

"Wages and Salary:"

Washington.—Priority payment to workman (under laws of Washington not exceeding $100) for services performed within sixty days preceding the appointment of a receiver or levy of execution upon the property of his employer, is exempt to the workman upon his afterwards going into bankruptcy. In re Holden, 12 A. B. R. 96, 127 Fed. 980 (D. C. Wash.).

"Wearing Apparel:"

Delaware—Wearing Apparel Exempt to Partners.—In re Evans & Co., 19 A. B. R. 752, 158 Fed. 153 (D. C. Del.).

Kentucky.—Ring as wearing apparel in re Leach, 22 A. B. R. 599, 171 Fed. 622 (C. C. A. Ky.).

Massachusetts.—Watch of one who keeps time of workmen for employer is exempt as a tool or implement of trade except as to any excess over appropriate value, in Massachusetts. In re Coller, 7 A. B. R. 131, 111 Fed. 503 (D. C. Mass.). But see In re Turnbull, 5 A. B. R. 549, 106 Fed. 666 (D. C. Mass., affirming 5 A. B. R. 231), that it is not generally speaking "necessary" wearing apparel.

New York.—Wearing apparel of single woman exempt in New York. In re Stokes, 4 A. B. R. 560 (Ref. N. Y.).

Ohio.—"Wearing apparel," in Ohio, gold watch and chain, of moderate value, habitually worn, exempt; but diamond ring, not. In re Henry, 14 A. B. R. 362 (Ref. Ohio).

Rhode Island.—Watch and chain of moderate value habitually worn are necessary wearing apparel in Rhode Island. In re Caswell, 6 A. B. R. 718 (Ref. R. I.). Also in Alabama, Sellers *v.* Bell, 2 A. B. R. 529, 94 Fed. 801 (C. C. A. Ala.). This case arose on discharge, however.

Texas.—Diamond shirt stud worth $250 is exempt as wearing apparel if customarily used to fasten shirt together. In re Smith, 3 A. B. R. 140, 96 Fed. 832 (D. C. Tex.).

Vermont.—But watch and chain of a barber are not exempt, in Vermont, either as "wearing apparel" or as "tools of trade" where he has a clock in his barber shop. In re Everleth, 12 A. B. R. 236, 129 Fed. 620 (D. C. Vt.).

Masonic regalia; only part exempt in Vermont is the hat. The belt and sword are not exempt. In re Everleth, 12 A. R. R. 236, 129 Fed. 620 (D. C. Vt.).

Wisconsin.—Watch, gold, carried on person is wearing apparel and exempt in Wisconsin. In re Jones, 3 A. B. R. 259, 97 Fed. 773 (D. C. Wis.).

Masonic regalia exempt in Wisconsin as "wearing apparel" although only occasionally worn. In re Jones, 3 A. B. R. 259, 97 Fed. 773 (D. C. Wis.).

Failure "to act in good faith," in Georgia. In re West, 8 A. B. R. 564, 116 Fed. 767 (D. C. Ga.). Also in re Waxelbaum, 4 A. B. R. 120, 101 Fed. 228 (D. C. Ga.). Also, In re Williamson, 8 A. B. R. 42, 114 Fed. 190 (D. C. Ga.). Also, In re Stephens, 8 A. B. R. 53, 114 Fed. 192 (D. C. Ga.). Also, In re Boorstein, 8 A. B. R. 89, 114 Fed. 696 (D. C. Ga.). Also, In re Castleberry, 16 A. B. R. 159, 143 Fed. 821 (D. C. Ga.); In re Dobbs, 22 A. B. R. 801, 172 Fed. 682 (D. C. Ga.); In re Dobbs, 23 A. B. R. 596, 175 Fed. 319 (D. C. Ga.).

No exemptions in property obtained by bankrupt through fraud in North Carolina. In re Wolcott, 15 A. B. R. 386, 140 Fed. 460 (D. C. N. Car.). Impliedly, In re Hennis, 17 A. B. R. 889 (Ref. N. Car.), wherein the fraud consisted in the willful disregard of an agreement to give a contemporaneous mortgage on purchase of goods. In re Cotton & Preston, 23 A. B. R. 586 (Ref. Ga.).

The making of a materially false statement in writing to obtain credit, whilst a bar to the bankrupt's discharge, is not, in and of itself, a valid objection to the allowance of the homestead exemption in Georgia. In re Cotton & Preston, 23 A. B. R. 586 (Ref. Ga.).

Failure to make "full and fair disclosure" in Georgia refers only to personal property, not to real estate. In re Cotton & Preston, 23 A. B. R. 586 (Ref. Ga.).

"Reconveyance of Fraudulently Transferred Property:"

But where fraudulently conveyed property is reconveyed to the bankrupt before bankruptcy he is entitled to his exemptions therein. In re Thompson, 8 A. B. R. 283, 112 Fed. 924 (D. C. Ga.).

Even though the reconveyance be made pending a suit in the State court to set aside the fraudulent conveyance. In re Allen & Co., 13 A. B. R. 518, 134 Fed. 620 (D. C. Va.).

"Exemption Applies to All Incidents of Property:"

Iowa, Wisconsin and Oregon.—The exemption applies to all incidents of the property; as, rents accruing after adjudication. In re Oleson, 7 A. B. R. 22, 110 Fed. 796 (D. C. Iowa). But compare, In re Hoag, 3 A. B. R. 290, 97 Fed. 543 (D. C. Wis.). Also, compare, In re Daubner, 3 A. B. R. 368, 96 Fed. 805 (D. C. Ore.). But does not apply to crops growing on the homestead in Oregon, see, In re Daubner, 3 A. B. R. 368, 96 Fed. 805 (D. C. Ore.); nor in Wisconsin, see In re Hoag, 3 A. B. R. 290, 97 Fed. 543 (D. C. Wis.); nor in Iowa, see In re Sullivan, 16 A. B. R. 87, 142 Fed. 620 (D. C. Iowa), and also, In re Sullivan, 17 A. B. R. 578 (C. C. A. Iowa, affirming 16 A. B. R. 87).

Miscellaneous:

Meaning of "Town" in Arkansas. —Exemption law. In re Overstreet, 2 A. B. R. 486 (Ref. Ark.).

Arkansas.—"The Constitution of Arkansas, art. IX., §§ 1 and 2, after ordaining that personal property of the amount of $500 belonging to any man the head of a family should be exempt from sale on execution, contains the following proviso: 'That no property shall be exempt from execution for

debts contracted for the purchase money thereof, *while in the hands of the vendee.'*" Mulinix v. Simon, 28 A. B. R. 1, 196 Fed. 775 (C. C. A. Ark.).

Massachusetts.—Where article claimed as exempt is of excessive value, the trustee may take it for creditors upon giving the bankrupt money to buy one of proper value, so it is held in Massachusetts. In re Coller, 7 A. B. R. 131, 111 Fed. 503 (D. C. Mass.). This would not probably be a safe precedent to follow elsewhere for it would seem that the article either is or is not exempt, and if not exempt the trustee need not concern himself with the procuring of an exempt substitute, and if exempt he has no right to it. And compare, In re Manning, 7 A. B. R. 571, 112 Fed. 948 (D. C. Penn.). "* * * and what the law of the State does not give, cannot be set aside by the trustee."

Idaho.—Bank of Nez Perce v. Pindel, 28 A. B. R. 69, 193 Fed. 917 (C. C. A. Idaho).

Iowa.—Exemptions to bankrupt heir out of decedent's estate. In re Eash, 19 A. B. R. 738, 157 Fed. 996 (D. C. Iowa).

Alabama.—Waiver of exemptions not available in Alabama until claim reduced to judgment, ascertaining extent of exemption waiver in mode prescribed by statute. In re Moore, 7 A. B. R. 285, 112 Fed. 289 (D. C. Ala., overruling In re Garden, 1 A. B. R. 582, 93 Fed. 423).

Household Goods Purchased with Wife's and Children's Earnings.—In re Diamond, 19 A. B. R. 811, 158 Fed. 370 (D. C. Ala.).

Oklahoma.—No exemptions out of partnership assets as against partnership debts. In re Rushmore, 24 A. B. R. 55 (Ref. Okla.).

No Exemption against Purchase Price.—Refers only to original sellers, not to one who has loaned the money to make the purchase. In re Bailes, 23 A. B. R. 789, 176 Fed. 460 (D. C. S. C.). See, also, ante, § 1035.

Supplementing statutory specific exemptions in Georgia by value of those articles not in possession that might have been claimed. In re Reinhart, 12 A. B. R. 78, 129 Fed. 510 (D. C. Ga.). But compare, In re Manning, 7 A. B. R. 571, 112 Fed. 948 (D. C. Penn.): "* * * and what the law of the State does not give, cannot be set apart by the trustee."

New York.—Waiver of exemptions. Failure to protest at time exempt

SUBDIVISION "C."

CLAIMING OF EXEMPTIONS.

§ 1048. But Time and Manner of Claiming and Setting Apart Exemptions Fixed by Act Itself.—While it is true that the State law fixes the kind and the amount of the exemptions and the persons entitled thereto, yet the time and manner of claiming them and of setting them apart are fixed by the provisions of the bankruptcy act itself wherever the bankruptcy act speaks at all.[59]

property was sold on execution prior to bankruptcy is no waiver where subsequently the property is surrendered to the trustee in bankruptcy. In re Osborn, 5 A. B. R. 111, 104 Fed. 780 (D. C. N. Y.).

Mining claim exemption in California. In re Diller, 4 A. B. R. 45, 100 Fed. 931 (D. C. Calif.).

Membership in Chamber of Commerce not exempt in Wisconsin. In re Neimann, 10 A. B. R. 739, 124 Fed. 738 (D. C. Wis.).

Pennsylvania.—Property Not Subject to Levy, Not Exempt.—Where the State statute gives exemptions only as to property subject to levy of execution or attachment, property not subject to levy, though reachable by other process, such as a liquor license, is not exempt. In re Myers, 4 A. B. R. 536, 102 Fed. 869 (D. C. Pa.).

Life Insurance Policies.—See ante, § 1003.

Vermont.—None in tenement house owned by bankrupt but not occupied by him or his family except one room for storage. In re Dawley, 2 A. B. R. 496, 94 Fed. 795 (D. C. Vt.).

"Team" exemption in Vermont. In re Grady, 14 A. B. R. 738, 138 Fed. 935 (D. C. Vt.).

Team horse intended for use but not actually yet in use exempt. In re Alfred, 1 A. B. R. 243 (Ref. Vt.).

Exemptions in South Carolina.—In re McCutchen, 4 A. B. R. 81, 100 Fed. 779 (D. C. S. Car.).

Virginia.—Exemptions are allowed in shifting stock of goods in Virginia but the articles must be specifically described else claim is insufficient. In re Wilson, 6 A. B. R. 287, 108 Fed. 197 (D. C. Va.).

Virginia.—No exemptions in Virginia in property where fraudulent conveyance set aside. Exemptions in reconveyed property previously fraudulently transferred in Virginia, pending suit in State Court to set aside conveyance, not yet gone to decree,

not contrary to Virginia Statute, since conveyance not yet "set aside." In re Allen & Co., 13 A. B. R. 518, 134 Fed. 620 (D. C. Va.).

Georgia.—No power to waive statutory exemptions in advance in Georgia, but power to waive constitutional exemptions. In re Reinhart, 12 A. B. R. 78, 129 Fed. 510 (D. C. Ga.).

Unmarried woman supporting aged grandfather entitled. In re Jackson, 18 A. B. R. 216 (Ref. Ga.).

Allowance from proceeds of sale. In re Hargraves, 20 A. B. R. 186, 160 Fed. 758 (D. C. Ga.); In re Hargraves, 19 A. B. R. 238 (Ref. Ga.); Citizens Bk. of Douglas v. Hargraves, 21 A. B. R. 323, 164 Fed. 613 (C. C. A. Ga., reversing District Court and affirming referee, In re Hargraves).

Mortgage Waiving Exemptions, Lien Not Lost by Selling Free from Liens by Consent, Rights Being Transferred to Proceeds.—Citizens Bk. v. Hargraves, 21 A. B. R. 323, 164 Fed. 613 (C. C. A. Ga.).

Federal Homestead—When Title Thereto Is Acquired, etc.—In re Cohn, 22 A. B. R. 761, 171 Fed. 568 (D. C. N. Dak.).

Application of proceeds of sale of former homestead. Ibid.

Exemptions May Be Waived but Not Assigned.—In Pennsylvania. In re Pfeiffer, 19 A. B. R. 230, 155 Fed. 892 (D. C. Pa.).

"Laborer" under California Statute.—In re Hindman, 5 A. B. R. 20, 104 Fed. 331 (C. C. A. Calif.).

Land used for burial purposes. Burdette v. Jackson, 24 A. B. R. 127, 179 Fed. 229 (C. C. A. Md.).

Aliens, not entitled to exemptions in Mississippi, In re Kaplan, 24 A. B. R. 376, 186 Fed. 242 (D. C. Miss.).

59. Burke v. Title & Trust Co., 14 A. B. R. 31, 134 Fed. 562 (C. C. A. Pa.); In re Friedrich, 3 A. B. R. 801, 100 Fed. 294 (C. C. A. Wis.); In re Groves, 6 A. B. R. 728 (Ref. Ohio, affirmed by D. C.); In re McClintock,

Lipman *v.* Stein, 14 A. B. R. 30, 134 Fed. 235 (C. C. A. Pa., affirming In re Stein, 12 A. B. R. 384): "That a bankrupt's right to exemption must be deduced from the state law is unquestionable; but it is no less true that, where the right exists, it is to be asserted in the manner which the Bankruptcy Act itself prescribes."

In re Gerber, 26 A. B. R. 608, 186 Fed. 693 (C. C. A. Wash.): "While the exemption right in the case at hand depends upon the statutes of Washington, as has already been said, the manner of claiming such exemptions and of setting apart and awarding them is regulated by the Bankruptcy Act."

In re LeVay, 11 A. B. R. 114, 125 Fed. 990 (D. C. Pa.): "But while it is no doubt true that the right of the bankrupt to his exemptions depends on the State law by which it is primarily given, the analogies derived from the practice upon execution process are not to be carried too far. The time and manner of obtaining it in this court are necessarily regulated by the Bankrupt Act, and it is there provided that the bankrupt shall claim in his schedules the exemptions to which he is entitled (§ 7a [8]); and that they are to be set apart to him by the trustee, who is to report to the court the items and estimated value thereof. Section 47a (11). Where this course has been pursued it must be regarded as effective and in time."

In re Lucius, 10 A. B. R. 653, 124 Fed. 455 (D. C. Ala.): "The Bankrupt Law allows to the bankrupt the exemption provided by the law of the State, but the manner in which the exemption is to be claimed, set apart and awarded is regulated by the Bankrupt Law. The voluntary bankrupt must claim the exemption to which he is entitled at the time of filing his petition."

In re Kane, 11 A. B. R. 533, 127 Fed. 552 (C. C. A. Ills.): "The Bankruptcy Act allows the exemptions which the State laws provided, and these laws, from motives of public policy, should be liberally construed. Courts of bankruptcy are not controlled as to the time or the manner in which claims for exemptions may be preferred in bankruptcy. The exemptions provided by the law of the State are allowed by the Bankruptcy Act, but the manner of claiming such exemptions, and of setting apart and awarding them, is regulated by the Bankruptcy Act."

But statutory regulations of a State requisite to the perfecting of the claim of exemption, such as the filing of a declaration of homestead with some officer, must also be complied with.[60]

---

13 A. B. R. 606 (Ref. Ohio, affirmed by D. C.); In re Jennings & Co., 22 A. B. R. 160, 166 Fed. 639 (D. C. Ga.); In re Kelly, 28 A. B. R. 730, 199 Fed. 984 (D. C. Pa.); In re Prince & Walter, 12 A. B. R. 680, 131 Fed. 546 (D. C. Pa.); In re Von Kerm. 14 A. B. R. 403, 135 Fed. 447 (D. C. Pa.); In re Sharp, 15 A. B. R. 491 (Ref. Ohio, affirmed by D. C.); inferentially, In re Royal, 7 A. B. R. 106, 112 Fed. 135 (D. C. N. Car.); inferentially, In re Nunn, 2 A. B. R. 664 (Ref. Ga.); inferentially, In re Grimes, 2 A. B. R. 730, 96 Fed. 529 (D. C. N. Car.); inferentially, In re Lynch, 4 A. B. R. 262, 101 Fed. 579 (D. C. Ga.); inferentially, In re Kaufmann, 16 A. B. R. 121, 142 Fed. 898 (D. C. Wis.). And the debtor will be held by his voluntary bankruptcy to have waived his right to prevent the creditors fiom entering on exempt land to seize more exempt property. Obiter, In re Coffman, 1 A. B. R. 530, 93 Fed. 422 (D. C. Tex.). But compare, inferentially, contra (that the State law must be complied with), as to the manner of claiming exemptions, In re Wilson, 6 A. B. R. 287, 108 Fed. 197 (D. C. Va.). Inferentially, contra, In re Wunder, 13 A. B. R. 701, 133 Fed. 821 (D. C. Penn.); inferentially, contra, In re Ogilvie, 5 A. B. R. 374 (Ref. Ga.); In re Jennings & Co., 22 A. B. R. 160, 166 Fed. 639 (D. C. Ga.); In re Gerber, 26 A. B. R. 608, 186 Fed. 693 (C. C. A. Wash.); In re Kelly, 28 A. B. R. 730, 199 Fed. 984 (D. C. Pa.).

60. In re Fisher, 15 A. B. R. 652, 142 Fed. 205 (D. C. Va.). In re Eash, 19

In re Youngstrom, 18 A. B. R. 572, 153 Fed. 97 (C. C. A. Colo.): "The premises in controversy were not so designated until after the time of the filing of the petition and after the time when the owner was adjudged a bankrupt, so neither he nor his family was entitled to a homestead exemption therein at either of these times."

Likewise, where the State statute requires itemization of the articles demanded as exempt, they must also be itemized in the bankrupt's schedules.[61]

But this rule is simply confirmatory of the provisions of the Bankruptcy Act requiring such particular description. Even were a general description sufficient in State practice it would not necessarily be sufficient in bankruptcy, for the Bankruptcy Act controls the manner of claiming exemptions.

But probably, in most States, regulations as to the designation of the homestead, etc., may be complied with after the bankruptcy.[61a]

In re Culwell, 21 A. B. R. 614, 165 Fed. 828 (D. C. Mont.): "I do not construe the Bankrupt Act as meaning that upon the trustee's qualifying, the bankrupt is deprived of all right to perfect his homestead exemption, provided in his schedules he claims a designated piece of realty as a homestead and as exempt, and provided he proceeds, under the State statutes, without delay, and provided always there is no fraud involved in the matter of the claim. * * * Yet the act does not make it a precedent to having a homestead allowed to the bankrupt claiming the same in the bankruptcy court, that the homestead shall have been designated pursuant to the State statute, prior to the date of adjudication."

As a consequence of this rule, the bankrupt must claim his exemptions, if he wishes them, as directed by § 7 of the act, which prescribes the duties of bankrupts.[62]

And if he claim his exemptions in writing, duly sworn to and filed with his schedules, his claim cannot be held to be "fatally" defective,[63] although amendment may be required to make them conform to the Supreme court's prescribed form in bankruptcy.

Burke v. Title & Trust Co., 14 A. B. R. 31, 134 Fed. 562 (C. C. A. Pa.): "The learned referee (whose action the court simply approved) was of opinion that this claim 'is fatally defective, in that it does not specifically enumerate the

---

A. B. R. 738, 157 Fed. 996 (D. C. Iowa): In re Mathews, 20 A. B. R. 369 (Rep. Okla.); In re Gardner, 8 A. B. R. 263 (D. C. Va.); In re Tobias, 4 A. B. R. 555, 103 Fed. 68 (D. C. Va.). Compare analogous rule, post, § 2199.

61. In re Mathews, 20 A. B. R. 369 (Ref. Okla.).

61a. Compare ante, § 1025; also see In re Fisher, 15 A. B. R. 652 (D. C. Va.). But compare, In re Gardner, 8 A. B. R. 263 (D. C. Va.) and In re Tobias, 4 A. B. R. 555, 103 Fed. 68 (D. C. Va.).

62. Bankr. Act, § 7 (8): "The bankrupt shall * * * (8) prepare, make oath to and file in court within ten days, unless further time is granted, after the adjudication, if an involuntary bankrupt, and with the petition if a voluntary bankrupt, a schedule of his property, etc., * * * and a list of his creditors. etc., * * * and a claim for such exemptions as he may be entitled to, all in triplicate, one copy of each for the clerk, one for the referee, and one for the trustee." In re [Jonas B.] Baughman, 25 A. B. R. 167, 183 Fed. 668 (D. C. Pa.), quoted at § 1026.

63. Lipman v. Stein, 14 A. B. R. 30, 134 Fed. 235 (C. C. A. Pa., affirming In re Stein, 12 A. B. R. 384). See post, § 1064, et seq.

articles claimed as exempt under the exemption law of the State of Pennsylvania.' But, as we have said in an opinion delivered to-day in the case of Lipman v. Stein, 14 Am. B. R. 30, 134 Fed. 235, though a bankrupt's right to exemption must be deduced from the State law, yet it is to be asserted in the manner prescribed by § 7 of the Bankruptcy Act itself; and that section does not require that he shall enumerate the articles claimed as exempt, but only that 'the claim for such exemption as he may be entitled to' shall appear in the schedule which he is required to file. The claim in this case was for $300 'of the * * * property * * * set out in schedule B, No. 2, under head of C,' and that the bankrupt was entitled to the exemption of that property to the amount stated is unquestionable. This was his right, and its denial was not justified by the fact that, in setting out the entire property, he seems to have excessively estimated its value. What he meant to claim was so much of that property as was of the value of $300, and this, we think, he made clearly apparent. The law imposed no further condition upon him. It nowhere exacted a specification and appraisement by him of the articles claimed. Having given notice of his claim, it was not his duty, but that of the trustee (§ 47, subd. 11, 30 Stat. 557 [U. S. Comp. St. 1901, p. 3439]), to 'set apart' the bankrupt's exemptions and report the items and estimated value thereof to the court. And there is not a word in the statute to warrant the conjecture that Congress intended that the bankrupt himself should make an itemization and estimate which the trustee, in performing the function expressly assigned to him, might wholly disregard.

"It is true that amongst the forms promulgated by the Supreme Court is 'Schedule B (5),' in which is contained the words: 'property claimed to be exempted by the State laws, its valuation,' etc. But, waiving the question whether in this instance the property claimed and its valuation were not stated in substantial accordance with this direction, it is enough to say that we do not understand it to be anything more than a direction. It could not have been intended to be mandatory. These forms were not designed to effect any change in the law. They are 'forms,' and nothing more. As was said by the Supreme Court (General Order 38, 89 Fed. xiv, 32 C. C. A. xxxvii), they are to be 'observed and used with such alterations as may be necessary to suit the circumstances of any particular case;' and, under the circumstances of this case, we decline to hold that the failure of the bankrupt to precisely observe one of them was fatal to his claim, because we could not do so without subordinating substance to form, and refusing a legal right, merely on account of a defect in procedure, which has caused no injury to any one, and which, if requisite, might be cured by amendment."

But the claim for exemptions also should conform to the Supreme Court's orders and prescribed form "Schedule 'B' (5)," and should specify each article in detail and its location and estimated value.[64]

In re Gerber, 26 A. B. R. 608, 186 Fed. 693 (C. C. A. Wis.): "The rules and forms so prescribed by the Supreme Court under and by virtue of the Bankruptcy Act have the force and effect of law, and it therefore seems to us to result necessarily that the bankrupt here * * * lost any right he may have had to the exemptions claimed, by his failure to make the claim in the manner and within the time legally prescribed therefor."

In re Von Kerm, 14 A. B. R. 403, 135 Fed. 447 (D. C. Pa.): "While a notice

64. In re Groves, 6 A. B. R. 728 (Ref. Ohio, affirmed by D. C.)· In re Mc-   Clintock, 13 A. B. R. 606 (Ref. Ohio, affirmed by D. C.).

in general language, both in a voluntary and involuntary petition, of an intention to claim the exemption may be amended if done in time * * * yet where the notice in either case is so general as not to indicate to the trustee what specific articles the bankrupt claims as his exemption, and the bankrupt files no schedule or makes no request upon the trustee to set aside specific articles of exemption until after the sale, he must be regarded as having waived his right of exemption, and he cannot claim three hundred dollars ($300) out of the proceeds of sale. In re Wunder, 13 Am. B. R. 701, 133 Fed. 821; In re Prince & Walter, 12 Am. B. R. 675, 131 Fed. 546; In re Manning, 7 Am. B. R. 571, 112 Fed. 948; In re Haskin, 6 Am. B. R. 485."

In re Duffy, 9 A. B. R. 358, 118 Fed. 926 (D. C. Pa.): "Besides that, the schedules prescribed by the Supreme Court call for a particular description of the property claimed, which of itself is controlling. * * * But this is a curable defect, and the petitioner asks leave to amend his schedules accordingly."

The decisions in Burke v. Title and Trust Co., 14 A. B. R. 31, 134 Fed. 562 (C. C. A. Pa.) and in Lipman v. Stein, 14 A. B. R. 30, 134 Fed. 235 (C. C. A. Pa.), must not be taken to lay down the rule that the bankrupt need not itemize his claim for exemptions in accordance with the Supreme Court's Form of Schedule "B" (5). Those decisions simply hold that failure to so itemize the claim will not be fatally defective; that the bankrupt's right to exemptions conferred by § 6 of the Act will not be thereby lost, so long as the statutory requirements are satisfied; that otherwise the mere forms prescribed as part of the remedy would override the statute as to substantive rights. They do not at all imply that it will be sufficient, much less that it is good practice, for the bankrupt to disregard the requirements of the form prescribed for claiming exemptions known as Schedule "B" 5. Indeed, the concluding words of the court carry the implication that failure to itemize the claim is a defect, but that it is one remediable by amendment, the court saying:

"We decline to hold that the failure of the bankrupt to precisely observe one of them was fatal to his claim, because we could not do so without subordinating substance to form, and refusing a legal right, merely on account of a defect in procedure, which has caused no injury to any one, and which, if requisite, might be cured by amendment."

The Supreme Court's Orders and Forms are made in conformity with the Act and in certain circumstances indeed are held to be in the nature of advance interpretations of its provisions, especially of its remedial provisions. Nowhere does the Statute, in so many words, declare what shall amount to a sufficient "claim" of exemptions to satisfy the requirements of § 7; and the Supreme Court's Form "Schedule 'B' (5)" amounts simply to an advance interpretation of the words "claim for exemptions." And such interpretation is not only reasonable but necessary, for, without such itemization it is impossible to determine what property passes to the trustee and what the bankrupt retains. In the practical administration of estates it is absolutely essential that the bankrupt, at some time, in some place, shall indicate precisely the articles he claims as exempt, and the law very reasonably points out the time and place while the forms point out the precise description requisite. The decisions adverted to might, quite as well, have been expressly placed on the error of the court below in failing to require amendment, as upon the ground mentioned therein, and thus not have seemed to give a qualified license to bankrupts to disregard the wisely framed forms prescribed by the Supreme Court.

Thus, the bankrupt should make his claim for exemptions at the time and in the manner prescribed by the bankruptcy act in § 7 (8) and the Supreme Court's Schedule "B" 5.

§ 1049. First Requirement of Exemption Claim—To Be in Writing and Sworn to.

—The claim must be in writing and the facts therein stated must be sworn to.[65]

And no additional demand is requisite other than the bankrupt's "claim" in his Schedule "B" (5).[66]

§ 1050. Exempt Property to Be Scheduled as Assets Elsewhere in Schedule "B" as Well as in Schedule "B" (5).

—Exempt property must, however, be scheduled as assets elsewhere in Schedule "B" as well as "claimed" in Schedule "B" (5).[67]

§ 1051. Second Requirement—To Be Filed with Schedules.

—The claim must be filed with the schedule of assets and list of debts of the bankrupt.[68]

The bankrupt is not to be permitted to defer his claim for exemptions. Thus, he may not make it "at any time before sale" of the property claimed, as may be done under some State statutes.[69]

But an extension of time for filing schedules, of course extends the time for filing the claim for exemptions.[70]

§ 1052. Third Requirement—Property to Be Particularly Described.

—The claim must describe in apt language the particular property claimed as exempt, with its location, present use, and estimated value.[70a] The description need not be minute, but should be apt enough to identify the property claimed.[71]

It will not suffice to make the claim in general terms, as for instance, "Bankrupt claims $500.00 worth of property in lieu of a homestead."

65. Bankr. Act, § 7 (8).
66. See post, § 1072½; and compare § 1083.
67. In re Todd, 7 A. B. R. 770, 112 Fed. 315 (D. C. Vt.); In re White, 6 A. B. R. 451, 109 Fed. 635 (D. C. Mo.); In re Bean, 4 A. B. R. 53, 100 Fed. 262 (D. C. Vt.).
68. Bankr. Act, § 7 (8).
69. In re Groves, 6 A. B. R. 728 (Ref. Ohio, affirmed by D. C.); In re McClintock, 13 A. B. R. 606 (Ref. Ohio, affirmed by D. C.); In re Von Kerm, 14 A. B. R. 403, 135 Fed. 447 (D. C. Pa.); In re Kane, 11 A. B. R. 533, 127

Fed. 552 (C. C. A. Ills.); In re Nunn, 2 A. B. R. 664 (Ref. Ga.); In re Royal, 7 A. B. R. 106, 112 Fed. 135 (D. C. N. Car.); In re Lucius, 10 A. B. R. 653, 124 Fed. 455 (D. C. Ala.); In re Prince & Walter, 12 A. B. R. 680, 131 Fed. 546 (D. C. Pa.); In re Le Vay, 11 A. B. R. 114, 125 Fed. 990 (D. C. Pa.).
70. In re O'Hara, 20 A. B. R. 714, 162 Fed. 325 (D. C. Pa.).
70a. In re Gerber, 26 A. B. R. 608, 186 Fed. 693 (C. C. A. Wis.).
71. Form of Schedule "B" (5) of the Supreme Court's prescribed Forms in Bankruptcy.

Such manner of claiming does not aid the trustee to set apart the property claimed at all, and it fails utterly to mark off the bankrupt's property from the property of the creditors. Moreover, such claim does not conform to the form prescribed by the Supreme Court.[72]

In re Wunder, 13 A. B. R. 701, 133 Fed. 821 (D. C. Pa.): "The fact that he has given notice, in his schedule filed, that he will claim $300 worth of property to be appraised, will not entitle him to the amount of $300 in cash out of the proceeds, or to property of that value, where he has not specified the articles, as claimed by the State law."

Nevertheless, as noted above, failure so to claim exemptions will not absolutely defeat them, for that would be to make the forms and orders override the provisions of the statute itself.[73] The court. would simply require amendment or grant leave to amend.[74]

§ 1053. Fourth Requirement—Description to Be as of Date of Filing Bankruptcy Petition.

—The claim must describe the property claimed as exempt in the condition the property was in at the date of the filing of the petition or of the adjudication, or at any rate at the time when, by law, the schedules should be filed.[75]

But compare, as to amending schedule "B" (5) after the trustee has recovered a preference, so as to claim the property recovered, In re Falconer, 6 A. B. R. 557, 110 Fed. 111 (C. C. A. Ark.): "In making his claim for exemption in the first instance his choice was necessarily confined to such property as he could himself lay claim to, at the time, as forming a part of his estate. His right to select other property then held by third parties, whose title could only be challenged by the trustee, arose, and in the nature of things could be exercised only, when the title by which it was held was vacated and the property became actually, as well as potentially, a part of his estate."

§ 1054. Claiming Money When No Actual Money, but Only Goods in Estate.

—Thus, if there was no actual money in the estate at the date of the filing of the petition or of the adjudication, it would not be proper to claim "$500 in lieu of a homestead," for the simple reason there were no "dollars" then to be set apart to the bankrupt. "Goods" are not "dollars" although they may be convertible into dollars; therefore, when the bankrupt

---

72. In re Neal, 14 A. B. R. 554 (Ref. Ohio); In re Von Kerm, 14 A. B. R. 403, 135 Fed. 447 (D. C. Pa.); In re Prince & Walter, 12 A. B. R. 680, 131 Fed. 546 (D. C. Pa.); In re Groves, 6 A. B. R. 728 (Ref. Ohio, affirmed by D. C.); In re McClintock, 13 A. B. R. 606 (Ref. Ohio, affirmed by D. C.); In re Duffy, 9 A. B. R. 358, 118 Fed. 926 (D. C. Pa.), quoted, § 1048; apparently contra, when property mortgaged, In re Kane, 11 A. B. R. 533, 127 Fed. 552 (C. C. A. Ills.), In re Mathews, 20 A. B. R. 369 (Ref. Okla.). But see ante, § 491; post, § 1056.

73. Lipman v. Stein, 14 A. B. R. 30, 134 Fed. 235 (C. C. A. Pa., affirming In re Stein, 12 A. B. R. 384); Burke v. Guarantee Title & Trust Co., 14 A. B. R. 31, 134 Fed. 562 (C. C. A. Pa.). See post, § 1064.

74. In re Duffy, 9 A. B. R. 358, 118 Fed. 926 (D. C. Pa.); In re Kelly, 28 A. B. R. 730, 199 Fed. 984 (D. C. Pa.).

75. In re Neal, 14 A. B. R. 554 (Ref. Ohio). Compare, impliedly, ante, § 1025; also, see impliedly contra, obiter, In re O'Hara, 20 A. B. R. 714, 162 Fed. 325 (D. C. Pa.).

is trying to describe what is his property as distinct from what is his creditors', he should be required to describe existing property—"goods," if it be goods; "dollars," if it be dollars.[76]

§ 1055. Claiming So Much Worth Out of Mass.

—Thus, it is not sufficient simply to claim that property to the "amount of" a certain named sum should be set off to him; the exact property which he elects to take should be specified.[77]

Analogously, In re White, 6 A. B. R. 451 (D. C. Mo.): "Under Rule 17 of General Orders in Bankruptcy, * * * it is made the duty of the trustee to report to the court, within 20 days after receiving notice of his appointment, the articles set off to the bankrupt by him, with the estimated value of each article. How could the trustee comply with this requirement of the law in respect of the property in question. * * * He made no selection of $300 worth of property out of any particular property."

§ 1056. Where Exemptions Claimed in Mortgaged Property.

—And if there be a mortgage on the property, then the claim should be of the "equity of redemption in the following described property," the particular description not being any the less necessary simply because the bankrupt claims only a qualified and not an absolute title therein.[78]

---

76. In re Groves, 6 A. B. R. 728 (Ref. Ohio, affirmed by D. C.); In re McClintock, 13 A. B. R. 606 (Ref. Ohio, affirmed by D. C.); In re Neal, 14 A. B. R. 554 (Ref. Ohio); In re Berman, 15 A. B. R. 464, 140 Fed. 761 (D. C. Ohio); In re Donahey, 23 A. B. R. 796, 176 Fed. 458 (D. C. Pa.).

77. In re Neal, 14 A. B. R. 554 (Ref. Ohio); compare, In re Hoyt, 9 A. B. R. 574, 119 Fed. 987 (D. C. N. Car.); In re Wunder, 13 A. B. R. 701, 133 Fed. 821 (D. C. Penn.); In re Duffy, 9 A. B. R. 358, 118 Fed. 926 (D. C. Pa.); In re Prince & Walter, 12 A. B. R. 680, 131 Fed. 546 (D. C. Pa.); compare, In re Staunton, 9 A. B. R. 79, and In re Wunder, 13 A. B. R. 701, 133 Fed. 821 (D. C. Pa.), where the court says this same rule prevails in the State practice in Pennsylvania. See also, In re Manning, 7 A. B. R. 571, 112 Fed. 948 (D. C. Pa.); compare also, In re Bessie Stein, 12 A. B. R. 384, 130 Fed. 377 (D. C. Penn.); In re Le Vay, 11 A. B. R. 114, 125 Fed. 990 (D. C. Pa.); In re Mathews, 20 A. B. R. 369 (Ref. Okla.).

78. Compare, In re Kane, 11 A. B. R. 533, 127 Fed. 552 (C. C. A. Ills.). This decision should not be considered as authority for claiming exemptions in general terms. Although the language of the court is somewhat misleading and the reasoning subject to criticism, yet the decision itself is correct. What the bankrupt in that case was claiming, or should be held to have been claiming, was the equity of redemption in the certain specified chattels that were covered by the mortgage. He had a perfect right to claim the equity of redemption in the certain specified chattels that were covered by the mortgage. He had a perfect right to claim the equity of redemption as exempt. It was a chose in action or interest in property or right that was quite as much a proper subject for exemption as would have been any other right or intangible interest in specific property. The bankrupt, however, should have been required to describe the articles in which he claimed the exempt equity of redemption, as they existed at the date of the adjudication or at the time the law required his claim to be made. He should not have been permitted to claim the "proceeds" of property. "Proceeds" implies a selling, and the trustee cannot be obliged to sell exempt property, nor to convert property into money for the benefit of the mortgagee and the bankrupt. He must be given a chance to set apart exemptions, and it is no part of his functions to do more—to manage exempt property, marshal liens thereon and sell it and disburse the proceeds. No title to exempt property vests in him and it is a cardinal principle of the present bankruptcy law that he must

And the bankruptcy court may sell the property clear and free from encumbrances and give the bankrupt his exemptions after payment of the prior mortgage.[79]

§ 1057. Claiming "Proceeds," Where Property Still in Specie.—
Thus a claim of the "proceeds" of certain specified property is improper, the property still being in specie.[80]

In re Donahey, 23 A. B. R. 796, 176 Fed. 458 (D. C. Pa.): "It is further objected, however, that the exemption was not properly claimed, money and not property having been asked for. As it appears in the schedules, the claim is in terms 'for the proceeds of personal property, $300;' which does not conform to the requirement of the statute. The debtor is called upon to designate the particular property which he desires to retain, which he has the right to do to the value of $300, as determined by a due appraisement. But it is goods and not the proceeds of them that he is entitled to, and it is these, therefore, that he must specify and demand. Hammer v. Freeze, 19 Pa. 257; In re Haskins (D. C.), 6 Am. B. R. 485; In re Wunder, 13 Am. B. R. 701; In re Peiffer, 18 Am. B. R. 230; In re Blanchard, 20 Am. B. R. 417. He cannot, as here, claim money resulting from a sale. The case is not like In re Renda, 17 Am. B. R. 521, where, after the bankrupt had designated the goods which he desired to have set aside, they were sold by arrangement with the trustee, which, it was held, did not prevent him from coming in on the fund. Neither is it like Burke v. Guarantee Title and Trust Co., 14 Am. B. R. 31, where specified property was claimed, the only objection to it being that it was not properly itemized."

§ 1058. But Where Not in Specie.—
But it is not improper if the property has been sold by order of court *before* the time for filing schedules has expired.[81]

Lipman v. Stein, 14 A. B. R. 30, 134 Fed. 235 (C. C. A. Pa.): "The fact that a receiver was appointed by the court, who, by its authorization, sold all the

not meddle with it, except to set it apart. The wording of the opinion in In re Kane is misleading in that it seems to give authority to a bankrupt to claim the "proceeds" of property not yet sold. The bankrupt would have received all that was due him, and that was in fact given him in that case, had he claimed simply the equity of redemption in certain specified articles and have been required to specify the articles for the guidance of the trustee.

Failure to note the distinction made in this paragraph was the evident origin of the decision in In re Luby, 18 A. B. R. 801, 155 Fed. 659 (D. C. Ohio).

79. In re Paramour & Ricks, 19 A. B. R. 126, 156 Fed. 208 (D. C. N. Car.); compare, also, In re Paramour & Ricks, 19 A. B. R. 130, 156 Fed. 211 (D. C. N. Car.).

80. In re Haskin, 6 A. B. R. 485, 109 Fed. 789 (D. C. Penn.); In re Berman, 15 A. B. R. 463 (D. C. Ohio); In re Wunder, 13 A. B. R. 701, 133 Fed. 821

(D. C. Penn.); In re Von Kerm, 14 A. B. R. 403, 404, 135 Fed. 447 (D. C. Pa.); compare, In re Diller, 4 A. B. R. 45, 100 Fed. 931 (D. C. Penn.), distinguished in In re Haskin, 6 A. B. R. 486, 109 Fed. 789 (D. C. Penn.). But compare, inferentially, contra, In re Falconer, 6 A. B. R. 557, 110 Fed. 111 (C. C. A. Ark.); In re Pfeiffer, 19 A. B. R. 230, 155 Fed. 892 (D. C. Pa.). But compare, contra, In re Luby, 18 A. B. R. 801, 155 Fed. 659 (D. C. Ohio), but in this case the bankrupt [or rather his wife] might have claimed as exempt the equity of redemption, describing the property and claiming merely the equity therein.

81. In re Stein, 12 A. B. R. 384, 130 Fed. 629 (D. C. Penn.), affirmed sub nom. Lipman v. Stein, 14 A. B. R. 30, 134 Fed. 235 (C. C. A. Penn.); In re Le Vay, 11 A. B. R. 114, 125 Fed. 990 (D. C. Penn.); In re Zack, 28 A. B. R. 138, 196 Fed. 909 (D. C. Pa.).

assets of the bankrupt's estate before her claim was made or the time allowed for making it had expired, rendered it impossible to appropriate specific property to its liquidation; but her right to its allowance was not thereby extinguished."

Obiter, In re Sloan, 14 A. B. R. 435, 135 Fed. 873 (D. C. Pa.): "As the bankrupt's property in this case was sold by order of court, by a receiver appointed the day after the petition in bankruptcy was filed, and prior to the filing of the schedule by the bankrupt, and in view of the fact that he notified the receiver that he claimed his exemption and specified the property at the date of sale, he would be entitled to claim his exemption from the proceeds."

Apparently, In re Renda, 17 A. B. R. 522, 151 Fed. 614 (D. C. Pa.): "The bankrupt having made claim for his exemption within the time fixed by the Act, is not debarred because the goods were sold." But perhaps this was a case where the exemptions were properly described and then sold by agreement.

§ 1059. Fifth Requirement —Estimated Values to Be Given.—The claim should give the estimated values of the articles.[82]

§ 1060. Sixth Requirement—State Statute to Be Mentioned.— The claim should mention the state statute under which the bankrupt claims.[83]

§ 1061. Seventh Requirement—Who to Make Claim?—Bankrupt Exclusively, or May Mortgagee, Assignee, Agent, etc., Claim?— The statute, in § 7 (8), might seem to require that the bankrupt himself make the claim for the exemptions. And some decisions have held that the right to claim exemptions, being a purely personal right, can not be exercised by third parties, such as mortgagees;[84] nor by assignees;[85] although, undoubtedly, after exemptions have been duly claimed, and at any rate after they have been set off by the trustee, they may be assigned.

In re Schuller, 6 A. B. R. 278, 108 Fed. 591 (D. C. Wis.): "The right of exemption is a personal privilege granted to the debtor, which he can exercise or waive, and, unless otherwise provided by the statute, it cannot be exercised by any other person; and the Wisconsin statute (supra) requires the claim

---

82. Schedule "B" (5). In re Mc-Clintock, 13 A. B. R. 606 (Ref. Ohio, affirmed by D. C.).

83. Schedule "B" (5).

84. Mitchell v. Mitchell, 17 A. B. R. 386 (D. C. N. Car.); In re Sloan, 14 A. B. R. 435, 135 Fed. 873 (D. C. Pa.).

85. **Whether Claim of Exemptions May Validate Fraudulent or Preferential Transfers.**—It has been held that a fraudulent transferee may not validate the transfer by setting up that the property was exempt, anyway. Mitchell v. Mitchell, 17 A. B. R. 389 (D. C. N. Car.); [1867] Edmondson v. Hyde, Fed. Cas. No. 4,285. And the same ruling has been made with

reference to a preferential transfer, In re Soper, 22 A. B. R. 860, 173 Fed. 116 (D. C. Neb.). In re Schuller, 6 A. B. R. 278, 108 Fed. 591 (D. C. Wis.). Compare facts, In re Vickerman Co., 29 A. B. R. 298, 199 Fed. 589 (D. C. S. Dak.). But it is possible under state rulings, that such claims, if made by the bankrupt himself may be effectual to validate the transfer. Compare ante, §§ 1031, 1093¾; post, §§ 1292, 1293.

And it has been expressly held, under the Michigan law, that creditors cannot complain of the transfer of exempt property. In re Hastings, 24 A. B. R. 360, 181 Fed. 34 (C. C. A. Mich.), quoted supra, § 1061.

and selection to be made by the debtor, or on his behalf, with an exception in favor of a wife, and confers no such right on a mortgagee."

[1867] Edmonson *v.* Hyde, Fed. Cas. 4,285: "If the bankrupt does not choose to assert any claim to have it exempted, * * * the mortgagee is in no position to claim it as against the assignee (in bankruptcy)."

But, it was held by the Circuit Court of Appeals, reversing a decision of the lower court, that, under the Michigan statute, which authorizes the claim also to be made by a "duly authorized agent," a mortgagee who was also empowered by the instrument to make selection of the exemptions was competent to make the selection in bankruptcy, notwithstanding the facts that the mortgage failed to particularly describe the exempt goods, that the goods had not been selected as exempt by the debtor at the time of the mortgage and that the bankrupt expressly waived exemptions in his schedule; the court holding that the mortgaging, pledging or waiving of exemptions that might be claimed in the future was not contrary to the public policy of Michigan, that the bankrupt by his assigning of the exemptions *had* claimed and not waived them and had so effectually claimed them that his subsequent attempted waiver was ineffectual as against the agent whose agency had been coupled with an interest, and that, finally, since Michigan law permitted the mortgaging of property not yet acquired, it permitted the mortgaging of exempt property not yet claimed as exempt.[85a]

In re Hastings, 24 A. B. R. 360, 181 Fed. 34 (C. C. A. Mich.): "And on the question of the validity of an instrument reserving the mortgagor's exemptions under the laws of the State, the settled local law controls * * *. The mortgaging or conveying of exempt property to a creditor is not against the public policy of the State of Michigan * * * Creditors cannot complain of transfers of exempt property * * * and a transfer which is good against the transferror is equally valid as against the trustee.

"It is clear, under the foregoing decisions, that the bankrupt had the power to convey to petitioner his existing exemptions; and as under the law of Michigan one may lawfully mortgage or convey property thereafter to be acquired, it is plain that the lien in question was not rendered invalid from the fact that it was made to apply to the stock as it should exist at the time the lien was sought to be enforced.

"It is urged by the trustee that the description of the exemptions is inadequate in that the exact property so intended to be exempted was not specified * * *. In our judgment, however, the case is ruled, with respect to this proposition, by the decision of this court in Wilson *v.* Perrin, 62 Fed. 629, 631.

"It is urged, however, that even if it be conceded that the assignment of the exemptions in question was originally valid, it was defeated by the failure of the bankrupt to select his exemptions under the bankruptcy proceedings, and especially by his express waiver thereof in his petition for adjudication in bankruptcy. It is argued, first, that the provisions of the Bankruptcy Act, impliedly at least, forbid recognition of any right to exemptions except upon a specific claim thereto presented by the bankrupt himself. The provisions of the Act which are thought to produce this result are § 2, subdiv. 11, which authorizes courts of bankruptcy to 'determine all claims of bankrupts to their exemptions,' and general order No. 17, which requires a trustee to report to the court 'the articles set off to the bankrupt by him.' In our opinion, the sections invoked

85a. But compare post, § 1062¼.

cannot be construed as denying the power of the court to recognize the right
of a party other than the bankrupt, holding under a valid and effective assignment, conferring in express terms authority to make the selection in the name
of the assignor. If the exemptions in question were lawfully assigned by the
bankrupt the trustee obtained no title thereto; and as the selection was made
according to an appraisement had under the direction of the trustee there is
no apparent difficulty in allowing the selection to be made by any one representing the bankrupt.

"We are thus brought to determine the second objection to the enforceability of the assignment, and upon which the court below held the petitioner
not entitled to enforce the attempted lien, viz., that the attempted delegation
of the right to select exempt property is against public policy and void. It is
true, as contended by the bankrupt, that the right to exemption is a personal
privilege, and may be waived by the debtor, and that such privilege cannot be
claimed for him by another. But this proposition is not decisive of the question before us, because the debtor did not in this case waive his privilege, but,
on the contrary, took advantage of it in making the assignment in question.
The assignment was based upon a valuable consideration, viz.: the giving of
future credit; and the authority to the assignee to make the selection, if originally valid, was irrevocable, as being coupled with an interest. Baker *v.*
Baird, 79 Mich. 255, 259."

But the bankrupt, of course, is not obliged to claim his exemptions, nor
is he bound to proceed with a claim therefor after he has made it.[86]

And whether a mortgagee, assignee or other transferee, in order to validate an otherwise fraudulent or preferential transfer may claim that the
property mortgaged or otherwise transferred was exempt is a question
variously decided.[87]

§ 1062. Wife Claiming Where Bankrupt Fails or Refuses to Claim.

—Failure of the bankrupt to claim exemptions may, in States where
a wife or child is entitled to make the claim in the event of the debtor's
failure to do so, entitle the wife or child to make the claim in the bankruptcy court.[88]

In re Youngstrom, 18 A. B. R. 572, 153 Fed. 97 (C. C. A. Colo.): "The bankrupt had been a merchant and part of his estate consisted of a stock in trade
used and kept for the purpose of carrying on his business, the stock exceeding
$200 in value. As before stated, the referee found that shortly before the filing
of the petition the bankrupt suddenly left the State with the apparent intention
of never returning and of deserting his wife, who with him had constituted the
family. The only reason assigned or advanced for the denial of this exemption
is that one person, such as the wife here, could not be 'the said family' within
the meaning of § 2563. It is quite true that a person residing alone is not, gen-

---

86. In re [Jonas B.] Baughman, 25
A. B. R. 167, 183 Fed. 668 (D. C. Pa.).
87. Compare post, §§ 1093¾, 1292,
1293. Also compare Mitchell *v.* Mitchell, 17 A. B. R. 389 (D. C. N. Car.);
In re Soper, 22 A. B. R. 860, 173 Fed.
116 (D. C. Neb.); In re Schuller, 6 A.
B. R. 278, 108 Fed. 591 (D. C. Wis.);

[1867] Edmondson *v.* Hyde, Fed.
Cases No. 4285.
88. In re Luby, 18 A. B. R. 801, 155
Fed. 659 (D. C. Ohio). Compare, In
re Tollett, 5 A. B. R. 305, 105 Fed. 425
(D. C. Tenn.); contra, that such right
cannot be exercised by wife, In re
Sharp, 15 A. B. R. 491 (Ref. Ohio, affirmed by D. J.). See ante, § 1045.

erally speaking, a family, but that does not answer the question here presented. Without doubt, there was a family prior to the husband's desertion. Of that family he was the head and so was entitled, under § 2562, to an exemption of $200 in his stock in trade. We think the other section in providing that, whenever the head of a family shall die, desert, or cease to reside with the same, 'the said family' shall succeed to the right of exemption, plainly means that this right shall pass to the remaining portion of the family; that is, to the family as it was before, but minus the head, whether what remains be one or several persons. In this view the wife, as the remaining portion of the family, was entitled to this exemption."

In re Maxson, 22 A. B. R. 424, 170 Fed. 356 (D. C. Iowa): "It seems clear, therefore, that under the Iowa statute, the homestead right of the husband or wife in property occupied by either as a home cannot be defeated by any act of the other in whose name the legal title may be held. If the bankrupt in this case, therefore, had declared in her petition that she expressly waived the right to the homestead in the property scheduled by her, and thereafter made no effort to have the property set apart to her as exempt, this would not defeat the right of the husband to have the homestead set apart to him, so long as he continued to occupy the same as such. If this be not so, then the spouse who happens to hold the legal title to the home may deprive the other, and other members of the family, thereof by proceedings in bankruptcy, and thus directly evade the provisions of the Iowa statute. Surely it was not intended that the Bankruptcy Act should have any such effect."

Compare, inferentially, In re Seabolt, 8 A. B. R. 62, 63 (D. C. N. Car.): "The law is well settled, therefore, that, although the owner of a homestead or a person entitled thereto die without having the same allotted in his lifetime, the same can be allotted at the instance of his minor child or children, if he leave such, or in the absence of minor children, at the instance of his widow."

There being no form prescribed for such an exigency, any reasonable manner would probably suffice, so it would seem. It has been held proper to make the claim by way of an intervening petition.

In re Maxson, 22 A. B. R. 424, 170 Fed. 356 (D. C. Iowa): "But if it should be held that the bankrupt has thus waived her right to the homestead, does this prevent the husband, who was one of the family occupying the homestead with her, from claiming it? On October 24th he also filed with the referee a petition in which he set forth that he was the husband of the bankrupt, a resident of Iowa, and as such was entitled to a homestead under the laws of that state in the real estate scheduled by the bankrupt. This was in effect an intervening petition by him claiming an interest in property in the custody of the court of bankruptcy, and is the proper method of making such claim."

Yet this claim must be made promptly, at any rate, wherever the right exists at all.

§ 1062¼. Withdrawal or Abandonment of Claim.—The bankrupt may withdraw and abandon a claim which he has made for the exemption, and he cannot be prevented from so doing by a creditor in whose favor the exemption has been waived.[89]

89. In re [Jonas B.] Baughman, 25 A. B. R. 167, 183 Fed. 668 (D. C. Pa.). But compare, § 1061; also compare,

inferentially, contra, In re Hastings, 24 A. B. R. 360, 181 Fed. 34 (C. C. A. Mich.), quoted at § 1061.

§ 1062½. Non-Bankrupt Partner in Partnership Bankruptcy.— Where the firm alone had been adjudicated bankrupt, it has been held that the bankruptcy court has no jurisdiction to set apart exemptions to an individual partner, who has not been adjudged bankrupt individually, out of his individual estate; that "the bankrupt" in such instances is the partnership, and that the sole power of the bankruptcy court to set apart exemptions is to set them apart to "the bankrupt."[90] But this seems an unnecessarily narrow construction.

In some jurisdictions neither the firm nor any of its members are entitled to exemptions out of the partnership's property.[91]

§ 1063. Failure to Claim Exemptions Deemed, Prima Facie, Waiver.—The failure to claim exemptions at all will (if unrebutted), be deemed a waiver of them;[92] but the presumption may be rebutted and the failure be cured.

§ 1064. Failure to Claim, or to Describe Particularly, Not Necessarily Fatal.—Failure to claim exemptions at all, or to claim them specifically, will not necessarily defeat them, for the failure may operate as authority to the trustee to convert all the property into money and to set aside the amount later asked for or later specifically demanded, after deduction of expenses; or the claim may later be inserted or corrected by amendment.[93]

As heretofore noted, failure to describe with particularity the property claimed, certainly will not defeat the exemptions, if there be a "claim" for exemptions made in the schedules, since otherwise it would be to hold that the forms and orders override the statute itself.[94]

Thus, where failure to claim exemptions has been through advice of counsel, under a mistaken notion of the law, it will not be fatal.[95]

§ 1065. Claim of "Proceeds," etc., May Authorize Trustee to Sell Exemptions with Remainder as Entirety.—Where the bankrupt claims a certain amount "out of the proceeds" of the property, he undoubtedly thereby authorizes the trustee to convert the property into money for his benefit, and he should not be heard to complain if the trustee deducts the

---

90. In re Blanchard & Howard, 20 A. B. R. 422, 161 Fed. 797 (D. C. N. Car.).

91. In re Vickerman & Co., 29 A. B. R. 298, 199 Fed. 589 (D. C. So. Dak.); see also, § 1047 note 157 for further instances occurring in bankruptcy.

92. Moran v. King, 7 A. B. R. 176, 111 Fed. 730 (C. C. A. W. Va.); obiter, In re Bolinger, 6 A. B. R. 171, 108 Fed. 374 (D. C. Penn.); In re Von Kerm, 14 A. B. R. 403, 135 Fed. 447 (D. C. Pa.); In re [Jonas B.] Baugh-man, 25 A. B. R. 167, 183 Fed. 668 (D. C. Pa.); In re Gerber, 26 A. B. R. 608, 186 Fed. 693 (C. C. A. Wash.); In re Harrington, 29 A. B. R. 666, 200 Fed. 1010 (D. C. N. Y.). Compare. In re Gerber, 26 A. B. R. 608, 186 Fed. 693 (C. C. A. Wash.). See editor's note to Sharpe v. Woolslare, 12 A. B. R. 396, 401.

93. In re [Jonas B.] Baughman, 25 A. B. R. 167, 183 Fed. 668 (D. C. Pa.).

94. See ante, § 1052.

95. In re Goodman, 23 A. B. R. 504, 174 Fed. 644 (C. C. A. Ala.), quoted at § 1070½.

proportionate expenses of the operation, even though thereby the bankrupt does not receive the full amount of his demand.[96] And undoubtedly the same rule would apply where he claims simply so much in value, or so much worth, "out of" a certain mass of property, without designating the particular articles claimed.[97]

§ 1066. Claim May Be Inserted or Corrected by Amendment.—
Thus the omitted or defective claim for exemptions may be inserted or corrected by amendment.[98]

In re Wunder, 13 A. B. R. 701, 133 Fed. 821 (D. C. Penna.): "He could, no doubt, have filed a schedule of property claimed, as an amendment to his notice in the schedule, * * * if done in time, and before the creditors have gone to the trouble and expense of a meeting for the purpose of passing upon the advisability of a sale, and have carried the sale into execution."

Thus, leave may be granted to amend to include property preferentially transferred, when it is subsequently recovered by the trustee where exemptions are allowable on recovery of property preferentially transferred.[99]

But the court will not permit a waiver to be withdrawn and a claim for exemptions to be reasserted repeatedly; the bankrupt must not play battledore and shuttlecock with the exemption claim.[1]

Amendment may even be allowed where an estate has been reopened on the discovery of more assets, provided the bankrupt has not been guilty of bad faith.[2]

§ 1067. Leave or Order to Amend Requisite.—
It can be amended only by order or leave of court; that is to say, by leave of the referee, in practice.

§ 1068. Amendment Required by Court, Where Exemptions Claimed Improperly.—
If there be a "claim" of exemptions but it be made

---

96. In re Berman, 15 A. B. R. 465, 140 Fed. 761 (D. C. Ohio); inferentially, In re Kane, 11 A. B. R. 533, 127 Fed. 552 (C. C. A. Ills.); contra, In re Von Kerm, 14 A. B. R. 403, 135 Fed. 447 (D. C. Pa.).

97. In re Berman, 15 A. B. R. 465, 140 Fed. 761 (D. C. Ohio).

98. Obiter, In re Neal, 14 A. B. R. 554 (Ref. Ohio); In re Berman, 15 A. B. R. 465, 140 Fed. 761 (D. C. Ohio); In re Kaufmann, 16 A. B. R. 121, 142 Fed. 898 (D. C. Wis.); obiter, In re Von Kerm, 14 A. B. R. 303, 135 Fed. 447 (D. C. Pa.); In re Duffy, 9 A. B. R. 358, 118 Fed. 926 (D. C. Penn.); In re Bean, 4 A. B. R. 53, 100 Fed. 262 (D. C. Vt.); In re Fisher, 15 A. B. R. 652, 142 Fed. 205 (D. C. Va.). Instance, In re White, 11 A. B. R. 556

(D. C. Penn.), in which instance "none" was written in the schedule for claiming exemptions; after a long delay of more than a year leave to amend was asked for; the referee refused because there was "nothing to amend by;" held, refusal to be improper. In re Maxson, 22 A. B. R. 424, 170 Fed. 356 (D. C. Iowa); General Order No. 11; obiter, In re Donahey, 23 A. B. R. 796, 176 Fed. 458 (D. C. Pa.); impliedly, In re Goodman, 23 A. B. R. 504, 174 Fed. 644 (C. C. A. Ala.), quoted post, § 1070½.

99. In re Falconer, 6 A. B. R. 557, 110 Fed. 111 (C. C. A. Ark.).

1. In re Pfeiffer, 19 A. B. R. 230, 155 Fed. 892 (D. C. Pa.).

2. In re Irwin, 22 A. B. R. 165, 177 Fed. 284 (D. C. Pa.).

improperly, as for instance, if it be made in general terms, the court may and indeed should, of its own motion, require amendment.[3]

§ 1069. Leave Liberally Granted.—Leave is liberally granted, as is usual in regard to exemption proceedings.[4]

Impliedly, In re Falconer, 6 A. B. R. 557, 110 Fed. 111 (C. C. A. Ark.): "No bankrupt should be deprived of his exemption by a narrow and strict interpretation of laws which were passed for his benefit and prompted by a wise and humane public policy."

Obiter, In re Royal, 7 A. B. R. 106, 112 Fed. 135 (D. C. N. Car.): "The filing of a petition in bankruptcy is as a rule a deliberate act. Under some circumstances when pressed to the wall, which does not seem to have been the case in the present instance, haste is necessary and errors occur in making up schedules. When attention is called to such errors leave to amend and correct is always granted."

And leave should not, in general, be refused where the original omission or defect was not in bad faith and where the parties can be put in statu quo. Thus, even after sale, if the proceeds of the exempt property can be definitely distinguished, the bankrupt should be allowed to amend upon reimbursing the trustee for his expenses incurred by reason of the original failure to claim exemptions or to claim them specifically.

Thus, too, even after an estate has been reopened on the discovery of more assets, the bankrupt may amend to claim exemptions therefrom, if he is not guilty of bad faith.[5]

§ 1070. Leave Refused Where Omission with Fraudulent Intent or Third Parties Injured.—But leave should be refused where the omission to mention the property in the first place was intentional.[6]

Thus, sometimes a bankrupt fails altogether to schedule fraudulently conveyed property, held on secret trust for him, in the hope that the cred-

---

3. Bankr. Act, § 39 (a) (2): "Referees shall * * * examine all schedules of property and lists of creditors filed by bankrupts and cause such as are incomplete or defective to be amended."

4. Impliedly, In re Kaufmann, 16 A. B. R. 121, 142 Fed. 898 (D. C. Wis.); impliedly, In re Berman, 15 A. B. R. 465, 140 Fed. 761 (D. C. Ohio); impliedly, In re Fisher, 15 A. B. R. 653, 142 Fed. 205 (D. C. Va.); In re Irwin, 22 A. B. R. 165, 177 Fed. 284 (D. C. Pa.); In re Maxson, 22 A. B. R. 424, 170 Fed. 356 (D. C. Iowa); obiter leave refused. In re Irwin, 23 A. B. R. 487, 174 Fed. 642 (C. C. A. Pa.), quoted at § 1070½.

Where the receiver, in an involuntary case, before the filing of schedules by the bankrupt, sells the property as perishable, including in the sale prop-erty later claimed as exempt when the schedules are filed, no part of the expenses can be taken out of the property thus later claimed; for the later filed schedules must be taken to have been in due time and not to have impaired the bankrupt's right to have his exemptions clear. In re Le Vay, 11 A. B. R. 114, 125 Fed. 990 (D. C. Pa.); In re Bessie Stein, 12 A. B. R. 384, 130 Fed. 377 (D. C. Penn., affirmed sub nom. Lipman v. Stein, 14 A. B. R. 30, 134 Fed. 235, C. C. A. Penn.). See post, § 1093.

5. In re Irwin, 22 A. B. R. 165, 177 Fed. 284 (D. C. Pa.).

6. In re Bean, 4 A. B. R. 53, 100 Fed. 262 (D. C. Vt.); In re Nunn, 2 A. B. R. 664 (Ref. Ga.); compare, to same effect, In re Gross, 5 A. B. R. 271 (Ref. N. Y., affirmed by D. C.); In re Neal, 14 A. B. R. 554 (Ref. Ohio).

itors will pass it over unnoticed and he be allowed to resume its enjoyment afterward. Then, on examination, the hidden property is revealed. Thereupon the bankrupt asks for it as exempt and files his application for leave to amend his claim for exemptions. Such an application should be refused; the trustee should not be robbed of the fruits of his work nor should the bankrupt be permitted to play fast and loose with his creditors. It is too late to claim the property as exempt then.

Leave to amend may be refused where the rights of third parties have intervened.[7] And amendment should be refused where, after the trustee has obtained possession of property not claimed as exempt on the plea that the lien of a creditor thereon as to the trustee is void under § 67 (f), although not void as to the bankrupt, the bankrupt asks leave to amend to claim it as exempt, thus attempting to assert the trustee's rights to enable himself to defraud the lienholder out of property to which, as between the bankrupt and the lienholder, the lienholder is entitled.[8]

And leave to amend may be refused where the bankrupt has not specifically described the property and the property has been sold.[9]

In re Wunder, 13 A. B. R. 701, 133 Fed. 821 (D. C. Penna.): "He could, no doubt, have filed a schedule of property claimed as an amendment to his notice in the schedule, as was done in In re Duffy (D. C.), 9 Am. B. R. 358, 118 Fed. 926, if done in time, and before the creditors have gone to the trouble and expense of a meeting for the purpose of passing upon the advisability of a sale, and have carried the sale into execution."

Amendment will not be permitted where the benefit will not accrue to the debtor or his family but solely to certain creditors holding waivers of exemptions in the property thus sought to be added or as to whom such property is not exempt;[10] or where it will accrue solely to a vendor of the article, who had failed to record his conditional sale contract thereon.[10a]

§ 1070½. Whether for Mere Laches.—It has been held that leave to amend may be refused for laches of the bankrupt.

In re Irwin, 23 A. B. R. 487, 174 Fed. 642 (C. C. A. Pa.): "While the rule allowing claims for exemptions to be amended is a liberal one, we think it ought not to be allowed after discharge in bankruptcy has been granted. In re Kean, 2 Hughes, 322 Fed. Cas. No. 7,630. In any event, an application to amend a claim for exemption should be made within a reasonable time after discovering the facts which will justify the amendment. The record of this case fails to show why the bankrupts, who discovered their additional assets in June, 1908, waited until the following December before applying for leave to amend their schedules."

7. In re McClintock, 13 A. B. R. 606 (Ref. Ohio, affirmed by D. C.).

8. See remarks to similar effect in In re J. C. Winship Co., 9 A. B. R. 638, 120 Fed. 93 (C. C. A. Ills.). However, compare practice as to recovery of preferences, post, § 1094, et seq.

9. In re Von Kerm, 14 A. B. R. 403, 135 Fed. 447 (D. C. Pa.).

10 Moran v. King, 7 A. B. R. 176, 111 Fed. 730 (C. C. A. Va., affirming In re Moran, 5 A. B. R. 472, 105 Fed. 901).

10a. In re Merry, 29 A. B. R. 829, 201 Fed. 369 (D. C. Me.).

But, it would seem, on principle, that such laches must involve more than mere delay; that there should be either fraud or third parties' rights involved.

Compare, In re Goodman, 23 A. B. R. 504, 174 Fed. 644 (C. C. A. Ala.): "In this case the bankrupt did not waive his exemptions, and he had notwithstanding his omission to set forth his claim in the schedules a clear legal right to the exemptions allowed by the laws of the State of Alabama; and we think he had a legal right to prefer his claim in the bankruptcy proceedings at any seasonable time while the property remained in the hands of the trustee unaffected by adverse rights. * * * There is no contention, aside from the omission in the schedules, that the claim was not asserted seasonably; in fact, reservation in the original petition suggested the right. * * * The mere failure to claim them in the schedules, which are amendable by the equity practice in General Order No. 11, ought not to be treated either as a legal or equitable estoppel. See Burke v. Title & Trust Co. (C. C. A.), 14 Am. B. R. 31, 134 Fed. 562, and Remington on Bankruptcy, §§ 1063-1070, inclusive. In this particular case it seems that the failure to specifically claim the exemptions in the schedules arose from the fact that the attorney who prepared the schedules for the bankrupt was ill informed as to the textual provisions of § 70 of the bankruptcy law, and advised his client that the claim for exemptions should be made later when the trustee should be appointed."

§ 1071. Amendment Reverts to Date of Filing Original Claim.—

Of course amendments of schedules and claims for exemptions, when made, revert to the date of the filing of the originals, and the rights of the parties should be passed on precisely as if the amended part had always been in the original schedules.[11]

SUBDIVISION "D".

SETTING APART OF EXEMPTIONS.

§ 1072. Setting Apart of Exemptions Governed by Bankruptcy Act Itself.—

Likewise the manner of setting apart exempt property is governed by the bankruptcy act, and not by the provisions of state law.[12] The exempt property must be set apart to the bankrupt by the trustee, and it must be so set apart as soon as practicable, and report thereof be made within twenty days after the trustee has received notice of his appointment.[13]

§ 1072½. No Demand to Set Apart Requisite.—

No additional demand for setting apart of exemptions need be made by the bankrupt; his

---

11. Inferentially. In re Neal, 14 A. B. R. 554 (Ref. Ohio).

12. In re Grimes, 2 A. B. R. 730, 96 Fed. 529 (D. C. N. Car.). But the "setting aside" must not involve the dislocating of valid liens, In re Thomas, 3 A. B. R. 99, 96 Fed. 828 (D. C. Wash.). In re Gerber, 26 A. B. R. 608, 186 Fed. 693 (C. C. A. Wash.), quoted ante, § 1048.

13. Bankr. Act, § 47 (11): "Trus-tees shall respectively * * * set apart the bankrupt's exemptions and report the items and estimated value thereof to the court as soon as practicable after their appointment." In re Black, 4 A. B. R. 776, 104 Fed. 289 (D. C. Pa.); In re Camp, 1 A. B. R. 165, 91 Fed. 745 (D. C. N. Car.); In re McClintock, 13 A. B. R. 606 (Ref. Ohio, affirmed by D. C.); In re Finkelstein, 27 A. B. R. 229, 192 Fed. 738 (D. C. Pa.).

simple claim for exemptions which he is required to file with his schedules is enough.[14]

§ 1073. Trustee to Set Apart.

—The trustee seems to be the only one qualified to perform the duty of setting apart the exemptions.[15]

In re Grimes, 2 A. B. R. 730, 96 Fed. 529 (D. C. N. Car.): "This duty cannot be performed by any other party. It is wholly and entirely the duty of the trustee, and any agreement on the part of the bankrupt or the creditors that the exemptions shall be allotted in any other manner than that presented by the Bankruptcy Law, or through other agencies than that of the trustee of the bankrupt, is a nullity."

Yet in an obiter in Smalley v. Laugenour, 13 A. B. R. 694, 196 U. S. 92, the United States Supreme Court says: "Where there is a trustee he sets apart the exemptions, and reports thereon to the court, § 47, cl. 11; where no trustee has been appointed, under General Order XV, the court acts in the first instance."

§ 1074. Must Set Aside "Soon as Practicable," and within Twenty Days.

—And it is the trustee's duty to set apart exempted property as soon as "practicable" after his appointment.[16]

General Order XVII[17] follows up the statutory provision of § 47 (11) by laying down the rule that "the trustee shall make report to the court," etc.

"The trustee shall make report to the court, within twenty days after receiving the notice of his appointment, of the articles set off to the bankrupt by him, according to the provisions of the 47th section of the act, with the estimated value of each article."

For this purpose the Supreme Court has prescribed a form Number 47, termed "Trustee's Report of Exempted Property;" and one court has held that if the trustee fails to file such report, he will not be allowed for exemptions paid out by him.[18]

---

14. See ante, § 1049; inferentially, McGahan v. Anderson, 7 A. B. R. 641, 113 Fed. 115 (C. C. A. S. C.); inferentially, In re Friedrich, 3 A. B. R. 801, 100 Fed. 284 (C. C. A. Wis.).

15. In re Friedrich, 3 A. B. R. 801, 100 Fed. 284 (C. C. A. Wis.). Compare, In re Smith, 2 A. B. R. 190, 93 Fed. 791 (D. C. Texas), to the point that there can be no review unless a trustee has been appointed and has set apart the exemptions. Compare, on same point, post, § 1111. The receiver may set aside property claimed as exempt when he is about to sell perishable property to await the determination of the bankrupt's exemption rights. In re Joyce, 11 A. B. R. 716, 128 Fed. 985 (D. C. Penn.); In re Shaffer & Son, 11 A. B. R. 717, 128 Fed. 986 (D. C. Penn.); obiter, In re Le Vay, 11 A. B. R. 115, 125 Fed. 990 (D. C. Penn.). But this setting aside is not the setting apart of exempt property to the bankrupt contemplated by the bankruptcy act, for such duty can only be performed by the trustee. Such property thus set aside to await the determination of the bankrupt's claim for exemptions may be delivered to the bankrupt upon the giving of security for its redelivery upon such determination. In re Shaffer & Son, 11 A. B. R. 717, 128 Fed. 986 (D. C. Penn.).

16. Bankr. Act, § 47 (11). Obiter, McGahan v. Anderson, 7 A. B. R. 645, 113 Fed. 115 (C. C. A. S. C.); In re Camp, 1 A. B. R. 165, 91 Fed. 745 (D. C. N. Car.); In re Goodman, 23 A. B. R. 504, 174 Fed. 644 (C. C. A. Ala.); In re Andrews & Simonds, 27 A. B. R. 116, 193 Fed. 776 (D. C. Mich.).

17. In re Soper, 22 A. B. R. 863, 173 Fed. 116 (D. C. Neb.).

18. In re Hoyt, 9 A. B. R. 574, 119 Fed. 987 (D. C. N. Car.).

The trustee is not only to file the report of exempted property, but is also under duty to give possession, as much as he himself has at any rate, to the bankrupt.[19]

But he is under no obligation to proceed against third parties in behalf of the bankrupt to gain possession of exempt property from them; unless perchance, such possession were obtained from the trustee himself.

§ 1075. Trustee's Report to Be Itemized, with Estimated Values. —The trustee's report must be itemized and a separate valuation put upon each item.[20]

§ 1076. Statutory Method of Bankruptcy Act to Be Followed—No Different Manner Proper.—No other nor different manner of setting apart exemptions than that prescribed in the Act itself is proper.[21]

§ 1077. Not to Set Aside Property Not Exempt by State Law.— The trustee must not set apart as exempt property not exempted by the law of the State.[22]

In re Manning, 7 A. B. R. 571, 112 Fed. 948 (D. C. Penn.): "* * * what the law of the State does not give, cannot be set aside by the trustee."

Inferentially, In re Gerber, 26 A. B. R. 608, 186 Fed. 693 (C. C. A. Wis.): "While it is a well-established law that exemptions in behalf of unfortunate debtors are to be liberally construed in furtherance of the object of such statutes, it should never be forgotten that courts have not the power to legislate, and can no more add an exemption not fairly within the statute than they can take from the statute."

§ 1078. Nor Property Not Claimed.—The trustee must not set apart as exempt property not claimed as exempt by the bankrupt; his act is beyond his lawful powers if he does so.[23]

§ 1079. Not Bound to Set Aside, if Bankrupt Not Entitled.—The trustee is not bound in the first instance to set apart all the property claimed

---

19. In re Soper, 22 A. B. R. 863, 173 Fed. 116 (D. C. Neb.).
20. Bankr. Act, § 47 (11). Rule XVII. In re Manning, 7 A. B. R. 571, 112 Fed. 948 (D. C. Penn.); In re McClintock, 13 A. B. R. 606 (Ref. Ohio, affirmed by D. C.); In re Black, 4 A. B. R. 776, 104 Fed. 28 (D. C. Pa.); obiter, McGahan v. Anderson, 7 A. B. R. 645, 113 Fed. 115 (C. C. A. S. C.).
21. In re Grimes, 2 A. B. R. 730, 96 Fed. 529 (D. C. N. Car.). But compare contra practice, In re Lynch, 4 A. B. R. 262, 101 Fed. 579 (D. C. Ga.). And compare, In re Park, 4 A. B. R. 432, 102 Fed. 602 (D. C. Ark.).
22. In re Ogilvie, 5 A. B. R. 374 (Ref. Ga.). But in practice, what is to be done with the clothing on the person of an unmarried man who is

not entitled to exemptions? The trustee would hardly invoke the authority of the bankruptcy court to denude the bankrupt.

And compare, In re Coller, 7 A. B. R. 131, 111 Fed. 508 (D. C. Mass.), where the court rules that where an article claimed as exempt is of excessive value the trustee might take it for creditors upon giving the bankrupt money with which to buy one of proper value.

Also compare, In re Reinhart, 12 A. B. R. 78, 129 Fed. 510 (D. C. Ga.), where the court permitted the supplementing of statutory specific exemptions by the value of those not in possession that might have been claimed.
23. In re Nunn, 2 A. B. R. 664 (Ref. Ga.).

by the bankrupt as exempt, nor any of it, if he considers the bankrupt is not entitled to it.[24]

But should the trustee, without good cause, refuse to set aside the exemptions, the bankrupt may bring the matter of his claim therefor to the attention of the referee, who has ample authority to act in the premises.[25]

§ 1080. Appraisal Not Binding.—The appraisal is not binding upon either the trustee, bankrupt or creditors as to exempt property, and it is not necessary to follow it, nor is it necessary to have a reappraisal, before the trustee may refuse to set aside the exemptions in accordance with the values placed on the articles by the appraisers. Indeed, the requirement of appraisal simply goes to the appraisal of the property belonging to the estate and therefore does not cover exempt property. Where the trustee is satisfied that the property is exempt, he would not be justified in having it appraised.[26]

§ 1081. Who May Except to Trustee's Report of Exempted Property—Bankrupt and Creditors.—Both the bankrupt and any of his creditors may take exceptions to the report of the trustee setting apart exemptions;[27] whereupon the court (the referee) will hear the exceptions and determine their validity, and order the trustee to set apart whatever is determined to be exempt.[28]

§ 1082. Creditor Must File Exceptions within Twenty Days.—If a creditor takes the exception, he must file his exception within twenty days after the trustee has filed his report setting apart the exempted property.[29]

---

24. In re Ellis, 10 A. B. R. 754 (Ref. Ohio); impliedly, In re Friedrich, 3 A. B. R. 801, 100 Fed. 284 (C. C. A. Wis.). Also see inferentially, Huenergardt v. Brittain Dry Goods Co., 8 A. B. R. 341, 116 Fed. 31 (C. C. A. Kas.); In re Irwin, 9 A. B. R. 689, 120 Fed. 733 (C. C. A. Ark.); contra, In re Campbell, 10 A. B. R. 723, 124 Fed. 417 (D. C. Va.). But compare, In re Rice, 21 A. B. R. 202, 164 Fed. 509 (D. C. Pa.).

25. In re Finkelstein, 27 A. B. R. 229, 192 Fed. 738 (D. C. Pa.).

26. But compare, In re McCutcheon, 4 A. B. R. 81, 100 Fed. 779 (D. C. S. C.). Where, however, exempt property is appraised, the appraisal should follow the ordinary rules, and sacrifice values should not be the criterion, In re Prager, 8 A. B. R. 356 (Ref. Colo.).

Wife's furniture appraised as husband's, both being in bankruptcy; wife not estopped from claiming ownership although present at appraisal and knowing appraisers were acting in husband's case. In re Jamieson, 6 A. B. R. 601 (D. C. R. I.).

27. In re Ellis, 10 A. B. R. 754 (Ref. Ohio).

In one case, In re Rice, 21 A. B. R. 202, 164 Fed. 509 (D. C. Pa.), it was held that the trustee must set apart the exemptions as claimed but might except—except to his own report! This would seem a violation of the maxim that the law does not require the doing of a vain thing.

28. Gen. Ord. No. XVII: "The referee may require the exceptions to be argued before him and shall certify them to the court for final determination at the request of either party."

Inferentially, In re Carmichael, 5 A. B. R. 552, 108 Fed. 789 (D. C. Ky.). The point was not raised in this case but was involved.

29. Gen. Ord. No. XVII: "Any creditor may take exceptions to the determination of the trustee within twenty days after the filing of the report." McGahan v. Anderson. 7 A. B. R. 641, 113 Fed. 115 (C. C. A. S. C.); In re Ellis, 10 A. B. R. 754 (Ref. Ohio). To same effect, obiter, In re Allen & Co., 13 A. B. R. 521, 134 Fed. 620 (D. C. Va.). In re Amos, 19 A.

And exceptions filed afterwards will be dismissed.[30]

Certain text books and decisions [see In re Campbell, 10 A. B. R. 723, 124 Fed. 417 (D. C. Va.), In re Rice, 21 A. B. R. 202, 164 Fed. 509 (D. C. Pa.), and In re White, 4 A. B. R. 613, 103 Fed. 774 (D. C. Vt.)], have laid down the rule that the trustee has no discretion in the matter of setting apart exemptions at all; that so long as the bankrupt has observed the proper formalities in making his claim for exemptions, the trustee is bound to set apart the property claimed, no matter if in fact the bankrupt is not entitled to them; in effect, that the trustee is a mere automaton and that only creditors may take exceptions; one decision,[30a] going to the absurd length of saying that if the trustee is dissatisfied he may file exceptions to his own report! This is not a correct idea and is founded upon a misapprehension of the real purport of that part of Rule XVII quoted.

Apparently the rule of statutory construction "expressio unius, exclusio alterius" is thought to be applicable and the mention of creditors alone, and the limitation of twenty days for them to file exceptions, is taken to mean that only creditors may file such exceptions. This would be a serious defect in bankruptcy practice were it the rule. For nothing is more helpless than an insolvent estate. The administration of such an estate is far different from an adversary lawsuit. In an adversary lawsuit there are two sides in opposition—each one alert to take advantage of the mistake or error of the opponent. In the administration of insolvent estates, on the contrary, after the first assembling of creditors and the election of trustee, the activity of creditors at once subsides. After that, the trustee is left wholly in charge and the individual creditor is little inclined to take part, probably because the benefit from his work goes to all and not to himself alone. It would be strange, indeed, if in such an important matter as the setting apart of exemptions, the trustee should be a mere automaton and creditors could not have him to watch over their interests. The Supreme Court's General Order does not mean this at all. Nor does it mean that the bankrupt may not also file exceptions. It simply means that creditors will not be absolutely bound by their trustee's acts in regard to the important matter of exemptions, although in other matters relating to third parties the trustee's acts may be binding on creditors; but that, on the con-

---

B. R. 804 (Ref. Ga.); In re Cotton & Preston, 23 A. B. R. 586 (Ref. Ga.).

Filing Additional Grounds of Objection after Twenty Days.—It has been held, also, that a creditor may not come in after the expiration of the twenty days and file additional objections. In re Cotton & Preston, 23 A. B. R. 586. But this holding should be carefully scrutinized.

See further, In re Cotton & Preston (No. 2), 25 A. B. R. 532, 183 Fed. 181, 190 (D. C. Ga.): "A creditor desiring to object to a trustee's report setting apart the bankrupt's exemption should file all of his objections within the time fixed by law, and cannot come in after the expiration of that time, and add new and additional grounds to his objections already on file. It is otherwise as to the enlargement or amplification of grounds originally taken."

30. In re Amos, 19 A. B. R. 804 (Ref. Ga.).

30a. In re Rice, 21 A. B. R. 202, 164 Fed. 509 (D. C. Pa.).

trary, the creditors, as well as the bankrupt, may except to the trustee's report setting apart exempted property, and that the creditors in doing so must file their exceptions within twenty days so that the trustee may have the question set at rest as to whether the beneficiaries of his trust—the creditors—will find fault with him in that particular. This, evidently, is the correct construction of the rule.

§ 1082½. Grounds of Exception.

The making of false statements in writing to obtain credit, is not a sufficient ground of exception to the allowance of the bankrupt's exemption.[31] Nor is it sufficient ground for refusing to set apart exemptions.

§ 1083. Schedule (b) 5, Trustee's Report and Written Exceptions, Only Pleadings Necessary.

The schedule claiming exemptions (Schedule (b) 5) and the trustee's report of exempted property and the subsequent exceptions thereto, are sufficient pleadings to raise the issue, and nothing more is requisite.[32]

§ 1084. Whether Exceptions to Be Verified.

Exceptions probably need not be verified; it is doubtful that they are "pleadings."

Query, In re Campbell, 10 A. B. R. 723, 124 Fed. 417 (D. C. Va.): "While an exception to a trustee's report is in some sense a pleading, in that it makes an issue, and while such an exception may be treated as a pleading, 'setting up matters of fact,' yet I doubt if Congress, in enacting clause 'c' of § 18 of the Bankrupt Act (Act July 1, 1898, ch. 541, 30 Stat. 551 [U. S. Comp. St. 1901, p. 3429]) had the intent to require that exceptions to a trustee's report should be verified."

But lack of verification is at any rate waivable.[33]

Certainly, unless allegations or denials of facts are made in the exceptions there would be no sense in requiring verification—verification of legal conclusions.

§ 1085. Burden of Proof on Bankrupt, if Exceptions Amount to General Denial.

The burden of proof of showing that an article, alleged to be exempt, is so, rests upon the bankrupt, if the exceptions amount to a general denial not affirming new matter.[34] But the bankrupt is not entitled to a jury trial of the issues raised.[35]

---

31. In re Cotton & Preston (No. 2), 25 A. B. R. 532, 183 Fed. 181, 190 (D. C. Ga.).

32. McGahan v. Anderson, 7 A. B. R. 641, 133 Fed. 115 (C. C. A. S. C.).

33. In re Campbell, 10 A. B. R. 723, 124 Fed. 417 (D. C. Va.). Compare rule that exceptions to receiver's accounts are to be verified. In re Ketterer Mfg. Co., 19 A. B. R. 646, 156 Fed. 719 (D. C. Pa.).

34. In re Turnbull, 5 A. B. R. 549, 106 Fed. 667 (D. C. Mass.).

No Reopening to Permit Contest of Exemptions Where Laches Exists.—After discharge has been granted and exemptions set off, it has been held that the matter will not be reopened to let in a creditor to file exceptions to exemptions where the creditor was duly scheduled and presumably had notice. In re Reese, 8 A. B. R. 411, 115 Fed. 993 (D. C. Ala.).

35. In re Thedford, 27 A. B. R. 354 (D. C. Tex.).

§ 1086. Res Judicata—Order Approving or Disapproving Trustee's Report of Exempted Property Res Judicata Elsewhere.

—The order of the bankruptcy court setting aside or approving the report of the trustee setting aside property as exempt is res judicata in the State courts as elsewhere as to all creditors properly notified of the bankruptcy.[36]

> Smalley v. Laugenour, 13 A. B. R. 692, 196 U. S. 93: "The State court was of opinion that Laugenour and his wife might have pleaded and proved facts showing that the property was exempt from execution at the time of the sale, making the issue directly in the State court, but, as they chose to rely on the principle of res judicata, that is, on the adjudication by the bankruptcy court, having jurisdiction of person and estate, in a proceeding in bankruptcy in which the judgment of Smalley and McLellan was provable, the court gave due force and effect to that adjudication. * * *
>
> "All that was determined, and all that the State court was called on to determine, was the question of exemption under the State statutes. Its acceptance of the judgment of the Federal court in that regard does not bring the case within § 709.
>
> "Writ of error dismissed."
>
> Evans v. Rounsaville, 8 A. B. R. 236 (Sup. Ct. Ga.): "An exemption assigned and set apart by the bankrupt court * * * is no more subject to levy and sale than if it has been set aside by the ordinary of a county having proper jurisdiction."

§ 1087. Conversely, Judgment of State Court as to Exemptions in Same Fund, Res Judicata.

—A judgment or decree of the State court as to exemption rights in the same fund have been held res adjudicata and binding on the bankruptcy court.[87]

But, of course, this could not be the rule where the State court proceedings were utterly without jurisdiction, as in cases of State bankruptcy or State Insolvency proceedings, and not simply valid until superseded as in cases of mere assignments for the benefit of creditors, or receiverships.

> In re Anderson, 6 A. B. R. 555, 110 Fed. 141 (D. C. Mass.): "Upon the whole, though with considerable doubt, I think that the allowances made by § 99 are not properly exemptions within the purview of § 6 of the Bankrupt Act, but are concerned with that part of the insolvency law which is suspended in its operation by the passage of the Bankrupt Act."

Nor could such be the rule where all creditors were not bound by the judgment, as, for instance, in a suit brought by one creditor for his own benefit, where the property eventually was turned over to the bankruptcy court.

§ 1088. No Second Exemption Out of Same Fund.

—No second ex-

---

36. Smith v. Zachry, 8 A. B. R. 240 (Sup. Ct. Ga.).

37. In re Rhodes, 6 A. B. R. 173, 109 Fed. 117 (D. C. Ohio), assignment; also, compare, In re Overstreet, 2 A. B. R. 486 (Ref. Ark.); compare, In re McBryde, 3 A. B. R. 729, 99 Fed. 686

(D. C. N. Car.); compare, In re Nunn, 2 A. B. R. 664 (Ref. Ga.).

In re Eash, 19 A. B. R. 738, 157 Fed. 996 (D. C. Iowa), administration of decedent's estate where heirs entitled to exemptions.

emption out of the same fund will be allowed by the Bankruptcy Court, where the State Court has previously allowed and set aside exemptions therefrom while the property was in its custody prior to bankruptcy.[38]

§ 1089. Selling Exemptions with Other Assets as Entirety and Allowance Out of Proceeds.—By agreement between the bankrupt and the trustee, the exempt property may be sold along with the remainder of the property as an entirety, and the bankrupt be allowed exemptions out of the proceeds.[39] Such agreement, however, does not dispense with the requirements of § 7, as to the proper time and manner of claiming exemptions.[40] And where the exempted property is not separable from the assets belonging to the estate without manifest injury, it is held, in accordance with the laws of some States, that the entire lot may be sold and the exemptions be transferred to the proceeds of sale;[41] in which event the trustee and not the bankrupt should pay the expenses of the sale.[42] And where a homestead is of a value in excess of that limited by statute, the bankrupt may—according to the rulings in the same cases—be permitted to retain the homestead on payment of the excess to the trustee.[43]

38. In re Miller, 1 A. B. R. 647 (Ref. Mo.); compare, In re Jeffers, 17 A. B. R. 368 (Ref. Ga.); compare, In re Hoag, 3 A. B. R. 290, 97 Fed. 543 (D. C. Wis.); compare obiter, In re Buckingham, 2 N. B. N. & Rep. 620 (Ref. Ohio): "It is undoubtedly true that successive allowances in lieu of a homestead at unreasonably short intervals of time would not be allowed, nor would more than one allowance be made out of the same property."

39. In re Richard, 2 A. B. R. 506, 94 Fed. 633 (D. C. N. Car.); In re Brown, 4 A. B. R. 46, 106 Fed. 441 (D. C. Penn.); In re Mayer, 6 A. B. R. 117, 108 Fed. 599, 600 (C. C. A. Wis.); In re Woodard, 2 A. B. R. 692, 95 Fed. 955 (D. C. N. Car.); instance, In re Renda, 17 A. B. R. 522, 149 Fed. 614 (D. C. Penn.); inferentially, McGahan v. Anderson, 7 A. B. R. 647, 113 Fed. 115 (C. C. A. S. C.); inferentially, In re Prince & Walter, 12 A. B. R. 675, 131 Fed. 546 (D. C. Pa.); inferentially, In re Kane, 11 A. B. R. 533, 127 Fed. 552 (C. C. A. Ills.); compare, In re Diller, 4 A. B. R. 45, 100 Fed. 931 (D. C. Calif.); In re Bolinger, 6 A. B. R. 171, 108 Fed. 374 (D. C. Penn.); compare, In re Bessie Stein, 12 A. B. R. 384, 130 Fed. 629 (D. C. Penn.); contra, and that such agreement is unlawful, In re Haskin, 6 A. B. R. 485, 109 Fed. 789 (D. C. Penn.); also contra, In re Grimes, 2 A. B. R. 730, 96 Fed. 529 (D. C. N. Car., reversing 2 A. B. R. 610); compare, In re Hoyt, 9 A. B. R. 574, 119 Fed. 987 (D. C. N. Car.).

Such agreement by a tax collector, however, will not bind a municipality. In re Prince & Walter, 12 A. B. R. 675, 131 Fed. 546 (D. C. Penn.); In re Ansley Bros., 18 A. B. R. 457, 153 Fed. 983 (D. C. N. Car.); In re Arnold, 22 A. B. R. 392, 169 Fed. 1000 (D. C. Ga.); obiter, In re Donahey, 23 A. B. R. 796, 176 Fed. 458 (D. C. Pa.); In re Finkelstein, 27 A. B. R. 229, 192 Fed. 738 (D. C. Pa.); In re Hutchinson, 28 A. B. R. 405, 197 Fed. 1021 (D. C. Mich). "It is immaterial whether the property sold for its appraised value or not."

40. In re Woodard, 2 A. B. R. 692, 95 Fed. 955 (D. C. N. Car.); In re Prince & Walter, 12 A. B. R. 675, 131 Fed. 546 (D. C. Penn.); In re Ansley Bros., 18 A. B. R. 457, 153 Fed. 983 (D. C. N. Car.); In re Donahey, 23 A. B. R. 796, 176 Fed. 458 (D. C. Pa.).

41. In re Oderkirk, 4 A. B. R. 617, 103 Fed. 779 (D. C. Vt.); In re Diller, 4 A. B. R. 45, 100 Fed. 931 (D. C. Penn.); In re Andrews & Simonds, 27 A. B. R. 116, 193 Fed. 776 (D. C. Mich.); Bank of Nez Perce v. Pindel, 28 A. B. R. 69, 193 Fed. 916 (C. C. A. Idaho); compare, In re Donahey, 23 A. B. R. 796, 176 Fed. 458 (D. C. Pa.).

42. In re Hopkins, 4 A. B. R. 619, 103 Fed. 781 (D. C. Vt.). But compare, In re Castleberry, 16 A. B. R. 431, 143 Fed. 1021 (D. C. Ga.).

43. In re Manning, 10 A. B. R. 498, 123 Fed. 180 (D. C. S. C.).

And it has been held, in some cases, that where the exempt property is sold at the bankrupt's request or consent along with the remainder of the assets, in bulk, he will be charged his percentage of the difference between the appraised value of the property and what it actually brought at the sale.[44]

In re Arnold, 22 A. B. R. 392, 169 Fed. 1000 (D. C. Ga.): "What the bankrupt would have received if he had not consented to the sale of the stock of merchandise as a whole would have been the particular articles designated and set apart for him by the trustee. On account of the expected benefit he would receive from the sale of the stock as a whole, he agreed to it, and I do not think he can now, as against the creditors of the estate, claim anything more than the proportion that the purchase price bears to the inventory value of the stock. To hold otherwise would be to allow the bankrupt to take several hundred dollars from the proceeds of that portion of the stock of goods which was left in the hands of the trustee for the benefit of creditors after the goods allowed the bankrupt as an exemption had been separated therefrom. I do not think this would be right."

On the other hand it has been held that where, with a bankrupt's consent, his entire estate is converted into cash after notice to the creditors and without objection on their part, they can not be heard to complain of an allowance to him of a homestead exemption from the proceeds of the sale without deduction of the costs of administration.[45]

§ 1090. **Trustee Not Entitled to Indemnity before Delivering Exemptions.**—The trustee probably may not demand indemnity from the bankrupt for the twenty days allotted for filing exceptions to the trustee's report as a condition of delivering over the exemptions before the expiration of the twenty days.[46] Therefore, since creditors have twenty days time within which to file exceptions to the trustee's report of exempted property, it follows that either the trustee must retain the property for twenty days, which it is doubtful that he may do, else set it apart and assume the risk of the filing and sustaining of exceptions. At any rate the trustee may not demand indemnity after the referee has decided that the bankrupt is entitled to them.[47] But the receiver may demand indemnity for setting aside perishable property as exempt pending the determination of the bankrupt's exemption rights therein.[48]

§ 1091. **Nor to Refuse to Set Apart until Costs Paid.**—The trustee must not refuse to set apart exemptions until costs or expenses of administration are paid.[49]

---

44. Also, see In re Ansley, 18 A. B. R. 457, 153 Fed. 983 (D. C. N. Car.).

45. Hardw. Co. v. Huddleston. 21 A. B. R. 731, 167 Fed. 433 (C. C. A. Ga.).

46. Inferentially, In re Brown, 4 A. B. R. 46, 100 Fed. 441 (D. C. Pa.).

47. In re Brown, 4 A. B. R. 46, 106 Fed. 441 (D. C. Penn.).

48. In re Shaffer, 11 A. B. R. 717, 128 Fed. 986 (D. C. Penn.).

49. Inferentially, In re LeVay, 11 A. B. R. 115, 125 Fed. 990 (D. C. Penn.); contra, In re Jackson, 18 A. B. R. 216 (Ref. Ga.).

Hardware Co. v. Huddleston, 21 A. B. R. 731, 167 Fed. 433 (C. C. A. Ga.): "It is contended in the petition for revision that the costs of the administration should be deducted from the allowance to the bankrupt. This contention cannot be sustained, for the reason that the homestead exemption is not subject to tax or charge of any character and to the extent of the burden which may be imposed in the way of costs in bankruptcy proceedings would be a diminution of the constitutional provision relating to homestead exemptions."

But, it has been held that he may be ordered to pay the necessary cost of administration out of funds in his hands, although the funds may be otherwise exempt.[50] And the suggested rule in Lockwood's Case, 10 A. B. R. 107, 190 U. S. 294, will not permit the withholding of the setting apart until the determination of a suit in tort against the bankrupt for the conversion of a note containing a waiver of exemptions.[51] And as elsewhere noted (ante, §.1069), where the bankrupt has omitted to claim exemptions or has been indefinite in describing them, the court may impose as a condition to allowing amendment the payment of the cost or expenses necessary to put the parties in statu quo.

§ 1092. Bankrupt Not Entitled to Reimbursement for Care of Exempt Property Pending Setting Off.

—The bankrupt is not entitled to reimbursement for his expenses in taking care of exempt property pending its being set off to him.[52]

§ 1093. Rent, Storage and Other Charges Pending Setting Off.

—It has been held that the Bankruptcy Court has power to tax as costs against the bankrupt the rent and storage charges for the keep of the exempt property pending its being set apart to the bankrupt.[53]

---

50. In re Herbold, 14 A. B. R. 119 (D. C. Wash.); compare, In re Castleberry, 16 A. B. R. 431, 143 Fed. 1021 (D. C. Ga.).

51. In re Hartsell & Son, 15 A. B. R. 177, 140 Fed. 30 (D. C. Ala.).

52. In re Groves, 6 A. B. R. 728 (Ref. Ohio, affirmed by D. C.).

53. Compare, In re Castleberry, 16 A. B. R. 431, 143 Fed. 1021 (D. C. Ga.).

Exempt Property May Be Subject to Payment of Statutory Fees in Bankruptcy; but Not Other Costs of Administration. — But exempt property may be subject to the order of the court for the payment of the statutory fees. In re Bean, 4 A. B. R. 54, 100 Fed. 262 (D. C. Vt.): "And it may be subject to an order for payment of the statutory fees, which are primarily for services for the benefit of the bankrupt, and do not depend upon property not exempt, but upon absolute inability."

But compare, In re LeVay, 11 A. B. R. 115, 125 Fed. 990 (D. C. Penn.): "So far as the bankrupt was concerned, the whole proceedings, as well as this part of them, were an useless interference with her affairs. Conceding that an act of bankruptcy had been committed, it must have been evident from the start that the small stock of millinery which she had, even if it realized $519 (at which it was appraised), was little more than enough to cover her exemption and the probable costs, leaving only the barest fraction, if anything at all, for general creditors. As it turned out, it has fallen far short of this, and the expenses incurred must therefore be borne by those who made them. They cannot be allowed to still further reduce the bankrupt's already scanty claim."

Bankrupt Selling Goods after Filing of Bankruptcy Petition—Amounts Received Deducted from Exemptions.— It has been held in one case that, where a bankrupt, after the filing of the petition against him and before seizure by the marshal, has continued selling in the due course of trade, the amounts received by him are to be de-

In re Grimes, 2 A. B. R. 730, 96 Fed. 529 (D. C. N. Car.): "The bankrupts' property has been thus preserved; but the bankrupts insist that their exemp- tions must first be set apart to them, and, if there be anything left, Schouler's claim for rental since their adjudication, and the legal and necessary expenses incurred in closing up the estate, can be paid out of the remainder of the es- tate of the bankrupts. This contention cannot be maintained either on legal or equitable grounds. The rental for the storage of the goods of the bankrupt firm is part and parcel of the legitimate costs incurred in this case, and is a lien upon the estate of the bankrupts, or any assets that may be in the hands of the trustee, or that may hereafter come into his hands."

Contra, In re LeVay, 11 A. B. R. 116, 125 Fed. 990 (D. C. Pa.): "The title to that which is now claimed (as exempt) having, therefore, never passed out of the bankrupt, even though temporarily in abeyance, cannot be subjected to the costs made in the attempt to otherwise deal with it (§§ 62, 64b); and this is true even though the appointment of the receiver and the sale of the goods as perishable would ordinarily be regarded as preservative steps taken in the interest of all parties.

"But there was this peculiarity in this case—the value of the goods sold was appraised at only slightly more than the exemptions claimed and it was obvious that no necessity existed for such a sale, thus distinguishing this case from those where impliedly the bankrupt gave his permission."

In cases of the amendment of schedules such payments may be required as a condition, in order to put the parties in statu quo.[54]

§ 1093¾. **Whether Commissions on Exempt Property.**—The Amendment of 1910 to § 48 of the act provides for commissions of the trustee and receiver upon moneys "turned over" to "any person." It is doubtful whether "any person" should be construed to include the bankrupt, since this amendment is to be read in connection with other sections of the act in pari materia; for example, in conjunction with § 6 providing that "This act shall not affect the allowance to bankrupts of the exemptions which are prescribed by the State laws," etc., as well as in the light of the decisions and of the well-known policy of the law prescribing liberality towards the bank- rupt in the matter of exemptions. The words "any person" are to be con- strued in the light of the doctrine "noscitur a sociis," as referring to parties similar to "lienholders," as, for instance, adverse claimants to money or to the proceeds of property in the trustee's hands who are not lienholders but yet receive the aid of the court in tracing and preserving their property, con- verting it into money, etc.[55]

ducted from his exemptions. In re Ansley Bros., 18 A. B. R. 457, 153 Fed. 983 (D. C. N. Car.). But this is doubt- ful law; for the mere filing of the pe- tition against him does not convert him into a trustee for creditors, nor prevent him from doing business, un- der the present law [see § 1119, et seq.]. If creditors desire to protect themselves from waste they may im- pound the assets by some one of the provisional remedies open to them. See ante, § 335.

54. See ante, §§ 1064, 1069.

Laches Barring Additional Exemp- tions Out of Newly-Discovered As- sets.—Bankrupts have been refused leave to amend their schedules to claim additional exemptions sufficient to make up what they might have been entitled to originally, out of the newly-discovered assets, where guilty of laches. In re Irwin, 23 A. B. R. 487, 174 Fed. 642 (C. C. A. Pa.), quoted at § 1070½.

55. See post, § 2111.

SUBDIVISION "E."

EXEMPTIONS ON RECOVERY OF PREFERENTIAL AND FRAUDULENT TRANSFERS; UPON AVOIDANCE OF GENERAL ASSIGNMENTS, AND WHEN ASSETS CONCEALED.

§ 1093¾. Fraudulent or Preferential Transfers of Exempt Property.—As a general proposition, creditors cannot complain of the transfer or holding of exempt property as being fraudulent or preferential.[55a] Forming no part of the insolvent debtor's assets seizable by creditors, creditors are not harmed by a disposition of exempt property.[55b]

In re Hastings, 24 A. B. R. 360, 181 Fed. 34 (C. C. A. Mich.): "Creditors cannot complain of transfers of exempt property * * * and a transfer which is good against the transferror is equally valid as against the trustee."

However, it is held in some cases that the exemption of the property transferred cannot be claimed by the otherwise fraudulent[55c] nor preferential[55d] transferee himself, in order to validate the transaction, but may only be asserted by the bankrupt.

§ 1094. Exemptions, on Recovery of Preferences and Fraudulent Transfers; and in Cases of Assignment, etc.—Whether a bankrupt, after a preference or fraudulent transfer has been recovered by the trustee or surrendered to him, or a general assignment been set aside or concealed property been recovered, may come in and amend his schedules and claim his exemptions out of the property recovered, or even out of other property, is variously decided.

§ 1095. On Recovery of Preferences.—Thus, in cases where a preference has been recovered by the trustee or surrendered to him, it has been held by some courts that he may have exemptions;[56] and by others that he may not have exemptions.[57]

In re White, 6 A. B. R. 451, 109 Fed. 635 (D. C. Mo.): "The bankrupt in this case, prior to the institution of the suits by the trustee to recover from

55a. In re Bailey, 24 A. B. R. 201, 176 Fed. 990 (D. C. Utah), quoted at § 1292; compare, obiter, Mills v. Fisher & Co., 20 A. B. R. 239, 159 Fed. 397 (C. C. A. Texas), quoted at § 1292; Vitzthum v. Large, 20 A. B. R. 666, 162 Fed. 685 (D. C. Iowa), quoted at § 1292.

55b. See post, §§ 1292, 1293. Compare facts, In re Vickerman & Co., 29 A. B. R. 298, 199 Fed. 589 (D. C. S. Dak.).

55c. Mitchell v. Mitchell, 17 A. B. R. 389 (D. C. N. Car.); [1867] Edmondson v. Hyde Fed. Cas. No. 4285.

55d. In re Soper, 22 A. B. R. 860, 173 Fed. 116 (D. C. Neb.).

56. In re Falconer, 6 A. B. R. 557,

110 Fed. 111 (C. C. A. Ark.); In re Osborn, 5 A. B. R. 111, 104 Fed. 780 (D. C. N. Y.).

Even freed from the preferential lien itself. In re Soper, 22 A. B. R. 868, 173 Fed. 116 (D. C. Neb.), quoted at § 1292.

57. In re Long, 8 A. B. R. 591, 116 Fed. 113 (D. C. Penn.); In re Evans, 8 A. B. R. 730, 116 Fed. 909 (D. C. N. Car.); compare, dissenting opinion, In re Falconer, 6 A. B. R. 557, 110 Fed. 111 (C. C. Ark.); In re Sharp, 15 A. B. R. 493 (Ref. Ohio, affirmed by District Judge); In re Coddington, 11 A. B. R. 122 (D. C. Penn.); In re Wishnefsky, 24 A. B. R. 798, 181 Fed. 896 (D. C. N. J.).

the preferred creditors the money in question, made no selection of any property out of which his $300 was to come. He scheduled no other property than that which was absolutely exempt under said § 3159, and which he claimed as exempt, and which he withheld from the trustee. How was it possible for the trustee in bankruptcy to comply with the statute to set off to this bankrupt $300 worth of property as exempt which he did not schedule? Under Rule 17 of the General Orders in Bankruptcy * * *, it is made the duty of the trustee to report to the court, within 90 days after receiving notice of his appointment, the articles set off to the bankrupt by him with the estimated value of each article. How could the trustee comply with this requirement of the law in respect of the property in question? The bankrupt had not scheduled it. He made no selection of $300 worth of property out of any particular property. He did not even claim this property as a part of his assets. The law would be a mockery, and permit a party to take advantage of his own wrong, if after having transferred his property in fraud of the bankruptcy act, and compelling the trustee in bankruptcy, at the expense of the estate, to engage in protracted litigation, to uncover his fraud, and recover the proceeds of the property from the wrongtakers, the bankrupt could stand quietly by, and then come in and make his selection of $300 in money out of the fruits of the litigation necessitated by his wrong and fraud. He is within neither the letter nor the spirit of the law."

Generally, the courts have seemed to consider the question to be controlled by the varying laws of the several states on the subject. One decision, In re Coddington (Penna.), 11 A. B. R. 122, however, is based on the provisions of the Bankruptcy Act itself. By this decision the bankrupt is held not to be entitled to exemptions out of preferentially conveyed property upon recovery or surrender of the same to the trustee, the argument being that the title to exempt property never passes to the trustee at all, therefore, if the court does permit him to recover property preferentially conveyed by the bankrupt, it can only be on the theory that the title is not in the bankrupt but in himself, which is equivalent to saying the property is recoverable because not exempt. Whilst the bankrupt might shield the conveyance already made by him to the preferred creditor by claiming the property as exempt,[57a] yet this claim can redound to the benefit only of the preferred creditor and will operate simply to protect the conveyance from molestation [58] and cannot be made to operate indirectly to give back to the debtor property that he could not have recovered directly from the creditor himself; the fraudulent or preferential conveyance being voidable only at the instance of creditors. In effect, since the right to exemptions is to be determined as of the date of the filing of the petition, unless at that date the property belonged to the debtor and was recoverable by him, it cannot be exempt to him, for the ownership is not in him. But suppose the trustee should set it apart to him as being property not belonging to the state. What would be the situation? The bankrupt would have had his exemptions set apart to him in property which he never himself could recover, for of course a

57a. Compare ante, § 1093¾.
58. Obiter, In re Wishnefsky, 24 A. B. R. 798, 181 Fed. 896 (D. C. N. J.).

debtor cannot recover property which he himself has fraudulently or preferentially conveyed to another, it being only as to creditors that the title is not good. So therefore, if, after the trustee has recovered the property, the bankrupt may step in and take it away as exempt, an inconsistency arises; for, on the one hand, the trustee who never possesses title to exempt property, is thus held to be the only one to whom the courts will give the exempt property, whilst on the other hand, the bankrupt, in whom the title to exempt property is supposed to have remained all the time, is precisely the one who cannot maintain a suit for its recovery and who has absolutely no standing in court at all to recover it.

Were bankruptcy exemptions, to be sure, simply a *priority* claim upon the funds passing into the trustee's hands the case would be different; but they are not simply a priority claim on a fund [59]—they are not part of the fund at all; the title to them never passes to the trustee, they always remain the property of the bankrupt and the trustee cannot be obliged to surrender property to one who has not enough title himself to recover it in his own name.

In re Ogilvie, 5 A. B. R. 380: "The Supreme Court of this State (Georgia) has decided that a homestead in bankruptcy constitutes a different estate than one allowed by State law. * * * The estate obtained in bankruptcy is a fee simple."

Now whilst all this is true, yet § 67 (e) by its express provisions sets aside fraudulent (although not preferential) transfers as to the bankrupt as well as to the creditors, and permits the bankrupt to have exemptions from the property so recovered; so the case In re Coddington could not lay down the correct rule as to fraudulently transferred property although it might do so as to property merely preferentially transferred.

. Compare, In re Neal, 14 A. B. R. 550 (Ref. Ohio): "Under the laws of Ohio, a debtor may claim his exemptions out of fraudulently conveyed property recovered by a trustee, for the reason, that he never in fact parted with the title, and the recovery by the trustee and the trustee's title is under and by virtue of the debtor's title, and while the debtor by reason of his participation in the fraudulent conveyance cannot recover it himself, the law leaving the parties to the fraud as it finds them, yet when recovery is made, it is his property in the hands of the trustee to be administered and is subject to homestead.

"A debtor who makes a voluntary transfer of his property to a creditor, prior to bankruptcy, parts absolutely with all title thereto, and when the same, or

59. But see Fenley *v.* Poor, 10 A. B. R. 377, 121 Fed. 739 (C. C. A. Ky.); also, see, In re White, 6 A. B. R. 451, 109 Fed. 635 (D. C. Mo.).
In some States homestead exemptions approximate in their nature actual estates and interests and thus harmonize with the theory of the present bankruptcy act; but in other States, as, for instance, Ohio and Kentucky, they seem to partake more of the nature of priority demands; accordingly in such States it is hard to reconcile the State exemption practice with that in bankruptcy. See Schuler *v.* Miller, 45 Ohio St. 325. See, In re Fenley *v.* Poor, 10 A. B. R. 377, 121 Fed. 739 (C. C. A. Ky.); compare, In re Camp, 1 A. B. R. 168, 91 Fed. 749 (D. C. Ga.).

its value, is afterwards recovered by the trustee, he is not entitled to his exemptions out of the same; especially is this true where the preferred creditor had a lien on the property which as between himself and the bankrupt would have precluded the allowance of exemptions."

And although the argument in In re Coddington is very cogent, yet the weight of authority seems to be that the state law will govern and that the bankrupt may claim his exemptions out of fraudulently or preferentially conveyed property recovered by the trustee or surrendered to him where allowed so to do by state law;[60] one of the reasons assigned for the holding being that, as the property was exempt any way its transfer could not have depleted the creditors' fund and therefore could not have been fraudulent nor preferential.[61]

In re Falconer, 6 A. B. R. 557, 110 Fed. 111 (C. C. A. Ark.): "Under these circumstances, we think that the bankrupt was under no obligation at the time he filed his original schedule to claim his exemption out of the fund in controversy, or to indicate his intention to do so if the fund should be recovered by the trustee or surrendered voluntarily by the creditor. In making his claim for exemptions in the first instance his choice was necessarily confined to such property as he could himself lay claim to, at the time, as forming a part of his estate. His right to select other property then held by third parties, whose title could only be challenged by the trustee, arose, and in the nature of things could be exercised only, when the title by which it was held was vacated and the property became actually, as well as potentially, a part of his estate."

But such reasoning seems to ignore the fact that the very reason the property was recoverable was because the court setting aside the transfer had thereby held that the creditor's fund had been depleted by the transfer.

This would undoubtedly be the rule also in states where the doctrine is established that a debtor may claim exemptions out of fraudulently conveyed property when the property is recovered for the benefit of creditors; this doctrine being based upon the principle that the avoiding of the conveyance operates to reinvest the debtor with the title to the property although he might not have been able to avoid the conveyance himself.

§ 1096. On Recovery of Fraudulently Transferred Property.—So, also, there is a conflict of authority as to whether a bankrupt may have exemptions out of property recovered by the trustee that has been fraudulently conveyed by the bankrupt.[62]

60. Bashinski v. Talbott, 9 A. B. R. 513, 119 Fed. 337 (C. C. A. Ga.); In re Osborn, 5 A. B. R. 111, 104 Fed. 780 (D. C. N. Y.).

61. In re Tollett, 5 A. B. R. 404, 106 Fed. 866 (C. C. A. Tenn., reversing 5 A. B. R. 305). Where the homestead is indivisible and is of greater value than that allowed by law, it has been held in South Carolina that the bankrupt might retain it on paying to the trustee the excess. In re Manning, 10 A. B. R. 498, 123 Fed. 180 (D. C. S. C.).

62. Obiter, in re Bashinski v. Talbot, 9 A. B. R. 513, 119 Fed. 337 (C. C. A. Ga.), although here it is doubtful as to whether the conveyance was fraudulent or not. But where the fraudulently conveyed property is reconveyed to the bankrupt before bankruptcy, the bankrupt may have his exemptions therein. In re Thompson, 8 A. B. R. 283, 115 Fed. 924 (D. C. Ga.); In re Tollett, 5 A. B. R. 404, 106 Fed. 866 (C. C. A. Tenn., reversing 5 A. B. R. 305); inferentially, In re Allen & Co.,

That he may have exemptions therein.[63]

In re Thompson, 15 A. B. R. 287, 115 Fed. 924 (D. C. Wash.): "But it does not necessarily follow that, if the conveyance is set aside and the property is treated as a fund in the hands of a trustee for the payment of the bankrupt's debts, he has no interest in it. Counsel seek, if I apprehend their position correctly, to sustain the view that the transfer by Mrs. Oliver to the trustee passed the title to him whereby any interest of the bankrupt is cut off, and that inasmuch as he could not disturb her in her possession, or demand an accounting for the proceeds of the property, that he is also precluded from demanding that his exemptions be set aside by the trustee. The attempted transfer being void as to creditors, the property still remains that of the bankrupt for the purpose of paying his debts; otherwise, we would have the anomaly of the debts of a bankrupt being paid out of the property of a third person. The property, being subject to the debts of the bankrupt, could not be so upon any other theory than that of ownership by him. While it is true some courts have held that, where the bankrupt commits fraud in the conveyance of his property, which is recovered at the suit of creditors, he is precluded from making claim to exemptions, yet the weight of authority is the other way. Those authorities which hold that an act of fraud is sufficient to deprive one of exemptions, in my opinion, confound fraudulent transfers generally with statutory rights. There can be no such thing as fraud in claiming that which the law allows. The question under consideration does not appear to have been decided by the Supreme Court of the State. * * *

"There is another reason equally convincing. Congress in the Bankruptcy Act appears to have anticipated the contention made in this case. Section 67e declares that all conveyances, transfers, etc., made or given by a person adjudged a bankrupt under the provisions of the Act, with the intent and purpose on his part to hinder, delay and defraud his creditors, shall be null and void as against such creditors, 'and all property of the debtor conveyed, assigned or encumbered as aforesaid, shall, if he be adjudged a bankrupt and the same is not exempt from execution and liability for debts by the law of his domicile, be and remain a part of the assets and estate of the bankrupt, and shall pass to his said trustee, whose duty it shall be to recover and reclaim the same by legal proceedings or otherwise for the benefit of the creditors.'" In this case the fraudulent transferee voluntarily surrendered the property.

§ 1097. Where General Assignment Nullified by Bankruptcy.—

So, also, there is a conflict of authorities as to whether a bankrupt may have exemptions out of property recovered by the trustee that has been assigned

---

13 A. B. R. 518, 134 Fed. 620 (D. C. Va.).

For a peculiar instance, where, during the pendency of a suit in the State Court to set aside a fraudulent conveyance, the debtor obtained a reconveyance and then filed his statutory claim for homestead, but was afterwards declared bankrupt before the State Court had entered any decree, see In re Allen & Co., 13 A. B. R. 518 (D. C. Va.), where the court granted the exemptions.

But as to whether creditors may complain of a transfer of exempt property as being fraudulent, see ante, § 1093¾; also In re Hastings, 24 A. B. R. 360, 181 Fed. 34 (C. C. A. Mich.), quoted at §§ 1061, 1093¾.

63. In re Tollett, 5 A. B. R. 404, 106 Fed. 620 (C. C. A. Tenn., reversing 5 A. B. R. 305); inferentially, In re Rothschild, 6 A. B. R. 48 (Ref. Ga.); obiter, In re Cotton & Preston (No. 2), 25 A. B. R. 532, 183 Fed. 181, 190 (D. C. Ga.).

within four months of bankruptcy where the assignment has been declared void as being an assignment in trust for creditors.[64]

§ 1098. Forfeiting Exemptions by Fraudulent Concealments or Removals.

—So, also, there is a conflict of authority as to whether a bankrupt forfeits his right to exemptions where he fraudulently disposes of his property, conceals it or removes it from the jurisdiction. Some cases have held that he does forfeit them;[65] and such is the rule by statute in Georgia.[66]

Other cases have held that he does not forfeit them.[67]

Even where recognized as a bar to the allowance of exemptions, however, the fraud relied upon must inhere in the transaction itself.[68]

But a failure to schedule household goods purchased with the proceeds of the labor of the wife and children has been held not to be such a concealment as will forfeit exemptions, even if such goods belong to the bankrupt.[69]

And the bankruptcy court may not refuse to set apart a homestead exemption because the homestead deed was filed on the eve of bankruptcy with the evident purpose of preferring certain creditors by confessing judgment on "waiver notes" held by them.[70]

64. That he may have these exemptions, see Bashinski v. Talbott, 9 A. B. R. 513, 119 Fed. 337 (C. C. A. Ga., affirming In re Talbott, 8 A. B. R. 427, 116 Fed. 417, which in turn affirmed In re Talbott, 9 A. B. R. 788), although in this case it is not clear whether there was any acting upon the assignment or other recognition of it than as being a species of agency for holding custody. In re Falconer, 6 A. B. R. 557, 110 Fed. 115 (C. C. A. Ark.). That he may not have his exemptions, In re Staunton, 9 A. B. R. 79, 117 Fed. 507 (D. C. Penn.).

65. In re Duffy, 9 A. B. R. 358, 118 Fed. 926 (D. C. Penn.); In re Alex, 15 A. B. R. 451, 141 Fed. 483 (D. C. Penn.); In re Taylor, 7 A. B. R. 410, 114 Fed. 607 (D. C. Colo.). Also, see In re Yost, 9 A. B. R. 153, 117 Fed. 792 (D. C. Penn.); compare, to same effect, In re White, 6 A. B. R. 451, 109 Fed. 635 (D. C. Mo.); In re Gerber, 26 A. B. R. 608, 186 Fed. 693 (C. C. A. Wash.); In re Schafer, 18 A. B. R. 361, 151 Fed. 505 (D. C. Pa.); instance, In re O'Hara, 20 A. B. R. 714, 162 Fed. 325 (D. C. Pa.); In re Leverton, 19 A. B. R. 426, 155 Fed. 925 (D. C. Pa.). Compare, In re Ansley Bros., 18 A. B. R. 457, 153 Fed. 983 (D. C. N. Car.); In re Wolcott, 15 A. B. R. 386, 140 Fed. 460 (D. C. N. Car.).

66. In re Cochran, 26 A. B. R. 459, 185 Fed. 913 (D. C. Ga.); In re Dobbs, 22 A. B. R. 801, 172 Fed. 682, also 23 A. B. R. 569, 175 Fed. 319 (D. C. Ga.); In re Thompson, 8 A. B. R. 283, 115 Fed. 924 (D. C. Ga.); In re Stephens, 8 A. B. R. 53, 114 Fed. 192 (D. C. Ga.); In re West, 8 A. B. R. 564, 116 Fed. 767 (D. C. Ga.); In re Williamson, 8 A. B. R. 42, 114 Fed. 190 (D. C. Ga.); In re Boorstin, 8 A. B. R. 89, 114 Fed. 696 (D. C. Ga.); In re Waxelbaum, 4 A. B. R. 120, 101 Fed. 228 (D. C. Ga.); In re Cotton & Preston, 23 A. B. R. 586 (Ref. Ga.); apparently contra, In re Rothschild, 6 A. B. R. 43 (Ref. Ga.).

67. In re Park, 4 A. B. R. 432, 102 Fed. 602 (D. C. Ark.); In re Peterson, 1 A. B. R. 254 (Ref. Wis.). In those States where fraud bars exemptions, the creditors thus opposing exemptions must show specifically in what the misrepresentations consisted by which they were deceived, In re Tobias, 4 A. B. R. 555, 103 Fed. 68 (D. C. Va.). In re Denson, 28 A. B. R. 162, 195 Fed. 854, 857 (D. C. Ala.).

68. In re McUlta, 26 A. B. R. 480, 189 Fed. 250 (D. C. Pa.).

69. In re Diamond, 19 A. B. R. 811, 158 Fed. 370 (D. C. Ala.).

70. In re Batten, 22 A. B. R. 270, 170 Fed. 688 (D. C. Va.).

Fraudulent Transferee . Claiming Property to Be Exempt.—See ante, § 1093¾; post, §§ 1292, 1293.

§ 1099. Whether Concealing Other Assets Presumed Selection as Exempt, Warranting Refusal of Exemptions Claimed in Schedules.

—Where the bankrupt has concealed any of his assets, it may be presumed in accordance with the law of some States that he has selected those concealed as exempt and to the extent of their value other exemptions will be refused him;[71] but in some of the other states the rule does not obtain.[72]

In re Park, 4 A. B. R. 432, 102 Fed. 602 (D. C. Ark.): "The exceptions seem to be based upon the fact that the bankrupt has not accounted for all of his assets, and is in possession of portions of his assets which were not turned over to the trustee. This is no reason why he should not have his exemptions. If he has in his possession, or under his control, assets which he has not accounted for, the trustee has his remedy. If he has fraudulently transferred property to other persons, the trustee has his remedy, but the bankrupt should not be denied his exemptions on account thereof."

SUBDIVISION "F."

LIENS BY LEGAL PROCEEDINGS ON EXEMPT PROPERTY WITHIN THE FOUR MONTHS PRECEDING BANKRUPTCY.

§ 1100. Whether Liens by Legal Proceedings on Exempt Property within Four Months, Nullified.

—Liens obtained by legal proceedings within the four months preceding the bankruptcy and whilst the bankrupt is insolvent, upon property claimed by the bankrupt in his schedules as exempt, have been held by some courts to be dissolved by the bankruptcy and by other courts not to be so dissolved.

Some cases hold that § 67 (f) annulling liens obtained by legal proceedings within the four months before bankruptcy does not apply to property claimed by the bankrupt as exempt and that the levy remains unimpaired so far as the bankruptcy law annulling liens is concerned.[73]

McKenney v. Cheney, 11 A. B. R. 54, 118 Ga. 387: "The effect of § 67f of the Bankruptcy Act of 1898 is not to avoid the levies and liens therein referred to against all the world, but only as against the trustee in bankruptcy and those claiming under him, in order that the property may pass to and be distributed among the creditors of the bankrupt. It is applicable only as against such trustee, and was designed to prevent preferences between creditors."

71. See Hoover v. Haslage, 16 Ohio, C. C. Rep. 570. It probably lies at the base of the decision in In re Duffy, 9 A. B. R. 358, 118 Fed. 926 (D. C. Pa.), and In re Mayer, 6 A. B. R. 122, 108 Fed. 599 (C. C. A. Ohio), and In re Alex, 15 A. B. R. 450, 141 Fed. 483 (D. C. Pa.). And see In re Leverton, 19 A. B. R. 426, 155 Fed. 925 (D. C. Pa.); In re Denson, 28 A. B. R. 162, 195 Fed. 854, 857 (D. C. Ala.); instance, Cowan v. Burchfield, 25 A. B. R. 293, 180 Fed. 614 (D. C. Ala.).

72. In re Peterson, 1 A. B. R. 254 (Ref. Wis.).

73. In re Durham, 4 A. B. R. 760, 104 Fed. 231 (D. C. Ark.); impliedly, White v. Thompson, 9 A. B. R. 653, 119 Fed. 868 (C. C. A. Ala.); impliedly, In re Allen & Co., 13 A. B. R. 518, 134 Fed. 620 (D. C. Va.); In re Hopkins, 1 A. B. R. 209 (Ref. Ala.); obiter, In re Weaver, 16 A. B. R. 265, 144 Fed. 229 (D. C. Ga.).

Thus, as to exempt wages, whether earned or not. Impliedly, In re Driggs, 22 A. B. R. 621, 171 Fed. 897 (D. C. N. Y.). Compare, analogously, post, § 1292.

"A discharge in bankruptcy does not discharge the lien of a judgment obtained, within four months prior to the adjudication of bankruptcy, upon a note waiving the homestead exemption allowed by the laws of this State upon lands set aside by the bankrupt court as exempt."

Jewett Bros. v. Huffman, 13 A. B. R. 738 (Sup. Ct. N. Dak.): "The lien of an attachment is not dissolved by the bankruptcy of the attachment debtor, where the property attached is exempt as against the trustee in bankruptcy, but is not exempt from seizure for the debt upon which the attachment is based.

"Where it is conceded that part and possibly all of the property attached is exempt from the bankruptcy proceedings, the property may be held under the attachment until it has been determined in the bankruptcy proceedings what part, if any, of the attached property has passed to the trustee in bankruptcy, freed from the bankrupt's claim for exemptions."

Obiter, Powers Dry Goods Co. v. Nelson, 7 A. B. R. 506 (Sup. Ct. N. Dak.): "Having reached the conclusion that the lien of the attachment in this case was not discharged by the mere discharge of the debt the question next presented is whether the discharge [adjudication] in bankruptcy did not in itself operate as a discharge of the lien.' * * * Aside from the convincing reasons of the cases referred to, we find ample ground in the language of the statute relied upon for holding that the liens which are declared void by it do not include liens upon exempt property, over which, as we have seen, the State, and not the federal, courts have jurisdiction. Section 67f, after declaring that all attachments levied within four months prior to the filing of the petition shall be null and void, and discharged and released, declares that the effect of such a discharge shall be to pass the property covered by the lien 'to the trustee as a part of the estate of the bankrupt.' It is entirely plain that this section does not refer to liens upon property upon which the court does not undertake to administer, and over which it has no jurisdiction. Exempt property constitutes no part of the estate which passes to the trustee for the benefit of creditors. As before stated, under the plain policy of the Bankruptcy Act, as well as by its specific provisions, exempt property is not disturbed but is left to the debtor, to be held by him subject to the laws of the State, entirely freed from federal interference. If defendant's contention that the discharge in bankruptcy destroyed the lien created by the attachment upon his exempt property is true, then such exempt property would, under the section above referred to, pass to the trustee as a part of the estate of the bankrupt for the benefit of his creditors; thus entirely destroying the debtor's right to save the exemption allowed by the laws of the State from the reach of general creditors. No such absurd construction can be sustained. In this case the bankruptcy court had by an express order set apart the property levied upon before the attachment was levied. By that order it disclaimed further jurisdiction, even for the purpose of inventory and appraisement. Upon this state of facts, it seems clear the discharge in bankruptcy was without effect upon the lien theretofore created under the laws of this State upon property which was then subject exclusively to the jurisdiction of the State courts."

Sharp v. Woolslare, 12 A. B. R. 396 (Superior Ct. Penn.): "A trustee in bankruptcy is not entitled to the bankrupt's exemption of $300, against a creditor who has attached the same by an attachment execution issued and served within four months prior to the bankruptcy, on a judgment waiving exemptions." The facts stated in this case fail to disclose, however, whether the bankrupt claimed the junk as exempt. Of course, if he did not claim it, it was not exempt.

First Nat'l Bk. of Sayre v. Bartlett, 21 A. B. R. 88, 35 Pa. Super. Ct. 593: "Now, if this ruling is sound, subsection 67 of the Bankruptcy Act should be construed to mean that all levies shall be deemed null and void, only, as to the property which passes to the trustee for the benefit of the creditors of the bankrupt, but remain valid for enforcement under the State laws as to the bankrupt's exempted property. This construction seems to be in accordance with the real meaning of said section. No good reason is apparent for holding the judgment, execution and levy, void as to the bankrupt's exempted property."

Nor will the discharge in bankruptcy discharge the otherwise valid lien on the exempt property.[74]

In re Driggs, 22 A. B. R. 621, 171 Fed. 897 (D. C. N. Y.): "The question is, therefore, squarely presented as to whether the bankrupt should be protected from garnishment, complete before petition filed, levied as execution upon exempt property. If the garnishment be no more than an attachment, and if the attachment be valid, it is no answer to say that the debt will be discharged." Although, of course, the pending suit in personam to which the garnishment may be incident may be stayed to permit the interposition of the discharge by the bankrupt, and thus, ultimately, the attachment or garnishment lien be defeated.

Other cases hold that § 67 (f) annulling liens obtained by legal proceedings within the four months before bankruptcy, does apply to property claimed by the bankrupt as exempt, and so frees the bankrupt's exempt property from the levy precisely as it does the creditors' property, although, but for the bankruptcy, the right of exemption might not prevail against the levy.[75]

In re Tune, 8 A. B. R. 285, 115 Fed. 906 (D. C. Ala.): "Whatever benefit results from the annulment of attachment liens extends to exempt property as well as to that which is not exempt. It is the policy of the law to allow the bankrupt, as well as creditors, to benefit by the changed status."

Impliedly, In re Beals, 8 A. B. R. 639, 116 Fed. 530 (D. C. Ind.): "The moment that Thomas C. Beals was adjudged a bankrupt, the statue operated ex proprio vigore to nullify and render void the judgment set up in the answer of the Pennsylvania Company, and to wholly release and discharge the debt due the bankrupt from such judgment. On what principle can this court hold the judgment to be of any force and effect in the face of a valid statute which declares such a judgment to be a nullity? The adjudication under this statute wipes out the judgment of the justice as effectually as though it never existed, and releases and discharges the debt due the bankrupt from the garnishee judgment as completely and effectually as would a formal release executed by the judgment plaintiff. In obedience to the positive mandate of the statute, the court must deem the attachment null and void, and the wages due the bankrupt wholly released and discharged from the same. It is too firmly settled to be open to doubt that, if a garnishee pays over money on a void judgment,

---

74. McKenney v. Cheney, 11 A. B. R. 54, 118 Ga. 387; Powers Dry Goods Co. v. Nelson, 7 A. B. R. 506 (Sup. Ct. N. Dak.); obiter, In re Weaver, 16 A. B. R. 265, 144 Fed. 229 (D. C. Ga.); impliedly, Maas v. Kuhn, 22 A. B. R. 91 (N. Y. Sup. Ct. App. Div.), quoted at § 1102; Newberry Shoe Co. v. Collier, 25 A. B. R. 130 (Sup. Ct. Va.).

75. In re Downing, 15 A. B. R. 425, 139 Fed. 590 (D. C. Ky.); In re Arnold, 2 A. B. R. 180, 94 Fed. 1001 (D. C. Ky.); impliedly, In re McCartney, 6 A. B. R. 366, 109 Fed. 639 (D. C. Wis.); impliedly, In re Bolinger, 6 A. B. R. 171, 108 Fed. 374 (D. C. Penn.); In re Forbes, 26 A. B. R. 355, 186 Fed. 79 (C. C. A. Ariz.).

he must bear the loss. He will not be heard to say that he paid it in obedience to a valid judgment after notice and knowledge that the judgment has been rendered null and void by operation of law. The adjudication having rendered the judgment against the bankrupt and the Pennsylvania Company null and void, it must be treated as a nullity whenever and wherever drawn in question, either in a direct or in a collateral proceeding. Here the judgment is drawn in question collaterally, and its nullity results from the subsequent adjudication by this court of Thomas C. Beals as a bankrupt. The statute declares that such shall be the effect of the adjudication on the judgment of the justice of the peace. The argument ab invenienti is without force. The judgment having been rendered null and void by the adjudication, if the plaintiff in that judgment should procure the justice of the peace to issue an execution against the Pennsylvania Company, the plaintiff, the justice, and the constable to whom the writ was delivered would be wrongdoers, and, if the property of the company were seized on such execution, they would be liable to an action as trespassers. The law imposes on every person the duty of protecting himself against the tortious acts of third persons, and the duty to do so, in legal contemplation, casts no wrongful burden upon him. As the property of the bankrupt is in the custody of the court, it is the duty of the court to protect it until its final disposition. It is a matter of no concern to the Pennsylvania Company what disposition of it shall ultimately be made by the court."

It would seem that the correct rule is that such liens are not annulled by the bankruptcy, because the reason lying at the basis of the annulment of legal liens, as well as that of preferences, is the protection of the creditor's trust fund and not the bankrupt's own property. Otherwise, even levies made on exempt property or notes or other obligations wherein exemptions have been expressly waived, would be void if made within the four months preceding bankruptcy whilst the debtor was insolvent.[76] On the other hand, the mere fact that at the time of the levy the property was claimed as exempt or might have been so claimed, is not of moment, else a ready way of perpetrating preferences might exist. The question is material only when it concerns property claimed by the bankrupt in the bankruptcy proceedings as exempt.

§ 1101. **Property Claimable as Exempt, but Not Claimed, Levies Nullified.**—Where property, not exempt as to certain creditors (as, for instance, not as to judgments or levies for its unpaid purchase price, or wages as against levies on judgments for necessaries, etc.), is not claimed by the bankrupt as part of his exemptions, although it might have been so claimed, it would seem that such creditors would have no special rights therein and a levy thereon within the four months period would be void under the same circumstances as with other property.[77] Yet it has been held in some cases that an assignee, mortgagee or other transferee may make

---

76. Compare, In re Bolinger, 6 A. B. R. 171, 108 Fed. 374 (D. C. Penn.), where such a levy was held void as creating a preference.

77. In re Wilkes, 7 A. B. R. 574, 112 Fed. 975 (D. C. Ark.); inferentially, In re Jonas B. Baughman, 25 A. B. R. 167, 183 Fed. 668 (D. C. Pa.). Compare, however, In re Wells, 5 A. B. R. 308, 105 Fed. 762 (D. C. Ark.).

the claim where the bankrupt fails to do so, and that thus an otherwise fraudulent or preferential transfer may be validated.[77a]

But, in any event, where property is first claimed in the schedules as exempt, a subsequent waiver of the exemptions by the bankrupt will be too late where the sheriff has meanwhile sold the property and paid over the proceeds to the judgment creditor, though the levy was made within the four months period.

In re Edwards, 19 A. B. R. 632, 156 Fed. 794 (D. C. Ala.): "The bankrupt's general waiver of exemption on July 19, 1907, subsequent to his claim of exemption made when his schedule was filed, as required by the Bankrupt Act, and subsequent to the special waiver of exemption in favor of Kohlman Company, which had been made effective by a judgment, valid at the time rendered, and under which the $90 now claimed by the trustee was paid over to them, would not and ought not in any way affect the right of Kohlman Company thus secured and obtained. If before the money had been paid over to Kohlman Company and the property or proceeds of its sale were in the hands of the constable, the bankrupt or any of his creditors, in the absence of a trustee, may have enjoined the constable from disposing of the property, or, having done so, from paying over the proceeds until the rights of Kohlman Company could have been ascertained and adjudicated. This was not done, but subsequent to the sale of the property and the paying over the net proceeds thereof, the bankrupt attempts to waive generally his claim of exemptions to specific property, some of which—that in question—had passed beyond his possession and control."

SUBDIVISION "G."

LEVYING ON EXEMPT PROPERTY BEFORE OR AFTER DISCHARGE AND WITH-HOLDING DISCHARGE TO PERMIT LEVY.

§ 1102. Levying on Exempt Property before and after Discharge, and Withholding Discharge to Permit Levy.

—After discharge, judgment cannot be had on notes containing waivers of exemption nor upon other rights of action against which particular property is not exempt, as, for instance, in actions for the purchase price of property sold, or for necessaries, nor can execution be levied thereunder upon the property set apart to the bankrupt as exempt by the trustee; for the obligations are discharged for all purposes, and are not enforceable even against exempt property, although such property may not have been exempt therefrom or exemptions may have been waived; the debt is discharged though the property otherwise might not have been exempt from application by legal process to its payment.

Thus, as to notes containing waivers of exemptions.[78]

In re Sisler, 2 A. B. R. 769, 96 Fed. 402 (D. C. Va.): "It can no more survive a discharge, and be enforced in a State court, than if it were a debt due by open account."

77a. Compare ante, §§ 1061, 1093¾.   Realty Co. v. Gioshio, 27 A. B. R. 58
78. Claster v. Soble, 10 A. B. R.   (Com. Pleas Pa.).
446 (22 Pa. Super. Ct. 631). Contra,

Thus, as to purchase money levies.

Graham *v.* Richardson, 8 A. B. R. 700 (Sup. Ct. Ga.): "A discharge in bankruptcy releases a bankrupt from all his provable debts, except those expressly excepted by the Bankrupt Act, and a debt for purchase money is not among those excepted. It is true that, under the constitution of this State, an exemption is subject to levy and sale for the purchase money thereof, but our law gives a vendor no lien for purchase money, and before exempted property can be sold for its purchase money, judgment must be obtained against the debtor, and execution be levied on the property. If the debtor be discharged in bankruptcy, he is thereby absolutely released from the purchase money debt. * * * This is so, though he may, during the pendency of such proceeding, and before the discharge was granted, have sued out an attachment for the purchase money, and cause the same to be levied upon the property he had sold the bankrupt."

Thus, as to claims against which there are no exemptions;[79] for example, where the statute permits collection of ten per cent. of wages.

In re Van Buren, 20 A. B. R. 896, 21 A. B. R. 338, 164 Fed. 883 (D. C. N. Y.): "The judgment creditor moves to vacate the stay on the ground that the present salary of the bankrupt is the property of the bankrupt, that the trustee in bankruptcy has no interest in it, and that this court, therefore, cannot enjoin the collection of one-tenth of the salary under the provisions of the recent amendments of the law. But the judgment was recovered before the adjudication in bankruptcy. All the bankrupt's property down to the time of the adjudication is applicable to the payment of that judgment ratably with the bankrupt's other debts, but the discharge of the bankrupt, if it shall be granted, is a bar to the enforcement of that judgment against any property subsequently acquired. Under these circumstances I think that the enforcement of the judgment against any portion of the bankrupt's present salary should be enjoined until the question is determined whether he shall receive a discharge. But as, if the entire salary were paid to the bankrupt, the probability is that the judgment creditor would never collect the tenth to which he is entitled if a discharge is refused, an order will be made directing the bankrupt's employers to withhold a tenth of the salary until that question is determined."

Compare, Maas *v.* Kuhn, 22 A. B. R. 91 (N. Y. Sup. Ct. App. Div.): "Until such stay is obtained, however, parties have the right to prosecute action or enforce collection of judgments. Especially is this so where, as in the present case, the property levied upon is a portion of the current salary of the bankrupt which could not be applied to the payment of his general debts, and which would not pass to his trustee in bankruptcy."

Amendment of 1910.—What effect the Amendment of 1910 to § 47, by which the trustee is to be deemed vested with all the rights, powers and remedies of a creditor holding a lien by legal or equitable process on property in his custody, will have in this regard has not yet been determined. But there is strong reason for the view that such custody will be a sufficient levy in behalf of the creditors holding special rights upon exempt property.

---

79. Obiter, In re Brumbaugh, 12 A. B. R. 204 (D. C. Penn.), which was the case of a judgment for breach of promise of marriage, there being no exemptions against judgments for torts in Pennsylvania.

§ 1103. Bankrupt Staying Creditor Pending Hearing on Discharge.

—Before discharge and pending the bankruptcy proceedings neither judgment nor levy upon such property can be had, if the bankrupt is allowed to exercise the right of staying the proceedings.[80]

§ 1104. Withholding Discharge to Permit Creditor to Levy, Where Property Not Exempt as to Him.

—In such cases the bankruptcy court may withhold the discharge and stay proceedings until the creditor can assert his peculiar rights upon the exempt property by appropriate proceedings in the state courts, as by action in equity and the appointment of a receiver to apply to the bankruptcy court for the possession, or perhaps even by levy of execution or attachment.[81]

Obiter, Lockwood v. Exchange Bank, 10 A. B. R. 107, 190 U. S. 294: "The rights of creditors having no lien, * * * but having a remedy under the State law against the exempt property, may be protected by the court of bankruptcy, since, certainly, there would exist in favor of a creditor holding a waiver note, like that possessed by the petitioning creditor in the case at bar, an equity entitling him to a reasonable postponement of the discharge of the bankrupt in order to allow the institution in the State court of such proceedings as might be necessary to make effective the rights possessed by the creditor."

In re Jackson, 8 A. B. R. 594, 116 Fed. 46 (D. C. Penn.): "I think the

80. Bankr. Act, § 11 (a): "A suit which is founded upon a claim from which a discharge would be a release, and which is pending against a person at the time of the filing of a petition against him, shall be stayed until after adjudication or the dismissal of the petition; if such person is adjudged a bankrupt, such action may be further stayed until twelve months after the date of such adjudication, or, if within that time such person applies for a discharge, then until the question of such discharge is determined."

Also, see "Staying Proceedings in Behalf of Bankrupt," ante, § 475, and post, § 2414, et seq., subject of "Discharge." Also, see § 1105; Bell v. Dawson Grocery Co., 12 A. B. R. 159 (Sup. Ct. Ga.); instance, Roden Grocery Co. v. Bacon, 13 A. B. R. 251 (C. C. A. Ala.); instance, First Nat'l Bk. of Sayre v. Partlett, 21 A. B. R. 88, 35 Pa. Super. Ct. 593; instance, In re Van Buren, 21 A. B. R. 338, 20 A. B. R. 896, 164 Fed. 883 (D. C. N. Y.), quoted at § 1102. Compare, Mass v. Kuhn, 22 A. B. R. 91 (N. Y. Sup. Ct. App. Div.), quoted at § 1102.

81. In re Allen & Co., 13 A. B. R. 526, 134 Fed. 520 (D. C. Va.); In re Ogilvie, 5 A. B. R. 374 (Ref. Ga.). Compare, analogously, effect of discharge of corporation on secondary liability of stockholders when judg-

ment is necessary, In re Marshall Paper Co., 4 A. B. R. 463, 102 Fed. 872. (C. C. A. Mass.). Compare, analogously, the rule in N. Y. Federal Courts permitting creditors to proceed to judgment and levy after bankruptcy, in suits begun before, where unfiled chattel mortgages exist, In re Beede, 14 A. B. R. 697, 138 Fed. 441 (D. C. N. Y.). Obiter, In re Weaver, 16 A. B. R. 265, 144 Fed. 229 (D. C. Ga.); In re Meredith, 16 A. B. R. 336, 144 Fed. 230 (D. C. Ga.); obiter, In re Bender, 17 A. B. R. 895 (Ref. Ohio); obiter, Snyder v. Guthrie, 17 A. B. R. 903 (Penn. Com. Pleas); contra, In re Moore, 7 A. B. R. 289, 112 Fed. 289 (D. C. Ala.); contra, Woodruff v. Cheeves, 5 A. B. R. 296, 105 Fed. 601 (C. C. A. Ga.). Also, contra (inferentially), Graham v. Richardson, 8 A. B. R. 700 (Sup. Ct. Ga.); compare distinctions in In re Lucius, 10 A. B. R. 655, 124 Fed. 455 (D. C. Ala.); H. S. Meinhard v. Pincus, 200 Fed. 736 (C. C. A. Ga.). Obiter, Bowen & Thomas v. Keller, 22 A. B. R. 727, 130 Ga. 31. Compare, Maas v. Kuhn, 22 A. B. R. 91 (N. Y. Sup. Ct. App. Div.), quoted at § 1102; In re Mitchell, 23 A. B. R. 707, 175 Fed. 877 (D. C. Ga.). Compare, analogous doctrine "Qualified Stay to Permit Creditors to Perfect Rights against Third Parties," §§ 1524, 1914, 2711, 2712.

restraining order should be so modified as to permit the creditor to assert such right as he may have gained by his execution against such property as may be set aside to the bankrupt under his claim for exemption, and the clerk will so modify the order."

Bell *v.* Dawson Grocery Co., 12 A. B. R. 159, 120 Ga. 628: "In the Lockwood case it was held that in cases of this character the court of bankruptcy would withhold the discharge of the bankrupt until a reasonable time had elapsed to give the creditors an opportunity to assert their claims in the proper State tribunal. As the court of bankruptcy has no power to aid or assist the creditors holding waiver notes, it becomes our duty to determine whether the State courts have such power, and whether the proper remedy has been sought in the present case. It is clear that the creditor cannot obtain a common-law judgment against the debtor and levy it upon the property exempted by the trustee. The bankrupt is under the exclusive jurisdiction of the court of bankruptcy, and no creditor would be allowed by that court to prosecute a claim in the State court in order to procure a judgment against the bankrupt. Yet the creditor has legal rights which he is entitled to enforce if he can find a court to enforce them. Our Code declares (Civ. Code 1895, § 4929): 'For every right there shall be a remedy, and every court having jurisdiction of the one may, if necessary, frame the other.' Whenever a person in this State enters into a contract with another whereby he agrees, for a sufficient consideration, to pay money, and in his obligation waives his right of homestead and exemption, this waiver is valid, and the debtor will be thereafter estopped to claim that any of his property is exempt from the judgment founded upon this contract. The waiver becomes in the nature of a security, in that the debt may be made out of any property, owned by the debtor, without regard to any exemption rights which the debtor would have had but for the waiver. In other words where the debtor waives the homestead and exemption, he means that all of his property shall be a security to the creditor for the payment of that debt. This then gives the creditor a legal right to rely upon all of the debtor's property for the payment of the debt. In the present case, as before stated, the creditor could not enforce his claim by a common-law proceeding against the debtor. From this remedy he is precluded by the proceedings in bankruptcy. The debtor has $1,600 worth of property set apart to him. It is or will be in his possession. If it is personal property, he may dispose of it by mere delivery or it may be of such nature as to be consumed in the use. Much of it may be used or destroyed in his hands. In any event, the creditor would lose his rights unless the property could be protected by placing it in the hands of a receiver until the creditor can obtain a judgment which will bind the property. Civ. Code 1895, § 4904, declares: 'A court of equity may appoint a receiver to take possession of and hold subject to the direction of the court, any assets charged with the payment of debts, where there is manifest danger of loss, or destruction, or material injury to those interested.' In the present case it appears that there was great probability of loss and destruction, and consequent injury to the interests of the creditor, if the debtor were given possession of the exempted property. The debtor has no right to complain, for, so far as appears, he voluntarily signed the waiver, and estopped himself to claim any exemption as against the claims of the creditor. The plaintiff gave him credit for the goods, doubtless upon the faith of the waiver. By signing the waiver he obtained the goods. He cannot now say that because he has been adjudicated a bankrupt the waiver amounts to nothing. But it was contended that a court of equity will not appoint a receiver except on the petition of one claiming title or having a lien. This is undoubtedly the general rule, but there are several exceptions. One of these is contained in the section of the Code last above cited. Another will be found in the case of Sanford *v.* Fidelity & Guaranty Co., 116 Ga. 689, 43 S. E. 61, where the whole doctrine is ably discussed by Mr. Justice Chandler, and the cases in our reports collected. It seems to us that the peculiar facts of the present case are clearly such as to authorize a court of equity to grant relief to the creditor. The creditor has no remedy at law. By the proceeding in bankruptcy he has been deprived of his legal remedy, and he should be entitled to relief in a court of equity. The goods exempted are, as above stated, in the nature of a security for the payment of the debt. They were about to go into the hands of the debtor, and, unless equity took jurisdiction, the creditor would be entirely deprived of its rights. It would be inequitable and unconscionable to allow this debtor, after having waived all homestead and exemption, to take these goods as an exemption, sell or dispose of them, eat them up, or squander them while the creditor stood by without relief."

Roden Grocery Co. *v.* Bacon, 13 A. B. R. 251 (C. C. Ala.): In this case a creditor holding notes with waivers of exemption was allowed to prosecute an attachment suit instituted after the debtor's adjudication and to levy the same upon property claimed as exempt, the court saying: "While the creditor holding a waiver note given by a bankrupt has no lien on specified property—in fact, no lien at all—and the debt represented by such note is one within the purview of the Bankrupt Law, to be discharged by proper proceedings thereunder, yet the rights of said creditor are to be so far recognized as to require the withholding of the bankrupt's discharge a reasonable time to permit the creditor to assert in the proper State tribunal his alleged right to subject the exempt property to the satisfaction of his claim. Lockwood *v.* Exchange Bank, 190 U. S. 294, 10 Am. B. R. 107, 23 Sup. Ct. 751, 47 L. Ed. 1061. This being the case, it would seem that it is to the interest of the general creditors that such right should be prosecuted and enforced pending the bankruptcy, and prior to proof of debt to prevent the creditor holding the waiver from taking a dividend on his whole claim from the general assets, and thereafter availing himself of the right resulting from the waiver to proceed against the exempt property.

"As the creditor holding a waiver may proceed to assert his right in a State tribunal pending the proceedings in bankruptcy, it follows that the form his action may take in the State tribunal is of no concern in the bankruptcy court, unless such writs are issued and proceedings had as directly interfere with property passing to the trustee in bankruptcy, or with exempt property not claimed by the bankrupt and in actual custody of the bankruptcy court."

In re Wells, 5 A. B. R. 308, 105 Fed. 762 (D. C. Ark.): "The whole equity of this case, however, is with the vendor, and if he elects to proceed against the bankrupt to enforce the vendor's lien, the court, on application, will withhold the discharge of the bankrupt, if he be otherwise entitled thereto, until the proper tribunal may pass on the question."

Ingram *v.* Wilson, 11 A. B. R. 192, 125 Fed. 913 (C. C. A. Iowa): "A creditor like Wilson, who has the right, under certain conditions, to subject the homestead to the payment of his debt, must seek such relief as he is entitled to under local laws in the courts of the State; and if a discharge of the bankrupt from all his debts, when granted by the bankrupt court, will stand in the way of his obtaining relief, that court, after administering upon all the assets subject to its control, may withhold the bankrupt's discharge until a reasonable time has elapsed to enable Wilson to assert his rights in the proper form."

In re Brumbaugh, 12 A. B. R. 207, 128 Fed. 971 (D. C. Pa.): "There is ground, however, for the present in withholding final action on this sub-

ject. If it be as contended that the bankrupt is not entitled to retain the property which he has exempted, as against the Keim judgment, on the ground that
it is for a tort, the only way to test that question as already intimated, is by
proceedings in the State courts, by issuing execution and levying upon it. But
as the legal effect of a discharge in bankruptcy would be to wipe out the liability (assuming that it is not one of those that are excepted by the act)
the right to execution would be cut off if once the discharge went out. Claster
v. Soble, 10 Am. B. R. 446, 23 Pa. Sup. Ct. 631. The judgment creditor has
therefore a right to ask that a discharge be withheld for the present in order
to enable her to test her rights in the way suggested. This was the course
pointed out and sanctioned in Lockwood v. Exchange Bank, 190 U. S. 294, 10
Am. B. R. 107, already referred to and it will be followed here.

"* * * But the discharge is withheld until the further order of the court,
for the purpose of allowing the excepting creditor to assert in the State court
by appropriate proceedings her alleged right to subject the property exempted
to execution upon the judgment which she has recovered."

In re Castleberry, 16 A. B. R. 161, 143 Fed. 108 (D. C. Ga.): "But under the
ruling of the Supreme Court in Lockwood v. Exchange Bk. the court will refuse a discharge until opportunity can be given to the creditors whose debts are
good against the exemptions, to enforce the same in a court of competent jurisdiction. Of course, where the exemption claimed, as in this case, is in money
held by the trustee, the bankruptcy court would hold the fund and protect it
until proper proceedings can be instituted and the money sequestered by a
court of competent jurisdiction, for the benefit of parties in interest."

Contra, In re Richardson, 11 A. B. R. 379 (Ref. Ala.): "Petition of creditor
praying for stay of bankruptcy proceedings and for leave to prosecute suit in
State Court to establish a lien in his favor upon property claimed by the bankrupt as exempt denied on the ground that the bankruptcy court would afford
the petitioner all the relief it could obtain in a State Court at a great saving
of time and expense; the referee distinguishing the Lockwood case."

And the rule will be the same whether the exemptions have already been
set apart;[82] or have not yet been set apart.[83]

Compare, In re Hartsell & Son, 15 A. B. R. .177, 140 Fed. 30 (D. C. Ala.):
"The reason of the rule in Lockwood's Case, 190 U. S. 294, 10 Am. B. R. 107,
requiring the court to withhold the discharge of a bankrupt, who would otherwise be entitled to it, pending a suit against him on a written obligation for
the payment of. money, which contains a waiver of exemptions of personal
property, has no application whatever to this case. We have here no suit to
enforce any contract as to which there is a waiver of exemptions of personal
property. On the contrary, the suit is in tort for the conversion of a note which
contained a waiver of exemptions.

Such withholding of discharge does not deprive the bankrupt of the benefit
of the discharge when the judgment thereafter is sought to be enforced
against him in personam because the judgment is itself discharged, being, by

---

82. Instance, Lockwood v. Exchange
Bank, 10 A. B. R. 107, 190 U. S. 294;
contra (but before the dictum in the
Lockwood case), Woodruff v. Cheeves,
5 A. B. R. 296, 105 Fed. 601 (C. C. A.
Ga.), in which such stay to permit the
creditor to take action was denied.

83. Contra, In re Richardson, 11 A.
B. R. 379 (Ref. Ala.), in which the referee held the bankruptcy court could
determine such rights before the exemptions were set off.

the express words of § 63 (b) (5), a "provable" debt and hence a discharged debt. Any attempt thereafter to enforce the judgment against the bankrupt could be enjoined.

But the creditor must obtain a stay of the discharge, otherwise the proceedings in rem to fasten a lien on the exempt property will be barred.

Bowen & Thomas *v.* Keller, 22 A. B. R. 727, 130 Ga. 31: "But, if the debtor succeeds in obtaining his discharge and pleads it prior to the fastening of a specific lien on such property, the effect is to release the debtor from the payment of the debt upon which the proceedings are based, and the creditor's right of action is destroyed." Quoted further at § 1106.

Groves *v.* Osburn, 46 Oregon 173, 79 Pac. 500: "After a debtor has been discharged in bankruptcy, a debt cannot be enforced in equity by a proceedings in rem against the homestead set apart in the proceedings in bankruptcy."

Although it has been held in a case where no stay evidently was obtained that the creditor might levy attachment for the purchase price directly on property thus set apart as exempt, it being not exempt as to him.[84]

§ 1105. No Withholding if Exemptions Good against Levy.—Manifestly, the court would not withhold a discharge where the exemptions would prevail, anyway, against the judgment.[85]

§ 1106. Subjecting Exempt Property While in Trustee's Hands, by Equitable Action in State Court.—If the property sought to be subjected is still in the trustee's hands, the proper practice, perhaps, is for the creditor, as to whose judgment it would not be exempt, to subject the property by an equitable action, in which a receiver could be appointed; who then could obtain possession of the property from the trustee, upon application to the bankruptcy court.[87]

Compare, Bell *v.* Dawson Grocery Co., 12 A. B. R. 159, 120 Ga. 628: "As the court of bankruptcy has no power to aid or assist the creditor holding waiver notes, it becomes our duty to determine whether the State courts have such power, and whether the proper remedy has been sought in the present case. It is clear that the creditor cannot obtain a common-law judgment against the debtor and levy it upon the property exempted by the trustee. The bankrupt is under the exclusive jurisdiction of the court of bankruptcy, and no creditor would be allowed by that court to prosecute a claim in the State Court

---

84. Northern Shoe Co. *v.* Cecka, 28 A. B. R. 935, 22 N. Dak. 631; but the court's attention does not seem to have been drawn to the doctrine of this section. Compare *post,* §§ 1107, 1108.

85. But if liens by legal proceedings on exempt property are vacated by bankruptcy (as is sometimes contended to be the rule), then there could be no such advantage given to holders of waivers. Compare reasoning in Klipstein *v.* Allen Miles, 14 A. B. R. 15, 136 Fed. 385 (C. C. A. Ga.).

87. In re Ogilvie, 5 A. B. R. 374 (Ref. Ga.); obiter, In re Brumbaugh, 12 A. B. R. 204 (D. C. Penn.); In re Meredith, 16 A. B. R. 336, 144 Fed. 230 (D. C. Ga.); In re Strickland, 21 A. B. R. 734, 167 Fed. 867 (D. C. Ga.); Bowen & Thomas *v.* Keller, 22 A. B. R. 727, 130 Ga. 31; Brooks *v.* Britt-Carson Shoe Co., 133 Ga. 191, 65 Southeastern 411. Compare, In re Mitchell, 23 A. B. R. 707, 175 Fed. 877 (D. C. Ga.).

in order to procure a judgment against the bankrupt. Yet the creditor has legal rights which he is entitled to enforce if he can find a court to enforce them. * * * It seems to us that the peculiar facts of the present case are clearly such as to authorize a court of equity to grant relief to the creditor. The creditor has no remedy at law. By the proceeding in bankruptcy he has been deprived of his legal remedy, and he should be entitled to relief in a court of equity. The goods exempted are, as above stated, in the nature of a security for the payment of the debt. They were about to go into the hands of the debtor, and, unless equity took jurisdiction, the creditor would be entirely deprived of its rights. It would be inequitable and unconscionable to allow this debtor, after having waived all homestead and exemption, to take these goods as an exemption, sell or dispose of them, eat them up, or squander them, while the creditor stood by without relief. * * * Of course, the State court is without power to take the property out of the hands of the court of bankruptcy, but it can, as was done in the present case, appoint a receiver to take charge of the property as soon as the trustee is ready to turn it over."

Bowen & Thomas v. Keller, 22 A. B. R. 727, 130 Ga. 31: "Whenever creditors of a bankrupt seek, by action in a State court, to subject the exempted property to the payment of debts for which they claim it is liable, the bankruptcy court will withhold the granting of a discharge for the purpose of enabling such creditors to enforce their rights in the State court, when the discharge of the debtor would be a bar to such enforcement. * * * Pending the bankruptcy proceedings, a creditor cannot maintain a suit at law against the debtor to obtain a judgment against him in personam, and the plaintiffs in this case properly brought their action on the equity side of the court for the purpose of obtaining a decree in rem subjecting the property to their debt." Quoted further at § 1104.

Thus it has been held that where the exemption is in cash, and it appears that there are creditors desirous of enforcing liens thereon, it may be retained by the trustee for a reasonable time to enable such creditors to proceed against it.[88]

Amendment of 1910.—What effect the Amendment of 1910 to § 47, by which the trustee is to be deemed vested with all the rights, powers and remedies of a creditor holding a lien by legal or equitable process on property in his custody will have in this regard, has not yet been determined. But there is strong reason for the view that such custody will be a sufficient levy in behalf of the creditors holding special rights upon exempt property.

§ 1107. Levying Attachment or Ordering Surrender to Sheriff Holding Writ.—But, possibly, the bankruptcy court may, by order, permit levy of execution or attachment; or turn the property over to the sheriff holding writs of execution or attachment.[89]

88. In re [J. E.] Maynard & Co., 25 A. B. R. 732, 183 Fed. 823 (D. C. Ga.).

89. In re Durham, 4 A. B. R. 760, 104 Fed. 231 (D. C. Ark.); compare, inferentially, In re Jackson, 8 A. B. R. 596 (D. C. Penn.); compare, inferentially, obiter, Snyder v. Guthrie, 17 A. B. R. 903 (Penn. Com. Pleas). Compare, obiter, In re MacKissac, 22 A. B. R. 817, 171 Fed. 259 (D. C. Pa.); Snyder v. Guthrie, 24 A. B. R. 58 (Pa. Court of Common Pleas). Compare, post, "Dividends Not to Be Subjected by Garnishment," § 2224.

Zumpfe v. Schultz, 20 A. B. R. 916, 35 Pa. Super. Ct. 106: "If the title to the bankrupt's exemption does not pass to the trustee in bankruptcy but remains in the bankrupt and if for this reason, as is pointed out * * * in Sharp v. Woolslare, * * * the trustee is not entitled to the $300 exemption which has been attached within four months preceding bankruptcy, on the ground that the trustee is not entitled thereto, it would seem to follow necessarily that the $300 exemption in the hands of the trustee in bankruptcy, although, as he declares in his answers to interrogatories, it is deposited to the credit of his account as trustee, does not belong to the creditors but is still the property of the bankrupt. If this be so, and we think a consideration of the authorities referred to in the case last cited leads to such a conclusion, we are unable to see why the attachment execution attaching the money in the hands of the trustee in bankruptcy, as garnishee, upon a judgment in which the bankrupt waived the benefit of the exemption, is not good and, if so, why the entry of judgment in favor of the plaintiff, against the garnishee, upon his answers admitting that the money was in his hands allowed the defendant in lieu of his exemption was deposited to his credit as trustee, was not proper and legal."

Under the doctrine of one case, indeed, it was held, before the Amendment of 1910 to Bankr. Act., § 47 (a), (2), that the bankruptcy itself operated as a levy upon exempt property in its actual custody in behalf of the creditors holding waiver claims, or claims for unpaid purchase price.[90]

In re Campbell, 10 A. B. R. 731, 124 Fed. 417 (D. C. Va.): "I have not overlooked the contention that the excepting creditors have no standing, because they are not armed with executions against the bankrupt. This contention is founded on the language of the State Homestead Law 'shall hold exempt from levy, seizure, garnishment or sale under any execution, order or process.' Under proceedings in bankruptcy the property is in effect seized or levied upon as much in behalf of non-judgment creditors as of any party in interest. In a voluntary case the debtor surrenders his property, and when he claims some or all of it as exempt, he is asking that such property be not 'sold' under judicial 'process' or 'order.'"

Amendment of 1910.—However, the Amendment of 1910 to § 47, whereby the trustee is to be deemed vested with all the rights, remedies and powers of a creditor holding a lien by legal or equitable proceedings upon property in his custody, or coming into his custody, may sufficiently operate as a levy in behalf of the creditors holding waiver claims or claims for unpaid purchase price.

§ 1108. Levying Direct Execution, after Exempt Property Set Apart.

—And, perhaps, after the exempt property has been set apart, levy of execution may be made directly on the property, if judgment has already been obtained; at least, that seems to be the holding in some jurisdictions.[91]

First Nat'l Bk. v. Bartlett, 21 A. B. R. 88, 35 Pa. Super. Ct. 593: "After such appraisal and setting apart, it is very clear that the execution issued like the

90. See discussion, post, § 1212. See ante, § 1035.

91. Gregory Co. v. Cale, 27 A. B. R. 131 (Sup. Ct. Minn.).

one in the present case is under the control of the State courts, and we cannot see that it is material whether such execution issued before or after the proceedings in bankruptcy."

In re Weaver, 16 A. B. R. 265, 144 Fed. 229 (D. C. Ga.): "* * * as determined in McKenney v. Cheney, supra, and rightly determined, I think, the discharge in bankruptcy would be no bar to the enforcement of such judgment against exempt property. * * * Besides this, it is manifest that the intention of the court, in Lockwood v. Exchange Bank, was to give the creditors holding waiver notes, and without judgment, an opportunity to reduce their claims to judgment. For this purpose, it was indicated that a postponement of the discharge would be proper. It does not apply in my opinion, to judgment creditors whose rights, whatever they may be, have already been fixed by the rendition of a judgment, when that judgment appears to have become as in this case, a finality between the parties. In this case the judgment creditor came into the bankruptcy court, proved his debt, and then, by leave of the court, was allowed to withdraw his debt from proof in the bankruptcy proceeding, for the express purpose of enforcing his judgment outside of the bankruptcy court."

But if the judgment were obtained before the adjudication of bankruptcy it is difficult to see why the bankrupt could not interpose his discharge.

But it has been held, in a case where there was no judgment first obtained, that the property set apart might be attached, as, for example, for its purchase price.

Northern Shoe Co. v. Cecka, 28 A. B. R. 935 (Sup. Ct. N. Dak.): "The fact that the plaintiff, after the adjudication in bankruptcy, abandoned attachment proceedings instituted by him within four months prior thereto and filed his claim thereafter as a general creditor does not constitute a waiver of his right to attach, or estop him from subsequently attaching property, in an action for the purchase price, after the same has been set apart to the debtor by the bankruptcy court as exempt."

SUBDIVISION "H."

REVIEW OF EXEMPTION MATTERS.[92]

§ 1109. "Appeal" Not Proper in Exemption Matters.—Appeal will not lie to revise an order relative to exemptions, for the disposition of exempted property is a "proceedings in bankruptcy" proper, and is not a mere "controversy arising in bankruptcy proceedings," and hence, not being within those cases of bankruptcy proceedings enumerated in § 25 wherein appeal is allowable, can be revised only by petition for review, under § 24 (b).

Ingram v. Wilson, 11 A. B. R. 192, 125 Fed. 913 (C. C. A. Iowa): "We are of opinion, however, that the order in question is an order made in the course

92. As to appeal or error proceedings in general relative to exemptions, see post, § 2864, et seq., subject, "Appeal and Error Proceedings." Also, §§ 2906, 2930.

of a bankruptcy proceeding, which this court is empowered to revise on a petition for review by virtue of § 24 of the Bankruptcy Act. It is not one of those cases in which an appeal in the ordinary form is expressly authorized by § 25 of the Bankrupt Act."

Likewise an order of the District Court allowing or refusing an exemption claim is not a "final decision allowing or rejecting a claim" within the meaning of § 25 (b) and an appeal from the Circuit Court of Appeals to the Supreme Court does not lie;[93] nor does direct appeal from the District Court to the Supreme Court lie;[94] nor is a judgment of the Supreme Court of a State giving due force to an order of the bankruptcy court setting apart exemptions reviewable by the United States Supreme Court.[95]

§ 1110. But "Review" under § 24 (b) Proper.—But review under § 24 (b) is a proper remedy.[96]

§ 1111. No Review unless Trustee Appointed Who Has Set Apart or Refused to Set Apart.—It would seem that there can be no review unless a trustee has been appointed;[96a] has set apart the exemptions;[97] or has refused to set apart any exemption.

§ 1111½. Miscellaneous Rulings on Review of Exemption Matters.—A bankrupt will not be heard on review of an order disallowing exemptions where he himself takes no exceptions but a creditor takes exception as to the distribution of the abandoned exemptions between prior and subsequent creditors; for review by one party upon one point does not necessarily bring up the entire case as to all parties.[98]

---

93. Holden v. Stratton, 10 A. B. R. 786, 191 U. S. 115.

94. Lucius v. Cawthon-Coleman Co., 13 A. B. R. 696, 196 U. S. 149.

95. Smalley v. Langenour, 13 A. B. R. 692, 196 U. S. 93.

96. See §§ 2866, 2906, 2930. Duncan v. Ferguson-McKinney Co., 18 A. B. R. 156, 150 Fed. 269 (C. C. A. Tex.); Smalley v. Langenour, 13 A. B. R. 692, 196 U. S. 93; Ingram v. Wilson, 11 A. B. R. 192, 125 Fed. 913 (C. C. A. Iowa); instance, Citizens Bk. of Douglas v. Hargraves, 21 A. B. R. 323, 164 Fed. 613 (C. C. A. Ga.); In re Goodman, 23 A. B. R. 504, 174 Fed. 644 (C. C. A. Ala.).

96a. Compare ante, § 1073.

97. In re Smith, 2 A. B. R. 190, 93 Fed. 791 (D. C. Tex.). An appeal, without cross appeal only brings up the grievance of the party appealing, so where the court sustains in part and overrules in part the creditor's exceptions to the trustee's report of exempt property and the creditor alone appeals, the bankrupt filing no cross appeal, the case can only be considered upon the points wherein the court has overruled the creditor's exceptions. McGahan v. Anderson, 7 A. B. R. 641, 113 Fed. 115 (C. C. A. S. C.).

98. In re Cohn, 22 A. B. R. 761, 171 Fed. 568 (D. C. N. Dak.). Compare also, post, § 2834, "Appeal by One Party Does Not Necessarily Bring Up Case as to All."

CHAPTER XXVIII.

How Title Vests in Trustee.

Synopsis of Chapter.

§ 1112. Title Vests in Trustee by Operation of Law.—Title vests in the trustee by operation of law;[1] that is to say, in every part of the world over which the laws of the United States are paramount, the bankrupt's adjudication, in and of itself, without any assignment, transfer or other act of the bankrupt, operates to divest him of all title and to vest it in the trustee of his creditors.[2]

In re Friedrich, 3 A. B. R. 803, 100 Fed. 284 (C. C. A. Wis.): "The title to the property of the bankrupt is vested in the trustee, not by conveyance but by operation of the law."

Under the law of 1841 title also vested by operation of law; but under the law of 1867 a formal conveyance or deed of assignment was requisite to vest title in the assignee in bankruptcy.[3]

As to the statute of 1867, Hiscock v. Varick Bk., 206 U. S. 28, 18 A. B. R. 9: "By the Act of 1867, it was provided that as soon as an assignee was appointed and qualified the judge or register should, by instrument, assign or convey to him all of the property of the bankrupt, and such assignment shall relate back to the commencement of the proceedings in bankruptcy, and by operation of law shall vest the title to such estate both real and personal, in the assignee."

§ 1113. Scheduling by Bankrupt Not Essential to Passing of Title.—Title passes even if the property is not scheduled, so that failure of the bankrupt to schedule property will not prevent its title passing to the trustee and the bankrupt does not retain title by omitting it from the sched-

---

1. Bankr. Act, § 70 (a); Hiscock v. Varick Bank, 18 A. B. R. 9, 206 U. S. 28; (1867) Markson & Spalding v. Heaney, 4 N. B. Reg. 165; In re Wiseman & Wallace, 20 A. B. R. 293, 159 Fed. 236 (D. C. Pa.); Fourth St. Nat. Bk. v. Millbourne Mills Co., 22 A. B. R. 442, 172 Fed. 177 (C. C. A. Pa.), quoted at § 1253½; In re Frazin & Oppenheim, 23 A. B. R. 289, 174 Fed. 713 (D. C. N. Y.), quoted at § 1120.

In the case In re Baird, 11 A. B. R. 435, 126 Fed. 845 (D. C. Va.), the court seems to think that where the trustee is subrogated to the lien of attaching creditors in behalf of the estate under § 67 "f," the title is not conferred by operation of law but by order of court. Yet the order of court is merely supplementary to § 67 (e), rendering effective the provisions of § 67 (e), giving to the trustee the right to avoid any transfer which any creditor might have avoided.

2. Hull v. Burr, 26 A. B. R. 897 (Sup. Ct. Fla.).

3. Rand v. Iowa Cent. Ry. Co., 12 A. B. R. 164, 96 App. Div. (N. Y.) 413 (reversed, on other grounds, in 16 A. B. R. 692).

ules.[4] But the defendant, sued by the bankrupt on a cause of action belonging to the estate, but omitted from the schedules, may not, where no trustee has yet been appointed plead that the bankrupt is not the real party in interest.[5]

§ 1114. Property in Foreign Countries Requires Assignment by Bankrupt.

—Of course property outside of the jurisdiction of the United States is controlled by the laws of the country where it is situated. The law of nations, whilst recognizing the common contractual obligations of men and enforcing the ordinary voluntary agreements and conveyances of men, pays no heed to the provisions of the various bankruptcy laws of the several nations and does not oblige one nation to recognize the bankruptcy laws of another nation. And title by operation of law naturally is not to be recognized out of the territory wherein the law is operative. So it is that when it comes to property located in foreign countries the courts of those countries do not recognize the passing of the title by the mere adjudication of bankruptcy in this country. Consequently they require evidence by way of the more common and universal instruments of voluntary conveyances such as deeds, bills of sale, etc., recognized all over the world, before they will acknowledge the title of the bankruptcy trustee. To that end, therefore, as also to aid in the transfer of title to property in this country, the bankrupt may be required to execute papers of transfer.[6]

§ 1115. Bankrupt Compelled to Execute Assignments and Other Papers to Aid Passing of Title.

—Thus it is that the bankrupt may be required to execute assignments and other papers to aid in effecting the transfer of title to the trustee.[7]

Fisher v. Cushman, 4 A. B. R. 646, 103 Fed. 867 (C. C. A. Mass.): "There can be no question of jurisdiction, inasmuch as the proceedings have taken

4. See ante. § 483. Rand v. Iowa Cent. Ry. Co., 12 A. B. R. 164, 96 App. Div. 413 (reversed, on other grounds, in 16 A. B. R. 692, 186 N. Y. 58); instance, In re Kranich, 23 A. B. R. 550, 174 Fed. 908 (D. C. Pa.).

5. Rand v. Iowa Cent. Ry. Co., 16 A. B. R. 692, 186 N. Y. 58 (reversing 12 A. B. R. 164, 96 App. Div. 413); First Nat'l Bk. v. Lasater, 13 A. B. R. 698, 196 U. S. 115, quoted at § 935.
Concealed Property Does Not Revest in Bankrupt on Closing of Estate. —Assets, concealed by the bankrupt do not, on the closing of the estate, revest in him. Fowler v. Jenks, 11 A. B. R. 255 (Minn.).

6. Bankr. Act, § 7 (a) (5).

7. Bankr. Act, § 7 (a): "The bankrupt shall * * * (4) execute and deliver such papers as shall be ordered by the court; (5) execute to his trustee transfers of all his property in foreign countries." See ante, §§ 460, 969, 1009; post, § 1835.

Instances.—1. Order to assign insurance policy to trustee when bankrupt previous to the bankruptcy had already assigned it to a third person. The order is not reviewable. In re Madden, 6 A. B. R. 614, 110 Fed. 348 (C. C. A. N. Y.). This case was decided long prior to the Supreme Court's ruling that policies of life insurance are not assets, see ante, § 1002, et seq.

2. Order to assign commissions on renewal premiums accruing after bankruptcy, although original contract one involving personal trust and not itself assignable. In re Wright, 18 A. B. R. 198, 202, 151 Fed. 361 (D. C. N. Y.).

3. Order on bankrupt to assign his contingent interest in an insurance policy to the trustee to enable the trustee to give title upon a sale. In

place in the case in which she was adjudged bankrupt, and the court therefore clearly had the power to proceed summarily for the purpose of merely compelling her to give her signature on the transfer of the license."

In re Hurlbutt, Hatch & Co., 13 A. B. R. 54, 135 Fed. 504 (C. C. A. N. Y.): "The general power of courts of equity to compel a transfer and sale of such personal privileges as patents and trade marks is asserted in Ager *v.* Murray, 105 U. S. 126, 131. The power of the court to require a bankrupt to execute the instruments necessary to effectuate the sale of a personal and exclusive right has been exercised in the cases of the transfer of liquor licenses * * * of a license of a stall in a market * * * and of a seat in the New York Stock Exchange under the Bankruptcy Act of 1867. * * *

"If there were any doubt as to the general power of the District Court to make such order, it would be resolved by the provisions of the Bankruptcy Act empowering courts of bankruptcy to * * * § 2 (7); * * * § 2 (15); * * * § 7 (4)."

In re Wright, 18 A. B. R. 198, 292, 151 Fed. 361 (D. C. N. Y.): "* * * this court has power to compel the bankrupt to execute a transfer thereof to the trustee in bankruptcy for the benefit of his creditors."

re Coleman, 14 A. B. R. 461, 136 Fed. 818 (C. C. A. N. Y.); In re Diack, 3 A. B. R. 723, 100 Fed. 770 (D. C. N. Y.); In re Wolff, 21 A. B. R. 452, 165 Fed. 984 (D. C. N. Y.).

4. Order to assign contingent interest in tontine policy payable to wife if bankrupt dies before expiration of tontine period and also to execute power of attorney to exercise options at end of tontine period. In re Phelps, 15 A. B. R. 170 (Ref. N. Y.).

5. Order to assign cause of action for wrongful death subject to lien for funeral expenses advanced on faith of it by wife where bankrupt is the beneficiary. In re Burnstine, 12 A. B. R. 596, 131 Fed. 828 (D. C. Mich.).

6. Order to sign request to Stock Exchange for sale of seat and payment of proceeds to trustee in bankruptcy. In re Hurlbutt, Hatch & Co., 13 A. B. R. 50, 135 Fed. 504 (C. C. A. N. Y.); (1867) In re Ketcham, 1 Fed. 840.

7. Transfer of liquor license. In re Fisher, 3 A. B. R. 406, 98. Fed. 89 (D. C. Mass., affirmed in 4 A. B. R. 646); In re Becker, 3 A. B. R. 412, 98 Fed. 407 (D. C. Penn.); In re Wiesel & Knaup, 23 A. B. R. 59, 173 Fed. 718 (D. C. Pa.).

8. Transfer of license to stall in market. In re Emrich, 4 A. B. R. 89, 101 Fed. 231 (D. C. Penn.).

9. No right to order third person, joint owner with bankrupt, to join in making transfer. In re Brodbine, 2 A. B. R. 53, 93 Fed. 643 (D. C. Mass.).

Third persons claiming interest in the subject and entering appearance in opposition to the application for an order requiring the bankrupt so to execute assignments or other papers, thereby consent to the jurisdiction and are bound. In re Emrich, 4 A. B. R. 89, 101 Fed. 231 (D. C. Penn.): "In determining the nature of this license, and whether it should be transferred to the trustee, it had the right to call before it all parties concerned in that question, and dispose of all incidental questions. * * * Whatever her answer to the rule might be, it is clear it could not divest the court's jurisdiction of the original subject-matter. Whether she could thus be brought in by rule, and her claim determined by this means, if objected to, is a question not now before us, and upon which we express no opinion. Suffice it to say, she has submitted herself to the jurisdiction of the court, has invited its action upon her rights, and, having taken the chance of a favorable decision by the referee, she cannot now for the first time complain of lack of jurisdiction when the decision is adverse." Compare, inferentially, Fisher *v.* Cushman, 4 A. B. R. 646, 103 Fed. 867 (C. C. A. Mass.).

The bankrupt may also be required to disclose to the trustee the combination of his safe. So, also, may the officer of a bankrupt corporation. In re Smelting Co., 15 A. B. R. 83, 138 Fed. 954 (D. C. Penn.).

10. Requiring individual partner not adjudicated bankrupt to transfer his individual interest in real estate of bankrupt firm to firm trustee. In re Latimer, 23 A. B. R. 388, 174 Fed. 824 (D. C. Pa.).

CHAPTER XXIX.

WHEN TITLE VESTS; AND STATUS OF PROPERTY AFTER FILING OF PETITION.

Synopsis of Chapter.

DIVISION 1.

DIVISION 2.

DIVISION 3.

SUBDIVISION "A".

DIVISION 1.

WHEN TITLE VESTS.

§ 1116. Title Vests in Trustee upon Appointment, etc., but Relates Back to Adjudication.—Title vests in the trustee for creditors, upon his appointment and qualification, but then relates back to the date of the bankrupt's adjudication.[1]

1. Bankr. Act, § 70 (a). Hiscock v. Varick Bk., 18 A. B. R. 9, 206 U. S. 28; In re Burka, 5 A. B. R. 12, 104 Fed. 326 (D. C. Mo.); obiter, Van Kirk v. Slate Co., 15 A. B. R. 239, 140 Fed. 38 (D. C. N. Y.). In re Elmira Steel Co., 5 A. B. R. 487, 109 Fed. 486 (Special Master N. Y.); In re Harris, 2 A. B. R. 359 (Ref. Ills.); In re Letson, 19 A. B. R. 506, 157 Fed. 78 (C. C. A. Okla.); In re Frazin & Oppenheim, 23 A. B. R. 289, 174 Fed. 713 (D. C. N. Y.), quoted at § 1120; Crowe v. Baumann, 27 A. B. R. 100, 190 Fed. 399 (D. C. N. Y.); Lovell v. Newman & Son, 27 A. B. R. 746, 188 Fed. 534 (C. C. La.); In re Hurley, 26 A. B. R. 434, 185 Fed. 851 (D. C. Mass.).

And a chattel mortgagee will be too late to take possession of after-acquired property after adjudication of bankruptcy though before the appointment of the trustee. In re Hurley, 26 A. B. R. 434, 185 Fed. 851 (D. C. Mass.).

Under English Bankruptcy Law Trustee's Title Relates to Date of Commission of Act of Bankruptcy.— Under English law, from the very beginning, the title of the trustee vests upon his appointment and qualification, but then relates back to the date of the commission of the act of bankruptcy on which the adjudication was based. If there are several acts of bankruptcy, then it relates back to the first act of bankruptcy. Indeed, upon actual proof of an even earlier act of bankruptcy than that upon which the adjudication is based, the title of the trustee will be held to relate back to that earlier (and unadjudicated) act of bankruptcy, although the commission of such earlier act of bankruptcy will be disputable. Where the act of bankruptcy is a continuing act, the trustee's title will relate back to the conclusion of the act. See Ex parte Learoyd, In re Foulds, L. R. 10 Chancery Div. (1878-9) 3; The singer, L. J.: "The question in dispute is as to the time in which the title of the trustee in the bankruptcy properly and legally relates back. If it relates back to the 31st of December it is admitted that the title of the trustee is good as against the holder of the bill of sale, he having taken no apparent possession of the property until the 1st of January. I am of the opinion that we a e bound by the terms of the Act of

1869 to hold that the bankruptcy did commence on the 31st of December. The adjudication was made on the 3rd day of January and it was made upon a petition which stated that the debtor being a trader, departed from his dwelling house on the 31st day of December with intent to defeat or delay his creditors. * * *

"In language clear and distinct the Legislature has said by § 11 [Act of 1883, § 43] that 'the bankruptcy of a debtor shall be deemed to have relation back to and to commence at the time of the act of bankruptcy being completed on which the order is made adjudging him to be bankrupt.'

"It has been suggested that this does not relate to outsiders. If it does not, it has not been pointed out to whom it does relate, nor how, if we are not to construe the words literally, we are to construe them. But the latter part of the section shows clearly that it must relate to outsiders, for it shows that it refers to any case of dispute between the trustee and a person against whom there may be a claim on behalf of the bankrupt's estate. * * *

"The Legislature, for the general convenience of the administration of the bankrupt's estate, has fixed a datum line for the commencement of the trustee's title—viz, the act of bankruptcy on which the adjudication is founded, leaving it open to the trustee to prove, if he can, earlier acts of bankruptcy. No doubt a certain amount of hardship will result from this construction. But the answer to that is, that it is open to any person aggrieved by the adjudication to apply to the Court to annul it. And there is this further answer that in the administration of bankruptcy the interests of individual creditors have to bow to the interests of the general body of creditors, and we must, therefore, expect to find some cases of hardship."

Also see Eden on Bankrupt Law (Eng.) 258, reprinted in 1841, from the edition of 1826: Chapter XV. "Relation to the Act of Bankruptcy," § 1.

Former Enactments.—By the doctrine of relation according to its original severity, as established by the 13 Eliz. C. 7, from the moment of committing an act of bankruptcy, the trader was deprived of all power of charging or disposing of his property to the prej-

§ 1117. Date of Cleavage of Estates.

§ **1117. Date of Cleavage of Estates.**—The date of cleavage between the old and new estates of the bankrupt is the date of the filing of the petition.[1a]

Everett *v.* Judson, 228 U. S. 474, 30 A. B. R. 1: "We think that the purpose of the law was to fix the line of cleavage with reference to the condition of the bankrupt estate as of the time at which the petition was filed, and that the property which vests in the trustee at the time of adjudication is that which the bankrupt owned at the time of the filing of the petition. And it is of that date that the surrender value of the insurance policy mentioned in § 70(a) should be ascertained. The subsequent suicide of the bankrupt before the adjudication was an unlooked for circumstance which does not change the result in the light of the construction which we give the statute."

In re Judson, 27 A. B. R. 704, 192 Fed. 834 (C. C. A. N. Y., affirmed sub nom Everett *v.* Judson, 228 U. S. 474, 30 A. B. R. 1): "Referring to the language of the provision in question as shown in the footnote [§ 70 (a)] it seems clear that a trustee in bankruptcy takes title as of the date of the adjudication, not to the property owned by the bankrupt at that time, but to the property owned at the time of the filing of the petition. The trustee's title vests, it is true, as of the date of the adjudication, but the title which vests is limited to the property belonging to the bankrupt at the time of the commencement of the proceedings—the filing of the petition. The one date determines when the title vests; the other, the property to which the title vests. Property acquired by the bankrupt after the filing of the petition is not—to use the language of the act—property which 'prior to the filing of the petition he could by any means have transferred.' We think it clear that the time of the filing of the petition in this case should be taken as the date of cleavage determining the property passing to the trustee and through him to the creditors."

Pratt *v.* Bothe, 12 A. B. R. 533, 130 Fed. 670 (C. C. A. Mich.): "The Bank-

udice of his creditors. After the commission issued, though no property vested in the commissioners, yet they had power of assigning everything he had in himself, or such interest as he might part with at the time he became bankrupt. When this power was executed by assignment the property became vested in the assignees by relation from the time of the act of bankruptcy. The consequence was, that all alienations or dispositions of property made after that time were void. * * * "The hardship of a doctrine like this was so great, that the legislature has been from time to time relaxing its severity; and by the new act (1861) a still further relief has been afforded to persons dealing bona fide with the bankrupt. * * *

"The chronological account of these enactments is as follows:

"By the 1 Joe. 1 C. 15, s. 14, no debtor to the bankrupt was to be endangered for the payment of his debt to the bankrupt without notice of an act of bankruptcy.

"By the 21 Joe. * * * .

"By the 19 George 2 c. 19 s. 14 pay-

ments by the bankrupt to creditors in respect of goods really and bona fide sold to such bankrupt, or in respect of any bills of exchange, in the usual or ordinary course of trade or dealing, were protected, provided the party had no notice of an act of bankruptcy, or that he was in insolvent circumstances.

"By the 46 Geo. 3 C. 135, S. 1 and the 49 Geo. 2 C. 121, S. 2 all conveyances by, all payments to, and all contracts and other dealings and transactions by and with the bankrupt, and all executions and attachments two months before a commission were declared valid."

1a. Burlingham *v.* Crouse, 228 U S. 459, 30 A. B. R. 6 (affirming 24 A. B. R. 632, 181 Fed. 479), quoted ante at §§ 1002, 1003, 1016; also, Andrews *v.* Partridge, 228 U. S. 479, 30 A. B. R. 4 (reversing Partridge *v.* Andrews, 27 A. B. R. 388, 191 Fed. 325, C. C. A. N. J.); compare, instructive obiter, In re Youngstrom, 18 A. B. R. 572, 153 Fed. 97 (C. C. A. Colo.), quoted at § 1025; In re Waite-Robbins Motor Co., 27 A. B. R. 541, 192 Fed. 47 (D. C. Mass.).

ruptcy Act makes a final and sharply determined line in respect of the power
of the bankrupt over his estate and the distribution of it as of the date of the
filing of the petition against him.   From that time his assets are in gremio
legis, and he cannot, unless he compounds with his creditors, bind his assets.
He may, of course, make new contracts and incur new obligations, but they
are not chargeable to the funds which have become vested in the trustee until
they have subserved the purpose of the bankruptcy proceedings, when, if anything remains, he reacquires it."

In re Waite Robbins Motor Co., 27 A. B. R. 541, 192 Fed. 47 (D. C. Mass.):
"The bankrupt's property passed to the trustee as it stood on January 13th,
1911, under the adjudication made January 30th, 1911, upon the involuntary petition in this case filed January 13th, 1911."

By some decisions before the Supreme Court announced its conclusions
in Everett v. Judson, etc., the date was held to be the date of adjudication.[2]

Under the law of 1867 the date of cleavage was the date of the filing of
the petition.[3]

Upon the filing of the petition, in general, all power of inchoate rights to
become consummated or vested rights ceases;[4] save and except dower rights
which constitute, in law, actual though inchoate interests in land and which
are specially excepted by § 8.[5] At the day of adjudication, however, and not
until then does the title to the property leave the bankrupt and vest in his
creditors though then it relates only to such property as was in existence
at the date of the filing of the petition.

§ 1118. Contractual Relations Not Dissolved.—But, as already
noted, merely contractual relations are not dissolved nor put an end to by
the adjudication in bankruptcy, nor by the bankrupt's discharge; they continue in full force, except in so far as they may have become merged in
"provable" claims.[6]

§ 1118½. Disregarding Fractions of Day.—It has been held that
fractions of a day are not to be disregarded when it comes to the acquisi-

---

2. Impliedly, Hiscock v. Varick Bk.,
18 A. B. R. 9, 206 U. S. 28; inferen-
tially, In re McKensie, 13 A. B. R.
229, 132 Fed. 986 (D. C. Ark.); In re
Burka, 5 A. B. R. 12, 104 Fed. 326 (D.
C. Mo.); compare, State Bank v. Cox,
16 A. B. R. 36, 143 Fed. 91 (C. C. A.
Ills.); In re Elmira Steel Co., 5 A. B.
R. 487, 109 Fed. 486 (Special Master
N. Y.); In re Duncan, 17 A. B. R. 289,
148 Fed. 464 (D. C. S. Car.); In re
Harris, 2 A. B. R. 359 (Ref. Ills.);
impliedly, Atchison, etc., R. Co. v.
Hurley, 18 A. B. R. 396, 153 Fed. 503
(C. C. A. Kans.), quoted at § 1144;
impliedly, In re Hurley, 26 A. B. R.
434, 185 Fed. 851 (D. C. Mass.); Bank
of Nez Perce v. Pindel, 28 A. B. R. 69,
193 Fed. 917 (C. C. A. Idaho).

Fines falling due under a building

and loan association mortgage after
adjudication cannot be collected from
the mortgagor's trustee in bankruptcy.
In re Davis, 25 A. B. R. 1, 180 Fed.
148 (D. C. N. Y.), quoted at § 451.

3. In re Rennie, 2 A. B. R. 182 (Ref.
Ind. Ter.); Hiscock v. Varick Bk., 18
A. B. R. 9, 206 U. S. 28.

4. Compare Hawk v. Hawk, 4 A.
B. R. 463, 102 Fed. 679 (D. C. Ark.),
where the court refused to enjoin distribution of a bankrupt's estate until
the bankrupt's wife could get a divorce, she being entitled, under the
State law to one-third absolutely of
his personal property on divorce.

5. See ante, § 99, et seq.

6. See ante, §§ 451, 653. See post,
§ 2662, et seq., "Effect of Discharge
on the Rights of the Parties."

tion of property; thus, not to be disregarded but to reserve to the bankrupt property acquired by him on the day he filed his voluntary petition, but before the hour of filing; as, for example, legacies.[7]

Yet it has been held proper in favor of the trustee in bankruptcy to disregard fractions of a day where a bank claimed the right of offsetting a deposit against the bankrupt's note, notwithstanding the deposit actually was made more than an hour before the filing of the bankruptcy petition, the right of offset being thus held not to have arisen, since the debts were not mutually existent before the filing.[8]

DIVISION 2.

STATUS OF PROPERTY AFTER FILING OF PETITION.

§ 1119. Filing of Petition an Assertion of Jurisdiction.—The filing of the petition is an assertion of jurisdiction and operates as an attachment upon all property in the control of the bankrupt and also as a caveat and injunction.[9]

Acme Harvester Co. *v.* Beekman Co., 27 A. B. R. 262, 222 U. S. 300: "The filing of the petition is an assertion of jurisdiction with a view to the determination of the status of the bankrupt and a settlement and distribution of his estate. The exclusive jurisdiction of the bankruptcy court is so far *in rem* that the estate is regarded as in *custodia legis* from the filing of the petition. It is true that under § 70a of the act of 1898 the trustee of the estate, on his appointment and qualification, is vested by operation of law with the title of the bankrupt as of the date he was adjudicated a bankrupt; but there are many provisions of the law which show its purpose to hold the property of the bankrupt intact from the time of the filing of the petition, in order that it may be administered under the law if an adjudication in bankruptcy shall follow the beginning of the proceedings." Quoted further at § 1126.

§ 1120. But Title Does Not Vest until Trustee's Qualification, Title Meanwhile in Bankrupt.—But title does not vest until the trustee's qualification;[10] meanwhile in law the title, although defeasible, remains in the bankrupt.[11]

In re Enge, 5 A. B. R. 372, 105 Fed. 893 (D. C. Pa.): "While it is true that during the interval between the adjudication and the appointment of the trustee the title to the property remains in the bankrupt, but liable to be divested

---

7. See ante, analogously, § 188; also, see In re Stoner, 5 A. B. R. 402, 105 Fed. 752 (D. C. Pa.); In re McKenna, 15 A. B. R. 4, 137 Fed. 611 (D. C. N. Y.), in which case the bankrupt's father died at 8:45 A. M. and the bankrupt filed his petition at 10:00 A. M. of the same day, although the petition had been sworn to several days prior thereto.

8. Compare, post, § 1172. Also Moore *v.* Third Natl. Bk. of Phila., 24 A. B. R. 568 (Pa. Super. Ct.).

9. Compare post, § 1270 9-10. Maxim, That Filing of Petition. A "Caveat, Attachment and Injunction;" also, see Sexton *v.* Dreyfus, 219 U. S. 339, 25 A. B. R. 363.

10. Bankr. Act, § 70 (a). Rand *v.* Iowa Cent. Ry. Co., 16 A. B. R. 697, 186 N. Y. 58.

11. Whittlesay *v.* Becker & Co., 25 A. B. R. 672 (Sup. Ct. N. Y.).

upon the appointment of such trustee, and no permanent lien can be acquired upon it."

Rand *v.* Railway Co., 16 A. B. R. 697, 186 N. Y. 58 (reversing Rand *v.* Railway Co., 12 A. B. R. 164): "It is apparent from the record that the omission to appoint a trustee must have been due to the failure of the plaintiff to disclose the existence either of this claim or any other property in the bankruptcy proceedings. While the concealment of any property on the part of a bankrupt must be deemed a reprehensible act as toward his creditors it by no means follows that such concealment has any bearing upon the question as to whether the bankruptcy proceedings have gone far enough to divest the bankrupt of title. In our judgment the proceedings in the case of the plaintiff had not progressed sufficiently to deprive him of the right to maintain an action in his own name in the State Court upon the claim in suit. The Bankruptcy Act of 1898 (§ 70) provides that the trustee of the estate of a bankrupt upon his appointment and qualification shall be vested by operation of law with the title of the bankrupt as of the date he was adjudged bankrupt. It is plain that this provision can never become effective until a trustee in bankruptcy shall have been appointed. Here none was appointed, hence the conditions did not exist which were requisite to render this provision of § 70 operative."

Gordon *v.* Mech. & Traders Ins. Co., 22 A. B. R. 649, 120 La. Ann. 441, 45 So. 384: "Under the bankruptcy law there is no change of title until the trustee is actually appointed and qualified, whatever may be its retroactive effect when it is actually accomplished."

Compare, Boonville Bk. *v.* Blakey, 6 A. B. R. 13, 107 Fed. 891: "If in any sense a trustee, he [the receiver] is trustee for the bankrupt, in whom is the title of the property until it passes by operation of law, as of the date of adjudication to the trustee selected by the creditors."

Compare, In re Frazin & Oppenheim, 23 A. B. R. 289, 174 Fed. 713 (D. C. N. Y.): "I think that the correct view in this matter is that the condition of a bankrupt's property, after the adjudication and before the appointment of a trustee, is analogous to the condition of the personal property of a decedent before the appointment of an executor or administrator. Bankruptcy [adjudication] like death divests the owner of the title. It becomes thereupon in custodia legis. Upon the appointment of a trustee he takes title by relation back, as of the date of the adjudication."

But the creditors acquire a right *in rem* against the assets the moment the petition in bankruptcy has been filed.[12]

§ 1121. Bankrupt Quasi Trustee until Receiver or Trustee Appointed.

—The bankrupt himself is quasi trustee of the property and its custodian and caretaker until a trustee, receiver or some other officer of the court is appointed.[13]

12. Sexton *v.* Dreyfus, 25 A. B. R. 363, 219 U. S. 339. To same effect, Acme Harvester Co. *v.* Beekman, 222 U. S. 300, 27 A. B. R. 262, quoted at § 1119; also to same effect compare discussion ante, §§ 1002, 1003, 1004 and 1117.

13. See ante, § 383. Impliedly, Acme Harvester Co. *v.* Beekman, 222 U. S. 300, 27 A. B. R. 262, quoted at § 1119; also to same effect, ante, §§ 1002, 1003, 1004 and 1117; In re Wil-

son. 6 A. B. R. 287, 289, 108 Fed. 197 (D. C. Va.); inferentially, In re Allen, 3 A. B. R. 38, 96 Fed. 512 (D. C. Calif.); impliedly, State Bank *v.* Cox, 16 A. B. R. 36, 143 Fed. 91 (C. C. A. Ills.); compare, Rand *v.* Iowa Central Ry. Co., 12 A. B. R. 164, 96 App. Div. 413 (reversed on ground that bankrupt nevertheless not divested of sufficient title to maintain suit in own name, 16 A. B. R. 692, 186 N. Y. 58).

Johnson v. Collier, 222 U. S. 538, 27 A. B. R. 454: "While for many purposes the filing of the petition operates in the nature of an attachment upon choses in action and other property of the bankrupt, yet his title is not thereby divested. He is still the owner, though holding in trust until the appointment and qualification of the trustee, who thereupon becomes 'vested by operation of law with the title of the bankrupt' as of the date of adjudication." Quoted further at § 1123.

In re Potteiger, 24 A. B. R. 648, 181 Fed. 640 (D. C. Pa.): "When the petition was filed against the bankrupt and when the subpœna was served, he was in possession of a horse and wagon and was using them in his business. Asserting that he was only a bailee and that a third person was the real owner, he delivered the property to such person two or three days afterwards, and failed to comply with a subsequent order of the court directing him to turn it over to the receiver. It needs neither discussion nor citation to establish the proposition that a bankrupt has no lawful authority thus to deal with goods in his possession after a petition has been filed and a subpœna has been served. If the horse and wagon really belonged to another person, application to the court would have brought immediate protection, and complete relief after his ownership had been proved; but it was not for the bankrupt and the claimant to decide the question of ownership summarily, and dispose of property that was in the bankrupt's exclusive possession when the proceedings were begun. It may be that the claimant is in fact the owner, but the title was apparently in the bankrupt, and his creditors have a right to be heard upon the question whether he was the owner as he seemed to be, or was only a bailee for hire. It is therefore adjudged, after hearing testimony and argument, that the bankrupt has been guilty of contempt in delivering to John C. Kunberger the horse and wagon in dispute."

Inferentially and obiter, Blake v. Valentine, 1 A. B. R. 378, 89 Fed. 691 (D. C. Calif.): " * * * before the appointment of an assignee (or trustee), proceeding for an injunction to protect the property of the bankrupt may be instituted by the bankrupt or the petitioning creditor. After an assignee or trustee has been appointed, he is the only person who could institute such proceedings on behalf of the bankrupt estate."

Compare, Rand v. Railway Co., 16 A. B. R. 698, 186 N. Y. 58: "It may very well be that any sum recovered by the plaintiff [bankrupt after adjudication but before appointment of trustee] in the present action will be held by him as trustee for his creditors."

Property or debts belonging to him before bankruptcy but coming into his hands after adjudication, must be turned over by him to the trustee ;[14] and if his receipt thereof is conceded, it would seem that the burden would rest upon him to prove he has turned it over to the trustee.[15]

But the bankrupt certainly is not a quasi trustee nor bailee for creditors before the filing of the petition, even within the four months period.[16]

Nevertheless, creditors must protect themselves by resort to some one or more of the provisional remedies available.[17] Summary proceedings are

14. Impliedly, In re Leslie, 9 A. B. R. 561, 119 Fed. 406 (D. C. N. Y.).

15. In re Leslie, 9 A. B. R. 561, 119 Fed. 406 (D. C. N. Y.).

16. In re Letson, 19 A. B. R. 506, 157 Fed. 78 (C. C. A. Okla.).

17. Compare post, §§ 1133, 1134, 1807. Contra, and that the bankrupt may be punished for contempt for surrendering property to an adverse claimant though no injunction had been issued upon him and no receiver

available to require the surrender of property unlawfully delivered or disposed of in the meantime,[18] the property having been taken from custodia legis.[19]

§ 1122. Destruction of Property Meanwhile.

—However, the *title* remains in the bankrupt, so that if the property is destroyed meanwhile by fire the insurance company may not raise the defense that the title had been transferred.[20]

Gordon *v.* Mech. & Traders Ins. Co., 22 A. B. R. 649, 120 La. Ann. 441, 45 So. 384: "A fire insurance policy contained the following stipulation: 'The entire policy, unless otherwise provided by agreement herein indorsed or added hereto, shall be void * * * if the interest of the insured be other than unconditional and sole ownership * * * or if any change other than death of an assured takes place in the interest, title or possession of the subject of insurance whether by legal process or judgment, or by voluntary act of the assured, or otherwise, or if this policy be assigned before a loss.' On February 1, 1905, the assured filed a petition in the United States District Court for the Eastern District of Kentucky in voluntary bankruptcy, and on the same day he was adjudged a bankrupt. On February 2d the stock of merchandise insured was (at Ruston, La.) destroyed by fire. On February 3d a receiver was appointed, and on February 13th the same person was appointed as trustee and qualified as such. On May 13th the District Court confirmed a composition which had been entered into between the bankrupt and his creditors. The assured thereafter sued the insurance company, pleading that the policy had become void by reason of the proceedings in bankruptcy. The court rendered judgment in favor of the plaintiff, and the correctness of that judgment has been brought up for review. Held, the judgment is correct and is affirmed. The property insured was destroyed before either a receiver or a trustee was appointed. In the interim between the adjudication in bankruptcy and the appointment and qualification of the trustee, the title to the property, with the incidents of interest and possession, continued in the bankrupt. When the trustee was appointed, there was no property in existence to which the title in the trustee could vest. The trustee of a bankrupt is not obliged to accept title to the property surrendered by the bankrupt, if to do so would not benefit the creditors, or would prejudice them. The creditors deemed it to their interest to make a composition with the bankrupt, and depend upon his personal obligation to them, and did so. The court confirmed the composition. The composition did away with the effect of the bankruptcy proceedings, and the assured had the right to sue on the policy with his rights intact."

Although, if the bankrupt is required by the court actually *to assign* any of the assets, the policy will cease to cover such property.

placed in charge. In re Potteiger, 24 A. B. R. 548, 181 Fed. 640 (D. C. Pa.) quoted supra this same section.

18. In re Denson, 28 A. B. R. 158, 195 Fed. 854 (D. C. Ala.). Compare, post, §§ 1800, 1807, et seq.

19. Acme Harvester Co. *v.* Beekman Lumber Co., 27 A. B. R. 262, 222 U. S. 307.

20. Fuller *v.* Jameson, 184 N. Y. 605; S. C., on review, 98 App. Div. 53, 90 N. Y. Supp. 456, 16 A. B. R. 693, note; Fuller *v.* N. Y. Fire Ins. Co., 185 Mass. 12 (Compare Tefft *v.* Providence Washington Ins. Co., 25 Ins. Law Journ. 226, on cognate proposition); obiter, Rand *v.* Ry. Co., 16 A. B. R. 697, 186 N. Y. 58. But compare, apparently but not really contra, In re Hamilton, 4 A. B. R. 543, 102 Fed. 683 (D. C. Ark.), where special terms of the particular policy were involved.

§ 1123. Institution of Suits by Bankrupt Meanwhile.

—In the meantime the bankrupt has sufficient title to maintain suits in his own name, at any rate where no receiver has been appointed or where title and not merely possessory right is essential to maintenance of the suit.[21]

Johnson *v.* Collier, 27 A. B. R. 454, 222 U. S. 538: "Until such election (of the trustee) the bankrupt has title—defeasible, but sufficient to authorize the institution and maintenance of a suit on any cause of action otherwise possessed by him. It is to the interest of all concerned that this should be so. There must always some time elapse between the filing of the petition and the meeting of the creditors. During that period it may frequently be important that action should be commenced, attachments and garnishments issued, and proceedings taken to recover what would be lost if it were necessary to wait until the trustee was elected. The institution of such suit will result in no harm to the estate. For if the trustee prefers to begin a new action in the same or another court, in his own name, the one previously brought can be abated. If, however, he is of opinion that it would be to the benefit of the creditors, he may intervene in the suit commenced by the bankrupt and avail himself of rights and priorities thereby acquired. Thatcher *v.* Rockwell, 105 U. S. 469, 26 L. Ed. 950.

"If, because of the disproportionate expense, or uncertainty as to the result, the trustee neither sues nor intervenes, there is no reason why the bankrupt himself should not continue the litigation. He has an interest in making the dividend for creditors as large as possible and in some states the more direct interest of creating a fund which may be set apart to him as an exemption. If the trustee will not sue and the bankrupt cannot sue, it might result in the bankrupt's debtor being discharged of an actual liability. The statute indicates no such purpose, and if money or property is finally recovered, it will be for the benefit of the estate. Nor is there any merit in the suggestion that this might involve a liability to pay both the bankrupt and the trustee. The defendant in any such suit can, by order of the bankrupt court, be amply protected against any danger of being made to pay twice." Further quoted at § 1121.

§ 1123½. Suits against Bankrupt.

—A suit brought against the bankrupt after adjudication will not bind the trustee, who was not a party thereto, even though the bankruptcy proceeding takes place in another state, and the suit was brought prior to the trustee's appointment.[22]

§ 1124. Whether Liens Given in Meantime Subject to Creditors' Rights.

—It has been held that any lien which the bankrupt attempts to create upon the property, pending the hearing on the bankruptcy petition or before the qualification of the trustee, is subject to the right of the creditors in bankruptcy.[23] This is particularly so where the lien would result in a preference.[24]

---

21. Rand *v.* Ry. Co., 16 A. B. R. 697, 186 N. Y. 58.
22. Hull *v.* Burr, 26 A. B. R. 897 (Sup. Ct. Fla.), suit in ejectment.
23. In re Austin, 13 A. B. R. 133 (D. C. Hawaii), where an attempt to give a lien to the bankrupt's attorney for legal services (not connected with the bankruptcy) was declared futile. In re Hurley, 26 A. B. R. 434, 185 Fed. 850 (D. C. Mass.).
24. Impliedly, Pratt *v.* Bothe, 12 A. B. R. 529, 130 Fed. 570 (C. C. A. Mich.). Bankr. Act, § 60 (a); instance, In re Hurley, 26 A. B. R. 434, 185 Fed. 850 (D. C. Mass.).

And a mortgagee will be too late to take possession of after-acquired property after adjudication of bankruptcy though before a trustee has been appointed.[25]

But such rule cannot divest bona fide liens on presently passing consideration created in the meantime;[26] nor other transactions on presently passing consideration that would not result in depleting the estate, since such transactions would be quite consistent with the quasi trusteeship of the bankrupt.

Thus artisans' liens for repairs done in the meantime are valid.

§ 1125. No Liens by Legal Proceedings after Adjudication.—Nor can a lien by legal proceedings be meanwhile obtained thereon after the adjudication.[27]

§ 1126. As to Legal Liens between Filing of Petition and Adjudication.—Nor if obtained before the adjudication, if after the filing of the petition;[28] even upon fraudulently conveyed property.

Such a lien obtained by a creditor on the bankrupt's property after the filing of the petition but before adjudication is not null and void, however, under § 67 (f) for that section annuls only liens obtained *before* the filing of the petition.[29] It is null and void on the theory that the property is in custodia legis—even though no receiver has been appointed and the marshal has made no seizure; the custody of the bankrupt being held that of the bankruptcy court after the filing of the petition and until a receiver is appointed.

Moreover, suits being ipso facto stayed until the date of the adjudication (see post, § 2695) such stay would prevent any lien being acquired meantime by legal proceedings.

In any event, no lien by legal proceeding can be meantime obtained thereon.

Compare Acme Harvester Co. *v.* Beekman Co., 27 A. B. R. 262, 222 U. S. 300: "To permit creditors to attach the bankrupt's property between the filing of the petition and the time of adjudication would be to encourage a race of diligence to defeat the purposes of the act and prevent the equal distribution of the estate among all creditors of the same class, which is the policy of the law. The filing of the petition asserts the jurisdiction of the Federal court, the issuing of its process brings the defendant into court, the selection of the trustee is to

---

25. In re Hurley, 26 A. B. R. 434, 185 Fed. 850 (D. C. Mass.).
26. In re Rich, 17 A. B. R. 893 (Ref. Ohio).
27. In re Engle, 5 A. B. R. 372, 105 Fed. 893 (D. C. Pa.). But compare, Evans *v.* Staalle, 11 A. B. R. 182 (Minn.), where the State court permitted a judgment creditor after the adjudication and before discharge to acquire a lien by a suit to declare a fraudulent trust in property bought for the bankrupt's benefit in the name of

another. Inferentially, In re Torchia, 26 A. B. R. 579, 188 Fed. 207 (C. C. A. Pa.).
28. Kinmouth *v.* Braeutigam, 10 A. B. R. 83, 52 Atl. 226 (N. J.). Cox *v.* State Bk., 11 A. B. R. 112, 125 Fed. 654 (D. C. Ills.). Recovery of proceeds of attachment sale in suit started after the filing of the petition, State Bank *v.* Cox, 16 A. B. R. 33, 143 Fed. 91 (C. C. A. Ills.).
29. Compare post, § 1452.

follow upon the adjudication, and thereupon the estate belonging to the bankrupt, held by him or for him, vests in the trustee. Pending the proceedings the law holds the property to abide the decision of the court upon the question of adjudication as effectively as if an attachment had been issued, and prevents creditors from defeating the purposes of the law by bringing separate attachment suits which would virtually amount to preferences in favor of such creditors." Quoted further at § 1119.

§ 1127. Query, if No Trustee Ever Appointed, Where Does Title to Concealed Assets Rest?

—But if no trustee at all is appointed, as the Supreme Court's General Order XV seems to permit in certain cases, the question arises in whom does the title to concealed property vest? [30]

§ 1128. Whether Bankrupt Retains Power of Disposal before Adjudication, unless Receiver or Marshal Takes Possession or Injunction Issues.

—Unless the bankrupt's property be sequestrated by a receiver or marshal or the bankrupt himself be enjoined, the bankrupt retains the power to dispose of the property, after the filing of the petition, even until the date of adjudication,[31] only to the extent, however, of dealing with it on presently passing consideration and in good faith, that is to say, only to an extent consistent with his quasi trusteeship.

In re Milk Co., 16 A. B. R. 730, 145 Fed. 1013 (D. C. Pa.): "* * * the filing of an involuntary petition does not, ipso facto take from him his dominion over it. It no doubt puts the property within the control of the court, if it sees fit to exercise the power, but pending and prior to an adjudication, it is still his own, title only vesting in the trustee, as of that date, after an adjudication has been obtained. (Section 70.) If this is not sufficient to protect the interests of creditors, in any case, upon a proper showing they may have the marshal put in possession or a receiver may be appointed, which will. Sections 2 (3) (5); 69.

"Subject, then, to the right of the trustee to avoid it as a preference, an honest disposition of his property by the bankrupt, even after proceedings have been instituted, therefore stands."

This power therefore is subject to the right of the trustee, subsequently appointed, to recover such transfers as were preferential,[32] or otherwise improper.

§ 1129. Remedies of Creditors Holding Securities, etc., Meantime Unimpaired.

—Likewise, the remedies of creditors holding securities, meantime are unimpaired.[33]

---

30. Compare, Rand *v.* Iowa Cent. Ry. Co., 16 A. B. R. 692, 186 N. Y. 58 (reversing 12 A. B. R. 164), quoted supra. Also, compare, as to title to concealed assets where estate closed. Fowler *v.* Jenks, 11 A. B. R. 255, 90 Minn. 74 (Sup. Ct. Minn.).

31. American Trust Co. *v.* Wallis, 11 A. B. R. 360, 126 Fed. 464 (C. C. A. Penn.); In re Benjamin, 15 A. B. R. 353, 140 Fed. 320 (D. C. Pa.); In re Mertens, 15 A. B. R. 369, 144 Fed. 818 (C. C. A. N. Y.); In re Pease, 4 A. B. R. 578 (Ref. N. Y.).

32. In re Milk Co., 16 A. B. R. 730, 145 Fed. 1013 (D. C. Penn.).

33. Hiscock *v.* Varick Bk., 18 A. B. R. 9, 206 U. S. 28.

DIVISION 3.

STATUS OF PROPERTY ACQUIRED AFTER ADJUDICATION.

§ 1130. Property Acquired after Adjudication Does Not Pass.— Property acquired after adjudication does not pass to the trustee at all, but belongs to the debtor's new estate, and is subject only to the claims of new creditors.[34]

§ 1131. After-Acquired Property Transferable at Date of Bankruptcy Passes, Though Incident to Property Not Passing to Trustee. —It is undoubtedly true that after-acquired property, which is merely the earnings, profit or incident of property existing beforehand and passing to the trustee, will itself pass to the trustee. The property with all its increments, earnings and rights passes to the trustee.

And if after-acquisitions are capable of assignment at the time of the filing of the petition, they will pass, though they flow from property itself not passing. Thus, commissions on insurance premiums, accruing after the agent's bankruptcy under an insurance agency contract existing before the bankruptcy, will pass, even though the agency contract itself does not pass.[85]

SUBDIVISION "A."

PROPERTY ACQUIRED DURING PENDENCY OF PETITION.

§ 1132. Property Acquired after Filing of Petition but before Adjudication.— Property acquired after the filing of the bankruptcy petition but before the adjudication, if the proceeds of property transferable or seizable at the time of the filing, vests in the trustee; if it be independently acquired or be bought on credit, it does not vest in the trustee.[36]

---

34. In re Smith, 1 A. B. R. 37 (Ref. N. Y.), claim against another bankrupt before claimant's own discharge. In re LeClaire, 10 A. B. R. 733, 124 Fed. 655 (D. C. Iowa); In re Wetmore, 6 A. B. R. 210, 108 Fed. 520 (C. C. A. Penn., affirming 3 A. B. R. 700, 99 Fed. 703, and 4 A. B. R. 335, 102 Fed. 290); In re Rennie, 2 A. B. R. 182 (Ref. Ind. Terr.); In re Parish, 10 A. B. R. 548, 122 Fed. 553 (D. C. Iowa); compare, analogously. In re Hoadley, 3 A. B. R. 780 (D. C. N. Y.). Instance. In re Polakoff, 1 A. B. R. 358 (Master's Report affirmed by D. C. N. Y.), which was a case of wages earned subsequent to adjudication. Instance, held not after-acquired property, McNaboe v. Marks, 16 A. B. R. 767 (N. Y. Sup. Ct.), which instance was that of a dis-

tributive share in a decedent's estate where the decree was entered after adjudication of bankruptcy, but "as of" a date anterior thereto. See, in addition, Whitlock's License, 22 A. B. R. 262, 39 Pa. Super. Ct. Rep. 34, liquor license granted to bankrupt after adjudication.

35. See ante, § 994; In re Wright, 18 A. B. R. 199, 151 Fed. 361 (D. C. N. Y., reversing 16 A. B. R. 778).

36. Compare. In re Harris, 2 A. B. R. 359 (Ref. Ills.), where the rule is laid down broadly that property acquired after the filing of the petition, but before adjudication, does not pass. As a general rule such would be the case, yet the rule may be complicated by certain circumstances.

§ 1133. Evils of Old Law Vesting Title as of Date of Filing Petition.

—The subject of the status of property acquired after the filing of the petition but before adjudication, is somewhat difficult.

It has been noted that the date of the vesting of the title, even by relating back, is not the date of the filing of the petition. Were it otherwise, the mere filing of a petition against a bankrupt would tend to drive him out of business; for no one would take the risk of buying from him, because, were he finally adjudged bankrupt, the title to all the goods he had meanwhile been selling or otherwise dealing in would be in doubt—the title to them would have been in the trustee and the bankrupt's sales would all have been null and void, except perhaps as to purchasers without notice. Under such circumstances ultimate victory would be of little avail to the unfortunate debtor—his business would nevertheless have been ruined.[87]

In re Pease, 4 A. B. R. 578 (N. Y. Ref.), 2 N. B. N. & R. 1108: "There was no such difficulty under the law of 1867. By § 14 of that statute the assignee's title vested by relation as of the date the proceedings were commenced. As a result, a merchant against whom a petition in bankruptcy was pending could not do business—the title being in the air until adjudication or dismissal. There seems little doubt that the insertion of the words 'as of the date of the adjudication' in the present law was intended to meet the difficulty. * * * It meets the difficulty complained of under the law of 1867, and applies to business the doctrine that the debtor is innocent of bankruptcy until proved guilty. It protects ad interim purchasers and keeps going concerns alive, for the benefit of the creditors, if adjudications follow and the benefit of the debtors themselves, if dismissals result. Nor can it be said that, by recognizing a valid title in the bankrupt until adjudication, creditors may be at the mercy of a dishonest debtor; Congress, foreseeing that, also enacted § 69, by which creditors may take possession of the property of debtors likely to take advantage of the situation, a privilege emphasized by the almost identical words of § 3e.

"This view also comports with well-established principles of bankruptcy legislation in the United States. Our policy has been to establish a day of cleavage, that is, a day before which the relation of debtor and creditor exists, but after which, at the debtor's option, it ceases; a day before which all the debtor has becomes his creditors', but after which that which he acquires is his, subject only to his new trusteeship to new creditors. With us that day has always been the day proceedings are commenced, and the present law repeatedly recognizes it. Compare §§ 1 (10), e-b, 9b, 11a, 29b (4), 60b, 63a (1), (2), (3), (5), 64b (4), 67 c-e-f, 68b. * * *

"The English Bankruptcy Act distinguishes sharply between the time of vesting and the property which vests. Section 54 vests the title in the trustee 'immediately on the debtor being adjudged a bankrupt.' But, by § 44, the property divisible among the creditors is defined as 'all such property as may belong to or be vested in the bankrupt at the commencement of the bankruptcy, or may be acquired by or devolve on him before his discharge;' while by § 43, 'the

37. Compare, under present law, obiter, In re Krinsky Bros., 7 A. B. R. 535, 112 Fed. 972 (D. C. N. Y.): "Those who deal with a bankrupt's property in the interval between the filing of the petition and the final adjudication do so at their peril." Compare, to same effect, note to In re Rennie, 2 A. B. R. 182 (Ref. Ind. Terr.).

commencement of the bankruptcy' is defined as the day on which the voluntary petition is filed, or, if involuntary, the day on which the first act of bankruptcy (not earlier than three months prior) relied on was committed. In other words, in England, while the title vests on the date of the adjudication, it may relate backward to three months before the petition, and may also include everything acquired before the discharge. It is a little difficult to understand the justice of this, especially as by §§ 30 and 37 of the same act, a discharge operates only on debts existent or obligations created prior to the date of the 'receiving order,' i. e., in actual practice, the date of filing the petition. In other words, it would seem that in England creditors may share in after-acquisitions prior to the discharge, though their debts post-date the beginning of the proceedings, and yet, if not paid in full, still have undischarged debts for the deficit. But the point to which attention is called is that, in spite of this period of probation, during which the English bankrupt must continue to surrender all that he may acquire, the English law, like ours, and probably for the same reason, distinguishes between the time of vesting and the title which vests, and further fixes the time on the day we fix it."

Compare analogously as to transactions on presently passing considerations not being preferences, In re Davidson, 5 A. B. R. 528-532, 109 Fed. 882 (D. C. Iowa): "The statute certainly cannot be invoked to put an end to legitimate business. And if the statute does mean, as is contended by objecting creditors, then it is readily seen that no business can be transacted with a merchant from the moment he becomes embarrassed."

Under the Act of 1867, title reverted to the date of the filing of the petition as a result of which a merchant against whom a petition in bankruptcy was pending could not do business—the title being in the air until adjudication or dismissal.[38]

In re Mertens, 15 A. B. R. 369, 142 Fed. 445 (C. C. A. N. Y.): "The change in the present Act, by which the trustee's title is that only which exists at the date of the adjudication, removes any uncertainty which arose under the Act of 1867. It was intended, we think, to permit all legitimate business transactions between a debtor and those dealing with him to be carried out and consummated as freely until he has been adjudicated a bankrupt as though no proceedings were pending. In many cases the proceedings against an alleged bankrupt are unfounded, and for this and other reasons never culminate in adjudication. While the filing of a petition in bankruptcy is a caveat to all the world, the notice ought not to have the effect of paralyzing all business dealings with the debtor, or to prevent lienors or pledgees from enforcing their contracts. This is its practical effect if the rights and remedies of all concerned are in suspense until it can be ascertained whether an adjudication is or is not to follow the commencement of the proceedings."

§ 1134. Bona Fide Transactions on Present Consideration Not Affected.

—Such a condition as above related would be intolerable and was found to be so under the law of 1867. So the present law says in effect: Let the creditors file their petition, if they will; although such filing places the property in the custody of the court, under the quasi trusteeship of the

---

38. In re Pease, 4 A. B. R. 578 (N. Y. Ref.), 2 N. B. N. & R. 1108; also, to same effect, In re Rennie, 2 A. B. R. 182 (Ref. Ind. Terr.).

bankrupt, yet people may continue in good faith to buy of the debtor and deal with him with impunity, on presently passing consideration that would not result in depleting the estate, until he is adjudged bankrupt or a receiver or marshal makes seizure of the property dealt with, even though they know of the petition, subject, only, to the right of the trustee to avoid preferences or other improper transactions, if any are effected meanwhile.[39]

Perhaps, In re Benjamin, 15 A. B. R. 353 (D. C. Pa.): "And even up to the moment of bankruptcy, a party may make a valid disposition of his property, where it is done for a fair consideration and with an honest motive."

As heretofore mentioned, if the debtor is suspected of making way with his property after the petition is filed against him, his creditors may have his property seized on process similar to levy of attachment, upon filing an affidavit and giving a bond; and thus the property may be held pending the trial of the debtor as to his bankruptcy. This remedy is amply sufficient also to protect the debtor, for if he be not adjudged bankrupt on the final hearing his property is returned to him and the bond becomes liable for all damages for the seizure and detention.[40]

Moreover, § 2 in clause 5 empowers the court to authorize the business of the bankrupt to be continued for a limited period by the marshal, if he has seized it, or by a receiver if one has been appointed, and thus, notwithstanding the seizure, the business may be kept intact as a going concern, contracts may be completed, goods manufactured and sold and everything kept in operation precisely as the bankrupt might have done, pending the hearing as to

39. In re Mertens, 15 A. B. R. 369, 142 Fed. 445 (C. C. A. N. Y.), supra. Perhaps, Githens v. Schiffler, 7 A. B. R. 453, 112 Fed. 505. Perhaps, In re Duffy, 9 A. B. R. 358, 118 Fed. 926 (D. C. Penn.). Perhaps, In re Milk Co., 16 A. B. R. 730, 145 Fed. 1013 (D. C. Penn.). But compare, obiter, contra, In re Krinsky Bros., 7 A. B. R. 535, 112 Fed. 972 (D. C. N. Y.). The debtor may pay his attorney for services to be rendered in bankruptcy by transferring property to him meanwhile. Inferentially, In re Corbett, 5 A. B. R. 224, 104 Fed. 872 (D. C. Wis.); In re Habegger, 15 A. B. R. 198, 139 Fed. 123 (C. C. A. Minn.); contra, Pratt v. Bothe, 12 A. B. R. 529 (C. C. A. Mich.); contra, In re Austin, 13 A. B. R. 136 (D. C. Hawaii). The transfer must be complete to pass title, however, In re Corbett, 5 A. B. R. 224, 104 Fed. 872 (D. C. Wis.).

Of course no lien can be obtained in the meantime by levy under legal proceedings that will avail against the bankrupt's creditors. Kinmouth v. Braeutigan, 10 A. B. R. 83, 52 Atl. 226

(N. J.); In re Engle, 5 A. B. R. 372, 105 Fed. 893 (D. C. Pa.).

Effect of Refusal of Discharge on Title to Property.—Even if his discharge be refused, creditors' rights have attached, and none of them can deal with his old estate, either in satisfaction of any of his old debts, or his new debts—the estate must be administered in accordance with the proceedings prescribed by the Bankrupt Act. Of course, in such event any new property he may acquire may be levied upon by any creditor in satisfaction of the unpaid balance of his claim. Kinmouth v. Braeutigam, 10 A. B. R. 85, 52 Atl. 226 (N. J.): "In case of the failure of the bankrupt to obtain his discharge the judgment remains. But even in the latter event it can never be enforceable against any property owned by the bankrupt at the time he filed his petition in bankruptcy, but can only be used against after-acquired property.

40. In re Milk Co., 16 A. B. R. 730, 145 Fed. 1013 (D. C. Penn.). Compare, to same effect, note to In re Rennie, 2 A. B. R. 182 (Ref. Ind. Terr.).

whether the debtor shall or shall not be adjudged to be a bankrupt. So the provisions of the present law are quite complete for protecting the creditor, as well as the debtor, pending the hearing of the petition, notwithstanding the statute makes the title vest as of the date of the adjudication instead of the date of the filing of the petition.

Nevertheless, a peculiar situation presents itself upon that very account when we come to the consideration of the broadest and most important class of assets that pass to the trustee, namely, class (5) of § 70, namely, property which prior to the filing of the petition the bankrupt could by any means have transferred or which might have been levied upon and sold under judicial process against him.

Are we to infer that the property acquired after the filing of the petition will not pass to the trustee, but will remain in the debtor notwithstanding the debtor may finally be adjudged bankrupt? The answer on analysis divides itself into two parts:

§ 1135. First, Property Acquired Meantime by Gift, Inheritance or Services, or Bought on Credit.

—As to property given to the debtor or inherited by him meanwhile and property bought by him on credit meanwhile and not paid for with property or proceeds of property owned by him at the time the petition was filed, such property is the property of the bankrupt absolutely and does not pass to the trustee at all. There is no escape from the plain words of the statute, for such property could not "have been transferred by him by any means before the filing of the petition" nor could it have been levied on before that time nor was it the proceeds of any property that could have been transferred or levied on before the filing of the petition. His old creditors have no share in it and no right to touch it. It goes along with the property acquired after the adjudication to form the nucleus of the bankrupt's new estate, freed by his discharge, later granted, from the claims of his old creditors.[41]

In re Pease, 4 A. B. R. 578 (Ref. N. Y.): "Creditors who become such before the filing of the petition cannot compel a bankrupt to account for profits in business after the petition and before the adjudication, or for goods sold in the interval which were purchased of other dealers and not taken from the bankrupt's stock, but can for moneys collected in that interval, or even thereafter, for goods sold either before or after the petition out of the stock with which the trustee became vested on the adjudication."

In re Burka, 5 A. B. R. 12, 104 Fed. 326 (D. C. Mo.): "In other words, the property which the trustee acquires must have been property or rights which so existed prior to the filing of the petition that the bankrupt might have transferred them."

---

41. In re Rennie, 2 A. B. R. 182 (Ref. Ind. Terr.); see, In re Harris, 2 A. B. R. 359 (Ref. Ills.), although in this case the character and origin of the property are not apparent. In re Stoner, 5 A. B. R. 402, 105 Fed. 752 (D. C. Pa.).

Similarly, it is a question whether the right to a government reward for information leading to the detection of smugglers will pass to the trustee where the award has not been made by the Secretary of the Treasury until after the filing of the bankruptcy petition, even though the services were performed beforehand, the question being whether there existed an assignable right or merely an inchoate right in the nature of a prospective gift.[42] Nor would wages earned in the meantime pass.[43]

Property bought on credit since the filing of the petition and before the adjudication it will be noted has been excepted, although doubtingly. It would seem on theory that *such property, neither having been in existence before the filing of the petition nor being the proceeds of such pre-existing property would not pass to the trustee,* and would not go to swell the fund for the payment of creditors.

As bearing out this conclusion, it is to be noted that in case such property were bought during that period, then the debt would not have been a provable debt in bankruptcy and consequently would not have been discharged by the bankrupt's discharge, not being "owing" at the date of the filing of the petition.

Thus, as to property bought on credit between the filing of the petition and the adjudication in bankruptcy, such property and the debt arising therefor are both taken out of the operation of the bankruptcy proceedings; the property does not pass to the trustee for the creditors, nor does the debt participate in the dividends, nor, for that matter is it released by the bankrupt's discharge.

This lends additional strength to the conclusion. And the property so purchased would not come within the operation of the bankruptcy act nor pass to the trustee for creditors, since it would be inequitable to have the property pass, if the debt could not participate.

In re Burka, 5 A. B. R. 12, 104 Fed. 326 (D. C. Mo.): "It is argued by claimant's counsel that because the trustee is vested with the title not only to property which the bankrupt had at the time of the filing of the petition against him, but also to such property as he may have acquired after that, and prior to the date of adjudication, and because all such property goes into the fund for creditors, therefore all creditors having claims which originated at any time prior to the actual adjudication should participate in the fund; in other words, that, as the property which the bankrupt acquires after the filing of the petition enhances the fund for the benefit of creditors, all creditors whose rights accrued at any time before actual adjudication should participate in it. This is a plausible argument, and I presume it would be true that, if the property acquired by the bankrupt after the filing of the petition and before the adjudication did vest in the trustee, creditors whose rights accrued between those dates should share in the property of the bankrupt, like other creditors; but the argument, in my opinion,

---

42. Obiter, In re Ghazal, 20 A. B. R. 807, 163 Fed. 602 (D. C. N. Y.), reversed in 23 A. B. R. 178, 174 Fed. 809 (C. C. A.).

43. Obiter, Sibley *v.* Nason, 22 A. B. R. 712, 196 Mass. 125.

is based on false premises. * * * Properly interpretated, the trustee is by operation of law vested with the title as of the date the bankrupt was adjudged to be a bankrupt. The further provisions of the section, already quoted, undertake to point out the property of which by operation of law he is to become the owner, namely, all property which prior to the filing of the petition the bankrupt could have transferred. In other words, the property which the trustee acquires must have been property or rights which so existed prior to the filing of the petition that the bankrupt might have transferred them. This clearly means the property or rights of property which existed at that time. Such being the true interpretation of § 70, it affords no ground for the argument made by claimant's counsel. Inasmuch as no property which the bankrupt may have acquired after the filing of the petition and before the date of adjudication is taken by the trustee, there is no ground for the argument that the claimant, holding a claim accrued since the filing of the petition, and before adjudication, should participate in the assets."

A still further complication arises where the property is bought meanwhile and bought on credit, but is paid for partly although not wholly out of funds belonging to the creditors. Certainly at any rate the creditors would have a lien on such property to the amount of such payment even if the property itself were not property in existence at the time of the filing of the petition.

§ 1136. Second, Property Purchased Meantime with Proceeds of Property Which Was in Existence at Time of Filing Petition.—As to property acquired in the meantime between the filing of the petition and the adjudication but purchased with property or the proceeds of property that was in existence at the time the petition was filed and that could then have been transferred or levied on at that time, such property if still in existence does pass to the trustee on adjudication although the identical property itself was not in existence at the time the petition was filed and therefore could not itself then have been transferred or levied on; and this is so because the bankrupt got the property by selling his creditors' property and it is impressed with the consequent trust in his hands for their benefit. In other words, it passes to the trustee not because it is property that was in existence at the time of the filing of the petition and could have been transferred or levied on at that time, but because it is the proceeds of such property and because such property belonged, by the latter adjudication, to his creditors and yet had been sold by the bankrupt: the bankrupt holding the proceeds as quasi trustee or agent for the real owner of the original property, precisely as would the marshal or a receiver had either of them held possession of the property during that meantime.

Although this precise course of reasoning does not appear to have been elaborated in any of the reported cases, yet it seems to be the course of reasoning actually adopted by the courts in arriving at their conclusions. The trustee may not be required to surrender property acquired by the bankrupt between the filing of the petition and the adjudication simply because it was not in existence when the petition was filed, so long as it is the proceeds of property that had belonged to the bankrupt at that time. Absolutely independent acquisitions during that period, however, belong unquestionably to the bankrupt, as, for instance, property acquired by gift from another, or by the death of an ancestor, or testator, or bought on credit meanwhile and not paid for, or the earnings of personal services in the meantime.[44]

44. Life Insurance Where Bankrupt Dies Whilst Bankruptcy Petition Pending.—Policies of life insurance on the bankrupt's life payable to the bankrupt himself or to his estate, are unquestionably property which at the time of the filing of the petition the bankrupt could by some means have transferred, and so, naturally, if he should die after the filing of the petition but before adjudication the whole amount of the insurance presumably would pass to the trustee, being so clearly the proceeds of the contract in existence at the time of the filing of the petition; and such would be the case were it not for the proviso contained in § 70 (a) (5), which the Supreme Court has construed to take the entire subject of life insurance out of Class 5 and to place the policies named into a separate class by themselves. Compare ante, §§ 1002, 1003, 1004, et seq.